The Philosophy of Science

The Philosophy of Science

edited by Richard Boyd, Philip Gasper, and J.D. Trout

A Bradford Book
The MIT Press
Cambridge, Massachusetts
London, England

Fifth printing, 1995

© 1991 Massachusetts Institute of Technology

This book was set in Palatino by Asco Trade Typesetting Ltd., Hong Kong and printed and bound in the United States of America.

Library of Congress Cataloging-in-Publication Data

The philosophy of science / edited by Richard Boyd, Philip Gasper, and J.D. Trout.
    p. cm.
"A Bradford book."
Includes bibliographical references and index.
ISBN 0-262-02315-6.—ISBN 0-262-52156-3 (pbk.)
1. Science—Philosophy. 2. Social sciences—Philosophy. I. Boyd, Richard.
II. Gasper, Philip. III. Trout, J.D.
Q175.3.P47 1991
121—dc20

90-20350
CIP

Contents

Introduction

Our model for this anthology was Feigl and Brodbeck's *Readings in the Philosophy of Science* (New York: Appleton-Century-Crofts, 1953), now long out of print. During the 1950s and early 1960s, when sophisticated developments in logical positivist philosophy of science dominated the field, Feigl and Brodbeck's anthology represented an almost ideal collection of readings for any serious introductory philosophy of science course for undergraduates or beginning graduate students. Its chief virtue was that it afforded the student (and her instructor) a remarkably synoptic overview of the literature in the philosophy of science.

As we know from our experience with it as students and teachers, Feigl and Brodbeck was a marvelous textbook. Because of its breadth and synoptic character, it could serve as the sole textbook for a serious philosophy of science course. It contained a sufficient number of articles so that those not assigned as readings in a course could be made the subject of term papers, and the variety of its contents was such that almost any student could find material relevant to her own special scientific or social scientific interests. Because its contents were so well selected, it remained a valuable resource for students long after the course was over. Indeed, it proved an important volume for faculty members as well, making it possible for philosophers who were not specialists in the philosophy of science to prepare courses that would nevertheless adequately survey the most important problems and approaches.

Feigl and Brodbeck was a product of a brief period of (late positivist) consensus in the philosophy of science—a consensus that reflected both a fundamentally verificationist conception of theory confirmation and of the semantics of theoretical terms and a conception of the sciences according to which physics (as positivists understood it) was to be taken as the paradigm science. Its success in providing so synoptic and so well integrated an overview of the issues in the field no doubt depended upon the strength of that consensus.

But Feigl and Brodbeck's book is now outdated and out of print. And no subsequent collection of readings has quite approached it either in scope or in the extent to which it provided an integrated view of the field. One reason is that, until recently, there had not emerged a new consensus in the philosophy of science that could serve as the programmatic basis for such a collection.

But recent developments in the philosophy of science and related areas of philosophy, and in the philosophies of the various special sciences, have progressed to a point where a new "post-positivist" consensus has emerged. This new consensus is not doctrinal; it is not the case that one general philosophical conception of scientific knowledge, of scientific language, or of causation and explanation has emerged as the consensus position. Instead, there has evolved a consensus about which more specific philosophical and scientific matters any adequate general philosophical conception of science must account for, along with a consensus about the broad outlines of the relevant philosophical positions, options, and argumentative strategies.

Roughly, the recent developments that have led to the new consensus are:

1. The emergence of sophisticated realist and neo-Kantian alternatives to traditional empiricist conceptions of science, and of more sophisticated post-positivist versions of empiricism in response to them.

2. The development of "naturalistic" or "causal" conceptions of reference and of the definitions of natural kind (magnitude, property, . . .) terms as alternatives to the standard empiricist conceptions of such matters.

3. Corresponding naturalistic developments in epistemology.

4. Critiques (and consequent reformulations) of the Humean conception of causal relations and of the associated covering-law account of explanation.

5. A greatly increased emphasis on the relevance of the history of science for work in the philosophy of science and a consequent de-emphasis on the alleged distinction between "context of invention (or discovery)" and "context of confirmation (or justification)."

6. The emergence of a distinct and philosophically important post-positivist literature in the philosophies of the various "special sciences" (especially biology, psychology, and history), particularly the emergence of a nonreductionist account of the relation between the special sciences and the more basic physical sciences.

7. A similar post-positivist reevaluation of issues in the philosophy of physics.

The resulting picture of scientific knowledge, of scientific language, and of causation and explanation is vastly more complex than the simple account dictated by traditional logical positivism and, consequently, is philosophically much richer. The newly emerging consensus resulting from this picture appears to have roughly the following components:

a. Scientific methodology is ineliminably theory-dependent, and the depth of its theory-dependence rules out any simple verificationist conception of science. The serious contenders among general positions in the philosophy of science are scientific realism and neo-Kantian constructivism—both of which arose as responses to the apparent theory-dependence of scientific methods—and sophisticated post-positivist versions of empiricism that arose as responses to these positions.

b. Foundationalist conceptions of knowledge in general, and of scientific knowledge in particular, are untenable in many of the ways suggested by defenders of causal or naturalistic conceptions of knowledge, both because of the theory-dependence of scientific methods and for independent reasons arising from causal theories of perception. Any account of scientific knowledge must embody at least some naturalistic elements, whatever its author's ultimate position on epistemological matters.

c. For similar reasons, we must acknowledge that the definitions of scientific concepts and of terms in scientific language are theory-dependent; any adequate account of the semantics of scientific terms must reflect this fact and must—whatever its author's ultimate position on semantic matters—reflect some of the insights of causal or naturalistic conceptions of definition and of reference.

d. Because of the importance of "naturalistic" considerations in the philosophy of science, the "natural history" of scientific theorizing—the history of science—provides a very important constraint on theories in the philosophy of science. The distinction between context of discovery and context of confirmation is correspondingly less important than positivists imagined.

e. The Humean conception of causation and the associated covering-law conception of explanation are by no means obviously correct; they must compete with both constructivist and naturalistic alternatives.

f. Materialist conceptions of both biological and psychological matters are well confirmed, but materialism within a special science does not require the sort of syntactic reducibility to physics anticipated by logical positivists. The biological and social sciences can be "autonomous" from the physical sciences even on the assumption of materialism. A reductionist approach in a special science requires a defense in terms of the special features of that science rather than in terms of an appeal to a generally reductionist analysis of materialism.

g. Because they are arguably autonomous, the various special sciences (and their histories) are as relevant for the philosopher of science as are the physical sciences.

h. Because of the importance of naturalistic approaches in the philosophy of science, and because many methodological disputes within the various special sciences have a heavily philosophical component, there is an important and appropriate dialectical interaction between research in the philosophy of science and research in the various special sciences.

It will be apparent that the new consensus is much more complex than that achieved in late positivism. In part this is simply a reflection of the fact that there is no doctrinal consensus but rather a consensus that identifies three distinct alternative general approaches—scientific realism, neo-Kantian constructivism, and post-positivist empiricism—as the major competitors.

Two other factors are also important. In the first place, positivist philosophy of science interacted little with the rest of philosophy (outside of logic) in any very fruitful way. Given the positivist rejection of metaphysics and the positivist tendency to treat all epistemological questions as special cases of questions in the foundations of science, it could hardly have been otherwise. By contrast, the recent literature in the philosophy of science reflects a much deeper and more vigorous interaction between philosophy of science and other areas of philosophy. The emerging naturalistic conceptions of knowledge and of semantics, for example, owe as much to the work of philosophers studying nonscientific examples as they do to work clearly internal to the philosophy of science. Similarly, the pioneering work that led to the current conception of the possibility of nonreductionist materialism was done by functionalist philosophers of mind, many of whom had a deeper interest in more general metaphysical issues than in the philosophy of science, or even the philosophy of psychology. Again, recent critiques of the Humean conception of causation have often arisen as much from similar metaphysical concerns as they have from issues specific to the philosophy of science.

The post-positivist recognition of the relevance of the various special sciences and their histories introduces an analogous source of complexity. To cite one example, one could not understand the source of recent antireductionist treatments of materialism either in the general literature in the philosophy of science or in, say, the philosophy of biology without understanding not only the initial, more metaphysically motivated, functionalist critiques of reductionism about the mental but also subsequent functionalist developments within the philosophy of psychology. Similarly, one could not understand the more abstract literature on "inductive inference to the best explanation" without recognizing the role that appeal to this sort of inference has played in discussions of methodology in evolutionary biology and in history.

These complexities of the current consensus do, of course, contribute to making the philosophy of science more interesting for students as well as for professionals. A good course in the philosophy of science is likely to refer to issues in some science or social science with which the student is familiar, and it is likely to serve as an introduction to broader issues within the rest of philosophy as well. The problem for the teacher of such a course is to assemble readings that will permit the student to see as much as possible of the complexity of the current state of the field and to present the material they contain in a way that draws out the relevant connections.

Moreover, it is also true that, although the existence of the consensus described here would be almost uncontroversial (even among the few philosophers who do not participate in it), there is no very clear statement of what the consensus is and of how it arose to guide the instructor who is not a specialist in the recent history of the philosophy of science. (Frederick Suppe's *The Structure of Scientific Theories* [University of Illinois Press, 2nd edition, 1977] provides a first-rate account of the central themes of twentieth-century philosophy of science up until the early 1970s, but was written before the new consensus had fully emerged.)

In this anthology, we attempt to remedy both deficiencies. We include sections consisting of both historical and contemporary readings on several broad areas, both theoretical and applied: theory confirmation; the semantics of theories and the dispute between empiricists, constructivists, and realists; causation and explanation; reductionism and the unity of science; the philosophy of physics; the philosophy of biology; the philosophy of psychology; and the philosophy of the social sciences. We hope that the introductions to the various sections will facilitate teaching and learning.

In choosing the more theoretical readings, our aim has been to select articles accessible to the nonspecialist in a way that clarifies both the historical development and the current status of the relevant doctrines and disputes and emphasizes the connection of issues in the philosophy of science to related issues in other areas of philosophy. In selecting readings in the philosophies of the various particular sciences, we have tried (1) to avoid significant duplication of articles already available in more specialized anthologies, (2) to include material that will be accessible to, and will interest, students from a wide range of disciplines (and thus provide material for possible term papers for a variety of students), and (3) to choose articles in the philosophies of particular sciences that illustrate and develop the general post-positivist themes discussed in the more theoretical readings. These constraints have limited our choices substantially. In compensation, our extensive bibliography includes articles and books dealing with a broader range of topics in the philosophies of each of the sciences in question, and we have provided suggestions for further reading at the end of the introductory essay to each section.

We believe this anthology will provide sufficient readings for a number of quite different introductory philosophy of science courses at the undergraduate and graduate levels. We hope that the volume will also be a useful reference book both for philosophers and for specialists in related areas. We also hope that teachers and students who use this anthology will write to us with ideas about how it might be improved.

While compiling this collection, we have incurred many debts. We would like to thank Arthur Fine, Philip Kitcher, Jon Jarrett, Dick Miller, Peter Railton, Elliott Sober, and Alison Wylie for suggestions about selections; Richard Farr and Janice Nadler for commenting on introductory material from various sections; James Anderson and Jon Jarrett for providing comments on the philosophy of physics introduction; Jim McClellan for bibliographical aid in the history of science; and Carol Sampson for help with proofreading. Finally, Betty Stanton, Joanna Poole, and Melissa Vaughn of The MIT Press deserve special mention for their patience and encouragement while we were working on this project.

Contributors

Richard Boyd
Department of Philosophy and
Department of Science and
Technology Studies
Cornell University
Ithaca, NY 14853

Percy Bridgman (1882–1961)
formerly Professor of Mathematics
and Natural History
Harvard University

Tyler Burge
Department of Philosophy
University of California at Los Angeles
Los Angeles, CA 90042

Rudolf Carnap (1891–1971)
formerly Professor of Philosophy
University of California at Los Angeles
University of Chicago

Nancy Cartwright
Department of Philosophy, Logic, and
Scientific Method
London School of Economics and
Political Science
Houghton Street
London, England WC2A 2AE

Paul Churchland
Department of Philosophy
University of California at San Diego
La Jolla, CA 92093

Daniel Dennett
Department of Philosophy
Tufts University
Medford, MA 02155

Arthur Fine
Department of Philosophy
Northwestern University
Evanston, IL 60208

Jerry Fodor
Department of Philosophy
Rutgers University
New Brunswick, NJ 08903

Evelyn Fox Keller
Department of Rhetoric
University of California
Berkeley, CA 94720

Alan Garfinkel
Philosophy Department
California State University
Northridge, CA 91330

Philip Gasper
Department of Philosophy
Middlebury College
Middlebury, VT 05753

Clark Glymour
Department of Philosophy
Carnegie-Mellon University
Pittsburgh, PA 15213

Ian Hacking
Department of Philosophy
University of Toronto
Toronto, Ontario M5S 1A1

Carl Hempel
Department of Philosophy
Princeton University
Princeton, NJ 08544

Patricia Kitcher
Department of Philosophy
University of California at San Diego
La Jolla, CA 92093

Philip Kitcher
Department of Philosophy
University of California at San Diego
La Jolla, CA 92093

Thomas Kuhn
Department of Linguistics and
Philosophy
Massachusetts Institute of Technology
Cambridge, MA 02139

Larry Laudan
Department of Philosophy
University of Hawaii at Manoa
Honolulu, HI 96822

Richard Lewontin
Museum of Comparative Zoology
Harvard University
Cambridge, MA 02138

N. David Mermin
Laboratory of Atomic and Solid State
Physics
Cornell University
Ithaca, NY 14853

Richard W. Miller
Sage School of Philosophy
Cornell University
Ithaca, NY 14853

Paul Oppenheim (1886–1977) lived in
Princeton, NJ, and collaborated with
other philosophers on a variety of
projects in the philosophy of science.

Karl Popper
Department of Philosophy, Logic, and
Scientific Method
London School of Economics and
Political Science
Houghton Street
London, England WC2A 2AE

Hilary Putnam
Department of Philosophy
Harvard University
Cambridge, MA 02138

W. V. O. Quine
Department of Philosophy
Harvard University
Cambridge, MA 02138

Peter Railton
Department of Philosophy
University of Michigan
Ann Arbor, MI 48109

Hans Reichenbach (1891–1953)
formerly Professor of Philosophy
University of California at Los Angeles

Moritz Schlick (1882–1936)
formerly Professor of Philosophy
University of Vienna

Abner Shimony
Department of Philosophy
Boston University
Boston, MA 02215

Elliott Sober
Department of Philosophy
University of Wisconsin
Madison, WI 53796

Kim Sterelny
Department of Philosophy
Victoria University
Wellington, New Zealand

J.D. Trout
Department of Philosophy
Loyola University of Chicago
6525 North Sheridan Road
Chicago, IL 60626

John Watkins
Department of Philosophy, Logic, and
Scientific Method
London School of Economics and
Political Science
Houghton Street
London, England WC2A 2AE

Max Weber (1864–1920)
formerly Professor of Economics
University of Heidelberg

Bas van Fraassen
Department of Philosophy
Princeton University
Princeton, NJ 08544

Part I

Section I

Confirmation, Semantics, and the Interpretation of Scientific Theories

Richard Boyd

Logical Empiricism and the Centrality of Foundational Issues

Some research in the philosophy of science addresses foundational questions—general questions about the nature and extent of scientific knowledge, of scientific concepts and categories, and of scientific language. Other studies address themselves to issues in applied philosophy of science: issues about the findings, concepts, and methods of particular sciences. Of course these two sorts of research are closely related: good philosophical method dictates that what one says about, for example, scientific methods or scientific language generally should be consistent with what one says about the methods or the language of particular sciences, and vice versa.

As a matter of fact, the interaction between general foundational considerations on the one hand and applied philosophy of science on the other has been in a way one-sided. Although what philosophers have written about philosophical issues arising in particular sciences has been influenced, often in deep and subtle ways, by their understanding of the history, findings, and methods of those sciences, it remains true that the broad outlines of the philosophical analyses they have offered have been largely determined by their views regarding foundational questions about scientific language and scientific knowledge. Indeed, even in the case of quite general foundational issues about the nature of explanation or reduction, proposed answers have been largely determined by commitments regarding these still more basic issues.

In part this primacy of foundational concerns may be a reflection of a general philosophical predilection for abstraction and generality. What is certain is that it is also a reflection of the influence within the philosophy of science of a particular philosophical tradition—*logical empiricism*—and of its emphasis on just those foundational concerns. Almost all work, foundational or applied, in English-language philosophy of science during the present century has either been produced within the tradition of logical empiricism or has been written in response to it. Indeed it is arguable that philosophy of science as an academic discipline is essentially a creation of logical empiricists and (derivatively) of the philosophical controversies that they sparked. It is thus impossible to understand the literature in this area without an understanding of logical empiricism and of the most prominent philosophical responses to it: scientific realism and social constructivism. It is with these philosophical doctrines and the dispute between them that the chapters in this section are chiefly concerned.

Getting Started: Some Basic Notions

One presupposition of the literature on these matters is so basic and so uncontroversial that it is typically not made explicit. By an *inference* philosophers and logicians mean a set of premises and a conclusion drawn from them. Thus, for example, someone who concluded that a fruit is sweet because it is round and green would have made an inference, as would someone who concluded, from the observations that a bird has sharp talons and a sharp curved beak, that it is flesh-eating. As you can see, some inferences are better than others.

A *deductively valid inference* is one that, in a certain sense, is best possible: an inference such that there is no possible way in which the premises could be true and the conclusion false. For example, the inference whose premises are "The number of balls in the urn is prime" and "The number of balls in the urn is greater than ten" and whose conclusion is "The number of balls in the urn is odd" is deductively valid, whereas the inference with the same premises and the conclusion "The number of balls in the urn is 13" is not deductively valid. Many people are familiar with the notion of deductive validity from their experience with Euclidean geometry: a Euclidean theorem is just a statement that can be derived from Eucledean axioms by a deductively valid inference.

Inductive inferences are the sorts of inferences scientists make when they take particular observations or experimental results to justify the acceptance of general conclusions about the behavior of natural (or social) phenomena. They are thus central to all empirical science. For example, a biologist who has observed, about a large number of birds with sharp talons and sharp curved beaks, that they are flesh-eaters and who, on the basis of premises reflecting those observations, concludes that birds with sharp talons and sharp curved beaks are always (or almost always) flesh-eaters, will have made an inductive inference.

Now here is the basic and uncontroversial presupposition of the literature: *inductive inferences are never deductively valid*. This point, first made explicit by Hume, is easily illustrated by the example just considered: no matter how many sharp-taloned-and-sharp-curved-beaked birds have been examined and found to be flesh-eating, it will remain conceivable, if unlikely, that arbitrarily many unobserved birds of this sort exist, or will come to exist, which are not flesh-eating. Inductive inferences, the sort of inferences upon which empirical science depends, necessarily involve a certain sort of risk of error.[1]

The last point can be made in a slightly different way, which will introduce a related presupposition. It is quite commonly held that, in most instances at least, the observations that tend to confirm a general principle or putative law are those that confirm predictions about observable phenomena that have been *deduced* from the general principle or putative law, together with additional premises (called *auxiliary hypotheses* or *auxiliary statements*) that are independently well confirmed.[2] On this assumption the point that inductive inferences cannot be deductively valid can be put this way: no matter how many successful predictions have been deduced from a generalization or putative law together with suitable auxiliary hypotheses, it remains logically possible that its predictions will be (sometimes or always) false in the future and/or that they have already been false about unexamined cases.

Again on the assumption that theories are tested by testing their deductive observational predictions, one additional concept proves to be important.[3] Two theories, or collections of theories, are said to be *empirically equivalent* just in case exactly the same observational predictions can be deduced from each of them.

Closely related to the concept of a deductively valid inference is another notion central to the way in which issues in the philosophy of science have been formulated: the distinction between *analytic statements* and *synthetic statements*. A statement is said to be analytic if it is true just in virtue of the meanings of its constituent words. A statement is synthetic if neither it nor its denial are analytic. Thus the truth or falsity (the technical term is the *truth-value*) of an analytic statement or a statement that is the denial of an analytic statement is determined solely by the meanings of words, whereas the truth-value of a synthetic statement depends on the way the world is. Analyticity and deductive validity are closely related: an inference with premises $p_1, \ldots, p_n$ and conclusion c is deductively valid if and only if the statement "If p_1 and $\ldots$ and p_n, then c" is analytic. "All bachelors are unmarried" is the standard example of an analytic statement. "All bachelors are happy" and "Some bachelors are not happy" are synthetic.[4]

With these concepts and presuppositions understood, we can turn our attention to the controversies about scientific knowledge, scientific language, and scientific evidence.

Verificationism and the Elimination of 'Metaphysics'

Our understanding of these papers first requires that we understand something of the development of the approach to the philosophy of science called *logical empiricism* or *logical positivism* (for reasons that are obscure, the former term seems to be preferred by those sympathetic to the approach, the latter by its detractors). Logical empiricism arose in the twentieth century as a result of efforts by scientifically inclined philosophers to articulate the insights of traditional empiricism, especially the views of Hume (1739, 1748), using newer developments in mathematical logic.[5]

There are several ways to characterize the logical empiricist project in the philosophy of science. Perhaps the best is to see logical empiricists as addressing the problem of demarcation—the problem of distinguishing between science and nonscience. Logical empiricists were especially concerned to find standards for distinguishing scientific theories from metaphysical theories of the sort philosophers and theologians often discuss. The central component in the logical empiricist solution to this problem was *verificationism*.

Traditional logical empiricist verificationism has two components. One is the *verifiability theory of meaning*, according to which understanding the meaning of a statement or theory consists in understanding the circumstances under which one would be justified in believing it, or in believing its negation. According to this conception, the meaning of a statement or theory is to be identified with the set of procedures by which it can be tested and thus verified or disconfirmed. The second component, which (following Bennett 1971) we can call *knowledge empiricism*, is an especially plausible interpretation of the doctrine that all synthetic knowledge is empirical knowledge: knowledge is grounded in the evidence of the senses. According to knowledge empiricism, evidence for (or against) a synthetic statement is provided solely by observations that confirm the truth (or falsity) of observational predictions deduced from it. Verificationists interpret this to mean, in particular, that rational justification for believing one of two synthetic statements while rejecting another can only be provided by something like a crucial experiment: an observation that disconfirms an observational prediction deduced from one of the statements while not contradicting any observational prediction of the other.[6]

The verifiability theory of meaning has striking consequences when it is interpreted in the light of knowledge empiricism. Suppose that S is a statement that is not analytic and from which no predictions about observable phenomena can be deduced. According to knowledge empiricism, there can be no justification for believing either S or its negation. Thus, according to the verifiability theory of meaning, S is *literally meaningless*. Likewise, suppose that two statements or theories are *empirically equivalent*. No crucial experiment will be possible in which one of these theories is found predictively superior to the other: they are exactly equally reliable as predictors of observable phenomena. According to knowledge empiricism, there cannot be any justification for accepting (or rejecting) one of the statements that is not a justification for accepting (or rejecting) the other. If the verifiability theory of meaning is taken as an additional premise, it follows that two such statements or theories *say the same thing*.

The two components of traditional verificationism, and the two consequences we have just derived, are central components in a philosophical project that defines the fundamental motivation for logical empiricism, and indeed for much of earlier empiricism as well: *the elimination of 'metaphysics'*. By 'metaphysics', which they employed as a term of abuse, logical empiricists understood most of what we ordinarily think of as metaphysics—e.g., doctrines about the fundamental nature of substances (like dualism and materialism), or about theological matters (like theism in its various forms and atheism), or about our relation to external objects (like idealism or realism)—as well as other doctrines similarly vulnerable to a verificationist critique. The idea of such a critique, of course, is that most metaphysical doctrines, as they have been understood by their defenders as well as by their traditional critics, seem neither to be analytic nor to have observational consequences. They are thus, on a traditional verificationist account, *literally meaningless*.

Some object to the verificationist analysis of a traditional metaphysical doctrine because the doctrine in question does indeed yield observational predictions. Thus, for example, someone concerned to defend the meaningfulness of traditional theism might argue that when traditional theism is spelled out in appropriate detail, it does make testable predictions. For instance, when it is fully spelled out, traditional theism holds that God created life in the world, so it predicts that living things exist. This prediction is, of course confirmed by many observations; theism is thus testable and its predictions are, in this regard at least, confirmed.

In response to this sort of objection, logical empiricists appealed to the second of the consequences of verificationism discussed earlier. Consider any suitably spelled-out version of theism that makes testable predictions of the sort in question. It will always be possible to formulate a suitably spelled-out version of, say, atheism that is rigged to make just the same predictions as its theist rival. Since the two metaphysical theories are empirically equivalent, according to the verifiability theory of meaning they say the same thing. Suitably spelled out, both theories are literally meaningful, but their distinctly metaphysical features disappear when the verifiability theory of meaning is applied. This analysis of theism and competing metaphysical doctrines is an example of what logical empiricists called *rational reconstruction*: an application of verificationism that results in the elimination of the metaphysical features of a concept or theory while preserving its empirically testable content. Moritz Schlick's "Positivism and Realism" (reprinted in this section) provides an excellent illustration of the elimination of metaphysics by rational reconstruction.

The analysis of theism illustrates nicely two important features of traditional verificationism. First, the philosophical machinery employed in the empiricist rational reconstruction of theism is extremely general. It depends solely on the possibility of constructing an atheistic but empirically equivalent alternative to any given theological conception. That possibility in turn depends only on the fact that gods are supposed to be *unobservable*. In fact, for any theory that is apparently about unobservable phenomena, there are always infinitely many alternative theories that contradict the first conception of unobservable phenomena but that are empirically equivalent to it. Thus it follows from knowledge empiricism that *no knowledge of unobservable phenomena is possible*, and thus from traditional verificationism that no statements about "unobservables" are even meaningful, unless they are rationally reconstructed to purge them of reference to unobservables.

Logical empiricism is thus an essentially *instrumentalist* position: it holds that the synthetic content of a scientific (or other) theory or doctrine is exhausted by the set of observable predictions deducible from it. It purchases its critique of metaphysics at the cost (if it is a cost) of denying, for example, that in confirming the atomic theory of matter scientists have confirmed a theory about unobservable atomic constituents of matter! Scientific theories are, according to logical empiricists, "merely models" in precisely the sense that, at best, they correctly predict the behavior of observable phenomena; they never succeed in representing knowledge of unobservable determinants of such phenomena.

Second, the rational reconstruction of theism reflects a fact about scientific (and metaphysical) theories that indicates that the project of verificationism cannot be carried out in exactly the way logical empiricists first intended. The traditional verifiability theory of meaning aimed at *individualistic* assessments of meaning: individual theories or doctrines were supposed to be assessed as meaningful or meaningless depending on whether or not they made observational predictions. Likewise, two individual theories or doctrines were supposed to have the same meaning (or *cognitive* content, to use standard logical empiricist terminology) just in case they made the same observational predictions.

In fact, however, as the example of the rational reconstruction of theism illustrates, the observational consequences of a doctrine are determined *holistically*: they depend on how it is spelled out—that is, on which auxiliary hypotheses are taken to be operative together with it. The empirical equivalence of theories or doctrines likewise depends holistically on the auxiliary hypotheses assumed to be operative. Thus the project of the elimination of metaphysics cannot be carried out in exactly the way initially anticipated by the defenders of verificationism.

Some terminology will help in characterizing the way in which the holistic features of the derivation of observational predictions compromises the project of rational reconstruction as it was initially conceived. Logical empiricists thought of the nonlogical terms occurring in scientific theories as belonging to two classes: *observation terms* and *theoretical terms*. Observation terms refer to observable phenomena or their observable properties ("observables" in logical empiricist terminology). Theoretical terms do not refer to observables; they are the terms that, if taken to refer to anything, would have to be taken to refer to unobservable phenomena (or "theoretical entities"). *Observation sentences* are sentences formulated solely in observational terms; *theoretical sentences* contain theoretical terms.

The initial verificationist conception identified the cognitive content of a theory with the set of observational consequences deducible from the theory alone. Had that conception proved viable, then the *theoretical structure* of a scientific theory (the particular theoretical sentences from which its observational consequences are to be deduced) might have been seen as methodologically irrelevant: any two empirically equivalent theories, however great the difference in their theoretical structures, would have the same methodological import. Instead, with respect to one important methodological role—being a source of observational predictions—the import of a theory depends both on its own theoretical structure and on the theoretical structures of the *background theories* available as auxiliary hypotheses.

Scientific methods for employing theories in making observational predictions are thus *theory-dependent* methods: the result of their applications depends on the theoretical structure of the theories in question. It is an important fact, now universally accepted, that many or all of the central methods of science are theory-dependent. This *theory-dependence of method* was initially surprising for philosophers attracted to logical empiricism, and most of the recent innovations within the empiricist tradition have arisen from attempts to accommodate the fact that scientific methods are theory-dependent while continuing to deny that knowledge of unobservable theoretical entities is possible. Likewise, most of the sustained criticism of logical empiricist philosophy of science has arisen from the conviction that the actual theory-dependence of scientific methods cannot be accounted for within a verificationist framework.

The various logical empiricist responses to the phenomenon of theory-dependence of scientific methods are discussed at length in the papers reprinted in this section and in other papers in this anthology, and a broad outline of these developments is provided in subsequent sections of this introductory essay. One response, however, was so nearly universal that it deserves note here. At least by the 1950s the holistic implications of the role of auxiliary hypotheses were so widely recognized that the initial empiricist project of establishing a criterion of meaningfulness for sentences or theories considered in isolation was almost entirely abandoned (see Hempel's "Empiricist Criteria of Cognitive Significance: Problems and Changes," reprinted in this volume). What remained as definitive of logical empiricism was the acceptance of some version of the doctrine of knowledge empiricism with its conclusion that knowledge of unobservables is impossible, together with a corresponding verificationist strategy of antimetaphysical rational reconstruction. It is with this sort of reconstruction that we next concern ourselves.

The Rational Reconstruction of Actual Science

As the example of the atomic theory of matter indicates, scientists and scientific theories apparently refer to unobservables routinely, and it is central to the empiricist project in the philosophy of science to offer verificationist rational reconstructions of apparent reference to unobservables that make sense of the rationality of actual scientific practice. Two proposed reconstructions are especially important in recent philosophy of science, one because its apparent failure led to important developments both within empiricist philosophy of science and within its principal rivals, the other because its apparent success has made it the most durable of empiricist rational reconstructions.

The first empiricist reconstruction, *operationalism*, represents the twentieth-century version of the standard empiricist account of classification and the meanings of classificatory terms first proposed by Locke (1689) as the doctrine of *nominal essences*. Operationalism arose in response to a serious challenge to the verificationist project of antimetaphysical rational reconstruction of science. Modern chemists seem to classify substances precisely in terms of the basic physical properties of their unobservable constituents. Likewise, physicists routinely classify physical conditions in terms that appear to refer to the values of various unobservable magnitudes like electromagnetic or gravitational field strength; geneticists appear to appeal to similarities and differences in unobservable genetic structures; microbiologists distinguish between conditions caused, as they appear to say, by different sorts of unobservable organisms, etc. In almost every science sound methodological practice seems to reflect just the sort of metaphysical concern with the unobservable that empiricists deplore.

In response to this fact, logical empiricists proposed that the theoretical terms that scientists employed in classifying substances, states of affairs, space-time regions, etc., be thought of, on rational reconstruction, as having *stipulative operational definitions* in terms of the laboratory procedures associated in practice with the terms in question. Thus, for example, the term "electrical field strength" is associated in practice with various procedures that physicists would describe as procedures for measuring field strength. On the proposed reconstruction these procedures would instead be thought of as the purely stipulative definition of the notion of electrical field strength. If we call the relevant procedures O, then the proposal is that all statements of the form "The electrical field strength at space-time point p is q" should be rationally reconstructed as asserting the claim *purely about observables* that if O were performed at p the result would be q. This style of analysis was for a while greatly influential and remains so today outside professional philosophical circles. It had many defenders. Bridgman's *The Logic of Modern Physics*, excerpted here, is perhaps the most famous and most influential of its many expositions. Its influence was enhanced not only by the clear style in which it was written but also by Bridgman's reputation as a distinguished physicist and Nobel laureate.

Almost all philosophers of science—including those most sympathetic to the verificationist project—agree that operationalism failed as a reconstruction of sound scientific practice. The reason is simple: scientists in practice, indeed in what seems the methodologically most exemplary practice, routinely modify or revise (they would say correct, extend, or improve) the laboratory procedures for, as they say, measuring or detecting the sorts of theoretical entities or properties reference to which operationalism is supposed to eliminate.

Thus, for example, laboratory procedures for the measurement of temperature are routinely modified either to improve their accuracy or to provide for temperature measurements under circumstances in which no previous procedure was available. According to operationalism, indeed according to any standard empiricist account of language, such changes would have to be counted as changes in the magnitude to which the term "temperature" refers, and the same is true for countless other cases in which the laboratory procedures associated with a theoretical term are improved. In fact good scientific practice does not appear to require that such modifications be treated as reflecting a change in subject matter. Instead, scientists treat the new procedures as improvements or extensions of the old ones and successfully employ the new laboratory procedures in applying theories initially developed in the experimental framework provided by the earlier ones. Scientists behave, that is, exactly as they should if the new laboratory procedures were improved or extended procedures for measuring, detecting, or otherwise assessing a previously studied unobservable feature of the world. Operationalism seems to dictate inappropriate methodology.

Here again we have a case of an initial verificationist analysis failing because of the theory-dependence of scientific methods: measurement and detection procedures associated with theoretical terms are determined not by linguistic convention but instead by theoretical considerations that change with new discoveries and frequently require revision of such procedures. In response to this challenge, logical empiricists offered a variety of alternative antimetaphysical accounts of the semantics of theoretical terms. Hempel's "Empiricist Criteria of Cognitive Significance" and Carnap's "Empiricism, Semantics, and Ontology," both reprinted here, are important examples of such responses.

Although logical empiricists offered a variety of reconstructions of the theory-dependence of the methods for applying theoretical terms, there is one systematic tendency in the development of their thought. The general empiricist strategy in semantic matters is to treat those fundamental principles that regulate the use of linguistic expressions as reflections of linguistic conventions. As theoretical considerations were recognized as being more and more deeply involved in the principles that regulate the use of theoretical terms, the tendency within logical positivism was to treat as matters of linguistic convention increasingly general theoretical considerations.

This tendency reaches a pinnacle of its development in "Empiricism, Semantics, and Ontology," in which Carnap advances an early version of what has come to be called the *law-cluster theory of meaning for theoretical terms*. According to this theory, the most basic laws containing a theoretical term are to be understood as analytic truths and as together constituting the definition of the term. As we shall see, the development of this and other logical empiricist alternatives to operationalism, and of anti-empiricist alternatives to those alternatives, has proven to be a major factor in recent philosophy of science.

The second and more durable logical empiricist reconstruction is the twentieth-century version of the Humean analysis of causal relations.[7] By empiricist standards, talk about causal relations *seems* to be both scientifically necessary and irreducibly metaphysical. Hume's response to this problem was to reconstruct the notion of causality in terms of *constant conjunction*: an event is the cause of a subsequent event if and only if events like the first are always followed by events like the second. As it stands, however, Hume's analysis fails, even by empiricist standards, to specify a determinate relation between events; it requires further specification of the respects of event similarity that are understood to be relevant.

In practice, scientists identify relevant respects of similarity in a theory-dependent way: typically they count observable respects of similarity as relevant if they are identified by currently accepted theories as symptoms of appropriate (and often unobservable) causal mechanisms. The logical empiricists' twentieth-century version of Hume's analysis incorporates a reference to this feature of scientific practice into the rational reconstruction of the notion of causation: one event causes a subsequent event just in case the second event is deductively predictable from the first, given laws of nature and suitable statements of antecedent conditions.[8]

For present purposes, two features of the contemporary Humean analysis of causal relations are important. First, like the law-cluster theory of meaning for theoretical terms, the contemporary Humean analysis of causal relations follows the standard empiricist pattern in coping with a potentially embarrassing theory-dependence of scientific methodology by treating it as a matter of convention. Instead of offering a metaphysical explanation of appeals to theoretical considerations in identifying causal relations, the empiricist offers a conception according to which reference to laws of nature is part of the conventional definition of causal relations, and the theory-dependence of methods is simply a manifestation of scientists' efforts to identify those laws.

Second, the durability of the contemporary Humean analysis illustrates in an indirect way the point that the principal challenge to logical empiricism arises from the theory-dependence of scientific methods. Almost certainly the primary explanation for the durability of the contemporary empiricist version of the Humean analysis of causal statements is that, by incorporating the notion of a law of nature into the very definition of causal relations, it gives the appearance of being able to accommodate, within an empiricist analysis, whatever sort of theory-dependence there might be in scientists' assessments of causal relations. Whether or not this appearance is reality is an issue raised by the critics of logical empiricism, to whose philosophical views we turn after a brief investigation of a variation on the verificationist theme.

Falsificationism

No discussion of twentieth-century philosophy of science is complete without an account of a variant version of verificationism which, although it has had rather little impact on recent philosophy of science, has had a deep influence on the thinking of many philosophically inclined scientists and other thinkers. I refer to the proposed solution to the demarcation problem proposed by Karl Popper and called *falsificationism*. Popper, whose views on this matter were published in German in 1934 but only became available in English translation in 1959, shared with early logical empiricists the conception that it was the testability of scientific theories that distinguished them from unscientific theories. He rejected, however, the verificationist conception that the possibility of confirmation or disconfirmation is the mark of the scientific. Instead, he was led by reflection on the fact that no inductive inferences are deductively valid to the conclusion that, strictly speaking, observations never *confirm* any general theories, but only refute or fail to refute them.

In consequence, Popper proposed a variation on the empiricist solution to the demarcation problem: a theory is potentially a scientific theory if and only if there are possible observations that would falsify (refute) it. The special role of auxiliary hypotheses in theory testing poses a challenge to this account of demarcation just as it does to traditional verificationism; but despite these technical difficulties, it remains deeply influential outside professional philosophical circles, perhaps because of its apparent commitment to an antidogmatic conception of scientific inquiry. The selections from Popper's *The Logic of Scientific Discovery* provide a classic statement of falsificationism; Hilary Putnam's "The 'Corroboration' of Theories" is a spirited critique.

Irreducible Metaphysics: Alternatives to Verificationism

Logical empiricism aims at the elimination of metaphysics—the elimination of reference to unobservables—by verificationist rational reconstruction. Both of the important alternatives in the philosophy of science, *scientific realism* and *social constructivism*, reflect the estimate that the elimination of metaphysics from scientific theories and methods is impossible: the rationality of scientific inquiry cannot be accounted for without acknowledging that successful scientific theories typically embody knowledge of "unobservables."

Of the two alternatives, scientific realism, although less influential outside of professional philosophical circles, is the easier doctrine to state. Scientific realists insist that scientific theories should be interpreted "at face value" rather than philosophically reconstructed. According to realists, when a well-confirmed scientific theory *appears* to describe unobservable "theoretical entities," it is almost always appropriate to think of its "theoretical terms" as *really* referring to real unobservable features of the world, *which exist independently of our theorizing about them*, and of which the theory is probably approximately true. Thus, for example, according to realists the molecular theory of gases says that gases are made up of very small unobservable particles with various properties, the evidence we have for that theory is evidence that such particles exist independently of our theorizing about them, and the descriptions of them embodied in the theory of gases are approximately true.

The component of scientific realism that emphasizes the independence of the reality described by scientific theories from our theorizing is significant because it is with respect to the claimed theory-independence of the reality studied by scientists that realists and social constructivists disagree. Constructivists and realists are equally impressed by the theory-dependence of scientific methods and hold that empiricist reconstructions that aim at a nonmetaphysical conception of the scientific enterprise are inadequate to the facts of scientific practice and the history of science. But the key figures in the constructivist tradition—N. R. Hanson (see Hanson 1958) and Thomas Kuhn (whose work is represented in this volume)—drew a different lesson from theory-dependence of methods. They were struck by, among other things, the *theory-dependence of observation*. The phenomenon is this: observations, as they are reported in actual science, are reported in theoretical language ("the pH was found to be ..."; "the magnetic field strength was found to vary between ... and ..."; "the particles were observed to be deflected at an angle of ... when passing between the charged plates") rather than in terms of observationally characterized features of laboratory equipment, and this feature of scientific observations seems essential to the way in which observational evidence is rationally assessed.

We have already discussed essentially the same phenomenon when we examined the reasons for the failure of operationalism: the way in which theoretical terms function in actual laboratory practice is determined by theoretical considerations. Constructivists drew from this fact—and from facts like it—more than the lesson that operationalism was not viable. Instead they concerned themselves with the methodological situation of scientists who initially hold fundamentally different theories and who might seek to resolve the issue between them by reference to observations. Pretty plainly, if their theoretical disagreements are sufficiently great, then they might fail to agree about the appropriate descriptions of the results of some observations. They would not (or at any rate not always) be able to appeal to observation as a kind of *neutral court* in which their dispute could be adjudicated.

Kuhn envisioned the possibility of situations in which two theoretical conceptions are so different that, because of the irremediable theory-dependence of observation and other methodological features of science, there is no rational method acceptable to defenders of each conception that could serve to ground the resolution of the dispute between them. In such situations, the two traditions are said to be *incommensurable*. Indeed Kuhn held not merely that this situation is logically possible, but that it has been actual in several cases in the history of modern science during periods of *scientific revolution*—for example, during the transition between Ptolemaic and Copernican astronomy and during the transition between Newtonian mechanics and special relativity. From the fact of the theory-dependence of scientific methods and the alleged phenomenon of incommensurability (it is a matter of controversy whether or not there have been any actual cases of incommensurability), Kuhn and other constructivists have drawn some striking philosophical conclusions.

First, the pattern of theory-dependence of methods, especially the theory-dependence of observation and the incommensurability of successive theoretical conceptions within the actual history of science, precludes any account of science according to which scientists achieve objective knowledge about a single theory-independent world. Realism cannot be defended. Second, the depth of the theory-dependence of methods similarly precludes any empiricist rational reconstruction: scientists must be understood as engaged in a metaphysical project whose very rules are irretrievably determined by theoretical conceptions regarding largely unobservable phenomena.

These two conclusions might seem incompatible. For the constructivist, however, there seems to be a viable philosophical conception that "splits the difference" between realism and empiricism. According to this conception, the fundamental theoretical principles that scientists accept, and the fundamental methodological principles that those theoretical principles largely determine, are imposed on the world by a sort of convention or social construction.[9] But knowledge of these principles is not to be understood as *merely* or *trivially* conventional; instead scientific theories really do embody knowledge of unobservable causal mechanisms, subatomic particles, etc. Socially constructed causal and metaphysical phenomena are, according to the constructivist, *real*: they are as real as anything scientists can study ever gets. The impression that there is some sort of socially unconstructed reality that is somehow deeper than the socially constructed variety rests, the constructivist maintains, on a failure to appreciate the theory-dependence of all of our methods. The only sort of reality any of our methods are good for studying is a theory-dependent reality.

As Kuhn spells out this view, modern scientific work comes in two sorts of historical episodes. There are long periods of *normal science* during which the prevailing theoretical conception and its associated set of methodological practices—the *paradigm*—is *articulated*. The fundamental features of the paradigm are matters of social convention; articulation of a paradigm consists of using experimental and observational techniques in spelling out those details (like the values of various physical parameters) that are left unspecified in the initial formulation of the paradigm. Normal science does not result in deep changes in theoretical conception; indeed it cannot, since deep features of the prevailing theoretical conception are imposed on the world in paradigm-governed research.

Periods of normal science are punctuated by brief periods of *revolutionary science*, which arise when researchers have recognized a significant body of experimental or observational *anomalies*: observations that resist explanation or assimilation within the developing paradigm. When sufficiently many anomalies have emerged, some researchers propose radically new theoretical conceptions to accommodate them. These radical proposals are *methodologically incommensurable* from each other and from the paradigm they challenge, in the sense described earlier. Eventually one of them may prove successful enough to recruit enough new adherents (typically from among younger scientists) to emerge as the basis of a new paradigm, and a new period of normal science then ensues.

The transition between the old paradigm and its replacement is not, according to Kuhn, determined by rational scientific methods: because the old paradigm and its new rivals are incommensurable, there are no rational scientific methods to adjudicate between them. Instead, what happens in the transition is the establishment of a new world of scientific study, socially constructed by the adoption of the new paradigm.

We have already seen a similarity between constructivism and later logical empiricism in their shared view that fundamental laws are matters of convention. In fact the similarity runs a bit deeper. Kuhn, like Carnap, takes the fundamental laws containing a theoretical term to constitute its conventional definition. In consequence, he has an additional argument for the incommensurability of paradigms separated by a period of scientific revolution. What characterizes scientific revolutions is that fundamental laws are revised; but revisions of those laws amount to changes in the definitions of the fundamental theoretical terms in science. Scientists before and after a scientific revolution are not talking about the same theoretical entities even when they use the same terms. Thus they are really talking past each other in their disputes and no rational method can effect a choice between their competing conceptions. This phenomenon is called *semantic incommensurability*. Semantic incommensurability implies methodological incommensurability.

We have come to understand social constructivism largely by understanding the sorts of arguments that have led philosophers to adopt it. Similarly, we understood logical empiricism largely by exploring the implications of the verificationist argumentative strategy that underwrites it. With respect to realism, however, we have a definition of its characteristic doctrines, but no account yet of the arguments for it. Now realism is, in a certain sense, the commonsense philosophical position about scientific theorizing, and it is sometimes very hard to formulate explicitly one's reasons for accepting commonsense positions. In fact, it was some time before philosophers of science sympathetic to realism were able to articulate arguments in its defense beyond the important observation that lots of scientific theories and practices seemed to be about unobservables and many empiricist rational reconstructions of them had proven inadequate. The formulation of detailed arguments for scientific realism—and the articulation of deep empiricist and constructivist responses to them—has been one of the main driving forces in very recent philosophy of science. It is to those arguments and the responses to them that we now turn our attention.

Metaphysics and the Success of Science: Arguments for Scientific Realism

Scientists appear to be studying unobservables as well as observables, and it is not easy to give a rational reconstruction of their practice to eliminate their apparent concern for metaphysics. That is some argument for realism (or, perhaps, for constructivism) since realists (and constructivists) can explain the difficulties in rational reconstruction by explaining why such reconstructions are impossible. But how good is this argument? How does it address the basic epistemological concerns that motivate logical empiricism?

As realists have examined these questions, a central theme has emerged that represents an attempt to articulate in philosophically appropriate detail ways in which the theory-dependence of scientific practices might support realism. According to this central theme, the case for scientific realism is best put by arguing that the methods of science are so theory-dependent that it is impossible to explain *scientifically* the *instrumental* success of scientific methods except on the hypothesis that in mature sciences the background theories that determine methods are approximately true of unobservable (as well as of observable) entities, and that the operation of the methods they determine tends to produce subsequent improvements in such approximations to the truth. Scientific realism is thus to be defended as a scientific hypothesis—an empirical claim about the way in which scientific methods work in the world. This argument for scientific realism is represented here in Putnam's "Explanation and Reference" and in the articles by Boyd.[10]

The view that philosophy is largely continuous with the natural sciences—*philosophical naturalism*—is relevant to the arguments for and against realism in another way. One way to frame the argument for realism is in terms of the notion of *projectibility*.[11] Consider the situation of a scientist trying to identify a general law of nature. She has access to a body of observations of phenomena of some sort and is considering a proposed generalization about such phenomena. Suppose that the observations in question all confirm predictions from the generalization in question. Does that mean that they provide (at least some) confirmatory evidence for the generalization? It is natural to suppose that the answer is "yes," but Goodman made the point that in any such case there will be *infinitely many* generalizations incompatible with the proposal under consideration that would have also made just the same predictions about all observed cases. If the observations provide equally good evidence for each of these generalizations, then they provide no significant evidence for any of them. If they do not, then we need to know what distinguishes the generalizations that are supported by the observations from those that are not. (Note that the answer is *not* to be framed in terms of "fit" with existing data; each of the generalizations fits equally well.)

Goodman introduced the term "projectibility" for the property that distinguishes the generalizations that are to some extent confirmed by their predictive success from those that are not. Almost all of the theory-dependent methodological considerations considered by scientific realists and their critics can be seen as judgments of projectibility, or as closely related judgments. The realist's claim, then, is that the success of projectibility judgments is to be explained by the hypothesis that the background theories upon which they depend are approximately true of unobservable (as well as observable) entities. Projectibility judgments are matters of empirical science.

Now, projectibility judgments are pretty fundamental epistemological judgments, so realism defended in this way seems committed to the view that at least parts of epistemology are continuous with the empirical sciences. This view—*the naturalistic conception of epistemology*—is defended in Quine's famous paper "Natural Kinds," reprinted in this section. Quine makes explicit an important connection between the theory of projectibility and the theory of the definitions of scientific terms: If projectibility judgments, which are matters of classification, are theory-dependent empirical matters, then so are the fundamental principles of classification that are reflected in the definitions of the terms scientists use. The correct definitions of a scientific term is an a posteriori theoretical matter, not a matter of linguistic convention or stipulation. Scientifically respectable kinds (magnitudes, relations, etc.) are defined by reference to the (sometimes unobservable) causal structure of the world.

So, scientific realism (defended in the standard way) implies a *naturalistic epistemology*, which in turn implies a rejection of nominalism about kind definitions and a *naturalistic conception of the definitions of kind terms*. The realist must hold that the definitions of fundamental terms in science are theoretical discoveries, revisable in the light of empirical findings!

But, of course, we knew that already. Recall that one of the central arguments against realism (but this time for constructivism instead of empiricism) is that changes in fundamental theory of the sort that occur during scientific revolutions involve changes in definition of theoretical terms *and thus changes in subject matter*. The realist cannot, given the historical evidence, disagree that there are historical developments that involve changes in the definitions that scientists offer for theoretical terms. Unless the constructivist conclusion that there is a corresponding change in subject matter is to be accepted, the realist must maintain that our definitions of scientific terms are properly revisable in the light of new data or new theoretical developments.

But how can a term—scientific or otherwise—continue to refer to the same phenomenon, if the definition people actually use changes? Here is why there is a puzzle. On the dominant empiricist conception of language, the nominal definition of a kind term does two quite different things: (1) it determines, by convention, the boundaries of the kind to which the term refers, and (2) by being associated with the term by convention, it brings it about that the term refers to the kind to which it does refer. If the term "human" has the conventional definition "featherless biped," then the boundaries of the class of humans is defined by the criteria of being featherless and bipedal, *and* the word "human" comes to refer to that class because the conceptions of featherlessness and bipedality are conventionally associated with it.

Suppose now that someone proposes, as a scientific realist certainly might, that the definition of the kind human being, and thus of the term "human," is really given by certain historical continuities in the recent evolution of a particular hominid lineage. That proposal would say what the boundaries of the kind are. But what could then be said about how the term "human" comes to refer to the kind thereby defined? The answer can no longer be that it is the employment of the definition in practice that makes the connection, because most users of the term have never heard of the real definition, and until a rather short time ago no one had heard of it. How could, for example, pre-Darwinian uses of the term "human" have referred to a kind defined in terms of a theory that hadn't been invented yet?

The standard realist answer—*the causal or naturalistic theory of reference*—was initially proposed in its current form by Kripke (1971, 1972) and Putnam (1970, and "Explanation and Reference," reprinted here) and has subsequently been considerably refined and developed (see, for example, Field 1973, Boyd 1979, Devitt 1981). According to this view, the connection between a natural kind term (or other theoretical term) and the class (relation, magnitude, etc.) to which it refers is established by causal relations of the right sort between actual uses of the term and instantiations of the kind (relation, etc.) in question. The articulation and development of this conception of reference represents the principal basis for the realist's response to social constructivism. Most realists now hold that methodological incommensurability is not a phenomenon sufficiently common in the relevant parts of the history of science to undermine the realistic picture of the growth of theoretical knowledge. They are able to maintain this doctrine only because a naturalistic conception of reference permits them to deny the semantic incommensurability of prerevolutionary and postrevolutionary theories. The causal theory of reference is developed and applied against constructivism in this way in Putnam's "Explanation and Reference."

Naturalistic and realist accounts of definition, of reference, and of knowledge have indisputably represented important contributions not only to philosophy of science but also to metaphysics, epistemology, and the philosophy of language. It would be a mistake, however, to conclude that such sophisticated developments are limited to the work of scientific realists and their allies. There are a number of recent antirealist philosophical proposals that pose serious challenges to realism and raise significant and deep philosophical issues. To understand these proposals and the responses to them, it is necessary to understand what is probably the most important piece of philosophical analysis of the first half of this century, Tarski's definition of truth.

Tarski on Truth

In 1935, Alfred Tarski published a paper that was a major contribution to metaphysics and the philosophy of language, and at the same time was certainly one of the two most important developments in mathematical logic in the first half of this century (the other is Gödel's incompleteness theorem [Gödel 1931]). Tarski set out to provide a mathematical analysis of the notion of truth. He proposed a definition of truth for certain formalized languages (those of the *first-order predicate calculus*) that are simpler in structure than natural languages but resemble them in important respects. It is very widely accepted that his definition provides the basis for an understanding of truth in natural as well as formal languages. (See the appendix for technical details of Tarski's position.)

The conception of truth that formed the basis for Tarski's analysis is usually called the *correspondence theory of truth*. According to this conception, what makes a sentence true or false is whether or not it *corresponds to the facts*, or *corresponds with reality*. Now, for many philosophers and logicians—not all of them verificationists or otherwise critics of metaphysics generally—the notion of correspondence with reality has seemed to be an example of dubious metaphysical speculation. What Tarski did was to break this conception of truth down into more basic components, define truth in terms of them, and suggest less speculative ways of understanding the resulting definition.

Let us (following Field 1972) call the relation that a predicate symbol in a formal language bears to its extension (i.e., the set of objects to which the predicate applies) and that an individual constant (a term denoting an individual) bears to its denotation, "primitive denotation." What Tarski showed is that truth for sentences in first-order languages is unproblematically definable in terms of primitive denotation. Recall that for many philosophers the notion of truth, especially the notion of truth as correspondence with reality, seemed suspect. What we may call the *correspondence interpretation of Tarski* corrects this impression: for those portions of natural languages for which languages of first-order quantification theory provide an adequate model (most philosophers of science believe that this includes all or most of scientific language), the notion of correspondence truth is no more mysterious than the notion of primitive denotation from which truth can be defined. Thus for any part of a natural language for which primitive denotation is unproblematical, correspondence truth is unproblematical as well.

The correspondence interpretation of Tarski's theory underwrites the naturalistic conceptions of reference and of natural definitions advanced by many scientific realists: such theories are intended to provide an appropriate account of primitive denotation from which truth for theoretical claims (among others) is definable.[12] The correspondence interpretation is, of course, available to empiricists as well. For logical empiricists this conception would entail that if they could give a nonmetaphysical account of primitive denotation for observational terms (as they certainly thought they could), then they could appeal to the notion of truth as correspondence to reality in the case of observation sentences. Correspondence truth for theoretical sentences would, presumably, remain objectionably metaphysical. But for a variety of reasons, empiricists and other nonrealist philosophers rarely accepted the correspondence interpretation of Tarski in the form adopted by realists. Instead, they typically defended another interpretation of Tarski.

Tarski's theory defines truth for sentences of a formal language, *L*, in terms of a specification of primitive denotation for the terms of that language. We can think of that specification as being provided by sentences in some language, *L**, adequate to describe the structure of *L* (a *metalanguage* for *L*). For sufficiently powerful metalanguages of this sort, the definition of truth for *L* can itself be formalized in *L**. Tarski concerned himself with the properties such a formal definition of truth should have, in the special case in which all of the sentences in *L* can be translated into *L**, and he proposed the following constraint on theories of truth for formalized languages, which he called "Convention T":

> If *L* is a formal language and *L** is a metalanguage for *L* within which a definition of truth for *L* is proposed, then for every sentence *s* of *L*, if "*s*" is the name of *s* in *L** and *True* is the formula in *L** which defines truth in *L*, and *t* is the translation of *s* into *L**, the following sentence of *L** must be deducible from the truth definition for *L*: *True* ("*s*") if and only if *t*.

We may illustrate the import of Convention T by ignoring for a moment the fact that natural languages are more complex and messy than formal languages and seeing what Convention T dictates about, say, a theory of truth for German formulated in English. What it requires is that all sentences of the following form be deducible from the theory (formulated in English) of the predicate "... is true in German":

"Schnee ist weiss" is true in German if and only if snow is white.

Similarly, consider the special case in which the *object* language (the language for which a truth definition is proposed) is a sublanguage of the relevant metalanguage. For example, consider the case in which we construct a metalanguage English* for English by adding the predicate "... is true in English" to the resources of ordinary English, together with whatever technical notions we need for the definition in English* of truth for sentences in English. Let us imagine (as before) that the resources English* uses to name words and sentences in English is to put quotation marks around them. Then what Convention T requires of the definition in English* of truth in English is that such sentences as the following sentence of English* should be deducible from the truth definition:

"Snow is white" is true in English if and only if snow is white.

Not surprisingly, Tarski's own definition of truth satisfies Convention T. Interestingly, however, Tarski's articulation of Convention T led many philosophers to reject the correspondence conception of truth. In the first place, alternative (noncorrespondence) theories of truth can easily be formulated so as to satisfy Convention T, the condition Tarski set as a criterion for an acceptable theory of truth. For example, either the coherence conception of truth (according to which a sentence is true just in case it appropriately "coheres" with some antecedently specified body of sentences) or various versions of the pragmatic conception (according to which sentences are true just in case they satisfy some specified set of pragmatic criteria) can be formulated so as to satisfy Convention T.

Second, Tarski's own definition of truth—which on its face appears to reflect a correspondence conception of truth—can be understood as undermining that very conception. Here is why: The definition proposed by Tarski defines truth in terms of primitive denotation—in terms, that is, of what looks like the most basic *correspondence* between features of language and the world. But it is a consequence of that definition that the truth of the sentence "Snow is white" comes to nothing more than snow being white. Insofar as we can offer a conception of the meaning of the latter claim in terms that do not appear to invoke "correspondence with reality," as coherence theorists and pragmatists, for example, think they can, then Tarski's own theory says that the meaning of '"Snow is white" is true' has also been captured without recourse to a conception of correspondence with reality. To many philosophers used to the notion that objectionable metaphysical commitments might be eliminated by rational reconstruction, this result seemed an especially nice example of such reconstruction.

Tarski started, it might be argued, with an informal conception of truth that is as metaphysical as any correspondence theorist could want, but the very logic of working out that conception leads to a theory satisfying Convention T in which the notion of correspondence is inessential. Even without application of distinctively verificationist analytical techniques, it seemed, the notion of correspondence had been eliminated from the notion of truth. For philosophers who accepted this last interpretation of Tarski, even those basic semantic notions (like reference and extension) that *seemed* to reflect a correspondence conception were available to those who rejected the correspondence theory of truth *just as Tarski had shown.*

The view that when the correspondence conception of truth is elaborated it rationally reconstructs itself into a theory for which a conception of correspondence with reality is *optional* had a profound effect on empiricist and later constructivist philosophers of science. They typically took themselves to be able to employ the notion of truth, and the subsidiary notions of reference and of predicate expressions having determinate extensions, without thereby making any concessions to realism *even when the sentences and terms to which they applied those notions were theoretical rather than observational!* From the perspective that thus emerged from Tarski's work, a new option became available for antirealist philosophy of science: the antirealist might accept, for example, that we know that there are electrons, that electrons are unobservable entities to which the term "electron" refers, and that electrons are not merely social constructions, while denying that the truth claims she thus accepts about them should be understood with respect to a realist correspondence conception of truth.[13]

Another class of antirealist options arises from a different feature of Tarski's definition of truth. It is a feature of that definition that it does not give rise in any natural way to a *general* characterization of approximate truth or of what it is for one claim to be more nearly true than another. It follows that realists who accept the correspondence interpretation of Tarski's theory of truth still lack a general realist theory of approximate truth. Since realism entails a picture of the growth of approximate knowledge in science, the absence of a general realist theory of approximate truth has led some philosophers to deny about realism, or at least about traditional versions of realism, that they rest on a non-question-begging conception of approximation.

The first of these antirealist options has been developed by a number of philosophers influenced by the most recent work of Hilary Putnam (1981, 1983). In his recent work Putnam defends what he calls (borrowing a term from Carnap's "Empiricism, Semantics, and Ontology") *internal realism*, but rejects *external realism*. Internal realism accepts the realist account of theory-dependent scientific methods and accepts a causal or naturalistic conception of the semantics of scientific terms, but is grounded in a conception of truth not as correspondence with reality but as the ideal limit of scientific inquiry. External realism, by contrast, treats truth claims as correspondence claims. One important thread in Fine's "The Natural Ontological Attitude" (reprinted here) is a version of this same critique of standard or external realism.

The second line of criticism is reflected in several papers reprinted in this volume. It represents part of the theme of Fine's paper and is a central point in Laudan's "A Confutation of Convergent Realism," in which it is maintained that the historical record provides numerous cases in which (contrary to the expectations of realists) successful science is grounded in theoretical conceptions that are in no interesting sense approximately true.

A quite different criticism of traditional scientific realism rests on concerns about approximate truth. Nancy Cartwright has argued in a number of papers that although realists are right that we can and do know that there are unobservable entities, they err in believing that scientific theories reveal truths or approximate truths about them.[14] The "entity realism" for which she argues is also a theme in the work of Hacking, whose "Experimentation and Scientific Realism" (reprinted here) reflects a tradition of realist analysis in the philosophy of science in which the emphasis is on detection and manipulation of "theoretical entities" rather than on theoretical knowledge.

A related criticism of scientific realism is reflected in the recent work of Bas van Fraassen (including "To Save the Phenomena," reprinted here). According to van Fraassen, realists are correct in their emphasis on the ways in which theoretical considerations guide scientific practice, but they are mistaken in holding that the acceptance of a scientific theory—even in its capacity as a guide to research—rationally requires that one accepts its theoretical claims as true (or approximately true) rather than as pragmatically useful. One way to think of claims like those of van Fraassen is that they reflect the idea that, in addition to embodying the obvious sort of knowledge about the behavior of observable things, scientific theories should be understood to embody methodologically relevant knowledge that is reflected in their theoretical structure, just as realists maintain. This additional knowledge should not, however, be understood as knowledge of unobservables; rather it should be seen as knowledge about success-making features of scientific practice, where the relevant notions of success and practice are formulated in observational terms.

Each of these lines of criticism has met with realist rebuttals. In a reply to Laudan, for example, Hardin and Rosenberg (1982) have indicated the direction in which a suitable realist conception of approximation might be developed. With respect to the other criticisms, the argumentative situation is quite complex, but one thing seems clear: a significant part of the appeal of such criticisms lies in the continuing appeal of (extremely sophisticated versions of) the empiricist critique of metaphysics. A defense of realism against such criticisms would require the articulation of a more distinctly realist epistemology—in particular, a better account of what is supposed to be wrong with the evidential indistinguishability thesis. According to this thesis, two empirically equivalent theories must always be equally well supported or refuted by any possible body of observational data; it is just this thesis that underwrites the empiricist claim that knowledge of unobservables is impossible.

As we have already noted, moves toward the articulation of a distinctly realist epistemology have typically embodied the insistence that epistemology itself is continuous with the natural sciences and that the appropriate standards for the assessment of scientific research are determined by a posteriori theoretical considerations. Boyd's "On the Current Status of Scientific Realism" extends this sort of naturalism to a critique of the evidential indistinguishability thesis, arguing that the evidence for or against a theory is provided not only by observational data but also by considerations of theoretical plausibility that reflect inductive inferences from previously established theoretical knowledge. If this is right, then considerations of theoretical plausibility are evidential. It is a consequence of this conception that scientific realism itself is a scientific hypothesis confirmed, if it is confirmed, by its capacity to explain certain features of the methods of science, especially their reliability in generating empirical knowledge.

Against the idea that the epistemology of science should itself be grounded in science—and especially against the acceptance of realism as a scientific hypothesis—Fine argues that such a conception of the issue of scientific realism begs the question in favor of realism and rests on an inappropriate conception of the nature of foundational studies in science (see Boyd for a reply). What seems to emerge from these disputes, which connect issues in the philosophy of science to broader issues in epistemology and metaphysics, is that in general foundational issues in philosophy of science must be understood in the broader context of related issues in the rest of philosophy. In the final paper in this section, Evelyn Fox Keller explores one way in which wider concerns relate to the philosophy of science in a discussion of recent feminist criticisms of science.[15]

Notes

1. For a useful introductory discussion, see Hempel 1966, chapter 2.
2. See Hempel 1966, chapter 3.
3. The assumption, incidentally, can't be *exactly* right. For one thing, purely stochastic laws never predict any particular set of outcomes with certainty, so one must acknowledge some sort of nondeductive relation between stochastic theories and statements reporting observations that confirm them; see Hempel 1965 on "inductive statistical explanations." For another, some theories (e.g., Darwin's theory

of descent with modification) don't seem to predict, even stochastically, the observations that confirm them; see Harman 1965. Still, it's an almost universal presupposition of the literature that something like the account mentioned is true about many sciences. For a dissenting view see Boyd, "Observations, Explanatory Power, and Simplicity," in part I, section 2.

4. The terminology "analytic" and "synthetic" is borrowed from Kant, but the exposition offered here reflects the by now standard logical empiricist reconstruction of the original Kantian notions. Almost nothing about the analytic-synthetic distinction is uncontroversial. Quine (1951), for example, argues that there are no analytic statements.

5. For a discussion of traditional empiricism, see Bennett 1971. The introduction to Ayer 1959 provides a short historical account of logical positivism.

6. Despite its naturalness, this is not the only possible interpretation of the doctrine that all synthetic knowledge is empirical knowledge; for alternatives to a knowledge empiricist interpretation see Harman 1965; Kitcher, "Explanatory Unification" (this volume, part I, section 2); Boyd "On the Current Status of Scientific Realism" (this volume, part I, section 1), and "Observations, Simplicity, and Explanatory Power" (this volume, part I, section 2).

7. The Humean analysis is discussed further in the introduction to part I, section 2.

8. We ignore here complications introduced by the case in which the relevant laws are nondeterministic. See part 2 for discussion of the model of explanation associated with the Humean account of causation.

9. A similar view had earlier been suggested by those logical empiricists who defended a law-cluster conception of the meanings of theoretical terms.

10. Putnam no longer accepts scientific realism in the sense defined here. For his more recent views see the articles in Putnam 1983.

11. The term was introduced by Goodman (1954), who first formulated the problem of projectibility in explicit terms.

12. See Field 1972 for a very nice discussion of this point.

13. It should be mentioned, however, that some realists have argued that realism can be defended without accepting a correspondence theory of truth. See Devitt 1984 for an elaboration of this view and Gasper 1986 for some criticisms.

14. Collected in Cartwright 1983. Cartwright's "The Reality of Causes in a World of Instrumental Laws" is reprinted in part I, section 2 of this volume.

15. In any anthology practical limitations of length require that some interesting themes and topics be omitted. Regarding the foundational issues upon which the present section focuses, there is one important approach that is neither advanced nor criticized in the papers reprinted: Bayesianism. Bayesianism represents a sophisticated and elaborate attempt to characterize rational inferences in science in terms of canons of probabilistic inference. Its mathematical foundations rest on a theorem (Bayes's theorem) which under suitable conditions assigns a probability, called its "degree of confirmation," to a theory B given evidence A ($P(B \backslash A)$) as a function of the "prior probability" of B($P(B)$), and the probability of the evidence A given a theory T($P(A \backslash T)$), for each of the alternative theoretical possibilities, including B. The theorem says:

$$P(B \backslash A) = \frac{P(A \backslash B)P(B)}{P(A \backslash B) + P(A \backslash B_1) + \ldots . P(A \backslash B_n)}$$

where B, B_1, ..., B_n are mutually exclusive and exhaust all possibilities. The theorem provides a method for starting with an initial assignment of prior probabilities to the members of a mutually exclusive and exhaustive set of possibilities and then obtaining values for their respective degrees of confirmation as new evidence is forthcoming.

Several features of Bayes's theorem help to explain its importance in the philosophy of science. In the first place, it seems to give formal expression to several important truisms about confirmation: (i) the initial plausibility of a theory determines the extent to which we take new evidence to support it; (ii) evidence tends to support a theory to the extent to which the theory would lead us to expect the evidence to obtain; (iii) conversely, evidence supports a theory to the extent that it is unexpected from the perspective of rival theories. The initial assignments of prior probabilities to hypotheses can be thought of as indications of judgments of their respective degrees of projectibility.

Two other features of Bayesianism make it especially important in the tradition of logical empiricism and its variants. In the first place, there has been a long Bayesian tradition of treating prior probabilities as subjective, and not as reflections of comparisons of any objective properties of the various alternative hypotheses. Since the projectibility judgments that prior probabilities reflect are among the theory-dependent aspects of scientific methods which pose prima facie difficulties for empiricism, the Bayesean proposal to treat them as merely subjective has proven attractive to many empiricists.

Its attractiveness is enhanced by another feature of Bayes's theorem. Imagine a situation in which scientists must choose between a set of independent and mutually exclusive theories. They begin with an assignment to each alternative of a prior probability that reflects, let us say, a theory-dependent projectibility judgment, and they then proceed to collect data relevant to the choice between the alternative theories, applying Bayes's theorem to recalculate degrees of confirmation as new data come in. One possibility is that during the conduct of their investigation independent theoretical developments in the relevant field(s) will lead them to revise their initial assignments of prior probabilities and employ the new values in their application of Bayes's theorem. They might, for instance, decide on the basis of new insights that they had erred in assigning a high probability to one of the alternative theories and base their calculations of degrees of confirmation on a lower assignment of a prior probability to that alternative.

Despite the plausibility of such a development, several philosophers of science have thought it a reasonable idealization to assume that in particular episodes of theory testing, initial assignments of prior probabilities remain fixed, so that values of the degrees of confirmation of various alternatives are just those given by applying Bayes's theorem to an ever-increasing body of data, updating one's calculations of degrees of confirmation as new data come in. On such an assumption it is possible to prove that eventually the work done by the data in fixing degrees of confirmation will almost completely outstrip the work done by the assignments of prior probabilities. That is, it is possible to show, on very reasonable assumptions, that for any two different assignments of prior probabilities to the various alternative theories, the degrees of confirmation that will be assigned to those theories on the basis of those assignments will converge as the body of available data becomes sufficiently large. The import of this result for the defense of empiricism in the philosophy of science is clear: Not only are theory-dependent judgments of projectibility to be interpreted as purely subjective, they don't matter in the long run anyway.

Despite the simplicity of the Bayesian theory of confirmation in its basic outline, it has given rise to an extensive literature both articulating and defending Bayesianism and rebutting it. For introductory expositions of Bayes's theorem, see Kyburg 1970, Salmon 1967, and Skyrms 1986. For sophisticated recent defenses of Bayesianism, see Horwich 1982 and Jeffrey 1983. For criticisms of Bayesianism, see Glymour 1980, Miller 1987, and Pollock 1986. Earman 1983 is a useful collection of articles on both sides of the issue.

References

Ayer, A. J., ed., 1959, *Logical Positivism*, Free Press, New York.

Bennett, J., 1971, *Locke, Berkeley, Hume*, Oxford University Press, New York.

Boyd, R., 1979, "Metaphor and Theory Change," in A. Ortony, ed., *Metaphor and Thought*, Cambridge University Press, New York.

Cartwright, N., 1983, *How the Laws of Physics Lie*, Oxford University Press, New York.

Devitt, M., 1981, *Designation*, Columbia University Press, New York.

Devitt, M., 1984, *Realism and Truth*, Princeton University Press, Princeton, NJ.

Earman, J., 1983, ed., *Testing Scientific Theories*, University of Minnesota Press, Minneapolis.

Field, H., 1972, "Tarski's Theory of Truth," *Journal of Philosophy* 69: 347–375.

Field, H., 1973, "Theory Change and the Indeterminacy of Reference," *Journal of Philosophy* 70: 462–481.

Gasper, P., 1986, Review of Devitt 1984, *Philosophical Review* 95: 446–451.

Glymour, C., 1980, *Theory and Evidence*, Princeton University Press, Princeton, NJ.

Gödel, K., 1931, "Über formal unentscheidbare Sätze der *Principia Mathematica* und verwandter Systeme, I," *Monatshefte für Mathematik und Physik* 38: 173–198.

Goodman, N., 1954, *Fact, Fiction and Forecast*, Bobbs-Merrill, Indianapolis.

Hanson, N. R., 1958, *Patterns of Discovery*, Cambridge University Press, New York.

Harman, G., 1965, "Inference to the Best Explanation," *Philosophical Review* 74: 88–95.

Hardin, C., and Rosenberg, A., 1982, "In Defense of Convergent Realism," *Philosophy of Science* 49: 604–615.

Hempel, C., 1965, "Aspects of Scientific Explanation," in *Aspects of Scientific Explanation*, Free Press, New York.

Hempel, C., 1966, *Philosophy of Natural Science*, Prentice-Hall, Englewood Cliffs, NJ.

Horwich, P., 1982, *Probability and Evidence*, Cambridge University Press, New York.

Hume, D., 1739, *A Treatise of Human Nature*.

Hume, D., 1748, *An Enquiry Concerning Human Understanding*.

Jeffrey, R., 1983, *The Logic of Decision*, 2nd ed., University of Chicago Press, Chicago.

Kripke, S., 1971, "Identity and Necessity," in M. Munitz, ed., *Identity and Individuation*, New York University Press, New York.

Kripke, S., 1972, "Naming and Necessity," in D. Davidson and G. Harman, eds., *Semantics of Natural Language*, Reidel, Dordrecht.

Kyburg, H., 1970, *Probability and Inductive Logic*, Macmillan, New York.

Locke, J., 1689/1975, *An Essay Concerning Human Understanding*, Oxford Univeristy Press, Oxford, England.

Miller, R., 1987, *Fact and Method*, Princeton University Press, Princeton, NJ.

Pollock, J., 1986, *Contemporary Theories of Knowledge*, Rowman and Littlefield, Totowa, NJ.

Popper, K., 1934/1959, *The Logic of Scientific Discovery*, Harper & Row, New York.

Putnam, H., 1970, "Is Semantics Possible?" in H. Keifer and M. Munitz, eds., *Language, Belief, and Metaphysics*, SUNY Press, Albany, NY.

Putnam, H., 1981, *Reason, Truth and History*, Cambridge University Press, New York.

Putnam, H., 1983, *Realism and Reason*, Cambridge University Press, New York.

Quine, W. V., 1951, "Two Dogmas of Empiricism," *Philosophical Review* 60: 20–43.

Salmon, W. 1967, *The Foundations of Scientific Inference*, University of Pittsburgh Press, Pittsburgh.

Skyrms, B., 1986, *Choice and Chance*, 3rd ed., Wadsworth, Belmont, CA.

Tarski, A., 1935, "Der Wahrheitsbegriff in den formalisierten Sprachen," *Studia Philosophica* I: 261–405.

Appendix: Tarski on Truth

In 1935, Alfred Tarski published a paper (Tarski 1935) that was a major contribution to metaphysics and the philosophy of language and at the same time was certainly one of the two most important developments in mathematical logic in the first half of this century (the other is Gödel's incompleteness theorem [Gödel 1931]). Tarski set out to provide a mathematical analysis of the notion of truth. He proposed a definition of truth for certain formalized languages (those of the *first-order predicate calculus*) that are simpler in structure than natural languages but resemble them in important respects. It is almost universally accepted that his definition provides the basis for an understanding of truth in natural as well as formal languages.

In order to understand Tarski's proposal, we need some terminology and some philosophical background. The conception of truth that formed the basis for Tarski's analysis is usually called *the correspondence theory of truth*. According to this conception, what makes a sentence true or false is whether or not it *corresponds to the facts*, or *corresponds with reality*. For many philosophers and logicians, not all of them verificationists or otherwise critics of metaphysics generally, the notion of correspondence with reality has seemed to be an example of dubious metaphysical speculation. What Tarski did was to break this conception of truth down into more basic components, define truth in terms of them, and suggest less speculative ways of understanding the resulting definition.

In order to understand Tarski's analysis, we need first to understand some basic semantic notions that apply both to natural languages and to the formal languages to which Tarski's definition directly applies. We are all familiar with the notion of a sentence in a natural language. Sentences in such languages may be in several moods: declarative, interrogative, imperative, etc. Tarski concerned himself with formal languages in which sentences are all analogs of declarative sentences in natural languages, which makes sense since it is just these sentences that can be true or false. In examining basic semantic notions we will likewise be concerned here only with declarative sentences and their formal analogs, and with their logical structures and constituent parts.

The first technical notion we need to understand is that of an *open sentence*. Logicians and philosophers of language are often interested in the components of meaning that two sentences have in common even thought the sentences differ in some respects. For example, the sentences "The cat is on the mat" and "The dog is on the mat" have important elements of meaning in common, even though they have different nouns as subjects. The open sentence "... is on the mat" represents that common meaning: the meaning common to all of the sentences that can be derived from that open sentence by substituting a noun or noun phrase for the dots.

When logicians and philosophers employ the notion of an open sentence to examine the semantic features of more complex sentences, they find it necessary to employ a notation more complicated than the dots we used above to indicate the place where a noun or noun phrase might be inserted. Here's why. Consider the following sentences:

(1) John bought a ticket and John went to town.

(2) Jane bought a ticket and Jane went to town.

(3) Bill bought a ticket and Sally went to town.

Clearly, all three sentences share some important elements of meaning in common, but (1) and (2) share a component of meaning that neither shares with (3), because in each of these sentences (but not in (3)) the same noun occurs in each clause. If we try to use the notation of dots for omitted nouns to write open sentences that reflect these various elements of common meaning, we find that we get the same result for each of the sentences:

(4) ... bought a ticket and ... went to town.

However (4) is interpreted—whether the two lines of dots are thought of as to be filled by the same noun or noun phrase or whether, instead, they are thought of as to be filled by two different nouns or noun phrases—one of the two elements of meaning is not represented. To have a way of representing each of these elements of meaning, logicians employ special symbols called *variables* in place of the dots. Variables are usually represented by the letters x, y, and/or z, sometimes with numerical subscripts. The way open sentences containing variables are understood is this: Whenever the same variable occurs in more than one place in an open sentence, it is understood that all occurrences of this variable are to be replaced by the *same* noun or noun phrase in making a complete sentence. Occurrences of different variables within an open sentence may be replaced either by the same noun or noun phrase *or* by different nouns or noun phrases.

Using variables in formulating open sentences allows us to represent each of the two components of meaning we identified in (1)–(3). For example, (5) and (6) represent the component of meaning that (1) and (2) share with each other but not with (3), whereas (7) and (8) represent the component of meaning that all three share. (Note that the variables have been selected randomly.)

(5) x bought a ticket and x went to town.

(6) y_3 bought a ticket and y_3 went to town.

(7) z bought a ticket and x_9 went to town.

(8) y bought a ticket and x went to town.

Consider the open sentence "x, y, and z are whole numbers and $x + y = z$." By the *extension* of that open sentence we mean the set of all sequences $\langle o_1, o_2, o_3 \rangle$ of things such that each of them is a whole number and $o_1 + o_2 = o_3$. *Extensions* of other open sentences are defined in the same way: If an open sentence has n different variables, then its extension is the set of all sequences of n objects such that if names for those objects are substituted for the relevant variables in the open sentence, then the resulting complete sentence is true. Sequences of two objects are called *ordered pairs*, sequences of three objects are called *triples*, of four objects *quadruples*, of five, *quintuples*, and so forth. In order to have a convenient name for sequences of n objects, no matter how big the number n, logicians introduce the notion of an *n-tuple*, where n is a whole number. A one-tuple is a single object, a two-tuple is an ordered pair, a three-tuple is a triple, etc.

Our understanding of sentences and open sentences requires us to have some concepts for describing their internal structure. Each of the sentences (1)–(3) is a *conjunction* of two shorter sentences: each is constructed from two such sentences by inserting the word "and" between them. From the two sentences which are *conjoined* to make (3) we can also make (among others) these additional sentences:

(9) Sally went to town *and* Bill bought a ticket.

(10) Bill bought a ticket *or* Sally went to town.

(11) *If* Bill bought a ticket, *then* Sally went to town.

(12) *If* Sally went to town, *then* Bill bought a ticket.

We can also make more complex open sentences by combining simpler open sentences in the same way, and we can make an open sentence by combining it with an (ordinary) sentence as these examples illustrate:

(13) x bought a ticket *or* y went to town.

(14) *If* Bill bought a ticket, *then* x went to town.

The italicized terms "and" and "or" and the pair of terms "if ... then ..." function in these sentences as logical terms. Since they function to combine sentences or open sentences to make bigger sentences or open sentences they are called *sentential connectives*. "And," as we have already seen, operates to produce the *conjunction* of two sentences or open sentences. When two sentences or open sentences are connected by "or," the result is said to be their *disjunction*. When two sentences or open sentences are connected by the terms "if" and "then," the result is called a *conditional*. The sentence or open sentence that immediately follows "if" is called the *antecedent* of the conditional; the sentence or open sentence following "then" is called the *consequent*. Sentences (11) and (12) are constructed from the same component sentences—the difference in their meaning is a reflection of the fact that the antecedent of (11) is the consequent of (12) and vice versa.

There is one other important way in which a term like a sentential connective can be employed to generate a new sentence or open sentence from a simpler one. Consider (15) and (16):

(15) Jane is hungry.

(16) Jane is not hungry.

(16) is the *denial* (or the *negation*) of (15), and the word "not" serves as a logical term that expresses the operation of denial or negation. Sometimes "not" and other terms that express negation are also called logical connectives. It is important to understand that in English, or in any other natural language, the logical operations associated

with the sentential connectives can be represented by a variety of different words or symbols; for example, (17) and (18) express the same content as (13) and (16) respectively.

(17) *Either* x bought a ticket *or* y went to town.

(18) It is not the case that Jane is hungry.

In the formal languages philosophers and mathematical logicians study, this redundancy is eliminated by the introduction of a unique logical symbol for each of these operations. Here we will use the following symbols:

for conjunction: &
for disjunction: v
for the conditional: →
for negation: ∼

Thus, for example, a partially formalized representation of *both* (13) and (17) would be

(19) x bought a ticket **v** y went to town.

One other notational device is required to avoid not redundancy but ambiguity. Consider (20):

(20) Sally went to town and Bill bought a ticket or Janet bought a car.

(20) is ambiguous in English. It could mean either (21) or (22):

(21) Sally went to town and either Bill bought a ticket or Janet bought a car.

(22) Either Sally went to town and Bill bought a ticket or Janet bought a car.

In English we use complicated constructions like (21) and (22) to resolve the ambiguity. Since logicians and philosophers use only very simple symbolic means to indicate the operation of sentential connectives, they employ a different and quite simple notational device that automatically makes each formalized sentence or open sentence unambiguous. Whenever, in formalized or partially formalized languages, two sentences or open sentences are united by a sentential connective, a pair of parentheses is put around the result to indicate which sentences or open sentences the particular instance of a sentential connective is to be thought of as connecting. Thus a more precisely formalized version of (19) would be (23), and (21) and (22) would be partially formalized as (24) and (25)

(23) (x bought a ticket **v** y went to town)

(24) (Sally went to town & (Bill bought a ticket **v** Janet bought a car))

(25) ((Sally went to town & Bill bought a ticket) **v** Janet bought a car)

Other features of declarative sentences in natural languages that are also important in the formal languages logicians study are *quantifiers*. Consider the following English sentences:

(26) There are one or more apples in the basket.

(27) There are one or more pears in the tree.

(28) Everything in the basket is an apple.

(29) Everything in the tree is a pear.

There are semantically relevant similarities and differences between any two of these sentences. Some important ones can be revealed if we partially formalize each of these sentences using the symbolic resources we have developed thus far. (26)–(29) might then be represented by (30)–(33) respectively.

(30) *There is an x such that* (x is an apple & x is in the basket)

(31) *There is a y such that* (y is a pear & y is in the tree)

(32) *For all x* (x is in the basket → x is an apple)

(33) *For all y* (y is in the tree → y is a pear)

The expressions *some* and *there is a ... such that* (and lots of other expressions in English) express the operation of *existential quantification* and are called *existential quantifiers*. The expressions *all* and *for all* (and lots of others) are used to express the operation of *universal quantification* and are called *universal quantifiers*. In The formal languages studied by logicians—and in partly formalized quantified sentences in natural languages—each of these operations is expressed by a unique term. Here we will use the expression ∃ followed by a variable to express existential quantification, and we will use the expression ∀ followed by a variable to express universal quantification. Thus (30)–(33) would be more formally expressed as (34)–(37).

(34) ∃x (x is an apple & x is in the basket)

(35) ∃y (y is a pear & y is in the tree)

(36) ∀x (x is in the basket → x is an apple)

(37) ∀y (y is in the tree → y is a pear)

We need two technical notions regarding the use of quantifiers. By the *scope* of a particular quantifier, logicians mean the part of a sentence or open sentence to which it applies. Consider for example the partly formalized English expression (38).

(38) There is an x such that x is an apple and x is good.

As it is written, (38) is ambiguous. It could either be a *sentence* that says that there is something that is both an apple and is good, or it could be an *open sentence* obtained by the conjunction of the *sentence* "There is an x such that x is an apple" with the *open sentence* "x is good." Note that this ambiguity is avoided if parentheses are used to indicate how sentential connectives work. The rule is then that the scope of a quantifier is the properly formulated sentence or open sentence immediately following it. The two different interpretations of (38) are then unambiguously provided by (39) and (40):

(39) ∃x (x is an apple & x is good)

(40) (∃x x is an apple & x is good)

An occurrence of a variable in a sentence or open sentence is said to be *bound* if it occurs in the scope of a quantifier involving that variable; it is said to be *free* otherwise. All of the occurrences of the variable x in (39) are bound, whereas the second occurrence (not counting the occurrence involved in the specification of the quantifier itself) is free in (40). If an occurrence of a variable within a sentence or open sentence lies within the scope of more than one quantifier involving that variable, the nearest of those quantifiers is said to *bind* or *govern* that occurrence and determines how the variable is to be interpreted. Thus, for example, while (39) says that there is a good apple, (41) says only that there is an apple and there is some (perhaps different) good thing.

(41) $\exists x(\exists x\ x$ is an apple & x is good)

A convention logicians adopt for convenience in interpreting formal languages and partly formalized sentences in natural languages is worth mentioning. Suppose that in a sentence or open sentence there are no free occurrences of some variable (either because all of the occurrences of that variable in the sentence or open sentence are bound or because there are no occurrences of it whatsoever). Prefixing a quantifier with respect to that variable to the sentence or open sentence makes no sense. It would be possible but technically messy to define the notion of a well-formed sentence or open sentence in such a way that the result of such a quantification is ill-formed. Instead, what logicians do is to treat such quantifications as having no effect on what the sentence or open sentence says. Thus for example (42) and (43) say the same thing as (41).

(42) $\forall x \exists x(\exists x\ x$ is an apple & x is good)

(43) $\exists y \exists x(\exists x\ x$ is an apple & x is good)

Thus far we have examined technical notions that apply both to natural languages and to formal ones, and we have seen how formal symbols corresponding to those notions can be employed to partially formalize sentences and open sentences in English. It remains to examine the features that are distinct to formal languages.

Consider the following partly formalized English sentences:

(44) (John is good $\rightarrow \forall x \exists y$ (x is a prime number $\rightarrow$ (y is a prime number & y is greater than x)))

(45) John is good.

(46) (Jane is tall $\rightarrow \forall x \exists y$ (x is a negative number $\rightarrow$ (y is a negative number & y is less than x)))

(47) Jane is tall.

(44) and (46) have fundamentally similar logical structures, as do (45) and (47); in consequence of these similarities, (44) and (45) are logically related in just the same way that (46) and (47) are. For example, from either of these pairs it is possible to deduce the second clause of its first member. Languages of the *first-order predicate calculus*, the sort for which Tarski's theory was developed, provide the machinery for representing these important similarities. One way to represent the common structure of (44) and (46), and of (45) and (47) respectively, would be (48) and (49).

(48) (c is $P \rightarrow \forall x \exists y(x$ is $Q \rightarrow (y$ is Q & yRx)))

(49) c is P

In (48) and (49), the particular names that occur in (44)–(47) have been replaced by the symbol c; such a symbol that functions in a formal language the way a name does in a natural one is called an *individual constant*. The adjectival expressions employed to formulate the predicate expressions in (44)–(47) have been replaced by the formal symbols P, Q, and R. Symbols of this sort are called *predicate symbols*. In formal languages each predicate symbol is an *n-place predicate symbol* for some whole number n. What this means is that it is to be thought of as having n places or "slots" that need to be filled with variables or individual constants (or a mixture of both) to construct a *well-formed formula* (or *wff*), the formal analog of a sentence or an open sentence. One remaining technical device and one remaining technical concept are required to make clear the way in which languages of the first-order predicate calculus are developed.

First the technical device: In English and in other natural languages the nouns or variables to which predicate expressions apply sometimes come before the relevant adjectival expressions and sometimes after them, and forms of the verb "to be" are employed to indicate that adjectival expressions apply to nouns and variables. In formal languages the convention is adopted that the n-tuple of individual constants and/or variables to which an n-place predicate symbol applies are written to its right and the forms of the verb "to be" are omitted. Thus, for example, (48) and (49) are fully formalized as (50) and (51).

(50) $(Pc \rightarrow \forall x \exists y(Qx \rightarrow (Qy \ \& \ Ryx)))$

(51) Pc

Now for the last technical notion. We have seen that the notion of a *well-formed formula* is the analog in formal languages for the notion of a grammatical sentence or open sentence in a natural language. In fact the term *sentence* has a technical use in describing expressions in a formal language: a sentence is a well-formed formula with no free occurrences of any variable. Thus, somewhat more precisely, the notion of a wff corresponds to the notion in a natural language of a declarative sentence or an open sentence derived from a declarative sentence, whereas the formal notion of a sentence corresponds to the notion of a declarative sentence.

We are now in a position to summarize our construction of formal languages by providing a *recursive definition* of the notion of a well-formed formula. For any particular formal language L of the first-order predicate calculus, the *vocabulary of L* consists of the individual constants and predicate expressions from which wffs of L are to be constructed. In defining the set of wffs, we must also specify some set of special symbols to serve as the variables of L. Logicians choose some infinite set of variables because, even though no single wff will contain infinitely many variables, there will be no upper limit to the finite number of variables that might be required to formulate a wff. Once the vocabulary of L and the set of variables are specified, we may precisely define the set of wffs of L as follows:

1. *Atomic (basic) well-formed formulas of L*: If W is an n-place predicate symbol in the vocabulary of L and $t_1, \ldots t_n$ is a n-tuple of symbols each of which is either an individual constant of L or a variable in L, then $Wt_1, \ldots, t_n$ is a wff of L.

2. *Forming wffs in L using sentential connectives*: If P and W are wffs in L, then so are the following:

(a) $(P \ \& \ W)$

(b) $(P \ \mathbf{v} \ W)$

(c) $(P \rightarrow W)$

(d) both $\sim P$ and $\sim W$.

3. *Forming wffs in L using quantifiers*: If P is a wff of L and $\mathbf{v}$ is a variable, then each of the following is a wff of L:

(a) $\exists \mathbf{v} \ P$

(b) $\forall \mathbf{v} \ P$.

4. Nothing is a wff of L unless it qualifies by virtue of 1.–3.

We now have a precise characterization of the wffs of any given language L of the first-order predicate calculus. One consequence of the way in which parentheses are used to disambiguate such wffs is that for any wff of L there is only one way in which it could have been constructed following principles 1.–3. Definitions like 1.–4., which define a set (or relation) by identifying some of its simpler members (as in clause 1.) and then by indicating how membership for more complex objects is defined in terms of membership for simpler objects, are called *recursive definitions*. Tarski's accomplishment was to show how truth can be defined for sentences in L by employing a set of recursive definitions closely related to that which defines the wffs in L.

One obvious fact about a wff of a formal language L is that without further interpretation it is neither true nor false because it expresses no definite proposition. Consider the wffs (50) and (51). They were constructed precisely so as to express the logical form that two pairs of English sentences ((44), (45) and (46), (47)) have in common with each other *and with infinitely many different pairs of sentences*. Because they are constructed by ignoring the particular content that each of these pairs express, neither (50) nor (51) says anything; instead each expresses the underlying logical form of infinitely many different sentences. Why, one might ask, is it useful to begin the study of truth by examining languages constructed in such a way that their sentences are neither true nor false rather than by examining natural languages at least some of whose declarative sentences are true or false?

The answer comes in two parts. First, while formal sentences like (50) and (51) are not true or false by themselves, if we provide an *interpretation* of their vocabulary, then *as interpreted* they will be true or false. Thus, for example, if we specify which person is referred to by the name "John" in (44), then we can frame an interpretation for (50) and (51) that assigns them the same truth-values as (44) and (45) respectively. But why, one might ask, is this roundabout procedure appropriate? Why not just consider natural language declarative sentences like (44) and (45)?

The answer lies in the recognition of two philosophical problems about the notion of truth. First there is the seeming mysteriousness of "correspondence with reality" and the suspicion on the part of antimetaphysical empiricists that any understanding of that notion would require accepting objectionably "metaphysical" conceptions. Second, the notion of the "interpretation" of a sentence in a natural language is complex: Are interpretations individual or social? Do they include just what is specified by the "meanings" of the constituent words or do they include features of the social role of the sentence as a rhetorical device? How stable are interpretations over time, and what are the conditions that define stability?

Because the formal languages to which it applies initially lack any interpretation, Tarski's theory of truth necessarily addresses two questions: "Which features of the interpretation of sentences in a language determine the truth-values for its sentences (i.e., determine whether they are true or false)?" and "How is the truth of a sentence defined in terms of those features?" The answer to the first of these questions is provided by the definition of an interpretation for an first-order language L. An interpretation of such a language consists of two parts: the specification of a non-empty set, U, called the *universe of discourse* of the the interpretation, and the specification of an *interpretation function, I, for the vocabulary of L*. The interpretation function must (a) assign to each individual constant of L some element of U, and (b) assign to each n-place predicate symbol of L a set (perhaps null) of n-tuples from U.

The function of these two components of an interpretation is straightforward. The universe of discourse specifies what—under the interpretation in question—the language L is supposed to be about. Consider someone who says, in the ordinary course of a conversation, "Everything is either animal, vegetable, or mineral." We might count what they said as false because of symbiotic systems that combine both animal and plant material, but it would be perverse under ordinary circumstances to object that the Bach B-minor Mass is something that is neither animal nor vegetable nor mineral. Under ordinary circumstances we would interpret what was said on the understanding that the speaker was talking about natural objects and not (also) musical compositions. What is implicit in natural language use is explicit in the interpretation of formal languages, so it is required that it be specified what the interpreted sentences are about. In particular, the universe of discourse fixes the interpretation of the quantifiers: if v is a variable then "$\forall v$" means "for all elements v of U" and "$\exists v$" means "there is an element v of U such that."

Even more obviously, the interpretation function assigns to each individual constant its *denotation*—the element of U for which it is a name—and to each predicate symbol its *extension*—the set of n-tuples in U to which it is correctly applied. It remains to see how the truth of sentences in a formal language is defined in terms of its interpretation.

For simplicity let us first consider how to define truth for languages of a simpler sort: those in which there are neither variables nor quantifiers. Wffs for such *first-order languages without quantifiers* are defined just like wffs for full first-order languages except that the clause regarding quantifiers (3. above) is omitted, and the places after predicate symbols are to be filled only by individual constants. For a quantifier-free language L, wffs are thus defined as follows:

1*. *Atomic (basic) well-formed formulas of L:* If W is an n-place predicate symbol in the vocabulary of L and $\langle t_1, \ldots t_n \rangle$ is a n-tuple of symbols each of which is an individual constant of L, then $Wt_1, \ldots t_n$ is a wff.

2*. *Forming wffs in L using sentential connectives:* If P and W are wffs in L, then so are the following:

(a) $(P \;\&\; W)$

(b) $(P \vee W)$

(c) $(P \rightarrow W)$

(d) both $\sim P$ and $\sim W$.

3*. Nothing is a wff of L unless it qualifies in virtue of 1*.–2*.

We can think of an interpretation for a quantifier-free first-order language as being just the same sort of thing as an interpretation for a first-order language with quantifiers (strictly speaking we could eliminate the specification of the universe of discourse, but let's keep the cases as much alike as possible). On that understanding we can now define truth relative to an interpretation I for sentences in a formal language L of the sort in question as follows:

I*. (*Truth for atomic (basic) sentences.*) If W is an n-place predicate symbol in the vocabulary of L and $t_1, \ldots t_n$ is a n-tuple of symbols each of which is an individual constant of L, let $\langle o_1, \ldots o_n \rangle$ be the n-tuple of elements of the universe of the interpretation I which I assigns to $\langle t_1, \ldots t_n \rangle$ respectively. The sentence $Wt_1, \ldots, t_n$ is true under I just in case the n-tuple $o_1, \ldots, o_n$ is an element of the extension assigned to W by I.

II*. If P and W are wffs of L, then

(a) $(P \;\&\; W)$ is true under I just in case both P and W are true under I.

(b) $(P \mathbf{v} W)$ is true under I just in case either P is true under I or W is true under I or both are true under I.

(c) $(P \to W)$ is true under I just in case either P is false under I or W is true under I.

(d) $\sim P$ is true under I just in case P is not true under I.

Note that I*.–II*. provide a recursive definition of truth for L and that for each clause in the definition of wffs in L (except the last "recursion" clause) there is a clause in the definition of truth for L that indicates how the truth or falsity of a wff with the structure indicated by the clause in the definition of a wff is determined by the truth or other semantic properties of the smaller constituents from which it is composed. In consequence, for any wff of L and any I, the definition of truth provided above uniquely assigns to that wff the truth-value "true" or "false." (Strictly speaking this latter claim is a theorem requiring a proof, but we will omit the details.)

Suppose now that we want to define truth recursively in the same way for a language, L, of the full predicate calculus, in whose wffs variables and quantifiers appear. The first clause in the definition of a wff for such a language is, of course:

1. *Atomic (Basic) well-formed formulas of L*: If W is an n-place predicate symbol in the vocabulary of L and $t_1, \ldots t_n$ is a n-tuple of symbols each of which is either an individual constant of L or a variable in L, then $Wt_1, \ldots, t_n$ is a wff of L.

Corresponding to 1. we would like to have a clause in the truth definition for L that indicates how the truth or falsity of an atomic wff in L is determined by an interpretation of the symbols in L. Immediately we face a difficulty: some atomic wffs—those with at least one free occurrence of a variable—are the analogs of open sentences in natural languages rather than of (ordinary) sentences and are not the sort of things that can be either true or false under an interpretation.

Suppose, for example, that L has one three-place relation symbol, R, and individual constants c_1, c_2, and c_3. Suppose that I is an interpretation whose universe of discourse is the set of non-negative integers, which assigns to R the set of triples $\langle a, b, c \rangle$ such that $a + b = c$, and which assigns the denotations 3, 10, and 20 to c_1, c_2, and c_3, respectively. We then know that the first clause of the truth definition for L should assign a value of "true" to the wff $Rc_2c_2c_3$, since $10 + 10 = 20$, and that it should assign false to $Rc_1c_2c_3$ (which means that a subsequent clause will assign "true" to $\sim Rc_1c_2c_3$). But what about the equally good wff $Rc_1x_3x_{34}$ (where x_3 and x_{34} are arbitrarily chosen variables)? I assigns 3 as the denotation of c_1 but, because variables are place-holders that indicate the structure of open sentences and specify the operation of quantifiers rather than names of things, I makes no assignment of denotata for x_3 and x_{34}, and the truth-value of $Rc_1x_3x_{34}$ is undetermined.

Tarski's solution to the problem of how to define truth for languages of the full predicate calculus can be understood by further reflection on the example at hand. x_3 and x_{34} don't denote anything under I, but if we *pretend*, for a moment, that x_3 denotes 12 and x_{34} denotes 15 then, subject to that pretense, we can assign $Rc_1x_3x_{34}$ the value "true" under I. Similarly, if we pretend that x_3 denotes 300 and that x_{34} denotes 55, then $Rc_1x_3x_{34}$ would be false under I. By a *pretense* for an interpretation let us mean a function that assigns to every variable some object in the universe of discourse of the interpretation. We have just been exploring the question of what it is for a wff to be true under an interpretation *with respect to a pretense*. It was Tarski's idea to offer a recursive definition of truth under an interpretation with respect to a pretense and to use that definition as a stepping stone toward a definition of truth for sentences in a formal language.

To understand the motivation for Tarski's definitions, let us consider, informally, how the notion of truth under an interpretation with respect to a pretense ought to work for wffs containing occurrences of variables bound by quantifiers. Consider the wff $\exists x_3 R c_1 x_3 x_{34}$. Suppose that the interpretation for L is the one we have been examining and that we have a pretense that assigns x_3 to 300 and x_{34} to 55. How should we interpret the occurrence of x_3 in the wff—an occurrence that is bound by an existential quantifier? Should we still think of it as denoting 300, and take the formula to be false under the interpretation with respect to the pretense, or should we instead treat the formula as saying (truly as it happens) that there is some number (not necessarily 300) which when added to 3 (the denotation of c_1) gives the sum 55 (the denotation assigned to x_{34} by the pretense)? Pretty obviously we should do the latter, otherwise quantifiers would play no role in the definition of truth toward which we are working.

Tarski's definition of truth for a wff, W, under an interpretation I, with respect to a pretense $\mathscr{P}$ was thus intended to capture the notion that W would be true under I if all of the *free* occurrences of variables in W were temporarily treated as denoting the objects assigned to them by $\mathscr{P}$. We will look at that definition in a moment, but there are two points about it that we can already see before looking at the formal details.

First, consider how this concept of truth under an interpretation with respect to a pretense applies to a wff W in L that is a *sentence* in L—that is to a wff with no free variables. Since only *free* variables in a wff are assigned denotations by a pretense, the truth-value assigned to a *sentence* under an interpretation with respect to a pretense depends only on the interpretation and not on the pretense. Thus, for example if we add a quantifier to the wff we have been considering to get the sentence $\exists x_{34} \exists x_3 R c_1 x_3 x_{34}$, we will have a formula that is true under the interpretation we have been considering (it says that there are two non-negative whole numbers such that the sum of the first of them and 12 equals the second) *no matter what pretense is supplied*. We no longer need the pretense to determine the truth-value because all of the variables in the formula are serving in their truth-defining roles of indicating the scope of quantifiers rather than just serving as place-holders. A sentence is true under an interpretation with respect to a given pretense just in case it is true under that interpretation with respect to every pretense.

It follows that if we have a recursive definition of the relation that holds between a wff of L and an interpretation and a pretense just in case that wff is true under the interpretation with respect to the pretense (as we shall shortly), then we can (non-recursively) define truth (simpliciter) for *sentences* of L by saying that a sentence of L is true under an interpretation just in case it is true under that interpretation with respect to every possible pretense.

One further observation will put us in a position to understand how Tarski defined truth under an interpretation with respect to a pretense. Consider the somewhat different wff $\exists x_3 \exists x_{34} R x_3 x_{34} x_{19}$, and the shorter wff $\exists x_{34} R x_3 x_{34} x_{19}$ from which it is derived by an application of clause 3(a). Let us continue to apply the interpretation we have been discussing and consider both of these formulas under that interpretation and with respect to a pretense that assigns x_3 to 300, x_{34} to 55, and x_{19} to 10. Under the interpretation in question the longer wff is true with respect to the pretense (it says that there are two non-negative whole numbers whose sum is 10), but the shorter wff is false (it says that there is a positive whole number that, when added to 300—the denotation assigned to x_3 by the pretense—gives the sum 10). How did adding the quantifier $\exists x_3$ to the shorter wff make it true rather than false?

One answer is that the pretense tells us that x_3 in the shorter formula must stand for

300—and there is no non-negative whole number which added to 300 yields 10—but when we assess the longer formula with the existential quantifier added, we are to ask whether there is some such number, not necessarily 300, which when added to another such number yields 10. Another way of putting the same question is this: Could we change what the pretense assigns to x_3 (but not what it assigns to other variables) in such a way that the *shorter* formula is true under the interpretation with respect to the changed pretense? If the answer is yes, as it is in this case, then the *longer* formula is true. This example illustrates the important general point that we can define the conditions under which a formula beginning with an existential quantifier is true, under an interpretation, with respect to a pretense, in terms of the conditions under which the *shorter* formula without the quantifier is true under the same interpretation with respect to closely related pretenses: A formula beginning with an existential quantifier is true under an interpretation with respect to a pretense just in case there is some pretense that is just like the first one *except perhaps in what it assigns to the variable of quantification* with respect to which the shorter formula without the quantifier is true under the same interpretation.

Exactly similar considerations allow us to formulate a related principle regarding universal quantification: a formula beginning with a universal quantifier is true under an interpretation with respect to a pretense just in case for every pretense that is just like the first one *except perhaps in what it assigns to the variable of quantification* the shorter formula without the quantifier is true under the same interpretation with respect to that pretense. These two insights about the effects of quantification on truth-conditions are just what Tarski required to formulate a recursive definition of truth under an interpretation with respect to a pretense whose clauses mirror those of the recursive definition of a wff. Here is Tarski's definition of truth for wffs in L under an interpretation I with respect to a pretense $\mathscr{P}$:

I. (*Truth for atomic (basic) sentences.*) If W is an n-place predicate symbol in the vocabulary of L and $\langle t_1, \ldots, t_n \rangle$ is a n-tuple of symbols each of which is either an individual constant of L or a variable of L, let $\langle o_1, \ldots, o_n \rangle$ be the n-tuple of elements of the universe of the interpretation I that are assigned to $t_1, \ldots, t_n$ respectively by I or by $\mathscr{P}$ (whichever is applicable). The wff $W t_1, \ldots, t_n$ is true under I with respect to $\mathscr{P}$ just in case the n-tuple $\langle o_1, \ldots, o_n \rangle$ is an element of the extension assigned to W by I.

II. If Q and W are wffs of L, then:

(a) $(Q \,\&\, W)$ is true under I with respect to $\mathscr{P}$ just in case both Q and W are true under I with respect to $\mathscr{P}$.

(b) $(Q \mathbf{\,v\,} W)$ is true under I with respect to $\mathscr{P}$ just in case either Q is true under I *with respect to $\mathscr{P}$* or W is true under I with respect to $\mathscr{P}$ or both are true under I with respect to $\mathscr{P}$.

(c) $(Q \rightarrow W)$ is true under I with respect to $\mathscr{P}$ just in case either Q is false under I with respect to $\mathscr{P}$ or W is true under I with respect to $\mathscr{P}$.[1]

(d) $\sim Q$ is true under I with respect to $\mathscr{P}$ just in case Q is not true under I with respect to $\mathscr{P}$.

III. If Q is a wff, and v is a variable in L, then:

(a) $\exists v\, Q$ is true under I with respect to $\mathscr{P}$ just in case there is some pretense $\mathscr{P}^*$ that makes the same assignments as $\mathscr{P}$, *except perhaps to v*, such that Q is true under I with respect to $\mathscr{P}^*$.

(b) $\forall v\, Q$ is true under I with respect to $\mathscr{P}$ just in case, for every pretense $\mathscr{P}^*$ that makes the same assignment as $\mathscr{P}$, *except perhaps to v*, Q is true under I with respect to $\mathscr{P}^*$.

We may now also formulate the definition of truth for sentences of L:

IV. If Q is a *sentence* of L, then Q is true under I just in case Q is true under I with respect to every pretense $\mathscr{P}$.

Tarski's definition of truth proved extremely important both for mathematical logicians and for philosophers. For logicians, it gave rise to a whole subdiscipline of mathematical logic called "model theory" (interpretations are sometimes called "models"; incidentally, what I have called a pretense is usually called an "assignment" or a "sequence"). Our concern is with the philosophical implications of the theory of truth, which are discussed in the preceding introduction.

Note

1. The treatment of the conditional "if ... then ..." may seem unusual, since a wff of the form $(A \to B)$ is said to be true under an interpretation with respect to a pretense just in case either A is false or B is true (or both) with respect to the interpretation and pretense. The conditional so defined is called the indicative conditional and it is meant to capture one of the senses of English sentences of the form "If A is true, then B is true," but it is not meant to capture any causal or counterfactual conditional notion. It is not, for example, supposed to capture the notion expressed in English by sentences of the form "If A were true, then B would be true" or "If A is (were) true, that causes (would cause) B to be true." That there is at least one meaning of "if ... then ..." whose meaning is captured by the clause for "$\to$" is suggested by the following considerations.

   Suppose that, either informally or in defining truth for a formal language, we want to say what it is for a sentence of the form "$\forall x$ (If Ax, then Bx)" to be true. One obvious suggestion is that the sentence is true just in case every relevant thing (everything in the universe of discourse, if we are being formal) which is an A (lies within the extension of A) is a B (lies within the extension of B). The other suggestion, captured by the clause of the definition of truth for the universal quantifier, is that the sentence in question should be true just in case the open sentence (wff) "(If Ax, then Bx)" is true no matter what we pretend that the variable x stands for. The only way to satisfy both of these obvious suggestions simultaneously is to make wffs of the form "(If Ax, then Bx)" true whenever x stands for some non-A, or when x stands for something that is both an A and a B, and to make it false only when x stands for an A that is a non-B. If we are to have a uniform treatment of the conditional "if ... then ..." of which this pattern of truth-value assignments is a special case, then the required treatment is just that which Tarski's definition of truth employs for "$\to$".

Chapter 1

Positivism and Realism

Moritz Schlick

I. Preliminary Questions

Every philosophical movement is defined by the principles that it regards as fundamental, and to which it constantly recurs in its arguments. But in the course of
historical development, the principles are apt not to remain unaltered, whether it be
that they acquire new formulations, and come to be extended or restricted, or that
even their meaning gradually undergoes noticeable modifications. At some point the
question then arises as to whether we should still speak at all of the development of a
single movement, and retain its old name, or whether a new movement has not in fact
arisen.

If, alongside the evolved outlook, an 'orthodox' movement still continues to exist,
which clings to the first principles in their original form and meaning, then sooner or
later some terminological distinction of the old from the new will automatically come
about. But where this is not clearly so, and where, on the contrary, the most diverse
and perhaps contradictory formulations and interpretations of the principles are ban-
died about among the various adherents of a 'movement', then a hubbub arises,
whose result is that supporters and opponents of the view are found talking at cross
purposes; everyone seeks out from the principles what he can specifically use for the
defense of his own view, and everything ends in hopeless misunderstandings and
obscurities. They only disappear when the various principles are separated from each
other and tested individually for meaning and truth on their own account, in which
process we do best, at first, to disregard entirely the contexts in which they have
historically arisen, and the names that have been given to them.

I should like to apply these considerations to the modes of thought grouped under
the name of 'positivism'. From the moment when Auguste Comte invented the term,
up to the present day, they have undergone a development which provides a good-
example of what has just been said. I do this, however, not with the historical purpose
of establishing, say, a rigorous concept of positivism in its historical manifestation, but
rather in order to contribute to a real settlement of the controversy currently carried
on about certain principles which rank as positivist axioms. Such a settlement is all the
dearer to me, in that I subscribe to some of these principles myself. My only concern
here is to make the meaning of these principles as clear as possible; whether, after such
clarification, people are still minded to impute them to 'positivism' or not, is a question
of wholly subordinate importance.

If every view is to be labelled positivist, which denies the possibility of metaphysics,
then nothing can be said against it as a mere definition, and in *this* sense I would have

Originally appeared in *Erkenntnis III* (1932/33); translated by Peter Heath and reprinted in *Moritz Schlick:
Philosophical Papers, Volume II (1925–1936)* from *Vienna Circle Collection*, edited by Henk L. Mulder
(Kluwer, 1979), pp. 259–284. Reprinted by permission of the Schlick estate and the publisher. Copyright
1979 by Kluwer Academic Publishers.

to declare myself a strict positivist. But this, of course, is true only if we presuppose a particular definition of 'metaphysics'. What the definition of metaphysics is, that would have to be made basic here, does not need to interest us at present; but it scarcely accords with the formulations that are mostly current in the literature of philosophy; and closer definitions of positivism that adhere to such formulations lead straight into obscurities and difficulties.

For if, say—as has mostly been done from time immemorial—we assert that metaphysics is the doctrine of 'true being', of 'reality in itself', or of 'transcendent being', this talk of true, real being obviously presupposes that a non-true, lesser or apparent being stands opposed to it, as has indeed been assumed by all metaphysicians since the days of Plato and the Eleatics. This seeming being is said to be the realm of 'appearances', and while the true transcendent reality is held to be accessible with difficulty only to the efforts of the metaphysician, the special sciences are exclusively concerned with appearances, and the latter are also perfectly accessible to scientific knowledge. The contrast in the knowability of the two 'kinds of being' is then traced to the fact that appearances are 'given' and immediately known to us, whereas metaphysical reality has had to be inferred from them only by a circuitous route. With this we seem to have arrived at a fundamental concept of the positivists, for they, too, are always talking of the 'given', and state their basic principle mostly by saying that, like the scientist, the philosopher must abide throughout in the given, that an advance beyond it, such as the metaphysician attempts, is impossible or absurd.

It is natural, therefore, to take the given of positivism to be simply identical with the metaphysician's appearances, and to believe that positivism is at bottom a metaphysics from which the transcendent has been omitted or struck out; and such a view may often enough have inspired the arguments of positivists, no less than those of their adversaries. But with this we are already on the road to dangerous errors.

This very term 'the given' is already an occasion for grave misunderstandings. 'To give', of course, normally signifies a three-termed relation: it presupposes in the first place someone who gives, secondly someone given to, and thirdly something given. For the metaphysician this is quite in order, for the giver is transcendent reality, the receiver is the knowing consciousness, and the latter appropriates what is given to it as its 'content'. But the positivist, from the outset, will obviously have nothing to do with such notions; the given, for him, is to be merely a term for what is simplest and no longer open to question. Whatever term we may choose, indeed, it will be liable to occasion misconceptions; if we talk of 'acquaintance' ['Erlebnis'], we seem to presuppose the distinction between he who is acquainted and what he is acquainted with; in employing the term 'content of consciousness', we appear to burden ourselves with a similar distinction, and also with the complex concept of 'consciousness', first ex-cogitated, at all events, by philosophical thought.

But even apart from such difficulties, it is possibly still not yet clear what is actually meant by the given. Does it merely include such 'qualities' as 'blue', 'hot' and 'pain', or also, for example, relations between them, or the order they are in? Is the similarity of two qualities 'given' in the same sense as the qualities themselves? And if the given is somehow elaborated or interpreted or judged, is this elaboration or judgement not also in turn a given in some sense?

It is not obscurities of this type, however, which give occasion to present-day controversies; it is the question of 'reality' that first tosses among the parties the apple of discord.

If positivism's rejection of metaphysics amounts to a denial of transcendent reality, it seems the most natural thing in the world to conclude that in that case it attributes reality only to non-transcendent being. The main principle of the positivist then seems to run: 'Only the given is real'. Anyone who takes pleasure in plays upon words could even make use of a peculiarity of the German language in order to lend this proposition the air of being a self-evident tautology, by formulating it as: '*Es gibt nur das Gegebene*' [Only the given exists].

What are we to say of this principle?

Many positivists may have stated and upheld it (particularly those, perhaps, who have treated physical objects as 'mere logical constructions' or as 'mere auxiliary concepts'), and others have had it imputed to them by opponents—but we are obliged to say that anyone who asserts this principle thereby attempts to advance a claim that is metaphysical in the same sense, and to the same degree, as the seemingly opposite contention, that 'There is a transcendent reality'.

The problem at issue here is obviously the so-called question as to the reality of the external world, and on this there seem to be two parties: that of 'realism', which believes in the reality of the external world, and that of 'positivism', which does not believe in this. I am convinced that in fact it is quite absurd to set two views in contrast to one another in this fashion, since (as with all metaphysical propositions) both parties, at bottom, have not the least notion of what they are trying to say. But before explaining this I should like to show how the most natural interpretations of the proposition 'only the given is real' in fact lead at once to familiar metaphysical views.

As a question about the existence of the 'external' world, the problem can make its appearance only through drawing a distinction of some kind between inner and outer, and this happens inasmuch and insofar as the given is regarded as a 'content' of consciousness, as belonging to a subject (or several) to *whom* it is given. The immediate data are thereby credited with a conscious character, the character of presentations or ideas; and the proposition in question would then assert that *all* reality possesses this character: no being outside consciousness. But this is nothing else but the basic principle of meta-physical *idealism*. If the philosopher thinks he can speak only of what is given to himself, we are confronted with a solipsistic metaphysics; but if he thinks he may assume that the given is distributed to many subjects, we then have an idealism of the Berkeleyan type.

On this interpretation, positivism would thus be simply identical with the older idealist metaphysics. But since its founders were certainly seeking something quite other than a renewal of that idealism, this view must be rejected as inconsistent with the antimetaphysical purpose of positivism. Idealism and positivism do not go together. The positivist Ernst Laas[1] devoted a work in several volumes to demonstrating the irreconcilable opposition that exists between them in all areas; and if his pupil Hans Vaihinger gave his *Philosophy of As If* the subtitle of an 'idealist positivism', that is just one of the contradictions that infect this work. Ernst Mach has particularly emphasized that his own positivism has evolved in a direction away from the Berkeleyan metaphysics; he and Avenarius laid much stress on not construing the given as a content of consciousness, and endeavored to keep this notion out of their philosophy altogether.

In view of the uncertainty in the positivists' own camp, it is not surprising if the 'realist' ignores the distinctions we have mentioned and directs his arguments against the thesis that 'there are only contents of consciousness', or that 'there is only an internal world'. But this proposition belongs to the idealist metaphysics; it has no place in an antimetaphysical positivism, and these counter-arguments do not tell against such a view.

The 'realist' can, indeed, take the line that it is utterly inevitable that the given should be regarded as a content of consciousness, as subjective, or mental—or whatever the term may be; and he would consider the attempts of Avenarius and Mach to construe the given as neutral, and to do away with the inner-outer distinction, as a failure, and would think a theory without metaphysics to be simply impossible. But this line of argument is more rarely encountered. And whatever the position there, we are dealing in any case with a quarrel about nothing, since the 'problem of the reality of the external world' is a meaningless pseudo-problem. It is now time to make this clear.

II. On the Meaning of Statements

It is the proper business of philosophy to seek for and clarify the *meaning* of claims and questions. The chaotic state in which philosophy has found itself throughout the greatest part of its history is traceable to the unlucky fact that firstly it has accepted certain formulations with far too much naivete, as genuine problems, without first carefully testing whether they really possessed a sound meaning; and secondly, that it has believed the answers to certain questions to be discoverable by particular philosophical methods that differ from those of the special sciences. By philosophical analysis we are unable to decide of anything whether it is real; we can only determine what it *means* to claim that it is real; and whether this is then the case or not can only be decided by the ordinary methods of daily life and science, namely by *experience*. So here the task is to get clear whether a meaning can be attached to the question about the reality of the 'external world'.

When are we certain, in general, that the meaning of a question is clear to us? Obviously then, and only then, when we are in a position to state quite accurately the circumstances under which it can be answered in the affirmative—or those under which it would have to receive a negative answer. By these statements, and these alone, is the meaning of the question defined.

It is the first step in every kind of philosophizing, and the basis of all reflection, to realize that it is absolutely impossible to give the meaning of any claim save by describing the state-of-affairs that must obtain if the claim is to be true. If it does not obtain, then the claim is false. The meaning of a proposition obviously consists in this alone, that it expresses a particular state-of-affairs. This state-of-affairs must actually be pointed out, in order to give the meaning of the proposition. One may say, indeed, that the proposition itself already gives this state-of-affairs; but only, of course, for one who *understands* it. But when do I understand a proposition? When I know the meaning of the words that occur in it? This can be explained by definitions. But in the definitions new words occur, whose meaning I also have to know in turn. The business of defining cannot go on indefinitely, so eventually we come to words whose meaning cannot again be described in a proposition; it has to be pointed out directly; the meaning of the word must ultimately be *shown*, it has to be *given*. This takes place through an act of pointing or showing, and what is shown must be given, since otherwise it cannot be pointed out to me.

In order, therefore, to find the meaning of a proposition, we have to transform it by introduction of successive definitions, until finally only such words appear in it as can no longer be defined, but whose meanings can only be indicated directly. The criterion for the truth or falsity of the proposition then consists in this, that under specific conditions (stated in the definitions) certain data are, or are not, present. Once this is established, I have established everything that the proposition was talking about, and hence I know its meaning. If I am *not* capable, in principle, of verifying a proposition, that is, if I have absolutely no knowledge of how I should go about it, what I would have to do, in order to ascertain its truth or falsity, then I obviously have no idea at all of what the proposition is actually saying; for then I would be in no position to interpret the proposition, in proceeding, by means of the definitions, from its wording to possible data, since insofar as I *am* in a position to do this, I can also, by this very fact, point out the road to verification in principle (even though, for practical reasons, I may often be unable actually to tread it). To state the circumstances under which a proposition is true is *the same* as stating its meaning, and nothing else.

And these 'circumstances', as we have now seen, have ultimately to be found in the given. Different circumstances imply differences in the given. The *meaning* of every proposition is ultimately determined by the given alone, and by absolutely nothing else.

I do not know if this view should be described as positivistic; though I should like to believe that it has been in the background of all efforts that go under this name in the history of philosophy, whether, indeed, it has been clearly formulated or not. It may well be assumed to constitute the true core and driving force of many quite erroneous formulations that we find among the positivists.

Anyone who has once attained the insight, that the meaning of any statement can be determined only by the given, no longer even grasps the *possibility of another* opinion, for he sees that he has merely discerned the conditions under which opinions can be formulated at all. It would thus be quite erroneous as well to perceive in the foregoing any sort of 'theory of meaning' (in Anglo-Saxon countries the view outlined, that the meaning of a statement is wholly and solely determined by its verification in the given, is commonly called the 'experimental theory of meaning'); that which precedes all formation of theories cannot itself be a theory.

The content of our thesis is in fact entirely trivial (and that is precisely why it can give so much insight); it tells us that a statement only has a specifiable meaning if it makes some testable difference whether it is true or false. A proposition for which the world looks exactly the same when it is true as it does when it is false, in fact says nothing whatever about the world; it is empty, it conveys nothing, I can specify no meaning for it. But a *testable* difference is present only if there is a difference in the given, for to be testable certainly means nothing else but 'demonstrable in the given'.

It is self-evident that the term 'testability' is intended only *in principle*, for the meaning of a proposition does not, of course, depend on whether the circumstances under which we actually find ourselves at a given moment allow of, or prevent, actual verification. The statement that 'there are 10,000 ft mountains on the far side of the moon' is beyond doubt absolutely meaningful, although we lack the technical means for verifying it. And it would remain just as meaningful even if we knew for certain, on scientific grounds of some kind, that no man would ever reach the far side of the moon. Verification always remains *thinkable*, we are always able to say what sort of data we should have to encounter, in order to effect the decision; it is *logically* possible, whatever the situation may be as regards the actual possibility of doing it. And that is all that is at issue here.

But if someone advanced the claim, that within every electron there is a nucleus which is always present, but produces absolutely no effects outside, so that its existence in nature is discernible in no way whatever—then this would be a meaningless claim. For we should at once have to ask the fabricator of this hypothesis: What, then, do you actually *mean* by the presence of this 'nucleus'?, and he could only reply: I mean that something exists there in the electron. We would then go on to ask: What is that supposed to mean? How would it be if this something did not exist? And he would have to reply: In that case, everything else would be exactly as before. For according to his claim, no effects of any kind proceed from this something, and everything observable would remain absolutely unaltered, the realm of the given would not be touched. We would judge that he had not succeeded in conveying to us the meaning of his hypothesis, and that it is therefore vacuous. In this case the impossibility of verification is actually not a factual, but a *logical* impossibility, since the claim that this nucleus is totally without effects rules out, *in principle*, the possibility of deciding by differences in the given.

Nor can it be supposed that the distinction between essential impossibility of verification and a merely factual and empirical impossibility is not sharp, and therefore often hard to draw; for the 'essential' impossibility is simply a logical one, which differs from the empirical, not by degrees, but absolutely. What is merely empirically impossible still remains *thinkable*; but what is logically impossible is contradictory, and cannot, therefore, be thought at all. We also find, in fact, that with sure instinct, this distinction is always very clearly sensed in the practice of scientific thinking. The physicists would be the first to reject the claim in our example, concerning the eternally hidden nucleus of the electron, with the criticism that this is no hypothesis whatever, but an empty play with words. And on the question of the meaning of their statements, successful students of reality have at all times adopted the standpoint here outlined, in that they acted upon it, even though mostly unawares.

Thus our position does not represent anything strange and peculiar for science, but in a certain sense has always been a self-evident thing. It could not possibly have been otherwise, because only from this standpoint can the truth of a statement be tested at all; since all scientific activity consists in testing the truth of statements, it constantly acknowledges the correctness of our viewpoint by what it does.

If express confirmation be still needed, it is to be found with the utmost clarity at critical points in the development of science, where research is compelled to bring its self-evident presuppositions to consciousness. This situation occurs where difficulties of principle give rise to the suspicion that something may not be in order about these presuppositions. The most celebrated example of this kind, which will forever remain notable, is Einstein's analysis of the concept of time, which consists in nothing else whatever but a statement of the *meaning* of our assertions about the simultaneity of spatially separated events. Einstein told the physicists (and philosophers): you must first say what you *mean* by simultaneity, and this you can only do by showing how the statement 'two events are simultaneous' is verified. But in so doing you have then also established the meaning fully and *without remainder*. What is true of the simultaneity concept holds good of every other; every statement has a meaning only insofar as it can be verified; it only *signifies* what is verified and absolutely *nothing* beyond this. Were someone to maintain that it contains more, he would have to be able to say what this more is, and for this he must again say what in the world would be different if he was wrong; but he can say nothing of the kind, for by previous assumption all observable differences have already been utilized in the verification.

In the simultaneity example the analysis of meaning, as is right and proper for the physicist, is carried only so far that the decision about the truth or falsity of a temporal statement resides in the occurrence or non-occurrence of a certain physical event (for example, the coincidence of a pointer with a scale-mark); but it is clear that one may go on to ask: What, then, does it *mean* to claim that the pointer indicates a particular mark on the scale? And the answer to this can be nothing else whatever but a reference to the occurrence of certain data, or, as we are wont to say, of certain 'sensations'. This is also generally admitted, and especially by physicists. "For in the end, positivism will always be right in this", says Planck,[2] "that there is no other source of knowledge but sensations", and this statement obviously means that the truth or falsity of a physical assertion is quite solely dependent on the occurrence of certain sensations (which are a special class of the given).

But now there will always be many inclined to say that this grants only that the truth of a physical statement can be tested in absolutely no other way save by the occurrence of certain sensations, but that this, however, is a different thing from claiming that the very *meaning* of the statement is thereby exhaustively presented. The latter would have to be denied, for a proposition can contain *more* than allows of verification; that the pointer stands at a certain mark on the scale means *more* than the presence of certain sensations (namely, the 'presence of a certain state-of-affairs in the external world').

Of this denial of the identity of meaning and verification the following needs to be said:

1. Such a denial is to be found among physicists only where they leave the proper territory of physical statements and begin to philosophize. (In physics, obviously, we find only statements about the nature or behaviour of things and processes; an express assertion of their 'reality' is needless, since it is always presupposed.) In his own territory the physicist fully acknowledges the correctness of our point of view. We have already mentioned this earlier, and have since elucidated it by the example of the concept of simultaneity. There are, indeed, many philosophers who say: Only relative simultaneity can admittedly be established, but from this it does not follow that there is no such thing as absolute simultaneity, and we continue, as before, to believe in it! There is no way of demonstrating the falsity of this claim; but the great majority of physicists are rightly of the opinion that it is meaningless. It must be emphatically stressed, however, that in both cases we are concerned with exactly the same situation. It makes absolutely no difference, in principle, whether I ask: Does the statement 'two events are simultaneous' mean more than can be verified? Or whether I ask: Does the statement 'the pointer indicates the fifth scale-mark' signify more than can be verified? The physicist who treats the two cases differently is guilty of an inconsistency. He will justify himself by arguing that in the second case, where the 'reality of the external world' is concerned, there is philosophically far more at stake. This argument is too vague for us to be able to assign it any weight, but we shall shortly examine whether anything lies behind it.

2. It is perfectly true that every statement about a physical object or event says *more* than is verified, say, by the once-and-for-all occurrence of an experience. It is presupposed, rather, that this experience took place under quite specific conditions, whose fulfilment can, of course, be tested in turn only by something given; and it is further presupposed that still other and further verifications (after-tests, confirmations) are always possible, which themselves of course reduce to manifestations of some kind in the given. In this way we can and must make allowance for sense-deceptions and errors, and it is easy to see how we are to classify the cases in which we would say that the observer had merely dreamt that the pointer indicated a certain mark, or that he had not observed carefully, and so on. Blondlot's claims about the N-rays that he thought he had discovered were intended, after all, to say more than that he had had certain visual sensations under certain circumstances, and hence they could also be refuted.[3] Strictly speaking, the meaning of a proposition about physical objects is exhausted only by the provision of indefinitely many possible verifications, and the consequence of this is, that in the last resort such a proposition can never be proved absolutely true. It is generally acknowledged, indeed, that even the most assured

propositions of science have always to be regarded merely as hypotheses, which remain open to further definition and improvement. This has certain consequences for the logical nature of such propositions, but they do not concern us here.

Once again: the meaning of a physical statement is never defined by a single isolated verification; it must be conceived, rather, as of the form: If circumstances x are given, data y occur, where indefinitely many circumstances can be substituted for x, and the proposition remains correct on every occasion (this also holds, even if the statement refers to a once-and-for-all occurrence—a historical event—for such an event always has innumerable consequences whose occurrence can be verified). Thus the meaning of every physical statement ultimately lies always in an endless chain of data; the individual datum as such is of no interest in this connection. So if a positivist should ever have said that the individual objects of science are simply the given experiences themselves, he would certainly have been quite wrong; what every scientist seeks, and seeks alone, are rather the rules which govern the connection of experiences, and by which they can be predicted. Nobody denies that the sole verification of natural laws consists in the fact that they provide correct predictions of this type. The oft-heard objection, that the immediately given, which at most can be the object of psychology, is now falsely to be made into an object of physics, is thereby robbed of its force.

3. The most important thing to say, however, is this: If anyone thinks that the meaning of a proposition is not in fact exhausted by what can be verified in the given, but extends far beyond that, then he must at least admit that this surplus of meaning is utterly indescribable, unstatable in any way, and inexpressible by any language. For let him just try to state it! So far as he succeeds in *communicating* something of the meaning, he will find that the communication consists in the very fact that he has pointed out some circumstances that can serve for verification in the given, and he thereby finds our view confirmed. Or else he may believe, indeed, that he has stated a meaning, but closer examination shows that his words only signify that there is still 'something' there, though nothing whatever is said about its nature. In that case he has really communicated nothing; his claim is meaningless, for one cannot maintain the existence of something without saying *of what* one is claiming the existence. This can be brought out by reference to our example of the essentially indemonstrable 'nucleus of the electron'; but for the sake of clarity we shall analyze yet another example of a very fundamental kind.

I am looking at two pieces of green paper, and establish that they have the same color. The proposition asserting the likeness of colour is verified, *inter alia*, by the fact that I twice experience the same color at the same time. The statement 'two patches of the same color are now present' can no longer be reduced to others; it is verified by the fact that it describes the given. It has a good meaning: by virtue of the significance of the words occurring in the statement, this meaning is simply the existence of this similarity of color; by virtue of linguistic usage, the sentence expresses precisely this experience. I now show one of the two pieces of paper to a second observer, and pose the question: Does he see the green just as I do? Is his color-experience the *same* as mine? This case is *essentially* different from the one just examined. While there the statement was verifiable through the occurrence of an experience of similarity, a brief consideration shows that here such a verification is absolutely impossible. Of course (if he is not color-blind), the second observer also calls the paper *green*; and if I now describe this green to him more closely, by saying that it is more yellowish than this wallpaper, more bluish than this billiard-cloth, darker than this plant, and so on, he will also find it so each time, that is, he will agree with my statements. But even though all his judgments about colors were to agree entirely with mine, I can obviously never conclude from this that he experiences 'the same quality'. It might be that on looking at the green paper he has an experience that I should call 'red'; that conversely, in the cases where I see red, he experiences green, but of course calls it 'red', and so forth. It might even be, indeed, that my color sensations are matched in him by experiences of sound or data of some other kind; yet it would be impossible in principle ever to discover these differences between his experience and mine. We would agree completely, and could never differ about our surroundings, so long only (and this is absolutely the only precondition that has to be made) as the inner *order* of his experiences agrees with that of mine. Their 'quality' does not come into it at all; all that is required is that they can be brought into a *system* in the same fashion.

All this is doubtless uncontested, and philosophers have pointed out this situation often enough. They have mostly added, however, that such subjective differences are indeed theoretically possible, and that this possibility is in principle very interesting, but that nevertheless it is 'in the highest degree probable' that the observer and I actually experience the *same* green. We, however, must say: The claim that different individuals experierice the *same* sensation has this verifiable meaning alone, that all their statements (and of course all their other behavior as well) display certain agreements; hence the claim *means* nothing else whatever but this. It is merely another mode of expression if we say that it is a question of the likeness of two systems of order. The proposition that two experiences of different subjects not only occupy the same place in the order of a system, but *beyond that* are *also* qualitatively like each other, has no meaning for us. It is not false, be it noted, but meaningless: we have no idea at all what it is supposed to signify.

Experience shows that for the majority of people it is very difficult to agree with this. One has to grasp that we are really concerned here with a *logical* impossibility of verification. To speak of the likeness of two data in *the same* consciousness has an acceptable meaning; it can be verified through an immediate experience. But if we wish to talk of the likeness of two data in *different* consciousnesses, that is a new concept; it has to be defined anew, for propositions in which it occurs are no longer verifiable in the old fashion. The new definition is, in fact, the likeness of all reactions of the two individuals; no other can be found. The majority believe, indeed, that no definition is required here; we know straight off what 'like' means, and the meaning is in both cases the same. But in order to recognize this as an error, we have only to recall the concept of simultaneity, where the situation is precisely analogous. To the concept of 'simultaneity at the same place' there corresponds here the concept of 'likeness of experiences in the same individual'; and to 'simultaneity at different places' there corresponds here the 'likeness of experiences in different individuals'. The second is in each case something new in comparison with the first, and must be specially defined. A directly experienceable quality can no more be pointed out for the likeness of two greens in different consciousnesses than for simultaneity at different places; both must be defined by way of a system of relations.

Many philosophers have tried to overcome the difficulty that seemed to confront them here by all sorts of speculations and thought-experiments, in that they have spoken, say, of a universal consciousness (God) embracing all individuals, or have imagined that perhaps by an artificial linkage of the nerve-systems of two people the sensations of the one might be made accessible to the other and could be compared— but all this is useless, of course, since even by such fantastical methods it is in the end only contents of one and the same consciousness that are directly compared; but the question is precisely whether a comparison is possible between qualities insofar as they belong to different consciousnesses, and *not* the same one.

It must be admitted, therefore, that a proposition about the likeness of the experiences of two different persons has no other *stateable* meaning save that of a certain agreement in their reactions. Now it is open to anyone to believe that such a proposition also possesses another, more direct meaning; but it is certain that this meaning is not verifiable, and that there can be no way at all of stating or pointing out what this meaning is supposed to be. From this it follows, however, that there is absolutely no way at all in which such a meaning could be made a topic of discussion; there could be absolutely no talk about it, and it can in no way enter into any language whereby we communicate with each other.

And what has, we hope, become clear from this example, is of quite general application. All we can understand in a proposition is what it conveys; but a meaning can be communicated only if it is verifiable. Since propositions are nothing else but a vehicle of communication, we can assign to their meaning only what can be communicated. For this reason I should insist that 'meaning' can never signify anything but 'stateable meaning'.

But even if someone insisted that there was a nonverifiable meaning, this would actually be of no consequence whatever; for in everything he says and asks, and in everything that we ask him and reply to him, *such* a meaning can never in any way come to light. In other words, if such a thing were to exist, all our utterances and arguments and modes of behavior would still remain totally untouched by it, whether it was a question of daily life, of ethical or aesthetic attitude, of science of any kind, or of philosophy. Everything would be exactly as though there were no unverifiable meaning, for insofar as anything was different, it would in fact be verifiable through this very difference.

That is a serious situation, and we must absolutely demand that it be taken seriously. One must guard above all things against confusing the present logical impossibility with an empirical incapacity, just as though some technical difficulties and human imperfection were to blame for the fact that only the verifiable can be expressed, and as though there were still some little backdoor through which an unstateable meaning could slip into the daylight and make itself noticeable in our speech and behavior! No! The incommunicability is an absolute one; anyone who believes in a nonverifiable meaning (or more accurately, we shall have to say, imagines he believes in this) must still confess that only *one* attitude remains in regard to it: absolute silence. It would be of no use either to him or us, however often he asserted: 'but there is a non-verifiable meaning', for this statement is itself devoid of meaning, and says nothing.

III. What Does 'Reality' Mean? What Does 'External World' Mean?

We are now prepared to make application of the foregoing to the so-called problem of the reality of the external world.

Let us ask: What meaning has it, if the 'realist' says 'there is an external world'? or even: What meaning attaches to the claim (which the realist attributes to the positivist) 'there is no external world'?

To answer the question, it is necessary, of course, to clarify the significance of the words 'there is' and 'external world'. Let us begin with the first. 'There is x' amounts to saying 'x is real' or 'x is actual'. So what does it mean if we attribute actuality (or reality) to an object? It is an ancient and very important insight of logic or philosophy, that the proposition 'x is actual' is totally different in kind from a proposition that attributes any sort of *property* to x (such as 'x is hard'). In other words, actuality, reality or existence is not a property. The statement 'the dollar in my pocket is round' has a totally different logical form from the statement 'the dollar in my pocket is actual'. In modern logic this distinction is expressed by an altogether different symbolism, but it had already been very sharply emphasized by Kant, who, as we know, in his critique of the so-alled ontological proof of God's existence had correctly found the error of this proof in the fact that existence was treated like a property there.

In daily life we very often have to speak of actuality or existence, and for that very reason it cannot be hard to discover the meaning of this talk. In a legal battle it often has to be established whether some document really exists, or whether this has merely been falsely claimed, say, by one of the parties; nor is it wholly unimportant to me, whether the dollar in my pocket is merely imaginary or actually real. Now everybody knows in what way such a reality-claim is verified, nor can there be the least doubt about it; the reality of the dollar is proved by this, and this alone, that by suitable manipulations I furnish myself certain tactual or visual sensations, on whose occurrence I am accustomed to say: this is a dollar. The same holds of the document, only there we should be content, on occasion, with certain statements by others claiming to have seen the document, that is, to have had perceptions of a quite specific kind. And the 'statements of others' again consist in certain acoustic, or—if they were written utterances—visual perceptions. There is need of no special controversy about the fact that the occurrence of certain sense-perceptions among the data *always* constitutes the sole criterion for propositions about the reality of a 'physical' object or event, in daily life no less than in the most refined assertions of science. That there are okapis in Africa can be established only by observing such animals. But it is not necessary that the object or event 'itself' should have to be perceived. We can imagine, for example, that the existence of a trans-Neptunian planet might be inferred by observation of perturbations with just as much certainty as by direct perception of a speck of light in the telescope. The reality of the atom provides another example, as does the back side of the moon.

It is of great importance to state that the occurrence of some one particular experience in verifying a reality-statement is often not recognized as such a verification, but that it is throughout a question of regularities, of law-like connections; in this way true verifications are distinguished from illusions and hallucinations. If we say of some event or object—which must be marked out by a description—that it is *real*, this means, then, that there is a quite specific connection between perceptions or other experiences, that under given circumstances certain data are presented. By this alone is it verified, and hence this is also its only stateable meaning.

This, too, was already formulated, in principle, by Kant, whom nobody will accuse of 'positivism'. Reality, for him, is a category, and if we apply it anywhere, and claim of an object that it is real, then all this asserts, in Kant's opinion, is that it belongs to a law-governed connection of perceptions.

It will be seen that for us (as for Kant; and the same must apply to any philosopher who is aware of his task) it is merely a matter of saying what is meant when we ascribe real existence to a thing in life or in science; it is in no sense a matter of correcting the claims of ordinary life or of research. I must confess that I should charge with folly and reject *a limine* every philosophical system that involved the claim that clouds and stars, mountains and the sea, were not actually real, that the 'physical world' did not exist, and that the chair against the wall ceases to be every time I turn my back on it. Nor do I seriously impute such a claim to any thinker. It would, for example, be undoubtedly a quite mistaken account of Berkeley's philosophy if his system were to be understood in this fashion. He, too, in no way denied the reality of the physical world, but merely sought to explain what we mean when we attribute reality to it. Anyone who says here that unperceived things are ideas in the mind of God is not in fact denying their existence, but is seeking, rather, to understand it. Even John Stuart Mill was not wanting to deny the reality of physical objects, but rather to explain it, when he declared them to be 'permanent possibilities of sensation', although I do consider his mode of expression to have been very unsuitably chosen.

So if 'positivism' is understood to mean a view that denies reality to bodies, I should simply have to declare it absurd; but I do not believe that such an interpretation of positivist opinions, at least as regards their competent exponents, would be historically just. Yet, however that may be, we are concerned only with the issue itself. And on this we have established as follows: our principle, that the question about the meaning of a proposition is identical with the question about its verification, leads us to recognize that the claim that a thing is real is a statement about lawful connections of experiences; it does *not*, however, imply this claim to be false. (There is therefore no denial of reality to physical objects in favor of sensations.)

But opponents of the view presented profess themselves by no means satisfied with this assertion. So far as I can see, they would answer as follows: 'You do, indeed, acknowledge completely the reality of the physical world, but—as we see it—only in words. You simply *call* real what we should describe as mere conceptual constructions. When *we* use the word "reality", we mean by it something quite different from you. Your definition of the real reduces it to experiences; but we mean something quite independent of all experiences. We mean something that possesses the same independence that you obviously concede only to the data, in that you reduce everything else to them, as the not-further-reducible'.

Although it would be a sufficient rebuttal to request our opponents to reflect once more upon how reality-statements are verified, and how verification is connected with *meaning*, I do in fact recognize the need to take account of the psychological attitude from which this argument springs, and therefore beg attention to the following considerations, whereby a modification of this attitude may yet, perhaps, be effected.

Let us first enquire whether, on our view, a 'content of consciousness' is credited with a reality that is denied to a physical object. We ask, therefore: does the claim that a feeling or sensation is real have a meaning different from the claim that a physical object is real? For us, this can mean only: are different types of verification involved in the two cases? The answer is: no!

To clarify this, we need to enter a little into the logical form of reality-statements. The general logical recognition that an existence-statement can be made about a datum only if it is marked out by a description, but not if it is given by an immediate indication, is also valid, of course, for the 'data of consciousness'. In the language of symbolic logic, this is expressed by the fact that an existence-claim must contain an 'operator'. In Russell's notation, for example, a reality-statement has the form $(\exists x)fx$, or in words, 'there is an x that has the property f'. The form of words 'there is a', where 'a' is supposed to be the individual name of a directly indicated object, therefore means no more than 'this here'; this form of words is meaningless, and in Russell's symbolism it cannot even be written down. We have to grasp the idea that Descartes's proposition 'I am'—or, to put it better, 'contents of consciousness exist'—is absolutely meaningless; it express nothing, and contains no knowledge. This is due to the fact that 'contents of consciousness' occurs in this connection as a mere *name* for the given; no characteristic is asserted, whose presence could be tested. A proposition has meaning, and is verifiable, only if I can state under what circumstances it would be true, and under what circumstances it would be false. But how am I to describe the circumstances under which the proposition 'My contents of consciousness exist' would be false? Every attempt would lead to ridiculous absurdities, to such propositions, say, as 'It is the case that nothing is the case', or the like. Hence I am self-evidently unable to describe the circumstances that make the proposition true (just try it!). Nor is there any doubt whatever that Descartes, with his proposition, had really obtained no knowledge, and was actually no wiser than before.

No, the question about the reality of an experience has meaning only where this reality can also be meaningfully *doubted*. I can ask, for example: Is it really true that I felt joy on hearing that news? This can be verified or falsified exactly as when we ask, say: Is it true that Sirius has a companion (that this companion is real)? That I felt joy on a particular occasion can be verified, for example, by examination of other people's statements about my behaviour at the time, by my finding of a letter that I then wrote, or simply by the return to me of an exact memory of the emotion I experienced. Here, therefore, there is not the slightest difference of principle: to be real always means to stand in a definite connection with the given. Nor is it otherwise, say, with an experience that is present at this very moment. I can quite meaningfully ask, for example (in the course, say, of a physiological experiment): Do I now actually feel a pain or not? (Notice that 'pain', here, does not function as an individual name for a 'this here', but represents a conceptual term for a describable class of experiences.) Here, too, the question is answered by establishing that in conjunction with certain circumstances (experimental conditions, concentration of attention, etc.) an experience with certain describable properties occurs. Such describable properties would be, for example: similarity to an experience that has occurred under certain other circumstances; tendency to evoke certain reactions; and so on.

However we may twist and turn, it is impossible to interpret a reality-statement otherwise than as fitting into a perceptual context. It is absolutely the *same* kind of reality that we have to attribute to the data of consciousness and to physical events. Scarcely anything in the history of philosophy has created more confusion than the attempt to pick out one of the two as true 'being'. Wherever the term 'real' is intelligibly used, it has one and the same meaning.

Our opponent, perhaps, will still feel his position unshaken by what we have said, having the impression, rather, that the arguments here presented presuppose a starting-point at which he cannot, from the outset, station himself. He has to concede that the decision about the reality or unreality of anything in experience takes place, in every case, in the manner outlined, but he claims that in this way we only arrive at what Kant called *empirical* reality. It designates the area governed by the observations of daily life and of science, but beyond this boundary there lies something else, *transcendent* reality, which cannot be inferred by strict logic, and is thus no postulate of the understanding, though it is a postulate of sound *reason*. It is the only true *external world*, and this alone is at issue in the philosophical problem of the existence of the external world. The discussion thereupon abandons the question about the meaning of the term 'reality', and turns to that about the meaning of the term 'external world'.

The term 'external world' is obviously used in two different ways: firstly in the usage of daily life, and secondly as a technical term in philosophy.

Where it occurs in everyday life, it has, like the majority of expressions employed in practical affairs, an intelligibly stateable meaning. In contrast to the 'internal world', which covers memories, thoughts, dreams, wishes and feelings, the 'external world' means nothing else, here, but the world of mountains and trees, houses, animals and men. What it means to maintain the existence of a certain object in this world, is known to every child; and it was necessary to point out that it really means absolutely nothing *more* than what the child knows. We all know how to verify the proposition, say, that 'There is a castle in the park before the town'. We perform certain acts, and if certain exactly specifiable states-of-affairs come about, then we say: 'Yes, there really is a castle there'; otherwise we say: 'That statement was an error or a lie.' And if somebody now asks us: 'But was the castle there in the night as well, when nobody saw it?' we answer: 'Undoubtedly! for it would have been impossible to build it in the period from early this morning till now, and besides, the state of the building shows that it was not only already *in situ* yesterday, but has been there for a hundred years, and hence since before we were born'. We are thus in possession of quite specific empirical criteria for whether houses and trees were also there when we were not seeing them, and whether they already existed before our birth, and will exist after our death. That is to say, the claim that these things 'exist independently of us' has a perfectly clear, testable meaning, and is obviously to be answered in the affirmative. We are very well able to distinguish such things in a stateable way from those that only occur 'subjectively', 'in dependence upon ourselves'. If, owing to an eye defect, I see, for example, a dark speck when I look at the wall opposite me, I say of it that it is there only when I look, whereas I say of the wall that it is also there when I am not looking. The verification of this difference is in fact very easy, and both claims assert precisely what is contained in these verifications and nothing more.

So if the term 'external world' is taken in the everyday sense, the question about its existence simply means: Are there, in addition to memories, wishes and ideas, also stars, clouds, plants and animals, and my own body? We have just affirmed once more that it would be utterly absurd to say no to this question. There are obviously houses and clouds and animals existing independently of us, and I have already said earlier that a thinker who denied the existence of the external world in this sense would have no claim to our attention. Instead of telling us what we mean when we speak of mountains and plants, he wishes to persuade us that there are no such things at all!

But now how about science? When it speaks of the external world, does it, unlike daily life, mean something other than things such as houses and trees? It seems to me that this is by no means the case. For atoms and electric fields, or whatever else the physicist may speak of, are precisely what houses and trees consist of, according to his teaching; the one must therefore be real in the same sense as the other. The objectivity of mountains and clouds is just exactly the same as that of protons and energies; the latter stand in no greater contrast to the 'subjectivity' of feelings, say, or hallucinations, than do the former. We have long since convinced ourselves, in fact, that the existence of even the most subtle of the 'invisible' things postulated by the scientist is verified, in principle, in exactly the same way as the reality of a tree or a star.

In order to settle the dispute about realism, it is of the greatest importance to alert the physicist to the fact that his external world is nothing else but the *nature* which also surrounds us in daily life, and is not the 'transcendent world' of the metaphysicians. The difference between the two is again quite particularly evident in the philosophy of Kant. Nature, and everything of which the physicist can and must speak, belongs, in Kant's view, to empirical reality, and the meaning of this (as already mentioned) is explained by him exactly as we have also had to do. Atoms, in Kant's system, have no transcendent reality—they are not 'things-in-themselves'. Thus the physicist cannot appeal to the Kantian philosophy; his arguments lead only to the empirical external world that we all acknowledge, not to a transcendent one; his electrons are not metaphysical entities.

Many scientists speak, nonetheless, of the necessity of having to postulate the existence of an external world as a *metaphysical* hypothesis. They never do this, indeed, within their own science (although all the necessary hypotheses of a science ought to occur *within* it), but only at the point where they leave this territory and begin to philosophize. The transcendent external world is actually something that is referred to exclusively in philosophy, never in a science or in daily life. It is simply a technical term, whose meaning we now have to inquire into.

How does the transcendent or metaphysical external world differ from the empirical one? In philosophical systems it is thought of as subsisting somehow behind the empirical world, where the word 'behind' is also supposed to indicate that this world is not *knowable* in the same sense as the empirical, that it lies beyond a boundary that divides the accessible from the inaccessible.

This distinction originally has its ground in the view formerly shared by the majority of philosophers, that to know an object requires that it be immediately given, directly experienced; knowledge is a kind of intuition, and is perfect only if the known is directly present to the knower, like a sensation or a feeling. So what cannot be immediately experienced or intuited remains, on this view, unknowable, ungraspable, transcendent, and belongs to the realm of things-in-themselves. Here, as I have elsewhere had to state on numerous occasions, we simply have a confusion of knowing with mere acquaintance or experiencing. But such a confusion is certainly not committed by modern scientists; I do not believe that any physicist considers knowledge of the electron to consist in its entering bodily, by an act of intuition, into the scientist's consciousness; he will take the view, rather, that for complete knowledge the only thing needed is for the regularity of an electron's behaviour to be so exhaustively stated that all formulae in which its properties occur in any way are totally confirmed by experience. In other words, the electron, and all physical realities likewise, are *not* unknowable things-in-themselves, and do not belong to a transcendent, metaphysical reality, if this is characterized by the fact that it embraces the unknowable.

Thus we again return to the conclusion that all the physicist's hypotheses can relate only to *empirical* reality, if by this we mean the knowable. It would in fact be a self-contradiction to wish to assume something unknowable as a hypothesis. For there must always be specific *reasons* for setting up a hypothesis, since it is, after all, supposed to fulfil a specific purpose. What is assumed in the hypothesis must therefore have the property of fulfilling this purpose, and of being precisely so constituted as to be justified by these reasons. But in virtue of this very fact certain statements are made of it, and these contain *knowledge* of it. And they contain, indeed, *complete* knowledge of it, since *only* that can be hypothetically assumed for which there are reasons in experience.

Or does the scientific 'realist' wish to characterize the talk of not immediately experienced objects as a metaphysical hypothesis for some reason other than the nonexistent one of its unknowability? To this, perhaps, he will answer 'yes'. In fact it can be seen from numerous statements in the literature, that the physicist by no means couples his claim of a transcendent world with the claim that it is unknowable; on the contrary, he (quite rightly) takes the view that the nature of extra-mental things is reflected with perfect correctness in his equations. Hence the external world of the physical realist is not that of traditional metaphysics. He employs the technical term of the philosophers, but what he designates by means of it has seemed to us to be merely the external world of everyday life, whose existence is doubted by nobody, not even the 'positivist'.

So what is this other reason that leads the 'realist' to regard his external world as a metaphysical assumption? Why does he want to distinguish it from the empirical external world that we have described? The answer to this question leads us back again to an earlier point in our argument. For the 'realistic' physicist is perfectly content with our description of the external world, except on one point: he thinks that we have not lent it enough *reality*. It is not by its unknowability or any other feature that he takes his 'external world' to differ from the empirical one; it is simply and solely by the fact that another, higher reality attaches to it. This often finds expression even in the terminology; the word 'real' is often reserved for this external world, in contrast to the merely 'ideal', 'subjective' content of consciousness, and the mere 'logical constructions' into which 'positivism' is accused of dissolving reality.

But now even the physical realist has a dim feeling that, as we know, reality is not a 'property'; hence he cannot simply pass from our empirical external world to his transcendent one by attributing to it the feature of 'reality' over and above the features that we, too, ascribe to all physical objects; yet that is how he talks, and this illegitimate leap, whereby he leaves the realm of the meaningful, would in fact be 'metaphysical', and is also felt to be such by himself.

We now have a clear view of the situation, and can judge it on the basis of the preceding considerations.

Our principle, that the truth and falsity of all statements, including those about the reality of a physical object, can be tested only in the 'given', and that *therefore* the meaning of all statements can likewise be formulated and understood only by means of the given—this principle has been wrongly construed as if it claimed or presupposed that only the given is real. Hence the 'realist' feels compelled to contradict the principle, and to set up the counterclaim, that the meaning of a reality-statement is by no means exhausted in mere assertions of the form 'Under these particular circumstances this particular experience will occur' (where these assertions, on our view, are in any case an infinite multitude); the meaning, he says, in fact lies *beyond this* in something else, which must be referred to, say, as 'independent existence', 'transcendent being' or the like, and of which our principle provides no account.

To this we ask: Well, then, *how* does one give an account of it? What do these words 'independent existence' and 'transcendent being' mean? In other words, what testable difference does it make in the world, whether an object has transcendent being or not?

Two answers are given here. The first runs: It makes a quite enormous difference. For a scientist who believes in a 'real external world' will feel and work quite differently from one who merely aims at 'describing sensations'. The former will regard the starry heaven, whose aspect recalls to him the inconceivable sublimity and size of the universe, and his own human smallness, with feelings of awe and devotion quite different from those of the latter, to whom the most distant galactic systems are but 'complexes of his own sensations' The first will be devoted to his task with an enthusiasm, and will feel in his knowing of the objective world a satisfaction, that are denied to the second, since he takes himself to be concerned only with constructions of his own.

To this first answer we have this to say: If, in the behaviour of two thinkers, there should anywhere occur a difference such as has here been described—and it would in fact involve an observable state-of-affairs—and were we to insist upon so expressing this difference as to say that the first believes in a real external world, and the other not—well, even so, the *meaning* of our assertion still consists solely in what we observe in the behavior of the two. That is to say, the words 'absolute reality', or 'transcendent being', or whatever other terms we may use for it, now *signify* absolutely nothing else but certain states of feeling which arise in the two whenever they contemplate the universe, or make reality-statements, or philosophize. The fact of the matter is, that employment of the words 'independent existence', 'transcendent reality' and so on, is simply and solely the expression of a feeling, a psychological attitude of the speaker (which may in the end, moreover, apply to all metaphysical propositions). If someone assures us that there is a real external world in the supra-empirical sense of the term, he thinks, no doubt, that he has thereby conveyed a truth about the world; but in actuality his words express a quite different state-of-affairs, namely the mere presence of certain feelings, which provoke him to specific reactions of a verbal or other nature.

If the self-evident still needs to be specially dwelt on, I should like to underline— but in that case with maximum emphasis, and with stress upon the *seriousness* of what I am saying—that the nonmetaphysician does not differ from the metaphysician by the fact, say, that he lacks those feelings to which the other gives expression by way of the propositions of a 'realistic' philosophy, but only by the fact that he has recognized that these propositions by no means have the meaning that they seem to have, and are therefore to be avoided. He will give expression to the same feelings in a *different* way. In other words, this confrontation of the two types of thinker, set up in the 'realist's' first answer, was misleading and erroneous. If anyone is so unfortunate as not to feel the sublimity of the starry heaven, then the blame lies on something other than a logical analysis of the concepts of reality and the external world. To suppose that the opponent of metaphysics is incapable, say, of justly estimating the greatness of Copernicus, because in a certain sense the Ptolemaic view reflects the empirical situation just as well as the Copernican, seems to me no less strange than to believe that the 'positivist' cannot be a good father to his family, because according to his theory his children are merely complexes of his own sensations, and it is therefore senseless to make provision for their welfare after his death. No, the world of the non-metaphysician is the same world as that of everybody else; it lacks nothing that is needed in order to make meaningful all the statements of science and all the actions of daily life. He merely refuses to add meaningless statements to his description of the world.

We come to the *second* answer that can be given to the question about the meaning of the claim that there is a transcendent reality. It simply consists in admitting that it makes absolutely no difference for experience whether we postulate something else existing behind the empirical world or not; metaphysical realism cannot therefore be actually tested or verified. Thus it cannot be further stated what is meant by this claim; yet something *is* meant thereby, and the meaning can also be understood without verification.

This is nothing else but the view criticized in the previous Section, that the meaning of a proposition has nothing to do with its verification, and it only remains for us to repeat once more our earlier general criticism, as applied to this particular Case. We must reply, therefore: Well now! You are giving the name 'existence' or 'reality' here to something that is utterly inexpressible and cannot be explained or stated in any fashion. You think, nonetheless, that these words have a meaning. As to that, we shall not quarrel with you. But this much is certain: by the admission just made, this meaning cannot in any way become manifest, cannot be expressed by any oral or written communication, or by any gesture or act. For if this were possible, a testable empirical situation would exist; there would be something *different* in the world, if the proposition 'There is a transcendent world' were true, from if it were false. This differentness would then signify the meaning of the words 'real external world', and hence it would be an empirical meaning—that is, this real external world would again be merely the empirical world which we, too, acknowledge, like everyone else. Even to speak, merely, of another world, is logically impossible. There can be no discussion about it, for a nonverifiable existence cannot enter as meaning into any possible proposition. Anyone who still believes in such a thing—or imagines he believes—can only do so in silence. There are arguments only for something that can be said.

The results of our discussion can be summarized as follows:

1. The principle, that the meaning of every proposition is exhaustively determined by its verification in the given, seems to me a legitimate, unassailable core of the 'positivist' schools of thought.

But within these schools it has seldom come clearly to light, and has often been mingled with so many untenable principles, that a logical clean-up is necessary. If we want to call the result of this clean-up 'positivism', which might well be justified on historical grounds, we should have, perhaps, to affix a differentiating adjective: the term[4] 'logical' or 'logistic positivism' is often used; otherwise the expression 'consistent empiricism' has seemed to me appropriate.

2. This principle does not mean, nor does it follow from it, that only the given is real; such a claim would actually be meaningless.

3. Consistent empiricism, therefore, does *not* deny, either, the existence of an external world; it merely points out the empirical meaning of this existence-claim.

4. It is not an 'as if theory'. It does not say, for example, that everything behaves as if there were physical independent bodies; on the contrary, for it, too, everything is real that the nonphilosophizing scientist declares to be real. The subject matter of physics does not consist of sensations, but of laws. The formulation employed by some positivists, that bodies 'are mere complexes of sensations' is therefore to be rejected. The only correct view is that propositions about bodies can be transformed into propositions of like meaning about the regularity of occurrence of sensations.[5]

5. Logical positivism and realism are therefore not opposed; anyone who acknowledges our principle must actually be an empirical realist.

6. There is opposition only between consistent empiricism and the metaphysician, and it is directed as much against the realist as the idealist (the former is designated in our discussion as a 'realist', in quotation-marks).

7. The denial of the existence of a transcendent external world would be just as much a metaphysical proposition as its assertion; the consistent empiricist does not therefore deny the transcendent, but declares both its denial and its affimmation to be equally devoid of meaning.

This last distinction is of the greatest importance. I am convinced that the main resistances to our viewpoint stem from the fact that the difference between the falsity and the meaninglessness of a proposition is not heeded. The proposition 'Talk of a metaphysical external world is meaningless' does *not* say 'There is no metaphysical external world', but something *toto coelo* different. The empiricist does not say to the metaphysician: 'Your words assert something false', but 'Your words assert nothing at all!' He does not contradict the metaphysician, but says: 'I do not understand you'.

Notes

1. [E. Laas, *Idealismus und Positivismus. Eine kritische Auseinandersetzung*, Berlin 1879–1881.]
2. M. Planck, *Positivismus und reale Aussenwelt*, Leipzig 1931, p. 14.
3. Cf. *ibid.*, p. 11.
4. Cf. the article by A. E. Blumberg and H. Feigl ["Logical Positivism"] in *The Journal of Philosophy* **28** (1931); see also E. Kaila ['Der logistische Neupositinsmus. Eine kritische Studie'] in *Annales Universitatis Aboensis* **13** (1930), and A. Petzäll ["Logistischer Positivismus"] in *Göreborgs Högskolas Arsskrift* **37** (1931).
5. On this, as on the content of the whole essay, cf. the article by H. Cornelius ['Zur Kritik der wissenschaftlichen Grundbegriffe'] in *Erkenntnis* **2** (1931). The formulations there are admittedly not free from objection. Cf. also the outstanding discussion by Philipp Frank in chapter X of his book *Das Kausalgesetz und seine Grenzen*, Wien 1932, and Rudolf Carnap, *Scheinprobleme in der Philosophie*, Leipzig and Berlin 1928.

Chapter 2

The Operational Character of Scientific Concepts

Percy Bridgman

Whatever may be one's opinion as to our permanent acceptance of the analytical details of Einstein's restricted and general theories of relativity, there can be no doubt that through these theories physics is permanently changed. It was a great shock to discover that classical concepts, accepted unquestioningly, were inadequate to meet the actual situation, and the shock of this discovery has resulted in a critical attitude toward our whole conceptual structure which must at least in part be permanent. Reflection on the situation after the event shows that it should not have needed the new experimental facts which led to relativity to convince us of the inadequacy of our previous concepts, but that a sufficiently shrewd analysis should have prepared us for at least the possibility of what Einstein did.

Looking now to the future, our ideas of what external nature is will always be subject to change as we gain new experimental knowledge, but there is a part of our attitude to nature which should not be subject to future change, namely that part which rests on the permanent basis of the character of our minds. It is precisely here, in an improved understanding of our mental relations to nature, that the permanent contribution of relativity is to be found. We should now make it our business to understand so thoroughly the character of our permanent mental relations to nature that another change in our attitude, such as that due to Einstein, shall be forever impossible. It was perhaps excusable that a revolution in mental attitude should occur once, because after all physics is a young science, and physicists have been very busy, but it would certainly be a reproach if such a revolution should ever prove necessary again.

New Kinds of Experience Always Possible

The first lesson of our recent experience with relativity is merely an intensification and emphasis of the lesson which all past experience has also taught, namely, that when experiment is pushed into new domains, we must be prepared for new facts, of a entirely different character from those of our former experience. This is taught not only by the discovery of those unsuspected properties of matter moving with high velocities, which inspired the theory of relativity, but also even more emphatically by the new facts in the quantum domain. To a certain extent, of course, the recognition of all this does not involve a change of former attitude; the *fact* has always been for the physicist the one ultimate thin from which there is no appeal, and in the face of which the only possible attitude is a humility almost religious. The new feature in the present situation is an intensified conviction that in reality new orders of experience do exist, and that we may expect to meet them continually. We have already encountered new phenomena in going to high velocities, and in going to small scales of magnitude: we may similarly expect to find them, for example, in dealing with relations of cosmic magnitudes, or in dealing with the properties of matter of enormous densities, such as is supposed to exist in the stars.

Implied in this recognition of the possibility of new experience beyond our present range is the recognition that no element of a physical situation, no matter how apparently irrelevant or trivial, may be dismissed as without effect on the final result until proved to be without effect by actual experiment.

The attitude of the physicist must therefore be one of pure empiricism. He recognizes no *a priori* principles which determine or limit the possibilities of new experience. Experience is determined only by experience. This practically means that we must give up the demand that all nature be embraced in any formula, either simple or complicated. It may perhaps turn out eventually that as a matter of fact nature can be embraced in a formula, but we must so organize our thinking as not to demand it as a necessity.

The Operational Character of Concepts

Einstein's Contribution in Changing Our Attitude Toward Concepts

Recognizing the essential unpredictability of experiment beyond our present range, the physicist, if he is to escape continually revising his attitude, must use in describing and correlating nature concepts of such a character that our present experience does not exact hostages of the future. Now here it seems to me is the greatest contribution of Einstein. Although he himself does not explicitly state or emphasize it, believe that a study of what he has done will show that he has essentially modified our view of what the concepts useful in physics are and should be. Hitherto many of the concepts of physics have been defined in terms of their properties. An excellent example is afforded by Newton's concept of absolute time. The following quotation from the Scholium in Book I of the *Principia* is illuminating:

> I do not define Time, Space, Place or Motion, as being well known to all. Only I must observe that the vulgar conceive those quantities under no other notions but from the relation they bear to sensible objects. And thence arise certain prejudices, for the removing of which, it will be convenient to distinguish them into Absolute and Relative, True and Apparent, Mathematical and Common.
>
> (I) Absolute, True, and Mathematical Time, of itself, and from its own nature flows equably without regard to anything external, and by another name is called Duration.

Now there is no assurance whatever that there exists in nature anything with properties like those assumed in the definition, and physics, when reduced to concepts of this character, becomes as purely an abstract science and as far removed from reality as the abstract geometry of the mathematicians, built on postulates. It is a task for experiment to discover whether concepts so defined correspond to anything in nature, and we must always be prepared to find that the concepts correspond to nothing or only partially correspond. In particular, if we examine the definition of absolute time in the light of experiment, we find nothing in nature with such properties.

The new attitude toward a concept is entirely different. We may illustrate by considering the concept of length: what do we mean by the length of an object? We evidently know what we mean by length if we can tell what the length of any and every object is, and for the physicist nothing more is required. To find the length of an object, we have to perform certain physical operations. The concept of length is therefore fixed when the operations by which length is measured are fixed: that is, the concept of length involves as much as and nothing more than the set of operations by which length is determined. In general, we mean by any concept nothing more than a set of operations; *the concept is synonymous with the corresponding set of operations.* If the concept is physical, as of length, the operations are actual physical operations, namely, those by which length is measured; or if the concept is mental, as of mathematical continuity, the operations are mental operations, namely those by which we determine whether a given aggregate of magnitudes is continuous. It is not intended to imply that there is a hard and fast division between physical and mental concepts, or that one kind of concept does not always contain an element of the other; this classification of concept is not important for our future considerations.

We must demand that the set of operations equivalent to any concept be a unique set, for otherwise there are possibilities of ambiguity in practical applications which we cannot admit.

Applying this idea of "concept" to absolute time, we do not understand the meaning of absolute time unless we can tell how to determine the absolute time of any concrete event, *i.e.*, unless we can measure absolute time. Now we merely have to examine any of the possible operations by which we measure time to see that all such operations are relative operations. Therefore the previous statement that absolute time does not exist is replaced by the statement that absolute time is meaningless. And in making this statement we are not saying something new about nature, but are merely bringing to light implications already contained in the physical operations used in measuring time.

It is evident that if we adopt this point of view toward concepts, namely that the proper definition of a concept is not in terms of its properties but in terms of actual operations, we need run no danger of having to revise our attitude toward nature. For if experience is always described in terms of experience, there must always be correspondence between experience and our description of it, and we need never be embarrassed, as we were in attempting to find in nature the prototype of Newton's absolute time. Furthermore, if we remember that the operations to which a physical concept are equivalent are actual physical operations, the concepts can be defined only in the range of actual experiment, and are undefined and meaningless in regions as yet untouched by experiment. It follows that strictly speaking we cannot make statements at all about regions as yet untouched, and that when we do make such statements, as we inevitably shall, we are making a conventionalized extrapolation, of the looseness of which we must be fully conscious, and the justification of which is in the experiment of the future.

There probably is no statement either in Einstein or other writers that the change described above in the use of "concept" has been self-consciously made, but that such is the case is proved, I believe, by an examination of the way concepts are now handled by Einstein and others. For of course the true meaning of a term is to be found by observing what a man does with it, not by what he says about it. We may show that this is the actual sense in which concept is coming to be used by examining in particular Einstein's treatment of simultaneity.

Before Einstein, the concept of simultaneity was defined in terms of properties. It was a property of two events, when described with respect to their relation in time, that one event was either before the other, or after it, or simultaneous with it. Simultaneity was a property of the two events alone and nothing else; either two events were simultaneous or they were not. The justification for using this term in this way was that it seemed to describe the behavior of actual things. But of course experience then was restricted to a narrow range. When the range of experience was broadened, as by going to high velocities, it was found that the concepts no longer applied, because there was no counterpart in experience for this absolute relation between two events. Einstein now subjected the concept of simultaneity to a critique, which consisted essentially in showing that the operations which enable two events to be described as simultaneous involve measurements on the two events made by an observer, so that "simultaneity" is, therefore, not an absolute property of the two events and nothing else, but must also involve the relation of the events to the observer. Until therefore we have experimental proof to the contrary, we must be prepared to find that the simultaneity of two events depends on their relation to the observer, and in particular on their velocity. Einstein, in thus analyzing what is involved in making a judgment of simultaneity, and in seizing on the act of the observer as the essence of the situation, is actually adopting a new point of view as to what the concepts of physics should be, namely, the operational view.

Of course Einstein actually went much further than this, and found precisely how the operations for judging simultaneity change when the observer moves, and obtained quantitative expressions for the effect of the motion of the observer on the relative time of two events. We may notice, parenthetically, that there is much freedom of choice in selecting the exact operations; those which Einstein chose were determined by convenience and simplicity with relation to light beams. Entirely apart from the precise quantitative relations of Einstein's theory, however, the important point for us is that if we had adopted the operational point of view, we would, before the discovery of the actual physical facts, have seen that simultaneity is essentially a relative concept, and would have left room in our thinking for the discovery of such effects as were later found.

Detailed Discussion of the Concept of Length
We may now gain further familiarity with the operational attitude toward a concept and some of its implications by examining from this point of view the concept of length. Our task is to find the operations by which we measure the length of any concrete physical object. We begin with objects of our commonest experience, such as a house or a house lot. What we do is sufficiently indicated by the following rough description. We start with a measuring rod, lay it on the object so that one of its ends coincides with one end of the object, mark on the object the position of the other end of the rod, then move the rod along in a straight line extension of its previous position until the first end coincides with the previous position of the second end, repeat this process as often as we can, and call the length the total number of times the rod was applied. This procedure, apparently so simple, is in practice exceedingly complicated, and doubtless a full description of all the precautions that must be taken would fill a large treatise. We must, for example, be sure that the temperature of the rod is the standard temperature at which its length is defined, or else we must make a correction for it; or we must correct for the gravitational distortion of the rod if we measure a vertical length; or we must be sure that the rod is not a magnet or is not subject to electrical forces. All these precautions would occur to every physicist. But we must also go further and specify all the details by which the rod is moved from one position to the next on the object—its precise path through space and its velocity and acceleration in getting from one position to another. Practically of course, precautions such as these are not mentioned, but the justification is in our experience that variations of

procedure of this kind are without effect on the final result. But we always have to recognize that all our experience is subject to error, and that at some time in the future we may have to specify more carefully the acceleration, for example, of the rod in moving from one position to another, if experimental accuracy should be so increased as to show a measureable effect. In *principle* the operations by which length is measured should be *uniquely* specified. If we have more than one set of operations, we have more than one concept, and strictly there should be a separate name to correspond to each different set of operations.

So much for the length of a stationary object, which is complicated enough. Now suppose we have to measure a moving street car. The simplest, and what we may call the "naïve" procedure, is to board the car with our meter stick and repeat the operations we would apply to a stationary body. Notice that this procedure reduces to that already adopted in the limiting case when the velocity of the street car vanishes. But here there may be new questions of detail. How shall we jump on to the car with our stick in hand? Shall we run and jump on from behind, or shall we let it pick us up from in front? Or perhaps does now the material of which the stick is composed make a difference, although previously it did not? All these questions must be answered by experiment. We believe from present evidence that it makes no difference how we jump on to the car, or of what material the rod is made, and that the length of the car found in this way will be the same as if it were at rest. But the experiments are more difficult, and we are not so sure of our conclusions as before. Now there are very obvious limitations to the procedure just given. If the street car is going too fast, we can not board it directly, but must use devices, such as getting on from a moving automobile; and, more important still, there are limitations to the velocity that can be given to street cars or to meter sticks by any practical means in our control, so that the moving bodies which can be measured in this way are restricted to a low range of velocity. If we want to be able to measure the length of bodies moving with higher velocities such as we find existing in nature (stars or cathode particles), we must adopt another definition and other operations for measuring length, which also reduce to the operations already adopted in the static case. This is precisely what Einstein did. Since Einstein's operations were different from our operations above, *his "length" does not mean the same as our "length."* We must accordingly be prepared to find that the length of a moving body measured by the procedure of Einstein is not the same as that above; this of course is the fact, and the transformation formulas of relativity give the precise connection between the two lengths.

Einstein's procedure for measuring the length of bodies in motion was dictated not only by the consideration that it must be applicable to bodies with high velocities, but also by mathematical convenience, in that Einstein describes the world mathematically by a system of coördinate geometry, and the "length" of an object is connected simply with quantities in the analytic equations.

It is of interest to describe briefly Einstein's actual operations for measuring the length of a body in motion; it will show how operations which may be simple from a mathematical point of view may appear complicated from a physical viewpoint. The observer who is to measure the length of a moving object must first extend over his entire plane of reference (for simplicity the problem is considered two-dimensional) a system of time coördinates, *i.e.*, at each point of his plane of reference there must be a clock, and all these clocks must be synchronized. At each clock an observer must be situated. Now to find the length of the moving object at a specified instant of time (it is a subject for later investigation to find whether its length is a function of time), the two observers who happen to coincide in position with the two ends of the object at the specified time on their clocks are required to find the distance between their two positions by the procedure for measuring the length of a stationary object, and this distance is by definition the length of the moving object in the given reference system. This procedure for measuring the length of a body in motion hence involves the idea of simultaneity, through the simultaneous position of the two ends of the rod, and we have seen that the operations by which simultaneity are determined are relative, changing when the motion of the system changes. We hence are prepared to find a change in the length of a body when the velocity of the measuring system changes, and this in fact is what happens. The precise numerical dependence is worked out by Einstein, and involves other considerations, in which we are not interested at present.

The two sorts of length, the naïve one and that of Einstein, have certain features in common. In either case in the limit, as the velocity of the measuring system approaches zero, the operations approach those for measuring the length of a stationary object. This, of course, is a requirement in any good definition, imposed by considerations of convenience, and it is too obvious a matter to need elaboration. Another feature is that the operations equivalent to either concept both involve the motion of the system, so that we must recognize the possibility that the length of a moving object may be a function of its velocity. It is a matter of experiment, unpredictable until tried, that within the limits of present experimental error the naïve length is not affected by motion, and Einstein's length is.

So far, we have extended the concept of length in only one way beyond the range of ordinary experience, namely to high velocities. The extension may obviously be made in other directions. Let us inquire what are the operations by which we measure the length of a very large object. In practice we probably first meet the desirability of a change procedure in measuring large pieces of land. Here our procedure depends on measurments with a surveyor's theodolite. This involves extending over the surface of the land a system of coördinates, starting from a base line measured with a tape in the conventional way, sighting on distant points from the extremities of the line, and measuring the angles. Now in this extension we have made one very essential change: the angles between the lines connecting distant points are now angles between beams of light. We assume that a beam of light travels in a straight line. Furthermore, we assume in extending our system of triangulation over the surface of the earth that the geometry of light beams is Euclidean. We do the best we can to check the assumptions, but at most can never get more than a partial check. Thus Gauss[1] checked whether the angles of a large terrestrial triangle add to two right angles and found agreement within experimental error. We now know from the experiments of Michelson[2] that if his measurements had been accurate enough he would not have got a check, but would have had an excess or defect according to the direction in which the beam of light traveled around the triangle with respect to the rotation of the earth. But if the geometry of light beams is Euclidean, then not only must the angles of a triangle add to two right angles, but there are definite relations between the lengths of the sides and the angles, and to check these relations the sides should be measured by the old procedure with a meter stick. Such a check on a large scale has never been attempted, and is not feasible. It seems, then, that our checks on the Euclidean character of optical space are all of restricted character. We have apparently proved that up to a certain scale of magnitude optical space is Euclidean with respect to measures of angle, but this may not necessarily involve that space is also Euclidean with respect to measures of length, so that space need not be completely Euclidean. There is a further most important restriction in that our studies of non-Euclidean geometry have shown that the *percentage* excess of the angles of a non-Euclidean triangle over 180° may depend on the magnitude of the triangle, so that it may well be that we have not detected the non-Euclidean character of space simply because our measurements have not been on a large enough scale.

We thus see that the concept of length has undergone a very essential change of character even within the range of terrestrial measurements, in that we have sub-stituted for what I may call the tactual concept an optical concept, complicated by an assumption about the nature of our geometry. From a very direct concept we have come to a very indirect concept with a most complicated set of operations. Strictly speaking, length when measured in this way by light beams should be called by another name, since the operations are different. The practical justification for retaining the same name is that within our present experimental limits a numerical difference between the results of the two sorts operations has not been detected.

We are still worse off when we make the extension to solar and stellar distances. Here space is entirely optical in character, and we never have an opportunity of even partially comparing tactual with optical space. No direct measures of length have ever been made, nor can we even measure the three angles of a triangle and so check our assumption that the use of Euclidean geometry in extending the concept of space is justified. We never have under observation more than two angles of a triangle, as when we measure the distance of the moon by observation from the two ends of the earth's diameter. To extend to still greater distance our measures of length, we have to make still further assumptions, such as that inferences from the Newtonian laws of mechanics are valid. The accuracy of our inferences about lengths from such measure-ments is not high. Astronomy is usually regarded as a science of extraordinarily high accuracy, but its accuracy is very restricted in character, namely to the measurement of angles. It is probably safe to say that no astronomical distance, except perhaps that of the moon, is known with an accuracy greater than 0.1%. When we push our estimates to distances beyond the confines of the solar system in which we are assisted by the laws of mechanics, we are reduced in the first place to measurements of parallax, which at best have a quite inferior accuracy, and which furthermore fail entirely outside a rather restricted range. For greater stellar distances we are driven to other and much rougher estimates, resting for instance on the extension to great distances of connec-tions found within the range of parallax between brightness and spectral type of a star, or on such assumptions as that, because a group of stars looks as if it were all together in space and had a common origin, it actually is so. Thus at greater and greater distances not only does experimental accuracy become less, but the very nature of the operations by which length is to be determined becomes indefinite, so that the distances of the most remote stellar objects as estimated by different observers or by different methods may be very divergent. A particular consequence of the inaccuracy of the astronomical measures of great distances is that the question of whether large scale space is Euclidean or not is merely academic.

We thus see that in the extension from terrestrial to great stellar distances the concept of length has changed completely in character. To say that a certain star is 10^5 light years distant is actually and conceptually an entire different *kind* of thing from saying that a certain goal post is 100 meters distant. Because of our conviction that the character of our experience may change when the range of phenomena changes, we feel the importance of such a question as whether the space of distances of 10^5 light years is Euclidean or not, and are correspondingly dissatisfied that at present there seems no way of giving meaning to it.

We encounter difficulties similar to those above, and are also compelled to modify our procedures, when we go to small distances. Down to the scale of microscopic dimensions a fairly straightforward extension of the ordinary measuring procedure is sufficient, as when we measure a length in a micrometer eyepiece of a microscope. This is of course a combination of tactual and optical measurements, and certain assumptions, justified as far as possible by experience, have to be made about the behavior of light beams. These assumptions are of a quite different character from those which give us concern on the astronomical scale, because here we meet difficulty from interference effects due to the finite scale of the structure of light, and are not concerned with a possible curvature of light beams in the long reaches of space. Apart from the matter of convenience, we might also measure small distances by the tactual method.

As the dimensions become smaller, certain difficulties become increasingly important that were negligible on a larger scale. In carrying out physically the operations equivalent to our concepts, there are a host of practical precautions to be taken which could be explicitly enumerated with difficulty, but of which nevertheless any practical physicist is conscious. Suppose, for example, we measure length tactually by a combination of Johanssen gauges. In piling these together, we must be sure that they are clean, and are thus in actual contact. Particles of mechanical dirt first engage our attention. Then as we go to smaller dimensions we perhaps have to pay attention to adsorbed films of moisture, then at still smaller dimensions to adsorbed films of gas, until finally we have to work in a vacuum, which must be the more nearly complete the smaller the dimensions. About the time that we discover the necessity for a complete vacuum, we discover that the gauges themselves are atomic in structure, that they have no definite boundaries, and therefore no definite length, but that the length is a hazy thing, varying rapidly in time between certain limits. We treat this situation as best we can by taking a time average of the apparent positions of the boundaries, assuming that along with the decrease of dimensions we have acquired a corresponding extravagant increase in nimbleness. But as the dimensions get smaller continually, the difficulties due to this haziness increase indefinitely in percentage effect, and we are eventually driven to give up altogether. We have made the discovery that there are *essential* physical limitations to the operations which defined the concept of length. [We perhaps do not regard the substitution of optical for tactual space on the astronomical scale as compelled by the same sort of physical necessity, because I suppose the possible eventual landing of men in the moon will always be one of the dreams of humanity.] At the same time that we have come to the end of our rope with our Johanssen gauge procedure, companion with the microscope has been encountering difficulties due to the finite wave length of light; this difficulty he has been able to minimize by using light of progressively shorter wave lengths, but he has eventually had to stop on reaching X-rays. Of course this optical procedure with the microscope is more convenient, and is therefore adopted in practice.

Let us now see what is implied in our concept of length extended to ultramicroscopic dimensions. What, for instance, is the meaning of the statement that the distance between the planes of atoms in a certain crystal is 3×10^{-8} cm.? What we would like to mean is that $1/3 \times 10^8$ of these planes piled on top of each other give a thickness of 1 cm.; but of course such a meaning is not the actual one. The actual meaning may be found by examining the operations by which we arrived at the number 3×10^{-8}. As a matter of fact, 3×10^{-8} was the number obtained by solving a general equation derived from the wave theory of light, into which certain numerical data obtained by experiments with X-rays had been substituted. Thus not only has the character of the concept of length changed from tactual to optical, but we have gone much further in committing ourselves to a definite optical theory. If this were the whole story, we would be most uncomfortable with respect to this branch of physics, because we are so uncertain of the correctness of our optical theories, but actually a number of checks can be applied which greatly restore our confidence. For instance, from the density of the crystal and the grating space, the weight of the individual atoms may be computed, and these weights may then be combined with measurements of the dimensions of other sorts of crystal into which the same atoms enter to give values of the densities of these crystals, which may be checked against experiment. All such checks have succeeded within limits of accuracy which are fairly high. It is important to notice that, in spite of the checks, the character of the concept is changing, and begins to involve such things as the equations of optics and the assumption of the conservation of mass.

We are not content, however, to stop with dimensions of atomic order, but have to push on to the electron with a diameter of the order of 10^{-13} cm. What is the possible meaning of the statement that the diameter of an electron is 10^{-13} cm.? Again the only answer is found by examining the operations by which the number 10^{-13} was obtained. This number came by solving certain equations derived from the field equations of electrodynamics, into which certain numerical data obtained by experiment had been substituted. The concept of length has therefore now been so modified as to include that theory of electricity embodied in the field equations, and, most important, assumes the correctness of extending these equations from the dimensions in which they may be verified experimentally into a region in which their correctness is one of the most important and problematical of present-day questions in physics. To find whether the field equations are correct on a small scale, we must verify the relations demanded by the equations between the electric and magnetic forces and the space coördinates, to determine which involves measurement of lengths. But if these space coördinates cannot be given an independent meaning apart from the equations, not only is the attempted verification of the equations impossible, but the question itself is meaningless. If we stick to the concept of length by itself, we are landed in a vicious circle. As a matter of fact, the concept of length disappears as an independent thing, and fuses in a complicated way with other concepts, all of which are themselves altered thereby, with the result that the total number of concepts used in describing nature at this level is reduced in number. A precise analysis of the situation is difficult, and I suppose has never been attempted, but the general character of the situation is evident. Until at least a partial analysis is attempted, I do not see how any meaning can be attached to such questions as whether space is Euclidean in the small scale.

It is interesting to observe that any increased accuracy in knowledge of large scale phenomena must, as far as we now can see, arise from an increase in the accuracy of measurement of small things, that is, in the measurement of small angles or the analysis of minute differences of wave lengths in the spectra. To know the very large takes us into the same field of experiment as to know the very small, so that operationally the large and the small have features in common.

This somewhat detailed analysis of the concept of length brings out features common to all our concepts. If we deal with phenomena outside the domain in which we originally defined our concepts, we may find physical hindrances to performing the operations of the original definition, so that the original operations have to be replaced by others. These new operations are, of course, to be so chosen that they give, within experimental error, the same numerical results in the domain in which the two sets of operations may be both applied; but we must recognize in principle that in changing the operations we have really changed the concept, and that to use the same name for these different concepts over the entire range is dictated only by considerations of convenience, which may sometimes prove to have been purchased at too high a price in terms of unambiguity. We must always be prepared some day to find that an increase in experimental accuracy may show that the two different sets of operations which give the same results in the more ordinary part of the domain of experience, lead to measurably different results in the more unfamiliar parts of the domain. We must remain aware of these joints in our conceptual structure if we hope to render unnecessary the services of the unborn Einsteins.

The second feature common to all concepts brought out by the detailed discussion of length is that, as we approach the experimentally attainable limit, concepts lose their individuality, fuse together, and become fewer in number, as we have seen that at dimensions of the order of the diameter of an electron the concepts of length and the electric field vectors fuse into an amorphous whole. Not only does nature as experienced by us become different in character on its horizons, but it becomes simpler, and therefore our concepts, which are the building stones of our descriptions, become fewer in number. This seem to be an entirely natural state of affairs. How the number of concepts is often kept formally the same as we approach the horizon will be discussed later in special cases.

A precise analysis of our conceptual structure has never been attempted, except perhaps in very restricted domains, and it seems to me that there is room here for much important future work. Such an analysis is not to be attempted in this essay, but only some of the more important qualitative aspects are be pointed out. It will never be possible to give a clean-cut logical analysis of the conceptual situation, for the nature of our concepts, according to our operational point of view, is the same as the nature of experimental knowledge, which is often hazy. Thus in the transition regions where nature is getting simpler and the number of operationally independent concepts changes, a certain haziness is inevitable, for the actual change in our conceptual structure in these transition regions is continuous, corresponding to the continuity of our experimental knowledge, whereas formally the number of concepts should be an integer.

The Relative Character of Knowledge

Two other consequences of the operational point of view must now be examined. First is the consequence that all our knowledge is relative. This may be understood in a general or a more particular sense. The general sense is illustrated in Haldane's book on the *Reign of Relativity*. Relativity in the general sense is the merest truism if the operational definition of concept is accepted, for experience is described in terms of concepts, and since our concepts are constructed of operations, all our knowledge must unescapably be relative to the operations selected. But knowledge is also relative in a narrower sense, as when we say there is no such thing as absolute rest (or motion) or absolute size, but rest and size are relative terms. Conclusions of this kind are involved in the specific character of the operations in terms of which rest or size are defined. An examination of the operations by which we determine whether a body is at rest or in motion shows that the operations are relative operations: rest or motion is determined with respect to some other body selected as the standard. In saying that there is no such thing as absolute rest or motion we are not making a statement about nature in the sense that might be supposed, but we are merely making a statement about the character of our descriptive processes. Similarly with regard to size: examination of the operations of the measuring process shows that size is measured relative to the fundamental measuring rod.

The "absolute" therefore disappears in the original meaning of the word. But the "absolute" may usefully return with an altered meaning, and we may say that a thing has absolute properties if the numerical magnitude is the same when measured with the same formal procedure by all observers. Whether a given property is absolute or not can be determined only by experiment, landing us in the paradoxical position that the absolute is absolute only relative to experiment. In some cases, the most superficial observation shows that a property is not absolute, as, for example, it is at once obvious that measured velocity changes with the motion of the observer. But in other cases the decision is more difficult. Thus Michelson thought he had an absolute procedure for measuring length, by referring to the wave length of the red cadmium line as standard;[3] it required difficult and accurate experiment to show that this length varies with the motion of the observer. Even then, by changing the definition of the length of a moving object, we believe that length might be made to reassume its desired absolute character.

To stop the discussion at this point might leave the impression that this observation of the relative character of knowledge is of only a very tenuous and academic interest, since it appears to be concerned mostly with the character of our descriptive processes, and to say little about external nature. [What this means we leave to the metaphysician to decide.] But I believe there is a deeper significance to all this. It must be remembered that all our argument starts with the concepts as given. Now these concepts involve physical operations; in the discovery of what operations may be usefully employed in describing nature is buried almost all physical experience. In erecting our structure of physical science, we are building on the work of all the ages. There is then this purely physical significance in the statement that all motion is relative, namely that no operations of measuring motion have been found to be useful in describing simply the behavior of nature which are not operations relative to a single observer; in making this statement we are stating something about nature. It takes an enormous amount of real physical experience to discover relations of this sort. The discovery that the number obtained by counting the number of times a stick may be applied to an object can be simply used in describing natural phenomena was one of the most important and fundamental discoveries ever made by man.

Meaningless Questions

Another consequence of the operational character of our concepts, almost a corollary of that considered above, is that it is quite possible, nay even disquietingly easy, to invent expressions or to ask questions that are meaningless. It constitutes a great advance in our critical attitude toward nature to realize that a great many of the questions that we uncritically ask are without meaning. If a specific question has meaning, it must be possible to find operations by which an answer may be given to it. It will be found in many cases that the operations cannot exist, and the question therefore has no meaning. For instance, it means nothing to ask whether a star is at rest or not. Another example is a question proposed by Clifford, namely, whether it is not possible that as the solar system moves from one part of space to another the absolute scale of magnitude may be changing, but in such a way as to affect all things equally, so that the change of scale can never be detected. An examination of the operations by which length is measured in terms of measuring rods shows that the operations do not exist (because of the nature of our definition of length) for answering the question. The question can be given meaning only from the point of view of some imaginary superior being watching from an external point of vantage. But the operations by which such a being measures length are different from the operations of our definition of length, so that the question acquires meaning only by changing the significance of our terms—in the original sense the question means nothing.

To state that a certain question about nature is meaningless is to make a significant statement about nature itself, because the fundamental operations are determined by nature, and to state that nature cannot be described in terms of certain operations is a significant statement.

It must be recognized, however, that there is a sense in which no serious question is entirely without meaning, because doubtless the questioner had in mind some intention in asking the question. But to give meaning in this sense to a question, one must inquire into the meaning of the concepts as used by the questioner, and it will often be found that these concepts can be defined only in terms of fictitious properties, as Newton's absolute time was defined by its properties, so that the meaning to be ascribed to the question in this way has no connection with reality. I believe that it will enable us to make more significant and interesting statements, and therefore will be more useful, to adopt exclusively the operational view, and so admit the possibility of questions entirely without meaning.

This matter of meaningless questions is a very subtle thing which may poison much more of our thought than that dealing with purely physical phenomena. I believe that many of the questions asked about social and philosophical subjects will be found to be meaningless when examined from the point of view of operations. It would doubtless conduce greatly to clarity of thought if the operational mode of thinking were adopted in all fields of inquiry as well as in the physical. Just as in the physical domain, so in other domains, one is making a significant statement about his subject in stating that a certain question is meaningless.

In order to emphasize this matter of meaningless questions, I give here a list of questions, with which the reader may amuse himself by finding whether they have meaning or not.

1. Was there ever a time when matter did not exist?
2. May time have a beginning or an end?
3. Why does time flow?
4. May space be bounded?
5. May space or time be discontinuous?
6. May space have a fourth dimension, not directly detectible, but given indirectly by inference?
7. Are there parts of nature forever beyond our detection?
8. Is the sensation which I call blue really the *same* as that which my neighbor calls blue? Is it possible that a blue object may arouse in him the same sensation that a red object does in me and *vice versa*?
9. May there be missing integers in the series of natural numbers as we know them?
10. Is a universe possible in which $2 + 2 \neq 4$?
11. Why does negative electricity attract positive?
12. Why does nature obey laws?
13. Is a universe possible in which the laws are different?
14. If one part of our universe could be *completely* isolated from the rest, would it continue to obey the same laws?
15. Can we be sure that our logical processes are valid?

General Comments on the Operational Point of View

To adopt the operational point of view involves much more than a mere restriction of the sense in which we understand "concept," but means a far-reaching change in all our habits of thought, in that we shall no longer permit ourselves to use as tools in our thinking concepts of which we cannot give an adequate account in terms of operations. In some respects thinking becomes simpler, because certain old generalizations and idealizations become incapable of use; for instance, many of the speculations of the early natural philosophers become simply unreadable. In other respects, however, thinking becomes much more difficult, because the operational implications of a concept are often very involved. For example, it is most difficult to grasp adequately all that is contained in the apparently simple concept of "time," and requires the continual correction of mental tendencies which we have long unquestioningly accepted.

Operational thinking will at first prove to be an unsocial virtue; one will find oneself perpetually unable to understand the simplest conversation of one's friends, and will make oneself universally unpopular by demanding the meaning of apparently the simplest terms of every argument. Possibly after every one has schooled himself to this better way, there will remain a permanent unsocial tendency, because doubtless much of our present conversation will then become unnecessary. The socially optimistic may venture to hope, however, that the ultimate effect will be to release one's energies for more stimulating and interesting interchange of ideas.

Not only will operational thinking reform the social art of conversation, but all our social relations will be liable to reform. Let any one examine in operational terms any popular present-day discussion of religious or moral questions to realize the magnitude of the reformation awaiting us. Wherever we temporize or compromise in applying our theories of conduct to practical life we may suspect a failure of operational thinking.

Notes

1. C. F. Gauss, *Gesammelte Werke*, especially vol. IV.
2. See a discussion of the theory of this experiment by L. Silberstein, *Jour. Opt. Soc. Amer.* 5, 291–307, 1921.
3. A. A. Michelson, *Light Waves and Their Uses*, University of Chicago Press, 1903, Chap. V.

Chapter 3

Empiricist Criteria of Cognitive Significance:
Problems and Changes

Carl Hempel

1. The General Empiricist Conception of Cognitive and Empirical Significance

It is a basic principle of contemporary empiricism that a sentence makes a cognitively significant assertion, and thus can be said to be either true or false, if and only if either (1) it is analytic or contradictory—in which case it is said to have purely logical meaning or significance—or else (2) it is capable, at least potentially, of test by experiential evidence—in which case it is said to have empirical meaning or significance. The basic tenet of this principle, and especially of its second part, the so-called testability criterion of empirical meaning (or better: meaningfulness), is not peculiar to empiricism alone: it is characteristic also of contemporary operationism, and in a sense of pragmatism as well; for the pragmatist maxim that a difference must make a difference to be a difference may well be construed as insisting that a verbal difference between two sentences must make a difference in experiential implications if it is to reflect a difference in meaning.

How this general conception of cognitively significant discourse led to the rejection, as devoid of logical and empirical meaning, of various formulations in speculative metaphysics, and even of certain hypotheses offered within empirical science is too well known to require recounting. I think that the general intent of the empiricist criterion of meaning is basically sound, and that notwithstanding much oversimplification in its use, its critical application has been, on the whole, enlightening and salutary. I feel less confident, however, about the possibility of restating the general idea in the form of precise and general criteria which establish sharp dividing lines (a) between statements of purely logical and statements of empirical significance, and (b) between those sentences which do have cognitive significance and those which do not.

In the present paper, I propose to reconsider these distinctions as conceived in recent empiricism, and to point out some of the difficulties they present. The discussion will concern mainly the second of the two distinctions; in regard to the first, I shall limit myself to a few brief remarks.

2. The Earlier Testability Criteria of Meaning and Their Shortcomings

Let us note first that any general criterion of cognitive significance will have to meet certain requirements if it is to be at all acceptable. Of these, we note one which we shall consider here as expressing a necessary, though by no means sufficient *condition of adequacy* for criteria of cognitive significance.

(A) If under a given criterion of cognitive significance, a sentence N is non-significant, then so must be all truth-functional compound sentences in which N occurs nonvacuously as a component. For if N cannot be significantly assigned a truth value, then it is impossible to assign truth values to the compound sentences containing N; hence, they should be qualified as nonsignificant as well.

We note two corollaries of requirement (A):

(A1) If under a given criterion of cognitive significance, a sentence S is non-significant, then so must be its negation, $\sim S$.

(A2) If under a given criterion of cognitive significance, a sentence N non-significant, then so must be any conjunction $N \cdot S$ and any disjunction $N \vee S$, no matter whether S is significant under the given criterion or not.

We now turn to the initial attempts made in recent empiricism to establish general criteria of cognitive significance. Those attempts were governed by the consideration that a sentence, to make an empirical assertion must be capable of being borne out by, or conflicting with, phenomena which are potentially capable of being directly observed. Sentences describing such potentially observable phenomena—no matter whether the latter do actually occur or not—may be called observation sentences. More specifically, an *observation sentence* might be construed as a sentence—no matter whether true or false—which asserts or denies that a specified object, or group of objects, of macroscopic size has a particular *observable characteristic*, i.e., a characteristic whose presence or absence can, under favorable circumstances, be ascertained by direct observation.[1]

The task of setting up criteria of empirical significance is thus transformed into the problem of characterizing in a precise manner the relationship which obtains between a hypothesis and one or more observation sentences whenever the phenomena described by the latter either confirm or disconfirm the hypothesis in question. The ability of a given sentence to enter into that relationship to some set of observation sentences would then characterize its testability-in-principle, and thus its empirical significance. Let us now briefly examine the major attempts that have been made to obtain criteria of significance in this manner.

One of the earliest criteria is expressed in the so-called *verifiability requirement*. According to it, a sentence is empirically significant if and only if it is not analytic and is capable, at least in principle, of complete verification by observational evidence; i.e., if observational evidence can be described which, if actually obtained, would conclusively establish the truth of the sentence.[2] With the help of the concept of observation sentence, we can restate this requirement as follows: A sentence S has empirical meaning if and only if it is possible to indicate a finite set of observation sentences, O_1, O_2, ..., O_n, such that if these are true, then S is necessarily true, too. As stated, however, this condition is satisfied also if S is an analytic sentence or if the given observation sentences are logically incompatible with each other. By the following formulation, we rule these cases out and at the same time express the intended criterion more precisely:

(2.1) Requirement of complete verifiability in principle.   A sentence has empirical meaning if and only if it is not analytic and follows logically from some finite and logically consistent class of observation sentences.[3] These observation sentences need not be true, for what the criterion is to explicate is testability by "potentially observable phenomena," or testability "in principle."

In accordance with the general conception of cognitive significance outlined earlier, a sentence will now be classified as cognitively significant if either it is analytic or contradictory, or it satisfies the verifiability requirement.

This criterion, however, has several serious defects. One of them has noted by several writers:

a. Let us assume that the properties of being a stork and of being red-legged are both observable characteristics, and that the former does not logically entail the latter. Then the sentence

(S1)   All storks are red-legged

is neither analytic nor contradictory; and clearly, it is not deducible from a finite set of observation sentences. Hence, under the contemplated criterion, S1 is devoid of empirical significance; and so are all other sentences purporting to express universal regularities or general laws. And since sentences of this type constitute an integral part of scientific theories, the verifiability requirement must be regarded as overly restrictive in this respect.

Similarly, the criterion disqualifies all sentences such as 'For any substance there exists some solvent', which contain both universal and existential quantifiers (i.e., occurrences of the terms 'all' and 'some' or their equivalents); for no sentences of this kind can be logically deduced from any finite set of observation sentences.

Two further defects of the verifiability requirement do not seem to have been widely noticed:

b. As is readily seen, the negation of S1

($\sim S1$)   There exists at least one stork that is not red-legged

is deducible from any two observation sentences of the type 'a is a stork' and 'a is not red-legged'. Hence, $\sim S1$ is cognitively significant under our criterion but S1 is not, and this constitutes a violation of condition (A1).

c. Let S be a sentence which does, and N a sentence which does not satisfy the verifiability requirement. Then S is deducible from some set of observation sentences; hence, by a familiar rule of logic, $S \lor N$ is deducible from the same set, and therefore cognitively significant according to our criterion. This violates condition (A2) above.[4]

Strictly analogous considerations apply to an alternative criterion, which makes complete falsifiability in principle the defining characteristic of empirical significance. Let us formulate this criterion as follows:

(2.2) *Requirement of complete falsifiability in principle.*   A sentence has empirical meaning if and only if its negation is not analytic and follows logically from some finite logically consistent class of observation sentences.

This criterion qualifies a sentence as empirically meaningful if its negation satisfies the requirement of complete verifiability; as it is to be expected, it is therefore inadequate on similar grounds as the latter:

(a) It denies cognitive significance to purely existential hypotheses, such as 'There exists at least one unicorn', and all sentences whose formulation calls mixed—i.e., universal and existential—quantification, such as 'For every compound there exists some solvent', for none of these can possibly be conclusively falsified by a finite number of observation sentences.

(b) If 'P' is an observation predicate, then the assertion that all things have the property P is qualified as significant, but its negation, being equivalent to a purely existential hypothesis, is disqualified [cf. (a)]. Hence, criterion (2.2) give rise to the same dilemma as (2.1).

(c) If a sentence S is completely falsifiable whereas N is a sentence which is not, then their conjunction, $S \cdot N$ (i.e., the expression obtained by connecting the two sentences by the word 'and') is completely falsifiable; for if the negation of S is entailed by a class of observation sentences, then the negation of $S \cdot N$ is, *a fortiori*, entailed by the same class. Thus, the criterion allows empirical significance to many sentences which an adequate empiricist criterion should rule out, such as 'All swans are white and the absolute is perfect.'

In sum, then, interpretations of the testability criterion in terms of complete verifiability or of complete falsifiability are inadequate because they are overly restrictive in one direction and overly inclusive in another, and because both them violate the fundamental requirement A.

Several attempts have been made to avoid these difficulties by construing the testability criterion as demanding merely a partial and possibly indirect confirmability of empirical hypotheses by observational evidence.

A formulation suggested by Ayer[5] is characteristic of these attempts to up a clear and sufficiently comprehensive criterion of confirmability. It states, in effect, that a sentence S has empirical import if from S in conjunction with suitable subsidiary hypotheses it is possible to derive observation sentences which are not derivable from the subsidiary hypotheses alone.

This condition is suggested by a closer consideration of the logical structure of scientific testing; but it is much too liberal as it stands. Indeed, as Ayer himself has pointed out in the second edition of his book, *Language, Truth, and Logic*,[6] his criterion allows empirical import to any sentence whatever. Thus, e.g., if S is the sentence 'The absolute is perfect', it suffices to choose as a subsidiary hypothesis the sentence 'If the absolute is perfect then this apple is red' in order to make possible the deduction of the observation sentence 'This apple is red', which clearly does not follow from the subsidiary hypothesis alone.

To meet this objection, Ayer proposed a modified version of his testability criterion. In effect, the modification restricts the subsidiary hypotheses mentioned in the previous version to sentences which either are analytic or can independently be shown to be testable in the sense of the modified criterion.[7]

But it can readily be shown that this new criterion, like the requirement of complete falsifiability, allows empirical significance to any conjunction $S \cdot N$ where S satisfies Ayer's criterion while N is a sentence such as 'The absolute is perfect', which is to be disqualified by that criterion. Indeed, whatever consequences can be deduced from S with the help of permissible subsidiary hypotheses can also be deduced from $S \cdot N$ by means of the same subsidiary hypotheses; and as Ayer's new criterion is formulated essentially in terms of the deducibility of a certain type of consequence from the given sentence, it countenances $S \cdot N$ together with S. Another difficulty has been pointed out by Church, who has shown[8] that if there are any three observation sentences none of which alone entails any of the others, then it follows for any sentence S whatsoever that either it or its denial has empirical import according to Ayer's revised criterion.

All the criteria considered so far attempt to explicate the concept of empirical significance by specifying certain logical connections which must obtain between a significant sentence and suitable observation sentences. It seems now that this type of approach offers little hope for the attainment of precise criteria of meaningfulness: this conclusion is suggested by the preceding survey of some representative attempts, and it receives additional support from certain further considerations, some of which will be presented in the following sections.

3. Characterization of Significant Sentences by Criteria for Their Constituent Terms

An alternative procedure suggests itself which again seems to reflect well the general viewpoint of empiricism: It might be possible to characterize cognitively significant sentences by certain conditions which their constituent term have to satisfy. Specifically, it would seem reasonable to say that all extralogical terms[9] a significant sentence must have experiential reference, and that therefore their meanings must be capable of explication by reference to observable exclusively.[10] In order to exhibit certain analogies between this approach and the previous one, we adopt the following terminological conventions:

Any term that may occur in a cognitively significant sentence will be called a *cognitively significant term*. Furthermore, we shall understand by an *observation term* any term which either (a) is an *observation predicate*, i.e., signifies some observable characteristic (as do the terms 'blue', 'warm', 'soft', 'coincident with', 'of greater apparent brightness than') or (b) names some physical object of macroscopic size (as do the terms 'the needle of this instrument'. 'the moon', 'Krakatoa Volcano', 'Greenwich, England', 'Julius Caesar').

Now while the testability criteria of meaning aimed at characterizing the cognitively significant sentences by means of certain inferential connections in which they must stand to some observation sentences, the alternative approach under consideration would instead try to specify the vocabulary that may be used in forming significant sentences. This vocabulary, the class of significant terms, would be characterized by the condition that each of its elements is either a logical term or else a term with empirical significance; in the latter case, it has to stand in certain definitional or explicative connections to some observation terms. This approach certainly avoids any violations of our earlier conditions of adequacy. Thus, e.g., if S is a significant sentence, i.e., contains cognitively significant terms only, then so is its denial, since the denial sign, and its verbal equivalents, belong to the vocabulary of logic and are thus significant. Again, if N is a sentence containing a nonsignificant term, then so is any compound sentence which contains N.

But this is not sufficient, of course. Rather, we shall now have to consider a crucial question analogous to that raised by the previous approach: Precisely how are the logical connections between empirically significant terms and observation terms to be construed if an adequate criterion of cognitive significance is to result ? Let us consider some possibilities.

(3.1) The simplest criterion that suggests itself might be called the *requirement of definability*. It would demand that any term with empirical significance must be explicitly definable by means of observation terms.

This criterion would seem to accord well with the maxim of operationism that all significant terms of empirical science must be introduced by operational definitions. However, the requirement of definability is vastly too restrictive, for many important terms of scientific and even prescientific discourse cannot be explicitly defined by means of observation terms.

In fact, as Carnap[11] has pointed out, an attempt to provide explicit definitions in terms of observables encounters serious difficulties as soon as disposition terms, such as 'soluble', 'malleable', 'electric conductor', etc., have to be accounted for; and many of these occur even on the prescientific level of discourse.

Consider, for example, the word 'fragile'. One might try to define it by saying that an object x is fragile if and only if it satisfies the following condition: If at any time t the object is sharply struck, then it breaks at that time. But if the statement connectives in this phrasing are construed truth-functionally, so that the definition can be symbolized by

(D) $Fx \equiv (t)(Sxt \supset Bxt)$

then the predicate 'F' thus defined does not have the intended meaning. For let a be any object which is not fragile (e.g., a raindrop or a rubber band), but which happens not to be sharply struck at any time throughout its existence. Then 'Sat' is false and hence '$Sat \supset Bat$' is true for all values of 't'; consequently, 'Fa' is true though a is not fragile.

To remedy this defect, one might construe the phrase 'if . . . then . . .' in the original definiens as having a more restrictive meaning than the truth-functional conditional. This meaning might be suggested by the subjunctive phrasing 'If x were to be sharply struck at any time t, then x would break at t.' But a satisfactory elaboration of this construal would require a clarification of the meaning and the logic of counterfactual and subjunctive conditionals, which is a theory problem.[12]

An alternative procedure was suggested by Carnap in his theory of reduction sentences.[13] These are sentences which, unlike definitions, specify the meaning of a term only conditionally or partially. The term 'fragile', for example, might be introduced by the following reduction sentence:

(R) $(x)(t)[Sxt \supset (Fx \equiv Bxt)]$

which specifies that if x is sharply struck at any time t, then x is fragile if and, if x breaks at t.

Our earlier difficulty is now avoided, for if a is a nonfragile object that is never sharply struck, then that expression in R which follows the quantifiers is true of a; but this does not imply that 'Fa' is true. But the reduction sentence R specifies the meaning of 'F' only for application to those objects which meet to "test condition" of being sharply struck at some time; for these it states fragility then amounts to breaking. For objects that fail to meet the test condition, the meaning of 'F' is left undetermined. In this sense, reduction sentences have the character of partial or conditional definitions.

Reduction sentences provide a satisfactory interpretation of the experiential import of a large class of disposition terms and permit a more adequate formulation of so-called operational definitions, which, in general, are not complete definitions at all. These considerations suggest a greatly liberalized alternative the requirement of definability:

(3.2) *The requirement of reducibility.* Every term with empirical significance must be capable of introduction, on the basis of observation terms, through chains of reduction sentences.

This requirement is characteristic of the liberalized versions of positivism and physicalism which, since about 1936, have superseded the older, overly narrow conception of a full definability of all terms of empirical science by mean. observables,[14] and it avoids many of the shortcomings of the latter. Yet, reduction sentences do not seem to offer an adequate means for the introduction of central terms of advanced scientific theories, often referred to as theoretical constructs. This is indicated by the following considerations: A chain of reduction sentences provides a necessary and a sufficient condition for the applicability the term it introduces. (When the two conditions coincide, the chain is tantamount to an explicit definition.) But now take, for example, the concept of length as used in classical physical theory. Here, the length in centimeters of the distance between two points may assume any positive real number as its value; yet it is clearly impossible to formulate, by means of observation terms, a sufficient condition for the applicability of such expressions as "having a length of $\sqrt{2}$ cm" and "having a length of $\sqrt{2} + 10^{-100}$ cm"; for such conditions would provide a possibility for discrimination, in observational terms, between two lengths which differ by only 10^{-100} cm.[15]

It would be ill-advised to argue that for this reason, we ought to permit only such values of the magnitude, length, as permit the statement of sufficient conditions in terms of observables. For this would rule out, among others, all irrational numbers and would prevent us from assigning, to the diagonal of a square with sides of length 1, the length $\sqrt{2}$, which is required by Euclidean geometry. Hence, the principles of Euclidean geometry would not be universally applicable in physics. Similarly, the principles of the calculus would become inapplicable, and the system of scientific theory as we know it today would be reduced to a clumsy, unmanageable torso. This, then, is no way of meeting the difficulty. Rather, we shall have to analyze more closely the function of constructs in scientific theories, with a view to obtaining through such an analysis a more adequate characterization of cognitively significant terms.

Theoretical constructs occur in the formulation of scientific theories. These may be conceived of, in their advanced stages, as being stated in the form of deductively developed axiomatized systems. Classical mechanics, or Euclidean or some non-Euclidean form of geometry in physical interpretation, present examples of such systems. The extralogical terms used in a theory of this kind may be divided, in familiar manner, into primitive or basic terms, which are not defined within the theory, and defined terms, which are explicitly defined by means of the primitives. Thus, e.g., in Hilbert's axiomatization of Euclidean geometry, the terms 'point', 'straight line', 'between' are among the primitives, while 'line segment', 'angle', 'triangle', 'length' are among the defined terms. The basic and the defined terms together with the terms of logic constitute the vocabulary out of which all the sentences of the theory are constructed. The latter are divided, in an axiomatic presentation, into primitive statements (also called postulates or basic statements) which, in the theory, are not derived from any other statements, and derived ones, which are obtained by logical deduction from the primitive statements.

From its primitive terms and sentences, an axiomatized theory can be developed by means of purely formal principles of definition and deduction, without any consideration of the empirical significance of its extralogical terms. Indeed, this is the standard procedure employed in the axiomatic development of uninterpreted mathematical theories such as those of abstract groups or rings or lattices, or any form of pure (i.e., noninterpreted) geometry.

However, a deductively developed system of this sort can constitute a scientific theory only if it has received an empirical interpretation[16] which renders it relevant to the phenomena of our experience. Such interpretation is given by assigning a meaning, in terms of observables, to certain terms or sentences of the formalized theory. Frequently, an interpretation is given not for the primitive terms or statements but rather for some of the terms definable by means of the primitives, or for some of the sentences deducible from the postulates.[17] Furthermore, interpretation may amount to only a partial assignment of meaning. Thus, e.g., the rules for the measurement of length by means of a standard rod may be considered as providing a *partial* empirical interpretation for the term 'the length, in centimeters, of interval i', or alternatively, for some sentences of the form 'the length of interval i is r centimeters'. For the method is applicable only to intervals of a certain medium size, and even for the latter it does not constitute a full interpretation since the use of a standard rod does not constitute the only way of determining length: various alternative procedures are available involving the measurement of other magnitudes which are connected, by general laws, with the length that is to be determined.

This last observation, concerning the possibility of an indirect measurement of length by virtue of certain laws, suggests an important reminder. It is not correct to speak, as is often done, of "the experiential meaning" of a term or a sentence in isolation. In the language of science, and for similar reasons even in prescientific discourse, a single statement usually has no experiential implications. A single sentence in a scientific theory does not, as a rule, entail any observation sentences; consequences asserting the occurrence of certain observation phenomena can be derived from it only by conjoining it with a set of other, subsidiary, hypotheses. Of the latter, some will usually be observation sentences, others will be previously accepted theoretical statements. Thus, e.g., the relativistic theory of the deflection of light rays in the gravitational field of the sun entails assertions about observable phenomena only if it is conjoined with a considerable body of astronomical and optical theory, as well as a large number of specific statements about the instruments used in those observations of solar eclipses which serve to test the hypothesis in question.

Hence, the phrase, 'the experiential meaning of expression E' is elliptical: What a given expression "means" in regard to potential empirical data is relative to two factors, namely:

I. *the linguistic framework $\mathscr{L}$* to which the expression belongs. Its rules determine, in particular, what sentences—observational or otherwise—may be inferred from a given statement or class of statements;
II. the theoretical context in which the expression occurs, i.e., the class of those statements in $\mathscr{L}$ which are available as subsidiary hypotheses.

Thus, the sentence formulating Newton's law of gravitation has no experiential meaning by itself; but when used in a language whose logical apparatus permits the development of the calculus, and when combined with a suitable system of other hypotheses—including sentences which connect some of the theoretical terms with observation terms and thus establish a partial interpretation—then it has a bearing on observable phenomena in a large variety of fields. Analogous considerations are applicable to the term 'gravitational field', for example. It can be considered as having experiential meaning only within the context of a theory, which must be at least partially interpreted; and the experiential meaning of the term—as expressed, say, in the form of operational criteria for its application—will depend again on the theoretical system at hand, and on the logical characteristics of the language within which it is formulated.

4. Cognitive Significance as a Characteristic of Interpreted Systems

The preceding considerations point to the conclusion that a satisfactory criterion of cognitive significance cannot be reached through the second avenue of approach here considered, namely by means of specific requirements for the terms which make up significant sentences. This result accords with a general characteristic of scientific (and, in principle, even prescientific) theorizing: Theory formation and concept formation go hand in hand; neither can be carried on successfully in isolation from the other.

If, therefore, cognitive significance can be attributed to anything, then only to entire theoretical systems formulated in a language with a well-determined structure. And the decisive mark of cognitive significance in such a system appears to be the existence of an interpretation for it in terms of observables. Such an interpretation might be formulated, for example, by means of conditional or biconditional sentences connecting nonobservational terms of the system with observation terms in the given language; the latter as well as the connecting sentences may or may not belong to the theoretical system.

But the requirement of partial interpretation is extremely liberal; it is satisfied, for example, by the system consisting of contemporary physical theory combined with some set of principles of speculative metaphysics, even if the latter have no empirical interpretation at all. Within the total system, these metaphysical principles play the role of what K. Reach and also O. Neurath liked to call *isolated sentences*: They are neither purely formal truths or falsehoods, demonstrable or refutable by means of the logical rules of the given language system; nor do they have any experiential bearing; i.e., their omission from the theoretical system would have no effect on its explanatory and predictive power in regard to potentially observable phenomena (i.e., the kind of phenomena described by observation sentences). Should we not, therefore, require that a cognitively significant system contain no isolated sentences? The following criterion suggests itself:

(4.1) A theoretical system is cognitively significant if and only if it is partially interpreted to at least such an extent that none of its primitive sentences is isolated.

But this requirement may bar from a theoretical system certain sentences which might well be viewed as permissible and indeed desirable. By way of a simple illustration, let us assume that our theoretical system T contains the primitive sentence

$$(S1) \quad (x)[P_1x \supset (Qx \equiv P_2x)]$$

where 'P_1' and 'P_2' are observation predicates in the given language $\mathscr{L}$, 'Q' functions in T somewhat in the manner of a theoretical construct and occurs in only one primitive sentence of T, namely $S1$. Now $S1$ is not a truth or falsehood of formal logic; and furthermore, if $S1$ is omitted from the set of primitive sentences of T, then the resulting system, T', possesses exactly the same systematic, i.e., explanatory and predictive, power as T. Our contemplated criterion would therefore qualify $S1$ as an isolated sentence which has to be eliminated—excised by means of Occam's razor, as it were—if the theoretical system at hand is to be cognitively significant.

But it is possible to take a much more liberal view of $S1$ by treating it as a partial definition for the theoretical term 'Q'. Thus conceived, $S1$ specifies that in all cases where the observable characteristic P_1 is present, 'Q' is applicable if and only if the observable characteristic P_2 is present as well. In fact, $S1$ is an instance of those partial, or conditional, definitions which Carnap calls bilateral reduction sentences. These sentences are explicitly qualified by Carnap as analytic (though not, of course, as truths of formal logic), essentially on the ground that all their consequences which are expressible by means of observation predicates (and logical terms) alone are truths of formal logic.[18]

Let us pursue this line of thought a little further. This will lead us to some observations on analytic sentences and then back to the question of the adequacy of (4.1).

Suppose that we add to our system T the further sentence

$$(S2) \quad (x)[P_3x \supset (Qx \equiv P_4x)]$$

where 'P_3', 'P_4' are additional observation predicates. Then, on the view that "every bilateral reduction sentence is analytic,"[19] S2 would be analytic as well as S1. Yet, the two sentences jointly entail nonanalytic consequences which are expressible in terms of observation predicates alone, such as[20]

$$(O) \quad (x)[\sim (P_1 x \cdot P_2 x \cdot P x_3 \cdot \sim P_4 x) \cdot \sim (P_1 x \cdot \sim P_2 x \cdot P_3 x \cdot P_4 x)]$$

But one would hardly want to admit the consequence that the conjunction of two analytic sentences may be synthetic. Hence if the concept of analyticity can be applied at all to the sentences of interpreted deductive systems, then it will have to be relativized with respect to the theoretical context at hand. Thus, e.g., S1 might be qualified as analytic relative to the system T, whose remaining postulates do not contain the term 'Q', but as synthetic relative to the system T enriched by S2. Strictly speaking, the concept of analyticity has to be relativized also in regard to the rules of the language at hand, for the latter determine what observational or other consequences are entailed bs a given sentence. This need for at least a twofold relativization of the concept of analyticity was almost to be expected in view of those considerations which required the same twofold relativization for the concept of experiential meaning of a sentence.

If, on the other hand, we decide not to permit S1 in the role of a partial definition and instead reject it as an isolated sentence, then we are led to an analogous conclusion: Whether a sentence is isolated or not will depend on the linguistic frame and on the theoretical context at hand: While S1 is isolated relative to T (and the language in which both are formulated), it acquires definite experiential implications when T is enlarged by S2.

Thus we find, on the level of interpreted theoretical systems, a peculiar rapprochement, and partial fusion, of some of the problems pertaining to the concepts of cognitive significance and of analyticity: Both concepts need to be relativized; and a large class of sentences may be viewed, apparently with equal right, as analytic in a given context, or as isolated, or nonsignificant, in respect to it.

In addition to barring, as isolated in a given context, certain sentences which could just as well be construed as partial definitions, the criterion (4.1) has another serious defect. Of two logically equivalent formulations of a theoretical system it may qualify one as significant while barring the other as containing an isolated sentence among its primitives. For assume that a certain theoretical system T1 contains among its primitive sentences S', S'', ... exactly one, S', which is isolated. Then T1 is not significant under (4.1). But now consider the theoretical system T2 obtained from T1 by replacing the two first primitive sentences, S, S'', by one, namely their conjunction. Then, under our assumptions, none of the primitive sentences of T2 is isolated, and T2, though equivalent to T1, is qualified as significant by (4.1). In order to do justice to the intent of (4.1), we would therefore have to lay down the following stricter requirement:

(4.2) A theoretical system is cognitively significant if and only if it is partially interpreted to such an extent that in no system equivalent to it at least one primitive sentence is isolated.

Let us apply this requirement to some theoretical system whose postulates include the two sentences S1 and S2 considered before, and whose other postulates do not contain 'Q' at all. Since the sentences S1 and S2 together entail the sentence O, the set consisting of S1 and S2 is logically equivalent to the set consisting of S1, S2, and O. Hence, if we replace the former set by the latter, we obtain a theoretical system equivalent to the given one. In this new system, both S1 and S2 are isolated since, as can be shown, their removal does not affect the explanatory and predictive power of the system in reference to observable phenomena. To put it intuitively, the systematic power of $S1$ and $S2$ is the same as that of O. Hence, the original system is disqualified by (4.2). From the view-point of a strictly sensationalist positivism as perhaps envisaged by Mach, this result might be hailed as a sound repudiation of theories making reference to fictitious entities, and as a strict insistence on theories couched exclusively in terms of observables. But from a contemporary vantage point, we shall have to say that such a procedure overlooks or misjudges the important function of constructs in scientific theory: The history of scientific endeavor shows that if we wish to arrive at precise, comprehensive, and well-confirmed general laws, we have to rise above the level of direct observation. The phenomena directly accessible to our experience are not connected by general laws of great scope and rigor. Theoretical constructs are needed for the formulation of such higher-level laws. One of the most important functions of a well-chosen construct is its potential ability to serve as a constituent in ever new general connections that may be discovered; and to such connections we would blind ourselves if we insisted on banning from scientific theories all those terms and sentences which could be "dispensed with" in the sense indicated in (4.2). In following such a narrowly phenomenalistic or positivistic course, we would deprive ourselves of the tremendous fertility of theoretical constructs, and we would often render the formal structure of the expurgated theory clumsy and inefficient.

Criterion (4.2), then, must be abandoned, and considerations such as those outlined in this paper seem to lend strong support to the conjecture that no adequate alternative to it can be found; i.e., that it is not possible to formulate general and precise criteria which would separate those partially interpreted systems whose isolated sentences might be said to have a significant function from those in which the isolated sentences are, so to speak, mere useless appendages.

We concluded earlier that cognitive significance in the sense intended by recent empiricism and operationism can at best be attributed to sentences forming a theoretical system, and perhaps rather to such systems as wholes. Now, rather than try to replace (4.2) by some alternative, we will have to recognize further that cognitive significance in a system is a matter of degree: Significant systems range from those whose entire extralogical vocabulary consists of observation terms, through theories whose formulation relies heavily on theoretical constructs, on to systems with hardly any bearing on potential empirical findings. Instead of dichotomizing this array into significant and nonsignificant systems it would seem less arbitrary and more promising to appraise or compare different theoretical systems in regard to such characteristics as these:

a. the clarity and precision with which the theories are formulated, and with which the logical relationships of their elements to each other and to expressions couched in observational terms have been made explicit;
b. the systematic, i.e., explanatory and predictive, power of the systems in regard to observable phenomena;
c. the formal simplicity of the theoretical system with which a certain systematic power is attained;
d. the extent to which the theories have been confirmed by experiential evidence.

Many of the speculative philosophical approaches to cosmology, biology or history, for example, would make a poor showing on practically all of these counts and would thus prove no matches to available rival theories, or would be recognized as so unpromising as not to warrant further study or development.

If the procedure here suggested is to be carried out in detail, so as to become applicable also in less obvious cases, then it will be necessary, of course, to develop general standards, and theories pertaining to them, for the appraisal and comparison of theoretical systems in the various respects just mentioned. To what extent this can be done with rigor and precision cannot well be judged in advance. In recent years, a considerable amount of work has been done towards a definition and theory of the concept of degree of confirmation, or logical probability, of a theoretical system;[21] and several contributions have been made towards the clarification of some of the other ideas referred to above.[22] The continuation of this research represents a challenge for further constructive work in the logical and methodological analysis of scientific knowledge.

Notes

This essay combines, with certain omissions and some other changes, the contents of two articles: "Problems and Changes in the Empiricist Criterion of Meaning." *Revue Internationale de Philosophie* No. 11, pp. 41–63 (January, 1950); and "The Concept of Cognitive Significance: A Reconsideration," *Proceedings of the American Academy of Arts and Sciences* 80, No. 1, pp. 61–77 (1951). This material is reprinted with kind permission of the Director of *Revue Internationale de Philosophie* and of the American Academy of Arts and Sciences.

1. Observation sentences of this kind belong to what Carnap has called the thing-language, cf., e.g., (1938), pp. 52–53. That they are adequate to formulate the data which serve as the basis for empirical tests is clear in particular for the intersubjective testing procedures used in science as well as in large areas of empirical inquiry on the commonsense level. In epistemological discussions, it is frequently assumed that the ultimate evidence for beliefs about empirical matters consists in perceptions and sensations whose description calls for a phenomenalistic type of language. The specific problems connected with the phenomenalistic approach cannot be discussed here; but it should be mentioned that at any rate all the critical considerations presented in this article in regard to the testability criterion are applicable, *mutatis mutandis*, to the case of a phenomenalistic basis as well.

2. Originally, the permissible evidence was meant to be restricted to what is observable by the speaker and perhaps his fellow beings during their lifetimes. Thus construed, the criterion rules out, as cognitively meaningless, all statements about the distant future or the remote past, as has been pointed out, among others, by Ayer (1946), chapter I; by Pap (1949), chapter 13, esp. pp. 333 ff.; and by Russell (1948), pp. 445–47. This difficulty is avoided, however, if we permit the evidence to consist of any finite set of "logically possible observation data," each of them formulated in an observation sentence. Thus, e.g., the sentence S_1, "The tongue of the largest dinosaur in New York's Museum of Natural History was blue or black" is completely verifiable in our sense; for it is a logical consequence of the sentence S_2, "The tongue of the largest dinosaur in New York's Museum of Natural History was blue"; and this is an observation sentence, in the sense just indicated.

And if the concept of *verifiability in principle* and the more general concept of *confirmability in principle*, which will be considered later, are construed as referring to *logically possible evidence* as expressed by observation sentences, then it follows similarly that the class of statements which are verifiable, or at least confirmable, in principle include such assertions as that the planet Neptune and the Antarctic continent existed before they were discovered, and that atomic warfare, if not checked, will lead to the extermination of this planet. The objections which Russell (1948), pp. 445 and 447, raises against the verifiability criterion by reference to those examples do not apply therefore if the criterion is understood in the manner here suggested. Incidentally, statements of the kind mentioned by Russell, which are not actually verifiable by any human being, were explicitly recognized as cognitively significant already by Schlick (1936), Part V, who argued that the impossibility of verifying them was "merely empirical." The characterization of verifiability with the help of the concept of observation sentence as suggested here might serve as a more explicit and rigorous statement of that conception.

3. As has frequently been emphasized in the empiricist literature, the term "verifiability" is to indicate, of course, the conceivability, or better, the logical possibility, of evidence of an observational kind which, if actually encountered, would constitute conclusive evidence for the given sentence; it is not intended to mean the technical possibility of performing the tests needed to obtain such evidence, and even less the possibility of actually finding directly observable phenomena which constitute conclusive evidence for that sentence—which would be tantamount to the actual existence of such evidence and would thus imply the truth of the given sentence. Analogous remarks apply to the terms "falsifiability" and "confirmability." This point has clearly been disregarded in some critical discussions

of the verifiability criterion. Thus, e.g., Russell (1948), p. 448 construes verifiability as the actual existence of a set of conclusively verifying occurrences. This conception, which has never been advocated by any logical empiricist, must naturally turn out to be inadequate since according to it the empirical meaningfulness of a sentence could not be established without gathering empirical evidence, and moreover enough of it to permit a conclusive proof of the sentence in question! It is not surprising, therefore, that his extraordinary interpretation of verifiability leads Russell to the conclusion: "In fact, that a proposition is verifiable is itself not verifiable" (*l.c.*). Actually, under the empiricist interpretation of complete verifiability, any statement asserting the verifiability of some sentence *S* whose text is quoted, is either analytic or contradictory; for the decision whether there exists a class of observation sentences which entail *S*, i.e., whether such observation sentences can be formulated, no matter whether they are true or false—that decision is a purely logical matter.

4. The arguments here adduced against the verifiability criterion also prove the inadequacy of a view closely related to it, namely that two sentences have the same cognitive significance if any set of observation sentences which would verify one of them would also verify the other, and conversely. Thus, e.g., under this criterion, any two general laws would have to be assigned the same cognitive significance, for no general law is verified by any set of observation sentences. The view just referred to must be clearly distinguished from a position which Russell examines in his critical discussion of the positivistic meaning criterion. It is "the theory that two propositions whose verified consequences are identical have the same significance" (1948), p. 448. This view is untenable indeed, for what consequences of a statement have actually been verified at a given time is obviously a matter of historical accident which cannot possibly serve to establish identity of cognitive significance. But I am not aware that any logical empiricist ever subscribed to that "theory."

5. (1936, 1946), Chap. I. The case against the requirements of verifiability and of falsifiability, and in favor of a requirement of partial confirmability and disconfirmability, is very clearly presented also by Pap (1949), chapter 13.

6. (1946), 2d ed., pp. 11–12.

7. This restriction is expressed in recursive form and involves no vicious circle. For the full statement of Ayer's criterion, see Ayer (1946), p. 13.

8. Church (1949). An alternative criterion recently suggested by O'Connor (1950) as a revision of Ayer's formulation is subject to a slight variant of Church's stricture: It can be shown that if there are three observation sentences none of which entails any of the others, and if *S* is any noncompound sentence, then either *S* or ∼ *S* is significant under O'Connor's criterion.

9. An extralogical term is one that does not belong to the specific vocabulary of logic. The following phrases, and those definable by means of them, are typical examples of logical terms: 'not', 'or', 'if . . . then', 'all', 'some', '. . . is an element of class . . .'. Whether it is possible to make a sharp theoretical distinction between logical and extra-logical terms is a controversial issue related to the problem of discriminating between analytic and synthetic sentences. For the purpose at hand, we may simply assume that the logical vocabulary is given by enumeration.

10. For a detailed exposition and critical discussion of this idea, see H. Feigl's stimulating and enlightening article (1950).

11. Cf. (1936–37), especially section 7.

12. On this subject, see for example Langford (1941); Lewis (1946), pp. 210–30; Chisholm (1946); Goodman (1947); Reichenbach (1947), Chapter VIII; Hempel and Oppenheim (1948), Part III; Popper (1949); and especially Goodman's further analysis (1955).

13. Cf. Carnap, *loc. cit.* note 11. For a brief elementary presentation of the main idea, see Carnap (1938), Part III. The sentence *R* here formulated for the predicate '*F*' illustrates only the simplest type of reduction sentence, the so-called bilateral reduction sentence.

14. Cf. the analysis in Carnap (1936–37), especially section 15; also see the briefer presentation of the liberalized point of view in Carnap (1938).

15. This is not strictly correct. For a more circumspect statement, see note 12 in "A Logical Appraisal of Operationism" and the fuller discussion in section 7 of the essay "The Theoretician's Dilemma."

16. The interpretation of formal theories has been studied extensively by Reichenbach, especially in his pioneer analyses of space and time in classical and in relativistic physics. He describes such interpretation as the establishment of *coordinating definitions* (*Zuordnungsdefintionen*) for certain terms of the formal theory. See, for example, Reichenbach (1928). More recently, Northrop [cf. (1947), Chap. VII, and also the detailed study of the use of deductively formulated theories in science, ibid., Chaps. IV, V, VI] and H. Margenau [cf., for example, (1935)] have discussed certain aspects of this process under the title of *epistemic correlation*.

17. A somewhat fuller account of this type of interpretation may be found in Carnap (1939), §24. The articles by Spence (1944) and by MacCorquodale and Meehl (1948) provide enlightening illustrations

of the use of theoretical constructs in a field outside that of the physical sciences, and of the difficulties encountered in an attempt to analyze in detail their function and interpretation.

18. Cf. Carnap (1936–37), especially sections 8 and 10.

19. Carnap (1936–37), p. 452.

20. The sentence O is what Carnap calls the *representative sentence* of the couple consisting of the sentences $S1$ and $S2$; see (1936–37), pp. 450–53.

21. Cf., for example, Carnap (1945)1 and (1945)2, and especially (1950). Also see Helmer and Oppenheim (1945).

22. On simplicity, cf. especially Popper (1935), Chap. V; Reichenbach (1938), § 42; Goodman (1949)1, (1949)2, (1950); on explanatory and predictive power, cf. Hempel and Oppenheim (1948), Part IV.

References

Ayer, A. J., *Language, Truth and Logic*, London, 1936; 2nd ed. 1946.

Carnap, R., "Testability and Meaning," *Philosophy of Science*, 3 (1936) and 4 (1937).

Carnap, R., "Logical Foundations of the Unity of Science," in *International Encyclopedia of Unified Science*, I, 1; Chicago, 1938.

Carnap, R., *Foundations of Logic and Mathematics*, Chicago, 1939.

Carnap, R., "On Inductive Logic," *Philosophy of Science*, 12 (1945). Referred to as (1945)1 in this article.

Carnap, R., "The Two Concepts of Probability," *Philosophy and Phenomenological Research*, 5 (1945). Referred to as (1945)2 in this article.

Carnap, R., *Logical Foundations of Probability*, Chicago, 1950.

Chisholm, R. M., "The Contrary-to-Fact Conditional," *Mind*, 55 (1946).

Church, A., Review of Ayer (1946), *The Journal of Symbolic Logic*, 14 (1949), 52–53.

Feigl, H., "Existential Hypotheses: Realistic vs. Phenomenalistic Interpretations," *Philosophy of Science*, 17 (1950).

Goodman, N., "The Problem of Counterfactual Conditionals," *The Journal of Philosophy*, 44 (1947).

Goodman, N., "The Logical Simplicity of Predicates," *The Journal of Symbolic Logic*, 14 (1949). Referred to as (1949)1 in this article.

Goodman, N., "Some Reflections on the Theory of Systems," *Philosophy and Phenomenological Research*, 9 (1949). Referred to as (1949)2 in this article.

Goodman, N., "An Improvement in the Theory of Simplicity," *The Journal of Symbolic Logic*, 15 (1950).

Goodman, N., *Fact, Fiction, and Forecast*, Cambridge, Massachusetts, 1955.

Helmer, O., and P. Oppenheim, "A Syntactical Definition of Probability and of Degree of Confirmation." *The Journal of Symbolic Logic*, 10 (1945).

Hempel, C. G., and P. Oppenheim, "Studies in the Logic of Explanation, *Philosophy of Science*, 15 (1948).

Langford, C. H., Review in *The Journal of Symbolic Logic*, 6 (1941), 67–68.

Lewis, C. I., *An Analysis of Knowledge and Valuation*, La Salle, Ill., 1946.

MacCorquodale, K., and P. E. Meehl, "On a Distinction Between Hypothetical Constructs and Intervening Variables," *Psychological Review*, 55 (1948).

Margenau, H., "Methodology of Modern Physics," *Philosophy of Science*, 2 (1935).

Northrop, F. S. C., *The Logic of the Sciences and the Humanities*, New York, 1947.

O'Connor, D. J., "Some Consequences of Professor A. J. Ayer's Verification Principle," *Analysis*, 10 (1950).

Pap, A., *Elements of Analytic Philosophy*, New York, 1949.

Popper, K., *Logik der Forschung*, Wien, 1935.

Popper, K., "A Note on Natural Laws and So-Called 'Contrary-to-Fact Conditionals'," *Mind*, 58 (1949).

Reichenbach, H., *Philosophie der Raum-Zeit-Lehre*, Berlin, 1928.

Reichenbach, H., *Elements of Symbolic Logic*, New York, 1947.

Russell, B., *Human Knowledge*, New York, 1948.

Schlick, M., "Meaning and Verification," *Philosophical Review*, 45 (1936). Also reprinted in Feigl, H. and W. Sellars, (eds.) *Readings in Philosophical Analysis*, New York, 1949.

Spence, Kenneth W., "The Nature of Theory Construction in Contemporary Psychology," *Psychological Review*, 51 (1944).

Chapter 4

Empiricism, Semantics, and Ontology

Rudolf Carnap

1. The Problem of Abstract Entities

Empiricists are in general rather suspicious with respect to any kind of abstract entities like properties, classes, relations, numbers, propositions, etc. They usually feel much more in sympathy with nominalists than with realists (in the medieval sense). As far as possible they try to avoid any reference to abstract entities and to restrict themselves to what is sometimes called a nominalistic language, i.e., one not containing such references. However, within certain scientific contexts it seems hardly possible to avoid them. In the case of mathematics, some empiricists try to find a way out by treating the whole of mathematics as a mere calculus, a formal system for which no interpretation is given or can be given. Accordingly, the mathematician is said to speak not about numbers, functions, and infinite classes, but merely about meaningless symbols and formulas manipulated according to given formal rules. In physics it is more difficult to shun the suspected entities, because the language of physics serves for the communication of reports and predictions and hence cannot be taken, as a mere calculus. A physicist who is suspicious of abstract entities may perhaps try to declare a certain part of the language of physics as uninterpreted and uninterpretable, that part which refers to real numbers as space-time coordinates or as values of physical magnitudes, to functions, limits, etc. More probably he will just speak about all these things like anybody else but with an uneasy conscience, like a man who in his everyday life does with qualms many things which are not in accord with the high moral principles he professes on Sundays. Recently the problem of abstract entities has arisen again in connection with semantics, the theory of meaning and truth. Some semanticists say that certain expressions designate certain entities, and among these designated entities they include not only concrete material things but also abstract entities, e.g., properties as designated by predicates and propositions as designated by sentences.[1] Others object strongly to this procedure as violating the basic principles of empiricism and leading back to a metaphysical ontology of the Platonic kind.

It is the purpose of this article to clarify this controversial issue. The nature and implications of the acceptance of a language referring to abstract entities will first be discussed in general; it will be shown that using such a language does not imply embracing a Platonic ontology but is perfectly compatible with empiricism and strictly scientific thinking. Then the special question of the role of abstract entities in semantics will be discussed. It is hoped that the clarification of the issue will be useful to those who would like to accept abstract entities in their work in mathematics, physics, semantics, or any other field; it may help them to overcome nominalistic scruples.

Reprinted from *Meaning and Necessity*, enlarged edition (Chicago: University of Chicago Press, 1956), pp. 205–221, by permission of the publisher. Copyright 1956 by University of Chicago Press.

2. Linguistic Frameworks

Are there properties, classes, numbers, propositions? In order to understand more clearly the nature of these and related problems, it is above all necessary to recognize a fundamental distinction between two kinds of questions concerning the existence or reality of entities. If someone wishes to speak in his language about a new kind of entities, he has to introduce a system of new ways of speaking, subject to new rules; we shall call this procedure the construction of a linguistic *framework* for the new entities in question. And now we must distinguish two kinds of questions of existence: first, questions of the existence of certain entities of the new kind *within the framework*; we call them *internal questions*; and second, questions concerning the existence or reality *of the system of entities as a whole*, called *external questions*. Internal questions and possible answers to them are formulated with the help of the new forms of expressions. The answers may be found either by purely logical methods or by empirical methods, depending upon whether the framework is a logical or a factual one. An external question is of a problematic character which is in need of closer examination.

The world of things.   Let us consider as an example the simplest kind of entities dealt with in the everyday language: the spatio-temporally ordered system of observable things and events. Once we have accepted the thing language with its framework for things, we can raise and answer internal questions, e.g., "Is there a white piece of paper on my desk?", "Did King Arthur actually live?", "Are unicorns and centaurs real or merely imaginary?", and the like. These questions are to be answered by empirical investigations. Results of observations are evaluated according to certain rules as confirming or disconfirming evidence for possible answers. (This evaluation is usually carried out, of course, as a matter of habit rather than a deliberate, rational procedure. But it is possible, in a rational reconstruction, to lay down explicit rules for the evaluation. This is one of the main tasks of a pure, as distinguished from a psychological, epistemology.) The concept of reality occurring in these internal questions is an empirical, scientific, nonmetaphysical concept. To recognize something as a real thing or event means to succeed in incorporating it into the system of things at a particular space-time position so that it fits together with the other things recognized as real, according to the rules of the framework.

From these questions we must distinguish the external question of the reality of the thing world itself. In contrast to the former questions, this question is raised neither by the man in the street nor by scientists, but only by philosophers. Realists give an affirmative answer, subjective idealists a negative one, and the controversy goes on for centuries without ever being solved. And it cannot be solved because it is framed in a wrong way. To be real in the scientific sense means to be an element of the system; hence this concept cannot be meaningfully applied to the system itself. Those who raise the question of the reality of the thing world itself have perhaps in mind not a theoretical question as their formulation seems to suggest, but rather a practical question, a matter of a practical decision concerning the structure of our language. We have to make the choice whether or not to accept and use the forms of expression in the framework in question.

In the case of this particular example, there is usually no deliberate choice because we all have accepted the thing language early in our lives as a matter of course. Nevertheless, we may regard it as a matter of decision in this sense: we are free to choose to continue using the thing language or not; in the latter case we could restrict ourselves to a language of sense-data and other "phenomenal" entities, or construct an alternative to the customary thing language with another structure, or, finally, we could refrain from speaking. If someone decides to accept the thing language there is no objection against saying that he has accepted the world of things. But this must not be interpreted as if it meant his acceptance of a *belief* in the reality of the thing world; there is no such belief or assertion or assumption, because it is not a theoretical question. To accept the thing world means nothing more than to accept a certain form of language, in other words, to accept rules for forming statements and for testing, accepting, or rejecting them. The acceptance of the thing language leads, on the basis of observations made, also to the acceptance, belief, and assertion of certain statements. But the thesis of the reality of the thing world cannot be among these statements, because it cannot be formulated in the thing language or, it seems, in any other theoretical language.

The decision of accepting the thing language, although itself not of a cognitive nature, will nevertheless usually be influenced by theoretical knowledge, just like any other deliberate decision concerning the acceptance of linguistic or other rules. The purposes for which the language is intended to be used, for instance, the purpose of communicating factual knowledge, will determine which factors are relevant for the decision. The efficiency, fruitfulness, and simplicity of the use of the thing language may be among the decisive factors. And the questions concerning these qualities are indeed of a theoretical nature. But these questions cannot be identified with the question of realism. They are not yes-no questions but questions of degree. The thing language in the customary form works indeed with a high degree of efficiency for most purposes of everyday life. This is a matter of fact, based upon the content of our experiences. However, it would be wrong to describe this situation by saying: "The fact of the efficiency of the thing language is confirming evidence for the reality of the thing world"; we should rather say instead: "This fact makes it advisable to accept the thing language".

The system of numbers.   As an example of a system which is of a logical rather than a factual nature let us take the system of natural numbers. The framework for this system is constructed by introducing into the language new expressions with suitable rules: (1) numerals like "five" and sentence forms like "there are five books on the table"; (2) the general term "number" for the new entities, and sentence forms like "five is a number"; (3) expressions for properties of numbers (e.g., "odd", "prime"), relations (e.g., "greater than"), and functions (e.g., "plus"), and sentence forms like "two plus three is five"; (4) numerical variables ("m", "n", etc.) and quantifiers for universal sentences ("for every n, . . .") and existential sentences ("there is an n such that . . .") with the customary deductive rules.

Here again there are internal questions, e.g., "Is there a prime number greater than a hundred?" Here, however, the answers are found, not by empirical investigation based on observations, but by logical analysis based on the rules for the new expressions. Therefore the answers are here analytic, i.e., logically true.

What is now the nature of the philosophical question concerning the existence or reality of numbers? To begin with, there is the internal question which, together with the affirmative answer, can be formulated in the new terms, say, by "There are numbers" or, more explicitly, "There is an n such that n is a number". This statement follows from the analytic statement "five is an number" and is therefore itself analytic. Moreover, it is rather trivial (in contradistinction to a statement like "There is a prime number greater than a million", which is likewise analytic but far from trivial), because it does not say more than that the new system is not empty; but this is immediately seen from the rule which states that words like "five" are substitutable for the new variables. Therefore nobody who meant the question "Are there numbers?" in the internal sense would either assert or even seriously consider a negative answer. This makes it plausible to assume that those philosophers who treat the question of the existence of numbers as a serious philosophical problem and offer lengthy arguments on either side do not have in mind the internal question. And, indeed, if we were to ask them: "Do you mean the question as to whether the framework of numbers, *if* we were to accept it, would be found to be empty or not?", they would probably reply: "Not at all; we mean a question *prior* to the acceptance of the new framework". They might try to explain what they mean by saying that it is a question of the ontological status of numbers; the question whether or not numbers have a certain metaphysical characteristic called reality (but a kind of ideal reality, different from the material reality of the thing world) or subsistence or status of "independent entities." Unfortunately, these philosophers have so far not given a formulation of their question in terms of the common scientific language. Therefore our judgment must be that they have not succeeded in giving to the external question and to the possible answers any cognitive content. Unless and until they supply a clear cognitive interpretation, we are justified in our suspicion that their question is a pseudo-question, that is, one disguised in the form of a theoretical question while in fact it is nontheoretical; in the present case it is the practical problem whether or not to incorporate into the language the new linguistic forms which constitute the framework of numbers.

The system of propositions.   New variables, "p", "q", etc., are introduced with a rule to the effect that any (declarative) sentence may be substituted for a variable of this kind; this includes, in addition to the sentences of the original thing language, also all general sentences with variables of any kind which may have been introduced into the language. Further, the general term "proposition" is introduced. "p is a proposition" may be defined by "p or not p" (or by any other sentence form yielding only analytic sentences). Therefore, every sentence of the form "... is a proposition" (where any sentence may stand in the place of the dots) is analytic. This holds, for example, for the sentence:

(a) "Chicago is large is a proposition".

(We disregard here the fact that the rules of English grammar require not a sentence but a that-clause as the subject of another sentence; accordingly, instead of (a) we should have to say "That Chicago is large is a proposition".) Predicates may be admitted whose argument expressions are sentences; these predicates may be either extensional (e.g., the customary truth-functional connectives) or not (e.g., modal predicates like "possible", "necessary", etc.). With the help of the new variables, general sentences may be formed, e.g.,.

(b) "For every p, either p or not-p".

(c) "There is a p such that p is not necessary and not-p is not necessary."

(d) "There is a p such that p is a proposition".

(c) and (d) are internal assertions of existence. The statement "There are propositions" may be meant in the sense of (d); in this case it is analytic (since it follows from (a)) and even trivial. If, however, the statement is meant in an external sense, then it is noncognitive.

It is important to notice that the system of rules for the linguistic expressions of the propositional framework (of which only a few rules have here been briefly indicated) is sufficient for the introduction of the framework. Any further explanations as to the nature of the propositions (i.e., the elements of the system indicated, the values of the variables "p", "q", etc.) are theoretically unnecessary because, if correct, they follow from the rules. For example, are propositions mental events (as in Russell's theory)? A look at the rules shows us that they are not, because otherwise existential statements would be of the form: "If the mental state of the person in question fulfills such and such conditions, then there is a p such that ...". The fact that no references to mental conditions occur in existential statements (like (c), (d), etc.) shows that propositions are not mental entities. Further, a statement of the existence of linguistic entities (e.g., expressions, classes of expressions, etc.) must contain a reference to a language. The fact that no such reference occurs in the existential statements here, shows that propositions are not linguistic entities. The fact that in these statements no reference to a subject (an observer or knower) occurs (nothing like: "There is a p which is necessary for Mr. X"), shows that the propositions (and their properties, like necessity, etc.) are not subjective. Although characterizations of these or similar kinds are, strictly speaking, unnecessary, they may nevertheless be practically useful. If they are given, they should be understood, not as ingredient parts of the system, but merely as marginal notes with the purpose of supplying to the reader helpful hints or convenient pictorial associations which may make his learning of the use of the expressions easier than the bare system of the rules would do. Such a characterization is analogous to an extrasystematic explanation which a physicist sometimes gives to the beginner. He might, for example, tell him to imagine the atoms of a gas as small balls rushing around with great speed, or the electromagnetic field and its oscillations as quasi-elastic tensions and vibrations in an ether. In fact, however, all that can accurately be said about atoms or the field is implicitly contained in the physical laws of the theories in question.[2]

The system of thing properties.   The thing language contains words like "red", "hard", "stone", "house", etc., which are used for describing what things are like. Now we may introduce new variables, say "f", "g", etc., for which those words are substitutable and furthermore the general term "property". New rules are laid down which admit sentences like "Red is a property", "Red is a color", "These two pieces of paper have at least one color in common" (i.e., "There is an f such that f is a color, and ..."). The last sentence is an internal assertion. It is of an empirical, factual nature. However, the external statement, the philosophical statement of the reality of properties—a special case of the thesis of the reality of universals—is devoid of cognitive content.

The systems of integers and rational numbers.   Into a language containing the framework of natural numbers we may introduce first the (positive and negative) integers as relations among natural numbers and then the rational numbers as relations among integers. This involves introducing new types of variables, expressions substitutable for them, and the general terms "integer" and "rational number".

The system of real numbers.   On the basis of the rational numbers, the real numbers may be introduced as classes of a special kind (segments) of rational numbers (according to the method developed by Dedekind and Frege). Here again a new type of variables is introduced, expressions substitutable for them (e.g., "$\sqrt{2}$") and the general term "real number".

The spatio-temporal coordinate system for physics.   The new entities are the space-time points. Each is an ordered quadruple of four real numbers, called its coordinates, consisting of three spatial and one temporal coordinates. The physical state of a spatio-temporal point or region is described either with the help of qualitative predicates (e.g., "hot") or by ascribing numbers as values of a physical magnitude (e.g., mass, temperature, and the like). The step from the system of things (which does not contain space-time points but only extended objects with spatial and temporal relations between them) to the physical coordinate system is again a matter of decision. Our choice of certain features, although itself not theoretical, is suggested by theoretical knowledge, either logical or factual. For example, the choice of real numbers rather than rational numbers or integers as coordinates is not much influenced by the facts of experience but mainly due to considerations of mathematical simplicity. The restriction to rational coordinates would not be in conflict with any experimental knowledge we have, because the result of any measurement is a rational number. However, it would prevent the use of ordinary geometry (which says, e.g., that the diagonal of a square with the side I has the irrational value $\sqrt{2}$) and thus lead to great complications. On the other hand, the decision to use three rather than two or four spatial coordinates is strongly suggested, but still not forced upon us, by the result of common observations. If certain events allegedly observed in spiritualistic séances, e.g., a ball moving out of a sealed box, were confirmed beyond any reasonable doubt, it might seem advisable to use four spatial coordinates. Internal questions are here, in general, empirical questions to be answered by empirical investigations. On the other hand, the external questions of the reality of physical space and physical time are pseudo-questions. A question like "Are there (really) space-time points?" is ambiguous. It may be meant as an internal question; then the affirmative answer is, of course, analytic and trivial. Or it may be meant in the external sense: "Shall we introduce such and such forms into our language?"; in this case it is not a theoretical but a practical question, a matter of decision rather than assertion, and hence the proposed formulation would be misleading. Or finally, it may be meant in the following sense: "Are our experiences such that the use of the linguistic forms in question will be expedient and fruitful?" This is a theoretical question of a factual, empirical nature. But it concerns a matter of degree; therefore a formulation in the form "real or not?" would be inadequate.

3. What Does Acceptance of a Kind of Entities Mean?

Let us now summarize the essential characteristics of situations involving the introduction of a new kind of entities, characteristics which are common to the various examples outlined above.

The acceptance of a new kind of entities is represented in the language by the introduction of a framework of new forms of expressions to be used according to a new set of rules. There may be new names for particular entities of the kind in question; but some such names may already occur in the language before the introduction of the new framework. (Thus, for example, the thing language contains certainly words of the type of "blue" and "house" before the framework of properties is introduced; and it may contain words like "ten" in sentences of the form "I have ten fingers" before the framework of numbers is introduced.) The latter fact shows that the occurrence of constants of the type in question—regarded as names of entities of the new kind after the new framework is introduced—is not a sure sign of the acceptance of the new kind of entities. Therefore the introduction of such constants is not to be regarded as an essential step in the introduction of the framework. The two essential steps are rather the following. First, the introduction of a general term, a predicate of higher level, for the new kind of entities, permitting us to say of any particular entity that it belongs to this kind (e.g., "Red is a *property*", "Five is a *number*"). Second, the introduction of variables of the new type. The new entities are values of these variables; the constants (and the closed compound expressions, if any) are substitutable for the variables.[3] With the help of the variables, general sentences concerning the new entities can be formulated.

After the new forms are introduced into the language, it is possible to formulate with their help internal questions and possible answers to them. A question of this kind may be either empirical or logical; accordingly a true answer is either factually true or analytic.

From the internal questions we must clearly distinguish external questions, i.e., philosophical questions concerning the existence or reality of the total system of the new entities. Many philosophers regard a question of this kind as an ontological question which must be raised and answered *before* the introduction of the new language forms. The latter introduction, they believe, is legitimate only if it can be justified by an ontological insight supplying an affirmative answer to the question of reality. In contrast to this view, we take the position that the introduction of the new ways of speaking does not need any theoretical justification because it does not imply any assertion of reality. We may still speak (and have done so) of "the acceptance of the new entities" since this form of speech is customary; but one must keep in mind that this phrase does not mean for us anything more than acceptance of the new framework, i.e., of the new linguistic forms. Above all, it must not be interpreted as referring to an assumption, belief, or assertion of "the reality of the entities". There is no such assertion. An alleged statement of the reality of the system of entities is a pseudo-statement without cognitive content. To be sure, we have to face at this point an important question; but it is a practical, not a theoretical question; it is the question of whether or not to accept the new linguistic forms. The acceptance cannot be judged as being either true or false beause it is not an assertion. It can only be judged as being more or less expedient, fruitful, conducive to the aim for which the language is intended. Judgments of this kind supply the motivation for the decision of accepting or rejecting the kind of entities.[4]

Thus it is clear that the acceptance of a linguistic framework must not be regarded as implying a metaphysical doctrine concerning the reality of the entities in question. It seems to me due to neglect of this important distinction that some contemporary nominalists label the admission of variables of abstract types as "Platonism"[5] This is, to say the least, an extremely misleading terminology. It leads to the absurd consequence, that the position of everybody who accepts the language of physics with its real number variables (as a language of communication, not merely as a calculus) would be called Platonistic, even if he is a strict empiricist who rejects Platonic metaphysics.

A brief historical remark may here be inserted. The non-cognitive character of the questions which we have called here external questions was recognized and emphasized already by the Vienna Circle under the leadership of Moritz Schlick, the group from which the movement of logical empiricism originated. Influenced by ideas of Ludwig Wittgenstein, the Circle rejected both the thesis of the reality of the external world and the thesis of its irreality as pseudo-statements;[6] the same was the case for both the thesis of the reality of universals (abstract entities, in our present terminology) and the nominalistic thesis that they are not real and that their alleged names are not names of anything but merely *flatus vocis*. (It is obvious that the apparent negation of a pseudo-statement must also be a pseudo-statement.) It is therefore not correct to classify the members of the Vienna Circle as nominalists, as is sometimes done. However, if we look at the basic anti-metaphysical and proscientific attitude of most nominalists (and the same holds for many materialists and realists in the modern sense), disregarding their occasional pseudo-theoretical formulations, then it is, of course, true to say that the Vienna Circle was much closer to those philosophers than to their opponents.

4. Abstract Entities in Semantics

The problem of the legitimacy and the status of abstract entities has recently again led to controversial discussions in connection with semantics. In a semantical meaning analysis certain expressions in a language are often said to designate (or name or denote or signify or refer to) certain extralinguistic entities.[7] As long as physical things or events (e.g., Chicago or Caesar's death) are taken as designata (entities designated), no serious doubts arise. But strong objections have been raised, especially by some empiricists, against abstract entities as designata, e.g., against semantical statements of the following kind:

(1) "The word 'red' designates a property of things";

(2) "The word 'color' designates a property of properties of things";

(3) "The word 'five' designates a number";

(4) "The word 'odd' designates a property of numbers";

(5) "The sentence 'Chicago is large' designates a proposition".

Those who criticize these statements do not, of course, reject the use of the expressions in question, like "red" or "five"; nor would they deny that these expressions are meaningful. But to be meaningful, they would say, is not the same as having a meaning in the sense of an entity designated. They reject the belief, which they regard as implicitly presupposed by those semantical statements, that to each expression of the types in question (adjectives like "red", numerals like "five", etc.) there is a particular real entity to which the expression stands in the relation of designation. This belief is rejected as incompatible with the basic principles of empiricism or of scientific thinking. Derogatory labels like "Platonic realism", "hypostatization", or "'Fido'-Fido principle" are attached to it. The latter is the name given by Gilbert Ryle (in his review of my *Meaning and Necessity* [*Philosophy*, 24(1949), 69–76]) to the criticized belief, which, in his view, arises by a naïve inference of analogy: just as there is an entity well known to me, viz. my dog Fido, which is designated by the name "Fido", thus there must be for every meaningful expression a particular entity to which it stands in the relation of designation or naming, i.e., the relation exemplified by "Fido"-Fido. The belief criticized is thus a case of hypostatization, i.e., of treating as names expressions which are not names. While "Fido" is a name, expressions like "red", "five", etc., are said not to be names, not to designate anything.

Our previous discussion concerning the acceptance of frameworks enables us now to clarify the situation with respect to abstract entities as designata. Let us take as an example the statement:

(a) "'Five' designates a number".

The formulation of this statement presupposes that our language L contains the forms of expressions which we have called the framework of numbers, in particular, numerical variables and the general term "number." If L contains these forms, the following is an analytic statement in L:

(b) "Five is a number".

Further, to make the statement (a) possible, L must contain an expression like "designates" or "is a name of" for the semantical relation of designation. If suitable rules for this term are laid down, the following is likewise analytic

(c) "'Five' designates five".

(Generally speaking, any expression of the form "'...' designates ..." is an analytic statement provided the term "..." is a constant in an accepted framework. If the latter condition is not fulfilled, the expression is not a statement.) Since (a) follows from (c) and (b), (a) is likewise analytic.

Thus it is clear that *if* someone accepts the framework of numbers, then he must acknowledge (c) and (b) and hence (a) as true statements. Generally speaking, if someone accepts a framework for a certain kind of entities, then he is bound to admit the entities as possible designata. Thus the question of the admissibility of entities of a certain type or of abstract entities in general as designata is reduced to the question of the acceptability of the linguistic framework for those entities. Both the nominalistic critics, who refuse the status of designators or names to expressions like "red", "five", etc., because they deny the existence of abstract entities and the skeptics, who express doubts concerning the existence and demand evidence for it, treat the question of existence as a theoretical question. They do, of course, not mean the internal question; the affirmative answer to *this* question is analytic and trivial and too obvious for doubt or denial as we have seen. Their doubts refer rather to the system of entities itself; hence they mean the external question. They believe that only after making sure that there really is a system of entities of the kind in question are we justified in accepting the framework by incorporating the linguistic forms into our language. However, we have seen that the external question is not a theoretical question but rather the practical question whether or not to accept those linguistic forms. This acceptance is not in need of a theoretical justification (except with respect to expediency and fruitfulness), because it does not imply a belief or assertion. Ryle says that the "Fido"-Fido principle is "a grotesque theory". Grotesque or not, Ryle is wrong in calling it a theory. It is rather the practical decision to accept certain frameworks. Maybe Ryle is historically right with respect to those whom he mentions as previous representatives of the principle, viz., John Stuart Mill, Frege, and Russell. If these philosophers regarded the acceptance of a system of entities as a theory, an assertion, they were victims of the same old, metaphysical confusion. But it is certainly wrong to regard *my* semantical method as involving a belief in the reality of abstract entities, since I reject a thesis of this kind as a metaphysical pseudo-statement.

The critics of the use of abstract entities in semantics overlook the fundamental difference between the acceptance of a system of entities and an internal assertion, e.g., an assertion that there are elephants or electrons or prime numbers greater than a million. Whoever makes an internal assertion is certainly obliged to justify it by providing evidence, empirical evidence in the case of electrons, logical proof in the case of the prime numbers. The demand for a theoretical justification, correct in the case of internal assertions, is sometimes wrongly applied to the acceptance of a system of entities. Thus, for example, Ernest Nagel (in his review of my *Meaning and Necessity* [*Journal of Philosophy*, 45 (1948), 467−472]) asks for "evidence relevant for affirming with warrant that there are such entities as infinitesimals or propositions". He characterizes the evidence required in these cases—in distinction to the empirical evidence in the case of electrons—as "in the broad sense logical and dialectical." Beyond this no hint is given as to what might be regarded as relevant evidence. Some nominalists regard the acceptance of abstract entities as a kind of superstition or myth, populating the world with fictitious or at least dubious entities, analogous to the belief in centaurs or demons. This shows again the confusion mentioned, because a superstition or myth is a false (or dubious) internal statement.

Let us take as example the natural numbers as cardinal numbers, i.e., in contexts like "Here are three books". The linguistic forms of the framework of numbers, including variables and the general term "number", are generally used in our common language of communication; and it is easy to formulate explicit rules for their use. Thus the logical characteristics of this framework are sufficiently clear (while many internal questions, i.e., arithmetical questions, are, of course, still open). In spite of this, the controversy concerning the external question of the ontological reality of the system of numbers continues. Suppose that one philosopher says: "I believe that there are numbers as real entities. This gives me the right to use the linguistic forms of the numerical framework and to make semantical statements about numbers as designata of numerals". His nominalistic opponent replies: "You are wrong; there are no numbers. The numerals may still be used as meaningful expressions. But they are not names, there are no entities designated by them. Therefore the word "number" and numerical variables must not be used (unless a way were found to introduce them as merely abbreviating devices, a way of translating them into the nominalistic thing language)." I cannot think of any possible evidence that would be regarded as relevant by both philosophers, and therefore, if actually found, would decide the controversy or at least make one of the opposite theses more probable than the other. (To construe the numbers as classes or properties of the second level, according to the Frege-Russell method, does, of course, not solve the controversy, because the first philosopher would affirm and the second deny the existence of the system of classes or properties of the second level.) Therefore I feel compelled to regard the external question as a pseudo-question, until both parties to the controversy offer a common interpretation of the question as a cognitive question; this would involve an indication of possible evidence regarded as relevant by both sides.

There is a particular kind of misinterpretation of the acceptance of abstract entities in various fields of science and in semantics, that needs to be cleared up. Certain early British empiricists (e.g., Berkeley and Hume) denied the existence of abstract entities on the ground that immediate experience presents us only with particulars, not with universals, e.g., with this red patch, but not with Redness or Color-in-General; with this scalene triangle, but not with Scalene Triangularity or Triangularity-in-General. Only entities belonging to a type of which examples were to be found within immediate experience could be accepted as ultimate constituents of reality. Thus, according to this way of thinking, the existence of abstract entities could be asserted only if one could show either that some abstract entities fall within the given, or that abstract entities can be defined in terms of the types of entity which are given. Since these empiricists found no abstract entities within the realm of sense-data, they either denied their existence, or else made a futile attempt to define universals in terms of particulars. Some contemporary philosophers, especially English philosophers following Bertrand Russell, think in basically similar terms. They emphasize a distinction between the data (that which is immediately given in consciousness, e.g., sense-data, immediately past experiences, etc.) and the constructs based on the data. Existence or reality is ascribed only to the data; the constructs are not real entities; the corresponding linguistic expressions are merely ways of speech not actually designating anything (reminiscent of the nominalists' *flatus vocis*). We shall not criticize here this general conception. (As far as it is principle of accepting certain entities and not accepting others, leaving aside any ontological, phenomenalistic, and nominalistic pseudo-statements, there cannot be any theoretical objection to it.) But if this conception leads to the view that other philosophers or scientists who accept abstract entities thereby assert or imply their occurrence as immediate data, then such a view must be rejected as a misinterpretation. References to space-time points, the electromagnetic field, or electrons in physics, to real or complex numbers and their functions in mathematics, to the excitatory potential or unconscious complexes in psychology, to an inflationary trend in economics, and the like, do not imply the assertion that entities of these kinds occur as immediate data. And the same holds for references to abstract entities as designata in semantics. Some of the criticisms by English philosophers against such references give the impression that, probably due to the misinterpretation just indicated, they accuse the semanticist not so much of bad metaphysics (as some nominalists would do) but of bad psychology. The fact that they regard a semantical method involving abstract entities not merely as doubtful and perhaps wrong, but as manifestly absurd, preposterous, and grotesque, and that they show a deep horror and indignation against this method, is perhaps to be explained by a misinterpretation of the kind described. In fact, of course, the semanticist does not in the least assert or imply that the abstract entities to which he refers can be experienced as immediately given either by sensation or by a kind of rational intuition. An assertion of this kind would indeed be very dubious psychology. The psychological question as to which kinds of entities do and which do not occur as immediate data is entirely irrelevant for semantics, just as it is for physics, mathematics, economics, etc., with respect to the examples mentioned above.[8]

5. Conclusion

For those who want to develop or use semantical methods, the decisive question is not the alleged ontological question of the existence of abstract entities but rather the question whether the use of abstract linguistic forms or, in technical terms, the use of variables beyond those for things (or phenomenal data), is expedient and fruitful for the purposes for which semantical analyses are made, viz., the analysis, interpretation, clarification, or construction of languages of communication, especially languages of science. This question is here neither decided nor even discussed. It is not a question simply of yes or no, but a matter of degree. Among those philosophers who have carried out semantical analyses and thought about suitable tools for this work, beginning with Plato and Aristotle and, in a more technical way on the basis of modern logic, with C. S. Peirce and Frege, a great majority accepted abstract entities. This does, of course, not prove the case. After all, semantics in the technical sense is still in the initial phases of its development, and we must be prepared for possible fundamental changes in methods. Let us therefore admit that the nominalistic critics may possibly be right. But if so, they will have to offer better arguments than they have so far. Appeal to ontological insight will not carry much weight. The critics will have to show that it is possible to construct a semantical method which avoids all references to abstract entities and achieves by simpler means essentially the same results as the other methods.

The acceptance or rejection of abstract linguistic forms, just as the acceptance or rejection of any other linguistic forms in any branch of science will finally be decided by their efficiency as instruments, tbe ratio of the results achieved to the amount and complexity of the efforts required. To decree dogmatic prohibitions of certain linguistic forms instead of testing them by their success or failure in practical use, is worse than futile it is positively harmful because it may obstruct scientific progress. The history of science shows examples of such prohibitions based on prejudices deriving from religious, mythological, metaphysical, or other irrational sources, which slowed up the developments for shorter or longer periods of time. Let us learn from the lessons of history. Let us grant to those who work in any special field of investigation the freedom to use any form of expression which seems useful to them; the work in the field will sooner or later lead to the elimination of those forms which have no useful function. *Let us be cautious in making assertions and critical in examining them, but tolerant in permitting linguistic forms.*

Notes

1. The terms "sentence" and "statement" are here used synonymously for declarative (indicative, propositional) sentences.
2. In my book *Meaning and Necessity* (Chicago, 1947) I have developed a semantical method which takes propositions as entities designated by sentences (more specifically, as intensions of sentences). In order to facilitate the understanding of the systematic development, I added some informal, extrasystematic explanations concerning the nature of propositions. I said that the term "proposition" "is used neither for a linguistic expression nor for a subjective, mental occurrence, but rather for something objective that may or may not be exemplified in nature . . . . We apply the term 'proposition' to any entities of a certain logical type, namely, those that may be expressed by (declarative) sentences in a language" (p. 27). After some more detailed discussions concerning the relation between propositions and facts, and the nature of false propositions, I added: "It has been the purpose of the preceding remarks to facilitate the understanding of our conception of propositions. If, however, a reader should find these explanations more puzzling than clarifying, or even unacceptable, he may disregard them" (p. 31) (that is, disregard these extrasystematic explanations, not the whole theory of the propositions as intensions of sentences, as one reciewer understood). In spite of this warning, it seems that some of those readers who were puzzled by the explanations, did not disregard them but thought that by raising objections against them they could refute the theory. This is analogous to the procedure of some laymen who by (correctly) criticizing the ether picture or other visualizations of physical theories, thought they had refuted those theories. Perhaps the discussions in the present paper will help in clarifying the role of the system of linguistic rules for the introduction of a framework for entities on the one hand, and that of extrasystematic explanations concerning the nature of the entities on the other.
3. W. V. Quine was the first to recognize the importance of the introduction of variables as indicating the acceptance of entities. "The ontology to which one's use of language commits him comprises simply the objects that he treats as falling . . . within the range of values of his variables" "Notes on Existence and Necessity," *Journal of Philosophy*, 40 (1943), 118. Compare Quine, "Designation and Existence," *Journal of Philosophy*, 36 (1939), 701–709, and "On Universals," *Journal of Symbolic Logic*, 12 (1947), 74–84.
4. For a closely related point of view on these questions see the detailed discussions in Herbert Feigl, "Existential Hypotheses," *Philosophy of Science*, 17 (1950), 35–62.
5. Paul Bernays, "Sur le platonisme dans les mathématiques," *L'Enseignement math.*, 34 (1935), 52–69. W. V. Quine, see previous footnote and a recent paper ["On What There Is," *Review of the Metaphysics*, 2 (1948), 21–38.]. Quine does not acknowledge the distinction which I emphasize above, because according to his general conception there are no sharp boundary lines between logical and factual truth, between questions of meaning and questions of fact, between the acceptance of a language structure and the acceptance of an assertion formulated in the language. This conception, which seems to deviate considerably from customary ways of thinking, will be explained in his article [Semantics]. When Quine in the article [What] classifies my logicistic conception of mathematics (derived from Frege and Russell) as "platonic realism" (p. 33), this is meant (according to a personal communication from him) not as ascribing to me agreement with Plato's metaphysical doctrine of universals, but merely as referring to the fact that I accept a language of mathematics containing variables of higher levels. With respect to the basic attitude to take in choosing a language form (an "ontology" in Quine's terminology, which seems to me misleading), there appears now to be agreement between us: "the obvious counsel is tolerance and an experimental spirit" ([What], p. 38).
6. See Carnap, *Scheinprobleme in der Philosophie; das Fremdpsychische und der Realismusstreit*, Berlin, 1928. Moritz Schlick, *Positivismus and Realismus*, reprinted in *Gesammelte Aufsätze*, Wien, 1938.
7. See [I]; *Meaning and Necessity* (Chicago, 1947). The distinction I have drawn in the latter book between the method of the name-relation and the method of intension and extension is not essential for our present discussion. The term "designation" is used in the present article in a neutral way; it may be

understood as referring to the name-relation or to the intension-relation or to the extension-relation or to any similar relations used in other semantical methods.

8. Wilfrid Sellars ("Acquaintance and Description Again," in *Journal of Philos.*, 46 (1949), 496–504; see pp. 502 f.) analyzes clearly the roots of the mistake "of taking the designation relation of semantic theory to be a reconstruction of *being present to an experience*".

Chapter 5

Selections from *The Logic of Scientific Discovery*

Karl Popper

A. SCIENTIFIC METHOD (1934)

The theory to be developed in the following pages stands directly opposed to all attempts to operate with the ideas of inductive logic. It might be described as the theory of *the deductive method of testing*, or as the view that a hypothesis can only be empirically *tested*—and only *after* it has been advanced.

Before I can elaborate this view (which might be called 'deductivism', in contrast to 'inductivism'[1]) I must first make clear the distinction between the *psychology of knowledge* which deals with empirical facts, and the *logic of knowledge* which is concerned only with logical relations. For the belief in inductive logic is largely due to a confusion of psychological problems with epistemological ones. It may be worth noticing, by the way, that this confusion spells trouble not only for the logic of knowledge but for its psychology as well.

1 Elimination of Psychologism

I said above that the work of the scientist consists in putting forward and testing theories.

The initial stage, the act of conceiving or inventing a theory, seems to me neither to call for logical analysis nor to be susceptible of it. The question how it happens that a new idea occurs to a man—whether it is a musical theme, a dramatic conflict, or a scientific theory—may be of great interest to empirical psychology; but it is irrelevant to the logical analysis of scientific knowledge. This latter is concerned not with *questions of fact* (Kant's *quid facti?*), but only with questions of *justification* or *validity* (Kant's *quid juris?*). Its questions are of the following kind. Can a statement be justified? And if so, how? Is it testable? Is it logically dependent on certain other statements? Or does it perhaps contradict them? In order that a statement may be logically examined in this way, it must already have been presented to us. Someone must have formulated it, and submitted it to logical examination.

Accordingly I shall distinguish sharply between the process of conceiving a new idea, and the methods and results of examining it logically. As to the task of the logic of knowledge—in contradistinction to the psychology of knowledge—I shall proceed on the assumption that it consists solely in investigating the methods employed in those systematic tests to which every new idea must be subjected if it is to be seriously entertained.

Some might object that it would be more to the purpose to regard it as the business of epistemology to produce what has been called a 'rational reconstruction' of the steps that have led the scientist to a discovery—to the finding of some new truth. But the question is: what, precisely, do we want to reconstruct? If it is the processes involved in the stimulation and release of an inspiration which are to be reconstructed, then I should refuse to take it as the task of the logic of knowledge. Such processes are the concern of empirical psychology but hardly of logic. It is another matter if we want to reconstruct rationally the *subsequent tests* whereby the inspiration may be discovered to be a discovery, or become known to be knowledge. In so far as the scientist critically judges, alters, or rejects his own inspiration we may, if we like, regard the methodological analysis undertaken here as a kind of 'rational reconstruction' of the corresponding thought processes. But this reconstruction would not describe these processes as they actually happen: it can give only a logical skeleton of the procedure of testing. Still, this is perhaps all that is meant by those who speak of a 'rational reconstruction' of the ways in which we gain knowledge.

It so happens that my arguments here are quite independent of this problem. However, my view of the matter, for what it is worth, is that there is no such thing as a logical method of having new ideas, or a logical reconstruction of this process. My view may be expressed by saying that every discovery contains 'an irrational element', or 'a creative intuition', in Bergson's sense. In a similar way Einstein speaks of the 'search for those highly universal laws ... from which a picture of the world can be obtained by pure deduction. There is no logical path', he says, 'leading to these ... laws. They can only be reached by intuition, based upon something like an intellectual love ('*Einfühlung*') of the objects of experience.'[2]

II Deductive Testing of Theories

According to the view that will be put forward here, the method of critically testing theories, and selecting them according to the results of tests, always proceeds on the following lines. From a new idea, put up tentatively, and not yet justified in any way— an anticipation, a hypothesis, a theoretical system, or what you will—conclusions are drawn by means of logical deduction. These conclusions are then compared with one another and with other relevant statements, so as to find what logical relations (such as equivalence, derivability, compatibility, or incompatibility) exist between them.

We may if we like distinguish four different lines along which the testing of a theory could be carried out. First there is the logical comparison of the conclusions among themselves, by which the internal consistency of the system is tested. Secondly, there is the investigation of the logical form of the theory, with the object of determining whether it has the character of an empirical or scientific theory, or whether it is, for example, tautological. Thirdly, there is the comparison with other theories, chiefly with the aim of determining whether the theory would constitute a scientific advance should it survive our various tests. And finally, there is the testing of the theory by way of empirical applications of the conclusions which can be derived from it.

The purpose of this last kind of test is to find out how far the new consequences of the theory—whatever may be new in what it asserts—stand up to the demands of practice, whether raised by purely scientific experiments, or by practical technological applications. Here too the procedure of testing turns out to be deductive. With the help of other statements, previously accepted, certain singular statements—which we may call 'predictions'—are deduced from the theory; especially predictions that are easily testable or applicable. From among these statements, those are selected which are not derivable from the current theory, and more especially those which the current theory contradicts. Next we seek a decision as regards these (and other) derived statements by comparing them with the results of practical applications and experiments. If this decision is positive, that is, if the singular conclusions turn out to be acceptable, or *verified*, then the theory has, for the time being, passed its test: we have found no reason to discard it. But if the decision is negative, or in other words, if the conclusions have been *falsified*, then their falsification also falsifies the theory from which they were logically deduced.

It should be noticed that a positive decision can only temporarily support the theory, for subsequent negative decisions may always overthrow it. So long as a theory withstands detailed and severe tests and is not superseded by another theory in the course of scientific progress, we may say that it has 'proved its mettle' or that it is '*corroborated*'[3] by past experience.

Nothing resembling inductive logic appears in the procedure here outlined. I never assume that we can argue from the truth of singular statements to the truth of theories. I never assume that by force of 'verified' conclusions, theories can be established as 'true', or even as merely 'probable'. And a more detailed analysis of the methods of deductive testing shows that all the problems can be dealt with that are usually called '*epistemological*'. Those problems, more especially, to which inductive logic gives rise, can be eliminated without creating new ones in their place.

III   *Why Methodological Decisions Are Indispensable*

In accordance with my proposal made above, epistemology, or the logic of scientific discovery, should be identified with the theory of scientific method. The theory of method, in so far as it goes beyond the purely logical analysis of the relations between scientific statements, is concerned with *the choice of methods*—with decisions about the way in which scientific statements are to be dealt with. These decisions will of course depend in their turn upon the aim which we choose from among a number of possible aims. The decision here proposed for laying down suitable rules for what I call the 'empirical method' is closely connected with my criterion of demarcation [see selection 8 section I above]: I propose to adopt such rules as will ensure the testability of scientific statements; which is to say, their falsifiability.

What are rules of scientific method, and why do we need them? Can there be a theory of such rules, a methodology?

The way in which one answers these questions will largely depend upon one's attitude to science. Those who, like the positivists, see empirical science as a system of statements which satisfy certain *logical criteria*, such as meaningfulness or verifiability, will give one answer. A very different answer will be given by those who tend to see (as I do) the distinguishing characteristic of empirical statements in their susceptibility to revision—in the fact that they can be criticized, and superseded by better ones; and who regard it as their task to analyse the characteristic ability of science to advance, and the characteristic manner in which a choice is made, in crucial cases, between conflicting systems of theories.

I am quite ready to admit that there is a need for a purely logical analysis of theories, for an analysis which takes no account of how they change and develop. But this kind of analysis does not elucidate those aspects of the empirical sciences which I, for one, so highly prize. A system such as classical mechanics may be 'scientific' to any degree you like; but those who uphold it dogmatically—believing, perhaps, that it is their business to defend such a successful system against criticism as long as it is not *conclusively disproved*—are adopting the very reverse of that critical attitude which in my view is the proper one for the scientist. In point of fact, no conclusive disproof of a theory can ever be produced; for it is always-possible to say that the experimental results are not reliable, or that the discrepancies which are asserted to exist between the experimental results and the theory are only apparent and that they will disappear with the advance of our understanding. (In the struggle against Einstein, both these arguments were often used in support of Newtonian mechanics, and similar arguments abound in the field of the social sciences.) If you insist on strict proof (or strict disproof) in the empirical sciences, you will never benefit from experience, and never learn from it how wrong you are.

If therefore we characterize empirical science merely by the formal or logical structure of its statements, we shall not be able to exclude from it that prevalent form of metaphysics which results from elevating an obsolete scientific theory into an incontrovertible truth.

Such are my reasons for proposing that empirical science should be characterized by its methods: by our manner of dealing with scientific systems: by what we do with them and what we do to them. Thus I shall try to establish the rules, or if you will the norms, by which the scientist is guided when he is engaged in research or in discovery, in the sense here understood.

IV *The Naturalistic Approach to the Theory of Method*

The hint I gave in the previous section as to the deepseated difference between my position and that of the positivists is in need of some amplification.

The positivist dislikes the idea that there should be meaningful problems outside the field of 'positive' empirical science—problems to be dealt with by a genuine philosophical theory. He dislikes the idea that there should be a genuine theory of knowledge, an epistemology or a methodology.[4] He wishes to see in the alleged philosophical problems mere 'pseudoproblems' or 'puzzles'. Now this wish of his—which, by the way, he does not express as a wish or a proposal but rather as a statement of fact—can always be gratified. For nothing is easier than to unmask a problem as 'meaningless' or 'pseudo'. All you have to do is to fix upon a conveniently narrow meaning for 'meaning', and you will soon be bound to say of any inconvenient question that you are unable to detect any meaning in it. Moreover, if you admit as meaningful none except problems in natural science, any debate about the concept of 'meaning' will also turn out to be meaningless. The dogma of meaning, once enthroned, is elevated forever above the battle. It can no longer be attacked. It has become (in Wittgenstein's own words) 'unassailable and definitive'.[5]

The controversial question whether philosophy exists, or has any right to exist, is almost as old as philosophy itself. Time and again an entirely new philosophical movement arises which finally unmasks the old philosophical problems as pseudoproblems, and which confronts the wicked nonsense of philosophy with the good sense of meaningful, positive, empirical, science. And time and again do the despised defenders of 'traditional philosophy' try to explain to the leaders of the latest positivistic assault that the main problem of philosophy is the critical analysis of the appeal to the authority of 'experience'[6]—precisely that 'experience' which every latest discoverer of positivism is, as ever, artlessly taking for granted. To such objections, however, the positivist only replies with a shrug: they mean nothing to him, since they do not belong to empirical science, which alone is meaningful. 'Experience' for him is a programme, not a problem (unless it is studied by empirical psychology).

I do not think positivists are likely to respond any differently to my own attempts to analyse 'experience' which I interpret as the method of empirical science. For only two kinds of statement exist for them: logical tautologies and empirical statements. If methodology is not logic, then, they will conclude, it must be a branch of some empirical science—the science, say, of the behaviour of scientists at work.

This view, according to which methodology is an empirical science in its turn—a study of the actual behaviour of scientists, or of the actual procedure of 'science'—may be described as *'naturalistic'*. A naturalistic methodology (sometimes called an 'inductive theory of science'[7]) has its value, no doubt. A student of the logic of science may well take an interest in it, and learn from it. But what I call 'methodology' should not be taken for an empirical science. I do not believe that it is possible to decide, by using the methods of an empirical science, such controversial questions as whether science actually uses a principle of induction or not. And my doubts increase when I remember that what is to be called a 'science' and who is to be called a 'scientist' must always remain a matter of convention or decision.

I believe that questions of this kind should be treated in a different way. For example, we may consider and compare two different systems of methodological rules; one with, and one without, a principle of induction. And we may then examine whether such a principle, once introduced, can be applied without giving rise to inconsistencies; whether it helps us; and whether we really need it. It is this type of inquiry which leads me to dispense with the principle of induction: not because such a principle is as a matter of fact never used in science, but because I think that it is not needed; that it does not help us; and that it even gives rise to inconsistencies.

Thus I reject the naturalistic view. It is uncritical. Its upholders fail to notice that whenever they believe themselves to have discovered a fact, they have only proposed a convention.[8] Hence the convention is liable to turn into a dogma. This criticism of the naturalistic view applies not only to its criterion of meaning, but also to its idea of science, and consequently to its idea of empirical method.

v *Methodological Rules as Conventions*

Methodological rules are here regarded as *conventions*. They might be described as the rules of the game of empirical science. They differ from the rules of pure logic rather as do the rules of chess, which few would regard as part of *pure* logic: seeing that the rules of pure logic govern transformations of linguistic formulae, the result of an inquiry into the rules of chess could perhaps be entitled 'The Logic of Chess', but hardly 'Logic' pure and simple. (Similarly, the result of an inquiry into the rules of the game of science—that is, of scientific discovery—may be entitled 'The Logic of Scientific Discovery'.)

Two simple examples of methodological rules may be given. They will suffice to show that it would be hardly suitable to place an inquiry into method on the same level as a purely logical—inquiry.

> (1) The game of science is, in principle, without end. He who decides one day that scientific statements do not call for any further test, and that they can be regarded as finally verified, retires from the game.

> (2) Once a hypothesis has been proposed and tested, and has proved its mettle, it may not be allowed to drop out without 'good reason'. A 'good reason' may be, for instance: replacement of the hypothesis by another which is better testable; or the falsification of one of the consequences of the hypothesis.[9]

These two examples show what methodological rules look like. Clearly they are very different from the rules usually called 'logical'. Although logic may perhaps set up criteria for deciding whether a statement is testable, it certainly is not concerned with the question whether anyone exerts himself to test it.

[In selection 8] I tried to define empirical science with the help of the criterion of falsifiability; but as I was obliged to admit the justice of certain objections, I provided a methodological supplement to my definition. Just as chess might be defined by the rules proper to it, so empirical science may be defined by means of its methodological rules. In establishing these rules we may proceed systematically. First a supreme rule is laid down which serves as a kind of norm for deciding upon the remaining rules, and which is thus a rule of a higher type. It is the rule which says that the other rules of scientific procedure must be designed in such a way that they do not protect any statement in science against falsification.

Methodological rules are thus closely connected both with other methodological rules and with our criterion of demarcation. But the connection is not a strictly deductive or logical one.[10] It results, rather, from the fact that the rules are constructed with the aim of ensuring the applicability of our criterion of demarcation; thus their formulation and acceptance proceed according to a practical rule of a higher type. An example of this has been given above (rule 1): theories which we decide not to submit to any further test would no longer be falsifiable. It is this systematic connection between the rules which makes it appropriate to speak of a *theory* of method. Admittedly the pronouncements of this theory are, as our examples show, for the most part conventions of a fairly obvious kind. Profound truths are not to be expected of methodology.[11] Nevertheless it may help us in many cases to clarify the logical situation, and even to solve some far-reaching problems which have hitherto proved intractable. One of these, for example, is the problem of deciding whether a probability statement should be accepted or rejected.[12]

It has often been doubted whether the various problems of the theory of knowledge stand in any systematic relation to one another, and also whether they can be treated systematically. I hope to show that these doubts are unjustified. The point is of some importance. My only reason for proposing my criterion of demarcation is that it is fruitful: that a great many points can be clarified and explained with its help. 'Definitions are dogmas; only the conclusions drawn from them can afford us any new insight', says Menger.[13] This is certainly true of the definition of the concept 'science'. It is only from the consequences of my definition of empirical science, and from the methodological decisions which depend upon this definition, that the scientist will be able to see how far it conforms to his intuitive idea of the goal of his endeavours. [See also selection 12 below.]

The philosopher too will accept my definition as useful only if he can accept its consequences. We must satisfy him that these consequences enable us to detect inconsistencies and inadequacies in older theories of knowledge, and to trace these back to the fundamental assumptions and conventions from which they spring. But we must also satisfy him that our own proposals are not threatened by the same kind of difficulties. This method of detecting and resolving contradictions is applied also within science itself, but it is of particular importance in the theory of knowledge. It is by this method, if by any, that methodological conventions might be justified, and might prove their value.[14]

Whether philosophers will regard these methodological investigations as belonging to philosophy is, I fear, very doubtful, but this does not really matter much. Yet it may be worth mentioning in this connection that not a few doctrines which are metaphysical, and thus certainly philosophical, could be interpreted as typical hypostatizations of methodological rules. An example of this is what is called 'the principle of causality'.[15] Another example is the problem of objectivity. For the requirement of scientific objectivity can also be interpreted as a methodological rule: the rule that only such statements may be introduced into science as are intersubjectively testable [see selection 10, section II, selection 11, section II, and selection 30]. It might indeed be said that the majority of the problems of theoretical philosophy, and the most interesting ones, can be reinterpreted in this way as problems of method.

Notes

1. J. Liebig, *Induktion und Deduktion*, 1865, was probably the first to reject the inductive method from the standpoint of natural science; his attack is directed against Bacon. P. Duhem, *The Aim and Structure of Physical Theory*, 1906 (English translation, 1954), held pronounced deductivist views. But there are also inductivist views to be found in Duhem's book, for example in the third chapter of Part I, where we are told that only experiment, induction, and generalization have produced Descartes's law of refraction (p. 34). See also V. Kraft, *Die Grundformen der Wissenschaftlichen Methoden*, 1925; and R. Carnap, *The Unity of Science*, 1934.

2. Address on Max Planck's sixtieth birthday. The passage quoted begins with the words, 'The supreme task of the physicist is to search for those highly universal laws ...'. See A. Einstein, *The World As I See It*, 1935 (translation by A. Harris), p. 125. The German word '*Einfühlung*' is difficult to translate. Harris translates as 'sympathetic understanding of experience' . Similar ideas are found earlier in J. Liebig, *op. cit.*; see also E. Mach, *Principien der Wärmerlehre*, 1896, pp. 443ff.

3. For this term see chapter X of *The Logic of Scientific Discovery*, and *Realism and the Aim of Science*, Part I, chapter IV.

4. In the two years before the first publication of *The Logic of Scientific Discovery* in 1934 it was the standing criticism raised by members of the Vienna Circle against my ideas that a theory of method which was neither an empirical science nor pure logic was impossible: what was outside these two fields was sheer nonsense. (The same view was still maintained by Wittgenstein in 1946; see note 8 on p. 69 of *Conjectures and Refutations*, and *Unended Quest*, section 26.) Later, the standing criticism became anchored in the legend that I proposed to replace the verifiability criterion by a falsifiability criterion of *meaning*. See *Realism and the Aim of Science*, Part I, sections 19–22, and 'Replies to My Critics', sections 1–4.

5. [See note 17 to selection 6 above.]

6. H. Gomperz, *Weltanschauungslehre*, volume I, 1905, p. 35, writes: 'If we consider how infinitely problematic the concept of *experience* is ... we may well be forced to believe that ... enthusiastic affirmation is far less appropriate in regard to it ... than the most careful and guarded criticism ...'

7. H. Dingler, *Physik und Hypothesis*, 1921; similarly, V. Kraft, *op. cit.*

8. The view, only briefly set forth here, that it is a matter for decision what is to be called 'a genuine statement' and what 'a meaningless pseudostatement' is one that I have held for years. (Also the view that the esclusion of metaphysics is likewise a matter of decision.) However, my present criticism of positivism (and of the naturalistic view) no longer applies, as far as I can see, to Carnap's *Logical Syntax of Language*, 1934, in which he too adopts the standpoint that all such questions rest upon decisions (the 'principle of tolerance'). According to Carnap's preface, Wittgenstein has for years propounded a similar view in unpublished works. Carnap's *Logical Syntax* was published while *The Logic of Scientific Discovery* was in proof. I regret that I was unable to discuss it in my text

9. Regarding the translation 'to prove one's mettle' for '*sich bewähren*' see the first footnote to chapter X of *The Logic of Scientific Discovery*. The concept 'better testable' is analysed in *op. cit.*, chapter VI.

10. See pp. 58ff. of K. Menger, *Moral, Wille, und Weltgestaltung*, 1934.

11. I am still inclined to uphold something like this, even though such theorems as '*degree of corroboration* ≠ *probability*' or my 'theorem on truth content' (see pp. 343–53 of P. K. Feyerabend & G. Maxwell, editors, *Mind, Matter, and Method*, 1966) are perhaps unexpected and not quite on the surface.

12. See *The Logic of Scientific Discovery*, chapter VIII, especially section 68 [and also selection 15 below].

13. See p. 76 of K. Menger, *Dimensionstheorie*, 1928.

14. In *The Logic of Scientific Discovery* I relegated the critical—or, if you will, the 'dialectical'—method of resolving contradictions to second place, since I was concerned with the attempt to develop the practical methodological aspects of my views. In *Die beiden Grundprobleme der Erkennlnistheorie* I

have tried to take the critical path; and I have tried to show that the problems of both the classical and the modern theory of knowledge (from Hume via Kant to Russell and Whitehead) can be traced back to the problem of demarcation, that is to the problem of finding the criterion of the empirical character of science.

15. See *The Logic of Scientific Discovery*, sections 12 and 79.

B. FALSIFICATIONISM VERSUS CONVENTIONALISM (1934)

The question whether there is such a thing as a falsifiable singular statement (or a 'basic statement') will be examined later. Here I shall assume a positive answer to this question; and I shall examine how far my criterion of demarcation is applicable to theoretical systems—if it is applicable at all. A critical discussion of a position usually called 'conventionalism' will raise first some problems of method, to be met by taking certain *methodological decisions*. Next I shall try to characterize the logical properties of those systems of theories which are falsifiable—falsifiable, that is, if our methodological proposals are adopted.

I Some Conventionalist Objections

Objections are bound to be raised against my proposal to adopt falsifiability as our criterion for deciding whether or not a theoretical system belongs to empirical science. They will be raised, for example, by those who are influenced by the school of thought known as 'conventionalism'.[1] Some of these objections have already been touched upon [in section V of the previous selection] they will now be considered a littie more closely.

The source of the conventionalist philosophy would seem to be wonder at the austerely beautiful *simplicity of the world* as revealed in the laws of physics. Conventionalists seem to feel that this simplicity would be incomprehensible, and indeed miraculous, if we were bound to believe, with the realists, that the laws of nature reveal to us an inner, a structural, simplicity of our world beneath its outer appearance of lavish variety. Kant's idealism sought to explain this simplicity by saying that it is our own intellect which imposes its laws upon nature. Similarly, but even more boldly, the conventionalist treats this simplicity as our own creation. For him, however, it is not the effect of the laws of our intellect imposing themselves upon nature, thus making nature simple; for he does not believe that nature is simple. Only the '*laws of nature*' are simple; and these, the conventionalist holds, are our own free creations; our inventions; our arbitrary decisions and conventions. For the conventionalist, theoretical natural science is not a picture of nature but merely a logical construction. It is not the properties of the world which determine this construction; on the contrary it is this construction which determines the properties of an artificial world: a world of concepts implicitly defined by the natural laws which we have chosen. It is only *this* world of which science speaks.

According to this conventionalist point of view, laws of nature are not falsifiable by observation; for they are needed to determine what an observation and, more especially, what a scientific measurement is. It is these laws, laid down by us, which form the indispensable basis for the regulation of our clocks and the correction of our so-called 'rigid' measuring rods. A clock is called 'accurate' and a measuring rod 'rigid' only if the movements measured with the help of these instruments satisfy the axioms of mechanics which we have decided to adopt.[2]

The philosophy of conventionalism deserves great credit for the way it has helped to clarify the relations between theory and experiment. It recognized the importance, so little noticed by inductivists, of the part played by our actions and operations, planned in accordance with conventions and deductive reasoning, in conducting and interpreting our scientific experiments. I regard conventionalism as a system which is self-contained and defensible. Attempts to detect inconsistencies in it are not likely to succeed. Yet in spite of all this I find it quite unacceptable. Underlying it is an idea of science, of its aims and purposes, which is entirely different from mine. Whilst I do not demand any final certainty from science (and consequently do not get it), the conventionalist seeks in science 'a system of knowledge based upon ultimate grounds', to use a phrase of Dingler's. This goal is attainable; for it is possible to interpret any given scientific system as a system of implicit definitions. And periods when science develops slowly will give little occasion for conflict—unless purely academic—to arise between scientists inclined towards conventionalism and others who may favour a view like the one I advocate. It will be quite otherwise in a time of crisis. Whenever the 'classical' system of the day is threatened by the results of new experiments which might be interpreted as falsifications according to my point of view, the system will appear unshaken to the conventionalist. He will explain away the inconsistencies which may have arisen; perhaps by blaming our inadequate mastery of the system. Or he will eliminate them by suggesting *ad hoc* the adoption of certain auxiliary hypotheses, or perhaps of certain corrections to our measuring instruments.

In such times of crisis this conflict over the aims of science will become acute. We, and those who share our attitude, will hope to make new discoveries; and we shall hope to be helped in this by a newly erected scientific system. Thus we shall take the greatest interest in the falsifying experiment. We shall hail it as a success, for it has opened up new vistas into a world of new experiences. And we shall hail it even if these new experiences should furnish us with new arguments against our own most recent theories. But the newly rising structure, the boldness of which we admire, is seen by the conventionalist as a monument to the 'total collapse of science', as Dingler puts it. In the eyes of the conventionalist one principle only can help us to select a system as the chosen one from among all other possible systems: it is the principle of selecting the simplest system—the simplest system of implicit definitions; which of course means in practice the 'classical' system of the day.[3]

Thus my conflict with the conventionalists is not one that can be ultimately settled merely by a detached theoretical discussion. And yet it is possible I think to extract from the conventionalist mode of thought certain interesting arguments against my criterion of demarcation; for instance the following. I admit, a conventionalist might say, that the theoretical systems of the natural sciences are not verifiable, but I assert that they are not falsifiable either. For there is always the possibility of '... attaining, for any chosen axiomatic system, what is called its "correspondence with reality"';[4] and this can be done in a number of ways (some of which have been suggested above). Thus we may introduce *ad hoc* hypotheses. Or we may modify the so-called 'ostensive definitions' (or the 'explicit definitions' which may replace them). Or we may adopt a sceptical attitude as to the reliability of the experimenter whose observations, which threaten our system, we may exclude from science on the ground that they are insufficiently supported, unscientific, or not objective, or even on the ground that the experimenter was a liar. (This is the sort of attitude which the physicist may sometimes quite rightly adopt towards alleged occult phenomena.) In the last resort we can always cast doubt on the acumen of the theoretician (for example if he does not believe, as does Dingler, that the theory of electricity will one day be derived from Newton's theory of gravitation).

Thus, according to the conventionalist view, it is not possible to divide systems of theories into falsifiable and non-falsifiable ones; or rather, such a distinction will be ambiguous. As a consequence, our criterion of falsifiability must turn out to be useless as a criterion of demarcation.

II Methodological Rules

These objections of an imaginary conventionalist seem to me incontestable, just like the conventionalist philosophy itself. I admit that my criterion of falsifiability does not lead to an unambiguous classification. Indeed, it is impossible to decide, by analysing its logical form, whether a system of statements is a conventional system of irrefutable implicit definitions, or whether it is a system which is empirical in my sense; that is, a refutable system. Yet this only shows that my criterion of demarcation cannot be applied immediately to a *system of statements*—a fact I have already pointed out [in selection 8, section II, and selection 9, section V]. The question whether a given system should as such be regarded as a conventionalist or an empirical one is therefore misconceived. *Only with reference to the methods applied* to a theoretical system is it at all possible to ask whether we are dealing with a conventionalist or an empirical theory. The only way to avoid conventionalism is by taking a *decision*: the decision not to apply its methods. We decide that if our system is threatened we will never save it by any kind of *conventionalist stratagem*. Thus we shall guard against exploiting the ever open possibility just mentioned of '... attaining, for any chosen ... system, what is called its "correspondence with reality"'.

A clear appreciation of what may be gained (and lost) by conventionalist methods was expressed, a hundred years before Poincaré, by Black who wrote: 'A nice adaptation of conditions will make almost any hypothesis agree with the phenomena. This will please the imagination but does not advance our knowledge.'[5]

In order to formulate methodological rules which prevent the adoption of conventionalist stratagems, we should have to acquaint ourselves with the various forms these stratagems may take, so as to meet each with the appropriate anticonventionalist countermove. Moreover we should agree that, whenever we find that a system has been rescued by a conventionalist stratagem, we shall test it afresh, and reject it, as circumstances may require.

The four main conventionalist stratagems have already been listed at the end of the previous section. The list makes no claim to completeness: it must be left to the investigator, especially in the fields of sociology and psychology (the physicist may hardly need the warning) to guard constantly against the temptation to employ new conventionalist stratagems—a temptation to which psychoanalysts, for example, often succumb.

As regards *auxiliary hypotheses* we propose to lay down the rule that only those are acceptable whose introduction does not diminish the degree of falsifiability or testability of the system in question, but, on the contrary, increases it.[6] If the degree of falsifiability is increased, then introducing the hypothesis has actually strengthened the theory: the system now rules out more than it did previously: it prohibits more. We can also put it like this. The introduction of an auxiliary hypothesis should always be regarded as an attempt to construct a new system; and this new system should then always be judged on the issue of whether it would, if adopted, constitute a real advance in our knowledge of the world. An example of an auxiliary hypothesis which is eminently acceptable in this sense is Pauli's exclusion principle. An example of an unsatisfactory auxiliary hypothesis would be the contraction hypothesis of Fitzgerald and Lorentz which had no falsifiable consequences but merely[7] served to restore the agreement between theory and experiment—mainly the findings of Michelson and Morley. An advance was here achieved only by the theory of relativity which predicted new consequences, new physical effects, and thereby opened up new possibilities for testing, and for falsifying, the theory. Our methodological rule may be qualified by the remark that we need not reject, as conventionalistic, every auxiliary hypothesis that fails to satisfy these standards. In particular, there are *singular* statements which do not really belong to the theoretical system at all. They are sometimes called 'auxiliary hypotheses', and although they are introduced to assist the theory, they are quite harmless. (An example would be the assumption that a certain observation or measurement which cannot be repeated may have been due to error. [See selection 11, section II.])

Changes in *explicit definitions*, whereby the concepts of an axiom system are given a meaning in terms of a system of lower level universality, are permissible if useful; but they must be regarded as modifications of the system, which thereafter has to be re-examined as if it were new. As regards undefined universal names, two possibilities must be distinguished. (1) There are some undefined concepts which only appear in statements of the highest level of universality, and whose use is established by the fact that we know in what logical relation other concepts stand to them. They can be eliminated in the course of deduction (an example is 'energy')'.[8] (2) There are other undefined concepts which occur in statements of lower levels of universality also, and whose meaning is established by usage (e.g. 'movement', 'mass point', 'position'). In connection with these, we shall forbid surreptitious alterations of usage, and otherwise proceed in conformity with our methodological decisions, as before.

As to the two remaining points (which concern the competence of the experimenter or theoretician) we shall adopt similar rules. Intersubjectively testable experiments are either to be accepted, or to be rejected in the light of counterexperiments. The bare appeal to logical derivations to be discovered in the future can be disregarded.

III Logical Investigation of Falsifiability

Only in the case of systems which would be falsifiable if treated in accordance with our rules of empirical method is there any need to guard against conventionalist stratagems. Let us assume that we have successfully banned these stratagems by our rules: we may now ask for a *logical* characterization of such falsifiable systems. We shall attempt to characterize the falsifiability of a theory by the logical relations holding between the theory and the class of basic statements.

The character of the singular statements which I call 'basic statements' will be discussed more fully [in the next selection], and also the question whether they, in their turn, are falsifiable. Here we shall assume that falsifiable basic statements exist. It should be borne in mind that when I speak of 'basic statements', I am not referring to a system of *accepted* statements. The system of basic statements, as I use the term, is to include, rather, *all self-consistent singular statements* of a certain logical form—all conceivable singular statements of fact, as it were. Thus the system of all basic statements will contain many statements which are mutually incompatible.

As a first attempt one might perhaps try calling a theory 'empirical' whenever singular statements can be deduced from it. This attempt fails, however, because in order to deduce singular statements from a theory, we always need other singular statements—the initial conditions that tell us what to substitute for the variables in the theory. As a second attempt, one might try calling a theory 'empirical' if singular statements are derivable with the help of other singular statements serving as initial conditions. But this will not do either; for even a nonempirical theory' for example a tautological one, would allow us to derive some singular statements from other singular statements. (According to the rules of logic we can for example say: from the conjunction of 'Twice two is four' and 'Here is a black raven' there follows, among other things, 'Here is a raven'.) It would not even be enough to demand that from the theory together with some initial conditions we should be able to deduce *more* than we could deduce from those initial conditions alone. This demand would indeed exclude tautological theories, but it would not exclude synthetic metaphysical statements. (For example from 'Every occurrence has a cause' and 'A catastrophe is occurring here', we can deduce 'This catastrophe has a cause'.)

In this way we are led to the demand that the theory should allow us to deduce, roughly speaking, more *empirical* singular statements than we can deduce from the initial conditions alone.[9] This means that we must base our definition upon a particular class of singular statements; and this is the purpose for which we need the basic statements. Seeing that it would not be very easy to say in detail how a complicated theoretical system helps in the deduction of singular or basic statements, I propose the following definition. A theory is to be called 'empirical' or 'falsifiable' if it divides the class of all possible basic statements unambiguously into the following two nonempty subclasses. First, the class of all those basic statements with which it is inconsistent (or which it rules out, or prohibits): we call this the class of the *potential falsifers* of the theory; and secondly, the class of those basic statements which it does not contradict (or which it 'permits'). We can put this more briefly by saying: a theory is falsifiable if the class of its potential falsifiers is not empty.

It may be added that a theory makes assertions only about its potential falsifiers. (It asserts their falsity.) About the 'permitted' basic statements it says nothing. In particular, it does not say that they are true.[10]

IV *Falsifiability and Falsification*

We must clearly distinguish between falsifiability and falsification. We have introduced falsifiability solely as a criterion for the empirical character of a system of statements. As to falsification, special rules must be introduced which will determine under what conditions a system is to be regarded as falsified.

We say that a theory is falsified only if we have accepted basic statements which contradict it. [See selection 9, section V.] This condition is necessary, but not sufficient; for non-reproducible single occurrences are of no significance to science. Thus a few stray basic statements contradicting a theory will hardly induce us to reject it as falsified. We shall take it as falsified only if we discover a *reproducible effect* which refutes the theory. In other words, we only accept the falsification if a low-level empirical hypothesis which describes such an effect is proposed and corroborated. This kind of hypothesis may be called a *falsifying hypothesis*. The requirement that the falsifying hypothesis must be empirical, and so falsifiable, only means that it must stand in a certain logical relationship to possible basic statements; thus this requirement only concerns the logical form of the hypothesis. The rider that the hypothesis should be corroborated refers to tests which it ought to have passed—tests which confront it with accepted basic statements.[11]

Thus the basic statements play two different roles. On the one hand, we have used the system of all *logically possible* basic statements in order to obtain with its help the logical characterization for which we were looking—that of the form of empirical statements. On the other hand, the *accepted* basic statements are the basis for the corroboration of hypotheses. If accepted basic statements contradict a theory, then we take them as providing sufficient grounds for its falsification only if they corroborate a falsifying hypothesis at the same time.

Notes

1. The chief representatives of the school are Poincaré and Duhem (*The Aim and Structure of Physical Theory*, 1906; English translation, 1954). A recent adherent is H. Dingler (among his numerous works may be mentioned: *Das Experiment*, and *Der Zusammenbruch der Wissenschaft und das Primat der Philosophie*, 1926). The German Hugo Dingler should not be confused with the Englishman Herbert Dingle. The chief representative of conventionalism in the English-speaking world is Eddington. It may be mentioned here that Duhem denies (p. 188) the possibility of crucial experiments, because he thinks of them as verifications, while I assert the possibility of crucial *falsifying* experiments. See *Conjectures and Refutations*, chapter 3, especially section v.

2. This view can also be regarded as an attempt to solve the problem of induction; for the problem would vanish if natural laws were definitions, and therefore tautologies. Thus according to the views of H. Cornelius, 'Zur Kritik der Wissenschaftlichen Grundbegriffe', *Erkenntnis* **2**, 1931, pp. 191–218, the statement 'The melting point of lead is about 335°C' is part of the definition of the concept 'lead' (suggested by inductive experience) and cannot therefore be refuted. A substance otherwise resembling lead but with a different melting point would simply not be lead. But according to my view the statement of the melting point of lead is, *qua* scientific statement, synthetic. It asserts, among other things, that an element with a given atomic structure (atomic number 82) always has this melting point, whatever name we may give to this element.

    K. Ajdukiewicz appears to agree with Cornelius (see 'Sprache und Sinn', *Erkenntnis* **4**, 1934, pp. 100–38, as well as the work there announced, 'Das Weltbild und die Begriffsapparatur', ibid., pp. 259–87); he calls his standpoint 'radical conventionalism'.

3. For the problem of simplicity see *The Logic of Scientific Discovery*, chapter VII, especially section 46.

4. R. Carnap, 'Über die Aufgabe der Physik und die Anwendung des Grundsatzes der Einfachtsheit', *Kant-Studien* **28**, 1923, pp. 90–107, especially p. 100.

5. See p. 193 of J. Black, *Lectures on the Elements of Chemistry*, volume I, 1803.

6. How degrees of falsifiability are to be estimated is explained in *The Logic of Scientific Discovery*, chapter VI.

7. *This is a mistake*, as pointed out by A. Grünbaum, 'The Falsifiability of the Lorentz-Fitzgerald Contraction Hypothesis', *British Journal for the Philosophy of Science* **10**, 1959, pp. 48–50. Yet as this hypothesis is less testable than special relativity, it may illustrate *degrees of adhocness*.

8. See, for instance, pp. 22ff. of H . Hahn, *Logik, Mathetmatik, und Naturerkennen (Einheitswissenschaft* **2**), 1933. In this connection, I only wish to say that in my view 'constituable' (i.e. empirically definable) terms do not exist at all. I am using in their place undefinable universal names which are established only by linguistic usage. [See also p. 97 above, and the end of section I of selection 11.]

9. Formulations equivalent to the one given here have been put forward as criteria of the *meaningfulness of sentences* (rather than as criteria of *demarcation* applicable to theoretical *systems*) again and again after the publication of my book, even by critics who pooh-poohed my criterion of falsifiability. But it is easily seen that, if used as a criterion of *demarcation*, our present formulation is equivalent to falsifiability. For if the basic statement b_2 does not follow from b_1, but follows from b_1 in conjunction with the theory t (this is the present formulation) then this amounts to saying that the conjunction of b_1 with the negation of b_2 contradicts the theory t. But the conjunction of b_1, with the negation of b_2 is a basic statement [see section III of the next selection]. Thus our criterion demands the existence of a faisifying basic statement, i.e. it demands falsifiability in precisely my sense.

    As a criterion of *meaning* (or of 'weak verifiability') it breaks down, however, for various reasons. First, because the negations of some meaningful statements would become meaningless, according to this criterion. Secondly, because the conjunction of a meaningful statement and a 'meaningless pseudosentence' would become meaningful—which is equally absurd.

    If we now try to apply these two criticisms to our criterion of *demarcation*, they both prove harmless. As to the first, see *The Logic of Scietnific Discovery*, section 15, especially note *2 (and *Realism* *and the Aim of Science*, Part I, section 22) As to the second, empirical theories (such as Newton's) may contain 'metaphysical' elements. But these cannot be eliminated by a hard and fast rule; though if we succeed in so presenting the theory that it becomes a conjunction of a testable and a non-testable part, we know, of course, that we can now eliminate one of its metaphysical components.

The preceding paragraph of this note may be taken as illustrating another *rule of method*: that after having produced some criticism of a rival theory, we should always make a serious attempt to apply this or a similar criticism to our own theory.

10. In fact, many of the 'permitted' basic statements will, in the presence of the theory, contradict each other. For example, the universal law 'All planets move in circles' (i.e., 'Any set of positions of one planet is co-circular') is trivially 'instantiated' by any set of no more than three positions of one planet; but two such 'instances' together will in most cases contradict the law.

11. The falsifying hypothesis can be of a very low level of universality (obtained, as it were, by generalizing the individual coordinates of a result of observation). Even though it is to be intersubjectively testable, it need not in fact be a strictly universal statement. Thus to falsify the statement 'All ravens are black' the intersubjectively testable statement that there is a family of white ravens in the zoo at New York would suffice. All this shows the urgency of replacing a falsified hypothesis by a better one. In most cases we have, before falsifying a hypothesis, another one up our sleeves; for the falsifying experiment is usually a *crucial experiment* designed to decide between the two. That is to say, it is suggested by the fact that the two hypotheses differ in some respect; and it makes use of this difference to refute (at least) one of them.

The reference to accepted basic statements may seem to contain the seeds of an infinite regress. For our problem here is this. Since a hypothesis is falsified by *accepting* a basic statement, we need *methodological rules for the acceptance of basic statements*. Now if these rules in their turn refer to accepted basic statements, we may get involved in an infinite regress. To this I reply that the rules we need are merely rules for accepting basic statements that falsify a well-tested and so far successful hypothesis; and the accepted basic statements to which the rule has recourse need not be of this character. Moreover, the rule formulated in the text is far from exhaustive; it only mentions an important aspect of the acceptance of basic statements that falsify an otherwise successful hypothesis, and it will be expanded [in the next selection (especially section IV)].

Professor J. H. Woodger, in a personal communication, has raised the question: how often has an effect to be actually reproduced in order to be a *'reproducible effect'* (or a *'discovery'*)? The answer is: in some cases *not even once*. If I assert that there is a family of white ravens in the New York zoo, then I assert something which can be tested *in principle*. If somebody wishes to test it and is informed, upon arrival, that the family has died, or that it has never been heard of, it is left to him to accept or reject my falsifying basic statement. As a rule, he will have means for forming an opinion by examining witnesses, documents, etc.; that is to say, by appealing to other intersubjectively testable and reproducible facts.

C. THE EMPIRICAL BASIS (1934)

We have now reduced the question of the falsifiability of theories to that of the falsifiability of those singular statements which I have called basic statements. But what kind of singular statements are these basic statements? How can they be falsified? To the practical research worker, these questions may be of little concern. But the obscurities and misunderstandings which surround the problem make it advisable to discuss it here in some detail.

I *Perceptual Experiences as Empirical Basis: Psychologism*

The doctrine that the empirical sciences are reducible to sense perceptions, and thus to our experiences, is one which many accept as obvious beyond all question. However, this doctrine stands or falls with inductive logic, and is here rejected along with it. I do not wish to deny that there is a grain of truth in the view that mathematics and logic are based on thinking, and the factual sciences on sense perceptions. But what is true in this view has little bearing on the epistemological problem. And indeed, there is hardly a problem in epistemology which has suffered more severely from the confusion of psychology with logic than this problem of the basis of statements of experience.

The problem of the basis of experience has troubled few thinkers so deeply as Fries.[1] He taught that, if the statements of science are not to be accepted *dogmatically*, we must be able to *justify* them. If we demand justification by reasoned argument, in the logical sense, then we are committed to the view that *statements can be justified only statements*. The demand that all statements are to be logically justified (described by Fries as a 'predilection for proofs') is therefore bound to lead to an *infinite regress*. Now, if we wish to avoid the danger of dogmatism as well as an infinite regress, then it seems as if we could only have recourse to *psychologism*, i.e. the doctrine that statements can be justified not only by statements but also by perceptual experience. Faced with this *trilemma*—dogmatism vs. infinite regress vs. psychologism—Fries, and with him almost all epistemologists who wished to account for our empirical knowledge, opted for psychologism. In sense experience, he taught, we have 'immediate knowledge':[2] by this immediate knowledge, we may justify our 'mediate knowledge'— knowledge expressed in the symbolism of some language. And this mediate knowledge includes, of course, the statements of science.

Usually the problem is not explored as far as this. In the epistemologies of sensationalism and positivism it is taken for granted that empirical scientific statements 'speak of our experiences'.[3] For how could we ever reach any knowledge of facts if not through sense perception? Merely by taking thought a man cannot add an iota to his knowledge of the world of facts . Thus perceptual experience must be the sole 'source of knowledge' of all the empirical sciences. All we know about the world of facts must therefore be expressible in the form of statements *about our experiences*. Whether this table is red or blue can be found out only by consulting our sense experience. By the immediate feeling of conviction which it conveys, we can distinguish the true statement, the one whose terms agree with experience, from the false statement, whose terms do not agree with it. Science is merely an attempt to classify and describe this perceptual knowledge, these immediate experiences whose truth we cannot doubt; *it is the systematic presentation of our immediate convictions*.

This doctrine founders in my opinion on the problems of induction and of universals. For we can utter no scientific statement that does not go far beyond what can be known with certainty 'on the basis of immediate experience'. (This fact may be referred to as the 'transcendence inherent in any description'.) Every description uses *universal* names (or symbols, or ideas); every statement has the character of a theory, of a hypothesis. The statement, 'Here is a glass of water' cannot be verified by any observational experience. The reason is that the universals which appear in it cannot be correlated with any specific sense experience. (An 'immediate experience' is *only once* 'immediately given'; it is unique.) By the word 'glass', for example, we denote physical bodies which exhibit a certain *lawlike behaviour*, and the same holds for the word 'water'. Universals cannot be reduced to classes of experiences; they cannot be 'constituted'.[4]

II *The Objectivity of the Empirical Basis*

I propose to look at science in a way which is slightly different from that favoured by the various psychologistic schools: I wish to *distinguish sharply between objective science on the one hand, and 'our knowledge' on the other*.

I readily admit that only observation can give us 'knowledge concerning facts', and that we can (as Hahn says) 'become aware of facts only by observation'. But this awareness, this knowledge of ours, does not justify or establish the truth of any statement. I do not believe, therefore, that the question which epistemology must ask is, '. . . on what does our *knowledge* rest? . . . or more exactly, how can I, having had the *experience S*, justify my description of it, and defend it against doubt?'[5] This will not do, even if we change the term 'experience' into 'protocol sentence'. In my view, what epistemology has to ask is, rather: how do we test scientific statements by their deductive consequences? (Or, more generally: how can we best criticize our theories (our hypotheses, our guesses), rather than defend them against doubt?) [See also selection 3, section III.]) And *what kind* of consequences can we select for thus purpose if they in their turn are to be intersubjectively testable?

By now, this kind of objective and non-psychological approach is pretty generally accepted where logical or tautological statements are concerned. Yet not so long ago it was held that logic was a science dealing with mental processes and their laws—the laws of our thought. On this view there was no other justification to be found for logic than the alleged fact that we just could not think in any other way. A logical inference seemed to be justified because it was experienced as a necessity of thought, as a feeling of being compelled to think along certain lines. In the field of logic, this kind of psychologism is now perhaps a thing of the past. Nobody would dream of justifying the validity of a logical inference, or of defending it against doubts, by writing beside it in the margin the following protocol sentence. 'Protocol: In checking this chain of inferences today, I experienced an acute feeling of conviction.'

The position is very different when we come to *empirical statements of science*. Here everybody believes that these are grounded on experiences such as perceptions; or in the formal mode of speech, on protocol sentences. Most people would see that any attempt to base logical statements on protocol sentences is a case of psychologism. But curiously enough, when it comes to empirical statements, the same kind of thing goes today by the name of 'physicalism'. Yet whether statements of logic are in question or statements of empirical science, I think the answer is the same: our *knowledge*, which may be described vaguely as a system of *dispositions*, and which may be of concern to psychology, may be in both cases linked with feelings of belief or of conviction: in the one case, perhaps, with the feeling of being compelled to think in a certain way; in the other with that of 'perceptual assurance'. But all this interests only the psychologists. It does not even touch upon problems like those of the logical connections between scientific statements, which alone interest the epistemologist.

(There is a widespread belief that the statement 'I see that this table here is white', possesses some profound advantage over the statement 'This table here is white', from the point of view of epistemology. But from the point of view of evaluating its possible objective tests, the first statement, in speaking about me, does not appear more secure than the second statement, which speaks about the table here.)

There is only one way to make sure of the validity of a chain of logical reasoning. This is to put it in the form in which it is most easily testable: we break it up into many small steps, each easy to check by anybody who has learnt the mathematical or logical technique of transforming sentences. If after this anybody still raises doubts then we can only beg him to point out an error in the steps of the proof, or to think the matter over again. In the case of the empirical sciences, the situation is much the same. Any empirical scientific statement can be presented (by describing experimental arrangements, etc.) in such a way that anyone who has learnt the relevant technique can test it. If, as a result, he rejects the statement, then it will not satisfy us if he tells us all about his feelings of doubt or about his feelings of conviction as to his perceptions. What he must do is to formulate an assertion which contradicts our own, and give us his instructions for testing it. If he fails to do this we can only ask him to take another and perhaps a more careful look at our experiment, and think again.

An assertion which owing to its logical form is not testable can at best operate, within science, as a stimulus: it can suggest a problem. In the field of logic and mathematics, this may be exemplified by Fermat's problem, and in the field of natural history, say, by reports about seaserpents. In such cases science does not say that the reports are unfounded; that Fermat was in error or that all the records of observed seaserpents are lies. Instead, it suspends judgement.

Science can be viewed from various standpoints, not only from that of epistemology; for example, we can look at it as a biological or as a sociological phenomenon. As such it might be described as a tool, or an instrument, comparable perhaps to some of our industrial machinery. Science may be regarded as a means of production—as the last word in 'roundabout production'.[6] Even from this point of view science is no more closely connected with 'our experience' than other instruments or means of production. And even if we look at it as gratifying our intellectual needs, its connection with our experiences does not differ in principle from that of any other objective structure. Admittedly it is not incorrect to say that science is '... an instrument' whose purpose is '... to predict from immediate or given experiences later experiences, and even as far as possible to control them'.[7] But I do not think that this talk about experiences contributes to clarity. It has hardly more point than, say, the not incorrect characterization of an oil derrick by the assertion that its purpose is to give us certain experiences: not oil, but rather the sight and smell of oil; not money, but rather the feeling of having money.

III Basic Statements

It has already been briefly indicated what role the basic statements play within the epistemological theory I advocate. We need them in order to decide whether a theory is to be called falsifiable, i.e. empirical. And we also need them for the corroboration of falsifying hypotheses, and thus for the falsification of theories. [See selection 10, sections III and IV respectively.]

Basic statements must therefore satisfy the following conditions. (1) From a universal statement without initial conditions, no basic statement can be deduced.[8] On the other hand, (2) a universal statement and a basic statement can contradict each other. Condition (2) can only be satisfied if it is possible to derive the negation of a basic statement from the theory which it contradicts. From this and condition (1) it follows that a basic statement must have a logical form such that its negation cannot be a basic statement in its turn.

There is a familiar example of statements whose logical form is different from that of their negations. These are universal statements and existential statements: they are negations of one another, and they differ in their logical form. *Singular* statements can be constructed in an analogous way. The statement: 'There is a raven in the spacetime region k' may be said to be different in its logical form—and not only in its linguistic form—from the statement 'There is no raven in the spacetime region k'. A statement of the form 'There is a so-and-so in the region k' or 'Such-and-such an event is occurring in the region k' may be called a '*singular* existential statement' or a '*singular* there-is statement'. And the statement which results from negating it, i.e. 'There is no so-and-so in the region k' or 'No event of such-and-such a kind is occurring in the region k', may be called a '*singular* nonexistence statement', or a '*singular* there-is-not statement'.

We may now lay down the following rule concerning basic statements: *basic statements have the form of singular existential statements*. This rule means that basic statements will satisfy condition (1), since a singular existential statement can never be deduced from a strictly universal statement, i.e. from a strict nonexistence statement. They will also satisfy condition (2), as can be seen from the fact that from every singular existential statement a purely existential statement can be derived simply by omitting any reference to any individual spacetime region; and as we have seen, a purely existential statement may indeed contradict a theory.

It should be noticed that the conjunction of two basic statements, d and r, which do not contradict each other, is in turn a basic statement. Sometimes we may even obtain a basic statement by joining one basic statement to another statement which is not basic. For example, we may form the conjunction of the basic statement, r, 'There is a pointer at the place k' with the singular non-existence statement $\bar{p}$, 'There is no pointer in motion at the place k'. For clearly, the conjunction $r \cdot \bar{p}$ ('*r-and-non-p*') of the two statements is equivalent to the singular existential statement 'There is a pointer at rest at the place k'. This has the consequence that, if we are given a theory t and the initial conditions r, from which we deduce the prediction p, then the statement $r \cdot \bar{p}$ will be a falsifier of the theory, and so a basic statement. (On the other hand, the conditional statement '$r \rightarrow p$' i.e. 'If r then p', is no more basic than the negation p, since it is equivalent to the negation of a basic statement, viz. to the negation of $r \cdot \bar{p}$.)

These are the formal requirements for basic statements; they are satisfied by all singular existential statements . In addition to these, a basic statement must also satisfy a material requirement—a requirement concerning the event which, as the basic statement tells us, is occurring at the place k. This event must be an '*observable*' event; that is to say, basic statements must be testable, intersubjectively, by 'observation'. Since they are singular statements, this requirement can of course only refer to observers who are suitably placed in space and time (a point which I shall not elaborate).

No doubt it will now seem as though in demanding observability, I have, after all, allowed psychologism to slip back quietly into my theory. But this is not so. Admittedly, it is possible to interpret the concept of an *observable event* in a psychologistic sense. But I am using it in such a sense that it might just as well be replaced by 'an event involving position and movement of macroscopic physical bodies'. Or we might lay it down, more precisely, that every basic statement either must be itself a statement about relative positions of physical bodies, or must be equivalent to some basic statement of this 'mechanistic' or 'materialistic' kind. (That this stipulation is practicable is connected with the fact that a theory which is intersubjectively testable will also be intersensually[9] testable. This is to say that tests involving the perception of one of our senses can, in principle, be replaced by tests involving other senses.) Thus the charge that, in appealing to observability, I have stealthily re-admitted psychologism would have no more force than the charge that I have admitted mechanism or materialism. This shows that my theory is really quite neutral and that neither of these labels should be pinned to it. I say all this only so as to save the term 'observable', as I use it, from the stigma of psychologism. (Observations and perceptions may be psychological but observability is not.) I have no intention of *defining* the term 'observable' or 'observable event', though I am quite ready to elucidate it by means of either psychologistic or mechanistic examples. I think that it should be introduced as an undefined term which becomes sufficiently precise in use: as a primitive concept whose use the epistemologist has to learn, much as he has to learn the use of the term 'symbol', or as the physicist has to learn the use of the term 'mass point'.

Basic statements are therefore—in the material mode of speech—statements asserting that an observable event is occurring in a certain individual region of space and time.

IV *The Relativity of Basic Statements: Resolution of Fries's Trilemma*

Every test of a theory, whether resulting in its corroboration or falsification, must stop at some basic statement or other which we *decide to accept*. If we do not come to any decision, and do not accept some basic statement or other, then the test will have led nowhere. But considered from a logical point of view, the situation is never such that it compels us to stop at this particular basic statement rather than at that, or else give up the test altogether. For any basic statement can again in its turn be subjected to tests, using as a touchstone any of the basic statements which can be deduced from it with the help of some theory, either the one under test, or another. This procedure has no natural end. Thus if the test is to lead us anywhere, nothing remains but to stop at some point or other and say that we are satisfied, for the time being.

It is fairly easy to see that we arrive in this way at a procedure according to which we stop only at a kind of statement that is especially easy to test. For it means that we are stopping at statements about whose acceptance or rejection the various investigators are likely to reach agreement. And if they do not agree, they will simply continue with the tests, or else start them all over again. If this too leads to no result, then we might say that the statements in question were not intersubjectively testable, or that we were not, after all, dealing with observable events. If some day it should no longer be possible for scientific observers to reach agreement about basic statements this would amount to a failure of language as a means of universal communication. It would amount to a new 'Babel of Tongues': scientific discovery would be reduced to absurdity. In this new Babel, the soaring edifice of science would soon lie in ruins.

Just as a logical proof has reached a satisfactory shape when the difficult work is over, and everything can be easily checked, so, after science has done its work of deduction or explanation, we stop at basic statements which are easily testable. Statements about personal experiences—i.e., protocol sentences—are clearly *not* of this kind; thus they will not be very suitable to serve as statements at which we stop. We do of course make use of records or protocols, such as certificates of tests issued by a department of scientific and industrial research. These, if the need arises, can be re-examined. Thus it may become necessary, for example, to test the reaction times of the experts who carry out the tests (i.e. to determine their personal equations). But in general, and especially '. . . in critical cases' we do stop at easily testable statements, and not, as Carnap recommends, at perception or protocol sentences; i.e., we *do not* '. . . stop just at these . . . because the intersubjective' testing of statements about perceptions . . . is relatively complicated and difficult'.[10]

'What is our position now in regard to Fries's trilemma, the choice between dogmatism, infinite regress, and psychologism? [See section I above.] The basic statements at which we stop, which we decide to accept as satisfactory, and as sufficiently tested, have admittedly the character of *dogmas*, but only in so far as we may desist from justifying them by further arguments (or by further tests). But this kind of dogmatism is innocuous since, should the need arise, these statements can easily be tested further.

I admit that this too makes the chain of deduction in principle infinite. But this kind of *infinite regress* is also innocuous since in our theory there is no question of trying to prove any statements by means of it. And finally, as to *psychologism*: I admit, again, that the decision to accept a basic statement, and to be satisfied with it, is causally connected with our experiences—especially with our *perceptual experiences*. But we do not attempt to *justify* basic statements by these experiences. Experiences can *motivate a decision*, perhaps decisively, and hence an acceptance or a rejection of a statement, but a basic statement cannot be justifed by them—no more than by thumping the table.[11]

Notes

1. J. F. Fries, *Neue oder anthropologische Kritik der Vernunft*, 1828–31.
2. See, for example, pp. 102f. of J. Kraft, *Von Husserl zu Heidegger*, 1932; 2nd edition, 1957, pp. 108f.
3. I am following here almost word for word the expositions of P. Frank and H. Hahn (see notes 7 and 5 below).
4. [See note 8 of the previous selection.] 'Constituted' is Carnap's term.
5. The first two quotations are from pp. 19 and 24 of H. Hahn, *Logik, Mathematik, und Naturerkennen* (*Einheitswissenschaft* **2**), 1933. The third is from p. 15 of R. Carnap, Pseudoproblems of Philosophy, 1928; English translation, 1967, p. 314 (the italics are not in the original).
6. The expression is Böhm-Bawerk's ('*Produktionsumweg*').
7. See p. 1 of P. Frank, *Das Kausalgesetz und seine Grenzen*, 1932. For instrumentalism, see *Conjectures and Refutations*, chapter 3, and *Realism and the Aim of Science*, Part I, sections 12–14.
8. When writing this, I believed that it was plain enough that from Newton's theory alone, without initial conditions, nothing of the nature of an observation statement can be deducible (and therefore certainly no basic statements). Unfortunately, it turned out that this fact, and its consequences for the problem of observation statements or 'basic statements', were not appreciated by some of the critics of *The Logic of Scientific Discovery*. I may therefore add here a few remarks.

    First, nothing observable follows from any pure allstatement—'All swans are white', say. This is easily seen if we contemplate the fact that 'All swans are white' and 'All swans are black' do not, of course, contradict each other, but together merely imply that there are no swans—clearly not an observation statement, and not even one that can be 'verified'. (A unilaterally falsifiable statement like 'All swans are white', by the way, has the same logical form as 'There are no swans', for it is equivalent to 'There are no non-white swans'.)

    Now if this is admitted, it will be seen at once that the singular statements which *can* be deduced from purely universal statements cannot be basic statements. I have in mind statements of the form: 'If there is a swan at the place k, then there is a white swan at the place k.' (Or, 'At k, there is either no swan or a white swan.') We see now at once why these 'instantial statements' (as they may be called) are not basic statements. The reason is that these instantial statements *cannot play the role of test statements* (or of potential falsifiers) which is precisely the role which basic statements are supposed to play. If we were to accept instantial statements as test statements, we should obtain for any theory (and thus both for 'All swans are white' *and* for 'All swans are black') an overwhelming number of verifications—indeed, an infinite number, once we accept as a fact that the overwhelming part of the world is empty of swans.

    Since 'instantial statements' are derivable from universal ones, their negations must be potential falsifiers, and *may* therefore be basic statements (if the conditions stated below in the text are satisfied). Instantial statements, vice versa, will then be of the form of negated basic statements. It is interesting to note that basic statements (which are too strong to be derivable from universal Laws alone) will have a greater informative content than their instantial negations; which means that *the content of basic statements exceeds their logical probability* (since it must exceed 1/2).

    These were some of the considerations underlying my theory of the logical form of basic statements. (See *Conjectures and Refutations*, pp. 386f.)
9. See p. 445 of R. Carnap, 'Die physikalische Sprsche als Universalsprache der Wissenschaft', *Erkennmis* **2**, 1932, pp. 432–65; translated into English as *The Unity of Science*, 1934.
10. See p. 224 of R. Carnap, 'Über Protokollsätze', *Erkenntnis* **3**, 1932, pp. 215–28. This paper of Carnap's contained the first published report of my theory of tests; and the View here quoted from it was there erroneously attributed to me.
11. It seems to me that the view here upheld is closer to that of the 'critical' (Kantian) school of philosophy (perhaps in the form represented by Fries) than to positivism. Fries in his theory of our

'predilection for proofs' emphasizes that the (logical) relations holding between statements are quite different from the relation between statements and sense experiences; positivism on the other hand always tries to abolish the distinction: either all science is made part of my knowing, 'my' sense experience (monism of sense data); or sense experiences are made part of the objective scientific network of arguments in the form of protocol statements (monism of statements).

Chapter 6

The 'Corroboration' of Theories

Hilary Putnam

Sir Karl Popper is a philosopher whose work has influenced and stimulated that of virtually every student in the philosophy of science. In part this influence is explainable on the basis of the healthy-mindedness of some of Sir Karl's fundamental attitudes: 'There is no method peculiar to philosophy'. 'The growth of knowledge can be studied best by studying the growth of scientific knowledge.'

> Philosophers should not be specialists. For myself, I am interested in science and in philosophy only because I want to learn something about the riddle of the world in which we live, and the riddle of man's knowledge of that world. And I believe that only a revival of interest in these riddles can save the sciences and philosophy from an obscurantist faith in the expert's special skill and in his personal knowledge and authority.

These attitudes are perhaps a little narrow (can the growth of knowledge be studied without also studying nonscientific knowledge? Are the problems Popper mentions of merely theoretical interest—just 'riddles'?), but much less narrow than those of many philosophers, and the 'obscurantist faith' Popper warns against is a real danger. In part this influence stems from Popper's realism, his refusal to accept the peculiar meaning-theories of the positivists, and his separation of the problems of scientific methodology from the various problems about the 'interpretation of scientific theories' which are internal to the meaning-theories of the positivists and which positivistic philosophers of science have continued to wrangle about.[1]

In this paper I want to examine his views about scientific methodology—about what is generally called 'induction', although Popper rejects the concept—and, in particular, to criticize assumptions that Popper has in common with received philosophy of science, rather than assumptions that are peculiar to Popper. For I think that there are a number of such common assumptions, and that they represent a mistaken way of looking at science.

1. Popper's View of 'Induction'

Popper himself uses the term 'induction' to refer to any method for verifying or showing to be true (or even probable) general laws on the basis of observational or experimental data (what he calls 'basic statements'). His views are radically Humean: no such method exists or can exist. A principle of induction would have to be either

Reprinted from The Library of Living Philosophers, Vol. XIV, *The Philosophy of Karl Popper*, edited by Paul A. Schilpp, by permission of the author and the publisher (LaSalle, IL: Open Court Publishing Company, 1974), pp. 221–240; the postscript is reprinted from *Philosophy As It Is*, ed. T. Honderich and M. Burnyeat, by permission of the author and the publisher (New York: Penguin Books, 1978), pp. 377–380.

synthetic a *priori* (a possibility that Popper rejects) or justified by a higher-level principle. But the latter course necessarily leads to an infinite regress.

What is novel is that Popper concludes neither that empirical science is impossible nor that empirical science rests upon principles that are themselves incapable of justification. Rather, his position is that empirical science does not really rely upon a principle of induction!

Popper does not deny that scientists state general laws, nor that they test these general laws against observational data. What he say is that when a scientist 'corroborates' a general law, that scientist does not thereby assert that law to be true or even probable. 'I have corroborated this law to a high degree' only means 'I have subjected this law to severe tests and it has withstood them'. Scientific laws are *falsifiable*, not verifiable. Since scientists are not even trying to *verify* laws, but only to falsify them, Hume's problem does not arise for empirical scientists.

2. A Brief Criticism of Popper's View

It is a remarkable fact about Popper's book, *The Logic of Scientific Discovery* that it contains but a half-dozen brief references to the *application* of scientific theories and laws; and then all that is said is that application is yet another *test* of the laws. 'My view is that ... the theorist is interested in explanations as such, that is to say, in testable explanatory theories: applications and predictions interest him only for theoretical reasons—because they may be used as *tests* of theories' (*Logic of Scientific Discovery*, p. 59).

When a scientist accepts a law, he is recommending to other men that they rely on it—rely on it, often, in practical contexts. Only by wrenching science altogether out of the context in which it really arises—the context of men trying to change and control the world—can Popper even put forward his peculiar view on induction. Ideas are not *just* ideas; they are guides to action. Our notions of 'knowledge', 'probability', 'certainty', etc., are all linked to and frequently used in contexts in which action is at issue: may I confidently rely upon a certain idea? Shall I rely upon it tentatively, with a certain caution? Is it neccssary to check on it?

If 'this law is highly corroborated', 'this law is scientifically accepted', and like locutions merely meant 'this law has withstood severe tests'—and there were no suggestion at all that a law which has to withstood severe tests is likely to withstand further tests, such as the tests involved in an application or attempted application, then Popper would be right; but then science would be a wholly unimportant activity. It would be practically unimportant, because scientists would never tell us that any law or theory is safe to rely upon for practical purposes; and it would be unimportant for the purpose of understanding, since on Popper's view, scientists never tell us that any law or theory is true or even probable. Knowing that certain 'conjectures' (according to Popper all scientific laws are 'provisional conjectures') have not yet been refuted is *not understanding anything*.

Since the application of scientific laws does involve the anticipation of future successes, Popper is not right in maintaining that induction is unnccessary. Even if scientists do not inductively anticipate the future (and, of course, they do), men who apply scientific laws and theories do so. And 'don't make inductions' is hardly reasonable advice to give these men.

The advice to regard all knowledge as 'provisional conjectures' is also not reasonable. Consider men striking against sweat-shop conditions. Should they say 'it is only a provisional conjecture that the boss is a bastard. Let us call off our strike and try appealing to his better nature'. The distinction between *knowledge* and *conjecture* does real work in our lives; Popper can maintain his extreme skepticism only because of his extreme tendency to regard theory as an end for itself.

3. Popper's View of Corroboration

Although scientists, on Popper's view, do not make inductions, they do 'corroborate' scientific theories. And although the statement that a theory is highly corroborated does not mean, according to Popper, that the theory may be accepted as true, or even as approximately true,[2] or even as probably approximately true, still, there is no doubt that most readers of Popper read his account of corroboration as an account of something like the verification of theories, in spite of his protests. In this sense, Popper has, *contre lui* a theory of induction. And it is this theory, or certain presuppositions of this theory, that I shall criticize in the body of this paper.

Popper's reaction to this way of reading him is as follows:

> My reaction to this reply would be regret at my continued failure to explain my main point with sufficient clarity. For the sole purpose of the elimination advocated by all these inductivists was to *establish as firmly as possible the surviving theory* which, they thought, must be the *true* one (or, perhaps, only a *highly probable* one, in so far as we may not have fully succeeded in eliminating every theory except the true one).
>
> As against this, I do not think that we can ever seriously reduce by elimination, the number of the competing theories, since this number remains always infinite. What we do—or should do—is to *hold on, for the time being, to the most improbable of the surviving theories* or, more precisely, to the one that can be most severely tested. We tentatively 'accept' this theory—but only in the sense that we select it as worthy to be subjected to further criticism, and to the severest tests we can design.
>
> On the positive side, we may be entitled to add that the surviving theory is the best theory—and the best tested theory—of which we know. (*Logic of Scientific Discovery*, p. 419)

If we leave out the last sentence, we have the doctrine we have been criticizing in pure form: when a scientist 'accepts' a theory, he does not assert that it is probable. In fact, he 'selects' it as most improbable! In the last sentence, however, am I mistaken, or do I detect an inductivist quaver? What does 'best theory' mean? Surely Popper cannot mean 'most likely'?

4. The Scientific Method—The Received Schema

Standard 'inductivist' accounts of the confirmation[3] of scientific theories go somewhat like this: Theory implies prediction (basic sentence, or observation sentence); if prediction is false, theory is falsified; if sufficiently many predictions are true, theory is confirmed. For all his attack on inductivism, Popper's schema is not *so* different: Theory implies prediction (basic sentence); if prediction is false, theory is falsified; if sufficiently many predictions are true, and certain further conditions are fulfilled, theory is highly corroborated.

Moreover, this reading of Popper does have certain support. Popper does say that the 'surviving theory' is *accepted*—his account is, therefore, an account of the logic of accepting theories. We must separate two questions: is Popper right about what the scientist means—or should mean—when he speaks of a theory as 'acccpted'; and is Popper right about the methodology involved in according a theory that status? What I am urging is that his account of that methodology fits the received schema, even it his interpretation of the status is very different.

To be sure there are some important conditions that Popper adds. Predictions that one could have made on the basis of background knowledge do not test a theory; it is only predictions that are *improbable* relative to background knowledge that test a theory. And a theory is not corroborated, according, to Popper, unless we make sincere attempts to derive false predictions from it. Popper regards these further conditions as anti-Bayesian;[4] but this seems to me to be a confusion, at least in part. A theory which implies an improbable prediction is improbable, that is true, but it may be the most probable of all theories which imply that prediction. If so, and the prediction turns out true, then Bayes's theorem itself explains why the theory receives a high probability. Popper says that we select the most improbable of the *surviving* theories—i.e., the accepted theory is most improbable even *after* the prediction has turned out true; but, of course, this depends on using 'probable' in a way no other philosopher of science would accept. And a Bayesian is not committed to the view that *any* true prediction significantly confirms a theory. I share Popper's view that quantitative measures of the probability of theories are not a hopeful venture in the philosophy of science;[5] but that does not mean that Bayes's theorem does not have a certain *qualitative* rightness, at least in many situations.

Be all this as it may, the heart of Popper's schema is the theory-prediction link. It is because theories imply basic sentences in the sense of 'imply' associated with deductive logic—because basic sentences are *deducible* from theories—that, according to Popper, theories and general laws can be falsifiable by basic sentences. And this same link is the heart of the 'inductivist' schema. Both schemes say: *look at the predictions that a theory implies; see if those predictions are true.*

My criticism is going to be a criticism of this link, of this one point on which Popper and the 'inductivists' agree. I claim: in a great many important cases, scientific theories do not imply predictions at all. In the remainder of this paper I want to elaborate this point, and show its significance for the philosophy of science.

5. The Theory of Universal Gravitation

The theory that I will use to illustrate my points is one that the reader will be familiar with: it is Newton's theory of universal gravitation. The theory consists of the law that every body a exerts on every other body b a force F_{ab} whose direction is towards a and whose magnitude is a universal constant g times $M_a M_b / d^2$, together with Newton's three laws. The choice of this particular theory is not essential to my case: Maxwell's theory, or Mendel's, or Darwin's would have done just as well. But this one has the advantage of familiarity.

Note that this theory does not imply a single basic sentence! Indeed, any motions whatsoever are compatible with this theory, since the theory says nothing about what forces other than gravitations may be present. The forces F_{ab} are not themselves directly measurable; consequently not a single *prediction* can be deduced from the theory.

What do we do, then, when we apply this theory to an astronomical situation? Typically we make certain simplifying assumptions. For example, if we are deducing the orbit of the earth we might assume as a first approximation:

(I) No bodies exist except the sun and the earth.

(II) The sun and the earth exist in a hard vacuum.

(III) The sun and the earth are subject to no forces except mutually induced gravitational forces.

From the conjunction of the theory of universal gravitation (U.G.) and these auxiliary statements (A.S.) we can, indeed, deduce certain predictions—e.g., Kepler's laws. By making (I), (II), (III) more 'realistic'—i.e., incorporating further bodies in our model solar system—we can obtain better predictions. But it is important to note that these predictions do not come from the theory alone, but from the conjunction of the theory with A.S. As scientists actually use the term 'theory', the statements A.S. are hardly part of the 'theory' of gravitation.

6. Is the Point Terminological?

I am not interested in making a merely *terminological* point, however. The point is not just that scientists don't use the term 'theory' to refer to the conjunction of U.G. with A.S., but that such a usage would obscure profound methodological issues. A *theory*, as the term is actually used, is a set of *laws*. Laws are statements that we hope to be *true* they are supposed to be true by the nature of things, and not just by accident. None of the statements (I), (II), (III) has this character. We do not really believe that *no* bodies except the sun and the earth exist, for example, but only that all other bodies exert forces small enough to be neglected. This statement is not supposed to be a law, of nature: it is a statement about the 'boundary conditions' which obtain as a matter of fact in a particular system. To blur the difference between A.S. and U.G. is to blur the difference between *laws* and *accidental statements*, between statements the scientist wishes to establish as *true* (the laws), and statements he already knows to be false (the oversimplifications (I), (II), (III)).

7. Uranus, Mercury, 'Dark Companions'

Although the statements A.S. *could* be more carefully worded to avoid the objection that they are known to be false, it is striking that they are not in practice. In fact, they are not 'worded' at all. Newton's calculation of Kepler's laws makes the assumptions (I), (II), (III) without more than a casual indication that this is what is done. One of the most striking indications of the difference between a theory, (such as U.G.) and a set of A.S. is the great care which scientists use in stating the theory, as contrasted with the careless way in which they introduce the various assumptions which make up A.S.

The A.S. are also far more subject to revision than the theory. For over two hundred years the law of universal gravitation was accepted as unquestionably true, and used as a premise in countless scientific arguments. If the standard kind of A.S. had not had to successful prediction in that period, they would have been modified, not the theory. In fact, we have an example of this. When the predictions about the orbit of Uranus that were made on the basis of the theory of universal gravitation and the assumption that the known planets were all there were turned out to be wrong, Leverrier in France and Adams in England simultaneously predicted that there must be another planet. In fact, this planet was discovered—it was Neptune. Had this modification of the A.S. not been successful, still others might have been tried—e.g., postulating a medium through which the planets are moving, instead of a hard vacuum or postulating significant nongravitational forces.

It may be argued that it was crucial that the new planet should itself be observable. But this is not so. Certain stars, for example, exhibit irregular behavior. This has been explained by postulating companions. When those companions are not visible through a telescope, this is handled by suggesting, that the stars have *dark companions*—companions which cannot be seen through a telesope. The fact is that many of the assumptions made in the sciences cannot be directly tested—there are many 'dark companions' in scientific theory.

Lastly, of course, there is the case of Mercury. The orbit of this planet can almost but not quite be successfully explained by Newton's theory. Does this show that Newton's theory is wrong? *In the light of an alternative theory*, say the General Theory of Relativity, one answers 'yes' But, in the absence of such a theory, the orbit of Mercury is just a slight anomaly, cause: unknown.

What I am urging is that all this is perfectly good scientific practice. The fact that any of the statements A.S. may be false—indeed, they are false, as stated, and even more careful and guarded statements might well be false—is important. We do not know for sure all the bodies in the solar system; we do not know for sure that the medium through which they move is (to a sufficiently high degree of approximation in all cases) a hard vacuum; we do not know that nongravitational forces can be neglected in all cases. Given the over-whelming success of the Law of Universal Gravitation in almost all cases, one or two anomalies are not reason to reject it. It is more *likely* that the A.S. are false than that the theory is false, at least when no alternative theory has seriously been put forward.

8. The Effect on Popper's Doctrine

The effect of this fact on Popper's doctrine is immediate. The Law of Universal Gravitation is *not* strongly falsifiable at all; yet it is surely a paradigm of a scientific theory. Scientists for over two hundred years did not derive predictions from U.G. in order to falsify U.G.; they derived predictions from U.G. in order to explain various astronomical facts. If a fact proved recalcitrant to this sort of explanation it was put aside as an anomaly (the case of Mercury). Popper's doctrine gives a correct account of neither the nature of the scientific theory nor of the practice of the scientific community in this case.

Popper might reply that he is not describing what scientists do, but what they *should* do. Should scientists then not have put forward U.G.? Was Newton a bad scientist? Scientists did not try to falsify U.G. because they could not try to falsify it; laboratory tests were excluded by the technology of the time and the weakness of the gravitational interactions. Scientists were thus limited to astronomical data for a long time. And, even in the astronomical cases, the problem arises that one cannot be absolutely sure that no nongravitational force is relevant in a given situation (or that one has summed *all* the gravitational forces). It is for this reason that astronomical data can *support* U.G., but they can hardly *falsify* it. It would have been incorrect to reject U.G. because of the deviancy of the orbit of Mercury; given that U.G. predicted the other orbits, to the limits of measurement error, the possibility could not be excluded that the deviancy in this one case was due to an unknown force, gravitational or nongravitational, and in putting the case aside as they could neither explain nor attach systematic significance to, scientists *were* acting as they 'should'.[6]

So far we have said that (1) theories do not imply predictions; it is only the conjunction of a theory with certain 'auxiliary statements' (A.S.) that, in general, implies a prediction. (2) The A.S. are frequently suppositions about boundary conditions (including initial conditions as a special case of 'boundary conditions'), and highly risky suppositions at that. (3) Since we are very unsure of the A.S., we cannot regard a false prediction as definitively falsifying a theory; theories are *not* strongly falsifiable.

All this is not to deny that scientists do sometimes derive predictions from theories and A.S. in order to test the theories. If Newton had not been able to derive Kepler's laws, for example, he would not have even put forward U.G. But even if the predictions Newton had obtained from U.G. had been wildly wrong, U.G. might still have been true: the A.S. might have been wrong. Thus, even if a theory is 'knocked out' by an experimental test, the theory may still be right, and the theory may come back in at a later stage when it is discovered the A.S. were not useful approximations to the true situation. As has previously been pointed out,[7] falsification in science is no more conclusive than verification.

All this refutes Popper's view that what the scientist does is to put forward 'highly falsifiable' theories, derive predictions from them, and then attempt to falsify the theories by falsifying the predictions. But it does not refute the standard view (what Popper calls the 'inductivist' view) that scientists try to *confirm* theories *and* A.S. by deriving predictions from them and verifying the predictions. There is the objection that (in the case of U.G.) the A.S. were known to be false, so scientists could hardly have been trying to confirm them; but this could be met by saying that the A.S. could, in principle, have been formulated in a more guarded way, and would not have been false if sufficiently guarded[8] I think that, in fact, there is some truth in the 'inductivist' view: scientific theories are shown to be correct be their successes, just as all human ideas are shown to be correct, to the extent that they are, by their successes in practice. But the inductivist schema is still inadequate, except as a picture of one aspect of scientific I procedure. In the next sections, I shall try to show that scientific activity cannot, in general, be thought of as a matter of deriving predictions from the conjunction of theories and A.S., whether for the purpose of confirmation or for the purpose of falsification.

9. Kuhn's View of Science

Recently a number of philosophers have begun to put forward a rather new view of scientific activity. I believe that I anticipated this view about ten years ago when I urged that some scientific theories cannot be overthrown by experiments and obserçatiors *alone*, but only by alternative theories.[9] The view is also anticipated by Hanson,[10] but it reaches its sharpest expression in the writings of Thomas Kuhn[11] and Louis Althusser.[12] I believe that both of these philosophers commit errors; but I also believe that the tendency they represent (and that I also represent, for that matter) is a needed corrective to the deductivism we have been examining. In this section. I shall present some of Kuhn's views, and then try to advance on them in the direction of a sharper formulation.

The heart of Kuhn's account is the notion of a *paradigm*. Kuhn has been legitimately criticized for some inconsistencies and unclarities in the use of this notion; but at least one of his explanations of the notion seems to me to be quite clear and suitable for his purposes. On this explanation, a paradigm is simply a scientific theory together with an example of a successful and striking application. It is important that the application—say, a successful explanation of some fact, or a successful and novel prediction—be *striking*; what this means is that the success is sufficiently impressive that scientists—especially young scientists choosing a career—are led to try to emulate that success by seeking further explanations, predictions, or whatever on the same model. For example, once U.G. had been put forward and one had the example of Newton's derivation of Kepler's laws together with the example of the derivation of, say, a planetary orbit or two, then one had a paradigm. The most important paradigms are the ones that generate scientific fields; the field generated by the Newtonian paradigm was, in the first instance, the entire field of celestial mechanies. (Of course, this field was only a part of the larger field of Newtonian mechanies, and the paradigm on which celestial mechanics is based is only one of a number of paradigms which collectively structure Newtonian mechanics.)

Kuln maintains that the paradigm that structures a field is highly immune to falsification—in particular, it can only be overthrown by a new paradigm. In one sense, this is an exaggeration: Newtonian physics would probably have been abandoned, even in the absence of a new paradigm, if the world had started to act in a markedly non-Newtonian way. (Although even then—would we have concluded that Newtonian physics was false, or just that we didn't know what the devil was going, on?) But then even the old successes, the successes which were paradigmatic for Newtonian physics, would have ceased to be available. What is true, I believe, is that in the absence of such a drastic and unprecedented change in the world, and in the absence of its turning out that the paradigmatic successes had something 'phony' about them (e.g., the data were faked, or there was a mistake in the deductions), a theory which is paradigmatic is not given up because of observational and experimental results by themselves, but because and when a better theory is available.

Once a paradigm has been set up, and a scientific field has grown around that paradigm, we get an interval of what Kuhn calls 'normal science'. The activity of scientists during such an interval is described by Kuhn as 'puzzle solving'—a notion I shall return to.

In general, the interval of normal science continues even though not all the puzzles of the field can be successfully solved (after all, it is only human experience that some problems are too hard to solve), and even though some of the solutions may look *ad hoc*. What finally terminates the interval is the introduction of a new paradigm which manages to supersede the old.

Kuhn's most controversial assertions have to do with the process whereby a new paradigm supplants an older paradigm. Here he tends to be radically subjectivistic (overly so, in my opinion): data, in the usual sense, cannot establish the superiority of one paradigm over another because data themselves are perceived through the spectacles of one paradigm or another. Changing from one paradigm to another requires a 'Gestalt switch'. The history and methodology of science get rewritten when there are major paradigm changes; so there are no 'neutral' historical and methodological canons to which to appeal. Kuhn also holds views on meaning and truth which are relativistic and, on my view, incorrect; but I do not wish to discuss these here.

What I want to explore is the interval which Kuhn calls 'normal science'. The term 'puzzle solving' is unfortunately trivializing; searching for explanations of phenomena and for ways to harness nature is too important a part of human life to be demeaned (here Kuhn shows the same tendency that leads Popper to call the problem of the nature of knowledge a 'riddle'). But the term is also striking: clearly, Kuln sees normal science as neither an activity of trying to falsify one's paradigm nor as an activity of trying to confirm it, but as something else. I want to try to advance on Kuhn by presenting a schema for normal science, or rather for one aspect of normal science; a schema which may indicate why a major philosopher and historian of science would use the metaphor of solving puzzles in the way Kuhn does.

10. *Schemata for Scientific Problems*

Consider the following two schemata:

SCHEMA I
_____

THEORY
AUXILIARY STATEMENTS
_____

PREDICTION—TRUE OR FALSE?

SCHEMA II
_____

THEORY
???????????????
_____

FACT TO BE EXPLAINED

These are both schemata for scientific problems. In the first type of problem we have a theory, we have some A.S., we have derived a prediction, and our problem is to see if the prediction is true or false: the situation emphasized by standard philosophy of science. The second type of problem is quite different. In this type of problem we have a theory, we have a fact to be explained, but the A.S. are missing: the problem is to find A.S., if we can, which are true, or approximately true (i.e., useful oversimplifications of the truth), and which have to be conjoined to the theory to get an explanation of the fact.

We might, in passing, mention also a third schema which is neglected by standard philosophy of science:

SCHEMA III
_____

THEORY
AUXILIARY STATEMENTS
_____

???????????????

This represents the type of problem in which we have a theory, we have some A.S., and we want to know what consequences we can derive. This type of problem is neglected because the problem is 'purely mathematical'. But knowing whether a set of statements has testable consequences at all depends upon the solution to this type of problem, and the problem is frequently of great difficulty—e.g., little is known to this day concerning just what the physical consequences of Einstein's 'unified field theory' are, precisely because the mathematical problem of deriving those consequences is too difficult. Philosophers of science frequently write as if it is *clear*, given a set of statements, just what consequences those statements do and do not have.

Let us, however, return to Schema II. Given the known facts concerning the orbit of Uranus, and given the known facts (prior to 1846) concening what bodies make up the solar system, and the standard A.S. that those bodies are moving in a hard vacuum, subject only to mutual gravitational forces, etc., it was clear that there was a problem: the orbit of Uranus could not be successfully calculated if we assumed that Mercury, Venus, Earth, Mars, Saturn, Jupiter, and Uranus were all the planets there are, and that these planets together with the sun make up the whole solar system. Let S_1 be the conjunction of the various A.S. we just mentioned, including the statement that the solar system consists of at least, but not necessarily of only, the bodies mentioned. Then we have the following problem:

Theory: U.G.
A.S.: S_1
Further A.S.: ???????

Explanandum: The orbit of Uranus

Note that the problem is not to find further explanatory laws (although sometimes it may be, in a problem of the form of Schema II); it is to find further assumptions about the initial and boundary conditions governing the solar system which, together with the Law of Universal Gravitation and the other laws which make up U.G. (i.e., the laws of Newtonian mechanics) will enable one to explain the orbit of Uranus. If one does not require that the missing statements be true, or approximately true, then there are an infinite number of solutions, mathematically speaking. Even if one includes in S_1 that no nongravitational forces are acting on the planets or the sun, there are still an infinite number of solutions. But one tries first the simplest assumption, namely:

(S_2) There is one and only one planet in the solar system in addition to the planets mentioned in S_1.

Now one considers the following problem:

Theory: U.G.
A.S.: S_1, S_2

Consequence ???—turns out to be that the unknown
planet must have a certain orbit O.

This problem is a mathematical problem—the one Leverrier and Adams both solved (an instance of Schema III). Now one considers the following empirical problem:

Theory: U.G.
A.S.: S_1, S_2

Prediction: A planet exists moving
in orbit O—TRUE OR FALSE?

This problem is an instance of Schema I—an instance one would not normally consider, because one of the A.S., namely the statement S_2, is not at all known to be true S_2 is, in fact, functioning as a low-level hypothesis which we wish to test. But the test is not an inductive one in the usual sense, because a verification of the prediction is also a verification of S_2—or rather, of the approximate truth of S_2, (which is all that is of interest in this context). Neptune was not the only planet unknown in 1846; there was also Pluto to be later discovered. The fact is that we are interested in the above problem in 1846, because we know that if the prediction turns out to be true, then that prediction is precisely the statement S_3 that we need for the following deduction:

Theory: U.G.
A.S.: S_1, S_2, S_3

Explanandum: the orbit of Uranus

—i.e., the statement S_3 (that the planet mentioned in S_2 has precisely the orbit O)[13] is the solution to the problem with which we started. In this case we started with a problem of the Schema II type: we introduced the assumption S_2 as a simplifying assumption in the hope of solving the original problem thereby more easily; and we had the good luck to be able to deduce S_3—the solution to the original problem—from U.G. together with S_1, S_2, and the more important good luck that S_3 turned out to be true when the Berlin Observatory looked. Problems of the Schema II-type are sometimes mentioned by philosophers of science when the missing A.S. are laws; but the case just examined, in which the missing A.S. was just a further contingent fact about the particular system, is almost never discussed. I want to suggest that Schema II exhibits the logical form of what Kuhn calls a 'puzzle'.

If we exmine Schema II, we can see why the term 'puzzle' is so appropriate. When one has a problem of this sort, one is looking for something to fill a 'hole'—often a thing of rather underspecified sort—and that *is* a sort of *puzzle*. Moreover, this sort of problem is extremely widespread in science. Suppose one wants to explain the fact that water is a liquid (under the standard conditions), and one is given the laws of physics; the fact is that the problem is extremely hard. In fact, quantum mechanical laws are needed. But that does not mean that from classical physics one can deduce that water is *not* a liquid; rather the classical physicist would give up this problem at a certain point as 'too hard'—i.e., he would conclude that he could not find the right A.S.

The fact that Schema II is the logical form of the 'puzzles' of ' normal science explains a number of facts. When one is tackling, a Schema II-type problem, there is no question of deriving a prediction from U.G. plus given A.S., the whole problem is to find the A.S. The theory—U.G., or whichever—is *unfalsifiable in the context*. It is also not up for 'confirmation' any more than for 'falsification'; *it is not function in a hypothetical role*. Failures do not falsify a theory, because the failure is not a false prediction from a theory together with known and trusted facts, but a failure to *find* something—in fact, a failure to find an A.S. Theories, during their tenure of office, are highly immune to falsification; that tenure of office is ended by the appearance on the scene of a better theory (or a whole new explanatory technique), not by a basic sentence. And successes do not 'confirm' a theory, once it has become paradigmatic, because the theory is not a 'hypothesis' in need of confirmation, but the basis of a whole explanatory and predictive technique, and possibly of a technology as well.

To sum up: I have suggested that standard philosophy of science, both 'Popperian' and non-Popperian, has fixated on the situation in which we derive predictions from a theory and test those predictions in order to falsify or confirm the theory —i.e., on the situation represented by Schema I. I have suggested that, by way of contrast, we see the 'puzzles' of 'normal science' as exhibiting the pattern represented by Schema II, the pattern in which we take a theory as fixed, take the fact to be explained as fixed, and seek further facts—frequently contingent[14] facts about the particular system—which will enable us to fill out the explanation of the particular fact on the basis of the theory. I suggest that adopting this point of view will enable us better to appreciate both the relative unfalsifiability of theories which have attained paradigm status, and the fact that the 'predictions' of physical theory are frequently facts which were known beforehand and not things which are surprising relative to background knowledge.

To take Schema II as describing everything that goes on between the introduction of a paradigm and its eventual replacement by a better paradigm would be a gross error in the opposite direction, however. The fact is that normal science exhibits a dialectic between two conflicting (at any rate, potentially conflicting) but interdependent tendencies, and that it is the conflict of these tendencies that drives normal science forward. The desire to solve a Schema II-type problem—explain the orbit of Uranus—led to a new hypothesis (albeit a very low-level one) namely, S_2. Testing S_2

involved deriving S_3 from it, and testing S_3 a Schema I-type situation. S_3 in turn served as the solution to the original problem. This illustrates the two tendencies, and also the way in which they are interdependent and the way in which their interaction drives science forward.

The tendency represented by Schema I is the *critical* tendency. Popper is right to emphasize the importance of this tendency, and doing this is certainly a contribution on his part—one that has influenced many philosophers. Scientists do want to know if their ideas are wrong, and they try to find out if their ideas are wrong by deriving predictions from them and testing those predictions—that is, they do this *when they can*. The tendency represented by Schema II is the *explanatory* tendency. The element of conflict arises because in a Schema II-type situation one tends to regard the given theory as something *known*, whereas in a Schema I-type situation one tends to regard it as *problematic*. The interdependence is obvious: the theory which serves as the major premise in Schema II *may* itself have been the survivor of a Popperian test (although it need not have been—U.G. was accepted on the basis of its explanatory successes, not on the basis of its surviving attempted falsifications). And the solution to a Schema II-type problem must itself be confirmed, frequently by a Schema I-type test. If the solution is a general law, rather than a singular statement, that law may itself become a paradigm, leading to new Schema II-type problems. In short, attempted falsifications do 'corroborate' theories—not just in Popper's sense, in which this is a tautology, but in the sense he denies, of showing that they are true, or partly true—and explanations on the basis of laws which are regarded as *known* frequently require the introduction of *hypotheses*. In this way, the tension between the attitudes of explanation and criticism drives science to progress.

11. *Kuhn versus Popper*

As might be expected, there are substantial differences between Kuhn and Popper on the issue of the falsifiability of scientific theories. Kuhn stresses the way in which a scientific theory may be immune from falsification, whereas Popper stresses falsifiability as the *sine qua non* of a scientific theory. Popper's answers to Kuhn depend upon two notions which must now be examined: the notion of an auxiliary hypothesis and the notion of a *conventionalist stratagem*.

Popper recognizes that the derivation of a prediction from a theory may require the use of auxiliary hypotheses (though the term 'hypothesis' is perhaps misleading, in suggesting something like putative laws rather than assumptions about, say, boundary conditions). But he regards these as part of the total 'system' under test. A 'conventionalist stratagem' is to save a theory from a contrary experimental result by making an *ad hoc* change in the auxiliary hypotheses. And Popper takes it as a fundamental methodological rule of the empirical method to avoid conventionalist stratagems.

Does this do as a reply to Kuhn's objections? Does it contravene our own objections, in the first part of this paper? It does not. In the first place, the 'auxiliary hypotheses' A.S. are not fixed, in the case of U.G., but depend upon the context. One simply cannot think of U.G. as part of a fixed 'system' whose other part is a fixed set of auxiliary hypotheses whose function is to render U.G. 'highly testable'.

In the second place, an alteration in one's beliefs, may be *ad hoc* without being unreasonable. 'Ad hoc' merely means 'to this specific purpose'. Of course, 'ad hoc' has acquired the connotation of 'unreasonable'—but that is a different thing. The assumption that certain stars have dark companions is *ad hoc* in the literal sense: the assumption is made for the specific purpose of accounting for the fact that no companion is visible. It is also highly reasonable.

It has already been pointed out that the A.S. are not only context-dependent but highly uncertain, in the case of U.G. and in many other cases. So, changing the A.S., or even saying in a particular context 'we don't know what the right A.S. are' may be *ad hoc* in the literal sense just noted, but is not *'ad hoc'* in the extended sense of 'unreasonable'.

12. Paradigm Change

How does a paradigm come to be accepted in the first place? Popper's view is that a theory becomes corroborated by passing severe tests: a prediction (whose truth value is not antecedently known) must be derived from the theory and the truth or falsity of that prediction must be ascertained. The severity of the test depends upon the set of basic sentences excluded by the theory, and also upon the improbability of the prediction relative to background knowledge. The ideal case is one in which a theory which rules out a great many basic sentences implies a prediction which is very improbable relative to background knowledge.

Popper points out that the notion of the number of basic sentences ruled out by a theory cannot be understood in the sense of cardinality; he proposes rather to measure it by means of concepts of *improbability* or *content*. It does not appear true to me that improbability (in the sense of logical [im]probability)[15] measures fasifiability, in Popper's sense: U.G. excludes *no* basic sentences, for example, but has logical probability *zero*, on any standard metric. And it certainly is not true that the scientist always selects 'the most improbable of the surviving hypotheses' on *any* measure of probability, except in the trivial sense that all strictly universal laws have probability zero. But my concern here is not with the technical details of Popper's scheme, but with the leading idea.

To appraise this idea, let us see how U.G. came to be accepted. Newton first derived Kepler's laws from U.G. and the A.S. we mentioned at the outset: this was not a 'test' in Popper's sense, because Kepler's laws were already known to be true. Then he showed that U.G. would account for the tides on the basis of the gravitational pull of the moon: this also was not a 'test', in Popper's sense, because the tides were already known. Then he spent many years showing that small perturbations (which were already known) in the orbits of the planets could be accounted for by U.G. By this time the whole civilized world had accepted—and, indeed, acclaimed—U.G.; but it had not been 'corroborated' at all in Popper's sense!

If we look for a Popperian 'test' of U.G.—a derivation of a new prediction, one risky relative to background knowledge—we do not get one until the Cavendish experiment of 1787, roughly a hundred years after the theory had been introduced! The prediction of S_3 (the orbit of Neptune) from U.G. and the auxiliary statements S_1 and S_2 can also be regarded as a confirmation of U.G. (in 1846!); although it is difficult to regard it as a severe test of U.G. in view of the fact that the assumption S_2 had a more tentative status than U.G.

It is easy to see what has gone wrong. A theory is not accepted unless it has real explanatory successes. Although a theory may legitimately be preserved by changes in the A.S. which are, in a sense, 'ad hoc' (although not *unreasonable*), its *successes* must not be *ad hoc*. Popper requires that the predictions of a theory must not be antecedently known to be true in order to rule out *ad hoc* 'successes'; but the condition is too strong.

Popper is right in thinking that a theory runs a risk during the period of its establishment. In the case of U.G., the risk was not a risk of definite falsification; it was the risk that Newton would not find reasonable A.S. with the aid of which he could obtain real (non-*ad hoc*) explanatory successes for U.G. A failure to explain the tides by the gravitational pull of the moon alone would not, for example, have falsified U.G.; but the success did strongly support U.G.

In sum, a theory is only accepted if the theory has substantial, non-*ad hoc*, explanatory successes. This is in accordance with Popper; unfortunately, it is in even better accordance with the 'inductivist' accounts that Popper rejects, since these stress *support* rather than *falsification*.

13. On Practice

Popper's mistake here is no small isolated failing. What Popper consistently fails to see is that *practice is primary*: ideas are not just an end in themselves (although they are *partly* an end in themselves), nor is the selection of ideas to 'criticize' just an end in itself. The primary importance of ideas is that they guide practice, that they structure whole forms of life. Scientific ideas guide practice in science, in technology, and sometimes in public and private life. We are concerned in science with trying to discover correct ideas: Popper to the contrary, this is not *obscurantism* but *responsibility*. We obtain our ideas—our correct ones, and many of our incorrect ones—by close study of the world. Popper denies that the accumulation of perceptual experience leads to theories: he is right that it does not lead to theories in a mechanical or algorithmic sense; but it does lead to theories in the sense that it is a regularity of methodological significance that (1) lack of experience with phenomena and with previous knowledge about phenomena decreases the probability of correct ideas in a marked fashion; and (2) extensive experience increases the probability of correct, or partially correct, ideas in a marked fashion. 'There is no logic of discovery'—in that sense, there is no logic of *testing*, either; all the formal algorithms proposed for testing, by Carnap, by Popper, by Chomsky, etc., are, to speak impolitely, *ridiculous*; if you don't believe this, program a computer to employ one of these algorithms and see how well it does at testing theories! There are *maxims* for discovery and maxims for testing: the idea that correct ideas just come from the sky, while the methods for testing them are highly rigid and predetermined, is one of the worst legacies of the Vienna Circle.

But the correctness of an idea is not certified by the fact that it came from close and concrete study of the relevant aspects of the world; in this sense, Popper is right. We judge the correctness of our ideas by applying them and seeing if they succeed; in general, and in the long run, correct ideas lead to success, and ideas lead to failures where and insofar as they are incorrect. Failure to see the importance of practice leads directly to failure to see the importance of success.

Failure to see the primacy of practice also leads Popper to the idea of a sharp 'demarcation' between science, on the one hand, and political, philosophical, and ethical ideas, on the other. This 'demarcation' is pernicious, in my view; fundamentally, it corresponds to Popper's separation of theory from practice, and his related separation of the critical tendency in science from the explanatory tendency in science. Finally, the failure to see the primacy of practice leads Popper to some rather reactionary political conclusions. Marxists believe that there are laws of society; that these laws can be known; and that men can and should act on this knowledge. It is not my purpose here to argue that this Marxist view is correct; but surely any view that rules this out *a priori* is reactionary. Yet this is precisely what Popper does—and in the name of an anti-*a priori* philosophy of knowledge!

In general, and in the long run, true ideas are the ones that succeed—how do we know this? This statement too is a statement about the world; a statement we have come to from experience of the world; and we believe in the practice to which this idea corresponds, and in the idea as informing that kind of practice, on the basis that we believe in any good idea—it has proved successful! In this sense 'induction is circular'. But of course it is! Induction has no deductive justification; induction is not deduction. Circular justifications need not be totally self-protecting nor need they be totally uninformative:[16] the past success of 'induction' increases our confidence in it, and its past failure tempers that confidence. The fact that a justification is circular only means that that justification has no power to serve as a *reason*, unless the person to whom it is given as a reason already has some propensity to accept the conclusion. We do have a propensity—an *a priori* propensity, if you like—to reason 'inductively', and the past success of 'induction' increases that propensity.

The method of testing ideas in practice and relying on the ones that prove successful (for that is what 'induction' is) is not unjustified. That is an *empirical* statement. The method does not have a 'justification'—if by a justification is meant a proof from eternal and formal principles that justifies reliance on the method. But then, nothing does—not even, in my opinion, pure mathematics and formal logic. Practice is primary.

Notes

1. I have discussed positivistic meaning theory in "What Theories Are Not," published in *Logic, Methodology, and Philosophy of Science,* ed. by A. Tarski, E. Nagel, and P. Suppes (Stanford: Stanford University Press, 1962), pp. 240–51, and also in "How Not to Talk about Meaning," published in *Boston Studies in the Philosophy of Science,* Vol. II, ed. by R. S. Coehn and M. W. Wartofsky (New York: Humanities Press, 1965), pp. 205–22.

2. For a discussion of 'approximate truth', see the second of the papers mentioned in the preceding note.

3. 'Confirmation' is the term in standard use for *support* a positive experimental or observational result gives to a hypothesis; Popper uses the term 'corroboration' instead, as a rule, because he objects to the connotations of 'showing to be true' (or at least probable) which he sees as attaching to the former term.

4. *Bayes's theorem* asserts, roughly, that the probability of a hypothesis H on given evidence E is directly proportional to the probability of E on the hypothesis H, and also directly proportional to the antecedent probability of H—i.e., the probability of H if one doesn't know that E. The theorem also asserts that the probability of H on the evidence E is less, other things being equal, if the probability of E on the assumption—(*not*-H) is greater. Today probability theorists are divided between those who accept the notion of "antecedent probability of a hypothesis," which is crucial to the theorem, and those who reject this notion, and therefore the notion of the probability of a hypothesis on given evidence. The former school are called 'Bayeseans'; the latter 'anti-Bayeseans'.

5. Cf. my paper "'Degree of Confirmation' and Inductive Logic," in *The Philosophy of Rudolf Carnap* (The Library of Living Philosophers, Vol. II), ed. by Paul A. Schilpp (La Salle, Ill.: Open Court Publishing Co., 1963), pp. 761–84.

6. Popper's reply to this sort of criticism is discussed below in the section titled "Kuhn versus Popper."

7. This point is made by many authors. The point that is often missed is that, in case such as the one discussed, the auxiliary statements are much less certain than the theory under test; without this remark, the criticism that one *might* preserve a theory by revising the A.S. looks like a bit of formal logic, without real relation to scientific practice. (See below, "Kuhn versus Popper.")

8. I have in mind saying 'the planets exert forces on each other which are more than .999 (or whatever) gravitational', rather than 'the planets exert *no* nongravitational forces on each other'. Similar changes in the other A.S. could presumably turn them into true statements—though it is not methodologically unimportant that no scientist, to my knowledge, has bothered to calculate exactly what changes in the A.S. would render them true while preserving their usefulness.

9. Hilary Putnam, "The Analytic and the Synthetic," in *Minnesota Studies in the Philosophy of Science*, Vol. III, ed. by H. Feigl and G. Maxwell (Minneapolis: University of Minnesota Press, 1962), pp. 358–97.
10. N. R. Nanson, in *Patterns of Discovery* (Cambridge: Cambridge University Press, 1958).
11. Thomas S. Kuhn, *The Structure of Scientific Revolutions*, Vol. II, No. 2 of *International Encyclopedia of Unified Science* (Chicago: University of Chicago Press, 1962).
12. Louis Althusser, *Pour Marx* and *Lire le Capital* (Paris: Maspero, 1965).
13. I use 'orbit' in the sense of space-time trajectory, not just spatial path.
14. By 'contingent' I mean *not physically necessary*.
15. 'Logical probability' is probability assigning equal weight (in some sense) to logically possible worlds.
16. This has been emphasized by Professor Max Black in a number of papers: e.g., "Self-supporting Inductive Arguments," *Journal of Philosophy* 55 (1958), pp. 718–25; reprinted in Richard Swinburne (ed.), *The Justification of Induction* (Oxford Readings in Philosophy, Oxford University Press, 1974).

Retrospective Note (1978): A Critic Replies to his Philosopher

Popper's reply[1] to my criticism consists of two main charges: (1) that I misrepresent him to such an extent that I must not have read his main book, *The Logic of Scientific Discovery*; and (2) that I commit an outright logical blunder. Both of these charges are false and unfounded.

The Charge of Textual Misrepresentation

The charge that I misrepresented Popper's doctrine itself rests on two claims: that I say of Popper that he neglects the need for *auxiliary statements*; and that Popper in fact talked about auxiliary statements at length (under the name 'initial conditions') in *The Logic of Scientific Discovery*.

The first claim is false: nowhere in my essay does there appear one sentence which says Popper denies the existence of, ignores, or neglects auxiliary statements. In fact, my section on the Kuhn-Popper debate talks explicitly about Popper's treatment of auxiliary hypotheses (which is (1) that they are part of 'the total system' under test; and (2) that one must not preserve the total system by *adjusting* this part—to do so is a 'conventionalist stratagem' and *bad*). What I *did* say is that Popper *blurs the distinction* between auxiliary statements and theory, and this, I still maintain, is true.

The second claim is also false. The auxiliary statements I was talking about, the ones I was taking as examples and on which my argument turned, were *not* 'initial conditions'.

'Initial conditions', in Popper's sense, are *singular* statements (as he stresses again and again in *The Logic of Scientific Discovery*). Moreover whenever he treats the question of their testability; he treats them as *verifiable* ('true basic statements', in his terminology).

The auxiliary statements I gave as examples were:

(1) The solar system consists of only the following bodies (list).

(2) *No* nongravitational forces (or gravitational forces from outside the solar system) are acting on the solar system (to a certain small ε of accuracy).

Both of these statements are *universal* statements, not singular statements. Neither can be verified as a basic statement can—indeed, to verify the second one would *already* have to know the true theory of gravitation! Popper's charge of textual misrepresentation is unfounded, and, in fact, I was very careful to present his doctrine *accurately*.[2]

The Charge of Logical Blunder

What I contended in my criticism is that as scientists actually use the term 'theory' (and, as argued, they *should* use it), Newton's theory of universal gravitation is *not* falsifiable: only its conjunction with the two auxiliary statements just listed is falsifiable.

Popper claims that this is a logical blunder. His proof that this is a logical blunder—that U.G. is falsifiable *without A.S.* (auxiliary statements)—*is a quotation from me*, a quotation in which I say we would give up U.G. if the world started acting in a 'markedly non-Newtonian manner'.

Now the logical situation is precisely this: *any trajectories whatsoever of all the observed bodies are compatible with U.G. without A.S.* Moreover, this is so for a number of reasons:

(1) U.G. without A.S. says nothing at all about what *non*gravitational forces there might be! By assuming nongravitational forces perturbing the system, we can account for any trajectories at all, even if U.G. is true.

(2) Even if we assume the system is acted on only by *gravitational* forces, we can still account for any trajectories at all, to any finite degree of accuracy, by assuming gravitational fields *in addition* to the ones caused by the observed bodies (e.g. there might be bodies too small and too rapid to be observed which are so massive that they give rise to significant fields).

Of course, such *ad hoc* assumptions as would be required to preserve U.G. if the trajectories did 'crazy' things (e.g., if we got *square* orbits), would be enormously *inductively implausible*— which is why we would give up U.G. in such a case. But I was not conceding that square orbits (or whatever) would *deductively* falsify U.G.—which is what Popper takes me to be conceding. The logical blunder is his, not mine.

Main Point

Since the reader has my article available, I do not have to expand on what I actually said there. The main points are two: that Popper's prohibition on saving a successful theory by modifying the A.S. is *bad methodological advice* (as Imre Lakatos and others also pointed out); and that successful predictions *can* confirm a theory plus A.S. even when they are not potential falsifiers in Popper's sense. My distinction between a theory in the canonical sense and A.S. is not the same as Popper's distinction between theory and initial conditions, as has already been pointed out, but it is closely related to, if not quite the same as, Lakatos's distinction between a 'theory core' and a 'protective belt'. The importance of such a distinction has become widely recognized in recent years.

Notes

1. See "Initial Conditions," in P. Schilpp, ed., *The Philosophy of Karl Popper* (La Salle, Ill.: Open Court, 1974).

2. For example, I say that Popper says that a 'theory' implies predictions. 'Predictions' is a nontechnical word which covers what Popper himself calls *instantial sentences* (conditionals whose antecedent and consequent are both basic sentences) as well as basic sentences, and the claim that a theory by itself implies instantial sentences occurs in many places in *The Logic of Scientific Discovery*. I did, unfortunately, write 'basic sentence' instead of 'instantial sentence' in the article in a number of places.

Chapter 7
Scientific Revolutions
Thomas Kuhn

A. THE ESSENTIAL TENSION: TRADITION AND INNOVATION IN SCIENTIFIC
RESEARCH

I am grateful for the invitation to participate in this important conference, and I
interpret it as evidence that students of creativity themselves possess the sensitivity to
divergent approaches that they seek to identify in others. But I am not altogether
sanguine about the outcome of your experiment with me. As most of you already
know, I am no psychologist, but rather an ex-physicist now working in the history of
science. Probably my concern is no less with creativity than your own, but my goals,
my techniques, and my sources of evidence are so very different from yours that I am
far from sure how much we do, or even *should*, have to say to each other. These
reservations imply no apology: rather they hint at my central thesis. In the sciences, as
I shall suggest below, it is often better to do one's best with the tools at hand than to
pause for contemplation of divergent approaches.

If a person of my background and interests has anything relevant to suggest to this
conference, it will not be about your central concerns, the creative personality and its
early identification. But implicit in the numerous working papers distributed to participants in this conference is an image of the scientific process and of the scientist; that
image almost certainly conditions many of the experiments you try as well as the
conclusions you draw; and about it the physicist-historian may well have something to
say. I shall restrict my attention to one aspect of this image—an aspect epitomized as
follows in one of the working papers: The basic scientist "must lack prejudice to a
degree where he can look at the most 'self-evident' facts or concepts without necessarily accepting them, and, conversely, allow his imagination to play with the most
unlikely possibilities" (Selye, 1959). In the more technical language supplied by other
working papers (Getzels and Jackson), this aspect of the image recurs as an emphasis
upon "divergent thinking, the freedom to go off in different directions, ... rejecting the
old solution and striking out in some new direction."

I do not at all doubt that this description of "divergent thinking" and the concomitant search for those able to do it are entirely proper. Some divergence characterizes all scientific work, and gigantic divergences lie at the core of the most significant
episodes in scientific development. But both my own experience in scientific research
and my reading of the history of sciences lead me to wonder whether flexibility and
open-mindedness have not been too exclusively emphasized as the characteristics
requisite for basic research. I shall therefore suggest below that something like "con-

Reprinted by permission of the author and publisher from (A) *The Third (1959) University of Utah Research
Conference on the Identification of Scientific Talent*, ed. C. W. Taylor (Salt Lake City: University of Utah Press,
1959), pp. 162–174. Copyright 1959 by the University of Utah Press; (B) *The Structure of Scientific
Revolutions* 2nd ed. (Chicago: University of Chicago Press, 1970), Chapter IX, pp. 92–110. Copyright
1962, 1970 by the University of Chicago Press.

vergent thinking" is just as essential to scientific advance as is divergent. Since these two modes of thought are inevitably in conflict, it will follow that the ability to support a tension that can occasionally become almost unbearable is one of the prime requisites for the very best sort of scientific research.

I am elsewhere studying these points more historically, with emphasis on the importance to scientific development of "revolutions."[1] These are episodes—exemplified in their most extreme and readily recognized form by the advent of Copernicanism, Darwinism, or Einsteinianism—in which a scientific community abandons one time-honored way of regarding the world and of pursuing science in favor of some other, usually incompatible, approach to its discipline. I have argued in the draft that the historian constantly encounters many far smaller but structurally similar revolutionary episodes and that they are central to scientific advance. Contrary to a prevalent impression, most new discoveries and theories in the sciences are not merely additions to the existing stockpile of scientific knowledge. To assimilate them the scientist must usually rearrange the intellectual and manipulative equipment he has previously relied upon, discarding some elements of his prior belief and practice while finding new significances in and new relationships between many others. Because the old must be revalued and reordered when assimilating the new, discovery and invention in the sciences are usually intrinsically revolutionary. Therefore, they do demand just that flexibility and open-mindedness that characterize, or indeed define, the divergent thinker. Let us henceforth take for granted the need for these characteristics. Unless many scientists possessed them to a marked degree, there would be no scientific revolutions and very little scientific advance.

Yet flexibility is not enough, and what remains is not obviously compatible with it. Drawing from various fragments of a project still in progress, I must now emphasize that revolutions are but one of two complementary aspects of scientific advance. Almost none of the research undertaken by even the greatest scientists is designed to be revolutionary, and very little of it has any such effect. On the contrary, normal research, even the best of it, is a highly convergent activity based firmly upon a settled consensus acquired from scientific education and reinforced by subsequent life in the profession. Typically, to be sure, this convergent or consensus-bound research ultimately results in revolution. Then, traditional techniques and beliefs are abandoned and replaced by new ones. But revolutionary shifts of a scientific tradition are relatively rare, and extended periods of convergent research are the necessary preliminary to them. As I shall indicate below, only investigations firmly rooted in the contemporary scientific tradition are likely to break that tradition and give rise to a new one. That is why I speak of an 'essential tension' implicit in scientific research. To do his job the scientist must undertake a complex set of intellectual and manipulative commitments. Yet his claim to fame, if he has the talent and good luck to gain one, may finally rest upon his ability to abandon this net of commitments in favor of another of his own invention. Very often the successful scientist must simultaneously display the characteristics of the traditionalist and of the iconoclast.[2]

The multiple historical examples upon which any full documentation of these points must depend are prohibited by the time limitations of the conference. But another approach will introduce you to at least part of what I have in mind—an examination of the nature of education in the natural sciences. One of the working papers for this conference (Getzels and Jackson) quotes Guilford's very apt description of scientific education as follows: "[It] has emphasized abilities in the areas of convergent thinking and evaluation, often at the expense of development in the area of divergent thinking. We have attempted to teach students how to arrive at 'correct' answers that our civilization has taught us are correct.... Outside the arts [and I should include most of the social sciences] we have generally discouraged the development of divergent-thinking abilities, unintentionally." That characterization seems to me eminently just, but I wonder whether it is equally just to deplore the product that results. Without defending plain bad teaching, and granting that in this country the trend to convergent thinking in all education may have proceeded entirely too far, we may nevertheless recognize that a rigorous training in convergent thought has been intrinsic to the sciences almost from their origin. I suggest that they could not have achieved their present state or status without it.

Let me try briefly to epitomize the nature of education in the natural sciences, ignoring the many significant yet minor differences between the various sciences and between the approaches of different educational institutions. The single most striking feature of this education is that, to an extent totally unknown in other creative fields, it is conducted entirely through textbooks. Typically, undergraduate *and* graduate students of chemistry, physics, astronomy, geology, or biology acquire the substance of their fields from books written especially for students. Until they are ready, or very nearly ready, to commence work on their own dissertations, they are neither asked to attempt trial research projects nor exposed to the immediate products of research done by others, that is, to the professional communications that scientists write for each other. There are no collections of "readings" in the natural sciences. Nor are science students encouraged to read the historical classics of their fields—works in which they might discover other ways of regarding the problems discussed in their textbooks, but in which they would also meet problems, concepts, and standards of solution that their future professions have long since discarded and replaced.

In contrast, the various textbooks that the student does encounter display different subject matters, rather than, as in many of the social sciences, exemplifying different approaches to a single problem field. Even books that compete for adoption in a single course differ mainly in level and in pedagogic detail, not in substance or conceptual structure. Last, but most important of all, is the characteristic technique of textbook presentation. Except in their occasional introductions, science textbooks do not describe the sorts of problems that the professional may be asked to solve and the variety of techniques available for their solution. Rather, these books exhibit concrete problem solutions that the profession has come to accept as paradigms, and they then ask the student, either with a pencil and paper or in the laboratory, to solve for himself problems very closely related in both method and substance to those through which the textbook or the accompanying lecture has led him. Nothing could be better calculated to produce "mental sets" or *Einstellungen*. Only in their most elementary courses do other academic fields offer as much as a partial parallel.

Even the most faintly liberal educational theory must view this pedagogic technique as anathema. Students, we would all agree, must begin by learning a good deal of what is already known, but we also insist that education give them vastly more. They must, we say, learn to recognize and evaluate problems to which no unequivocal solution has yet been given; they must be supplied with an arsenal of techniques for approaching these future problems; and they must learn to judge the relevance of these techniques and to evaluate the possibly partial solutions which they can provide. In many respects these attitudes toward education seem to me entirely right, and yet we must recognize two things about them. First, education in the natural sciences seems to have been totally unaffected by their existence. It remains a dogmatic initiation in a pre-established tradition that the student is not equipped to evaluate. Second, at least in the period when it was followed by a term in an apprenticeship relation, this technique of exclusive exposure to a rigid tradition has been immensely productive of the most consequential sorts of innovations.

I shall shortly inquire about the pattern of scientific practice that grows out of this educational initiation and will then attempt to say why that pattern proves quite so successful. But first, an historical excursion will reinforce what has just been said and prepare the way for what is to follow. I should like to suggest that the various fields of natural science have not always been characterized by rigid education in exclusive paradigms, but that each of them acquired something like that technique at precisely the point when the field began to make rapid and systematic progress. If one asks about the origin of our contemporary knowledge of chemical composition, of earthquakes, of biological reproduction, of motion through space, or of any other subject matter known to the natural sciences, one immediately encounters a characteristic pattern that I shall here illustrate with a single example.

Today, physics textbooks tell us that light exhibits some properties of a wave and some of a particle: both textbook problems and research problems are designed accordingly. But both this view and these textbooks are products of an early twentieth-century revolution. (One characteristic of scientific revolutions is that they call for the rewriting of science textbooks.) For more than half a century before 1900, the books employed in scientific education had been equally unequivocal in stating that light was wave motion. Under those circumstances scientists worked on somewhat different problems and often embraced rather different sorts of solutions to them. The nineteenth-century textbook tradition does not, however, mark the beginning of our subject matter. Throughout the eighteenth century and into the early nineteenth, Newton's *Opticks* and the other books from which men learned science taught almost all students that light was particles, and research guided by this tradition was again different from that which succeeded it. Ignoring a variety of subsidiary changes within these three successive traditions, we may therefore say that our views derive historically from Newton's views by way of two revolutions in optical thought, each of which replaced one tradition of convergent research with another. If we make appropriate allowances for changes in the locus and materials of scientific education, we may say that each of these three traditions was embodied in the sort of education by exposure to unequivocal paradigms that I briefly epitomized above. Since Newton, education and research in physical optics have normally been highly convergent.

The history of theories of light does not, however, begin with Newton. If we ask about knowledge in the field before his time, we encounter a significantly different pattern—a pattern still familiar in the arts and in some social sciences, but one which has largely disappeared in the natural sciences. From remote antiquity until the end of the seventeenth century there was no single set of paradigms for the study of physical optics. Instead, many men advanced a large number of different views about the nature of light. Some of these views found few adherents, but a number of them gave rise to continuing schools of optical thought. Although the historian can note the emergence of new points of view as well as changes in the relative popularity of older ones, there was never anything resembling consensus. As a result, a new man entering the field was inevitably exposed to a variety of conflicting viewpoints; he was forced to examine the evidence for each, and there always was good evidence. The fact that he made a choice and conducted himself accordingly could not entirely prevent his awareness of other possibilities. This earlier mode of education was obviously more suited to produce a scientist without prejudice, alert to novel phenomena, and flexible in his approach to his field. On the other hand, one can scarcely escape the impression that, during the period characterized by this more liberal educational practice, physical optics made very little progress.[3]

The preconsensus (we might here call it the divergent) phase in the development of physical optics is, I believe, duplicated in the history of all other scientific specialties, excepting only those that were born by the subdivision and recombination of pre-existing disciplines. In some fields, like mathematics and astronomy, the first firm consensus is prehistoric. In others, like dynamics, geometric optics, and parts of physiology, the paradigms that produced a first consensus date from classical antiquity. Most other natural sciences, though their problems were often discussed in antiquity, did not achieve a first consensus until after the Renaissance. In physical optics, as we have seen, the first firm consensus dates only from the end of the seventeenth century; in electricity, chemistry, and the study of heat, it dates from the eighteenth; while in geology and the nontaxonomic parts of biology no very real consensus developed until after the first third of the nineteenth century. This century appears to be characterized by the emergence of a first consensus in parts of a few of the social sciences.

In all the fields named above, important work was done before the achievement of the maturity produced by consensus. Neither the nature nor the timing of the first consensus in these fields can be understood without a careful examination of both the intellectual and the manipulative techniques developed before the existence of unique paradigms. But the transition to maturity is not less significant because individuals practiced science before it occurred. On the contrary, history strongly suggests that, though one can practice science—as one does philosophy or art or political science— without a firm consensus, this more flexible practice will not produce the pattern of rapid consequential scientific advance to which recent centuries have accustomed us. In that pattern, development occurs from one consensus to another, and alternate approaches are not ordinarily in competition. Except under quite special conditions, the practitioner of a mature science does not pause to examine divergent modes of explanation or experimentation.

I shall shortly ask how this can be so—how a firm orientation toward an apparently unique tradition can be compatible with the practice of the disciplines most noted for the persistent production of novel ideas and techniques. But it will help first to ask what the education that so successfully transmits such a tradition leaves to be done. What can a scientist working within a deeply rooted tradition and little trained in the perception of significant alternatives hope to do in his professional career? Once again limits of time force me to drastic simplification, but the following remarks will at least suggest a position that I am sure can be documented in detail.

In pure or basic science—that somewhat ephemeral category of research undertaken by men whose most immediate goal is to increase understanding rather than control of nature—the characteristic problems are almost always repetitions, with minor modifications, of problems that have been undertaken and partially resolved before. For example, much of the research undertaken within a scientific tradition is an attempt to adjust existing theory or existing observation in order to bring the two into closer and closer agreement. The constant examination of atomic and molecular spectra during the years since the birth of wave mechanics, together with the design of theoretical approximations for the prediction of complex spectra, provides one important instance of this typical sort of work. Another was provided by the remarks about the eighteenth-century development of Newtonian dynamics in the paper on measurement supplied to you in advance of the conference.[4] The attempt to make existing theory and observation conform more closely is not, of course, the only standard sort of research problem in the basic sciences. The development of chemical thermodynamics or the continuing attempts to unravel organic structure illustrate another type—the extension of existing theory to areas that it is expected to cover but in which it has never before been tried. In addition, to mention a third common sort of research problem, many scientists constantly collect the concrete data (e.g., atomic weights, nuclear moments) required for the application and extension of existing theory.

These are normal research projects in the basic sciences, and they illustrate the sorts of work on which all scientists, even the greatest, spend most of their professional lives and on which many spend all. Clearly their pursuit is neither intended nor likely to produce fundamental discoveries or revolutionary changes in scientific theory. Only if the validity of the contemporary scientific tradition is assumed do these problems make much theoretical or any practical sense. The man who suspected the existence of a totally new type of phenomenon or who had basic doubts about the validity of existing theory would not think problems so closely modeled on textbook paradigms worth undertaking. It follows that the man who does undertake a problem of this sort—and that means all scientists at most times—aims to elucidate the scientific tradition in which he was raised rather than to change it. Furthermore, the fascination of his work lies in the difficulties of elucidation rather than in any surprises that the work is likely to produce. Under normal conditions the research scientist is not an innovator but a solver of puzzles, and the puzzles upon which he concentrates are just those which he believes can be both stated and solved within the existing scientific tradition.

Yet—and this is the point—the ultimate effect of this tradition-bound work has invariably been to change the tradition. Again and again the continuing attempt to elucidate a currently received tradition has at last produced one of those shifts in fundamental theory, in problem field, and in scientific standards to which I previously referred as scientific revolutions. At least for the scientific community as a whole, work within a well-defined and deeply ingrained tradition seems more productive of tradition-shattering novelties than work in which no similarly convergent standards are involved. How can this be so? I think it is because no other sort of work is nearly so well suited to isolate for continuing and concentrated attention those loci of trouble or causes of crisis upon whose recognition the most fundamental advances in basic science depend.

As I have indicated in the first of my working papers, new theories and, to an increasing extent, novel discoveries in the mature sciences are not born *de novo*. On the contrary, they emerge from old theories and within a matrix of old beliefs about the phenomena that the world does *and does not* contain. Ordinarily such novelties are far too esoteric and recondite to be noted by the man without a great deal of scientific training. And even the man with considerable training can seldom afford simply to go out and look for them, let us say by exploring those areas in which existing data and theory have failed to produce understanding. Even in a mature science there are always far too many such areas, areas in which no existing paradigms seem obviously to apply and for whose exploration few tools and standards are available. More likely than not the scientist who ventured into them, relying merely upon his receptivity to new phenomena and his flexibility to new patterns of organization, would get nowhere at all. He would rather return his science to its preconsensus or natural history phase.

Instead, the practitioner of a mature science, from the beginning of his doctoral research, continues to work in the regions for which the paradigms derived from his education and from the research of his contemporaries seem adequate. He tries, that is, to elucidate topographical detail on a map whose main outlines are available in advance, and he hopes—if he is wise enough to recognize the nature of his field—that he will some day undertake a problem in which the anticipated does *not* occur, a problem that goes wrong in ways suggestive of a fundamental weakness in the paradigm itself. In the mature sciences the prelude to much discovery and to all novel theory is not ignorance, but the recognition that something has gone wrong with existing knowledge and beliefs.

What I have said so far may indicate that it is sufficient for the productive scientist to adopt existing theory as a lightly held tentative hypothesis, employ it *faute de mieux* in order to get a start in his research, and then abandon it as soon as it leads him to a trouble spot, a point at which something has gone wrong. But though the ability to recognize trouble when confronted by it is surely a requisite for scientific advance, trouble must not be too easily recognized. The scientist requires a thoroughgoing commitment to the tradition with which, if he is fully successful, he will break. In part this commitment is demanded by the nature of the problems the scientist normally undertakes. These, as we have seen, are usually esoteric puzzles whose challenge lies less in the information disclosed by their solutions (all but its details are often known in advance) than in the difficulties of technique to be surmounted in providing any solution at all. Problems of this sort are undertaken only by men assured that there is a solution which ingenuity can disclose, and only current theory could possibly provide assurance of that sort. That theory alone gives meaning to most of the problems of normal research. To doubt it is often to doubt that the complex technical puzzles which constitute normal research have any solutions at all. Who, for example, would have developed the elaborate mathematical techniques required for the study of the effects of interplanetary attractions upon basic Keplerian orbits if he had not assumed that Newtonian dynamics, applied to the planets then known, would explain the last details of astronomical observation? But without that assurance, how would Neptune have been discovered and the list of planets changed?

In addition, there are pressing practical reasons for commitment. Every research problem confronts the scientist with anomalies whose sources he cannot quite identify. His theories and observations never quite agree; successive observations never yield quite the same results; his experiments have both theoretical and phenomenological by-products which it would take another research project to unravel. Each of these anomalies or incompletely understood phenomena could conceivably be the clue to a fundamental innovation in scientific theory or technique, but the man who pauses to examine them one by one never completes his first project. Reports of effective research repeatedly imply that all but the most striking and central discrepancies could be taken care of by current theory if only there were time to take them on. The men who make these reports find most discrepancies trivial or uninteresting, an evaluation that they can ordinarily base only upon their faith in current theory. Without that faith their work would be wasteful of time and talent.

Besides, lack of commitment too often results in the scientist's undertaking problems that he has little chance of solving. Pursuit of an anomaly is fruitful only if the anomaly is more than nontrivial. Having discovered it, the scientist's first efforts and those of his profession are to do what nuclear physicists are now doing. They strive to generalize the anomaly, to discover other and more revealing manifestations of the same effect, to give it structure by examining its complex interrelationships with phenomena they still feel they understand. Very few anomalies are susceptible to this sort of treatment. To be so they must be in explicit and unequivocal conflict with some structurally central tenet of current scientific belief. Therefore, their recognition and evaluation once again depend upon a firm commitment to the contemporary scientific tradition.

This central role of an elaborate and often esoteric tradition is what I have principally had in mind when speaking of the essential tension in scientific research. I do not doubt that the scientist must be, at least potentially, an innovator, that he must possess mental flexibility, and that he must be prepared to recognize troubles where they exist. That much of the popular stereotype is surely correct, and it is important accordingly to search for indices of the corresponding personality characteristics. But what is no part of our stereotype and what appears to need careful integration with it is the other face of this same coin. We are, I think, more likely fully to exploit our potential scientific talent if we recognize the extent to which the basic scientist must also be a firm traditionalist, or, if I am using your vocabulary at all correctly, a convergent thinker. Most important of all, we must seek to understand how these two superficially discordant modes of problem solving can be reconciled both within the individual and within the group.

Everything said above needs both elaboration and documentation. Very likely some of it will change in the process. This paper is a report on work in progress. But, though I insist that much of it is tentative and all of it incomplete, I still hope that the paper has indicated why an educational system best described as an initiation into an unequivocal tradition should be thoroughly compatible with successful scientific work. And I hope, in addition, to have made plausible the historical thesis that no part of science has progressed very far or very rapidly before this convergent education and correspondingly convergent normal practice became possible. Finally, though it is beyond my competence to derive personality correlates from this view of scientific development, I hope to have made meaningful the view that the productive scientist must be a traditionalist who enjoys playing intricate games by pre-established rules in order to be a successful innovator who discovers new rules and new pieces with which to play them.

As first planned, my paper was to have ended at this point. But work on it, against the background supplied by the working papers distributed to conference participants, has suggested the need for a postscript. Let me therefore briefly try to eliminate a likely ground of misunderstanding and simultaneously suggest a problem that urgently needs a great deal of investigation.

Everything said above was intended to apply strictly only to basic science, an enterprise whose practitioners have ordinarily been relatively free to choose their own problems. Characteristically, as I have indicated, these problems have been selected in areas where paradigms were clearly applicable but where exciting puzzles remained about how to apply them and how to make nature conform to the results of the application. Clearly the inventor and applied scientist are not generally free to choose puzzles of this sort. The problems among which they may choose are likely to be largely determined by social, economic, or military circumstances external to the sciences. Often the decision to seek a cure for a virulent disease, a new source of household illumination, or an alloy able to withstand the intense heat of rocket engines must be made with little reference to the state of the relevant science. It is, I think, by no means clear that the personality characteristics requisite for pre-eminence in this more immediately practical sort of work are altogether the same as those required for a great achievement in basic science. History indicates that only a few individuals, most of whom worked in readily demarcated areas, have achieved eminence in both.

I am by no means clear where this suggestion leads us. The troublesome distinctions between basic research, applied research, and invention need far more investigation.

Nevertheless, it seems likely, for example, that the applied scientist, to whose problems no scientific paradigm need be fully relevant, may profit by a far broader and less rigid education than that to which the pure scientist has characteristically been exposed. Certainly there are many episodes in the history of technology in which lack of more than the most rudimentary scientific education has proved to be an immense help. This group scarcely needs to be reminded that Edison's electric light was produced in the face of unanimous scientific opinion that the arc light could not be "subdivided," and there are many other episodes of this sort.

This must not suggest, however, that mere differences in education will transform the applied scientist into a basic scientist or vice versa One could at least argue that Edison's personality, ideal for the inventor and perhaps also for the "oddball" in applied science, barred him from fundamental achievements in the basic sciences. He himself expressed great scorn for scientists and thought of them as wooly-headed people to be hired when needed. But this did not prevent his occasionally arriving at the most sweeping and irresponsible scientific theories of his own. (The pattern recurs in the early history of electrical technology: both Tesla and Gramme advanced absurd cosmic schemes that they thought deserved to replace the current scientific knowledge of their day.) Episodes like this reinforce an impression that the personality requisites of the pure scientist and of the inventor may be quite different, perhaps with those of the applied scientist lying somewhere between.[5]

Is there a further conclusion to be drawn from all this? One speculative thought forces itself upon me. If I read the working papers correctly, they suggest that most of you are really in search of the *inventive* personality, a sort of person who does emphasize divergent thinking but whom the United States has aleady produced in abundance. In the process you may be ignoring certain of the essential requisites of the basic scientist, a rather different sort of person, to whose ranks America's contributions have as yet been notoriously sparse. Since most of you are, in fact, Americans, this correlation may not be entirely coincidental.

Notes

1. *The Structure of Scientific Revolutions* (Chicago, 1962).
2. Strictly speaking, it is the professional group rather than the individual scientist that must display both these characteristics simultaneously. In a fuller account of the ground covered in this paper that distinction between individual and group characteristics would be basic. Here I can only note that, though recognition of the distinction weakens the conflict or tension referred to above, it does not eliminate it. Within the group some individuals may be more traditionalistic, others more iconoclastic, and their contributions may differ accordingly. Yet education, institutional norms, and the nature of the job to be done will inevitably combine to insure that all group members will, to a greater or lesser extent, be pulled in both direction.
3. The history of physical optics before Newton has recently been well described by Vasco Ronchi in *Histoire de la lumière*, trans. J. Taton (Paris, 1956). His account does justice to the element I elaborate too little above. Many fundamental contributions to physical optics were made in the two millennia before Newton's work. Consensus is not prerequisite to a sort of progress in the natural sciences, any more than it is to progress in the social sciences or the arts. It is, however, prerequisite to the sort of progress that we now generally refer to when distinguishing the natural sciences from the arts and from most social sciences.
4. A revised version appeared in *Isis* 52 (1961): 161–93.
5. For the attitude of scientists toward the technical possibility of the incandescent light see Francis A. Jones, *Thomas Alva Edison* (New York, 1908), pp. 99–100, and Harold C. Passer, *The Electrical Manufacturers, 1875–1900* (Cambridge, Mass., 1953). pp. 82–83. For Edison's attitude toward scientists see Passer, ibid., pp. 180–81. For a sample of Edison's theorizing in realms otherwise subject to scientific treatments see Dagobert D. Runes, ed., *The Diary and Sundry Observatons of Thomas Alva Edison* (New York, 1948), pp. 205–44, passim.

B. THE NATURE AND NECESSITY OF SCIENTIFIC REVOLUTIONS

... What are scientific revolutions, and what is their function in scientific development? ... [S]cientific revolutions are here taken to be those noncumulative developmental episodes in which an older paradigm is replaced in whole or in part by an incompatible new one. There is more to be said, however, and an essential part of it can be introduced by asking one further question. Why should a change of paradigm be called a revolution? In the face of the vast and essential differences between political and scientific development, what parallelism can justify the metaphor that finds revolutions in both?

One aspect of the parallelism must already be apparent. Political revolutions are inaugurated by a growing sense, often restricted to a segment of the political community, that existing institutions have ceased adequately to meet the problems posed by an environment that they have in part created. In much the same way, scientific revolutions are inaugurated by a growing sense, again often restricted to a narrow subdivision of the scientific community, that an existing paradigm has ceased to function adequately in the exploration of an aspect of nature to which that paradigm itself had previously led the way. In both political and scientific development the sense of malfunction that can lead to crisis is prerequisite to revolution. Furthermore, though it admittedly strains the metaphor, that parallelism holds not only for the major paradigm changes, like those attributable to Copernicus and Lavoisier, but also for the far smaller ones associated with the assimilation of a new sort of phenomenon, like oxygen or X-rays. Scientific revolutions ... need seem revolutionary only to those whose paradigms are affected by them. To outsiders they may, like the Balkan revolutions of the early twentieth century, seem normal parts of the developmental process. Astronomers, for example, could accept X-rays as a mere addition to knowledge, for their paradigms were unaffected by the existence of the new radiation. But for men like Kelvin, Crookes, and Roentgen, whose research dealt with radiation theory or with cathode ray tubes, the emergence of X-rays necessarily violated one paradigm as it created another. That is why these rays could be discovered only through something's first going wrong with normal research.

This genetic aspect of the parallel between political and scientific development should no longer be open to doubt. The parallel has, however, a second and more profound aspect upon which the significance of the first depends. Political revolutions aim to change political institutions in ways that those institutions themselves prohibit. Their success therefore necessitates the partial relinquishment of one set of institutions in favor of another, and in the interim, society is not fully governed by institutions at all. Initially it is crisis alone that attenuates the role of political institutions as we have already seen it attenuate the role of paradigms. In increasing numbers individuals become increasingly estranged from political life and behave more and more eccentrically within it. Then, as the crisis deepens, many of these individuals commit themselves to some concrete proposal for the reconstruction of society in a new institutional framework. At that point the society is divided into competing camps or parties, one seeking to defend the old institutional constellation, the others seeking to institute some new one. And, once that polarization has occurred, *political recourse fails*. Because they differ about the institutional matrix within which political change is to be achieved and evaluated, because they acknowledge no supra-institutional framework for the adjudication of revolutionary difference, the parties to a revolutionary conflict must finally resort to the techniques of mass persuasion, often including force. Though revolutions have had a vital role in the evolution of political institutions, that role depends upon their being partially extrapolitical or extra-institutional events.

The remainder of this essay aims to demonstrate that the historical study of paradigm change reveals very similar characteristics in the evolution of the sciences. Like the choice between competing political institutions, that between competing paradigms proves to be a choice between incompatible modes of community life. Because it has that character, the choice is not and cannot be determined merely by the evaluative procedures characteristic of normal science, for these depend in part upon a particular paradigm, and that paradigm is at issue. When paradigms enter, as they must, into a debate about paradigm choice, their role is necessarily circular. Each group uses its own paradigm to argue in that paradigm's defense.

The resulting circularity does not, of course, make the arguments wrong or even ineffectual. The man who premises a paradigm when arguing in its defense can nonetheless provide a clear exhibit of what scientific practice will be like for those who adopt the new view of nature. That exhibit can be immensely persuasive, often compellingly so. Yet, whatever its force, the status of the circular argument is only that of persuasion. It cannot be made logically or even probabilistically compelling for those who refuse to step into the circle. The premises and values shared by the two parties to a debate over paradigms are not sufficiently extensive for that. As in political revolutions, so in paradigm choice—there is no standard higher than the assent of the relevant community. To discover how scientific revolutions are effected, we shall therefore have to examine not only the impact of nature and of logic, but also the techniques of persuasive argumentation effective within the quite special groups that constitute the community of scientists.

To discover why this issue of paradigm choice can never be unequiocally settled by logic and experiment alone, we must shortly examine the nature of the differences that separate the proponents of a traditional paradigm from their revolutionary successors. That examination is the principal object of this section and the next. We have, however, already noted numerous examples of such differences, and no one will doubt that history can supply many others. What is more likely to be doubted than their existence—and what must therefore be considered first—is that such examples provide essential information about the nature of science. Granting that paradigm rejection has been a historic fact, does it illuminate more than human credulity and confusion? Are there intrinsic reasons why the assimilation of either a new sort of phenomenon or a new scientific theory must demand the rejection of an older paradigm?

First notice that if there are such reasons, they do not derive from the logical structure of scientific knowledge. In principle, a new phenomenon might emerge without reflecting destructively upon any part of past scientific practice. Though discovering life on the moon would today be destructive of existing paradigms (these tell us things about the moon that seem incompatible with life's existence there), discovering life in some less well-known part of the galaxy would not. By the same token, a new theory does not have to conflict with any of its predecessors. It might deal exclusively with phenomena not previously known, as the quantum theory deals (but, significantly, not exclusively) with subatomic phenomena unknown before the twentieth century. Or again, the new theory might be simply a higher level theory than those known before, one that linked together a whole group of lower level theories without substantially changing any. Today, the theory of energy conservation provides just such links between dynamics, chemistry, electricity, optics, thermal theory, and so on. Still other compatible relationships between old and new theories can be conceived. Any and all of them might be exemplified by the historical process through which science has developed. If they were, scientific development would be genuinely cumulative. New sorts of phenomena would simply disclose order in an aspect of nature where none had been seen before. In the evolution of science new knowledge would replace ignorance rather than replace knowledge of another and incompatible sort.

Of course, science (or some other enterprise, perhaps less effective) might have developed in that fully cumulative manner. Many people have believed that it did so, and most still seem to suppose that cumulation is at least the ideal that historical development would display if only it had not so often been distorted by human idiosyncrasy. There are important reasons for that belief ... Nevertheless, despite the immense plausibility of that ideal image, there is increasing reason to wonder whether it can possibly be an image of *science*. After the pre-paradigm period the assimilation of all new theories and of almost all new sorts of phenomena has in fact demanded the destruction of a prior paradigm and a consequent conflict between competing schools of scientific thought. Cumulative acquisition of unanticipated novelties proves to be an almost nonexistent exception to the rule of scientific development. The man who takes historic fact seriously must suspect that science does not tend toward the ideal that our image of its cumulativeness has suggested. Perhaps it is another sort of enterprise.

If, however, resistant facts can carry us that far, then a second look at the ground we have already covered may suggest that cumulative acquisition of novelty is not only rare in fact but improbable in principle. Normal research, which *is* cumulative, owes its success to the ability of scientists regularly to select problems that can be solved with conceptual and instrumental techniques close to those already in existence. (That is why an excessive concern with useful problems, regardless of their relation to existing knowledge and technique, can so easily inhibit scientific development.) The man who is striving to solve a problem defined by existing knowledge and technique is not, however, just looking around. He knows what he wants to achieve, and he designs his instruments and directs his thoughts accordingly. Unanticipated novelty, the new discovery, call emerge only to the extent that his anticipations about nature and his instruments prove wrong. Often the importance of the resulting discovery will itself be proportional to the extent and stubbornness of the anomaly that foreshadowed it. Obviously, then, there must be a conflict between the paradigm that discloses anomaly and the one that later renders the anomaly law-like ... There is no other effective way in which discoveries might be generated.

The same argument applies even more clearly to the invention of new theories. There are, in principle, only three types of phenomena about which a new theory might be developed. The first consists of phenomena already well explained by existing paradigms, and these seldom provide either motive or point of departure for theory construction. When they do, ... the theories that result are seldom accepted, because nature provides no ground for discrimination. A second class of phenomena consists of those whose nature is indicated by existing paradigms but whose details can be understood only through further theory articulation. These are the phenomena to which scientists direct their research much of the time, but that research aims at the articulation of existing paradigms rather than at the invention of new ones. Only when these attempts at articulation fail do scientists encounter the third type of phenomena, the recognized anomalies whose characteristic feature is their stubborn refusal to be assimilated to existing paradigms. This type alone gives rise to new theories. Paradigms provide all phenomena except anomalies with a theory-determined place in the scientist's field of vision.

But if new theories are called forth to resolve anomalies in the relation of an existing theory to nature, then the successful new theory must somewhere permit predictions that are different from those derived from its predecessor. That difference could not occur if the two were logically compatible. In the process of being assimilated, the second must displace the first. Even a theory like energy conservation, which today seems a logical superstructure that relates to nature only through independently established theories, did not develop historically without paradigm destruction. Instead, it emerged from a crisis in which an essential ingredient was the incompatibility between Newtonian dynamics and some recently formulated consequences of the caloric theory of heat. Only after the caloric theory had been rejected could energy conservation become part of science.[1] And only after it had been part of science for some time could it come to seem a theory of a logically higher type, one not in conflict with its predecessors. It is hard to see how new theories could arise without these destructive changes in beliefs about nature. Though logical inclusiveness remains a permissible view of the relation between successive scientific theories, it is a historical implausibility.

A century ago it would, I think, have been possible to let the case for the necessity of revolutions rest at this point. But today, unfortunately, that cannot be done because the view of the subject developed above cannot be maintained if the most prevalent contemporary interpretation of the nature and function of scientific theory is accepted. That interpretation, closely associated with early logical positivism and not categorically rejected by its successors, would restrict the range and meaning of an accepted theory so that it could not possibly conflict with any later theory that made predictions about some of the same natural phenomena. The best-known and the strongest case for this restricted conception of a scientific theory emerges in discussions of the relation between contemporary Einsteinian dynamics and the older dynamical equations that descend from Newton's *Principia*. From the viewpoint of this essay these two theories are fundamentally incompatible in the sense illustrated by the relation of Copernican to Ptolemaic astronomy: Einstein's theory can be accepted only with the recognition that Newton's was wrong. Today this remains a minority view.[2] We must therefore examine the most prevalent objections to it.

The gist of these objections can be developed as follows. Relativistic dynamics cannot have shown Newtonian dynamics to be wrong, for Newtonian dynamics is still used with great success by most engineers and, in selected applications, by many physicists. Furthermore, the propriety of this use of the older theory can be proved from the very theory that has, in other applications, replaced it. Einstein's theory can be used to show that predictions from Newton's equations will be as good as our measuring instruments in all applications that satisfy a small number of restrictive conditions. For example, if Newtonian theory is to provide a good approximate solution, the relative velocities of the bodies considered must be small compared with the velocity of light. Subject to this condition and a few others, Newtonian theory seems to be derivable from Einsteinian, of which it is therefore a special case.

But, the objection continues, no theory can possibly conflict with one of its special cases. If Einsteinian science seems to make Newtonian dynamics wrong, that is only because some Newtonians were so incautious as to claim that Newtonian theory yielded entirely precise results or that it was valid at very high relative velocities. Since they could not have had any evidence for such claims, they betrayed the standards of science when they made them. In so far as Newtonian theory was ever a truly scientific theory supported by valid evidence, it still is. Only extravagant claims for the theory

—claims that were never properly parts of science—can have been shown by Einstein to be wrong. Purged of these merely human extravagances, Newtonian theory has never been challenged and cannot be.

Some variant of this argument is quite sufficient to make any theory ever used by a significant group of competent scientists immune to attack. The much-maligned phlogiston theory, for example, gave order to a large number of physical and chemical phenomena. It explained why bodies burned—they were rich in phlogiston—and why metals had so many more properties in common than did their ores. The metals were all compounded from different elementary earths combined with phlogiston, and the latter, common to all metals, produced common properties. In addition, the phlogiston theory accounted for a number of reactions in which acids were formed by the combustion of substances like carbon and sulphur. Also, it explained the decrease of volume when combustion occurs in a confined volume of air—the phlogiston released by combustion "spoils" the elasticity of the air that absorbed it, just as fire "spoils" the elasticity of a steel spring.[3] If these were the only phenomena that the phlogiston theorists had claimed for their theory, that theory could never have been challenged. A similar argument will suffice for any theory that has ever been successfully applied to any range of phenomena at all.

But to save theories in this way, their range of application must be restricted to those phenomena and to that precision of observation with which the experimental evidence in hand already deals.[4] Carried just a step further (and the step can scarcely be avoided once the first is taken), such a limitation prohibits the scientist from claiming to speak "scientifically" about any phenomenon not already observed. Even in its present form the restriction forbids the scientist to rely upon a theory in his own research whenever that research enters an area or seeks a degree of precision for which past practice with the theory offers no precedent. These prohibitions are logically unexceptionable. But the result of accepting them would be the end of the research through which science may develop further.

By now that point too is virtually a tautology. Without commitment to a paradigm there could be no normal science. Furthermore, that commitment must extend to areas and to degrees of precision for which there is no full precedent. If it did not, the paradigm could provide no puzzles that had not already been solved. Besides, it is not only normal science that depends upon commitment to a paradigm. If existing theory binds the scientist only with respect to existing applications, then there can be no surprises, anomalies, or crises. But these are just the signposts that point the way to extraordinary, science. If positivistic restrictions on the range of a theory's legitimate applicability are taken literally, the mechanism that tells the scientific community what problems may lead to fundamental change must cease to function. And when that occurs, the community will inevitably return to something much like its pre-paradigm state, a condition in which all members practice science but in which their gross product scarcely resembles science at all. Is it really any wonder that the price of significant scientific advance is a commitment that runs the risk of being wrong?

More important, there is a revealing logical lacuna in the positivist's argument, one that will reintroduce us immediately to the nature of revolutionary change. Can Newtonian dynamics really be *derived* from relativistic dynamics? What would such a derivation look like? Imagine a set of statements, E_1, E_2, ..., E_n, which together embody the laws of relativity theory. These statements contain variables and parameters representing spatial position, time, rest mass, etc. From them, together with the apparatus of logic and mathematics, is deducible a whole set of further statements including some that can be checked by observation. To prove the adequacy of New-tonian dynamics as a special case, we must add to the E_i's additional statements, like $(v/c)^2 \ll 1$, restricting the range of the parameters and variables. This enlarged set of statements is then manipulated to yield a new set, $N_1, N_2, \ldots N_m$, which is identical in form with Newton's laws of motion, the law of gravity, and so on. Apparently Newtonian dynamics has been derived from Einsteinian, subject to a few limiting conditions.

Yet the derivation is spurious, at least to this point. Though the N_i's are a special case of the laws of relativistic mechanics, they are not Newton's laws. Or at least they are not unless those laws are reinterpreted in a way that would have been impossible until after Einstein's work. The variables and parameters that in the Einsteinian E_i's represented spatial position, time, mass, etc., still occur in the N_i's; and they there still represent Einsteinian space, time, and mass. But the physical referents of these Ein-steinian concepts are by no means identical with those of the Newtonian concepts that bear the same name. (Newtonian mass is conserved; Einsteinian is convertible with energy. Only at low relative velocities may the two be measured in the same way, and even then they must not be conceived to be the same.) Unless we change the definitions of the variables in the N_i's, the statements we have derived are not New-tonian. If we do change them, we cannot properly be said to have *derived* Newton's laws, at least not in any sense of "derive" now generally recognized. Our argument has, of course, explained why Newton's laws ever seemed to work. In doing so it has justified, say, an automobile driver in acting as though he lived in a Newtonian universe. An argument of the same type is used to justify teaching earth-centered astronomy to surveyors. But the argument has still not done what it purported to do. It has not, that is, shown Newton's laws to be a limiting case of Einstein's. For in the passage to the limit it is not only the forms of the laws that have changed. Simultan-eously we have had to alter the fundamental structural elements of which the universe to which they apply is composed.

This need to change the meaning of established and familiar concepts is central to the revolutionary impact of Einstein's theory. Though subtler than the changes from geocentrism to heliocentrism, from phlogiston to oxygen, or from corpuscles to waves, the resulting conceptual transformation is no less decisively destructive of a previously established paradigm. We may even come to see it as a prototype for revo-lutionary reorientations in the sciences. Just because it did not involve the introduc-tion of additional objects or concepts, the transition from Newtonian to Einsteinian mechanics illustrates with particular clarity the scientific revolution as a displacement of the conceptual network through which scientists view the world.

These remarks should suffice to show what might, in another philosophical climate, have been taken for granted. At least for scientists, most of the apparent differences between a discarded scientific theory and its successor are real. Though an out-of-date theory can always be viewed as a special case of its up-to-date successor, it must be transformed for the purpose. And the transformation is one that can be undertaken only with the advantages of hindsight, the explicit guidance of the more recent theory. Furthermore, even if that transformation were a legitimate device to employ in inter-preting the older theory, the result of its application would be a theory so restricted that it could only restate what was already known. Because of its economy, that restatement would have utility, but it could not suffice for the guidance of research.

Let us, therefore, now take it for granted that the differences between successive paradigms are both necessary and irreconcilable. Can we then say more explicitly what sorts of differences these are? The most apparent type has already been illustrated repeatedly. Successive paradigms tell us different things about the population of the universe and about that population's behavior. They differ, that is, about such questions as the existence of subatomic particles, the materiality of light, and the conservation of heat or of energy. These are the substantive differences between successive paradigms, and they require no further illustration. But paradigms differ in more than substance, for they are directed not only to nature but also back upon the science that produced them. They are the source of the methods, problem-field, and standards of solution accepted by any mature scientific community at any given time. As a result, the reception of a new paradigm often necessitates a redefinition of the corresponding science. Some old problems may be relegated to another science or declared entirely "unscientific." Others that were previously nonexistent or trivial may, with a new paradigm, become the very archetypes of significant scientific achievement. And as the problems change, so, often, does the standard that distinguishes a real scientific solution from a mere metaphysical speculation, word game, or mathematical play. The normal-scientific tradition that emerges from a scientific revolution is not only incompatible but often actually incommensurable with that which has gone before.

The impact of Newton's work upon the normal seventeenth-century tradition of scientific practice provides a striking example of these subtler effects of paradigm shift. Before Newton was born the "new science" of the century had at last succeeded in rejecting Aristotelian and scholastic explanations expressed in terms of the essences of material bodies. To say that a stone fell because its "nature" drove it toward the center of the universe had been made to look a mere tautological word-play, something it had not previously been. Henceforth the entire flux of sensory appearances, including color, taste, and even weight, was to be explained in terms of the size, shape, position, and motion of the elementary corpuscles of base matter. The attribution of other qualities to the elementary atoms was a resort to the occult and therefore out of bounds for science. Molière caught the new spirit precisely when he ridiculed the doctor who explained opium's efficacy as a soporific by attributing to it a dormitive potency. During the last half of the seventeenth century many scientists preferred to say that the round shape of the opium particles enabled them to sooth the nerves about which they moved.[5]

In an earlier period explanations in terms of occult qualities had been an integral part of productive scientific work. Nevertheless, the seventeenth century's new commitment to mechanico-corpuscular explanation proved immensely fruitful for a number of sciences, ridding them of problems that had defied generally accepted solution and suggesting others to replace them. In dynamics, for example, Newton's three laws of motion are less a product of novel experiments than of the attempt to reinterpret well-known observations in terms of the motions and interactions of primary neutral corpuscles. Consider just one concrete illustration. Since neutral corpuscles could act on each other only by contact, the mechanico-corpuscular view of nature directed scientific attention to a brand-new subject of study, the alteration of particulate motions by collisions. Descartes announced the problem and provided its first putative solution. Huyghens, Wren, and Wallis carried it still further, partly by experimenting with colliding pendulum bobs, but mostly by applying previously well-known characteristics of motion to the new problem. And Newton embedded their results in his laws of motion. The equal "action" and "reaction" Of the third law are the changes in quantity of motion experienced by the two parties to a collision. The same change of motion supplies the definition of dynamical force implicit in the second law. In this case, as in many others during the seventeenth century, the corpuscular paradigm bred both a new problem and a large part of that problem's solution.[6]

Yet, though much of Newton's work was directed to problems and embodied standards derived from the mechanico-corpuscular world view, the effect of the paradigm that resulted from his work was a further and partially destructive change in the problems and standards legitimate for science. Gravity, interpreted as an innate attraction between every pair of particles of matter, was an occult quality in the same sense as the scholastics' "tendency to fall" had been. Therefore, while the standards of corpuscularism remained in effect, the search for a mechanical explanation of gravity was one of the most challenging problems for those who accepted the *Principia* as paradigm. Newton devoted much attention to it and so did many of his eighteenth-century successors. The only apparent option was to reject Newton's theory for its failure to explain gravity, and that alternative, too, was widely adopted. Yet neither of these views ultimately triumphed. Unable either to practice science without the *Principia* or to make that work conform to the corpuscular standards of the seventeenth century, scientists gradually accepted the view that gravity was indeed innate. By the mid-eighteenth century that interpretation had been almost universally accepted, and the result was a genuine reversion (which is not the same as a retrogression) to a scholastic standard. Innate attractions and repulsions joined size, shape, position, and motion as physically irreducible primary properties of matter.[7]

The resulting change in the standards and problem-field of physical science was once again consequential. By the 1740s, for example, electricians could speak of the attractive "virtue" of the electric fluid without thereby inviting the ridicule that had greeted Molière's doctor a century before. As they did so, electrical phenomena increasingly displayed an order different from the one they had shown when viewed as the effects of a mechanical effluvium that could act only by contact. In particular, when electrical action-at-a-distance became a subject for study in its own right, the phenomenon we now call charging by induction could be recognized as one of its effects. Previously, when seen at all, it had been attributed to the direct action of electrical "atmospheres" or to the leakages inevitable in any electrical laboratory. The new view of inductive effects was, in turn, the key to Franklin's analysis of the Leyden jar and thus to the emergence of a new and Newtonian paradigm for electricity. Nor were dynamics and electricity the only scientific fields affected by the legitimization of the search for forces innate to matter. The large body of eighteenth-century literature on chemical affinities and replacement series also derives from this supramechanical aspect of Newtonianism. Chemists who believed in these differential attractions between the various chemical species set up previously unimagined experiments and searched for new sorts of reactions. Without the data and the chemical concepts developed in that process, the later work of Lavoisier and, more particularly, of Dalton would be incomprehensible.[8] Changes in the standards governing permissible problems, concepts, and explanations can transform a science . . .

Other examples of these nonsubstantive differences between successive paradigms can be retrieved from the history of any science in almost any period of its development. For the moment let us be content with just two other and far briefer illustrations. Before the chemical revolution, one of the acknowledged tasks of chemistry was to account for the qualities of chemical substances and for the changes these qualities under vent during chemical reactions. With the aid of a small number of elementary "principles"—of which phlogiston was one—the chemist was to explain why some substances are acidic, others metalline, combustible, and so forth. Some success in this direction had been achieved. We have already noted that phlogiston explained why the metals were so much alike, and we could have developed a similar argument for the acids. Lavoisier's reform, however, ultimately did away with chemical "principles," and thus ended by depriving chemistry of some actual and much potential explanatory power. To compensate for this loss, a change in standards was required. During much of the nineteenth century failure to explain the qualities of compounds was no indictment of a chemical theory.[9]

Or again, Clerk Maxwell shared with other nineteenth-century proponents of the wave theory of light the conviction that light waves must be propagated through a material ether. Designing a mechanical medium to support such waves was a standard problem for many of his ablest contemporaries. His own theory, however, the electromagnetic theory of light, gave no account at all of a medium able to support light waves, and it clearly made such an account harder to provide than it had seemed before. Initially, Maxwell's theory was widely rejected for those reasons. But, like Newton's theory, Maxwell's proved difficult to dispense with, and as it achieved the status of a paradigm, the community's attitude toward it changed. In the early decades of the twentieth century Maxwell's insistence upon the existence of a mechanical ether looked more and more like lip service, which it emphatically had not been, and the attempts to design such an ethereal medium were abandoned. Scientists no longer thought it unscientific to speak of an electrical "displacement" without specifying what was being displaced. The result, again, was a new set of problems and standards, one which, in the event, had much to do with the emergence of relativity theory.[10]

These characteristic shifts in the scientific community's conception of its legitimate problems and standards would have less significance to this essay's thesis if one could suppose that they always occurred from some methodologically lower to some higher type. In that case their effects, too, would seem cumulative. No wonder that some historians have argued that the history of science records a continuing increase in the maturity and refinement of man's conception of the natule of science.[11] Yet the case for cumulative development of science's problems and standards is even harder to make than the case for cumulation of theories. The attempt to explain gravity, though fruitfully abandoned by most eighteenth-century scientists, was not directed to an intrinsically illegitimate problem; the objections to innate forces were neither inherently unscientific nor metaphysical in some pejorative sense. There are no external standards to permit a judgment of that sort. What occurred was neither a decline nor a raising of standards, but simply a change demanded by the adoption of a new paradigm. Furthermore, that change has since been reversed and could be again. In the twentieth century Einstein succeeded in explaining gravitational attractions, and that explanation has returned science to a set of canons and problems that are, in this particular respect, more like those of Newton's predecessors than of his successors. Or again, the development of quantum mechanics has reversed the methodological prohibition that originated in the chemical revolution. Chemists now attempt, and with great success, to explain the color, state of aggregation, and other qualities of the substances used and produced in their laboratories. A similar reversal may even be underway in electromagnetic theory. Space, in contemporary physics, is not the inert and homogenous substratum employed in both Newton's and Maxwell's theories; some of its new properties are not unlike those once attributed to the ether; we may someday come to know what an electric displacement is.

By shifting emphasis from the cognitive to the normative functions of paradigms, the preceding examples enlarge our understanding of the ways in which paradigms give form to the scientific life. Previously, we had principally examined the paradigm's role as a vehicle for scientific theory. In that role it functions by telling the scientist about the entities that nature does and does not contain and about the ways in which those entities behave. That information provides a map whose details are elucidated by mature scientific research. And since nature is too complex and varied to be explored at random, that map is as essential as observation and experiment to science's continuing development. Through the theories they embody, paradigms prove to be constitutive of the research activity. They are also, however, constitutive of science in other respects, and that is now the point. In particular, our most recent examples show that paradigms provide scientists not only with a map but also with some of the directions essential for map-making. In learning a paradigm the scientist acquires theory, methods, and standards together, usually in an inextricable mixture. Therefore, when paradigms change, there are usually significant shifts in the criteria determining the legitimacy both of problems and of proposed solutions.

That observation returns us to the point from which this section began, for it provides our first explicit indication of why the choice between competing paradigms regularly raises questions that cannot be resolved by the criteria of normal science. To the extent, as significant as it is incomplete, that two scientific schools disagree about what is a problem and what a solution, they will inevitably talk through each other when debating the relative merits of their respective paradigms. In the partially circular arguments that regularly result, each paradigm will be shown to satisfy more or less the criteria that it dictates for itself and to fall short of a few of those dictated by its opponent. There are other reasons, too, for the incompleteness of logical contact that consistently characterizes paradigm debates. For example, since no paradigm ever solves all the problems it defines and since no two paradigms leave all the same problems unsolved, paradigm debates always involve the question: Which problems is it more significant to have solved? Like the issue of competing standards, that question of values can be answered only in terms of criteria that lie outside of normal science altogether, and it is that recourse to external criteria that most obviously makes paradigm debates revolutionary. Something even more fundamental than standards and values is, however, also at stake. I have so far argued only that paradigms are constitutive of science. Now I wish to display a sense in which they are constitutive of nature as well.

Notes

1. Silvanus P. Thompson, *Life of William Thomson Baron Kelvin of Largs* (London, 1910), I, 266–81.
2. See, for example, the remarks by P. P. Wiener in *Philosophy of Science*, XXV (1958), 298.
3. James B. Conant, *Overthrow of the Phlogiston Theory* (Cambridge, 1950), pp. 13–16; and J. R. Partington, *A Short History of Chemistry* (2d ed.; London, 1951), pp. 85–88. The fullest and most sympathetic account of the phlogiston theory's achievements is by H. Metzger, *Newton, Stahl, Boerhaave et la doctrine chimique* (Paris, 1930), Part II.
4. Compare the conclusions reached through a very different sort of analysis by R. B. Braithwaite, *Scientific Explanation* (Cambridge, 1953), pp. 50–87, esp. p. 76.
5. For corpuscularism in general, see Marie Boas, "The Establishment of the Mechanical Philosophy," *Osiris*, X (1952), 412–541. For the effect of particle shape on taste, see *ibid.*, p. 483.
6. R. Dugas, *La mécanique au XVIIe siècle* (Neuchatel, 1954), pp. 177–85, 284–98, 345–56.
7. I. B. Cohen, *Franklin and Newton: An Inquiry into Speculative Newtonian Experimental Science and Franklin's Work in Electricity as an Example Thereof* (Philadelphia, 1956), chaps. vi–vii.
8. For electricity, see *ibid.*, chaps. viii–ix. For chemistry, see Metzger, *op. cit.*, Part I.
9. E. Meyerson, *Identity and Reality* (New York, 1930), chap. x.
10. E. T. Whittaker, *A History of the Theories of Aether and Electricity*, II (London, 1953), 28–30.
11. For a brilliant and entirely up-to-date attempt to fit scientific development into this Procrustean bed, see C. C. Gillispie, *The Edge of Objectivity: An Essay in the History of Scientific Ideas* (Princeton, 1960).

Chapter 8
Natural Kinds
W. V. O. Quine

What tends to confirm an induction? This question has been aggravated on the one hand by Hempel's puzzle of the non-black non-ravens,[1] and exacerbated on the other by Goodman's puzzle of the grue emeralds.[2] I shall begin my remarks by relating the one puzzle to the other, and the other to an innate flair that we have for natural kinds. Then I shall devote the rest of the chapter to reflections on the nature of this notion of natural kinds and its relation to science.

Hempel's puzzle is that just as each black raven tends to confirm the law that all ravens are black, so each green leaf, being a non-black non-raven, should tend to confirm the law that all non-black things are non-ravens, that is, again, that all ravens are black. What is paradoxical is that a green leaf should count toward the law that all ravens are black.

Goodman propounds his puzzle by requiring us to imagine that emeralds, having been identified by some criterion other than color, are now being examined one after another and all up to now are found to be green. Then he proposes to call anything *grue* that is examined today or earlier and found to be green or is not examined before tomorrow and is blue. Should we expect the first one examined tomorrow to be green, because all examined up to now were green? But all examined up to now were also grue; so why not expect the first one tomorrow to be grue, and therefore blue?

The predicate "green," Goodman says,[3] is *projectible*; "grue" is not. He says this by way of putting a name to the problem. His step toward solution is his doctrine of what he calls entrenchment,[4] which I shall touch on later. Meanwhile the terminological point is simply that projectible predicates are predicates ζ and η whose shared instances all do count, for whatever reason, toward confirmation of [All ζ are η].

Now I propose assimilating Hempel's puzzle to Goodman's by inferring from Hempel's that the complement of a projectible predicate need not be projectible. "Raven" and "black" are projectible; a black raven does count toward "All ravens are black." Hence a black raven counts also, indirectly, toward "All non-black things are non-ravens," since this says the same thing. But a green leaf does not count toward "All non-black things are non-ravens," nor, therefore, toward "All ravens are black"; "non-black" and "non-raven" are not projectible. "Green" and "leaf" are projectible, and the green leaf counts toward "All leaves are green" and "All green things are leaves"; but only a black raven can confirm "All ravens are black," the complements not being projectible.

If we see the matter in this way, we must guard against saying that a statement [All ζ are η] is lawlike only if ζ and η are projectible. "All non-black things are non-ravens" is a law despite its nonprojectible terms, since it is equivalent to "All ravens are black."

Reprinted from *Ontological Relativity and Other Essays* (New York: Columbia University Press, 1969), pp. 114–138, by permission of the publisher and the author. Copyright 1969 by Columbia University Press.

Any statement is lawlike that is logically *equivalent* to [All ζ are η] for some projectible ζ and η.[5]

Having concluded that the complement of a projectible predicate need not be projectible, we may ask further whether there is *any* projectible predicate whose complement is projectible. I can conceive that there is not, when complements are taken strictly. We must not be misled by limited or relative complementation; "male human" and "nonmale human" are indeed both projectible.

To get back now to the emeralds, why do we expect the next one to be green rather than grue? The intuitive answer lies in similarity, however subjective. Two green emeralds are more similar than two grue ones would be if only one of the grue ones were green. Green things, or at least green emeralds, are a kind.[6] A projectible predicate is one that is true of all and only the things of a kind. What makes Goodman's example a puzzle, however, is the dubious scientific standing of a general notion of similarity, or of kind.

The dubiousness of this notion is itself a remarkable fact. For surely there is nothing more basic to thought and language than our sense of similarity; our sorting of things into kinds. The usual general term, whether a common noun or a verb or an adjective, owes its generality to some resemblance among the things referred to. Indeed, learning to use a word depends on a double resemblance: first, a resemblance between the present circumstances and past circumstances in which the word was used, and second, a phonetic resemblance between the present utterance of the word and past utterances of it. And every reasonable expectation depends on resemblance of circumstances, together with our tendency to expect similar causes to have similar effects.

The notion of a kind and the notion of similarity or resemblance seem to be variants or adaptations of a single notion. Similarity is immediately definable in terms of kind; for, things are similar when they are two of a kind. The very words for "kind' and "similar" tend to run in etymologically cognate pairs. Cognate with "kind" we have "akin" and "kindred." Cognate with "liken we have "ilk." Cognate with "similar" and "same" and "resemble" there are "*sammeln*" and "assemble," suggesting a gathering into kinds.

We cannot easily imagine a more familiar or fundamental notion than this, or a notion more ubiquitous in its applications. On this score it is like the notions of logic: like identity, negation, alternation, and the rest. And yet, strangely, there is something logically repugnant about it. For we are baffled when we try to relate the general notion of similarity significantly to logical terms. One's first hasty suggestion might be to say that things are similar when they have all or most or many properties in common. Or, trying to be less vague, one might try defining comparative similarity— "*a* is more similar to *b* than to *c*"—as meaning that *a* shares more properties with *b* than with *c*. But any such course only reduces our problem to the unpromising task of settling what to count as a property.

The nature of the problem of what to count as a property can be seen by turning for a moment to set theory. Things are viewed as going together into sets in any and every combination, describable and indescribable. Any two things are joint members of any number of sets. Certainly then we cannot define "*a* is more similar to *b* than to *c*" to mean that *a* and *b* belong jointly to more sets than *a* and *c* do. If properties are to support this line of definition where sets do not, it must be because properties do not, like sets, take things in every random combination. It must be that properties are shared only by things that are significantly similar. But properties in such a sense are no clearer than kinds. To start with such a notion of property, and define similarity on that basis, is no better than accepting similarity as undefined.

The contrast between properties and sets which I suggested just now must not be confused with the more basic and familiar contrast between properties, as intensional, and sets as extensional. Properties are intensional in that they may be counted as distinct properties even though wholly coinciding in respect of the things that have them. There is no call to reckon kinds as intensional. Kinds can be seen as sets, determined by their members. It is just that not all sets are kinds.

If similarity is taken simple-mindedly as a yes-or-no afair, with no degrees, then there is no containing of kinds within broader kinds. For, as remarked, similarity now simply means belonging to some one same kind. If all colored things comprise a kind, then all colored things count as similar, and the set of all red things is too narrow to count as a kind. If on the other hand the set of all red things counts as a kind, then colored things do not all count as similar, and the set of all colored things is too broad to count as a kind. We cannot have it both ways. Kinds can, however, overlap; the red things can comprise one kind, the round another.

When we move up from the simple dyadic relation of similarity to the more serious and useful triadic relation of comparative similarity, a correlative change takes place in the notion of kind. Kinds come to admit now not only of overlapping but also of containment one in another. The set of all red things and the set of all colored things can now both count as kinds; for all colored things can now be counted as resembling one another more than some things do, even though less, on the whole, than red ones do.

At this point, of course, our trivial definition of similarity as sameness of kind breaks down; for almost any two things could count now as common members of some broad kind or other, and anyway we now want to define comparative or triadic similarity. A definition that suggests itself is this: a is more similar to b than to c when a and b belong jointly to more kinds than a and c do. But even this works only for finite systems of kinds.

The notion of kind and the notion of similarity seemed to be substantially one notion. We observed further that they resist reduction to less dubious notions, as of logic or set theory. That they at any rate be definable each in terms of the other seems little enough to ask. We just saw a somewhat limping definition of comparative similarity in terms of kinds. What now of the converse project, definition of kind in terms of similarity?

One may be tempted to picture a kind, suitable to a comparative similarity relation, as any set which is "qualitatively spherical" in this sense: it takes in exactly the things that differ less than so-and-so much from some central norm. If without serious loss of accuracy we can assume that there are one or more actual things (*paradigm cases*) that nicely exemplify the desired norm, and one or more actual things (*foils*) that deviate just barely too much to be counted into the desired kind at all, then our definition is easy: *the kind with paradigm a and foil b* is the set of all the things to which a is more similar than a is to b. More generally, then, a set may be said to be a *kind* if and only if there are a and b, known or unknown, such that the set is the kind with paradigm a and foil b.

If we consider examples, however, we see that this definition does not give us what we want as kinds. Thus take red. Let us grant that a central shade of red can be picked as norm. The trouble is that the paradigm cases, objects in just that shade of red, can come in all sorts of shapes, weights, sizes, and smells. Mere degree of overall similarity to any one such paradigm case will afford little evidence of degree of redness, since it will depend also on shape, weight, and the rest. If our assumed relation of comparative similarity were just comparative chromatic similarity, then our paradigm-and-foil definition of kind would indeed accommodate redkind. What the definition will not do is distill purely chromatic kinds from mixed similarity.

A different attempt, adapted from Carnap, is this: a set is a kind if all its members are more similar to one another than they all are to any one thing outside the set. In other words, each nonmember differs more from some member than that member differs from any member. However, as Goodman showed in a criticism of Carnap,[7] this construction succumbs to what Goodman calls the difficulty of imperfect community. Thus consider the set of all red round things, red wooden things, and round wooden things. Each member of this set resembles each other member somehow: at least in being red, or in being round, or in being wooden, and perhaps in two or all three of these respects or others. Conceivably, moreover, there is no one thing outside the set that resembles every member of the set to even the least of these degrees. The set then meets the proposed definition of kind. Yet surely it is not what anyone means by a kind. It admits yellow croquet balls and red rubber balls while excluding yellow rubber balls.

The relation between similarity and kind, then, is less clear and neat than could be wished. Definition of similarity in terms of kind is halting, and definition of kind in terms of similarity is unknown. Still the two notions are in an important sense correlative. They vary together. If we reassess something a as less similar to b than to c, where it had counted as more similar to b than to c, surely we will correspondingly permute a, b, and c in respect of their assignment to kinds; and conversely.

I have stressed how fundamental the notion of similarity or of kind is to our thinking, and how alien to logic and set theory. I want to go on now to say more about how fundamental these notions are to our thinking, and something also about their nonlogical roots. Afterward I want to bring out how the notion of similarity or of kind changes as science progresses. I shall suggest that it is a mark of maturity of a branch of science that the notion of similarity or kind finally dissolves, so far as it is relevant to that branch of science. That is, it ultimately submits to analysis in the special terms of that branch of science and logic.

For deeper appreciation of how fundamental similarity is, let us observe more closely how it figures in the learning of language. One learns by *ostension* what presentations to call yellow; that is, one learns by hearing the word applied to samples. All he has to go on, of course, is the similarity of further cases to the samples. Similarity being a matter of degree, one has to learn by trial and error how reddish or brownish or greenish a thing can be and still be counted yellow. When he finds he has applied the word too far out, he can use the false cases as samples to the contrary; and then he can proceed to guess whether further cases are yellow or not by considering whether they are more similar to the in-group or the out-group. What one thus uses, even at this primitive stage of learning, is a fully functioning sense of similarity, and relative similarity at that: a is more similar to b than to c.

All these delicate comparisons and shrewd inferences about what to call yellow are, in Sherlock Holmes's terminology, elementary. Mostly the process is unconscious. It is the same process by which an animal learns to respond in distinctive ways to his master's commands or other discriminated stimulations.

The primitive sense of similarity that underlies such learning has, we saw, a certain complexity of structure: a is more similar to b than to c. Some people have thought that it has to be much more complex still: that it depends irreducibly on *respects*, thus similarity in color, similarity in shape, and so on. According to this view, our learning of yellow by ostension would have depended on our first having been told or somehow apprised that it was going to be a question of color. Now hints of this kind are a great help, and in our learning we often do depend on them. Still one would like to be able to show that a single general standard of similarity, but of course comparative similarity, is all we need, and that respects can be abstracted afterward. For instance, suppose the child has learned of a yellow ball and block that they count as yellow, and of a red ball and block that they do not, and now he has to decide about a yellow cloth. Presumably he will find the cloth more similar to the yellow ball and to the yellow block than to the red ball or red block; and he will not have needed any prior schooling in colors and respects. Carnap undertook to show long ago how some respects, such as color, could by an ingenious construction be derived from a general similarity notion;[8] however, this development is challenged, again, by Goodman's difficulty of imperfect community.

A standard of similarity is in some sense innate. This point is not against empiricism; it is a commonplace of behavioral psychology. A response to a red circle, if it is rewarded, will be elicited again by a pink ellipse more readily than by a blue triangle; the red circle resembles the pink ellipse more than the blue triangle. Without some such prior spacing of qualities, we could never acquire a habit; all stimuli would be equally alike and equally different. These spacings of qualities, on the part of men and other animals, can be explored and mapped in the laboratory by experiments in conditioning and extinction.[9] Needed as they are for all learning, these distinctive spacings cannot themselves all be learned; some must be innate.

If then I say that there is an innate standard of similarity, I am making a condensed statement that can be interpreted, and truly interpreted, in behavioral terms. Moreover, in this behavioral sense it can be said equally of other animals that they have an innate standard of similarity too. It is part of our animal birthright. And, interestingly enough, it is characteristically animal in its lack of intellectual status. At any rate we noticed earlier how alien the notion is to mathematics and logic.

This innate qualitative spacing of stimulations was seen to have one of its human uses in the ostensive learning of words like "yellow." I should add as a cautionary remark that this is not the only way of learning words, nor the commonest; it is merely the most rudimentary way. It works when the question of the reference of a word is a simple question of spread: how much of our surroundings counts as yellow, how much counts as water, and so on. Learning a word like "apple" or "square" is more complicated, because here we have to learn also where to say that one apple or square leaves off and another begins. The complication is that apples do not add up to an apple, nor squares, generally, to a square. "Yellow" and "water" are mass terms, concerned only with spread; "apple" and "square" are terms of divided reference, concerned with both spread and individuation. Ostension figures in the learning of terms of this latter kind too, but the process is more complex:[10] And then there are all the other sorts of words, all those abstract and neutral connectives and adverbs and all the recondite terms of scientific theory; and there are also the grammatical constructions themselves to be mastered. The learning of these things is less direct and more complex still. There are deep problems in this domain, but they lie aside from the present topic.

Our way of learning "yellow," then, gives less than a full picture of how we learn language. Yet more emphatically, it gives less than a full picture of the human use of an innate standard of similarity, or innate spacing of qualities. For, as remarked, every reasonable expectation depends on similarity. Again on this score, other animals are like man. Their expectations, if we choose so to conceptualize their avoidance movements and salivation and pressing of levers and the like, are clearly dependent on their appreciation of similarity. Or, to put matters in their methodological order, these avoidance movements and salivation and pressing of levers and the like are typical of what we have to go on in mapping the animals' appreciation of similarity, their spacing of qualities.

Induction itself is essentially only more of the same: animal expectation or habit formation. And the ostensive learning of words is an implicit case of induction. Implicitly the learner of "yellow" is working inductively toward a general law of English verbal behavior, though a law that he will never try to state; he is working up to where he can in general judge when an English speaker would assent to "yellow" and when not.

Not only is ostensive learning a case of induction; it is a curiously comfortable case of induction, a game of chance with loaded dice. At any rate this is so if, as seems plausible, each man's spacing of qualities is enough like his neighbor's. For the learner is generalizing on his yellow samples by similarity considerations, and his neighbors have themselves acquired the use of the word "yellow", in their day, by the same similarity considerations. The learner of "yellow" is thus making his induction in a friendly world. Always, induction expresses our hope that similar causes will have similar effects; but when the induction is the ostensive learning of a word, that pious hope blossoms into a foregone conclusion. The uniformity of people's quality spaces virtually assures that similar presentations will elicit similar verdicts.

It makes one wonder the more about other inductions, where what is sought is a generalization not about our neighbor's verbal behavior but about the harsh impersonal world. It is reasonable that our quality space should match our neighbor's, we being birds of a feather; and so the general trustworthiness of induction in the ostensive learning of words was a put-up job. To trust induction as a way of access to the truths of nature, on the other hand, is to suppose, more nearly, that our quality space matches that of the cosmos. The brute irrationality of our sense of similarity, its irrelevance to anything in logic and mathematics, offers little reason to expect that this sense is somehow in tune with the world—a world which, unlike language, we never made. Why induction should be trusted, apart from special cases such as the ostensive learning of words, is the perennial philosophical problem of induction.

One part of the problem of induction, the part that asks why there should be regularities in nature at all, can, I think, be dismissed. *That* there are or have been regularities, for whatever reason, is an established fact of science; and we cannot ask better than that. *Why* there have been regularities is an obscure question, for it is hard to see what would count as an answer. What does make clear sense is this other part of the problem of induction: why does our innate subjective spacing of qualities accord so well with the functionally relevant groupings in nature as to make our inductions tend to come out right? Why should our subjective spacing of qualities have a special purchase on nature and a lien on the future?

There is some encouragement in Darwin. If people's innate spacing of qualities is a gene-linked trait, then the spacing that has made for the most successful inductions will have tended to predominate through natural selection.[11] Creatures inveterately wrong in their inductions have a pathetic but praiseworthy tendency to die before reproducing their kind.

At this point let me say that I shall not be impressed by protests that I am using inductive generalizations, Darwin's and others, to justify induction, and thus reasoning in a circle. The reason I shall not be impressed by this is that my position is a naturalistic one; I see philosophy not as an *a priori* propaedeutic or groundwork for science, but as continuous with science. I philosophy and science as in the same boat—a boat which, to revert to Neurath's figure as I so often do, we can rebuild only at sea while staying afloat in it. There is no external vantage point, no first philosophy. All scientific findings, all scientific conjectures that are at present plausible, are therefore in my view as welcome for use in philosophy as elsewhere. For me then the problem of induction is a problem about the world: a problem of how we, as we now are (by our present scientific lights), in a world we never made, should stand better than random or coin-tossing chances of coming out right when we predict by inductions which are based on our innate, scientifically unjustified similarity standard. Darwin's natural selection is a plausible partial explanation.

It may, in view of a consideration to which I next turn, be almost explanation enough. This consideration is that induction, after all, has its conspicuous failures. Thus take color. Nothing in experience, surely, is more vivid and conspicuous than color and its contrasts. And the remarkable fact, which has impressed scientists and philosophers as far back at least as Galileo and Descartes, is that the distinctions that matter for basic physical theory are mostly independent of color contrasts. Color impresses man; raven black impresses Hempel; emerald green impresses Goodman. But color is cosmically secondary. Even slight differences in sensory mechanisms from species to species, Smart remarks,[12] can make overwhelming differences in the grouping of things by color. Color is king in our innate quality space, but undistinguished in cosmic circles. Cosmically, colors would not qualify as kinds.

Color is helpful at the food-gathering level. Here it behaves well under induction, and here, no doubt, has been the survival value of our color-slanted quality space. It is just that contrasts that are crucial for such activities can be insignificant for broader and more theoretical science. If man were to live by basic science alone, natural selection would shift its support to the color-blind mutation.

Living as he does by bread and basic science both, man is torn. Things about his innate similarity sense that are helpful in the one sphere can be a hindrance in the other. Credit is due man's inveterate ingenuity, or human sapience, for having worked around the blinding dazzle of color vision and found the more significant regularities elsewhere. Evidently natural selection has dealt with the conflict by endowing man doubly: with both a color-slanted quality space and the ingenuity to rise above it.

He has risen above it by developing modified systems of kinds, hence modified similarity standards for scientific purposes. By the trial-and-error process of theorizing he has regrouped things into new kinds which prove to lend themselves to many inductions better than the old.

A crude example is the modification of the notion of fish by excluding whales and porpoises. Another taxonomic example is the grouping of kangaroos, opossums, and marsupial mice in a single kind, marsupials, while excluding ordinary mice. By primitive standards the marsupial mouse is more similar to the ordinary mouse than to the kangaroo; by theoretical standards the reverse is true.

A theoretical kind need not be a modification of an intuitive one. It may issue from theory full-blown, without antecedents; for instance the kind which comprises positively charged particles.

We revise our standards of similarity or of natural kinds on the strength, as Goodman remarks,[13] of second-order inductions. New groupings, hypothetically adopted at the suggestion of a growing theory, prove favorable to inductions and so become "entrenched." We newly establish the projectibility of some predicate, to our satisfaction, by successfully trying to project it. In induction nothing succeeds like success.

Between an innate similarity notion or spacing of qualities and a scientifically sophisticated one, there are all gradations. Sciences, after all, differs from common sense only in degree of methodological sophistication. Our experiences from earliest infancy are bound to have overlaid our innate spacing of qualities by modifying and supplementing our grouping habits little by little, inclining us more and more to an appreciation of theoretical kinds and similarities, long before we reach the point of studying science systematically as such. Moreover, the later phases do not wholly supersede the earlier; we retain different similarity standards, different systems of kinds, for use in different contexts. We all still say that a marsupial mouse is more like an ordinary mouse than a kangaroo, except when we are concerned with genetic matters. Something like our innate quality space continues to function alongside the more sophisticated regroupings that have been found by scientific experience to facilitate induction.

We have seen that a sense of similarity or of kinds is fundamental to learning in the widest sense—to language learning, to induction, to expectation. Toward a further appreciation of how utterly this notion permeates our thought, I want now to point out a number of other very familiar and central notions which seem to depend squarely on this one. They are notions that are definable in terms of similarity, or kinds, and further irreducible.

A notable domain of examples is the domain of dispositions, such as Carnap's example of solubility in water. To say of some individual object that it is soluble in water is not to say merely that it always dissolves when in water, because this would be true by default of any object, however insoluble, if it merely happened to be destined never to get into water. It is to say rather that it *would* dissolve if it were in water; but this account brings small comfort, since the device of a subjunctive conditional involves all the perplexities of disposition terms and more. Thus far I simply repeat Carnap.[14] But now I want to point out what could be done in this connection with the notion of kind. Intuitively, what qualifies a thing as soluble though it never gets into water is that it is of the same kind as the things that actually did or will dissolve; it is similar to them. Strictly we can't simply say "*the* same kind," nor simply "similar," when we have wider and narrower kinds, less and more similarity. Let us then mend our definition by saying that the soluble things are the common members of *all* such kinds. A thing is soluble if *each* kind that is broad enough to embrace all actual victims of solution embraces it too.

Graphically the idea is this: we make a set of all the sometime victims, all the things that actually did or will dissolve in water, and then we add just enough other things to round the set out into a kind. This is the water-soluble kind.

If this definition covers just the desired things, the things that are really soluble in water, it owes its success to a circumstance that could be otherwise. The needed circumstance is that a sufficient variety of things actually get dissolved in water to assure their not all falling under any one kind narrower than the desired water-soluble kind itself. But it is a plausible circumstance, and I am not sure that its accidental character is a drawback. If the trend of events had been otherwise, perhaps the solubility concept would not have been wanted.

However, if I seem to be defending this definition, I must now hasten to add that of course it has much the same fault as the definition which used the subjunctive conditional. This definition uses the unreduced notion of kind, which is certainly not a notion we want to rest with either; neither theoretical kind nor intuitive kind. My purpose in giving the definition is only to show the link between the problem of dispositions and the problem of kinds.

As between theoretical and intuitive kinds, certainly the theoretical ones are the ones wanted for purposes of defining solubility and other dispositions of scientific concern. Perhaps "amiable" and "reprehensible" are disposition terms whose definitions should draw rather on intuitive kinds.[15]

Another dim notion, which has intimate connections with dispositions and subjunctive conditionals, is the notion of cause; and we shall see that it too turns on the notion of kinds. Hume explained cause as invariable succession, and this makes sense as long as the cause and effect are referred to by general terms. We can say that fire causes heat, and we can mean thereby, as Hume would have it, that each event classifiable under the head of fire is followed by an event classifiable under the head of heat, or heating up. But this account, whatever its virtues for these general causal statements, leaves singular causal statements unexplained.

What does it mean to say that the kicking over of a lamp in Mrs. Leary's barn caused the Chicago fire? It cannot mean merely that the event at Mrs. Leary's belongs to a set, and the Chicago fire belongs to a set, such that there is invariable succession between the two sets: every member of the one set is followed by a member of the other. This paraphrase is trivially true and too weak. Always, if one event happens to be followed by another, the two belong to *certain* sets between which there is invariable succession. We can rig the sets arbitrarily. Just put any arbitrary events in the first set, including the first of the two events we are interested in; and then in the other set put the second of those two events, together with other events that happen to have occurred just after the other members of the first set.

Because of this way of trivialization, a singular causal statement says no more than that the one event was followed by the other. That is, it says no more if we use the definition just now contemplated; which, therefore, we must not. The trouble with that definition is clear enough: it is the familiar old trouble of the promiscuity of sets. Here, as usual, kinds, being more discriminate, enable us to draw distinctions where sets do not. To say that one event caused another is to say that the two events are of *kinds* between which there is invariable succession. If this correction does not yet take care of Mrs. Leary's cow, the fault is only with invariable succession itself, as affording too simple a definition of general causal statements; we need to hedge it around with provisions for partial or contributing causes and a good deal else. That aspect of the causality problem is not my concern. What I wanted to bring out is just the relevance of the notion of kinds, as the needed link between singular and general causal statements.

We have noticed that the notion of kind, or similarity, is crucially relevant to the notion of disposition, to the subjunctive conditional, and to singular causal statements. From a scientific point of view these are a pretty disreputable lot. The notion of kind, or similarity, is equally disreputable. Yet some such notion, some similarity sense, was seen to be crucial to all learning, and central in particular to the processes of inductive generalization and prediction which are the very life of science. It appears that science is rotten to the core.

Yet there may be claimed for this rot a certain undeniable fecundity. Science reveals hidden mysteries, predicts successfully, and works technological wonders. If this is the way of rot, then rot is rather to be prized and praised than patronized.

Rot, actually, is not the best model here. A better model is human progress. A sense of comparative similarity, I remarked earlier, is one of man's animal endowments. Insofar as it fits in with regularities of nature, so as to afford us reasonable success in our primitive inductions and expectations, it is presumably an evolutionary product of natural selection. Secondly, as remarked, one's sense of similarity or one's system of kinds develops and changes and even turns multiple as one matures, making perhaps for increasingly dependable prediction. And at length standards of similarity set in which are geared to theoretical science. This development is a development away from the immediate, subjective, animal sense of similarity to the remoter objectivity of a similarity determined by scientific hypotheses and posits and constructs. Things are similar in the later or theoretical sense to the degree that they are interchangeable parts of the cosmic machine revealed by science.

This progress of similarity standards, in the course of each individual's maturing years, is a sort of recapitulation in the individual of the race's progress from muddy savagery. But the similarity notion even in its theoretical phase is itself a muddy notion still. We have offered no definition of it in satisfactory scientific terms. We of course have a behavioral definition of what counts, for a given individual, as similar to what, or as more similar to what than to what; we have this for similarity old and new, human and animal. But it is no definition of what it means really for a to be more similar to b than to c; really, and quite apart from this or that psychological subject.

Did I already suggest a definition to this purpose, metaphorically, when I said that things are similar to the extent that they are interchangeable parts of the cosmic machine? More literally, could things be said to be similar in proportion to how much of scientific theory would remain true on interchanging those things as Objects of reference in the theory? This only hints a direction; consider for instance the dimness of "how much theory." Anyway the direction itself is not a good one; for it would make similarity depend in the wrong way on theory. A man's judgments of similarity do and should depend on his theory, on his beliefs; but similarity itself, what the man's judgments purport to be judgments of, purports to be an objective relation in the world. It belongs in the subject matter not of our theory of theorizing about the world, but of our theory of the world itself. Such would be the acceptable and reputable sort of similarity concept, if it could be defined.

It does get defined in bits: bits suited to special branches of science. In this way, on many limited fronts, man continues his rise from savagery, sloughing off the muddy old notion of kind or similarity piecemeal, a vestige here and a vestige there. Chemistry, the home science of water-solubility itself, is one branch that has reached this stage. Comparative similarity of the sort that matters for chemistry can be stated outright in chemical terms, that is, in terms of chemical composition. Molecules will be said to *match* if they contain atoms of the same elements in the same topological combinations. Then, in principle, we might get at the comparative similarity of objects a and b by considering how many pairs of matching molecules there are, one molecule from a and one from b each time, and how many unmatching pairs. The ratio gives even a theoretical measure of relative similarity, and thus abundantly explains what it is for a to be more similar to b than to c. Or we might prefer to complicate our definition by allowing also for degrees in the matching of molecules; molecules having almost equally many atoms, or having atoms whose atomic numbers or atomic weights are almost equal, could be reckoned as matching better than others. At any rate a lusty chemical similarity concept is assured.

From it, moreover, an equally acceptable concept of kinds is derivable, by the paradigm-and-foil definition noted early in this paper. For it is a question now only of distilling purely chemical kinds from purely chemical similarity; no admixture of other respects of similarity interferes. We thus exonerate water-solubility, which, the last time around, we had reduced no further than to an unexplained notion of kind. Therewith also the associated subjunctive conditional, "If this were in water it would dissolve," gets its bill of health.

The same scientific advances that have thus provided a solid underpinning for the definition of solubility in terms of kinds, have also, ironically enough, made that line of definition pointless by providing a full understanding of the mechanism of solution. One can redefine water-solubility by simply describing the structural conditions of that mechanism. This embarrassment of riches is, I suspect, a characteristic outcome. That is, once we can legitimize a disposition term by defining the relevant similarity standard, we are apt to know the mechanism of the disposition, and so bypass the similarity. Not but that the similarity standard is worth clarifying too, for its own sake or for other purposes.

Philosophical or broadly scientific motives can impel us to seek still a basic and absolute concept of similarity, along with such fragmentary similarity concepts as suit special branches of science. This drive for a cosmic similarity concept is perhaps identifiable with the age-old drive to reduce things to their elements. It epitomizes the scientific spirit, though dating back to the pre-Socratics: to Empedocles with his theory of four elements, and above all to Democritus with his atoms. The modern physics of elementary particles, or of hills in space-time, is a more notable effort in this direction.

This idea of rationalizing a single notion of relative similarity, throughout its cosmic sweep, has its metaphysical attractions. But there would remain still need also to rationalize the similarity notion more locally and superficially, so as to capture only such similarity as is relevant to some special science. Our chemistry example is already a case of this, since it stops short of full analysis into neutrons, electrons, and the other elementary particles.

A more striking example of superficiality, in this good sense, is afforded by taxonomy, say in zoology. Since learning about the evolution of species, we are in a position to define comparative similarity suitably for this science by consideration of family trees. For a theoretical measure of the degree of similarity of two individual animals we can devise some suitable function that depends on proximity and frequency of their common ancestors. Or a more significant concept of degree of similarity might be devised in terms of genes. When kind is construed in terms of any such similarity concept, fishes in the corrected, whale-free sense of the word qualify as a kind while fishes in the more inclusive sense do not.

Different similarity measures, or relative similarity notions, best suit different branches of science; for there are wasteful complications in providing for finer gradations of relative similarity than matter for the phenomena with which the particular science is concerned. Perhaps the branches of science could be revealingly classified by looking to the relative similarity notion that is appropriate to each. Such a plan is reminiscent of Felix Klein's so-called *Erlangerprogramm* in geometry, which involved characterizing the various branches of geometry by what transformations were irrelevant to each. But a branch of science would only qualify for recognition and classification under such a plan when it had matured to the point of clearing up its similarity notion. Such branches of science would qualify further as unified, or integrated into our inclusive systematization of nature, only insofar as their several similarity concepts were *compatible*; capable of meshing, that is, and differing only in the fineness of their discriminations.

Disposition terms and subjunctive conditionals in these areas, where suitable senses of similarity and kind are forthcoming, suddenly turn respectable; respectable and, in principle, superfluous. In other domains they remain disreputable and practically indispensable. They may be seen perhaps as unredeemed notes; the theory that would clear up the unanalyzed underlying similarity notion in such cases is still to come. An example is the disposition called intelligence—the ability, vaguely speaking, to learn quickly and to solve problems. Sometime, whether in terms of proteins or colloids or nerve nets or overt behavior, the relevant branch of science may reach the stage where a similarity notion can be constructed capable of making even the notion of intelligence respectable. And superfluous.

In general we can take it as a very special mark of the maturity of a branch of science that it no longer needs an irreducible notion of similarity and kind. It is that final stage where the animal vestige is wholly absorbed into the theory. In this career of the similarity notion, starting in its innate phase, developing over the years in the light of accumulated experience, passing then from the intuitive phase into theoretical similarity, and finally disappearing altogether, we have a paradigm of the evolution of unreason into science.

Notes

1. C. G. Hempel, *Aspects of Scientific Explanation and Other Essays* (New York: Free Press, 1965), p. 15.
2. Nelson Goodman, *Fact, Fiction, and Forecast* (Cambridge, Mass., 1955, or New York: Bobbs-Merrill, 1965), p. 74. I am indebted to Goodman and to Burton Dreben for helpful criticisms of earlier drafts of the present paper.
3. Goodman, *Fact*, pp. 82 f.
4. *Ibid.*, pp 95 ff.
5. I mean this only as a sufficient condition of lawlikeness. See Donald Davidson, "Emeroses by other names," *Journal Of Philosophy* 63 (1966), 778–780.
6. This relevance of kind is noted by Goodman, *Fact*, first edition, pp. 119 f; second edition, pp. 121 f.
7. Nelson Goodman, *The Structure of Appearance*, 2d ed. (New York: Bobbs-Merrill, 1966), pp. 163 f.
8. Rudolf Carnap, *The Logical Structure of the World* (California, 1967), pp. 141–147. (German edition 1928).
9. See my *Word and Object*, pp. 83 f, for further discussion and references.
10. See *Word and Object*, pp. 90–95.
11. This was noted by S. Watanabe on the second page of his paper "Une explication mathématique du classement d'objets," in S. Dockx and P. Bernays, eds., *Information and Prediction in Science* (New York: Academy Press, 1965).
12. J. J. C. Smart, *Philosophy and Scientific Realism* (New York: Humanities, 1963), pp. 68–72.
13. Goodman, *Fact*, pp. 95 ff.
14. Carnap, "Testability and meaning," *Philosophy of Science* 3 (1936), 419–471; 4 (1937), 1–40.
15. Here there followed, in previous printings, 26 lines which I have deleted. They were concerned with explaining certain subjunctive conditionals on the basis of the notion of kind. Paul Berent pointed out to me that the formulation was wrong, for it would have equated those conditionals to their converses.

Chapter 9

Explanation and Reference

Hilary Putnam

I. General Significance of the Topic

In this paper I try to contrast Marxist (and more broadly realist) theories of meaning with what may be called 'idealist' theories of meaning. But a word of explanation is clearly in order.

There is no Marxist 'theory of meaning' as such, but there are a series of remarks on the correspondence between concepts and things, on concepts, and on the impossibility of a priori knowledge in the writings of Engels and Lenin[1] which clearly bear on problems of meaning and reference, and which constitute the starting point for such a theory. In particular, there is a passage[2] in which Engels makes the point that a concept may contain elements which are not true of the things which correspond to that concept. Engels's example is the concept *fish*. A contemporary scientific characterization of fish would include, Engels says, such properties as life under water and breathing through gills; yet lungfish and other anomalous species which lack these properties are classified as fish for scientific purposes. And Engels argues, I think correctly, that to stick to the letter of the 'definition' in applying the concept *fish* would be bad science. In short, Engels contends that:

(1) Our scientific conception (I would say 'stereotype') of a fish includes the property 'breathing through gills', but

(2) 'All fish breath through gills' is not true! (and, *a fortiori*, not analytic).

I do not wish to ascribe to Engels an anachronistic sophistication about contemporary logical issues, but without doing this it is fair to say on the basis of this argument that Engels *rejects* the model according to which such a concept as *fish* provides anything like analytically necessary and sufficient conditions for membership in a natural kind. Two further points are of importance: (1) The fact that the concept "natural kind *all* of whose members live under water, breath through gills, etc." does not strictly fit the natural kind Fish does not mean that the concept does not *correspond* to the natural kind Fish. As Engels puts it, the concept is not exactly correct (as a description of the corresponding natural kind) but that does not make it a *fiction*. (2) The concept is continually changing as a result of the impact of scientific discoveries, but that does not mean that it ceases to correspond to the same natural kind (which is itself, of course, also changing). Again, without attributing to Engels a sophisticated theory of meaning and reference, it is fair, I think, to restate the essential gist of these two points in the following way: concepts which are not strictly true of anything may yet refer to something; and concepts in different theories may refer to the same thing. Of these two points, the second is obvious for most realists; with a few possible

Reprinted from *Conceptual Change*, ed. G. Pearce and P. Maynard (Dordrecht: Reidel, 1973), pp. 199–221, by permission of the author and the publisher. Copyright 1973 by Kluwer Academic Publishers.

exceptions (e.g., Paul Feyerabend), realists have held that there are successive scientific theories about the *same* things: about heat, about electricity, about electrons, and so forth; and this involves treating such terms as 'electricity' as *transtheoretical* terms, as Dudley Shapere has called them,[3] i.e., as terms that have the same reference in different theories. The first point is more controversial; the idea that concepts provide necessary and sufficient conditions for class membership has often been attacked but, nonetheless, constantly reappears. Without it, however, the other point is moot. Bohr took it for granted that there are (at every time) numbers p and q such that the (one dimensional) position of a particle is q and the (one dimensional) momentum is p; if this was part of the meaning of "particle" for Bohr, and in addition, "part of the meaning" means "necessary condition for membership in the extension of a term," then electrons are *not* particles in Bohr's sense, and, indeed, there are *no* particles "in Bohr's sense". (And no "electrons" in Bohr's sense of 'electron', etc.) In fact, none of the terms in Bohr's theory referred! It follows on this account that we cannot say that present electron theory is a better theory of the same particles that Bohr was referring to. I take it that this is the line of thinking that Paul Feyerabend represents. On an account like Engels's, however, Bohr would have been referring to electrons when he used the word 'electron', notwithstanding the fact that some of his beliefs about electrons were mistaken, and *we* are referring to those same particles notwithstanding the fact that some of our beliefs—even beliefs included in our scientific "definition" of the term 'electron'—may very likely turn out to be equally mistaken. This seems right to me, and likewise Shapere's recent emphasis on the idea that such terms as 'electron' are *transtheoretical* seems to me right and important. The main technical contribution of this paper will be a sketch of a theory of meaning which supports Engels's and Shapere's insights.

An "idealist" theory of meaning, as I am using the term, might go like this (in its simplest form): the meaning of such a sentence as 'electrons exist' is a function of certain *predictions* that can be derived from it (in a pure idealist theory, these would have to be predictions about *sensations*); these predictions are clearly a function of the *theory* in which the sentence occurs; thus 'electrons exist' has no meaning apart from this, that or the other theory, and it has a different meaning in different theories.

The question of "reference" is a harder one for an idealist: the essence of idealism is to view scientific theories and concepts as instruments for predicting sensations and not as representatives of real things and magnitudes. But a sophisticated idealist is likely to say that the question of reference is "trivial",[4] if one has a scientific language L containing the term 'electron', then one can certainly construct a metalanguage ML over it *a là* Tarski, and define "reference" in such a way that "'electron' refers to electrons" is a trivial theorem. But if different scientific theories T_1 and T_2 are associated with different formal languages L_1 and L_2 (as they must be if the words have different meanings in T_1 and T_2), then they will be associated with different *meta*languages ML_1 and ML_2. In ML_1 we can say "'electron' refers to electrons," meaning that 'electron' in the sense of T_1 refers to electrons *in the sense of* T_1, and in ML_2 we can say "'electron' refers to electrons" meaning that 'electron' in the sense of T_2 refers to electrons *in the sense of* T_2; but there is no ML in which we can even express the statement that "electron" refers to the same entities in T_1 and T_2—or, at least, no prescription for constructing such an ML has been provided by positivist philosophers of science. In short, just as the idealist regards 'electron' as *theory dependent*, so does he regard the semantical notions of reference and truth as theory dependent; just as the Marxist (and, more generally, the realist) regards 'electron' as *transtheoretical*, so does he regard truth and reference as *transtheoretical*.

II. The Meaning of Physical Magnitude Terms

A. A Causal Account of Meaning

My purpose here is to sketch an account of the meaning of physical magnitude terms (e.g. 'temperature', 'electrical charge'); not an account of meaning in general, although I will try to indicate similarities between what is said here about these terms and what Kripke has said about proper names and what I have said elsewhere about natural kind words. (Kripke's work has come to me second hand; even so, I owe him a large debt for suggesting the idea of causal chains as the mechanism of reference.)

On a traditional view, any term has an intension and an extension. "Knowing the meaning" is having knowledge of the intension; what it is to "know" an intension (construed, usually, as an abstract entity of some kind) is never explained. The extension of the color term 'red', for example, is the class of red things; the intension, according to Carnap, is the property Red. Carnap spoke of "grasping" the intension of terms; what it would be the "grasp" the property Red was never explained; probably Carnap would have equated it with knowing how to verify sentences of the form "x is red," but this comes from his theory of knowledge, not his writings on semantics. In any case, understanding words is a matter of having knowledge. Full linguistic competence in connection with a word may require more knowledge than just the intension; for example, syntactical knowledge, knowledge of co-occurence regularities, etc.; but linguistic competence, like understanding, is a matter of *knowledge*—not necessarily explicit knowledge—knowledge in the wide sense, implicit as well as explicit, "knowing how" as well as "knowing that," skills and abilities as well as facts, but all *knowledge* none the less.

According to the theory I shall present this is fundamentally wrong. Linguistic competence and understanding are not just *knowledge*. To have linguistic competence in connection with a term it is not sufficient, in general, to have the full battery of usual linguistic knowledge and skills; one must, in addition, be in the right sort of relationship to certain distinguished situations (normally, though not necessarily, situations in which the *referent* of the term is present). It is for this reason that this sort of theory is called a "causal theory" of meaning.

Coming to physical magnitude terms, what every user of the term 'electricity' knows is that electricity is a magnitude of some sort—and, in fact, not even that: electricity was thought at one time to possibly be a sort of substance, and so was heat. At any rate, speakers know that "electricity" and "heat" are putative physical *quantities* —capable of more and less, and capable of location. (I do not think that even these statements are *analytic*, but I think they have a kind of *linguistic* association with the terms in question.) In a developed semantic theory one might introduce a special semantic marker, e.g., 'physical quantity', for terms of this sort. I cannot, however, think of anything that *every* user of the term 'electricity' *has* to know except that electricity is (associated with the notion of being) a physical magnitude of some sort, and, possibly, that "electricity" (or electrical charge or charges) is capable of flow or motion. Benjamin Franklin knew that "electricity" was manifested in the form of sparks and lightning bolts; someone else might know about currents and electromagnets; someone else might know about atoms consisting of positively and negatively charged particles. They could all use the term 'electricity' without there being a discernible "intension" that they all share. I want to suggest that what they do have in common is this: that each of them is connected by a certain kind of causal chain to a situation in which a *description* of electricity is given, and generally a *causal* description

—that is, one which singles out electricity as *the* physical magnitude *responsible* for certain effects in a certain way.

Thus, suppose I were standing next to Ben Franklin as he performed his famous experiment. Suppose he told me that "electricity" is a physical quantity which behaves in certain respects like a liquid (if he were a mathematician he might say "obeys an equation of continuity"); that it collects in clouds, and then, when a critical point of some kind is reached, a large quantity flows from the cloud to the earth in the form of a lightning bolt; that it runs along (or perhaps "through") his metal kite string; etc. He would have given me an *approximately correct definite description* of a physical magnitude. I could now use the term 'electricity' myself. Let us call this event—my acquiring the ability to use the term 'electricity' in this way—an *introducing event*. It is clear that each of my later uses will be causally connected to this introducing event, as long as those uses exemplify the ability I acquired in that introducing event. Even if I use the term so often that I forget when I first learned it, the intention to refer to the same magnitude that I referred to in the past by using the word links my present use to those earlier uses, and indeed the word's being in my present vocabulary at all is a causal product of earlier events—ultimately of the introducing event. If I teach the word to someone else by telling him that the word 'electricity' is the name of a physical magnitude, and by telling him certain facts about it which do not constitute a causal description—e.g., I might tell him that like charges repel and unlike charges attract, and that atoms consist of a nucleus with one kind of charge surrounded by satellite electrons with the opposite kind of charge—even if the facts I tell him do not constitute a definite description of any kind, let alone a causal description—still, the word's being in his vocabulary will be causally linked to its being in my vocabulary, and hence, ultimately, to an introducing event.

I said before that different speakers use the word 'electricity' without their being a discernible "intension" that they all share. If an "intension" is anything like a necessary and sufficient condition, then I think that this is right. But it does not follow that there are no ideas about electricity which are in some way linguistically associated with the word. Just as the idea that tigers are striped is linguistically associated with the word 'tiger', so it seems that some idea that "electricity" (i.e., electric charge or charges) is capable of flow or motion *is* linguistically associated with 'electricity'. And perhaps this is all—apart from being a physical magnitude or quantity in the sense described before—that is linguistically associated with the word.

Now then, if anyone knows that 'electricity' is the name of a physical quantity, and his use of the word is connected by the sort of causal chain I described before to an introducing event in which the causal description given was, in fact, a causal description of electricity, then we have a clear basis for saying that he uses the word to refer to electricity. Even if the causal description failed to describe electricity, if there is good reason to treat it as a misdescription *of electricity* (rather than as a description of nothing at all)—for example, if electricity was described as the physical magnitude with such-and-such properties which is responsible for such-and-such effects, where in fact electricity is not responsible for the effects in question, and the speaker intended to refer to the magnitude responsible for those effects, but mistakenly added the incorrect information "electricity has such-and-such properties" because he mistakenly thought that the magnitude responsible for those effects had those further properties—we still have a basis for saying that both the original speaker and the persons to whom he teaches the word use the word to refer to electricity.

If a number of speakers use the word 'electricity' to refer to electricity, and, in addition, they have the standard sorts of associations with the word—that it refers to a magnitude which can move or flow—then, I suggest, the question of whether it has "the same meaning" in their various idiolects simply does not arise. If a word is linguistically associated with a necessary and sufficient condition in the way that 'bachelor' is, then that sort of question *can* arise; but it does not arise, for example, in the case of proper names, and it does not arise, for a similar reason, in the case of physical magnitude terms. Thus if you know that 'Quine' is a name and I know that 'Quine' is a name and, in addition, we both refer to the same person when we use the word (even if the causal chains linking us to the referent are quite different) then the question of whether 'Quine' has the same meaning in my idiolect and in yours does not arise. More precisely: if the referent is the same, and we both associate the same minimal linguistic information with the word 'Quine', namely that it is a person's name, then the word is treated as the same word whether it occurs in your idiolect or in mine. Similarly, 'electricity' is the same word in Ben Franklin's idiolect and in mine. Of course, if you had wrong linguistic ideas about the name 'Quine'—for example, if you thought 'Quine' was a female name (not just that Quine was a woman, but that the name was restricted to females)—then there would be a difference in meaning.

This account stresses causal descriptions because physical magnitudes are invariably discovered through their effects, and so the natural way to first single out a physical magnitude is as the magnitude responsible for certain effects. Of course, the words 'responsible', 'causes', etc., do not literally have to occur in the description: *spin*, for example, was introduced by describing it as a physical magnitude having half-integral values characteristic of certain elementary particles, and giving a *law* connecting it with magnitudes previously introduced; I intend the notion of a causal description to include this case. And it is not a "necessary truth" that the description introducing a new physical magnitude should involve a notion of cause or law; but I am not trying in this paper to state "necessary truths".

Once the term 'electricity' has been introduced into someone's vocabulary (or into his "idiolect", as the dialect of a single speaker is called) whether by an introducing event, or by his learning the word from someone who learned it via an introducing event, or by his learning the word from someone linked by a chain of such transmissions to an introducing event, the referent in that person's idiolect is also fixed, even if no knowledge that that person has fixed it. And once the referent is fixed, one can use the word to formulate any number of theories about that referent (and even to formulate theoretical definitions of that referent which may be correct or incorrect scientific characterizations of that referent), without the word's being in any sense a different word in different theories. Thus the account just given fulfills the desideratum with which we started—it makes such terms as 'electricity' transtheoretical. The "operational criteria" you can give for the presence of electricity will depend strongly on what theory you accept; but, without the illicit identification of meaning with operational criteria, it does not follow at all that *meaning* depends on the theory you accept.

The possibility of formulating definite descriptions (or even misdescriptions) of physical magnitudes depends upon the availability in our language of such "broad spectrum" notions as *physical magnitude* and *causes*; that these play a crucial role in the introduction of physical magnitude terms was argued in a previous paper.[5] In that paper, however, I did not distinguish between *defining* what I then called theoretical terms and *introducing* them. Of course, if we have available a language in which we can formulate descriptions of the referents of our various physical magnitude terms, then we can consider the various theories that we have containing those terms as so many different systems of sentences in that one language. To the extent that we can do this, we can treat the notions of reference and truth appropriate to that language as transtheoretical notions also.

B. Kripke's Theory of Proper Names

I have already acknowledged a heavy indebtedness to Kripke's (unpublished) work on proper names. Since I have heard mainly secondhand reports of that work, I shall not attempt to describe it here in any great detail. But, as it has come down to me, the key idea is that a person may use a proper name to refer to a thing or person X even though he has *no* true beliefs about X. For example, suppose someone asks me who Quine is, and I falsely tell him that Quine was a Roman emperor. If he believes me, and if he goes on to use the word 'Quine' with the intention of referring to the person to whom *I* refer as Quine, then he will say such things as "Quine was a Roman emperor" —and he will be referring to a contemporary logician. Of course, he still has some true beliefs about Quine (beyond the belief that Quine is or was a person); for example, that Quine is or was named 'Quine'; but Kripke has more elaborate examples to show that even this is not always the case. On Kripke's view, the essential thing is this: that the use of a proper name to refer involves the existence of a causal chain of a certain kind connecting the user of the name (and the particular event of his using the name) to the bearer of the name.

Now then, I do not feel that one should be quite as liberal as Kripke is with respect to the causal chains one allows. I do not see much point, for example, in saying that someone is referring to Quine when he uses the name 'Quine' if he thinks that "Quine" was a Roman emperor, and that is all he "knows" about Quine; unless one has *some* beliefs about the bearer of the name which are true or approximately true, then it is at best idle to consider that the name refers to that bearer in one's idiolect. But what seems right about Kripke's account is that the knowledge an individual user of a language has need not at all fix the reference of the proper names in that individual's idiolect; the reference is fixed by the fact that that individual is causally linked to other individuals who were in a position to pick out the bearer of the name, or of some names from which the name descended. Indeed, what is important about Kripke's theory is not that the use of proper names is "causal"—what is not?—but that the use of proper names is *collective*. Anyone who uses a proper name to refer is, in a sense, a member of a collective which had "contact" with the bearer of the name: If it is surprising that a particular member of the collective need not have had such contact, and need not even have any good idea of the bearer of the name, it is only surprising because we think of language as private property.

The relationship of this theory of Kripke's to the above theory of physical magnitude terms should be obvious. Indeed, one might say that physical magnitude terms *are* proper names: they are proper names of *magnitudes* not *things*—however, this would be wrong, I think, since some physical magnitude terms (e.g., 'heat') are linguistically associated with rather rich information about the referent. The important thing about proper names is that it would be ridiculous to think that having linguistic competence can be equated in their case with knowledge of a necessary and sufficient condition—thus one is led to search for something other than the knowledge of the speaker which fixes the referent in their case.

It will be noted that I required a causal chain from the use of the physical magnitude term back to an introducing event—not back to an event in which the physical magnitude played a significant role. The reason is that, although no one in practice is going to be in a position to give a definite description of a physical magnitude unless he is causally connected to such an event, the nature of *that* causal chain seems not to matter. As long as one is in a position to give a definite description (or even a misdescription), one is in a position to introduce the term; and the chain from there on is something about which much more definite statements can be made. (In my opinion, it would be good to make a similar modification in Kripke's theory of proper names.)

C. Natural Kind Words

In an earlier paper[6] I presented an account of natural kind words (e.g. 'lemon') which has some relation to the present account of physical magnitude terms. I suggested that anyone who has linguistic competence in connection with "lemon" satisfies three conditions: (1) He has implicit knowledge of such facts as the fact that 'lemon' is a concrete noun, that it is the "name of a fruit", etc.—information given by classifing the word under certain natural syntactic and semantic "markers." I criticized Jerrold Katz for the view that natural systems of semantic markers can enable us to give the exact meaning of each term (or of *any* natural kind term); but *some* of the information associated with a word can naturally be represented by classifying the word under such familiar headings as 'noun', 'concrete', etc. (2) He associates the word with a certain "stereotype"—yellow color, tart taste, thick peel, etc. (3) He uses the word to *refer* to a certain natural kind—say, a natural kind of fruit whose most essential feature, from a biologist's point of view, might be a certain kind of DNA.

Two points were most important in the argument of that paper. The first was that the properties mentioned in the stereotype (and, I would add, the properties indicated by the semantic markers) are not being analytically predicated of each member of the extension, or, indeed, of any members of the extension. It is not analytic that all tigers have stripes, nor that some tigers have stripes; it is not analytic that all lemons are yellow, nor that some lemons are yellow; it is not even analytic that tigers are animals or that lemons are fruits. The stereotype is *associated* with the word; it is not a necessary and sufficient condition for membership in the corresponding class, nor even for being a normal member of the corresponding class. Engels's example of the word 'fish' fits right in here: what Engels was pointing out was precisely that the stereotype associated with the term 'fish' even in scientific, as opposed to lay, usage is not a necessary and sufficient condition. The second point was that speakers must be refer-ring to a particular natural kind for us to treat them as using the same word 'lemon', or 'aluminum', or whatever. The weakness of that paper, apart from being very poorly organized and presented, is that nothing positive is said about the conditions under which a speaker who uses a word (say 'aluminum' or 'elm tree') is referring to one set of things rather than another. Clearly, the speaker who uses the word 'aluminum' need not be able to tell aluminum from molybdenum, and the speaker who use the term 'elm tree' cannot tell elm trees from beech trees if he happens to be me. But then what does determine the reference of the terms 'aluminum' and 'molybdenum' in my idiolect? In the previous paper, I suggested that the reference is fixed by a test known to experts; it now seems to me that this is just a special case of my use being causally connected to an introducing event. For natural kind words too, then, linguistic competence is a matter of knowledge plus causal connection to introducing events (and ultimately to members of the natural kind itself). And this is so for the same reason as in the case of physical magnitude terms; namely, that the use of a natural kind word involves in many cases membership in a "collective" which has contact with the natural kind, which knows of tests for membership in the natural kind, etc., only as a collective. The idea that linguistic competence in connection with a natural kind word involves more than just having the right extension or reference (where this is now explained via a causal account), but also associating the right stereotype seems to me to carry over to physical magnitude words. Natural kind words can be associated with "strong" stereotypes (stereotypes that give a strong picture of a stereotypical member—even to the point of enabling one to tell, in most cases, if something belongs to the natural kind), as in the case of 'lemon' or 'tiger', or with "weak" stereotypes (stereotypes that give no idea of what a sufficient condition for membership in the class would be) as in the case of 'molybdenum' or (unless I am a very atypical speaker) 'elm'. Similarly, it seems to me that the physical magnitude term 'temperature' is associated with a very strong stereotype, and "electricity" with a weak one.

D. Objections and Questions

It is obvious that the account presented here must face certain hard questions. Without attempting to think of all of them myself, I should like to list a few that may help to launch discussion.

(1) One question that must be faced by all causal theories of meaning is how to make more precise the notion of a causal chain of the appropriate kind. How precisely can we describe the sorts of causal chains that must exist from one use of a word to a later use of the same word if we are to say that the referent or referents are the same in the two cases? And how much of a defect in these sorts of theories is it if one cannot be more precise on this point?

(2) It may seem counterintuitive that a natural kind word such as 'horse' is sharply distinguished from a term for a fictitious or nonexistent natural kind such as 'unicorn', and that a physical magnitude term such as 'electricity' is sharply distinguished from a term for a fictitious or nonexistent physical magnitude or substance such as 'phlogiston." Indeed, I myself believe that if unicorns were found to exist and people began to discover facts about them, give nonobvious definite descriptions or approximately correct descriptions of the class of unicorns, etc., then the linguistic character of the word unicorn would change; and similarly with "phlogiston"; but this is certain to be controversial.

(3) Some people will argue that definitions of such terms as 'electricity' (or, more precisely, 'charge') are crucial in the exact sciences, and further that such definitions should be regarded as *meanings stipulations*. I agree with the first part of this—that definitions are important in science, provided one remembers what Quine has pointed out, that "definition" is relative to a particular text or presentation, and that there is no such thing, in general, as the definition of a term "in physics" or "in biology"—only the definition in X, Y, or Z's presentation or axiomatization. I disagree with the last part—that "definitions" in science are meaning stipulations—but, again, this is certain to be controversial.

(4) Finally, there will be objections to my use of causal notions, from Humeans who expect them to be reduced away, and to my use of the term 'physical magnitude' from extensionalists and nominalists. Here I can only plead guilty to the belief that talk about what causes what, or what the laws of nature are, or what would happen if other things happened is *not* highly derived talk about mere regularities, and to the belief that the real world requires for its description not only reference to things but reference to physical magnitudes[7]—in a sense of 'physical magnitude' in which physical magnitudes exist contingently, not as a matter of logical necessity, and in which magnitudes can be synthetically identical (e.g., temperature is the same magnitude as mean molecular kinetic energy).

III. Why Positivistic Theory of Science is Wrong

My contention in this paper is not that what is wrong with positivist theory of science is positivist theory of meaning. What is wrong with positivist theory of science today, as it was wrong with the Machian theories that Lenin criticized in 1908,[8] is that it is based on an idealist or idealist-tending worldview, and that that worldview does not correspond to reality. However, the idealist element in contemporary positivism enters precisely through the theory of meaning; thus part of any realist critique of positivism has to include at least a sketch of rival theory. In the present section, I want to turn from the task of sketching such a rival theory, which was just completed, to the task of showing that positivistic theory of explanation broadly construed—that is, positivist theory of scientific theory—does not correspond to reality any better than the older and less sophisticated idealist theories to which it is historically the successor.

Let us for a moment review some of those older theories. The oldest theory is Bishop Berkeley's. Here one already meets what might be called the *adequacy claim*: that is, the claim that a convinced Berkelian is *entitled* to accept standard scientific theory and practice, that Berkeley can give an account of the scientific method which would justify this. Indeed, I have heard philosophers argue that acceptance of Berkeley's metaphysics would not make any difference to the scientific theories one would accept. Here one already meets an important ambiguity. One can be claiming that a Berkelian can make the move of "accepting" scientific theory in some sense other than accepting as true or approximately-true: say, accepting as a useful prediction heuristic. If this is what one means, then the claim is trivial. To be sure, Berkeley can "accept" Newtonian physics in the Pickwickian sense of "accept" as a useful scheme for making predictions. But Berkeley, to do him justice, was interested in much more: What he claimed was that an idealist could *reinterpret* (only he would not consider it *re*interpretation, but rather correct interpretation) the notion of object so as to square both the layman's and the scientist's talk of objects with the idealist claim that reality consists of minds and their sensations ("spirits" and their "ideas"). The difference between the two claims is the difference between accepting the idea that social practice is the test of truth and rejecting it, between accepting the idea that the overwhelming success of scientific theory offers some reason for accepting that theory as true or approximately-true, and claiming that success in practice is *no* indication of truth. Machian positivism fails for the same reason that Berkelian idealism does: although Mach makes the claim that his construction of the world out of sensations ("Empfindungen") is compatible with lay and scientific object-talk, no demonstration at all is given that this is so. The first philosopher to both precisely state and to undertake the task of *translating* thing-language into phenomenalistic language was Carnap (in *Logische Aufbau der Welt*). And what does Carnap do? He devotes the entire book to *preliminaries*, to "reconstructions" *within* sensationalistic language (i.e., reductions of some sensation-concepts to others, not of thing-concepts to sensation-concepts), and then in the last chapter gives a sketch of the relation of thing-language to sensation-language which is *not* a translation, and which, indeed, amounts to no more than the old claim that we pick the thing-theory that is "simplest" and most useful. In short, no demonstration is given at all that the positivist is entitled to quantify over (or refer to) material things.

It is with the failure of the phenomenalist translation enterprise, that is, with the failure to find *any* interpretation of object-concepts under which the prima facie incompatibility between an idealist worldview and a materialist worldview, between a world consisting of "spirits and their ideas", or of "*Empfindungen*", or of total experience slices in one "specious present", and a world consisting of fields and particles, simply *disappears*—it is with this failure that contemporary positivistic philosophy of science begins. Basically, two moves were made by the positivists after the failure of phenomenalist translation. The first was to give up construing scientific theories as systems of statements each of which had to have an intelligible interpretation (intelligible from the standpoint of what was taken as "completely understood" or "fully interpreted"), and to construe them rather as mere calculi, whose objective was to give successful predictions and otherwise to be as "simple" as possible. "Scientific theories are partially interpreted calculi".[9] The second move was to shift from phenomenalist language to "observable thing language" as one's reduction-base—i.e., to say that one was seeking an interpretation or "partial interpretation" of physical theory in "observable thing language", not in "sensationalistic language".

The second move may make it appear questionable whether positivism is still correctly characterized as an "idealist" tendency—i.e., as a tendency which regards or tends to regard the "hard facts" as just facts about actual and potential *experiences*, and all other talk as somehow just highly derived talk about actual and potential experiences. I, myself, think this characterization *is* still fundamentally correct despite the shift to "observable thing predicates" for two reasons: (1) The cut between observable things and "theoretical entities" was historically introduced as a substitute for the thing/sensation dichotomy. Indeed, the reduction of "theoretical entities" to "observable things and qualities" would hardly seem to be a natural problem to someone who did not have in the back of his head the older problem of reduction to *sensations*. The reduction of things to sensations is both a historically motivated problem and one which rests upon the sharpness of the distinction between a material thing and a sensation (of course, even this sharpness is partly an illusion, on a materialist view—substitute "material process" for material thing!), as well as the supposed "certainty" one has concerning one's own sensations. But the reduction of electrons to tables and chairs, or, more generally, of "unobservable" things to "observable" things is not historically motivated, the distinction is not sharp (Grover Maxwell asked years ago if a dust mote is something "given" when it is just big enough to see and a "construct" when it is just too small to see—can the distinction between data and constructs be a matter of size?), and one is not supposed to have certainty concerning observable things. (2) The positivists themselves frequently say that one could carry their analysis back down to the level of sensations, and that stopping with "observable thing predicates" is a matter of *convenience*.[10]

In the remainder of this section I want to show that the first move—construing scientific theories as partially interpreted calculi—does not solve the adequacy problem at all. The positivist today is no more entitled than Berkeley was to accept scientific theory and practice—that is, his own story leads to no reason to think either that scientific theory is true, or that scientific practice tends to discover truth. In a sense, this is immediate. The positivist does not claim that scientific theory is "true" in any transtheoretic sense of "true"; the only transtheoretic notions he has are of the order of "leads to successful prediction" and "is simple". Like the Berkelian, he has to fall back on the position that scientific theory is *useful* rather than true or approximately-true. But he does try to provide some account of the acceptability of scientific theories, even some account of their "interpretation." And he wants to maintain that in some sense the principle on which Marx says realist philosophy of science rests—that social practice is the test of truth, that the success of scientific theories is reason to think they are true or approximately-true—is right. What I want to show is that the notion of "truth" that the positivist can give us is not the one on which scientific practice is based.

A. *Truth*

When a realistically minded scientist—that is to say, a scientist *whose practice* is realistic, not one whose official "philosophy of science" is realistic—accepts a theory, he accepts it as true (or probably true, or approximately-true, or probably approximately-true). Since he also accepts *logic*[11] he knows that certain moves *preserve truth*. For example, if he accepts a theory T_1 as true and he accepts a theory T_2 as true, then he knows that T_1 & T_2—the *conjunction* of T_1 and T_2—is also true, by logic, and so he accepts T_1 & T_2. If we talk about probability, we have to say that if T_1 is very highly, probably true and T_2 is very highly probably true, then the conjunction T_1 & T_2 is also highly probable (though not as highly as the conjuncts separately), provided that T_1 is not negatively relevant to T_2—i.e., provided that T_2 is not only highly probable on the evidence, but also no less probable on the added assumption of T_1 (this is a judgment that must be made on the basis of what T_1 says and of background knowledge, of course). If we talk about approximate-truth, then we have to say that the approximations probably involved in T_1 and T_2 need to be compatible for us to pass from the approximate-truth of T_1 and T_2 to the approximate-truth of their conjunction. None of these matters is at all deep, from a realist point of view. But even if we confine ourselves to the simplest case, the case in which we can neglect the chances of error and the presence of approximations, and treat the acceptance of T_1 and T_2 as simply the acceptance of them as true, I want to suggest that the move from this acceptance to the acceptance of the conjunction is one to which one is not entitled on positivist philosophy of science. One of the simplest moves that scientists daily make, a move they make as a matter of propositional logic, a move which is central if scientific inquiry is to have any *cumulative* character at all, is totally *arbitrary* if positivist philosophy of science is right.

The difficulty is very simple. Acceptance of T_1, for a positivist, means acceptance of the calculus T_1 as leading to successful predictions (i.e., .all *observation sentences* which are theorems of T_1 are true; not all *sentences* which are theorems of T_1 are "true" in any fixed transtheoretic sense). Similarly. the acceptance of T_2 means the acceptance of T_2 as leading to successful predictions. But from the fact that T_1 leads to successful predictions and the fact that T_2 leads to successful predictions it does not follow at all that the conjunction T_1 & T_2 leads to successful predictions. The difficulty, in a nutshell, is that the predicate which plays the *role* of truth—the predicate "leads to successful predictions"—does not have the *properties* of truth. The positivist may teach in his philosophy seminar that acceptance of a scientific theory is acceptance of it as "simple" and leading to true predictions', and then go out and do science (or his students may go out and do science) by verifying theories T_1 and T_2, conjoining theories which have been previously verified, etc.—but then there is just as great a discrepancy between what he teaches in his philosophy seminar and his *practice* as there was between Berkeley's teaching that the world consisted of spirits and their ideas and continuing in practice to daily rely on the material object conceptual system.

Nor does it help to bring in "simplicity". It is not obvious that the conjunction of simple theories is simple; and even if simplicity is preserved by conjunction, the conjunction of simple theories which separately lead to no false predictions may even be *inconsistent* (examples are easy to construct). More sophisticated moves have indeed been made. Thus, for Carnap truth of a theory is the same as truth of its "Ramsey sentence"[12]. But exactly the same objection applies: "truth of the Ramsey sentence" does not have the properties of truth: if T_1 has a true Ramsey sentence and T_2 has a true Ramsey sentence it does not at all follow that the conjunction does.

(For those readers farmiliar with Carnap's use of the Hilbert epsilon symbol, it may be pointed out that the difficulty comes out in very sharp form in Carnap's symbolization of his interpretation of individual theoretical terms. Thus let $T_1(P)$, $T_2(P)$ be two theories containing exactly one theoretical term P. On Carnap's own symbolization of his view,[12] what P means in T_1 is $\varepsilon PT_1(P)$; what P means in T_2 is $\varepsilon PT_2(P)$; and what P means in T_1 & T_2 is $\varepsilon P[T_1(P) \& T_2(P)]$; this makes it explicit that P has different meanings in T_1 and T_2 and *yet a third meaning* in their conjuntion.)

B. Simplicity

It is easy to construct a "theory" in the positivist sense (a calculus containing some observation terms) which leads to no false predictions but which no scientist would dream of accepting. This is usually handled by saying that scientists only choose "simple" theories. Also, a simple theory may mess up science as a whole: So it is said that scientists are trying to maximize the simplicity of "total science". "Theory" means, then, "formalization of total science, or of some piece which is independent of the rest of total science". Unfortunately, no one has ever written down or ever will write down a "theory" in this sense. The fact is, that positivist philosophy of science depends on a constant slide between giving the impression that one is talking about "theories" in the customary sense—Newton's theory, Maxwell's theory, Darwin's theory, Mendel's theory—and saying, at key points of difficulty such as the one just alluded to, that one is *really* talking about a "formalization of total science", or some such thing.

The difficulty with the rule "choose the simplest theory compatible with the evidence" is that it is probably not *right*, or would probably not be right, even if one *could* formalize "total science" (at a given time). Scientists are not trying to maximize some formal property of "simplicity"; they are trying to maximize *truth* (or improve their approximation to truth, or increase the amount of approximate-truth they know without decreasing the goodness of the approximation, and so forth).

Of course, a realist might accept the rule "chose the simplest hypothesis", if it could be shown that the simplest hypothesis is always the most *probable* on the basis of the rest of his knowledge. But this is not so on any usual measure of simplicity. For example, suppose I know just three points on interstate highway 40, and those three points lie on a straight line. Suppose also that the statement 'IS 40 is straight' is logically consistent with my total knowledge. Then accepting 'IS 40 is straight' would, on the usual simplicity metrics, be accepting the simplest hypothesis. Yet I would not in fact accept 'IS 40 straight', nor would anyone with our background knowledge. Given that every other interstate highway has curves, and given the enormous length of IS 40 and the enormous impracticality of making a straight highway across the entire United States, it is overwhelmingly probable that IS 40 is *not* straight.

Can we not say that my *total* "knowledge" is less simple if I accept 'IS 40 is straight'? Not, it seems to me, on the basis of any criterion of *simplicity* that I know of. What is obviously involved here is not *simplicity* but plausibility: What introducing the word "simplicity" does is make it look as if a calculation which is in fact the calculation of the probability of a state of affairs is in reality just a calculation of a formal property (such as number of argument places, number of primitive symbols, length and number of the axioms, perhaps shape of the curves mentioned) of an uninterpreted or semi-interpretcd *calculus*. Even if the property of being the most probable hypothesis on background knowledge could be *represented* syntactically, omitting to mention that the representing property was the syntactic representation of a *probability measure*, and pretending that it was just a formal property (like having simple axioms), would be a way of disguising rather than revealing what was going on.

C. Confirmation

Indeed, positivist philosophers of science have made attempts at formalizing the logic of confirmation. These attempts are interesting (though so far unsuccessful) researches on any philosophy of science. But not only do they have nothing to do with positivist theory of meaning; they are in fact *incompatible* with it. Thus when they write about meaning, positivists tell us that "theoretical terms" have different meanings in different theories; when they formalize confirmation theory, they invariably treat theories as systems of sentences in *one* language, and assume that all semantic concepts are *trans*theoretic. Thus the positivists are engaged in formalizing *realistic* confirmation theory, not the confirmation theory (if there is one!) to which their own theory of meaning should lead.

What is going on here should be evident from Carnap's work on the foundations of mathematics. Carnap has a consistent tendency to *identify* concepts with their syntactic representations: thus, mathematical truth with theoremhood (after the discovery of Gödel's theorem, he either allowed "non-constructive rules of proof," or simply assumed set theory, and took "logical consequence" rather than derivability as the basic notion, although this trivialized the "analysis" of mathematical truth). In the same way he would have liked to identify a state of affairs having a probability of, say, .9, with the corresponding sentences having a c-value of .9 (where "c" would be a syntactically defined measure on sentences in a formalized language). Even if Carnap had found a successful "c-function", the fact is that it would have been successful because it corresponded to a reasonable probability measure over some collection of states of affairs; but this is just what Carnap's positivism did not allow him to say.

D. Auxiliary Hypotheses

Sometimes, as we mentioned, the positivists make it explicit that the "theories" to which their theory of science applies are "formalizations of total science," and not theories in the usual sense; but their readers do, I think, tend to come away with the impression that their model is a model of a scientific theory in the usual sense—especially, a physical theory. Believing this involves believing that a physical theory is a calculus, or could easily be formalized as a calculus, and that its predictions are *self-contained*—that they are deduced from, the explicitly stated assumptions of the theory itself. This leads to a comparison with social sciences which is derogatory to the social sciences—for the classic social science theories are clearly *not* self-contained in this sense. For example, when Marxists write that the capitalist class controls the state—that the army and the police intervene on the side of capitalists, that the politicians who have a chance of obtaining state power through elections are tied to capitalists, etc.—what they do is make a series of generalizations about ways in which this control allegedly takes place: what happens in elections, when the army intervenes, etc. But these generalizations do not lead to predictions about specific political events (or, not to predictions in the positivist's "observation language", without very substantive auxiliary assumptions. These auxiliary assumptions, if they could be spelled out, would be numerous and would be highly context dependent. Thus Marxist theory must either be ignored or treated as not a scientific theory at all, but only a theory sketch, and likewise for such classic theories as those of Weber or even Mill. In short, the positivist attitude tends to be that social science is science only when and to the extent that it apes *physics*. And this for the reason that the mathematical model of a scientific theory provided by the positivists is thought to clearly fit *physical* theories.

But, in fact, it fits physical theories very badly, and this for the reason that even physical theories in the usual sense—e.g., Newton's theory of universal gravitation, Maxwell's theory—lead to no predictions at all without a host of auxiliary assumptions, and moreover without auxiliary assumptions that are not at all law-like, but that are, in fact, assumptions about boundary conditions and initial conditions in the case of particular systems. Thus, if the claim that the term 'gravitation', for example, had a meaning which depended on the theory were true, and the theory included such auxiliary assumptions as that "space is a hard vacuum," and "there is no tenth planet in the solar system," then it would follow that discovery that space is *not* a hard vacuum or even that there is a tenth planet would change the meaning of 'gravitation'. I think one has to be pretty idealistic in one's intuitions to find this at all plausible! It is not so implausible that knowledge of the meaning of the term 'gravitation' involves some knowledge of the theory (although I think that this is wrong: the stereotype associated with 'gravitation' is not nearly as strong as a particular theory of gravitation), and this is probably what most readers think of when they encounter the claim that physical magnitude terms (usually called "theoretical terms" to prejudge just the issue this paper discusses) are "theory loaded"; but the actual meaning-dependence required by positivist meaning theory would be a dependence not just on the *laws* of the theory, but on the particular auxiliary assumptions—for, if these are not counted as part of the theory, then the whole theory-prediction scheme collapses at the outset.

Finally, neglect of the role that auxiliary assumptions actually play in science leads to a wholly incorrect idea of how a scientific theory is confirmed. Newton's theory of gravitation was not confirmed by checking predictions derived from it plus some set of auxiliary statements fixed in advance; rather the auxiliary assumptions had to be continually modified and expanded in the history of celestial mechanics. That scientific problems as often have the form of finding auxiliary hypotheses as they do of finding and checking predictions is something that has been too much neglected in philosophy of science.[13] This neglect is largely the result of the acceptance of the positivist model and its uncritical application to actual physical theories.

Notes

1. Cf. Engels (1959) and Lenin (1970).
2. In a letter written to Conrad Schmidt in 1895; cf. Marx and Engels (1942), pp. 527–30.
3. Cf. Shapere (1969).
4. See, for example, the discussion by Hempel (1965), pp. 217–18. A contrasting view is sketched in Putnam (1962).
5. Putnam (1962).
6. Putnam (1970a).
7. Cf. Putnam (1970b).
8. Cf. Lenin (1970).
9. Putnam (1962).
10. E.g., Carnap says this on p. 63 in Carnap (1956).
11. The role of logic in empirical science is discussed in Putnam (1971) and Putnam (1969).
12. For details see Hempel (1965).
13. I discuss this in "The 'Corroboration' of Theories," in *The Philosophy of Karl Popper* (ed., by P. A. Schilpp), Open Court, La Salle, IL, 1974, pp. 221–240. [This volume, pp. 121–137.]

Bibilography

Carnap, R., 1956, "The Methodological Character of Theoretical Concepts," in *Minnesotoa Studies in the Philosophy of Science*, Vol. I. (ed. by H. Feigl), Minneapolis.

Engels, F., 1959, *Anti-Dühring, Herr Eugen Dühring's Revolution in Science*, New York.

Hempel, C., 1965, "The Theoretician's Dilemma," *Aspects of Scientific Explanation*, New York.

Lenin, V., 1970 *Materialism and Empirio-Criticism*, New York.

Marx, K. and Engels, F., *Selected Correspondence 1846–1895*, New York.

Putnam, H., 1962, "What Theories Are Not," in *Logic Methodology and Philosophy of Science* (ed. by E. Nagel, P. Suppes, and A. Tarski), Stanford.

Putnam, H., 1969, "Is Logic Empirical?," in *Boston Studies in the Philosophy of Science*, Vol. V (ed. by R. Cohen and M. Wartofsky), New York.

Putnam, H., 1970a, "Is Semantics Possible?", in *Language, Belief and Metaphysics*, Vol. I of *Contemporary Philosophical Thought: The International Philosophy Year Conferences at Brockport*, Albany.

Putnam, H., 1970b, "On Properties," in *Eaasys in Honor of Carl G. Hempel* (ed. by N, Rescher), D. Reidel, Dordrecht, pp. 235–254.

Putnam, H., 1971, *Philosophy of Logic*, New York.

Shapere, D., 1969. "Towards a Post-Positivistic Interpretation of Science," in *The Legacy of Logical Positivism* (ed. by P. Achenstein and S. Barker), Baltimore.

Chapter 10

To Save the Phenomena

Bas van Fraassen

After the demise of logical positivism, scientific realism has once more returned as a major philosophical position. I shall not try here to criticize that position, but rather attempt to outline a comprehensive alternative.[1]

I

What exactly is scientific realism? Naively stated, it is the view that the picture science gives us of the world is true, and the entities postulated really exist. (Historically, it added that there are real necessities in nature; I shall ignore that aspect here.[2]) But that statement is too naive; it attributes to the scientific realist the belief that today's scientific theories are (essentially) right.

The correct statement, it seems to me, must indeed be in terms of epistemic attitudes, but not so directly. The aim of science is to give us *a literally true story of what the world is like*; and the proper form of acceptance of a theory is to believe that it is true. This is the statement of scientific realism: "To have good reason to accept a theory is to have good reason to believe that the entities it postulates are real," as Wilfrid Sellars has expressed it. Accordingly, all antirealism is a position according to which the aims of science can well be served without giving such a literally true story, and acceptance of a theory may properly involve something less (or other) than belief that it is true.

The idea of a literally true account has two aspects: the language is to be literally construed; and, so construed, the account is true. This divides the antirealists into two sorts. The first sort holds that science is or aims to be true, properly (but not literally) construed. The second holds that the language of science should be literally construed, but its theories need not be true to be good. The antirealism I advocate belongs to the second sort.

II

When Newton wrote his *Mathematical Principles of Natural Philosophy* and *System of the World*, he carefully distinguished the phenomena to be saved from the reality he postulated. He distinguished the "absolute magnitudes" that appear in his axioms from their "sensible measures" which are determined experimentally. He discussed carefully the ways in which, and extent to which, "the true motions of particular bodies [may be determined] from the apparent," via the assertion that "the apparent motions ... are the differences of true motions."[3]

Reprinted by permission of the author and *Journal of Philosophy* 73, no. 18 (October 21, 1976), pp. 623–32. Copyright 1976 by *Journal of Philosophy*.

The "apparent motions" form relational structures define by measuring relative distances, time intervals, and angles of separation. For brevity, let us call these relational structures *appearances*. In the mathematical model provided by Newton's theory, bodies are located in Absolute Space, in which they have real or absolute motions. But within these models we can define structures that are meant to be exact reflections of those appearances and are, as Newton says, identifiable as differences between true motions. These structures, defined in terms of the relevant relations between absolute locations and absolute times, which are the appropriate parts of Newton's models, I shall call *motions*, borrowing, Simon's term.[4]

When Newton claims empirical adequacy for his theory, he is claiming that his theory has some model such that *all actual appearances are identifiable with (isomorphic to)* motions in that model.

Newton's theory goes a great deal further than this. It is part of his theory that there is such a thing as Absolute Space, that absolute motion is motion relative to Absolute Space, that absolute acceleration causes certain stresses and strains; and thereby deformations in the appearances, and so on. He offered, in addition, the hypothesis (his term) that the center of gravity of the solar system is at rest in Absolute Space. But, as he himself noted, the appearances would be no different if that center were in any other state of constant absolute motion.

Let us call Newton's theory (mechanics and gravitation) TN, and $TN(v)$ the theory TN plus the postulate that the center of gravity of the solar system has constant absolute velocity. By Newton's own account, he claims empirical adequacy for $TN(0)$; and also claims that, if $TN(0)$ is empirically adequate, then so are all the theories $TN(v)$.

Recalling what it was to claim empirical adequacy, we see that all the theories $TN(v)$ are empirically equivalent exactly *if all the motions in a model of $TN(v)$ are isomorphic to motions in a model $TN(v + w)$*, for all constant velocities v and w. For now, let us agree that these theories are empirically equivalent, referring objections to a later section.

III

What exactly is the "empirical import" of $TN(0)$? Let us focus on a fictitious and anachronistic philosopher Leibniz*, whose only quarrel with Newton's theory is that he does not believe in the existence of Absolute Space. As a corollary, of course, he can attach no "physical significance" to statements about absolute motion. Leibniz* believes, like Newton, that $TN(0)$ is empirically adequate; but not that it is true. For the sake of brevity, let us say that Leibniz* *accepts* the theory but that he does not *believe* it; when confusion threatens we may expand that idiom to say that he *accepts the theory as empirically adequate*, but does not *believe it to be true*. What does Leibniz* believe, then?

Leibniz* believes that $TN(0)$ is empirically adequate, and hence, equivalently, that all the theories $TN(v)$ are empirically adequate. Yet we cannot identify the theory that Leibniz* holds about the world—call it TNE—with the common part of all the theories $TN(v)$. For each of the theories $TN(v)$ has such consequences as that the earth has *some* absolute velocity, and that Absolute Space exists. In each model of each theory $TN(v)$ there is to be found something other than motions, and there is the rub.

To believe a theory is to believe that one of its models correctly represents the world. A theory may have isomorphic models; that redundancy is easily removed. If it has been removed, then to believe the theory is to believe that exactly one of its models correctly represents the world. Therefore, if we believe of a family of theories that all are empirically adequate, but each goes beyond the phenomena, then we are still free to believe that each is false, and hence their common part is false. For that common part is phrasable as: one of the models of one of those theories correctly represents the world.

IV

It may be objected that theories will seem empirically equivalent only so long as we do not consider their possible extensions.[5] The equivalence may generally, or always, disappear when we consider their implications for some further domain of application. The usual example is Brownian motion; but this is imperfect, for it was known that phenomenological and statistical thermodynamics (disagreed even on macroscopic phenomena over sufficiently long periods of time. But there is a good, *fictional* example: the combination of electromagnetism with mechanics, if we ignore the unexpected null results that led to the replacement of classical mechanics.

Maxwell's theory was not developed as part of mechanics, but it did have mechanical models. This follows from a result of Koenig, as detailed by Poincaré in the preface of his *Electricité et Optique* and elsewhere. But the theory had the strange new feature that velocity itself, not just its derivative, appears in the equations. A spate of thought experiments was designed to measure absolute velocity, the simplest perhaps that of Poincaré:

> Consider two electrified bodies; though they are both carried along by the motion of the earth; ... therefore, equivalent to two parallel currents of the same sense and these two currents should attract each other. In measuring this attraction, we shall measures the velocity of the earth; not its velocity in relation to the sum or the fixed stars, but its absolute velocity.[6]

The null outcome of all experiments of this sort led to the replacement of classical by relativistic mechanics. But let us imagine that values *were* found for the absolute velocities; specifically for that of the center of the solar system. Then, surely, one of the theories $TN(v)$ would be confirmed and the others falsified?

This reasoning is spurious. Newton made the distinction between true and apparent motions without presupposing more than the basic mechanics in which Maxwell's theories had models. Each motion in a model oE $TN(v)$ is isomorphic to one in some model of $TN(v + w)$, for all constant velocities v and w. Could this assertion Of empirical equivalence possibly be controverted by those nineteenth-century reflections? The answer is *no*. The thought experiment, we may imagine, confirmed the theory that added to TN the hypothesis:

> HO. The center of gravity of the solar system is at absolute rest.
> EO. Two electrified bodies moving with absolute velocity v attract each other with force $F(v)$.

This theory has a consequence strictly about appearances:

> CON. Two electrified bodies moving with velocity v relative to the center of gravity of the solar system, attract each other with force $F(v)$.

However, that same consequence can be had by adding to TN the two alternative hypotheses:

H*w*. The center of gravity of the solar system has absolute velocity *w*.
E*w*. Two electrified bodies moving with absolute velocity $v + w$ attract each other with force $F(v)$.

More generally, for each theory $TN(v)$ there is an electromagnetic theory $E(v)$ such that $E(0)$ is Maxwell's and all the combined theories $TN(v)$ plus $E(v)$ are empirically equivalent.

There is no originality in this observation, of which Poincaré discusses the equivalent immediately after the passage I cited above. Only familiar examples, but rightly stated, are needed, it seems, to show the feasibility of concepts of empirical adequacy and equivalence. In the remainder of this paper I shall try to generalize these considerations, while showing that the attempts to explicate those concepts *syntactically* had to reduce them to absurdity.

V

The idea that theories may have hidden virtues by allowing successful extensions to new kinds of phenomena, is too pretty to be left. Nor is it a very new idea. In the first lecture of his *Cours de philosophie positive*, Comte referred to Fourier's theory of heat as showing the emptiness of the debate between partisans of calorific matter and kinetic theory. The illustrations of empirical equivalence have that regrettable tendency to date; calorifics lost. Federico Enriques seemed to place his finger on the exact reason when he wrote: "The hypotheses which are indifferent in the limited sphere of the actual theories acquire significance from the point of view of their possible extension."[7] To evaluate this suggestion, we must ask what exactly is an extension of a theory.

Suppose that experiments really had confirmed the combined theory $TN(0)$ plus $E(0)$. In that case mechanics would have won a *victory*. The claim that $TN(0)$ was empirically adequate would have been borne out by the facts. But such victorious extensions could never count for a theory as against one of its empirical equivalents.

Therefore, if Enriques' idea is to be correct, there must be another sort of extension, which is really a defeat—but qualified. For a theory T may have an easy or obvious modification which is empirically adequate, while another theory empirically equivalent to T does not. One example may be the superiority oE Newton's celestial mechanics over the variant produced by Brian Ellis; Ellis himself seems to be of this opinion.[8] This is a *pragmatic* superiority and cannot suggest that theories, empirically equivalent in the sense explained, can nevertheless have different empirical import.

VI

We still need a general account of empirical adequacy and equivalence. It is here that the syntactic approach has most conspicuously failed. A theory was conceived as identifiable with the set of its theorems in a specified language. This language has a vocabulary, divided into two classes—the observational and theoretical terms. Let the first class be E; then the empirical import of theory T was said to be its subtheory T/E—those theorems expressible in that subvocabulary. T and T' were declared empirically equivalent if T/E was the same as T'/E.

Obvious questions were raised and settled. Craig showed that, under suitable conditions, T/E is axiomatizable in the vocabulary E. Logicians attached importance to questions about restricted vocabularies, and this was apparently enough to make philosophers think them important too. The distinction between observational and theoretical terms was more debatable, and some changed the division into "old" and "newly introduced" terms.[9] But all this is mistaken. Empirical import cannot be isolated in this syntactic fashion. If that could be done, then then T/E would say exactly what T says about what is observable, and nothing else. But consider: the quantum theory, Copenhagen version, says that there are things which sometimes have a position in space and sometimes do not. This consequence I have just stated without using theoretical terms. Newton's theory TN implies that there is something (to wit, Absolute Space) which neither has a position nor occupies volume. As long as unobservable entities differ systemically from observation entities with respect to observable characteristics, T/E will say that there are such if T does.

The reduced theory T/E is not a description of the observable part of the world of T; rather, it is hobbled and hamstrung version of T's description of everything. Empirical equivalence fares as badly. In section II, $TN(0)$ and TNE *must* be empirically equivalent, but the above remark about TN shows that $TN(0)/E$ is not TNE/E. To eliminate such embarrassments, extensions of theories were considered in attempts to redefine empirical equivalence.[10] But these have similar absurd consequences.

The worst consequence of the syntactic approach was surely the way it focused philosophical attention on irrelevant technical question. The expressions 'theoretical object' and 'observational predicate' mark category mistakes. Terms may be theoretical, but 'observable' classifies putative entities. Hence there cannot be a "theoretical/observable distinction." It is true surely that elimination of all theory-laden terms would leave no usable language; also all that 'observable' is as vague as 'bald'. But these facts imply not at all the 'observable' marks on unreal distinction. It refers quite clearly to our limitations, the limits of observation, which are not incapacitating, but also not negligible.

VII

The phenomena are saved when they are exhibited as fragments of a larger unity. For that very reason it would be strange if scientific theories described the phenomena, the observable part, in different terms from the rest of the world they describe. And so an attempt to draw the conceptual line between phenomena and the transphenomenal by means of a distinction of vocabulary, must always have looked too simple to be good.

Not all philosophers who discussed unobservables, by any means, did so in terms of vocabulary. But there was a common assumption: that the distinction marked is philosophical. Hence it must be drawn, if at all, by philosophical analysis and, if attacked, by philosophical arguments. This attitude needs a Grand Reversal. If there are limits to observation, these are empirical, and must be described by empirical science. The classification marked by "observable" must be of entities in the world of science. And science, in giving content to the distinction, will reveal how much we believe when we accept it as empirically adequate.

A future Unified Science may detail the limits of observation exactly; meanwhile, extant theories are not silent on them. We saw Newton's delineation; for relativity theory, we have two revealing studies by Clark Glymour. The first shows that local (hence, I should think, measurable) quantities do not uniquely determine global features of space-time.[11] The second shows that these features also are not uniquely determined by structures each lying wholly within some absolute past cone—hence, I should think, by observable structures. It is the theory of relativity itself, after all, that places *all absolute* limit on the information we can gather, through the limiting function of the speed of light.

In the foundations of quantum mechanics much more attention has been given to measurement. Much of the discussion is about necessary limitations: the role of noise in amplification. the distinction between macro- and micro-observables.[12] Yet we have no such clarity as Glymour gave us for relativity theory, concerning the extent to which macro-structure determines micro-structure. The debate over scientific realism may at least have the virtue of directing attention to such questions.

Science itself distinguishes the observable that it postulates from the whole it postulates. The distinction, being in part a function of the limits science discloses on human observation, is anthropocentric. But, since science places human observers among the physical systems it means to describe, it also gives itself the task of describing anthropocentric distinctions. It is in this way that even the scientific realist must observe a distinction between the phenomena and the transphenomenal in the scientific world picture.

VIII

I have laid some philosophical misfortunes at the door of a mistaken orientation toward syntax. The alternative is to say that theories are presented directly by describing their models. But does this really introduce a new element? When you give the theorems of T, you give the set of models of T—namely, all those structures which satisfy the theorems. And, if you give the models, you give at least the set of theorems of T—namely all those sentences which are satisfied in all the models. Does it not follow that we can as advantageously identify T with its theorems as with its models?

But there is an ellipsis in the argument. It is being assumed that there is a specific language L which is the one language that belongs to T. And indeed, the theorems of T in L determine and are determined by the set of model structures of L (that is, structures in which L is interpreted) in which those theorems are satisfied. However, the assumption that there is a language L which plays this role for T places important restrictions on what the set of models of T can like.

A theory provides, among other things, a specification (more or less complete) of the parts of its models that are to be direct images of the structures described in measurement reports. In the case of Newton's mechanics, I called those parts *motions*; in general, let us call them *empirical substructures*. The structures described in measurement reports we may continue to call *appearances*. A theory is *empirically adequate* exactly if all appearances are isomorphic to empirical substructures in at least one of its models. Theory T is *empirically no stronger* than theory T' exactly if, for each model M of T, there is a model M' of T' such that all empirical substructures of M are isomorphic to empirical substructures of M'. Theories T and T' are *empirically equivalent* exactly if neither is empirically stronger than the other. In that case, as an easy corollary, each is empirically adequate if and only if the other is.

In section v, I distinguished two kinds of extensions, the first a sort of victory and the second a sort of defeat. Let us call the first a *proper extension*: this simply narrows the class of models. We may call a theory *empirically minimal* if it is not empirically equivalent to any of its proper extensions. Glymour has convincingly argued, in the work cited above, that General Relativity is not empirically minimal. The reason is, in my present terms, that only local properties of space-time enter the descriptions of the appearances, but models may differ in global properties. This is a further nontrivial example of empirical equivalence.

The second sort of extension I shall not try to define precisely. The idea is that models of the theory may differ in structure other than that of the empirical substructures. In that case the theory is not empirically minimal, but this may put it in the advantageous position of offering modeling possibilities when radically new phenomena come to light An example may yet be offered by hidden-variable theories in quantum mechanics.[13]

In terms of the concepts now at our disposal, and the examples given, we can conclude that there are indeed nontrivial cases of empirical equivalence, non-uniqueness, and extendability, both proper and improper. Such cases are now seen to be quite possible *even if the formulation of the theory has not a single term that cannot be called observationial, in some way.* And now it should be possible to state the issue of scientific realism, which concerns our epistemic attitude toward theories rather than their internal structure.

All the results of measurements are not in; they are never all in. Therefore we cannot know what all the appearances are. We can say that a theory is empirically adequate, that all the appearances will fit (the empirical substructures of) its models. Though we cannot know this with certainty, we can reasonably believe it. All this is the case not only for empirical adequacy but for truth as well. Yet there are two distinct epistemic attitudes that can be taken: we can *accept* a theory (accept it as empirically adequate) or *believe* the theory (believe it to be true). We can take it to be the aim of science to produce a literally true story about the world, or simply to produce accounts that are empirically adequate. This is the issue of scientific realism versus its (divided) opposition. The intrascientific distinction between the observable and the unobservable is an anthropocentric distinction; but it is reasonable that the distinction should be drawn in terms of *us*, when it is a question of *our* attitudes toward theories.

Notes

This paper was presented in an APA symposium on Scientific Realism, December 28, 1976. The research for this paper was supported by Canada Council Grant S74-0590. An earlier version was presented at the Western Division of the Canadian Philosophical Association (Calgary, October 1975).

I want to acknowledge my debt to Clark Glymour, Princeton University, for the challenge of his critiques of conventionalism in his dissertation and unpublished manuscripts.

1. For some criticisms, see my "Theoretical Entities: The Five Ways," *Philosophia* 4 (1974): 95–109, and "Wilfrid Sellars on Scientific Realism," *Dialogue*, XIV, 4 (December 1975): 606–616.
2. Cf. my "The Only Necessity Is Verbal Necessity," *Journal of Philosophy*, LXXIV, 2 (February 1977).
3. F. Cajori, ed. *Sir Isaac Newton's Mathematical Principles of Natural Philosophy and His System of the World* (Berkeley: University of California Press, 1960), p. 12.
4. Herbert A. Simon, "The Axiomatization of Classical Mechanics," *Philosophy of Science*, XXI, 4 (October 1954): 340–343.
5. See, for example, Richard N. Boyd, "Realism, Undetermination, and a Causal Theory of Evidence," *Noûs*, VII, 1 (March 1973): 1–12.
6. Henri Poincaré, *The Value of Science*, B. Halsted, tr. (New York: Dover, 1958), p. 98.
7. *Historical Development of Logic*, J. Rosenthal, tr. (New York: Holt, 1929), p. 230.
8. "The Origins and Nature of Newton's Laws of Motion," in R. Colodny, ed., *Beyond the Edge of Certainly* (Englewood Cliffs, N.J.: Prentice-Hall, 1965), pp. 29–68.
9. For example, David Lewis, "How to Define Theoretical Terms," *Journal of Philosophy*, LXVII, 13 (July 9, 1970): 427–446. This paper is not subject to my criticisms here; on the contrary, it provides independent reasons to conclude that the empirical import of a theory cannot be syntactically isolated.
10. See note 5, above. We could say that Boyd's paper, like Lewis's, provides independent evidence that empirical import cannot be syntactically isolated. But Boyd concludes also that there can be no distinction between truth and empirical adequacy for scientific theories.
11. Cosmology, Convention, and the Closed Universe," *Synthese*, XXIV, 1/2 (July/August 1972): 195–218; discussed in my "Earman on the Causal Theory of Time," *op. cit.*, pp. 87–95 (referred to therein by an earlier title).
12. See for example N. D. Cartwright, "Superposition and Macroscopic Observation," *Synthese*, XXIX (December 1974): 229–242, and references therein.

13. See Stanley Gudder, "Hidden Variables in Quantum Mechanics Reconsidered," *Review of Modern Physics*, XI (1968): 229–231; and section III of my "Semantic Analysis of Quantum Logic," in C. A. Hooker, ed., *Contemporary Research in the Foundations and Philosophy of Quantum Theory* (Dordrecht: Reidel, 1973), pp. 80–113.

Chapter 11

On the Current Status of Scientific Realism

Richard Boyd

1. Introduction

The aim of this essay is to assess the strengths and weaknesses of the various "traditional" arguments for and against scientific realism. I conclude that the typical realist rebuttals to empiricist or constructivist arguments against realism are in important ways inadequate; I diagnose the source of the inadequacies in these arguments as a failure to appreciate the extent to which scientific realism requires the abandonment of central tenets of modern epistemology; and I offer an outline of a defense of scientific realism which avoids the inadequacies in question.

2. Scientific Realism Defined

By "scientific realism" philosophers typically understand a doctrine which we may think of as embodying four central theses:

(i) "Theoretical terms" in scientific theories (i.e., nonobservational terms) should be thought of as putatively referring expressions; scientific theories should be interpreted "realistically"

(ii) Scientific theories, interpreted realistically, are confirmable *and in fact often confirmed* as approximately true by ordinary scientific evidence interpreted in accordance with ordinary methodological standards.

(iii) The historical progress of mature sciences is largely a matter of successively more accurate approximations to the truth about both observable and unobservable phenomena. Later theories typically build upon the (observational and theoretical) knowledge embodied in previous theories.

(iv) The reality which scientific theories describe is largely independent of our thoughts or theoretical commitments.

Critics of realism in the empiricist tradition typically deny (i) and (ii), and qualify their acceptance of (iii) so as to avoid commitment to the possibility of theoretical knowledge (but van Fraassen 1980 accepts (i)). Antirealists in the constructivist tradition, like Kuhn (1970) deny (iv); they may well affirm (i)–(iii) on the understanding that the "reality" which scientific theories describe is somehow a social and intellectual "construct". As Kuhn (1970) and Hanson (1958) both argue, a constructivist perspective limits, however, the scope of application of (iii), since successive theories can be understood as approximating the truth more closely only when they are part of the same general constructive tradition or "paradigm".

In any event, the principal challenge to scientific realism arise from quite deep epistemological criticisms of (i)–(iv). The key antirealist arguments, and standard

Reprinted (with emendations) by permission of the author and *Erkenntnis* 19 (1983), pp. 45–90. Copyright 1983 by Kluwer Academic Publishers.

Table 11.1
The Basic Antirealist Arguments, the Standard Rebuttals, and their Weaknesses

Antirealist Argument	Standard Rebuttal	Weakness
1. Empiricist argument: Empirically Equivalent theories are evidentially indistinguishable, so knowledge cannot extend to "unobservables."	1. a. No sharp distinction between "observables" and unobservables.	1. a. (i) Sharp distinction can be drawn in a well-motivated way. (ii) In any event, distinction need not be sharp.
	b. Empiricist argument ignores the role of "auxiliary hypotheses" in assessing empirical equivalence.	b. Empiricist argument can be reformulated to apply to "total sciences."
	c. The "no miracles" argument: If scientific theories weren't (approximately) true, it would be miraculous that they yield such accurate observational predictions.	c. Does not address the crucial epistemological claim of the empiricist argument: that since factual knowledge is grounded in experience, it can extend only to observable phenomena.
2. Constructivist arguments: a. Scientific methodology is so theory-dependent that it is at best a construction procedure, not a discovery procedure.	2. a Pair-wise theory-neutrality of method: for any two rival theories, there are experimental tests based on a method legitimized by both theories.	2. a. Does not address the epistemological point that theory-dependent methodology must be a construction procedure.
b. Consecutive "paradigms" in the history of science are not logically commensurable in the way they would be if they embodied theories about a paradigm-independent world. (Kuhn 1970)	b. It is possible to give an account of continuity or reference for theoretical terms which allows for commensurability of paradigms.	b. If the antirealist *epistemological* argument (2. a.) is sound, then such continuity of reference is itself a construct, or at best a matter of continuity of reference to constructs, so that the realist's conception of scientific knowledge of theory-independent reality is still not vindicated.

rebuttals to them in the literature, and certain weaknesses in these rebuttals are summarized in chart form in table 11.1.

3. Antirealism in the Empiricist Tradition

There is a single, simple, and very powerful epistemological argument which represents the basis for the rejection of scientific realism by philosophers in the empiricist tradition. Suppose that T is a proposed theory of unobservable phenomena, which can be subjected to experimental testing. A theory is said to be empirically equivalent to T just in case it makes the same predictions about observable phenomena that T does. Now it is always possible, given T, to construct arbitrarily many alternative theories which are empirically equivalent to T but which offer contradictory accounts of the nature of unobservable phenomena. Since scientific evidence for or against a theory consists in the confirmation or disconfirmation of one of its observational predictions, T and each of the theories empirically equivalent to it will be equally well confirmed or disconfirmed by any possible observational evidence. Therefore no scientific evidence can bear on the question of which of these theories provides the correct account of unobservable phenomena; at best, it might be possible to confirm or disconfirm the claim that each of these theories is a reliable instrument for the prediction of observable phenomena. Since this construction is possible for any theory T, it follows that scientific evidence can never decide the question between theories of unobservable phenomena and knowledge of unobservable phenomena is thus impossible. We may choose the "simplest" "model" for "pragmatic" reasons, but if evidence in science is experimental evidence, then pragmatic standards for theory-choice have nothing to do with truth or knowledge. Scientific realism promises theoretical knowledge of the world, where, at best, it can deliver only formal elegance, or computational convenience.

As I have indicated in table 11.1, the empiricist argument we have been considering depends on the epistemological principle that empirically equivalent theories are evidentially indistinguishable The evidential indistinguishability thesis (whether explicit or implicit) represents the key epistemological doctrine of contemporary empiricism and may be thought of as a precise formulation of the traditional empiricist doctrine ("knowledge empiricism" in the phrase of Bennett 1971) that factual knowledge must always be grounded in experiences; that there is no *a priori* factual knowledge. (As I shall argue in section 6, the evidential indistinguishability thesis is the wrong formulation of the important epistemological truth in that doctrine; still, it represents the way in which empiricist philosophers of science—and most other empiricists for that matter—have understood the fundamental doctrine of empiricist epictemology.)

Perhaps the most commonplace rebuttal to verificationist or empiricist arguments against realism is that the distinction between observable and unobservable phenomena is not a sharp one, and that the fundamental empiricist antirealist argument therefore rests upon an arbitrary distinction (see, for example, Maxwell 1962).[1] In assessing this rebuttal, it is important to distinguish between the question of the truth of the claim that the distinction between observable and "theoretical" entities is not sharp, and the question of the appropriateness of this claim as a rebuttal to empiricist antirealism. *If* scientific realism has somehow been established, then it may well be evident that the distinction in question is epistemologically arbitrary: *if* we are able to confirm theories of, say, electrons, then we may be able to employ such theories to design electron detecting instruments whose "readings" may have an epistemological status essentially like that of ordinary observations. If, on the other hand, it is scientific realism which is in dispute, then the considerations just presented would be inappropriately circular, even if their conclusion is ultimately sound. Only a non-question-begging demonstration that the distinction in question is arbitrary would constitute an adequate rebuttal to the empiricist's strong *prima facie* case that experimental knowledge cannot extend to the unobservable realm.

If we understand the rebuttal in question in this light, then several responses are available to the empiricist which indicate its weakness as a response to the central epistemological principle of empiricism. In the first place, it is by no means clear that the empiricist need hold that there is a *sharp* distinction between observable and unobservable phenomena in order to show that the distinction is epistemologically nonarbitrary. Suppose that there are entities which represent borderline cases of observability and suppose that there are cases in which it's not clear whether something is being observed or not. Then there will be some entities about which our knowledge will be limited by our capacity to observe them, and there will be cases in which the evidence is equivocal about whether there are entities of a certain sort at all. But the empiricist need hardly resist these conclusions: they are independently plausible, and—provided that there are some clear cases of putative unobservable entities (atoms, elementary particles, magnetic fields, etc.)—the antirealist claims of the empiricist are essentially unaffected.

Moreover, there are at least three ways in which the distinction in question can be made sharper in an epistemologically motivated way. In the first place, there is nothing obviously wrong with the traditional empiricist distinction between sense data and putative external objects. It is often claimed that the failure of logical positivists to construct a sense-datum language shows that the observation-theory dichotomy cannot be formulated in such terms, because it would be impossible to say of a theory that evidence for or against it consists in the confirmation or disconfirmation of observational (that is, sense datum) predictions which are *deduced* from the theory. Quite so, but the fact remains that some experiences are of the sort we expect on the basis of the acceptance of a given theory, and others are of the sort we would not expect. Whatever the relation of expectation is between theories and sensory experiences, we may define empirical equivalence with respect to it, and affirm the empiricist thesis of the evidential indistinguishability of empirically equivalent theories. The result is *the* classical empiricist formulation of "knowledge empiricism".

It is true, of course, that the sense-datum formulation of the evidential indistinguishability thesis leads to phenomenalism (at best) about physical objects and other persons. As early logical positivists recognized, this consequence makes it difficult to account for the apparent social and inter-subjective character of scientific knowledge. To be sure, this difficulty provides a reason to doubt the truth of the evidential indistinguishability thesis in its sense datum formulation. But it does not constitute a satisfactory *rebuttal* to that thesis, nor a satisfactory *rebuttal* to the antirealist argument we are considering. The sense-datum version of the indistinguishability thesis is, after all, the *obvious* precise formulation of the doctrine that factual knowledge is always grounded in experience. The empiricist argument against realism is a straightforward application of that thesis. The fact that the thesis in question has inconvenient consequences neither shows that factual knowledge is not grounded in experience nor that the (sense-datum version of) the indistinguishability thesis is not the appropriate explication of the doctrine that factual knowledge is grounded in this way. Considerations about the public character of science my provide us with reason to think that there must be *something* wrong with the phenomenalist's argument against scientific realism, but they do not provide us with any plausible account of *what* is wrong with it. If I am right, the rebuttal to the sense-datum version of the evidential indistinguishability thesis which we are considering displays a weakness which is common to all of the rebuttals to anti-empiricist arguments described in table 11.1. Each of the principal antirealist arguments raises deep questions in epistemology or semantic theory against scientific realism The standard rebuttals, insofar as they are effective at all, provide *some* reason to think that the antirealist arguments in question are unsound, or that realism is true, but they do not succeed in diagnosing the error in these arguments, nor do they point the way to alternative and genuinely realist conceptions of the central issues in epistemology or semantic theory.

It remains to examine the other two ways in which the dichotomy between observable and unobservable phenomena can be sharpened. On the one hand, phenomena might be classed as "observable" if they are quite plainly observable to persons with normal perceptual abilities. On the other hand, there is the proposal, which seems to be implicit in Maxwell 1962, that entities which may not be directly observable to the unaided senses should count as "observable" for the purposes of the epistemology of science if they can be detected by the senses when the senses have been "aided" by devices whose reliability can be previously established by procedures which do not beg the question between empiricists and scientific realists. Roughly at least, the latter proposal can be put this way: Let O_1 be the class of entities which are observable to the typical unaided senses: for any n, let O_{n+1} be the class of entities which are detectable by procedures whose legitimacy can be established on the basis of theories which can be established (and can be applied to justify those procedures) without presupposing the existence of entities not in O_n; the union of the sets O_n is the class of "observables" in the sense relevant to the epistemology of science.

Neither of these proposals is without difficulties. Either can be challenged from the perspective of traditional empiricism by a simple application of the sense-datum version of the evidential indistinguishability thesis. The proposal that observability should be defined in terms of what is plainly observable to the unaided senses may be challenged for failing to account, for example, for "observations" made through a simple light microscope or telescope. The more generous conception is open to the challenge that it fails to see the force of the evidential indistinguishability thesis with respect to its own conception of observability—that it fails, for example, to recognize that there are infinitely many different and evidentially indistinguishable hypotheses which could explain the intersubjectively observable *images* which are the objective data of light microscopy.

In any event, each of these proposals reflects an important aspect of the intuitive conception that experimental knowledge is grounded in observation. What is important for our purposes is that *either* account of unobservability is sufficient to sustain a significant antirealist application of the evidential indistinguishability thesis. That this is true for the less generous conception of observability is obvious. In regard to the more generous conception, it is important to recognize that what is proposed is not that one may treat as observable whatever phenomena can be identified by "inductive inference to the best explanation" (see Harman 1965) as causes of the results of laboratory "measurement" or "detection". A general appeal to a principle of inductive inference to *theoretical* explanations would beg the question against the empiricist in this context. Instead, the proposed account of observability depends crucially on the conception that theories whose confirmation by observations are unproblematical from an empiricist point of view can be employed to legitimize an additional level of "observables" and that this process can then be iterated. The example of light micro-scopy is illustrative here: The idea is that the lens-makers' equations can be confirmed in a fashion entirely acceptable to empiricism, and that these equations can then be used to legitimize interpreting the images observed through a microscope as images *of* other-wise unobservable entities.

It is not clear that this approach even gets off the ground as a non-question-begging account of observability. Arguably, the empiricist will hold that the lens-makers' equations, for example, are confirmable only insofar as they are understood to apply to unproblematically observable entities. The application of those equations which underlies the broader conception of observability requires that they be confirmed even when they are understood to apply to the very entities whose observability they are supposed to legitimize. It is by no means clear that objections such as this do not yield the conclusion that $O_n = O_{n+1}$ for all n.

Even if this problem is somehow circumvented, it is still true that the generous definition of observability is unlikely to legitimize knowledge of the standard "un-observables" which worry the philosopher of science. The reason is this: the account of observability we are considering cannot work to legitimize as "observable" putative entities which are such that the available procedures for (as a realist would say) measuring and detecting them depend upon explicit theories of those entities themselves, or (worse yet) upon theories of other (putative) entities as well which are equally "unobservable" in the traditional sense. In such cases only a question-begging inductive inference to a theoretical explanation of the results of the relevant "measure-ments" or "detections" would suffice to legitimize the entities in question. But it is almost certain that the basic unobservable putative features of matter (atoms, their constituent particles, electrical and magnetic fields, etc.) fall into the category of entities for which legitimization would be question-begging. Therefore the central claims of antirealist empiricism in the philosophy of science will be sustained even if the evidential indistinguishability thesis is so understood as not to rule out the use of, e.g., light microscopes in scientific observations.

We may apparently conclude the following about the rebuttal to empiricist anti-realist arguments which turns on the claim that the distinction between observable entities and unobservables ones is not sharp, and that the empiricist argument there-fore rests upon an epistemologically arbitrary distinction: The distinction in question need not be sharp in order to be nonarbitrary. Moreover, there are at least three epistemologically motivated ways of making it sharper. An examination of each of these refinements of the distinction indicates features which might make it reasonable to suppose that there is something problematical about the basic empiricist argument against realism, but none of these considerations provides any diagnosis of the error, nor do any of them allow us to foresee any alternative to the doctrine of the evidential indistinguishability of empirically equivalent theories upon which the empiricist argu-ment depends. The standard rebuttals are inadequate in the face of the serious epis-temological issues raised by the empiricist position.

I said that we may *apparently* reach these conclusions because it may seem that I have overlooked the real force of the rebuttal under consideration. The real force, it might seem, lies in the following consideration: it has often happened that scientists have postulated unobservable entities and have developed and confirmed, to their satisfaction, theories about them, and that they have much later been able, on the basis of those very theories, to measure or detect those very entities whose existence they earlier had postulated. Examples may include germs, viruses, atoms, neutrinos, etc. Surely this shows that the sort of inductive inference to theoretical explanations in which scientists engage are reliable, whatever empiricists may say.

Taken at face value, this argument is question-begging: it assumes at the outset that what scientific realists describe as "measurement" and "detection" of the entities in question are really measurement and detection. But there is an argument for realism lurking here. It does not turn on the claim that the empiricist has drawn the observable-unobservable dichotomy arbitrarily; such a reading makes the argument question-begging. Instead, what we have, is an example of the third anti-empiricist rebuttal indicated in table 11.1. In general, that rebuttal points to the astonishing predictive reliability of well-confirmed scientific theories as evidence that they must be approxi-mately true as descriptions of unobservable entities. The cases of predictive reliability which make this argument plausible are typically those in which predictions quite different from the ones which were involved in the initial confirmation of a theory— and especially predictions which are arrived at by calculations which take the theo-retical machinery of the theory quite seriously—turn out to be surprisingly accurate. In such cases it seems that miracles are the only alternative to a realist explanation of the success of scientific practice. (This may be the argument which Putnam 1978 attributes to Boyd, unpublished (b)). Cases in which what is predicted are the results of (what a realist would call) "measurement" or "detection" of the postulated unobserv-able entities are especially clear examples of the cases to which this argument applies.

This rebuttal to empiricist antirealism has considerable force (indeed it is probably the argument which reconstructs the reason why most scientific realists are realists). But it suffers from the same defect which we observed earlier in the case of the first rebuttal: while it provides good reason to think that there must be *something* wrong with the empiricists' argument, it affords us no diagnosis of *what* is wrong with it. No rebuttal to the basic epistemological principle of the empiricist argument (the evidential indistinguishability thesis) flows from this rebuttal; nor is there any rebuttal to the application of that basic principle to the issue of scientific realism. We are provided with a reason to suppose that realism is true, but we are not provided with any epistemology to go with that conclusion.

There remains one rebuttal among the standard responses to empiricist antirealism and it does seem to directly challenge the evidential indistinguishability thesis. The evidential indistinguishability thesis asserts that empirically equivalent theories are evidentially indistinguishable. But it has been widely recognized by philosophers of science that this is wrong. It might be right, they would argue, if the only predictions from a theory which are appropriate to test are those which can be deduced from the theory in isolation. But it is universally acknowledged that in theory testing we are permitted to use various well-confirmed theories as "auxiliary hypotheses" in the derivation of testable predictions. Thus two different theories might be empirically equivalent—they might have the same consequence about observable phenomena—but it might be easy to design a crucial experiment for deciding between the theories if one could find a suitable set of auxiliary hypotheses such that when they were brought into play as additional premises, the theories (so expanded) are no longer empirically equivalent.

There is almost no doubt that considerations of this sort rebut any verificationist attempt to classify individual statements or theories as literally meaningful or literally meaningless by the criterion of verifiability in principle. But there is no reason to suppose that the rebuttal based on the role of auxiliary hypotheses is fatal to the basic claim of the evidential indistinguishability thesis, or to its antirealistic application. The reason is this: we may reformulate the evidential indistinguishability thesis so that it applies, not to individual theories, but to "total sciences". The thesis, so understood. then asserts that empirically equivalent total sciences are evidentially indistinguishable. Since total sciences are self-contained with respect to auxiliary hypotheses, the rebuttal we have been considering does not apply, and the revised version of the evidential indistinguishability thesis entails that at no point in the history of science could we have knowledge that the theoretical claims of the existing total science are true or approximately true (see Boyd 1982).

One objection which has sometimes been offered against the employment of the notion of a "total science" is the observation that if, by a total science, one means the set of well-established theories at a particular time in the history of science, then total sciences are almost certainly always logically inconsistent and that they have therefore all possible observational consequences and cannot be experimentally confirmed. In this case, as in the case of the objection discussed earlier to the sense-datum version of the evidential indistinguishability thesis, there is an obvious reply. Somehow, scientists manage to cope with inconsistent total sciences; they have a good idea which tentatively accepted or merely approximate (as they might say) theories should not be employed together in making predictions. They have a pretty good idea which predictions not to trust. All we need to do is to define empirical equivalence with respect to the practice of scientists. The evidential indistinguishability thesis formulated with respect to total sciences in this way yields the antirealist conclusion of empiricists, and it certainly seems reasonable to hold that some such version of the evidential indistinguishability thesis represents the obvious interpretation of "knowledge empiricism" once the role of auxiliary hypotheses is acknowledged. Thus the fact that auxiliary hypotheses play a crucial role in theory confirmation does not constitute a significant rebuttal to a sophisticated version of the standard empiricist argument against scientific realism. There *is* a point regarding the use of auxiliary hypotheses which can be made the basis for a very strong defense of scientific realism. The use of auxiliary hypotheses, like other applications of what positivists called the "unity of science" principle, depends upon judgments of univocality regarding different occurrences of the same theoretical terms. It is possible to argue that only a realist conception of the semantics and epistemology of science can account for the role of such univocality judgments in contributing to the reliability of scientific methodology (Boyd 1979, 1982, unpublished (b)), but this argument is not anticipated in the standard rebuttals to empiricist antirealism.

We must conclude that the standard rebuttals to the central empiricist argument against scientific realism are significantly flawed. Where they do provide reason to suspect that the empiricist argument is unsound (or, more directly, that realism is true) they do not provide any effective rebuttal to the main epistemological principle (the evidential indistinguishability thesis) upon which the empiricist argument depends, nor do they indicate respects in which the application of that principle to the question of realism is unwarranted.

4. *Constructivist Antirealism*

There is a single basic empiricist argument against realism and it is an argument of striking simplicity and power. In the case of constructivist antirealism the situation is much more complex. In part, at least, this is so because constructivist philosophers of science have typically been led to antirealist conclusions by reflections upon the results of *detailed* examinations of the history and actual methodological practices of science as well as by reflections on the psychology of scientific understanding. Different philosophers have focused on different aspects of the complex procedures of actual science as a basis for antirealist conclusions. Nevertheless, it is possible, I believe, to identify the common thread in all of these diverse arguments. Roughly, the constructivist antirealist reasons as follows: The actual methodology of science is profoundly theory-dependent. What scientists count as an acceptable theory, what they count as an observation, which experiments they take to be well designed, which measurement procedures they consider legitimate, what problems they seek to solve, what sorts of evidence they require before accepting a theory, ... all of these features of scientific methodology are in practice determined by the theoretical tradition within which scientists work. What sort of world must there be, the constructivist asks, in order for this sort of theory-dependent methodology to constitute a vehicle for gaining knowledge? The answer, according to the constructivist, is that the world which scientists study must be, in some robust sense, defined or constituted by, or "constructed" from, the theoretical tradition in which the scientific community in question works. If the world which scientists study were not partly constituted by their theoretical tradition then, so the argument goes, there would be no way of explaining why the theory-dependent methods which scientists use are a way of finding out what's true.

To this argument, there is typically added another which addresses an apparent problem with constructivism. The problem is that scientists seem sometimes to be forced by new data to abandon important features of their current theories, and to adopt radically new theories in their place. This phenomenon, it would seem, must be an example of scientific theories being brought into conformity with a theory-independent world, rather than an example of the construction of reality within a theoretical tradition. In response to this problem, constructivism often asserts that successive theories in science which represent the sort of radical "breaks" in tradition at issue are "incommensurable" (Kuhn 1970). The idea here is that the standards of evidence, interpretation, and understanding dictated by the old theory on the one hand, and by the new theory on the other hand, are so different that the transition between them cannot be interpreted as having been dictated by any common standards of rationality. Since there are no significant theory-independent standards of rationality, it follows that the transition in question is not a matter of rationally adopting a new conception of (theory-independent) reality in the light of new evidence; instead, what is involved is the adoption of a wholly new conception of the world, complete with its own distinctive standards of rationality. In its most influential version (Kuhn 1970) this argument incorporates the claim that the semantics of the two consecutive theories changes to such an extent that those terms which they have in common should not be thought of as having the same referents in the two theories. Thus transitions of the sort we are discussing ("scientific revolutions" in Kuhn's terminology) involve a total change of theoretical subject matter.

There are two closely related standard rebuttals to these antirealist arguments. In the first place, against the claim that realism must be abandoned because scientific methodology is too theory-dependent to constitute a discovery (as opposed to a construction) procedure, it is often replied that for any two rival scientific theories it is always possible to find a methodology for testing them which is neutral with respect to the theories in question. Thus, so it is argued. the choice between rival scientific theories on the basis of experimental evidence can be rational even though experimental methodology is theory-dependent. The outcome of a "crucial experiment" which pits one rival theory against another need not be biased, since such an experiment can be conducted on the basis of a methodology which—however theory-dependent—is not committed to either of the two contesting theories.

Against the incommensurability claim, it is often argued that an account of reference for theoretical expressions can be provided which makes it possible to describe scientific revolutions as involving continuity in reference for the theoretical terms common to the laws of the earlier and later theoretical traditions or "paradigms". With such referential continuity comes a kind of continuity of methodology as well, because (assuming continuity of reference) the actual cases of scientific revolutions typically result in the preservation of some of the theoretical machinery of the earlier paradigm in the structure of the new one and this, in turn, guarantees a continuity of methodology.

Neither of these rebuttals is fully adequate as a response to constructivist anti-realism. Consider first the claim that for any two rival theories there is a methodology for testing them which is neutral with respect to the issues on which they differ ("pair-wise theory neutrality of method" in table 11.1). It is generally true that—for theoretical rivalries which arise in actual science—a relevantly neutral testing methodology will exist. Indeed, the use of such "neutral" testing methodologies is a routine part of what Kuhn calls "normal science" (Kuhn 1970). And indeed, the existence of such methodologies helps to explain how scientists can appeal to common standards of rationality even when they have theoretical differences of the sort which influence methodological judgments. Nevertheless, pair-wise theory neutrality of method does not provide a reason to reject the antirealist conclusions of the constructivist.

Remember that what the constructivist argues is that a general methodology which is predicated upon a particular theoretical tradition, and which is theory-determined to its core, cannot be understood as a methodology for discovering features of a world which is not in some significant way defined by that tradition. All that the doctrine of the existence of pair-wise theory neutral methods asserts is that—within the theoretical and methodological tradition in question—there are available experimental procedures which are neutral with respect to quite particular disputes between alternative ways of modifying or extending that very tradition. There is no suggestion of a procedure by which scientific methodology can escape from the presuppositions of the tradition and examine objectively the structure of a theory-independent world. Insofar as the profound theory-dependence of method raises an epistemological problem for realism, the pair-wise theory neutrality of methods does not provide an answer to it.

Perhaps surprisingly, it doesn't help either to demonstrate that successive paradigms are commensurable. Suppose that a satisfactory account of referential continuity for theoretical terms during scientific revolutions is available (see Boyd 1979). Suppose further (what is not implied by the former claim) that the theoretical continuity thus established during revolutionary periods is such that the transition between the prerevolutionary theory and the postrevolutionary one is governed by a continuously evolving standard of scientific rationality. If these suppositions are true, then much of what Kuhn, for example, had claimed about the history of science will be mistaken: postrevolutionary scientists will (contrary to Kuhn) be building on the theoretical achievements of their prerevolutionary predecessors; the adoption of new "paradigms" will be scientifically rational: and it will not involve a "Gestalt shift" in the scientific community's understanding of the world, whatever may be the case for some individual scientists. *But*, the basic constructivist epistemological objection to scientific realism will still be unrebutted. If the theory-dependence of methodology provides reason to doubt that scientific inquiry possesses the right sort of "objectivity" for the study of a theory-independent world, then the sort of historical continuity through scientific revolutions which we are considering will not address that doubt. Only if the transitional methodology during revolutions were largely theory-neutral would the fact of methodological and semantic continuity between revolutions provide, by itself, a rebuttal to the constructivist antirealist; but there is no chance that such theory-independence could be demonstrated by the sort of rebuttal to incommensurability we are considering. Indeed, there is no reason of any sort to suppose that such a theory-neutral method ever prevails.

In the present case, as in the case of the standard rebuttals to empiricist antirealism, it is by no means true that the standard rebuttals to the constructivist arguments are irrelevant to the issue of scientific realism. If there were no such phenomenon as pair-wise theory neutrality of method, then it would be hard to see how there could be any sort of scientific objectivity, realist or constructivist. If there is no way of defending the continuity of subject matter and methodology during most of the episodes which Kuhn calls scientific revolutions, then the realist conception of science is rendered most implausible. The point is that, even though these prorealist rebuttals to constructivist antirealism do provide some support for aspects of the realist position, they fail to offer any reason to reject the basic epistemological argument against realism which the constructivist offers.

5. Empiricism and Constructivism

Kuhn (1970) presents his constructivist account of science as an alternative to the tradition of logical empiricism and, indeed, there is much he says with which traditional positivists would disagree. There are, nevertheless, important similarities between the constructivist and the empiricist approach to the philosophy of science. Kuhn, for example, relies on the late positivist "law-cluster" account of the meaning of theoretical terms in his famous argument against the semantic commensurability of successive paradigms (Kuhn 1970, pp. 101–102; see Boyd 1979 for a discussion). Similarly, Carnap's mature positivism of the early 1950s has much in common with Kuhn's views. In particular, Carnap (1950) offers an account of the criteria for the rational acceptance of a linguistic framework which is surprisingly like a formalized version of Kuhn's view (see Schlick 1932/33 for an anticipation of Carnap's later position). We may say with some precision what the points of similarity between Kuhn and Carnap are. In the first place, they are agreed that the day-to-day business of the development and testing of scientific theories is governed by broader and more basic theoretical principles including the most basic laws and definitions of the relevant sciences.

There is a far deeper point of agreement. Kuhn, and constructivists generally, cannot consistently accept the principle of the evidential indistinguishability of empirically equivalent total sciences; they hold, after all, that "facts"—insofar as they are the subject matter of the sciences—are partly constituted or defined by the adoption of "paradigms" or theoretical traditions, so that there is a sort of *a priori* character to the scientist's knowledge of the fundamental laws in the relevant traditon or paradigm. But they agree with logical empiricists in holding that any rational constraint on theory acceptance which is not purely pragmatic and which does not accord with the evidential indistinguishability thesis must be essentially conventional. For Carnap and other positivists the conventions are essentially linguistic: they amount to the conventional adoption of one set of "L-truths" rather than another. For Kuhn and other constructivists, the conventions go far deeper: they amount to the social construction of reality and of experimental "facts". What neither empiricists nor constructivists accept is the idea that the regulation of theory acceptance by features (linguistic or otherwise) of the existing theoretical tradition can be reliable guide to the discovery of theory-independent matters of fact.

One further point of agreement between empiricists and constructivists is significant for our purposes. Empiricist philosophers of science deny that knowledge of theoretical entities is possible. But it is no part of contemporary empiricism to deny that the scientific method yields objective instrumental knowledge: knowledge of regularities in the behavior of observable phenomena. It is important to see that this point is not seriously contested by constructivist philosophers of science. It is true that constructivists insist that observation in science is significantly theory-determined, and that Kuhn, for example, emphasizes that experimental results which are anomalous in the light of the prevailing theoretical conceptions are typically ignored if they cannot readily be assimilated into the received theoretical framework. But no serious constructivist maintains that the predictive reliability of theories in mature science or the reliability of scientific methodology in identifying predictively reliable theories is largely an artifact of the tendency to ignore anomalous results. Such a view would be nonsensical in the light of the contributions of pure science to technological advance.

There is one point which, whether it is ultimately compatible with empiricism or not, is certainly emphasized by constructivists much more than by empiricists, and which is especially relevant when one considers the role of scientific methodology in producing instrumental knowledge. It was early recognized by logical empiricists that any account of the methodology of science requires some account of the way in which the "degree of confirmation" of a theory, given a body of observational evidence, is to be determined. More recently, Goodman (1973) has, following Locke, raised a question which is really a special case of the problem of determining "degree of confirmation". Any account of the methodology of science must account for judgments of "projectibility" of predicates or, to put the issue more broadly, it must provide an account of the standards by which scientists determine which general conclusions are even real candidates for acceptance given an (always finite) body of available data (for further discussion of this issue see Quine 1969; Boyd 1979, 1980, 1982). This question is interesting precisely because, given any finite body of data, there are infinitely many different general theories which are logically consistent with those data (indeed, there will be infinitely many such theories which are pairwise empirically in-equivalent, given the existing total science as a source of auxiliary hypotheses).

What Kuhn and other constructivists insist (correctly, I believe) is that judgments of projectibility and of degrees of confirmation are quite profoundly dependent upon the theories which make up the existing theoretical tradition or paradigm. The theoretical tradition dictates the terms in which questions are posed and the terms in which possible answers are articulated. In a similar way, theoretical considerations dictate the standards for experimental design and for the assessment of the experimental evidence. Assuming this to be true, and assuming, as reasonable constructivists must, that the reliability of scientific methodology in producing instrumental knowledge is not to be explained largely by the tendency to ignore anomalous data, we can see that an important epistemological issue emerges regarding judgments of projectibility and of degree of confirmation: why should so theory-dependent a methodology be reliable at producing knowledge about (largely theory-independent) observable phenomena?

A related question about what we might call the "instrumental reliability" of scientific method should prove challenging both to Kuhn, and to empiricists who share with Kuhn the "law-cluster" theory of the meaning of theoretical terms. Judgment of univocality for particular occurrences of (lexicographically) the same theoretical term play an important epistemological role in scientific methodology. This is evident since such commonplaces as the use of auxiliary hypotheses in theory-testing, or applications of the principle of "unity of science" in the derivation of observational predictions from theories which have already been accepted, depend upon prior assessments of univocality. This means that scientific standards for the assessment of univocality for token occurrences of theoretical terms must play a crucial epistemological role, and it must be the business of an adequate account of the language of science to say what those standards are *and* why they are such as to render instrumentally reliable the methodological principles in actual science which depend upon univocality judgments (see Boyd 1982, unpublished (b) for a discussion).

Unlike earlier positivist theories of meaning for theoretical terms (like operationalism for example) the law-cluster theory does not say what it is for two tokens of orthographically the same theoretical term to occur with the same meaning or reference. The meaning of a theoretical term is given by the most basic laws in which it occurs; this may possibly tell us something about diachronic questions about univocality of theoretical terms. But suppose that t and t' are two tokens of orthographically the same theoretical term, used at the same time, and that neither t nor t' occurs in a law which is fundamental in the sense relevant to the law-cluster theory. This latter condition describes the circumstances of almost all tokens of theoretical terms in actual scientific usage. Under the circumstances in question, the law-cluster theory says nothing about the question of whether t and t' have the same meaning or reference. Only when the synchronic problem of univocality in such cases is presumed to have already been solved does the law-cluster theory have anything to say about univocality for theoretical terms. The law-cluster theory is thus entirely without the resources to address the important question of the contribution which judgments of univocality for theoretical terms make to the instrumental reliability of scientific methodology.

We have thus identified two questions which pose especially sharp challenges to both empiricist and constructivist conceptions of science: why are theory-dependent standards for assessing projectibility and degrees of confirmation instrumentally reliable? and how do judgments of univocality for theoretical terms contribute to the instrumental reliability of scientific methodology? I shall argue in the next section that answers to these challenges provides the basis for a new and more effective defense of scientific realism

6. Defending Scientific Realism

I have elsewhere (Boyd 1972, 1973, 1979, 1982, unpublished (a), (b)) offered a defense of scientific realism against empiricist antirealism which proceeds by proposing that a realistic account of scientific theories is a component in the only scientifically plausible explanation for the instrumental reliability of scientific methodology. What I propose to do here is to summarize this defense very briefly and to indicate how it also constitutes a defense of scientific realism against constructivist criticisms, and how it avoids the weaknesses in the traditional rebuttals to antirealist arguments.

The proposal that scientific realism might be required in order to adequately explain the instrumental reliability of scientific methodology can be motivated by reexamining the principal constructivist argument against scientific realism (2a in table 11.1). The constructivist asks, "What must the world be like in order that a methodology so theory-dependent as ours could constitute a way of finding out what's true?" She answers: "The world would have to be largely defined or constituted by the theoretical tradition which defines that methodology". It is clear that another answer is at least possible: the world might be one in which the laws and theories embodied in our actual theoretical tradition are approximately true. In that case, the methodology of science might progress dialectically. Our methodology, based on approximately true theories, would be a reliable guide to the discovery of new results and the improvement of older theories. The resulting improvement in our knowledge of the world would result in a still more reliable methodology leading to still more accurate theories, and so on (see Boyd 1982).

What I have argued in the works cited above is that this conception of the enterprise of science provides the only scientifically plausible explanation for the instrumental reliability of the scientific method. In particular, I argue that the reliability of theory-dependent judgments of projectibility and degrees of confirmation can only be satisfactorily explained on the assumption that the theoretical claims embodied in the background theories which determine those judgments are relevantly approximately true, and that scientific methodology acts dialectically so as to produce in the long run an increasingly accurate theoretical picture of the world. Since logical empiricists accept the instrumental reliability of actual scientific methodology, this defense of realism represents a cogent challenge to logical empiricist antirealism. It remains to see whether it has the weaknesses of more traditional responses to empiricist antirealism. but let us first examine its relevance to constructivism.

First, it should be observed that the argument for realism which I have indicated is a direct response to the central constructivist argument against realism. If the argument for realism is correct, then we can see *what* is wrong with the central constructivist argument: the constructivist's epistemological challenge to scientific realism rests upon the wrong explanation for the reliability of the scientific method as a guide to truth.

It is equally important to see that there is no answer within a purely constructivist framework to the question of why the methods of science are *instrumentally* reliable. The instrumental reliability of particular scientific theories cannot be an artifact of the social construction of reality. Even within "pure" science this is acknowledged, for example by Kuhn. The anomalous observations which (sometimes) give rise to "scientific revolutions" cannot be reflections of a fully paradigm-dependent world: anomalies are defined as observations which are inexplicable within the relevant paradigm. It is even more evident that theory-dependent technological progress (the most striking example of the instrumental reliability of scientific *methods* as well as theories) cannot be explained by an appeal to social construction of reality. It cannot be that the explanation for the fact that airplanes, whose design rests upon enormously sophisticaled theory, do not often crash is that the paradigm *defines* the concept of an airplane in terms of crash-resistance. If the empiricist cannot offer a satisfactory account of the instrumental realiability of scientific method (as I have argued in the works cited), then the constructivist—who even more than the empiricist emphasizes the theory dependence of that method—cannot do so either. Thus, the epistemological thrust of constructivism is directly challenged by the argument for scientific realism under consideration.

It is, moreover, clear that if scientific realism is defended in this way, then the more traditional rebuttals to constructivist antirealism are rendered fully effective. If the fundamental epistemological thrust of constructivism is mistaken, then (as I indicated in section 4) the pair-wise theory neutrality of scientific methodology, and the continuity of reference of theoretical terms and methods across "revolutions" are crucial components in the defense of scientific realism.

Let us turn now to the question of whether the defense of realism we are considering has the weakness of the more traditional rebuttals to empiricist antirealism. Those rebuttals had the defect that, while they provided some reason to believe that scientific realism is true, they offered no insight into the question of what is wrong with the crucial empiricist argument against realism. Here the argument under consideration succeeds where the more traditional arguments fail. What is wrong with the fundamental empiricist argument is that the principle that empirically equivalent total sciences are evidentially indistinguishable is false, and it represents the wrong reconstruction of the perfectly true doctrine that factual knowledge is grounded in observation.

The point here is that, if the realist and dialectical conception of scientific methodology is right, then considerations of the theoretical plausibility of a proposed theory in the light of the *actual* (and approximately true) theoretical tradition are *evidential* considerations: results of such assessments of plausibility constitute evidence for or against proposed theories. Indeed, such considerations are a matter of theory-mediated empirical evidence, since the background theories with respect to which assessments of plausibility are made are themselves empirically tested (again, in a theory-mediated way). Theory-mediated evidence of this sort is no less empirical than more "direct" experimental evidence—largely because the evidential standards which apply to so-called direct experimental tests of theories are theory-determined in just the same way that judgments of plausibility are. In consequence, the *actual* theoretical traditon has an epistemically privileged position in the assessment of *empirical* evidence. Thus, a "total science" whose theoretical conception is significantly in conflict with the received theoretical tradition is, for that reason, subject to "indirect" but perfectly real *prima facie* disconfirmation relative to an empirically equivalent total science which reflects the existing tradition. The evidential indistinguishability thesis is therefore false, and the basic empiricist antirealist argument is fully rebutted. (See Boyd 1979, 1980, 1982, unpublished (a), (b) for discussion of these points.)

It might seem that this realist conception that theoretical considerations in science are evidential would reflect a weakening of ordinary standards of evidential rigor in science. After all, on the realist conception, a theory can get evidential support both from "direct" experimental evidence and from "indirect" theoretical considerations. Moreover, the realist proposal might seem to make it impossible to disconfirm traditional theories, treating them as *a priori* truths in much the same way that the constructivist conception does. Neither of these claims proves to be sound. In the first place, rigorous assessment of experimental evidence in science depends fundamentally upon just the principle that theoretical considerations are evidential: that is why a realist conception of theories is necessary to account for the instrumental reliability of our standards for assessing experimental evidence (Boyd 1972, 1973, 1979, 1982, forthcoming (a), forthcoming (b)). Secondly, the realist conception of theory-mediated experimental evidence does not have the consequence that any traditional laws are immune from refutation. Instead, it provides the explanation of how rigorous testing of these and oiher laws is possible. The dialectical process of improvement in the theoretical tradition does not preclude, but instead requires, that particular laws or principles in the tradition may have to be abandoned in the light of new evidence (see Boyd 1982, unpublished (a), (b)).

Let us turn now to the second puzzle about the instrumental reliability of scientific method which was raised at the end of the preceding section: how to account for the epistemic reliability of judgments of univocality for theoretical terms. The realistic account of the instrumental reliability of judgments of "projectibility" requires that the kinds or categories into which features of the world are sorted for the purpose of inductive inference be determined by theoretical considerations rather than being fixed by conventional definitions, however abstract (Boyd 1982, see also Quine 1969). In particular, the law-cluster theory of meaning, understood conventionally, is inadequate as an account of the "definitions" of theoretical terms in science. It has been widely recognized (Feigl 1956, Kripke 1972, Putnam 1975) that if theoretical terms in science are to refer to entities or kinds whose "essences" are determined by empirical investigation rather than by stipulation, then the traditional conception of reference fixing by stipulatory conventions must be abandoned for such terms in favor of some "causal" or "naturalistic" theory of reference.

Given the distinctly realistic conception of scientific knowledge described previously, it is possible to offer a naturalistic theory of reference which is especially appropriate to an understanding of the role of theoretical considerations in scientific reasoning. Such a theory defines reference in terms of relations of "epistemic access" (Boyd 1979, 1982, unpublished (b)). Roughly, a (type) term t refers to some entity e just in the case where complex causal interactions between features of the world and human social practices bring it about that what is said of t is, generally speaking and over time, reliably regulated by the real properties of e. Because such regulation of what we say by the real features of the world depends upon the approximate truth of background theories, the approximate reliability of measurement and detection procedures, and the like, the epistemic access account of reference can explain the grains of truth in such previous accounts of reference as the law-cluster theory, or operationalism (Boyd 1979, 1982).

Consider now the question of univocality for two token occurrences of orthographically the same theoretical term. Such a pair of terms will be coreferential just in case the social history of each of their occurrences links them, by the relevant sort of causal relations, to a situation of reliable belief regulation by the actual properties of the same feature of the world. Which the relevant sorts of causal relations are is to be determined by epistemology, construed as an empirical investigation into the mechanisms of reliable belief regulation (Boyd 1982). It is thus an empirical question, not a "conceptual" one, whether two such tokens are univocal.

Because the epistemic access account of reference can account for the grains of truth in the other theories of reference for theoretical terms which have been advanced to explain the actual judgments of scientists and historians about issues of univocality (Boyd 1979, 1982), there is every reason to believe that the epistemic access account-can explain why the ordinary standards for judging univocality which prevail in science are reliable indicators of actual coreferentiality. Together uith the realist's conception that scientific methodology produces (typically and over time) approximately true beliefs about theoretical entities, the epistemic access account of reference provides an explanation of the contribution of univocality judgments to the reliability of scientific methodology which is fully in accord with the general realist conception of scientific methodology described here (see Boyd 1982, unpublished (b)).

Finally, the epistemic access account provides a precise formulation of the crucial realist claim that (perhaps despite changes in law-clusters) there is typically continuity of reference across "scientific revolutions" (Boyd 1979). Indeed, it permits us to integrate cases of what Field (1973) calls "partial denotation" into a general theory of reference and thus to treat cases of "denotational refinement" (Field 1973) as establishing referential continuity in the relevant sense (Boyd 1979).

If the dialectical and realistic conception of scientific methodology described here and the related epistemic access conception of reference are approximately correct, then together they constitute a rebuttal to both empiricist and constructivist antirealism which suffers none of the shortcomings of the more traditional rebuttals, while at the same time accommodating the insights which the more traditional rebuttals provide.

7. *Scientific Realism and Metaphilosophy*

If the conception of scientific knowledge and language which I have described here is correct, then it has implications for philosophical methodology which are sufficiently startling that they may help to explain why the dialectical and realist account of the reliability of scientific methodology was not put forward earlier as the epistemological foundation for scientific realism. I believe that it is fair to say that scientific realists have had a conception of their dispute with empiricist and (more recently) with constructivist antirealists according to which they shared with their opponents a general conception of the logic and methods of science, and according to which the dispute between realists and antirealists was over whether that logic and those methods were adequate to secure theoretical knowledge of a theory-independent reality. It was not anticipated that a new and distinctly realist general account of the methods of science would be necessary in order to defend scientific realism. This conception of a shared account of the logic and methods of science was advanced explicitly by Nagel, in discussing the realism-empiricist dispute:

> It is difficult to escape the conclusion that when the two opposing views on the cognitive status of theories are stated with some circumspection, each can assimilate into its formuation not only the racts concerning the primary subject matter explored by experimental inquiry but also the relevant facts concerning the logic and procedures of science. In brief, the opposition between these views is a conflict over preferred mode of speech. (Nagel 1961, pp. 151–152)

It is evident that the argument for scientific realism described in the preceding section departs from this understanding. According to that argument, no empiricist or constructivist account of the methods of science can explain the phenomenon of instrumental knowledge in science, the very kind of scientific knowledge about which realists, empiricists, and constructivists largely agree. Only on a distinctly realist conception of the logic and methods of science—a conception which empiricists and constructivists cannot share—can instrumental knowledge be explained.

At least since Descartes, the characteristic conception of epistemology in general has been that the most basic epistemological principles—the basic canons of reasoning or justification—should be defensible *a priori*. Thus, for example, almost all empiricists have thought that the most basic principles of inductive reasoning, whatever they are, can be defended *a priori*. What is striking is that, if the distinctly realist account of scientific knowledge is sound, then the most basic principles of inductive inference lack any *a priori* justification. That this is so can be seen by reflecting on what the scientific realist must say about the history of the scientific method.

According to the distinctly realist account of scientific knowledge, the reliability of the scientific method as a guide to (approximate) truth is to be explained only on the assumption that the theoretical tradition which defines our actual methodological principles reflects an approximately true account of the natural world. On that assumption, scientific methods will lead to successively more accurate theories and to successively more reliable methodological practices (for a discussion of limitations of this process of successive approximation see Boyd 1982, fn. 4). If we now inquire how the theoretical tradition came to embody sufficiently accurate theories in the first place, the scientific realist cannot appeal to the scientific method as an explanation, because that method is epistemically reliable only on the assumption that the relevant theoretical tradition *already* embodies a sufficiently good approximation to the truth. The realist, as I have portrayed her, must hold that the reliability of the scientific method rests upon the logically, epistemically, and historically contingent emergence of suitably approximately true theories. Like the causal theorist of perception or other "naturalistic" epistemologists, the scientific realist must deny that the most basic principles of inductive inference or justification are defensible *a priori*. In a word, the scientific realist must see epistemology as an *empirical* science (see Boyd 1982 for a discussion of the relation between scientific realism and other recent naturalistic trends in epistemology).

Closely analogous consequences follow from the epistemic access account of reference when it is applied in the light of scientific realism. The question of whether two tokens of a theoretical term are coreferential is, for example, a purely empirical question which cannot be resolved by conceptual analysis. If we think of the "meaning" of a theoretical term as comprising those features of its use in virtue of which it has whatever referent it in fact has, then meanings of theoretical terms are not given by *a priori* stipulations or social conventions. It is a logically, historically, and epistemically contingent matter which features of the use of a given term constitute its meaning in the sense of meaning relevant to referential semantics. There just are not going to be any important analytic or conceptual truths about any scientifically interesting subject matter (Boyd 1982).

If these controversial consequences of a thoroughgoing realist conception of scientific knowledge are sound, then it would be hard to escape a still more controversial conclusion: philosophy is itself a sort of empirical science. It may well be a normative science—epistemology, for example, may aim at understanding which belief regulating mechanisms are reliable guides to the truth—but it will be no less an empirical science for being normative in this way.

8. *Issues of Philosophical Method*

In this section, I shall discuss two issues of philosophical methodology raised by the arguments for scientific realism described in section 6. First, I shall discuss at some length an important challenge raised by Arthur Fine against the basic strategy of those arguments. I shall then discuss, somewhat more briefly, certain questions about the ways in which evidence from the history of science bears upon the arguments in question.

In a recent paper, Fine (1984) raises a number of interesting objections to the arguments for scientific realism which I have outlined in section 6. Of these objections one is particularly striking because it challenges not the details of the argument for realism, but its basic philosophical strategy. I shall now turn my attention to this objection.

Fine's objection is extremely simple and elegant. The proposed defense of realism precedes by an abductive argument: we are encouraged to accept realism because, realists maintain, realism provides the best explanation of the instrumental reliability of scientific methodology. Suppose for the sake of argument that this is true. We are still not justified in believing that realism is true. This is so because the issue between realists and empiricists is precisely over the question of whether or not abduction is an epistemologically justifiable inferential principle, especially when, as in the present case, the explanation postulated involves the operation of unobservable mechanisms. After all, if abductive inference is justifiable, then there is no epistemological problem about the theoretical postulation of "unobservables" in the first place. It is precisely abductive inference to unobservables which the standard empiricist arguments call into question. Thus, the abductive defense of realism we are considering is viciously circular.

It is reasonable to think of Fine's objection in the light of the previous discussion of the "no miracles" argument for realism discussed in section 3. Against the "no miracles" argument, I argued that, even if realism provides the best explanation for the predictive reliability of scientific theories, there remains for the realist the problem that this fact does not constitute a rebuttal to the very powerful epistemological considerations which form the basis for empiricist antirealism. Fine, in effect, presents a generalized version of this response to the "no miracles" argument. In the first place, Fine's version of the response in question applies not only to the "no miracles" argument but to any argument for realism which adduces realism as (a component of) the best explanation for some natural phenomenon. In particular. Fine's objection applies to the argument for realism offered in section 6. Suppose now that scientific realism provides the best explanation for the reliability (not just of individual theories but) of the methodology of science as a whole. This fact *by itself* does not constitute a rebuttal to the epistemological principles upon which the empiricist criticism of realism rests.

Moreover, Fine's objection diagnoses not only a weakness in such arguments for realism, but a circularity as well. The issue of scientific realism is—at least insofar as the dispute between realists and empiricists is concerned—a debate over the legitimacy of inductive inferences to the best explanation, at least in those cases in which the explanation in question postulates unobservable entities. Arguments for realism of the sort which Fine criticizes employ just this sort of inference, and thus simply beg the question between realists and empiricist antirealists.

Several things must be said in reply to Fine's subtle and elegant objection. In the first place, Fine's entirely correct insistence that the issue between empiricists and realists is over the legitimacy of abductive inferences is a double-edged sword. While it facilitates the identification of a sort of circularity in arguments for realism, it also highlights the epistemological oddity of consistent empiricism. The rejection of abduction or inference to the best explanation would place quite remarkable strictures on intellectual inquiry. In particular, it is by no means clear that students of the sciences—whether philosophers or historians—would have any methodology left if abduction were abandoned. If the fact that a theory provides the best available explanation for some important phenomenon is not a justification for believing that the theory is at least approximately true, then it is hard to see how intellectual inquiry could proceed. Of course, the antirealist might accept abductive inferences whenever their conclusions do not postulate unobservables, while rejecting such inferences to "theoretical" conclusions. In this case however the burden of proof will no longer lie exclusively on the realist's side: the antirealist must justify the proposed limitation on an otherwise legitimate principle of inductive inference.

This difficulty for the antirealist is exacerbated when one considers the issue of inductive inference in science itself. It must be remembered that empiricist philosophers of science do not intend to be fully skeptical: it is no part of standard empiricist philosophy of science to reject all nondeductive inferences. Instead, a selective skepticism is intended: (some) inductive generalizations about observables are to be epistemologically legitimate, while inferences to conclusions about unobservables are to be rejected. As Hanson, Kuhn and others have shown, the actual methods of science are profoundly theory-dependent. I have emphasized (Boyd 1972, 1973, 1979, 1980, 1982) that this theory-dependence extends to the methods which scientists employ in making inductive generalizations about observable phenomena. Both the choice of the generalizations which are seriously advanced and the assessment of the evidence for or against them rest upon theoretical inferences which manifest, or depend upon, the sort of abductive inferences to which the empiricist objects. In the terminology of recent empiricism, both the assessment of "projectability" of predicates, and the assessment of the "degree of confirmation" of generalizations about observables depend in practice upon inferences about "theoretical entities." Of course, acknowledging these facts about scientific practice would not commit the empiricist to agreeing that realism provides the best explanation for the instrumental reliability of scientific methodology nor, as Fine insists, would agreeing to that proposition commit the empiricist to holding that there is any reason to believe that realism is true. Nevertheless it certainly seems that, unless—as is very unlikely—the apparent theory-dependence of inductive inference about observables is really only apparent, the empiricist who rejects abductive inferences regarding unobservables must hold that even the inductive inferences which scientists make about observables are unjustified.

It might seem that there is an easy way out of this last difficulty for the empiricist. Suppose that inductive inferences about observables in science are genuinely theory-dependent and that, therefore, the (necessarily theoretical) justifications which scientists would ordinarily offer in defense of their inductive inferences about observables themselves rest on theoretical claims which are without justification. Still a philosopher might propose a sort of inductive justification of theory-dependent scientific inductions. Let the inductive procedures of science be as theory-dependent as you like, and let the justifications offered for individual inferences by scientists be as faulty as the empiricist claims. The fact remains that the (theory-dependent) methodology of science gives evidence of being instrumentally reliable. Let *that* constitute the justification for the inferences which scientists make. The thesis that the methodology of science is instrumentally reliable is, after all, a thesis about observable phenomena. It is moreover well confirmed by the observational evidence presented by the recent history of science and technology. Since no abductive inference objectionable from an empiricist perspective is required to establish the generalization that scientific methodology is instrumentally reliable, we may accept this generalization and then apply it to justify the acceptance of the inductive generalizations which scientists arrive at by employing the scientific method. Even though the theoretical reasoning which underlies inductive inferences about observables may not be justificatory, a second-order induction about the instrumental reliability of such reasoning might still afford a justification for that part of scientific practice which is supposed to be immune from the empiricist's selective skepticism.

It is very doubtful that this application of the inductive justification of induction can help the empiricist we are considering to avoid the conclusion that inductive generalizations in science about observables are unjustified. The hypothesis that scientific methodology is instrumentally reliable (henceforth the "reliability hypothesis") is itself an inductive generalization about observable phenomena. If, as I have suggested earlier, the confirmation or disconfirmation of such generalizations typically presupposes theoretical considerations of the sort our empiricist cannot accept. then we should expect that this might be true of the confirmation of the reliability hypothesis itself. If this is so, then the effort to circumvent the empiricist's conclusion that inductive generalizations in science are unjustified because they are theory-dependent. by appealing to the confirmation of the reliability hypothesis. will have failed. The reliability hypothesis will itself be unjustified by the standards of the empiricist we are considering.

I earlier suggested that theory-dependent considerations enter into the confirmation or disconfirmation of inductive generalizations in science in two related ways. In the first place, theoretical considerations are decisive in solving what Goodman (1973) calls the problem of "projectability". Given any finite body of observational data, there are infinitely many different generalizations about observables which are logically compatible with them. Theoretical considerations dictate the choice of a relatively small finite number of these generalizations as "projectable", that is, as worthy of serious scientific and experimental consideration. Moreover, when the experimental evidence for or against such projectively appropriate generalizations is assessed, theoretical considerations are crucial in determining the degree of confirmation or disconfirmation which those generalizations receive, given any particular body of observational evidence. If this is so. then we might expect to be able to discern the effects of both sorts of theory-dependent judgments in the special case of the confirmation of the reliability hypothesis.

Consider first the issue of the degree of confirmation of the reliability hypothesis. The hypothesis that the scientific method is instrumentally reliable asserts that that method tends to produce acceptance of instrumentally reliable theories. The reliability of a theory in turn is a matter not only of its past predictive successes but also of its *future* predictive success. Now the observational evidence which supports the reliability hypothesis consists of the past and present predictive successes of (many of) the theories whose acceptance has been dictated by the scientific method. In order for these past successes to count as evidence for the instrumental reliability of the scientific method, they surely must be understood first as counting as evidence for the future (approximate) instrumental reliability of most of the theories in question. Our conviction that the methods of science are instrumentally reliable turns on our conviction that those methods have led us to accept theories which tended themselves to be instrumentally reliable. We can make this latter judgment only if we take the past predictive successes of the relevant theories as evidence for their future instrumental reliability; that is, only if we are *already* prepared to make the ordinary scientific judgment that past predictive successes *of the sort actually available* warrant our belief in the inductive generalizations about observables embodied in the theories in question. But this is just the sort of theory-dependent judgment which the reliability hypothesis is supposed to justify. If the ordinary scientific justifications for assigning the generalizations in question a high degree of confirmation are inadequate because they depend upon abductions to theoretical explanations, then the second-order inductive justification of scientists' inductions by appeal to the reliability hypothesis fails to help. The decision to assign the reliability hypothesis a high degree of confirmation on the available evidence rests upon the very theory-dependent judgments about the degree of confirmation of ordinary scientific theories which the empiricist we are considering cannot accept as justificatory.

We may also see how theoretical considerations regarding "projectability" are involved in the confirmation of the reliability hypothesis. When philosophers of whatever persuasion assert that the methods of science are instrumentally (or theoretically, for that matter) reliable, their claim is of very little interest if nothing can be said about which methods are the methods in question. Indeed, without at least a preliminary specification of the methods in question, it would be difficult to have any evidence whatsoever for the reliability thesis. Moreover, it will not do to countenance as "methods of science" just any regularities which may be discerned in the practice of scientists. If the reliability thesis is to be correctly formulated, one must identify those features of scientific practice which contribute to its instrumental reliability. This is a nontrivial intellectual problem, as one may see by examining the various different attempts—behaviorist, reductionist and functionalist—to explain what a *scientific* foundation for psychology would look like.

In so far as the confirmation of the reliability hypothesis is concerned, the issue is not so much over how easy or difficult it is to identify the reliability-making features of scientific practice, but rather over what sorts of considerations would have to go into a justification for a proposed identification of those features. Recall that we are considering the options open to the empiricist who rejects abductive inferences as nonjustificatory but who agrees that the actual inductive methods of science (the instrumentally reliable methods) are theory-dependent and rest in practice upon abductive inferences. It is reasonble to ask of this empiricist—as it would be reasonable to ask of any other philosopher who had identified the same theory-dependent methods as the methods of sciences—what justification can be offered for the identification of these particular methods as the reliability-making features of scientific practice.

The problem of providing a justification for a particular proposed identification of such features represents, as regards the formulation of the reliability hypothesis, a special case of the problem of projectability. This may be easily seen if we employ a variant of the empiricists' favorite argument that theory choice is underdetermined by observational data. Suppose that you believe that past scientific practice has certain reliability-making general features which should form the basis for a suitable formulation of the reliability hypothesis. There have been only finitely many methodological judgments in the whole history of science to date. Even if you know which of these judgments have contributed to the reliability of past scientific practice, there will still be infinitely many different "methodologies"—infinitely many different sets of principles for theory-choice, experimental design, data assessment, etc.—which would have dictated the conclusions of those finitely many past methodological judgments. The choice of any one of these infinitely many "methodologies" represents a particular solution to the problem of projectability for the investigator interested in finding an appropriate formulation of the reliability hypothesis. Alternative choices yield different versions of the reliability hypothesis and represent different estimates of what the reliability-making *general* features of past scientific practice have been.

If what I have suggested earlier is true then the solution to this particular case of the problem of projectability might be expected to depend upon *theoretical* considerations. Indeed, this proves to be the case. Remember that the empiricist we are considering accepts the ordinary theory-dependent methods of the working scientist as the reliability-making features of scientific practice. Let us consider an illustrative example of such methods. It is by now widely acknowledged that sound scientific methodology dictates that "measurement procedures" for physical magnitudes should be revised in the light of new theoretical "discoveries". [I use quotation marks to indicate that the empiricist need not take the notions of measurement or theoretical discovery at face value. What is important is that the application of this principle in practice has a significant effect upon the inductive generalizations about observables which scientists accept.] Let P be the methodological principle which says that one should follow the dictates of the best confirmed theory in (re)designing measurement procedures. What justifies us in taking P to be one of the reliability-making features of scientific practice? Why should we not subsume the finitely many cases to date of successful applications of this principle under some other quite different maxim with which they are all consistent?

Recalling that an appeal to the reliability hypothesis is inappropriate here, since what is at issue is the formulation and confirmation of that hypothesis, it is hard to see how our reasons for accepting P as reliability-making could he other than a summary of the ordinary reasons which scientists have for accepting various applications of P. But these are theory-dependent reasons—roughly, they amount to the idea that the best theories represent results of the best (abductive) inferences regarding the unobservable magnitudes in question, and that therefore these theories are likely to provide approximately true accounts of how to measure those magnitudes. But theoretical reasons of this sort are just those which the empiricist considers nonjustificatory. Worse yet if we are to accept P, and not just some particular applications of P, as reliability-making it would seem that our justification for accepting P must involve not just the scientists' theoretical reasons for particular applications of P but the scientific realist's reasons for thinking P generally reliable (see Boyd 1982). If the empiricist forgoes appeals to the abductive inferences of ordinary scientific practice, on the grounds that such inferences are nonjustificatory then it is hard to see how she can make scientifically sound judgments about which methods are scientific or about how to even formulate the reliability hypothesis.

It is worth noting that the empiricist we are considering gets into this particular difficulty largely because she accepts the results of recent philosophical and historical scholarship, which strongly suggest that the real methods of science are theory-dependent and rest in practice on abductive inferences of the sort unacceptable to empiricists. What appears to be true is that the consistent empiricists cannot both (a) hold that the inductive methods of scientists are justified insofar as generalizations about observables are concerned, and (b) accept the best recent work on the question of what those methods actually are.

I conclude that the empiricist who rejects abductive inferences is probably unable to avoid—in any philosophically plausible way—the conclusion that the inductive inferences which scientists make about observables are unjustified. Nevertheless, even if this is so, Fine's criticism of abductive arguments for realism still has force. If what is at issue is the legitimacy of abductive inferences to theoretical explanations in general, then there is a kind of circularity in the appeal to a particular abduction of this sort in the defense of scientific realism. I suggested earlier in this paper that standard rebuttals to empiricist antirealism, while they provide some reason to believe that scientific realism is true, fail to respond to the strong epistemological challenge which empiricist antirealism offers. Should we take the circularity which Fine discerns to indicate that the same is true for the abductive argument for scientific realism as a component in the best explanation for the instrumental reliability of scientific method? I want to argue that the answer should be no.

If abduction were *prima facie* suspect, in the way that palm reading or horoscope casting now are, then surely it would be inappropriate to appeal to some particular abductive inference in defense of abductive inference in general. Abduction is, however, *prima facie* legitimate: it is seen as suspect only in the light of certain distinctly empiricist epistemological considerations. In order to assess the import of the circularity of appealing to abduction in replying to empiricist antirealism. we must examine more closely the relation between the particular abductive inferences in question, and the empiricist's arguments against realism.

I suggest that our assessment of the import of the circularity in question should focus not on the legitimacy of the realist's abductive inference considered in isolation, but rather on the relative merits of the overall accounts of scientific knowledge which the empiricist and the realist defend. Such an assessment strategy is familiar from many areas of intellectual inquiry, scientific and scholarly: defenders of rival positions often reach their distinctive conclusions *via* forms of inference which their rivals think unjustified. The "pair-wise theory neutral" procedure for addressing such disputes typically consists in an assessment of the overall adequacy of the theories put forward rather than in an assessment of the particular controversial inference forms considered in isolation.

If we consider the present dispute in this light, then there are two considerations which are especially important. First, the empiricist's objection to abductive inferences (at least to those which yield conclusions about unobservable phenomena) rests upon the powerful and sophisticated epistemological argument rehearsed in section 3. That argument depends upon the evidential indistinguishability thesis. Moreover, the evidential indistinguishability thesis itself is put forward by empiricists (tacitly or explicitly) on the understanding that it captures the truth reflected in the doctrine of "knowledge empiricism": the doctrine that all factual knowledge must be grounded in observation. If either knowledge empiricism is basically false, or if the indistinguish-ability thesis represents a seriously misleading interpretation of it, then the empiricist's argument against abduction to theoretical explanation fails.

Secondly, the empiricist aims at a selectively skeptical account of scientific know-ledge: knowledge of unobservables is impossible, but inductive generalizations about observables are sometimes epistemologically legitimate. It turns out however that the empiricist's commitment to knowledge empiricism, together with her adoption of the evidential indistinguishability thesis as an interpretation of it, threaten to dictate the unwelcome and implausible conclusion that even inductive inferences regarding ob-servables are always unjustified.

The rebuttals to empiricist antirealism discussed in section 3 strengthen the case for realism as an account of the structure of scientific knowledge, but they provide no direct argument either against knowledge empiricism or against the evidential in-distinguishability thesis as an interpretation of it. The situation of the abductive argument for scientific realism sketched in section 6 is quite different. If we accept the abductive inference to a distinctly realistic account of scientific methodology then we can see *why* the evidential indistinguishability thesis is false. Moreover we can see that the distinctly realistic conception of scientific methodology retains the central core of the doctrine of knowledge empiricism: all factual knowledge *does* depend upon ob-servation; there are no *a priori* factual statements immune from empirical refutation.

I think that it is fair to say that, given the difficulties which plague empiricist antirealism in the philosophy of science, the only philosophically cogent reason for rejecting scientific realism in favor of instrumentalism, or some other variant of empiri-cism, lies in the conviction that only from an empiricist perspective can one be faithful to the basic idea that factual knowledge must be experimental knowledge, that is, to the grain of truth in knowledge empiricism. The abductive argument for scientific realism that we are considering is best thought of as a component of an alternative realistic conception of scientific knowledge which preserves the empiricist insight that factual knowledge rests on the senses without the cost of an inadequate and potentially wholly skeptical treatment of scientific inquiry.

I have suggested in section 7 (see also Boyd 1982) that the crucial feature of this alternative conception of knowledge is its naturalism. In particular, the special relation of the senses to knowledge is seen in this conception as resting on logically con-tingent facts about the role of the senses in the reliable production or regulation of belief. Here an analogy between the naturalistic defense of scientific realism against empiricist antirealism and the naturalistic defense of knowledge of external objects against empiricist phenomenalism is revealing. The phenomenalist rejects realism about ("observable") external objects, relying on an application of the sense-datum version of the evidential indistinguishability thesis. The indistinguishability thesis itself is understood as the appropriate interpretation of the fundamental truth embodied in the doctrine of knowledge empiricism. The causal theorist of knowledge does not reject the basic doctrine of the epistemic primacy of the senses, but instead insists that the truth of that doctrine, in so far as it concerns perceptual knowledge, is really a reflection of the logically contingent fact that the senses are causally reliable detectors of external objects. Sensory experience provides reliable evidence for propositions only when it arises from suitable causal connections to the subject matter of the propositions in question. The sense-datum form of the indistinguishability thesis is therefore false, and inadequately expresses the fundamental truth of knowledge empiricism.

The causal theorist's critique of phenomenalism rests upon what her empiricist opponent would characterize as an illegitimate abductive inference to external objects, as the explanation for facts about sensations. The causal theorist's position does not, however, stand or fall on the strength of that abduction taken in isolation. Instead the alternative empiricist and naturalist conceptions of knowledge and especially of the epistemic role of the senses must be evaluated as rival philosophical theories. The very grave difficulties which phenomenalism faces in explaining ordinary perceptual knowledge strongly suggest that the naturalist's causal theory of perceptual knowledge is preferable.

The situation with respect to the dispute between the empiricist antirealist and the scientific realist who subscribes to the argument sketched in section 6 is exactly analogous. The antirealist's position rests upon an application of the indistinguishability thesis, which in turn is offered as an explication of knowledge empiricism. The scientific realist—like the causal theorist of perception—accepts the insight of knowledge empiricism while denying that the indistinguishability thesis captures that insight. The causal theorist maintains that the truth of knowledge empiricism, insofar as it applies to perceptual knowledge, is a reflection of a logically contingent fact about the reliability of the senses as detectors. Analogously, the scientific realist maintains that the truth of knowledge empiricism, insofar as experimental knowledge in the sciences is concerned, is a reflection not only of the logically contingent reliability of the senses as detectors, but also of the logically and historically contingent emergence of a theoretical tradition relevantly approximately true enough to make theory-dependent experimental practice a reliable mechanism for belief regulation (see Boyd 1982). Like the causal theorist's rebuttal to phenomenalism, the scientific realist's rebuttal to empiricist antirealism rests upon what her opponent would regard as an illegitimate abductive inference. In this case, like the previous one, however, the scientific realist's position does not stand or fall on the strength of that abduction considered in isolation. Rather what is to be assessed are the relative merits of empiricist epistemology and the emerging naturalistic epistemology of which the realist's conception of scientific knowledge is one of the more distinctive and controversial parts.

In this regard it is worth remarking that the plausibility of knowledge empiricism has no doubt always rested upon two considerations: a recognition of the central causal role of the senses in information-gathering and a recognition of the success of experimental science. It is doubtful if consistent empiricism can recognize either of these phenomena. If this proves to be the case, then the alternative realistic and naturalistic conception of the epistemic role of the senses must surely capture what truth there is in knowledge empiricism.

Let us turn now to the question of the way in which evidence from the history of science bears upon the arguments for scientific realism which we have been discussing. I have emphasized the important role which, according to the version of naturalistic and realistic epistemology discussed in this paper, was played by the historically contingent emergence of research traditions embodying suitably approximately true theories of unobservables. If I am right, it is to the successive development of the approximate truths (theoretical as well as instrumental) embodied in these traditions that we owe the instrumental reliability of current scientific practice. Although it is no part of my thesis that this development was progressive in all particular instances, or occurred uniformly with respect to different disciplines, subdisciplines, or even problem areas within subdisciplines, it is essential to the thesis I am defending that there be some measure of referential continuity and successive approximation to the truth in the history of recent science (Boyd 1982). I emphasized in section 4 that if continuity of reference and methodology could not be established in many cases in the history of modern science, the sort of realism I am defending would be strongly undermined.

Because of the centrality of considerations of historical continuity to the abductive argument for scientific realism which we are considering here, I think it important to indicate ways in which historical continuity is *not* involved in that argument. In the first place, it is not a consequence of the position advocated here on behalf of the realist that a successful pattern of inductive generalization at the observational level must *always* rest upon the acceptance of relevantly approximately true background theories. In order for any inductive enterprise to be successful, there must be an appropriate correspondence between the categories in terms of which phenomena are classified, and their relevant causal powers. There is however nothing to prevent scientists or others from hitting upon categories appropriate to some limited class of generalizations by chance rather than as a result of theoretical understanding.

In mature sciences, however, scientists do not solve the problem of "projectability" by the specification of some relatively fixed sets of projectable properties or predicates, theoretical or observational. Instead we possess a *methodology* for exploiting the full descriptive resources of our *theoretical* concepts to guide inductive inferences at the observational level. Instead of assessing the projectability of particular predicates, we are able to assess the projectability of theoretically characterizable patterns in observational data: we count as projectable any pattern in observational data which corresponds to a theoretical hypothesis which is plausible in the light of the current "total science." Moreover, we take such a hypothesis to represent the inductive generalization about observables which corresponds to the observational consequences derivable from the hypothesis itself, *together with* the theories which constitute the existing total science. Once such a hypothesis has been accepted, we countenance *further* expansion and modification of the inductive generalizations about observables which it warrants as our "total science" itself changes and develops (for a more precise discussion see Boyd 1982). We are thus able to identify as projectable an extraordinary variety of patterns among observables representing empirical generalizations of great power, scope, and precision.

In addition to the methods for identifying inductively appropriate empirical generalizations, the methods employed in mature sciences for the experimental and observational testing of such generalizations—methods for the design of experiments and of instrumentation for the establishment of appropriate control, and for the assessment of "degrees of confirmation"—are also profoundly theory-dependent. It is the instrumental reliability of all of these various theory-dependent methods—methods whose characteristic reliability is displayed typically only in mature (and, often, relatively recent) science—for which according to the argument we are considering the only plausible explanation rests upon a realistic conception of scientific knowledge. What is claimed is that when, in the historical development of any particular science, its theory-dependent methodological practices come to display the sort of intricacy *and* instrumental reliability characteristic say of modern physical or chemical practice, only the realistic account of scientific knowledge described in section 6 will provide an adequate explanation of that reliability. No claim is made that the more limited inductive success of earlier scientific practice must always be explained in the same way.

The positive evidence for scientific realism thus rests primarily on features of scientific practice which would be discernible even if one limited one's examination to very recent science. According to the realist, realism provides the only acceptable explanation for the current instrumental reliability of scientific methodology in mature sciences. Realism does however entail interesting conclusions about historical development within mature sciences—that is, within those sciences in which theoretical considerations contribute significantly to a high level of instrumental reliability of method. For many sciences, especially the physical sciences the period of maturity in this sense begins long before the recent past. Historical studies of such sciences—of, for example, the extent of semantic and methodological continuity in the history of those sciences—are thus evidentally relevant to the issue of realism. Insofar as a realist perspective proves fruitful in understanding the history of mature sciences, that would provide further evidence for realism, but the primary role of historical studies in this area is to subject the claims of realists to possible disconfirmation by historical evidence rather than to provide new kinds of positive evidence favoring realism over its rivals.

Note

Earlier versions of this paper were presented at Rice University, Hobart and William Smith College, Franklin and Marshall College, and Cornell University. I am grateful to the audiences at these institutions for helpful comments and criticisms. I am especially grateful to Professor Nicholas Sturgeon and Dr. Kristin Guyot.

References

Bennett, Jonathan: 1971, *Locke, Berkeley, Hume*, Oxford: Oxford University Press.

Boyd, R.: 1972, "Deteriminism, Laws and Predictability in Principle," *Philosophy of Science* **39**

Boyd, R.: 1973, "Realism, Underdetermination and A Causal Theory of Evidence," *Noûs* 7: 1–12.

Boyd, R.: 1979, "Metaphor and Theory Change," in Andrew Ortony (ed.), *Metaphor and Thought*, Cambridge: Cambridge University Press.

Boyd, R.: 1980 "Materialism Without Reductionism: What Physicalism Does Not Entail," in Ned Bock (ed.), *Reading in Philosophy of Psychology*, vol. 1, Cambridge: Harvard University Press.

Boyd, R.: 1982, "Scientific Realism and Naturalistic Epistemology," *PSA 80*, vol. 2, East Lansing: Philosophy of Science Association.

Boyd, R.: unpublished (a), "Materialism Without Reductionism: Non-Humean Causation and the Evidence for Physicalism."

Boyd, R.: unpublished (b), *Realism and Scientific Epistemology*.

Carnap, R.: 1950, *Meaning and Necessity*, Chicago: University of Chicago Press.

Feigl, H.: 1956, "Some Major Issues and Developments in the Philosophy of Science of Logical Empiricism," in H. Feigl and M. Scriven (eds.), *Minnesota Studies in the Philosophy of Science*. vol. 1, Minneapolis: University of Minnesota Press.

Field, H.: 1973, "Theory Change and the Indeterminacy of Reference," *Journal of Philosophy* **70**: 462–481.

Fine, A.: 1984, "The Natural Ontological Attitude," in J. Leplin (ed.), *Scientific Realism*, Berkeley: University of California Press.

Goodman, N.: 1973, *Fact, Fiction and Forecast*, 3rd ed., Indianapolis and New York: Bobbs-Merrill Co.

Hanson, N. R.: 1958, *Patterns of Discovery*, Cambridge: Cambridge Univeristy Press.

Harman, G.: 1965, "The Inference to the Best Explanation," *Philosophical Review* **74**: 88–95.

Kripke, S.: 1972, "Naming and Necessity," in G. Harman and D. Davidson (eds.), *The Semantics of Natural Language*, Dordrecht: D. Reidel.

Kuhn, T.: 1970, *The Structure of Scientific Revolution*, 2nd ed., Chicago: University of Chicago Press.

Maxwell, G.: 1963, "The Ontological Status of Theoretical Entities," in H. Feigl and G. Maxwell (eds.), *Scientific Explanation, Space and Time*, Minneapolis: University of Minnesota Press.

Nagel, E.: 1961, *The Structure of Science*, New York: Harcourt, Brace.

Putnam, H.: 1975, "The Meaning of 'Meaning'," in Putnam, *Mind, Language and Reality*, Cambridge: Cambridge University Press.

Putnam, H.: 1978, *Meaning and the Moral Sciences*, London: Routledge and Kegan Paul.

Quine, W. V. O.: 1969, "Natural Kinds," in Quine, *Ontological Relativity and Other Essays*, New York: Columbia University Press.

Schlick, M.: 1932/33, "Positivism and Realism," *Erkenntnis* 3 (1932/33), translated by D. Rynin in A. J. Ayer (ed.), *Logical Positivism*, New York: Free Press, 1959.

Smart, J. J. C.: 1963, *Philosophy and Scientific Realism*, London: Routledge and Kegan Paul.

van Fraassen, B.: 1980, *The Scientific Image*, Oxford: The Clarendon Press.

Chapter 12

A Confutation of Convergent Realism

Larry Laudan

The positive argument for realism is that it is the only philosophy that doesn't make the success of science a miracle.
H. Putnam (1975)

The Problem

It is becoming increasingly common to suggest that epistemological realism is an empirical hypothesis, grounded in, and to be authenticated by, its ability to explain the workings of science. A growing number of philosophers (including Boyd, W. Newton-Smith, A. Shimony, Putnam, and I. Niiniluoto) have argued that the theses of epistemic realism are open to empirical test.[1] The suggestion that epistemological doctrines have much the same empirical status as the sciences is a welcome one; for, whether it stands up to detailed scrutiny or not, this suggestion marks a significant facing-up by the philosophical community to one of the most neglected (and most notorious) problems of philosophy: the status of epistemological claims.

There are, however, potential hazards as well as advantages associated with the "scientizing" of epistemology. Specifically, once one concedes that epistemic doctrines are to be tested in the court of experience, it is possible that one's favorite epistemic theories may be refuted rather than confirmed. It is the thesis of this paper that precisely such a fate afflicts a form of realism advocated by those who have been in the vanguard of the move to show that realism is supported by an empirical study of the development of science. Specifically, I will show that epistemic realism, at least in certain of its extant forms, is neither supported by, nor has it made sense of, much of the available historical evidence.

Convergent Realism

Like other philosophical "isms," the term 'realism' covers a variety of sins. Many of these will not be at issue here. For instance, 'semantic realism' (in brief, the claim that all theories have truth values and that some theories are true, although we know not which) is not in dispute. Nor shall I discuss what one might call 'intentional realism' (i.e., the view that theories are generally intended by their proponents to assert the existence of entities corresponding to the terms in those theories). What I will focus on instead are certain forms of epistemological realism. As Hilary Putnam has pointed out, although such realism has become increasingly fashionable, "very little is said

Reprined from *Philosophy of Science* 48 (1981), pp. 19–48, by permission of the author and the Philosophy of Science Association.

about what realism is.[2] The lack of specificity about what realism asserts makes it difficult to evaluate its claims, since many formulations are too vague and sketchy to get a grip on. At the same time, any efforts to formulate the realist position with greater precision lay the critic open to charges of attacking a straw man. In the course of this paper, I shall attribute several theses to the realists. Although there is probably no realist who subscribes to all of them, most of them have been defended by some self-avowed realist or other; taken together, they are perhaps closest to that version of realism advocated by Putnam, Boyd, and Newton-Smith. Although I believe the views I shall be discussing can be legitimately attributed to certain contemporary philosophers (and I will cite the textual evidence for such attributions), it is not crucial to my case that such attributions can be made. Nor will I claim to do justice to the complex epistemologies of those whose work I will criticize. Rather, my aim is to explore certain epistemic claims which those who are realists might be tempted (and in some cases have been tempted) to embrace. If my arguments are sound, we will discover that some of the most intuitively tempting versions of realism prove to be chimeras.

The form of realism I shall discuss involves variants of the following claims:

(R1) Scientific theories (at least in the 'mature' sciences) are typically approximately true, and more recent theories are closer to the truth than older theories in the same domain.

(R2) The observational and theoretical terms within the theories of a mature science genuinely refer (roughly, there are substances in the world that correspond to the ontologies presumed by our best theories).

(R3) Successive theories in any mature science will be such that they preserve the theoretical relations and the apparent referents of earlier theories, that is, earlier theories will be limiting cases of later theories.[3]

(R4) Acceptable new theories do and should explain why their predecessors were successful insofar as they were successful.

To these semantic, methodological, and epistemic theses is conjoined an important metaphilosophical claim about how realism is to be evaluated and assessed. Specifically, it is maintained that:

(R5) Theses (R1) to (R4) entail that ("mature") scientific theories should be successful; indeed, these theses constitute the best, if not the only, explanation for the success of science. The empirical success of science (in the sense of giving detailed explanations and accurate predictions) accordingly provides striking empirical confirmation for realism.

I shall call the position delineated by (R1) to (R5) *convergent epistemological realism,* or CER for short. Many recent proponents of CER maintain that (R1), (R2), (R3), and (R4) are empirical hypotheses that, via the linkages postulated in (R5), can be tested by an investigation of science itself. They propose two elaborate abductive arguments. The structure of the first (argument 1) which is germane to (R1), is something like this:

1. If scientific theories are approximately true, then they typically will be empirically successful.

2. If the central terms in scientific theories genuinely refer, then those theories generally will be empirically successful.

3. Scientific theories are empirically successful.

4. (Probably) theories are approximately true and their terms genuinely refer.

The structure of the second abductive argument (argument 2), which is relevant to (R3), is of slightly different form, specifically:

1. If the earlier theories in a "mature" science are approximately true, and if the central terms of those theories genuinely refer, then later, more successful theories in the same science will preserve the earlier theories as limiting cases.
2. Scientists seek to preserve earlier theories as limiting cases and generally succeed in doing so.
3. (Probably) earlier theories in a "mature" science are approximately true and genuinely referential.

Taking the success of present and past theories as givens, proponents of CER claim that *if* CER were true, it would follow, as a matter of course, that science would be successful and progressive. Equally, they allege that if CER were false, the success of science would be "miraculous" and without explanation.[4] Because (on their view) CER explains the fact that science is successful, the theses of CER are thereby confirmed by the success of science, and nonrealist epistemologies are discredited by the latter's alleged inability to explain both the success of current theories and the progress which science historically exhibits.

As Putnam and certain others (e.g., Newton-Smith) see it, the fact that statements about reference (R2, R3) or about approximate truth (R1, R3) function in the explanation of a contingent state of affairs, establishes that "the notions of 'truth' and 'reference' have a causal explanatory role in epistemology."[5] In one fell swoop, both epistemology and semantics are 'naturalized' and, to top it all off, we get an explanation of the success of science thrown into the bargain!

The central question before us is whether the realist's assertions about the interrelations between truth, reference, and success are sound. It will be the burden of this paper to raise doubts about both arguments 1 and 2. Specifically, I will argue that four of the five premises of those abductions are either false or too ambiguous to be acceptable. I will also seek to show that, even if the premises were true, they would not warrant the conclusions that realists draw from them. The next three sections of this essay deal with the first abductive argument. Then I turn to the second.

Reference and Success

The specifically referential side of the empirical argument for realism has been developed chiefly by Putnam, who talks explicitly of reference rather more than most realists. However, reference is usually implicitly smuggled in, since most realists subscribe to the (ultimately referential) thesis that "the world probably contains entities very like those postulated by our most successful theories."

If (R2) is to fulfill Putnam's ambition that reference can explain the success of science, and that the success of science establishes the presumptive truth of (R2), it seems he must subscribe to claims similar to these:

(S1) The theories in the advanced or mature sciences are successful.
(S2) A theory whose central terms genuinely refer will be a successful theory.
(S3) If a theory is successful, we can reasonably infer that its central terms genuinely refer.
(S4) All the central terms in theories in the mature sciences do refer.

There are complex interconnections here. (S2) and (S4) explain (S1), while (S1) and (S3) provide the warrant for (S4). Reference explains success, and success warrants a presumption of reference. The arguments are plausible, given the premises. But there is the rub, for with the possible exception of (S1), none of the premises is acceptable.

The first and toughest problem involves getting clearer about the nature of that "success" which realists are concerned to explain. Although Putnam, W. Sellars, and Boyd all take the success of certain sciences as a given, they say little about what this success amounts to. So far as I can see, they are working with a largely *pragmatic* notion to be couched in terms of a theory's workability or applicability. On this account, we would say that a theory is successful if it makes substantially correct predictions, if it leads to efficacious interventions in the natural order, and if it passes a battery of standard tests. One would like to be able to be more specific about what success amounts to, but the lack of a coherent theory of confirmation makes further specificity very difficult.

Moreover, the realist must be wary, at least for these purposes, of adopting too strict a notion of success, for a highly robust and stringent construal of "success" would defeat the realist's purposes. What he wants to explain, after all, is why science in general has worked so well. If he were to adopt a very demanding characterization of success (such as those advocated by inductive logicians or Popperians), then it would probably turn out that science has been largely "unsuccessful" (because it does not have high confirmation), and the realist's avowed explanandum would thus be a nonproblem. Accordingly, I will assume that a theory is successful so long as it has worked well, that is, so long as it has functioned in a variety of explanatory contexts, has led to confirmed predictions, and has been of broad explanatory scope. As I understand the realist's position, his concern is to explain why certain theories have enjoyed this kind of success.

If we construe 'success' in this way, (S1) can be conceded. Whether one's criterion of success is broad explanatory scope, possession of a large number of confirming instances, or conferring manipulative or predictive control, it is clear that science, by and large, is a successful activity .

What about (S2)? 1 am not certain that any realist would or should endorse it, although it is a perfectly natural construal of the realist's claim that "reference explains success." The notion of reference that is involved here is highly complex and unsatisfactory in significant respects. Without endorsing it, I shall use it frequently in the ensuing discussion. The realist sense of reference is a rather liberal one, according to which the terms in a theory may be genuinely referring even if many of the claims the theory makes about the entities to which it refers are false. Provided that there are entities that "approximately fit" a theory's description of them, Putnam's charitable account of reference allows us to say that the terms of a theory genuinely refer.[6] On this account (and these are Putnam's examples), Bohr's 'electron', Newton's 'mass', Mendel's 'gene', and Dalton's 'atom' are all referring terms, while 'phlogiston' and 'ether' are not.[7]

Are genuinely referential theories (i.e., theories whose central terms genuinely refer) invariably or even generally successful at the empirical level, as (S2) states? There is ample evidence that they are not. The chemical atomic theory in the eighteenth century was so remarkably unsuccessful that most chemists abandoned it in favor of a more phenomenological, elective affinity chemistry. The Proutian theory that the atoms of heavy elements are composed of hydrogen atoms had, through most of the nineteenth century, a strikingly unsuccessful career, confronted by a long string of apparent refutations. The Wegenerian theory that the continents are carried by large subterranean objects moving laterally across the earth's surface was, for some thirty years in the recent history of geology, a strikingly unsuccessful theory until, after major modifications, it became the geological orthodoxy of the 1960s and 1970s. Yet all of these theories postulated basic entities which (according to Putnam's "principle of charity") genuinely exist.

The realist's claim that we should expect referring theories to be empirically successful is simply false. And, with a little reflection, we can see good reasons why it should be. To have a genuinely referring theory is to have a theory that "cuts the world at its joints," a theory that postulates entities of a kind that really exist. But a genuinely referring theory need not be such that all—or even most—of the specific claims it makes about the properties of those entities and their modes of interaction are true. Thus, Dalton's theory makes many false claims about atoms; Bohr's early theory of the electron was similarly flawed in important respects. Contra-(S2), genuinely referential theories need not be strikingly successful, since such theories may be 'massively false' (i.e., have far greater falsity content than truth content).

(S2) is so patently false that it is difficult to imagine that the realist need be committed to it. But what else will do? The (Putnamian) realist wants attributions of reference to a theory's terms to function in an explanation of that theory's success. The simplest and crudest way of doing that involves a claim like (S2). A less outrageous way of achieving the same end would involve the weaker:

(S2′) A theory whose terms refer will usually (but not always) be successful.

Isolated instances of referring but unsuccessful theories, sufficient to refute (S2), leave (S2′) unscathed. But, if we were to find a broad range of referring but unsuccessful theories, that would be evidence against (S2′). Such theories can be generated at will. For instance, take any set of terms which one believes to be genuinely referring. In any language rich enough to contain negation, it will be possible to construct indefinitely many unsuccessful theories, all of whose substantive terms are genuinely referring. Now, it is always open to the realist to claim that such "theories" are not really theories at all, but mere conjunctions of isolated statements—lacking that sort of conceptual integration we associate with "real" theories. Sadly, a parallel argument can be made for genuine theories. Consider, for instance, how many inadequate versions of the atomic theory there were in the 2,000 years of atomic speculating, before a genuinely successful theory emerged. Consider how many unsuccessful versions there were of the wave theory of light before the 1820s, when a successful wave theory first emerged. Kinetic theories of heat in the seventeenth and eighteenth century, and developmental theories of embryology before the late nineteenth century, sustain a similar story. (S2′), every bit as much as (S2), seems hard to reconcile with the historical record.

As Richard Burian has pointed out to me (personal communication), a realist might attempt to dispense with both of those theses and simply rest content with (S3) alone. Unlike (S2) and (S2′), (S3) is not open to the objection that referring theories are often unsuccessful, for it makes no claim that referring theories are always or generally successful. But (S3) has difficulties of its own. In the first place, it seems hard to square with the fact that the central terms of many relatively successful theories (e.g., ether theories or phlogistic theories) are evidently nonreferring. I shall discuss this tension in detail below. More crucial for our purposes here is that (S3) is *not strong enough* to permit the realist to utilize reference to explain success. Unless genuineness of reference entails that all or most referring theories will be successful, then the fact that a theory's terms refer scarcely provides a convincing explanation of that theory's success. If, as (S3) allows, many (or even most) referring theories can be unsuccessful, how can the fact that a successful theory's terms refer be taken to explain why it is successful? (S3) may or may not be true; but in either case it arguably gives the realist no explanatory access to scientific success.

A more plausible construal of Putnam's claim that reference plays a role in explaining the success of science involves a rather more indirect argument. It might be said (and Putnam does say this much) that we can explain why a theory is successful by assuming that the theory is true or approximately true. Since a theory can only be true or nearly true (in any sense of those terms open to the realist) if its terms genuinely refer, it might be argued that reference gets into the act willy-nilly when we explain a theory's success in terms of its truthlike status. On this account, reference is piggy-backed on approximate truth. The viability of this indirect approach is treated at length in the next section, so I will not discuss it here except to observe that if the only contact point between reference and success is provided through the medium of approximate truth, then the link between reference and success is extremely tenuous.

What about (S3), the realist's claim that success creates a rational presumption of reference? We have already seen that (S3) provides no explanation of the success of science, but does it have independent merits? The question specifically is whether the success of a theory provides a warrant for concluding that its central terms refer. Insofar as this is, as certain realists suggest, an empirical question, it requires us to inquire whether past theories which have been successful are ones whose central terms genuinely referred (according to the realist's own account of reference).

A proper empirical test of this hypothesis would require an extensive sifting of the historical record that is not possible to perform here. What I can do is to mention a range of once successful, but (by present lights) nonreferring, theories. A fuller list will come later, but for now we will focus on a whole family of related theories, namely, the subtle fluids and ethers of eighteenth- and nineteenth-century physics and chemistry.

Consider specifically the state of etherial theories in the 1830s and 1840s. The electrical fluid, a substance that was generally assumed to accumulate on the surface rather than to permeate the interstices of bodies, had been utilized to explain inter alia the attraction of oppositely charged bodies, the behavior of the Leyden jar, the similarities between atmospheric and static electricity, and many phenomena of current electricity. Within chemistry and heat theory, the caloric ether had been widely utilized since H. Boerhaave (by, among others, A. L. Lavoisier, P. S. Laplace, J. Black, Count Rumford, J. Hutton, and H. Cavendish) to explain everything from the role of heat in chemical reactions to the conduction and radiation of heat and several standard problems of thermometry. Within the theory of light, the optical ether functioned centrally in explanations of reflection, refraction, interference, double refraction, diffraction, and polarization. (Of more than passing interest, optical ether theories had also made some very startling predictions, e.g., A. Fresnel's prediction of a bright spot at the center of the shadow of a circular disc; a surprising prediction which, when tested, proved correct. If that does not count as empirical success, nothing does!) There were also gravitational (e.g., G. LeSage's) and physiological (e.g., D. Hartley's) ethers which enjoyed some measure of empirical success. It would be difficult to find a family of theories in this period as successful as ether theories; compared with them, nineteenth-century atomism (for instance), a genuinely referring theory (on realist accounts), was a dismal failure. Indeed, on any account of empirical success which I can conceive of, nonreferring nineteenth-century ether theories were more successful than contemporary, referring atomic theories. In this connection, it is worth recalling the remark of the great theoretical physicist, J. C. Maxwell, to the effect that the ether was better confirmed than any other theoretical entity in natural philosophy.

What we are confronted with in nineteenth-century ether theories, then, is a wide variety of once successful theories, whose central explanatory concept Putnam singles out as a prime example of a nonreferring one.[8] What are (referential) realists to make of this historical case? On the face of it, this case poses two rather different kinds of challenges to realism: first, it suggests that (S3) is a dubious piece of advice in that *there can be* (and have been) *highly successful theories some central terms of which are nonreferring;* and second, it suggests that *the realist's claim that he can explain why science is successful is false at least insofar as a part of the historical success of science has been success exhibited by theories whose central terms did not refer.*

But perhaps I am being less than fair when I suggest that the realist is committed to the claim that *all* the central terms in a successful theory refer. It is possible than when Putnam, for instance, says that "terms in a mature [or successful] science typically refer,"[9] he only means to suggest that *some* terms in a successful theory or science genuinely refer. Such a claim is fully consistent with the fact that certain other terms (e.g., 'ether') in certain successful, mature sciences (e.g., nineteenth-century physics) are nonetheless nonreferring. Put differently, the realist might argue that the success of a theory warrants the claim that at least some (but not necessarily all) of its central concepts refer.

Unfortunately, such a weakening of (S3) entails a theory of evidential support which can scarcely give comfort to the realist. After all, part of what separates the realist from the positivist is the former's belief that the evidence for a theory is evidence for *everything* the theory asserts. Where the stereotypical positivist argues that the evidence selectively confirms only the more 'observable' parts of a theory, the realist generally asserts (in the language of Boyd) that:

> the sort of evidence which ordinarily counts in favor of the acceptance of a scientific law or theory is, ordinarily, evidence for the (at least approximate) truth of the law or theory as an account of the causal relations obtaining between the entities ["observational or theoretical"] quantified over in the law or theory in question.[10]

For realists such as Boyd, either all parts of a theory (both observational and non-observational) are confirmed by successful tests or none are. In general, realists have been able to utilize various holistic arguments to insist that it is not merely the lower-level claims of a well-tested theory that are confirmed but its deep-structural assumptions as well. This tactic has been used to good effect by realists in establishing that inductive support 'flows upward' so as to authenticate the most 'theoretical' parts of our theories. Certain latter-day realists (e.g., Glymour) want to break out of this holist web and argue that certain components of theories can be 'directly' tested. This approach runs the very grave risk of undercutting what the realist desires most: a rationale for taking our deepest-structure theories seriously, and a justification for linking reference and success. After all, if the tests to which we subject our theories only test *portions* of those theories, then even highly successful theories may well have central terms that are nonreferring and central tenets that, because untested, we have no grounds for believing to be approximately true. Under those circumstances, a theory might be highly successful and yet contain important constituents that were patently false. Such a state of affairs would wreak havoc with the realist's presumption (thesis R1) that success betokens approximate truth. In short, to be less than a holist about theory testing is to put at risk precisely that predilection for deep-structure claims which motivates much of the realist enterprise.

There is, however, a rather more serious obstacle to this weakening of referential realism. It is true that by weakening (S3) to only certain terms in a theory, one would immunize it from certain obvious counterexamples. But such a maneuver has debilitating consequences for other central realist theses. Consider the realist's thesis (R3) about the retentive character of intertheory relations (discussed below in detail). The realist both recommends as a matter of policy and claims as a matter of fact that successful theories are (and should be) rationally replaced only by theories that preserve reference for the central terms of their successful predecessors. The rationale for the normative version of this retentionist doctrine is that the terms in the earlier theory, *because it was successful, must have been referential,* and thus a constraint on any successor to that theory is that reference should be retained for such terms. This makes sense just in case success provides a blanket warrant for presumption of reference. But if (S3) were weakened so as to say merely that it is reasonable to assume that *some* of the terms in a successful theory genuinely refer, then the realist would have no rationale for his retentive theses (variants of R3), which have been a central pillar of realism for several decades.[11]

Something apparently has to give. A version of (S3) strong enough to license (R3) seems incompatible with the fact that many successful theories contain nonreferring central terms. But any weakening of (S3) dilutes the force of, and removes the rationale for, the realist's claims about convergence, retention, and correspondence in intertheory relations.[12] If the realist once concedes that some unspecified set of the terms of a successful theory may well not refer, then his proposals for restricting "the class of candidate theories" to those that retain reference for the prima facie referring terms in earlier theories is without foundation.[13]

More generally, we seem forced to say that such linkages as there are between reference and success are rather murkier than Putnam's and Boyd's discussions would lead us to believe. If the realist is going to make his case for CER, it seems that it will have to hinge on approximate truth, (R1), rather than reference, (R2).

Approximate Truth and Success: The Downward Path

Ignoring the referential turn among certain recent realists, most realists continue to argue that, at bottom, epistemic realism is committed to the view that successful scientific theories, even if strictly false, are nonetheless 'approximately true' or 'close to the truth' or 'verisimilar'.[14] The claim generally amounts to this pair:

(T1)   If a theory is approximately true, then it will be explanatorily successful.

(T2)   If a theory is explanatorily successful, then it is probably approximately true.

What the realist would *like* to be able to say, of course, is:

(T1')   If a theory is true, then it will be successful.

(T1') is attractive because self-evident. Most realists, however, balk at invoking (T1') because they are (rightly) reluctant to believe that we can reasonably presume of any given scientific theory that it is true. If all the realist could explain was the success of theories that were true *simpliciter,* his explanatory repertoire would be acutely limited. As an attractive move in the direction of broader explanatory scope, (T1) is rather more appealing. After all, presumably many theories which we believe to be false (e.g., Newtonian mechanics, thermodynamics, wave optics) were—and still are—highly successful across a broad range of applications.

Perhaps, the realist evidently conjectures, we can find an *epistemic* account of that pragmatic success by assuming such theories to be 'approximately true'. But we must be wary of this potential sleight of hand. It may be that there is a connection between success and approximate truth; *but if there is such a connection it must be independently argued for*. The acknowledgedly uncontroversial character of (T1') must not be surreptitiously invoked —as it sometimes seems to be—in order to establish T1. When the antecedent of (T1') is appropriately weakened by speaking of approximate truth, it is by no means clear that (T1) is sound.

Virtually all the proponents of epistemic realism take it as unproblematic that if a theory were approximately true, it would deductively follow that the theory would be a relatively successful predictor and explainer of observable phenomena. Unfortunately, few of the writers of whom I am aware have defined what it means for a statement or theory to be 'approximately true'. Accordingly, it is impossible to say whether the alleged entailment is genuine. This reservation is more than perfunctory. Indeed, on the best known account of what it means for a theory to be approximately true, it does *not* follow that an approximately true theory will be explanatorily successful.

Suppose, for instance, that we were to say in a Popperian vein that a theory, T_1, is approximately true if its truth content is greater than its falsity content, that is,

$$Ct_T(T_1) \gg Ct_F(T_1),[15]$$

where $Ct_T(T_1)$ is the cardinality of the set of true sentences entailed by T_1, and $Ct_F(T_1)$ is the cardinality of the set of false sentences entailed by T_1. When approximate truth is so construed, it does *not* logically follow that an arbitrarily selected class of a theory's entailments (namely, some of its observable consequences) will be true. Indeed, it is entirely conceivable that a theory might be approximately true in the indicated sense and yet be such that *all* of its consequences tested thus far are *false*.[16]

Some realists concede their failure to articulate a coherent notion of approximate truth or verisimilitude but insist that this failure in no way compromises the viability of (T1). Newton-Smith, for instance, grants that "no one has given a satisfactory analysis of the notion of verisimilitude,"[17] but insists that the concept can be legitimately invoked "even if one cannot at the time give a philosophically satisfactory analysis of it." He quite rightly points out that many scientific concepts were explanatorily useful long before a philosophically coherent analysis was given for them. But the analogy is unseemly, for what is being challenged is not whether the concept of approximate truth is philosophically rigorous, but rather whether it is even clear enough for us to ascertain whether it entails what it purportedly explains. Until someone provides a clearer analysis of approximate truth than is now available, it is not even clear whether truthlikeness would explain success, let alone whether, as Newton-Smith insists,[18] "the concept of verisimilitude is *required* in order to give a satisfactory theoretical explanation of an aspect of the scientific enterprise." If the realist would demystify the "miraculousness" (Putnam) or the "mysteriousness" (Newton-Smith) of the success of science, he needs more than a promissory note that somehow, someday, someone will show that approximately true theories must be successful theories.[19]

It is not clear whether there is some definition of approximate truth that does indeed entail that approximately true theories will be predictively successful (and yet still probably false).[20] What can be said is that, promises to the contrary notwithstanding, none of the proponents of realism has yet articulated a coherent account of approximate truth which entails that approximately true theories will, across the range where we can test them, be successful predictors. Further difficulties abound. Even if the realist had a semantically adequate characterization of approximate or partial truth, and even if that semantics entailed that most of the consequences of an approximately true theory would be true, he would still be without any criterion that would *epistemically* warrant the ascription of approximate truth to a theory. As it is, the realist seems to be long on intuitions and short on either a semantics or an epistemology of approximate truth.

These should be urgent items on the realists' agenda since, until we have a coherent account of what approximate truth is, central realist theses such as (R1), (T1), and (T2) are just so much mumbo jumbo.

Approximate Truth and Success: The Upward Path

Despite the doubts voiced in the previous section, let us grant for the sake of argument that if a theory is approximately true, then it will be successful. Even granting (T1), is there any plausibility to the suggestion of (T2) that explanatory success can be taken as a rational warrant for a judgment of approximate truth? The answer seems to be "no."

To see why, we need to explore briefly one of the connections between "genuinely referring" and being "approximately true." However the latter is understood, I take it that *a realist would never want to say that a theory was approximately true if its central terms failed to refer.* If there were nothing like genes, then a genetic theory, no matter how well confirmed it was, would not be approximately true. If there were no entities similar to atoms, no atomic theory could be approximately true; if there were no subatomic particles, then no quantum theory of chemistry could be approximately true. In short, a necessary condition, especially for a scientific realist, for a theory being close to the truth is that its central explanatory terms genuinely refer. (An *instrumentalist*, of course, could countenance the weaker claim that a theory was approximately true so long as its directly testable consequences were close to the observable values. But as I argued above, the realist must take claims about approximate truth to refer alike to the observable and the deep-structural dimensions of a theory.)

Now, what the history of science offers us is a plethora of theories that were both successful and (so far as we can judge) nonreferential with respect to many of their central explanatory concepts. I discussed earlier one specific family of theories that fits this description. Let me add a few more prominent examples to the list:

- the crystalline spheres of ancient and medieval astronomy;
- the humoral theory of medicine;
- the effluvial theory of static electricity;
- "catastrophist" geology, with its commitment to a universal (Noachian) deluge;
- the phlogiston theory of chemistry;
- the caloric theory of heat;
- the vibratory theory of heat;
- the vital force theories of physiology;
- the electromagnetic ether;
- the optical ether;

- the theory of circular inertia; and
- theories of spontaneous generation.

This list, which could be extended ad nauseam, involves in every case a theory that was once successful and well confirmed, but which contained central terms that (we now believe) were nonreferring. Anyone who imagines that the theories that have been successful in the history of science have also been, with respect to their central concepts, genuinely referring theories has studied only the more whiggish versions of the history of science (i.e., the ones which recount only those past theories that are referentially similar to currently prevailing ones).

It is true that proponents of CER sometimes hedge their bets by suggesting that their analysis applies exclusively to "the mature sciences" (e.g., Putnam and W. Krajewski). This distinction between mature and immature sciences proves convenient to the realist since he can use it to dismiss any prima facie counterexample to the empirical claims of CER on the grounds that the example is drawn from a so-called immature science. But this insulating maneuver is unsatisfactory in two respects. In the first place, it runs the risk of making CER vacuous since these authors generally define a mature science as one in which correspondence or limiting-case relations obtain invariably between any successive theories in the science once it has passed "the threshold of maturity." Krajewski grants the tautological character of this view when he notes that "the thesis that there is [correspondence] among successive theories becomes, indeed, analytical."[21] Nonetheless, he believes that there is a version of the maturity thesis which "may be and must be tested by the history of science." That version is that "every branch of science crosses at some period the threshold of maturity." But the testability of this hypothesis is dubious at best. There is no historical observation that could conceivably *refute* it since, even if we discovered that no sciences yet possessed "corresponding" theories, it could be maintained that eventually every science will become corresponding. It is equally difficult to *confirm* it since, even if we found a science in which corresponding relations existed between the latest theory and its predecessor, we would have no way of knowing whether that relation will continue to apply to subsequent changes of theory in that science. In other words, the much-vaunted empirical testability of realism is seriously compromised by limiting it to the mature sciences.

But there is a second unsavory dimension to the restriction of CER to the mature sciences. The realists' avowed aim, after all, is to explain why science is successful: that is the "miracle" they allege the nonrealists leave unaccounted for. The fact of the matter is that parts of science, including many immature sciences, have been successful for a very long time; indeed, many of the theories I alluded to above were empirically successful by any criterion I can conceive of (including fertility, intuitively high confirmation, successful prediction, etc.). If the realist restricts himself to explaining only how the mature sciences work (and recall that very few sciences indeed are yet mature as the realist sees it), then he will have completely failed in his ambition to explain why science in general is successful. Moreover, several of the examples I have cited above come from the history of mathematical physics in the last century (e.g., electromagnetic and optical ethers) and, as Putnam himself concedes, "*physics* surely counts as a 'mature' science if any science does."[22] Since realists would presumably insist that many of the central terms of the theories enumerated above do not genuinely refer, it follows that none of those theories could be approximately true (recalling that the former is a necessary condition for the latter). Accordingly, cases of this kind cast very grave doubts on the plausibility of (T2), that is, the claim that nothing succeeds like approximate truth.

I daresay that for every highly successful theory in the history of science that we now believe to be a genuinely referring theory, one could find half a dozen once successful theories that we now regard as substantially nonreferring. If the proponents of CER are the empiricists they profess to be about matters epistemological, cases of this kind and this frequency should give them pause about the well-foundedness of (T2).

But we need not limit our counterexamples to nonreferring theories. There were many theories in the past that (so far as we can tell) were both genuinely referring and empirically successful which we are nonetheless loathe to regard as approximately true. Consider, for instance, virtually all those geological theories prior to the 1960s which denied any lateral motion to the continents. Such theories were, by any standard, highly successful (and apparently referential); but would anyone today be prepared to say that their constituent theoretical claims—committed as they were to laterally stable continents—are almost true? Is it not the fact of the matter that structural geology was a successful science between (say) 1920 and 1960, even though geologists were fundamentally mistaken about many (perhaps even most) of the basic mechanisms of tectonic construction? Or what about the chemical theories of the 1920s which assumed that the atomic nucleus was structurally homogenous? Or those chemical and physical theories of the late nineteenth century which explicitly assumed that matter was neither created nor destroyed? I am aware of no sense of approximate truth (available to the realist) according to which such highly successful, but evidently false, theoretical assumptions could be regarded as "truthlike."

More generally, the realist needs a riposte to the prima facie plausible claim that there is no necessary connection between increasing the accuracy of our deep-structural characterizations of nature and improvements at the level of phenomenological explanations, predictions, and manipulations. It *seems* entirely conceivable intuitively that the theoretical mechanisms of a new theory, T_2, might be closer to the mark than those of a rival T_1, and yet T_1 might be more accurate at the level of testable predictions. In the absence of an argument that greater correspondence at the level of unobservable claims is more likely than not to reveal itself in greater accuracy at the experimental level, one is obliged to say that the realist's hunch that increasing deep-structural fidelity must manifest itself pragmatically in the form of heightened experimental accuracy has yet to be made cogent. (Equally problematic, of course, is the inverse argument to the effect that increasing experimental accuracy betokens greater truthlikeness at the level of theoretical, i.e., deep-structural, commitments.)

Confusions about Convergence and Retention

Thus far, I have discussed only the static or synchronic versions of CER, versions that make absolute rather than relative judgments about truth likeness. Of equal appeal have been those variants of CER that invoke a notion of what is variously called "convergence," "correspondence," or "cumulation." Proponents of the diachronic version of CER supplement the arguments discussed above [(S1)–(S4) and (T1)–(T2)] with an additional set. They tend to be of this form:

(C1) If earlier theories in a scientific domain are successful and thereby, according to realist principles [e.g., (S3) above], approximately true, then scientists should only accept later theories that retain appropriate portions of earlier theories.

(C2) As a matter of fact, scientists do adopt the strategy of (C1) and manage to produce new, more successful theories in the process.

(C3) The "fact" that scientists succeed at retaining appropriate parts of earlier theories in more successful successors shows that the earlier theories did genuinely refer and that they are approximately true. And thus, the strategy propounded in (C1) is sound.[23]

Perhaps the prevailing view here is Putnam's and (implicitly) Popper's, according to which rationally warranted successor theories in a mature science must contain reference to the entities apparently referred to in the predecessor theory (since, by hypothesis, the terms in the earlier theory refer), and also contain the theoretical laws and mechanisms of the predecessor theory as limiting cases. As Putnam tells us, a realist should insist that *any* viable successor to an old theory T_1 must "contain the laws of T as a limiting case."[24] John Watkins, a like-minded convergentist, puts the point this way:

> It typically happens in the history of science that when some hitherto dominant theory T is superseded by T^1, T^1 is in the relation of correspondence to T [i.e., T is a 'limiting case' of T^1].[25]

Numerous recent philosophers of science have subscribed to a similar view, including Popper, H. R. Post, Krajewski, and N. Koertge.[26]

This form of retention is not the only one to have been widely discussed. Indeed, realists have espoused a wide variety of claims about what is or should be retained in the transition from a once successful predecessor (T_1) to a successor theory (T_2). Among the more important forms of realist retention are the following cases: (1) T_2 entails T_1 (W. Whewell); (2) T_2 retains the true consequences or truth content of T_1 (Popper); (3) T_2 retains the "confirmed" portions of T_1 (Post, Koertge); (4) T_2 preserves the theoretical laws and mechanisms of T_1 (Boyd, McMullin, Putnam); (5) T_2 preserves T_1 as a limiting case (J. Watkins, Putnam, Krajewski); (6) T_2 explains why T_1 succeeded insofar as T_1 succeeded (W. Sellars); and (7) T_2 retains reference for the central terms of T_1 (Putnam, Boyd).

The question before us is whether, when retention is understood in *any* of these senses, the realist's theses about convergence and retention are correct.

Do Scientists Adopt the Retentionist Strategy of CER?

One part of the convergent realist's argument is a claim to the effect that scientists generally adopt the strategy of seeking to preserve earlier theories in later ones. As Putnam puts it:

> preserving the mechanisms of the earlier theory as often as possible, which is what scientists try to do.... That scientists try to do this ... is a fact, and that this strategy has led to important discoveries ... is also a fact.[27]

In a similar vein, I. Szumilewicz (although not stressing realism) insists that many eminent scientists made it a main heuristic requirement of their research programs that a new theory stand in a relation of 'correspondence' with the theory it supersedes.[28] If Putnam and the other retentionists are right about the strategy that most scientists have adopted, we should expect to find the historical literature of science abundantly provided with proofs that later theories do indeed contain earlier theories as limiting cases, or outright rejections of later theories that fail to contain earlier theories. Except on rare occasions (coming primarily from the history of mechanics), one finds neither of these concerns prominent in the literature of science. For instance, to the best of my knowledge, literally no one criticized the wave theory of light because it did not preserve the theoretical mechanisms of the earlier corpuscular theory; no one faulted C. Lyell's uniformitarian geology on the grounds that it dispensed with several causal processes prominent in catastrophist geology; Darwin's theory was not criticized by most geologists for its failure to retain many of the mechanisms of Lamarckian evolutionary theory.

For all the realist's confident claims about the prevalence of a retentionist strategy in the sciences, I am aware of *no* historical studies that would sustain as a *general* claim his hypothesis about the evaluative strategies utilized in science. Moreover, insofar as Putnam and Boyd claim to be offering "an explanation of the retentionist behavior of scientists,"[29] they have the wrong explanandum, for if there is any widespread strategy in science, it is one that says, "accept an empirically successful theory, regardless of whether it contains the theoretical laws and mechanisms of its predecessors."[30] Indeed, one could take a leaf from the realist's (C2) and claim that the success of the strategy of assuming that earlier theories do not generally refer shows that it is true that earlier theories generally do not!

(One might note in passing how often, and on what evidence, realists imagine that they are speaking for the scientific majority. Putnam, for instance, claims that "realism is, so to speak, 'science's philosophy of science'" and that "science taken at 'face value' *implies* realism."[31] C. A. Hooker insists that to be a realist is to take science "seriously,"[32] as if to suggest that conventionalists, instrumentalists, and positivists such as Duhem, Poincaré, and Mach did not take science seriously. The willingness of some realists to attribute realist strategies to working scientists—on the strength of virtually no empirical research into the principles which *in fact* have governed scientific practice—raises doubts about the seriousness of their avowed commitment to the empirical character of epistemic claims.)

Do Later Theories Preserve the Mechanisms, Models, and Laws of Earlier Theories?
Regardless of the explicit strategies to which scientists have subscribed, are Putnam and several other retentionists right that later theories "typically" entail earlier theories, and that "earlier theories are, very often, limiting cases of later theories?"[33] Unfortunately, answering this question is difficult, since 'typically' is one of those weasel words that allows for much hedging. I shall assume that Putnam and Watkins mean that "most of the time (or perhaps in most of the important cases) successor theories contain predecessor theories as limiting cases." So construed, the claim is patently false. Copernican astronomy did not retain all the key mechanisms of Ptolemaic astronomy (e.g., motion along an equant); Newton's physics did not retain all (or even most of) the theoretical laws of Cartesian mechanics, astronomy, and optics; Franklin's electrical theory did not contain its predecessor (J. A. Nollet's) as a limiting case. Relativistic physics did not retain the ether, nor the mechanisms associated with it; statistical mechanics does not incorporate all the mechanisms of thermodynamics; modern genetics does not have Darwinian pangenesis as a limiting case; the wave theory of light did not appropriate the mechanisms of corpuscular optics; modern embryology incorporates few of the mechanisms prominent in classical embryological theory. As I have shown elsewhere,[34] loss occurs at virtually every level: the confirmed predictions of earlier theories are sometimes not explained by later ones; even the 'observable' laws explained by earlier theories are not always retained, not even as limiting cases; theoretical processes and mechanisms of earlier theories are, as frequently as not, treated as flotsam.

The point is that some of the most important theoretical innovations have been due to a willingness of scientists to violate the cumulationist or retentionist constraint which realists enjoin 'mature' scientists to follow.

There is a deep reason why the convergent realist is wrong about these matters. It has to do, in part, with the role of ontological frameworks in science and with the nature of limiting case relations. As scientists use the term 'limiting case', T_1 can be a limiting case of T_2 only if *all* the variables (observable and theoretical) assigned a value in T_1 are assigned a value by T_2 and if the values assigned to every variable of T_1 are the same as, or very close to, the values T_2 assigns to the corresponding variable when certain initial and boundary conditions—consistent with T_2[35]—are specified. This seems to require that T_1 can be a limiting case of T_2 only if *all* the entities postulated by T_1 occur in the ontology of T_2. Whenever there is a change of ontology accompanying a theory transition such that T_2 (when conjoined with suitable initial and boundary conditions) fails to capture the ontology of T_1, then T_1 cannot be a limiting case of T_2. Even where the ontologies of T_1 and T_2 overlap appropriately (i.e., where T_2's ontology embraces all of T_1's), T_1 is a limiting case of T_2 only if *all* the laws of T_1 can be derived from T_2, given appropriate limiting conditions. It is important to stress that *both* these conditions (among others) must be satisfied before one theory can be a limiting case of another. Where "closet" positivists might be content with capturing only the formal mathematical relations or only the observable consequences of T_1 within a successor T_2, any genuine realist must insist that T_1's underlying ontology is preserved in T_2's, *for it is that ontology above all which he alleges to be approximately true.*

Too often, philosophers (and physicists) infer the existence of a limiting-case relation between T_1 and T_2 on substantially less than this. For instance, many writers have claimed one theory to be a limiting case of another when only some, but not all, of the laws of the former are derivable from the latter. In other cases, one theory has been said to be a limiting case of a successor when the mathematical laws of the former find homologies in the latter but where the former's ontology is not fully extractable from the latter's.

Consider one prominent example which has often been misdescribed, namely, the transition from the classical ether theory to relativistic and quantum mechanics. It can, of course, be shown that *some* law of classical mechanics are limiting cases of relativistic mechanics. But there are other laws and general assertions made by the classical theory (e.g., claims about the density and fine structure of the ether, general laws about the character of the interaction between ether and matter, models and mechanisms detailing the compressibility of the ether) which could not conceivably be limiting cases of modern mechanics. The reason is a simple one: a theory cannot assign values to a variable that does not occur in that theory's language (or, more colloquially, it cannot assign properties to entities whose existence it does not countenance). Classical ether physics contained a number of postulated mechanisms for dealing inter alia with the transmission of light through the ether. Such mechanisms could not possibly appear in a successor theory like the special theory of relativity which denies the very existence of an etherial medium and which accomplishes the explanatory tasks performed by the ether via very different mechanisms.

Nineteenth-century mathematical physics is replete with similar examples of evidently successful mathematical theories which, because some of their variables refer to entities whose existence we now deny, cannot be shown to be limiting cases of our physics. As Adolf Grünbaum has cogently algued, when we are confronted with two incompatible theories, T_1 and T_2, such that T_2 does not "contain" all of T_1's ontology, then not all the mechanisms and theoretical laws of T_1 that involve those entities of T_1 not postulated by T_2 can possibly be retained—not even as limiting cases—in T_2.[36] This result is of some significance. What little plausibility convergent or retentive realism has enjoyed derives from the presumption that it correctly describes the relationship between classical and postclassical mechanics and gravitational theory. Once we see that even in this prima facie most favorable case for the realist (where some of the laws of the predecessor theory are genuinely limiting cases of the successor), changing ontologies or conceptual frameworks make it impossible to capture many of the central theoretical laws and mechanisms postulated by the earlier theory, then we can see how misleading Putnam's claim is that "what scientists try to do [is to preserve] the *mechanisms* of the earlier theory as often as possible—or to show that they are 'limiting cases' of new mechanisms."[37] Where the mechanisms of the earlier theory involve entities whose existence the later theory denies, no scientist does (or should) feel any compunction about wholesale repudiation of the earlier mechanisms.

But even where there is no change in basic ontology, many theories (even in mature sciences such as physics) fail to retain all the explanatory successes of their predecessors. It is well known that statistical mechanics has yet to capture the irreversibility of macrothermodynamics as a genuine limiting case. Classical continuum mechanics has not yet been reduced to quantum mechanics or relativity. Contemporary field theory has yet to replicate the classical thesis that physical laws are invariant under reflection in space. If scientists had accepted the realist's constraint (namely, that new theories must have old theories as limiting cases), neither relativity nor statistical mechanics would have been viewed as viable theories. It has been said before, but it needs to be reiterated over and again: *a proof of the existence of limiting relations between selected componets of two theories is a far cry from a systematic proof that one theory is a limiting case of the other.* Even if classical and modern physics stood to one another in the manner in which the convergent realist erroneously imagines they do, his hasty generalization that theory successions in all the advanced sciences show limiting-case relations is patently false.[38] But, as this discussion shows, not even the realist's paradigm case will sustain the claims he is apt to make about it.

What this analysis underscores is just how reactionary many forms of convergent epistemological realism are. If one took seriously CER's advice to reject any new theory that did not capture existing mature theories as referential and existing laws and mechanisms as approximately authentic, then any prospect for deep-structure, ontological changes in our theories would be foreclosed. Equally outlawed would be any significant repudiation of our theoretical models. In spite of his commitment to the growth of knowledge, the realist would unwittingly freeze science in its present state by forcing all future theories to accommodate the ontology of contemporary (mature) science and by foreclosing the possibility that some future generation may come to the conclusion that some (or even most) of the central terms in our best theories are no more referential than was 'natural place', 'phlogiston', 'ether', or 'caloric'.

Could Theories Converge in Ways Required by the Realist?
These violations, within genuine science, of the sorts of continuity usually required by realists are by themselves sufficient to show that the form of scientific growth which the convergent realist takes as his explicandum is often absent, even in the mature sciences. But we can move beyond these specific cases to show in principle that the kind of cumulation demanded by the realist is unattainable. Specifically, by drawing on some results established by David Miller and others, the following can be shown:

1. The familiar requirement that a successor theory, T_2, must both preserve as true the true consequences of its predecessor, T_1, and explain T_1's anomalies is contradictory.

2. If a new theory, T_2, involves a change in the ontology or conceptual framework of a predecessor, T_1, then T_1 will have true and determinate consequences not possessed by T_2.

3. If two theories, T_1 and T_2, disagree, then each will have true and determinate consequences not exhibited by the other.

To establish these conclusions, one needs to utilize a "syntactic" view of theories according to which a theory is a conjunction of statements and its consequences are defined a la Tarski in terms of content classes. Needless to say, this is neither the only, nor necessarily the best, way of thinking about theories; but it happens to be the way in which most philosophers who argue for convergence and retention (e.g., Popper, Watkins, Post, Krajewski, and I. Niiniluoto) tend to conceive of theories. What can be said is that if one utilizes the Tarskian conception of a theory's content and its consequences as they do, then the familiar convergentist theses alluded to in conclusions 1 through 3 make no sense.

The elementary but devastating consequences of Miller's analysis establish that virtually any effort to link scientific progress or growth to the wholesale retention of a predecessor theory's Tarskian content *or* logical consequences *or* true consequences *or* observed consequences *or* confirmed consequences, is evidently doomed. Realists have not only got their history wrong insofar as they imagine that cumulative retention has prevailed in science, but we can also see that, given their views on what should be retained through theory change, history could not possibly have been the way their models require it to be. The realist's strictures on cumulativity are as ill advised normatively as they are false historically.

Along with many other realists, Putnam has claimed that "the mature sciences do converge ... and that that convergence has great explanatory value for the theory of science."[39] As this section should show, Putnam and his fellow realists are arguably wrong on *both* counts. Popper once remarked that "no theory of knowledge should attempt to explain why we are successful in our attempts to explain things."[40] Such a dogma is too strong. But what the foregoing analysis shows is that an occupational hazard of recent epistemology is imagining that convincing explanations of our success come easily or cheaply.

Should New Theories Explain Why Their Predecessors Were Successful?

An apparently more modest realism than that outlined above is familiar in the form of the requirement (R4) often attributed to Sellars—that every satisfactory new theory must be able to explain why its predecessor was successful insofar as it was successful. On this view, viable new theories need not preserve all the content of their predecessors, nor capture those predecessors as limiting cases. Rather, it is simply insisted that a viable new theory, T_N, must explain why, when we conceive of the world according to the old theory T_O, there is a range of cases where our T_O-guided expectations are correct or approximately correct.

What are we to make of this requirement? In the first place, it is clearly *gratuitous*. If T_N has more confirmed consequences (and greater conceptual simplicity) than T_O, then T_N is preferable to T_O even if T_N cannot explain why T_O is successful. Contrariwise, if T_N has fewer confirmed consequences than T_O, then T_N cannot be rationally preferred to T_O even if T_N explains why T_O is successful. In short, a theory's ability to explain why a rival is successful is neither a necessary nor a sufficient condition for saying that it is better than its rival.

Other difficulties likewise confront the claim that new theories should explain why their predecessors were successful. Chief among them is the ambiguity of the notion itself. One way to show that an older theory, T_O, was successful is to show that it shares many confirmed consequences with a newer theory, T_N, which is highly successful. But this is not an "explanation" that a scientific realist could accept, since it makes no reference to, and thus does not depend upon, an epistemic assessment of either T_O or T_N. (After all, an instrumentalist could quite happily grant that if T_N "saves the phenomena" then T_O—insofar as some of its observable consequences overlap with or are experimentally indistinguishable from those of T_N—should also succeed at saving the phenomen.)

The intuition being traded on in this persuasive account is that the pragmatic success of a new theory, combined with a partial comparison of the respective consequences of the new theory and its predecessor, will sometimes put us in a position to say when the older theory worked and when it failed. But such comparisons as can be made in this manner do not involve *epistemic* appraisals of either the new or the old theory qua theories. Accordingly, the possibility of such comparisons provides no argument for epistemic realism.

What the realist apparently needs is an epistemically robust sense of "explaining the success of a predecessor." Such an epistemic characterization would presumably begin with the claim that T_N, the new theory, was approximately true and would proceed to show that the 'observable' claims of its predecessor, T_O, deviated only slightly from (some of) the 'observable' consequences of T_N. It would then be alleged that the (presumed) approximate truth of T_N and the partially overlapping consequences of T_O and T_N jointly explained why T_O was successful insofar as it was successful. But this is a non sequitur. As I have shown above, the fact that a T_N is approximately true does not even explain why it is successful; how, under those circumstances, can the approximate truth of T_N explain why some theory different from T_N is successful? Whatever the nature of the relations between T_N and T_O (entailment, limiting case, etc.), the epistemic ascription of approximate truth to either T_O or T_N (or both) apparently leaves untouched questions of how successful T_O or T_N are.

The idea that new theories should explain why older theories were successful (insofar as they were) originally arose as a rival to the "levels" picture of explanation according to which new theories fully explained, because they entailed, their predecessors. It is clearly an improvement over the levels picture (for it does recognize that later theories generally do not entail their predecessors). But when it is formulated as a general thesis about intertheory relations, designed to buttress a realist epistemology, it is difficult to see how this position avoids difficulties similar to those discussed in earlier sections.

The Realists' Ultimate Petitio Principii

It is time to step back a moment from the details of the realists' argument to look at its general strategy. Fundamentally, the realist is utilizing, as we have seen, an abductive inference which proceeds from the success of science to the conclusion that science is approximately true, verisimilar, or referential (or any combination of these). This argument is meant to show the skeptic that theories are not ill gotten, the positivist that theories are not reducible to their observational consequences, and the pragmatist that classical epistemic categories (e.g., "truth" and "falsehood") are a relevant part of metascientific discourse.

It is little short of remarkable that realists would imagine that their critics would find the argument compelling. As I have shown elsewhere,[41] ever since antiquity critics of epistemic realism have based their skepticism upon a deep-rooted conviction that the fallacy of affirming the consequent is indeed fallacious. When E. Sextus or R. Bellarmine or Hume doubted that certain theories which saved the phenomena were warrantable as true, their doubts were based on a belief that the exhibition that a theory had some true consequences left entirely open the truth-status of the theory. Indeed, many nonrealists have been nonrealists precisely because they believed that false theories, as well as true ones, could have true consequences.

Now enters the new breed of realist (e.g., Putnam, Boyd, Newton-Smith) who wants to argue that epistemic realism can reasonably be presumed true by virtue of the fact that it has true consequences. But this is a monumental case of begging the question. The nonrealist refuses to admit that a *scientific* theory can be warrantedly judged to be true simply because it has some true consequences. Such nonrealists are not likely to be impressed by the claim that a philosophical theory such as realism can be warranted as true because it arguably has some true consequences. If nonrealists are chary about first-order abductions to avowedly true conclusions, they are not likely to be impressed by second-order abductions, particularly when, as I have tried to show above, the premises and conclusions are so indeterminate.

But, it might be argued, the realist is not out to convert the intransigent skeptic or the determined instrumentalist.[42] Perhaps, he is seeking to show that realism can be tested like any other scientific hypothesis, and that realism is at least as well confirmed as some of our best scientific theories. Such an analysis, however plausible initially, will not stand up to scrutiny. I am aware of no realist who is willing to say that a scientific theory can be reasonably presumed to be true or even regarded as well confirmed just on the strength of the fact that its thus-far-tested consequences are true. Realists have long been in the forefront of those opposed to ad hoc and post hoc theories. Before a realist accepts a scientific hypothesis, he generally wants to know whether it has explained or predicted more than it was devised to explain, whether it has been subjected to a battery of controlled tests, whether it has successfully made novel predictions, and whether there is independent evidence for it.

What, then, of realism itself as a "scientific" hypothesis?[43] Even if we grant (contrary to what I argued in the section on "Approximate Truth and Success") that realism entails and thus explains the success of science, ought that (hypothetical) success warrant, by the realist's own construal of scientific acceptability, the acceptance of realism? Since realism was devised to explain the success of science, it remains purely ad hoc with respect to that success. If realism has made some novel predictions or has been subjected to carefully controlled tests, one does not learn about it from the literature of contemporary realism. At the risk of apparent inconsistency, the realist repudiates the instrumentalist's view that saving the phenomena is a significant form of evidential support while endorsing realism itself on the transparently instrumentalist grounds that it is confirmed by those very facts it was invented to explain. No proponent of realism has sought to show that realism satisfies those stringent empirical demands which the realist himself minimally insists on when appraising scientific theories. The latter-day realist often calls realism a "scientific" or "well-tested" hypothesis but seems curiously reluctant to subject it to those controls he otherwise takes to be a sine qua non for empirical well-foundedness.

Conclusion

The arguments and cases discussed above seem to warrant the following conclusions:

1. The fact that a theory's central terms refer does not entail that it will be successful, and a theory's success is no warrant for the claim that all or most of its central terms refer.

2. The notion of approximate truth is presently too vague to permit one to judge whether a theory consisting entirely of approximately true laws would be empirically successful. What is clear is that a theory may be empirically successful even if it is not approximately true.

3. Realists have no explanation whatever for the fact that many theories which are not approximately true and whose "theoretical" terms seemingly do not refer are, nonetheless, often successful.

4. The convergentist's assertion that scientists in a "mature" discipline usually preserve, or seek to preserve, the laws and mechanisms of earlier theories in later ones is probably false. His assertion that when such laws are preserved in a successful successor, we can explain the success of the latter by virtue of the truthlikeness of the preserved laws and mechanisms, suffers from all the defects noted above confronting approximate truth.

5. Even if it could be shown that referring theories and approximately true theories would be successful, the realist's argument that successful theories are approximately true and genuinely referential takes for granted precisely what the nonrealist denies, namely, that explanatory success betokens truth.

6. It is not clear that acceptable theories either *do* or *should* explain why their predecessors succeeded or failed. If a theory is better supported than its rivals and predecessors, then it is not epistemically decisive whether it explains why its rivals worked.

7. If a theory has once been falsified, it is unreasonable to expect that a successor should retain either all of its content *or* its confirmed consequences or its theoretical mechanisms.

8. Nowhere has the realist established, except by fiat, that nonrealist epistemologists lack the resources to explain the success of science.

With these specific conclusions in mind, we can proceed to a more global one: it is not yet established—Putnam, Newton-Smith, and Boyd notwithstanding—that realism can explain any part of the successes of science. What is very clear is that realism *cannot*, even by its own lights, explain the success of those many theories whose central terms have evidently not referred and whose theoretical laws and mechanisms were not approximately true. The inescapable conclusion is that insofar as many realists are concerned with explaining how science works and with assessing the adequacy of their epistemology by that standard, they have, thus far, failed to explain very much. Their epistemology is confronted by anomalies that seem beyond its resources to grapple with.

It is important to guard against a possible misinterpretation of this essay. Nothing I have said here refutes the possibility, in principle, of a realistic epistemology of science. To conclude as much would be to fall prey to the same inferential prematurity with which many realists have rejected in principle the possibility of explaining science in a nonrealist way. My task here is, rather, that of reminding ourselves that there is a difference between wanting to believe something and having good reasons for believing it. All of us would like realism to be true; we would like to think that science works because it has got a grip on how things really are. But such claims have yet to be made out. Given the present state of the art, it can only be wish fulfillment that gives rise to the claim that realism, and realism alone, explains why science works.

Notes

1. R. Boyd, "Realism, Underdetermination, and a Causal Theory of Evidence," *Nous* 7 (1973): 1–12; W. Newton-Smith, "The Underdetermination of Theories by Data," *Proceedings of the Aristotelian Society* (1978), 71–91; H. Putnam, *Mathematics, Matter, and Method*, vol. 1 (Cambridge: Cambridge University Press, 1975); Ilkka Niiniluoto, "On the Truthlikeness of Generalizations," in *Basic Problems in Methodology and Linguistics*, ed. R. Butts and J. Hintikka (Dordrecht: D. Reidel, 1977), 121–147.
2. See Putnam's essay in this volume (ed.).
3. Putnam, evidently following Boyd, sums up theses R1 and R3 in these words:

    1) Terms in a mature science typically *refer*.
    2) The laws of a theory belonging to a mature science are typically approximately rule.
       ... I will only consider [new] theories ... which have this property—[they] contain the [theoretical] laws of [their predecessors] as a limiting case.

    H. Putnam, *Meaning and the Moral Sciences* (London: Routledge and Kegan Paul, 1978), 20–21.
4. Putnam insists, for instance, that if the realist is wrong about theories being referential, then "the success of science is a miracle" (Putnam, *Mathematics, Matter, and Method*, 1: 69).
5. Boyd remarks: "Scientific realism offers an *explanation* for the legitimacy of ontological commitment to theoretical entities" (Putnam, *Meaning and the Moral Sciences*, 2). It allegedly does so by explaining why theories containing theoretical entities work so well: because such entities genuinely exist.
6. Whether one utilizes Putnam's earlier or later versions of realism is irrelvant for the central arguments of this eassy.
7. Putnam, *Meaning and the Moral Sciences*, 20–22.
8. Ibid., 22.
9. Ibid., 20.
10. "Realism, Underdeterminism, and a Causal Theory of Evidence," 1. See also p. 3: "experimental evidence for a theory is evidence for the truth of even its non-observational laws." See also W. Sellars, *Science, Perception and Reality* (New York: The Humanities Press, 1963), 97.
11. A caveat is in order here. *Even* if all the central terms in some theory refer, it is not obvious that every rational successor to that theory must preserve all the referring terms of its predecessor. One can easily imagine circumstances when the new theory is preferable to the old one even though the range of application of the new theory is less broad than the old. When the range is so restricted, it may well be entirely appropriate to drop reference to some of the entities that figured in the earlier theory.
12. For Putnam and Boyd both, "it will be a constraint on T_2 [i.e., any new theory in a domain] ... that T_2 must have this property, the property that *from its standpoint* one can assign referents to the terms of T_1 [i.e., an earlier theory in the same domain]" (Putnam, "What is Realism?" this volume). For Boyd, see "Realism, Underdeterminism, and a Causal Theory of Evidence," 8: "new theories should, *prima facie*, resemble current theories with respect to their accounts of causal relations among theoretical entities."
13. Putnam, *Mathematics, Matter, and Method*, 22.
14. For just a small sampling of this view, consider the following: "the claim of a realist ontology of science is that the only way of explaining why the models of science function so successfully ... is that they approximate in some way the structure of the object" (Ernan McMullin, "The History and Philosophy of Science: A Taxonomy," in *Minnesota Studies in the Philosophy of Science*, ed. R. Stuewer, 5 [1970]: 63–64); "the continued success of confirmed theories can be *explained* by the hypothesis that they are in fact close to the truth" (Niiniluoto); and the claim that "the laws of a theory belonging to a mature science are typically approximately *true* ... [provides] an explanation of the behavior of scientists and the success of science" (Putnam, *Meaning and the Moral Sciences*, 20–21). J. J. Smart, W. Sellars, and Newton-Smith, among others, share a similar view.
15. Although Popper is generally careful not to assert that actual historical theories exhibit ever-increasing truth content (for an exception, see his *Conjectures and Refutations* [London: Routledge and Kegan Paul, 1963], 220), other writers have been more bold. Thus, Newton-Smith writes that "the historically generated sequence of theories of a mature science is a sequence in which succeeding theories are increasing in truth content without increasing in falsity content" (W. Newton-Smith, "In Defense of Truth," forthcoming).

16. On the more technical side, Niiniluoto has shown that a theory's degree of corroboration covaries with its "estimated verisimilitude" (Niiniluoto, "On the Truthlikeness of Generalizations," 121–147). Roughly speaking, "estimated truthlikeness" is a measure of how closely (the content of) a theory corresponds to *what we take to be* the best conceptual systems that, so far, we have been able to find (Ilkka Niiniluoto, "Scientific Progress," *Synthese* 45 (1980): 443 ff.). If Niiniluoto's measures work, it follows from the above-mentioned covariance that an empirically successful theory will have a high degree of estimated truthlikeness. But because estimated truthlikeness and genuine verisimilitude are not necessarily related (the former being parasitic on existing evidence and available conceptual systems), it is an open question whether, as Niiniluoto asserts, the continued success of highly confirmed theories can be *explained* by the hypothesis that they in fact are so close to the truth, at least in the relevant respects. Unless I am mistaken, this remark of his betrays a confusion between "true verisimilitude" (to which we have no epistemic access) and "estimated verisimilitude" (which is accessible but nonepistemic.).

17. Newton-Smith, "In Defense of Truth," 16.

18. Newton-Smith claims that the increasing predictive success of science through time "would be totally mystifying ... if it were not for the fact that theories are capturing more and more truth about the world" (Newton-Smith, "In Defense of Truth," 15).

19. I must stress again that I am *not* denying that there *may* be a connection between approximate truth and predictive success. I am only observing that until the realists show us what that connection is, they should be more reticent than they are about claiming that realism can explain the success of science.

20. A *nonrealist* might argue that a theory is approximately true just in case all its *observable* consequences are true or within a specified interval from the true value. Theories that were "approximately true" in this sense would indeed be demonstrably successful. But, the realist's (otherwise commendable) commitment to taking seriously the theoretical claims of a theory precludes him from utilizing any such construal of approximate truth, since he wants to say that the theoretical as well as the observational consequences are approximately true.

21. W. Krajewski, *Correspondence Principle and Growth of Science* (Dordrecht: D. Reidel, 1977), 91.

22. Putnam, *Meaning and the Moral Sciences*, 21.

23. If this argument, which I attribute to the realists, seems a bit murky, I challenge any reader to find a more clear-cut one in the literature! Overt formulations of this position can be found in Putnam, Boyd, and Newton-Smith.

24. Putnam, *Meaning and the Moral Sciences*, 21.

25. John Watkins, "Corroboration and the Problem of Content-Comparison," in *Progress and Rationality in Science*, ed. G. Radnitzky and G. Anderson (Dordrecht: D. Reidel, 1978), 376–377.

26. Popper: "A theory which has been well-corroborated can only be superseded by one ... [which] *contains* the old well-corroborated theory—or at least a good approximation to it." K. Popper, *Logic of Scientific Discovery* (New York: Basic Books, 1959), 276.

    Post: "I shall even claim that, as a matter of empirical historical fact, [successor] theories [have] always explained the *whole* of [the well-confirmed part of their predecessors]." H. R. Post, "Correspondence, Invariance and Heuristics: In Praise of Conservative Induction," *Studies in the History and Philosophy of Science* 2 (1971): 229.

    Koertge: "Nearly all part of successive theories in the history of science stand in a correspondence relation and ... where there is no correspondence to begin with, the new theory will be developed in such a way that it comes more nearly into correspondence with the old." N. Koertge, "Theory Change in Science," in *Conceptual Change*, ed. G. Pearce and P. Maynard (Dordrecht: D. Reidel, 1973), 176–177.

    Among other authors who have defended a similar view, one should mention A. Fine, "Consistency, Derivability and Scientific Change," *Journal of Philosophy* 64 (1967): 231 ff.; C. Kordig, "Scientific Transitions, Meaning Invariance, and Derivability," *Southern Journal of Philosophy* (1971): 119–125; H. Margenau, *The Nature of Physical Reality* (New York: McGraw-Hill, 1950); and L. Sklar, "Types of Inter-Theoretic Reductions," *British Journal for Philosophy of Science* 18 (1967): 190–224.

27. Putnam fails to point out that it is also a fact that many scientists do *not* seek to preserve earlier theoretical mechanisms and that theories which have not preserved earlier theoretical mechanisms (whether the germ theory of disease, plate tectonics, or wave optics) have led to important discoveries is also a fact.

28. I. Szumilewicz, "Incommensurability and the Rationality of the Development of Science," *British Journal for the Philosophy of Science* 28 (1977): 348.

29. Putnam, *Meaning and the Moral Sciences*, 21.

30. I have written a book about this strategy. See Larry Laudan, *Progress and Its Problems* (Berkeley, Los Angeles, London: University of California Press, 1977).

31. After the epistemological and methodological battles about science during the last three hundred years, it should be fairly clear that science, taken at its face value, implies no particular epistemology.

32. Clifford Hooker, "Systematic Realism," *Synthese* 26 (1974): 409–497.

33. Putnam, *Meaning and the Moral Sciences*, 20, 123.

34. Larry Laudan, "Two Dogmas of Methodology," *Philosophy of Science* 43 (1976): 467–472.

35. This matter of limiting conditions consistent with the "reducing" theory is curious. Some of the best-known expositions of limiting-case relations depend (as Krajewski has observed) upon showing an earlier theory to be a limiting case of a later theory only by adopting limiting assumptions *explicitly denied by the later theory*. For instance, several standard textbook discussions present (a portion of) classical mechanics as a limiting case of special relativity, provided c approaches infinity. But special relativity is committed to the claim that c is a constant. Is there not something suspicious about a "derivation" of T_1 from a T_2 which essentially involves an assumption inconsistent with T_2? If T_2 is correct, then it forbids the adoption of a premise commonly used to derive T_1 as a limiting case. (It should be noted that must such proofs can be reformulated unobjectionably, e.g., in the relativity case, by letting $v \to 0$ rather than $v \to \infty$.)

36. Adolf Grünbaum, "Can a Theory Answer More Questions than One of Its Rivals?" *British Journal of Philosophy of Science* 27 (1976): 1–23.

37. Putnam, *Meaning and the Moral Sciences*, 20.

38. As Mario Bunge has cogently put it: "The popular view on inter-theory relations . . . that every new theory includes (as regards its extension) its predecessors . . . is philosophically superficial . . . and it is false as a historical hypothesis concerning the advancement of science. "M. Bunge, "Problems Concerning Intertheory Relations," In *Induction, Physics and Ethics*, ed. P. Weingartner and G. Zecha (Dordrecht: D. Reidel, 1970), 309–310.

39. Putnam, *Meaning and the Moral Sciences*, 37.

40. K. Popper, *Conjectures and Refutations* (London: Routlege and Kegan Paul, 1963), Introduction.

41. Larry Laudan, "Ex-Huming Hacking," *Erkenntis* 13 (1978).

42. I owe the suggestion of this realist response to Andrew Lugg.

43. I find Putnam's views on the "empirical" or "scientific" character of realism rather perplexing. At some points, he seems to suggest that realism is both empirical and scientific. Thus, he writes: "If realism is an explanation of this fact [namely, that science is successful], realism must itself be an over-arching scientific *hypothesis*" ("What is Realism?"). Since Putnam clearly maintains the antecedent, he seems committed to the consequent. Elsewhere he refers to certain realist tenets are being "our highest level empirical generalizations about knowledge" (*Meaning and the Moral Sciences*, 37). He says, moreover, that realism "could be false," and that "facts are relevant to its support (or to criticize it)" (pp. 78–79). Nonetheless, for reasons he has not made clear, Putnam wants to deny that realism is either scientific or a hypothesis (p. 79). How realism can consist of doctrines which explain facts about the world, are empirical generalizations about knowledge, and can be confirmed or falsified by evidence, and *yet* be neither scientific nor hypothetical, is left opaque.

Chapter 13

Experimentation and Scientific Realism

Ian Hacking

Experimental physics provides the strongest evidence for scientific realism. Entities that in principle cannot be observed are regularly manipulated to produce new phenomena and to investigate other aspects of nature. They are tools, instruments not for thinking but for doing.

The philosopher's standard "theoretical entity" is the electron. I will illustrate how electrons have become experimental entities, or experimenter's entities. In the early stages of our discovery of an entity, we may test hypotheses about it. Then it is merely a hypothetical entity. Much later, if we come to understand some of its causal powers and use it to build devices that achieve well-understood effects in other parts of nature, then it assumes quite a different status.

Discussions about scientific realism or antirealism usually talk about theories, explanation, and prediction. Debates at that level are necessarily inconclusive. Only at the level of experimental practice is scientific realism unavoidable—but this realism is not about theories and truth. The experimentalist need only be a realist about the entities used as tools.

A Plea for Experiments

No field in the philosophy of science is more systematically neglected than experiment. Our grade school teachers may have told us that scientific method is experimental method, but histories of science have become histories of theory. Experiments, the philosophers say, are of value only when they test theory. Experimental work, they imply, has no life of its own. So we lack even a terminology to describe the many varied roles of experiment. Nor has this one-sidedness done theory any good, for radically different types of theory are used to think about the same physical phenomenon (e.g., the magneto-optical effect). The philosophers of theory have not noticed this and so misreport even theoretical enquiry.

Different sciences at different times exhibit different relationships between "theory" and "experiment." One chief role of experiment is the creation of phenomena. Experimenters bring into being phenomena that do not naturally exist in a pure state. These phenomena are the touchstones of physics, the keys to nature, and the source of much modern technology. Many are what physicists after the 1870s began to call "effects": the photoelectric effect, the Compton effect, and so forth.[1] A recent high-energy extension of the creation of phenomena is the creation of "events," to use the jargon of the trade. Most of the phenomena, effects, and events created by the experimenter are like plutonium: they do not exist in nature except possibly on vanishingly rare occasions.[2]

Reprinted from *Philosophical Topics* 13 (1982), pp. 71–87, by permission of the author and the publisher.

In this paper I leave aside questions of methodology, history, taxonomy, and the purpose of experiment in natural science. I turn to the purely philosophical issue of scientific realism. Simply call it "realism" for short. There are two basic kinds: realism about entities and realism about theories. There is no agreement on the precise definition of either. Realism about theories says that we try to form true theories about the world, about the inner constitution of matter and about the outer reaches of space. This realism gets its bite from optimism: we think we can do well in this project and have already had partial success. Realism about entities—and I include processes, states, waves, currents, interactions, fields, black holes, and the like among entities— asserts the existence of at least some of the entities that are the stock in trade of physics.[3]

The two realisms may seem identical. If you believe a theory, do you not believe in the existence of the entities it speaks about? If you believe in some entities, must you not describe them in some theoretical way that you accept? This seeming identity is illusory. *The vast majority of experimental physicists are realists about entities but not about theories.* Some are, no doubt, realists about theories too, but that is less central to their concerns.

Experimenters are often realists about the entities that they investigate, but they do not have to be so. R. A. Millikan probably had few qualms about the reality of electrons when he set out to measure their charge. But he could have been skeptical about what he would find until he found it. He could even have remained skeptical. Perhaps there is a least unit of electric charge, but there is no particle or object with exactly that unit of charge. Experimenting on an entity does not commit you to believing that it exists. Only manipulating an entity, in order to experiment on something else, need do that,

Moreover, it is not even that you use electrons to experiment on something else that makes it impossible to doubt electrons. Understanding some causal properties of electrons, you guess how to build a very ingenious, complex device that enables you to line up the electrons the way you want, in order to see what will happen to something else. Once you have the right experimental idea, you know in advance roughly how to try to build the device, because you know that this is the way to get the electrons to behave in such and such a way. Electrons are no longer ways of organizing our thoughts or saving the phenomena that have been observed. They are now ways of creating phenomena in some other domain of nature. Electrons are tools.

There is an important experimental contrast between realism about entities and realism about theories. Suppose we say that the latter is belief that science aims at true theories. Few experimenters will deny that. Only philosophers doubt it. Aiming at the truth is, however, something about the indefinite future. Aiming a beam of electrons is using present electrons. Aiming a finely tuned laser at a particular atom in order to knock off a certain electron to produce an ion is aiming at present electrons. There is, in contrast, no present set of theories that one has to believe in. If realism about theories is a doctrine about the aims of science, it is a doctrine laden with certain kinds of values. If realism about entities is a matter of aiming electrons next week or aiming at other electrons the week after, it is a doctrine much more neutral between values. The way in which experimenters are scientific realists about entities is entirely different from ways in which they might be realists about theories.

This shows up when we turn from ideal theories to present ones. Various properties are confidently ascribed to electrons, but most of the confident properties are expressed in numerous different theories or models about which an experimenter can be rather agnostic. Even people in a team, who work on different parts of the same large experiment, may hold different and mutually incompatible accounts of electrons. That is because different parts of the experiment will make different uses of electrons. Models good for calculations on one aspect of electrons will be poor for others. Occasionally, a team actually has to select a member with a quite different theoretical perspective simply to get someone who can solve those experimental problems. You may choose someone with a foreign training, and whose talk is well-nigh incommensurable with yours, just to get people who can produce the effects you want.

But might there not be a common core of theory, the intersection of everybody in the group, which is the theory of the electron to which all the experimenters are realistically committed? I would say common lore, not common core. There are a lot of theories, models, approximations, pictures, formalisms, methods, and so forth involving electrons, but there is no reason to suppose that the intersection of these is a theory at all. Nor is there any reason to think that there is such a thing as "the most powerful nontrivial *theory* contained in the intersection of all the theories in which this or that member of a team has been trained to believe." Even if there are a lot of shared beliefs, there is no reason to suppose they form anything worth calling a theory. Naturally, teams tend to be formed from like-minded people at the same institute, so there is usually some real shared theoretical basis to their work. That is a sociological fact, not a foundation for scientific realism.

I recognize that many a scientific realism concerning theories is a doctrine not about the present but about what we might achieve, or possibly an ideal at which we aim. So to say that there is no present theory does not count against the optimistic aim. The point is that such scientific realism about theories has to adopt the Peircean principles of faith, hope, and charity. Scientific realism about entities needs no such virtues. It arises from what we can do at present. To understand this, we must look in some detail at what it is like to build a device that makes the electrons sit up and behave.

Our Debt to Hilary Putnam

It was once the accepted wisdom that a word such as 'electron' gets its meaning from its place in a network of sentences that state theoretical laws. Hence arose the infamous problems of incommensurability and theory change. For if a theory is modified, how could a word such as 'electron' go on meaning the same? How could different theories about electrons be compared, since the very word 'electron' would differ in meaning from theory to theory?

Putnam saved us from such questions by inventing a referential model of meaning. He says that meaning is a vector, refreshingly like a dictionary entry. First comes the syntactic marker (part of speech); next the semantic marker (general category of thing signified by the word); then the stereotype (cliches about the natural kind, standard examples of its use, and present-day associations. The stereotype is subject to change as opinions about the kind are modified). Finally, there is the actual referent of the word, the very stuff, or thing, it denotes if it denotes anything. (Evidently dictionaries cannot include this in their entry, but pictorial dictionaries do their best by inserting illustrations whenever possible.)[4]

Putnam thought we can often guess at entities that we do not literally point to. Our initial guesses may be jejune or inept, and not every naming of an invisible thing or stuff pans out. But when it does, and we frame better and better ideas, then Putnam says that, although the stereotype changes, we refer to the same kind of thing or stuff all along. We and Dalton alike spoke about the same stuff when we spoke of (inorganic) acids. J. J. Thomson, H. A. Lorentz, Bohr, and Millikan were, with their different theories and observations, speculating about the same kind of thing, the electron.

There is plenty of unimportant vagueness about when an entity has been successfully "dubbed," as Putnam puts it. 'Electron' is the name suggested by G. Johnstone Stoney in 1891 as the name for a natural unit of electricity. He had drawn attention to this unit in 1874. The name was then applied to the subatomic particles of negative charge, which J. J. Thomson, in 1897, showed cathodes rays consist of. Was Johnstone Stoney referring to the electron? Putnam's account does not require an unequivocal answer. Standard physics books say that Thomson discovered the electron. For once I might back theory and say that Lorentz beat him to it. Thomson called his electrons 'corpuscles', the subatomic particles of electric charge. Evidently, the name does not matter much. Thomson's most notable achievement was to measure the mass of the electron. He did this by a rough (though quite good) guess at e, and by making an excellent determination of e/m, showing that m is about $1/1800$ the mass of the hydrogen atom. Hence it is natural to say that Lorentz merely postulated the existence of a particle of negative charge, while Thomson, determining its mass, showed that there is some such real stuff beaming off a hot cathode.

The stereotype of the electron has regularly changed, and we have at least two largely incompatible stereotypes, the electron as cloud and the electron as particle. One fundamental enrichment of the idea came in the 1920s. Electrons, it was found, have angular momentum, or "spin." Experimental work by O. Stern and W. Gerlach first indicated this, and then S. Goudsmit and G. E. Uhlenbeck provided the theoretical understanding of it in 1925. Whatever we think, Johnstone Stoney, Lorentz, Bohr, Thomson, and Goudsmit were all finding out more about the same kind of thing, the electron.

We need not accept the fine points of Putnam's account of reference in order to thank him for giving us a new way to talk about meaning. Serious discussion of inferred entities need no longer lock us into pseudo-problems of incommensurability and theory change. Twenty-five years ago the experimenter who believed that electrons exist, without giving much credence to any set of laws about electrons, would have been dismissed as philosophically incoherent. Now we realize it was the philosophy that was wrong, not the experimenter. My own relationship to Putnam's account of meaning is like the experimenter's relationship to a theory. I do not literally believe Putnam, but I am happy to employ his account as an alternative to the unpalatable account in fashion some time ago.

Putnam's philosophy is always in flux. His account of reference was intended to bolster scientific realism. But now, at the time of this writing (July 1981), he rejects any "metaphysical realism" but allows "internal realism."[5] The internal realist acts, in practical affairs, as if the entities occurring in his working theories did in fact exist. However, the direction of Putnam's metaphysical antirealism is no longer scientific. It is not peculiarly about natural science. It is about chairs and livers too. He thinks that the world does not naturally break up into our classifications. He calls himself a transcendental idealist. I call him a transcendental nominalist. I use the word 'nominalist' in the old-fashioned way, not meaning opposition to "abstract entities" like sets, but meaning the doctrine that there is no nonmental classification in nature that exists over and above our own human system of naming.

There might be two kinds of internal realist, the instrumentalist about science and the scientific realist. The former is, in practical affairs where he uses his present scheme of concepts, a realist about livers and chairs but thinks that electrons are only mental constructs. The latter thinks that livers, chairs, and electrons are probably all in the same boat, that is, real at least within the present system of classification. I take Putnam to be an internal scientific realist rather than an internal instrumentalist. The fact that either doctrine is compatible with transcendental nominalism and internal realism shows that our question of scientific realism is almost entirely independent of Putnam's internal realism.

Interfering

Francis Bacon, the first and almost last philosopher of experiments, knew it well: the experimenter sets out "to twist the lion's tail." Experimentation is interference in the course of nature; "nature under constraint and vexed; that is to say, when by art and the hand of man she is forced out of her natural state, and squeezed and moulded."[6] The experimenter is convinced of the reality of entities, some of whose causal properties are sufficiently well understood that they can be used to interfere *elsewhere* in nature. One is impressed by entities that one can use to test conjectures about other, more hypothetical entities. In my example, one is sure of the electrons that are used to investigate weak neutral currents and neutral bosons. This should not be news, for why else are we (nonskeptics) sure of the reality of even macroscopic objects, but because of what we do with them, what we do to them, and what they do to us?

Interference and interaction are the stuff of reality. This is true, for example, at the borderline of observability. Too often philosophers imagine that microscopes carry conviction because they help us see better. But that is only part of the story. On the contrary, what counts is what we can do to a specimen under a microscope, and what we can see ourselves doing. We stain the specimen, slice it, inject it, irradiate it, fix it. We examine it using different kinds of microscopes that employ optical systems that rely on almost totally unrelated facts about light. Microscopes carry conviction because of the great array of interactions and interferences that are possible. When we see something that turns out to be unstable under such play, we call it an artifact and say it is not real.[7]

Likewise, as we move down in scale to the truly unseeable, it is our power to use unobservable entities that makes us believe they are there. Yet, I blush over these words 'see' and 'observe'. Philosophers and physicists often use these words in different ways. Philosophers tend to treat opacity to visible light as the touchstone of reality, so that anything that cannot be touched or seen with the naked eye is called a theoretical or inferred entity. Physicists, in contrast, cheerfully talk of observing the very entities that philosophers say are not observable. For example, the fermions are those fundamental constituents of matter such as electron neutrinos and deuterons and, perhaps, the notorious quarks. All are standard philosophers' "unobservable" entities. C. Y. Prescott, the initiator of the experiment described below, said in a recent lecture, that "of these fermions, only the t quark is yet unseen. The failure to observe $t\bar{t}$ states in $e + e^-$ annihilation at PETRA remains a puzzle."[8] Thus, the physicist distinguishes among the philosophers' "unobservable" entities, noting which have been observed and which not. Dudley Shapere has just published a valuable study of this fact.[9] In his example, neutrinos are used to see the interior of a star. He has ample quotations such as "neutrinos present the only way of directly observing" the very hot core of a star.

John Dewey would have said that fascination with seeing-with-the-naked-eye is part of the spectator theory of knowledge that has bedeviled philosophy from earliest times. But I do not think Plato or Locke or anyone before the nineteenth century was as obsessed with the sheer opacity of objects as we have been since. My own obsession with a technology that manipulates objects is, of course, a twentieth-century counterpart to positivism and phenomenology. Its proper rebuttal is not a restriction to a narrower domain of reality, namely, to what can be positivistically seen with the eye, but an extension to other modes by which people can extend their consciousness.

Making

Even if experimenters are realists about entities, it does not follow that they are right. Perhaps it is a matter of psychology: maybe the very skills that make for a great experimenter go with a certain cast of mind which objectifies whatever it thinks about. Yet this will not do. The experimenter cheerfully regards neutral bosons as merely hypothetical entities, while electrons are real. What is the difference?

There are an enormous number of ways in which to make instruments that rely on the causal properties of electrons in order to produce desired effects of unsurpassed precision. I shall illustrate this. The argument—it could be called the 'experimental argument for realism'—is not that we infer the reality of electrons from our success. We do not make the instruments and then infer the reality of the electrons, as when we test a hypothesis, and then believe it because it passed the test. That gets the time-order wrong. By now we design apparatus relying on a modest number of home truths about electrons, in order to produce some other phenomenon that we wish to investigate.

That may sound as if we believe in the electrons because we predict how our apparatus will behave. That too is misleading. We have a number of general ideas about how to prepare polarized electrons, say. We spend a lot of time building prototypes that do not work. We get rid of innumerable bugs. Often we have to give up and try another approach. Debugging is not a matter of theoretically explaining or predicting what is going wrong. It is partly a matter of getting rid of "noise" in the apparatus. "Noise" often means all the events that are not understood by any theory. The instrument must be able to isolate, physically, the properties of the entities that we wish to use, and damp down all the other effects that might get in our way. *We are completely convinced of the reality of electrons when we regularly set to build—and often enough succeed in building—new kinds of device that use various well understood causal properties of electrons to interfere in other more hypothetical parts of nature.*

It is not possible to grasp this without an example. Familiar historical examples have usually become encrusted by false theory-oriented philosophy or history, so I will take something new. This is a polarizing electron gun whose acronym is PEGGY II. In 1978, it was used in a fundamental experiment that attracted attention even in the *New York Times*. In the next section I describe the point of making PEGGY II. To do that, I have to tell some new physics. You may omit reading this and read only the engineering section that follows. Yet it must be of interest to know the rather easy-to-understand significance of the main experimental results, namely, that parity is not conserved in scattering of polarized electrons from deuterium, and that, more generally, parity is violated in weak neutral-current interactions.[10]

Parity and Weak Neutral Currents

There are four fundamental forces in nature, not necessarily distinct. Gravity and electromagnetism are familiar. Then there are the strong and weak forces (the fulfillment of Newton's program, in the *Optics*, which taught that all nature would be understood by the interaction of particles with various forces that were effective in attraction or repulsion over various different distances, i.e., with different rates of extinction).

Strong forces are 100 times stronger than electromagnetism but act only over a minuscule distance, at most the diameter of a proton. Strong forces act on "hadrons," which include protons, neutrons, and more recent particles, but not electrons or any other members of the class of particles called "leptons."

The weak forces are only 1/10,000 times as strong as electromagnetism, and act over a distance 100 times greater than strong forces. But they act on both hadrons and leptons, including electrons. The most familiar example of a weak force may be radioactivity.

The theory that motivates such speculation is quantum electrodynamics. It is incredibly successful, yielding many predictions better than one part in a million, truly a miracle in experimental physics. It applies over distances ranging from diameters of the earth to 1/100 the diameter of the proton. This theory supposes that all the forces are "carried" by some sort of particle: photons do the job in electromagnetism. We hypothesize "gravitons" for gravity.

In the case of interactions involving weak forces, there are charged currents. We postulate that particles called "bosons" carry these weak forces.[11] For charged currents, the bosons may be either positive or negative. In the 1970s, there arose the possibility that there could be weak "neutral" currents in which no charge is carried or exchanged. By sheer analogy with the vindicated parts of quantum electrodynamics, neutral bosons were postulated as the carriers in weak neutral interactions.

The most famous discovery of recent high-energy physics is the failure of the conservation of parity. Contrary to the expectations of many physicists and philosophers, including Kant,[12] nature makes an absolute distinction between right-handedness and left-handedness. Apparently, this happens only in weak interactions.

What we mean by right- or left-handed in nature has an element of convention. I remarked that electrons have spin. Imagine your right hand wrapped around a spinning particle with the fingers pointing in the direction of spin. Then your thumb is said to point in the direction of the spin vector. If such particles are traveling in a beam, consider the relation between the spin vector and the beam. If all the particles have their spin vector in the same direction as the beam, they have right-handed (linear) polarization, while if the spin vector is opposite to the beam direction, they have left-handed (linear) polarization.

The original discovery of parity violation showed that one kind of product of a particle decay, a so-called muon neutrino, exists only in left-handed polarization and never in right-handed polarization.

Parity violations have been found for weak *charged* interactions. What about weak *neutral* currents? The remarkable Weinberg-Salam model for the four kinds of force was proposed independently by Stephen Weinberg in 1967 and A. Salam in 1968. It implies a minute violation of parity in weak neutral interactions. Given that the model is sheer speculation, its success has been amazing, even awe-inspiring. So it seemed worthwhile to try out the predicted failure of parity for weak neutral interactions. That would teach us more about those weak forces that act over so minute a distance.

The prediction is: slightly more left-handed polarized electrons hitting certain targets will scatter, than right-handed electrons. Slightly more! The difference in relative frequency of the two kinds of scattering is 1 part in 10,000, comparable to a difference in probability between 0.50005 and 0.49995. Suppose one used the standard equipment available at the Stanford Linear Accelerator Center in the early 1970s, generating 120 pulses per second, each pulse providing one electron event. Then you would have to run the entire SLAC beam for twenty-seven years in order to detect so small a difference in relative frequency. Considering that one uses the same beam for lots of experiments simultaneously, by letting different experiments use different pulses, and considering that no equipment remains stable for even a month, let alone twenty-seven years, such an experiment is impossible. You need enormously more electrons coming off in each pulse. We need between 1000 and 10,000 more electrons per pulse than was once possible. The first attempt used an instrument now called PEGGY I. It had, in essence, a high-class version of J. J. Thomson's hot cathode. Some lithium was heated and electrons were boiled off. PEGGY II uses quite different principles.

Peggy II

The basic idea began when C. Y. Prescott noticed (by chance!) an article in an optics magazine about a crystalline substance called gallium arsenide. GaAs has a curious property; when it is struck by circularly polarized light of the right frequencies, it emits lots of linearly polarized electrons. There is a good, rough and ready quantum understanding of why this happens, and why half the emitted electrons will be polarized, three-fourths of these polarized in one direction and one-fourth polarized in the other.

PEGGY II uses this fact, plus the fact that GaAs emits lots of electrons owing to features of its crystal structure. Then comes some engineering—it takes work to liberate an electron from a surface. We know that painting a surface with the right stuff helps. In this case, a thin layer of cesium and oxygen is applied to the crystal. Moreover, the less air pressure around the crystal, the more electrons will escape for a given amount of work. So the bombardment takes place in a good vacuum at the temperature of liquid nitrogen.

We need the right source of light. A laser with bursts of red light (7100 Ångstroms) is trained on the crystal. The light first goes through an ordinary polarizer, a very old-fashioned prism of calcite, or Iceland spar[13]—this gives linearly polarized light. We want circularly polarized light to hit the crystal, so the polarized laser beam now goes through a cunning device called a Pockel's cell, which electrically turns linearly polarized photons into circularly polarized ones. Being electric, it acts as a very fast switch. The direction of circular polarization depends on the direction of current in the cell. Hence, the direction of polarization can be varied randomly. This is important, for we are trying to detect a minute asymmetry between right- and left-handed polarization. Randomizing helps us guard against any systematic "drift" in the equipment.[14] The randomization is generated by a radioactive decay device, and a computer records the direction of polarization for each pulse.

A circularly polarized pulse hits the GaAs crystal, resulting in a pulse of linearly polarized electrons. A beam of such pulses is maneuvered by magnets into the accelerator for the next bit of the experiment. It passes through a device that checks on a proportion of polarization along the way. The remainder of the experiment requires other devices and detectors of comparable ingenuity, but let us stop at PEGGY II.

Bugs

Short descriptions make it all sound too easy; therefore, let us pause to reflect on debugging. Many of the bugs are never understood. They are eliminated by trial and error. Let me illustrate three different kinds of bugs: (1) the essential technical limitations that, in the end, have to be factored into the analysis of error; (2) simpler mechanical defects you never think of until they are forced on you, and (3) hunches about what might go wrong.

Here are three examples of bugs:

1. Laser beams are not as constant as science fiction teaches, and there is always an irremediable amount of "jitter" in the beam over any stretch of time.

2. At a more humdrum level, the electrons from the GaAs crystal are back-scattered and go back along the same channel as the laser beam used to hit the crystal. Most of them are then deflected magnetically. But some get reflected from the laser apparatus and get back into the system. So you have to eliminate these new ambient electrons. This is done by crude mechanical means, making them focus just off the crystal and, thus, wander away.

3. Good experimenters guard against the absurd. Suppose that dust particles on an experimental surface lie down flat when a polarized pulse hits it, and then stand on their heads when hit by a pulse polarized in the opposite direction. Might that have a systematic effect, given that we are detecting a minute asymmetry? One of the team thought of this in the middle of the night and came down next morning frantically using anti-dust spray. They kept that up for a month, just in case[15]

Results

Some 10^{11} events were needed to obtain a result that could be recognized above systematic and statistical error. Although the idea of systematic error presents interesting conceptual problems, it seems to be unknown to philosophers. There were systematic uncertainties in the detection of right- and left-hand polarization, there was some jitter, and there were other problems about the parameters of the two kinds of beam. These errors were analyzed and linearly added to the statistical error. To a student of statistical inference, this is real seat-of-the-pants analysis with no rationale whatsoever. Be that as it may, thanks to PEGGY II the number of events was big enough to give a result that convinced the entire physics community.[16] Left-handed polarized electrons were scattered from deuterium slightly more frequently than right-handed electrons. This was the first convincing example of parity-violation in a weak neutral current interaction.

Comment

The making of PEGGY II was fairly nontheoretical. Nobody worked out in advance the polarizing properties of GaAs—that was found by a chance encounter with an unrelated experimental investigation. Although elementary quantum theory of crystals explains the polarization effect, it does not explain the properties of the actual crystal used. No one has got a real crystal to polarize more than 37 percent of the electrons, although in principle 50 percent should be polarized.

Likewise, although we have a general picture of why layers of cesium and oxygen will "produce negative electron affinity," that is, make it easier for electrons to escape, we have no quantitative understanding of why this increases efficiency to a score of 37 percent.

Nor was there any guarantee that the bits and pieces would fit together. To give an even more current illustration, future experimental work, briefly described later in this paper, makes us want even more electrons per pulse than PEGGY II can give. When the aforementioned parity experiment was reported in the *New York Times*, a group at Bell Laboratories read the newspaper and saw what was going on. They had been constructing a crystal lattice for totally unrelated purposes. It uses layers of GaAs and a related aluminum compound. The structure of this lattice leads one to expect that virtually all the electrons emitted would be polarized. As a consequence, we might be able to double the efficiency of PEGGY II. But, at present, that nice idea has problems. The new lattice should also be coated in work-reducing paint. The cesium-oxygen compound is applied at high temperature. Hence the aluminum tends to ooze into the neighboring layer of GaAs, and the pretty artificial lattice becomes a bit uneven, limiting its fine polarized-electron-emitting properties.[17] So perhaps this will never work. Prescott is simultaneously reviving a souped up new thermionic cathode to try to get more electrons. Theory would not have told us that PEGGY II would beat out thermionic PEGGY I. Nor can it tell if some thermionic PEGGY III will beat out PEGGY II.

Note also that the Bell people did not need to know a lot of weak neutral current theory to send along their sample lattice. They just read the *New York Times*.

Moral

Once upon a time, it made good sense to doubt that there were electrons. Even after Thomson had measured the mass of his corpuscles, and Millikan their charge, doubt could have made sense. We needed to be sure that Millikan was measuring the same entity as Thomson. Thus, more theoretical elaboration was needed, and the idea had to be fed into many other phenomena. Solid state physics, the atom, and superconductivity all had to play their part.

Once upon a time, the best reason for thinking that there are electrons might have been success in explanation. Lorentz explained the Faraday effect with his electron theory. But the ability to explain carries little warrant of truth. Even from the time of J. J. Thomson, it was the measurements that weighed in, more than the explanations. Explanations, however, did help. Some people might have had to believe in electrons because the postulation of their existence could explain a wide variety of phenomena. Luckily, we no longer have to pretend to infer from explanatory success (i.e., from what makes our minds feel good). Prescott and the team from the SLAC do not explain phenomena with electrons. They know how to use them. Nobody in his right mind thinks that electrons "really" are just little spinning orbs about which you could, with a small enough hand, wrap your fingers and find the direction of spin along your thumb. There is, instead, a family of causal properties in terms of which gifted experimenters describe and deploy electrons in order to investigate something else, for example, weak neutral currents and neutral bosons. We know an enormous amount about the behavior of electrons. It is equally important to know what does *not* matter to electrons. Thus, we know that bending a polarized electron beam in magnetic coils does not affect polarization in any significant way. We have hunches, too strong to ignore although too trivial to test independently: for example, dust might dance under changes of directions of polarization. Those hunches are based on a hard-won sense of the kinds of things electrons are. (It does not matter at all to this hunch whether electrons are clouds or waves or particles.)

When Hypothetical Entities Become Real

Note the complete contrast between electrons and neutral bosons. Nobody can yet manipulate a bunch of neutral bosons, if there are any. Even weak neutral currents are only just emerging from the mists of hypothesis. By 1980, a sufficient range of convincing experiments had made them the object of investigation. When might they lose their hypothetical status and become commonplace reality like electrons?—when we use them to investigate something else.

I mentioned the desire to make a better electron gun than PEGGY II. Why? Because we now "know" that parity is violated in weak neutral interactions, Perhaps by an even more grotesque statistical analysis than that involved in the parity experiment, we can isolate just the weak interactions. For example, we have a lot of interactions, including electromagnetic ones, which we can censor in various ways. If we could also statistically pick out a class of weak interactions, as precisely those where parity is not conserved, then we would possibly be on the road to quite deep investigations of matter and antimatter. To do the statistics, however, one needs even more electrons per pulse than PEGGY II could hope to generate. If such a project were to succeed, we should then be beginning to use weak neutral currents as a manipulable tool for looking at something else. The next step toward a realism about such currents would have been made.

The message is general and could be extracted from almost any branch of physics. I mentioned earlier how Dudley Shapere has recently used "observation" of the sun's hot core to illustrate how physicists employ the concept of observation. They collect neutrinos from the sun in an enormous disused underground mine that has been filled with old cleaning fluid (i.e., carbon tetrachloride). We would know a lot about the inside of the sun if we knew how many solar neutrinos arrive on the earth. So these are captured in the cleaning fluid. A few neutrinos will form a new radioactive nucleus (the number that do this can be counted). Although, in this study, the extent of neutrino manipulation is much less than electron manipulation in the PEGGY II experiment, we are nevertheless plainly using neutrinos to investigate something else. Yet not many years ago, neutrinos were about as hypothetical as an entity could get. After 1946 it was realized that when mesons disintegrate giving off, among other things, highly energized electrons, one needed an extra nonionizing particle to conserve momentum and energy. At that time this postulated "neutrino" was thoroughly hypothetical, but now it is routinely used to examine other things.

Changing Times

Although realisms and antirealisms are part of the philosophy of science well back into Greek prehistory, our present versions mostly descend from debates at the end of the nineteenth century about atomism. Antirealism about atoms was partly a matter of physics; the energeticists thought energy was at the bottom of everything, not tiny bits of matter. It also was connected with the positivism of Comte, Mach, K. Pearson, and even J. S. Mill. Mill's young associate Alexander Bain states the point in a characteristic way, apt for 1870:

> Some hypotheses consist of assumptions as to the minute structure and operation of bodies. From the nature of the case these assumptions can never be proved by direct means. Their merit is their suitability to express phenomena. They are Representative Fictions.[18]

"All assertions as to the ultimate structure of the particles of matter," continues Bain, "are and ever must be hypothetical.... The kinetic theory of heat serves an important intellectual function." But we cannot hold it to be a true description of the world. It is a representative fiction.

Bain was surely right a century ago, when assumptions about the minute structure of matter could not be proved. The only proof could be indirect, namely, that hypotheses seemed to provide some explanation and helped make good predictions. Such inferences, however, need never produce conviction in the philosopher inclined to instrumentalism or some other brand of idealism.

Indeed, the situation is quite similar to seventeenth-century epistemology. At that time, knowledge was thought of as correct representation. But then one could never get outside the representations to be sure that they corresponded to the world. Every test of a representation is just another representation. "Nothing is so much like an idea as an idea," said Bishop Berkeley. To attempt to argue to scientific realism at the level of theory, testing, explanation, predictive success, convergence of theories, and so forth is to be locked into a world of representations. No wonder that scientific antirealism is so permanently in the race. It is a variant on "the spectator theory of knowledge."

Scientists, as opposed to philosophers, did, in general, become realists about atoms by 1910. Despite the changing climate, some antirealist variety of instrumentalism or fictionalism remained a strong philosophical alternative in 1910 and in 1930. That is what the history of philosophy teaches us. The lesson is: think about practice, not theory. Antirealism about atoms was very sensible when Bain wrote a century ago. Antirealism about *any* submicroscopic entities was a sound doctrine in those days. Things are different now. The "direct" proof of electrons and the like is our ability to manipulate them using well-understood low-level causal properties. Of course, I do not claim that reality is constituted by human manipulability. Millikan's ability to determine the charge of the electron did something of great importance for the idea of electrons, more, I think, than the Lorentz theory of the electron. Determining the charge of something makes one believe in it far more than postulating it to explain something else. Millikan got the charge on the electron; but better still, Uhlenbeck and Goudsmit in 1925 assigned angular momentum to electrons, brilliantly solving a lot of problems. Electrons have spin, ever after. The clincher is when we can put a spin on the electrons, and thereby get them to scatter in slightly different proportions.

Surely, there are innumerable entities and processes that humans will never know about. Perhaps there are many in principle we can never know about, since reality is bigger than us. The best kinds of evidence for the reality of a postulated or inferred entity is that we can begin to measure it or otherwise understand its causal powers. The best evidence, in turn, that we have this kind of understanding is that we can set out, from scratch, to build machines that will work fairly reliably, taking advantage of this or that causal nexus. Hence, engineering, not theorizing, is the best proof of scientific realism about entities. My attack on scientific antirealism is analogous to Marx's onslaught on the idealism of his day. Both say that the point is not to understand the world but to change it. Perhaps there are some entities which in theory we can know about only through theory (black holes). Then our evidence is like that furnished by Lorentz. Perhaps there are entities which we shall only measure and never use. The experimental argument for realism does not say that only experimenter's objects exist.

I must now confess a certain skepticism, about, say, black holes. I suspect there might be another representation of the universe, equally consistent with phenomena, in which black holes are precluded. I inherit from Leibniz a certain distaste for occult powers. Recall how he inveighed against Newtonian gravity as occult. It took two centuries to show he was right. Newton's ether was also excellently occult—it taught us lots: Maxwell did his electromagnetic waves in ether, H. Hertz confirmed the ether by demonstrating the existence of radio waves. Albert A. Michelson figured out a way to interact with the ether. He thought his experiment confirmed G. G. Stoke's ether drag theory, but, in the end, it was one of many things that made ether give up the ghost. A skeptic such as myself has a slender induction: long-lived theoretical entities which do not end up being manipulated commonly turn out to have been wonderful mistakes.

Notes

1. C. W. E. Everitt suggests that the first time the word 'effect' is used this way in English is in connection with the Peltier effect, in James Clerk Maxwell's 1873 *Electricity and Magnetism*, par. 249, p. 301. My interest in experiment was kindled by conversation with Everitt some years ago, and I have learned much in working with him on our joint (unpublished) paper, "Theory or Experiment, Which Comes First?"
2. Ian Hacking, "Spekulation, Berechnung und die Erschaffung der Phänomenen," in *Versuchungen: Aufsätze zur Philosophie, Paul Feyerabends*, no. 2, ed. P. Duerr (Frankfort, 1981), 126–158.
3. Nancy Cartwright makes a similar distinction in her book, *How the Laws of Physics Lie* (Oxford: Oxford University Press, 1983). She approaches realism from the top, distinguishing theoretical laws (which do not state the facts) from phenomenological laws (which do). She believes in some "theoretical" entities and rejects much theory on the basis of a subtle analysis of modeling in physics. I proceed in the opposite direction, from experimental practice. Both approaches share an interest in real life physics as opposed to philosophical fantasy science. My own approach owes an enormous amount to Cartwright's parallel developments, which have often preceded my own. My use of the two kinds of realism is a case in point.
4. Hilary Putnam, "How Not to Talk About Meaning," "The Meaning of 'Meaning,'" and other papers in *Mind, Language and Reality*, Philosophical Papers, vol. 2 (Cambridge: Cambridge University Press, 1975).
5. These terms occur in, e.g., Hilary Putnam, *Meaning and the Moral Sciences* (London: Routlege and Kegan Paul, 1978), 123–130.
6. Francis Bacon, *The Great Instauration*, in *The Philosophical Works of Francis Bacon*, trans. Ellis and Spedding, ed. J. M. Roberston (London, 1905), 252.
7. Ian Hacking, "Do We See Through a Microscope?" *Pacific Philosophical Quarterly* 62 (1981): 305–322.
8. C. Y. Prescott, "Prospects for Polarized Electrons at High Energies," SLAC-PUB-2630, Stanford Linear Accelerator, October 1980, p. 5.
9. "The Concept of Observation in Science and Philosophy," *Philosophy of Science* 49 (1982): 485–526. See also K. S. Shrader-Frechette, "Quark Quantum Numbers and the Problem of Microphysical Observation," Synthese 50 (1982): 125–146, and ensuing discussion in that issue of the journal.
10. I thank Melissa Franklin, of the Stanford Linear Accelerator, for introducing me to PEGGY II and telling me how it works. She also arranged discussion with members of the PEGGY II group, some of whom are mentioned below. The report of experiment E-122 described here is "Parity Nonconservation in Inelastic Electron Scattering," C. Y. Prescott et al., in *Physics Letters*. I have relied heavily on the in-house journal, the *SLAC Beam Line*, report no. 8, October 1978, "Parity Violation in Polarized Electron Scattering." This was prepared by the in-house science writer Bill Kirk.
11. The odd-sounding bosons are named after the Indian physicist S. N. Bose (1894–1974), also remembered in the name "Bose-Einstein statistics" (which bosons satisfy).
12. But excluding Leibniz, who "knew" there had to be some real, natural difference between right- and left-handedness.
13. Iceland spar is an elegant example of how experimental phenomena persist even while theories about them undergo revolutions. Mariners brought calcite from Iceland to Scandinavia. Erasmus Bartholinus experimented with it and wrote it up in 1609. When you look through these beautiful crystals you see double, thanks to the so-called ordinary and extraordinary rays. Calcite is a natural polarizer. It was our entry to polarized light which for three hundred years was the chief route to improved theoretical and experimental understanding of light and then electromagnetism. The use of calcite in PEGGY II is a happy reminder of a great tradition.
14. It also turns GaAs, a 3/4 to 1/4 left-hand/right-hand polarizer, into a 50–50 polarizer.
15. I owe these examples to conversation with Roger Miller of SLAC.

16. The concept of a "convincing experiment" is fundamental. Peter Gallison has done important work on this idea, studying European and American experiments on weak neutral currents conducted during the 1970s.
17. I owe this information on Charles Sinclair of SLAC.
18. Alexander Bain, *Logic, Deductive and Inductive* (London and New York, 1870), 362.

Chapter 14

The Natural Ontological Attitude

Arthur Fine

Let us fix our attention out of ourselves as much as possible; let us chace our imagination to the heavens, or to the utmost limits of the universe; we never really advance a step beyond ourselves, nor can conceive any kind of existence, but those perceptions, which have appear'd in that narrow compass. This is the universe of the imagination, nor have we any idea but what is there produced.

Hume, *Treatise*, book 1, part II, section VI

Realism is dead. Its death was announced by the neopositivists who realized that they could accept all the results of science, including all the members of the scientific zoo, and still declare that the questions raised by the existence claims of realism were mere pseudo-questions. Its death was hastened by the debates over the interpretation of quantum theory, where Bohr's nonrealist philosophy was seen to win out over Einstein's passionate realism. Its death was certified, finally, as the last two generations of physical scientists turned their backs on realism and have managed, nevertheless, to do science successfully without it. To be sure, some recent philosophical literature has appeared to pump up the ghostly shell and to give it new life. I think these efforts will eventually be seen and understood as the first stage in the process of mourning, the stage of denial. But I think we shall pass through this first stage and into that of acceptance, for realism is well and truly dead, and we have work to get on with, in identifying a suitable successor. To aid that work I want to do three things in this essay. First, I want to show that the arguments in favor of realism are not sound, and that they provide no rational support for belief in realism. Then, I want to recount the essential role of nonrealist attitudes for the development of science in this century, and thereby (I hope) to loosen the grip of the idea that only realism provides a progressive philosophy of science. Finally, I want to sketch out what seems to me a viable nonrealist position, one that is slowly gathering support and that seems a decent philosophy for postrealist times.[1]

1. Arguments for Realism

Recent philosophical argument in support of realism tries to move from the success of the scientific enterprise to the necessity for a realist account of its practice. As I see it, the arguments here fall on two distinct levels. On the ground level, as it were, one attends to particular successes; such as novel, confirmed predictions, striking unifications of disparate-seeming phenomena (or fields), successful piggybacking from

Reprinted from *Scientific Realism*, ed. J. Leplin (Berkeley: University of California Press, 1984), pp. 83–107, by permission of the author and the publisher. Copyright 1984 by the Regents of the University of California.

one theoretical model to another, and the like. Then, we are challenged to account for such success, and told that the best and, it is slyly suggested, perhaps, the *only* way of doing so is on a realist basis. I do not find the details of these ground-level arguments at all convincing. Neither does Larry Laudan (1984) and, fortunately, he has provided a forceful and detailed analysis which shows that not even with a lot of handwaving (to shield the gaps in the argument) and charity (to excuse them) can realism itself be used to explain the very successes to which it invites our attention. But there is a second level of realist argument, the methodological level, that derives from Popper's (1972) attack on instrumentalism, which he attacks as being inadequate to account for the details of his own, falsificationist methodology. Arguments on this methodological level have been skillfully developed by Richard Boyd (1981, 1984), and by one of the earlier Hilary Putnams (1975). These arguments focus on the methods embedded in scientific practice, methods teased out in ways that seem to me accurate and perceptive about ongoing science. We are then challenged to account for why these methods lead to scientific success and told that the best and, (again) perhaps, the only truly adequate way of explaining the matter is on the basis of realism.

I want to examine some of these methodological arguments in detail to display the flaws that seem to be inherent in them. But first I want to point out a deep and, I think, insurmountable problem with this entire strategy of defending realism, as I have laid it out above. To set up the problem, let me review the debates in the early part of this century over the foundations of mathematics, the debates that followed Cantor's introduction of set theory. There were two central worries here, one over the meaningfulness of Cantor's hierarchy of sets insofar as it outstripped the number-theoretic content required by Kronecker (and others); the second worry, certainly deriving in good part from the first, was for the consistency (or not) of the whole business. In this context, Hilbert devised a quite brilliant program to try to show the consistency of a mathematical theory by using only the most stringent and secure means. In particular, if one were concerned over the consistency of set theory, then clearly a set-theoretic proof of consistency would be of no avail. For if set theory were inconsistent, then such a consistency proof would be both possible and of no significance. Thus, Hilbert suggested that finite constructivist means, satisfactory even to Kronecker (or Brouwer) ought to be employed in metamathematics. Of course, Hilbert's program was brought to an end in 1931, when Gödel showed the impossibility of such a stringent consistency proof. But Hilbert's idea was, I think, correct even though it proved to be unworkable. Metatheoretic arguments must satisfy more stringent requirements than those placed on the arguments used by the theory in question, for otherwise the significance of reasoning about the theory is simply moot. I think this maxim applies with particular force to the discussion of realism.

Those suspicious of realism, from Osiander to Poincaré and Duhem to the "constructive empiricism" of van Fraassen,[2] have been worried about the significance of the explanatory apparatus in scientific investigations. While they appreciate the systematization and coherence brought about by scientific explanation, they question whether acceptable explanations need to be true and, hence, whether the entities mentioned in explanatory principles need to exist.[3] Suppose they are right. Suppose, that is, that the usual explanation-inferring devices in scientific practice do not lead to principles that are reliably true (or nearly so), nor to entities whose existence (or near existence) is reliable. In that case, the usual abductive methods that lead us to good explanations (even to "the best explanation") cannot be counted on to yield results even approximately true. But the strategy that leads to realism, as I have indicated, is just such an ordinary sort of abductive inference. Hence, if the nonrealist were correct in his doubts, then such an inference to realism as the best explanation (or the like), while possible, would be of no significance exactly as in the case of a consistency proof using the methods of an inconsistent system. It seems, then, that Hilbert's maxim applies to the debate over realism: to argue for realism one must employ methods more stringent than those in ordinary scientific practice. In particular, one must not beg the question as to the significance of explanatory hypotheses by assuming that they carry truth as well as explanatory efficacy.

There is a second way of seeing the same result. Notice that the issue over realism is precisely the issue of whether we should believe in the reality of those individuals, properties, relations, processes, and so forth, used in well-supported explanatory hypotheses. Now what *is* the hypothesis of realism, as it arises as an explanation of scientific practice? It is just the hypothesis that our accepted scientific theories are approximately true, where "being approximately true" is taken to denote an extratheoretical relation between theories and the world. Thus, to address doubts over the reality of relations posited by explanatory hypotheses, the realist proceeds to introduce a further explanatory hypothesis (realism), itself positing such a relation (approximate truth). Surely anyone serious about the issue of realism, and with an open mind about it, would have to behave inconsistently if he were to accept the realist move as satisfactory.

Thus, both at the ground level and at the level of methodology, no support accrues to realism by showing that realism is a good hypothesis for explaining scientific practice. If we are open-minded about realism to begin with, then such a demonstration (even if successful) merely begs the question that we have left open ("need we take good explanatory hypotheses as true?"). Thus, Hilbert's maxim applies, and we must employ patterns of argument more stringent than the usual abductive ones. What might they be? Well, the obvious candidates are patterns of induction leading to empirical generalizations. But, to frame empirical generalizations, we must first have some observable connections between observables. For realism, this must connect theories with the world by way of approximate truth. But no such connections are observable and, hence, suitable as the basis for an inductive inference. I do not want to labor the points at issue here. They amount to the well-known idea that realism commits one to an unverifiable correspondence with the world. So far as I am aware, no recent defender of realism has tried to make a case based on a Hilbert strategy of using suitably stringent grounds and, given the problems over correspondence, it is probably just as well.

The strategy of arguments for realism as a good explanatory hypothesis, then, *cannot* (logically speaking) be effective for an open-minded nonbeliever. But what of the believer? Might he not, at least, show a kind of internal coherence about realism as an overriding philosophy of science, and should that not be of some solace, at least for the realist?[4] Recall, however, the analogue with consistency proofs for inconsistent systems. That sort of harmony should be of no solace to anyone. But for realism, I fear, the verdict is even harsher. For, so far as I can see, the arguments in question just do not work, and the reason for that has to do with the same question-begging procedures that I have already identified. Let me look closely at some methodological arguments in order to display the problems.

A typical realist argument on the methodological level deals with what I shall call the problem of the "small handful." It goes like this. At any time, in a given scientific area, only a small handful of alternative theories (or hypotheses) are in the field. Only such a small handful are seriously considered as competitors, or as possible successors to some theory requiring revision. Moreover, in general, this handful displays a sort of family resemblance in that none of these live options will be too far from the previously accepted theories in the field, each preserving the well-confirmed features of the earlier theories and deviating only in those aspects less confirmed. Why? Why does this narrowing down of our choices to such a small handful of cousins of our previously accepted theories work to produce good successor theories?

The realist answers this as follows. Suppose that the already existing theories are themselves approximately true descriptions of the domain under consideration. Then surely it is reasonable to restrict one's search for successor theories to those whose ontologies and laws resemble what we already have, especially where what we already have is well confirmed. And if these earlier theories were approximately true, then so will be such conservative successors. Hence, such successors will be good predictive instruments; that is, they will be successful in their own right.

The small-handful problem raises three distinct questions: (1) why only a small handful out of the (theoretically) infinite number of possibilities? (2) why the conservative family resemblance between members of the handful? and (3) why does the strategy of narrowing the choices in this way work so well? The realist response does not seem to address the first issue at all, for even if we restrict ourselves just to successor theories resembling their progenitors, as suggested, there would still, theoretically, always be more than a small handful of these. To answer the second question, as to why conserve the well-confirmed features of ontology and laws, the realist must suppose that such confirmation is a mark of an approximately correct ontology and approximately true laws. But how could the realist possibly justify such an assumption? Surely, there is no valid inference of the form, "T is well-confirmed; therefore, there exist objects pretty much of the sort required by T and satisfying laws approximating those of T. "Any of the dramatic shifts of ontology in science show the invalidity of this schema. For example, the loss of the ether from the turn-of-the-century electrodynamic theories demonstrates this at the level of ontology, and the dynamics of the Rutherford-Bohr atom vis-à-vis the classical energy principles for rotating systems demonstrates it at the level of laws. Of course, the realist might respond that there is no question of a strict inference between being well confirmed and being approximately true (in the relevant respects), but there is a probable inference of some sort. But of what sort? Certainly there is no probability relation that rests on inductive evidence here. For there is no independent evidence for the relation of approximate truth itself: at least, the realist has yet to produce any evidence that is independent of the argument under examination. But if the probabilities are not grounded inductively, then how else? Here, I think the realist may well try to fall back on his original strategy and suggest that being approximately true provides the best explanation for being well confirmed. This move throws us back to the ground-level realist argument, the argument from specific success to an approximately true description of reality, which Laudan (1984) has criticized. I should point out, before looking at the third question, that if this last move is the one the realist wants to make, then his success at the methodological level can be no better than his success at the ground level. If he fails there, he fails across the board.

The third question, and the one I think the realist puts most weight on, is why does the small-handful strategy work so well. The instrumentalist, for example, is thought to have no answer here. He must just note that it does work well and be content with that. The realist, however, can explain why it works by citing the transfer of approximate truth from predecessor theories to the successor theories. But what does this explain? At best, it explains why the successor theories cover the same ground as well as their predecessors, for the conservative strategy under consideration assures that.

But note that here the instrumentalist can offer the same account: if we insist on preserving the well-confirmed components of earlier theories in later theories, then, of course, the later ones will do well over the well-confirmed ground. The difficulty, however, is not here at all but rather in how to account for the successes of the later theories in new ground, or with respect to novel predictions, or in overcoming the anomalies of the earlier theories. And what can the realist possibly say in this area except that the theorist, in proposing a new theory, has happened to make a good guess? For nothing in the approximate truth of the old theory can guarantee (or even make it likely) that modifying the theory in its less-confirmed parts will produce a progressive shift. The history of science shows well enough how such tinkering succeeds only now and again, and fails for the most part. This history of failures can scarcely be adduced to explain the occasional success. The idea that by extending what is approximately true one is likely to bring new approximate truth is chimera. It finds support neither in the logic of approximate truth nor in the history of science. The problem for the realist is how to explain the *occasional success* of a strategy that *usually fails.*[5] I think he has no special resources with which to do this. In particular, his usual fallback onto approximate truth provides nothing more than a gentle pillow. He may rest on it comfortably, but it does not really help to move his cause forward.

The problem of the small handful raises three challenges: why small? why narrowly related? and why does it work? The realist has no answer for the first of these, begs the question as to the truth of explanatory hypotheses on the second, and has no resources for addressing the third. For comparison, it may be useful to see how well his archenemy the instrumentalist, fares on the same turf. The instrumentalist, I think, has a substantial basis for addressing the questions of smallness and narrowness, for he can point out that it is extremely difficult to come up with alternative theories that satisfy the many empirical constraints posed by the instrumental success of theories already in the field. Often it is hard enough to come up with even one such alternative. Moreover, the common apprenticeship of scientists working in the same area certainly has the effect of narrowing down the range of options by channeling thought into the commonly accepted categories. If we add to this the instrumentally justified rule, "If it has worked well in the past, try it again," then we get a rather good account, I think, of why there is usually only a small and narrow handful. As to why this strategy works to produce instrumentally successful science, we have already noted that for the most part it does not. Most of what this strategy produces are failures. It is a quirk of scientific memory that this fact gets obscured, much as do the memories of bad times during a holiday vacation when we recount all our "wonderful" vacation adventures to a friend. Those instrumentalists who incline to a general account of knowledge as a social construction can go further at this juncture and lean on the sociology of science to explain how the scientific community "creates" its knowledge. I am content just to back off here and note that over the problem of the small handful, the instrumentalist scores at least two out of three, whereas the realist, left to his own devices, has struck out.[6]

I think the source of the realist's failure here is endemic to the methodological level, infecting all of his arguments in this domain It resides, in the first instance, in his repeating the question-begging move from explanatory efficacy to the truth of the explanatory hypothesis. And in the second instance, it resides in his twofold mishandling of the concept of approximate truth: first, in his trying to project from some body of assumed approximate truths *to* some further and novel such truths, and second, in his needing genuine access to the relation of correspondence. There are no general connections of this first sort, however, sanctioned by the logic of approximate truth, nor secondly, any such warranted access. However, the realist must pretend that there are in order to claim explanatory power for his realism. We have seen those two agents infecting the realist way with the problem of the small handful. Let me show them at work in another methodological favorite of the realist, the "problem of conjunctions."

The problem of conjunctions is this. If T and T' are independently well-confirmed, explanatory theories, and if no shared term is ambiguous between the two, then we expect the conjunction of T and T' to be a reliable predictive instrument (provided, of course, that the theories are not mutually inconsistent). Why? challenges the realist, and he answers as follows. If we make the realist assumption that T and T', being well confirmed, are approximately true of the entities (etc.) to which they refer, and if the unambiguity requirement is taken realistically as requiring a domain of common reference, then the conjunction of the two theories will also be approximately true and, hence, it will produce reliable observational predictions. Q.E.D.

But notice our agents at work. First, the realist makes the question-begging move from explanations to their approximate truth, and then he mistreats approximate truth. For nothing in the logic of approximate truth sanctions the inference from "T is approximately true" and "T' is approximately true" to the conclusion that the conjunction "$T \cdot T'$" is approximately true. Rather, in general, the tightness of an approximation dissipates as we pile on further approximations. If T is within ε, in its estimation of some parameter, and T' is also within ε, then the only general thing we can say is that the conjunction will be within 2ε of the parameter. Thus, the logic of approximate truth should lead us to the opposite conclusion here; that is, that the conjunction of two theories is, in general, less reliable than either (over their common domain). But this is neither what we expect nor what we find. Thus, it seems quite implausible that our actual expectations about the reliability of conjunctions rest on the realist's stock of approximate truths.

Of course, the realist could try to retrench here and pose an additional requirement of some sort of uniformity on the character of the approximations, as between T and T'.[7] It is difficult to see how the realist could do this successfully without making reference to the distance between the approximations and "the truth." For what kind of internalist requirement could possibly insure the narrowing of this distance? But the realist is in no position to impose such requirements, since neither he nor anyone else has the requisite access to "the truth." Thus, whatever uniformity-of-approximation condition the realist might impose, we could still demand to be shown that this leads closer to the truth, not farther away. The realist will have no demonstration, except to point out to us that it all works (sometimes!). But that was the original puzzle.[8] Actually, I think the puzzle is not very difficult. For surely, if we do not entangle ourselves with issues over approximation, there is no deep mystery as to why two compatible and successful theories lead us to expect their conjunction to be successful. For in forming the conjunction, we just add the reliable predictions of one onto the reliable predictions of the other, having antecedently ruled out the possibility of conflict.

There is more to be said about this topic. In particular, we need to address the question of why we expect the logical gears of the two theories to mesh. However, I think that a discussion of the realist position here would only bring up the same methodological and logical problems that we have already uncovered at the center of the realist argument.

Indeed, this schema of knots in the realist argument applies across the board and vitiates every single argument at the methodological level. Thus my conclusion here is harsh, indeed. The methodological arguments for realism fail, even though, were they successful, they would still not support the case. For the general strategy they are supposed to implement is just not stringent enough to provide rational support for realism. In the next two sections, I will try to show that this situation is just as well, for realism has not always been a progressive factor in the development of science and, anyway, there is a position other than realism that is more attractive

2. Realism and Progress

If we examine the two twentieth-century giants among physical theories, relativity and the quantum theory, we find a living refutation of the realist's claim that only his view of science explains its progress, and we find some curious twists and contrasts over realism as well. The theories of relativity are almost single-handedly the work of Albert Einstein. Einstein's early positivism and his methodological debt to Mach (and Hume) leap right out of the pages of the 1905 paper on special relativity.[9] The same positivist strain is evident in the 1916 general relativity paper as well, where Einstein (in section 3 of that paper) tries to justify his requirement of general covariance by means of a suspicious-looking verificationist argument which, he says, "takes away from space and time the last remnants of physical objectivity" (Einstein et al. 1952, p. 117). A study of his tortured path to general relativity[10] shows the repeated use of this Machist line, always used to deny that some concept has a real referent. Whatever other, competing strains there were in Einstein's philosophical orientation (and there certainly were others), it would be hard to deny the importance of this instrumentalist/positivist attitude in liberating Einstein from various realist commitments. Indeed, on another occasion, I would argue in detail that without the "freedom from reality" provided by his early reverence for Mach, a central tumbler necessary to unlock the secret of special relativity would never have fallen into place.[11] A few years after his work on general relativity, however, roughly around 1920, Einstein underwent a philosophical conversion, turning away from his positivist youth (he was forty-one in 1920) and becoming deeply committed to realism (see chapter 6). In particular, following his conversion, Einstein wanted to claim genuine reality for the central theoretical entities of the general theory, the four-dimensional space-time manifold and associated tensor fields. This is a serious business, for if we grant his claim, then not only do space and time cease to be real but so do virtually all of the usual dynamical quantities.[12] Thus motion, as we understand it, itself ceases to be real. The current generation of philosophers of space and time (led by Howard Stein and John Earman) have followed Einstein's lead here. But, interestingly, not only do these ideas boggle the mind of the average man in the street (like you and me), they boggle most contemporary scientific minds as well.[13] That is, I believe the majority opinion among working, knowledgeable scientists is that general relativity provides a magnificent organizing tool for treating certain gravitational problems in astrophysics and cosmology. But few, I believe, give credence to the kind of realist existence and nonexistence claims that I have been mentioning. For relativistic physics, then, it appears that a nonrealist attitude was important in its development, that the founder nevertheless espoused a realist attitude to the finished product, but that most who actually use it think of the theory as a powerful instrument, rather than as expressing a "big truth."

With quantum theory, this sequence gets a twist. Heisenberg's seminal paper of 1925 is prefaced by the following abstract, announcing, in effect, his philosophical stance: "In this paper an attempt will be made to obtain bases for a quantum-theoretical mechanics based exclusively on relations between quantities observable in principle"

(Heisenberg 1925, p. 879). In the body of the paper, Heisenberg not only rejects any reference to unobservables, he also moves away from the very idea that one should try to form any picture of a reality underlying his mechanics. To be sure, Schrodinger, the second father of quantum theory, seems originally to have had a vague picture of an underlying wavelike reality for his own equation. But he was quick to see the difficulties here and, just as quickly, although reluctantly, abandoned the attempt to interpolate any reference to reality.[14] These instrumentalist moves away from a realist construal of the emerging quantum theory were given particular force by Bohr's so-called philosophy of complementarity. This nonrealist position was consolidated at the time of the famous Solvay Conference, in October 1927, and is firmly in place today. Such quantum nonrealism is part of what every graduate physicist learns and practices. It is the conceptual backdrop to all the brilliant successes in atomic, nuclear, and particle physics over the past fifty years. Physicists have learned to think about their theory in a highly nonrealist way, and doing just that has brought about the most marvelous predictive success in the history of science.

The war between Einstein, the realist, and Bohr, the nonrealist, over the interpretation of quantum theory was not, I believe, just a sideshow in physics, nor an idle intellectual exercise. It was an important endeavor undertaken by Bohr on behalf of the enterprise of physics as a progressive science. For Bohr believed (and this fear was shared by Heisenberg, Sommerfeld, Pauli, and Born—and all the big guys) that Einstein's realism, if taken seriously, would block the consolidation and articulation of the new physics and, thereby, stop the progress of science. They were afraid, in particular, that Einstein's realism would lead the next generation of the brightest and best students into scientific dead ends. Alfred Landé, for example, as a graduate student, was interested in spending some time in Berlin to sound out Einstein's ideas. His supervisor was Sommerfeld, and recalling this period, Landé (1974, p. 460) writes, "The more pragmatic Sommerfeld ... warned his students, one of them this writer, not to spend too much time on the hopeless task of "explaining" the quantum but rather to accept it as fundamental and help work out its consequences."

The task of "explaining" the quantum, of course, is the realist program for identifying a reality underlying the formulas of the theory and thereby explaining the predictive success of the formulas as approximately true descriptions of this reality. It is this program that I have criticized in the first part of this chapter, and this same program that the builders of quantum theory saw as a scientific dead end. Einstein knew perfectly well that the issue was joined right here. In the summer of 1935, he wrote to Schrödinger, "The real problem is that physics is a kind of metaphysics; physics describes 'reality.' But we do not know what 'reality' is. We know it only through physical description.... But the Talmudic philosopher sniffs at 'reality,' as at a frightening creature of the naive mind."[15]

By avoiding the bogey of an underlying reality, the "Talmudic" originators of quantum theory seem to have set subsequent generations on precisely the right path. Those inspired by realist ambitions have produced no predictively successful physics. Neither Einstein's conception of a unified field, nor the ideas of the de Broglie group about pilot waves, nor the Bohm-inspired interest in hidden variables has made for scientific progress. To be sure, several philosophers of physics, including another Hilary Putnam and myself, have fought a battle over the last decade to show that the quantum theory is at least consistent with some kind of underlying reality. I believe that Hilary has abandoned the cause, perhaps in part on account of the recent Bell-inequality problem over correlation experiments, a problem that van Fraassen (1982) calls "the Charybdis of realism." My own recent work in the area suggests that we may still be able to keep realism afloat in this whirlpool.[16] But the possibility (as I still see it) for a realist account of the quantum domain should not lead us away from appreciating the historical facts of the matter.

One can hardly doubt the importance of a nonrealist attitude for the development and practically infinite success of the quantum theory. Historical counterfactuals are always tricky, but the sterility of actual realist programs in this area at least suggests that Bohr and company were right in believing that the road to scientific progress here would have been blocked by realism. The founders of quantum theory never turned on the nonrealist attitude that served them so well. Perhaps that is because the central underlying theoretical device of quantum theory, the densities of a complex-valued and infinite-dimensional wave function, are even harder to take seriously than is the four-dimensional manifold of relativity. But now there comes a most curious twist. For just as the practitioners of relativity, I have suggested, ignore the *realist* interpretation in favor of a more pragmatic attitude toward the space/time structure, the quantum physicists would appear to make a similar reversal and to forget their nonrealist history and allegiance when it comes time to talk about new discoveries.

Thus, anyone in the business will tell you about the exciting period, in the fall of 1974, when the particle group at Brookhaven, led by Samuel Ting, discovered the J particle, just as a Stanford team at the Stanford Linear Accelerator Center, under Burton Richter, independently found a new particle they called ψ. These turned out to be one and the same, the so-called ψ/J particle (Mass 3,098 MeV, Spin 1, Resonance 67 keV, Strangeness 0). To explain this new entity, the theoreticians were led to introduce a new kind of quark, the so-called charmed quark. The ψ/J particle is then thought to be made up out of a charmed quark and an anticharmed quark, with their respective spins aligned. But if this is correct, then there ought to be other such pairs antialigned, or with variable spin alignments, and these ought to make up quite new observable particles. Such predictions from the charmed-quark model have turned out to be confirmed in various experiments.

I have gone on a bit in this story in order to convey the realist feel to the way scientists speak in this area. For I want to ask whether this is a return to realism or whether, instead, it can somehow be reconciled with a fundamentally nonrealist attitude.[17] I believe that the nonrealist option is correct.

3. Nonrealism

Even if the realist happens to be a talented philosopher, I do not believe that, in this heart, he relies for his realism on the rather sophisticated form of abductive argument that I have examined and rejected in the first section of this chapter, and which the history of twentieth-century physics shows to be fallacious. Rather, if his heart is like mine, then I suggest that a more simple and homely sort of argument is what grips him. It is this, and I will put it in the first person. I certainly trust the evidence of my senses, on the whole, with regard to the existence and features of everyday objects. And I have similar confidence in the system of "check, double-check, check, triple-check" of scientific investigation, as well as the other safeguards built into the institutions of science. So, if the scientists tell me that there really are molecules, and atoms, and ψ/J particles, and, who knows, maybe even quarks, then so be it. I trust them and, thus, must accept that there really are such things with their attendant properties and relations. Moreover, if the instrumentalist (or some other member of the species "nonrealistica") comes along to say that these entities and their attendants are just fictions (or the like), then I see no more reason to believe him than to believe that *he is* a fiction, made up (somehow) to do a job on me; which I do not believe. It seems, then, that I had better be a realist. One can summarize this homely and compelling line as follows: it is possible to accept the evidence of one's senses and to accept, *in the same way*, the confirmed results of science only for a realist; hence, I should be one (and so should you!).

What is it to accept the evidence of one's senses and, *in the same way*, to accept confirmed scientific theories? It is to take them into one's life as true, with all that implies concerning adjusting one's behavior, practical and theoretical, to accommodate these truths. Now, of course, there are truths. and truths. Some are more central to us and our lives, some less so. I might be rnistaken about anything, but were I mistaken about where I am right now, that might affect me more than would my perhaps mistaken belief in charmed quarks. Thus, it is compatible with the homely line of argument that some of the scientific beliefs that I hold are less central than some, for example, perceptual beliefs. Of course, were I deeply in the charmed-quark business, giving up that belief might be more difficult than giving up some at the perceptual level. (Thus we get the phenomenon of "seeing what you believe," well known to all thoughtful people.) When the homely line asks us, then, to accept the scientific results "in the same way" in which we accept the evidence of our senses, I take it that we are to accept them both as true. I take it that we are being asked not to distinguish between kinds of truth or modes of existence or the like, but only among truths themselves in terms of centrality, degrees of belief, or such.

Let us suppose this understood. Now, do you think that Bohr, the archenemy of realism, could toe the homely line? Could Bohr, fighting for the sake of science (against Einstein's realism) have felt compelled either to give up the results of science, or else to assign its "truths" to some category different from the truths of everyday life? It seems unlikely. And thus, unless we uncharitably think Bohr inconsistent on this basic issue, we might well come to question whether there is any necessary connection moving us from accepting the results of science as true to being a realist.[18]

Let me use the term "antirealist" to refer to any of the many different specific enemies of realism: the idealist, the instrumentalist, the phenomenalist, the empiricist (constructive or not), the conventionalist, the constructivist, the pragmatist, and so forth. Then, it seems to me that both the realist and the antirealist must toe what I have been calling "the homely line." That is, they must both accept the certified results of science as on par with more homely and familiarly supported claims. That is not to say that one party (or the other) cannot distinguish more from less well-confirmed claims at home or in science; nor that one cannot single out some particular mode of inference (such as inference to the best explanation) and worry over its reliability, both at home and away. It is just that one must maintain parity. Let us say, then, that both realist and antirealist accept the results of scientific investigations as "true," on par with more homely truths. (I realize that some antirealists would rather use a different word, but no matter.) And call this acceptance of scientific truths the "core position."[19] What distinguishes realists from antirealists, then, is what they add onto this core position.

The antirealist may add onto the core position a particular analysis of the concept of truth, as in the pragmatic and instrumentalist and conventionalist conceptions of truth. Or the antirealist may add on a special analysis of concepts, as in idealism, constructivism, phenomenalism, and in some varieties of empiricism. These addenda will then issue in a special meaning, say, for existence statements. Or the antirealist may add on certain methodological strictures, pointing a wary finger at some particular inferential tool, or constructing his own account for some particular aspects of science (e.g., explanations or laws). Typically, the antirealist will make several such additions to the core.

What then of the realist, what does he add to his core acceptance of the results of science as really true? My colleague, Charles Chastain, suggested what I think is the most graphic way of stating the answer—namely, that what the realist adds on is a desk-thumping, foot-stamping shout of "Really!" So, when the realist and antirealist agree, say, that there really are electrons and that they really carry a unit negative charge and really do have a small mass (of about 9.1×10^{-28} grams), what the realist wants to add is the emphasis that all this is really so. "There really are electrons, really!" This typical realist emphasis serves both a negative and a positive function. Negatively, it is meant to deny the additions that the antirealist would make to that core acceptance which both parties share. The realist wants to deny, for example, the phenomenalistic reduction of concepts or the pragmatic conception of truth. The realist thinks that these addenda take away from the substantiality of the accepted claims to truth or existence. "No," says he, "they *really* exist, and not in just your diminished antirealist sense." Positively, the realist wants to explain the robust sense in which *he* takes these claims to truth or existence; namely, as claims about reality—what is really, really the case. The full-blown version of this involves the conception of truth as correspondence with the world, and the surrogate use of approximate truth as near-correspondence. We have already seen how these ideas of correspondence and approximate truth are supposed to explain what *makes* the truth *true* whereas, in fact, they function as mere trappings, that is, as superficial decorations that may well attract our attention but do not compel rational belief. Like the extra "really," they are an arresting foot thump and, logically speaking, of no more force.

It seems to me that when we contrast the realist and the antirealist in terms of what they each want to add to the core position, a third alternative emerges—and an attractive one at that. It is the core position itself, *and all by itself*. If I am correct in thinking that, at heart, the grip of realism only extends to the homely connection of everyday truths with scientific truths, and that good sense dictates our acceptance of the one on the same basis as our acceptance of the other, then the homely line makes the core position, all by itself, a compelling one, one that we ought to take to heart. Let us try to do so and see whether it constitutes a philosophy, and an attitude toward science, that we can live by.

The core position is neither realist nor antirealist; it mediates between the two. It would be nice to have a name for this position, but it would be a shame to appropriate another "ism" on its behalf, for then it would appear to be just one of the many contenders for ontological allegiance. I think it is not just one of that crowd but rather, as the homely line behind it suggests, it is for commonsense epistemolog—the natural ontological attitude. Thus, let me introduce the acronym NOA (pronounced as in "Noah"), for *natural ontological attiude*, and, henceforth, refer to the core position under that designation.

To begin showing how NOA makes for an adequate philosophical stance toward science, let us see what it has to say about ontology. When NOA counsels us to accept the results of science as true, I take it that we are to treat truth in the usual referential way, so that a sentence (or statement) is true just in case the entities referred to stand in the referred-to relations. Thus, NOA sanctions ordinary referential semantics and commits us, via truth, to the existence of the individuals, properties, relations, processes, and so forth referred to by the scientific statements that we accept as true. Our belief in their existence will be just as strong (or weak) as our belief in the truth of the bit of science involved, and degrees of belief here, presumably, will be tutored by ordinary relations of confirmation and evidential support, subject to the usual scientific canons. In taking this referential stance, NOA is not committed to the progressivism that seems inherent in realism. For the realist, as an article of faith, sees scientific success, over the long run, as bringing us closer to the truth. His whole explanatory enterprise, using approximate truth, forces his hand in this way. But, a "NOAer" (pronounced as "knower") is not so committed. As a scientist, say, within the context of the tradition in which he works, the NOAer, of course, will believe in the existence of those entities to which his theories refer. But should the tradition change, say, in the manner of the conceptual revolutions that Kuhn dubs "paradigm shifts," then nothing in NOA dictates that the change be assimilated as being progressive, that is, as a change where we learn more accurately about *the same things*. NOA is perfectly consistent with the Kuhnian alternative, which counts such changes as wholesale changes of reference. Unlike the realist, adherents to NOA are free to examine the facts in cases of paradigm shift, and to see whether or not a convincing case for stability of reference across paradigms can be made without superimposing on these facts a realist-progressivist superstructure. I have argued elsewhere (Fine 1975) that if one makes oneself free, as NOA enables one to do, then the facts of the matter will not usually settle the case; and that this is a good reason for thinking that cases of so-called incommensurability are, in fact, genuine cases where the question of stability of reference is indeterminate. NOA, I think, is the right philosophical position for such conclusions. It sanctions reference and existence claims, but it does not force the history of science into prefit molds.

So far I have managed to avoid what, for the realist, is the essential point: what of the "external world"? How can I talk of reference and of existence claims unless I am talking about referring to things right out there in the world? And here, of course, the realist, again, wants to stamp his feet.[20] I think the problem that makes the realist want to stamp his feet. shouting "Really!" (and invoking the external world) has to do with the stance the realist tries to take vis-à-vis the game of science. The realist, as it were, tries to stand outside the arena watching the ongoing game and then tries to judge (from this external point of view) what the point is. It is, he says, *about* some area external to the game. The realist, I think, is fooling himself. For he cannot (really!) stand outside the arena, nor can he survey some area off the playing field and mark it out as what the game is about.

Let me try to address these two points. How are we to arrive at the judgment that, in addition to, say, having a rather small mass, electrons are objects "out there in the external world"? Certainly, we can stand off from the electron game and survey its claims, methods, predictive success, and so forth. But what stance could we take that would enable us to judge what the theory of electrons is *about*, other than agreeing that it is about electrons? It is not like matching a blueprint to a house being built, or a map route to a country road. For we are in the world, both physically and conceptually.[21] That is, *we* are among the objects of science, and the concepts and procedures that we use to make judgments of subject matter and correct application are themselves part of that same scientific world. Epistemologically, the situation is very much like the situation with regard to the justification of induction. For the problem of the external world (so-called) is how to satisfy the realist's demand that we justify the existence claims sanctioned by science (and, therefore, by NOA) as claims to the existence of entities "out there." In the case of induction, it is clear that only an inductive justification will do, and it is equally clear that no inductive justification will do at all. So too with the external world, for only ordinary scientific inferences to existence will do, and yet none of them satisfies the demand for showing that the existent is really "out there." I think we ought to follow Hume's prescription on induction with regard to the external world. There is no possibility for justifying the kind of externality that realism requires, yet it may well be that. in fact, we cannot help yearning for just such a comforting grip on reality.

If I am right, then the realist is chasing a phantom, and we cannot actually do more, with regard to existence claims, than follow scientific practice, just as NOA suggests. What then of the other challenges raised by realism? Can we find in NOA the resources for understanding scientific practice? In particular (since it was the topic of the first part of this chapter), does NOA help us to understand the scientific method, say, the problems of the small handful or of conjunctions? The sticking point with the small handful was to account for why the few and narrow alternatives that we can come up with, result in successful novel predictions, and the like. The background was to keep in mind that most such narrow alternatives are not successful. I think that NOA has only this to say. If you believe that guessing based on some truths is more likely to succeed than guessing pure and simple, then if our earlier theories were in large part true and if our refinements of them conserve the true parts, then guessing on this basis has some relative likelihood of success. I think this is a weak account, but then I think the phenomenon here does not allow for anything much stronger since, for the most part, such guesswork fails. In the same way, NOA can help with the problem of conjunctions (and, more generally, with problems of logical combinations). For if two consistent theories in fact have overlapping domains (a fact, as I have just suggested, that is not so often decidable), and if the theories also have true things to say about members in the overlap, then conjoining the theories just adds to the truths of each and, thus, *may*, in conjunction, yield new truths. Where one finds other successful methodological rules, I think we will find NOA's grip on the truth sufficient to account for the utility of the rules.

Unlike the realist, however, I would not tout NOA's success at making science fairly intelligible as an argument in its favor, vis-à-vis realism or various antirealisms. For NOA's accounts are available to the realist and the antirealist, too, provided what they add to NOA does not negate its appeal to the truth, as does a verificationist account of truth or the realist's longing for approximate truth. Moreover, as I made plain enough in the first section of this chapter, I am sensitive to the possibility that explanatory efficacy call be achieved without the explanatory hypothesis being true. NOA may well make science seem fairly intelligible and even rational, but NOA could be quite the wrong view of science for all that. If we posit as a constraint on philosophizing about science that the scientific enterprise should come out in our philosophy as not too unintelligible or irrational, then, perhaps, we can say that NOA passes a minimal standard for a philosophy of science.

Indeed, perhaps the greatest virtue of NOA is to call attention to just how minimal an adequate philosophy of science can be. (In this respect, NOA might be compared to the minimalist movement in art.) For example, NOA helps us to see that realism differs from various antirealisms in this way: realism adds an outer direction to NOA, that is, the external world and the correspondence relation of approximate truth; antirealisms (typically) add an inner direction, that is, human-oriented reductions of truth, or concepts, or explanations (as in my opening citation from Hume). NOA suggests that the legitimate features of these additions are already contained in the presumed equal status of everyday truths with scientific ones, and in our accepting them both as *truths*. No other additions are legitimate, and none are required.

It will be apparent by now that a distinctive feature of NOA, one that separates it from similar views currently in the air, is NOA's stubborn refusal to amplify the concept of truth by providing a theory or analysis (or even a metaphorical picture). Rather, NOA recognizes in "truth" a concept already in use and agrees to abide by the standard rules of usage. These rules involve a Davidsonian-Tarskian referential semantics, and they support a thoroughly classical logic of inference. Thus NOA respects the customary "grammar" of "truth" (and its cognates). Likewise, NOA respects the customary epistemology, which grounds judgments of truth in perceptual judgments and various confirmation relations. As with the use of other concepts. disagreements are bound to arise over what is true (for instance, as to whether inference to the best explanation is always truth-conferring). NOA pretends to no resources for settling these disputes, for NOA takes to heart the great lesson of twentieth-century analytic and continental philosophy, namely, that there *are* no general methodological or philosophical resources for deciding such things. The mistake common to realism and all the antirealisms alike is their commitment to the existence of such nonexistent resources. If pressed to answer the question of what, then, does it *mean* to say that something is true (or to what does the truth of so-and-so commit one), NOA will reply by pointing out the logical relations engendered by the specific claim and by focusing, then, on the concrete historical circumstances that ground that particular judgment of truth. For, after all, there *is* nothing more to say.[22]

Because of its parsimony, I think the minimalist stance represented by NOA marks a revolutionary approach to understanding science. It is, I would suggest, as profound in its own way as was the revolution in our conception of morality, when we came to see that founding morality on God and his order was *also* neither legitimate nor necessary. Just as the typical theological moralist of the eighteenth century would feel bereft to read, say, the pages of *Ethics*, so I think the realist must feel similarly when NOA removes that "correspondence to the external world" for which he so longs. I too have regret for that lost paradise, and too often slip into the realist fantasy. I use my understanding of twentieth-century physics to help me firm up my convictions about NOA, and I recall some words of Mach, which I offer as a comfort and as a closing. With reference to realism, Mach writes,

> It has arisen in the process of immeasurable time without the intenional assistance of man. It is a product of nature, and preserved by nature. Everything that philosophy has accomplished ... is, as compared with it, but an insignificant and ephemeral product of art. The fact is, every thinker, every philosopher, the moment he is forced to abandon his one-sided intellectual occupation ..., immediately returns [to realism].
>
> Nor is it the purpose of these "introductory remarks" to discredit the standpoint [of realism]. The task which we have set ourselves is simply to show why and for what purpose we hold that standpoint during most of our lives, and why and for what purpose we are ... obliged to abandon it.

These lines are taken from Mach's *The Analysis of Sensations* (sec. 14). I recommend that book as effective realism-therapy, a therapy that works best (as Mach suggests) when accompanied by historicophysical investigations (real versions of the breakneck history of my second section). For a better philosophy, however, I recommend NOA.

Notes

My thanks to Charles Chastain, Gerald Dworkin, and Paul Teller for useful preliminary conversations about realism and its rivals, but especially to Charles—for only he, then, (mostly) agreed with me, and surely that deserves special mention. This paper was written by me, but cothought by Micky Forbes. I don't know any longer whose ideas are whose. That means that the responsibility for errors and confusions is at least half Micky's (and she is two-thirds responsible for "NOA"). Finally, I am grateful to the many people who offered comments and criticisms at the conference on realism sponsored by the Department of Philosophy, University of North Carolina at Greensboro in March 1982, where an earlier version of this chapter was first presented under the title "Pluralism and Scientific Progress." I am also grateful to the National Science Foundation for a grant in support of this research.

1. In the final section, I call this postrealism "NOA." Among recent views that relate to NOA, I would include Hilary Putnam's "internal realism," Richard Rorty's "epistemological behaviorism," the "semantic realism" espoused by Paul Horwich, parts of the "Mother Nature" story told by Wiliam Lycan, and the defense of common sense worked out by Joseph Pitt (as a way of reconciling W. Sellars's manifest and scientific images). For references, see Putnam (1981). Rorty (1979), Horwich (1982), Lycan (1985, 1988), and Pitt (1981).

2. Van Fraassen (1980). See especially pp. 97–101 for a discussion of the truth of explanatory theories. To see that the recent discussion of realism is joined right here, one should contrast van Fraassen with Newton-Smith (1981), especially chap. 8.

3. Cartwright (1983) includes some marvelous essays on these issues.

4. Some realists may look for genuine support, and not just solace, in such a coherentist line. They may see in their realism a basis for general epistemology, philosophy of language, and so forth (as does Boyd 1981, 1984). If they find in all this a coherent and comprehensive worldview, then they might want to argue for their philosophy as Wilhelm Wien argued (in 1909) for special relativity, "What speaks for it most of all is the inner consistency which makes it possible to lay a foundation having no self-contradictions, one that applies to the totality of physical appearances." (Quoted by Gerald Holton, "Einstein's Scientific Program: Formative Years," in H. Woolf (1980), p. 58.) Insofar as the realist moves away from the abductive defense of realism to seek support, instead, from the merits of a comprehensive philosophical system with a realist core, he marks as a failure the bulk of recent defenses of realism. Even so, he will not avoid the critique pursued in the text. For although my argument above has been directed, in particular, against the abductive strategy, it is itself based on a more general maxim; namely, that the form of argument used to support realism must be more stringent than the form of argument embedded in the very scientific practice that realism itself is supposed to ground—on pain of begging the question. Just as the abductive strategy fails because it violates this maxim, so too would the coherentist strategy, should the realist turn from one to the other. For, as we see from the words of Wien, the same coherentist line that the realist would appropriate for his own support is part of ordinary scientific practice in framing judgments about competing theories. It is, therefore, not a line of defense available to the realist. Moreover, just as the truth-bearing status of abduction is an issue dividing realists from various nonrealists, so too is the status of coherence-based inference. Turning from abduction to coherence, therefore, still leaves the realist begging the question. Thus, when we bring out into the open the character of arguments *for* realism, we see quite plainly that they do not work. See Fine (1986a) for a more detailed discussion.

   In support of realism there seem to be only those "reasons of the heart" which, as Pascal says, reason does not know. Indeed, I have long felt that belief in realism involves a profound leap of faith, not at all dissimilar from the faith that animates deep religious convictions. I would welcome engagement with realists on this understanding, just as I enjoy conversation on a similar basis with my religious friends. The dialogue will proceed more fruitfully. I think, when the realists finally stop pretending to a rational support for their faith, which they do not have. Then we can all enjoy their intricate and sometimes beautiful philosophical constructions (of, e.g., knowledge, or reference, etc.), even though to us, as nonbelievers, they may seem only wonder-full castles in the air.

5. I hope all readers of this essay will take this idea to heart. For in formulating the question as how to explain why the methods of science lead to instrumental success, the realist has seriously misstated the explanandum. Overwhelmingly, the results of the conscientious pursuit of scientific inquiry are failures: failed theories, failed hypotheses, failed conjectures, inaccurate measurements, incorrect estimations of parameters, fallacious causal inferences, and so forth. If explanations are appropriate here, then what requires explaining is why the very same methods produce an overwhelming background of failures and, occasionally, also a pattern of successes. The realist literature has not yet begun to address this question, much less to offer even a hint of how to answer it.

6. Of course, the realist can appropriate the devices and answers of the instrumentalist, but that would be cheating, and anyway, it would not provide the desired support of realism per se.

7. Paul Teller has made this suggestion to me in conversation.

8. Niiniluoto (1982) contains interesting formal constructions for "degree of truthlikeness," and related versimilia. As conjectured above, they rely on an unspecified correspondence relation to the truth and on measures of the "distance" from the truth. Moreover, they fail to sanction that projection, from some approximate truths to other, novel truths, which lies at the core of realist rationalizations.

9. See Gerald Holton, "Mach, Einstein, and the Search for Reality," in Holton (1973), pp. 219–59. I have tried to work out the precise role of this positivist methodology in chapter 2 of Fine 1986b. See also Fine (1981).

10. Earman and Glymour (1978). The tortuous path detailed by Earman is sketched by B. Hoffmann (1972), pp. 116–28. A nontechnical and illuminating account is given by John Stachel (1979).

11. I have in mind the role played by the analysis of simultaneity in Einstein's path to special relativity. Despite the important study by Arthur Miller (1981) and an imaginative pioneering work by John Earman et al. (1983), I think the role of positivist analysis in the 1905 paper has yet to be properly understood.

12. Roger Jones in "Realism about What?" (forthcoming) explains very nicely some of the difficulties here.

13. I think the ordinary, deflationist attitude of working scientists is much like that of Steven Weinberg (1972).

14. See Wessels (1979), and chapter 5 of Fine 1986b.

15. Letter to Schrödinger, June 19, 1935.

16. See my (1982) for part of the discussion and also Chapter 9 of Fine 1986b.

17. The nonrealism that I attribute to students and practitioners of the quantum theory requires more discussion and distinguishing of cases and kinds than I have room for here. It is certainly not the all-or-nothing affair I make it appear in the text. I carry out some of the required discussion in chapter 9 of Fine 1986b. My thanks to Paul Teller and James Cushing, each of whom saw the need for more discussion.

18. I should be a little more careful about the historical Bohr than I am in the text. For Bohr himself would seem to have wanted to truncate the homely line somewhere between the domain of chairs and tables and atoms, whose existence he plainly accepted, and that of electrons, where he seems to have thought the question of existence (and of realism, more generally) was no longer well defined. An illuminating and provocative discussion of Bohr's attitude toward realism is given by Paul Teller (1981). Thanks, again, to Paul for helping to keep me honest.

19. In this context, for example, van Fraassen's "constructive empiricism" would prefer the concept of empirical adequacy, reserving "truth" for an (unspecified) literal interpretation and believing in that truth only among observables. I might mention here that in this classification Putnam's internal realism comes out as antirealist. For Putnam accepts the core position, but he would add to it a Peircean construal of truth as ideal rational acceptance. This is a mistake, which I expect that Putnam will realize and correct in future writings. He is criticized for it by Horwich (1982) whose own "semantic realism" turns out, in my classification, to be neither realist nor antirealist. Indeed, Horwich's views are quite similar to what is called "NOA" below, and could easily be read as sketching a philosophy of language compatible with NOA. Finally, the "epistemological behaviorism" espoused by Rorty (1979) is a form of antirealism that seems to me very similar to Putnam's position, but achieving the core parity between science and common sense by means of an acceptance that is neither ideal nor especially rational, at least in the normative sense. (I beg the reader's indulgence over this summary treatment of complex and important positions. I have been responding to Nancy Cartwright's request to differentiate these recent views from NOA.) See chapter 8 of Fine 1986b for a discussion of these antirealisms.

20. In his remarks at the Greensboro conference, my commentator, John King, suggested a compelling reason to prefer NOA over realism: namely, because NOA is less percussive! My thanks to John for this nifty idea, as well as for other comments.

21. "There is, I think, no theory-independent way to reconstruct phrases like 'really there'; the notion of a match between the ontology of a theory and its 'real' counterpart in nature now seems to me illusive in principle." T. S. Kuhn (1970), p. 206. The same passage is cited for rebuttal by Newton-Smith (1981). But the "rebuttal" sketched there in chapter 8, sections 4 and 5, not only runs afoul of the objections stated here in my first section, it also fails to provide for the required theory-independence. For Newton-Smith's explication of verisimilitude (p. 204) makes explicit reference to some unspecified background theory. (He offers either current science or the Peircean limit as candidates). But this is not to rebut Kuhn's challenge (and mine); it is to concede its force.

22. No doubt I am optimistic, for one can always think of more to say. In particular, one could try to fashion a general, descriptive framework for codifying and classifying such answers. Perhaps there would be something to be learned from such a descriptive, semantical framework. But what I am afraid of is that this enterprise, once launched, would lead to a proliferation of frameworks not so carefully descriptive. These would take on a life of their own, each pretending to ways (better than its rivals) to settle disputes over truth claims, or their import. What we need, however, is less bad philosophy, not more. So here, I believe, silence is indeed golden.

References

Boyd, R. 1981. Scientific realism and naturalistic epistemology. In *PSA: 1980*, vol. 2, edited by P. Asquith and R. Giere, 613–62. East Lansing, Mich: Philosophy of Science Association.

Boyd, R. 1984. The current status of scientific realism. [Reprinted in this volume.]

Cartwright, N. 1983. *How the laws of physics lie.* New York: Clarendon Press.

Earman, J., and C. Glymour. 1978. Lost in the tensors. *Studies in History and Philosophy of Science* 9: 251–78.

Earman, J., et al. 1983. On writing the history of special relativity. In *PSA: 1982*, vol.2, edited by P. Asquith and T. Nichols, 403–16. East Lansing, Mich.: Philosophy of Science Association.

Einstein, A., et al. 1952. *The principle of relativity.* Translated by W. Perrett and G.B. Jeffrey. New York: Dover.

Fine, A. 1975. How to compare theories: Reference and change. Nous 9: 17–32.

Fine, A. 1981. Conceptual change in mathematics and science: Lakatos' stretching refined. In *PSA: 1978*, vol. 2, edited by P. Asquith and I. Hacking, 328–41. East Lansing, Mich.: Philosophy of Science Association.

Fine, A. 1982. Antinomies of entanglement: The puzzling case of the tangled statistics. *Journal of philosophy* 79: 733–47

Fine, A. 1986a. Unnatural attitudes: Realist and instrumentalist attachments to science. *Mind* 95: 149–79.

Fine, A. 1986b. *The shaky game.* Chicago: University of Chicago Press.

Heisenberg, W. 1925. Uber den anschaulichen Inhalt der quantentheoretischen Kinematik und Mechanik. *Zeitschrift für Physik* 33: 879–93.

Hoffman, B. 1972. *Albert Einstein, creator and rebel.* New York: Viking Press.

Holton, G. 1973. *Thematic origins of scientific thought.* Cambridge: Harvard University Press.

Horwich, P. 1982.Three forms of realism. *Synthese* 51: 181–201.

Kuhn, T.S. 1970. *The structure of scientific revolutions.* 2d ed. Chicago: University of Chicago Press.

Lande, A. 1974. Albert Einstein and the quantum riddle. *American journal of Physics* 42: 459–64.

Laudan, L. 1984. A confutation of convergent realism. [Reprinted in this volume.]

Lycan, W. 1985. Epistemic value. *Synthese* 64: 137–64.

Lycan, W. 1988. *Judgment and justification.* New York: Cambridge University Press.

Miller, A. 1981. *Albert Einstein's special theory of relativity.* Reading, Mass.: Addison-Wesley.

Newton-Smith, W.H. 1981. *The rationality of science.* London: Routledge and Kegan Paul.

Niiniluoto, I. 1982. What shall we do with verisimilitude? *Philosophy of Science* 49: 181–97.

Pitt, J. 1981. *Pictures, images and conceptual change.* Dordrecht: Reidel.

Popper, K. 1972. *Conjectures and refutations.* London: Routledge and Kegan Paul.

Putnam, H. 1975. The meaning of "Meaning." In *Language, mind and knowledge*, edited by K. Gunderson, 131–93. Minneapolis: University of Minnesota Press.

Putnam, H. 1981. *Reason truth and history.* Cambridge: Cambridge University Press.

Rorty, R. 1979. *Philosophy and the mirror of nature.* Princeton: Princeton University Press.

Stachel, J. 1979. The genesis of general relativity. In *Einstein symposium Berlin*, edited by H. Nelkowski, 428–42. Berlin: Springer-Verlag.

Teller, P. 1981. The projection postulate and Bohr's interpretation of quantum mechanics. In *PSA: 1980*, vol. 2, edited by P. Asquith and R. Giere, 201–23. East Lansing, Mich.: Philosophy of Science Association.

van Fraassen, B. 1980. *The scientific image.* Oxford: Clarendon Press.

van Fraassen, B. 1982. The Charbydis of realism: Epistemological implications of Bell's inequality. *Synthese* 52: 25–38.

Weinberg, S. 1972. *Gravitation and cosmology: Principles and applications of the general theory of relativity.* New York: Wiley.

Wessels, L. 1979. Schrödinger's route to wave mechanics. *Studies in History and Philosophy of Science* 10: 311–40.

Woolf, H., ed. 1980. *Some strangeness in the proportion.* Reading, Mass.: Addison-Wesley.

Chapter 15

Feminism and Science

Evelyn Fox Keller

In recent years, a new critique of science has begun to emerge from a number of feminist writings. The lens of feminist politics brings into focus certain masculinist distortions of the scientific enterprise, creating, for those of us who are scientists, a potential dilemma. Is there a conflict between our commitment to feminism and our commitment to science? As both a feminist and a scientist, I am more familiar than I might wish with the nervousness and defensiveness that such a potential conflict evokes. As scientists, we have very real difficulties in thinking about the kinds of issues that, as feminists, we have been raising. These difficulties may, however, ultimately be productive. My purpose in the present essay is to explore the implications of recent feminist criticism of science for the relationship between science and feminism. Do these criticisms imply conflict? If they do, how necessary is that conflict? I will argue that those elements of feminist criticism that seem to conflict most with at least conventional conceptions of science may, in fact, carry a liberating potential for science. It could therefore benefit scientists to attend closely to feminist criticism. I will suggest that we might even use feminist thought to illuminate and clarify part of the substructure of science (which may have been historically conditioned into distortion) in order to preserve the things that science has taught us, in order to be more objective. But first it is necessary to review the various criticisms that feminists have articulated.

The range of their critique is broad. Though they all claim that science embodies a strong androcentric bias, the meanings attached to this charge vary widely. It is convenient to represent the differences in meaning by a spectrum that parallels the political range characteristic of feminism as a whole. I label this spectrum from right to left, beginning somewhere left of center with what might be called the liberal position. From the liberal critique, charges of androcentricity emerge that are relatively easy to correct. The more radical critique calls for correspondingly more radical changes; it requires a reexamination of the underlying assumptions of scientific theory and method for the presence of male bias. The difference between these positions is, however, often obscured by a knee-jerk reaction that leads many scientists to regard all such criticism as a unit—as a challenge to the neutrality of science. One of the points I wish to emphasize here is that the range of meanings attributed to the claim of androcentric bias reflects very different levels of challenge, some of which even the most conservative scientists ought to be able to accept.

First, in what I have called the liberal critique, is the charge that is essentially one of unfair employment practices. It proceeds from the observation that almost all scientists are men. This criticism is liberal in the sense that it in no way conflicts either with

Reprinted from *Sex & Scientific Inquiry*, ed. S. Harding and J. O'Barr (Chicago: University of Chicago Press, 1987), pp. 233–246, by permission of the author and the publisher. Copyright 1987 by University of Chicago Press.

traditional conceptions of science or with current liberal, egalitarian politics. It is, in fact, a purely political criticism, and one which can be supported by all of us who are in favor of equal opportunity. According to this point of view, science itself would in no way be affected by the presence or absence of women.

A slightly more radical criticism continues from this and argues that the predominance of men in the sciences has led to a bias in the choice and definition of problems with which scientists have concerned themselves. This argument is most frequently and most easily made in regard to the health sciences. It is claimed, for example, that contraception has not been given the scientific attention its human importance warrants and that, furthermore, the attention it has been given has been focused primarily on contraceptive techniques to be used by women. In a related complaint, feminists argue that menstrual cramps, a serious problem for many women, have never been taken seriously by the medical profession. Presumably, had the concerns of medical research been articulated by women, these particular imbalances would not have arisen.[1] Similar biases in sciences remote from the subject of women's bodies are more difficult to locate—they may, however, exist. Even so, this kind of criticism does not touch our conception of what science is, nor our confidence in the neutrality of science. It may be true that in some areas we have ignored certain problems, but our definition of science does not include the choice of problem—that, we can readily agree, has always been influenced by social forces. We remain, therefore, in the liberal domain.

Continuing to the left, we next find claims of bias in the actual design and interpretation of experiments. For example, it is pointed out that virtually all of the animal-learning research on rats has been performed with male rats.[2] Though a simple explanation is offered—namely, that female rats have a four-day cycle that complicates experiments—the criticism is hardly vitiated by the explanation. The implicit assumption is, of course, that the male rat represents the species. There exist many other, often similar, examples in psychology. Examples from the biological sciences are somewhat more difficult to find, though one suspects that they exist. An area in which this suspicion is particularly strong is that of sex research. Here the influence of heavily invested preconceptions seems all but inevitable. In fact, although the existence of such preconceptions has been well documented historically,[3] a convincing case for the existence of a corresponding bias in either the design or interpretation of experiments has yet to be made. That this is so can, I think, be taken as testimony to the effectiveness of the standards of objectivity operating.

But evidence for bias in the interpretation of observations and experiments is very easy to find in the more socially oriented sciences. The area of primatology is a familiar target. Over the past fifteen years women working in the field have undertaken an extensive reexamination of theoretical concepts, often using essentially the same methodological tools. These efforts have resulted in some radically different formulations. The range of difference frequently reflects the powerful influence of ordinary language in biasing our theoretical formulations. A great deal of very interesting work analyzing such distortions has been done.[4] Though I cannot begin to do justice to that work here, let me offer, as a single example, the following description of a single-male troop of animals that Jane Lancaster provides as a substitute for the familiar concept of "harem": "For a female, males are a resource in her environment which she may use to further the survival of herself and her offspring. If environmental conditions are such that the male role can be minimal, a one-male group is likely. Only one male is necessary for a group of females if his only role is to impregnate them."[5]

These critiques, which maintain that a substantive effect on scientific theory results from the predominance of men in the field, are almost exclusively aimed at the "softer," even the "softest," sciences. Thus they can still be accommodated within the traditional framework by the simple argument that the critiques, if justified, merely reflect the fact that these subjects are not sufficiently scientific. Presumably, fair-minded (or scientifically minded) scientists can and should join forces with the feminists in attempting to identify the presence of bias—equally offensive, if for different reasons, to both scientists and feminists—in order to make these "soft" sciences more rigorous.

It is much more difficult to deal with the truly radical critique that attempts to locate androcentric bias even in the "hard" sciences, indeed in scientific ideology itself. This range of criticism takes us out of the liberal domain and requires us to question the very assumptions of objectivity and rationality that underlie the scientific enterprise. To challenge the truth and necessity of the conclusions of natural science on the grounds that they too reflect the judgment of men is to take the Galilean credo and turn it on its head. It is not true that "the conclusions of natural science are true and necessary, and the judgement of man has nothing to do with them";[6] it is the judgment of woman that they have nothing to do with.

The impetus behind this radical move is twofold. First, it is supported by the experience of feminist scholars in other fields of inquiry. Over and over, feminists have found it necessary, in seeking to reinstate women as agents and as subjects, to question the very canons of their fields. They have turned their attention, accordingly, to the operation of patriarchal bias on ever deeper levels of social structure, even of language and thought.

But the possibility of extending the feminist critique into the foundations of scientific thought is created by recent developments in the history and philosophy of science itself.[7] As long as the course of scientific thought was judged to be exclusively determined by its own logical and empirical necessities. there could be no place for any signature, male or otherwise, in that system of knowledge. Furthermore, any suggestion of gender differences in our thinking about the world could argue only too readily for the further exclusion of women from science. But as the philosophical and historical inadequacies of the classical conception of science have become more evident, and as historians and sociologists have begun to identify the ways in which the development of scientific knowledge has been shaped by its particular social and political context, our understanding of science as a social process has grown. This understanding is a necessary prerequisite, both politically and intellectually, for a feminist theoretic in science.

Joining feminist thought to other social studies of science brings the promise of radically new insights, but it also adds to the existing intellectual danger a political threat. The intellectual danger resides in viewing science as pure social product; science then dissolves into ideology and objectivity loses all intrinsic meaning. In the resulting cultural relativism, any emancipatory function of modern science is negated, and the arbitration of truth recedes into the political domain.[8] Against this background, the temptation arises for feminists to abandon their claim for representation in scientific culture and, in its place, to invite a return to a purely "female" subjectivity, leaving rationality and objectivity in the male domain, dismissed as products of a purely male consciousness.[9]

Many authors have addressed the problems raised by total relativism;[10] here I wish merely to mention some of the special problems added by its feminist variant. They are several. In important respects, feminist relativism is just the kind of radical move that transforms the political spectrum into a circle. By rejecting objectivity as a masculine ideal, it simultaneously lends its voice to an enemy chorus and dooms women to residing outside of the realpolitik modern culture; it exacerbates the very problem it wishes to solve. It also nullifies the radical potential of feminist criticism for our understanding of science. As I see it, the task of a feminist theoretic in science is twofold: to distinguish that which is parochial from that which is universal in the scientific impulse, reclaiming for women what has historically been denied to them; and to legitimate those elements of scientific culture that have been denied precisely because they are defined as female.

It is important to recognize that the framework inviting what might be called the nihilist retreat is in fact provided by the very ideology of objectivity we wish to escape. This is the ideology that asserts an opposition between (male) objectivity and (female) subjectivity and denies the possibility of mediation between the two. A first step, therefore, in extending the feminist critique to the foundations of scientific thought is to reconceptualize objectivity as a dialectical process so as to allow for the possibility of distinguishing the objective effort from the objectivist illusion. As Piaget reminds us:

> Objectivity consists in so fully realizing the countless intrusions of the self in everyday thought and the countless illusions which result—illusions of sense, language, point of view, value, etc.—that the preliminary step to every judgement is the effort to exclude the intrusive self. Realism, on the contrary, consists in ignoring the existence of self and thence regarding one's own perspective as immediately objective and absolute. Realism is thus anthropocentric illusion, finality—in short, all those illusions which teem in the history of science. So long as thought has not become conscious of self, it is a prey to perpetual confusions between objective and subjective, between the real and the ostensible.[11]

In short, rather than abandon the quintessentially human effort to understand the world in rational terms, we need to refine that effort. To do this, we need to add to the familiar methods of rational and empirical inquiry the additional process of critical self-reflection. Following Piaget's injunction, we need to "become conscious of self." In this way, we can become conscious of the features of the scientific project that belie its claim to universality.

The ideological ingredients of particular concern to feminists are found where objectivity is linked with autonomy and masculinity, and in turn, the goals of science with power and domination. The linking of objectivity with social and political autonomy has been examined by many authors and shown to serve a variety of important political functions.[12] The implications of joining obectivity with masculinity are less well understood. This conjunction also serves critical political functions. But an understanding of the sociopolitical meaning of the entire constellation requires an examination of the psychological processes through which these connections become internalized and perpetuated. Here psychoanalysis offers us an invaluable perspective, and it is to the exploitation of that perspective that much of my own work has been directed. In an earlier paper, I tried to show how psychoanalytic theories of development illuminate the structure and meaning of an interacting system of associations linking objectivity (a cognitive trait) with autonomy (an affective trait) and masculinity (a gender trait).[13] Here, after a brief summary of my earlier argument, I want to explore the relation of this system to power and domination.

Along with Nancy Chodorow and Dorothy Dinnerstein, I have found that branch of psychoanalytic theory known as object relations theory to be especially useful.[14] In seeking to account for personality development in terms of both innate drives and actual relations with other objects (i.e., subjects), it permits us to understand the ways in which our earliest experiences—experiences in large part determined by the socially structured relationships that form the context of our developmental processes—help to shape our conception of the world and our characteristic orientations to it. In particular, our first steps in the world are guided primarily by the parents of one sex—our mothers; this determines a maturational framework for our emotional, cognitive, and gender development, a framework later filled in by cultural expectations.

In brief, I argued the following: Our early maternal environment, coupled with the cultural definition of masculine (that which can never appear feminine) and of autonomy (that which can never be compromised by dependency) leads to the association of female with the pleasures and dangers of merging, and of male with the comfort and loneliness of separateness. The boy's internal anxiety about both self and gender is echoed by the more widespread cultural anxiety, thereby encouraging postures of autonomy and masculinity, which can, indeed may, be designed to defend against that anxiety and the longing that generates it. Finally, for all of us, our sense of reality is carved out of the same developmental matrix. As Piaget and others have emphasized, the capacity for cognitive distinctions between self and other (objectivity) evolves concurrently and interdependently with the development of psychic autonomy; our cognitive ideals thereby become subject to the same psychological influences as our emotional and gender ideals. Along with autonomy the very act of separating subject from object—objectivity itself—comes to be associated with masculinity. The combined psychological and cultural pressures lead all three ideals—affective, gender, and cognitive—to a mutually reinforcing process of exaggeration and rigidification.[15] The net result is the entrenchment of an objectivist ideology and a correlative devaluation of (female) subjectivity.

This analysis leaves out many things. Above all it omits discussion of the psychological meanings of power and domination, and it is to those meanings I now wish to turn. Central to object relations theory is the recognition that the condition of psychic autonomy is double edged: it offers a profound source of pleasure, and simultaneously of potential dread. The values of autonomy are consonant with the values of competence, of mastery. Indeed competence is itself a prior condition for autonomy and serves immeasurably to confirm one's sense of self. But need the development of competence and the sense of mastery lead to a state of alienated selfhood, of denied connectedness, of defensive separateness? To forms of autonomy that can be understood as protections against dread? Object relations theory makes us sensitive to autonomy's range of meanings; it simultaneously suggests the need to consider the corresponding meanings of competence. Under what circumstances does competence imply mastery of one's own fate and under what circumstances does it imply mastery over another's? In short, are control and domination essential ingredients of competence, and intrinsic to selfhood, or are they correlates of an alienated selfhood?

One way to answer these questions is to use the logic of the analysis summarized above to examine the shift from competence to power and control in the psychic economy of the young child. From that analysis, the impulse toward domination can be understood as a natural concomitant of defensive separateness—as Jessica Benjamin has written. "A way of repudiating sameness, dependency and closeness with another person, while attempting to avoid the consequent feelings of aloneness."[16] Perhaps no one has written more sensitively than psychoanalyst D. W. Winnicott of the rough waters the child must travel in negotiating the transition from symbiotic union to the recognition of self and other as autonomous entities. He alerts us to a danger that others have missed—a danger arising from the unconscious fantasy that the subject has actually destroyed the object in the process of becoming separate.

Indeed, he writes, "It is the destruction of the object that places the object outside the area of control.... After 'subject relates to object' comes 'subject destroys object' (as it becomes external); then may come *'object survives* destruction by the subject.' But there may or may not be survival." When there is, "because of the survival of the object, the subject may now have started to live a life in the world of objects, and so the subject stands to gain immeasurably; but the price has to be paid in acceptance of the ongoing destruction in unconscious fantasy relative to object-relating."[17] Winnicott, of course, is not speaking of actual survival but of subjective confidence in the survival of the other. Survival in that sense requires that the child maintain relatedness; failure induces inevitable guilt and dread. The child is poised on a terrifying precipice. On one side lies the fear of having destroyed the object, on the other side, loss of self. The child may make an attempt to secure this precarious position by seeking to master the other. The cycles of destruction and survival are reenacted while the other is kept safely at bay, and as Benjamin writes, "the original self assertion is ... converted from innocent mastery to mastery over and against the other."[18] In psychodynamic terms, this particular resolution of preoedipal conflicts is a product of oedipal consolidation. The (male) child achieves his final security by identification with the father—an identification involving simultaneously a denial of the mother and a transformation of guilt and fear into aggression.

Aggression, of course, has many meanings, many sources, and many forms of expression. Here I mean to refer only to the form underlying the impulse toward domination. I invoke psychoanalytic theory to help illuminate the forms of expression that impulse finds in science as a whole, and its relation to objectification in particular. The same questions I asked about the child I can also ask about science. Under what circumstances is scientific knowledge sought for the pleasures of knowing, for the increased competence it grants us, for the increased mastery (real or imagined) over our own fate, and under what circumstances is it fair to say that science seeks actually to dominate nature? Is there a meaningful distinction to be made here?

In his work *The Domination of Nature* William Leiss observes, "The necessary correlate of domination is the consciousness of subordination in those who must obey the will of another; thus properly speaking only other men can be the objects of domination."[19] (Or women, we might add.) Leiss infers from this observation that it is not the domination of physical nature we should worry about but the use of our knowledge of physical nature as an instrument for the domination of human nature. He therefore sees the need for correctives, not in science but in its uses. This is his point of departure from other authors of the Frankfurt school, who assume the very logic of science to be the logic of domination. I agree with Leiss's basic observation but draw a somewhat different inference. I suggest that the impulse toward domination does find expression in the goals (and even in the theories and practice) of modern science, and argue that where it finds such expression the impulse needs to be acknowledged as projection. In short, I argue that not only in the denial of interaction between subject and other but also in the access of domination to the goals of scientific knowledge, one finds the intrusion of a self we begin to recognize as partaking in the cultural construct of masculinity.

The value of consciousness is that it enables us to make choices—both as individuals and as scientists. Control and domination are in fact intrinsic neither to selfhood (i.e., autonomy) nor to scientific knowledge. I want to suggest, rather, that the particular emphasis Western science has placed on these functions of knowledge is twin to the objectivist ideal. Knowledge in general, and scientific knowledge in particular, serves two gods: power and transcendence. It aspires alternately to mastery over and union with nature.[20] Sexuality serves the same two gods, aspiring to domination and ecstatic communion—in short, aggression and eros. And it is hardly a new insight to say that power, control, and domination are fueled largely by aggression, while union satisfies a more purely erotic impulse.

To see the emphasis on power and control so prevalent in the rhetoric of Western science as projection of a specifically male consciousness requires no great leap of the imagination. Indeed, that perception has become a commonplace. Above all, it is invited by the rhetoric that conjoins the domination of nature with the insistent image of nature as female, nowhere more familiar than in the writings of Francis Bacon. For Bacon, knowledge and power are one, and the promise of science is expressed as "leading to you Nature with all her children to bind her to your service and make her your slave,"[21] by means that do not "merely exert a gentle guidance over nature's course; they have the power to conquer and subdue her, to shake her to her foundations."[22] In the context of the Baconian vision, Bruno Bettelheim's conclusion appears inescapable: "Only with phallic psychology did aggressive manipulation of nature become possible."[23]

The view of science as an oedipal project is also familiar from the writings of Herbert Marcuse and Norman O. Brown.[24] But Brown's preoccupation, as well as Marcuse's, is with what Brown calls a "morbid" science. Accordingly, for both authors the quest for a nonmorbid science, an "erotic" science, remains a romantic one. This is so because their picture of science is incomplete: it omits from consideration the crucial, albeit less visible, erotic components already present in the scientific tradition. Our own quest, if it is to be realistic rather than romantic, must be based on a richer understanding of the scientific tradition, in all its dimensions, and on an understanding of the ways in which this complex, dialectical tradition becomes transformed into a monolithic rhetoric. Neither the oedipal child nor modern science has in fact managed to rid itself of its preoedipal and fundamentally bisexual yearnings. It is with this recognition that the quest for a different science, a science undistorted by masculinist bias, must begin.

The presence of contrasting themes, of a dialectic between aggressive and erotic impulses, can be seen both within the work of individual scientists and, even more dramatically, in the juxtaposed writings of different scientists. Francis Bacon provides us with one model;[25] there are many others. For an especially striking contrast, consider a contemporary scientist who insists on the importance of "letting the material speak to you," of allowing it to "tell you what to do next"—one who chastises other scientists for attempting to "impose an answer" on what they see. For this scientist, discovery is facilitated by becoming "part of the system," rather than remaining outside; one must have a "feeling for the organism."[26] It is true that the author of these remarks is not only from a different epoch and a different field (Bacon himself was not actually a scientist by most standards), she is also a woman. It is also true that there are many reasons, some of which I have already suggested, for thinking that gender (itself constructed in an ideological context) actually does make a difference in scientific inquiry. Nevertheless, my point here is that neither science nor individuals are totally bound by ideology. In fact, it is not difficult to find similar sentiments expressed by male scientists. Consider, for example, the following remarks: "I have often had cause to feel that my hands are cleverer than my head. That is a crude way of characterizing the dialectics of experimentation. When it is going well, it is like a quiet conversation with Nature."[27] The difference beween conceptions of science as "dominating" and as "conversing with" nature may not be a difference primarily between epochs, nor between the sexes. Rather, it can be seen as representing a dual theme played out in the work of all scientists, in all ages. But the two poles of this dialectic do not appear with equal weight in the history of science. What we therefore need to attend to is the evolutionary process that selects one theme as dominant.

Elsewhere I have argued for the importance of a different selection process.[28] In part, scientists are themselves selected by the emotional appeal of particular (stereotypic) images of science. Here I am arguing for the importance of selection within scientific thought—first of preferred methodologies and aims, and finally of preferred theories. The two processes are not unrelated. While stereotypes are not binding (i.e., they do not describe all or perhaps any individuals), and this fact creates the possibility for an ongoing contest within science, the first selection process undoubtedly influences the outcome of the second. That is, individuals drawn by a particular ideology will tend to select themes consistent with that ideology.

One example in which this process is played out on a theoretical level is in the fate of interactionist theories in the history of biology. Consider the contest that has raged throughout this century between organismic and particulate views of cellular organization—between what might be described as hierarchical and nonhierarchical theories. Whether the debate is over the primacy of the nucleus or the cell as a whole, the genome or the cytoplasm, the proponents of hierarchy have won out. One geneticist has described the conflict in explicitly political terms:

> Two concepts of genetic mechanisms have persisted side by side throughout the growth of modern genetics, but the emphasis has been very strongly in favor of one of these.... The first of these we will designate as the "Master Molecule" concept.... This is in essence the Theory of the Gene, interpreted to suggest a totalitarian government.... The second concept we will designate as the "Steady State" concept. By this term ... we envision a dynamic self-perpetuating organization of a variety of molecular species which owes its specific properties not to the characteristic of any one kind of molecule, but to the functional interrelationships of these molecular species.[29]

Soon after these remarks, the debate between "master molecules" and dynamic interactionism was foreclosed by the synthesis provided by DNA and the "central dogma." With the success of the new molecular biology such "steady state" (or egalitarian) theories lost interest for almost all geneticists. But today, the same conflict shows signs of reemerging—in genetics, in theories of the immune system, and in theories of development.

I suggest that method and theory may constitute a natural continuum, despite Popperian claims to the contrary, and that the same processes of selection may bear equally and simultaneously on both the means and aims of science and the actual theoretical descriptions that emerge. I suggest this in part because of the recurrent and striking consonance that can be seen in the way scientists work, the relation they take to their object of study, and the theoretical orientation they favor. To pursue the example cited earlier, the same scientist who allowed herself to become "part of the system," whose investigations were guided by a "feeling for the organism," developed a paradigm that diverged as radically from the dominant paradigm of her field as did her methodological style.

In lieu of the linear hierarchy described by the central dogma of molecular biology, in which the DNA encodes and transmits all instructions for the unfolding of a living cell, her research yielded a view of the DNA in delicate interaction with the cellular environment—an organismic view. For more important than the genome as such (i.e., the DNA) is the "overall organism." As she sees it, the genome functions "only in respect to the environment in which it is found."[30] In this work the program encoded by the DNA is itself subject to change. No longer is a master control to be found in a single component of the cell; rather, control resides in the complex interactions of the entire system. When first presented, the work underlying this vision was not understood, and it was poorly received.[31] Today much of that work is undergoing a renaissance, although it is important to say that her full vision remains too radical for most biologists to accept.[32]

This example suggests that we need not rely on our imagination for a vision of what a different science—a science less restrained by the impulse to dominate—might be like. Rather, we need only look to the thematic pluralism in the history of our own science as it has evolved. Many other examples can be found, but we lack an adequate understanding of the full range of influences that lead to the acceptance or rejection not only of particular theories but of different theoretical orientations. What I am suggesting is that if certain theoretical interpretations have been selected against, it is precisely in this process of selection that ideology in general, and a masculinist ideology in particular, can be found to effect its influence. The task this implies for a radical feminist critique of science is, then, first a historical one, but finally a transformative one. In the historical effort, feminists can bring a whole new range of sensitivities, leading to an equally new consciousness of the potentialities lying latent in the scientific project.

Notes

1. Notice that the claim is not mere presence of women in medical research is sufficient to right such imbalances, for it is understood how readily women, or any "outsiders" for that matter, come to internalize the concerns and values of a world to which they aspire to belong.
2. I would like to thank Lila Braine for calling this point to my attention.
3. D. L. Hall and Diana Long, "The Social Implications of the Scientific Study of Sex," *Scholar and the Feminist* 4 (1977): 11–21.
4. See, e.g., Donna Haraway, "Animal Sociology and a Natural Economy of the Body Politic, Part I: A Political Physiology of Dominance"; and "Animal Sociology and a Natural Economy of the Body Politic, Part II: The Past Is the Contested Zone: Human Nature and Theories of Production and Reproduction in Primate Behavior Studies," *Signs: Journal of Women in Culture and Society* 4, no. 1 (Autumn 1978): 21–60.
5. Jane Lancaster, *Primate Behavior and the Emergence of Human Culture* (New York: Holt, Rinehart & Winston, 1975), p. 34.
6. Galileo Galilei, *Dialogue on the Great World Systems*, trans. T. Salusbury, ed. G. de Santillana (Chicago: University of Chicago Press, 1953), p. 63.
7. The work of Russell Hanson and Thomas S. Kuhn was of pivotal importance in opening up our understanding of scientific thought to a consideration of social, psychological, and political influences.
8. See, e.g., Paul Feyerabend, *Against Method* (London: New Left Books, 1975); and *Science in a Free Society* (London: New Left Books, 1978).
9. This notion is expressed most strongly by some of the French feminists (see Elaine Marks and Isabelle de Courtivron, eds., *New French Feminisms: An Anthology* [Amherst: University of Massachusetts Press, 1980]), and is currently surfacing in the writings of some American feminists. See, e.g., Susan Griffin, *Woman and Nature: The Roaring Inside Her* (New York: Harper & Row, 1978).
10. See, e.g., Steven Rose and Hilary Rose, "Radical Science and Its Enemies," *Socialist Register 1979*, ed. Ralph Miliband and John Saville (Atlantic Highlands, H.J.: Humanities Press, 1979), pp. 317–35. A number of the points made here have also been made by Elizabeth Fee in "Is Feminism a Threat to Objectivity?" (paper presented at the American Association for the Advancement of Science meeting. Toronto, January 4, 1981).
11. Jean Piaget, *The Child's Conception of the World* (Totowa, N.J.: Littlefield, Adams & Co., 1972).

12. Jerome R. Ravetz, *Scientific Knowledge and Its Social Problems* (London: Oxford University Press, 1971); and Hilary Rose and Steven Rose, *Science and Society* (London: Allen Lane, 1969).

13. Evelyn Fox Keller, "Gender and Science," *Psychoanalysis and Contemporary Thought* 1 (1978): 409–33.

14. Nancy Chodorow, *The Reproduction of Mothering: Psychoanalysis and the Sociology of Gender* (Berkeley: University of California Press, 1978); and Dorothy Dinnerstein, *The Mermaid and the Minotaur: Sexual Arrangements and Human Malaise* (New York: Harper & Row, 1976).

15. For a fuller development of this argument, see n. 12 above. By focusing on the contributions of individual psychology, I in no way mean to imply a simple division of individual and social factors, or to set them up as alternative influences. Individual psychological traits evolve in a social system and, in turn, social systems reward and select for particular sets of individual traits. Thus if particular options in science reflect certain kinds of psychological impulses or personality traits, it must be understood that it is in a distinct social framework that those options, rather than others, are selected.

16. Jessica Benjamin has discussed this same issue in an excellent analysis of the place of domination in sexuality. See "The Bonds of Love: Rational Violence and Erotic Domination." *Feminist Studies* 6, no. 1 (Spring 1980): 144–74, esp. 150.

17. D. W. Winnicott, *Playing and Reality* (New York: Basic Books, 1971), pp. 89–90.

18. Benjamin, p. 165.

19. William Leiss, *The Domination of Nature* (Boston: Beacon Press, 1974), p. 122.

20. For a discussion of the different roles these two impulses play in Platonic and in Baconian images of knowledge, see Evelyn Fox Keller, "Nature as 'Her'" (paper delivered at the Second Sex Conference, New York Institute for the Humanities, September 1979).

21. B. Farrington, "*Temporis Partus Masculus*: An Untranslated Writing of Francis Bacon." *Centaurus* 1 (1951): 193–205, esp. 197.

22. Francis Bacon, "Description of the Intellectual Globe," in *The Philosophical Works of Francis Bacon*, ed. J. H. Robertson (London: Routledge & Sons, 1905), p. 506.

23. Quoted in Norman O. Brown, *Life against Death* (New York: Random House, 1959), p. 280.

24. Brown; and Herbert Marcuse, *One Dimensional Man* (Boston: Beacon Press, 1964).

25. For a discussion of the presence of the same dialectic in the writings of Francis Bacon, see Evelyn Fox Keller, "Baconian Science: A Hermaphrodite Birth," *Philosophical Forum* 11, no. 3 (Spring 1980): 299–308.

26. Barbara McClintock, private interviews, December 1, 1978, and January 13, 1979.

27. G. Wald, "The Molecular Basis of Visual Excitation," *Les Prix Nobel en 1967* (Stockholm: Kungliga Boktryckerlet, 1968), p. 260.

28. Keller, "Gender and Science."

29. D. L. Nanney, "The Role of the Cyctoplasm in Heredity," in *The Chemical Basis of Heredity*, ed. William D. McElroy and Bentley Glass (Baltimore: Johns Hopkins University Press, 1957), p. 136.

30. McClintock, December 1, 1978.

31. McClintock, "Chromosome Organization and Genic Expression," *Cold Spring Harbor Symposium of Quantitative Biology* 16 (1951): 13–44.

32. McClintock's most recent publication on this subject is "Modified Gene Expressions Induced by Transposable Elements," in *Mobilization and Reassembly of Genetic Information*, ed. W. A. Scott, R. Werner, and J. Schultz (New York: Academic Press, 1980).

Section II

Causation and Explanation

Philip Gasper

Explanation is an important goal of scientific inquiry. We seek explanations not only of particular events but also of recurring types of phenomena, and we look to science to provide them for us. Moreover, after we have developed scientific theories that yield such explanations, we even look for explanations of why our theories are themselves true (or why they are empirically adequate)—explanations couched in terms of more fundamental or encompassing theories. Thus valency theory explains why chemical substances combine in various proportions, while valency theory itself can be explained in terms of the more fundamental theories of atomic physics.

The search for explanation is clearly an important motivation for engaging in scientific research. But it seems to be more than just this. Scientists often claim that judgments of explanatory power play an important (sometimes crucial) role in assessing the acceptability of new theories. So acceptable scientific theories not only yield explanations, their potential for providing us with such explanations often seems to be part of the ground for accepting them in the first place. If this is true, then explanatory power must be recognized as a legitimate factor in theory choice, alongside such other theoretical virtues as predictive content and simplicity. In other words, explanatory power must be recognized as evidential.

Given this, a satisfactory account of scientific explanation must answer two questions. First, it must tell us what an explanation is and how we are to judge the satisfactoriness of proposed explanations. Second, it must explain (or perhaps explain away) the apparent connection between explanatory power and theory acceptance.

A precise account of what counts as an explanation is essential if we are to have objective criteria for assessing when something has been explained. A satisfactory explanation of an event or phenomenon should provide us with understanding of what has been explained (the "explanandum"). But understanding is a notoriously vague and subjective state. Different inquirers may disagree about what is sufficient for understanding and whether or not understanding has actually been achieved. If the search for explanation has a central role in scientific reasoning, then it is important to ensure that our concept of explanation is free from this kind of vagueness. We want to be able to tell accurately when the goal of scientific explanation has been reached and when a new theory has sufficient explanatory resources to be accepted or preferred over its competitors.

It has seemed to many philosophers that our central, pre-analytic, commonsense view of what an explanation is does little to help us achieve these aims. On such a view, to explain some phenomenon is simply to say how it was caused. But this view of explanation is only as satisfactory as the notion of causation that goes along with it, and the notion of causation has traditionally been a worry for philosophers, particularly those of a verificationist bent. Many philosophers have seen causation as a problematic relation, one that science should abandon or at the very least reconstruct. What is it for one thing to be the cause of another? How can we tell when a causal relation exists? In the absence of answers to questions like these, we will not have given a satisfactory account of what it is to explain something.

It seems clear that both rational commonsense and rational scientific inquiry require a distinction between, on the one hand, the case of two events in which the first is the (or a) cause of the second and, on the other, the case in which one event merely precedes another but is not the (or a) cause of it. But most of the obvious accounts of the difference seem to require reference to the unobservable. Thus, for example, it is sometimes suggested that the two cases differ in that in the first case, but not in the second, the first event *necessitates* (or, perhaps, *naturally necessitates*) the latter. Alternatively, the first event may be said to have the *power* or *dispositional capacity* to bring about (or tend to bring about) the second. Finally, it is sometimes suggested that the difference lies in the fact that in the first case but not the second, there are *mechanisms* by which the first event produces (or helps to produce) the second. Now, *necessitation*, *powers*, *capacities*, and for that matter *production* are all unobservable, and so are at least some of the alleged *mechanisms* to which the last analysis appeals. This raises an uncomfortable problem for empiricists: talk about causal relations *seems* to be both scientifically necessary and irreducibly metaphysical by empiricist standards.

The Scotish empiricist David Hume discussed this problem in the eighteenth century in section VII of his *Enquiry Concerning Human Understanding*. Hume's solution was to reconstruct the distinction in terms of *constant conjunction*. Hume argued that if we examine our idea of causality, we will find that the claim that one event is the cause of another amounts to saying no more than that events like the first one are always (or usually, or typically) followed by events like the second. As it stands, however, Hume's analysis fails to specify a determinate relation between events, since we have not yet been told what it is for one event to be relevantly similar to another. For Hume, similarity was to be spelled out in psychological terms: two events are similar if we have a psychological propensity to class them together. Modern empiricists have taken a different tack, since it hardly seems satisfactory to leave the notion of causality on so subjective a footing. They look to the practice of the scientific community to explicate the relevant notion of similarity.

In practice scientists identify relevant respects of similarity in a theory-dependent way: observable respects of similarity are relevant if they are identified by currently accepted theories as symptoms of appropriate (and often unobservable) causal mechanisms. What the logical empiricists' twentieth-century version of Hume's analysis does is to incorporate a reference to this feature of scientific practice into the rational reconstruction of the notion of causation: one event causes a subsequent event just in case the second event is deductively predictable from the first given laws of nature and suitable statements of antecedent conditions.[1] On this reconstruction the theory-dependence of scientists' standards for identifying causes and effects is not mysterious: causation is defined in terms of laws of nature, so of course scientists will employ the best confirmed theories in recognizing causal relations because these theories represent their best estimate of what the laws of nature are.

Two features of the contemporary Humean analysis of causal relations are worth noting. First, the analysis follows the standard empiricist pattern in coping with a potentially embarrassing example of the theory-dependence of scientific methodology by treating it as a matter of convention. Instead of offering a verificationistically unacceptable metaphysical explanation of appeals to theoretical considerations in identifying causal relations (according to which knowledge of unobservable causal mechanisms is being applied), the empiricist offers a conception according to which reference to laws of nature is part of the conventional definition of causal relations and the theory-dependence of methods is simply a manifestation of scientists' efforts to identify those laws.

Second, the durability of the contemporary Humean analysis illustrates in an indirect way a point made in the introduction to the previous section of this anthology: the principal challenge to logical empiricism arises from the theory-dependence of scientific methods. Almost certainly the primary explanation for the durability of the contemporary version of the Humean analysis of causal statements is that, by incorporating the notion of a law of nature into the very definition of causal relations, it gives the appearance of being able to accommodate, within an empiricist analysis, whatever sort of theory-dependence there might be in scientists' assessments of causal relations.

Given this reconstrucion of the notion of causation, we are led directly to an account of explanation based on our pre-analytic view. According to that view, to explain something is to specify how it was caused. If we now develop this view in the light of a sophisticated Humean account of causation, we arrive at the following account: an event of a certain kind is explained by citing a general law (or laws) that relates events of that kind to events or conditions of some other kind and showing that events or conditions of the latter kind took place or were in effect. This is the classic *covering-law model* of explanation, which can be set out schematically as follows:

$$\frac{L_1, L_2, \ldots, L_n \quad \text{(General laws)}}{C_1, C_2, \ldots, C_n \quad \text{(Background conditions)}}$$
$$E \qquad \text{(Explanandum)}$$

The general laws and background conditions that jointly do the explaining are known as the *explanans*. In the limiting case, the explanans deductively entails the explanandum, and the covering-law model is then sometimes known as the *deductive-nomological* model of explanation.[2]

In recent times, the most prominent and sophisticated defender of the covering-law model of explanation has been Carl Hempel (see chapter 16 in this section), but the idea of explanation as nomic subsumption goes back at least as far as Newton. Indeed, we can see Hume's explicit worries about unobservable causal powers prefigured in Newton's dislike of "occult powers" and in his famous claim "hypotheses non fingo".

The covering-law model of explanation is thus no mere philosophical abstraction. It has had an important influence on the conduct of the sciences, particularly the social sciences. As Richard Miller points out (in part II, section 4), for example, the model was one of the motivations behind structuralism in social anthropology. If explanation requires general laws, but no such laws are available couched in terms of familiar social roles such as mother or brother, then such laws must be formulated in terms of increasingly abstract structural relations, such as "binary opposition".

We arrived at the covering-law model by considering the first question that a theory of explanation must address: what is an explanation and what makes it satisfactory? But the model not only provides an answer to this question, it also neatly answers our second question: why is explanatory power evidential? On the covering-law model, a satisfactory explanation turns out to have exactly the same logical structure as deriving a prediction on the basis of a scientific theory. If we have an adequate explanation of some occurrence, then, in principle, we could have predicted it before it actually took place (or before we knew that it had taken place). Now, for obvious reasons, we value theories that make accurate predictions; accurate prediction is important evidence in favor of a theory. It follows that we should value explanatory theories for exactly the same reasons. A theory that provides us with good explanations is confirmed in exactly the same way as one that yields true predictions.

So the covering-law model of explanation nicely addresses both of the questions with which we began: it lays down criteria that a satisfactory explanation should meet, and it explains why we should value theories with explanatory power. But unfortunately matters are not so simple. In fact, the covering-law model faces a number of serious problems, widely (though by no means universally) regarded by contemporary philosophers of science as decisive. One general background question (which I will simply mention in passing here) is whether it is possible to specify which general statements count as genuine laws (or as lawlike statements) without reference to unobservables or to causal factors. If this isn't possible (and a strong case can be made that it is not), then the epistemological motivation for the covering-law model—which is predicated on the assumption that reference to unobservables, and in particular unobservable causal relations, is problematical—would be completely undercut.[3]

In addition to this general problem, however, the covering-law model can be confronted with a large number of specific counterexamples. Broadly, these fall into two classes: First, cases in which an event is not explained, even though its occurrence has been derived from general laws and background conditions; and second, cases in which an event *is* explained, even though its occurrence has *not* been derived in the appropriate way.

Included in the first set of cases are the so-called asymmetries of explanation. Many mathematical laws link events in such a way that, given information about either one, information about the other can be derived. Thus, given the laws of optics, the position of the sun and the height of a certain flagpole, we can calculate the length of the shadow that the flagpole will cast. Here, the covering-law model conforms with our intuition that the height of the flagpole explains the length of the shadow. But, given the length of the shadow and the other information, we can equally calculate the height of the flagpole. In terms of the covering-law model, the two cases are parallel, yet it seems that we would not want to say that the length of the shadow explains the height of the flagpole.[4]

We can also find examples of derivation without explanation that involve no asymmetry. For instance, from the laws of biology together with the fact that there are mammals on the earth, we can deduce that there is oxygen in the atmosphere. We clearly have not explained the presence of oxygen in this way, but neither does the presence of oxygen explain the existence of mammal life.

One particularly important class of cases of this kind involves examples in which the derivation fails to provide an explanation due to what might be called "lack of depth". For example, suppose it were possible, given suitable general laws and knowledge of background conditions, to predict the outbreak of the First World War on the basis of information about the assassination of the Archduke Ferdinand in Sarajevo. Such a prediction would still not constitute a satisfactory explanation of the outbreak of war—the events it cites were at best the immediate triggers of the conflict, not its underlying cause. It is likely that, had the war not broken out in this way, then underlying causes would have brought about war in some other way instead. A satisfactory explanation should appeal to these causes, but a derivation that meets the standards of the covering-law model may nevertheless fail to do so.

Not only are there cases of covering-law derivations that fail to explain, there also appear to be explanations that fail to meet the standards of the covering-law model. For example, an explanation of the absence of a mass-based working-class political organization in the United States (a phenomenon known as "American exceptionalism") in terms of such factors as constitutional design, geography and natural resources, uneven economic development, racism, ethnic and religious divisions, and state repression has been defended by Joshua Cohen and Joel Rogers (1986, part 1) and seems worth taking seriously. Yet there are no general laws connecting the cited factors with the phenomenon to be explained, and no reason to think that the presence of such factors would always be incompatible with the emergence of class-based politics. Moreover, it is not obvious that Cohen and Rogers's explanation is merely a sketch waiting to be filled out in a manner that fits the covering-law model. Indeed, it looks like it would be bad methodological advice to suggest that political scientists should try to fill out the explanation to fit the model. If Cohen and Rogers's explanation is deficient, it is surely because it ignores salient factors (e.g., the political weaknesses of the U.S. working-class movement during crucial periods[5]), not because it fails to provide a covering law. If we demand a covering law in cases of this sort, then it seems likely that we will only end up with a tautology: when factors of this sort are strong enough and not outweighed by other factors, they produce the effect in question.[6] But tautologies are not explanatory.

Problems of the kinds just mentioned have persuaded many philosophers that the covering-law model of explanation is fundamentally flawed.[7] But in that case, what do we put in its place? The papers by Bas van Fraassen, Philip Kitcher, and Richard Boyd in this section each sketches a different way of going beyond the old account of explanation. Van Fraassen argues that the correct approach is to treat explanation as a completely pragmatic matter. Kitcher makes the case for an account of explanation as unification. Finally, Boyd develops a view of the nature and role of scientific explanation consistent with a realist construal of scientific theories and designed to account for the puzzling fact that considerations of explanatory power seem to be evidential.

According to van Fraassen, explaining an event typically involves describing some of the events leading up to it. But which ones? Van Fraassen argues that the choice of events is a pragmatic matter, determined by our particular interests. With the help of some technical devices, he tries to make the pragmatic dimension of explanation clearer and show how the problems facing the old covering-law model can be overcome.

The first of these devices is what van Fraassen calls an explanation's *contrast class*. He claims that we do not explain the occurrence of an event simpliciter, but only its occurrence in contrast to some specified set of other possible occurrences. Thus we are supposed to ask not simply why the First World War broke out but, rather, why it broke out in August 1914 rather than September 1914, or why there was a war rather than an attempt to set up international institutions designed to solve major power conflicts by negotiations. Van Fraassen makes the plausible claim that paying attention to the contrast class allows a solution to the problem of explanatory depth. Thus the Archduke's assassination is not completely irrelevant—it simply provides an answer to a less interesting question (why war in August rather than September?) than the question we want to ask (why war rather than negotiations?).

Appeal to contrast classes also clarifies cases of explanation without general laws, according to van Fraassen. If we want to know why there is no mass-based labor party in the United States in contrast to Britain, then mentioning factors of the sort cited above may be relevant, since at least some of them (geography and natural resources, and uneven economic development) are unique to the United States. However, if Canada is included in our contrast class, then the factors may cease to be explanatory, since there is a Canadian labor party (the New Democratic Party) with a significant base even though, to one degree or another, the cited factors are all present in Canada as well.

The notion of an explanation's contrast class may have some value in cases such as the ones just discussed. But does the fact that explanations have contrast classes make explanation pragmatic in any deep sense? Contrast classes can be seen as a way of specifying identity conditions for the event to be explained (indeed, when the identity conditions are already clear, it is hard to specify an informative contrast class for the explanandum), and it is not a surprise that it is up to us to choose what we want explained. The existence of this kind of pragmatic element in explanation gives no support to the claim that standards for assessing explanations are, for instance, merely matters of convenience. Moreover, as Alan Garfinkel points out, even when it comes to choosing what we want to be explained, there can be good choices and bad ones: "We can stipulate equivalences at will, but the result will be a good piece of science only if the way *we* are treating things as inessentially different corresponds to the way *nature* treats things as inessentially different" (Garfinkel 1981, p. 32).

What does van Fraassen have to say about the asymmetries of explanation, though? Here he appeals to a new notion: the *relevance relation* of an explanation. The relevance relation specifies the form of the explanation that we are looking for. We might be interested in the events leading up to the event to be explained, or in a standing condition that preceded the event, or in the event's function or purpose, and so on. Van Fraassen claims that we may choose whichever relevance relation we like, and that as a consequence there is no such thing as *the* cause of an event, independent of our particular interests. And he argues that the asymmetries of explanation can therefore be reversed—there are occasions on which the length of the shadow explains the height of the flagpole, for instance, when the pole was chosen to cast a shadow of a certain length.

But one may doubt whether van Fraassen has shown that the asymmetries can be reversed. Is it the length of the shadow or, rather, the *plan* that the shadow should be a certain length that explains the flagpole's height? It is also an open question whether there is any independent role for relevance relations to play in the assessment of explanations. Once we have decided what is to be explained (perhaps by specifying a contrast class), can we always go on to specify independently the form that the explanation is to have? Having said that I want to know why the First World War began in August rather than in September, can I then require that I be given an explanation in terms of, say, a standing condition? In many cases, there may simply be no explanation of a certain form to be had, once a contrast class has been specified. And in some cases there may be no explanation of a certain form available no matter what contrast class is chosen. Choose what contrast class you like, it seems improbable that the fact that the sky is blue can be explained in terms of any purpose that this may serve.

Van Fraassen's pragmatic account of explanation may also leave questions concerning the relation between explanatory power and theory choice. Van Fraassen claims that the search for explanatory theories is ipso facto a search for empirically adequate theories, but he offers no argument for this claim. He also considers whether explanatory power is evidential when choosing between two theories each of which is known to be empirically adequate (i.e., compatible with the data). Van Fraassen answers this question in the negative, arguing that explanatory power gives us only a pragmatic reason for preferring one theory to the other.

In fact, it is not clear that scientists are very often faced with choices of this second kind; but consider an actual example—the choice between Darwinian theory and creationism in the 1860s. Nineteenth-century creationism was empirically adequate in van Fraassen's sense (at any rate, it would not have been hard to modify it to make it consistent with the known data), so was it rejected merely on pragmatic grounds? On the one hand, creationist "explanations" don't seem to fail on pragmatic grounds while, on the other hand, Darwin's own assessment of his theory seems compelling:

> It can hardly be supposed that a false theory would explain, in so satisfactory a manner as does the theory of natural selection, the several large classes of facts above specified. (Darwin 1859, p. 476; cited in Thagard 1978, p. 77)

Darwin's argument is by no means an unusual one. Darwin himself noted this in defending his reasoning:

> It has recently been objected that this is an unsafe method of arguing; but it is a method used in judging of the common events of life, and has often been used by the greatest natural philosophers. (Darwin 1859, p. 476)

Paul Thagard cites other important instances of scientists taking explanatory power as a guide to at least approximate truth—Lavoisier's argument for the oxygen theory of combustion, Huygens's arguments for the wave theory of light, and Fresnel's later arguments for the same theory—and claims that such examples are "common in the history of science" (Thagard 1978, p. 77). Yet if van Fraassen's account of the value of explanation as purely pragmatic were right, it seems that Darwin's claim and others like it would have to be rejected.[8]

In this volume, both Kitcher and Boyd defend accounts of explanation that allow them to accept Darwin's claim. According to Kitcher,

> There are certain context-independent features of arguments which distinguish them for application in response to explanation-seeking why questions, and ... we can assess theories (including embryonic theories) by their ability to provide us with such arguments.... [H]istorical appeals to the explanatory power of theories involve recognition of a virtue over and beyond considerations of simplicity and predictive power.

The feature that Kitcher discusses is the capacity of a theory to provide a small number of explanatory patterns that can unify a wide variety of apparently disparate phenomena. Kitcher attempts to sketch a rigorous and formal account of explanation as unification and argues that this conception of explanation helps solve the main problems facing the covering-law model. Consider, for example, the following asymmetry: we can explain the period of a pendulum in terms of the pendulum's length, but not the length in terms of the period. Why is this? According to Kitcher, allowing the latter derivation to count as an explanation would require that we have one pattern of explanation for the length of swinging bodies and another for the length of stationary ones, which would be less unified than allowing only a single pattern for both sorts. To the objection that "we can construct derivations of the dimensions of bodies from specifications of their dispositional periods, thereby generating an argument pattern which can be applied ... generally," Kitcher replies that "[t]here are some objects ... which *could not* be pendulums, and for which the notion of a dispositional period makes no sense."

Kitcher's account of explanation as unification has a number of promising features, but also some problems. Some of these stem from the fact that Kitcher develops his account in a formal manner that ignores the specific content of the theories he is discussing, in particular the specific causal processes and powers they postulate. Consider, for instance, a world in which every object *could* be a pendulum—a world consisting only of objects that are potentially swinging bodies. In such a world, would Kitcher say that the period of a pendulum does explain its length? That would seem to ignore the fact that there is a causal mechanism in virtue of which the pendulum's length determines its period, but no mechanism which operates in the opposite direction.

A second problem for Kitcher's account is that, while he recognizes explanatory power as relevant to theory choice, he provides no explanation of the link. Why should the fact that a theory is able to explain disparate phenomena in a unified way give us any (nonpragmatic) reason for accepting it? What is the connection between unification and truth (or between unification and empirical adequacy)?

In his contribution to the discussion, Boyd argues that a satisfactory account of explanation requires an explicit rejection of the Humean analysis of causation and the development of a non-Humean alternative. Just as a realist construal of scientific theories is required to give an adequate explanation of the experimental and observational testing of hypotheses, so we must be realists about causal relations to give a satisfactory account of the role of explanation in science. Boyd develops a complex account of explanatory procedures on this basis and attempts to show how such an account makes the apparent connection between explanatory power and truth less puzzling.

One question that anyone who rejects the Humean analysis of causation must face is "what do we put in its place?" Boyd replies as follows:

> What causation is and what causal interaction amounts to are theoretical questions about natural phenomena (to reject the Humean project is just to admit that causal relations, powers, and interactions really are features of nature), so it is hardly surprising that answers to them should depend more upon the empirically confirmed theoretical findings of the various sciences than should answers to more abstract (and more typically philosophical) questions about the nature of knowledge, reference, or explanation.

But this response is unlikely to satisfy an empiricist, who will no doubt see it as merely labeling a problem, not solving it.

Perhaps the only way of making progress on these questions lies in examining scientific practice in greater detail. The final essay in this section represents one attempt to do just that. In "The Reality of Causes in a World of Instrumental Laws," Nancy Cartwright argues that the traditional empiricist belief that laws are a more secure part of science than talk of underlying causes reverses the way that these notions are treated by practicing physicists. If Cartwright's intriguing argument is sound, then the traditional empiricist effort to analyze causal notions in terms of laws must be seen as radically misguided. This issue, like the others discussed in this section, remains a question of lively current debate.

Notes

Some of the material in this introduction previously appeared in Gasper 1990 and is used here with permission.

1. I ignore here complications introduced by the case in which the relevant laws are nondeterministic.

2. For simplicity, I will ignore those cases in which the relation between the explanans and the explanandum is probabilistic and not deductive, as well as cases in which the explanandum is not some specific event, but is itself a general law or scientific theory. See the article by Hempel reprinted in this section for discussion of probabilistic explanation. See part I, section 3 for discussion of the relation between the laws of different theories.

3. For further discussion of this issue, see the article by Boyd reprinted here. In addition to the articles in this section, see the article by Miller in part II, section 4 for further discussion of the covering-law model.
4. Bromberger 1966 discusses a number of similar examples. The argument goes back to Aristotle, who points out in *Posterior Analytics* I 13 that while the proximity of the planets explains why they (unlike the stars) do not twinkle, the fact that the planets do not twinkle does not explain their proximity, even though the relationship is symmetrical.
5. See, for instance, the discussion in Davis 1986.
6. See Miller 1987, chapter 1.
7. Not all philosophers are convinced by counterexamples of the sort I have discussed. Railton 1978 is one sophisticated attempt to defend the covering-law model. Railton's views are discussed in Miller 1987, pp. 40–43. Also see Michael Redhead's essay in Knowles 1990.
8. Van Fraassen might claim that explanatory power is a guide to empirical adequacy, but, as noted above, this claim needs to be supported, and no argument has been offered for it.

References

Bromberger, S., 1966, "Why-Questions," in Colodny, R., ed., *Mind and Cosmos*, University of Pittsburgh Press, Pittsburgh.

Cohen, J., and Rogers, J., 1986, *The Rules of the Gam*, South End Press, Boston.

Darwin, C., 1859, *The Origin of Species*. Sixth edition reprinted 1962, Collier, New York.

Davis, M., 1986, *Prisoners of the American Dream*, Verso, London.

Garfinkel, A., 1981, *Forms of Explanation*, Yale University Press, New Haven, CT.

Gasper, P., 1990, "Explanation and Scientific Realism," in Knowles, *Explanation and its Limits*.

Hume, D., 1748, "An Enquiry Concerning Human Understanding," in Flew, A., ed., 1962, *On Human Nature and the Understanding*, Macmillan, New York.

Knowles, D., 1990, ed., *Explanation and its Limits*, Cambridge University Press, New York.

Miller, R., 1987, *Fact and Method*, Princeton University Press, Princeton, NJ.

Railton, P., 1978, "A Deductive-Nomological Model of Probabilistic Explanation," *Philosophy of Science* 45: 206–226.

Thagard, P., 1978, "The Best Explanation: Criteria for Theory Choice," *Journal of Philosophy* 75: 76–92.

Further Reading

Achinstein, P., 1983, *The Nature of Explanation*, Oxford University Press, New York.

Beauchamp, T., and Rosenberg, A., 1981, *Hume and the Problem of Causation*, Oxford University Press, New York.

Cartwright, N., 1983, *How the Laws of Physics Lie*, Oxford University Press, New York.

Davidson, D., 1980, *Essays on Actions and Events*, Oxford University Press, New York.

Glymour, C., et al. 1987, *Discovering Causal Structure*, Academic Press, San Diego.

Hempel, C., 1965, *Aspects of Scientific Explanation*, Free Press, New York.

Kitcher, P., and Salmon, W., 1989, eds., *Scientific Explanation*, University of Minnesota Press, Minneapolis.

Körner, S., 1975, ed., *Explanation*, Blackwell, Oxford, England.

Lewis, D., 1986, "Causal Explanation," in *Philosophical Papers*, Volume II, Oxford University Press, New York.

Mackie, J., 1974, *The Cement of the Universe*, Oxford University Press, New York.

Nagel, E., 1961, *The Structure of Science*, Harcourt, Brace and World, New York.

Pitt, J., 1988, ed., *Theories of Explanation*, Oxford University Press, New York.

Salmon, W., 1971, ed., *Statistical Explanation and Statistical Relevance*, University of Pittsburgh Press, Pittsburgh.

Salmon, W., 1978, "Why ask "Why?" An Inquiry Concerning Scientific Explanation," *Proceedings and Addresses of the American Philosophical Association* 51: 683–705.

Salmon, W., 1984, *Scientific Explanation and the Causal Structure of the World*, Princeton University Press, Princeton, NJ.

Sosa, E., 1975, ed., *Causation and Conditionals*, Oxford University Press, New York.

Strawson, G., 1989, *The Secret Connexion: Causation, Realism and David Hume*, Oxford University Press, New York.

van Fraassen, B., 1980, *The Scientific Image*, Oxford University Press, New York.

Chapter 16

Laws and Their Role in Scientific Explanation

Carl Hempel

Two Basic Requirements for Scientific Explanations

To explain the phenomena of the physical world is one of the primary objectives of the natural sciences. Indeed, almost all of the scientific investigations that served as illustrations in the preceding chapters were aimed not at ascertaining some particular fact but at achieving some explanatory insight; they were concerned with questions such as how puerperal fever is contracted, why the water-lifting capacity of pumps has its characteristic limitation, why the transmission of light conforms to the laws of geometrical optics, and so forth. In this chapter ... we will examine in some detail the character of scientific explanations and the kind of insight they afford.

That man has long and persistently been concerned to achieve some understanding of the enormously diverse, often perplexing, and sometimes threatening occurrences in the world around him is shown by the manifold myths and metaphors he has devised in an effort to account for the very existence of the world and of himself, for life and death, for the motions of the heavenly bodies, for the regular sequence of day and night, for the changing seasons, for thunder and lightning, sunshine and rain. Some of these explanatory ideas are based on anthropomorphic conceptions of the forces of nature, others invoke hidden powers or agents, still others refer to God's inscrutable plans or to fate.

Accounts of this kind undeniably may give the questioner a sense of having attained some understanding; they may resolve his perplexity and in this sense "answer" his question. But however satisfactory these answers may be psychologically, they are not adequate for the purposes of science, which, after all, is concerned to develop a conception of the world that has a clear, logical bearing on our experience and is thus capable of objective test. Scientific explanations must, for this reason, meet two systematic requirements, which will be called the requirement of explanatory relevance and the requirement of testability.

The astronomer Francesco Sizi offered the following argument to show why, contrary to what his contemporary, Galileo, claimed to have seen through his telescope, there could be no satellites circling around Jupiter:

> There are seven windows in the head, two nostrils, two ears, two eyes and a mouth; so in the heavens there are two favorable stars, two unpropitious, two luminaries, and Mercury alone undecided and indifferent. From which and many other similar phenomena of nature such as the seven metals, etc., which it were tedious to enumerate, we gather that the number of planets is necessarily seven.... Moreover, the satellites are invisible to the naked eye and therefore can have no influence on the earth and therefore would be useless and therefore do not exist.[1]

The crucial defect of this argument is evident: the "facts" it adduces, even if accepted without question, are entirely irrelevant to the point at issue; they do not afford the slightest reason for the assumption that Jupiter has no satellites; the claim of relevance suggested by the barrage of words like 'therefore', 'it follows', and 'necessarily' is entirely spurious.

Consider by contrast the physical explanation of a rainbow. It shows that the phenomenon comes about as a result of the reflection and refraction of the white light of the sun in spherical droplets of water such as those that occur in a cloud. By reference to the relevant optical laws, this account shows that the appearance of a rainbow is to be expected whenever a spray or mist of water droplets is illuminated by a strong white light behind the observer. Thus, even if we happened never to have seen a rainbow, the explanatory information provided by the physical account would constitute good grounds for expecting or believing that a rainbow will appear under the specified circumstances. We will refer to this characteristic by saying that the physical explanation meets the *requirement of explanatory relevance*: the explanatory information adduced affords good grounds for believing that the phenomenon to be explained did, or does, indeed occur. This condition must be met if we are to be entitled to say: "That explains it—the phenomenon in question was indeed to be expected under the circumstances!"

The requirement represents a necessary condition for an adequate explanation, but not a sufficient one. For example, a large body of data showing a red-shift in the spectra of distant galaxies provides strong grounds for believing *that* those galaxies recede from our local one at enormous speeds, yet it does not explain *why*.

To introduce the second basic requirement for scientific explanations, let us consider once more the conception of gravitational attraction as manifesting a natural tendency akin to love. As we noted earlier, this conception has no test implications whatever. Hence, no empirical finding could possibly bear it out or disconfirm it. Being thus devoid of empirical content, the conception surely affords no grounds for expecting the characteristic phenomena of gravitational attraction: it lacks objective explanatory power. Similar comments apply to explanations in terms of an inscrutable fate: to invoke such an idea is not to achieve an especially profound insight, but to give up the attempt at explanation altogether. By contrast, the statements on which the physical explanation of a rainbow is based do have various test implications; these concern, for example, the conditions under which a rainbow will be seen in the sky, and the order of the colors in it; the appearance of rainbow phenomena in the spray of a wave breaking on the rocks and in the mist of a lawn sprinkler; and so forth. These examples illustrate a second condition for scientific explanations, which we will call the *requirement of testability*: the statements constituting a scientific explanation must be capable of empirical test.

It has already been suggested that since the conception of gravitation in terms of an underlying universal affinity has no test implications, it can have no explanatory power: it cannot provide grounds for expecting that universal gravitation will occur, nor that gravitational attraction will show such and such characteristic features; for if it did imply such consequences either deductively or even in a weaker, inductive-probabilistic sense, then it would be testable by reference to those consequences. As this example shows, the two requirements just considered are interrelated: a proposed explanation that meets the requirement of relevance also meets the requirement of testability. (The converse clearly does not hold.)

Now let us see what forms scientific explanations take, and how they meet the two basic requirements.

Deductive-Nomological Explanation

Consider once more Périer's finding in the Puy-de-Dôme experiment, that the length of the mercury column in a Torricelli barometer decreased with increasing altitude. Torricelli's and Pascal's ideas on atmospheric pressure provided an explanation for this phenomenon; somewhat pedantically, it can be spelled out as follows:

> (a) At any location, the pressure that the mercury column in the closed branch of the Torricelli apparatus exerts upon the mercury below equals the pressure exerted on the surface of the mercury in the open vessel by the column of air above it.
>
> (b) The pressures exerted by the columns of mercury and of air are proportional to their weights; and the shorter the columns, the smaller their weights.
>
> (c) As Périer carried the apparatus to the top of the mountain, the column of air above the open vessel became steadily shorter.
>
> (d) (Therefore,) the mercury column in the closed vessel grew steadily shorter during the ascent.

Thus formulated, the explanation is an argument to the effect that the phenomenon to be explained, as described by the sentence (d), is just what is to be expected in view of the explanatory facts cited in (a), (b), and (c); and that, indeed, (d) follows deductively from the explanatory statements. The latter are of two kinds; (a) and (b) have the character of general laws expressing uniform empirical connections; whereas (c) describes certain particular facts. Thus, the shortening of the mercury column is here explained by showing that it occurred in accordance with certain laws of nature, as a result of certain particular circumstances. The explanation fits the phenomenon to be explained into a pattern of uniformities and shows that its occurrence was to be expected, given the specified laws and the pertinent particular circumstances.

The phenomenon to be accounted for by an explanation will henceforth also be referred to as the *explanandum phenomenon*; the sentence describing it, as the *explanandum sentence*. When the context shows which is meant, either of them will simply be called the explanandum. The sentences specifying the explanatory information— (a), (b), (c) in our example—will be called the *explanans sentences*; jointly they will be said to form the *explanans*.

As a second example, consider the explanation of a characteristic of image formation by reflection in a spherical mirror; namely, that generally $1/u + 1/v = 2/r$, where u and v are the distances of object-point and image-point from the mirror, and r is the mirror's radius of curvature. In geometrical optics, this uniformity is explained with the help of the basic law of reflection in a plane mirror, by treating the reflection of a beam of light at any one point of a spherical mirror as a case of reflection in a plane tangential to the spherical surface. The resulting explanation can be formulated as a deductive argument whose conclusion is the explanandum sentence, and whose premisses include the basic laws of reflection and of rectilinear propagation, as well as the statement that the surface of the mirror forms a segment of a sphere.[2]

A similar argument, whose premises again include the law for reflection in a plane mirror, offers an explanation of why the light of a small light source placed at the focus of a paraboloidal mirror is reflected in a beam parallel to the axis of the paraboloid (a principle technologically applied in the construction of automobile headlights, searchlights, and other devices).

The explanations just considered may be conceived, then, as deductive arguments whose conclusion is the explanandum sentence, E, and whose premiss-set, the explanans, consists of general laws, L_1, L_2, ..., L_r and of other statements, C_1, C_2, ..., C_k, which make assertions about particular facts. The form of such arguments, which thus constitute one type of scientific explanation, can be represented by the following schema:

$$\text{D-N]} \quad \left. \begin{array}{l} L_1,\ L_2,\ \ldots,\ L_r \\ C_1,\ C_2,\ \ldots,\ C_k \end{array} \right\} \quad \text{Explanans sentences}$$

$$\overline{\hspace{2cm} E \hspace{2cm}} \quad \text{Explanandum sentence}$$

Explanatory accounts of this kind will be called explanations by deductive subsumption under general laws, or *deductive-nomological explanation*. (The root of the term 'nomological' is the Greek word 'nomos', for law.) The laws invoked in a scientific explanation will also be called *covering laws* for the explanandum phenomenon, and the explanatory argument will be said to subsume the explanandum under those laws.

The explanandum phenomenon in a deductive-nomological explanation may be an event occurring at a particular place and time, such as the outcome of Périer's experiment. Or it may be some regularity found in nature, such as certain characteristics generally displayed by rainbows; or a uniformity expressed by an empirical law such as Galileo's or Kepler's laws. Deductive explanations of such uniformities will then invoke laws of broader scope, such as the laws of reflection and refraction, or Newton's laws of motion and of gravitation. As this use of Newton's laws illustrates, empirical laws are often explained by means of theoretical principles that refer to structures and processes underlying the uniformities in question. ....

Deductive-nomological explanations satisfy the requirement of explanatory relevance in the strongest possible sense: the explanatory information they provide implies the explanandum sentence deductively and thus offers logically conclusive grounds why the explanandum phenomenon is to be expected. (We will soon encounter other scientific explanations, which fulfill the requirement only in a weaker, inductive, sense.) And the testability requirement is met as well, since the explanans implies among other things that under the specified conditions, the explanandum phenomenon occurs.

Some scientific explanations conform to the pattern (D-N) quite closely. This is so, particularly, when certain quantitative features of a phenomenon are explained by mathematical derivation from covering general laws, as in the case of reflection in spherical and paraboloidal mirrors. Or take the celebrated explanation, propounded by Leverrier (and independently by Adams), of peculiar irregularities in the motion of the planet Uranus, which on the current Newtonian theory could not be accounted for by the gravitational attraction of the other planets then known. Leverrier conjectured that they resulted from the gravitational pull of an as yet undetected outer planet, and he computed the position, mass, and other characteristics which that planet would have to possess to account in quantitative detail for the observed irregularities. His explanation was strikingly confirmed by the discovery, at the predicted location, of a new planet, Neptune, which had the quantitative characteristics attributed to it by Leverrier. Here again, the explanation has the character of a deductive argument whose premises include general laws—specifically Newton's laws of gravitation and of motion—as well as statements specifying various quantitative particulars about the disturbing planet.

Not infrequently, however, deductive-nomological explanations are stated in an elliptical form: they omit mention of certain assumptions that are presupposed by the explanation but are simply taken for granted in the given context. Such explanations are sometimes expressed in the form 'E because C', where E is the event to be explained and C is some antecedent or concomitant event or state of affairs. Take, for example, the statement: 'The slush on the sidewalk remained liquid during the frost because it had been sprinkled with salt'. This explanation does not explicitly mention any laws, but it tacitly presupposes at least one: that the freezing point of water is lowered whenever salt is dissolved in it. Indeed, it is precisely by virtue of this law that the sprinkling of salt acquires the explanatory, and specifically causative, role that the elliptical because-statement ascribes to it. That statement, incidentally, is elliptical also in other respects; for example, it tacitly takes for granted, and leaves unmentioned, certain assumptions about the prevailing physical conditions, such as the temperature's not dropping to a very low point. And if nomic and other assumptions thus omitted are added to the statement that salt had been sprinkled on the slush, we obtain the premises for a deductive-nomological explanation of the fact that the slush remained liquid.

Similar comments apply to Semmelweis's explanation that childbed fever was caused by decomposed animal matter introduced into the bloodstream through open wound surfaces. Thus formulated, the explanation makes no mention of general laws; but it presupposes that such contamination of the bloodstream generally leads to blood poisoning attended by the characteristic symptoms of childbed fever, for this is implied by the assertion that the contamination *causes* puerperal fever. The generalization was no doubt taken for granted by Semmelweis, to whom the cause of Kolletschka's fatal illness presented no etiological problem: given that infectious matter was introduced into the bloodstream, blood poisoning would result. (Kolletschka was by no means the first one to die of blood poisoning resulting from a cut with an infected scalpel. And by a tragic irony, Semmelweis himself was to suffer the same fate.) But once the tacit premise is made explicit, the explanation is seen to involve reference to general laws.

As the preceding examples illustrate, corresponding general laws are always presupposed by an explanatory statement to the effect that a particular event of a certain kind G (e.g., expansion of a gas under constant pressure; flow of a current in a wire loop) was *caused* by an event of another kind F (e.g., heating of the gas; motion of the loop across a magnetic field). To see this, we need not enter into the complex ramifications of the notion of cause; it suffices to note that the general maxim "Same cause, same effect", when applied to such explanatory statements, yields the implied claim that whenever an event of kind F occurs, it is accompanied by an event of kind G.

To say that an explanation rests on general laws is not to say that its discovery required the discovery of the laws. The crucial new insight achieved by an explanation will sometimes lie in the discovery of some particular fact (e.g., the presence of an undetected outer planet; infectious matter adhering to the hands of examining physicians) which, by virtue of antecedently accepted general laws, accounts for the explanandum phenomenon. In other cases, such as that of the lines in the hydrogen spectrum, the explanatory achievement does lie in the discovery of a covering law (Balmer's) and eventually of an explanatory theory (such as Bohr's); in yet other cases, the major accomplishment of an explanation may lie in showing that, and exactly how, the explanandum phenomenon can be accounted for by reference to laws and data about particular facts that are already available: this is illustrated by the explanatory derivation of the reflection laws for spherical and paraboloidal mirrors from the basic law of geometrical optics in conjunction with statements about the geometrical characteristics of the mirrors.

An explanatory problem does not by itself determine what kind of discovery is required for its solution. Thus, Leverrier discovered deviations from the theoretically expected course also in the motion of the planet Mercury; and as in the case of Uranus, he tried to explain these as resulting from the gravitational pull of an as yet undetected planet, Vulcan, which would have to be a very dense and very small object between the sun and Mercury. But no such planet was found, and a satisfactory explanation was provided only much later by the general theory of relativity, which accounted for the irregularities not by reference to some disturbing particular factor, but by means of a new system of laws.

Universal Laws and Accidental Generalizations

As we have seen, laws play an essential role in deductive-nomological explanations. They provide the link by reason of which particular circumstances (described by C_1, C_2, ..., C_k) can serve to explain the occurrence of a given event. And when the explanandum is not a particular event, but a uniformity such as those represented by characteristics mentioned earlier of spherical and paraboloidal mirrors, the explanatory laws exhibit a system of more comprehensive uniformities, of which the given one is but a special case.

The laws required for deductive-nomological explanations share a basic characteristic: they are, as we shall say, statements of universal form. Broadly speaking, a statement of this kind asserts a uniform connection between different empirical phenomena or between different aspects of an empirical phenomenon. It is a statement to the effect that whenever and wherever conditions of a specified kind F occur, then so will, always and without exception, certain conditions of another kind, G. (Not all scientific laws are of this type. In the sections that follow, we will encounter laws of probabilistic form, and explanations based on them.)

Here are some examples of statements of universal form: whenever the temperature of a gas increases while its pressure remains constant, its volume increases; whenever a solid is dissolved in a liquid, the boiling point of the liquid is raised; whenever a ray of light is reflected at a plane surface, the angle of reflection equals the angle of incidence; whenever a magnetic iron rod is broken in two, the pieces are magnets again; whenever a body falls freely from rest in a vacuum near the surface of the earth, the distance it covers in t seconds is $16t^2$ feet. Most of the laws of the natural sciences are quantitative: they assert specific mathematical connections between different quantitative characteristics of physical systems (e.g., between volume, temperature, and pressure of a gas), or of processes (e.g., between time and distance in free fall in Galileo's law; between the period of revolution of a planet and its mean distance from the sun, in Kepler's third law; between the angles of incidence and refraction in Snell's law).

Strictly speaking, a statement asserting some uniform connection will be considered a law only if there are reasons to assume it is true: we would not normally speak of false laws of nature. But if this requirement were rigidly observed, then the statements commonly referred to as Galileo's and Kepler's laws would not qualify as laws; for according to current physical knowledge, they hold only approximately; and as we shall see later, physical theory explains why this is so. Analogous remarks apply to the laws of geometrical optics. For example, even in a homogeneous medium, light does not move strictly in straight lines: it can bend around corners. We shall therefore use the word 'law' somewhat liberally, applying the term also to certain statements of the kind here referred to, which, on theoretical grounds, are known to hold only approximately and with certain qualifications. . . .

We saw that the laws invoked in deductive-nomological explanations have the basic form: 'In all cases when conditions of kind *F* are realized, conditions of kind *G* are realized as well'. But, interestingly, not all statements of this universal form, even if true, can qualify as laws of nature. For example, the sentence 'All rocks in this box contain iron' is of universal form (*F* is the condition of being a rock in the box, *G* that of containing iron); yet even if true, it would not be regarded as a law, but as an assertion of something that "happens to be the case", as an "accidental generalization". Or consider the statement: 'All bodies consisting of pure gold have a mass of less than 100,000 kilograms'. No doubt all bodies of gold ever examined by man conform to it; thus, there is considerable confirmatory evidence for it and no disconfirming instances are known. Indeed, it is quite possible that never in the history of the universe has there been or will there be a body of pure gold with a mass of 100,000 kilograms or more. In this case, the proposed generalization would not only be well confirmed, but true. And yet, we would presumably regard its truth as accidental, on the ground that nothing in the basic laws of nature as conceived in contemporary science precludes the possibility of there being—or even the possibility of our producing—a solid gold object with a mass exceeding 100,000 kilograms.

Thus, a scientific law cannot be adequately defined as a true statement of universal form: this characterization expresses a necessary, but not a sufficient, condition for laws of the kind here under discussion.

What distinguishes genuine laws from accidental generalizations? This intriguing problem has been intensively discussed in recent years. Let us look briefly at some of the principal ideas that have emerged from the debate, which is still continuing.

One telling and suggestive difference, noted by Nelson Goodman,[3] is this: a law can, whereas an accidental generalization cannot, serve to support *counterfactual conditionals*, i.e., statements of the form 'If *A* were (had been) the case, then *B* would be (would have been) the case', where in fact *A* is not (has not been) the case. Thus, the assertion 'If this paraffin candle had been put into a kettle of boiling water, it would have melted' could be supported by adducing the law that paraffin is liquid above 60 degrees centigrade (and the fact that the boiling point of water is 100 degrees centigrade). But the statement 'All rocks in this box contain iron' could not be used similarly to support the counterfactual statement 'If this pebble had been put into the box, it would contain iron'. Similarly, a law, in contrast to an accidentally true generalization, can support *subjunctive conditionals*, i.e., sentences of the type 'If *A* should come to pass, then so would *B*', where it is left open whether or not *A* will in fact come to pass. The statement 'If this paraffin candle should be put into boiling water then it would melt' is an example.

Closely related to this difference is another one, which is of special interest to us: a law can, whereas an accidental generalization cannot, serve as a basis for an explanation. Thus, the melting of a particular paraffin candle that was put into boiling water can be explained, in conformity with the schema (D-N), by reference to the particular facts just mentioned and to the law that paraffin melts when its temperature is raised above 60 degrees centigrade. But the fact that a particular rock in the box contains iron cannot be analogously explained by reference to the general statement that all rocks in the box contain iron.

It might seem plausible to say, by way of a further distinction, that the latter statement simply serves as a conveniently brief formulation of a finite conjunction of this kind: 'Rock r_1 contains iron, and rock r_2 contains iron, . . . , and rock r_{63} contains iron'; whereas the generalization about paraffin refers to a potentially infinite set of particular cases and therefore cannot be paraphrased by a finite conjunction of statements describing individual instances. This distinction is suggestive, but it is overstated. For to begin with, the generalization 'All rocks in this box contain iron' does not in fact tell us how many rocks there are in the box, nor does it name any particular rocks r_1, r_2, etc. Hence, the general sentence is not logically equivalent to a finite conjunction of the kind just mentioned. To formulate a suitable conjunction, we need additional information, which might be obtained by counting and labeling the rocks in the box. Besides, our generalization 'All bodies of pure gold have a mass of less than 100,000 kilograms' would not count as a law even if there were infinitely many bodies of gold in the world. Thus, the criterion we have under consideration fails on several grounds.

Finally, let us note that a statement of universal form may qualify as a law even if it actually has no instances whatever. As an example, consider the sentence: 'On any celestial body that has the same radius as the earth but twice its mass, free fall from rest conforms to the formula $s = 32t^2$'. There might well be no celestial object in the entire universe that has the specified size and mass, and yet the statement has the character of a law. For it (or rather, a close approximation of it, as in the case of Galileo's law) follows from the Newtonian theory of gravitation and of motion in conjunction with the statement that the acceleration of free fall on the earth is 32 feet per second per second; thus, it has strong theoretical support, just like our earlier law for free fall on the moon.

A law, we noted, can support subjunctive and counterfactual conditional statements about potential instances, i.e., about particular cases that might occur, or that might have occurred but did not. In similar fashion, Newton's theory supports our general statement in a subjunctive version that suggests its lawlike status, namely: 'On any celestial body that there may be which has the same size as the earth but twice its mass, free fall would conform to the formula $s = 32t^2$'. By contrast, the generalization about the rocks cannot be paraphrased as asserting that any rock that might be in this box would contain iron, nor of course would this latter claim have any theoretical support.

Similarly, we would not use our generalization about the mass of gold bodies—let us call it H—to support statements such as this: 'Two bodies of pure gold whose individual masses add up to more than 100,000 kilograms cannot be fused to form one body; or if fusion should be possible, then the mass of the resulting body will be less than 100,000 kg', for the basic physical and chemical theories of matter that are currently accepted do not preclude the kind of fusion here considered, and they do not imply that there would be a mass loss of the sort here referred to. Hence, even if the generalization H should be true, i.e., if no exceptions to it should ever occur, this would constitute a mere accident or coincidence as judged by current theory, which permits the occurrence of exceptions to H.

Thus, whether a statement of universal form counts as a law will depend in part upon the scientific theories accepted at the time. This is not to say that "empirical generalizations"—statements of universal form that are empirically well confirmed but have no basis in theory—never qualify as laws: Galileo's, Kepler's, and Boyle's laws, for example, were accepted as such before they received theoretical grounding. The relevance of theory is rather this: a statement of universal form, whether empirically confirmed or as yet untested, will qualify as a law if it is implied by an accepted theory (statements of this kind are often referred to as theoretical laws); but even if it is empirically well confirmed and presumably true in fact, it will not qualify as a law if it rules out certain hypothetical occurrences (such as the fusion of two gold bodies with a resulting mass of more than 100,000 kilograms, in the case of our generalization *H*) which an accepted theory qualifies as possible.[4]

Probabilistic Explanation: Fundamentals

Not all scientific explanations are based on laws of strictly universal form. Thus, little Jim's getting the measles might be explained by saying that he caught the disease from his brother, who had a bad case of the measles some days earlier. This account again links the explanandum event to an earlier occurrence, Jim's exposure to the measles; the latter is said to provide an explanation because there is a connection between exposure to the measles and contracting the disease. That connection cannot be expressed by a law of universal form, however; for not every case of exposure to the measles produces contagion. What can be claimed is only that persons exposed to the measles will contract the disease with high probability, i.e., in a high percentage of all cases. General statements of this type, which we shall soon examine more closely, will be called *laws of probabilistic form* or *probabilistic laws*, for short.

In our illustration, then, the explanans consists of the probabilistic law just mentioned and the statement that Jim was exposed to the measles. In contrast to the case of deductive-nomological explanation, these explanans statements do not deductively imply the explanandum statement that Jim got the measles; for in deductive inferences from true premises, the conclusion is invariably true, whereas in our example, it is clearly possible that the explanans statements might be true and yet the explanandum statement false. We will say, for short, that the explanans implies the explanandum, not with "deductive certainty", but only with near-certainty or with high probability.

The resulting explanatory argument may be schematized as follows:

> The probability for persons exposed to the measles
> to catch the disease is high.
>
> Jim was exposed to the measles.
> ======================================= [makes highly probable]
> Jim caught the measles.

In the customary presentation of a deductive argument, which was used, for example, in the schema (D-N) above, the conclusion is separated from the premises by a single line, which serves to indicate that the premises logically imply the conclusion. The double line used in our latest schema is meant to indicate analogously that the "premises" (the explanans) make the "conclusion" (the explanandum sentence) more or less probable; the degree of probability is suggested by the notation in brackets.

Arguments of this kind will be called *probabilistic explanations*. As our discussion shows, a probabilistic explanation of a particular event shares certain basic characteristics with the corresponding deductive-nomological type of explanation. In both cases, the given event is explained by reference to others, with which the explanandum event is connected by laws. But in one case, the laws are of universal form; in the other, of probabilistic form. And while a deductive explanation shows that, on the information contained in the explanans, the explanandum was to be expected with "deductive certainty", an inductive explanation shows only that, on the information contained in the explanans, the explanandum was to be expected with high probability, and perhaps with "practical certainty"; it is in this manner that the latter argument meets the requirement of explanatory relevance.

Statistical Probabilities and Probabilistic Laws

We must now consider more closely the two differentiating features of probabilistic explanation that have just been noted: the probabilistic laws they invoke and the peculiar kind of probabilistic implication that connects the explanans with the explanandum.

Suppose that from an urn containing many balls of the same size and mass, but not necessarily of the same color, successive drawings are made. At each drawing, one ball is removed, and its color is noted. Then the ball is returned to the urn, whose contents are thoroughly mixed before the next drawing takes place. This is an example of a so-called random process or random experiment, a concept that will soon be characterized in more detail. Let us refer to the procedure just described as experiment U, to each drawing as one performance of U, and to the color of the ball produced by a given drawing as the result, or the outcome, of that performance.

If all the balls in an urn are white, then a statement of strictly universal form holds true of the results produced by the performance of U: every drawing from the urn yields a white ball, or yields the result W, for short. If only some of the balls—say, 600 of them—are white, whereas the others—say 400—are red, then a general statement of probabilistic form holds true of the experiment: the probability for a performance of U to produce a white ball, or outcome W, is .6; in symbols:

$$P(W, U) = .6. \tag{5a}$$

Similarly, the probability of obtaining heads as a result of the random experiment C of flipping a fair coin is given by

$$P(H, C) = .5, \tag{5b}$$

and the probability of obtaining an ace as a result of the random experiment D of rolling a regular die is

$$P(A, D) = 1/6. \tag{5c}$$

What do such probability statements mean? According to one familiar view, sometimes called the "classical" conception of probability, the statement (5a) would have to be interpreted as follows: each performance of the experiment U effects a choice of one from among 1,000 basic possibilities, or basic alternatives, each represented by one of the balls in the urn; of these possible choices, 600 are "favorable" to the outcome W; and the probability of drawing a white ball is simply the ratio of the number of favorable choices available to the number of all possible choices, i.e., 600/1,000. The classical interpretation of the probability statements (5b) and (5c) follows similar lines.

Yet this characterization is inadequate, for if before each drawing, the 400 red balls in the urn were placed on top of the white ones, then in this new kind of urn experiment—let us call it U'—the ratio of favorable to possible basic alternatives would remain the same, but the probability of drawing a white ball would be smaller than in the experiment U, in which the balls are thoroughly mixed before each drawing. The classical conception takes account of this difficulty by requiring that the basic alternatives referred to in its definition of probability must be "equipossible" or "equiprobable"—a requirement presumably violated in the case of experiment U'.

This added proviso raises the question of how to define equipossibility or equiprobability. We will pass over this notoriously troublesome and controversial issue, because—even assuming that equiprobability can be satisfactorily characterized—the classical conception would still be inadequate, since probabilities are assigned also to the outcomes of random experiments for which no plausible way is known of marking off equiprobable basic alternatives. Thus, for the random experiment D of rolling a regular die, the six faces might be regarded as representing such equiprobable alternatives; but we attribute probabilities to such results as rolling an ace, or an odd number of points, etc., also in the case of a loaded die, even though no equiprobable basic outcomes can be marked off here.

Similarly—and this is particularly important—science assigns probabilities to the outcomes of certain random experiments or random processes encountered in nature, such as the step-by-step decay of the atoms of radioactive substances, or the transition of atoms from one energy state to another. Here again, we find no equiprobable basic alternatives in terms of which such probabilities might be classically defined and computed.

To arrive at a more satisfactory construal of our probability statements, let us consider how one would ascertain the probability of the rolling of an ace with a given die that is not known to be regular. This would obviously be done by making a large number of throws with the die and ascertaining the *relative frequency*, i.e., the proportion, of those cases in which an ace turns up. If, for example, the experiment D' of rolling the given die is performed 300 times and an ace turns up in 62 cases, then the relative frequency, 62/300, would be regarded as an approximate value of the probability $p(A, D')$ of rolling an ace with the given die. Analogous procedures would be used to estimate the probabilities associated with the flipping of a given coin, the spinning of a roulette wheel, and so on. Similarly, the probabilities associated with radioactive decay, with the transitions between different atomic energy states, with genetic processes, etc., are determined by ascertaining the corresponding relative frequencies; however, this is often done in highly indirect ways rather than by simply counting individual atomic or other events of the relevant kinds.

The interpretation in terms of relative frequencies applies also to probability statements such as (5b) and (5c), which concern the results of flipping a fair (i.e., homogeneous and strictly cylindrical) coin or tossing a regular (homogeneous and strictly cubical) die: what the scientist (or the gambler, for that matter) is concerned with in making a probability statement is the relative frequency with which a certain outcome O can be expected in long series of repetitions of some random experiment R. The counting of "equiprobable" basic alternatives and of those among them which are "favorable" to O may be regarded as a heuristic device for guessing at the relative frequency of O. And indeed when a regular die or a fair coin is tossed a large number of times, the different faces tend to come up with equal frequency. One might expect this on the basis of symmetry considerations of the kind frequently used in forming physical hypotheses, for our empirical knowledge affords no grounds on which to expect any of the faces to be favored over any other. But while such considerations often are heuristically useful, they must not be regarded as certain or as self-evident truths: some very plausible symmetry assumptions, such as the principle of parity, have been found not to be generally satisfied at the subatomic level. Assumptions about equiprobabilities are therefore always subject to correction in the light of empirical data concerning the actual relative frequencies of the phenomena in question. This point is illustrated also by the statistical theories of gases developed by Bose and Einstein and by Fermi and Dirac, respectively, which rest on different assumptions concerning what distributions of particles over a phase space are equiprobable.

The probabilities specified in the probabilistic laws, then, represent relative frequencies. They cannot, however, be strictly defined as relative frequencies in long series of repetitions of the relevant random experiment. For the proportion, say, of aces obtained in throwing a given die will change, if perhaps only slightly, as the series of throws is extended; and even in two series of exactly the same length, the number of aces will usually differ. We do find, however, that as the number of throws increases, the relative frequency of each of the different outcomes tends to change less and less, even though the results of successive throws continue to vary in an irregular and practically unpredictable fashion. This is what generally characterizes a random experiment R with outcomes O_1, O_2, ..., O_n: successive performances of R yield one or another of those outcomes in an irregular manner; but the relative frequencies of the outcomes tend to become stable as the number of performances increases. And the probabilities of the outcomes, $p(O_1, R)$, $p(O_2, R)$, ..., $p(O_n, R)$, may be regarded as ideal values that the actual frequencies tend to assume as they become increasingly stable. For mathematical convenience, the probabilities are sometimes defined as the mathematical *limits* toward which the relative frequencies converge as the number of performances increases indefinitely. But this definition has certain conceptual shortcomings, and in some more recent mathematical studies of the subject, the intended empirical meaning of the concept of probability is deliberately, and for good reasons, characterized more vaguely by means of the following so-called *statistical interpretation of probability*:[5]

The statement

$$p(O, R) = r$$

means that in a long series of performances of random experiment R, the proportion of cases with outcome O is almost certain to be close to r.

The concept of *statistical probability* thus characterized must be carefully distinguished from the concept of *inductive or logical probability*. Logical probability is a quantitative logical relation between definite *statements*; the sentence

$$c(H, K) = r$$

asserts that the hypothesis H is supported, or made probable, to degree r by the evidence formulated in statement K. Statistical probability is a quantitative relation between repeatable *kinds of events*: a certain kind of outcome, O, and a certain kind of random process, R; it represents, roughly speaking, the relative frequency with which the result O tends to occur in a long series of performances of R.

What the two concepts have in common are their mathematical characteristics: both satisfy the basic principles of mathematical probability theory:

a) The possible numerical values of both probabilities range from 0 to 1:

$$0 \leq p(O, R) \leq 1,$$

$$0 \leq c(H, K) \leq 1.$$

b) The probability for one of two mutually exclusive outcomes of R to occur is the sum of the probabilities of the outcomes taken separately; the probability, on any evidence K, for one or the other of two mutually exclusive hypotheses to hold is the sum of their respective probabilities:

If O_1, O_2 are mutually exclusive, then
$$p(O_1 \text{ or } O_2, R) = p(O_1, R) + p(O_2, R).$$

If H_1, H_2 are logically exclusive hypotheses, then
$$c(H_1 \text{ or } H_2, K) = c(H_1, K) + c(H_2, K).$$

c) The probability of an outcome that necessarily occurs in all cases—such as *O* or not *O*—is 1; the probability, on any evidence, of a hypothesis that is logically (and in this sense necessarily) true, such as *H* or not *H*, is 1:

$$p(0 \text{ or not } 0, R) = 1,$$

$$c(H \text{ or not } H, K) = 1.$$

Scientific hypotheses in the form of statistical probability statements can be, and are, tested by examining the long-run relative frequencies of the outcomes concerned; and the confirmation of such hypotheses is then judged, broadly speaking, in terms of the closeness of the agreement between hypothetical probabilities and observed frequencies. The logic of such tests, however, presents some intriguing special problems, which call for at least brief examination.

Consider the hypothesis, *H*, that the probability of rolling an ace with a certain die is .15; or briefly, that $p(A, D) = .15$, where *D* is the random experiment of rolling the given die. The hypothesis *H* does not deductively imply any test implications specifying how many aces will occur in a finite series of throws of the die. It does not imply, for example, that exactly 75 among the first 500 throws will yield an ace, nor even that the number of aces will lie between 50 and 100, say. Hence, if the proportion of aces actually obtained in a large number of throws differs considerably from .15, this does not refute *H* in the sense in which a hypothesis of strictly universal form, such as 'All swans are white', can be refuted, in virtue of the *modus tollens* argument, by reference to one counter-instance, such as a black swan. Similarly, if a long run of throws of the given die yields a proportion of aces very close to .15, this does not confirm *H* in the sense in which a hypothesis is confirmed by the finding that a test sentence *I* that it logically implies is in fact true. For in this latter case, the hypothesis asserts *I* by logical implication, and the test result is thus confirmatory in the sense of showing that a certain part of what the hypothesis asserts is indeed true; but nothing strictly analogous is shown for *H* by confirmatory frequency data; for *H* does *not* assert by implication that the frequency of aces in some long run will definitely be very close to .15.

But while *H* does not logically preclude the possibility that the proportion of aces obtained in a long series of throws of the given die may depart widely from .15, it does logically imply that such departures are highly improbable in the statistical sense; i.e., that if the experiment of performing a long series of throws (say, 1,000 of them per series) is repeated a large number of times, then only a tiny proportion of those long series will yield a proportion of aces that differs considerably from .15. For the case of rolling a die, it is usually assumed that the results of successive throws are "statistically independent"; this means roughly that the probability of obtaining an ace in a throw of the die does not depend on the result of the preceding throw. Mathematical analysis shows that in conjunction with this independence assumption, our hypothesis *H* deductively determines the statistical probability for the proportion of aces obtained in *n* throws to differ from .15 by no more than a specified amount. For example, *H* implies that for a series of 1,000 throws of the die here considered, the probability is about .976 that the proportion of aces will lie between .125 and .175; and similarly, that for a run of 10,000 throws the probability is about .995 that the proportion of aces will be between .14 and .16. Thus, we may say that if *H* is true, then it is practically certain that in a long trial run the observed proportion of aces will differ by very little from the hypothetical probability value .15. Hence, if the observed long-run frequency of an outcome is not close to the probability assigned to it by a given probabilistic hypothesis, then that hypothesis is very likely to be false. In this case, the frequency data count as disconfirming the hypothesis, or as reducing its credibility; and if sufficiently strong disconfirming evidence is found, the hypothesis will be considered as practically, though not logically, refuted and will accordingly be rejected. Similarly, close agreement between hypothetical probabilities and observed frequencies will tend to confirm a probabilistic hypothesis and may lead to its acceptance.

If probabilistic hypotheses are to be accepted or rejected on the basis of statistical evidence concerning observed frequencies, then appropriate standards are called for. These will have to determine (a) what deviations of observed frequencies from the probability stated by a hypothesis are to count as grounds for rejecting the hypothesis, and (b) how close an agreement between observed frequencies and hypothetical probability is to be required as a condition for accepting the hypothesis. The requirements in question can be made more or less strict, and their specification is a matter of choice. The stringency of the chosen standards will normally vary with the context and the objectives of the research in question. Broadly speaking, it will depend on the importance that is attached, in the given context, to avoiding two kinds of error that might be made: rejecting the hypothesis under test although it is true, and accepting it although it is false. The importance of this point is particularly clear when acceptance or rejection of the hypothesis is to serve as a basis for practical action. Thus, if the hypothesis concerns the probable effectiveness and safety of a new vaccine, then the decision about its acceptance will have to take into account not only how well the statistical test results accord with the probabilities specified by the hypothesis, but also how serious would be the consequences of accepting the hypothesis and acting on it (e.g., by inoculating children with the vaccine) when in fact it is false, and of rejecting the hypothesis and acting accordingly (e.g., by destroying the vaccine and modifying or discontinuing the process of manufacture) when in fact the hypothesis is true. The complex problems that arise in this context form the subject matter of the theory of statistical tests and decisions, which has been developed in recent decades on the basis of the mathematical theory of probability and statistics[6]

Many important laws and theoretical principles in the natural sciences are of probabilistic character, though they are often of more complicated form than the simple probability statements we have discussed. For example, according to current physical theory, radioactive decay is a random phenomenon in which the atoms of each radioactive element possess a characteristic probability of disintegrating during a specified period of time. The corresponding probabilistic laws are usually formulated as statements giving the "half-life" of the element concerned. Thus, the statements that the half-life of radium[226] is 1,620 years and that of polonium[218] is 3.05 minutes are laws to the effect that the probability for a radium[226] atom to decay within 1,620 years, and for an atom of polonium[218] to decay within 3.05 minutes, are both one-half. According to the statistical interpretation cited earlier, these laws imply that of a large number of radium[226] atoms or of polonium[218] atoms given at a certain time, very close to one-half will still exist 1,620 years, or 3.05 minutes, later; the others having disintegrated by radioactive decay.

Again, in the kinetic theory various uniformities in the behavior of gases, including the laws of classical thermodynamics, are explained by means of certain assumptions about the constituent molecules; and some of these are probabilistic hypotheses concerning statistical regularities in the motions and collisions of those molecules.

A few additional remarks concerning the notion of a probabilistic law are indicated. It might seem that all scientific laws should be qualified as probabilistic since the supporting evidence we have for them is always a finite and logically inconclusive body of findings, which can confer upon them only a more or less high probability. But this argument misses the point that the distinction between laws of universal form and laws of probabilistic form does not refer to the strength of the evidential support for the two kinds of statements, but to their form, which reflects the logical character of the claim they make. A law of universal form is basically a statement to the effect that in *all* cases where conditions of kind F are realized, conditions of kind G are realized as well; a law of probabilistic form asserts, basically, that under certain conditions, constituting the performance of a random experiment R, a certain kind of outcome will occur in a specified percentage of cases. No matter whether true or false, well supported or poorly supported, these two types of claims are of a logically different character, and it is on this difference that our distinction is based.

As we saw earlier, a law of the universal form 'Whenever F then G' is by no means a brief, telescoped equivalent of a report stating for each occurrence of F so far examined that it was associated with an occurrence of G. Rather, it implies assertions also for all unexamined cases of F, past as well as present and future; also, it implies counterfactual and hypothetical conditionals which concern, so to speak "possible occurrences" of F: and it is just this characteristic that gives such laws their explanatory power. Laws of probabilistic form have an analogous status. The law stating that the radioactive decay of radium^{226} is a random process with an associated half-life of 1,620 years is plainly not tantamount to a report about decay rates that have been observed in certain samples of radium^{226}. It concerns the decaying process of any body of radium^{226}—past, present, or future; and it implies subjunctive and counterfactual conditionals, such as: if two particular lumps of radium^{226} were to be combined into one, the decay rates would remain the same as if the lumps had remained separate. Again, it is this characteristic that gives probabilistic laws their predictive and their explanatory force.

The Inductive Character of Probabilistic Explanation

One of the simplest kinds of probabilistic explanation is illustrated by our earlier example of Jim's catching the measles. The general form of that explanatory argument may be stated thus:

$$p(O, R) \text{ is close to } 1$$
$$i \text{ is a case of } R$$
$$\overline{\qquad\qquad\qquad\qquad} \text{ [makes highly probable]}$$
$$i \text{ is a case of } O$$

Now the high probability which, as indicated in brackets, the explanans confers upon the explanandum is surely not a statistical probability, for it characterizes a relation between sentences, not between (kinds of) events. We might say that the probability in question represents the rational credibility of the explanandum, given the information provided by the explanans; and as we noted earlier, in so far as this notion can be construed as a probability, it represents a logical or inductive probability.

In some simple cases, there is a natural and obvious way of expressing that probability in numerical terms. In an argument of the kind just considered, if the numerical value of $p(O, R)$ is specified, then it is reasonable to say that the inductive probability that the explanans confers upon the explanandum has the same numerical value. The resulting probabilistic explanation has the form:

$$p(O, R) = r$$
$$i \text{ is a case of } R$$
$$\overline{\hspace{3cm}} \ [r]$$
$$i \text{ is a case of } O$$

If the explanans is more complex, the determination of corresponding inductive probabilities for the explanandum raises difficult problems, which in part are still unsettled. But whether or not it is possible to assign definite numerical probabilities to all such explanations, the preceding considerations show that when an event is explained by reference to probabilistic laws, the explanans confers upon the explanandum only more or less strong inductive support. Thus, we may distinguish deductive-nomological from probabilistic explanations by saying that the former effect a deductive subsumption under laws of universal form, the latter an inductive subsumption under laws of probabilistic form.

It is sometimes said that precisely because of its inductive character, a probabilistic account does not explain the occurrence of an event, since the explanans does not logically preclude its nonoccurrence. But the important, steadily expanding role that probabilistic laws and theories play in science and its applications, makes it preferable to view accounts based on such principles as affording explanations as well, though of a less stringent kind than those of deductive-nomological form. Take, for example, the radioactive decay of a sample of one milligram of polonium^{218}. Suppose that what is left of this initial amount after 3.05 minutes is found to have a mass that falls within the interval from .499 to .501 milligrams. This finding can be explained by the probabilistic law of decay for polonium^{218}; for that law, in combination with the principles of mathematical probability, deductively implies that given the huge number of atoms in a milligram of polonium^{218}, the probability of the specified outcome is overwhelmingly large, so that in a particular case its occurrence may be expected with "practical certainty".

Or consider the explanation offered by the kinetic theory of gases for an empirically established generalization called Graham's law of diffusion. The law states that at fixed temperature and pressure, the rates at which different gases in a container escape, or diffuse, through a thin porous wall are inversely proportional to the square roots of their molecular weights; so that the amount of a gas that diffuses through the wall per second will be the greater, the lighter its molecules. The explanation rests on the consideration that the mass of a given gas that diffuses through the wall per second will be proportional to the average velocity of its molecules, and that Graham's law will therefore have been explained if it can be shown that the average molecular velocities of different pure gases are inversely proportional to the square roots of their molecular weights. To show this, the theory makes certain assumptions broadly to the effect that a gas consists of a very large number of molecules moving in random fashion at different speeds that frequently change as a result of collisions, and that this random behavior shows certain probabilistic uniformities—in particular, that among the molecules of a given gas at specified temperature and pressure, different velocities will occur with definite, and different, probabilities. These assumptions make it possible to compute the probabilistically expected values—or, as we might briefly say, the "most probable" values—that the average velocities of different gases will possess at equal temperatures and pressures. These most probable average values, the theory shows, are indeed inversely proportional to the square roots of the molecular weights of the gases. But the actual diffusion rates, which are measured experimentally and are the subject of Graham's law, will depend on the actual values that the average velocities have in the large but finite swarms of molecules constituting the given bodies of gas. And the actual average values are related to the corresponding probabilistically estimated, or "most probable", values in a manner that is basically analogous to the relation between the proportion of aces occurring in a large but finite series of tossings of a given die and the corresponding probability of rolling an ace with that die. From the theoretically derived conclusion concerning the probabilistic estimates, it follows only that in view of the very large number of molecules involved, it is overwhelmingly *probable* that at any given time the actual average speeds will have values very close to their probability estimates and that, therefore, it is *practically certain* that they will be, like the latter, inversely proportional to the square roots of their molecular masses, thus satisfying Graham's law.[7]

It seems reasonable to say that this account affords an explanation, even though "only" with very high associated probability, of why gases display the uniformity expressed by Graham's law; and in physical texts and treatises, theoretical accounts of this probabilistic kind are indeed very widely referred to as explanations.

Notes

1. From Holton and Roller, *Foundations of Modern Physical Science*, p. 160.
2. The derivation of the laws of reflection for the curved surfaces referred to in this example and in the next one is simply and lucidly set forth in Chap. 17 of Morris Kline, *Mathematics and the Physical World* (New York: Thomas Y. Crowell Company, 1959).
3. In his essay, "The Problem of Counterfactual Conditionals," reprinted as the first chapter of his book, *Fact, Fiction, and Forecast*, 2nd ed. (Indianapolis: The Bobbs-Merrill Co., Inc., 1965). This work raises fascinating basic problems concerning laws, counterfactual statements, and inductive reasoning, and examines them from an advanced analytic point of view.
4. For a fuller analysis of the concept of law, and for further bibliographic references, see E. Nagel, *The Structure of Science* (New York: Harcourt, Brace & World, Inc., 1961), Chap. 4.
5. Further details on the concept of statistical probability and on the limit-definition and its shortcomings will be found in E. Nagel's monograph, *Principles of the Theory of Probability* (Chicago: University of Chicago Press, 1939). Our version of the statistical interpretation follows that given by H. Cramér on pp. 148–49 of his book, *Mathematical Methods of Statistics* (Princeton: Princeton University Press, 1946).
6. On this subject, see R. D. Luce and H. Raiffa, *Games and Decisions* (New York: John Wiley & Sons, Inc., 1957).
7. The "average" velocities here referred to are technically defined as root-mean-square velocities. Their values do not differ very much from those of average velocities in the usual sense of the arithmetic mean. A succinct outline of the theoretical explanation of Graham's law can be found in Chap. 25 of Holton and Roller, *Foundations of Modern Physical Science*. The distinction, not explicitly mentioned in that presentation, between the average value of a quantity for some finite number of cases and the probabilistically estimated or expected value of that quantity is briefly discussed in Chap. 6 (especially section 4) of R. P. Feynman, R. B. Leighton, and M. Sands, *The Feynman Lectures on Physics* (Reading, Mass.: Addison-Wesley Publishing Co., 1963).

Chapter 17

The Pragmatics of Explanation

Bas van Fraassen

There are two problems about scientific explanation. The first is to describe it: when is something explained? The second is to show why (or in what sense) explanation is a virtue. Presumably we have no explanation unless we have a good theory; one which is independently worthy of acceptance. But what virtue is there in explanation over and above this? I believe that philosophical concern with the first problem has been led thoroughly astray by mistaken views on the second.

I. False Ideals

To begin I wish to dispute three ideas about explanation that seem to have a subliminal influence on the discussion. The first is that explanation is a relation simply between a theory or hypothesis and the phenomena or facts, just like truth for example. The second is that explanatory power cannot be logically separated from certain other virtues of a theory, notably truth or acceptability. And the third is that explanation is the overriding virtue, the end of scientific inquiry.

When is something explained? As a foil to the above three ideas, let me propose the simple answer: *when we have a theory which explains*. Note first that "have" is not "have on the books"; I cannot claim to have such a theory without implying that this theory is acceptable all told. Note also that both "have" and "explain" are tensed; and that I have allowed that we can have a theory which does not explain, or "have on the books" an unacceptable one that does. Newton's theory explained the tides but not the advance in the perihelion of mercury; we used to have an acceptable theory, provided by Newton, which bore (or bears timelessly?) the explanation relationship to some facts but not to all. My answer also implies that we can intelligibly say that the theory explains, and not merely that people can explain by means of the theory. But this consequence is not very restrictive, because the former could be an ellipsis for the latter.

There are questions of usage here. I am happy to report that the history of science allows systematic use of both idioms. In Huygens and Young the typical phrasing seemed to be that phenomenon may be explained *by means* of principles, laws, and hypotheses, or *according to* a view.[1] On the other hand, Fresnel writes to Arago in 1815 "Tous ces phénomènes ... sont réunis et expliqués par la même théorie des vibrations," and Lavoisier says that the oxygen hypothesis he proposes *explains* the phenomena of combustion.[2] Darwin also speaks in the latter idiom: "In scientific investigations it is permitted to invent any hypothesis, and if it explains various large and independent classes of facts it rises to the rank of a well-grounded theory"; though

Reprinted from *American Philosophical Quarterly* 14 (1977), pp. 143–150, by permission of the author and the publisher.

elsewhere he says that the facts of geographical distribution are *explicable* on the theory of migration.[3]

My answer did separate acceptance of the theory from its explanatory power. Of course, the second can be a reason for the first; but *that* requires their separation. Various philosophers have held that explanation logically requires true (or acceptable) theories as premises. Otherwise, they hold, we can at most mistakenly believe that we have an explanation.

This is also a question of usage, and again usage is quite clear. Lavoisier said of the phlogiston hypothesis that it is too vague and consequently "s'adapte a toutes les explications dans lesquelles on veut le faire entrer."[4] Darwin explicitly allows explanation by false theories when he says "It can hardly be supposed that a false theory would explain, in so satisfactory a manner as does the theory of natural selection, the several large classes of facts above specified."[5] More recently, Gilbert Harman has argued similarly: that a theory explains certain phenomena is part of the evidence that leads us to accept it. But that means that the explanation-relation is visible beforehand. Finally, we criticize theories selectively: a discussion of celestial mechanics around the turn of the century would surely contain the assertion that Newton's theory does explain many planetary phenomena, though not the advance in the perihelion of Mercury.

There is a third false ideal, which I consider worst: that explanation is the *summum bonum* and exact aim of science. A virtue could be overriding in one of two ways. The first is that it is a minimal criterion of acceptability. Such is consistency with the facts in the domain of application (though not necessarily with all data, if these are dubitable!). Explanation is not like that, or else a theory would not be acceptable at all unless it explained all facts in its domain. The second way in which a virtue may be overriding is that of being required when it can be had. This would mean that if two theories pass other tests (empirical adequacy, simplicity) equally well, then the one which explains more must be accepted. As I have argued elsewhere,[6] and as we shall see in connection with Salmon's views below, a precise formulation of this demand requires hidden variables for indeterministic theories. But of course, hidden variables are rejected in scientific practice as so much "metaphysical baggage" when they make no difference in empirical predictions.

II. A Biased History

I will outline the attempts to characterize explanation of the past three decades, with no pretense of objectivity. On the contrary, the selection is meant to illustrate the diagnosis, and point to the solution, of the next section.

1. Hempel

In 1966, Hempel summarized his views by listing two main criteria for explanation. The first is the criterion of *explanatory relevance*: "the explanatory information adduced affords good grounds for believing that the phenomenon to be explained did, or does, indeed occur."[7] That information has two components, one supplied by the scientific theory, the other consisting of auxiliary factual information. The relationship of providing good grounds is explicated as (a) implying (D-N case), or (b) conferring a high probability (I-S case), which is not lowered by the addition of other (available) evidence.

As Hempel points out, this criterion is not a sufficient condition for explanation: the red-shift gives us good grounds for believing that distant galaxies are receding from us, but does not explain why they do. The classic case is the *barometer example*: the storm will come exactly if the barometers fall, which they do exactly if the atmospheric conditions are of the correct sort; yet only the last factor explains. Nor is the criterion a necessary condition; for this the classic case is the *paresis example*. We explain why the mayor, alone among the townsfolk, contracted paresis by his history of latent, contracted syphilis; yet such histories are followed by paresis in only a small percentage of cases.

The second criterion is the requirement of *testability*; but since all serious candidates for the role of scientific theory meet this, it cannot help to remove the noted defects.

2. Beckner, Putnam, and Salmon

The criterion of explanatory relevance was revised in one direction, informally by Beckner and Putnam and precisely by Salmon. Morton Beckner, in his discussion of evolution theory, pointed out that this often explains a phenomenon only by showing how it could have happened, given certain possible conditions.[8] Evolutionists do this by constructing models of processes which utilize only genetic and natural selection mechanisms, in which the outcome agrees with the actual phenomenon. Parallel conclusions were drawn by Hilary Putnam about the way in which celestial phenomena are explained by Newton's theory of gravity: celestial motions could indeed be as they are, given a certain possible (though not, known) distribution of masses in the universe.[9]

We may take the paresis example to be explained similarly. Mere consistency with the theory is of course much too weak, since that is implied by logical irrelevance. Hence Wesley Salmon made this precise as follows: to explain is to exhibit (the) statistically relevant factors.[10] (I shall leave till later the qualifications about "screening off.") Since this sort of explication discards the talk about modeling and mechanisms of Beckner and Putnam, it may not capture enough. And indeed, I am not satisfied with Salmon's arguments that his criterion provides a sufficient condition. He gives the example of an equal mixture of uranium[238] atoms and polonium[214] atoms, which makes the Geiger counter click in interval $(t, t + m)$. This means that one of the atoms disintegrated. Why did it? The correct answer will be: because it was a uranium[238] atom, if that so—although the probability of its disintegration is much higher relative to the previous knowledge that the atom belonged to the described mixture.[11] The problem with this argument is that, on Salmon's criterion, we can explain not only why there was a disintegration, but also why *that* atom disintegrated *just then*. And surely that is exactly one of those facts which atomic physics leaves unexplained?

But there is a more serious general criticism. Whatever the phenomenon is, we can amass the statistically relevant factors, as long as the theory does not rule out the phenomenon altogether. "What more could one ask of an explanation?" Salmon inquires.[12] But in that case, as soon as we have an empirically adequate theory, we have an explanation of every fact in its domain. We may claim an explanation as soon as we have shown that the phenomenon can be embedded in some model allowed by the theory—that is, does not throw doubt on the theory's empirical adequacy.[13] But surely that is too sanguine?

3. Global Properties

Explanatory power cannot be identified with empirical adequacy; but it may still reside in the performance of the theory as a whole. This view is accompanied by the conviction that science does not explain individual facts but general regularities and was developed in different ways by Michael Friedman and James Greeno. Friedman says explicitly that in his view, "the kind of understanding provided by science is global rather than local" and consists in the simplification and unification imposed on our world picture.[14] That S_1 explains S_2 is a conjunction of two facts: S_1 implies S_2 relative to our background knowledge (and/or belief) K, *and* S_1 unifies and simplifies the set of its consequences relative to K. Friedman will no doubt wish to weaken the first condition in view of Salmon's work.

The precise explication Friedman gives of the second condition does not work, and is not likely to have a near variant that does.[15] But here we may look at Greeno's proposal.[16] His abstract and closing statement subscribe to the same general view as Friedman. But he takes as his model of a theory one which specifies a single probability space Q as the correct one, plus two partitions (or random variables) of which one is designated *explanandum* and the other *explanans*. An example: sociology cannot explain why Albert, who lives in San Francisco and whose father has a high income, steals a car. Nor is it meant to. But it does explain delinquency in terms of such other factors as residence and parental income. The degree of explanatory power is measured by an ingeniously devised quantity which measures the information I the theory provides of the explanandum variable M on the basis of explanans S. This measure takes its maximum value if all conditional probabilities $P(M_i/S_j)$ are zero or one (D-N case), and its minimum value zero if S and M are statistically independent.

Unfortunately, this way of measuring the unification imposed on our data abandons Friedman's insight that scientific understanding cannot be identified as a function of grounds for rational explanatory power cannot be identified with expectation. For if we let S and M describe the empirical adequacy; but it may still reside in the behavior of the barometer and coming storms, with $P(\text{barometer falls}) = P(\text{storm comes}) = 0.2$, $P(\text{storm comes/barometer falls}) = 1$, and $P(\text{storm comes/barometer does not fall}) = 0$, then the quantity I takes its maximum value. Indeed, it does so whether we designate M or S as explanans.

It would seem that such asymmetries as exhibited by the red-shift and barometer examples must necessarily remain recalcitrant for any attempt to strengthen Hempel's or Salmon's criteria by global restraints on theories alone.

4. The Major Difficulties

There are two main difficulties, illustrated by the old paresis and barometer examples, which none of the examined positions can handle. The first is that there are cases, clearly in a theory's domain, where the request for explanation is nevertheless rejected. We can explain why John, rather than his brothers contracted paresis, for he had syphilis; but not why he, among all those syphilitics, got paresis. Medical science is incomplete, and hopes to find the answer some day. But the example of the uranium atom disintegrating just then rather than later, is formally similar and we believe the theory to be complete. We also reject such questions as the Aristotelians asked the Galileans: why does a body free of impressed forces retain its velocity? The importance of this sort of case, and its pervasive character, has been repeatedly discussed by Adolf Grünbaum.

The second difficulty is the asymmetry revealed by the barometer: even if the theory implies that one condition obtains when and only when another does, it may be that it explains the one in terms of the other and not vice versa.; An example which combines both the first and second difficulty is this: according to atomic physics, each chemical element has a characteristic atomic structure and a characteristic spectrum (of light emitted upon excitation). Yet the spectrum is explained by the atomic structure, and the question why a substance has that structure does not arise at all (except in the trivial sense that the questioner may need to have the terms explained to him).

5. Causality

Why are there no longer any Tasmanian natives? Well, they were a nuisance, so the white settlers just kept shooting them till there were none left. The request was not for population statistics, but for the story; though in some truncated way, the statistics "tell" the story.

In a later paper Salmon gives a primary place to causal mechanisms in explanation.[17] Events are bound into causal chains by two relations: spatio-temporal continuity and statistical relevance. Explanation requires the exhibition of such chains. Salmon's point of departure is Reichenbach's *principle of the common cause*: every relation of statistical relevance ought to be explained by one of causal relevance. This means that a correlation of simultaneous values must be explained by a prior common cause. Salmon gives two statistical conditions that must be met by a common cause C of events A and B:

(a) $P(A \text{ \& } B/C) = P(A/C)P(B/C)$

(b) $P(A/B \text{ \& } C) = P(A/C)$ "C screens off B from A."

If $P(B/C) \neq 0$ these are equivalent, and symmetric in A and B.

Suppose that explanation is typically the demand for a common cause. Then we still have the problem: when does this arise? Atmospheric conditions explain the correlation between barometer and storm, say; but are still prior causes required to explain the correlation between atmospheric conditions and falling barometers?

In the quantum domain, Salmon says, causality is violated because "causal influence is not transmitted with spatio-temporal continuity." But the situation is worse. To assume Reichenbach's principle to be satisfiable, continuity aside, is to rule out all genuinely indeterministic theories. As example, let a theory say that C is invariably followed by one of the incompatible events A, B, or D, each with probability $1/3$. Let us suppose the theory complete, and its probabilities irreducible, with C the complete specification of state. Then we will find a correlation for which only C could be the common cause, but it is not. Assuming that A, B, D are always preceded by C and that they have low but equal prior probabilities, there is a statistical correlation between $\phi = (A \text{ or } D)$ and $\psi = (B \text{ or } D)$, for $P(\phi/\psi) = P(\psi/\phi) = 1/2 \neq P(\phi)$. But C, the only available candidate, does not screen off ϕ from ψ: $P(\phi/C \text{ \& } \psi) = P(\phi/\psi) = 1/2 \neq P(\phi/C)$ which is $2/3$. Although this may sound complicated, the construction is so general that almost any irreducibly probabilistic situation will give a similar example. Thus Reichenbach's *principle of the common cause* is in fact a demand for hidden variables.

Yet we retain the feeling that Salmon has given an essential clue to the asymmetries of explanation. For surely the crucial point about the barometer is that the atmospheric conditions screen off the barometer fall from the storm? The general point that the asymmetries are totally bound up with causality was argued in a provocative article by B. A. Brody.[18] Aristotle certainly discussed examples of asymmetries: the planets do not twinkle because they are near, yet they are near if and only if they do not twinkle (*Posterior Analytics*, I, 13). Not all explanations are causal, says Brody, but the others use a second Aristotelian notion, that of essence. The spectrum angle is a clear case: sodium has that spectrum because it has this atomic structure, which is its essence.

Brody's account has the further advantage that he can say when questions do not arise: other properties are explained in terms of essence, but the request for an explanation of the essence does not arise. However, I do not see how he would distinguish between the questions why the uranium atom disintegrated and why it disintegrated just then. In addition there is the problem that modern science is not formulated in terms of causes and essences, and it seems doubtful that these concepts can be redefined in terms which do occur there.

6. Why-Questions

A why-question is a request for explanation. Sylvain Bromberger called P the *presupposition* of the question *Why-P?* and restated the problem of explanation as that of giving the conditions under which proposition Q is a correct answer to a why-question with presupposition P.[19] However, Bengt Hannson has pointed out that "Why was it John who ate the apple?" and "Why was it the apple which John ate?: are different why-questions, although the comprised proposition is the same.[20] The difference can be indicated by such phrasing, or by emphasis ("Why did *John* ...?") or by an auxiliary clause ("Why did John rather than ...?"). Hannson says that an explanation is requested, not of a proposition or fact, but of an *aspect* of a proposition.

As is at least suggested by Hannson, we can cover all these cases by saying that we wish an explanation of why P is true in contrast to other members of a set X or propositions. This explains the tension in our reaction to the paresis-example. The question why the mayor, in contrast to other townfolk generally, contracted paresis *has* a true correct answer: because of his latent syphilis. But the question why he did in contrast to the other syphilitics in his country club, has no true correct answer. Intuitively we may say: Q is a correct answer to *Why P in contrast to X?* only if Q gives reasons to expect that P, in contrast to the other members of X. Hannson's proposal for a precise criterion is: the probability of P given Q is higher than the average of the probabilities of R given Q, for members R of X.

Hannson points out that the set X of alternatives is often left tacit; the two questions about paresis might well be expressed by the same sentence in different contexts. The important point is that explanations are not requested of propositions, and consequently a distinction can be drawn between answered and rejected requests in a clear way. However, Hannson makes Q a correct answer to *Why P in contrast to X?* when Q is statistically irrelevant, when P is already more likely than the rest; or when Q implies P but not the others. I do not see how he can handle the barometer (or red shift, or spectrum) asymmetries. On his precise criterion, that the barometer fell is a correct answer to why it will storm as opposed to be calm. The difficulty is very deep: if P and R are necessarily equivalent, according to our accepted theories, how can *Why P in contrast to X?* be distinguished from *Why R in contrast to X?*

III. The Solution

1. Prejudices

Two convictions have prejudiced the discussion of explanation, one methodological and one substantive.

The first is that a philosophical account must aim to produce necessary and sufficient conditions for theory T explaining phenomenon E. A similar prejudice plagued the discussion of counter-factuals for twenty years, requiring the exact conditions under which, if A were the case, B would be. Stalnaker's liberating insight was that these conditions are largely determined by context and speaker's interest. This brings the central question to light: what *form* can these conditions take?

The second conviction is that explanatory power is a virtue of theories by them-selves, or of their relation to the world, like simplicity, predictive strength, truth, empirical adequacy. There is again an analogy with counterfactuals: it used to be thought that science contains, or directly implies, counterractuals. In all but limiting cases, however, the proposition expressed is highly context-dependent, and the impli-cation is there at most relative to the determining contextual factors, such as speakers' interest.

2. Diagnosis

The earlier accounts lead us to the format: C explains E relative to theory T exactly if (a) T has certain global virtues, and (b) T implies a certain proposition $\phi(C, E)$ expres-sible in the language of logic and probability theory. Different accounts directed themselves to the specification of what should go into (a) and (b). We may add, following Beckner and Putnam, that T explains E exactly if there is a proposition C consistent with T (and presumably, background beliefs) such that C explains E relative to T.

The significant modifications were proposed by Hannson and Brody. The former pointed out that the explanadum E cannot be reified as a proposition: we request the explanation of something F in contrast to its alternatives X (the latter generally tacitly specified by context). This modification is absolutely necessary to handle some of our puzzles. It requires that in (b) above we replace "$\phi(C, E)$" by the formula form "$\psi(C, F, X)$." But the problem of asymmetries remains recalcitrant, because if T implies the necessary equivalence of F and F' (say, atomic structure and characteristic spec-trum), then T will also imply $\psi(C, F', X)$ if and only if it implies $\psi(C, F, X)$.

The only account we have seen which grapples at all successfully with this, is Brody's. For Brody points out that even properties which we believe to be constantly conjoined in all possible circumstances, can be divided into essences and accidents, or related as cause and effect. In this sense, the asymmetries were no problem for Aristotle.

3. The Logical Problem

We have now seen exactly what logical problem is posed by the asymmetries. To put it in current terms: how can we distinguish propositions which are true in exactly the same possible worlds?

There are several known approaches that use impossible worlds. David Lewis, in his discussion of causality, suggests that we should look not only to the worlds theory T allows as possible, but also to those it rules out as impossible, and speaks of counterractuals which are counterlegal. Relevant logic and entailment draw distinc-tions between logically equivalent sentences and their semantics devised by Routley and Meyer use both inconsistent and incomplete worlds. I believe such approaches to be totally inappropriate for the problem of explanation, for when we look at actual explanations of phenomena by theories, we do not see any detours through circum-stances or events ruled out as impossible by the theory.

A further approach, developed by Rolf Schock, Romane Clark, and myself distin-guishes sentences by the facts that make them true. The idea is simple. That it rains, that it does not rain, that it snows, and that it does not snow, are four distinct facts. The disjunction that it rains or does not rain is made true equally by the first and second, and not by the third or fourth, which distinguishes it from the logically equivalent disjunction that it snows or does not snow.[21] The distinction remains even if there is also a fact of its raining or not raining, distinct or identical with that of its snowing or not snowing.

This approach can work for the asymmetries of explanation. Such asymmetries are possible because, for example, the distinct facts that light is emitted with wavelengths λ, μ, ... conjointly make up thc characteristic spectrum, while quite different facts conjoin to make up the atomic structure. So we have shown how such asymmetries *can* arise, in the way that Stalnaker showed how failures of transitivity in counterfactuals *can* arise. But while we have the distinct facts to classify asymmetrically, we still have the non-logical problem: whence comes the classification? The only suggestion so far is that it comes from Aristotle's concepts of cause and essence; but if so, modern science will not supply it.

4. *The Aristotelian Sieve*

I believe that we should return to Aristotle more thoroughly, and in two ways. To begin, I will state without argument how I understand Aristotle's theory of science. Scientific activity is divided into two parts, *demonstration* and *explanation*, the former treated mainly by the *Posterior Analytics* and the latter mainly by Book II of the *Physics*. Illustrations in the former are mainly examples of explanations in which the results of demonstration are *applied*; this is why the examples contain premises and conclusions which are not necessary and universal principles, although demonstration is only to and from such principles. Thus the division corresponds to our pure versus applied science. There is no reason to think that principles and demonstrations have such words as "cause" and "essence" in them, although looking at pure science from outside, Aristotle could say that its principles state causes and essences. In applications, the principles may be filtered through a conceptual sieve originating outside science.

The doctrine of the four "causes" (*aitiai*) allows for the systematic ambiguity or context-dependence of why-questions.[22] Aristotle's example (Physics II, 3; 195a) is of a lantern. In a modern example, the question why the porch light is on may be answered "because I flipped the switch" or "because we are expecting company," and the context determines which is appropriate. Probabilistic relations cannot distinguish these. Which factors are explanatory is decided not by features of the scientific theory but by concerns brought from outside. This is true even if we ask specifically for an "efficient cause," for how far back in the chain should we look, and which factors are merely auxiliary contributors?

Aristotle would not have agreed that essence is context-dependent. The essence is what the thing *is*, hence, its sum of classificatory properties. Realism has always asserted that ontological distinctions determine the "natural" classification. But which property is counted as explanatory and which as explained seems to me clearly context dependent. For consider Bromberger's flagpole example: the shadow is so long because the pole has this height, and not conversely. At first sight, no contextual factor could reverse this asymmetry, because the pole's height is a property it has in and by itself, and its shadow is a very accidental feature. The general principle linking the two is that its shadow is a function $f(x, t)$ of its height x and the time t (the latter determining the sun's elevation). But imagine the pole is the pointer on a giant sundial. Then the values of f have desired properties for each time t, and we appeal to these to explain why it is (had to be) such a tall pole.

We may again draw a parallel to counterfactuals. Professor Geach drew my attention to the following spurious argument: If John asked his father for money, then they would not have quarreled (because John is too proud to ask after a quarrel). Also if John asked and they hadn't quarreled, he would receive. By the usual logic of counterfactuals, it follows that if John asked his father for money, he would receive. But we know that he would not, because they have in fact quarreled. The fallacy is of equivocation, because "what was kept constant" changed in the middle of the monologue. (Or if you like, the aspects by which worlds are graded as more or less similar to this one.) Because science cannot dictate what speakers decide to "keep constant" it contains no counterfactuals By exact parallel, *science contains no explanations*.

5. The Logic of Why-Questions

What remains of the problem of explanation is to study its logic, which is the logic of why-questions. This can be put to some extent, but not totally, in the general form developed by Harrah and Belnap and others.[23]

A question admits of three classes of response, *direct answer, corrections,* and *comments*. A *presupposition*, it has been held, is any proposition implied by all direct answers, or equivalently, denied by a correction. I believe we must add that the question "Why P, in contrast to X?" also presupposes that (a) P is a member of X, (b) P is true and the majority of X are not. This opens the door to the possibility that a question may not be uniquely determined by its set of direct answers. The question itself should decompose into factors which determine that set: the *topic P*, the *alternatives X*, and a *request specification* (of which the doctrine of the four "causes" is perhaps the first description).

We have seen that the propositions involved in question and answer must be individuated by something more than the set of possible worlds. I propose that we use the facts that make them true (see footnote 21). The context will determine an asymmetric relation among these facts, of *explanatory relevance*; it will also determine the theory or beliefs which determine which worlds are *possible*, and what is *probable* relative to what.

We must now determine what direct answers are and how they are evaluated. They must be made true by facts (and only by facts forcing such) which are explanatorily relevant to those which make the topic true. Moreover, these facts must be statistically relevant, telling for the topic in contrast to the alternatives generally; this part I believe to be explicable by probabilities, combining Salmon's and Hannson's account. How strongly the answers count for the topic should be part of their evaluation as better or worse answers.

The main difference from such simple questions as "Which cat is on the mat ?" lies in the relation of a why-question to its presuppositions. A why-question may fail to arise because it is ill-posed (P is false, or most of X is true), or because only question-begging answers tell probabilistically for P in contrast to X generally, or because none of the factors that do tell for P are explanatorily relevant in the question-context. Scientific theory enters mainly in the evaluation of possibilities and probabilities, which is only part of the process, and which it has in common with other applications such as prediction and control.

IV. Simple Pleasures

There are no explanations in science. How did philosophers come to mislocate explanation among semantic rather than pragmatic relations? This was certainly in part because the positivists tended to identify the pragmatic with subjective psychological features. They looked for measures by which to evaluate theories. Truth and empirical adequacy are such, but they are weak, being preserved when a theory is watered down. Some measure of "goodness of fit" was also needed, which did not reduce to a purely internal criterion such as simplicity, but concerned the theory's relation to the world. The studies of explanation have gone some way toward giving us such a measure, but it was a mistake to call this explanatory power. The fact that seemed to confirm this error was that we do not say that we *have* an explanation unless we have a theory which is acceptable, and victorious in its competition with alternatives, whereby we can explain. Theories are applied in explanation, but the peculiar and puzzling features of explanation are supplied by other factors involved. I shall now redescribe several familiar subjects from this point of view.

When a scientist campaigns on behalf of an advocated theory, he will point out how our situation will change if we accept it. Hitherto unsuspected factors become relevant, known relations are revealed to be strands of an intricate web, some terribly puzzling questions are laid to rest as not arising at all. We shall be in a much better position to explain. But equally, we shall be in a much better position to predict and control. The features of the theory that will make this possible are its empirical adequacy and logical strength, not special "explanatory power" and "control power." On the other hand, it is also a mistake to say explanatory power is nothing but those other features, for then we are defeated by asymmetries having no "objective" basis in science.

Why are *new* predictions so much more to the credit of a theory than agreement with the old? Because they tend to bring to light new phenomena which the older theories cannot explain. But of course, in doing so, they throw doubt on the empirical adequacy of the older theory: they show that a precondition for explanation is not met. As Boltzmann said of the radiometer, "the theories based on older hydrodynamic experience can never describe" these phenomena.[24] The failure in explanation is a by-product.

Scientific inference is inference to the best explanation. That does not rule at all for the supremacy of explanation among the virtues of theories. For we evaluate how good an explanation is given by how good a theory is used to give it, how close it fits to the empirical facts, how internally simple and coherent the explanation. There is a further evaluation in terms of a prior judgment of which kinds of factors are explanatorily relevant. If this further evaluation took precedence, overriding other considerations, explanation would be the peculiar virtue sought above all. But this is not so: instead, science schools our imagination so as to revise just those prior judgments of what satisfies and eliminates wonder.

Explanatory power is something we value and desire. But we are as ready, for the sake of scientific progress, to dismiss questions as not really arising at all. Explanation is indeed a virtue; but still, less a virtue than an anthropocentric pleasure.[25]

Notes

1. I owe these and following references to my student Paul Thagrad. For instance see C. Huygens, *Treatise on Light*, tr. by S. P. Thompson (New York, 1962), pp. 19, 20, 22, 63; Thomas Young, *Miscellaneous* Works, ed. by George Peacock (London, 1855), Vol. I, pp. 168, 170.

2. Augustin Fresnel, *Oeuvres Complètes* (Paris, 1866), Vol. I, p. 36 (see also pp. 254, 355); Antoine Lavoisier, *Oeuvres* (Paris, 1862), Vol. II, p. 233.

3. Charles Darwin, *The Variation of Animals and Plants* (London, 1868), Vol. I, p. 9; *On the Origin of the Species* (Facs. of first edition, Cambridge, Mass., 1964), p. 408.

4. Antoine Lavoisier, *op. cit.*, p. 640.

5. *Origin* (sixth ed., New York, 1962), p. 476.

6. "Wilfrid Sellars on Scientific Realism," *Dialogue*, vol. 14 (1975), pp. 606–616.

7. C. G. Hempel, *Philosophy of Natural Science* (Englewood Cliffs, New Jersey, 1966), p. 48.

8. *The Biological Way of Thought* (Berkeley, 1968), p. 176; this was first published in 1959.

9. In a paper of which a summary is found in Frederick Suppe (ed.), *The Structure of Scientific Theories* (Urbana, Ill., 1974).

10. "Statistical Explanation," pp. 173–231 in R. G. Colodny (ed.) *The Nature and Function of Scientific Theories* (Pittsburgh, 1970); reprinted also in Salmon's book cited below.

11. *Ibid.*, pp. 207–209. Nancy Cartwright has further, unpublished, counterexamples to the necessity and sufficiency of Salmon's criterion.

12. *Ibid.*, p. 222.

13. These concepts are discussed in my "To Save the Phenomena," this volume, chapter 10.

14. "Explanation and Scientific Understanding," *The Journal of Philosophy*, vol. 71 (1974), pp. 5–19.

15. See Philip Kitcher, "Explanation, Conjunction, and Unification," *The Journal of Philosophy*, vol. 73 (1976), pp. 207–212.

16. "Explanation and Information," pp. 89–103 in Wesley Salmon (ed.), *Statistical Explanation and Statistical Relevance* (Pittsburgh, 1971). This paper was originally published with a different title in *Philosophy of Science*, vol. 37 (1970), pp. 279–293.

17. "Theoretical Explanation," pp. 118–145 in Stephan Körner (ed.), *Explanation* (Oxford, 1975).

18. "Towards an Aristotelian Theory of Scientific Explanation," *Philosophy of Science*, vol. 39 (1972), pp. 20–31.

19. "Why-Questions," pp. 86–108 in R. G. Colodny (ed.), *Mind and Cosmos* (Pittsburgh, 1966).

20. "Explanations—Of What?" (mimeographed: Stanford University, 1974).

21. Cf. my "Facts and Tautological Entailments," *The Journal of Philosophy*, vol. 66 (1969), pp. 477–487 and in A. R. Anderson, *et al*, (ed.), *Entailment* (Princeton, 1975); and "Extension, Intension, and Comprehension" in Milton Munitz (ed.), *Logic and Ontology* (New York, 1973).

22. Cf. Julius Moravcik, "Aristotle on Adequate Explanations," *Synthese*, vol. 28 (1974), pp. 3–18.

23. Cf. N. D. Belnap, Jr., "Questions: Their Presuppositions, and How They Can Fail to Arise," *The Logical Way of Doing Things*, ed. by Karel Lambert (New Haven, 1969), pp. 23–39.

24. Ludwig Boltzmann, *Lectures on Gas Theory*, tr. by S. G. Brush (Berkeley, 1964), p. 25.

25. The author wishes to acknowledge helpful discussions and correspondence with Professors N. Cartwright, B. Hannson, K. Lambert, and W. Salmon, and the financial support of the Canada Council.

Chapter 18

Explanatory Unification

Philip Kitcher

1. The Decline and Fall of the Covering Law Model

One of the great apparent triumphs of logical empiricism was its official theory of explanation. In a series of lucid studies (Hempel 1965, Chapters 9, 10, 12; Hempel 1962; Hempel 1966), C. G. Hempel showed how to articulate precisely an idea which had received a hazy formulation from traditional empiricists such as Hume and Mill. The picture of explanation which Hempel presented, the *covering law model*, begins with the idea that explanation is derivation. When a scientist explains a phenomenon, he derives (deductively or inductively) a sentence describing that phenomenon (the *explanandum* sentence) from a set of sentences (the *explanans*) which must contain at least one general law.

Today the model has fallen on hard times. Yet it was never the empiricists' whole story about explanation. Behind the official model stood an unofficial model, a view of explanation which was not treated precisely, but which sometimes emerged in discussions of theoretical explanation. In contrasting scientific explanation with the idea of reducing unfamiliar phenomena to familiar phenomena, Hempel suggests this unofficial view: "What scientific explanation, especially theoretical explanation, aims at is not an intuitive and highly subjective kind of understanding, but an objective kind of insight that is achieved by a systematic unification, by exhibiting the phenomena as manifestations of common, underlying structures and processes that conform to specific, testable, basic principles" (Hempel 1966, p. 83; see also Hempel 1965, pp. 345, 444). Herbert Feigl makes a similar point: "The aim of scientific explanation throughout the ages has been *unification*, that is, the comprehending of a maximum of facts and regularities in terms of a minimum of theoretical concepts and assumptions" (Feigl 1970, p. 12).

This unofficial view, which regards explanation as unification, is, I think, more promising than the official view. My aim in this paper is to develop the view and to present its virtues. Since the picture of explanation which results is rather complex, my exposition will be programmatic, but I shall try to show that the unofficial view can avoid some prominent shortcomings of the covering law model.

Why should we want an account of scientific explanation? Two reasons present themselves. Firstly, we would like to understand and to evaluate the popular claim that the natural sciences do not merely pile up unrelated items of knowledge of more or less practical significance, but that they increase our understanding of the world. A theory of explanation should show us *how* scientific explanation advances our understanding. (Michael Friedman cogently presents this demand in his (1974)). Secondly, an account of explanation ought to enable us to comprehend and to arbitrate

Reprinted from *Philosophy of Science* 48, (1981) pp. 507–531, by permission of the author and the Philosophy of Science Association.

disputes in past and present science. Embryonic theories are often defended by appeal to their explanatory power. A theory of explanation should enable us to judge the adequacy of the defense.

The covering law model satisfies neither of these *desiderata*. Its difficulties stem from the fact that, when it is viewed as providing a set of necessary *and sufficient* conditions for explanation, it is far too liberal. Many derivations which are intuitively non-explanatory meet the conditions of the model. Unable to make relatively gross distinctions, the model is quite powerless to adjudicate the more subtle considerations about explanatory adequacy which are the focus of scientific debate. Moreover, our ability to derive a description of a phenomenon from a set of premises *containing a law* seems quite tangential to our understanding of the phenomenon. Why should it be that exactly those derivations which employ laws advance our understanding?

The unofficial theory appears to do better. As Friedman points out, we can easily connect the notion of unification with that of understanding. (However, as I have argued in my (1976), Friedman's analysis of unification is faulty; the account of unification offered below is indirectly defended by my diagnosis of the problems for his approach.) Furthermore, as we shall see below, the acceptance of some major programs of scientific research—such as, the Newtonian program of eighteenth-century physics and chemistry, and the Darwinian program of nineteenth-century biology—depended on recognizing promises for unifying, and thereby explaining, the phenomena. Reasonable skepticism may protest at this point that the attractions of the unofficial view stem from its unclarity. Let us see.

2. Explanation: Some Pragmatic Issues

Our first task is to formulate the problem of scientific explanation clearly, filtering out a host of issues which need not concern us here. The most obvious way in which to categorize explanation is to view it as an activity. In this activity we answer the actual or anticipated questions of an actual or anticipated audience. We do so by presenting reasons. We draw on the beliefs we hold, frequently using or adapting arguments furnished to us by the sciences.

Recognizing the connection between explanations and arguments, proponents of the covering law model (and other writers on explanation) have identified explanations as special types of arguments. But although I shall follow the covering law model in employing the notion of argument to characterize that of explanation, I shall not adopt the ontological thesis that explanations are arguments. Following Peter Achinstein's thorough discussion of ontological issues concerning explanation in his (1977), I shall suppose that an explanation is an ordered pair consisting of a proposition and an act type.[1] The relevance of arguments to explanation resides in the fact that what makes an ordered pair (p, explaining q) an explanation is that a sentence expressing p bears an appropriate relation to a particular argument. (Achinstein shows how the central idea of the covering law model can be viewed in this way.) So I am supposing that there are acts of explanation which draw on arguments supplied by science, re-formulating the traditional problem of explanation as the question: What features should a scientific argument have if it is to serve as the basis for an act of explanation?[2]

The complex relation between scientific explanation and scientific argument may be illuminated by a simple example. Imagine a mythical Galileo confronted by a mythical fusilier who wants to know why his gun attains maximum range when it is mounted on a flat plain, if the barrel is elevated at 45° to the horizontal. Galileo reformulates this question as the question of why an ideal projectile, projected with fixed velocity from a perfectly smooth horizontal plane and subject only to gravitational acceleration, attains maximum range when the angle of elevation of the projection is 45°. He defends this reformulation by arguing that the effects of air resistance in the case of the actual projectile, the cannonball, are insignificant, and that the curvature of the earth and the unevenness of the ground can be neglected. He then selects a kinematical argument which shows that, for fixed velocity, an ideal projectile attains maximum range when the angle of elevation is 45°. He adapts this argument by explaining to the fusilier some unfamiliar terms ("uniform acceleration," let us say), motivating some problematic principles (such as the law of composition of velocities). and by omitting some obvious computational steps. Both Galileo and the fusilier depart satisfied.

The most general problem of scientific explanation is to determine the conditions which must be met if science is to be used in answering an explanation-seeking question Q. I shall restrict my attention to explanation-seeking why-questions, and I shall attempt to determine the conditions under which an argument whose conclusion is S can be used to answer the question "Why is it the case that S?" More colloquially, my project will be that of deciding when an argument explains why its conclusion is true.[3]

We leave on one side a number of interesting, and difficult issues. So, for example, I shall not discuss the general relation between explanation-seeking questions and the arguments which can be used to answer them, nor the pragmatic conditions governing the idealization of questions and the adaptation of scientific arguments to the needs of the audience. (For illuminating discussions of some of these issues, see Bromberger 1962.) Given that so much is dismissed, does anything remain?

In a provocative article. (van Fraassen 1977) Bas van Fraassen denies, in effect, that there are any issues about scientific explanation other than the pragmatic questions I have just banished. After a survey of attempts to provide a theory of explanation he appears to conclude that the idea that explanatory power is a special virtue of theories is a myth. We accept scientific theories on the basis of their empirical adequacy and simplicity, and, having done so, we use the arguments with which they supply us to give explanations. This activity of applying scientific arguments in explanation accords with extra-scientific, "pragmatic," conditions. Moreover, our views about these extra-scientific factors are revised in the light of our acceptance of new theories: "... science schools our imagination so as to revise just those prior judgments of what satisfies and eliminates wonder" (van Fraassen 1977, p. 150). Thus there are no context-independent conditions, beyond those of simplicity and empirical adequacy which distinguish arguments for use in explanation.

Van Fraassen's approach does not fit well with some examples from the history of science—such as the acceptance of Newtonian theory of matter and Darwin's theory of evolution—examples in which the explanatory promise of a theory was appreciated in advance of the articulation of a theory with predictive power. (See pp. 170–172.) Moreover, the account I shall offer provides an answer to skepticism that no "global constraints" (van Fraassen 1977, p. 146) on explanation can avoid the familiar problems of asymmetry and irrelevance, problems which bedevil the covering law model. I shall try to respond to van Fraassen's challenge by showing that there are certain context-independent features of arguments which distinguish them for application in response to explanation-seeking why-questions, and that we can assess theories (including embryonic theories) by their ability to provide us with such arguments. Hence I think that it is possible to defend the thesis that historical appeals to the explanatory power of theories involve recognition of a virtue over and beyond considerations of simplicity and predictive power.

Resuming our main theme, we can use the example of Galileo and the fusilier to achieve a further refinement of our problem. Galileo selects and adapts an argument from his new kinematics—that is, he draws an argument from a set of arguments available for explanatory purposes, a set which I shall call the *explanatory store*. We may think of the sciences not as providing us with many unrelated individual arguments which can be used in individual acts of explanation, but as offering a reserve of explanatory arguments, which we may tap as need arises. Approaching the issue in this way, we shall be led to present our problem as that of specifying the conditions which must be met by the explanatory store.

The set of arguments which science supplies for adaptation acts of explanation will change with our changing beliefs. Therefore the appropriate *analysandum* is the notion of the store of arguments relative to a set of accepted sentences. Suppose that, at the point in the history of inquiry which interests us, the set of accepted sentences is K. (I shall assume, for simplicity's sake, that K is consistent. Should our beliefs be inconsistent then it is more appropriate to regard K as some tidied version of our beliefs.) The general problem I have set is that of specifying $E(K)$, the *explanatory store over K*, which is the set of arguments acceptable as the basis for acts of explanation by those whose beliefs are exactly the members of K. (For the purposes of this paper I shall assume that, for each K there is exactly one $E(K)$.)

The unofficial view answers the problem: for each K, $E(K)$ is the set of arguments which best unifies K. My task is to articulate the answer. I begin by looking at two historical episodes in which the desire for unification played a crucial role. In both cases, we find three important features: (i) prior to the articulation of a theory with high predictive power, certain proposals for theory construction are favored on grounds of their explanatory promise; (ii) the explanatory power of embryonic theories is explicitly tied to the notion of unification; (iii) particular features of the theories are taken to support their claims to unification. Recognition of (i) and (ii) will illustrate points that have already been made. while (iii) will point towards an analysis of the concept of unification.

3. A Newtonian Program

Newton's achievements in dynamics, astronomy, and optics inspired some of his successors to undertake an ambitious program which I shall call "dynamic corpuscularianism."[4] *Principia* had shown how to obtain the motions of bodies from a knowledge of the forces acting on them, and had also demonstrated the possibility of dealing with gravitational systems in a unified way. The next step would be to isolate a few basic force laws, akin to the law of universal gravitation, so that, applying the basic laws to specifications of the dispositions of the ultimate parts of bodies, all of the phenomena of nature could be derived. Chemical reactions, for example, might be understood in terms of the rearrangement of ultimate parts under the action of cohesive and repulsive forces. The phenomena of reflection, refraction and diffraction of light might be viewed as resulting from a special force of attraction between light corpuscles and ordinary matter. These speculations encouraged eighteenth-century Newtonians to construct very general hypotheses about inter-atomic forces—even in the absence of any confirming evidence for the existence of such forces.

In the preface to *Principia*, Newton had already indicated that he took dynamic corpuscularianism to be a program deserving the attention of the scientific community:

I wish we could derive the rest of the phenomena of Nature by the same kind of reasoning from mechanical principles, for I am induced by many reasons to suspect that they may all depend upon certain forces by which the particles of bodies, by some causes hitherto unknown, are either mutually impelled towards one another, and cohere in regular figures, or are repelled and recede from one another (Newton 1962, p. xviii. See also Newton 1952, pp. 401–2).

This, and other influential passages, inspired Newton's successors to try to complete the unification of science by finding further force laws analogous to the law of universal gravitation. Dynamic corpuscularianism remained popular so long as there was promise of signifcant unification. Its appeal began to fade only when repeated attempts to specify force laws were found to invoke so many different (apparently incompatible) attractive and repulsive forces that the goal of unification appeared unlikely. Yet that goal could still motivate renewed efforts to implement the program. In the second half of the eighteenth-century Boscovich revived dynamic corpuscularian hopes by claiming that the whole of natural philosophy can be reduced to "one law of forces existing in nature."[5]

The passage I have quoted from Newton suggests the nature of the unification that was being sought. *Principia* had exhibited how one style of argument, one "kind of reasoning from mechanical principles," could be used in the derivation of descriptions of many, diverse, phenomena. The unifying power of Newton's work consisted in its demonstration that one *pattern* of argument could be used again and again in the derivation of a wide range of accepted sentences. (I shall give a representation of the Newtonian pattern in section 5.) In searching for force laws analogous to the law of universal gravitation, Newton's successors were trying to generalize the pattern of argument presented in *Principia*, so that one "kind of reasoning" would suffice to derive all phenomena of motion. If, furthermore, the facts studied by chemistry, optics, physiology and so forth, could be related to facts about particle motion, then one general pattern of argument would be used in the derivation of all phenomena. I suggest that this is the ideal of unification at which Newton's immediate successors aimed, which came to seem less likely to be attained as the eighteenth century wore on, and which Boscovich's work endeavored, with some success, to reinstate.

4. The Reception of Darwin's Evolutionary Theory

The picture of unification which emerges from the last section may be summarized quite simply: a theory unifies our beliefs when it provides one (or more generally, a few) pattern(s) of argument which can be used in the derivation of a large number of sentences which we accept. I shall try to develop this idea more precisely in later sections. But first I want to show how a different example suggests the same view of unification.

In several places, Darwin claims that his conclusion that species evolve through natural selection should be accepted because of its explanatory power, that "... the doctrine must sink or swim according as it groups and explains phenomena" (F. Darwin 1887; vol. 2. p. 155, quoted in Hull 1974, p. 292). Yet, as he often laments, he is unable to provide any complete derivation of any biological phenomenon—our ignorance of the appropriate facts and regularities is "profound." How, then, can he contend that the primary virtue of the new theory is its explanatory power?

The answer lies in the fact that Darwin's evolutionary theory promises to unify a host of biological phenomena (C. Darwin 1964, pp. 243–44). The eventual unification would consist in derivations of descriptions of these phenomena which would instantiate a common pattern. When Darwin expounds his doctrine what he offers us is the pattern. Instead of detailed explanations of the presence of some particular trait in some particular species, Darwin presents two "imaginary examples" (C. Darwin 1964, pp. 90–96) and a diagram. which shows, in a general way, the evolution of species *represented by schematic letters* (1964, pp. 116–26). In doing so, he exhibits a pattern of argument, which. he maintains, can be instantiated, *in principle*, by a complete and rigorous derivation of descriptions of the characteristics of any current species. The derivation would employ the principle of natural selection—as well as premises describing ancestral forms and the nature of their environment and the (unknown) laws of variation and inheritance. In place of detailed evolutionary stories, Darwin offers *explanation-sketches*. By showing how a particular characteristic would be advantageous to a particular species, he indicates an explanation of the emergence of that characteristic in the species, suggesting the outline of an argument instantiating the general pattern.

From this perspective, much of Darwin's argumentation in the *Origin* (and in other works) becomes readily comprehensible. Darwin attempts to show how his pattern can be applied to a host of biological phenomena. He claims that, by using arguments which instantiate the pattern, we can account for analogous variations in kindred species, for the greater variability of specific (as opposed to generic) characteristics, for the facts about geographical distribution. and so forth. But he is also required to resist challenges that the pattern cannot be applied in some cases, that premises for arguments instantiating the pattern will not be forthcoming. So, for example, Darwin must show how evolutionary stories, fashioned after his pattern, can be told to account for the emergence of complex organs. In both aspects of his argument, whether he is responding to those who would limit the application of his pattern or whether he is campaigning for its use within a realm of biological phenomena. Darwin has the same goal. He aims to show that his theory should be accepted because it unifies and explains.

5. Argument Patterns

Our two historical examples[6] have led us to the conclusion that the notion of an argument pattern is central to that of explanatory unification. Quite different considerations could easily have pointed us in the same direction. If someone were to distinguish between the explanatory worth of two arguments instantiating a common pattern, then we would regard that person as an explanatory deviant. To grasp the concept of explanation is to see that if one accepts an argument as explanatory, one is thereby committed to accepting as explanatory other arguments which instantiate the same pattern.

To say that members of a set of arguments instantiate a common pattern is to recognize that the arguments in the set are similar in some interesting way. With different interests, people may fasten on different similarities, and may arrive at different notions of argument pattern. Our enterprise is to characterize the concept of argument pattern which plays a role in the explanatory activity of scientists.

Formal logic, ancient and modern, is concerned in one obvious sense with patterns of argument. The logician proceeds by isolating a small set of expressions (the logical vocabulary), considers the schemata formed from sentences by replacing with dummy letters all expressions which do not belong to this set, and tries to specify which sequences of these schemata are valid patterns of argument. The pattern of argument which is taught to students of Newtonian dynamics is not a pattern of the kind which interests logicians. It has instantiations with different logical structures. (A rigorous derivation of the equations of motion of different dynamical systems would have a logical structure depending on the number of bodies involved and the mathematical details of the integration.) Moreover, an argument can only instantiate the Newtonian pattern if particular *non*logical terms, 'force,' 'mass,' and 'acceleration,' occur in it in particular ways. However, the logician's approach can help us to isolate the notion of argument pattern which we require.

Let us say that a *schematic sentence* is an expression obtained by replacing some, but not necessarily all, the non-logical expressions occurring in a sentence with dummy letters. A set of *filling instructions* for a schematic sentence is a set of directions for replacing the dummy letters of the schematic sentence, such that, for each dummy letter, there is a direction which tells us how it should be replaced. A *schematic argument* is a sequence of schematic sentences. A *classification* for a schematic argument is a set of sentences which describe the inferential characteristics of the schematic argument: its function is to tell us which terms in the sequence are to be regarded as premises, which are to be inferred from which, what rules of inference are to be used, and so forth.

We can use these ideas to define the concept of a *general argument pattern*. A general argument pattern is a triple consisting of a schematic argument, a set of sets of filling instructions containing one set of filling instructions for each term of the schematic argument, and a classification for the schematic argument. A sequence of sentences instantiates the general argument pattern just in case it meets the following conditions:

(i) The sequence has the same number or terms as the schematic argument of the general argument pattern.

(ii) Each sentence in the sequence is obtained from the corresponding schematic sentence in accordance with the appropriate set of filling instructions.

(iii) It is possible to construct a chain of reasoning which assigns to each sentence the status accorded to the corresponding schematic sentence by the classification.

We can make these definitions more intuitive by considering the way in which they apply to the Newtonian example. Restricting ourselves to the basic pattern used in treating systems which contain one body (such as the pendulum and the projectile) we may represent the schematic argument as follows:

(1) The force on α is β.
(2) The acceleration of α is γ.
(3) Force = mass $\cdot$ acceleration.
(4) (Mass of α) $\cdot$ (γ) $= \beta$
(5) $\delta = \theta$

The filling instructions tell us that all occurrences of 'α' are to be replaced by an expression referring to the body under investigation; occurrences of 'β' are to be replaced by an algebraic expression referring to a function of the variable coordinates and of time; 'γ' is to be replaced by an expression which gives the acceleration of the body as a function of its coordinates and their time-derivatives (thus, in the case of a one-dimensional motion along the x-axis of a Cartesian coordinate system, 'γ' would be relaced by the expression 'd^2x/dt^2'); 'δ' is to be replaced by an expression referring to the variable coordinates of the body, and 'θ' is to be replaced by an explicit function of time (thus the sentences which instantiate (5) reveal the dependence of the variable coordinates on time, and so provide specifications of the positions of the body in question throughout the motion). The classification of the argument tells us that (1)–(3) have the status of premises, that (4) is obtained from them by substituting identicals, and that (5) follows from (4) using algebraic manipulation and the techniques of the calculus.

Although the argument patterns which interest logicians are general argument patterns in the sense just defined, our example exhibits clearly the features which distinguish the kinds of patterns which scientists are trained to use. Whereas logicians are concerned to display all the schematic premises which are employed and to specify exactly which rules of inference are used, our example allows for the use of premises (mathematical assumptions) which do not occur as terms of the schematic argument, and it does not give a complete description of the way in which the route from (4) to (5) is to go. Moreover, our pattern does not replace all nonlogical expressions by dummy letters. Because some non-logical expressions remain, the pattern imposes special demands on arguments which instantiate it. In a different way, restrictions are set by the instructions for replacing dummy letters. The patterns of logicians are very liberal in both these latter respects. The conditions for replacing dummy letters in Aristotelian syllogisms, or first-order schemata, require only that some letters be relaced with predicates, others with names.

Arguments may be similar either in terms of their logical structure or in terms of the non-logical vocabulary they employ at corresponding places. I think that the notion of similarity (and the corresponding notion of pattern) which is central to the explanatory activity of scientists results from a compromise in demanding these two kinds of similarity. I propose that scientists are interested in *stringent* patterns of argument, patterns which contain some non-logical expressions and which are fairly similar in terms of logical structure. The Newtonian pattern cited above furnishes a good example. Although arguments instantiating this pattern do not have exactly the same logical structure, the classification imposes conditions which ensure that there will be similarities in logical structure among such arguments. Moreover, the presence of the non-logical terms sets strict requirements on the instantiations and so ensures a different type of kinship among them. Thus, without trying to provide an exact analysis of the notion of stringency, we may suppose that the stringency of a pattern is determined by two different constraints: (1) the conditions on the substitution of expressions for dummy letters, jointly imposed by the presence of non-logical expressions in the pattern and by the filling instructions; and, (2) the conditions on the logical structure, imposed by the classification. If both conditions are relaxed completely then the notion of pattern degenerates so as to admit *any* argument. If both conditions are simultaneously made as strict as possible, then we obtain another degenerate case, a "pattern" which is its own unique instantiation. If condition (2) is tightened at the total expense of (1), we produce the logician's notion of pattern. The use of condition (1) requires that arguments instantiating a common pattern draw on a common non-logical vocabulary. We can glimpse here that ideal of unification through the use of a few theoretical concepts which the remarks of Hempel and Feigl suggest.

Ideally, we should develop a precise account of how these two kinds of similarity are weighted against one another. The best strategy for obtaining such an account is to see how claims about stringency occur in scientific discussions. But scientists do not make explicit assessments of the stringency of argument patterns. Instead they evaluate the ability of a theory to explain and to unify. The way to a refined account of stringency lies through the notions of explanation and unification.

6. Explanation as Unification

As I have posed it, the problem of explanation is to specify which set of arguments we ought to accept for explanatory purposes given that we hold certain sentences to be true. Obviously this formulation can encourage confusion: we must not think of a scientific community as *first* deciding what sentences it will accept and *then* adopting the appropriate set of arguments. The Newtonian and Darwinian examples should convince us that the promise of explanatory power enters into the modification of our beliefs. So, in proposing that $E(K)$ is a function of K, I do not mean to suggest that the acceptance of K must be temporally prior to the adoption of $E(K)$.

$E(K)$ is to be that set of arguments which best unifies K. There are, of course, usually many ways of deriving some sentences in K from others. Let us call a set of arguments which derives some members of K from other members of K a *systematization* of K. We may then think of $E(K)$ as the best systematization of K.

Let us begin by making explicit an idealization which I have just made tacitly. A set of arguments will be said to be *acceptable relative* to K just in case every argument in the set consists of a sequence of steps which accord with elementary valid rules of inference (deductive or inductive) and if every premise of every argument in the set belongs to K. When we are considering ways of systematizing K we restrict our attention to those sets of arguments which are acceptable relative to K. This is an idealization because we sometimes use as the basis of acts of explanation arguments furnished by theories whose principles we no longer believe. I shall not investigate this practice nor the considerations which justify us in engaging in it. The most obvious way to extend my idealized picture to accommodate it is to regard the explanatory store over K, as I characterize it here, as being supplemented with an extra class of arguments meeting the following conditions: (a) from the perspective of K, the premises of these arguments are approximately true; (b) these arguments can be viewed as approximating the structure of (parts of) arguments in $E(K)$; (c) the arguments are simpler than the corresponding arguments in $E(K)$. Plainly, to spell out these conditions precisely would lead into issues which are tangential to my main goal in this paper.

The moral of the Newtonian and Darwinian examples is that unification is achieved by using similar arguments in the derivation of many accepted sentences. When we confront the set of possible systematizations of K we should therefore attend to the *patterns* of argument which are employed in each systematization. Let us introduce the notion of a *generating set*: if Σ is a set of arguments then a generating set for Σ is a set of argument patterns Π such that each argument in Σ is an instantiation of some pattern in Π. A generating set for Σ will be said to be *complete with respect to K* if and only if every argument which is acceptable relative to K and which instantiates a pattern in Π belongs to Σ. In determining the explanatory store $E(K)$ we first narrow our choice to those sets of arguments which are acceptable relative to K, the systematizations of K. Then we consider, for each such set of arguments, the various generating sets of argument patterns which are complete with respect to K. (The importance of the requirement of completeness is to debar explanatory deviants who use patterns selectively.) Among these latter sets we select that set with the greatest unifying power (according to criteria shortly to be indicated) and we call the selected set the *basis* of the set of arguments in question. The explanatory store over K is that systematization whose basis does best by the criteria of unifying power.

This complicated picture can be made clearer, perhaps, with the help of a diagram.

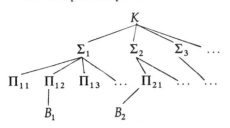

Systematizations. sets of arguments acceptable relative to K.

Complete generating sets. Π_{ij}, is a generating set for Σ_i which is complete with respect to K.

If B_k is the basis with the greatest unifying power then $E(K) = \Sigma_k$.

Bases. B_i is the basis for Σ_i, and is selected as the best of the Π_{ij} on the basis of unifying power.

The task which confronts us is now formulated as that of specifying the factors which determine the unifying power of a set of argument patterns. Our Newtonian and Darwinian examples inspire an obvious suggestion: unifying power is achieved by generating a large number of accepted sentences as the conclusions of acceptable arguments which instantiate a few, stringent patterns. With this in mind, we define the *conclusion set* of a set of arguments Σ, $C(\Sigma)$, to be the set of sentences which occur as conclusions of some argument in Σ. So we might propose that the unifying power of a basis B_i with respect to K varies directly with the size of $C(\Sigma_i)$, varies directly with the stringency of the patterns which belong to B_i, and varies inversely with the number of members of B_i. This proposal is along the right lines, but it is, unfortunately, too simple.

The pattern of argument which derives a specification of the positions of bodies as explicit functions of time from a specification of the forces acting on those bodies is, indeed, central to Newtonian explanations. But not every argument used in Newtonian explanations instantiates this pattern. Some Newtonian derivations consist of an argument instantiating the pattern followed by further derivations from the conclusion. Thus, for example, when we explain why a pendulum has the period it does we may draw on an argument which *first* derives the equation of motion of the pendulum and *then* continues by deriving the period. Similarly, in explaining why projectiles projected with fixed velocity obtain maximum range when projected at 45° to the horizontal, we first show how the values of the horizontal and vertical coordinates can be found as functions of time and the angle of elevation, use our results to compute the horizontal distance traveled by the time the projectile returns to the horizontal, and then show how this distance is a maximum when the angle of elevation of projection is 45°. In both cases we take further steps beyond the computation of the explicit equations of motion—and the further steps in each case are different.

If we consider the entire range of arguments which Newtonian dynamics supplies for explanatory purposes, we find that these arguments instantiate a number of different patterns. Yet these patterns are not entirely distinct, for all of them proceed by using the computation of explicit equations of motion as a prelude to further derivation. It is natural to suggest that the pattern of computing equations of motion is the *core* pattern provided by Newtonian theory, and that the theory also shows how conclusions generated by arguments instantiating the core pattern can be used to derive further conclusions. In some Newtonian explanations, the core pattern is supplemented by a *problem-reducing pattern*, a pattern of argument which shows how to obtain a further type of conclusion from explicit equations of motion.

This suggests that our conditions on unifying power should be modified, so that, instead of merely counting the number of different patterns in a basis, we pay attention to similarities among them. All the patterns in the basis may contain a common core pattern, that is, each of them may contain some pattern as a subpattern. The unifying power of a basis is obviously increased if some (or all) of the patterns it contains share a common core pattern.

As I mentioned at the beginning of this chapter, the account of explanation as unification is complicated. The explanatory store is determined on the basis of criteria which pull in different directions, and I shall make no attempt here to specify precisely the ways in which these criteria are to be balanced against one another. Instead, I shall show that some traditional problems of scientific explanation can be solved without more detailed specification of the conditions on unifying power. For the account I have indicated has two impontant corollaries.

(A) Let Σ, Σ' be sets of arguments which are acceptable relative to K and which meet the following conditions:

> (i) the basis of Σ' is as good as the basis of Σ in terms of the criteria of stringency of patterns, paucity of patterns, presence of core patterns and so forth.
> (ii) $C(\Sigma)$ is a proper subset of $C(\Sigma')$.

Then $\Sigma \neq E(K)$.

(B) Let Σ, Σ' be sets of arguments which are acceptable relative to K and which meet the following conditions:

> (i) $C(\Sigma) = C(\Sigma')$
> (ii) the basis of Σ' is a proper subset of the basis of Σ.

Then $\Sigma \neq E(K)$.

(A) and (B) tell us that sets of arguments which do equally well in terms of some of our conditions are to be ranked according to their relative ability to satisfy the rest. I shall try to show that (A) and (B) have interesting consequences.

7. Asymmetry, Irrelevance, and Accidental Generalization

Some familiar difficulties beset the covering law model. The *asymmetry problem* arises because some scientific laws have the logical form of equivalences. Such laws can be used "in either direction." Thus a law asserting that the satisfaction of a condition C_1 is equivalent to the satisfaction of a condition C_2 can be used in two different kinds of argument. From a premise asserting that an object meets C_1, we can use the law to infer that it meets C_2; conversely, from a premise asserting that an object meets C_2, we can use the law to infer that it meets C_1. The asymmetry problem is generated by noting that in many such cases one of these derivations can be used in giving explanations while the other cannot.

Consider a hoary example, (For further examples, see Bromberger 1966.) We can explain why a simple pendulum has the period it does by deriving a specification of the period from a specification of the length and the law which relates length and period. But we cannot explain the length of the pendulum by deriving a specification of the length from a specification of the period and the same law. What accounts for our different assessment of these two arguments? Why does it seem that one is explanatory while the other "gets things backwards"? The covering law model fails to distinguish the two, and thus fails to provide answers.

The *irrelevance problem* is equally vexing. The problem arises because we can sometimes find a lawlike connection between an accidental and irrelevant occurrence and an event or state which would have come about independently of that occurrence. Imagine that Milo the magician waves his hands over a sample of table salt, thereby "hexing" it. It is true (and I shall suppose, lawlike) that all hexed samples of table salt dissolve when placed in water. Hence we can construct a derivation of the dissolving of Milo's hexed sample of salt by citing the circumstances of the hexing. Although this derivation fits the covering law model, it is, by our ordinary lights, non-explanatory. (This example is given by Wesley Salmon in his (1970); Salmon attributes it to Henry Kyburg. For more examples, see Achinstein 1971.)

The covering law model explicitly debars a further type of derivation which any account of explanation ought to exclude. Arguments whose premises contain no laws, but which make essential use of accidental generalizations are intuitively non-explanatory. Thus, if we derive the conclusion that Horace is bald from premises stating that Horace is a member of the Greenbury School Board and that all members of the Greenbury School Board are bald, we do not thereby explain why Horace is bald. (See Hempel 1965, p. 339.) We shall have to show that our account does not admit as explanatory derivations of this kind.

I want to show that the account of explanation I have sketched contains sufficient resources to solve these problems.[7] In each case we shall pursue a common strategy. Faced with an argument we want to exclude from the explanatory store we endeavor to show that any set of arguments containing the unwanted argument could not provide the best unification of our beliefs. Specifically, we shall try to show either that any such set of arguments will be more limited than some other set with an equally satisfactory basis, or that the basis of the set must fare worse according to the criterion of using the smallest number of most stringent patterns. That is, we shall appeal to the corollaries (A) and (B) given above. In actual practice, this strategy for exclusion is less complicated than one might fear, and, as we shall see, its applications to the examples just discussed brings out what is intuitively wrong with the derivations we reject.

Consider first the irrelevance problem. Suppose that we were to accept as explanatory the argument which derives a description of the dissolving of the salt from a description of Milo's act of hexing. What will be our policy for explaining the dissolving of samples of salt which have not been hexed? If we offer the usual chemical arguments in these latter cases then we shall commit ourselves to an inflated basis for the set of arguments we accept as explanatory. For, unlike the person who explains *all* cases of dissolving of samples of salt by using the standard chemical pattern of argument, we shall be committed to the use of two different patterns of argument in covering such cases. Nor is the use of the extra pattern of argument offset by its applicability in explaining other phenomena. Our policy employs one extra pattern of argument without extending the range of things we can derive from our favored set of arguments. Conversely, if we eschew the standard chemical pattern of argument (just using the pattern which appeals to the hexing) we shall find ourselves unable to apply our favored pattern to cases in which the sample of salt dissolved has not been hexed. Moreover, the pattern we use will not fall under the more general patterns we employ to explain chemical phenomena such as solution, precipitation and so forth. Hencc the unifying power of the basis for our preferred set of arguments will be less than that of the basis for the set of arguments we normally accept as explanatory.[8]

If we explain the dissolving of the sample of salt which Milo has hexed by appealing to the hexing then we are faced with the problems of explaining the dissolving of unhexed samples of salt. We have two options: (a) to adopt two patterns of argument corresponding to the two kinds of case: (b) to adopt one pattern of argument whose instantiations apply just to the cases of hexed salt. If we choose (a) then we shall be in conflict with (B), whereas choice of (b) will be ruled out by (A). The general moral is that appeals to hexing fasten on a local and accidental feature of the cases of solution. By contrast our standard arguments instantiate a pattern which can be generally applied.[9]

A similar strategy succeeds with the asymmetry problem. We have general ways of explaining why bodies have the dimensions they do. Our practice is to describe the circumstances leading to the formation or the object in question and then to show how it has since been modifed. Let us call explanations of this kind "origin and development derivations." (In some cases, the details of the original formation of the object are more imponant; with other objects, features of its subsequent modification are crucial.) Suppose now that we admit as explanatory a derivation of the length of a simple pendulum from a specification of the period. Then we shall either have to explain the lengths of *non*-swinging bodies by employing quite a different style of explanation (an origin and development derivation) or we shall have to forego explaining the lengths of such bodies. The situation is exactly parallel to that of the irrelevance problem. Admitting the argument which is intuitively non-explanatory saddles us with a set of arguments which is less good at unifying our beliefs than the set we normally choose for explanatory purposes.

Our approach also solves a more refined version of the pendulum problem (given by Paul Teller in his (1974)). Many bodies which are not currently executing pendulum motion *could* be making small oscillations, and, were they to do so, the period of their motion would be functionally related to their dimensions. For such bodies we can specify the *dispositional period* as the period which the body would have if it were to execute small oscillations. Someone may now suggest that we can construct derivations of the dimensions of bodies from specifications of their dispositional periods, thereby generating an argument pattern which can be applied as generally as that instantiated in origin and development explanations. This suggestion is mistaken. There are some objects—such as the earth and the Crab Nebula—which *could not* be pendulums, and for which the notion of a dispositional period makes of no sense. Hence the argument pattern proposed cannot entirely supplant our origin and development derivations, and, in consequence, acceptance of it would fail to achieve the best unification of our beliefs.

The problem posed by accidental generalizations can be handled in parallel fashion. We have a general pattern of argument, using principles of physiology, which we apply to explain cases of baldness. This pattern is generally applicable, whereas that which derives ascriptions of baldness using the principle that all members of the Greenbury School Board are bald is not. Hence, as in the other cases, sets which contain the unwanted derivation be ruled out by one of the conditions (A), (B).

Of course, this does not show that an account of explanation along the lines I have suggested would sanction only derivations which satisfy the conditions imposed by the covering law model. For I have not argued that an explanatory derivation need contain *any* sentence or universal form. What *does* seem to follow from the account of explanation as unification is that explanatory arguments must not use accidental generalization, and, in this respect, the new account appears to underscore and generalize an important insight of the covering law model. Moreover, our success with the problems of asymmetry and irrelevance indicates that, even in the absence or a detailed account of the notion of stringency and of the way in which generality of the consequence set is weighed against paucity and stringency of the patterns in the basis, the view of explanation as unification has the resources to solve some traditional difficulties for theories of explanation.

8. Spurious Unification

Unfortunately there is a fly in the ointment. One of the most aggravating problems for the covering law model has been its failure to exclude certain types of self-explanation. (For a classic source of difficulties see Eberle, Kaplan, and Montague 1961.) As it stands, the account of explanation as unification seems to be even more vulnerable on this score. The problem derives from a phenomenon which I shall call *spurious unification*.

Consider, first, a difficulty which Hempel and Oppenheim noted in a seminal article (Hempel 1965, Chapter 10). Suppose that we conjoin two laws. Then we can derive one of the laws from the conjunction, and the derivation conforms to the covering law model (unless, of course, the model is restricted to cover only the explanation of singular sentences: Hempel and Oppenheim do, in fact, make this restriction). To quote Hempel and Oppenheim:

> The core of the difficulty can be indicated briefly by reference to an example: Kepler's laws, K, may be conjoined with Boyle's law, B, to a stronger law $K \cdot B$; but derivation of K from the latter would not be considered as an explanation of the regularities stated in Kepler's laws; rather it would be viewed as representing, in effect, a pointless "explanation" of Kepler's laws by themselves. (Hempel 1965, p. 273, fn. 33.)

This problem is magnified for our account. For, why may we not unify our beliefs *completely* by deriving all of them using arguments which instantiate the one pattern?

$$\frac{\alpha \text{ and } \beta}{\alpha} \qquad [\text{'}\alpha\text{' is to be replaced by any sentence we accept.}]$$

Or, to make matters even more simple, why should we not unify our beliefs by using the most trivial pattern of self-derivation?

$$\alpha \qquad [\text{'}\alpha\text{' is to be replaced by any sentence we accept.}]$$

There is an obvious reply. The patterns just cited may succeed admirably in satisfying our criteria of using a few patterns of argument to generate many beliefs, but they fail dismally when judged by the criterion of stringency. Recall that the stringency of a pattern is assessed by adopting a compromise between two constraints: stringent patterns are not only to have instantiations with similar logical structures; their instantiations are also to contain similar nonlogical vocabulary at similar places. Now both of the above argument patterns are very lax in allowing any vocabulary whatever to appear in the place of 'α'. Hence we can argue that, according to our intuitive concept of stringency, they should be excluded as nonstringent.

Although this reply is promising, it does not entirely quash the objection. A defender of the unwanted argument patterns may *artificially* introduce restrictions on the pattern to make it more stringent. So, for example, if we suppose that one of *our* favorite patterns (such as the Newtonian pattern displayed above) is applied to generate conclusions meeting a particular condition C, the defender of the patterns just cited may propose that 'α' is to be replaced, not by any sentence, but by a sentence which meets C. He may then legitimately point out that his newly contrived pattern is as stringent as our favored pattern. Inspired by this partial success, he may adopt a general strategy. Wherever we use an argument pattern to generate a particular type of conclusion, he may use some argument pattern which involves self-derivation, placing an appropriate restriction on the sentences to be substituted for the dummy letters. In this way, he will mimic whatever unification we achieve. His "unification" is obviously spurious. How do we debar it?

The answer comes from recognizing the way in which the stringency of the unwanted patterns was produced. Any condition on the substitution of sentences for dummy letters would have done equally well, provided only that it imposed constraints comparable to those imposed by acceptable patterns. Thus the stringency of the restricted pattern seems accidental to it. This accidental quality is exposed when we notice that we can vary the filling instructions, while retaining the same syntactic structure, to obtain a host of other argument patterns with equally many instantiations. By contrast, the constraints imposed on the substitution of non-logical vocabulary in the Newtonian pattern (for example) cannot be amended without destroying the stringency of the pattern or without depriving it of its ability to furnish us with many instantiations. Thus the constraints imposed in the Newtonian pattern are essential to its functioning; those imposed in the unwanted pattern are not.

Let us formulate this idea as an explicit requirement. If the filling instructions associated with a pattern P could be replaced by different filling instructions, allowing for the substitution of a class of expressions or the same syntactic category, to yield a pattern P' and if P' would allow the derivation *any* sentence, then the unification achieved by P is spurious. Consider, in this light, any of the patterns which we have been trying to debar. In each case, we can vary the filling instructions to produce an even more "successful" pattern. So, for example, given the pattern:

α   ['α' is to be replaced by a sentence meeting condition C]

we can generalize the filling instructions to obtain

α   ['α' is to be replaced by any sentence].

Thus, under our new requirement, the unification achieved by the original pattern is spurious.

In a moment I shall try to show how this requirement can be motivated, both by appealing to the intuition which underlies the view or explanation as unification and by recognizing the role that something like my requirement has played in the history of science. Before I do so, I want to examine a slightly different kind of example which initially appears to threaten my account. Imagine that a group of religious fanatics decides to argue for the explanatory power of some theological doctrines by claiming that these doctrines unify their beliefs about the world. They suggest that their beliefs can be systematized by using the following pattern:

God wants it to be the case that α.   ['α' is to be replaced by any accepted
What God wants to be the case is the   sentence describing the physical world]
case.
_____
α

The new requirement will also identify as spurious the pattern just presented, and will thus block the claim that the theological doctrines that God exists and has the power to actualize his wishes have explanatory power. For it is easy to see that we can modify the filling instructions to obtain a pattern that will yield any sentence whatsoever.

Why should patterns whose filling instructions can be modified to accommodate any sentence be suspect? The answer is that, in such patterns, the non-logical vocabulary which remains is idling. The presence of that non-logical vocabulary imposes no constraints on the expressions we can substitute for the dummy symbols, so that, beyond the specification that a place be filled by expressions of a particular syntactic category, the structure we impose by means of filling instructions is quite incidental. Thus the patterns in question do not genuinely reflect the contents of our beliefs. The explanatory store should present the order of natural phenomena which is exposed by what we think we know. To do so, it must exhibit connections among our beliefs beyond those which could be found among any beliefs. Patterns of self-derivation and the type of pattern exemplified in the example of the theological community merely provide trivial, omnipresent connections, and, in consequence, the unification they offer is spurious.

My requirement obviously has some kinship with the requirement that the principles put forward in giving explanations be testable. As previous writers have insisted that genuine explanatory theories should not be able to cater to all possible evidence. I am demanding that genuinely unifying patterns should not be able to accommodate all conclusions. The requirement that I have proposed accords well with some of the issues which scientists have addressed in discussing the explanatory merits of particular theories. Thus several of Darwin's opponents complain that the explanatory benefits claimed for the embryonic theory of evolution are illusory, on the grounds that the style of reasoning suggested could be adapted to any conclusion. (For a particularly acute statement of the complaint, see the review by Fleeming Jenkin, printed in Hull 1974. especially p. 342.) Similarly, Lavoisier denied that the explanatory power of the phlogiston theory was genuine, accusing that theory of using a type of reasoning which could adapt itself to any conclusion (Lavoisier 1862, vol. II. p. 233). Hence I suggest that some problems of spurious unification can be solved in the way I have indicated, and that the solution conforms both to our intuitions about explanatory unification and to the considerations which are used in scientific debate.

However, I do not wish to claim that my requirement will debar all types of spurious unification. It may be possible to find other unwanted patterns which circumvent my requirement. A full characterization of the notion of a stringent argument pattern should provide a criterion for excluding the unwanted patterns. My claim in this section is that it will do so by counting as spurious the unification achieved by patterns which adapt themselves to any conclusion and by patterns which accidentally restrict such universally hospitable patterns. I have also tried to show how this claim can be developed to block the most obvious cases of spurious unification.

9. Conclusions

I have sketched an account of explanation as unification, attempting to show that such an account has the resources to provide insight into episodes in the history of science and to overcome some traditional problems for the covering law model. In conclusion, let me indicate very briefly how my view of explanation as unification suggests how scientific explanation yields understanding. By using a few patterns of argument in the derivation of many beliefs we minimize the number of *types* of premises we must take as underived. That is, we reduce, in so far as possible, the number of types of facts we must accept as brute. Hence we can endorse something close to Friedman's view of the merits of explanatory unification (Friedman 1974, pp. 18–19).

Quite evidently, I have only *sketched* an account of explanation. To provide precise analyses of the notions I have introduced, the basic approach to explanation offered here must be refined against concrete examples of scientific practice. What needs to be done is to look closely at the argument patterns favored by scientists and attempt to understand what characteristics they share. If I am right, the scientific search for explanation is governed by a maxim, once formulated succinctly by E. M. Forster. Only connect.

Notes

A distant ancestor of this paper was read to the Dartmouth College Philosophy Colloquium in the Spring of 1977. I would like to thank those who participated, especially Merrie Bergmann and Jim Moor, for their helpful suggestions. I am also grateful to two anonymous referees for *Philosophy of Science* whose extremely constructive criticisms have led to substantial improvements. Finally, I want to acknowledge the amount I have learned from the writing and teaching of Peter Hempel. The present essay is a token payment on an enormous debt.

1. Strictly speaking, this is one of two views which emerge from Achinstein's discussion and which he regards as equally satisfactory. As Achinstein goes on to point out, either of these ontological theses can be developed to capture the central idea of the covering law model.

2. To pose the problem in this way we may still invite the change that *arguments* should not be viewed as the bases for acts of explanation. Many of the criticisms leveled against the covering law model by Wesley Salmon in his seminal paper on statistical explanation (Salmon 1970) can be reformulated to support this charge. My discussion in section 7 will show how some of the difficulties raised by Salmon for the covering law model do not bedevil my account. However, I shall not respond directly to the points about statistical explanation and statistical inference advanced by Salmon and by Richard Jeffrey in his (1970). I believe that Peter Railton has shown how these specific difficulties concerning statistical explanation can be accommodated by an approach which takes explanations to be (or be based on) arguments (see Railton 1978), and that the account offered in section 4 of his paper can be adapted to complement my own.

3. Of course, in restricting my attention to why-questions I am following the tradition of philosophical discussion of scientific explanation: as Bromberger notes in section IV of his (1966) not all explanations are directed at why-questions, but attempts to characterize explanatory responses to why-questions have a special interest for the philosophy of science because of the connection to a range of methodological issues. I believe that the account of explanation offered in the present paper could be extended to cover explanatory answers to some other kinds of questions (such as how-questions). But I do want to disavow the claim that unification is relevant to all types of explanation. If one believes that explanations are sometimes offered in response to what-questions (for example), so that it is correct to talk of someone explaining what a gene is, then one should allow that some types of explanation can be characterized independently of the notions of unification or of argument. I ignore these kinds of explanation in part because they lack the methodological significance of explanations directed at why-questions and in part because the problem of characterizing explanatory answers to what-questions seems so much less recalcitrant than that of characterizing explanatory answers to why-questions (for a similar assessment, see Belnap and Steel 1976, pp. 86–87). Thus I would regard a full account of explanation as a heterogeneous affair, because the conditions required of adequate answers to different types of questions are rather different, and I intend the present essay to make a proposal about how *part* of this account (the most interesting part) should be developed.

4. For illuminating accounts of Newton's influence on eighteenth-century research see Cohen (1956) and Schofield (1969). I have simplified the discussion by considering only *one* of the programs which eighteenth-century scientists derived from Newton's work. A more extended treatment would reveal the existence of several different approaches aimed at unifying science, and I believe that the theory of explanation proposed in this paper may help in the historical task of understanding the divere aspirations of different Newtonians. (For the problems involved in this enterprise, see Heimann and McGuire 1971).

5. See Boscovich (1966) Part III, especially p. 134. For an introduction to Boscovich's work, see the essays by L. L. Whyte and Z. Markovic in Whyte (1961). For the influence of Boscovich on British science, see the essays of Pearce Williams and Schofield in the same volume, and Scholfield (1969).

6. The examples could easily be multiplied. I think it is possible to understand the structure and explanatory power of such theories as modern evolutionary theory, transmission genetics, plate tectonics, and sociobiology in the terms I develop here.

7. More exactly, I shall try to show that my account can solve some of the principal versions of these difficulties which have been used to discredit the covering law model. I believe that it can also overcome more refined versions of the problems than I consider here, but to demonstrate that would require a more lengthy exposition.

8. There is an objection this line of reasoning. Can't we view the arguments $\langle(x)((Sx \text{ and } Hx) \rightarrow Dx), Sa \text{ and } Ha, Da\rangle$, $\langle(x)((Sx \text{ and } \sim Hx) \rightarrow Dx), Sb \text{ and } \sim Hb, Db\rangle$ as instantiating a common pattern? I reply that, insofar as we can view these arguments as instantiating a common pattern, the standard pair of comparable (low-level) derivations—$\langle(x)(Sx \rightarrow Dx), Sa, Da\rangle$, $\langle(x)(Sx \rightarrow Dx), Sb, Db\rangle$—share a more stringent common pattern. Hence incorporating the deviant derivations in the explanatory store would give us an inferior basis. We can justify the claim that the pattern instantiated by the standard pair of derivations is more stringent than that shared by the devaint derivations, by noting that representation of the deviant pattern would compel us to broaden our conception of schematic sentence, and, even were we to do so, the deviant pattern would contain a "degree of freedom" which the standard pattern lacks. For a representation of the deviant "pattern" would take the form $\langle(x)((Sx \text{ and } \alpha Hx) \rightarrow Dx), Sa$ and $\alpha Ha, Da\rangle$, where 'α' is to be replaced uniformly either with the null symbol or with '$\sim$'. Even if we waive my requirement that, in schematic sentences, we substitute for *non*-logical vocabulary, it is evident that this "pattern" is more accommodating than the standard pattern.

9. However, the strategy I have recommended will not avail with a different type of case. Suppose that a deviant wants to explain the dissolving of the salt by appealing to some property which holds universally. That is, the "explanatory" arguments are to begin from some premise such as "$(x)((x$ is a sample of salt and x does not violate conservation of energy) $\rightarrow x$ dissolves in water)" or "$(x)((x$ is a sample of salt and $x = x) \rightarrow x$ dissolves in water)." I would handle these case somewhat differently. If the deviant's explanatory store were to be as unified as our own, then it would contain arguments corresponding to ours in which a redundant conjunct systematically occurred, and I think it would be plausible to invoke a criterion of simplicity to advocate dropping that conjunct.

References

Achinstein, P., *Law and Explanation*. Oxford University Press, 1971.

Achinstein, P., "What is an Explanation?," *American Philosophical Quarterly* 14(1977), pp. 1–15.

Belnap, N., and Steel, T. B., *The Logic of Questions and Answers*. New Haven: Yale University Press, 1976.

Boscovich, R. J., *A Theory of Natural Philosophy* (trans. J. M. Child). Cambridge: MIT Press, 1966.

Bromberger, S., "An Approach to Explanation," in R. J. Butler (ed.), *Analytical Philosophy* (First Series). Oxford: Blackwell, 1962.

Bromberger, S., "Why-Questions," in R. Colodny (ed.), *Mind and Cosmos*. Pittsburgh: University of Pittsburgh Press, 1966.

Cohen, I. B., *Franklin and Newton*. Philadelphia: American Philosophical Society, 1956.

Darwin, C., *On the Origin of Species*, Facsimile of the First Edition, ed. E. Mayr. Cambridge: Harvard University Press, 1964.

Darwin, F., *The Life and Letters of Charles Darwin*. London: John Murray, 1987.

Eberle, R., Kaplan, D., and Montague, R., "Hempel and Oppenheim on Explanation," *Philosophy of Science* 28(1961), pp. 418–28.

Feigl, H., "The 'Orthodox' View of Theories: Remarks in Defense as Well as Critique," in M. Radner. and S. Winokur (eds.), *Minnesota Studies in the Philosophy of Science*, vol. IV. Minneapolis: University of Minnesota Press, 1970.

Friedman, M., "Explanation and Scientific Understanding," *Journal of Philosophy*, vol. LXXI(1974), pp. 5–19.

Heimann, P., and McGuire, J. E., "Newtonian Forces and Lockean Powers," *Historical Studies in the Physical Sciences* 3(1971), pp. 233–306.

Hempel, C. G., *Aspects of Scientific Explanation*. New York: The Free Press, 1965.

Hempel, C. G., "Deductive-Nonlogical vs. Statistical Explanation," in H. Feigl and G. Maxwell (eds.) *Minnesota Studies in the Philosophy of Science*, vol. III. Minneapolis: University of Minnesota Press, 1962.

Hempel, C. G., *Philosophy of Natural Science*. Englewood Cliffs, N.J.: Prentice-Hall, 1966.

Hull, D. (ed.), *Darwin and his Critics*. Cambridge: Harvard University Press, 1974.

Jeffrey, R., "Statistical Explanation vs. Statistical Inference," in N. Rescher (ed.), *Essays in Honor of Carl G. Hempel*. Dordrecht: D. Reidel, 1970.

Kitcher, P. S., "Explanation, Conjunction and Unification," *Journal of Philosophy*, vol. LXXIII(1976), pp. 207–12.

Lavoisier, A., *Oeuvres*. Paris, 1862.

Newton, I., *The Mathematical Principles of Natural Philosophy* (trans. A. Motte and F. Cajori). Berkeley: University of California Press, 1962.

Newton, I., *Opticks*. New York Dover, 1952.

Railton, P., "A Deductive-Nomological Model of Probabilistic Explanation," *Philosophy of Science* 45(1978), pp. 206–26.

Salmon, W., "Statistical Explanation," in R. Colodny (ed.), *The Nature and Function of Scientific Theories*. Pittsburgh: University of Pittsburgh Press, 1970.

Schofield, R. E., *Mechanism and Materialism*. Princeton: Princeton University Press, 1969.

Teller, P., "On Why-Questions," *Noûs*, vol. VIII(1974), pp. 371–80.

van Fraassen, B., "The Pragmatics of Explanation," *American Philosphical Quarterly* 14(1977), pp. 143–50.

Whyte, L. L. (ed.), *Roger Joseph Boscovich*. London: Allen and Unwin, 1961.

Chapter 19

Observations, Explanatory Power, and Simplicity: Toward a Non-Humean Account

Richard Boyd

Introduction

Two Puzzles about Confirmation

Truisms from empiricist philosophy of science often turn out to be false, but one such truism is certainly true: Scientific knowledge is experimental knowledge. It is characteristic of scientific research that observational evidence plays a decisive role in the resolution of the issue between contending hypotheses, and whatever sort of objectivity scientific inquiry has depends crucially on this feature of the scientific method. It may be disputed what the limits of experimental knowledge are, or how theory-dependent observations are, or how conventional or "constructive" scientific objectivity is, but it is not a matter for serious dispute that the remarkable and characteristic capacity scientific methodology has for the resolution of disputed issues and for the establishment of instrumental knowledge is strongly dependent upon the special role it assigns to observation. In some way, observations permit scientists to use the world as a kind of court to which issues can be submitted for resolution. However "biased" the court may be, the striking success of scientific methodology in identifying predictively reliable theories must be in significant measure a reflection of that court's role. Call a theory *instrumentally reliable* if, and to the extent that, it yields approximately accurate predictions about observable phenomena. Similarly, call methodological practices instrumentally reliable if, and to the extent that, they contribute to the discovery and acceptance of instrumentally reliable theories. It is unproblematical that the crucial role of observation in science contributes profoundly to the instrumental reliability of scientific methodology.

Once this special epistemological role of observations is recognized, it is natural to investigate other features of scientific methodology by comparing or contrasting the role they play with the special role played by observation. In this chapter I apply this strategy to two features of scientific methodology. The first of these is the systematic preference that scientific methodology dictates in favor of explanatory theories. The second goes by several names; what I have in mind is the methodological preference for theories having the property or properties that philosophers typically call simplicity or parsimony and scientists often call elegance (or, perhaps, beauty) instead. The standards for theory assessment (call them the nonexperimental standards) required by these features of scientific methodology are, at least apparently, so different from those set by the requirement that the predictions of theories must be sustained by observational tests that it is, initially at least, puzzling what they have to do with the rational scientific assessment of theories or with scientific objectivity.

Reprinted (with emendations) from *Observation, Experiment, and Hypothesis in Modern Physical Science*, ed. P. Achinstein and O. Hannaway (Cambridge, MA: MIT Press, 1985), pp. 47–94, by permission of the author and the publisher.

Simplicity, Explanatory Power, and Projectability: Why the Puzzles Are Serious

When we think of scientific objectivity, two importantly different features of scientific practice seem to be at issue: *intersubjectivity* (the capacity of scientists to reach a stable consensus about the issues they investigate and to agree about revisions in that consensus in the light of new data or new theoretical developments) and *epistemic reliability* (the capacity of scientists to get it (approximately) right about the things they study). If we focus exclusively on the first component of scientific objectivity, then the role of the preference for explanatory theories and for simple theories may not seem especially puzzling. Suppose that, for whatever reason, scientists prefer simple and explanatory theories. Perhaps the preference for simplicity reflects a basic psychological law and the preference for explanatory theories reflects a feature of graduate training in science; the source of the preferences does not matter. Suppose as well that, as a result of common indoctrination in their professional training (a common "paradigm" in Kuhn's sense), scientists share basically the same standards of explanatory power and relative simplicity. Under these conditions, the methodological preference for explanatory and simple theories could as readily contribute to the production of a stable scientific consensus as could scientists' common recourse to the results of observation. Indeed, the contribution to the establishment of consensus might be greater, since the consensus-making effects of appeals to observations sometimes depend upon considerable luck or ingenuity in the design of experiments or in the making of relevant observations in nature.

Similarly, even if we focus on the second component of scientific objectivity (the capacity of scientists to get it right in their views about the world), some features of the contribution of the nonexperimental standards of theory assessment to scientific objectivity may seem unpuzzling. Suppose that we follow Kuhn (as we should) in holding that judgments of explanatory power and simplicity are determined by standards embodied in the current research tradition or "paradigm" (Kuhn 1970). Suppose, further, that we follow Kuhn (as we should not; see Boyd 1979, 1982, 1983) in holding that the theoretical structure of the world that scientists study (its fundamental ontology, basic laws, and so on) is constituted or constructed by the adoption of the paradigm. In that case the contribution of nonexperimental standards to the epistemic reliability of scientific methodology with respect to theoretical knowledge will seem unproblematical. After all, it would be hardly surprising that paradigm-determined standards of the acceptability of theories should be a reliable guide to the truth about a paradigm-determined world.

When we turn to the question of the contribution of such standards to the epistemic reliability of scientific methods with respect to our general knowledge of observable phenomena—that is, their contribution to the instrumental reliability of those methods—the situation is quite different. In the first place, the instrumental reliability of scientific methodology cannot be plausibly explained solely on the basis of the supposed paradigmatic construction of reality postulated by Kuhn and others. The fact that anomalous experimental results (results that contradict the expectations dictated by the theoretical tradition or "paradigm" in theoretically intractable ways) occur repeatedly in the history of science and are important in initiating "scientific revolutions" (Kuhn 1970) is sufficient to show that the capacity of scientists to set it right in their predictions about observable phenomena cannot be explained by assuming that the observable world is "constituted by" or "constructed from" the paradigm that determines their methodology. The data from the history of science simply do not permit such an interpretation (Boyd 1983).

Moreover, nonexperimental criteria of theory acceptability are absolutely crucial to the methodology by which scientists achieve instrumental knowledge (Boyd 1973, 1979, 1982, 1983, 1985). Briefly, this is so for two reasons. In the first place, nonexperimental criteria determine which theories are taken to be "projectable" in Goodman's (1973) sense. Of the infinitely many generalizations about observables that are logically compatible with any body of observational evidence, only the (typically quite small) finite number of generalizations that correspond to theories that are simple, are explanatory, and otherwise satisfy nonexperimental criteria are candidates for even tentative confirmation by those observations. Thus, many possible and experimentally unrefuted generalizations about observables are simply ruled out by such criteria (Boyd 1972, 1973, 1979, 1980, 1982, 1983, 1985; van Fraassen 1980).

To make matters more puzzling, in the testing of hypotheses that have been identified in this way as projectable, scientific methodology requires that a theory be tested under circumstances that are identified by other projectable rival theories as circumstances in which its observational predictions are likely to prove false. From the extraordinarily large body of predictive consequences of a proposed theory we identify those few whose testing is adequate for its confirmation by pitting the proposed theory against its few rivals that satisfy the nonexperimental criteria. To a very good first approximation this is the fundamental methodological principle governing the assessment of experimental evidence in science (Boyd 1972, 1973, 1979, 1980, 1982, 1983, 1985). Both judgments of projectability and assessments of experimental evidence for claims about observables thus depend on nonexperimental criteria of the sort that I am discussing. They play a crucial epistemic role in scientific methodology, and thus, like the practice of subjecting theories to observational tests, they contribute to the epistemic reliability that characterizes scientific objectivity.

The same point may be put in another way. Van Fraassen (1980, p. 88) discusses the various nonexperimental theoretical "virtues" and concludes that they should be treated as pragmatic rather than epistemic constraints on theory acceptability: "In so far as they go beyond consistency, empirical adequacy, and empirical strength, they do not concern the relation between theory and the world, but rather the use and usefulness of the theory; they provide reasons to prefer the theory independently of questions of truth." What we have just seen is that this approach is not tenable. We cannot think of the nonexperimental virtues as additional purely pragmatic criteria of theory acceptability above and beyond the criterion of empirical adequacy, for they are essential components in the methodology we have for assessing empirical adequacy. They may also be desirable "independently of questions of truth" (although I doubt it); however, what is striking about their methodological role is precisely that they are central to the ways we assess observational evidence for the truth of generalizations about observables .

We really do have an epistemological puzzle, then. On the one hand, it seems pretty clear that scientific objectivity depends crucially upon the practice of deciding scientific issues by referring those issues to adjudication by the world via experimental or observational testing of proposed theories. That this practice should contribute to both components of scientific objectivity seems unproblematical. On the other hand, it appears that judgments of the aesthetic or cognitive merits of theories play a role in establishing the epistemic reliability of scientific practice comparable to that played by the criterion of experimental confirmation—indeed, such considerations seem to be part of the very methodology by which adequate experimental confirmation is defined. We need to ask how nonexperimental criteria of this sort can play a role so similar to that played by observations in sound scientific practice.

Traditional Empiricist Approaches to the Puzzle

Traditional logical empiricist philosophy of science treats the two non-experimental criteria I am discussing quite differently. In the case of simplicity and related criteria, I think it would be fair to characterize the approach of logical empiricists as varying, depending upon whether they were doing abstract epistemology of science or applied philosophy of science. In the former case, simplicity was almost always treated as a purely pragmatic theoretical virtue. Often the rationality of preferring simple theories (all other things being equal) was explained in terms of rational allocation of time: It was more rational to investigate first the computationally less complex theories rather than those whose testing would require longer and more difficult computations. Variations on this theme of simplicity as a factor in intellectual economy are characteristic of the pragmatic treatment of the issue within twentieth-century logical empiricism.

In the context of applied philosophy of science—the examination of epistemological and logical issues surrounding particular issues in the various sciences—the situation was quite different. In general, logical empiricists treated issues of scientific methodology more descriptively when they undertook to do applied philosophy. That is, they identified methodologically important features of scientific practice, which they characterized in relatively nonanalytical terms (such as "simplicity," "parsimony," or "coherence"). They then cited the standards set by such features in offering solutions to philosophical problems in particular sciences. What they tended not to do, in such contexts, was emphasize the "rational reconstruction" of methodological principles in the light of the verificationist accounts of scientific knowledge and scientific language that formed the basis of their more abstract philosophical investigations. There is little doubt that this departure from verificationist strictures in applied philosophy of science was a reflection of the fact that the antirealist perspective dictated by verificationism cannot serve as the basis for an adequate account of the epistemology or the semantics of actual science (Boyd 1972, 1973, 1979, 1980, 1982, 1983, 1985). In any event, the general pattern of departure from strict verificationism in applied philosophy of science was clearly manifested in many applications of the methodological principle of preference for simpler theories. In dealing with actual disputes in science, logical empiricist philosophers of science typically took the preference for simpler theories as a basic principle in the epistemology of science and cheerfully cited it as relevant to the determination of answers to questions that were plainly substantive rather than pragmatic. If this practice admits a coherent philosophical rationalization within the empiricist tradition, its rationalization probably lies in positions like that of Carnap (1950), according to which many substantive questions are held to be intelligible only when they are understood as arising within a theoretical perspective that is itself purely conventional and is chosen on essentially pragmatic grounds. Positions of this sort are anticipations of "constructivist" positions in the philosophy of science, such as those of Hanson (1958) and Kuhn (1970), and they are probably best thought of as intermediate between verificationist antirealism and the antirealism of these latter positions (Boyd 1983). In any event, no matter how their philosophical practice might be rationalized, logical empiricists routinely treated the methodological preference for simple theories as though it were on a par with more obviously epistemic norms of the scientific method when they were dealing with philosophical issues arising out of actual scientific theories or scientific practices.

In the case of explanatory power, standard logical-empiricist accounts have all been variations on a single basic account, the deductive-nomological (D-N) theory of explanation, which has been employed both in the abstract analysis of scientific methodology and in applications to particular scientific issues. The key idea is that what it is for a theory to explain an event is that it is possible to carry out an *ex post facto* prediction of the event from the theory together with suitable specifications of conditions antecedent to the event in question. The explanatory power of a theory consists in its capacity to serve as the basis for such "retrodictions." As logical empiricists knew, the adoption of this sort of analysis of explanatory power affords what appears to be a neat (indeed, elegant and even simple) solution to the puzzle of the relationship between scientific objectivity and the methodological principle of preference for explanatory theories. A successful explanation by a theory of some fact has just the same logical form as the confirmation by that fact of an experimental prediction of the theory. An explanation amounts to a demonstration that some event that has occurred previously can be retrospectively interpreted as an experimental test of the theory on which the explanation is based—a test which the theory passes. Thus, it is hardly surprising that the observational testing of theories and the practice of preferring explanatory theories should play similar roles in establishing scientific objectivity; they are the same practice, except for the largely irrelevant retrospective character of the latter. The methodological preference for explanatory theories is just a special case of the more general preference for theories that have survived experimental testing.

Three features of the D-N account make it especially attractive and plausible:

- It has the consequence—plausible in the light of the integrative nature of scientific understanding—that the explanatory power of a theory depends upon the theoretical setting in which it is applied. That it has this consequence is a reflection of the acknowledged role of previously established "auxiliary hypotheses" in the derivation of testable (or applicable) observational consequences from a given scientific theory.
- It is appropriate to the conception of causation prevailing in the philosophical tradition in which it arises. This is so because the D-N account is simply a verificationist "Humean" gloss on the "unreconstructed" preanalytic conception that to explain an event is to say how it was caused.
- It portrays the methodological preference for explanatory theories as a special case of a general epistemic principle, of which the principle dictating a preference for theories whose observational predictions have been confirmed is also a special case.

To these we should add a feature that almost all logical empiricists intended as a feature not only of the D-N account of explanation but also of their accounts of all other features of scientific methodology:

- Philosophical accounts of scientific methodology should all honor the distinction between the "context of discovery" and the "context of justification." In particular, they should invoke principles of deductive logic and statistical reasoning, but not principles of inductive logic of the sort that might be thought to provide rational principles for the invention or discovery of scientific theories. Accounts of the nature of theory confirmation should be entirely independent of contingent empirical claims about how theories are invented.

Despite its attractiveness, the D-N account of explanation proved vulnerable to a number of *prima facie* objections. These fall into three rough categories. In the first place, there seem to be clear-cut cases of scientific theories that explain events even though they do not yield deterministic predictions of their occurrence. Second, there are retrodictions from laws that fit the D-N account of explanations but do not seem to be genuinely explanatory. Finally, even where the laws in question appear to be deterministic, there are clear-cut cases of explanations in which it seems doubtful that the explanation is founded on information sufficient to allow the deduction of a retrodiction of the explained event.

It will not be my aim here to examine in detail any of these objections to the D-N account, or the rebuttals to them, since I hope to raise difficulties for the D-N account of quite a different sort. Suffice it to say that the first of the objections has typically been met by requiring only that there be a statistical prediction of the explained event deduced from the laws in question. (For criticisms of this approach and a defense of a related alternative, see Salmon 1971.) The second objection has typically been met by holding that the apparently deficient D-N "explanations" are indeed explanations that their apparent deficiency reflects merely their failure to meet purely pragmatic standards of, for example, practical or current theoretical interest. Against the third sort of objection, the typical reply has been (depending on the case at issue) either to identify suitable "tacit" premises to make the deductive prediction of the event possible or to assimilate the case to the statistical version of the D-N account. I think it is a fair summary of the literature in the empiricist tradition to say that the first and the third of the objections we are considering have been seen as the more pressing and that the treatment of the second objection in terms of pragmatic considerations has typically been taken to have been largely successful. For the sake of argument, I will assume throughout the chapter that an adequate empiricist solution to the first of these problems exists. I will speak of "predictions" or of "retrodictions" deducible from scientific theories on the understanding that these terms cover the relevant sort of statistical prediction or retrodiction in cases where deterministic predictions or retrodictions are not possible.

The Aims of the Chapter
The D-N account of explanation and the "Humean" account of causation from which it derives are, in their numerous variants, the most durable legacy of the tradition of logical positivism within professional philosophy. (No doubt extreme noncognitivism in ethics is even more durable if we consider the thinking of those who are not professional philosophers.) What I intend to show here is, first, that these legacies of positivism are inadequate even as first approximations to the epistemic task of explaining how considerations of explanatory power are able to play a methodological role analogous to that played by observational testing in science. An adequate explanation of this phenomenon requires that we adopt an account of explanation appropriate to a scientific-realist conception of scientific theories and scientific knowledge (see Smart 1963; Putnam 1975b; Boyd 1972, 1973, 1979, 1980, 1982, 1983, 1985).

I shall argue that nevertheless logical empiricists were right in proposing an account of explanation having the first three features mentioned above: that it portray the explanatory power of a theory as depending upon the theoretical setting in which it is applied, that it be consonant with an appropriate account of causation, and that it treat explanatory power as epistemically relevant in the same way that success in making observational predictions is. I will offer a realist account of a wide class of scientific explanations that meet these criteria and that avoid the difficulties plaguing the D-N account and its variants.

I will indicate how the realist account of explanation can be extended to a closely analogous treatment of the other nonexperimental criterion of theory acceptability we are considering: simplicity. Indeed, I will argue that, in an extended but well-motivated sense of the term, both simplicity and explanatory power are "experimental" criteria of theory acceptability. They reflect indirect theory-mediated evidential considerations that can be accounted for only from the perspective of scientific realism.

Finally I shall argue that these realist treatments of the nonexperimental criteria show that the fourth feature of logical empiricist accounts of scientific methodology—the sharp distinction between context of invention and context of confirmation—cannot be sustained. An adequate account of the epistemic role of observations or of the nonexperimental criteria of theory acceptability requires that we countenance inductive inferences at the theoretical as well as the observational level. The epistemic reliability of such inferences depends both upon logically contingent facts about the particular theoretical tradition that human invention has produced and upon logically contingent psychological and social facts about the capacity of scientists to employ that tradition in the invention of future theories. No account of the epistemology of science that is independent of contingent claims about the social and psychological foundations of scientific practice can be adequate to the task of explaining how the epistemic evaluation of scientific theories works. The epistemology of science must be "naturalized" in a way that requires that the sharp distinction between theory invention and theory confirmation be rejected.

The Humean Conception of Explanation

The "Humean" Conception of Causation in Recent Empiricism

According to Hume's philosophical definition, a cause is "an object precedent and contiguous to another, and where all objects resembling the former are placed in like relations of precedency and contiguity to those objects that resemble the latter." Hume's reasons for adopting this definition are as close to twentieth-century verificationism as one can get in early empiricism. His account has the property (characteristic of later verificationist analyses of scientific notions) that, according to the analysis it provides, the cognitive content of a causal statement is a simple generalization of the cognitive content of the observation statements that are seen as providing evidence for it. No inference from observed regularities to natural necessities or causal powers is required for the confirmation of causal statements.

The version of Hume's account that prevails in twentieth-century empiricist philosophy is significantly different. Roughly, this account holds that an event e_1 causes an event e_2 just in case there are natural laws L and statements C describing conditions antecedent to e_2 such that from L and C, together with a statement reporting the occurrence of e_1, a statement describing the subsequent occurrence of e_2 can be deduced. This account, with variations intended to rule out "trick" cases and to accommodate statistical laws, has proved to be the most durable of the doctrines of logical positivism. The contemporary empiricist account is of course fundamentally verificationist in its content and its justification. "Metaphysical" commitment to such insensibilia as causal powers, underlying mechanisms, hidden essences, and natural necessity is eliminated in favor of the "rational reconstruction" of causal notions in terms of deductive subsumption under natural laws. As in the case of Hume's original formulation, the effect is to make the cognitive content of causal statements closely related to the cognitive content of the observation statements that support them. On an empiricist conception, the nonstipulative cognitive content of natural laws is exhausted by the observational predictions deducible from them, since scientific knowledge cannot extend to "unobservables." Moreover, confirmation of a body of laws consists solely in the experimental confirmation of just those predictions. Thus, the cognitive content of a body of laws consists in a predicted pattern in observations, and evidence for the laws consists in observations that instantiate the pattern in question. Just as in the case of Hume's analysis, events are causally related if they instantiate an appropriate pattern in observable phenomena and evidence for a causal claim consists of confirmation of instances of that pattern. What is different is the way the two "Humean" analyses of cause characterize the relevant patterns in observable phenomena.

The difference in formulation between Hume's account and the account that logical positivists adopted in his name reflects two important features of recent empiricist philosophy of science. In the first place, the contemporary formulations reflect the emphasis recent empiricists have placed on employing the results of modern logical theory in the "rational reconstruction" of scientific concepts. Where Hume's "natural" definition clarifies his philosophical definition by reference to the natural disposition of the mind to form associations of ideas, the contemporary definition refers instead to the logical integration of propositions into deductive systems. More important for our purposes is a special case of this sort of reconstruction: the syntactic conception of "lawlikeness." Hume's account of causation is incomplete without some answer to the question of what respects of resemblances are relevant in applying the definition he offers. It is rather plain that Hume's answer is provided by the "natural" definition of causation: The respects of resemblance that "count" are just those to which the mind naturally attends in forming general beliefs about property correlations. Logical positivists quite rightly rejected this particular form of philosophical naturalism. In its place they substituted an appeal to the notion of a natural law. Respects of resemblance "count" just in case they are the respects of similarity indicated as relevant by natural laws. Now, for any two nonsimultaneous events there will be some true general statement about events from which one can deduce a prediction of the occurrence of the subsequent event if one is given as an additional premise a statement reporting the occurrence of the antecedent event. If by a natural law one were to understand simply a true general statement about events, the contemporary "Humean" definition of causation would have the absurd consequence that causation amounts simply to temporal priority. The positivists' solution was to distinguish "lawlike" from non-'lawlike' generalizations and to understand the natural laws to be just the true lawlike generations. It was understood that lawlikeness should be a syntactic property of sentences—in particular, that it should be an *a priori* question which sentences were lawlike, although of course it would be an empirical question which of these were true (and thus laws). The problem of characterizing those generalizations that are lawlike is just the same problem as characterizing those generalizations that are "projectable" (Goodman 1973) or those kinds, relations, and categories that are "natural" (Quine 1969). In each case the question is which patterns in empirical data should be thought of *prima facie* as instantiations of causal regularities.

Within recent empiricist philosophy (see, e.g., Goodman 1973; Quine 1969) there have been proposed variations on the traditional positivist conception of lawlikeness according to which judgments of lawlikeness or projectability are not *a priori*. Successful inductive generalizations governed by particular judgments of projectability may be taken to provide empirical evidence in favor of the projectability judgments themselves, whereas unsuccessful inductive inferences may tend to disconfirm the projectability judgments upon which they depend. It will be important for us to establish just what variations on the traditional positivist conception of lawlikeness are compatible with the contemporary Humean conception of causation.

The Humean definition of causation, whether in its eighteenth-century or in its twentieth-century version, is essentially an eliminative definition. It is not an analysis of what we (as scientist or as laypersons) ordinarily take ourselves to mean when we talk about causal relations. No doubt we would ordinarily paraphrase causal statements in such terms as "makes happen," "brings about," or "necessitates," or in terms that refer to underlying mechanisms or processes. The Humean conception rejects definitions of causation in such terms not because they inadequately capture our preanalytic conceptions but rather because our preanalytic conceptions are held to be epistemologically defective. Neither natural necessitation nor most of the underlying mechanisms or processes to which we would ordinarily refer in paraphrasing causal statements are observable. Therefore, on the empiricist conception, knowledge of such phenomena —if there are any—is impossible. Our preanalytic conceptions of causation, if taken literally, would render knowledge of causal relations likewise impossible. The Humean definition of causation offers a remedy for this difficulty by "rationally reconstructing" our causal concepts in noncausal terms. Reference to suspect unobservable entities, powers, or necessitations is reduced to reference to patterns in observable data. This is the whole point of, and the sole justification for, the Humean definition. The appropriateness of various conceptions of lawlikeness must be assessed in the light of this essentially verificationist justification for the Humean definition. An analysis of lawlikeness—whatever its independent merits might be—is inappropriate for the formulation of a Humean definition of causation unless it is itself compatible with the verificationist project of reducing causal talk and other talk about insensibilia to talk about regularities in the behavior of observables.

This constraint is important because, just as our preanalytic inclination would be to paraphrase causal statements in terms of natural necessitation or underlying mechanisms, our preanalytic conception of the distinction between natural laws and accidental generalizations is probably equally infected with unreduced causal notions. We might, for example, propose to define as lawlike those generalizations that attribute the observable regularities they predict to the operation of a fixed set of underlying mechanisms, or perhaps to consider lawlike those generalizations that attribute the predicted observable regularities to underlying mechanisms that are relevantly similar to those already postulated in well-confirmed generalizations. Some such definition of lawlikeness might well be the correct one (indeed, I think that the latter proposal is very nearly right), but no such definition would be appropriate for the formulation of the contemporary version of the Humean definition of causation. If lawlikeness is already a causal notion, then the Humean definition fails to accomplish the desired eliminative reduction of causal notions to noncausal observational notions and is thus without any philosophical justification. It must be emphasized that any analysis of lawlikeness that referred to unobservable "theoretical entities" and "theoretical properties" or to unobservable underlying mechanisms or processes would be just as inappropriate for a formulation of the Humean definition as one that talked explicitly about "natural necessity." Such "secret powers" or hidden "inner constitutions" of matter have always been the paradigm cases of the sort of alleged causal phenomena reference to which the Humean definition of causation is designed to eliminate. To appeal to unobservable constituents of matter and their unobservable theoretical properties (such as mass, charge, and spin) is precisely to engage in a twentieth-century version of Locke's appeal to insensible corpuscles and their various "powers." Unreduced reference to, say, the charge of electrons *just is* reference to an unobservable causal power of one of the unobservable participants in the unobservable mechanisms underlying causal relations among observables. Reference to phenomena of this sort is precisely what the Humean definition must eliminate.

Similar considerations dictate a closely related additional constraint on definitions of lawlikeness suitable for formulations of the Humean definition. Suppose that a definition of lawlikeness were proposed that involved no unreduced reference to causal notions or to theoretical entities. Such a definition of lawlikeness might still prove inappropriate for the Humean definition of causation if in order to determine whether or not a statement fell under it one would have to rely on inferences from premises that themselves involve irreducible reference to causal notions or to theoretical entities. After all, the whole point of the Humean definition is to render causal statements confirmable even on the assumption that knowledge of unobservable phenomena is impossible. If judgments of lawlikeness can be made only on the basis of premises thus supposed to be unknowable, then the Humean project fails. As we shall see, this proves to be the case.

Explanation and the Humean Definition of Causation
For a wide class of cases, an explanation of an event is provided by a statement saying how the event was caused. On the Humean definition of causation, saying how an event was caused amounts to deductive subsumption of the event under natural laws together with specifications of antecedent conditions—in other words, deductive retrodiction of the event from initial condition statements and laws. The preanalytic conception of a wide class of explanations reduces to the deductive-nomological conception upon Humean rational reconstruction. This fact provides the only good reason there has ever been to accept the D-N account of explanation; to a good first approximation, the D-N account *just is* the Humean definition of causation.

As the recent empiricist conceptions of causation and lawlikeness depart significantly from our preanalytic conceptions, so the D-N account of explanation departs from our unreconstructed conception of explanation. Without doubt our preanalytic understanding of the central cases of scientific and everyday explanation would, if spelled out, invoke unreduced notions of causation and of causal processes and mechanisms. If unreconstructed causal talk were philosophically unobjectionable (as, I shall eventually argue, it should be), there would be no reason whatsoever to adopt the alternative D-N account. Indeed, the considerable difficulty defenders of the D-N account and its variants have had in accommodating paradigm cases of explanations (and of nonexplanations) to the definitions of explanation they have offered indicates just how far from compelling (or even plausible) the D-N account would be were it not for the verificationist objections to unreduced causal notions.

The Humean roots of the D-N account are evident in the literature, albeit in a somewhat unexpected way. A survey of the classical early papers defending and elaborating the D-N account and its variants (e.g., Hempel and Oppenheim 1948; Hempel 1965; Feigl 1945; Popper 1959) indicates that in the typical case Hume is never mentioned but it is taken for granted that the D-N account is appropriate for straightforward causal explanations. In Hempel and Oppenheim 1948 and in Hempel 1965 the Humean analysis (not so described) is very briefly appealed to in the case of causal explanations. Hempel and Oppenheim adduce the requirement that the explanans must have empirical content in support of the D-N account, and Feigl insists that it is possible to "retain the valuable anti-metaphysical point of view" in rival conceptions of explanation while adopting the D-N definition instead. None of the early authors, however, spend much time elaborating these plainly verificationist and Humean justifications for the D-N account. Instead, insofar as the account is defended in detail, they defend its extension to less clear-cut cases (teleological, motivational, or statistical explanations, for example). They take it for granted that, perhaps with the help of a few verificationist "reminders," the reader will agree that the D-N account of explanation is appropriate for ordinary causal explanations and will find controversial only its extension to other sorts of explanation. The unselfconscious Humeanism in these early papers is striking, but the fact that it is unselfconscious merely makes it clearer that the philosophical justification for the D-N account lies in the fact that it represents the Humean rational reconstruction of the notion of causal explanation. At least for the central case of causal explanation, no other philosophical justification is to be found.

This situation persists in the more recent literature on the D-N account. I think it is fair to say that, insofar as more recent philosophers have defended the D-N account or its variants, their strategy has been to offer rebuttals to a variety of putative counterexamples to the account. These rebuttals have often been extraordinarily ingenious. It is nevertheless true that if we had no Humean and verificationist reasons for accepting the D-N account in the first place these rebuttals to counterexamples would not by themselves constitute a good reason to accept the account. The situation remains that the D-N account of explanation is a preanalytically implausible analysis whose philosophical justification lies in the presumed need to rationally reconstruct causal notions in noncausal terms. Without this verificationist and anti-"metaphysical" premise, the D-N account would be philosophically indefensible.

Humean Explanation and Evidence

I suggested above that the D-N account of explanation has three philosophical virtues: that it portrays the explanatory power of a theory as depending upon the more general theoretical setting in which it is applied, that it rests on a theory of causation appropriate to the philosophical tradition in which it arises, and that it portrays the methodological preference for explanatory theories as a special case of the same methodological principle that dictates a preference for theories whose predictions have been observationally confirmed. We have just seen that the second of these claims is true, that at least for the central case of causal explanations the D-N account is the Humean definition of explanation. The first is true just because the D-N account was understood in light of the principle of "unity of science" according to which a variety of different well-confirmed theories may legitimately be employed conjointly in making observational predictions. This principle is exactly the principle that entails the employment of "auxiliary hypotheses" in deducing the observational predictions that are to be tested in order to confirm or disconfirm a proposed theory. It is worth remarking that the "unity of science" principle is ineliminable if the D-N account of explanation is to be even remotely plausible. Even in the most typical and straightforward cases of causal explanation it is usually true that the event explained will not be retrodictable from the primary explanatory theory unless additional well-confirmed theories are also employed as premises. This point is as unchallenged in the empiricist literature as the corresponding point about the necessity of "auxiliary hypotheses" in the testing of theories.

Let us now turn to the third of these features. When an event is explained, the theories that are said to be explanatory on the D-N account are those that are employed in the retrodiction of the event. Thus, every successful explanation of an observable event has just the same logical form as a successful observational test of the relevant explanatory theories. This happy result is no surprise. It is characteristic of Humean conceptions of causation that the occurrence of a cause followed by its effect should be an instance of, and thus evidence for, the law or regularity whose existence is asserted by the appropriate "rationally reconstructed" causal statement. It would thus appear that the D-N account of explanation solves the epistemological puzzle about the evidential relevance of explanatory power as a nonexperimental criterion of theory acceptance. Really, according to the D-N account, the methodological preference for explanatory theories is not a non-experimental criterion. Instead it is the special case of the criterion that dictates preference for experimentally tested theories —the case that applies to experimental (or observational) evidence whose epistemic relevance is recognized only after the relevant observation has been made. For one of the nonexperimental criteria, at least, the puzzle appears to be resolved. The elegance of this proposed solution is surely one of the most attractive features of the D-N account.

Nevertheless, it is extremely important to recognize that—even by empiricist standards—the D-N solution to the puzzle of the evidential role of explanatory power is incomplete. Recall that explanatory power is only one of a number of apparently nonexperimental criteria of theory acceptability. Even if it should turn out that the explanatory power of a theory is just a matter of its experimental confirmation by belatedly recognized observational tests of its own predictions, the fact remains that there are some genuinely nonexperimental criteria that are central to scientific methodology. This must be the case, since, as Goodman demonstrated, judgments regarding the confirmation of theories require prior (though perhaps tentative and revisable) judgments of their projectability. The genuine nonexperimental criteria are just those that legitimately play a role in projectability judgments. It follows, of course, that no account of the epistemology of science that does not say something about the epistemic (as opposed to the purely pragmatic) role of the genuine nonexperimental criteria can be complete. What is striking is that the D-N account presupposes an appropriate solution to this problem because the notion of projectability or lawlikeness is appealed to in the very formulation of the D-N account. There are two possibilities: Either judgments of lawlikeness are simply judgments of explanatory potential (a plausible enough view in light of actual scientific practice) or there are additional or different components of such judgments. In the first case, the D-N account of explanation cannot be a complete account of the epistemic role of judgments of explanatory power, since it presupposes a nonexperimental role for such judgments. In the second case, the D-N account succeeds in the project of providing a Humean anti-metaphysical analysis of the epistemic role of such judgments only if a similarly Humean reconstruction is possible for the genuinely nonexperimental criteria. In either case, the view that the D-N account of explanation succeeds in offering an account of the epistemic role of judgments of explanatory power presupposes the possibility of providing a similarly Humean account of whatever nonexperimental criteria of theory acceptability there are.

Thus, providing Humean accounts of the evidential relevance of nonexperimental criteria and of explanatory power are not two independent tasks of empiricist philosophy of science; success in the former is a prerequisite for success in the latter. Once this fact is recognized, one can see that there is a significant *prima facie* difficulty in the traditional empiricist program. The traditional empiricist treatment of nonexperimental criteria other than explanatory power has been to treat such criteria either as purely pragmatic and thus epistemically irrelevant (as is typical when such criteria are described as "simplicity" or "parsimony") or as purely syntactic and thus conventional (as in the case of typical treatments of lawlikeness or projectability). As we have seen, there is no reason to believe that the epistemic contribution of nonexperimental criteria to the instrumental reliability of scientific methodology can be accounted for on solely pragmatic or conventionalistic grounds. The question is thus raised whether an adequate treatment of nonexperimental criteria is possible within the empiricist tradition, as the D-N account of explanation requires. In the next section I shall argue that the answer is no.

Toward a Non-Humean Alternative

Why a Non-Humean Alternative Is Needed

There is an extraordinarily rich and interesting literature in which various versions of the D-N account of explanation are criticized and defended with respect to their applicability to a wide range of kinds of explanation. What is characteristic of this literature is that philosophers have debated the applicability of the D-N account with respect to particular examples of scientific, historical, or psychological explanations that might be thought to resist subsumption under the D-N conception. Many of the criticisms of the D-N account represented in this literature are extremely important, as are many of the replies in its defense. Nevertheless, what I propose to do here is not to review this important literature but instead to argue directly against the D-N account on the grounds that the Humean definition of causation—which is its only philosophical basis—can now be seen to be wholly inadequate. I propose to adopt this strategy for two reasons. In the first place, it seems to me that the fact that for causal explanations the D-N account is an utterly straightforward application of the Humean definition of causation means that, unless a critique of the Humean definition is developed, the effectiveness of any criticisms of the D-N account for such cases will necessarily be reduced in the light of the support the D-N account receives from so well established a philosophical doctrine as the Humean definition. Moreover, it seems to me that recent criticisms of empiricist philosophy of science (including, of course, criticisms of the D-N account) have permitted us to develop enough anti-empiricist insights in the philosophy of science that a useful direct criticism of the Humean roots of the D-N account is now possible. What I propose to do in the remainder of this section is offer two sorts of criticisms of the Humean definition of causation (one more technical and the other more epistemological), propose and defend alternative conceptions of causation and of explanation that are in the tradition of "scientific realism" rather than in the tradition of logical empiricism, and indicate briefly how the proposed alternative conception of explanation would apply to the problem of explaining the epistemic role of explanatory power in scientific methodology. Since my aim is to indicate how recent critiques of logical empiricism and its variants can be extended to a treatment of the issue of explanation, I will rely heavily on recent work (including some of my own) that is critical of empiricism. I will usually sketch the main philosophical arguments involved, but I will not attempt to defend in detail the anti-empiricist positions upon which my critique of the Humean conceptions of causation and explanation depends. The present work is intended as a contribution to a developing realist critique of empiricism, not as an entirely self-contained refutation of the empiricist conception of explanation.

A Technical Criticism

[We omit here a portion of the original paper in which Boyd argues against the Humean conception of causation by establishing the possibility of deterministic laws whose mathematical structure is such that not all of their causal consequences are deducible from them. The basic strategy is that rehearsed in Boyd 1972.]

A promising response might be to propose a natural revision in the formulation of the Humean definition itself. Suppose that, instead of requiring that the occurrence of the effect be deductively predictable from the laws together with relevant specifications of initial conditions, we require that statements completely specifying the effect hold in all of the intended models of the laws together with the specifications of initial conditions. At least for a great many cases (including all those discussed in Boyd 1972), a suitable notion of "intended interpretation" is available, and the Humean definition so modified will therefore identify causal relations in the appropriate way. The difficulties with this proposal are philosophical rather than mathematical. In order for the proposed definition of causation to be Humean, it would have to be the case that—on the conception of cause it advances—causal relations could be discerned in nature without recourse to knowledge of unobservable "theoretical entities" and their causal powers. There are extremely good reasons to believe that this is not so. The question of the confirmation of laws not all of whose observational consequences are deducible from them raises, in an especially clear way, a general problem in the experimental confirmation of theories. In general, when we accept the observational confirmation of finitely many of the infinitely many observational predictions of a theory as constituting sufficient evidence for its tentative confirmation, we are tacitly relying on some solution to what might be called the general problem of "sampling" in experimental design. By this I mean the problem of deciding, for any particular proposed theory, which reasonably small finite subsets from among the infinite set of observational predictions it makes are "representative samples" in the sense that observational confirmation of all their members would constitute good evidence for the approximate truth of the rest of the theory's observational consequences. The significance of this problem is especially easy to see when we consider the special case of theories not all of whose intended observational consequences are computationally available. In order to confirm such a theory, we would have to assure ourselves that from among the computationally available predictions of the theory a suitable representative sample can be formed.

I have argued (Boyd 1972, section 7) that for some theories with some computationally unavailable consequences it would be possible to reliably identify such representative samples by employing available theoretical knowledge of (typically unobservable) underlying mechanisms to determine under what various sorts of conditions the theory would be likely to fail, and by finding computationally available predictions of the theory regarding conditions of these various sorts. Such a strategy would permit confirmation of such theories, but it would not do so within the constraints required by a Humean conception of scientific knowledge. Prior theoretical knowledge of underlying unobservable causal mechanisms would be essential for the confirmation of such theories. Thus, the revised definition of causation we are considering would fail to be Humean, in that it would not portray causal knowledge as independent of knowledge of unobservable causal factors.

I have also argued (Boyd 1973, 1979, 1982, 1983, and especially Boyd 1985) that—for theories in general and not just for those theories whose causal consequences are not fully available deductively—no alternative to this procedure for solving the problem of sampling exists. I conclude, therefore, that the second response to the primarily technical objection to the Humean definition of causation also fails. The technical criticism is apparently successful.

It is, nevertheless, a good methodological practice in philosophy to be cautious in accepting primarily technical criticisms of broadly significant philosophical theses. Such theses often admit of unanticipated reformulations that are sufficient to avoid particular technical criticisms. The more important criticisms are those suggesting that the thesis in question rests upon a fundamental philosophical mistake. Such a criticism of the Humean definition is suggested by the epistemological rebuttal just offered to the possible revision we were considering. If the methods of actual scientific practice for resolving questions about sampling in experimental design rely upon prior (approximate) theoretical knowledge of unobservable causal factors, then, in particular, knowledge of such factors is actual and therefore possible. Thus, the empiricist conception that experimental knowledge cannot extend to unobservable causal powers and mechanisms must be mistaken and the philosophical justification of the Humean definition of causation rests upon a false epistemological premise. There is indeed considerable evidence that almost all the significant features of the methodology of recent science rest ultimately upon knowledge of unobservable causal powers and mechanisms (see Putnam 1975a, 1975b; Boyd 1973,1979, 1982, 1983, 1985), and thus that the empiricist reservations about experimental knowledge of unobservable causal powers and mechanisms are profoundly mistaken. In the next section, I will explore in greater detail the consequences for the Humean conception of causation and explanation of the failure of the empiricist conception of experimental knowledge.

The Epistemological Inadequacy of the Humean Definition
The Humean definition of causation and the associated D-N account of explanation require acceptance of the "unity of science" principle and presuppose a Humean (that is, nonrealistic) but nevertheless epistemic account of the nonexperimental criteria of theory acceptance that determine judgments of lawlikeness and projectability. In fact, no satisfactory epistemological account of the "unity of science" principle is compatible with the empiricist's denial that we can have knowledge of unobservable causal powers and mechanisms, and no Humean account of lawlikeness and projectability can be epistemogically adequate.

Consider first the "unity of science" principle. Neither the Humean definition of causation nor the D-N account of explanation is even remotely plausible unless it is understood that the laws under which the caused or explained event is to be subsumed can be drawn from several different scientific disciplines or subdisciplines and conjointly applied in predicting an event. It must be possible for two laws that have been quite independently confirmed by specialists working in different areas to both be premises in the sort of deductive prediction to which the Humean definition and the D-N account refer. Moreover, it must of course be epistemically legitimate that independently confirmed laws be conjointly applied in this way to make observational predictions....

There is a further Humean requirement that applications of the "unity of science" principle must meet if the Humean conceptions of causation and explanation are to be justified. We have already seen that the Humean conceptions are philosophically untenable if judgments of lawlikeness or projectability involve knowledge of unreduced causal factors. In a similar way, the Humean conceptions would be philosophically untenable if the applications of the "unity of science" principle upon which their plausibility depends themselves presupposed knowledge of unobservable causal factors. In fact this proves to be the case. The argument (see Putnam 1975b; Boyd 1982, 1983, 1985) can be summarized as follows: The principle that independently confirmed theories can legitimately be conjointly applied in making predictions about observables must presuppose some sort of judgments of univocality for the nonobservational (or "theoretical") terms occurring in the theories in question.... Moreover, the principle for assessing univocality cannot be that theoretical terms are nonunivocal whenever they occur in different theories; such a principle would result in a very significant underestimation of the scope of the "unity of science" principle in actual scientific practice and therefore would be inappropriate for the defense of the Humean conceptions we are considering.

Once it is recognized that theoretical terms from quite different theories are sometimes to be counted as occurring univocally, it becomes clear that the "unity of science" principle makes a striking epistemological claim. Suppose that T_1 and T_2 are two theories from quite different scientific disciplines in whose conjunction no theoretical terms occur ambiguously. Suppose further that in the experimental confirmation of these theories neither was ever employed as an "auxiliary hypothesis" in the testing of the other. There will thus have been no *direct* experimental test of the conjunction of the two theories, except insofar as the predictive reliability of each of them taken independently has been tested by prior experiments. Nevertheless, the "unity of science" principle maintains, we are justified in expecting the conjunction of the two theories to be instrumentally reliable even in the absence of direct experimental tests, provided only that the univocality constraint on their constituent theoretical terms is satisfied. The univocality constraint is thus supposed to do real epistemic work in making possible what may be thought of as the *indirect* confirmation of the instrumental reliability of the conjunction of T_1 and T_2.

A good way of seeing what is going on is to consider what an empiricist might plausibly take the confirmation of a theory to amount to. Since no knowledge of theoretical entities is supposed to be possible, it would be initially natural for the empiricist to hold that when a theory is confirmed all that is confirmed is the approximate instrumental reliability of the theory itself. Recognition of the crucial role of auxiliary hypotheses in the testing of theories suggests replacing this instrumentalist conception with a broader one according to which the experimental confirmation of a theory amounts to the confirmation of the conjoint reliability of the theory together with the other theories that have been employed as auxiliary hypotheses in testing it. The "unity of science" principle requires a much broader conception. Experimental confirmation of a theory is supposed to constitute evidence for its instrumental reliability even when it is applied conjointly with other well-confirmed theories not even discovered at the time the evidence for the first theory was assessed! Something over and above the instrumental reliability of the conjunction of the theory with actually employed auxiliary hypotheses—something over and above even the instrumental reliability of the theory taken conjointly with currently established theories—is supposed to be confirmed when the theory is properly tested. That "something," the knowledge over and above the instrumental knowledge that has been directly confirmed, is represented in the theoretical structure of the theory, and the rule for extracting it is to make deductive predictions from the theoretical sentences in the theory in question together with the theoretical sentences that represent the similar "excess knowledge" in other well-confirmed theories. There is no plausible explanation of the instrumental reliability of this sort of instrumental knowledge-extraction procedure other than that provided by a realist conception of theory confirmation according to which confirmation of theories involves confirmation of the approximate truth of their theoretical claims as well as their observational ones. On such a conception, judgments of univocality for theoretical terms are judgments of co-referentiality, and what the "unity of science" principle licenses is deductive inferences from the partly theoretical knowledge embodied in independently tested theories to conclusions about the behavior of observables. . . . (As a matter of fact, the situation is even more complicated: The unity of science also involves inductive inferences from theoretical knowledge. This additional consideration strengthens the case for a realist construal of both theory confirmation and univocality judgments; see Boyd 1985.)

It follows not only that knowledge of unobservable causal factors is possible but also that it is presupposed by the "unity of science" principle.... The "unity of science" principle thus presupposes just the sort of knowledge that the Humean conceptions are designed to "rationally reconstruct" away, and the Humean conceptions are thus philosophically indefensible.

Similar arguments show that judgments of lawlikeness and projectability are likewise infected with essentially non-Humean commitments to knowledge of unobservable causal factors. I have argued for this and related claims elsewhere (Boyd 1973, 1979, 1982, 1983, 1985); the basic argument can be summarized as follows.

We have seen that the solution to the problem of sampling in experimental design in mature sciences presupposes prior knowledge of unobservable "theoretical entities" or causal factors. In fact, the solution to this problem is intimately related to the solution to the problem of projectability. Roughly, theories are projectable just in case there is some *prima facie* reason to believe that they might be (approximately) true and thus some reason to treat them as live candidates for confirmation by observational evidence. The methodological rule for the solution to the sampling problem is this: Test a proposed theory under circumstances representative of those identified by other projectable theories about the same issues as those under which its predictions are most likely to be wrong. The theory-dependent judgments that go into solving the problem of sampling are just special cases of judgments of projectability.

In fact, as Kuhn (1970) has correctly maintained, this pattern of the dependence of scientific methodology on the ontological picture presented by the received theoretical tradition infects all the important principles of scientific methodology.... For each of the theory-dependent principles of scientific methodology we can ask what explains its contribution to the instrumental reliability of scientific practice. In each case, the only plausible explanation is given by the realist conception that in making such judgments we employ the approximate knowledge of observable and unobservable causal factors reflected in existing theories in order to establish methods for improving our knowledge of both observable and "theoretical" entities (Boyd 1973, 1979, 1982, 1983, 1985). Theoretical understanding of unobservable causal factors enjoys a dialectical relationship with the development and improvement of methods for improving theoretical understanding itself. In particular, judgments of projectability require knowledge of unobservable causal factors. Thus, the appeal to projectability in the Humean definition of causation deprives that definition of its Humean content and hence of its only philosophical justification.

It will be useful to consider one important rebuttal to the position I have just taken. In "Natural Kinds" (1969), Quine sometimes describes the natural kinds in mature sciences as issuing from theory "full-blown." When Quine writes in this way, his account of natural kinds (and thus of projectability) seems very close to the realist and anti-Humean conception just discussed. In other places he seems to prefer to treat the identification of projectable theories or predicates as involving "second-order induction about induction." He says: "We establish the projectability of some predicate, to our satisfaction, by trying to project it.... In induction, nothing succeeds like success" (p. 129). This formulation suggests that projectability judgments might be thought of as *a posteriori* judgments involving consideration only of observable phenomena. After all, the instrumental reliability thus far displayed by some particular inductive strategy (with its particular judgments of projectability) is an observable phenomenon, and Quine's suggestion appears to be that we can (at least tentatively) identify projectable theories or predicates by looking at which ones have figured in successful inductive inferences in the past. No consideration of unobservable phenomena appears to be involved.

It is important to see what the philosophical consequences would be if this conception of projectability judgments could be sustained. We have already seen that projectability judgments play an essential epistemic role in establishing the instrumental reliability of scientific methodology, and that therefore it is not adequate to treat projectability judgments as purely conventional or to offer a purely pragmatic account of their rationale. As Quine and Goodman both recognized, projectability judgments must have some sort of empirical basis in order for their epistemic role to be explicable. The proposal that Quine appears to be making would, if it were successful, provide an adequate account of that epistemic role without invoking knowledge of unobservable causal factors. The Humean conceptions of causation and explanation would therefore succeed in offering a reductive analysis of causal notions. Moreover, a nonrealist account of the epistemic role of projectability judgments would undermine the arguments rehearsed earlier in this section to the effect that experimental knowledge of unobservable causal factors is possible. The Humean definition of causation and the D-N account of explanation would indeed be philosophically justified, and the project of the present essay would be misconceived.

I have discussed the second-order induction about induction interpretation of projectability at length elsewhere (Boyd 1972, section 2.3; 1985, part III; and especially 1983, section 8). Roughly, the flaw in the proposal lies not in the claim that projectability judgments can be thought of as a species of second-order induction about induction but rather in the conception (which may not have been Quine's) that such inductions are independent of knowledge of unobservable causal factors. The problem is that such inductions—like all inductions—depend upon projectability judgments, and the projectability judgments upon which they depend involve just the appeals to knowledge of unobservable causal factors that (the version we are considering of) second-order induction about induction is supposed to eliminate. Thus second-order inductions about induction will not supply us with projectability judgments which are—as the Humean account requires—obtained independently of knowledge of unobservable causal factors. . . .

The Humean definition aims to rationally reconstruct causal notions in noncausal terms. The philosophical justification for this project rests upon the epistemological premise that experimental knowledge of unobservable causal factors is impossible. The epistemological premise is false, and the rational reconstruction is in any event unsuccessful. There is no reason to accept the Humean definition. The D-N account of explanation is—for those cases in which it is most plausible—simply an application of the Humean definition, and thus it is also without philosophical justification. There is no reason to reject the preanalytic conception that, for a wide and central class of cases, to explain an event or a recurring phenomenon is to say something about how it is caused. Nor is there any reason to think that the empiricist analyses of causation and explanation rest on, or provide, an even approximately accurate conception of the nature of causal knowledge in science or in any other area of inquiry.

The Semantics of "Cause" and "Explain"

It is a puzzling fact that many philosophers who reject the empiricist conclusion that knowledge of unobservables is impossible and who are sympathetic to scientific realism rather than to verificationism or instrumentalism nevertheless employ the Humean definition of causation or the D-N account of explanation, even in cases in which the phenomena caused or explained are unobservable. The principal explanation of this phenomenon, I believe, is that the Humean definition and the D-N account were so widely accepted during the time when empiricism dominated the philosophy of science that they now have the status of established philosophical maxims whose initial justification has been forgotten. The fact that the rejection of an empiricist conception of experimental knowledge in favor of a realist conception leaves these positions without any philosophical justification may have gone largely unnoticed. I am inclined to think, however, that there is an additional explanation for the durability of these two pieces of philosophical analysis in the face of widely accepted criticisms of their empiricist foundations. I think that philosophers may believe that we need to have some analysis of the meaning of terms such as "cause" and "explain" and that the definitions that arise from the Humean tradition may serve as good first approximations to such meaning analyses. Of course, that such definitions fail to be reductive and thus fail to meet empiricist standards would not, by itself, show that they are inappropriate as nonreductive philosophical analyses.

It nevertheless seems plain that the Humean definitions are strikingly inadequate. In the case of the Humean definition of cause, what seems to be the primary causal notion gets defined in terms of the highly derivative causal-epistemological notion of projectability. Instead, it would seem that the revealing definition would go more nearly in the opposite direction, projectability being defined in terms of knowledge of causal powers and mechanisms. The D-N account of explanation of course inherits these difficulties; moreover, there are notorious difficulties in assimilating clear-cut cases of explanation to the D-N model. It would appear that neither of these definitions is a very promising beginning for a philosophical analysis of the relevant concept. It might be thought that they have the advantage of reminding us that our concept of causation is related to something like a conception of determinism. (It had better not be exactly like one if our conception is to correspond to something real; that is why there are statistical versions of both definitions.) The D-N account of explanation might also be thought of as setting a standard for complete explanations appropriate to the conception that something like determinism is involved in causation.

Against these claims one may reply, first, that the technical criticism of the Humean definitions presented above show that in any event they embody the wrong analysis of determinism (see Boyd 1972). Moreover, in any event we want the question of the relationship between causation and determinism to be spelled out by research in the various sciences and social sciences rather than by so abstract a definitional specification. In a similar way, we should want the relevant methodological standards of completeness of explanations to be determined (in a theory-dependent way) by the aims and the findings of the various special sciences. (Indeed, it is difficult to imagine what scientific activity would, even with a suitable idealization, require us to seek explanations complete in the D-N sense even in a deterministic world.) Finally, as we shall see in the next section, in order to account for the evidential import of explanatory power we need not assimilate explanation to the sort of retrodiction provided by "complete" D-N explanations.

But, someone might ask, if the Humean definitions of causation and explanation are rejected in the name of scientific realism then what does the realist propose as an alternative account of the semantics of these and other causal notions? The answer dictated by the realist considerations offered here has several components. First, of course, it is not to be expected that any significant causal notions are adequately definable in noncausal terms. That is just what the critique of the Humean definition establishes. Second, it is quite doubtful that there are philosophically interesting analytic definitions of scientifically important causal notions, even in terms of each other. As the change in our conception of the relation between causation and determinism induced by the acceptance of quantum mechanics indicates, there is no reason to believe that proposed philosophical analyses or definitions of causal notions will be immune in principle from amendment in the light of new theoretical discoveries.

It is nevertheless clear that informative philosophical analyses of many causal or partly causal notions are possible. I take it that such analyses are in some sense empirical because they depend upon empirical facts about causal phenomena and about our practices regarding them and because they are revisable in the light of new discoveries in these areas. Nevertheless, they appear to lie squarely within the province of philosophy. Analyses of such causal notions as explanation, projectability, reference, and knowledge I take to be in this category. About the less derivative causal notions, such as "(total) cause," "causal power," "interaction," "mechanism," and "possibility," it seems less likely that informative analyses of the sort that philosophers typically seek are available; it might be that "cause" and "causal power" are somehow interdefinable, but it is doubtful that whatever definition might be available would prove very informative to someone who wanted to know, e.g., what causal powers are. Informative definitions or analyses in these latter cases, I suggest, are not primarily a matter of conceptual analysis, even on the understanding suggested above according to which conceptual analysis is a kind of empirical enterprise. Instead, the informative analyses or definitions of more basic causal notions are to be established by theoretical inquiry in the various sciences and social sciences. What causation is and what causal interaction amounts to are theoretical questions about natural phenomena (to reject the Humean project is just to admit that causal relations, powers, and interactions really are features of nature), so it is hardly surprising that answers to them should depend more upon the empirically confirmed theoretical findings of the various sciences than should answers to more abstract (and more typically philosophical) questions about the nature of knowledge, reference, or explanation.

The distinction between the two sorts of questions is one of degree. "Conceptual analysis," when done well, has an ineliminable empirical component, and the more foundational questions in the various sciences are typically philosophical questions as well, often requiring the special analytical techniques of philosophy for their resolution. But even though the distinction is one of degree, the fact that definitional questions about fundamental causal notions fall on the side nearer to the various empirical sciences dictates an important conclusion: that such notions as "(total) cause," "causal power," and "interaction" are like the notions of various natural kinds in that they possess no analytic definitions, no "nominal essences." They are defined instead by natural definitions or "real essences" whose features are dictated by logically contingent facts about the way the world is. From a realist perspective, this is hardly surprising. Natural kinds and categories lack stipulative *a priori* definitions precisely because, in order to play a reliable role in explanation and induction, natural kinds and categories must be defined in ways that reflect the particular causal structure the world happens to possess (Putnam 1975a, 1975b; Boyd 1979, 1982,1983, 1985). For exactly the same reason, of course, the definitions of our causal notions must also reflect *a posteriori* facts about the nature of causation.

It follows that the reference of terms referring to fundamental causal notions is not fixed by analytic definitions; there are none. Instead, such terms are like natural-kind terms, theoretical terms in the particular sciences, and other terms with "natural" rather than analytic definitions, in having their reference fixed by epistemically relevant causal relations between occasions of their use and instantiations of the causal phenomena to which they refer. (For discussions of the epistemic character of reference see Boyd

1979, 1982.) It follows that in order to account for the semantics of causal terms we need no such analyses of their meaning as the Humean definitions provide. To hold that some largely *a priori* conceptual analysis must provide definitions for such terms is to fall victim to an outmoded empiricist conception of the semantics of scientific and everyday language.

Explanation and Evidence

At least for many central cases (and for the cases the D-N account is designed to fit), an explanation of an event is an account of how it was caused. In all but the most atypical cases the account will be partial: Not all the causally determining factors will be indicated, nor will the relevant mechanisms be fully specified. The D-N account is typically extended to cover the cases of explanations for laws or regularities in nature. On the D-N conception, to explain a law or a regularity is to deduce the law or a statement of the regularity from other laws, together with statements of appropriate boundary conditions. It is not entirely clear that this standard extension of the D-N account is really appropriate to the Humean task of reducing causal notions to noncausal ones. One should argue that, inasmuch as the possible knowledge reflected in the explained theory is supposed to be exhausted by its observational predictions, all the consistent Humean should require by way of an explanation is the deduction of those observational consequences from the explaining theory. In any event, the realist conception of explanation also generalizes (even more naturally) to cases of the explanation of laws or regularities: To explain a law or a regularity is to give an account (presumably partial) of the causal factors, mechanisms, processes, and the like that bring about the regularity or the phenomena described in the law.

It is a consequence of the Humean account that all explanations of particular events have a certain level of generality "built in" in virtue of reference to the relevant laws; of course, this is just what the Humean conception of causation requires. The realist conception of causation and explanation does not rule out the possibility of singular causal relations that are not instances of more general patterns; it leaves such issues to the findings of the various special sciences. Nevertheless, it does appear that, given what we know about causal relations and about the sorts of causal explanations that are actually discovered, the Humean conception is in this respect right or very nearly right. Scientific explanations of individual events do, almost always, extend to cover similar cases, actual and counterfactual. In consequence, our conception will be appropriate for the central cases of causal explanation if we think of explanations as being provided by small theories describing the causal factors that determine, or the causal mechanisms or processes that underlie, some class of phenomena. I will use the term *explanation* to refer to such theories. Explanations will of course differ considerably in the extent to which they are complete in their identification of causative factors, in the specificity with which they describe underlying mechanisms or processes, in the level of numerical precision with which they characterize the relations between such factors, and in other respects. Part of the task of a theory of causal explanations is to say how the epistemological significance of an explanation is influenced by factors such as these.

Suppose that a theory E is an explanation for some phenomenon p. It would be natural to understand the terms "explains" and "explanatory power" so that it is just E that is therefore said to explain p and so that it is just the explanatory power of E that is thereby demonstrated. Neither scientific usage nor scientific practice conforms to this picture. E might well be said to explain p, but scientific practice dictates our taking the explanatory success of E as grounds for saying of other more general theories that they explain p. Indeed, under the circumstances envisioned, we would not ordinarily speak of the explanatory power of E being manifested at all; instead, E's being an explanation of p would ordinarily be taken to indicate the explanatory power of those other, more general theories and to provide evidential support for them.

Consider for example the explanation of the "law" of fixed combining ratios, according to which in a certain class of reactions chemical elements combine in fixed ratios by weight. An explanation is provided by a theory that says that this phenomenon is produced by the underlying tendency for atoms to combine in fixed ratios by number, together with the claim that atoms of an element all have the same weight. (I ignore here the issue of isotopes.) What chemists and historians of chemistry correctly say is that this explanation indicated that the atomic theory of matter could explain the phenomenon in question; it demonstrated the explanatory power of the atomic theory and thus provided evidence for it. Similarly, consider the occurrence of subcutaneous degenerate hind limbs in the larger constrictors. An explanation for this phenomenon is provided by a theory according to which these limbs are the vestigial remnants of the ordinary hind limbs of reptiles ancestral to the snakes, which were gradually lost through the process of natural selection. Insofar as this explanation is accepted, it indicates the explanatory power of the Darwinian conception of the origin of species and provides evidence for it.

In these cases we can see a pattern that is utterly typical. An explanation for a particular phenomenon will typically draw upon the resources of some more general theory. It will appropriate the theoretical resources of the broader theory (entities, mechanisms, processes, causal powers, physical magnitudes, and so on), and it will employ, and often elaborate upon, these resources in describing how the phenomenon in question is caused. The dependence of minor theories and explanations upon the theoretical resources of larger theories has been amply documented by Kuhn (1970), who describes the dependence of research in "normal science" upon the ontological picture dictated by the most general theories in the theoretical tradition or "paradigm." (Note that in thus agreeing with Kuhn one need not accept the constructivist conception of scientific knowledge he so ably defends; see Boyd 1979, 1983.) Adequate explanations of particular phenomena are taken to be indicative of the explanatory power of the more general theories whose resources they exploit and to provide additional evidence for those theories. The evidential relevance of explanations does not depend upon its being possible to retrodict or deductively subsume the explained phenomena from the explanation itself or from the explanation together with the relevant general theory(ies) (together with auxiliary hypotheses). The examples of explanations just mentioned illustrate the last point. In the case of the explanation of degenerate limbs in the large constrictors (as in the case of almost all similar evolutionary explanations) we lack altogether the resources for retrodiction, but the fact that the Darwinian theory provides the resources for explanations in such cases properly counts as evidence for it nevertheless.

The case of the "law" of fixed combining ratios is more complicated, because the more precise formulations of the "law" were developed simultaneously with its explanation. Nevertheless, it seems clear that the capacity to predict previously unnoticed instances of the "law" or to deduce an adequate formulation of it emerged quite slowly as the explanation became more detailed, and probably not until Mendelev's work on the periodic table was anything remotely approximating the sort of explanation anticipated by the D-N model available. Despite this fact, it is also clear that the cogency of earlier versions of the atomic explanation, from Dalton's early-nineteenth-century work on, were rightly taken to indicate the explanatory power of the atomic theory of matter and to constitute some evidence in its favor.

There are indeed cases in which the explained phenomenon (or rather a statement describing it) is better thought of as a premise than as a conclusion in the testing of the theory that constitutes its explanation and thereby indicates the (evidentially relevant) explanatory power of the theory upon which it itself is based. The following sort of situation is commonplace (though perhaps not typical): Some general theory T, which is projectable (and thus already supported by some theory-mediated empirical evidence), postulates mechanisms of a certain sort as causally relevant in a broad class of related phenomena; however, T is not sufficiently well developed to permit prediction of such phenomena. T itself does not specify in detail the mechanisms underlying particular cases of the phenomena in question, but it does specify theoretically important general descriptions under which (if T is right) such mechanisms will fall. For some phenomenon p of the relevant sort, an explanation E is proposed. E says that p is produced by certain more precisely specified mechanisms of the general sort prescribed by T. Despite its greater precision, even E is inadequate (given available auxiliary hypotheses) to reliably predict occurrences of p. Nevertheless, it is predictable from E that if an instance of p occurs then various experimentally distinguishable symptoms of the operation of the mechanisms specified by E will be present. Experimental confirmation of E consists in producing or finding occurrences of p and testing for the relevant symptoms. The experimental test of E consists, not in finding occurrences of p where and when E predicts their occurrence (since it makes no such predictions), but in finding the relevant symptoms when and where they are predicted to occur, given E and the occurrence of p (together, presumably, with other auxiliary hypotheses) as premises! The success of such predictions tends to confirm E and, less directly, T.

Cases of this sort are routine where T is a general chemical theory about complex and predictively intractable reaction mechanisms, E is a proposed application of T to the case of a particular sort of reaction, and the symptom in question indicates the presence of a reaction by-product that can, on the basis of well-established chemical theories, be taken to be distinctive of the particular reaction mechanisms postulated by E. What all the sorts of cases we have examined suggest is that when an explanation E of a phenomenon p provides evidence for a more general theory T by indicating that T has explanatory power, what is crucial is that E be testable largely independent of T and that the approximate truth of E constitute good reason for believing the approximate truth of T. It appears not to matter very much whether the occurrence of p is itself otherwise significantly confirmatory of E or T, much less whether it is predictable from E or T.

What we need to know is how this sort of confirmatory evidence for theories upon whose resources successful explanations are based is related to the sort of confirmatory evidence provided by the experimental confirmation of observational predictions made from the theories themselves. Understanding this will be easier if we understand better the confirmatory relationship between theories and those of their observational predictions whose experimental confirmation supports them.

In mature sciences all theory confirmation is theory-mediated. As we have seen, theories are not confirmable at all unless they are projectable, and projectability judgments are theory-dependent judgments of plausibility. The confirmation of an observational prediction of a projectable theory does not count significantly toward its confirmation unless theory-determined considerations indicate that it is a relevant test (that is, roughly, unless it tests the theory against a projectable rival). Particular experiments do not count as well designed (and thus are not potentially confirmatory or disconfirmatory) unless there are appropriate controls for the possible experimental artifacts that are indicated as relevant by previously established background theories.

No piece of experimental evidence counts for or against a theory except in the light of theoretical considerations dictated by previously established theories. (For discussions of these and the following points see Boyd 1972, 1973, 1979, 1982, 1983, 1985.)

The theoretical considerations that thus bear on theory confirmation are themselves evidential considerations. The fact that a theory is plausible in the light of well-confirmed theories is evidence that it is approximately true. This is so because the evidence for the well-confirmed theories that form the basis for the plausibility judgment is evidence for their approximate truth (as scientific realists insist) rather than just for their empirical adequacy (as empiricists typically maintain) and because the inferential principles by which conclusions about the plausibility of proposed theories are drawn from the previously established theories are themselves determined by previously acquired theoretical knowledge. The dialectical development of theoretical knowledge and of methodological principles extends to the principles by which plausible inferences are made from wholly or partly theoretical premises to theoretical conclusions. Judgments of theoretical plausibility reflect inductive inferences at the theoretical level (that is, inferences from previously acquired theoretical knowledge to inductively justified theoretical conclusions). These inferences proceed according to theory-determined assessments of projectability, just as inferences from observational data to theoretical conclusions do. (See especially Boyd 1983, Boyd 1985.)

The evidence for a theory provided by its being plausible in the light of previously established background theories is every bit as much empirical evidence as is the evidence provided by experimental tests of the theory's observational predictions; the empirical basis for this evidence consists of the various observations involved in the confirmation of the relevant background theories. Call empirical evidence for a theory *direct* if it is provided by experimental tests of observational predictions drawn from the theory itself, and *indirect* if it is obtained by *inductive* inferences at the theoretical level from other theories that have themselves been confirmed by experimental tests. The important consequence of a realist conception of scientific epistemology is that the distinction between direct and indirect empirical evidence is of no fundamental significance. The observations that provide direct experimental evidence for a theory provide significant evidence at all only because of indirect evidential considerations in support of the theory itself (viz. the bases of the judgment that it is projectable) and in support of various other theories (those of its logically possible rivals also judged projectable, the theoretically plausible accounts of possible experimental artifacts, and so on). Thus, direct experimental evidence is only superficially direct. Moreover, indirect empirical evidence can be very strong evidence indeed. The fact that a theory provides theoretically plausible accounts of a very large number of phenomena in a way in which none of its plausible rivals do can, under appropriate circumstances, constitute genuinely confirmatory evidence for it even though almost no evidence for it is provided by direct tests of its observational predictions. This was the situation of the Darwinian theory of the origin of species until very recently, and it is the current situation of many astronomical theories. Observations can often provide striking confirmation of a theory not by confirming a prediction of the theory but by ruling out its theoretically plausible alternatives. It may be true, nevertheless, that in many important cases direct empirical evidence for a theory plays an especially important confirmatory role, and there may even be some general methodological reason why this should be so. But the distinction between direct and indirect evidence cannot be an epistemologically fundamental one. They are two closely related and interpenetrating cases of the same epistemological phenomenon.

It will now be clear, I believe, how the evidence for a theory that arises from a demonstration of its explanatory power is to be understood. Let T be a theory, E an explanation that draws upon the resources of T and p the phenomenon that E explains. Evidence (direct or indirect) for E will demonstrate the explanatory power of T just in case (given the available background theoretical knowledge and the inductive standards it determines) the way in which E draws on the theoretical resources of T is such that E's being approximately true provides inductive reason to believe that T is also approximately true. It will not matter in any fundamental way whether or not the evidence for E includes successful prediction of p. In any event, the evidence thus provided for T will be a perfectly ordinary case of indirect empirical evidence of the sort we have just been examining. Assessments of explanatory power are just one species of assessment of indirect theory-mediated empirical evidence. There is nothing going on when we prefer explanatory theories over and above what goes on in all cases in which we prefer theories that are supported by (necessarily partly indirect) empirical evidence.

Let us return to the D-N account of explanation. Its three most attractive features were that it rested upon an appropriate account of causation, that it indicated that the explanatory power of a theory depends upon its integration into a larger body of well-confirmed theories, and that it portrays the preference for explanatory theories as a special case of the preference for theories supported by observational evidence. In all these respects the D-N account is right. What we have seen is that the weakness of the D-N account lies not in the unworkability of the above three features but in the mistaken Humean conceptions of causation and evidence upon which the D-N account rests. When we adopt a realist conception of causal relations and causal powers as real features of the world, an account of the integration of theories that countenances inductive integration of theoretical knowledge as well as conjoint deductive prediction, and an account of empirical evidence that recognizes the crucial methodological role of such inductive integration, we are able to preserve the best features of the D-N account while avoiding the insuperable difficulties to which empiricist accounts of scientific methodology invariably fall victim.

Other Epistemological Issues

Simplicity and Parsimony

Traditional logical-empiricist accounts assimilate the methodological preference for explanatory theories to a preference for empirically tested theories but typically treat the other nonexperimental standards for the acceptability of a theory as purely conventional or pragmatic. At least, that is the typical "official" empiricist position. In applied philosophy of science, logical empiricists often treated considerations of "simplicity" and "parsimony" as though they had evidential weight. In this latter case, I believe, empiricists were basically right.

One of the striking things about the methodological judgments philosophers of science assimilate to the categories of "simplicity" and "parsimony" is the extent to which they are more complex than those descriptions would suggest. Scientists do not, as a general rule, prefer the simplest from among the empirically unrefuted theories about some natural phenomenon. They quite often—and without any misgivings—reject theories as too simple (or perhaps as too simpleminded) even when they fit the data that have already been examined. There are whole disciplines in which "single-factor" theories are held up to methodological derision, and there are even more disciplines in which this would be true were single-factor theories seriously proposed. Similarly, the principle of parsimony, or Occam's razor, seems to be applied quite unevenly. In many fields, at particular moments in their histories, scientists quite cheerfully postulate new entities in order to account for new empirical discoveries rather than making other theoretical accommodations equally compatible with the data in question. What plainly happens in these cases is that theoretical reasons legitimate the unsimple or unparsimonious theoretical choices. Thus, judgments of simplicity and parsimony are—like judgments of explanatory power—theory-dependent.

We know, moreover, that if (as seems plausible) judgments identified as simplicity or parsimony judgments are important factors in judgments of projectability then such judgments cannot be merely conventional or pragmatic; they must play an epistemic role in scientific practice. What I suggest is that judgments of "simplicity" and of "parsimony" are simply special cases of judgments of theoretical plausibility. When a proposed theory assimilates new data into our existing theoretical framework via a modification that is (according to the evidential standards dictated by that framework) warranted by those data, we see the modification as a simple one (in the sense that it does not introduce epistemologically needless modifications into theories we already take to be well confirmed) and we somewhat misleadingly describe the theory itself as simple. Similarly, we reject proposed theories that accommodate new data by postulating theoretically implausible new entities, and we misleadingly characterize our preference as being for parsimonious theories in general.

If this suggestion is basically right (I invite the reader to consider various actual cases), then the methodological preferences we typically misdescribe in terms of simplicity and parsimony are simply special cases of the methodological preference for theories that are supported by inductive inferences at the theoretical level from the approximate theoretical knowledge we already have. But that principle, as we have seen, amounts to a preference for theories supported by indirect experimental evidence. In the case of the principles of "simplicity" and "parsimony" just as in the case of the principle that we should prefer explanatory theories, all that is really going on is a recognition of the role of indirect evidence in science. The nonexperimental criteria of theory acceptability, which initially appear puzzling, turn out to be nonexperimental only in the sense that they do not reflect the assessment of direct experimental evidence. The logical positivists were right in their applied philosophy of science when they took these principles to be evidentially relevant, but their anti-realist Humean conception of scientific knowledge prevented them from seeing why they were right.

Contexts of Discovery and Confirmation

I have suggested above that three characteristic features of the D-N conception of explanation that help to explain its philosophical plausibility actually represent important insights of the empiricist tradition in the philosophy of science—insights that can be extended to the cases of other nonexperimental criteria as well, but insights that an empiricist as opposed to a realist conception of scientific knowledge cannot successfully assimilate. The development of a consistent realist conception of the epistemic role of nonexperimental (or, better, indirectly experimental) criteria of theory acceptability permits us to examine the cogency of another distinctive feature of empiricist philosophy of science: the traditional logical-empiricist claim that the epistemology of science need concern itself with the logic of confirmation but not with the principles of reasoning by which scientific theories are invented or discovered. On the logical-empiricist conception, the latter issue belongs to psychology and to the social study of science but not to the philosophy of science.

Part of what empiricists meant when they held that issues about the context of discovery were irrelevant to the philosophy of science was that philosophers of science need not develop a formal inductive logic to account for the discovery of theories. No doubt they were right in this respect; there is no reason to believe that what is ordinarily meant by an inductive logic would provide an even remotely adequate account of theory discovery in science. They also meant that philosophers of science need not concern themselves with all the details of psychological theories about how theories are discovered. Here too they were no doubt right. What is striking, however, is that some quite important empirical issues about theory discovery are irremediably central to an adequate epistemology of science.

It is a central part of the business of the philosophy of science to answer the fundamental epistemological question of why the methods of science are epistemically reliable. We have just had the occasion to examine in some detail two important features of those methods. First, the problem of sampling in experimental design is solved by the requirement that a proposed theory be tested under experimental circumstances that pit it against those alternatives to it that are theoretically plausible (and thus evidentially supported by inductive inference) given the body of previously established theories. Second, it can sometimes count as overwhelmingly confirmatory evidence for a theory that it is the basis for theoretically plausible explanations of a wide variety of phenomena that none of its otherwise plausible rivals can explain equally well. In each of these sorts of cases, the epistemic reliability of the relevant methodological practice depends on its being true in the (not too) long run that, when a proposed theory is in fact seriously mistaken, among its theoretically plausible rivals there will be theories that are relevantly closer to the truth and that can serve to identify the errors in the first theory or to challenge its exclusive claim to explanatory power with respect to the relevant class of natural phenomena.

It is, of course, impossible to assess the theoretical plausibility of theoretical proposals unless someone thinks them up. Failures of theoretical imagination can thus render the methodological practices we are discussing epistemologically unreliable in particular cases. The scientists who test a proposed theory against all the available theoretically plausible alternative theories will be employing an epistemically reliable testing strategy only on the assumption that the imaginative capacity of the scientific community is sufficient, so that theories near the truth in relevant respects will appear among those theories. Similarly, the scientists who accept a theory because it displays an apparent explanatory capacity utterly unmatched by any of the available plausible rivals will be reasoning reliably only if the imaginative capacity of the scientific community is up to the task of inventing a rich enough class of theoretically plausible rivals. Rival theories that would be theoretically plausible if we were only able to invent them and to understand them well enough to assess their theoretical plausibility play no methodological role unless we actually possess and display the relevant imaginative and cognitive capacities.

It is true, even on an empiricist conception of the matter, that successful science depends upon facts about our intellectual and imaginative capacities. Even if theory confirmation did not depend upon those capacities, we would not succeed in science unless we were able to think up suitably accurate theories to test. What we have just seen is that the same dependence of success upon our imaginative and cognitive capacities infects our ability to reliably confirm or disconfirm the theories we have already invented. The epistemic reliability of our scientific practices depends not only upon our possession of a suitably approximately true body of background theories but also upon our having quite contingent psychological capacities for exploiting these theoretical resources. This fact has three quite different implications for the philosophy of science.

First, it seems plausible that something somewhat like an "inductive logic" of theory invention may be epistemically important in science. It is probably true that theory invention (and creativity in general) involves finding new combinations of previously understood ideas and concepts. It is also true that inductive inferences at the theoretical level favor theoretical proposals that are relevantly similar (where the relevant respects of similarity are themselves theory-determined) to proposals that have already been established. It would be quite surprising if the respects of similarity to previous theories involved in theory invention were not fairly closely related to the respects of similarity determined to be epistemically relevant by the previous theories themselves. Indeed, if there were no relevant relations between the two it would be hard to see how our methodological practices thus far would have been epistemically reliable. The "logic of confirmation" must be somehow related to psychologically real inductive procedures for theory invention if scientific practice is to be epistemically reliable at all. The question "Just what is the relationship?" is simultaneously a question in empirical psychology and a question in the epistemology of science.

Second, a recognition of the role of theoretical imagination in epistemically reliable scientific practice opens up important possibilities in applied philosophy of science. Consider the question of the role of social prejudice in the practice of scientists. It has been traditional, on discovering that some figure in the history of science reached conclusions on scientific matters that we can, in retrospect, see as having been determined by inaccurate racial or sexual stereotypes, to conclude that the figure in question must have failed to employ the scientific method conistently. No doubt this is right in many cases, but reflection upon the crucial epistemic role of theoretical imagination in the evidential assessment of theories suggests an alternative hypothesis that may prove more accurate in many actual historical cases. The scientist may well have adhered scrupulously to the dictates of sound scientific methodology; all the available theoretically plausible alternatives to the now objectionable conclusions may have been taken quite seriously in assessing the evidence for them. The epistemic unreliability of the scientist's procedures may have stemmed, not from a failure to be methodologically scrupulous, but rather from socially determined failures of imagination on the part of the scientific community as a whole. In cases where this explanation is the right one, there may be no culpable methodological failure at all. Avoidance of socially prejudiced conclusions in such cases will depend either on political and social changes affecting the imaginative capacity of researchers or (perhaps) on extraordinary leaps of imagination, which are not part of normal scientific practice. In important ways, then, good scientific methodology is not prejudice-proof even when practiced with the greatest possible care, which is not to say that good methodological practice does not in the very long run help to overcome social prejudice. It is an instructive exercise to see how well or badly this model fits the various cases of social prejudice in biology described by Gould (1981).

Third, the importance of scientists' imaginative capacity for the epistemic reliability of scientific methodology illustrates in a striking way what is perhaps the most surprising feature of the realist conception of scientific knowledge. The epistemic reliability of scientific methods is logically contingent. It depends upon the historically contingent emergence of relevantly approximately true theoretical traditions (Boyd 1982, 1983, 1985) and also upon logically contingent features of our individual and collective capacities for theoretical imagination. Thus, principles of scientific methodology are not defensible *a priori* but have empirical presuppositions. The philosophy of science is an empirical discipline, not an *a priori* one. Indeed, this is probably true of philosophical inquiry generally. Here again is a conclusion with which Hume might have agreed, altough it is true for distinctly non-Humean reasons.

References

Boyd, R. 1972. "Determinism, Laws and Predictability in Principle." *Philosophy of Science* 39: 431–450.

Boyd, R. 1973. "Realism, Underdetermination and a Causal Theory of Evidence." *Noûs* 7: 1–12.

Boyd, R. 1979. "Metaphor and Theory Change." In *Metaphor and Thought*, ed. A. Ortony. Cambridge University Press.

Boyd, R. 1980. "Materialism Without Reductionism: What Physicalism Does Not Entail." In *Readings in Philosophy of Psychology*, vol. 1, ed. N. Block. Cambridge, Mass.: Harvard University Press.

Boyd, R. 1982. "Scientific Realism and Naturalistic Epistemology." In *PSA 80*, vol. 2. East Lansing, Mich.: Philosophy of Science Association.

Boyd, R. 1983. "On the Current Status of the Issue of Scientific Realism." *Erkenntnis* 19: 45–90. Reprinted in this volume, chapter 11.

Boyd, R. 1985. "Lex Orendi est Lex Credendi." In *Images of Science: Scientific Realism Vc˜sus Constructive Empiricism*, ed. Churchland and Hooker. University of Chicago Press.

Carnap, R. 1950. "Empiricism, Semantics, and Ontology," this volume, chapter 4.

Feigl, H. 1945. "Operationism and Scientific Method." *Psychological Review* 52: 250–259.

Goodman, N. 1973. *Fact, Fiction and Forecast*, third edition. New York: Bobbs-Merrill.

Gould, S. J. 1981. *The Mismeasure of Man*. New York: Norton.

Hanson, N. R. 1958. *Patterns of Discovery*. Cambridge University Press.

Hempel, C. G. 1965. "Aspects of Scientific Explanation." In Hempel, *Aspects of Scientific Explanation*. New York: Free Press.

Hempel, C. G., and P. Oppenheim. 1948. "Studies in the Logic of Explanation." *Philosophy of Science* 15: 98–115.

Kripke, S. 1972. "Naming and Necessity." In *The Semantics of Natural Language*, ed. G. Harman and D. Davidson. Dordrecht: Reidel.

Kuhn, T. 1970. The Structure of Scientific Revolutions, second edition. University of Chicago Press.

Popper, K. 1959. *The Logic of Scientific Discovery*. London: Hutchinson.

Putnam, H. 1975a. "The Meaning of 'Meaning.'" In Putnam, *Mind, Language and Reality*. Cambridge University Press.

Putnam, H. 1975b. "Explanation and Reference." In Putnam, *Mind, Language and Reality*. Cambridge University Press. Reprinted in this volume, chapter 9.

Quine, W. V. O. 1969. "Natural Kinds," this volume, chapter 8.

Salmon, W. 1971. *Statistical Explanation and Statistical Relevance*. University of Pittsburgh Press.

Smart, J. J. C. 1963. *Philosophy and Scientific Realism*. London: Routledge and Kegan Paul.

van Fraassen, B. 1980. *The Scientific Image*. Oxford: Clarendon.

Chapter 20

The Reality of Causes in a World of Instrumental Laws

Nancy Cartwright

Empiricists are notoriously suspicious of causes. They have not been equally wary of laws. Hume set the tradition when he replaced causal facts with facts about generalizations. Modern empiricists do the same. But nowadays Hume's generalizations are the laws and equations of high level scientific theories. On current accounts, there may be some question about where the laws of our fundamental theories get their necessity; but it is no question that these laws are the core of modern science. Bertrand Russell is well known for this view:

> The law of gravitation will illustrate what occurs in any exact science ... Certain differential equations can be found, which hold at every instant for every particle of the system ... But there is nothing that could be properly called 'cause' and nothing that could be properly called 'effect' in such a system.[1]

For Russell, causes 'though useful to daily life and in the infancy of a science, tend to be displaced by quite different laws as soon as a science is successful'. It is convenient that Russell talks about physics and that the laws he praises are its fundamental equations—Hamilton's equations or Schroedinger's, or the equations of general relativity. That is what I want to discuss too. But I hold just the reverse of Russell's view. I am in favor of causes and opposed to laws. I think that, given the way modern theories of mathematical physics work, it makes sense only to believe their causal claims and not their explanatory laws.

1. Explaining by Causes

Following Bromberger, Scriven, and others, we know that there are various things one can be doing in explaining. Two are of importance here: in explaining a phenomenon one can cite the causes of that phenomenon; or one can set the phenomenon in a general theoretical framework. The framework of modern physics is mathematical, and good explanations will generally allow us to make quite precise calculations about the phenomena we explain. Rene Thom remarks the difference between these two kinds of explanation, though he thinks that only the causes really explain: 'DesCartes with his vortices, his hooked atoms, and the like explained everything and calculated nothing; Newton, with the inverse square of gravitation, calculated everything and explained nothing'.[2]

Unlike Thom, I am happy to call both explanation, so long as we do not illicitly attribute to theoretical explanation features that apply only to causal explanation. There is a tradition, since the time of Aristotle, of deliberately conflating the two. But

Reprinted from *PSA 1980*, Vol. 2, ed. P. Asquith and R. Giere (East Lansing, MI: Philosophy of Science Association, 1981), pp. 38–48, by permission of the author and the Philosophy of Science Association.

I shall argue that they function quite differently in modem physics. If we accept Descartes's causal story as adequate, we must count his claims about hooked atoms and vortices true. But we do not use Newton's inverse square law as if it were either true or false.

One powerful argument speaks against my claim and for the truth of explanatory laws—the *argument from coincidence*. Those who take laws seriously tend to subscribe to what Gilbert Harman has called inference to the best explanation. They assume that the fact that a law *explains* provides evidence that the law is true. The more diverse the phenomena that it explains, the more likely it is to be true. It would be an absurd coincidence if a wide variety of different kinds of phenomena were all explained by a particular law, and yet were not in reality consequent from the law. Thus the argument from coincidence supports a good many of the inferences we make to best explanations.

The method of inference to the best explanation is subject to an important constraint, however—the requirement of non-redundancy. We can infer the truth of an explanation only if there are no alternatives that account in an equally satisfactory way for the phenomena. In physics nowadays, I shall argue, an acceptable causal story is supposed to satisfy this requirement. But exactly the opposite is the case with the specific equations and models that make up our theoretical explanations. There is redundancy of theoretical treatment, but not of causal account.

There is, I think, a simple reason for this: causes make their effects happen. We begin with a phenomenon which, relative to our other general beliefs, we think would not occur unless something peculiar brought it about. In physics we often mark this belief by labeling the phenomena as effects—the Sorbet effect, the Zeeman effect, the Hall effect. An effect needs something to bring it about, and the peculiar features of the effect depend on the particular nature of the cause, so that—in so far as we think we have got it right—we are entitled to infer the character of the cause from the character of the effect.

But equations do not bring about the phenomenological laws we derive from them (even if the phenomenological laws are themselves equations). Nor are they used in physics as if they did. The specific equations we use to treat particular phenomena provide a way of casting the phenomena into the general framework of the theory. Thus we are able to treat a variety of disparate phenomena in a similar way, and to make use of the theory to make quite precise calculations. For both of these purposes it is an advantage to multiply theoretical treatments.

Pierre Duhem used the redundancy requirement as an argument against scientific realism, and recently Hilary Putnam uses it as an argument against realism in general. Both propose that, in principle, for any explanation of any amount of data there will always be an equally satisfactory alternative. The history of science suggests that this claim may be right: we constantly construct better explanations to replace those of the past. But such arguments are irrelevant here; they do not distinguish between causal claims and theoretical accounts. Both are likely to be replaced by better accounts in the future.

Here I am not concerned with alternatives that are at best available only in principle, but rather with the practical availability of alternatives within theories we actually have to hand. For this discussion, I want to take the point of view that Putnam calls 'internal realism'; to consider actual physical theories which we are willing to account as acceptable, even if only for the time being, and to ask, 'Relative to that theory, which of its explanatory claims are we to deem true?' My answer is that causal claims are to be deemed true, but to count the basic explanatory laws as true is to fail to take seriously how physics succeeds in giving explanations.

I will use two examples to show this. The first—quantum damping and its associated line broadening—is a phenomenon whose understanding is critical to the theory of lasers. Here we have a single causal story, but a fruitful multiplication of successful theoretical accounts. This contrasts with the unacceptable multiplication of causal stories in the second example.

There is one question we should consider before looking at the examples, a question pressed by two colleagues in philosophy of science, Dan Hausman and Robert Ennis. How are we to distinguish the explanatory laws, which I argue are not to be taken literally, from the causal claims and more pedestrian statements of fact, which are? The short answer is that there is no way. A typical way of treating a problem like this is to find some independent criterion—ideally syntactical, but more realistically semantical—which will divide the claims of a theory into two parts. Then it is argued that claims of one kind are to be taken literally whereas those of the other kind function in some different way.

This is not what I have in mind. I think of a physics theory as providing an explanatory scheme into which phenomena of interest can be fitted. I agree with Duhem here. The scheme simplifies and organizes the phenomena so that we can treat similarly happenings that are phenomenologically different, and differently ones that are phenomenologically the same. It is part of the nature of this organizing activity that it cannot be done very well if we stick too closely to stating what is true. Some claims of the theory must be literally descriptive (I think the claims about the mass and charge of the electron are a good example) if the theory is to be brought to bear on the phenomena; but I suspect that there is no general independent way of characterizing which these will be. What is important to realize is that if the theory is to have considerable explanatory power, most of its fundamental claims will not state truths, and that this will in general include the bulk of our most highly prized laws and equations.

2. Examples: Quantum Damping

In radiative damping, atoms de-excite, giving off photons whose frequencies depend on the energy levels of the atom. We know by experiment that the emission line observed in a spectroscope for a radiating atom is not infinitely sharp, but rather has a finite linewidth; that is, there is a spread of frequencies in the light emitted. What causes this natural linewidth? Here is the standard answer which physicists give, quoted from a good textbook on quantum radiation theory by William Louisell:

> There are many interactions which may broaden an atomic line, but the most fundamental one is the reaction of the radiation field on the atom. That is, when an atom decays spontaneously from an excited state radiatively, it emits a quantum of energy into the radiation field. This radiation may be reabsorbed by the atom. The reaction of the field on the atom gives the atom a linewidth and causes the original level to be shifted as we show. This is the source of the natural linewidth and the Lamb shift.[3]

Following his mathematical treatment of the radiative decay, Louisell continues:

> We see that the atom is continually emitting and reabsorbing quanta of radiation. The energy level shift does not require energy to be conserved while the damping requires energy conservation. Thus damping is brought about by the emission and absorption of real photons while the photons emitted and absorbed which contribute to the energy shift are called virtual photons.[4]

This account is universally agreed upon. Damping, and its associated line broadening, are brought about by the emission and absorption of real photons.

Here we have a causal story; but not a mathematical treatment. We have not yet set line broadening into the general mathematical framework of quantum mechanics. There are many ways to do this. One of the Springer Tracts by G. S. Agarwal[5] summarizes the basic treatments which are offered. He lists six different approaches in his table of contents: (1) Weisskopf-Wigner method; (2) Heitler-Ma method; (3) Goldberger-Watson method; (4) quantum statistical method: master equations; (5) Langevin equations corresponding to the master equation and a c-number representation; and (6) neoclassical theory of spontaneous emission.

Before going on to discuss these six approaches, I will give one other example. The theory of damping forms the core of current quantum treatments of lasers. Figure 20.1 is a diagram from a summary article by H. Haken on 'the' quantum theory of the laser.[6] We see that the situation I described for damping theory is even worse here. There are so many different treatments that Haken provides a 'family tree' to set straight their connections. Looking at the situation Haken himself describes it as a case of 'theory overkill'. Laser theory is an extreme case, but I think there is no doubt that this kind of redundancy of treatment, which Haken and Agarwal picture, is common throughout physics.

Agarwal describes six treatments of line broadening. All six provide precise and accurate calculations for the shape and width of the broadened line. How do they differ? All of the approaches employ the basic format of quantum mechanics. Each writes down a Schroedinger equation; but it is a *different* equation in each *different* treatment. (Actually among the six treatments there are really just three different equations.) The view that I am attacking takes theoretical explanations to provide, as best they can, statements of objective laws. On this view the six approaches that Agarwal lists compete with one another; they offer different laws for exactly the same phenomena.

But this is not Agarwal's attitude. Different approaches are useful for different purposes; they complement rather than compete. The Langevin and Master equations of (4) and (5), for instance, have forms borrowed from statistical mechanics. They were introduced in part because the development of lasers created an interest in photon correlation experiments. Clearly, if we have statistical questions, it is a good idea to start with the kind of equations from which we know how to get statistical answers.

Let us consider an objection to the point of view I have been urging. We all know that physicists write down the kinds of equations they know how to solve; if they cannot use one approximation, they try another; and when they find a technique that works, they apply it in any place they can. These are commonplace observations that remind us of the pragmatic attitude of physicists. Perhaps, contrary to my argument, the multiplication of theoretical treatments says more about this pragmatic orientation than it does about how explanatory laws ought to be viewed. I disagree. I think that it does speak about laws, and in particular shows how laws differ from causes. We do not have the same pragmatic tolerance of causal alternatives. We do not use first one causal story in explanation, then another, depending on the ease of calculation, or whatever.

The case of the radiometer illustrates. The radiometer was introduced by William Crookes in 1873 but it is still not clear what makes it work, ... There are three plausible theories. The first attributes the motion of the vanes to light pressure. This explanation is now universally rejected. As M. Goldman remarks in 'The Radiometer Revisited',

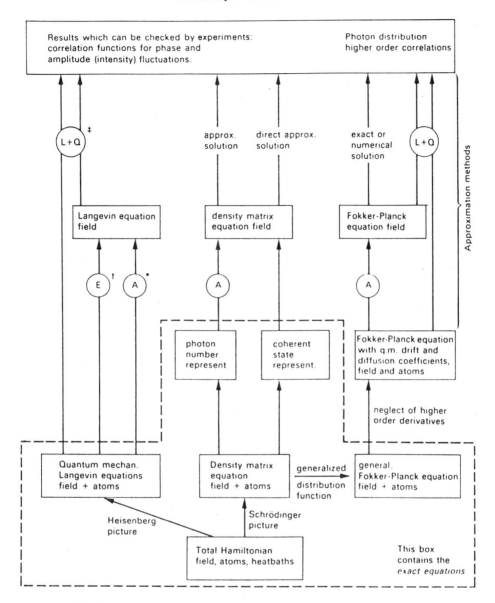

•A : adiabatic elimination of atomic variables

† E : exact elimination of atomic variables

‡ L + Q: linearization and quantum mechanical quasilinearization

Figure 20.1
Family tree of the quantum theory of the laser. (Source: Haken, "The Semiclassical and Quantum Theory of the Laser.")

A simple calculation shows that on a typical British summer day, when the sky is a uniform grey (equally luminous all over) the torque from the black and silver faces exactly balance, so that for a perfect radiometer [i.e., a radiometer with a perfect vacuum] no motion would be possible.[7]

Two explanations still contend. The first is the more standard, textbook account, which is supported by Goldman's calculations. It supposes that the motion is caused by the perpendicular pressure of the gas in the perfect vacuum against the vanes. But as we have seen, on Maxwell's account the motion must be due to the tangential stress created by the gas slipping around the edge of the vanes. There is a sense in which Maxwell and Goldman may both be right: the motion may be caused by a combination of tangential and perpendicular stress. But this is not what they claim. Each claims that the factor he cites is the single significant factor in bringing about the motion, and only one or the other of these claims can be accepted. This situation clearly constrasts with Agarwal's different theoretical treatments. Insofar as we are interested in giving a causal explanation of the motion, we must settle on one account or the other. We cannot use first one account, then the other, according to our convenience.

I know of this example through Francis Everitt, who thinks of building an experiment that would resolve the question. I mention Everitt's experiment again because it argues for the difference in objectivity which I urge between theoretical laws and causal claims. It reminds us that unlike theoretical accounts, which can be justified only by an inference to the best explanation, causal accounts have an independent test of their truth: we can perform controlled experiments to find out if our causal stories are right or wrong. Experiments of these kinds in fact play an important role in an example from which Wesley Salmon defends inferences to the best explanation.

3. The Argument from Coincidence

In a recent paper[8] Salmon considers Jean Perrin's arguments for the existence of atoms and for the truth of Avogadro's hypothesis that there are a fixed number of molecules in any gram mole of a fluid. Perrin performed meticulous experiments on Brownian motion in colloids from which he was able to calculate Avogadro's number quite precisely. His 1913 tract, in which he summarizes his experiments , and recounts the evidence for the existence of atoms, helped sway the community of physicists in favor of these hypotheses. Besides Brownian motion. Perrin lists thirteen quite different physical situations which yield a determination of Avogadro's number. So much evidence of such a variety of kinds all pointing to the same value must surely convince us urges Perrin, that atoms exist and that Avogadro's hypothesis is true.

For many, Perrin's reasoning is a paradigm of inference to the best explanation; and it shows the soundness of that method. I think this misdiagnoses the structure of the argument. Perrin does not make an inference to the best explanation, where explanation includes anything from theoretical laws to a detailed description of how the explanandum was brought about. He makes rather a more restricted inference—an inference to the most probable cause.

A well-designed experiment is constructed to allow us to infer the character of the cause from the character of its more readily observable effects. Prior to Perrin, chemists focused their attention on the size and velocities of the suspended particles. But this study was unrewarding; the measurements were difficult and the results did not signify much. Perrin instead studied the height distribution of the Brownian granules at equilibrium. From his results, with a relatively simple model for the collision interactions, he was able to calculate Avogadro's number. Perrin was a brilliant experimenter. It was part of his genius that he was able to find quite specific effects which were peculiarly sensitive to the exact character of the causes he wanted to study. Given his model, the fact that the carrier fluids had just 6×10^{23} atoms for every mole made precise and calculable differences to the distribution he observed.

The role of the model is important. It brings out exactly what part coincidence plays in the structure of Perrin's argument. Our reasoning from the character of the effect to the character of the cause is always against a background of other knowledge. We aim to find out about a cause with a particular structure. What effects appear as a result of that structure will be highly sensitive to the exact nature of the causal processes which connect the two. If we are mistaken about the processes that link cause and effect in our experiment, what we observe may not result in the way we think from the cause under study. Our results may be a mere artifact of the experiment, and our conclusions will be worthless.

Perrin explicitly has this worry about the first of the thirteen phenomena he cites: the viscosity of gases, which yields a value for Avogadro's number via Van der Waal's equation and the kinetic theory of gases. In his *Atoms* he writes that 'the probable error, for all these numbers is roughly 30 per cent, owing to the approximations made in the calculations that lead to the Clausius-Maxwell and Van der Waal's equations.' He continues: 'The Kinetic Theory justly excites our admiration. [But] it fails to carry complete conviction, because of the many hypotheses it involves.' (I take it he means 'unsubstantiated hypotheses'.) What sets Perrin's worries to rest? He tell us himself in the next sentence: 'If by entirely independent routes we are led to the same values for the molecular magnitudes, we shall certainly find our faith in the theory considerably strengthened.'[9]

Here is where coincidence enters. We have thirteen phenomena from which we can calculate Avogadro's number. Any one of these phenomena—if we were sure enough about the details of how the atomic behavior gives rise to it—would be good enough to convince us that Avogadro is right. Frequently we are not sure enough; we want further assurance that we are observing genuine results and not experimental artifacts. This is the case with Perrin. He lacks confidence in some of the models on which his calculations are based. But he can appeal to coincidence. Would it not be a coincidence if each of the observations was an artifact, and yet all agreed so closely about Avogadro s number? The convergence of results provides reason for thinking that the various models used in Perrin's diverse calculations were each good enough. It thus reassures us that those models can legitimately be used to infer the nature of the cause from the character of the effects.

In each of Perrin's thirteen cases we infer a concrete cause from a concrete effect. We are entitled to do so because we assume that causes make effects occur in just the way that they do, via specific, concrete causal processes. The structure of the cause physically determines the structure of the effect. Coincidence enters Perrin's argument, but not in a way that supports inference to the best explanation in general. There is no connection analogous to causal propagation between theoretical laws and the phenomenological generalizations which they bring together and explain. Explanatory laws summarize phenomenological laws; they do not make them true. Coincidence will not help with laws. We have no ground for inferring from any phenomenological law that an explanatory law must be just so; multiplying cases cannot help.

I mentioned that Gilbert Harman introduced the expression 'inference to the best explanation'. Harman uses two examples in his original paper.[10] The first is the example that we have just been discussing: coming to believe in atoms. The second is a common and important kind of example from everyday life: inferring that the butler did it. Notice that these are both cases in which we infer facts about concrete causes: they are not inferences to the laws of some general explanatory scheme. Like Perrin's argument, these do not vindicate a general method for inferring the truth of explanatory laws. What they illustrate is a far more restrictive kind of inference: inference to the best cause.

4. Conclusion

Perrin did not make an inference to the best explanation, only an inference to the most probable cause. This is typical of modern physics. 'Competing' theoretical treatments—treatments that write down different laws for the same phenomena—are encouraged in physics, but only a single causal story is allowed. Although philosophers generally believe in laws and deny causes, explanatory practice in physics is just the reverse.

Notes

1. Bertrand Russell, "On the Notion of Cause," *Mysticism and Logic* (London: Allen & Unwin, 1917), p. 194.
2. Rene Thom, *Structural Stability and Morphogenesis*, trans. C. H. Waddington (Reading, Mass.: W. A. Benjamin, 1972), p. 5.
3. William H. Louisell, *Quantum-Statistical Properties of Radiation* (New York: John Wiley & Sons, 1973), p. 285.
4. Ibid., p. 289.
5. See G. S. Agarwal, *Quantum-Statistical Theories of Spontaneous Emission and their Relation to Other Approaches* (Berlin: Springer-Verlag, 1974).
6. H. Haken, "The Semiclassical and Quantum Theory of the Laser," in S. M. Kay and A. Maitland (eds), *Quantum Optics* (London: Academic Press, 1970), p. 244.
7. M. Goldman, "The Radiometer Revisited," *Physics Education* 13 (1978), p. 428.
8. See W. Salmon, *Scientific Explanation and the Causal Structure of the World* (Princeton: Princeton University Press, 1984).
9. Jean Perrin, *Atoms*, trans. D. Ll. Hammick (New York: D. Van Nostrand Co., 1916), p. 82.
10. G. H. Harman, "Inference to the Best Explanation," *Philosophical Review* 74 (1965), pp. 88–95.

Section III

Reductionism and the Unity of Science

J.D. Trout

Reductionism is often formulated as the claim that some object, state, process, event, or property "is just" or "is nothing more than" the physical ingredients that compose it. Our best scientific theories would seem to support such proclamations. Evolutionary and biochemical theories of life have described the physical bases of life. Modern genetics specifies in physical terms some of the mechanisms of heritability. Neuroscience enumerates the chemical and electrical means by which nerve impulses propagate and affect locomotion. Biopsychology traces the influences of drugs on mental states of clinical interest, such as depression. These theories have had the collective effect of eliminating vitalistic accounts of life, along with dualistic theories of mentality, because they have provided convincing evidence in favor of physicalism—the view that all phenomena are physical or entirely composed of physical phenomena.

Reductionists, however, typically intend something even stronger than physicalism by their claim that some social system, organism, or mental state "is just" a physical thing. One version of reductionism states that the central terms of "higher-level" theories, from biology to sociology, will ultimately be defined in terms of, and thus eliminated in favor of, the more basic vocabulary of physics or chemistry. We might call this "predicate reductionism." Predicate reductionists reason that, since terms like 'finch' denote organisms, and organisms are just collections of cells, and cells are just collections of molecules, etc., then statements about finches should be (at least in principle) translatable into statements that use only the vocabulary of physics.

Another version of reductionism—law reductionism—is the view that the laws of higher-level theories such as those of economics and sociology can be explained in terms of, and thus replaced by, those of some lower-level theory like individual psychology, biology, chemistry, or physics. In other words, economic laws about market segmentation can be (at least in principle) replaced by complicated psychological laws about the ways in which attitudes and individual preference-orderings cause market segmentation, which in turn can be replaced by still more complicated biological laws about the ways in which individual physiologies ultimately produce the behavior in question, and so on.

Theories can also be the objects of a reduction. On the standard account, intertheoretic reduction proceeds as a formal deduction (Nagel 1961, chapter 11). A theory T_1 reduces theory T_2 if and only if T_1, along with a set of "correspondence rules" or "bridge laws" linking the ontologies of the two theories, logically entails T_2. The bridge laws are typically expressed as identity statements, such as 'temperature = mean kinetic energy'.

Purely formal criteria, however, prove to be insufficient to determine the direction of the reduction. First, bridge laws represent identities, and identity is a symmetric relation. Moreover, since the ontology as described by the reduced theory is seldom entirely retained, and thus strict identity claims are seldom warranted (consider the reduction of Newtonian mechanics to special relativity), we must weaken the identity restriction so that the ontology postulated by T_2 must only be in some way "isomorphic" with that of T_1. Unfortunately, merely formal criteria for reduction would permit, say, an economic theory to reduce a formally isomorphic chemical theory. The envisioned reduction therefore would fail to capture the physicalist's commitment that higher-level phenomena depend on the physical phenomena that compose them.[1]

Most reductionists introduce nonformal or "nonlogical" criteria, either tacitly or explicitly, in order to identify the relevant similarities between the reduced and reducing theories. Theoretical reduction seems to rest on prior assumptions concerning what each theory is about, and theory-dependent considerations about the reducing theory's greater explanatory power, simplicity, and plausibility play a central role in determining both the direction and the comprehensiveness of the reduction.[2]

The language, ontology, and methodology of a higher-level scientific theory (such as biology) frequently gets integrated with those of a neighboring, lower-level theory (such as chemistry). Many philosophers and scientists, reflecting upon this process of theoretical integration, extract reductionistic morals; consequently, reductionism of one form or another has become the model of theoretical unification, a picture of the unity of science.

This image of the unity of science is reflected in the work of the logical positivists, who denied that philosophical disputes about materialism, dualism, and other metaphysical issues had cognitive or theoretical content. In "The Logical Foundations of the Unity of Science," Carnap construes reductionism in typical antimetaphysical fashion, not as an *ontological* doctrine about the reduction of one domain of objects to another, but as a *semantic* doctrine about the reduction of certain types of linguistic expression to others. Carnap's unity of science program gives privileged epistemic status to the role of observation and attempts to carry out the envisioned reduction by defining scientific terms via observation terms and observation statements.

Some observation predicates, such as 'hot', 'blue', and 'heavy', are part of what Carnap calls the "observable-thing language," which designates "directly observable" properties of objects. Many important scientific terms, known as "theoretical terms," designate unobservable phenomena. According to Carnap, in order to define theoretical terms by observation we need to know two things: 1. the conditions and instrumentation appropriate for a particular experiment, and 2. the possible experimental results that would confirm the presence of the studied phenomenon. Knowledge of such conditions and activities provides operational definitions of theoretical terms. Theoretical terms such as 'electric current' are then said to be reducible to a variety of "reduction-sentences" that describe the observable detection of the presence of electric current, from 'x amount of heat produced in the conductor' to 'x period of deflection of a magnetic needle'.

It is a substantial hypothesis of Carnap's project that theoretical terms can be adequately defined in this manner, and one important class of scientific terms—disposition-predicates such as 'soluble' and 'fragile'—present the first problem for Carnap's program. These predicates designate properties of substances that can be directly observed only when they are actually dissolving or breaking, though the objects remain soluble or fragile in other circumstances.

Suppose that we try to define 'fragile', as Carnap would, in the following way: $Fx = (t)(Sxt \rightarrow Bxt)$; that is, if at any time x is sharply struck, then x breaks at that time. When '$\rightarrow$' is construed truth-functionally, the claim is true of nonfragile objects that are never sharply struck. Carnap recognizes this difficulty and proposes to characterize 'if ... then' non-truth-functionally. The resulting subjunctive account claims that if x

were sharply struck at time *t*, then *x* would break at time *t*. Unfortunately, there is no adequate theory of subjunctive conditionals to underwrite Carnap's proposal. Carnap therefore retreats to the earlier truth-functional analysis, resurrected in a more sophisticated form: $Fx = (x)(t)(Sxt \rightarrow [Fx = Bxt])$. This statement says that, for any object at any time, if it is sharply struck at any time, the object is fragile if and only if it breaks. From this statement, however, we are not entitled to infer, as scientists routinely do about unstruck objects, that some *particular* object (*Fa*) is fragile; the meaning of 'fragile' is specified here only for objects that are actually struck sharply at time *t*. For objects failing to satisfy this "test condition," the meaning of '*F*' is left undetermined. Despite this, Carnap concludes that "we can easily see that every term of the physical language is reducible to those of the thing-language and hence finally to observable thing-predicates." But far from demonstrating the unity of scientific language, the above considerations show that chains of reduction sentences provide, at best, only partial definitions for disposition terms.[3]

One might suppose that the failure of formal or "syntactic" reductions of theoretical to observation terms derives from nothing more than isolated technical problems in extensional logic. But it should be noted that despite considerable technical refinement and effort, the problems persist, and no adequate revisions have been proposed. In addition, operationalist efforts to define theoretical notions exclusively in observational terms (see the Bridgman article in part I, section 1 of this anthology) have also proven too restrictive (Byerly and Lazara 1973), so it may appear that it is the empiricist focus on solely observational conceptions of theoretical definition that is fundamentally misguided, along with the formal syntactic conception of reduction crucial to Carnap's program.

Difficulties with the program of "logical analysis" and with purely formal definitions of "reduction" proved so stubborn that philosophers of science ultimately proposed alternative accounts of the unity of science that were more openly metaphysical. In "Unity of Science as a Working Hypothesis," Oppenheim and Putnam understand reduction as a relation between the ontologies of two domains (rather than between the *sentences* describing them, as Carnap did). Following other prominent accounts (Kemeny and Oppenheim 1956), theory T_2 is reduced to T_1 if and only if three conditions are satisfied: 1. The vocabulary of T_2 contains terms not in the vocabulary of T_1, 2. Any observational data explainable by T_2 are explainable by T_1, and 3. T_1 is at least as well systematized as T_2.[4] According to Oppenheim and Putnam, this sense of "reduction" describes both an ideal state of science and a pervasive trend within science "to explain apparently dissimilar phenomena in terms of qualitatively identical parts and their spatiotemporal relations."

What is the evidence that reduction is a pervasive trend within science? Oppenheim and Putnam report a putative tendency among sociologists and economists to explain group phenomena in terms of individual psychology, psychologists to explain individual behavior in terms of underlying physiology, physiologists to explain motor functions in terms of neurochemical composition, etc. Oppenheim and Putnam are concerned only to establish the credibility of their working hypothesis, so it is perhaps no objection to their account that they merely *cite* experimental and theoretical work, rather than show that the theories in question have already been successfully reduced. Even so, they claim that biologists have advanced "hypothetical explanations on the cellular level for such phenomena as association, memory, motivation, emotional disturbance, and some of the phenomena connected with learning, intelligence, and perception," and that Hebb's theory of the brain "accounts for all of the above-mentioned phenomena." This claim to successful reduction would be striking even if it were made today, with reference to far more sophisticated theories of brain function. In the absence of any detailed account of how the two theories satisfy all of their conditions on reduction, such passages are best understood as a defense of the claim that sociological, economic, psychological, and biological processes are all physical processes; they should not be interpreted as supporting the stronger view that the one theory has reduced or replaced the other. Nonetheless, it has now become commonplace among philosophers and scientists to defend a rather strong version of reductionism on the basis of the evidence for physicalism alone.

Fodor develops this latter theme in "Special Sciences." As the original subtitle—"The Disunity of Science as a Working Hypothesis"—indicates, Fodor attempts to undermine the reductionist interpretation of the relation between the special and basic sciences that had dominated the philosophical literature. Fodor points out that the traditional motivation for reductionism was the belief in the generality of physics; that is, the view that all phenomena are physical. This doctrine has been conflated with the much stronger "unity of science" view, which states that all events (properties, states, processes, etc.) that are implicated in the laws of any special science fall under the laws of physics. He then argues that, on the one hand, a weak version of physicalism (token physicalism) captures all that is plausible about the generality of physics, and on the other, that the "unity of science" view fails to capture the causal taxonomies of the special sciences. Therefore, the history of science—the "natural history" of the philosophy of science—dictates that we should adopt a nonreductionist version of physicalism.

On the traditional account of reduction, the predicates of a special science are linked biconditionally to predicates of physics via "bridge laws." The unity of science version of physicalism requires that the natural kinds expressed by predicates in an ideally completed special science each correspond to a natural kind expressed by a predicate in an ideally completed physics. But when we consider a representative bridge law, it appears that no such reduction is likely to be forthcoming. For example, the event predicate "monetary exchange" is routinely implicated in economic generalizations, but the money exchanged can be in the form of copper, gold, wampam, shells, etc., making the set of biconditionally related physical predicates enormously disjunctive.

This example serves two important functions. First, it shows that we can be good physicalists without being reductionists, because we can claim that each token higher-level state is identical to a token physical state without claiming that there are smooth type-type identities.[5] Second, it represents a pervasive and representative counter-example to the common view that reductionism is a trend within science, because it involves an important higher-level kind that is rendered explanatorily impotent once defined in physical terms. As Fodor points out, if this version of the unity of science doctrine offered the appropriate understanding of physicalism, then "the more the special sciences succeed, the more they ought to disappear"; but, this trend has been demonstrably absent: "The development of science has witnessed the proliferation of specialized disciplines at least as often as it has witnessed their elimination."[6]

In "Reductionism," Alan Garfinkel provides an explanation for the apparent resistance of the special sciences to replacement by more basic sciences. Garfinkel asks us to consider an ecological case in which the rabbit population (the macrostate) fluctuates in response to changes in the fox population. Now, when an individual rabbit is caught and eaten (the microstate), we might appeal to the macrostate to explain this microstate: "The cause of the death of the rabbit was that the fox population was high."

Reductionists contend that the macro-explanation can be eliminated in favor of a micro-explanation. For example, "Rabbit r was eaten because he passed through the capture space of fox f" might be advanced as a micro-explanation for a particular rabbit being caught. On this reductionist proposal, once we fix such initial and boundary conditions as the physiology and reaction time of the two relevant actors, it follows that rabbit r would travel through the capture space of fox f. But does this micro-explanation actually eliminate the macro-explanation?

It appears that the micro- and macro-explanations have different objects. The object of the the macro-explanation is "the death of the rabbit," while the object of the micro-explanation is "the death of rabbit r by fox f at time t, etc." But we don't really want to know why the rabbit was eaten by *that* fox at *this* place and *this* time; we want to know why the rabbit was eaten *at all*. So the micro-explanation fails to tell us something we want to know. At the same time, the details provided in the micro-explanation do not merely represent an innocent embarrassment of informational riches; "the death of rabbit r by fox f at time t" suggests that, had the specific cause (rabbit r passing through fox f's capture space) not obtained, the effect would not have occurred. Thus, because of its exclusive focus on the *local* cause, the micro-explanation presents a misleading picture of the sensitivity of the rabbit-fox relation to changes in the system. The macro-explanation, on the other hand, captures the apparent fact that the event (the rabbit's death) was "overdetermined" by the fox population. Even if the circumstances were slightly different, the rabbit probably would have been eaten anyway because rabbit r's avoidance of fox f's capture space increases the likelihood that r is in (or will wander into) the capture space of some other fox. The existence of redundant causal factors (such as the fox population) raises serious doubts that higher-level explanations in biology, psychology, economics, and sociology ultimately will be reduced to, or eliminated by, micro-explanations.

Garfinkel does not extract any positive ontological morals from these observations about structural explanation. Instead, he focuses on the epistemically reliable explanatory practices of scientists and notes that, despite reductionist advertisements, explanations in the various sciences "seek their own level." Those who favor reductionism attempt to explain the multilevel accretion of theories in terms of our peculiar epistemic relation to the world. If we could directly observe the objects of the microstates and keep track of all of their relations, higher-level, structural explanations could be reconstructed according to reductionist strictures. But note that, by this time, the reductionist is no longer defending the version of the unity of science doctrine that attempts to claim a pervasive reductive trend within science. The nonreductionist, by contrast, is in a position to draw an ontological moral: causal features of the world determine which explanatory practices are appropriate. Therefore, we must take seriously the appropriateness of higher-level explanations so prevalent in the special sciences and interpret realistically the kinds implicated in their generalizations. If the nonreductionist is correct in extracting this realist moral from the explanatory practices cited by Garfinkel, then the unity of science doctrine depicts a state of science that is far from ideal.

The plausibility of reductionism for each of the special sciences will be a central theme in part II, but the importance of this issue is not exhausted by its application to the special sciences. Tacit stances on the issue of reductionism often influence more general metaphysical, epistemological, and semantic positions in the philosophy of science. In the two other sections of part I, we might ask whether and how a particular position on the realism/antirealism dispute, the nature of cause, rationality, and the meaning of theoretical terms, is motivated by independent conceptions about the nature and plausibility of reductionism that are not discussed explicitly in the particular reading.

Notes

1. This treatment of the standard account of reduction is obviously abbreviated. For an elaborate discussion of the classical empiricist conception of reduction and more recent developments, see Hooker 1981.
2. For a discussion of explanatory power, see the introduction to part I, section 2 of this anthology.
3. Carnap (1936–37) describes his position in greater detail, though his proposals there are subject to the same difficulties. For the relevant criticisms of Carnap's treatment of the cognitive content of theoretical discourse, see Hempel's "Empiricist Criteria of Cognitive Significance" (reprinted in part I, section 1), particularly section 3 of that article.
4. In fact, the satisfaction of these three conditions is not sufficient for successful reduction. We would not regard the reduction as successful unless the newer theory also explains the *unobservable* mechanisms proposed by the theory targeted for reduction.
5. For arguments to the effect that even the token-identity theory is an inappropriately strong analysis of physicalism, see Boyd (1980) and Haugeland (1982).
6. A reductionist response to Fodor's argument can be found in Causey (1977).

References

Boyd, R., 1980, "Materialism Without Reductionism: What Physicalism Does Not Entail," in Block, N., ed., *Readings in Philosophy of Psychology*, volume 1, Harvard University Press, Cambridge, MA.

Byerly, H., and Lazara, V., 1973, "Realist Foundations of Measurement," *Philosophy of Science* 40: 1–27.

Carnap, R., 1936–37, "Testability and Meaning," *Philosophy of Science*, vols. 3 and 4. Reprinted in Feigl, H. and Brodbeck, M. 1953, eds., *Readings in the Philosophy of Science*, Appleton-Century-Crofts, New York.

Causey, R., 1977, *Unity of Science*, Reidel, Dordrecht.

Haugeland, J., 1982, "Weak Supervenience," *American Philosophical Quarterly* 19: 93–103.

Hooker, C., 1981, "Towards a General Theory of Reduction," *Dialogue* XX, 1–3: 38–59; 201–236; 496–529.

Kemeny, J., and P. Oppenheim, 1956, "On Reduction," *Philosophical Studies* 7: 6–19.

Nagel, E., 1961, *The Structure of Science*, Harcourt Brace Jovanovich, New York.

Further Readings

Bechtel, W., 1986, ed., *Integrating Scientific Disciplines*, Martinus Nijhoff, Dordrecht.

Bonevac, D., 1982, *Reduction in the Abstract Sciences*, Hackett, Indianapolis.

Cohen, R. S., Hooker, C. A., Michalos, A. C., and van Evra, J. 1976, eds., *PSA 1976, Boston Studies in the Philosophy of Science*, Reidel, Dordrecht.

Darden. L., and Maull, N., 1977, "Interfield Theories," *Philosophy of Science* 43: 44–64.

Hellman, G., and Thompson, F., 1975, "Physicalism: Ontology, Determinism, and Reduction," *Journal of Philosophy* 72: 551–564.

Hellman, G., and Thompson, F., 1977, "Physicalist Materialism," *Noûs* 11: 309–345.

Hempel, C., 1966, *Philosophy of Natural Science*, Prentice–Hall, Englewood Cliffs, NJ, ch. 8.

Horgan, T., 1981, "Token Physicalism, Supervenience, and the Generality of Physics," *Synthese* 49: 395–413.

Kim, J., 1978, "Supervenience and Nomological Incommensurables," *American Philosophical Quarterly* 15: 149–156.

Schaffner, K., 1967, "Approaches to Reduction," *Philosophy of Science* 34:137–147.

Sklar, L., 1967, "Types of Inter-Theoretic Reduction," *British Journal for the Philosophy of Science* 18: 109–124.

Wimsatt, W., 1979, "Reduction and Reductionism," in Asquith, P. D. and Kyburg, H. eds., *Current Research in the Philosophy of Science*, Philosophy of Science Association, East Lansing, MI.

Chapter 21

Logical Foundations of the Unity of Science

Rudolf Carnap

I. What Is Logical Analysis of Science?

The task of analyzing science may be approached from various angles. The analysis of the subject matter of the sciences is carried out by science itself. Biology, for example, analyzes organisms and processes in organisms, and in a similar way every branch of science analyzes its subject matter. Mostly, however, by 'analysis of science' or 'theory of science' is meant an investigation which differs from the branch of science to which it is applied. We may, for instance, think of an investigation of scientific *activity*. We may study the historical development of this activity. Or we may try to find out in which way scientific work depends upon the individual conditions of the men working in science, and upon the status of the society surrounding them. Or we may describe procedures and appliances used in scientific work. These investigations of scientific activity may be called history, psychology, sociology, and methodology of science. The subject matter of such studies is science as a body of actions carried out by certain persons under certain circumstances. Theory of science in this sense will be dealt with at various other places in this *Encyclopedia*; it is certainly an essential part of the foundation of science.

We come to a theory of science in another sense if we study not the actions of scientists but their results, namely, science as a body of ordered knowledge. Here, by 'results' we do not mean beliefs, images, etc., and the behavior influenced by them. That would lead us again to psychology of science. We mean by 'results' certain linguistic expressions, viz., the statements asserted by scientists. The task of the theory of science in this sense will be to analyze such statements, study their kinds and relations, and analyze terms as components of those statements and theories as ordered systems of those statements. A statement is a kind of sequence of spoken sounds, written marks, or the like, produced by human beings for specific purposes. But it is possible to abstract in an analysis of the statements of science from the persons asserting the statements and from the psychological and sociological conditions of such assertions. The analysis of the linguistic expressions of science under such an abstraction is *logic of science*.

Within the logic of science we may distinguish between two chief parts. The investigation may be restricted to the forms of the linguistic expressions involved, i.e., to the way in which they are constructed out of elementary parts (e.g., words) without referring to anything outside of language. Or the investigation goes beyond this boundary and studies linguistic expressions in their relation to objects outside of language. A study restricted in the first-mentioned way is called *formal*; the field of

Reprinted from *International Encyclopedia of Unified Science: Volume I*, ed. O. Neurath, R. Carnap, and C. Morris (Chicago: University of Chicago Press, 1938–55), pp. 42–62. Copyright 1955 by University of Chicago Press.

such formal studies is called formal logic or *logical syntax*. Such a formal or syntactical analysis of the language of science as a whole or in its various branches will lead to results of the following kinds. A certain term (e.g., a word) is defined within a certain theory on the basis of certain other terms, or it is definable in such a way. A certain term, although not definable by certain other terms, is reducible to them (in a sense to be explained later). A certain statement is a logical consequence of (or logically deducible from) certain other statements; and a deduction of it, given within a certain theory, is, or is not, logically correct. A certain statement is incompatible with certain other statements, i.e., its negation is a logical consequence of them. A certain statement is independent of certain other statements, i.e., neither a logical consequence of them nor incompatible with them. A certain theory is inconsistent, i.e., some of its statements are incompatible with the other ones. The last sections of this essay will deal with the question of the unity of science from the logical point of view, studying the logical relations between the terms of the chief branches of science and between the laws stated in these branches; thus it will give an example of a syntactical analysis of the language of science.

In the second part of the logic of science, a given language and the expressions in it are analyzed in another way. Here also, as in logical syntax, abstraction is made from the psychological and sociological side of the language. This investigation, however, is not restricted to formal analysis but takes into consideration one important relation between linguistic expressions and other objects—that of designation. An investigation of this kind is called *semantics*. Results of a semantical analysis of the language of science may, for instance, have the following forms. A certain term designates a certain particular object (e.g., the sun), or a certain property of things (e.g., iron), or a certain relation between things (e.g., fathership), or a certain physical function (e.g., temperature); two terms in different branches of science (e.g., 'Homo sapiens' in biology and 'person' in economics, or, in another way, 'man' in both cases) designate (or: do not designate) the same. What is designated by a certain expression may be called its *designatum*. Two expressions designating the same are called *synonymous*. The term 'true,' as it is used in science and in everyday life, can also be defined within semantics. We see that the chief subject matter of a semantical analysis of the language of science are such properties and relations of expressions, and especially of statements, as are based on the relation of designation. (Where we say 'the designatum of an expression,' the customary phrase is 'the meaning of an expression.' It seems, however, preferable to avoid the word 'meaning' wherever possible because of its ambiguity, i.e., the multiplicity of its designata. Above all, it is important to distinguish between the semantical and the psychological use of the word 'meaning.')

It is a question of terminological convention whether to use the term 'logic' in the wider sense, including the semantical analysis of the designata of expressions, or in the narrower sense of logical syntax, restricted to formal analysis, abstracting from designation. And accordingly we may distinguish between logic of science in the narrower sense, as the syntax of the language of science, and logic of science in the wider sense, comprehending both syntax and semantics.

II. The Main Branches of Science

We use the word 'science' here in its widest sense, including all theoretical knowledge, no matter whether in the field of natural sciences or in the field of the social sciences and the so-called humanities, and no matter whether it is knowledge found by the application of special scientific procedures, or knowledge based on common sense in everyday life. In the same way the term 'language of science' is meant here to refer to the language which contains all statements (i.e., theoretical sentences as distinguished from emotional expressions, commands, lyrics, etc.) used for scientific purposes or in everyday life. What usually is called science is merely a more systematic continuation of those activities which we carry out in everyday life in order to know something.

The first distinction which we have to make is that between *formal science* and *empirical science*. Formal science consists of the analytic statements established by logic and mathematics; empirical science consists of the synthetic statements established in the different fields of factual knowledge. The relation of formal to empirical science will be dealt with at another place; here we have to do with empirical science, its language, and the problem of its unity.

Let us take 'physics' as a common name for the nonbiological field of science, comprehending both systematic and historical investigations within this field, thus including chemistry, mineralogy, astronomy, geology (which is historical), meteorology, etc. How, then, are we to draw the boundary line between physics and biology? It is obvious that the distinction between these two branches has to be based on the distinction between two kinds of things which we find in nature: organisms and nonorganisms. Let us take this latter distinction as granted; it is the task of biologists to lay down a suitable definition for the term 'organism,' in other words, to tell us the features of a thing which we take as characteristic for its being an organism. How, then, are we to define 'biology' on the basis of 'organism'? We could perhaps think of trying to do it in this way: biology is the branch of science which investigates organisms and the processes occurring in organisms, and physics is the study of nonorganisms. But these definitions would not draw the distinction as it is usually intended. A law stated in physics is intended to be valid universally, without any restriction. For example, the law stating the electrostatic force as a function of electric charges and their distance, or the law determining the pressure of a gas as a function of temperature, or the law determining the angle of refraction as a function of the coefficients of refraction of the two media involved, are intended to apply to the processes in organisms no less than to those in inorganic nature. The biologist has to know these laws of physics in studying the processes in organisms. He needs them for the explanation of these processes. But since they do not suffice, he adds some other laws, not known by the physicist, viz., the specifically biological laws. Biology presupposes physics, but not vice versa.

These reflections lead us to the following definitions. Let us call those terms which we need—in addition to logico-mathematical terms—for the description of processes in inorganic nature *physical terms*, no matter whether, in a given instance, they are applied to such processes or to processes in organisms. That sublanguage of the language of science, which contains—besides logico-mathematical terms—all and only physical terms, may be called *physical language*. The system of those statements which are formulated in the physical language and are acknowledged by a certain group at a certain time is called the physics of that group at that time. Such of these statements as have a specific universal form are called *physical laws*. The physical laws are needed for the explanation of processes in inorganic nature; but, as mentioned before, they apply to processes in organisms also.

The whole of the rest of science may be called *biology (in the wider sense)*. It seems desirable, at least for practical purposes, e.g., for the division of labor in research work, to subdivide this wide field. But it seems questionable whether any distinctions can be found here which, although not of a fundamental nature, are at least clear to about the same degree as the distinction between physics and biology. At present, it is scarcely possible to predict which subdivisions will be made in the future. The traditional distinction between bodily (or material) and mental (or psychical) processes had its origin in the old magical and later metaphysical mind-body dualism. The distinction as a practical device for the classification of branches of science still plays an important role, even for those scientists who reject that metaphysical dualism; and it will probably continue to do so for some time in the future. But when the aftereffect of such prescientific issues upon science becomes weaker and weaker, it may be that new boundary lines for subdivisions will turn out to be more satisfactory.

One possibility of dividing biology in the wider sense into two fields is such that the first corresponds roughly to what is usually called biology, and the second comprehends among other parts those which usually are called psychology and social science. The second field deals with the behavior of individual organisms and groups of organisms within their environment, with the dispositions to such behavior, with such features of processes in organisms as are relevant to the behavior, and with certain features of the environment which are characteristic of and relevant to the behavior, e.g., objects observed and work done by organisms.

The first of the two fields of biology in the wider sense may be called biology in the narrower sense, or, for the following discussions, simply *biology*. This use of the term 'biology' seems justified by the fact that, in terms of the customary classification, this part contains most of what is usually called biology, namely, general biology, botany, and the greater part of zoology. The terms which are used in this field in addition to logico-mathematical and physical terms may be called biological terms in the narrower sense, or simply *biological terms*. Since many statements of biology contain physical terms besides biological ones, the *biological language* cannot be restricted to biological terms; it contains the physical language as a sublanguage and, in addition, the biological terms. Statements and laws belonging to this language but not to physical language will be called *biological statements* and *biological laws*.

The distinction between the two fields of biology in the wider sense has been indicated only in a very vague way. At the present time it is not yet clear as to how the boundary line may best be drawn. Which processes in an organism are to be assigned to the second field? Perhaps the connection of a process with the processes in the nervous system might be taken as characteristic, or, to restrict it more, the connection with speaking activities, or, more generally, with activities involving signs. Another way of characterization might come from the other direction, from outside, namely, selecting the processes in an organism from the point of view of their relevance to achievements in the environment (see Brunswik and Ness). There is no name in common use for this second field. (The term 'mental sciences' suggests too narrow a field and is connected too closely with the metaphysical dualism mentioned before.) The term 'behavioristics' has been proposed. If it is used, it must be made clear that the word 'behavior' has here a greater extension than it had with the earlier behaviorists. Here it is intended to designate not only the overt behavior which can be observed from outside but also internal behavior (i.e., processes within the organism); further, dispositions to behavior which may not be manifest in a special case; and, finally certain effects upon the environment. Within this second field we may distinguish roughly between two parts dealing with individual organisms and with groups of organisms. But it seems doubtful whether any sharp line can be drawn between these two parts. Compared with the customary classification of science, the first part would include chiefly psychology, but also some parts of physiology and the humanities. The second part would chiefly include social science and, further, the greater part of the humanities and history, but it has not only to deal with groups of human beings but also to deal with groups of other organisms. For the following discussion, the terms 'psychology' and 'social science' will be used as names of the two parts because of lack of better terms. It is clear that both the question of boundary lines and the question of suitable terms for the sections is still in need of much more discussion.

III. Reducibility

The question of the unity of science is meant here as a problem of the logic of science, not of ontology. We do not ask: "Is the world one?" "Are all events fundamentally of one kind?" 'Are the so-called mental processes really physical processes or not?" "Are the so-called physical processes really spiritual or not?" It seems doubtful whether we can find any theoretical content in such philosophical questions as discussed by monism, dualism, and pluralism. In any case, when we ask whether there is a unity in science, we mean this as a question of logic, concerning the logical relationships between the terms and the laws of the various branches of science. Since it belongs to the logic of science, the question concerns scientists and logicians alike.

Let us first deal with the question of terms. (Instead of the word 'term' the word 'concept' could be taken, which is more frequently used by logicians. But the word 'term' is more clear, since it shows that we mean signs, e.g., words, expressions consisting of words, artificial symbols, etc., of course with the meaning they have in the language in question. We do not mean 'concept' in its psychological sense, i.e., images or thoughts somehow connected with a word; that would not belong to logic.) We know the meaning (designatum) of a term if we know under what conditions we are permitted to apply it in a concrete case and under what conditions not. Such a knowledge of the conditions of application can be of two different kinds. In some cases we may have a merely practical knowledge, i.e., we are able to use the term in question correctly without giving a theoretical account of the rules for its use. In other cases we may be able to give an explicit formulation of the conditions for the application of the term. If now a certain term x is such that the conditions for its application (as used in the language of science) can be formulated with the help of the terms y, z, etc., we call such a formulation a *reduction statement* for x in terms of y, z, etc., and we call x *reducible* to y, z, etc. There may be several sets of conditions for the application of x; hence x may be reducible to y, z, etc., and also to u, v, etc., and perhaps to other sets. There may even be cases of mutual reducibility, e.g., each term of the set x_1, x_2, etc., is reducible to y_1, y_2, etc.; and, on the other hand, each term of the set y_1, y_2, etc., is reducible to x_1, x_2, etc.

A *definition* is the simplest form of a reduction statement. For the formulation of examples, let us use '$\equiv$' (called the symbol of equivalence) as abbreviation for 'if and only if.' Example of a definition for 'ox': 'x is an ox $\equiv$ x is a quadruped and horned and cloven-footed and ruminant, etc.' This is also a reduction statement because it states the conditions for the application of the term 'ox,' saying that this term can be applied to a thing if and only if that thing is a quadruped and horned, etc. By that definition the term 'ox' is shown to be reducible to—moreover definable by—the set of terms 'quadruped,' 'horned,' etc.

A reduction statement sometimes cannot be formulated in the simple form of a definition, i.e., of an equivalence statement, '.... $\equiv$ ....,' but only in the somewhat more complex form 'If ...., then: .... $\equiv$ .....' Thus a reduction statement is either a simple (i.e., explicit) definition or, so to speak, a conditional definition. (The term reduction statement' is generally used in the narrower sense, referring to the second, conditional form.) For instance, the following statement is a reduction statement for the term 'electric charge' (taken here for the sake of simplicity as a nonquantitative term), i.e., for the statement form 'the body x has an electric charge at the time t': 'If a light body y is placed near x at t, then: x has an electric charge at $t \equiv y$ is attracted by x at t.' A general way of procedure which enables us to find out whether or not a certain term can be applied in concrete cases may be called a *method of determination* for the term in question. The method of determination for a quantitative term (e.g., 'temperature') is the method of measurement for that term. Whenever we know an experimental method of determination for a term, we are in a position to formulate a reduction statement for it. To know an experimental method of determination for a term, say 'Q_3,' means to know two things. First, we must know an experimental situation which we have to create, say the state Q_1, e.g., the arrangement of measuring apparatuses and of suitable conditions for their use. Second, we must know the possible experimental result, say Q_2, which, if it occurs, will confirm the presence of the property Q_3. In the simplest case—let us leave aside the more complex cases—Q_2 is also such that its nonoccurrence shows that the thing in question does not have the property Q_3. Then a reduction statement for 'Q_3,' i.e., for the statement form 'the thing (or space-time-point) x is Q_3 (i.e., has the property Q_3) at the time t,' can be formulated in this way: 'If x is Q_1 (i.e., x and the surroundings of x are in the state Q_1) at time t, then: x is Q_3 at $t \equiv x$ is Q_2 at t.' On the basis of this reduction statement, the term 'Q_3' is reducible to 'Q_1,' 'Q_2,' and spatio-temporal terms. Whenever a term 'Q_3' expresses the disposition of a thing to behave in a certain way (Q_2) to certain conditions (Q_1), we have a reduction statement of the form given above. If there is a connection of such a kind between Q_1, Q_2, and Q_3, then in biology and psychology in certain cases the following terminology is applied: 'To the stimulus Q_1 we find the reaction Q_2 as a symptom for Q_3.' But the situation is not essentially different from the analogous one in physics, where we usually do not apply that terminology.

Sometimes we know several methods of determination for a certain term. For example, we can determine the presence of an electric current by observing either the heat produced in the conductor, or the deviation of a magnetic needle, or the quantity of a substance separated from an electrolyte, etc. Thus the term 'electric current' is reducible to each of many sets of other terms. Since not only can an electric current be measured by measuring a temperature but also, conversely, a temperature can be measured by measuring the electric current produced by a thermo-electric element, there is mutual reducibility between the terms of the theory of electricity, on the one hand, and those of the theory of heat, on the other. The same holds for the terms of the theory of electricity and those of the theory of magnetism.

Let us suppose that the persons of a certain group have a certain set of terms in common, either on account of a merely practical agreement about the conditions of their application or with an explicit stipulation of such conditions for a part of the terms. Then a reduction statement reducing a new term to the terms of that original set may be used as a way of introducing the new term into the language of the group. This way of introduction assures conformity as to the use of the new term. If a certain language (e.g., a sublanguage of the language of science, covering a certain branch of science) is such that every term of it is reducible to a certain set of terms, then this language can be constructed on the basis of that set by introducing one new term after the other by reduction statements. In this case we call the basic set of terms a *sufficient reduction basis* for that language.

IV. The Unity of the Language of Science

Now we will analyze the logical relations among the terms of different parts of the language of science with respect to reducibility. We have indicated a division of the whole language of science into some parts. Now we may make another division cutting across the first, by distinguishing in a rough way, without any claims to exactness, between those terms which we use on a prescientific level in our everyday language, and for whose application no scientific procedure is necessary, and scientific terms in the narrower sense. That sublanguage which is the common part of this prescientific language and the physical language may be called physical thing-language or briefly *thing-language*. It is this language that we use in speaking about the properties of the observable (inorganic) things surrounding us. Terms like 'hot' and 'cold' may be regarded as belonging to the thing-language, but not 'temperature' because its determination requires the application of a technical instrument; further, 'heavy' and 'light' (but not 'weight'); 'red,' 'blue,' etc.; 'large,' 'small,' 'thick,' 'thin,' etc.

The terms so far mentioned designate what we may call observable properties, i.e., such as can be determined by a direct observation. We will call them *observable thing-predicates*. Besides such terms the thing-language contains other ones, e.g., those expressing the disposition of a thing to a certain behavior under certain conditions, e.g., 'elastic,' 'soluble,' 'flexible,' 'transparent,' 'fragile,' 'plastic,' etc. These terms—they might be called disposition-predicates—are reducible to observable thing-predicates because we can describe the experimental conditions and the reactions characteristic of such disposition-predicates in terms of observable thing-predicates. Example of a reduction statement for 'elastic': 'If the body x is stretched and then released at the time t, then: x is elastic at the time $t \equiv x$ contracts at t,' where the terms 'stretched,' 'released,' and 'contracting' can be defined by observable thing-predicates. If these predicates are taken as a basis, we can moreover introduce, by iterated application of definition and (conditional) reduction, every other term of the *thing-language*, e.g., designations of substances, e.g., 'stone,' 'water,' 'sugar,' or of processes, e.g., 'rain,' 'fire,' etc. For every term of that language is such that we can apply it either on the basis of direct observation or with the help of an experiment for which we know the conditions and the possible result determining the application of the term in question.

Now we can easily see that every term of the *physical language* is reducible to those of the thing-language and hence finally to observable thing-predicates. On the scientific level, we have the quantitative coefficient of elasticity instead of the qualitative term 'elastic' of the thing-language; we have the quantitative term 'temperature' instead of the qualitative ones 'hot' and 'cold'; and we have all the terms by means of which physicists describe the temporary or permanent states of things or processes. For any such term the physicist knows at least one method of determination. Physicists would not admit into their language any term for which no method of determination by observations were given. The formulation of such a method, i.e., the description of the experimental arrangement to be carried out and of the possible result determining the application of the term in question, is a reduction statement for that term. Sometimes the term will not be directly reduced by the reduction statement to thing-predicates, but first to other scientific terms, and these by their reduction statements again to other scientific terms, etc.; but such a reduction chain must in any case finally lead to predicates of the thing-language and, moreover, to observable thing-predicates because otherwise there would be no way of determining whether or not the physical term in question can be applied in special cases, on the basis of given observation statements.

If we come to *biology* (this term now always understood in the narrower sense), we find again the same situation. For any biological term the biologist who introduces or uses it must know empirical criteria for its application. This applies, of course, only to biological terms in the sense explained before, including all terms used in scientific biology proper, but not to certain terms used sometimes in the philosophy of biology—'a whole,' 'entelechy,' etc. It may happen that for the description of the criterion, i.e., the method of determination of a term, other biological terms are needed. In this case the term in question is first reducible to them. But at least indirectly it must be reducible to terms of the thing-language and finally to observable thing-predicates, because the determination of the term in question in a concrete case must finally be based upon observations of concrete things, i.e., upon observation statements formulated in the thing-language.

Let us take as an example the term 'muscle.' Certainly biologists know the conditions for a part of an organism to be a muscle; otherwise the term could not be used in concrete cases. The problem is: Which other terms are needed for the formulation of those conditions? It will be necessary to describe the functions within the organism which are characteristic of muscles, in other words, to formulate certain laws connecting the processes in muscles with those in their environment, or, again in still other words, to describe the reactions to certain stimuli characteristic of muscles. Both the processes in the environment and those in the muscle (in the customary terminology: stimuli and reactions) must be described in such a way that we can determine them by observations. Hence the term 'muscle,' although not definable in terms of the thing-language, is reducible to them. Similar considerations easily show the reducibility of any other biological term—whether it be a designation of a kind of organism, or of a kind of part of organisms, or of a kind of process in organisms.

The result found so far may be formulated in this way: The terms of the thing-language, and even the narrower class of the observable thing-predicates, supply a sufficient basis for the languages both of physics and of biology. (There are, by the way, many reduction bases for these languages, each of which is much more restricted than the classes mentioned.) Now the question may be raised whether a basis of the kind mentioned is sufficient even for the whole language of science. The affirmative answer to this question is sometimes called *physicalism* (because it was first formulated not with respect to the thing-language but to the wider physical language as a sufficient basis). If the thesis of physicalism is applied to biology only, it scarcely meets any serious objections. The situation is somewhat changed, however, when it is applied to psychology and social science (individual and social behavioristics). Since many of the objections raised against it are based on misinterpretations, it is necessary to make clear what the thesis is intended to assert and what not.

The question of the reducibility of the terms of psychology to those of the biological language and thereby to those of the thing-language is closely connected with the problem of the various methods used in psychology. As chief examples of methods used in this field in its present state, the physiological, the behavioristic, and the introspective methods may be considered. The *physiological approach* consists in an investigation of the functions of certain organs in the organism, above all, of the nervous system. Here, the terms used are either those of biology or those so closely related to them that there will scarcely be any doubt with respect to their reducibility to the terms of the biological language and the thing-language. For the *behavioristic approach* different ways are possible. The investigation may be restricted to the external behavior of an organism, i.e., to such movements, sounds, etc., as can be observed by other organisms in the neighborhood of the first. Or processes within the organism may also be taken into account so that this approach overlaps with the physiological one. Or, finally, objects in the environment of the organism, either observed or worked on or produced by it, may also be studied. Now it is easy to see that a term for whose determination a behavioristic method—of one of the kinds mentioned or of a related kind—is known, is reducible to the terms of the biological language, including the thing-language. As we have seen before, the formulation of the method of determination for a term is a reduction statement for that term, either in the form of a simple definition or in the conditional form. By that statement the term is shown to be reducible to the terms applied in describing the method, namely, the experimental arrangement and the characteristic result. Now, conditions and results consist in the behavioristic method either of physiological processes in the organism or of observable processes in the organism and in its environment. Hence they can be described in terms of the biological language. If we have to do with a behavioristic approach in its pure form, i.e., leaving aside physiological investigations, then the description of the conditions and results characteristic for a term can in most cases be given directly in terms of the thing-language. Hence the behavioristic reduction of psychological terms is often simpler than the physiological reduction of the same term.

Let us take as an example the term 'angry.' If for anger we knew a sufficient and necessary criterion to be found by a physiological analysis of the nervous system or other organs, then we could define 'angry' in terms of the biological language. The same holds if we knew such a criterion to be determined by the observation of the overt, external behavior. But a physiological criterion is not yet known. And the peripheral symptoms known are presumably not necessary criteria because it might be that a person of strong self-control is able to suppress these symptoms. If this is the case, the term 'angry' is, at least at the present time, not definable in terms of the biological language. But, nevertheless, it is reducible to such terms. It is sufficient for the formulation of a reduction sentence to know a behavioristic procedure which enables us—if not always, at least under suitable circumstances—to determine whether the organism in question is angry or not. And we know indeed such procedures; otherwise we should never be able to apply the term 'angry' to another person on the basis of our observations of his behavior, as we constantly do in everyday life and in scientific investigation. A reduction of the term 'angry' or similar terms by the formulation of such procedures is indeed less useful than a definition would be, because a definition supplies a complete (i.e., unconditional) criterion for the term in question, while a reduction statement of the conditional form gives only an incomplete one. But a criterion, conditional or not, is all we need for ascertaining reducibility. Thus the result is the following: If for any psychological term we know either a physiological or a behavioristic method of determination, then that term is reducible to those terms of the thing-language.

In psychology, as we find it today, there is, besides the physiological and the behavioristic approach, the so-called *introspective method*. The questions as to its validity, limits, and necessity are still more unclear and in need of further discussion than the analogous questions with respect to the two other methods. Much of what has been said about it, especially by philosophers, may be looked at with some suspicion. But the facts themselves to which the term 'introspection' is meant to refer will scarcely be denied by anybody, e.g., the fact that a person sometimes knows that he is angry without applying any of those procedures which another person would have to apply, i.e., without looking with the help of a physiological instrument at his nervous system or looking at the play of his facial muscles. The problems of the practical reliability and theoretical validity of the introspective method may here be left aside. For the discussion of reducibility an answer to these problems is not needed. It will suffice to show that in every case, no matter whether the introspective method is applicable or not, the behavioristic method can be applied at any rate. But we must be careful in the interpretation of this assertion. It is not meant as saying: 'Every psychological process can be ascertained by the behavioristic method.' Here we have to do not with the single processes themselves (e.g., Peter's anger yesterday morning) but with kinds of processes (e.g., anger). If Robinson Crusoe is angry and then dies before anybody comes to his island, nobody except himself ever knows of this single occurrence of anger. But anger of the same kind, occurring with other persons, may be studied and ascertained by a behavioristic method, if circumstances are favorable. (Analogy: if an electrically charged raindrop falls into the ocean without an observer or suitable recording instrument in the neighborhood, nobody will ever know of that charge. But a charge of the same kind can be found out under suitable circumstances by certain observations.) Further, in order to come to a correct formulation of the thesis, we have to apply it not to the kinds of processes (e.g., anger) but rather to the terms designating such kinds of processes (e.g., 'anger'). The difference might seem trivial but is, in fact, essential. We do not at all enter a discussion about the question whether or not there are kinds of events which can never have any behavioristic symptoms, and hence are knowable only by introspection. We have to do with psychological terms not with kinds of events. For any such term, say, 'Q,' the psychological language contains a statement form applying that term, e.g., 'The person.... is at the time.... in the state Q.' Then the utterance by speaking or writing of the statement 'I am now (or: I was yesterday) in the state Q,' is (under suitable circumstances, e.g., as to reliability, etc.) an observable symptom for the state Q. Hence there cannot be a term in the psychological language, taken as an intersubjective language for mutual communication, which designates a kind of state or event without any behavioristic symptom. Therefore, there is a behavioristic method of determination for any term of the psychological language. Hence every such term is reducible to those of the thing-language.

The logical nature of the psychological terms becomes clear by an analogy with those physical terms which are introduced by reduction statements of the conditional form. Terms of both kinds designate a state characterized by the disposition to certain reactions. In both cases the state is not the same as those reactions. Anger is not the same as the movements by which an angry organism reacts to the conditions in his environment, just as the state of being electrically charged is not the same as the process of attracting other bodies. In both cases that state sometimes occurs without these events which are observable from outside; they are consequences of the state according to certain laws and may therefore under suitable circumstances be taken as symptoms for it; but they are not identical with it.

The last field to be dealt with is *social science* (in the wide sense indicated before; also called social behavioristics). Here we need no detailed analysis because it is easy to see that every term of this field is reducible to terms of the other fields. The result of any investigation of a group of men or other organisms can be described in terms of the members, their relations to one another and to their environment. Therefore, the conditions for the application of any term can be formulated in terms of psychology, biology, and physics, including the thing-language. Many terms can even be defined on that basis, and the rest is certainly reducible to it.

It is true that some terms which are used in psychology are such that they designate a certain behavior (or disposition to behavior) within a group of a certain kind or a certain attitude toward a group, e.g., 'desirous of ruling,' 'shy,' and others. It may be that for the definition or reduction of a term of this kind some terms of social science describing the group involved are needed. This shows that there is not a clear-cut line between psychology and social science and that in some cases it is not clear whether a term is better assigned to one or to the other field. But such terms are also certainly reducible to those of the thing-language because every term referring to a group of organisms is reducible to terms referring to individual organisms.

The result of our analysis is that the class of observable thing-predicates is a sufficient reduction basis for the whole of the language of science, including the cognitive part of the everyday language.

V. The Problem of the Unity of Laws

The relations between the terms of the various branches of science have been considered. There remains the task of analyzing the relations between the laws. According to our previous consideration, a biological law contains only terms which are reducible to physical terms. Hence there is a common language to which both the biological and the physical laws belong so that they can be logically compared and connected. We can ask whether or not a certain biological law is compatible with the system of physical laws, and whether or not it is derivable from them. But the answer to these questions cannot be inferred from the reducibility of the terms. At the present state of the development of science, it is certainly not possible to derive the biological laws from the physical ones. Some philosophers believe that such a derivation is forever impossible because of the very nature of the two fields. But the proofs attempted so far for this thesis are certainly insufficient. This question is, it seems, the scientific kernel of the problem of vitalism; some recent discussions of this problem are, however, entangled with rather questionable metaphysical issues. The question of derivability itself is, of course, a very serious scientific problem. But it will scarcely be possible to find a solution for it before many more results of experimental investigation are available than we have today. In the meantime the efforts toward derivation of more and more biological laws from physical laws—in the customary formulation: explanation of more and more processes in organisms with the help of physics and chemistry—will be, as it has been, a very fruitful tendency in biological research.

As we have seen before, the fields of psychology and social science are very closely connected with each other. A clear division of the laws of these fields is perhaps still less possible than a division of the terms. If the laws are classified in some way or other, it will be seen that sometimes a psychological law is derivable from those of social science, and sometimes a law of social science from those of psychology. (An example of the first kind is the explanation of the behavior of adults—e.g., in the theories of A. Adler and Freud—by their position within the family or a larger group during childhood; an example of the second kind is the obvious explanation of an increase of the price of a commodity by the reactions of buyers and sellers in the case of a diminished supply.) It is obvious that, at the present time, laws of psychology and social science cannot be derived from those of biology and physics. On the other hand, no scientific reason is known for the assumption that such a derivation should be in principle and forever impossible.

Thus there is at present *no unity of laws*. The construction of one homogeneous system of laws for the whole of science is an aim for the future development of science. This aim cannot be shown to be unattainable. But we do not, of course, know whether it will ever be reached.

On the other hand, there is a *unity of language* in science, viz., a common reduction basis for the terms of all branches of science, this basis consisting of a very narrow and homogeneous class of terms of the physical thing-language. This unity of terms is indeed less far-reaching and effective than the unity of laws would be, but it is a necessary preliminary condition for the unity of laws. We can endeavor to develop science more and more in the direction of a unified system of laws only because we have already at present a unified language. And, in addition, the fact that we have this unity of language is of the greatest practical importance. The practical use of laws consists in making predictions with their help. The important fact is that very often a prediction cannot be based on our knowledge of only one branch of science. For instance, the construction of automobiles will be influenced by a prediction of the presumable number of sales. This number depends upon the satisfaction of the buyers and the economic situation. Hence we have to combine knowledge about the function of the motor, the effect of gases and vibration on the human organism, the ability of persons to learn a certain technique, their willingness to spend so much money for so much service, the development of the general economic situation, etc. This knowledge concerns particular facts and general laws belonging to all the four branches, partly scientific and partly commonsense knowledge. For very many decisions, both in individual and in social life, we need such a prediction based upon a combined knowledge of concrete facts and general laws belonging to different branches of science. If now the terms of different branches had no logical connection between one another, such as is supplied by the homogeneous reduction basis, but were of fundamentally different character, as some philosophers believe, then it would not be possible to connect singular statements and laws of different fields in such a way as to derive predictions from them. Therefore, the unity of the language of science is the basis for the practical application of theoretical knowledge.

Selected Bibliography

I. Logical Analysis

Carnap, R. *Philosophy and Logical Syntax*. London, 1955.
Carnap, R. *Logical Syntax of Language*. London, 1937.

II. Reducibility

Carnap, R. "Testability and Meaning," *Philosophy of Science*, Vols, III (1936) and IV (1937).

III. The Unity of the Language of Science; Physicalism

Papers by Neurath and Carnap, *Erkenntnis* Vol. II (1932); *ibid.*, Vol. III (1933). Translation of one of these papers: Carnap, *The Unity of Science*, London, 1934. Concerning psychology: papers by Schlick, Hempel, and Carnap, *Revue de synthèse*, Vol. X (1935).

Chapter 22

Unity of Science as a Working Hypothesis

Paul Oppenheim and Hilary Putnam

---

1. Introduction

1.1. The expression "unity of science" is often encountered, but its precise content is difficult to specify in a satisfactory manner. It is the *aim of this paper* to formulate a precise concept of unity of science; and to examine to what extent that unity can be attained.

A concern with unity of science hardly needs justification. We are guided especially by the conviction that science of science, i.e., the metascientific study of major aspects of science, is the natural means for counterbalancing specialization by promoting the integration of scientific knowledge. The desirability of this goal is widely recognized; for example, many universities have programs with this end in view; but it is often pursued by means different from the one just mentioned, and the conception of the unity of science might be especially suited as an organizing principle for an enterprise of this kind.

1.2. As a preliminary, we will distinguish, in order of increasing strength, three broad concepts of unity of science:

First, unity of science in the weakest sense is attained to the extent to which all the terms of science[1] are reduced to the terms of some one discipline (e.g., physics, or psychology). This concept of *unity of language* (12) may be replaced by a number of subconcepts depending on the manner in which one specifies the notion of "reduction" involved. Certain authors, for example, construe reduction as the *definition* of the terms of science by means of those in the selected basic discipline (reduction by means of biconditionals (47)); and some of these require the definitions in question to be analytic, or "true in virtue of the meanings of the terms involved" (epistemological reduction); others impose no such restriction upon the biconditionals effecting reduction. The notion of reduction we shall employ is a wider one, and is designed to include reduction by means of biconditionals as a special case.

Second, unity of science in a stronger sense (because it implies unity of language, whereas the reverse is not the case) is represented by *unity of laws* (12). It is attained to the extent to which the laws of science become reduced to the laws of some one discipline. If the ideal of such an all-comprehensive explanatory system were realized, one could call it *unitary science* (18, 19, 20, 80). The exact meaning of 'unity of laws' depends, again, on the concept of "reduction" employed.

Third, unity of science in the strongest sense is realized if the laws of science are not only reduced to the laws of some one discipline, but the laws of that discipline are in some intuitive sense "unified" or "connected." It is difficult to see how this last

Reprinted from *Minnesota Studies in the Philosophy of Science: Volume II*, ed. H. Feigl, M. Scriven, and G. Maxwell (Minneapolis, MN: University of Minnesota Press, 1958), pp. 3–36, by permission of the author and the publisher. Copyright 1958 by University of Minnesota Press.

requirement can be made precise; and it will not be imposed here. Nevertheless, trivial realizations of "unity of science" will be excluded, for example, the simple conjunction of several branches of science does not *reduce* the particular branches in the sense we shall specify.

1.3. In the present paper, the term 'unity of science' will be used in two senses, to refer, first, to an ideal state of science, and, second, to a pervasive *trend* within science, seeking the attainment of that ideal.

In the first sense, 'unity of science' means the state of unitary science. It involves the two constituents mentioned above: unity of vocabulary, or "unity of language"; and unity of explanatory principles, or "unity of laws." That unity of science, in this sense, can be fully realized constitutes an overarching metascientific hypothesis which enables one to see a unity in scientific activities that might otherwise appear disconnected or unrelated, and which encourages the construction of a unified body of knowledge.

In the second sense, unity of science exists as a trend within scientific inquiry, whether or not unitary science is ever attained, and notwithstanding the simultaneous existence, (and, of course, legitimacy) of other, even *incompatible*, trends.

1.4. The expression 'unity of science' is employed in various other senses, of which two will be briefly mentioned in order to distinguish them from the sense with which we are concerned. In the first place, what is sometimes referred to is something that we may call the *unity of method* in science. This might be represented by the thesis that all the empirical sciences employ the same standards of explanation, of significance, of evidence, etc.

In the second place, a radical reductionist thesis (of an alleged "logical," not an empirical kind) is sometimes referred to as the thesis of the unity of science. Sometimes the "reduction" asserted is the definability of all the terms of science in terms of *sensationalistic predicates* (10); sometimes the notion of "reduction" is wider (11) and predicates referring to *observable qualities of physical things* are taken as basic (12). These theses are epistemological ones, and ones which today appear doubtful. The epistemological uses of the terms 'reduction', 'physicalism', 'unity of science', etc., should be carefully distinguished from the use of these terms in the present paper.

2. Unity of Science and Microreduction

2.1. In this paper we shall employ a concept of reduction introduced by Kemeny and Oppenheim in their paper on the subject (47), to which the reader is referred for a more detailed exposition. The principal requirements may be summarized as follows: given two theories T_1 and T_2, T_2 is said to be *reduced* to T_1 if and only if:

(1) The vocabulary of T2 contains terms not in the vocabulary of T_1.

(2) Any observational data explainable by T_2 are explainable by T_1.

(3) T_1 is at least as well systematized as T_2. (T_1 is normally more complicated than T_2; but this is allowable, because the reducing theory normally explains more than the reduced theory. However, the "ratio," so to speak, of simplicity to explanatory power should be at least as great in the case of the reducing theory as in the case of the reduced theory.)[2]

Kemeny and Oppenheim also define the reduction of a branch of science B_2 by another branch B_1 (e.g., the reduction of chemistry to physics). Their procedure is as follows: take the accepted theories of B_2 at a given time t as T_2. Then B_2 *is reduced to* B_1 at time t if and only if there is some theory T_1 in B_1 at t such that T_1 reduces T_2 (47). Analogously, if *some* of the theories of B_2 are reduced by some T_1 belonging to branch

B_1 at t, we shall speak of a *partial reduction* of B_2 to B_2 at t. This approach presupposes (1) the familiar assumption that some division of the total vocabulary of both branches into theoretical and observational terms is given, and (2) that the two branches have the same observational vocabulary.

2.2. The essential feature of a *micro*reduction is that the branch B_1 deals with the parts of the objects dealt with by B_2. We must suppose that corresponding to each branch we have a specific universe of discourse U_{Bi};[3] and that we have a part-whole relation, Pt (75; 76, especially p. 91). Under the following conditions we shall say that the reduction of B_2 to B_1[4] is a *micro*reduction: B_2 is reduced to B_1; and the objects in the universe of discourse of B_2 are wholes which possess a decomposition (75; 76, especially p. 91) into proper parts all of which belong to the universe of discourse of B_1. For example, let us suppose B_2 is a branch of science which has multicellular living things as its universe of discourse. Let B_1 be a branch with cells as its universe of discourse. Then the things in the universe of discourse of B_2 can be decomposed into proper parts belonging to the universe of discourse of B_1. If, in addition, it is the case that B_1 reduces B_2 at the time t, we shall say that B_1 *microreduces* B_2 *at time t*.

We shall also say that a branch B_1 is a *potential microreducer* of a branch B_2 if the objects in the universe of discourse of B_2 are wholes which possess a decomposition into proper parts all of which belong to the universe of discourse of B_1. The definition is the same as the definition of 'microreduces' except for the omission of the clause 'B_2 is reduced to B_1.'

Any microreduction constitutes a step in the direction of *unity of language* in science. For, if B_1 reduces B_2, it explains everything that B_2 does (and normally, more besides). Then, even if we cannot define in B_1 analogues for some of the theoretical terms of B_2, we can *use B_1 in place of B_2*. Thus any reduction, in the sense explained, permits a "reduction" of the total vocabulary of science by making it possible to dispense with some terms.[5] Not every reduction moves in the direction of unity of science; for instance reductions *within* a branch lead to a simplification of the vocabulary of science, but they do not necessarily lead in the direction of unity of science as we have characterized it (although they may at times fit into that trend). However, *micro*reductions, and even partial microreductions, insofar as they permit us to replace some of the terms of one branch of science by terms of another, *do* move in this direction.

Likewise, the microreduction of B_2 to B_1 moves in the direction of *unity of laws*; for it "reduces" the total number of scientific laws by making it possible, in principle, to dispense with the laws of B_2 and explain the relevant observations by using B_1.

The relations 'microreduces' and 'potential microreducer' have very simple properties: (1) they are transitive (this follows from the transitivity of the relations 'reduces' and 'Pt'); (2) they are irreflexive (no branch can microreduce itself); (3) they are asymmetric (if B_1 microreduces B_2, B_2 never microreduces B_1). The two latter properties are not purely formal; however, they require for their derivation only the (certainly true) empirical assumption that there does not exist an infinite descending chain of proper parts, i.e., a series of things x_1, x_2, x_3 ... such that x_2 is a proper part of x_1, x_3 is a proper part of x_2, etc.

The just-mentioned *formal* property of the relation 'microreduces'—its transitivity —is of great importance for the program of unity of science. It means that microreductions have a *cumulative* character. That is, if a branch B_3 is microreduced to B_2, and B_2 is in turn microreduced to B_1, then B_3 is automatically microreduced to B_1. This simple fact is sometimes overlooked in objections[6] to the theoretical possibility of attaining unitary science by means of microreduction. Thus it has been contended that one manifestly cannot explain human behavior by reference to the laws of atomic physics. It would indeed be fantastic to suppose that the simplest regularity in the field of psychology could be explained directly—i.e., "skipping" intervening branches of science—by employing subatomic theories. But one may believe in the attainability of unitary science without thereby committing oneself to this absurdity. It is not absurd to suppose that psychological laws may eventually be explained in terms of the behavior of individual neurons in the brain; that the behavior of individual cells— including neurons—may eventually be explained in terms of their biochemical constitution; and that the behavior of molecules—including the macromolecules that make up living cells—may eventually be explained in terms of atomic physics. If this is achieved, then psychological laws will have, in *principle*, been reduced to laws of atomic physics, although it would nevertheless be hopelessly impractical to try to derive the behavior of a single human being directly from his constitution in terms of elementary particles.

2.3. *Unitary* science certainly does not exist today. But will it ever be attained? It is useful to divide this question into two subquestions: (1) If unitary science can be attained at all, *how* can it be attained? (2) *Can* it be attained at all?

First of all, there are various abstractly possible ways in which unitary science might be attained. Howvever, it seems very doubtful, to say the least, that a branch B_2 could be reduced to a branch B_1, if the things in the universe of discourse of B_2 are not themselves in the universe of discourse of B_1 and also do not possess a decomposition into parts in the universe of discourse of B_1. ("They don't speak about the same things.")

It does not follow that B_1 must be a potential *micro*reducer of B_2, i.e., that all reductions are microreductions.

There are many cases in which the reducing theory and the reduced theory belong to the same branch, or to branches with the same universe of discourse. When we come, however, to branches with different universes—say, physics and psychology— it seems clear that the possibility of reduction depends on the existence of a structural connection between the universes *via* the 'Pt' relation. Thus one cannot plausibly suppose—for the present at least—that the behavior of inorganic matter is explainable by reference to psychological laws; for inorganic materials do not consist of living parts. One supposes that psychology may be reducible to physics, but not that physics may be reducible to psychology!

Thus, the only method of attaining unitary science that appears to be seriously available at present is microreduction.

To turn now to our second question, can unitary science be attained? We certainly do not wish to maintain that it has been *established* that this is the case. But it does not follow, as some philosophers seem to think, that a tentative acceptance of the hypothesis that unitary science can be attained is therefore a mere "act of faith." We believe that this hypothesis is *credible*;[7] and we shall attempt to support this in the latter part of this paper, by providing empirical, methodological, and pragmatic reasons in its support. We therefore think the assumption that unitary science can be attained through cumulative microreduction recommends itself as a *working hypothesis*.[8] That is, we believe that it is in accord with the standards of reasonable scientific judgment to tentatively accept this hypothesis and to work on the assumption that further progress can be made in this direction, without claiming that its truth has been established, or denying that success may finally elude us.

3. Reductive Levels

3.1. As a basis for our further discussion, we wish to consider now the possibility of ordering branches in such a way as to indicate the major potential microreductions standing between the present situation and the state of unitary science. The most natural way to do this is by their universes of discourse. We offer, therefore, a system of *reductive levels* so chosen that a branch with the things of a given level as its universe of discourse will always be a potential microreducer of any branch with things of the next higher level (if there is one) as its universe of discourse.

Certain conditions of adequacy follow immediately from our aim. Thus:

(1) There must be several levels.

(2) The number of levels must be finite.

(3) There must be a unique lowest level (i.e., a unique "beginner" under the relation 'potential microreducer'); this means that success at transforming all the *potential* microreductions connecting these branches into *actual* microreductions must, *ipso facto*, mean reduction to a single branch.

(4) Any thing of any level except the lowest must possess a decomposition into things belonging to the next lower level. In this sense each level, will be as it were a "common denominator" for the level immediately above it.

(5) Nothing on any level should have a part on any higher level.

(6) The levels must be selected in a way which is "natural"[9] and justifiable from the standpoint of present-day empirical science. In particular, the step from any one of our reductive levels to the next lower level must correspond to what is, scientifically speaking, a crucial step in the trend toward over-all physicalistic reduction.

The accompanying list gives the levels we shall employ;[10] the reader may verify that the six conditions we have listed are all satisfied.

6	Social groups
5	(Multicellular) living things
4	Cells
3	Molecules
2	Atoms
1	Elementary particles

Any whole which possesses a decomposition into parts all of which are on a given level, will be counted as also belonging to that level. Thus each level includes all higher levels. However, the highest level to which a thing belongs will be considered the "proper" level of that thing.

This inclusion relation among our levels reflects the fact that scientific laws which apply to the things of a given level and to all combinations of those things also apply to all things of higher level. Thus a physicist, when he speaks about "all physical objects," is also speaking about living things—but not qua living things.

We maintain that each of our levels is *necessary* in the sense that it would be utopian to suppose that one might reduce all of the major theories or a whole branch concerned with any one of our six levels to a theory concerned with a lower level, *skipping* entirely the *immediately* lower level; and we maintain that our levels are *sufficient* in the sense that it would *not* be utopian to suppose that a major theory on any one of our levels *might* be directly reduced to the next lower level. (Although this is *not* to deny that it may be convenient, in special cases, to introduce intervening steps.)

However, this contention is significant only if we suppose some set of *predicates* to be associated with each of these levels. Otherwise, as has been pointed out,[11] *trivial* microreductions would be possible; e.g., we might introduce the property "Tran" (namely, the property of being an atom of a transparent substance) and then "explain the transparency of water in terms of properties on the atomic level," namely, by the hypothesis that all atoms of water have the property Tran. More explicitly, the explanation would consist of the statements

(a) (x) $(x$ is transparent $\equiv (y)$ $(y$ is an atom of $x \supset$ Tran $(y))$

(b) (x) $(x$ is water $\supset (y)$ $(y$ is an atom of $x \supset$ Tran $(y))$

To exclude such trivial "microreductions," we shall suppose that with each level there is associated a list of the theoretical predicates normally employed to characterize things on that level at present (e.g., with level 1, there would be associated the predicates used to specify spatiotemporal coordinates, mass-energy, and electric charge). And when we speak of a theory concerning a given level, we will mean not only a theory whose universe of discourse is that level, but one whose predicates belong to the appropriate list. Unless the hypothesis that theories concerning level $n + 1$ can be reduced by a theory concerning level n is restricted in this way, it lacks any clear empirical significance.

3.2. If the "part-whole" ('Pt') relation is understood in the wide sense, that x Pt y holds if x is spatially or temporally contained in y, then everything, continuous or discontinuous, belongs to one or another reductive level; in particular to level 1 (at least), since it is a whole consisting of elementary particles. However, one may wish to understand 'whole' in a narrower sense (as "structured organization of elements"[12]). Such a specialization involves two essential steps: (1) the construction of a calculus with such a narrower notion as its primitive concept, and (2) the definition of a particular 'Pt' relation satisfying the axioms of the calculus.

Then the problem will arise that some things do not belong to *any* level. Hence a theory dealing with such things might not be microreduced even if all the microreductions indicated by our system of levels were accomplished; and for this reason, unitary science might not be attained.

For a trivial example, "a man in a phone booth" is an aggregate of things on different levels which we would not regard as a whole in such a narrower sense. Thus, such an "object" does not belong to any reductive level; although the "phone booth" belongs to level 3 and the man belongs to level 5.

The problem posed by such aggregates is not serious, however. We may safely make the assumption that the behavior of "man in phone booths" (to be carefully distinguished from "men in phone booths") could be completely explained given (a) a complete physicochemical theory (i.e., a theory of levels up to 3, including "phone booths"), and (b) a complete individual psychology (or more generally, a theory of levels up to 5). With this assumption in force, we are able to say: If we can construct a theory that explains the behavior of all the objects in our system of levels, then it will also handle the aggregates of such objects.

4. The Credibility of Our Working Hypothesis

4.1. John Stuart Mill asserts (55, Book VI, Chapter 7) that since (in our wording) human social groups are wholes whose parts are individual persons, the "laws of the phenomena of society" are "derived from and may be resolved into the laws of the nature of individual man." In our terminology, this is to suggest that it is a logical truth that theories concerning social groups (level 6) can be *microreduced* by theories concerning individual living things (level 5); and, *mutatis mutandis*, it would have to be a logical truth that theories concerning any other level can be microreduced by theories concerning the next lower level. As a consequence, what we have called the "working hypothesis" that unitary science can be attained would likewise be a logical truth.

Mill's contention is, however, not so much *wrong* as it is vague. What is one to count as "the nature of individual man"? As pointed out above (section 3.1) the question whether theories concerning a given reductive level can be reduced by a theory concerning the next lower level has empirical content only if the theoretical vocabularies are specified; that is, only if one associates with each level, as we have supposed to be done, a particular set of theoretical concepts. Given, e.g., a sociological theory T_2, the question whether there exists a true psychological theory T_1 *in a particular vocabulary* which reduces T_2 is an empirical question. Thus our "working hypothesis" is one that can only be justified on empirical grounds.

Among the factors on which the degree of credibility of any empirical hypothesis depends are (45, p. 307) the *simplicity* of the hypothesis, the *variety* of the evidence, its *reliability*, and, last but not least, the *factual support* afforded by the evidence. We proceed to discuss each of these factors.

4.2. As for the *simplicity*[13] of the hypothesis that unitary science can be attained, it suffices to consider the traditional alternatives mentioned by those who oppose it. "Hypotheses" such as psychism and neovitalism assert that the various objects studied by contemporary science have special parts or attributes, unknown to present-day science, in addition to those indicated in our system of reductive levels. For example, men are said to have not only cells as parts; there is also an immaterial "psyche"; living things are animated by "entelechies" or "vital forces"; social groups are moved by "group minds." But, in none of these cases are we provided *at present* with postulates or coordinating definitions which would permit the derivation of testable predictions. Hence, the claims made for the hypothetical entities just mentioned lack any clear scientific meaning; and as a consequence, the question of supporting evidence cannot even be raised.

On the other hand, if the effort at microreduction should seem to fail, we cannot preclude the introduction of theories postulating presently unknown relevant parts or presently unknown relevant attributes for some or all of the objects studied by science. Such theories are perfectly admissible, provided they have genuine explanatory value. For example, Dalton's chemical theory of molecules might not be reducible to the best available theory of atoms at a given time if the latter theory ignores the existence of the electrical properties of atoms. Thus the hypothesis of microreducibility,[14] as the meaning is specified at a particular time, may be false because of the insufficiency of the theoretical apparatus of the reducing branch.

Of course, a new working hypothesis of microreducibility, obtained by enlarging the list of attributes associated with the lowest level, might then be correct. However, if there are presently unknown attributes of a more radical kind (e.g., attributes which are relevant for explaining the behavior of living, but not of nonliving things), then no such simple "repair" would seem possible. In this sense, unity of science is an alternative to the view that it will eventually be necessary to *bifurcate* the conceptual system of science, by the postulation of new entities or new attributes unrelated to those needed for the study of inanimate phenomena.

4.3. The requirement that there be *variety* of evidence assumes a simple form in our present case. If all the past successes referred to a single pair of levels, then this would be poor evidence indeed that theories concerning each level can be reduced by theories concerning a lower level. For example, if all the past successes were on the atomic level, we should hardly regard as justified the inference that laws concerning social groups can be explained by reference to the "individual psychology" of the members of those groups. Thus, the first requirement is that one should be able to provide examples of successful micreductions between several pairs of levels, preferably between all pairs.

Second, within a given level what is required is, preferably, examples of different kinds, rather than a repetition of essentially the same example many times. In short, one wants good evidence that *all* the phenomena of the given level can be microreduced.

We shall present below a survey of the past successes in each level. This survey is, of course, only a sketch; the successful microreductions and projected microreductions in biochemistry alone would fill a large book. But even from this sketch it will be apparent, we believe, how great the variety of these successful microreductions is in both the respects discussed.

4.4. Moreover, we shall, of course, present only evidence from authorities regarded as *reliable* in the particular area from which the theory or experiment involved is drawn.

4.5. The important factor *factual support* is discussed only briefly now, because we shall devote to it many of the following pages and would otherwise interrupt our presentation.

The first question raised in connection with any hypothesis is, of course, what *factual* support it possesses; that is, what confirmatory or disconfirmatory evidence is available. The evidence supporting a hypothesis is conveniently subdivided into that providing *direct* and that providing *indirect* factual support. By the direct factual support for a hypothesis we mean, roughly,[15] the proportion of confirmatory as opposed to disconfirmatory instances. By the indirect factual support, we mean the inductive support obtained from other well-confirmed hypotheses that lend credibility to the given hypothesis. While intuitively adequate quantitative measures of direct factual support have been worked out by Kemeny and Oppenheim,[16] no such measures exist for indirect factual support. The present paper will rely only on intuitive judgments of these magnitudes, and will not assume that quantitative explicata will be worked out.

As our hypothesis is that theories of each reductive level can be microreduced by theories of the next lower level, a "confirming instance" is simply any successful microreduction between any two of our levels. The *direct* factual support for our hypothesis is thus provided by the *past successes* at reducing laws about the things on each level by means of laws referring to the parts on lower (usually, the next lower) levels. In the sequel, we shall survey the past successes with respect to each pair of levels.

As *indirect* factual support, we shall cite evidence supporting the hypothesis that each reductive level is, in evolution and ontogenesis (in a wide sense presently to be specified) prior to the one above it. The hypothesis of *evolution* means here that (for n + 1 ... 5) there was a time when there were things of level n, but no things of any higher level. This hypothesis is highly speculative on levels 1 and 2; fortunately the microreducibility of the molecular to the atomic level and of the atomic level to the elementary particle level is relatively well established on other grounds.

Similarly, the hypothesis of ontogenesis is that, in certain cases, for any *particular* object on level n, there was a time when it did not exist, but when some of its parts on the next lower level existed; and that it developed or was causally produced out of these parts.[17]

The reason for our regarding evolution and ontogenesis as providing indirect factual support for the unity of science hypothesis may be formulated as follows:

Let us, as is customary in science, assume causal determination as a guiding principle; i.e., let us assume that things that appear later in time can be accounted for in terms of things and processes at earlier times. Then, if we find that there was a time when a certain whole did not exist, and that things on a lower level came together to form that whole, it is very natural to suppose that the characteristics of the whole can be causally explained by reference to these earlier events and parts; and that the theory of these characteristics can be microreduced by a theory involving only characteristics of the parts.

For the same reason, we may cite as further indirect factual support for the hypothesis of empirical unity of science the various successes at *synthesizing* things of each level out of things on the next lower level. Synthesis strongly increases the evidence that the characteristics of the whole in question are causally determined by the characteristics, including spatio-temporal arrangement, of its parts by showing that the object is produced, under controlled laboratory conditions, whenever parts with those characteristics are arranged in that way.

The consideration just outlined seems to us to constitute an argument against the view that, as objects of a given level combine to form wholes belonging to a higher level, there appear certain new phenomena which are "emergent" (35, p. 151; 76, p. 93) in the sense of being forever irreducible to laws governing the phenomena on the level of the parts. What our argument opposes is not, of course, the obviously true statement that there are many phenomena which are not reducible by currently available theories pertaining to lower levels; our working hypothesis rejects merely the claim of absolute irreducibility, unless such a claim is supported by a theory which has a sufficiently high degree of credibility; thus far we are not aware of any such theory. It is not sufficient, for example, simply to advance the claim that certain phenomena considered to be specifically human, such as the use of verbal language, in an abstract and generalized way, can never be explained on the basis of neurophysiological theories, or to make the claim that this conceptual capacity distinguishes man in principle and not only in degree from nonhuman animals.

4.6. Let us mention in passing certain *pragmatic* and *methodological* points of view which speak in favor of our working hypothesis:

> (1) It is of *practical* value, because it provides a good synopsis of scientific activity and of the relations among the several scientific disciplines.
>
> (2) It is, as has often been remarked, *fruitful* in the sense of stimulating many different kinds of scientific research. By way of contrast, I belief in the *irreducibility* of various phenomena has yet to yield a single accepted scientific theory.
>
> (3) It corresponds *methodologically* to what might be called the "Democritean tendency" in science; that is, the pervasive methodological tendency[18] to try, insofar as is possible, to explain apparently dissimilar phenomena in terms of qualitatively identical parts and their spatio-temporal relations.

5. Past Successes at Each Level

5.1 By comparison with what we shall find on lower levels, the microreduction of level 6 to lower ones has not yet advanced very far, especially in regard to human societies. This may have at least two reasons: First of all, the body of well-established theoretical knowledge on level 6 is still rather rudimentary, so that there is not much to *be* microreduced. Second, while various precise theories concerning certain special types of phenomena on level 5 have been developed, it seems as if a good deal of further theoretical knowledge concerning other areas on the same level will be needed before reductive success on a larger scale can be expected.[19] However, in the case of certain very primitive groups of organisms, astonishing successes have been achieved. For instance, the differentiation into social castes among certain kinds of insects has been tentatively explained in terms of the secretion of so-called social hormones (3).

Many writers[20] believe that there are some laws common to all forms of animal association, including that of humans. Of greater potential relevance to such laws are experiments dealing with "pecking order" among domestic fowl (29). In particular, experiments showing that the social structure can be influenced by the amount of male hormone in individual birds suggest possible parallels farther up the evolutionary scale.

With respect to the problems of human social organization, as will be seen presently, two things are striking: (1) the most developed body of theory is undoubtedly in the field of *economics*, and this is at present entirely microreductionistic in character; (2) the main approaches to *social* theory are *all* likewise of this character. (The technical term 'microreduction' is not, of course, employed by writers in these fields. However, many writers have discussed "the Principle of Methodological Individualism";[21] and this is nothing more than the special form our working hypothesis takes in application to human social groups.)

In economics, if very weak assumptions are satisfied, it is possible to represent the way in which an individual orders his choices by means of an individual preference function. In terms of these functions, the economist attempts to explain group phenomena, such as the market, to account for collective consumer behavior, to solve the problems of welfare economics, etc. As theories for which a microreductionistic derivation is accepted in economics we could cite all the standard macro-theories; e.g., the theories of the business cycle, theories of currency fluctuation (Gresham's law to the effect that bad money drives out good is a familiar example), the principle of marginal utility, the law of demand, laws connecting change in interest rate with changes in inventory, plans, equipment, etc. The relevant point is while the economist is no longer dependent on the oversimplified assumption of "economic man," the explanation of economic phenomena is still in terms of the preferences, choices, and actions available to *individuals*.

In the realm of *sociology*, one can hardly speak of any major theory as "accepted." But it is of interest to survey some of the major theoretical approaches from the standpoint of microreduction.

On the one hand, there is the *economic determinism* represented by Marx and Veblen. In the case of Marx the assumptions of classical economics are openly made: Individuals are supposed—at least on the average, and in the long run—to act in accordance with their material interests. From this assumption, together with a theory of the business cycle which, for all its undoubted originality, Marx based on the classical laws of the market, Marx derives his major laws and predictions. Thus Marxist sociology is microreductionistic in the same sense as classical economics, and shares the same basic weakness (the assumption of "economic man").

Veblen, although stressing class interests and class divisions as did Marx, introduces some noneconomic factors in his sociology. His account is ultimately in terms of individual psychology; his hypothesis of "conspicuous consumption" is a brilliant—and characteristic—example.

Max Weber produced a sociology strongly antithetical to Marx's. Yet each of his explanations of group phenomena is ultimately in terms of individual psychology; e.g., in his discussion of political parties, he argues that people *enjoy* working under a "charismatic" leader, etc.

Indeed the psychological (and hence microreductionistic) character of the major sociologies (including those of Mannheim, Simmel, etc., as well as the ones mentioned above (54, 86, 94, 103)) is often recognized. Thus one may safely say, that while there is no one accepted sociological theory, all of these theoretical approaches represent attempted microreductions.

5.2. Since Schleiden and Schwann (1838/9), it is known that all living things consist of cells. Consequently, explaining the laws valid on level 5 by those on the cell level means microreducing all phenomena of plants and animals to level 4.

As instances of past successes in connection with level 5 we have chosen to cite, in preference to other types of example, microreductions and projected microreductions dealing with *central nervous systems* as wholes and nerve cells as parts. Our selection of these examples has not been determined by anthropocentrism. First of all, substantially similar problems arise in the case of multicellular animals, as nearly all of them possess a nervous system; and, second, the question of microreducing those aspects of behavior that are controlled by the central nervous system in man and the higher animals is easily the most significative (85, p. 1) one at this level, and therefore most worth discussing.

Very great activity is, in fact, apparent in the direction of microreducing the phenomena of the central nervous system. Much of this activity is very recent; and most of it falls under two main headings: *neurology*, and the *logical design of nerve nets*. (Once again, the technical term 'microreduction' is not actually employed by workers in these fields. Instead, one finds widespread and lasting discussion concerning the advantages of "molecular" versus "molar"[22] explanations, and concerning "reductionism.[23]

Theories constructed by neurologists are the product of highly detailed experimental work in neuroanatomy, neurochemistry, and neurophysiology, including the study of electric activity of the nervous system, e.g., electroencephalography.[24]

As a result of these efforts, it has proved possible to advance more or less hypothetical explanations on the cellular level for such phenomena as association, memory, motivation, emotional disturbance, and some of the phenomena connected with learning, intelligence, and perception. For example, a theory of the brain has been advanced by Hebb (32) which accounts for all of the above-mentioned phenomena. A classical psychological law, the Weber-Fechner law (insofar as it seems to apply), has likewise been microreduced, as a result of the work of Hoagland (36).

We turn now to *the logical design* of nerve nets: The logician Turing[25] proposed (and solved) the problem of giving a characterization of *computing machines* in the widest sense—mechanisms for solving problems by effective series of logical operations. This naturally suggests the idea of seeing whether a "Turing machine" could consist of the elements used in neurological theories of the brain; that is, whether it could consist of a network of neurons. Such a nerve network could then serve as a hypothetical model for the brain.

Such a network was first constructed by McCulloch and Pitts.[26] The basic element is the neuron, which, at any instant, is either *firing* or *not firing* (quiescent). On account of the "all or none" character of the activity of this basic element, the *nerve* net designed by McCulloch and Pitts constitutes, as it were, a digital computer. The various relations of propositional logic can be represented by instituting suitable connections between neurons; and in this way the hypothetical net can be "programmed" to solve any problem that will yield to a predetermined sequence of logical or mathematical operations. McCulloch and Pitts employ approximately 10^4 elements in their net; in this respect they are well below the upper limit set by neurological investigation, since the number of neurons in the brain is estimated to be of the order of magnitude of 10^{10}. In other respects, their model was, however, unrealistic: no allowance is made for time delay, or for random error, both of which are important features of all biological processes.

Nerve nets incorporating both of these features have been designed by von Neumann. Von Neumann's model employs bundles of nerves rather than single nerves to form a network; this permits the simultaneous performance of each operation as many as 20,000 times as a check against error. This technique of constructing a computer is impractical at the level of present-day technology, von Neumann admits, "but quite practical for a perfectly conceivable, more advanced technology, and for the natural relay-organs (neurons). I.e., it merely calls for microcomponentry which is not at all unnatural as a concept on this level" (97, p. 87). Still further advances in the direction of adapting these models to neurological data are anticipated. In terms of such nerve nets it is possible to give hypothetical microreductions for *memory, exact thinking, distinguishing similarity or dissimilarity of stimulus patterns, abstracting* of "essential" components of a stimulus pattern, recognition of shape regardless of form and of chord regardless of pitch (phenomena of great importance in Gestalt psychology (5, pp. 128, 129, 152)), *purposeful behavior* as controlled by negative feedback, *adaptive behavior*, and *mental disorders*.

It is the task of the neurophysiologist to test these models by investigating the existence of such nets, scanning units, reverberating networks, and pathways of feedback, and to provide physiological evidence of their functioning. Promising studies have been made in this respect.

5.3. As past successes in connection with level 4 (i.e.,as cases in which phenomena involving whole cells[27] have been explained by theories concerning the molecular level) we shall cite microreductions dealing with three phenomena that have a fundamental character for all of biological science: the *decoding, duplication,* and *mutation* of the genetic information that is ultimately responsible for the development and maintenance of order in the cell. Our objective will be to show that at least one well-worked-out microreducing theory, has been advanced for each phenomenon.[28] (The special form taken by our working hypothesis on this level is "methodological mechanism.")

Biologists have long had good evidence indicating that the genetic information in the cell's nucleus—acting as an "inherited message"—exerts its control over cell biochemistry, through the production of specific protein catalysts (enzymes) that mediate particular steps (reactions) in the chemical order that is the cell's life. The problem of *"decoding"* the control information in the nucleus thus reduces to how the specific molecules that comprise it serve to specify the construction of specific protein catalysts. The problem of *duplication* (one aspect of the overall problem of inheritance) reduces to how the molecules of genetic material can be copied—like so many "blueprints."

And the problem of *mutation* (elementary step in the evolution of new inheritable messages) reduces to how "new" forms of the genetic molecules can arise.

In the last twenty years evidence has accumulated implicating *desoxyribose nucleic acid* (DNA) as the principal "message-carrying" molecule and constituting the genetic material of the chromosomes. Crick and Watson's[29] brilliant analysis of DNA structure leads to powerful microreducing theories that explain the decoding and duplication of DNA. It is known that the giant molecules that make up the nucleic acids have, like proteins (49, 66, 67), the structure of a backbone with side groups attached. But, whereas the proteins are polypeptides, or chains of amino-acid residues (slightly over 20 kinds of amino acids are known); the nucleic acids have a phosphate-sugar backbone, and there are only 4 kinds of side groups all of which are nitrogen bases (purines and pyrimidines). Crick and Watson's model contains a pair of DNA chains wound around a common axis in the form of two interlocking helices. The two helices are held together (forming a helical "ladder") by hydrogen bonds between pairs of the nitrogen bases, one belonging to each helix. Although 4 bases occur as side groups only 2 of 16 conceivable pairings are possible, for steric reasons. These 2 pairs of bases recur along the length of the DNA molecule and thus invite a picturesque analogy with the dots and dashes of the Morse code. They can be arranged in any sequence: there is enough DNA in a single cell of the human body to encode in this way 1,000 large textbooks. The model can be said to imply that the genetic "language" of the inherited control message is a "language of surfaces": the information in DNA structure is decoded as a sequence of amino acids in the proteins which are synthesized under ultimate DNA control. The surface structure of the DNA helix, dictated by the sequence of base pairs, specifies like a template[30] the sequence of amino acids laid down end to end in the fabrication of polypeptides.

Watson and Crick's model immediately suggests how the DNA might produce an exact copy of itself—for transmission as an inherited message to the succeeding generation of cells. The DNA molecule, as noted above, consists of two interwoven helices, each of which is the complement of the other. Thus each chain may act as a mold on which a complementary chain can be synthesized. The two chains of a DNA molecule need only unwind and separate. Each begins to build a new complement onto itself, as loose units, floating in the cell, attach themselves to the bases in the single DNA chain. When the process is completed, there are two pairs of chains where before there was only one![31]

Mutation of the genetic information has been explained in a molecular (microreduction) theory advanced some years ago by Delbrück.[32] Delbrück's theory was conceived long before the newer knowledge of DNA was available; but it is a very general model in no way vitiated by Crick and Watson's model of the particular molecule constituting the genetic material. Delbrück, like many others, assumed that the gene is a single large "nucleo-protein" molecule. (This term is used for macromolecules, such as viruses and the hypothetical "genes," which consist of protein and nucleic acid. Some recent theories even assume that an entire chromosome is a single such molecule.) According to Delbruck's theory, different quantum levels within the atoms of the molecule correspond to different hereditary characteristics. A mutation is simply a quantum jump of a rare type (i.e., one with a high activation energy). The observed variation of the spontaneous mutation rate with temperature is in good quantitative agreement with the theory.

Such hypotheses and models as those of Crick and Watson, and of Delbruck, are at present far from sufficient for a complete microreduction of the major biological generalization, e.g., evolution and general genetic theory (including the problem of the control of development). But they constitute an encouraging start towards this ultimate goal and, to this extent, an indirect support for our working hypothesis.

5.4. Only in the twentieth century has it been possible to microreduce to the atomic and in some cases directly to the subatomic level most of the *macrophysical* aspects of matter (e.g., the high fluidity of water, the elasticity of rubber, and the hardness of diamond) as well as the *chemical* phenomena of the elements, i.e. those changes of the peripheral electrons which leave the nucleus unaffected. In particular, electronic theories explain, e.g., the laws governing valence, the various types of bonds, and the "resonance" of molecules between several equivalent electronic structures. A complete explanation of these phenomena and those of the periodic table is possible only with the help of Pauli's exclusion principle which states in one form that no two electrons of the same atom can be alike in all of 4 "quantum numbers." While some molecular laws are not yet micro-reduced, there is every hope that further successes will be obtained in these respects. Thus Pauling (63, 64) writes:

> There are still problems to be solved, and some of them are great problems—an example is the problem of the detailed nature of catalytic activity. We can feel sure, however, that this problem will in the course of time be solved in terms of quantum theory as it now exists: there seems little reason to believe that some fundamental new principle remains to be discovered in order that catalysis be explained. (64)

5.5. Micro-reduction of level 2 to level 1 has been mentioned in the preceding section because many molecular phenomena are at present (skipping the atomic level) explained with reference to laws of elementary particles.[33] Bohr's basic (and now somewhat outdated) model of the atom as a kind of "solar system" of elementary particles is today part of everyone's conceptual apparatus; while the mathematical development of theory in its present form is formidable indeed! Thus we shall not attempt to give any details of this success. But the high rate of progress in this field certainly gives reason to hope that the unsolved problems, especially as to the forces that hold the nucleus together, will likewise be explained in terms of an elementary particle theory.

6. Evolution, Ontogenesis, and Synthesis

6.1. As pointed out in section 4.5, evolution provides indirect factual support for the working hypothesis that unitary science is attainable. Evolution (in the present sense) is an over-all phenomenon involving all levels, from 1 through 6; the mechansims of chance variation and "selection" operate throughout in ways characteristic for the evolutionary level involved.[34] Time scales have, indeed, been worked out by various scientists showing the times when the first things of each level first appeared.[35] (These times are, of course, the less hypothetical the higher the level involved.) But even if the hypothesis of evolution should fail to hold in the case of certain levels, it is important to note that whenever it does hold—whenever it can be shown that things of a given level existed before things of the next higher level came into existence—some degree of indirect support is provided to the particular special case of our working hypothesis that concerns those two levels.

The hypothesis of "evolution" is most speculative insofar as it concerns levels 1 to 3. Various cosmological hypothesis are at present undergoing lively discussion.[36] According to one of these, strongly urged by Gamow (24, 25, 26), the first nuclei did not form out of elementary particles until five to thirty minutes after the start of the universe's expansion; molecules may not have been able to exist until considerably later. Most present-day cosmologists still subscribe to such evolutionary views of the universe; i.e., there was a "zero point" from which the evolution of matter began, with diminishing density through expansion. However, H. Bondi, T. Gold, and F. Hoyle have advanced a conflicting idea, the "steady state" theory, according to which there is no "zero point" from which the evolution of matter began; but matter is continuously created, so that its density remains constant in spite of expansion. There seems to be hope that these rival hypotheses will be submitted to specific empirical tests in the near future. But, fortunately, we do not have to depend on hypotheses that are still so highly controverisal: as we have seen, the mircoreducibility of molecular and atomic phenomena is today not open to serious doubt.

Less speculative are theories concerning the origin of life (transition from level 3 to level 4). Calvin (9; Fox, 22) points out that four mechanisms have been discovered which lead to the formation of amino acids and other organic materials in a mixture of gases duplicating the composition of the primitive terrestrial atmosphere.[37] These have, in fact, been tested experimentally with positive results. Many biologists today accept with Oparin (61) the view that the evolution of life as such was not a single chance event but a long process possibly requiring as many as two billion years, until precellular living organisms first appeared.

According to such views, "chemical evolution" gradually leads in an appropriate environment to evolution in the familiar Darwinian sense. In such a process, it hardly has meaning to speak of a point at which "life appeared." To this day controversies exist concerning the "dividing line" between living and non-living things. In particular, viruses are classified by some biologists as living, because they exhibit self-duplication and mutability; but most biologists refuse to apply the term to them, because viruses exhibit these characteristic phenomena of life only due to activities of a living cell with which they are in contact. But, wherever one draws the line,[38] non-living molecules preceded primordial living substance, and the latter evolved gradually into highly organized living units, the unicellular ancestors of all living things. The "first complex molecules endowed with the faculty of reproducing their own kind" must have been synthesized—and with them the beginning of evolution in the Darwinian sense—a few billion years ago, Goldschmidt (27, p. 84) asserts: "all the facts of biology, geology, paleontology, biochemistry, and radiology not only agree with this statement but actually prove it."

Evolution at the next two levels (from level 4 to level 5, and from 5 to 6) is not speculative at all, but forms part of the broad line of Darwinian evolution, so well marked out by the various kinds of evidence referred to in the statement just quoted. The line of development is again a continuous one;[39] and it is to some extent arbitary (as in the case of "living" versus "non-living") to give a "point" at which true multicellulars first appeared, or at which an animal is "social" rather than "solitary." But in spite of this arbitrariness, it is safe to say that:

(a) Multicellulars evolved from what were originally competing single cells; the "selection" by the environment was in this case determined by the superior survival value of the cooperative structure.[40]

(b) Social animals evolved from solitary ones for similar reasons; and, indeed, there were millions of years during which there were only solitary animals on earth, and not yet their organization into social structures.[41]

6.2. To illustrate ontogenesis, we must show that particular things of a particular level have arisen out of particular things of the next lower level. For example, it is a consequence of most contemporary cosmological theories—whether of the evolutionary or of the "steady state" type—that each existent atom must have originally been formed by a union of elementary particles. (Of course an atom of an element may subsequently undergo "transmutation.") However, such theories are extremely speculative. On the other hand, the chemical union of atoms to form molecules is commonplace in nature.

Coming to the higher levels of the reductive hierarchy, we have unfortunately a hiatus at the level of cells. Individual cells do not, as far as our observations go, ever develop out of individual molecules; on the contrary, "cells come only from cells," as

Virchow stated about one hundred years ago. However, a characteristic example of ontogenesis of things of one level out of things of the next level is afforded by the development of multicellular organisms through the process of mitosis and cell division. All the hereditary characteristics of the organism are specified in the "genetic information" carried in the chromosomes of each individual cell, and are transmitted to the resultant organism through cell division and mitosis.

A more startling example of ontogenesis at this level is provided by the slime molds studied by Bonner (3). These are isolated amoebae; but, at a certain stage, they "clump" together chemotactically and form a simple multicellular organism, a sausage-like "slug"! This "slug" crawls with comparative rapidity and good coordination. It even has sense of a sort, for it is attracted by light.

As to the level of social groups, we have some ontogenetic data, however slight; for children, according to the well-known studies of Piaget (70, 71) (and other authorities on child behavior), acquire the capacity to cooperate with one another, to be concerned with each other's welfare, and to form groups in which they treat one another as peers, only after a number of years (not before seven years of age, in Piaget's studies). Here one has in a rudimentary form what we are looking for: the ontogenetic development of progressively more social behavior (level 6) by what begin as relatively "egocentric" and unsocialized individuals (level 5).

6.3. Synthesis affords factual support for microreduction much as ontogenesis does; however, the evidence is better because synthesis usually takes place under controlled conditions. Thus it enable one to show that one can obtain an object of the kind under investigation invariably by instituting the appropriate causal relations among the parts that go to make it up. For this reason, we may say that success in synthesizing is as strong evidence as one can have for the possibility of microreduction, short of actually finding the microreducing theory.

To begin on the lowest level of the reductive hierarchy, that one can obtain an atom by bringing together the appropriate elementary particles is a basic consequence of elementary nuclear physics. A common examples from the operation of atomic piles is the synthesis of deuterium. This proceeds as one bombards protons (in, e.g., hydrogen gas) with neutrons.

The synthesis of a molecule by chemically uniting atoms is an elementary laboratory demonstration. One familiar example is the union of oxygen and hydrogen gas. Under the influence of an electric spark one obtains the appearance of H_2O molecules.

The next level is that of life. "On the borderline" are the viruses. Thus success at synthesizing a virus out of non-living macro-molecules would count as a first step to the synthesis of cells (which at present seems to be an achievement for the far distant future).

While success at synthesizing a virus out of atoms is not yet in sight, synthesis out of non-living highly complex macro-molecules has been accomplished. At the University of California Virus Laboratory (23), protein obtained from viruses has been mixed with nucleic acid to obtain active virus. The protein does not behave like a virus—it is completely non-infectious. However, the reconstituted virus has the same structure as "natural" virus, and will produce the tobacco mosaic disease when applied to plants. Also new "artificial" viruses have been produced by combining the nucleic acid from one kind of virus with the protein from a different kind. Impressive results in synthesizing proteins have been accomplished. e.g., R. B. Woodward C. H. Schramm (107; see also Nogushi and Hayakawa, 60; and Oparin, 61) have synthesized "protein analogues"—giant polymers containing at least 10,000 amino-acid residues.

At the next level, no one has of course synthesized a whole multicellular organism out of individual cells; but here too there is an impressive partial success to report. Recent experiments have provided detailed descriptions of the manner in which cells organize themselves into whole multicellular tissues. These studies show that even isolated whole cells, when brought together in random groups, could effectuate the characteristic construction of such tissues.[42] Similar phenomena are well known in the case of sponges and fresh-water polyps.

Lastly, the "synthesis" of a new social group by bringing together previously separated individuals is extremely familiar; e.g., the organization of new clubs, trade unions, professional associations, etc. One has even the deliberate formation of whole new societies, e.g., the formation of the Oneida community of utopians, in the nineteenth century, or of the state of Israel by Zionists in the twentieth.

There have been experimental studies in this field; among them, the pioneer work of Kurt Lewin and his school is especially well known.[43]

7. Concluding Remarks

The possibility that all science may one day be reduced to microphysics (in the sense in which chemistry seems today to be reduced to it), and the presence of a unifying trend toward micro-reduction running through much of scientific activity, have often been noticed both by specialists in the various sciences and by metascientists. But these opinions have, in general, been expressed in a more or less vague manner and without very deep-going justification. It has been our aim, first, to provide precise definitions for the crucial concepts involved, and, second, to reply to the frequently made accusations that belief in the attainability of unitary science is "a mere act of faith." We hope to have shown that, on the contrary, a tentative acceptance of this belief, an acceptance of it as a working hypothesis, *justified*, and that the hypothesis is *credible*, partly on methodological grounds (e.g., the simplicity of the hypothesis, as opposed to the bifurcation that rival suppositions create in the conceptual system of science), and partly because there is really a large mass of direct and indirect evidence in its favor.

The idea of reductive levels employed in our discussion suggests what may plausibly be regarded as a *natural order of sciences*. For this purpose, it suffices to take as "fundamental disciplines" the branches corresponding to our levels. It is understandable that many of the well-known orderings of things[44] have a rough similarity to our reductive levels, and that corresponding orderings of sciences are more or less similar to our order of 6 "fundamental disciplines." Again, several successive levels may be grouped together (e.g., physics today conventionally deals at least with levels 1, 2, and 3; just as biology deals with at least levels 4 and 5). Thus we often encounter a division into simply physics, biology, and social sciences. But these other efforts to solve a problem which goes back to ancient times[45] have apparently been made on more or less intuitive grounds; it does not seem to have been realized that these orderings are "natural" in a deeper sense, of being based on the relation of *potential microreducer* obtaining between the branches of science.

It should be emphasized that these six "fundamental disciplines" are, largely, fictitious ones (e.g., there is no actual branch whose universe of discourse is *strictly* molecules and combinations thereof). If one wishes a less idealized approach, one may utilize a concept in semantical information theory which has been defined by one of us (3). This is the semantical functor: 'the amount of information the statement S contains about the class C' (or, in symbols: $inf\ (S, C)$). Then one can characterize any theory

S (or any branch, if we are willing to identify a branch with a conjunction of theories) by a sextuple: namely, inf(S, level 1), inf(S, level 2) ... inf(S, level 6). This sextuple can be regarded as the "locus" of the branch S in a six-dimensional space. The axes are the loci of the imaginary "fundamental disciplines" just referred to; any real branch (e.g., present-day biology) will probably have a position not quite on any axis, but nearer to one than to the others.

Whereas the orderings to which we referred above generally begin with the historically given branches, the procedure just described reverses this tendency. *First* a continuous order is defined in which any imaginable branch can be located; *then* one investigates the relations among the actually existing branches. These positions may be expected to change with time; e.g., as microreduction proceeds, "biology" will occupy a position closer to the "level 1" axis, and so will all the other branches. The continuous order may be described as "Darwinian" rather than "Linnean"; it derives its naturalness, not from agreement with intuitive or customary classifications, but from its high systematic import in the light of the hypothesis that unity of science is attainable.

Notes

1. Science, in the wider sense, may be understood as including the formal disciplines, mathematics, and logic, as well as the empirical ones. In this paper, we shall be concerned with science only in the sense of empirical disciplines, including the sociohumanistic ones.

2. By a "theory" (in the widest sense) we mean any hypothesis, generalization, or law (whether deterministic or statistical), or any conjunction of these; likewise by "phenomena" (in the widest sense) we shall mean either particular occurrences or theoretically formulated general patterns. Throughout this paper, "explanation" ("explainable" etc.) is used as defined in Hempel and Oppenheim (35). As to "explanatory power," there is a definite connection with "systematic power." See Kemeny and Oppenheim (46, 47).

3. If we are willing to adopt a "taxonomic system" for classifying all the things dealt with by science, then the various classes and subclasses in such a system could represent the possible "universes of discourse." In this case, the U_{Bi} of any branch would be associated with the extension of a taxonomic term in the sense of Oppenheim (62).

4. Henceforth, we shall as a rule omit the clause 'at time t'.

5. Oppenheim (62, section 3) has a method for measuring such a reduction.

6. Of course, in some cases, such "skipping" does occur in the process of microreduction, as shall be illustrated later on.

7. As to degree of *credibility*, see Kemeny and Oppenheim (45, especially p. 307).

8. The "acceptance, as an overall fundamental working hypothesis, of the reduction theory, with physical science as most general, to which all others are reducible; with biological science less general; and with social science least general of all," has been emphasized by Hockett (37, especially p. 571).

9. As to *natural*, see Hempel (33, p. 52), and Hempel and Oppenheim (34, pp. 107, 110).

10. Many well-known hierarchical orders of the same kind (including some compatible with ours) can be found in modern writings. It suffices to give the following quotation from an article by L. von Bertalanffy (95, p. 164): "Reality, in the modern conception, appears as a tremendous hierarchical order of organized entities, leading, in a superposition of many levels, from physical and chemical to biological and sociological systems. Unity of Science is granted, not by an utopian reduction of all sciences to physics and chemistry, but by the structural uniformities of the different levels of reality." As to the last sentence, we refer in the last paragraph of section 2.2 to the problem noted. Von Bertalanffy has done pioneer work in developing a General System Theory which, in spite of some differences of emphasis, is an interesting contribution to our problem.

11. The following example is a slight modification of the one given in Hempel and Oppenheim (35, p. 148). See also Rescher and Oppenheim (76, pp. 93, 94).

12. See Rescher and Oppenheim (76, p. 100), and Rescher (75). Of course, nothing is intrinsically a "true" whole; the characterization of certain things as "wholes" is always a function of the point of view, i.e. of the particular 'Pt' relation selected. For instance, if a taxonomic system is given, it is very natural to define 'Pt' so that the "wholes" will correspond to the things of the system. Similarly for *aggregate* see Rescher and Oppenheim (76, p. 90, n. 1).

13. See Kemeny and Oppenheim (47, n. 6). A suggestive characterization of *simplicity* in terms of the "entropy" of a theory has been put forward by Rothstein (78). Using Rothstein's terms, we may say that any microreduction moves in the direction of lower entropy (greater organization).

14. The statement that B_2 is *microreducible* to B_1 means (according to the analysis we adopt here) that some *true* theory belonging to B_1—i.e., some true theory with the appropriate vocabulary and universe of discourse, whether accepted or not, and whether it is ever even written down or not—microreduces every true theory of B_2. This seems to be what people have in mind when they assert that a given B_2 may not be reduced to a given B_1 at a certain time, but may nonetheless be reducible (microreducible) to it.

15. See Kemeny and Oppenheim (45, p. 307); also for "related concepts," like Carnap's "degree of confirmation" see Carnap (13).

16. As to degree of credibility see Kemeny and Oppenheim (45, especially p. 307).

17. Using a term introduced by Kurt Lewin (48), we can also say in such a case: any particular object on level n is *genidentical* with these parts.

18. Though we cannot accept Sir Arthur Eddington's idealistic implications, we quote from his *Philosophy of Physical Science* (17, p. 125): "I conclude therefore that our engrained form of thought is such that we shall not rest satisfied until we are able to represent all physical phenomena as an interplay of a vast number of structural units intrinsically alike. All the diversity of phenomena will be then seen to correspond to different forms of relatedness of these units or, as we should usually say, different configurations."

19. M. Scriven has set forth some suggestive considerations on this subject in his essay, "A Possible Distinction between Traditional Scientific Disciplines and the Study of Human Behavior" (79).

20. See e.g. Kartman (43), with many quotations, references, and notes, some of them microreductionistic.

21. This term has been introduced by F. A. Hayek (31). See also Watkins (98, especially pp. 729–732) and Watkins (99). We owe valuable information in economics to W. J. Baumol, Princeton University.

22. This distinction, first made by C. D. Broad (6, p. 616), adopted by E. C. Tolman (90), C. L. Hull (39), and others, is still in use, in spite of objections against this terminology.

23. This is the form our working hypothesis takes on this level in this field. See in this connection the often quoted paper by K. MacCorquodale and P. E. Meehl, "On a Distinction between Hypothetical Constructs and Intervening Variables" (52), and some of the discussions in the "Symposium on the Proability Approach in Psychology" (73), as well as references therein, to H. Feigl, W. Koehler, D. Krech, and C. C. Pratt.

24. As to *neuroanatomy*, see e.g. W. Penfield (69); as to *neurochemistry*, see e.g. Rosenblueth (77, especially Chapter 26 for acetylcholine and the summaries on pp. 134–135, 274–275); as to *The Electric Activity of the Nervous System*, see the book of this title by Brazier (5). See this last book also for neuroanatomy, neurophysiology, neurochemistry. See Brazier (5, pp. 128, 129, 152) for microreduction of *Gestalt phenomena* mentioned below.

25. Turing (91, 92). For an excellent popular presentation, see Kemeny (44).

26. See the often quoted paper by McCulloch and Pitts (53), and later publications by these authors, as well as other papers in this field in the same *Bulletin of Mathematical Biophysics*, e.g. by N. Rashevsky. See also Platt (72) for a "complementary approach which might be called amplifier theory." For more up to date details, see Shannon and McCarthy's (82) *Automata Studies*, including von Neumann's model, discussed by him (82, pp. 43–98).

27. Throughout this paper, "cell" is used in a wide sense, i.e., "Unicellular" organism or single cell in a multicellular organism.

28. For more details and much of the following, see Simpson, Pittendrigh and Tiffany (87), Goldschmidt (28), and Horowitz (38). For valuable suggestions we are indebted to C. S. Pittendrigh who also coined the terms "message carrying molecule" and "languages of surface" used in our text.

29. See in reference to the following discussion Watson and Crick (100), also (101), and (102), and Crick (15).

30. Pauling and Delbrück (68). A microreducing theory has been proposed for these activities using the "lock-key" model. See Pauling, Campbell, and Pressman (65), and Burnet (8).

31. For a mechanical model, see von Neumann (96) and Jacobson (40).

32. See Timoféeff-Ressovsky (89, especially pp. 108–138). It should, however, be noted that since Delbrück's theory was put forward, his model has proved inadequate for explaining genetic facts concerning mutation. And it is reproduced here only as a historical case of a microreducing theory that, in its day, served valuable functions.

33. We think that, throughout this paper, our usage of thing language also on this level is admissible in spite of well-known difficulties and refer e.g. to Born (4), and Johnson (42).

34. See e.g. Broad (6, espeically p. 93), as to "a general tendency of one order to combine with each other under suitable conditions to form complexes of the next order." See also Blum (1, and 2, especially p. 608); Needham (59, especially pp. 184–185); and Dodd (16).
35. This wording takes care of "regression," a reversal of trend, illustrated e.g. by parasitism.
36. For a clear survey of cosmological hypotheses see the 12 articles published in the issue of *Scientific American* cited under Gamow (26).
37. Perhaps the most sensational method is an experiment suggested by H. C. Urey and made by S. L. Miller (56, 57), according to which amino acids are formed when an electric discharge passes through a mixture of methane, hydrogen, ammonia, and water.
38. "Actually life has many attributes, almost any one of which we can reproduce in a nonliving system. It is only when they all appear to a greater or lesser degree in the same system simultaneously that we call it living" (Calvin, 9, p. 252). Thus the dividing line between "living" and "non-living" is obtained by transforming an underlying "multidimensional concept of order" (see Hempel and Oppenheim, 34, pp. 65–77), in a more or less arbitrary way, into a dichotomy. See also Stanley (88, especially pp. 15 and 16 of the reprint of this article).
39. See note 38 above.
40. For details, see Lindsey (50, especially pp. 136–139, 152–153, 342–344). See also Burkholder (7).
41. See e.g. the publications (104, 105, 106) by Wheeler. See also Haskins (30, especially pp. 30–36). Since we are considering evolution on level 6 as a whole, we can refrain from discussing the great difference between, on the one hand, chance mutations, natural selection, and "instinctive" choices and, on the other hand, the specific faculty of man of consciously and willfully directing social evolution in time stretches of specifically small orders of magnitude (see Zilsel, 108).
42. See Moscana (58) and his references, especailly to work by the same author and by Paul Weiss.
43. See Lippitt (51). For recent experiments, see Sherif and Sherif (84, Chapters 6 and 9), and Sherif (83).
44. See note 10 above.
45. For details, see Flint (21), and Vannerus (93), Auguste Comte in his *Cours de Philosophie Positive*, Première et Deuxième Leçons (14), has given a hierarchical order of 6 "fundamental disciplines" which, independently from its philosophical background, is amazingly modern in many respects, as several contemporary authors recognize.

References

1. Blum, H. F. *Time's Arrow and Evolution*. Princeton: Princeton Univ. Press, 1951.
2. Blum, H. F. "Perspectives in Evolution," *American Scientist*, 43:595–610 (1955).
3. Bonner, J. T. *Morphogenesis*. Princeton: Princeton Univ. Press, 1952.
4. Born, M. "The Interpretation of Quantum Mechanics," *British Journal for the Philosophy of Science*, 3: 95–106 (1953).
5. Brazier, M. A. B. *The Electric Activity of the Nervous System*. London: Sir Isaac Pitman & Sons, Ltd., 1951.
6. Broad, C. D. *The Mind and its Place in Nature*. New York: Harcourt, Brace, 1925.
7. Burkholder, P. R. "Cooperation and Conflict among Primitive Organisms," *American Scientist*, 40: 601–631 (1952).
8. Burnet, M. "How Antibodies are Made," *Scientific American*, 191: 74–78 (November 1954).
9. Calvin, M. "Chemical Evolution and the Origin of Life," *American Scientist*, 44: 248–263 (1956).
10. Carnap, R. *Der logische Aufbau der Welt*. Berlin-Schlachtensee: Im Weltkreis-Verlag, 1928. Summary in N. Goodman, *The Structure of Appearances*, pp. 114–146. Cambridge: Harvard Univ. Press, 1951.
11. Carnap, R. "Testability and Meaning," *Philosophy of Science*, 3: 419–471 (1936), and 4: 2–40 (1937). Reprinted by Graduate Philosophy Club, Yale University, New Haven, 1950.
12. Carnap, R. *Logical Foundations of the Unity of Science, International Encyclopedia of Unified Science*. Vol. 1, pp. 42–62. Chicago: Univ. of Chicago Press, 1938.
13. Carnap, R. *Logical Foundations of Probability*. Chicago: Univ. of Chicago Press, 1950.
14. Comte, Auguste. *Cours de Philosophie Positive*. 6 Vols. Paris: Bachelier, 1830–42.
15. Crick, F. H. C. "The Structure of Hereditary Material," *Scientific American*, 191: 54–61 (October 1954).
16. Dodd, S. C. "A Mass-Time Triangle" *Philosophy of Science*, 11: 233–244 (1944).
17. Eddington, Sir Arthur. *The Philosophy of Physical Science*. Cambridge: Cambridge University Press, 1949.
18. Feigl, H. "Logical Empiricism" in D. D. Runes (ed.), *Twentieth Century Philosophy*, pp. 371–416. New York: Philosophical Library, 1943. Reprinted in H. Feigl and W. Sellars (eds.), *Readings in Philosophical Analysis*. New York: Appleton-Century-Crofts, 1949.

19. Feigl, H. "Unity of Science and Unitary Science" in H. Feigl and M. Brodbeck (eds.), *Readings in the Philosophy of Science*, pp. 382–384. New York: Appleton-Century-Crofts, 1953.

20. Feigl, H. "Functionalism, Psychological Theory and the Uniting Sciences: Some Discussion Remarks," *Psychological Review*, 62: 232–235 (1955).

21. Flint, R. *Philosophy as Scientia Scientiarum and the History of the Sciences*. New York: Scribner, 1904.

22. Fox, S. W. "The Evolution of Protein Molecules and Thermal Synthesis of Biochemical Substances," *American Scientist*, 44: 347–359 (1956).

23. Fraenkel-Conrat, H. "Rebuilding a Virus," *Scientific American*, 194: 42–47 (June 1956).

24. Gamow, G. "The Origin and Evolution of the Universe," *American Scientist*, 39: 393– 406 (1951).

25. Gamow, G. *The Creation of the Universe*. New York: Viking Press, 1952.

26. Gamow, G. "The Evolutionary Universe," *Scientific American*, 195: 136–154 (September 1956).

27. Goldschmidt, R. B. "Evolution, as Viewed by One Geneticist," *American Scientist*, 40: 84–98 (1952).

28. Goldschmidt, R. B. *Theoretical Genetics*. Berkeley and Los Angeles: Univ. of California Press, 1955.

29. Guhl, A. M. "The Social Order of Chickens," *Scientific American*, 194: 42–46 (February 1956).

30. Haskins, C. P. *Of Societies and Man*. New York: Norton & Co., 1951.

31. Hayek, F. A. *Individualism and the Economic Order*. Chicago: Univ. of Chicago Press, 1948.

32. Hebb, D. O. *The Organization of Behavior*. New York: Wiley, 1949.

33. Hempel, C. G. *Fundamentals of Concept Formation in the Empirical Sciences*, Vol. II, No. 7 of *International Encyclopedia of Unified Science*. Chicago: Univ. of Chicago Press, 1952.

34. Hempel, C. G., and P. Oppenheim *Der Typusbegriff im Lichte der neuen Logik; wissenschaftstheoretische Untersuchungen zur Konstitutionsforschung und Psychologie*. Leiden: A. W. Sythoff, 1936.

35. Hempel, C. G, and P. Oppenheim. "Studies in the Logic of Explanation,," *Philosophy of Science*, 15: 135–175 (1948).

36. Hoagland, H. "The Weber-Fechner Law and the All-or-None Theory," *Journal of General Psychology*, 3: 351–373 (1930).

37. Hockett, C. H. "Biophysics, Linguistics, and the Unity of Science," *American Scientist*, 36: 558–572 (1948).

38. Horowitz, N. H. "The Gene," *Scientific American*, 195: 78–90 (October 1956).

39. Hull, C. L. *Principles of Animal Behavior*. New York: D. Appleton-Century, Inc., 1943.

40. Jacobson, H. "Information, Reproduction, and the Origin of Life," *American Scientist*, 43 :119–127 (1955).

41. Jeffress, L. A. *Cerebral Mechanisms in Behavior; the Hixon Symposium*. New York: Wiley, 1951.

42. Johnson, M. "The Meaning of Time and Space in Philosophies of Science," *American Scientist*, 39: 412–431 (1951).

43. Kartman, L. "Metaphorical Appeals in Biological Thought," *American Scientist*, 44: 296–301 (1956).

44. Kemeny, J. G. "Man Viewed as a Machine," *Scientific American*, 192: 58–66 (April 1955).

45. Kemeny, J. G., and P. Oppenheim. "Degree of Factual Support," *Philosophy of Science*, 19: 307–324 (1952).

46. Kemeny, J. G., and P. Oppenheim. "Systematic Power," *Philosophy of Science*, 22: 27–33 (1955).

47. Kemeny, J. G., and P. Oppenheim. "On Reduction," *Philosophical Studies*, 7: 6–19 (1956).

48. Lewin, Kurt. *Der Begriff der Genese*. Berlin: Verlag von Julius Springer, 1922.

49. Linderstrom-Lang, K. U. "How is a Protein Made?" *American Scientist*, 41: 100–106 (1953).

50. Lindsey, A. W. *Organic Evolution*. St. Louis: C. V. Mosbey Company, 1952.

51. Lippitt, R. "Field Theory and Experiment in Social Psychology," *American Journal of Sociology*, 45: 26–79 (1939).

52. MacCorquodale, K., and P. E. Meehl. "On a Distinction Between Hypothetical Constructs and Intervening Variables," *Psychological Review*, 55: 95–105 (1948).

53. McCulloch, W. S., and W. Pitts. "A Logical Calculus of the Ideas Immanent in Nervous Activity," *Bulletin of Mathematical Biophysics*, 5: 115–133 (1943).

54. Mannheim, K. *Ideology and Utopia*. New York: Harcourt, Brace, 1936.

55. Mill, John Stuart. *System of Logic*. New York: Harper, 1848 (1st ed. London, 1843).

56. Miller, S. L. "A Production of Amino Acids Under Possible Primitive Earth Conditions," *Science*, 117: 528–529 (1953).

57. Miller, S. L. "Production of Some Organic Compounds Under Possible Primitive Earth Conditions," *Journal of the American Chemical Society*, 77: 2351–2361 (1955).

58. Moscana, A. "Development of Heterotypic Combinations of Dissociated Embryonic Chick Cells," *Proceedings of the Society for Experimental Biology and Medicine*, 92: 410–416 (1956).

59. Needham, J. *Time*. New York: Macmillan, 1943.

60. Nogushi, J., and T. Hayakawa. Letter to the Editor, *Journal of the American Chemical Society*, 76: 2846–2848 (1954).

61. Oparin, A. I. *The Origin of Life*. New York: Macmillan, 1938 (Dover Publications, Inc. edition, 1953).

62. Oppenheim, P. "Dimensions of Knowledge," *Revue Internationale de Philosophie*, Fascicule 40, Section 7 (1957).

63. Pauling, L. "Chemical Achievement and Hope for the Future," *American Scientist*, 36: 51−58 (1948).

64. Pauling, L. "Quantum Theory and Chemistry," *Science*, 113: 92−94 (1951).

65. Pauling, L., D. H. Campbell, and D. Pressmann. "The Nature of Forces between Antigen and Antibody and of the Precipitation Reaction," *Physical Review*, 63: 203−219 (1943).

66. Pauling L., and R. B. Corey. "Two Hydrogen-Bonded Spiral Configurations of the Polypeptide Chain," *Journal of the American Chemical Society*, 72: 5349 (1950).

67. Pauling, L., and R. B. Corey. "Atomic Coordination and Structure Factors for Two Helical Configurations," *Proceedings of the National Academy of Science* (U.S.), 37: 235 (1951).

68. Pauling, L., and M. Delbrück. "The Nature of Intermolecular Forces Operative in Biological Processes," *Science*, 97: 585−586 (1940).

69. Penfield, W. "The Cerebral Cortex and the Mind of Man," in P. Laslett (ed.), *The Physical Basis of Mind*, pp. 56−64. Oxford: Blackwell, 1950.

70. Piaget, J. *The Moral Judgment of the Child*. London: Kegan Paul, Trench, Trubner and Company, Ltd., 1932.

71. Piaget, J. *The Language and Thought of the Child*. London: Kegan Paul, Trench, Trubner and Company; New York: Harcourt, Brace, 1926.

72. Platt, J. R. "Amplification Aspects of Biological Response and Mental Activity," *American Scientist*, 44: 180−197 (1956).

73. Probability Approach in Psychology (Symposium), *Psychological Review*, 62: 193−242 (1955).

74. Rashevsky, N. Papers in general of Rashevsky, published in the *Bulletin of Mathematical Biophysics*, 5 (1943).

75. Rescher, N. "Axioms of the Part Relation," *Philosophical Studies*, 6: 8−11 (1955).

76. Rescher, N. and P. Oppenheim. "Logical Analysis of Gestalt Concepts," *British Journal for the Philosophy of Science*, 6: 89−106 (1955).

77. Rosenblueth, A. *The Transmission of Nerve Impulses at Neuroeffector Junctions and Peripheral Synapses*. New York: Technological Press of MIT and Wiley, 1950.

78. Rothstein, J. *Communication, Organization, and Science*. Indian Hills, Colorado: Falcon's Wing Press, 1957.

79. Scriven, M. "A Possibe Distinction between Traditional Scientific Disciplines and the Study of Human Behavior," in H. Feigl and M. Scriven (eds.), Vol. I, *Minnesota Studies in the Philosophy of Science*, pp. 330−339. Minneapolis: Univ. of Minnesota Press, 1956.

80. Sellars, W. "A Semantical Solution of the Mind-Body Problem," *Methodos*, 5: 45−84 (1953).

81. Sellars, W. "Empiricism and the Philosophy of Mind," in H. Feigl and M. Scriven (eds.), *Minnesota Studies in the Philosophy of Science*, Vol. I, pp. 253−329. Minneapolis: Univ. of Minnesota Press, 1956.

82. Shannon, C. E., and J. McCarthy (eds.), *Automata Studies*. Princeton: Princeton Univ. Press, 1956.

83. Sherif, M. "Experiments in Group Conflict," *Scientific American*, 195: 54−58 (November 1956).

84. Sherif, M., and C. W. Sherif. *An Outline of Social Psychology*. New York: Harper, 1956.

85. Sherrington, Charles. *The Integrative Action of the Nervous System*. New Haven: Yale Univ. Press, 1948.

86. Simmel, G. *Sociologie*. Leipzig: Juncker und Humblot, 1908.

87. Simpson, G. G., C. S. Pittendrigh, and C. H. Tiffany. *Life*. New York: Harcourt, Brace, 1957.

88. Stanley, W. M. "The Structure of Viruses," reprinted from publication No. 14 of the *American Association for the Advancement of Science, The Cell and Protoplasm*, pp. 120−135 (reprint consulted) (1940).

89. Timoféeff Ressovsky, N. W. *Experimentelle Mutationsforschung in der Vererbungslehre*. Dresden und Leipzig: Verlag von Theodor Steinkopff, 1937.

90. Tolman, E. C. *Purposive Behavior in Animals and Men*. New York: The Century Company, 1932.

91. Turing, A. M. "On Computable Numbers, With an Application to the Entscheidungsproblem," *Proceedings of the London Mathematical Society*, Ser. 2, 42: 230−265 (1936).

92. Turing, A. M. "A Correction" *Proceedings of the London Mathematcial Society*, Ser. 2, 43: 544−546 (1937).

93. Vannerus, A. *Vetenskapssystematik*. Stockholm: Aktiebolaget Ljus, 1907.

94. Veblen, T. *The Theory of the Leisure Class*. London: Macmillan, 1899.

95. Von Bertalanffy, L. "An Outline of General System Theory," *The British Journal for the Philosophy of Science*, 1: 134−165 (1950).

96. Von Neumann, John. "The General and Logical Theory of Automata," in L. A. Jeffress (ed.), *Cerebral Mechanisms in Behavior; The Hixon Symposium*, pp 20–41. New York: John Wiley and Sons, Inc., 1951.

97. Von Neumann, John. "Probabilistic Logics and the Synthesis of Reliable Organisms from Unreliable Components," in C. E. Shannon and J. McCarthy (eds.), *Automata Studies*. Princeton: Princeton Univ. Press, 1956.

98. Watkins, J. W. N. "Ideal Types and Historical Explanation," in H. Feigl and M. Brodbeck (eds.), *Readings in the Philosophy of Science*, pp. 723–743. New York: Appleton-Century-Crofts, 1953.

99. Watkins, J. W. N. "A Reply," *Philosophy of Science*, 22: 58–62 (1955).

100. Watson, J. D., and F. H. C. Crick. "The Structure of DNA," *Cold Spring Harbor Symposium on Quantitative Biology*, 18: 123–131 (1953).

101. Watson, J. D., and F. H. C. Crick. "Molecular Structure of Nucleic Acids—A Structure for Desoxyribosenucleic Acid," *Nature*, 171: 737–738 (1953).

102. Watson, J. D., and F. H. C. Crick. "Genetical Implications of the Structure of Desoxyribosenucleic Acid," *Nature*, 171: 964–967 (1953).

103. Weber, M. *The Theory of Social and Economic Organization*, translated by A. M. Henderson and T. Persons. New York: Oxford Univ. Press, 1947.

104. Wheeler, W. M. *Social Life Among the Insects*. New York: Harcourt, Brace, 1923.

105. Wheeler, W. M. *Emergent Evolution and the Development of Societies*. New York: Norton & Co., 1928.

106. Wheeler, W. M. "Animal Societies," *Scientific Monthly*, 39: 289–301 (1934).

107. Woodward, R. B., and C. H. Schramm. Letter to the Editor, *Journal of the American Chemical Society*, 69: 1551 (1947).

108. Zilsel, E. "History and Biological Evolution," *Philosophy of Science*, 7: 121–128 (1940).

Chapter 23

Special Sciences

Jerry Fodor

A typical thesis of positivistic philosophy of science is that all true theories in the special sciences should reduce to physical theories in the 'long run'. This is intended to be an empirical thesis, and part of the evidence which supports it is provided by such scientific successes as the molecular theory of heat and the physical explanation of the chemical bond. But the philosophical popularity of the reductionist program cannot be explained by reference to these achievements alone. The development of science has witnessed the proliferation of specialized disciplines at least as often as it has witnessed their elimination, so the widespread enthusiasm for the view that there will eventually be only physics can hardly be a mere induction over past reductionist successes.

I think that many philosophers who accept reductionism do so primarily because they wish to endorse the generality of physics vis-à-vis the special sciences: roughly, the view that all events which fall under the laws of any science are physical events and hence fall under the laws of physics.[1] For such philosophers, saying that physics is basic science and saying that theories in the special sciences must reduce to physical theories have seemed to be two ways of saying the same thing, so that the latter doctrine has come to be a standard construal of the former.

In what follows, I shall argue that this is a considerable confusion. What has traditionally been called 'the unity of science' is a much stronger, and much less plausible, thesis than the generality of physics. If this is true, it is important. Though reductionism is an empirical doctrine, it is intended to play a regulative role in scienific practice. Reducibility to physics is taken to be a *constraint* upon the acceptability of theories in the special science with the curious consequence that the more the special sciences succeed, the more they ought to disappear. Methodological problems about psychology, in particular, arise in just this way: The assumption that the subject matter of psychology is part of the subject matter of physics is taken to imply that psychological theories must reduce to physical theories, and it is this latter principle that makes the trouble. I want to avoid the trouble by challenging the inference.

Reductionism is the view that all the special sciences reduce to physics. The sense of 'reduce to' is, however, proprietary. It can be characterized as follows:[2]

Let formula (1) be a law of the special science *S*.

(1) $S_1 x \rightarrow S_2 y$

Formula (1) is intended to be read as something like 'all events which consist of x's being S_1 bring about events which consist of y's being S_2.' I assume that a science is individuated largely by reference to its typical predicates (see note 2), hence that if S is a special science, 'S_1' and 'S_2' are not predicates of basic physics. (I also assume that

Reprinted from *Synthese* 28 (1974), pp. 77–115, originally appearing under the title "Special Sciences, or The Disunity of Science as a Working Hypothesis," by permission of the author and the publisher. Copyright 1974 by Kluwer Academic Publishers.

the 'all' which quantifies laws of the special sciences needs to be taken with a grain of salt. Such laws are typically *not* exceptionless. This is a point to which I shall return at length.) A necessary and sufficient condition for the reduction of formula (1) to a law of physics is that the formulae (2) and (3) should be laws, and a necessary and sufficient condition for the reduction

(2a) $S_1 x \rightleftharpoons P_1 x$
(2b) $S_2 y \rightleftharpoons P_2 y$
(3) $P_1 x \rightarrow P_2 y$

of S to physics is that all its laws should be so reduced.[3]

'P_1' and 'P_2' are supposed to be predicates of physics, and formula (3) is supposed to be a physical law. Formulae like (2) are often called 'bridge' laws. Their characteristic feature is that they contain predicates of both the reduced and the reducing science. Bridge laws like formula (2) are thus contrasted with 'proper' laws like formulae (1) and (3). The upshot of the remarks so far is that the reduction of a science requires that any formula which appears as the antecedent or consequent of one of its proper laws must appear as the reduced formula in some bridge law or other.[4]

Several points about the connective '$\rightarrow$' are now in order. First, whatever properties that connective may have, it is universally agreed that it must be transitive. This is important because it is usually assumed that the reduction of some of the special sciences proceeds via bridge laws which connect their predicates with those of intermediate reducing theories. Thus, psychology is presumed to reduce to physics via, say, neurology, biochemistry, and other local stops. The present point is that this makes no difference to the logic of the situation so long as the transitivity of '$\rightarrow$' is assumed. Bridge laws which connect the predicates of S to those of S^* will satisfy the constraints upon the reduction of S to physics so long as there are other bridge laws which, directly or indirectly, connect the predicates of S^* to physical predicates.

There are, however, quite serious open questions about the interpretation of '$\rightarrow$' in bridge laws. What turns on these questions is the extent to which reductionism is taken to be a physicalist thesis.

To begin with, if we read '$\rightarrow$' as 'brings about' or 'causes' in proper laws, we will have to have some other connective for bridge laws, since bringing about and causing are presumably asymmetric, while bridge laws express symmetric relations. Moreover, unless bridge laws hold by virtue of the *identity* of the events which satisfy their antecedents with those that satisfy their consequents, reductionism will guarantee only a weak version of physicalism, and this would fail to express the underlying ontological bias of the reductionist program.

If bridge laws are not-identity statements, then formulae like (2) claim at most that, by law, x's satisfaction of a P predicate and x's satisfaction of an S predicate are causally correlated. It follows from this that it is nomologically necessary that S and P predicates apply to the same things (i.e., that S predicates apply to a subset of the things that P predicates apply to). But, of course, this is compatible with a nonphysicalist ontology, since it is compatible with the possibility that x's satisfying S should not itself be a physical event. On this interpretation, the truth of reductionism does *not* guarantee the generality of physics vis-à-vis the special sciences, since there are some events (satisfactions of S predicates) which fall in the domain of a special science (S) but not in the domain of physics. (One could imagine, for example, a doctrine according to which physical and psychological predicates are both held to apply to organisms, but where it is denied that the event which consists of an organism's satisfying a psychological predicate is, in any sense, a physical event. The upshot would be a kind of psychophysical dualism of a non-Cartesian variety; a dualism of events and/or properties rather than substances.)

Given these sorts of considerations, many philosophers have held that bridge laws like formula (2) ought to be taken to express contingent event identities, so that one would read formula (2a) in some such fashion as 'every event which consists of an x's satisfying S_1 is identical to some event which consists of that x's satisfying P_1 and vice versa'. On this reading, the truth of reductionism would entail that every event that falls under any scientific law is a physical event, thereby simultaneously expressing the ontological bias of reductionism and guaranteeing the generality of physics vis-à-vis the special sciences.

If the bridge laws express event identities, and if every event that falls under the proper laws of a special science falls under a bridge law, we get classical reductionism, a doctrine that entails the truth of what I shall call 'token physicalism'. Token physicalism is simply the claim that all the events that the sciences talk about are physical events. There are three things to notice about token physicalism.

First, it is weaker than what is usually called 'materialism'. Materialism claims *both* that token physicalism is true *and* that every event falls under the laws of some science or other. One could therefore be a token physicalist without being a materialist, though I don't see why anyone would bother.

Second, token physicalism is weaker than what might be called 'type physicalism', the doctrine, roughly, that every *property* mentioned in the laws of any science is a physical property. Token physicalism does not entail type physicalism, if only because the contingent identity of a pair of events presumably does not guarantee the identity of the properties whose instantiation constitutes the events; not even when the event identity is nomologically necessary. On the other hand, if an event is simply the instantiation of a property, then type physicalism does entail token physicalism; two events will be identical when they consist of the instantiation of the same property by the same individual at the same time.

Third, token physicalism is weaker than reductionism. Since this point is, in a certain sense, the burden of the argument to follow, I shan't labor it here. But, as a first approximation, reductionism is the conjunction of token physicalism with the assumption that there are natural kind predicates in an ideally completed physics which correspond to each natural kind predicate in any ideally completed special science. It will be one of my morals that reductionism cannot be inferred from the assumption that token physicalism is true. Reductionism is a sufficient, but not a necessary, condition for token physicalism.

To summarize: I shall be reading reductionism as entailing token physicalism since, if bridge laws state nomologically necessary contingent event identities, a reduction of psychology to neurology would require that any event which consists of the instantiation of a psychological property is identical with some event which consists of the instantiation of a neurological property. Both reductionism and token physicalism entail the generality of physics, since both hold that any event which falls within the universe of discourse of a special science will also fall within the universe of discourse of physics. Moreover, it is a consequence of both doctrines that any prediction which follows from the laws of a special science (and a statement of initial conditions) will follow equally from a theory which consists only of physics and the bridge laws (together with the statement of initial conditions). Finally, it is assumed by both reductionism and token physicalism that physics is the *only* basic science; viz., that it is the only science that is general in the sense just specified.

I now want to argue that reductionism is too strong a constraint upon the unity of science, but that, for any reasonable purposes, the weaker doctrine will do.

Every science implies a taxonomy of the events in its universe of discourse. In particular, every science employs a descriptive vocabulary of theoretical and observation predicates, such that events fall under the laws of the science by virtue of satisfying those predicates. Patently, not every true description of an event is a description in such a vocabulary. For example, there are a large number of events which consist of things having been transported to a distance of less than three miles from the Eiffel Tower. I take it, however, that there is no science which contains 'is transported to a distance of less than three miles from the Eiffel Tower' as part of its descriptive vocabulary. Equivalently, I take it that there is no natural law which applies to events in virtue of their instantiating the property *is transported to a distance of less than three miles from the Eiffel Tower* (though I suppose it is just conceivable that there is some law that applies to events in virtue of their instantiating some distinct but coextensive property). By way of abbreviating these facts, I shall say that the property *is transported* . . . does not determine a *(natural) kind*, and that predicates which express that property are not (natural) kind predicates.

If I knew what a law is, and if I believed that scientific theories consist just of bodies of laws, then I could say that 'P' is a kind predicate relative to S if S contains proper laws of the form '$P_x \rightarrow \ldots y$' or '$\ldots y \rightarrow P_x'$': roughly, the kind predicates of a science are the ones whose terms are the bound variables in its proper laws. I am inclined to say this even in my present state of ignorance, accepting the consequence that it makes the murky notion of a kind viciously dependent on the equally murky notions of *law* and *theory*. There is no firm footing here. If we disagree about what a kind is, we will probably also disagree about what a law is, and for the same reasons. I don't know how to break out of this circle, but I think that there are some interesting things to say about which circle we are in.

For example, we can now characterize the respect in which reductionism is too strong a construal of the doctrine of the unity of science. If reductionism is true, then *every* kind is, or is coextensive with, a physical kind. (Every kind *is* a physical kind if bridge statements express nomologically necessary property identities, and every kind is coextensive with a physical kind if bridge statements express nomologically necessary event identities.) This follows immediately from the reductionist premise that every predicate which appears as the antecedent or consequent of a law of a special science must appear as one of the reduced predicates in some bridge law, together with the assumption that the kind predicates are the ones whose terms are the bound variables in proper laws. If, in short, some physical law is related to each law of a special science in the way that formula (3) is related to formula (1), then every kind predicate of a special science is related to a kind predicate of physics in the way that formula (2) relates 'S_1' and 'S_2' to 'P_1' and 'P_2' respectively.

I now want to suggest some reasons for believing that this consequence is intolerable. These are not supposed to be knock-down reasons; they couldn't be, given that the question of whether reductionism is too strong is finally an *empirical* question. (The world could turn out to be such that every kind corresponds to a physical kind, just as it could turn out to be such that the property *is transported to a distance of less than three miles from the Eiffel Tower* determines a kind in, say, hydrodynamics. It's just that, as things stand, it seems very unlikely that the world *will* turn out to be either of these ways.)

The reason it is unlikely that every kind corresponds to a physical kind is just that (a) interesting generalizations (e.g., counterfactual supporting generalizations) can often be made about events whose physical descriptions have nothing in common; (b) it is often the case that *whether* the physical descriptions of the events subsumed by such generalizations have anything in common is, in an obvious sense, entirely irrelevant to the truth of the generalizations, or to their interestingness, or to their degree of confirmation, or, indeed, to any of their epistemologically important properties; and (c) the special sciences are very much in the business of formulating generalizations of this kind.

I take it that these remarks are obvious to the point of self-certification; they leap to the eye as soon as one makes the (apparently radical) move of taking the existence of the special sciences at all seriously. Suppose, for example, that Gresham's 'law' really is true. (If one doesn't like Gresham's law, then any true and counterfactual supporting generalization of any conceivable future economics will probably do as well.) Gresham's law says something about what will happen in monetary exchanges under certain conditions. I am willing to believe that physics is general *in the sense that it implies that any event which consists of a monetary exchange* (hence any event which falls under Gresham's law) *has a true description in the vocabulary of physics and in virtue of which it falls under the laws of physics.* But banal considerations suggest that a physical description which covers all such events must be wildly disjunctive. Some monetary exchanges involve strings of wampum. Some involve dollar bills. And some involve signing one's name to a check. What are the chances that a disjunction of physical predicates which covers all these events (i.e., a disjunctive predicate which can form the right hand side of a bridge law of the form 'x is a monetary exchange $\rightleftharpoons$ ...') expresses a physical kind? In particular, what are the chances that such a predicate forms the antecedent or consequent of some proper law of physics? The point is that monetary exchanges have interesting things in common; Gresham's law, if true, says what one of these interesting things is. But what is interesting about monetary exchanges is surely not their commonalities under *physical* description. A kind like a monetary exchange *could* turn out to be coextensive with a physical kind; but if it did, that would be an accident on a cosmic scale.

In fact, the situation for reductionism is still worse than the discussion thus far suggests. For reductionism claims not only that all kinds are coextensive with physical kinds, but that the coextensions are nomologically necessary: bridge laws are *laws*. So, if Gresham's law is true, it follows that there is a (bridge) law of nature such that 'x is a monetary exchange $\rightleftharpoons x$ is P' is true for every value of x, and such that P is a term for a physical kind. But, surely, there is no such law. If there were, then P would have to cover not only all the systems of monetary exchange that there *are*, but also all the systems of monetary exchange that there *could be*; a law must succeed with the counterfactuals. What physical predicate is a candidate for P in 'x is a nomologically possible monetary exchange iff P_x'?

To summarize: An immortal econophysicist might, when the whole show is over, find a predicate in physics that was, in brute fact, coextensive with 'is a monetary exchange'. If physics is general—if the ontological biases of reductionism are true— then there must *be* such a predicate. But (a) to paraphrase a remark Professor Donald Davidson made in a slightly different context, nothing but brute enumeration could convince us of this brute coextensivity, and (b) there would seem to be no chance at all that the physical predicate employed in stating the coextensivity would be a physical kind term, and (c) there is still less chance that the coextension would be lawful (i.e., that it would hold not only for the nomologically possible world that turned out to be real, but for any nomologically possible world at all).[5]

I take it that the preceding discussion strongly suggests that economics is not reducible to physics in the special sense of reduction involved in claims for the unity of science. There is, I suspect, nothing peculiar about economics in this respect; the reasons why economics is unlikely to reduce to physics are paralleled by those which suggest that psychology is unlikely to reduce to neurology.

If psychology is reducible to neurology, then for every psychological kind predicate there is a coextensive neurological kind predicate, and the generalization which states this coextension is a law. Clearly, many psychologists believe something of the sort. There are departments of psychobiology or psychology and brain science in universities throughout the world whose very existence is an institutionalized gamble that such lawful coextensions can be found. Yet, as has been frequently remarked in recent discussions of materialism, there are good grounds for hedging these bets. There are no firm data for any but the grossest correspondence between types of psychological states and types of neurological states, and it is entirely possible that the nervous system of higher organisms characteristically achieves a given psychological end by a wide variety of neurological means. It is also possible that given neurological structures subserve many different psychological functions at different times, depending upon the character of the activities in which the organism is engaged.[6] In either event, the attempt to pair neurological structures with psychological functions could expect only limited success. Physiological psychologists of the stature of Karl Lashley have held this sort of view.

The present point is that the reductionist program in psychology is clearly *not* to be defended on ontological grounds. Even if (token) psychological events are (token) neurological events, it does not follow that the kind predicates of psychology are coextensive with the kind predicates of any other discipline (including physics). That is, the assumption that every psychological event is a physical event does not guarantee that physics (or, a fortiori, any other discipline more general than psychology) can provide an appropriate vocabulary for psychological theories. I emphasize this point because I am convinced that the make-or-break commitment of many physiological psychologists to the reductionist program stems precisely from having confused that program with (token) physicalism.

What I have been doubting is that there are neurological kinds coextensive with psychological kinds. What seems increasingly clear is that, even if there are such coextensions, they cannot be lawful. For it seems increasingly likely that there are nomologically possible systems other than organisms (viz., automata) which satisfy the kind predicates of psychology but which satisfy no neurological predicates at all. Now, as Putnam has emphasized (1960), if there are any such systems, then there must be vast numbers, since equivalent automata can, in principle, be made out of practically anything. If this observation is correct, then there can be no serious hope that the class of automata whose psychology is effectively identical to that of some organism can be described by *physical* kind predicates (though, of course, if token physicalism is true, that class can be picked out by some physical predicate or other). The upshot is that the classical formulation of the unity of science is at the mercy of progress in the field of computer simulation. This is, of course, simply to say that that formulation was too strong. The unity of science was intended to be an empirical hypothesis, defeasible by possible scientific findings. But no one had it in mind that it should be defeated by Newell, Shaw, and Simon.

I have thus far argued that psychological reductionism (the doctrine that every psychological natural kind is, or is coextensive with, a neurological natural kind) is not equivalent to, and cannot be inferred from, token physicalism (the doctrine that every psychological event is a neurological event). It may, however, be argued that one might as well take the doctrines to be equivalent since the only possible *evidence* one could have for token physicalism would also be evidence for reductionism: *viz.,* that such evidence would have to consist in the discovery of type-to-type psychophysical correlations.

A moment's consideration shows, however, that this argument is not well taken. If type-to-type psychophysical correlations would be evidence for token physicalism, so would correlations of other specifiable kinds.

We have type-to-type correlations where, for every n-tuple of events that are of the same psychological kind, there is a correlated n-tuple of events that are of the same neurological kind.[7] Imagine a world in which such correlations are *not* forthcoming. What is found, instead, is that for every n-tuple of type identical psychological events, there is a spatiotemporally correlated n-tuple of type *distinct* neurological events. That is, every psychological event is paired with some neurological event or other, but psychological events of the same kind are sometimes paired with neurological events of different kinds. My present point is that such pairings would provide as much support for token physicalism as type-to-type pairings do *so long as we are able to show that the type distinct neurological events paired with a given kind of psychological event are identical in respect of whatever properties are relevant to type identification in psychology.* Suppose, for purposes of explication, that psychological events are type identified by reference to their behavioral consequences.[8] Then what is required of all the neurological events paired with a class of type homogeneous psychological events is only that they be identical in respect of their behavioral consequences. To put it briefly, type identical events do not, of course, have *all* their properties in common, and type distinct events must nevertheless be identical in *some* of their properties. The empirical confirmation of token physicalism does not depend on showing that the neurological counterparts of type identical psychological events are themselves type identical. What needs to be shown is just that they are identical in respect of those properties which determine what kind of *psychological* event a given event is.

Could we have evidence that an otherwise heterogeneous set of neurological events have those kinds of properties in common? Of course we could. The neurological theory might itself explain why an n-tuple of neurologically type distinct events are identical in their behavioral consequences, or, indeed, in respect of any of indefinitely many other such relational properties. And, if the neurological theory failed to do so, some science more basic than neurology might succeed.

My point in all this is, once again, not that correlations between type homogeneous psychological states and type heterogeneous neurological states would prove that token physicalism is true. It is only that such correlations might give us as much reason to be token physicalists as type-to-type correlations would. If this is correct, then epistemological arguments from token physicalism to reductionism must be wrong.

It seems to me (to put the point quite generally) that the classical construal of the unity of science has really badly misconstrued the *goal* of scientific reduction. The point of reduction is *not* primarily to find some natural kind predicate of physics coextensive with each kind predicate of a special science. It is, rather, to explicate the physical mechanisms whereby events conform to the laws of the special sciences. I have been arguing that there is no logical or epistemological reason why success in the second of these projects should require success in the first, and that the two are likely to come apart *in fact* wherever the physical mechanisms whereby events conform to a law of the special sciences are heterogeneous.

I take it that the discussion thus far shows that reductionism is probably too strong a construal of the unity of science; on the one hand, it is incompatible with probable results in the special sciences, and, on the other, it is more than we need to assume if what we primarily want, from an ontological point of view, is just to be good token physicalists. In what follows, I shall try to sketch a liberalized version of the relation between physics and the special sciences which seems to me to be just strong enough in these respects. I shall then give a couple of independent reasons for supposing that the revised doctrine may be the right one.

The problem all along has been that there is an open empirical possibility that what corresponds to the kind predicates of a reduced science may be a heterogeneous and unsystematic disjunction of predicates in the reducing science. We do not want the unity of science to be prejudiced by this possibility. Suppose, then, that we allow that bridge statements may be of this form,

$$(4)\ \ S_x \rightleftharpoons P_1 x \lor P_2 x \lor \ldots \lor P_n x$$

where $P_1 \lor P_2 \lor \ldots \lor P_n$ is *not* a kind predicate in the reducing science. I take it that this is tantamount to allowing that at least some 'bridge laws' may, in fact, not turn out to be laws, since I take it that a necessary condition on a universal generalization being lawlike is that the predicates which constitute its antecedent and consequent should be kind predicates. I am thus assuming that it is enough, for purposes of the unity of science, that every law of the special sciences should be reducible to physics by bridge statements which express true empirical generalizations. Bearing in mind that bridge statements are to be construed as species of identity statements, formula (4) will be read as something like 'every event which consists of x's satisfying S is identical with some event which consists of x's satisfying some or other predicate belonging to the disjunction $P_1 \lor P_2 \lor \ldots \lor P_n'$.

Now, in cases of reduction where what corresponds to formula (2) is not a law, what corresponds to formula (3) will not be either, and for the same reason: viz., the predicates appearing in the antecedent and consequent will, by hypothesis, not be kind predicates. Rather, what we will have is something that looks like figure 23.1. That is, the antecedent and consequent of the reduced law will each be connected with a disjunction of predicates in the reducing science. Suppose, for the moment, that the reduced law is exceptionless, viz., that no S_1 events satisfy P'. Then there will be laws of the reducing science which connect the satisfaction of *each* member of the disjunction associated with the antecedent of the reduced law with the satisfaction of some member of the disjunction associated with the consequent of the reduced law. That is, if $S_1 x \rightarrow S_2 y$ is exceptionless, then there must be some proper law of the reducing science which either states or entails that $P_1 x \rightarrow P^*$ for some P^*, and similarly for $P_2 x$ through $P_n x$. Since there must be such laws, and since each of them is a 'proper law in the sense of which we have been using that term, it follows that each disjunct of $P_1 \lor P_2 \lor \ldots \lor P_n$ is a kind predicate, as is each disjunct of $P^*_1 \lor P^*_2 \lor \ldots \lor P^*_n$.

This, however, is where push comes to shove. For it might be argued that if each disjunct of the P disjunction is lawfully connected to some disjunct of the P^* disjunction, then it follows that formula (5) is itself a law.

$$(5)\ \ P_1 x \lor P_2 x \lor \ldots \lor P_n x \rightarrow P^*_1 y \lor P^*_2 y \lor \ldots \lor P^*_n y$$

The point would be that the schema in Figure 1 implies $P_1 x \rightarrow P^*_2 y$, $P_2 x \rightarrow P^*_m y$,

Law of special science:

Disjunctive predicate of
reducing science:

Laws of reducing science:

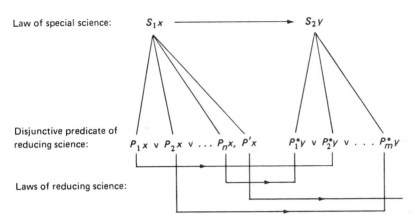

Figure 23.1
Schematic representation of the proposed relation between the reduced and the reducing science on a
revised account of the unity of science. If any S_1 events are of the type P', they will be exceptions to the
law $S_1x \rightarrow S_2y$. See text.

etc., and the argument from a premise of the form $(P \supset R)$ and $(Q \supset S)$ to a conclusion
of the form $(P \lor Q) \supset (R \lor S)$ is valid.

What I am inclined to say about this is that it just shows that 'it's a law that—'
defines a nontruth functional context (or, equivalently for these purposes, that not all
truth functions of kind predicates are themselves kind predicates); in particular, that one
may not argue from: 'it's a law that P brings about R' and 'it's a law that Q brings about
S' to 'it's a law that P or Q brings about R or S'. (Though, of course, the argument from
those premises to 'P or Q brings about R or S *simpliciter* is fine.) I think, for example,
that it is a law that the irradiation of green plants by sunlight causes carbohydrate
synthesis, and I think that it is a law that friction causes heat, but I do not think that it
is a law that (either the irradiation of green plants by sunlight or friction) causes (either
carbohydrate synthesis or heat). Correspondingly, I doubt that 'is either carbohydrate
synthesis or heat' is plausibly taken to be a kind predicate.

It is not strictly mandatory that one should agree with all this, but one denies it at
a price. In particular, if one allows the full, range of truth-functional arguments inside
the context 'it's a law that—', then one gives up the possibility of identifying the kind
predicates of a science with the ones which constitute the antecedents or consequents
of its proper laws. (Thus formula (5) would be a proper law of physics which fails to
satisfy that condition.) One thus inherits the need for an alternative construal of the
notion of a kind, and I don't know what that alternative would be like.

The upshot seems to be this. If we do not require that bridge statements must be
laws, then either some of the generalizations to which the laws of special sciences
reduce are not themselves lawlike, or some laws are not formulable in terms of kinds.
Whichever way one takes formula (5), the important point is that the relation between
sciences proposed by figure .1 is weaker than what standard reductionism requires. In
particular, it does not imply a correspondence between the kind predicates of the
reduced and the reducing science. Yet it does imply physicalism given the same
assumption that makes standard reductionism physicalistic: viz., that bridge statements
express token event identities. But these are precisely the properties that we wanted a
revised account of the unity of science to exhibit.

I now want to give two further reasons for thinking that this construal of the unity
of science is right. First, it allows us to see how the laws of the special sciences could

reasonably have exceptions, and, second, it allows us to see why there are special sciences at all. These points in turn.

Consider, again, the model of reduction implicit in formulae (2) and (3). I assume that the laws of basic science are strictly exceptionless, and I assume that it is common knowledge that the laws of the special sciences are not. But now we have a dilemma to face. Since '$\rightarrow$' expresses a relation (or relations) which must be transitive, formula (1) can have exceptions only if the bridge laws do. But if the bridge laws have exceptions, reductionism loses its ontological bite, since we can no longer say that every event which consists of the satisfaction of an S-predicate consists of the satisfaction of a P-predicate. In short, given the reductionist model, we cannot consistently assume that the bridge laws and the basic laws are exceptionless while assuming that the special laws are not. But we cannot accept the violation of the bridge laws unless we are willing to vitiate the ontological claim that is the main point of the reductionist program.

We can get out of this (*salve* the reductionist model) in one of two ways. We can give up the claim that the special laws have exceptions or we can give up the claim that the basic laws are exceptionless. I suggest that both alternatives are undesirable—the first because it flies in the face of fact. There is just no chance at all that the true, counterfactual supporting generalizations of, say, psychology, will turn out to hold in strictly each and every condition where their antecedents are satisfied. Even when the spirit is willing, the flesh is often weak. There are always going to be behavioral lapses which are physiologically explicable but which are uninteresting from the point of view of psychological theory. But the second alternative is not much better. It may, after all, turn out that the laws of basic science have exceptions. But the question arises whether one wants the unity of science to depend on the assumption that they do.

On the account summarized figure 23.1, however, everything works out satisfactorily. A nomologically sufficient condition for an exception to $S_1 x \rightarrow S_2 y$ is that the bridge statements should identify some occurrence of the satisfaction of S_1 with an occurrence of the satisfaction of a P^*-predicate which is not itself lawfully connected to the satisfaction of any P^*-predicate (i.e., suppose S_1 is connected to P' such that there is no law which connects P' to any predicate which bridge statements associate with S_2. Then any instantiation of S_1 which is contingently identical to an instantiation of P' will be an event which constitutes an exception to $S_1 x \rightarrow S_2 y$). Notice that, in this case, we need assume no exceptions to the laws of the *reducing* science since, by hypothesis, formula (5) is not a law.

In fact, strictly speaking, formula (5) has no status in the reduction at all. It is simply what one gets when one universally quantifies a formula whose antecedent is the physical disjunction corresponding to S_1 and whose consequent is the physical disjunction corresponding to S_2. As such, it will be true when $S_1 x \rightarrow S_2 y$ is exceptionless and false otherwise. What does the work of expressing the physical mechanisms whereby n-tuples of events conform, or fail to conform, to $S_1 x \rightarrow S_2 y$ is not formula (5) but the laws which severally relate elements of the disjunction $P_1 \vee P_2 \vee \ldots \vee P_n$ to elements of the disjunction $P^*_1 \vee P^*_2 \vee \ldots \vee P^*_m$. Where there *is* a law which relates an event that satisfies one of the P disjuncts to an event which satisfies one of the P^* disjuncts, the pair of events so related conforms to $S_1 x \rightarrow S_2 y$. When an event which satisfies a P-predicate is not related by law to an event which satisfies a P^*-predicate, that event will constitute an exception to $S_1 x \rightarrow S_2 y$. The point is that none of the laws which effect these several connections need themselves have exceptions in order that $S_1 x \rightarrow S_2 y$ should do so.

To put this discussion less technically: We could, if we liked, *require* the taxonomies of the special sciences to correspond to the taxonomy of physics by insisting upon distinctions between the kinds postulated by the former whenever they turn out to correspond to distinct kinds in the latter. This would *make* the laws of the special sciences exceptionless if the laws of basic science are. But it would also likely loose us precisely the generalizations which we want the special sciences to express. (If economics were to posit as many *kinds* of monetary systems as there are physical realizations of monetary systems, then the generalizations of economics *would* be exceptionless. But, presumably, only vacuously so, since there would be no generalizations left for economists to state. Gresham's law, for example, would have to be formulated as a vast, open disjunction about what happens in monetary system$_1$ or monetary system$_n$ under conditions which would themselves defy uniform characterization. We would not be able to say what happens in monetary systems *tout court* since, by hypothesis, 'is a monetary system' corresponds to no kind of predicate of physics.)

In fact, what we do is precisely the reverse. We allow the generalizations of the special sciences to *have* exceptions, thus preserving the kinds to which the generalizations apply, But since we know that the *physical* descriptions of the members of these kinds may be quite heterogeneous, and since we know that the physical mechanisms which connect the satisfaction of the antecedents of such generalizations to the satisfaction of their consequents may be equally diverse, we expect both that there will be exceptions to the generalizations and that these will be 'explained away' at the level of the reducing science. This is one of the respects in which physics really is assumed to be bedrock science; exceptions to *its* generalizations (if there are any) had better be random, because there is nowhere 'further down' to go in explaining the mechanism whereby the exceptions occur.

This brings us to why there are special sciences at all. Reductionism, as we remarked at the outset, flies in the face of the facts about the scientific institution: the existence of a vast and interleaved conglomerate of special scientific disciplines which often appear to proceed with only the most casual acknowledgment of the constraint that their theories must turn out to be physics 'in the long run'. I mean that the acceptance of this constraint often plays little or no role in the practical validation of theories. Why is this so? Presumably, the reductionist answer must be *entirely* epistemological. If only physical particles weren't so small (if only brains were on the *out*side, where one can get a look at them), *then* we would do physics instead of paleontology (neurology instead of psychology, psychology instead of economics, and so on down). There is an epistemological reply: viz., that even if brains were out where they could be looked *at*, we wouldn't, as things now stand, know what to look *for*. We lack the appropriate theoretical apparatus for the psychological taxonomy of neurological events.

If it turns out that the functional decomposition of the nervous system corresponds precisely to its neurological (anatomical, biochemical, physical) decomposition, then there are only epistemological reasons for studying the former instead of the latter. But suppose that there is no such correspondence? Suppose the functional organization of the nervous system cross-cuts its neurological organization. Then the existence of psychology depends not on the fact that neurons are so depressingly small, but rather on the fact that neurology does not posit the kinds that psychology requires.

I am suggesting, roughly, that there are special sciences not because of the nature of our epistemic relation to the world, but because of the way the world is put together: not all the kinds (not all the classes of things and events about which there are important, counterfactual supporting generalizations to make) are, or correspond to, physical kinds. A way of stating the classical reductionist view is that things which belong to different physical kinds ipso facto can have none of their projectable descriptions in common:[9] that if x and y differ in those descriptions by virtue of which they fall under the proper laws of physics, they must differ in those descriptions by virtue of which they fall under any laws at all. But why should we believe that this is so? Any pair of entities, however different their physical structure, must nevertheless converge in indefinitely many of their properties. Why should there not be, among those convergent properties, some whose lawful interrelations support the generalizations of the special sciences? Why, in short, should not the kind predicates of the special sciences *cross-classify* the physical natural kinds?

Physics develops the taxonomy of its subject matter which best suits its purposes: the formulation of exceptionless laws which are basic in the several senses discussed above. But this is not the only taxonomy which may be required if the purposes of science in general are to be served: e.g., if we are to state such true, counterfactual supporting generalizations as there are to state. So there are special sciences, with their specialized taxonomies, in the business of stating some of these generalizations. If science is to be unified, then all such taxonomies must apply to *the same things*. If physics is to be basic science, then each of these things had better be a physical thing. But it is not further required that the taxonomies which the special sciences employ must themselves reduce to the taxonomy of physics. It is not required, and it is probably not true.

Notes

1. For expository convenience, I shall usually assume that sciences are about events in at least the sense that it is the occurrence of events that makes the laws of a science true. Nothing, however, hangs on this assumption.

2. The version of reductionism I shall be concerned with is a stronger one than many philosophers of science hold, a point worth emphasizing, since my argument will be precisely that it is too strong to get away with. Still, I think that what I shall be attacking is what many people have in mind when they refer to the unity of science, and I suspect (though I shan't try to prove it) that many of the liberalized versions of reductionism suffer from the same basic defect as what I shall take to be the classical form of the doctrine.

3. There is an implicit assumption that a science simply *is* a formulation of a set of laws. I think that this assumption is implausible, but it is usually made when the unity of science is discussed, and it is neutral so far as the main argument of this chapter is concerned.

4. I shall sometimes refer to 'the predicate which constitutes the antecedent or consequent of a law'. This is shorthand for 'the predicate such that the antecedent or consequent of a law consists of that predicate, together with its bound variables and the quantifiers which bind them'.

5. Oppenheim and Putnam (1958) argue that the social sciences probably *can* be reduced to physics assuming that the reduction proceeds via (individual) psychology. Thus, they remark, "in economics, if very weak assumptions are satisfied, it is possible to represent the way in which an individual orders his choices by means of an individual preference function. In terms of these functions, the economist attempts to explain group phenomena, such as the market, to account for collective consumer behavior, to solve the problems of welfare economics, etc." (p. 17). They seem not to have noticed, however, that even if such explanations can be carried through, they would not yield the kind of *predicate-by-predicate* reduction of economics to psychology that Oppenheim and Putnam's own account of the unity of science requires.

   Suppose that the laws of economics hold because people have the attitudes, motives, goals, needs, strategies, etc., that they do. Then the fact that economics is the way it is can be explained by reference to the fact that people are the way that they are. But it doesn't begin to follow that the typical predicates of economics can be reduced to the typical predicates of psychology. Since bridge laws entail biconditionals, P_1 reduces to P_2 only if P_1 and P_2 are at least coextensive. But while the typical predicates of economics subsume (e.g.) monetary systems, cash flows, commodities, labor pools, amounts of capital invested, etc., the typical predicates of psychology subsume stimuli, responses, and mental states. Given the proprietary sense of 'reduction' at issue, to reduce economics to psychology would therefore involve a very great deal more than showing that the economic behavior of groups is determined by the psychology of the individuals that constitute them. In particular, it would involve showing that such notions as *commodity*, *labor pool*, etc., can be reconstructed in the vocabulary of stimuli, responses and mental states and that, moreover, the predicates which affect the reconstruction express psychological kinds (viz., occur in the proper laws of psychology). I think it's fair to say that there is no reason at all to suppose that such reconstructions can be provided; prima facie there is every reason to think that they cannot.

6. This would be the case if higher organisms really are interestingly analogous to general purpose computers. Such machines exhibit to detailed structure-to-function correspondence over time; rather, the function subserved by a given structure may change from instant to instant depending upon the character of the program and of the computation being performed.

7. To rule out degenerate cases, we assume that n is large enough to yield correlations that are significant in the statistical sense.

8. I don't think there is any chance at all that this is true. What is more likely is that type identification for psychological states can be carried out in terms of the 'total states' of an abstract automation which models the organism whose states they are.

9. For the notion of projectability, see Goodman (1965).

References

Goodman, N. (1965). *Fact, Fiction and Forecast*, Indianapolis, Bobbs-Merrill.

Oppenheim, P., and Putnam, H. (1958). "Unity of Science as a Working Hypothesis," in Feigl, H., Scriven, M., and Maxwell, G. (eds.), *Minnesota Studies in the Philosophy of Science*, Minneapolis, University of Minnesota Press, 2: 3–36 [this volume, chapter 22].

Putnam, H. (1960). "Minds and Machines," in Hook, S. (ed.), *Dimensions of Mind*, New York, New York University Press, pp. 138–164.

Chapter 24

Reductionism

Alan Garfinkel

Reduction

Reductionist claims are often expressed by saying that something "is just" (or "is really") something else. The claim that psychology is reducible to physics or chemistry is expressed as the statement that people "are just" physical objects. The claim that actions are reducible to primitive drives is put as the statement that human behavior "is just" the expression of those drives. There are claims that everything "is just" economics, while others say that everything "is just" biology. The claim that thermodynamics is reducible to statistical mechanics is expressed as the claim that a gas "is just" a collection of molecules, and the claim that social laws are reducible to the actions of individuals is expressed as the claim that society "is just" individuals.

The first problem with such claims is understanding what they could possibly mean. What does it mean to say that something "is just" (or "is really") something else?

The examples suggest that what is being claimed is a certain fact about *explanation*, namely, that the phenomena of the first kind are explainable from the theory of the second kind. The reducibility of psychology to physics and chemistry amounts to the claim that conduct can be explained wholly in terms of physical and chemical phenomena. Similarly in each of the other cases, the claim is that the one theory explains the other phenomena.

So reduction, which is on its face an ontological question, is really a question about the possibility of explanation: to say that something is reducible to something else is to say that certain kinds of explanations exist. This can be reconciled with more traditional conceptions, perhaps the best known of which is Quine's "ontological reduction." On his view an ontological reduction has been effected when one realm of discourse has been shown to be eliminable in favor of another:

> We have, to begin with, an expression or form of expression that is somehow troublesome ... But it also serves other purposes that are not to be abandoned. Then we find a way of accomplishing these same purposes through other channels, using other and less troublesome forms of expression. The old perplexities are solved.[1]

So one theory reduces another if it enables us to "accomplish the same purposes" as the other. Reducibility becomes relativized to a set of purposes. But there are some purposes for which almost any theory can replace any other (e.g., in serving as an exercise in penmanship) and other purposes for which nothing else will do. Therefore the question of reducibility turns on what the crucial purposes are, and here Quine

Chapter 2 from *Forms of Explanation* (New Haven, CT: Yale University Press, 1981), pp. 49–74, reprinted by permission of the author and the publisher. Copyright 1981 by Yale University Press. [Ed. note: All internal references in this chapter of the anthology are to *Forms of Explanation*.]

does not really tell us which we should insist on and which we should forgo. His pragmatism takes the purposes on which everything turns to be uncontroversial, given from the outside, or at any rate not themselves problematic. He does not offer a theory of what our purposes should be.

If we supply the missing purpose as explanation, the resulting account of reduction corresponds to our own: one realm of discourse is reducible to another if the reduction theory gives us all the explanatory power of the theory being reduced.

This gives us a criterion for assessing a reduction. Look at the explanations that are possible in the one realm of discourse and see whether we can explain the same phenomena in the other. If we can, the reduction is successful.

It is very important to note that this criterion depends on its being clear what "the same phenomena" are. But often we do not know when one term in one theory and another term in another are referring to the same phenomenon. If psychology speaks of "aggression" as hostility toward imagined castration, and sociobiology speaks of "aggression" as biological territoriality, is this the same phenomenon? It is not clear.

So in order to assess a claim of reduction, we need a notion of when two explanations are explaining the same thing ... In particular we can say that if the reduction is to be successful, the two explanations must have the same *object*. This means that they must be about the same phenomena and also that they must construe the problematic in the same way. Not only must they be talking about the same thing but they must have contrast spaces that line up in the right way. Otherwise the reduction will fail.

This gives us a simple test to apply to reductions: Do their objects correspond? My strategy will be to assess various claims of reduction by studying their objects, especially with respect to the relevant contrast spaces.

Microreduction: The Whole and Its Parts

I want to focus on one particular archetype of reduction: the reduction which is said to hold between a whole and its parts, between an object and the stuff or things which comprise it. In such claims, called *microreductions*, a certain object can be explained as just the sum of its parts. In microreduction the upper level object is explainable by the (lower level) microtheory. Therefore, the upperlevel explanations can in principle be eliminated in favor of the microexplanations.

The classic manifesto of microreduction was the 1958 paper by Oppenheim and Putnam, "Unity of Science as a Working Hypothesis."[2] It laid out seven levels of scientific phenomena. The objects at each level contain as their parts the objects of the next lower level. The level of the biology of the organism has as its objects whole organisms, which are composed of the objects of the next lower level, cells. Cells, in turn, are composed of biochemical molecules, which are in turn composed of atoms. The thesis of the "unity of science" is that each level is reducible to the next lower: organism biology to cell biology, cell biology to biochemistry, biochemistry to physics, and so forth.

But what does *reducible* mean? The notion they use is in some ways like ours. They say that theory A is reducible to theory B if B explains all the observation sentences that A does. This is like our criterion in holding that the successful reduction enables us to recapture explanations. It differs in having a specific notion of what the objects of explanation are: observation sentences. Their use of this notion comes from basic empiricism: a theory is divided into a "theoretical vocabulary" and an "observation vocabulary," with the observation vocabulary confronting experience directly. Because only observation statements had any transtheoretical cash value, if one theory captured all the observation statements of another, it captured all that was worth capturing and hence had achieved a successful reduction.

There are several problems with this view. The first stems from the idea that it is a *sentence*, a piece of syntax, that is the object of explanation. The problem is that looking at sentences will not tell you whether two sentences are talking about the same thing. If a term X appears in theory A, and a term X appears in theory B, and theory B explains all the sentences in which X occurs, is it a successful reduction? It will be only if the two terms X are really the same, that is, if they both *refer* to the same phenomenon. This means that we cannot limit ourselves to talking about the terms in question but must go beyond them to talk about that to which the terms refer, the phenomena themselves.

The second weakness of the positivist approach is the reliance on *observation*. Even if theory B explained all the observation sentences that theory A does, its status as a reduction would be in doubt unless it could also explain the mechanisms and postulated unobservables, the explaining entities, of theory A.[3]

If we negate these two aspects, we arrive at a more realist notion of reduction. This realist version of the Oppenheim-Putnam criterion would then correspond to the one I am proposing: that theory A is reducible to theory B if theory B explains the phenomena previously the province of theory A.

Taking this as our definition of reduction, we can return to the claims of microreduction, the reduction of the upper level to the underlying level, and ask, What reason are we given for thinking that the explanations of each level are reducible to the explanations of the underlying level? The answer is: not much. The authors really did think of it as a "working hypothesis" and were more concerned to evoke a method and show some examples than to give an argued presentation. In fact, arguments in this area seem hard to find. Most reductionists rely on the assertion that the underlying level is "all there really is," or that "there isn't anything but ...," or they warn that the denial of reductionism is somehow "mysterious," a belief in a holistic ectoplasm. Thus the economist Kenneth Arrow writes of reduction in social theory:

> A full characterization of each individual's behavior logically implies a knowledge of group behavior; there is nothing left out. The rejection of the organism approach to social problems has been a fairly complete, and to my mind salutary, rejection of mysticism.[4]

The reductionist's claim, then, is that the lower-level description is somehow all there is; such a description is complete. We can express this as a pair of slogans:

1. for every state, a microstate; and
2. for every microstate, a microexplanation.

In other words the claim is that the microlevel constitutes an *underlying determinism*, a complete causal picture. So far, so good, we think.

Let us suppose that there is indeed such an underlying determinism. To every upper-level state (macrostate) there corresponds a microstate, and for every microstate, there is a microexplanation. The question is, Does this imply that the explanations of the macrolevel are in any sense dispensable or reducible? I will argue that the answer is no.

We need a concrete example to use as a focus for this discussion, and I will use one from population ecology. Suppose we have an ecological system composed of foxes and rabbits. There are periodic fluctuations in the population levels of the two species, and the explanation turns out to be that the foxes eat the rabbits to such a point that there are too few rabbits left to sustain the fox population, so the foxes begin dying off. After a while, this takes the pressure off the rabbits. who then begin to multiply until there is plenty of food for the foxes, who begin to multiply, killing more rabbits, and so forth.

We can construct a simple global model of this process by taking as our basic variables the levels of the fox and rabbit populations:

$X(t) =$ level of fox population at time t.

$Y(t) =$ level of rabbit population at time t.

The main influences on the levels of the populations will be the frequency with which foxes encounter, and eat, rabbits. The number of encounters between foxes and rabbits will clearly be proportional both to the fox level and to the rabbit level. We use as an estimate the product, XY. This frequency of encounter will appear as a positive contribution to the fox level and as a negative contribution to the rabbit level. The fox level is also affected by the number of foxes itself because the more foxes there are, the more competition there is. So the dynamics of the fox level can be represented by the ordinary differential equation

$$\frac{dX}{dt} = aXY - bX,$$

which represents the sum of these two contributions. On the other hand, the rabbit level is determined by the frequency of encounter (negatively) and by the proverbial multiplication of rabbits (positively), so its law is

$$\frac{dY}{dt} = cY - dXY.$$

Jointly, these two determine a two-dimensional ordinary differential equation on the two-dimensional state space of population levels.[5]

Using this law or its ordinary language versions, we can then frame explanations for various phenomena. First of all, there is the basic explanation for the fluctuations which we saw above and various other explanations which derive from it. For example, if the fox population is high, this will place great pressure on the rabbits, and when one of them gets caught and eaten, it is reasonable to say:

The cause of the death of the rabbit was that the fox population was high,

This seems like an acceptable explanation although its form is that of an explanation of a microstate, the death of a rabbit, by appeal to another macrostate, the level of the fox population. Similarly, statements like

The cause of the low level of the rabbit population is the high level of foxes,

involve an explanation of a macrostate by appeal to another macrostate. So these are typical explanations from the upper level. Reductionism tells us that these can be eliminated in terms of microexplanations. Well, *which* ones?

Consider first the case of the explanation of the death of the rabbit. We are told that since this is a microstate we must look on the microlevel for its explanation. What do we see when we look there? Presumably, something like this: Rabbit r, hopping through the field one afternoon, passed closely, too closely, to a tree behind which fox f was lurking and so got eaten. The microexplanation is therefore something like

Rabbit r was eaten because he passed through the capture space of fox f,

because the overall nature of the microlevel is a huge-dimensional determinism, which, given a complete description of all the equations of interaction between individual foxes and individual rabbits (depending on such things as their physiology and reaction times) and given a complete specification of an initial distribution of foxes and rabbits, tells us the individual destiny of every one of them at every future time. Extracting from this mass the data relevant to rabbit r, we learn that, given certain initial positions and other factors, it follows that rabbit r was to pass through the capture space of fox f. This is our microexplanation.

The problem of reductionism is therefore: Do microexplanations such as this enable us to dispense with macroexplanations? This turns on what these explanations are really explanations *of*, in the sense of the previous chapter. When we consider this, we can see that their respective objects do not really correspond. The first explanation, for example, cited the high fox population as the cause of the death of the rabbit, and "the death of the rabbit" was also the micro-object. But this is not really true; the actual object of the microexplanation is not

the death of the rabbit,

but rather

the death of the rabbit at the hands of fox f, at place p, time t, and so on.

The microlevel has an extremely specific object of explanation and consequently an extremely specific antecedent to explain it. But we do not really want to know why the rabbit was eaten by that fox at that time and under those circumstances; we want to know why he was eaten (period). The object of the macroexplanation is why

$$\text{the rabbit was} \begin{Bmatrix} \text{eaten} \\ \text{not eaten} \end{Bmatrix},$$

while all the microexplanation tells us is why

$$\text{the rabbit was eaten} \begin{Bmatrix} \text{by fox at time } t \ldots \\ \text{by some other fox} \ldots \end{Bmatrix}.$$

The microexplanation, therefore, contains much that is irrelevant to why the rabbit got eaten and does not really answer that question at all.

There are several reasons for insisting on the autonomy of the higher-order question of why the rabbit got eaten. Obviously, there are pragmatic considerations recommending it. What the rabbit wants to know is why rabbits get eaten, not why they eaten by specific foxes. It is the higher-order explanation which provides the information that is of value to the rabbit. It is more valuable because if the circumstances had been slightly different, then, although the rabbit would not have been eaten by fox f, he probably (assuming the high fox population) would have been eaten by another fox. The microexplanation does not tell us this and does not tell us how sensitive the outcome is to changes in the conditions. Therefore, it does not tell us what things would have to be otherwise for the rabbit *not* to get eaten.

This difference makes the macro-object superior to the micro-object in several ways. The first is pragmatic. The microexplanation includes data that are irrelevant to the outcome and therefore bury the explanation unrecognizably. It delivers an embarrassment of riches and so is less useful. It also does not lend itself to a certain kind of practical reasoning, which the macroexplanation does. In many cases the point of asking for an explanation of something is that we are interested in eradicating or preventing it. Microexplanations, by their nature, cannot lend themselves to this use.

The difference between the micro- and macroexplanations is not only pragmatic. It centers on the requirement that an explanation tell us *what could have been otherwise*. This requirement has several sources. In addition to the pragmatic factors there are considerations from what could be called the pure theory of causality which suggest such a requirement. Basically, they stem from the idea that a causal explanation has as much to do with what is causally necessary as with what is causally sufficient. This conception of causality is gaining currency, and several contemporary philosophers have proposed an analysis of causation in term of a negative counterfactual, the same kind I have been recommending for "practical" reasons.[6]

These difficulties of the microexplanation are related to the requirement discussed in the previous chapter, that an explanation must have a certain amount of *stability* under perturbations of its conditions. Recall the discussion of the auto accident example: I argued that

auto accident at x, t, . . .

was not a good choice of object of explanation for the auto accident because it was extremely unstable under small perturbations. The crucial point there, as here, is: If things had been otherwise, what would have happened?

In both cases structural factors operate to ensure the stability of the object at the macrolevel. We know that the rabbit started out at place p and did certain things which led to its being eaten. But if it had not done those things, it would have done other things which also would have resulted in its being eaten. This often happens in the explanation of social phenomena. We may explain why a child has certain attitudes by pointing out that it had certain experiences. This teacher said that to them on such-and-such day, they saw such-and-such movie, all of which had the effect of engendering a certain attitude. But if the attitude is relatively important to a society, the means of generating that attitude will not be left to chance; there will be a multiplicity, a *redundancy*, of mechanisms to ensure that the child developed the "right" attitude.

So the causality with which the effect is produced has a strong resiliency. The very fact that the child did not have those experiences calls forth other experiences to do the job of producing the effect. The same is true in the foxes and rabbits case: the very fact that the rabbit did not wander into the capture space of fox f makes it likely that it will be eaten by another fox.

I want to call this "redundant causality." Systems which exhibit redundant causality therefore have, for every consequent Q, a bundle of antecedents (P_i) such that:

1. If any one of the P_i is true, so will be Q.
2. If one P_i should not be the case, some other will.

Obviously, in any system with redundant causality, citing the actual P_i that caused Q will be defective as an explanation. This will apply to many cases in which P_i is the microexplanation.

The motivation of reductionism then becomes clearer. If some structural fact is responsible for a redundant causality producing Q, then, as I said, it will be misleading to cite the P_i which actually occurred as the explanation of Q. But *some* P_i did have to occur. The macroexplanation tells us that some realization or other will be the case to bring about Q but is indifferent as to which. The microexplanation tells us the mechanism by which the macroexplanation operated. The structure gives the *why*, while the microexplanation gives the *how*.

We can see the force behind the reductionist's claim. Without some mechanism or other, without some realization of the effectivity of the structure, it really would be mysterious to talk about the structure's *causing* something. But merely citing the specific mechanism which brought about the effect does not tell us the important fact that had that particular mechanism not occurred, then some other would have, to accomplish the same end.[7] The crucial point here is that the particular mechanism was not necessary for the effect, and therefore it is not a good explanation to cite it as the cause.

And so, even if such underlying determinisms do exist, we need more than them in order to get an explanation. Microreduction is sometimes thought of as an ideal, something that is possible "in theory" though not "in practice." One can then be a reductionist while conceding a "practical" independence. But my claim is stronger than that: the explanations we want simply do not exist at the underlying level. It is not that the microreduction is an impractical ideal, too good to be true, but rather that it is, in a way, too true to be good.

Explanation Seeks Its Own Level

So the fact that something materially "is" something else does not mean that we can reduce the explanations involved.[8] From the point of view of explanation there is a relative independence from the nature of the substrate. A macrostate, a higher level state of the organization of a thing, or a state of the social relations between one thing and another can have a particular realization which, in some sense, "is" that state in this case. But the explanation of the higher order state will not proceed via the micro-explanation of the microstate which it happens to "be." Instead, the explanation will seek its own level, and typically this will not be the level of the underlying substratum. The level on which it occurs will be whatever one has the redundancies and structural factors, that make nontrivial explanation possible.

A number of different approaches to explanation share the assumption that explanation can be liberated from the nature of the substratum. For example, it is one of the fundamental themes of structuralism, characteristic of Saussure's work on sign systems and Lévi-Strauss's analyses of societies. Both try to find elementary structures, binary oppositions, for example, that occur in all different kinds of matter. The explanations given are in terms of the forms themselves and not in terms of the kind of thing which happens to be realizing this form.

It has recently become a theme in the writing of the mathematician René Thom. In an article called "Structuralism and Biology" he writes:

> A knowledge of the fine structure, molecules for a fluid, cells for an animal, is practically irrelevant for understanding the global structure ... of the total system. For instance, the final structure of a theory like Fluid Mechanics does not depend on whether one takes as the basic concept molecules or a continuous fluid.[9]

But the independence of levels of explanation is not limited to structuralists in any narrow sense; it can be found in Aristotle's remark that in explanation it is the form and not the matter that counts, or in Russell's remark that in mathematics we do not know what we are talking about. In each case its role is to license some form of antireductionism. What the particular subject matter is varies from case to case. It may be anything from fluid mechanics, as above, to music. Schoenberg took an anti-reductionist approach to music theory, where the independence of levels of explanation takes the form of an independence of the theory of harmony from the fine structure of the physics of tone:

> Should someone succeed in deriving the phenomena solely from the physical properties of tone and explaining them solely on that basis, then it would hardly matter whether our physical knowledge of the nature of tone is correct or not. It is entirely possible that in spite of an observation falsely construed as fundamental we may, by inference or through intuition, arrive at correct results; whereas it is not at all a proved fact that more correct or better observation would necessarily yield a more correct or better conclusion.[10]

One area in which this kind of antireductionism has been especially important is the question of the reducibility of human activity to biology. Here, reductionism takes the form of a claim that human action "is just" neurophysiology. So in order to assess this claim, we have to ask: Even if the actions have a neurophysiological substratum, will neurophysiology *explain* them?

In the *Phaedo* (99 E ff.), Socrates says no. The reason he gives is that the neurophysiological account ("nerves and bones and sinew"), although presumably true, does not give us an explanation (*aitia*) of human action. A true explanation must inevitably be in terms of *reasons*, not "nerves and bones and sinew." The latter are the necessary medium of any human action, but citing them does not suffice to explain action, because, he says, it does not explain why he does one thing (staying in jail) rather than another (escaping).

Recently, the same kind of independence of explanation has been argued against the identification of mental states with physical states. Hilary Putnam, in a series of papers, argues that mental states cannot be reduced to their material realizations in this or that organism. "Pain," for example, denotes a *functional* state, a relatively high-order property of the organization of a creature. The specific mechanisms which realize pain in one kind of organism (say, with a carbon-based biochemistry) may be very different from the ways that pain is realized in another kind or organism (say, with a silicon-based chemistry), or for that matter, the ways that pain is realized in some artificially created machine. Therefore the explanations which pain enters into (like "he cried out from the pain" or "the wound caused great pain") must be captured on the appropriate level, which in this case means the level of functional organization. It is a mistake, a kind of hyperspecificity, to try to explain this in terms of the specific mechanisms which realize pain in this particular creature. Hence statements about pain (or preferences) in various machines "are not logically equivalent to statements concerning the physical-chemical composition of these machines."[11] These explanations seek their own level.

Freeing explanation from the substrate produces new strategies of explanation, strategies which depend on the autonomy of levels. Perhaps the most sweeping approach of this sort is the one which the mathematician Thom has proposed as a new model for scientific explanation. He begins by rejecting reductionism:

> [The] ancient dream of the atomist—to reconstruct the universe and all its properties in one theory of combination of elementary particles and their interactions—has scarcely beon started (e.g., there is no satisfactory theory of the liquid state of matter).

As an alternative program, he suggests:

> If the biologist is to progress and to understand living processes, he cannot wait until physics and chemistry can give him a complete theory of all local phe-

nomena found in living matter; instead, he should try only to construct a model that is locally compatible with known properties of the environment and to separate off the geometricoalgebraic structure ensuring the stability of the system, without attempting a complete description of living matter. This methodology goes against the present dominant philosophy that the first step in revealing nature must be the analysis of the system and its ultimate constituents. We must reject this primitive and almost cannibalistic delusion about knowledge, that an understanding of something requires first that we dismantle it, like a child who pulls a watch to pieces and spreads out the wheels in order to understand the mechanism.[12]

Against Reduction

What all these approaches have in common is a style of explanation in which explanations of the upper-level phenomena proceed independently of any reduction. The idea is that no matter what the substratum turns out to be, we can proceed independently to construct upper-level explanations. So far, this is a fairly modest claim. It asserts only a declaration of independence for explanations. Most sober antireductionists stop at this assertion.

I want to make a stronger claim: that in many cases, the microlevel is inadequate, and we therefore *must* construct upper-level explanations. For this stronger claim, we need more than examples and plausibility arguments. My argument for the indispensability of upper-level explanations rests on a conception of what an explanation is.

In the second section of this chapter we saw one basic argument against microreduction: that microreduction fails as an explanation because its object is too specific. This hyperconcreteness, for example, in choosing

the death of the rabbit at the hands of fox f at place x at time $t, \ldots$

as the object of explanation has the consequence that the resulting explanation gives us a false picture of the sensitivity of the situation to change. It suggests that, had the specific cause not been the case, the effect would not have occurred. This is false in such cases because there is a redundant causality operating, the effect of which is to ensure that many *other* states, perturbations of the original microcause, would have produced the same result. Microreductions cannot take account of this redundancy and to that extent cannot replace upper-level explanations.

Consider the case of reducing human action to neurophysiology. Here reductionism says that the action of raising my arm "is just" the physical movement of the arm (the underlying state), together with its microexplanation (the neurophysiological causes of the movement of the arm). But the problem with such an identification is that we do not *want* an explanation of why my arm moved in *exactly* that way. Suppose my arm moved in some specific trajectory T. Then the underlying determinism explains why my arm moved precisely in trajectory T. But any such explanation will contain much that is irrelevant to why I moved my arm because the object

I moved my arm

is much more general, much more stable, than the object

my arm moved in trajectory T.

My arm did not have to move in exactly that trajectory for it to have been the same action, and thus an explanation of that specific trajectory will be subject to the same objections as the explanations we saw earlier of why the rabbit was eaten by *that* fox or why I had *that* (very) auto accident. In each case the stability of the upperlevel object under perturbations of the microstate demands an autonomous level of explanation appropriate to its own object. If, for example, the explanation of why my arm moved is that I was shaking hands with someone to whom I was being introduced, this explanation gives us what the underlying neurophysiology does not: a conception of what the allowable variation in the circumstances might have been.

This is worth examining in greater detail. In each of these cases there is an underlying substratum with its own local determinism, the principles that explain the causal succession of the microstates. For each microstate Y_0, we have another microstate X_0 and a microexplanation of Y_0 in terms of X_0. Such explanations are deficient in being hyperspecific. The occurrence of the specific microstate X_0 was not necessary for the occurrence of the qualitative outcome, and hence it is counter explanatory to include it in the explanation.

But, of course, not *all* perturbations of the underlying state produce the same outcome. *Some* will result in a quaitatively different outcome. It is crucial for the upper-level explanation that we get some account of what things really are relevant to the outcome. The underlying determinism also fails to supply this. It has no account of the sensitive aspects of the causal connection.

And that is, after all, what we really want to know: what is going to make a difference? Along what dimensions is the outcome *un*stable, that is, sensitive to variations in the underlying state?

We can imagine the space of the substratum as underlying the whole process. We have a complete set of microstates and a principle of microexplanation, V, which explains the microstate Y_0 in terms of X_0:

$$X_0 \overset{V}{\hookrightarrow} Y_0.$$

The rabbit was eaten by fox $f (= Y_0)$ because it was at a certain place, time, and so on $(= X_0)$. For most X_0, this evolution is smooth; small changes in X_0 do not make for qualitative changes. But at certain critical points, small perturbations *do* make a difference and will result in the rabbit's wandering out of the capture space of the fox. These critical points mark the boundaries of the regions of smooth change.

They partition the underlying space into equivalence classes within which the map is stable. The crucial thing we want to know is how this set of critical points is embedded in the substratum space, for that will tell us what is really relevant and what is not. Therefore, what is necessary for a true explanation is an account of how the underlying space is partitioned into basins of irrelevant differences, separated by ridge lines of critical points[13]

Consider an example. A car is stopped at a traffic light. The light changes, and the car proceeds. Now try to visualize this episode purely from the point of view of the underlying physics. The picture looks like this. We had a steady, stable distribution of mass and energy. Then there was a small change in the energy distribution (the light changing), a variation which was, from the physical point of view, negligible. This tiny variation then produced an enormous effect: a large mass was set into motion.

In other words the underlying physics gives us a physical relation:

$$\begin{Bmatrix} \text{red} \\ \text{green} \end{Bmatrix} \text{light} \Longrightarrow \text{car} \begin{Bmatrix} \text{stops} \\ \text{goes} \end{Bmatrix}.$$

Along most of its parameters this is a stable relationship. Small changes in the intensity of the light or its shape will not produce a qualitatively different outcome. There is, however, one dimension along which it is unstable: the red-green boundary.

The fact that there is such an instability means that we cannot simply cite the underlying physics as the explanation for the car's stopping or going. What we must supply in addition is an account of why these instabilities occur; this is something which is imposed on the underlying substratum not something which arises from it.

Discontinuities and instabilities mean that purely mechanical explanation fails at that point, and we must show why the qualitative outcome occurred by showing how the upper level partitions the underlying set of physical signals into two equivalence classes, "red light" and "green light." All red lights are equivalent to all others, and, conversely, all red lights are radically different from all green lights despite their physical similarity. So the underlying space is partitioned into equivalence classes within which differences do not make a difference but across which differences *do* make a difference.

This means that there is some kind of discontinuity in the underlying space. In the natural topology on the space of physical signals, the map from the signal input to the action output is discontinuous on the boundary between red and green.[14]

The resulting picture of qualitative changes intervening in an underlying determinism is a very attractive and useful one. Thom and his followers have already applied it to physical examples such as phase transitions, for example, liquid to gas, where the smooth relationships among pressure, volume, and temperature become discontinuous at the boundaries which mark the transitions from one phase to the other. Another example of Thom's is embryological development, in which each phase of development features smooth and continuous change, punctuated by symmetry-breaking changes that introduce new morphologies, new qualitative stages.

It is especially tempting to try to apply this picture to the development and change of large-scale social forms. Feudalism, mercantilism, the capitalism of small traders, and the capitalism of oligopolies would become phases in the morphological development of society, separated by revolutionary (sudden or gradual) phase transitions.

It is difficult at this point to say whether this picture has any real content. The phases of social history seem to lend themselves to this kind of dynamical description. Marx spoke of revolution as like the change from water to steam. Henry Adams, fascinated with Gibbs phase rule, which limits the number and kinds of phase changes that can occur in physical systems, made analogous claims about the phases in the development of Western thought (see "The Rule of Phase Applied to History" in his *The Degradation of the Democratic Dogma*).

It seems possible that such a program, a qualitative dynamics of history, can be carried out, perhaps even far enough to satisfy the conjecture of Thomas Pynchon:

> If tensor analysis is good enough for turbulence, it ought to be good enough for history. There ought to be nodes, critical points ... there ought to be super-derivatives of the crowded and insatiate flow that can be set equal to zero and these critical points found ... 1904 was one of them.[15]

To summarize, we began this discussion by considering the nature of reduction as a general claim about explanations. Specifically, we considered the claims of microreduction, that the underlying level is in some sense "all there really is." The notion of contrast spaces and the related concept of the object of explanation was then brought to bear: Do the upper-level theory and the would-be reduction have the same object of explanation? My answer was no. They generally have distinct objects; this, in turn, means that for certain basic purposes the underlying level cannot replace the upper-level theory.

I now want to extend the discussion by considering a very special class of cases of reductionism, the discussion of which takes up the rest of this work. It is the class of reductions in which the underlying level is *atomistic*, that is, in which the upper level is an aggregate of microindividuals, whose interaction is supposed to produce the upper-level phenomena.

Atomism

Let us therefore consider microreductions in which the underlying level is a collection of *atoms*. The term "atom" is meant here not in the narrow sense but as including all cases in which there is an aggregation of many similar individual entities, with the upper level said to arise from their interaction.

In such cases the overall structure appears as follows. We have, on the one hand, the atoms. Each atom has a nature, a possibility-space which is taken as initially given. Then we imagine many of these atoms being collected into the overall system, so that the possibility-space of the total system is the sum (the Cartesian product) of the possibility-spaces of the atomic constituents.

As a general style of explanation, atomism dates from Leucippus and Democritus. Aristotle criticizes atomism in the *De Generatione* and in the *Metaphysics*.[16] In its modern form it appeared as methodological doctrine in the seventeenth century. Most explicit was Hobbes, who based his political philosophy on atomism as a method of knowledge, a philosophy of science: "It is necessary that we know the things that are to be compounded before we can know the whole compound, (for) everything is best understood by its constitutive causes."[17] It received a tremendous impetus from the work of Newton, whose derivation of the elliptical orbits of the planets stands as one of the great paradigms of atomist reductionism. He showed that, given two "atoms," in this case, gravitational mass-points, with an individual "nature," given by the laws of motion and the law of universal gravitation, the overall system of elliptical orbits could be deduced and thereby explained.

This reduction served as the (conscious or unconscious) paradigm for much of the intellectual life of the seventeenth and eighteenth centuries. It had a tremendous impact even on social theory, but its influence was very broad. It is hard for us to imagine the force of its impact. The basic form of his explanation became the ideal toward which all explanation strived. We have nothing in the modem era to compare it with; no discovery or theory has spread to other fields or captured the general imagination the way Newton did.[18]

My interest here is in atomism as it functions in social theory, that is, in the doctrines of *individualism*. But I do not mean to suggest that individualism in social theory is simply the result of the application of the Newtonian paradigm. For one thing, this would be historically inaccurate. Hobbes's *Leviathan* was published in 1651, Newton's *Principia* in 1687 . But more important, Hobbes did not merely take a picture from physics and apply it to society. His atomism is as much a social conception as a natural one. Conceiving the social world as a collection of independent individuals became possible in this period because, for the first time, society itself came to have that structure. The breakdown of feudal socioeconomic forms and relations and the rise of individual entrepreneurs, dependent on and responsible to themselves only, produced a society which corresponded much more closely to the atomistic picture than previous societies had. The conception of a collection of atomized individuals expressed well the life form of this new capitalist class, for whom the old, feudal state forms and relations appeared as holistic entities imposed antagonistically on the pattern of their individual activities.

But as Hobbes saw it, individualism at its heart is really a very general kind of explanatory frame, much more general than simply a social or political doctrine. It is a deep methodological principle, from which economic individualism or political individualism emerges as a special case. What these individualisms have in common is their form: that there is an upper level possibility-space which "is" the sum of a set of individual possibility-spaces each with its own individual dynamic.

The general question I want to raise about such reductions is as follows. Is the overall possibility-space really just the sum of N copies of an individual space? Or are there, on the other hand, hidden presuppositions of a structural nature?

The essence of the criterion [for answering such questions] is to see what combinations of individual possibilities are jointly possible. If any combination of individual possibilities *is* jointly possible, we have a true case of reducibility. But in the typical case these generalized counterfactual conditionals (e.g., what if everyone had property P?) fail, and then we may infer that there are hidden structural presuppositions. In such cases a simpleminded atomism will fail, and we will have to focus on the structural presuppositions which are making the explanation possible.

This basic strategy is the foundation for what I will be doing in the rest of this work. I will be looking at a variety of examples of individualism in social theory and finding in each case hidden structural presuppositions. The nature of those presuppositions rules out the reductionist program in social theory.

But before going on to talk about social theory, I want first to discuss a case of "individualism" in natural science, one which is often held up as a paradigm for social individualism: the case of the reduction of the thermodynamics of gases to the statistical mechanics of the molecules which comprise it. This example is interesting in its own right but also as an example of certain anti-individualist principles that I will be using later on.

It was hailed as a great victory of mechanist reductionism when Boltzmann and others succeeded in deriving the laws governing the global properties of gases (temperature, pressure, volume) from a set of assumptions that amounted to postulating that the gas consisted of a large number of individual Newtonian molecules.

I think that the philosophical significance of this reduction has been misunderstood and that, when examined in detail, it does not support the kinds of claims that philosophers have made on its behalf. Here I want to look at that reduction as a paradigm for individualism, to see what kind of individualism it really is.

The gas is presented to us globally as an extended substance with various macroproperties: pressure, volume, and temperature. The most important law on this macrolevel is the Boyle-Charles law

$$PV = kT,$$

where P is the pressure of the gas, V is the volume, and T is the temperature (k is a constant). For the microlevel assume first that the gas is composed of tiny, hard, independent molecules; these are the "individuals." Assume further that these molecules collide with one another and with the walls of the box in a way describable by standard Newtonian mechanics. This is the microlevel. We will also need some connecting principles ("bridge laws") which enable us to identify P, V, and T with constructs on the microlevel. (For example, T is identified with the average kinetic energy of the gas molecules.) Having done all this, we can derive the Boyle-Charles law from the statistical theory of the behavior of the ensemble of molecules.

But there are some complications in this derivation that are important for our purposes. So let us consider it in detail, following a classic source, Nagel's *Structure of Science*. Nagel proceeds by postulating a microlevel of tiny Newtonian molecules and observes:

> A further assumption must be introduced ... that the probability of a molecule's occupying an assigned phase cell is the same for all molecules and is equal to the probability of a molecule's occupying any other phase cell and (subject to certain qualifications involving among other things the total energy of the system) the probability that one molecule occupies a phase cell is independent of the occupation of that cell by any other molecule.[19]

Let us set out carefully Nagel's independence assumptions. The key concept is that of a phase cell, a region in the state-space of a molecule, the product of a location interval with a velocity interval. Thus at every point in time every molecule is in one phase cell or another. If we represent such a phase cell by (X, V), Nagel's independence assumptions can be put this way:

> 1. For all molecules a, b, and all intervals (X, V), probability $[a\varepsilon(X, V)] = $ probability $[b\varepsilon (X, V)]$.

This assumption is unobjectionable; it postulates a homogeneity among the molecules. The others are:

> 2. For all molecules a, and intervals (X, V), (X', V'), probability $[a\varepsilon(X, V)] = $ probability $[a\varepsilon(X', V')]$.
> 3. For all molecules a, b, and intervals (X, V), probability $[b\varepsilon(X, V)]$ is independent of the probability $[a\varepsilon(X, V)]$.

Both of these are false. They are invalidated by those things that Nagel refers to as "certain qualifications involving among other things the total energy of the system." Let us see what those "qualifications" are.

First and foremost is *conservation of energy*. Obviously, energy must be conserved in all transactions affecting the gas or else PV could decrease relative to T if, for example, heat energy were allowed to dissipate. So energy must be conserved. But the total energy of the gas is the sum of the kinetic energies of the particles:

$$E = \tfrac{1}{2}(m_1 v_1{}^2 + \ldots + m_n v_n{}^2).$$

Assuming for convenience that all the masses have value 1, we get

$$(v_1{}^2 + \ldots + v_n{}^2) = \text{constant}.$$

This flatly contradicts assumption 3 above because you cannot say, "Pick n numbers at random, independently, but the sum of their squares must be a given constant." The overall requirement of conservation of energy, then, violates the independence of the "individuals," the molecules of the gas.

Assumption 2 is also false (even if we add the requirement that the intervals be the same size), for it is violated by the standard assumption of a normal distribution of velocities.

The failure of these independence assumptions tells us that we do not really have a case of a global property arising as a simple aggregate of independent individuals. There is, to be sure, a collection of individuals (the gas molecules) with an individual nature given by Newtonian mechanics, according to which they are essentially small elastic particles. But the properties of the gas, like the Boyle-Charles law, do not arise simply from this individual nature. We must make, in addition, strong assumptions about the *collective* possibilities of the system, assumptions which are imposed on the individual nature and do not in any sense follow from it. Their effect is exactly like the effect of the kinematical conditions discussed earlier: to restrict sharply the a priori possibilities of the system.

Because the effect of such additional assumptions is a reduction of the dimensions of the problem (a reduction in the degrees of freedom), we may expect that explanations taking place in the presence of such assumptions can take a greatly simplified form. In the foxes and rabbits example, the local equations were also of huge dimension. But we knew that on the global level all that is relevant to the level of the two populations are their previous levels. There the imposed kinematical condition tells us in effect: forget about the individual foxes and rabbits; especially, forget about differences among them; they are all irrelevant. Any state in which there are N foxes and M rabbits is "the same" as any other.[20]

Here too the passage to the statistical point of view, renouncing the possibility of explaining individual differences among the molecules, is the result of these imposed structural presuppositions.

In each case the test that brought out the nontrivial sociology was the formation of a generalized contrary-to-fact conditional, posed as a question:

If the rabbit had not been at x, t, would it have avoided being eaten?

Could everyone in the class have gotten an A?

Could all the molecules have velocity v?

In each case the answer is no. Generalizing this, we can formulate the principle: *Whenever a global property is not simply a sum of N individual properties (a fact revealed by the test above), the explanation of that global property will involve structural presuppositions.*

This idea, that the reduction of thermodynamics is not really to an "individualistic" level, is not widely recognized; in fact, I have been able to find it in only one treatment, A. I. Khinchin's excellent *Mathematical Foundations of Statistical Mechanics*. He develops there the notion of something's being a *component* of a mechanical system, which corresponds basically to what we have been calling an "individual." Suppose $E(x_1, \ldots, x_n)$ is the total energy of a system, and suppose further that E can be represented "as a sum of two terms E_1 and E_2, where the first term depends on some (not all) of the dynamical coordinates, and the second term depends on the remaining coordinates" (p. 38). We can therefore write $E = E_1 + E_2$, where

$$E_1 = E_1(x_1, \ldots, x_k),$$

$$E_2 = E_2(x_{k+1}, \ldots, x_n).$$

"In such a case we agree to say that the set ... of the dynamical coordinates of the given system is decomposed into two components."

In other words, in such a case we have the global property "energy" expressible as the sum of two independent individual properties, the energies of the two components. Now it is natural to think, reductionistically, that the molecules of the gas are its components in this sense, that is, that the total energy of the gas is the sum of the independent energies of the molecules. But there is a paradox here. Although this presentation assumes the independence of the energies of the particles, the assumptions of conservation of energy and the normal distribution of velocities absolutely require that the particles interact energetically! Khinchin writes:

> The statistical mechanics bases its method precisely on a possibility of such an exchange of energy between various particles constituting the matter. However, if we take the particles constituting the given physical system to be its components in the above defined sense [i.e., the individuals], we are excluding the possibility of any energetical interaction between them. Indeed, if the Hamiltonian function, which expresses the energy of our system, is a sum of functions each depending only on the dynamic coordinates of a single particle (and representing the Hamiltonian function of this particle), then, clearly, the whole system of equations [describing the overall dynamics of the system] splits into component systems each of which describes the motion of some separate particle and is not connected in any way with other particles. Hence the energy of each particle, which is expressed by its Hamiltonian function, appears as an integral of equations of motion, and therefore remains constant.[21]

In other words, because the sum of the energies is constant, if the particles really were independent, the individual energies would have to be constant too! But this is absurd, and so we must deny the fact that the total energy is simply the sum of the N independent individual energies. He continues immediately:

> The serious difficulty so created is resolved by the fact that we can consider particles of matter as only approximately isolated energetical components. There is no doubt that a precise expression for the energy of the system must contain also terms which depend simultaneously on the energy of several particles, and which assure the possibility of an energetical interaction between the particles (from a mathematical point of view, prevent the splitting of the system into systems referring to single particles).[22]

What Khinchin is saying here is what I am claiming about such individualisms in general. The "individuals" are not really separable (they are "only approximately isolated") and structural presuppositions are at work, so that the real microlevel consists of a set of individuals together with a nontrivial sociology.

The interaction effects, which are *quantitatively* negligible for the Boyle-Charles law, are nevertheless qualitatively important for under standing it. Moreover, as the gas begins to get highly compressed, these interaction effects become significant even quantitatively, and the Boyle-Charles law no longer holds. Thus, changes in certain parameters can change the structural conditions....

Notes

1. W. V. Quine, *Word and Object* (Cambridge: MIT Press, 1960), p. 260.
2. In H. Feigel, M. Scriven, and G. Maxwell, eds., *Minnesota Studies in the Philosophy of Science*, vol. 2 (Minneapolis: University of Minnesota Press, 1955) [reprinted here].
3. For this point see Richard Boyd, "Realism, Undetermination and a Causal Theory of the Evidence," *Noûs* 7 (1973): 1, and his *Realism and Scientific Epistemology* (New York: Cambridge University Press unpublished).
4. "Mathematical Models in the Social Sciences" in M. Brodbeck, ed., *Readings in the Philosophy of the Social Sciences* (New York: Macmillan, 1968), p. 641.
5. This is called the *Lotka-Volterra* equation. The classic sources are A. J. Lotka, *Elements of Mathematic Biology* (Baltimore: Williams and Wilkins, 1925), and V. Volterra, *Leçons sur la théorie mathématique de la lutte pour la vie* (Paris: Gauthier-Villars, 1931). Two contemporary treatments are Braun, *Differential Equations and Their Applications* (New York: Springer-Verlag, 1975), and E. C. Pielou, *An Introduction*

to *Mathematical Ecology* (New York: Wiley-Interscience, 1977). These works present the relevant biological and mathematical reasoning but do not draw philosophical conclusions.

6. See the discussion on p. 163 [of *Forms of Explanation* (New Haven: Yale University Press, 1981)].

7. Such systems act as if they are goal directed because, should one means to the end be blocked, the system will shift to an alternative.

8. It follows that the "is" of material identity is not the "is" of reduction.

9. In C. H. Waddington, ed., *Towards a Theoretical Biology* (Edinburgh: Edinburgh University Press, 1972), p. 78.

10. A. Schoenberg, *Theory of Harmony* (Berkeley: University of California Press, 1978), p. 42.

11. "The Mental Life of Some Machines," p. 420. A good account of anti-reductionism in the philosophy of mind can be found in W. A. Wimsatt, "Reductionism, Levels of Organization, and the Mind-Body Problem," in G. Globus, *Brain and Mind* (New York: Plenum, 1976).

12. *Structural Stability and Morphogenesis* (New York: W. A. Benjamin, 1975), p. 159.

13. This is the basic picture of Thom's *catastrophe theory*. See his *Structural Stability and Morphogenesis* for an account of catastrophes. Two good works on the mathematical foundations are M. Golubitsky and V. Guillemin, *Stable Mappings and Their Singularities* (New York: Springer-Verlag, 1973), and Y. C. Lu, *Singularity Theory and an Introduction to Catastrophe Theory* (New York: Springer-Verlag, 1976). A good popular account can be found in A. Woodcock and M. Davis, *Catastrophe Theory* (E. P. Dutton: New York, 1978). The basic picture stems ultimately from Poincaré's contribution to the problem of the stability of the solar system, for which see R. Abraham and J. Marsden, *Foundations of Mechanics* (Reading, Mass.: Benjamin/Cummings, 1978).

14. This is very much in the spirit of Thom. In his view every underlying space is stratified into regions within which there are no qualitative changes. The regions are separated by a boundary, called the catastrophe set, across which changes in parameters produce qualitative changes in the form of the outcome. The catastrophe set is just the set of singularities of the underlying map.

15. *Gravity's Rainbow* (New York: Viking Press, 1973), p. 451.

16. Vide *De Gen* I and *Met.* 1071 b 33.

17. *English Works of Thomas Hobbes*, vol. 1, p. 67; vol. 2, p. xiv (citation from Lukes, *Individualism*, p. 110).

18. Compare it, e.g., to the theory of relativity, whose cultural impact, so far, is limited to certain undergraduates who now think they have Einstein's blessing for thinking that "everything is relative" (and to whom it is useful to point that the fundamental postulate of the theory is that the speed of light is absolute).

19. E. Nagel, *The Structure of Science* (New York: Harcourt Brace, 1961), p. 344.

20. Well, *almost* any. We typically neglect statistically freakish distributions (e.g., all the foxes in one corner) which would invalidate the law. We suppose Maxwell's demon not to be at work.

21. A. I. Khinchin, *The Mathematical Foundations of Statistical Mechanics*, trans. G. Gamow (New York: Dover, 1949), p. 18.

22. Ibid.

Part II

Section 1

The Philosophy of Physics

J.D. Trout

Among the special sciences that philosophers have discussed, physics has enjoyed a favored position. In part this is because physics is regarded as the "basic" science; its subject matter includes the fundamental elements that make up our universe. If materialism is correct, then physics studies the phenomena that compose the entire proprietary domain of every other science, from molecular chemistry and geology to economics and cosmology. More important, the favored status of physics derives from its notable predictive and explanatory successes, compared to those of the other special sciences. We can have no better grounds for confidence in the methods and practices of a discipline than its actual production of instrumentally and explanatorily reliable theories.

Historically, the relationship between physics and philosophy has been exercised in two ways, in philosophical discussions of the *methods* of physics, and in the interaction between substantial views in physics (about, say, the nature of matter, cause, space, and time) on the one hand, and traditional philosophical doctrines regarding these phenomena on the other. We will be concerned primarily with topics of the second sort. Developments in two areas of physics have been particularly influential in philosophy: quantum mechanics and the physics of space-time. The present selections illustrate the variety of philosophical and scientific responses to these developments. The reader without a substantial background in physics or mathematics may find parts of the following essays dauntingly technical. But don't be daunted. The articles reprinted here (engaging philosophical issues such as causation, underdetermination, and conventionality) retain their novelty and force even when the reader is not in a position to appreciate those parts of the literature that are appropriately formal. Indeed, many of the central conceptual problems in physics are distinctive for the ease with which they can be depicted in homey illustrations and thought experiments, a technique that Einstein and others used with great facility. At the same time, the technically sophisticated reader will find reflected in these articles the standards of formal rigor that practitioners have come to expect in their own fields.

In part I of this anthology, we find one powerful argument in favor of an empiricist conception of scientific theories. Any claim about unobservable phenomena is underdetermined by all possible observational evidence. Thus, for any domain, it is always possible to construct infinitely many different "empirically equivalent" theories, theories that contradict each others' claims about unobservables but that all serve equally well as predictors of observable phenomena; here, no "crucial experiment" can help the scientist to decide between such theories. Therefore, the empiricist concludes, we have no knowledge of unobservable phenomena; indeed, such knowledge is impossible.

Although empiricists appealed to the impotence of crucial experiments in such cases in order to defend the claim that knowledge of unobservable phenomena is impossible, they were not, of course, suggesting that in practice scientists remain equally committed to all empirically equivalent theories. Scientists do decide between competing theories, and any adequate account of scientific practice must explain this fact. Empiricists reasoned that, since observational evidence underdetermines any particular theory, theory choice must be determined by factors that are fundamentally "extra-theoretical." These "pragmatic" features of a theory include simplicity, a priori plausibility, notational convenience, and so on. Any or all of these considerations may cause us to favor one theory over its rivals, but according to the traditional empiricist, such choices are recommended by prudence or convenience, not by the evidence.

In space-time physics, the issue of the conventionality of theoretical choices is raised most acutely in disputes about the large-scale structure of space. The selection by Reichenbach represents an empiricist application of the underdetermination argument to our understanding of the geometrical features of the universe. Reichenbach argues that our choice of a particular geometry by which to depict the nature of space is a matter of convention, not forced on us by the "intrinsic" nature of space itself, if there is such a nature.

Our philosophical analysis must be informed by a few basic mathematical and physical concepts. For the purposes of our discussion, space has two general sorts of properties. First, space has certain *topological* properties. The most important of these is *continuity*; that is, space can be subdivided in such a way that every point has a "neighborhood" that, no matter how many times it is subdivided or reduced, contains an infinite number of other points. Other topological features include *dimensionality, connectivity, and orientability.* Second, space has certain *geometrical* properties. Unlike topology, which depends only on the continuity of space, geometry depends on features such as size and shape. For example, there is a shortest path between any two points, and distances and angles between those points can be defined.

Until about 1915, most physicists and mathematicians believed that our universe had a metric structure constrained by the rules of Euclidean geometry. But with the earlier proliferation of non-Euclidean geometries and with the advent of general relativity, physicists were in a position to explore alternative possible characterizations of the metric of real space, characterizations that permit the construction of triangles whose interior angles sum to greater than 180 degrees, and that prohibit the construction of parallel lines. Descended from these explorations are modern theories that permit a metric structure that can vary from place to place (and from time to time).

Experimental and theoretical practices in astronomy and cosmology require that we calculate the size of objects or measure the distances of regions in space. Reichenbach parlays this fact into an interesting and potent argument for conventionalism. Suppose we take two measuring rods of equal length and transport them by different routes to a distant place, where they are once again laid down next to one another and determined to be of equal length. Now, if universal forces enlarged the two measuring rods—say, doubling their departure length—it would be impossible to detect the increase; after all, universal forces operate on all bodies in the same way, so any other measuring rod transported to detect the difference would also have doubled in length. Reichenbach argues that if we are to avoid the conclusion that nothing can be consistently measured, we must adopt a convention: The rods will be regarded as equal in length when they are in different places.

Scientific conventions are ratified by what Reichenbach calls "coordinative definitions." Coordinative definitions relate concepts to objects. In the case of the measuring rod, Reichenbach says, "A physical structure is coordinated to the concept unit of length." Either tacitly or explicitly, we stipulate the relation between concept and object (or theory and evidence), and thus coordinative definitions are analytic. It is by conventional means, bred by underdetermination and required by practice, that the mechanism of measurement (the measuring rod) is assigned a length.

In its initial formulation, Reichenbach's underdetermination argument makes no mention of the particular topology and metric structure of the space through which the measuring rods travel, so it may be appropriate to assume that Reichenbach intended his argument to hold at least under the Minkowski ("flat space-time") metric, according to which the metric properties of space are not influenced by the distribution of matter, energy, and momentum. The argument would therefore appear to hold for the flat space presupposed by classical physics and for the flat space-time of special relativity.

Reichenbach contends that the underdetermination argument for conventionality can be extended to address the choice of a metric for the representation of the large-scale structure of space. To illustrate the generality of the underdetermination strategy, Reichenbach proposes the following theorem: "Given a geometry G' to which the measuring instruments conform, we can imagine a universal force F that affects the instruments in such a way that the actual geometry is an arbitrary geometry G, while the observed deviation from G is due to a universal deformation of the measuring instruments." The same strategy is employed elsewhere in Reichenbach's work to argue that our choice of a topology of space is every bit as conventional as our selection of a metric. Different topologies for space-time can "save the phenomena" —that is, represent equally well the observable features of space—provided that we make appropriate revisions in our metric.[1]

Reichenbach was able to avail himself of this particular defense of conventionalism only because he recognized, long before many of his colleagues, the holistic nature of hypothesis confirmation. Hypotheses are normally tested in groups (as when, in this case, the hypothesis that space has such-and-such topological characteristics gets tested along with the hypothesis that it has such-and-such an intrinsic metric). The failure of a hypothesis to conform to predicted values, therefore, could result either from the falsity of the tested hypothesis *or* from the falsity of the other, "auxiliary" assumption.[2]

In "The Epistemology of Geometry," Clark Glymour addresses directly the source of Reichenbach's conventionalism. Glymour contends that underdetermination arguments would be decisive only if the empirically equivalent theories are also equally well tested. But they are not. On an appropriate account of confirmation, surviving theories that are better tested than their rivals are also better confirmed. Glymour constructs an instance of just such an alternative, "empirically equivalent" theory. Suppose you are teaching high school physics, and someone in your class states both that he has arrived at an alternative to Newtonian mechanics and that there is no reason to select Newtonian theory over this empirically equivalent rival. According to the rival, "there are two distinct quantities, gorce and morce; the sum of gorce and morce acts exactly as Newtonian force does. Thus the sum of gorce and morce acting on a body is equal to the mass of the body times its acceleration, and so on."

But is there really no reason to prefer Newtonian mechanics in this case? Glymour points out that the student's theory and the Newtonian theory have the same observational consequences, but the rival theory makes an *additional* claim—that Newtonian force is the sum of two distinct quantities, gorce and morce—a proposed distinction for which there is no evidence. If we sign on to the methodological principle that we should prefer a theory with fewer untested hypotheses to a theory with more untested hypotheses, then the natural thing to conclude in such cases, Glymour says, is that Newton's theory is to be preferred. Glymour then presents several reasons for thinking that conformity with this principle is itself evidential, not merely a pragmatic feature of theory choice.

Three aspects of Glymour's position are especially significant here. First, Glymour's considerations about the quality and frequency of testing may well be evidential, and thus two theories could be at once empirically equivalent and *evidentially distinguishable*. This result would undermine Reichenbach's position. As we saw in our earlier discussion, Reichenbach's chief motivation for conventionalism derived from his conviction that it is impossible to construct observationally equivalent space-time theories that are evidentially distinguishable.

Second, in his independently important account of confirmation and evidence, Glymour stops short of saying that real, causal features of the world constrain the number and kind of metrics that we can select, making our choices largely nonconventional. Nor does he state that the theory's relation to these features of the world can explain why certain results constitute "better evidence" for or a "reason for preferring" one theory rather than another. Some realists, however, have argued that sophisticated empiricist attempts to treat "preference principles" as purely pragmatic are bound to fail; pragmatic judgments (such as those of simplicity) in fact depend on further, theoretical commitments. Considerations of simplicity are indeed pragmatic, the realist might contend, but they are not *merely* pragmatic. A theory's simplicity, then, may be a reason for selecting one theory over rival, less simple theories. But once understood in realist terms, theoretical properties like simplicity constitute reasons for thinking that a particular theory *is true*.

Third, Glymour does *not* argue that our choice of a metric (or of a topology, for that matter) for space is in *no* way conventional; instead, he contends only that the geometry of space is not radically underdetermined in the way envisioned by Reichenbach and others. In general, realists need not reject some degree of conventionality in scientific practice. The question of whether space has an "intrinsic" geometry, however, invites disputes that appear to be patently metaphysical, and Reichenbach's use of the underdetermination argument can be understood as an instance of the more general empiricist tendency to see conventionality whenever a dispute engages a metaphysical issue.

A very different set of issues is raised by another branch of twentieth-century physics: quantum theory. It is sometimes thought that the results of quantum mechanics undermine determinism—the doctrine that the final state of a system is completely fixed by its initial state.[3] Although there is much controversy about the relation of quantum mechanics to the general metaphysical doctrine of determinism, it is specifically in the philosophy of science that the philosophical significance of quantum mechanics is receiving its due, raising questions about the plausibility of realist interpretations of science and about such long-honored principles as the "local" character of causation.

The curious features of subatomic phenomena immediately captured the interest of philosophers and scientists, in part because these features appear to differ so starkly from the classical conception of particles, as well as from our commonsense conception of objects. Experimental and theoretical work by Werner Heisenberg and others indicated that it is physically impossible to specify the exact position and exact momentum of a particle simultaneously. The very act of measurement interferes with the properties whose values we are trying to determine. To oversimplify: In order to reveal a particle's exact position, we must bounce a sufficient amount of light off of the particle, a procedure that affects the particle's momentum. Alternatively, revealing the exact momentum of the particle requires that we bounce so little light off of the

Heisenberg
= no determinism

particle that we are unable to specify its exact position.[4] Contemporary quantum theory captures this uncertainty by characterizing an electron as a "wave-function"—a mathematical expression of the probability that an electron will be detected in a certain region of space.

Broadly speaking, two different accounts of this fact were rendered. Proponents of the Copenhagen interpretation argued that the indeterminacy principle reflects the fact that the electron *has* neither position nor momentum. By contrast, early hidden-variable theorists believed this result to be a mere artifact of experimental intervention; as classical physics would suggest, the electron has a determinate position and a determinate momentum simultaneously, but these properties simply can't be *measured* simultaneously.

The Copenhagen theorists were not denying the *existence* of electrons, but only the classical account of the manner in which electrons possessed position, momentum, and other attributes. But the apparent dependence of the particle's properties on the act of measurement led many physicists and philosophers to draw elaborate metaphysical conclusions concerning the "mentally constructed" character of reality and to raise doubts about the traditional conception of how those properties are distributed in space. It now appears that simple versions of hidden variable interpretations of quantum theory are mistaken and that the evidence for this claim does not depend on the correctness of quantum theory. But hidden-variable interpretations face difficulties anyway, for reasons having to do with the nature of quantum state descriptions and Bell-type phenomena.

The background to the peculiarities of quantum theory is provided, in exceptionally clear terms, in N. David Mermin's, "Is the Moon There When Nobody Looks?" Mermin begins by describing Einstein's dissatisfaction with the curious uncertainty of such quantum descriptions, detailed in a paper Einstein published with Podolsky and Rosen in 1935. The paper (hereafter EPR) contains a thought experiment designed to clarify what they deemed as the unacceptable consequences of quantum indeterminacy. We are asked to imagine a quantum state consisting of two correlated particles in different regions. From our measurement of the position or momentum of the particle in region A, quantum theory permits us to predict with certainty the corresponding property of the particle in region B. However, if what it is that exists in region B is independent of measurements carried out at region A, then the particle in region B must have always had both a definite position and a definite momentum.

The EPR paper concludes that, because quantum theory is unable to assign definite values to both particles simultaneously, quantum theory provides at best an incomplete description of the physically real properties involved, properties that are causally relevant to the events that the theory tries to explain. The quantum theorist could claim, of course, that the particle in region B gets its position or momentum *because* of the measurement of the position or momentum of the particle in region A, but such a claim represents the very instantaneous "spooky action-at-a-distance" reviled by physicists on both sides of the hidden-variable dispute. In other words, we would seem to be rejecting the "locality" of physical causation, normally understood as the claim that no causal influence can propagate faster than the speed of light.[5]

Mermin introduces Bell's demonstration that "the nonexistence of these properties is a direct consequence of the quantitative predictions of the quantum theory" (Bell's theorem).[6] In effect, there are correlations between outcomes of experiments simultaneously run on two particles that have been prepared in a special way. On the basis of these experiments, the realist, said to be committed to an EPR-type "reality-criterion," is characterized as reasoning in the following way. Each particle must carry to the measurement device a certain set of instructions, specifying the response of the measurement device for each possible state of the device.[7] If each particle in fact possesses such "instruction sets," based on the experimental apparatus and on putatively real and determinate properties of quantum systems such as spin, position, and momentum, then we should expect a distribution of outcomes (for two possible outcomes based on all combinations of values within instruction sets) that deviates from the .5 predicted by quantum theory. However, actual experiments yield a .5 distribution. This result raises doubts about the existence of such instruction sets and, in turn, doubts about whether the reality criterion is appropriate and whether the relevant properties have determinate values prior to measurements in spatially distant regions.

If we take the results of quantum mechanics seriously, then, there would appear to be only two options. Either we 1. abandon locality, and insist that there is instantaneous action-at-a-distance, despite experimental and theoretical evidence from special and general relativity indicating that there is no superluminal signal transmission, or 2. abandon the version of realism associated with EPR, which states that any given physical system possesses an intrinsic set of properties independent of any observations that a scientist intends to run on the system.

After providing an elegant description of the EPR experiment and Bell inequality, Abner Shimony ("Metaphysical Problems in the Foundations of Quantum Mechanics") addresses the plausibility of, and problems with, both the rejection of locality and the rejection of EPR-type realism. Perhaps EPR-type realism is not the guilty premise, but the assumption of locality; we could then contend that, after all, there is action-at-a-distance. Shimony considers two versions of this contention. One might hold that the quantum state includes a "wormhole"—explicable in terms of topological features of space-time whereby "two points are close to each other by one route and remote by another." At the microscopic level, then, we might conjecture that two correlated events, apparently spatially separated, are actually close to one another and thus do not have a space-like separation at all. Alternatively, one might venture a "peaceful coexistence" between relativity theory and nonlocality, on the grounds that quantum-mechanical events have a hybrid (potentiality/actuality) character accommodated by neither the classical nor the quantum mechanical accounts of relativistic restrictions on causality. However, according to Shimony, the rejection of locality has a price as well. The "wormhole" proposal is wildly speculative. The second, "peaceful coexistence" proposal is not so much a solution as it is a temporary, tactical evasion of the original problem by the invocation of an unanalyzed (and perhaps artificial) distinction between "levels" or "modalities" of reality.

Shimony argues that the second alternative—the rejection of EPR-type realism—is unattractive for three reasons. First, the mind-dependence of experimental outcomes implied by the second alternative is at odds with the corrections to this sort of anthropocentrism in the history of science. Second, quantum nonseparability is presupposed in diverse experimental arrangements not directly concerned with Bell-type phenomena. Third, there is no coherent nonontological interpretation of quantum mechanics—that is, no interpretation of the objects of quantum mechanics as mind-dependent—and no proposals in the offing with the resources to evade even the most traditional and straightforward objections to formulations of scientific domains as mind-dependent. Therefore, our difficulty in rejecting EPR-type realism may indicate that, as Shimony puts it at one point, "these peculiarities of the quantum mechanical description are intrinsic characteristics of the things themselves and not just of our way of looking at or talking about the things."[8]

Elsewhere in Shimony's paper we find a skillful discussion of the relation between experimental physics and traditional metaphysics. In the same manner, Arthur Fine's "Is Scientific Realism Compatible with Quantum Physics?" explores the options available to the quantum realist, and argues for a metaphysically agnostic interpretation of the results of quantum theory: "Quantum theory neither supports that realism of atoms and molecules, etc., to which the old positivism was opposed, nor does it deny it. Thus I will urge the forgotten moral of the new positivism; namely, that realism is a metaphysical doctrine that finds neither support nor refutation in scientific theories or investigations."

Fine identifies two versions of quantum realism: *minimal realism* and *reductive realism*. According to minimal realism, "Quantum systems correspond to real objects. The observables of the theory (spin, position, momentum, etc.) will correspond to some generic feature of the real objects." Some realist accounts now in the literature (Miller 1987, 1989; Teller 1986) treat EPR-type correlations as aspects of a holistic, objective property of the quantum system. According to this account, locality need not be rejected. Since the correlation is an irreducibe property of an entire system, the correlation needn't be explained in terms of the transmission of a signal from one region (or system) to another. This is a route Fine himself suggests, though in the end, he argues, this account "only explains puzzling features of the theory (or of our observations) by invoking mysterious features of the world. I have considerable sympathy with that response, the general drift of which is to point to the sterility of realism as such."

The reductive realist position, like other reductive stances, attempts to eliminate appeals to one set of facts in favor of another, "more basic," set of facts. In this case, the reductive realist is an eliminativist in principle about the probabilities appealed to in quantum theory, treating them "as mere averages over a single well-determined ensemble." This view is *reductive* because of the type of demand it places on the treatment of physical probabilities: it requires that the joint probability for a pair of simultaneous outcomes in separate regions can always be expressed as the product of the probabilities of each outcome taken separately. According to Fine's reductive realist, we are pressed to take the eliminativist strategy "in the face of ignorance of the finer details of things. The probabilistic assertion, then, would signify merely a restriction on the epistemic accessibility of the world." And in so doing, the reductive realist is committed to the idea that there is a local hidden variable, as well as the very type of ensemble representation whose possibility Bell and others have argued against.[9]

Amidst the minimal, reductive, and holist varieties of realism described above, we must consider whether there is a version of realism not captured by the accounts presented here, which respects the traditional commitment to a mind-independent reality, but avoids unnecessarily strong causal principles. Whether such an alternative will prove tenable is unclear, but what is certain is that the classical conception of microphenomena is being revised in fundamental ways, and with it, the philosophical principles so indebted to the classical picture.

Notes

1. Reichenbach makes this point in a section not reprinted here; see Reichenbach 1958, section 12. It might be worth mentioning that now physicists typically don't believe that one can always "save the appearances" in this way. For one deft treatment of Reichenbach's conventionalism, as well as of other issues this topic engages, see "Facts, Conventions and Assumptions in the Theory of SpaceTime," in Sklar 1985.

2. It is, perhaps, ironic then that Quine 1951 should use the very considerations of underdetermination and holism to argue *against* the putative analytic character of theoretical choices advertised as "true by convention," though, the success of Quine's anticonventionalist arguments is still a matter of some dispute. See, for example, Sidelle 1989.

3. In light of the probabilistic character of quantum phenomena, incompatibilist advocates of free will embraced these results. This enthusiastic coopting of quantum mechanics now seems to have been premature, bred from an inadequate analysis of how quantum phenomena bear on issues of free will and from an overly simplistic understanding of the nature of deterministic systems.

4. This oversimplification is especially prominent in popularizations of quantum mechanics, but it is not entirely accurate; the inaccuracy will be dealt with shortly. For discussions of the superposition of states see d'Espagnat 1979 and Shimony 1988.

5. For an important clarification and qualification concerning the notion of locality, see Jarrett 1984, 1989.

6. It is important to note that Bell's theorem is a derivation of a constraint on any theory satisfying certain assumptions. Whether or not one of these assumptions must be abandoned is a question that is independent of the correctness of quantum theory. Since it would be difficult to improve upon the clarity and succinctness of Mermin's treatment, I won't rehearse the results here. For the reader interested in other clear, introductory treatments of Bell's inequality and the stunning experiments whose results conform to the statistical predictions of quantum theory, see Bell 1981, d'Espagnat 1979, and Shimony 1988, 1989.

7. As was the case in the original EPR argument, determinacy is not being used as an assumption, but instead, is being derived.

8. The fact that the mind-dependence of reality is regarded by many as a dispensable assumption is a testament to the powerful grip that locality has on contemporary physicists. Here I echo Nick Herbert's sentiment that 'It's difficult to convey to outsiders the distaste which the majority of physicists feel when they hear the word 'non-locality'. [M]ost physicists ... so treasure locality that they are willing to deny reality itself before accepting a world that's non-local (1985, p. 234).

9. It might be worth mentioning that this "single well-determined ensemble" view is no longer regarded as a live option in the literature. Another approach commits the realist to determinism, or to a certain causal principle such as that of "common cause," and then argues that this principle is incompatible with the results of quantum mechanics. For one application of this approach, see van Fraassen 1982.

References

Bell, J. S., 1981, "Bertlmann's Socks and the Nature of Reality," *Journal de Physique*, Colloque C2, 42(3): 41–61; reprinted in Bell 1987.

Bell, J. S., 1987, *Speakable and Unspeakable in Quantum Mechanics*, Cambridge University Press, New York.

Cushing, J., and McMullin, E., 1989, eds., *The Philosophical Consequences of Quantum Theory*, Notre Dame Press, Notre Dame, IN.

Earman, J., Glymour, C., and Stachel, J., 1977, eds., *Minnesota Studies in the Philosophy of Science VIII: Foundations of Space-Time Theories*, University of Minnesota Press, Minneapolis.

d'Espagnat, B., 1979, "The Quantum Theory and Reality," *Scientific American* 241(5): 158–181.

Einstein, A., Podolsky, B., and Rosen, N., 1935, "Can Quantum-Mechanical Description of Physical Reality be Considered Complete?" *Physical Review* 47: 777–780.

Herbert, N., 1985, *Quantum Reality*, Anchor, New York.

Jarrett, J., 1984, "On the Physical Significance of the Locality Conditions in the Bell Arguments," *Noûs* 18: 569–589.

Jarrett, J., 1989, "Bell's Theorem: A Guide to the Implications," in Cushing and McMullin.

Miller, R., 1987, *Fact and Method*, Princeton University Press, Princeton, NJ.

Miller, R., 1989, "In Search of Einstein's Legacy: A Critical Notice of *The Shaky Game: Einstein, Realism and the Quantum Theory*," *The Philosophical Review* 98: 215–238.

Quine, W. V., 1951, "Two Dogmas of Empiricism," *Philosophical Review* 60: 20–43.

Reichenbach, H., 1958, *The Philosophy of Space & Time*, Dover, New York.

Shimony, A., 1988, "The Reality of the Quantum World," *Scientific American* 258(1): 46–53.

Shimony, A., 1989, "Conceptual Foundations of Quantum Mechanics," in Davies, P., ed., *The New Physics*, Cambridge University Press, New York.

Sidelle, A., 1989, *Necessity, Essence, and Individuation: A Defense of Conventionalism*, Cornell University Press, Ithaca, NY.

Sklar, L., 1977, "Facts, Conventions, and Assumptions in the Theory of Space Time," in Earman, J. et al.; reprinted in Sklar 1985.

Sklar, L., 1985, *Philosophy and Space-Time Physics*, University of California Press, Berkeley, CA.

Teller, P., 1986, "Relational Holism and Quantum Mechanics," *British Journal for the Philosophy of Science* 37: 71–81.

van Fraassen, B., 1982, "The Charybdis of Realism: Epistemological Implications of Bell's Inequality," *Synthese* 52: 25–38.

Further Readings

On conventionality and the metric structure of Space-time:

Davies, P. C. W., 1974, *The Physics of Time Asymmetry*, University of California Press, Berkeley, CA.

Davies, P. C. W., 1977, *Space and Time in the Modern Universe*, Cambridge University Press, New York.

Earman, J., 1989, *World Enough and Space-Time*, MIT Press, Cambridge, MA.

Friedman, M., 1983, *Foundations of Space-Time Theories*, Princeton University Press, Princeton, NJ.

Glymour, C., 1980, *Theory and Evidence*, Princeton University Press, Princeton, NJ.

Grünbaum, A., 1963, *Philosophical Problems of Space and Time*, Knopf, New York.

Grünbaum, A., 1968, *Geometry and Chronometry in Philosophical Perspective*, University of Minnesota Press, Minneapolis.

Horwich, P., 1987, *Asymmetries in Time*, MIT Press, Cambridge, MA.

Malament, D., 1977, "Observationally Indistinguishable Space-Times," in Earman et al. 1977.

Poincaré, H., 1952, *Science and Hypothesis*, Dover, New York.

Putnam, H., 1975, "The Refutation of Conventionalism," in M. Munitz, ed., *Semantics and Meaning*, New York University Press, New York. Reprinted in Putnam 1975, vol. 2.

Sklar, L., 1974, *Space, Time, and Spacetime*, University of California Press, Berkeley, CA.

Suppes, P., 1973, ed., *Space, Time, and Geometry*, Reidel, Dordrecht.

van Fraassen, B., 1970, *An Introduction to the Philosophy of Time and Space*, Random House, New York, NY.

On the philosophical significance of quantum mechanics:

d'Espagnat, B., 1989, *Reality and the Physicist*, Cambridge University Press, New York.

Fine, A., 1986, *The Shaky Game*, University of Chicago Press, Chicago.

Gibbins, P., 1987, *Particles and Paradoxes*, Cambridge University Press, New York.

Healey, R., 1989, *The Philosophy of Quantum Mechanics: An Interactive Interpretation*, Cambridge University Press, New York.

Hughes, R. I. G., 1989, *The Structure and Interpretation of Quantum Mechanics*, Harvard University Press, Cambridge, MA.

Krips, H., 1988, *The Metaphysics of Quantum Theory*, Oxford University Press, New York.

Lockwood, M., 1989, *Mind, Brain and The Quantum*, Blackwell, Cambridge, MA.

Putnam, H., 1983, "Quantum Mechanics and the Observer," in *Philosophical Papers*, vol. III , Cambridge University Press, New York.

Redhead, M., 1987, *Incompleteness, Nonlocality and Realism*, Oxford University Press, New York.

Stein, H., 1972, "On the Conceptual Structure of Quantum Mechanics," in Colodny, R., ed., *Paradigms and Paradoxes: The Philosophical Challenge of the Quantum Domain*, University of Pittsburgh, Pittsburgh.

van Fraassen, B., 1989, *Laws and Symmetries*, Oxford University Press, New York.

Chapter 25

Selections from *The Philosophy of Space and Time*

Hans Reichenbach

A. Coordinative Definitions

Defining usually means reducing a concept to other concepts. In physics, as in all other fields of inquiry, wide use is made of this procedure. There is a second kind of definition, however, which is also employed and which derives from the fact that physics, in contradistinction to mathematics, deals with real objects. Physical knowledge is characterized by the fact that concepts are not only defined by other concepts, but are also coordinated to real objects. This coordination cannot be replaced by an explanation of meanings, it simply states that this *concept* is coordinated to *this particular thing*. In general this coordination is not arbitrary. Since the concepts are interconnected by testable relations, the coordination may be verified as true or false, if the requirement of uniqueness is added, i.e., the rule that the same concept must always denote the same object. The method of physics consists in establishing the uniqueness of this coordination, as Schlick[1] has clearly shown. But certain preliminary coordinations must be determined before the method of coordination can be carried through any further; these first coordinations are therefore definitions which we shall call *coordinative definitions*. They are *arbitrary*, like all definitions; on their choice depends the conceptual system which develops with the progress of science.

Wherever metrical relations are to be established, the use of coordinative definitions is conspicuous. If a distance is to be measured, the unit of length has to be determined beforehand by definition. This definition is a coordinative definition. Here the duality of conceptual definition and coordinative definition can easily be seen. We can define only by means of other concepts what we mean by a unit; for instance: "A unit is a distance which, when transported along another distance, supplies the measure of this distance." But this statement does not say anything about the size of the unit, which can only be established by reference to a physically given length such as the standard meter in Paris. The same consideration holds for other definitions of units. If the definition reads, for instance: "A meter is the forty-millionth part of the circumference of the earth," this, circumference is the physical length to which the definition refers by means of the insertion of some further concepts. And if the wavelength of cadmium light is chosen as a unit, cadmium light is the physical phenomenon to which the definition is related. It will be noticed in this example that the method of coordinating a unit to a physical object may be very complicated. So far nobody has seen a wave-length; only certain phenomena have been observed which are theoretically related to it, such as the light and dark bands resulting from interference. In principle, a unit of length can be defined in terms of an observation that does not include any

Reprinted from *The Philosophy of Space & Time*, sections 4, 7, and 8 (New York: Dover, 1958), pp. 14–19, 28–37, by permission of the publisher and Maria Reichenbach. [Ed. note: All internal references in this chapter are to *The Philosophy of Space & Time*.]

metrical relations, such as "that wave-length which occurs when light has a certain redness." In this case a sample of this red color would have to be kept in Paris in place of the standard meter. The characteristic feature of this method is the coordination of a concept to a physical object. These considerations explain the term "coordinative definition." If the definition is used for measurements, as in the case of the unit of length, it is a *metrical* coordinative definition.

The philosophical significance of the theory of relativity consists in the fact that it has demonstrated the necessity for metrical coordinative definitions in several places where empirical relations had previously been assumed. It is not always as obvious as in the case of the unit of length that a coordinative definition is required before any measurements can be made, and pseudo-problems arise if we look for truth where definitions are needed. The word "relativity" is intended to express the fact that the results of the measurements depend upon the choice of the coordinative definitions. It will be shown presently how this idea affects the solution of the problem of geometry.

After this solution of the problem of the unit of length, the next step leads to the comparison of two units of lengths at different locations. If the measuring rod is laid down, its length is compared only to that part of a body, say a wall, which it covers at the moment. If two separate parts of the wall are to be compared, the measuring rod will have to be transported. It is assumed that the measuring rod does not change during the transport. It is fundamentally impossible, however, to detect such a change if it is produced by universal forces. Assume two measuring rods which are equal in length. They are transported by different paths to a distant place; there again they are laid down side by side and found equal in length. Does this procedure prove that they did not change on the way? Such an assumption would be incorrect. The only observable fact is that the two measuring rods are always equal in length at the place where they are compared to each other. But it is impossible to know whether on the way the two rods expand or contract. An expansion that affects all bodies in the same way is not observable because a direct comparison of measuring rods at different places is impossible.

An optical comparison, for instance by measuring the angular perspective of each rod with a theodolite, cannot help either. The experiment makes use of light rays and the interpretation of the measurement of the lengths depends on assumptions about the propagation of light.

The problem does not concern a matter of *cognition* but of *defintion*. There is no way of knowing whether a measuring rod retains its length when it is transported to another place; a statement of this kind can only be introduced by a definition. For this purpose a coordinative definition is to be used, because two physical objects distant from each other are *defined* as equal in length. It is not the *concept* equality of length which is to be defined, but a *real object* corresponding to it is to be pointed out. A physical structure is coordinated to the concept equality of length, just as the standard meter is coordinated to the concept unit of length.

This analysis reveals how definitions and empirical statements are interconnected. As explained above, it is an observational fact, formulated in an empirical statement, that two measuring rods which are shown to be equal in length by local comparison made at a certain space point will be found equal in length by local comparison at every other space point, whether they have been transported along same or different paths. When we add to this empirical fact the definition that the rods shall be called equal in length when they are at *different places*, we do not make an inference from the observed fact; the addition constitutes an independent convention. There is, however, a certain relation between the two. The physical fact makes the convention unique, i.e., independent of the path of transportation. The statement about the uniqueness of the convention is therefore empirically verifiable and not a matter of choice. One can say that the factual relations holding for a local comparison of rods, though they do not require the definition of congruence in terms of transported rods, make this definition admissible. Definitions that are not unique are inadmissible in a scientific system.

This consideration can only mean that the factual relations may be used for the simple definition of congruence where any rigid measuring rod establishes the congruence. If the factual relations did not hold, a special definition of the unit of length would have to be given for every space point. Not only at Paris, but also at every other place a rod having the length of a "meter" would have to be displayed, and all these arbitrarily chosen rods would be called equal in length by definition. The requirement of uniformity would be satisfied by carrying around a measuring rod selected at random for the purpose of making copies and displaying these as the unit. If two of these copies were transported and compared locally, they would be different in length, but this fact would not "falsify" the definition. In such a world it would become very obvious that the concept of congruence is a definition; but we, in our simple world, are also permitted to choose a definition of congruence that does not correspond to the actual behavior of rigid rods. Thus we could arrange measuring rods, which in the ordinary sense are called equal in length, and, laying them end to end, call the second rod half as long as the first, the third one a third, etc. Such a definition would complicate all measurements, but epistemologically it is equivalent to the ordinary definition, which calls the rods equal in length. In this statement we make use of the fact that the definition of a unit at only one space point does not render general measurements possible. For the general case the definition of the unit has to be given in advance as a function of the place (and also of the time).[1] *It is again a matter of fact that our world admits of a simple definition of congruence because of the factual relations holding for the behavior of rigid rods; but this fact does not deprive the simple definition of its definitional character.*

The great significance of the realization that congruence is a matter of definition lies in the fact that by its help the epistemological problem of geometry is solved. The determination of the geometry of a certain structure depends on the definition of congruence. In the example of the surface E the question arose whether or not the distances AB and BC are equal; in the first case the surface E will have the same geometrical form as the surface G, in the second case it will be a plane. The answer to this question can now be given in terms of the foregoing analysis: whether $AB = BC$ is not a matter of cognition but of definition. If in E the congruence of widely separated distances is defined in such a way that $AB = BC$, E will be a surface with a hump in the middle; if the definition reads differently, E will be a plane. *The geometrical form of a body is no absolute datum of experience, but depends on a preceding coordinative definition;* depending on the definition, the same structure may be called a plane, or a sphere, or a curved surface. Just as the measure of the height of a tower does not constitute an absolute number, but depends on the choice of the unit of length, or as the height of a mountain is only defined when the zero level above which the measurements are to be taken is indicated, geometrical shape is determined only after a preceding definition. This requirement holds for the three-dimensional domain in the same way as it does for the two-dimensional. While in the two-dimensional case the observed non-Euclidean geometry can be interpreted as the geometry of a curved surface in a Euclidean three-dimensional space, we arrive at a three-dimensional non-Euclidean geometry when we measure a three-dimensional structure. A simple consideration will clarify this point. Let us choose as our coordinative definition that of practical surveying, i.e., let us define rigid measuring rods as congruent, when transported. If under these conditions a large circle, say with a radius of 100 meters, is measured on the surface of the earth, a very exact measurement will furnish a number smaller than $\pi = 3.14\ldots$ for the relation of circumference and diameter. This result is due to the curvature of the surface of the earth, which prevents us from measuring the real diameter going through the earth below the curved surface. In this case it would be possible to use the third dimension. If we add the third dimension, however, the situation becomes different. Imagine a large sphere made of tin which is supported on the inside by rigid iron beams; on the sphere and upon the iron scaffold people are climbing around who are measuring circumference and diameter at different points with the same measuring rods they used for the two-dimensional case. If this time the measuring result deviates from π, we must accept a three-dimensional non-Euclidean geometry which can no longer be interpreted as the curvature of a surface in three-dimensional Euclidean space. We obtain this result because the coordinative definition of congruence was chosen as indicated above. A different geometry would have been obtained, if we had used, for instance, the coordinative definition of the earlier example, in which we called the measuring rod half its length after putting it down twice, a third its length after putting it down three times, etc. The question of the geometry of real space, therefore, cannot be answered before the coordinative definition is given which establishes the congruence for this space.

We are now left with the problem: which coordinative definition should be used for physical space? Since we need a geometry, a decision has to be made for a definition of congruence. Although we must do so, we should never forget that we deal with an arbitrary decision that is neither true nor false. Thus the geometry of physical space is not an immediate result of experience, but depends on the choice of the coordinative definition.

In this connection we shall look for the most adequate definition, i.e., one which has the advantage of logical simplicity and requires the least possible change in the results of science. The sciences have implicitly employed such a coordinative definition all the time, though not always consciously; the results based upon this definition will be developed further in our analysis. It can be assumed that the definition hitherto employed possesses certain practical advantages justifying its use. In the discussion about the definition of congruence by means of rigid rods, this coordinative definition has already been indicated....

B. Technical Impossibility and Logical Impossibility

In the following section a criticism will be discussed which has been made against our theory of coordinative definitions. It has been objected that we base the arbitrariness in the choice of the definition on the impossibility of making measurements. Although it is admitted that certain differences cannot be *verified* by measurement, we should not infer from this fact that they do not *exist*. If we had no means of discovering the shape of surface E in figure 25.1 it would still be meaningful to ask what shape the surface has; although the possibility of making measurements is dependent on our human abilities, the objective fact is independent of them. Thus we are accused of having confused <u>subjective inability</u> with <u>objective indeterminacy</u>.

There are, indeed, many cases where physics is unable to make measurements. Does this mean that the magnitude to be measured does not exist? It is impossible, for instance, to determine exactly the number of molecules in a cubic centimeter of air; we can say with a high degree of certainty that we shall never succeed in counting every

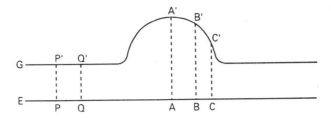

Figure 25.1
Projection of a non-Euclidean geometry on a plane.

individual molecule. But can we infer that this number does not exist? On the contrary, we must say that there will always be an integer which denotes this quantity exactly. The mistake of the theory of relativity is supposed to consist in the fact that it confuses the *impossibility of making measurements* with *objective indeterminacy*.

Whoever makes this objection overlooks an important distinction. There is an impossibility of making measurements which is due to the limitation of our technical means; I shall call it *technical impossibilty*. In addition, there is a *logical impossibility* of measuring. Even if we had a perfect experimental technique, we should not be able to avoid this logical impossibility. It is logically impossible to determine whether the standard meter in Paris is really a meter. The highest refinement of our geodetic instruments does not teach us anything about this problem, because the meter cannot be defined in absolute terms. This is the reason why the measuring rod in Paris is called the definition of a meter. It is arbitrarily defined as the unit, and the question whether it really represents this unit has lost its meaning. The same considerations hold for a comparison of units at distant places. Here we are not dealing with technical limitations, but with a logical impossibility. The impossibility of a determination of the shape of a surface, if universal forces are admitted, is not due to a deficiency of our instruments, *but is the consequence of an unprecise question*. The question concerning the shape of the surface has no precise formulation, unless it is preceded by a coordinative definition of congruence. What is to be understood by "the shape of a real surface"? Whatever experiments and measurements I make, they will never furnish a unique indication of the shape of the surface. If universal forces are admitted, the measurements may be interpreted in such a way that many different shapes of surfaces are compatible with the same observations. There is one definition which closes the logical gap and tells us which interpretations of our observations must be eliminated: this task is performed bv the coordinative definition. It gives a precise meaning to the question of the shape of the real surface and makes a unique answer possible, just as a question about length has a unique meaning only when the unit of measurerment is given. It is not a technical failure that prevents us from determining the shape of a surface without a coordinative definition of congruence, but a logical impossibility that has nothing to do with the limitations of human abilities.

The situation will be further clarified if we compare the last example with the case of the indeterminacy of the number of molecules in a given cubic centimeter of air. This number is precisely defined and it is only due to human imperfection that we cannot determine it exactly. But in this case an approximation is possible which will increase with increasing perfection of our technical instruments. When we are faced with a logical impossibility there are no approximations. We cannot decide approximately whether the surface *E* of figure 25.1 is a plane, or a surface with a hemispherical hump in the middle; there is no defined limit which the measurement could approach. Furthermore, once the coordinative definition is given, the technical impossibility of an exact measurement remains. Even our definition of the rigid body does not permit a strict determination of the structure of space; all our measurements will still contain some degree of inexactness which a progressive technique will gradually reduce but never overcome.

C. The Relativity of Geometry

With regard to the problem of geometry we have come to realize that the question which geometry holds for physical space must be decided by measurements, i.e., empirically. Furthermore, this decision is dependent on the assumption of an arbitrary coordinative definition of the comparison of length. Against this conception arguments have been set forth which endeavor to retain Euclidean geometry for physical space under any circumstances and thus give it a preference among all other geometries. On the basis of our results we can discuss these arguments; our analysis will lead to the relativity of geometry.

One of the arguments maintains it is a mistake to believe that the choice of the coordinative definition is a matter left to our discretion. The measurements of geometry as carried through in practice presuppose quite complicated measuring instruments such as the theodolite; therefore these measurements cannot be evaluated without a theory of the measuring instruments. The theory of the measuring instruments, however, presupposes the validity of Euclidean geometry and it constitutes a contradiction to infer a non-Euclidean geometry from the results.

This objection can be met in the following way. Our conception permits us to start with the assumption that Euclidean geometry holds for physical space. Under certain conditions, however, we obtain the result that there exists a universal force F that deforms all measuring instruments in the same way. However, we can invert the interpretation: we can set F equal to zero by definition and correct in turn the theory of our measuring instruments. We are able to proceed in this manner because a transformation of all measurements from one geometry into another is possible and involves no difficulties. It is correct to say that all measurements must be preceded by a definition; we expressed this fact by the indispensability of the coordinative definition. The mistake of the objection consists in the belief that this definition cannot be changed afterwards. Just as we can measure the temperature with a Fahrenheit thermometer and then convert the results into Celsius, measurements can be started under the assumption of Euclidean geometry and later converted into non-Euclidean measurements. There is no logical objection to this procedure.

In practice the method is much simpler. It turns out that the non-Euclidean geometry obtained under our coordinative definition of the rigid body deviates quantitatively only very little from Euclidean geometry when small areas are concerned. In this connection "small area" means "on the order of the size of the earth"; deviations from Euclidean geometry can be noticed only in astronomic dimensions. In practice, therefore, it is not necessary to correct the theory of the measuring instruments afterwards, because these corrections lie within the errors of observation. The following method of inference is permissible: we can prove by the assumption that Euclidean geometry holds for small areas that in astronomic dimensions a non-Euclidean geometry holds-which merges infinitesimally into Euclidean geometry. No logical objection can be advanced against this method, which is characteristic of the train of thought in modern physics. It is carried through in practice for astronomic measurements designed to confirm Einstein's theory of gravitation.

The objection is connected with the a *priori* theory of space that goes back to Kant and today is represented in various forms. Not only Kantians and neo-Kantians attempt to maintain the a *priori* character of geometry: the tendency is also pronounced in philosophical schools which in other respects are not Kantian. It is not my intention to give a critical analysis of Kant's philosophy. In the course of the discussion of the theory of relativity, it has become evident that the philosophy of Kant has been subject to so many interpretations by his disciples that it can no longer serve as a sharply defined basis for present day epistemological analysis. Such an analysis would clarify less the *epistemological* question of the structure of space than the *historical* question of the meaning and content of Kant's system. The author has presented his own views on this problem in another publication;[1] the present investigation is aimed at philosophical clarification and will not concern itself with historical questions. Therefore, I shall select only those arguments of Kant's theory of space, the refutation of which will further our understanding of the problem.

The ideas expressed in the preceding considerations attempted to establish Euclidean geometry as *epistemologically a priori*; we found that this *a priori* cannot be maintained and that Euclidean geometry is not an indispensable presupposition of knowledge. We turn now to the idea of the *visual a priori*; this Kantian doctrine bases the preference for Euclidean geometry upon the existence of a certain manner in which we visualize space.

The theory contends that an innate property of the human mind, the ability of visualization, demands that we adhere to Euclidean geometry. In the same way as a certain self-evidence compels us to believe the laws of arithmetic, a visual self-evidence compels us to believe in the validity of Euclidean geometry. It can be shown that this self-evidence is not based on logical grounds. Since mathematics furnishes a proof that the construction of non-Euclidean geometries does not lead to contradictions, no *logical* self-evidence can be claimed for Euclidean geometry. This is the reason why the self-evidence of Euclidean geometry has sometimes been derived, in Kantian fashion, from the human ability of visualization conceived as a source of knowledge.

Everybody has a more or less clear notion of what is understood by visualization. If we draw two points on a piece of paper, connect them by a straight line and add a curved connecting line, we "see" that the straight line is shorter than the curved line. We even claim to be certain that the straight line is shorter than any other line connecting the two points. We say this without being able to prove it by measurements, because it is impossible for us to draw and measure all the lines. The power of imagination compelling us to make this assertion is called the ability of *visualization*. Similarly, the Euclidean axiom of the parallels seems to be visually necessary. It remains for us to investigate this human quality and its significance for the problem of space.

The analysis will be carried through in two steps. Let us first assume it is correct to say that a special ability of visualization exists, and that Euclidean geometry is distinguished from all other geometries by the fact that it can easily be visualized. The question arises: what consequences does this assumption have for physical space? Only after this question has been answered can the assumption itself be tested. The second step of our analysis will therefore consist in the inquiry whether a special ability of visualization exists (§9 §11).

Let us turn to the first question, which has to be reformulated in order to relate it clearly to the epistemological problem.

Mathematics proves that every geometry of the Riemannian kind can be mapped upon another one of the same kind. In the language of physics this means the following:

Theorem θ: "Given a geometry G' to which the measuring instruments conform, we can imagine a universal force F which affects the instruments in such a way that the actual geometry is an arbitrary geometry G, while the observed deviation from G is due to a universal deformation of the measuring instruments."[4]

No epistemological objection can be made against the correctness of theorem θ. Is the visual *a priori* compatible with it?

Offhand we must say yes. Since the Euclidean geometry G_0 belongs to the geometries of the Riemannian kind, it follows from theorem θ that it is always possible to carry through the visually preferred geometry for physical space. Thus we have proved that we can always satisfy the requirement of visualization.

But something more is proved by theorem θ which does not fit very well into the theory of the visual *a priori*. The theorem asserts that Euclidean geometry is not preferable on epistemological grounds. Theorem θ shows all geometries to be equivalent; it formulates the *principle of the relativity of geometry*. It follows that it is meaningless to speak about one geometry as the *true* geometry. We obtain a statement about physical reality only if in addition to the geometry G of the space its universal field of force F is specified. Only the combination

$$G + F$$

is a testable statement.

We can now understand the significance of a decision for Euclidean geometry on the basis of a visual *a priori*. The decision means only the choice of a specific coordinative definition. In our definition of the rigid body we set $F = 0$; the statement about the resulting G is then a univocal description of reality. This definition means that in "$G + F$" the second factor is zero. The visual *a priori*, however, sets $G = G_0$. But then the empirical component in the results of measurements is represented by the determination of F; only through the combination

$$G_0 + F$$

are the properties of space exhaustively described.

There is nothing wrong with a coordinative definition established on the requirement that a certain kind of geometry is to result from the measurements. We ourselves renounced the simplest form of the coordinative definition, which consists in pointing to a measuring rod; instead we chose a much more complicated coordinative definition in terms of our distinction between universal and differential forces. A coordinative definition can also be introduced by the prescription what the result of the measurements is to be. "The comparison of length is to be performed in such a way that Euclidean geometry will be the result"—this stipulation is a possible form of a coordinative definition. It may be compared to the definition of the meter in terms of the circumference of the earth: "The unit is to be chosen in such a way that 40 million times this length will be equal to the circumference of the earth."

Although it may be admitted that Euclidean geometry is unique in that it can be easily visualized, the theory of the visual *a priori* does not disprove the theory of the relativity of geometry and of the necessity for coordinative definitions of the comparison of length. On the contrary, it is only this theory that can state precisely the epistemological function of visualization: the possibility of visualization is a ground for subjective preference of one particular coordinative definition. But the occurrence of visualization does not imply anything about the space of real objects.

In this connection another argument in support of the preference for Euclidean geometry is frequently adduced. To be sure, this argument is not related to the problem of visualization, but like the visual *a priori* it attributes a specific epistemological position to Euclidean geometry; therefore we shall consider it here. It is maintained that Euclidean geometry is the *simplest* geometry, and hence physics must choose the coordinative definition $G = G_0$ rather than the coordinative definition $F = 0$. This point of view can be answered as follows: physics is not concerned with the question which *geometry* is simpler, but with the question which *coordinative definition* is simpler. It seems that the coordinative definition $F = 0$ is simpler, because then the expression $G + F$ reduces to G. But even this result is not essential, since in this case simplicity is not a criterion for truth. Simplicity certainly plays an important part in physics, even as a criterion for choosing between physical hypotheses. The significance of simplicity as a means to knowledge will have to be carefully examined in connection with the problem of induction, which does not fall within the scope of this book.

Geometry is concerned solely with the simplicity of a *definition*, and therefore the problem of empirical significance does not arise. It is a mistake to say that Euclidean geometry is "more true" than Einstein's geometry or vice versa, because it leads to simpler metrical relations. We said that Einstein's geometry leads to simpler relations because in it $F = 0$. But we can no more say that Einstein's geometry is "truer" than Euclidean geometry, than we can say that the meter is a "truer" unit of length than the yard. The simpler system is always preferable; the advantage of meters and centimeters over yards and feet is only a matter of economy and has no bearing upon reality. *Properties of reality are discovered only by a combination of the results of measurement with the underlying coordinative definition.* Thus it is a characterization of objective reality that (according to Einstein) a three-dimensional non-Euclidean geometry results in the neighborhood of heavenly bodies, if we define the comparison of length by transported rigid rods. But only the *combination* of the two statements has objective significance. The same state of affairs can therefore be described in different ways. In our example it could just as well be said that in the neighborhood of a heavenly body a universal field of force exists which affects all measuring rods, while the geometry is Euclidean. Both combinations of statements are equally true, as can be seen from the fact that one can be transformed into the other. Similarly, it is just as true to say that the circumference of the earth is 40 million meters as to say that it is 40 thousand kilometers. The significance of this simplicity should not be exaggerated; this kind of simplicity, which we call *descriptive simplicity*, has nothing to do with truth.

Taken alone, the statement that a certain geometry holds for space is therefore meaningless. It acquires meaning only if we add the coordinative definition used in the comparison of widely separated lengths. The same rule holds for the geometrical shape of bodies. The sentence "The earth is a sphere" is an incomplete statement, and resembles the statement "This room is seven units long." Both statements say something about objective states of affairs only if the assumed coordinative definitions are added, and both statements must be changed if other coordinative definitions are used. These considerations indicate what is meant by *relativity of geometry*.

This conception of the problem of geometry is essentially the result of the work of Riemann, Helmholtz, and Poincaré and is known as *conventionalism*. While Riemann prepared the way for an application of geometry to physical reality by his mathematical formulation of the concept of space, Helmholtz laid the philosophical foundations. In particular, he recognized the connection of the problem of geometry, with that of rigid bodies and interpreted correctly the possibility of a visual representation of non-Euclidean spaces (cf. p. 63). It is his merit, furthermore, to have clearly stated that Kant's theory of space is untenable in view of recent mathematical developments.[5] Helmholtz's epistemological lectures must therefore be regarded as the source of modern philosophical knowledge of space.[6] It is Einstein's achievement to have applied the theory of the relativity of geometry to physics. The surprising result was the fact that the world is non-Euclidean, as the theorists of relativity are wont to say; in our language this means: if $F = 0$, the geometry G becomes non-Euclidean. This outcome had not been anticipated, and Helmholtz and Poincaré still believed that the geometry obtained could not be proved to be different from Euclidean geometry. Only Einstein's theory of gravitation predicted the non-Euclidean result which was confirmed by astronomical observations. The deviations from Euclidean geometry, however, are very small and not observable in everyday life.

Unfortunately, the philosophical discussion of conventionalism, misled by its ill-fitting name, did not always present the epistemological aspect of the problem with sufficient clarity.[7] From conventionalism the consequence was derived that it is impossible to make an objective statement about the geometry of physical space, and that we are dealing with subjective arbitrariness only; the concept of geometry of real space was called meaningless. This is a misunderstanding. Although the statement about the geometry is based upon certain arbitrary definitions, the statement itself does not become arbitrary: once the definitions have been formulated, it is determined through objective reality alone which is the actual geometry. Let us use our previous example: although we can define the scale of temperature arbitrarily, the indication of the temperature of a physical object does not become a subjective matter. By selecting a certain scale we can stipulate a certain arbitrary number of degrees of heat for the respective body, but this indication has an objective meaning as soon as the coordinative definition of the scale is added. On the contrary, it is the significance of coordinative definitions to lend an objective meaning to physical measurements. As long as it was not noticed at what points of the metrical system arbitrary definitions occur, all measuring results were undetermined; only by discovering the points of arbitrariness, by identifying them as such and by classifying them as definitions can we obtain objective measuring results in physics. *The objective character of the physical statement is thus shifted to a statement about relations.* As statement about the boiling point of water is no longer regarded as an absolute statement, but as a statement about a relation between the boiling water and the length of the column of mercury. There exists a similar objective statement about the geometry of real space: *it is a statement about a relation between the universe and rigid rods.* The geometry chosen to characterize this relation is only a mode of speech; however, our awareness of the relativity of geometry enables us to formulate the objective character of a statement about the geometry of the physical world as a statement about relations. In this sense we are permitted to speak of *physical geometry*. The description of nature is not stripped of arbitrariness by naive absolutism, but only by recognition and formulation of the points of arbitrariness. The only path to objective knowledge leads through conscious awareness of the role that subjectivity plays in our methods of research.

Notes

1. M. Schlick, *Allgemeine Erkenntnislehre*, Springer, Berlin 1918, Ziff. 10.
2. Cf. §39 and §46.
3. H. Reichenbach, *Relativitätstheorie und Erkenntnis a priori*, Springer, Berlin, 1920.

4. Generally the force F is a tensor. If $g'_{\mu\nu}$ are the metrical coefficients of the geometry G' and $g_{\mu\nu}$ those of G, the potentials $F_{\mu\nu}$ of the force F are given by

$$g'_{\mu\nu} + F_{\mu\nu} = g_{\mu\nu}$$
$$\mu\nu = 1, 2, 3$$

The measuring rods furnish directly the $g'_{\mu\nu}$; the $F_{\mu\nu}$ are the "correction factors" by which the $g'_{\mu\nu}$ are corrected so that $g_{\mu\nu}$ results. The universal force F influencing the measuring rod is usually dependent on the orientation of the measuring rod. About the mathematical limitation of theorem θ cf. §12.

5. The antithesis Kant-Helmholtz has been interpreted by Neo-Kantians (in particular by Riehl, *Kant-studien* 9, p. 261f., less plainly by Görland, *Natorp-Festschrift*, p. 94f) not as a contradiction but as a misunderstanding of Kant by Helmholtz. The same argument has been advanced by Neo-Kantians recently with respect to Einstein's theory. This conception is due to an underestimation of the differences between the points of view, and it would be in the interest of a general clarification if the patent contradiction between the only possible modern philosophy of space and Kant were admitted. Such an admission avoids the danger of an interpretation of Kant's philosophy too vague to retain any concrete content. The author presented his ideas on the subject in "Der gegenwärtige Stand der Relativitätsdiskussion," *Logos* X, 1922, section III, p. 341. Cf. also p. 31. (The English translation of this paper will be included in a forthcoming volume of *Selected Essays* by Hans Reichenbach, to be published by Routledge and Kegan Paul, London.)

6. Cf. the new edition by Hertz and Schlick, *Helmholtz' Erkenntnistheoretische Schriften*, Berlin 1921.

7. This is also true of the expositions by Poincaré, to whom we owe the designation of the geometrical axioms as conventions (*Science and Hypothesis*, Dover Publications, Inc. 1952, p. 50) and whose merit it is to have spread the awareness of the definitional character of congruence to a wider audience. He overlooks the possibility of making objective statements about real space in spite of the relativity of geometry and deems it impossible to "discover in geometric empiricism a rational meaning" (*op. cit.*, p. 79). Cf. §44.

Chapter 26

The Epistemology of Geometry

Clark Glymour

There is a philosophical tradition, going back at least to Poincaré [9], which argues that the geometrical features of the universe are underdetermined by all possible evidence, by all of the actual or possible coincidences and trajectories of material things, whatever they may be. Many different geometrical and physical theories can encompass the phenomena, can account for the motions of things. Poincaré supported his view with a parable, Reichenbach [11] with a sort of recipe for writing down alternative but empirically equivalent theories; later authors have repeated their arguments or given very similar ones. In his admirable book on space, time, and space-time [13], Lawrence Sklar has tried to catalog the possible philosophical attitudes toward the underdetermination arguments put forward by Poincaré, Reichenbach, and others: One can simply be skeptical about the possibility of knowing geometrical truths; one can maintain that in so far as there are any such, they are truths by convention; one can contend that certain theories are *a priori* more plausible than others and so should win any ties based on empirical evidence; one can insist that despite appearances all empirically equivalent theories say the same thing; or one can deny that there is any coherent notion of empirical equivalence and so lay the entire question aside. What one cannot do, if this catalog of options is complete, is to admit the notion of empirical equivalence, admit an account of sameness of meaning which permits that different theories may save the phenomena, deny that there are available *a priori* principles about what is most likely true, and still insist that arguments such as Poincaré and Reichenbach give do not establish the underdetermination of geometry. Of the options, listed and unlisted, I think this uncataloged view is the one closest to the truth.

I will concentrate on Reichenbach's argument, for it is more explicit and more general. My thesis is that even when it is sympathetically developed, Reichenbach's sort of argument does not establish the underdetermination of geometry or of anything else. The same is true for any other arguments for the underdetermination of geometry which use devices like those employed by Reichenbach to generate alternative theories. Since I do not deny that Reichenbach showed how to construct different but empirically equivalent theories, my thesis is perhaps a little puzzling. My idea is that the body of evidence which distinct theories hold in common, the phenomena which both theories save, may nonetheless provide differing support for the two theories, more reason to believe one than the other, more confirmation of one than the other. This is so not because one theory is *a priori* more plausible or probable than the other but, roughly, because one theory is better tested than the other by the body of evidence in question. I think this is the case with most of the putative examples of underdetermination in geometry. My view, then, is that the arguments for the underdetermination of geometry fail because they succeed only in producing different

Reprinted by permission of the author and the editor of *NOÛS*, Vol. XI (1977): 227–251.

theories which are empirically equivalent but which the imagined body of evidence does not equally well test or support. The particular view that evidence may discriminate among empirically adequate hypotheses without being inconsistent with any of them and without supposing that some of them are *a priori* likelier than others is not unprecedented. It is a view shared, I think, by Popper and by many Popperians; no doubt they would have little use for the rest of what I shall have to say about confirmation.

To address the question of the underdetermination of geometry requires several things. It requires a framework for the statement of alternative theories; it requires at least some necessary conditions for the synonymy of theories so expressed; it requires a characterization, however rough, of the states of affairs, actual or possible, which will serve as possible evidence; and it requires a theory of confirmation which will provide criteria for comparing and assessing competing theories. Most discussions of the underdetermination of geometry omit the specification of some of these elements; I shall try to make it clear, if not convincing, what I am supposing about these matters.

Space-Time Theories

Since arguments for underdetermination include relativistic theories, and since they involve geometry in the context of physical theory, I will just assume we are concerned with the underdetermination of features of space or of space-time in the context of space-time theories, whether classical or relativistic. I will assume that all such theories are formulated covariantly using a differentiable manifold and geometrical objects on that manifold, in order to state field equations relating sources to field quantities (such as the metric in general relativity or the gravitational potential in Newtonian theory) and to state equations of motion for material systems of various kinds. In addition there may be equations not containing source terms but which put restrictions on geometrical features of space-time. Further, the theories may contain principles not stated as equations which establish boundary conditions in certain situations or which establish symmetry properties (e.g., symmetric sources have symmetric fields) and so on. Such formulations are natural in the sense that actual theories are sometimes stated that way, they are reasonably clear, and we know how to write down a great many theories in such terms.[1] While any theory may imply, given a coordinate system, various coordinate dependent equations, and may sometimes be more easily tested in such a form, it is essential that the theory be stated covariantly; otherwise we become enormously confused about what each theory claims, about the synonymy of theories, and so on.

Synonomy

In dealing with formalized first-order theories there is a natural necessary condition for synonymy. First, identify any two theories if one can be obtained from the other simply by adding a predicate, but no new axioms, to its language. Second, make a lexicographic change in the theories so that no two theories considered have any nonlogical vocabulary in common. Then count two theories as synonymous only if their transmogrifications have a common definitional extention. That is, we can add a set of sentences of definitional form to one theory (or rather to its transmog) and another set of sentences of definitional form to the other theory (or rather its transmog) and the two results are logically equivalent. This condition not only catches the intuition that synonymous theories are those that with proper substitutions say the same thing, it also satisfies natural conditions about translation.[2] A much weaker condition is that the theories have at least one model in common: For at least one model of theory 1 it is possible to define in this model the quantities of theory 2 so as to form a model of theory 2, and, conversely, from the model of theory 2 so formed it is possible to define the quantities of the original model of theory 1.

I propose to use the best analogs I can for these first-order requirements, and especially for the second one. For the synonymy of theories formulated as covariant equations we will require at least that for any manifold and set of geometrical objects on that manifold which constitute a solution to the equations of one theory there be covariantly definable from the geometrical objects of this solution another set of geometrical objects which, together with the manifold, constitute a solution to the equations of the other theory, and symmetrically. In other words, if theory 1 is synonymous with theory 2, then given geometrical objects A, B, C which are distributed on manifold M so as to satisfy the equation of theory 1, we can write a covariant set of equations in appropriate variables, such that for A, B, C as values of some of the variables there are determined on M a unique set of geometrical objects, X, Y, Z as values for the other variables, and X, Y, Z satisfy the equations of theory 2. Furthermore, the equations which constitute the implicit definitions must contain only variables and operations occurring in one of the two theories. The only regard in which this condition might seem in the least too strong is the demand that the equations used to get one set of objects from another set be covariant; but this demand is no less plausible than the demand of covariance in general. To insist that non-covariant equations may establish the determination of one set of objects from another set is in effect to suppose that each of the theories ascribes "true" coordinates in the world. Charity forbids.

Evidence

There are a variety of objections to the supposition that talk of empirical equivalence makes sense at all. In discussions of space-time theories the states of affairs, actual or possible, that are ordinarily cited as the fundamental evidence for theoretical claims are coincidences of material bodies and the trajectories of bodies in space-time. The first are but a special feature of the second. It can be objected that these states of affairs are not "observational", that theoretical principles of various kinds are involved somehow in their determination. That is probably true, but irrelevant nonetheless. It is not claimed that the body of phenomena to be saved comprise some epistemic rock bottom, nor need it be. It is claimed only that there are a collection of states of affairs that can be ascertained, at least approximately, independently of the assumption of the truth or falsity of any of the space-time theories in question, and that these states of affairs are those for which such theories must account. The other sort of criticism apt to be made is that the supposed evidence is the wrong kind of thing to be evidence. Theories, it is said, tell us nothing or next to nothing about the trajectories of bodies subject to specified forces, or subject to specified fields. Thus classical physics says nothing about the motions of bodies but only about the motions of bodies if subjected to various kinds of forces and to no others. But, the objection continues, we cannot infer the forces from the motions, and the forces are most definitely theoretical quantities. So there is no theory-independent body of evidence that can adjudicate between space-time theories.

To reply: First of all, in special circumstances we *can* infer the forces from the motions; Newton did so and so did a number of later Newtonians. Second, there are built into our theories various principles which establish presumptions as to the forces acting in various situations; for example, in Newtonian theory there is built the presumption that the only significant force determining the trajectories of the major bodies of the solar system is gravity. Such presumptions are not, and perhaps cannot be, laws, but they are an essential part of our theories nonetheless.

What is at issue is something like this. Bodies of various identifiable kinds move in certain ways; Newtonian theory, say, accounts for these motions by supposing a limited class of forces acting on the various bodies, and providing principles which serve as guides to which forces are working on which bodies. We wish to know whether these motions, in turn, provide grounds for believing Newtonian theory as against other possible space-time theories, and to answer the question we ask whether there are other space-time theories, which may suppose whatever forces and force-laws may be imagined, that account both for the actual motions and for any other motions Newtonian theory could account for. Now Newtonian theory must explain any motion as the result of the action of some finite number of kinds of fields, and any of its competitors, if we imagine them to be field theories, must do the same. If then, for some competitor it can be shown that for every possible combination of Newtonian fields there is a combination of the fields of some competing theory such that the respective combinations of fields determine the same motions, we will be well along in demonstrating the existence of empirically equivalent alternatives. If, furthermore, the alternative theories are such that Newtonian principles for determining the forces (or fields) acting in any situation can be parodied by principles of the alternatives, there will be nothing remaining to show. Such a parody will be possible generally only when there is some systematic connection between the fields of the alternative theory and the fields of Newtonian theory. However, for the theories to be genuinely distinct, the connection must not be so systematic that values of the Newtonian quantities are uniquely determined by values of the non-Newtonian quantities, and conversely. Newtonian theory, of course, is just an example; the issue is the same for any other space-time theory.

Confirmation

I propose to look at confirmation in the following way.[3] An hypothesis in a theory is tested positively by producing an instance of the hypothesis by a procedure that does not guarantee that an instance rather than a counterinstance will result. Since the quantities or states of affairs (hereafter, simply quantities) that can be determined without use of the theory are not all of the quantities of the theory, many hypotheses will contain quantities whose values are not found among the empirical data. Values for such quantities are obtained by *using* other hypotheses of the theory to compute from them values of the empirically accessible quantities. Any hypotheses in the theory may be used in such a capacity. So a test of a hypothesis consists of a set of values of empirically available quantities, a set of hypotheses of the theory which determine from this empirical data a set of values for various quantities of the theory, and an hypothesis of the theory for which these values constitute either an instance or a counterinstance. To give a trivial example, suppose we have a theory consisting of Newton's second law and Hooke's law, and suppose we can measure, independently of this theory, length, acceleration, and mass. Then we can test, say, the second law by measuring the mass, extention, and acceleration of a spring, using Hooke's law to determine the force on the spring, and then seeing whether or not the values of mass, acceleration, and force so determined provide an instance of the second law. Equally trivial but more realistic examples of this strategy are provided by the use of data to determine arbitrary parameters in relations such as the gas laws and then using further data plus the parameter values to provide instances of the relations. It is essential that the computations of theoretical quantities from empirical ones not be so constructed that an instance of the hypothesis to be tested would result whatever the values of the empirical quantities might be. This does not prevent one from using the very hypothesis to be tested to determine values of certain theoretical quantities (one does that, legitimately, in curve-fitting), but it does prohibit using the hypothesis itself in certain ways.

The essentials of the strategy are ordinary enough that many people have hit upon them, but generally only to conclude that something must be wrong. Sneed (cf. [14]) and, following him, Stegmüller, for example, describe something very close to this strategy but claim that it cannot be correct because it is circular. The strategy is not circular at all, though it is a bit of a bootstrap operation. One claims that if certain principles of the theory are true, then certain empirical data in fact determine an instance of some theoretical relation, and moreover if the data had been otherwise a counterinstance of that relation would have been obtained. This is some reason to believe the hypothesis tested, but a reason with assumptions. Of course it is possible that the assumptions—the hypotheses used to determine values of theoretical quantities—are false and a positive instance of the hypothesis tested is therefore spurious, or a negative instance equally spurious. But this does not mean that the test is circular or of no account; it does not mean that the strategy can have no part in genuine scientific method. On the contrary, it is just this feature of the strategy which explains part of an important element of method, the demand for a variety of evidence. The hypotheses used in testing a hypothesis may themselves be in error, so that the instances or counterinstances obtained with them are spurious. The only means we have to guard against such error is to test the auxiliary hypotheses used in computing theoretical quantities and to test the original hypothesis using a different combination of auxiliary hypotheses to determine values of theoretical quantities. It is this need that determines part of what counts as a variety of evidence. One can see this aspect of evidential variety explicitly in some experimental research programs, for example in Jean Perrin's series of experiments to test the kinetic theory.[4]

The strategy is holistic in some ways and not in others. Given a definite theory, and some particular pieces of data, it will in general be possible to test some hypotheses of the theory from the data but not other hypotheses. That is because the structure of the theory may be such that there is no way to compute values of certain theoretical quantities from the data in such a way as to test some hypotheses of the theory. For example, from data about the positions of a single planet, Mars say, one can test, relative to the theory consisting of Kepler's three laws, Kepler's first and second laws, but one cannot test his third law. For using this theory, from data about one planet it is impossible to compute, independently, the period and orbital diameter of any *other* planet. Different hypotheses, then, may be tested by different data. It may even be that for certain bodies of possible data some hypotheses of a theory are not tested at all. It is exactly because of this nonholistic aspect of the strategy that the explanation just given of the demand for a variety of evidence makes sense. But the *assessment* of the hypotheses of a theory may be nearly holistic insofar as deciding to accept an hypothesis on the basis of the instances of it obtained involves making a decision about the truth of the auxiliary hypotheses used in testing it, which truth in turn. . . . Still, one can easily construct theories which contain hypotheses that are not tested at all and that are not needed to test other hypotheses of the theory.

There are a number of features that we can use in an inexact way to compare how well theories are supported by evidence. I will mention the most important and obvious ones.

First, it is better that the hypotheses of the theory be confirmed rather than disconfirmed; if one theory contains hypotheses disconfirmed by a given body of evidence, while another does not, then other things being equal that is a reason for preferring the latter.

Second, one theory may contain untested hypotheses whereas its competitor does not; or in some appropriate sense one theory may contain more untested hypotheses than another. As a special case, two theories may share a common hypothesis which is tested by the evidence with respect to one theory but not tested by that same evidence with respect to the other theory. (Such is the case, for instance, with Copernican and Ptolemaic astronomies.)

Third, the evidence may be more various for one theory than for another. One theory may, for example, contain pairs of hypotheses, A and B, such that every test of B must use A (or hypotheses that imply A) and every test of A must use B (or hypotheses that imply B), whereas the competing theory does not have hypotheses so interdependent. Again, there are real examples. Before 1680, tests of Kepler's first law had to use his second, and tests of his second law had to use his first, and astronomers thought this a difficulty with his laws (cf. [17]).

Fourth, some or all of the evidence may have the following feature: It tests one hypothesis of one theory repeatedly, whereas in the other theory it provides fewer tests for a larger number of hypotheses. Informally, the body of evidence may be explained in a uniform way in one theory but have to be explained in several different ways in the second theory. We prefer the first.

Fifth, not all hypotheses in a theory are of equal importance—some are central, others peripheral. There is often enough an historical distinction of this kind, the peripheral hypotheses being those which have resulted from a process of modification to fit the data, the central hypotheses being those which are applied to the data to produce the modifications. In many cases we might expect the historical distinction to correspond to one or more logical distinctions. (Try, for example, this one: Central hypotheses of the theory are the members of the smallest deductively closed set S of hypotheses such that all hypotheses of the theory, or all confirming instances of hypotheses that can be obtained from the data are logically entailed by S together with the set of data statements.) In any case, if a large part of the evidence tests hypotheses that are peripheral to one theory but tests hypotheses that are central to another competing theory, that is reason to prefer the second theory.

These grounds for discriminating among theories could in principle lead us to prefer one from among several competing theories on the basis of a body of evidence explained by all of the theories in the group. Such preferences are not founded, or rather need not be founded, on *a priori* conceptions about how the world is or likely is; they are founded on the preference for better tested theories, and the various modes of comparison are only aspects of that preference. It is true that the principles of comparison are vague, and further that there is no principle given that determines which of these considerations take precedence should they conflict, or how they are to be weighted. (I doubt that there are any principles of this kind which are both natural and explain pervasive features of scientific practice.) I think there is rigor enough, however, to distinguish unambiguously among candidates that are offered in demonstration of the underdetermination of geometry.

One of the puzzling things about the literature on the underdetermination of space-time theories is how little notice its authors have given to the matter of how such theories have been tested. Testing of space-time theories has typically (though not exclusively) proceeded through planetary theory, and the bootstrap strategy, while it can be found throughout science, is preeminently a strategy for planetary theory. The differences between Ptolemaic and Copernican theory, and the relative advantages of the latter, are made evident by the strategy. Many of Kepler's arguments seem to involve it, and such elementary facts as that his evidence for the second law is founded almost entirely on observations of one planet, Mars, whereas his evidence for the third law is founded on observations of many planets, are explained by it. The difficulties which post-Keplerian and pre-Newtonian astronomers found in testing his first and second laws are unintelligible without it. Newton's argument for universal gravitation, certainly the most fundamental nonmathematical argument of the *Principia*, employs the strategy as a central component.[5] The differing values placed on the classical tests of general relativity are difficult to understand without the strategy. The strategy I have described is, I maintain, not only a good strategy, it is one that has predominated in the testing of space-time theories.

We have the elements for an assessment of arguments for the underdetermination of geometry. To make the criteria for theory comparison more definite and at the same time to illustrate why alternative theories of the kind that Reichenbach envisioned are not as good as the theories they are supposed to undermine, imagine a situation. Suppose you find yourself teaching high school physics, Newtonian mechanics in fact. Suppose further that a bright and articulate student named Hans one day announces that he has an alternative theory which is absolutely as good as Newtonian theory, and there is no reason to prefer Newton's theory to his. According to his theory, there are two distinct quantities, gorce and morce; the sum of gorce and morce acts exactly as Newtonian force does. Thus the sum of the gorce and morce acting on a body is equal to the mass of the body times its acceleration, and so on. Hans demands to know why there is not quite as much reason to believe his theory as to believe Newton's. What do you answer?

I should tell him something like this. His theory is merely an extension of Newton's. If he admits that an algebraic combination of quantities is a quantity, then his theory is committed to the existence of a quantity, the sum of gorce and morce, which has all of the features of Newtonian force, and for which there is exactly the evidence there is for Newtonian forces. But in addition his theory claims that this quantity is the sum of two distinct quantities, gorce and morce. However, there is no evidence at all for this additional hypothesis, and Newton's theory is therefore to be preferred. That is roughly what I should say, and I believe it is a natural thing to say; but then I am, I admit, in the grip of a philosophical theory.

The gorce plus morce theory is obtained by replacing "force" wherever it occurs in Newtonian hypotheses by "gorce plus morce", and by further claiming that gorce and morce are distinct quantities neither of which is always zero. In general, a test of Newtonian hypotheses—for example the simple test of Newton's second law using Hooke's law described earlier—will not be a test of the corresponding gorce plus morce hypothesis. That is because the computations which give values for force will not give values either for gorce or for morce, but only for the sum of gorce and morce. Indeed, in general if we have a set of simultaneous equations such that using these equations, values for some of the variables in the equations may be determined from values of other variables, if each of the former variable are replaced systematically throughout the equations with an algebraic combination of two or more new variables, then values for the new variables will not be determined. If to the gorce plus morce theory we add the hypothesis that force is equal to the sum of gorce plus morce, then the theory, with this addition, entails Newtonian theory and every test of Newtonian theory is a test of the identical fragment of the expanded gorce plus morce theory. But there are no tests of the hypothesis that force equals the sum of gorce plus morce, nor are there any tests of those hypotheses that contain "gorce plus morce" in place of "force". The bootstrap strategy, then, gives formally what I should say informally. No surprise there.

My thesis is that the theories advanced to demonstrate the underdetermination of geometry bear a relation to ordinary theories very much like the relation the gorce plus morce theory bears to ordinary Newtonian theory, and are inferior for much the same reason. Implicit in the discussion is a certain articulation of the principle that we prefer a theory with fewer untested hypotheses to one with more untested hypotheses. Suppose there are two theories, T and Q, such that there are a set of axioms A of definitional form and $T\&A$ entail Q but there is no set of axioms B of definitional form such that $Q\&B$ entail T. Further suppose that every test of $T\&A$ from some body of evidence is a test only of hypotheses in Q. Then Q is better tested by that body of evidence than is T. Intuitively, T has whatever untested stuff Q has plus some more. This principle, though rather weak and applicable to only a very limited number of cases, enables us to see how some apparent cases of underdetermination are not that at all. Let us consider a case that might be taken to illustrate the underdetermination of affine geometry in the context of classical physics.

One formulation of Newtonian gravitational theory uses as geometrical objects two scalar fields, the mass density ρ and the gravitational potential ϕ. In addition, there is a scalar field t, the absolute time, and a $(2, 0)$ singular tensor field representing the metric, and, finally, an affine connection compatible with the metric. The field equations in component form are

1) $R^i_{jkl} = 0$

2) $t_{i;k} = 0$ where $t_i = \dfrac{2t}{2x^i}$

3) $g^{ir}_{;k\,k} = 0$

4) $g^{ik}t_i t_k = 0$

5) $g^{ik}\phi_{;i;k} = 4\pi\kappa\rho$

where the semicolon signifies covariant differentiation with respect to the index following it and, as usual, repeated indices are understood to be summed over. The equation of motion is

6) $\dfrac{d^2 x^i}{dt^2} + \Gamma^i_{jk}\dfrac{dx^j}{dt}\dfrac{dx^k}{dt} = -g^{ir}\phi_{;r}$

where the Γ^i_{jk} are the Christoffel symbols of the connection.

It is easy to prove that there are inertial coordinates in which the time scalar functions as one coordinate, and the components of the metric tensor are constant and the matrix of components of the tensor are $(g^{ij}) = \text{diag}\,(0, 1, 1, 1)$—see [2]. In such coordinates, equation 5 becomes just Poisson's equation

$\nabla^2\phi = 4\pi\kappa\rho$

Consider now how well Newtonian theory, so formulated, is tested by the kind of evidence generally in mind. Assume then, as part of the theory, that ordinary rigid rods determine congruences according to the metric and that mechanical clocks measure the absolute time function at least approximately. So we may take as data such congruences, time intervals, and the trajectories of freely falling bodies. The question is what parts of Newtonian theory are tested by such data. On the account of testing given earlier, the answer depends on what other quantities can be determined uniquely from such data by means of the theory itself, and in what ways such determinations can be carried out. By a model of Newtonian gravitational theory let us mean a tuple $\langle M, g, t, \rho, \phi, \Gamma, F \rangle$ where M is a four-dimensional differentiable manifold, g a $(2,0)$ metric field, t, ρ, and ϕ scalar fields, Γ an affine connection, and F a family of time-like trajectories on the manifold, such that these objects satisfy the equations of the theory if F is taken as the collection of free falls. Our question can be answered in part by asking whether such quantities as the affine connection and gravitational potential are uniquely determined in some models or in every model by g, t, ρ and the family of trajectories. The answer is that they are not so determined, not in any model. Let $\langle M, g, t, \rho, \phi, \Gamma, F \rangle$ be a model of the theory. Choose three linearly independent constant vector fields ${}_k\bigcup^a$ ($k = 1, 2, 3$) such that ${}_k\bigcup^a t_a = 0$ and let $f_k(t)$ ($K = 1, 2, 3$) be any three scalar fields which are constant on each constant time hypersurface. Denoting $g^{ar}\phi_{;r}$ by ϕ^a, define

$$\psi^a = \phi^a + f^k(t)\,{}_k\bigcup^a$$

$$°\Gamma^a_{bc} = \Gamma^a_{bc} - f^k(t)\,{}_k\bigcup^a t_b t_c$$

Then Trautman (see [16]) has shown that $\langle M, g, t, \rho, °\Gamma, \psi, F \rangle$ is a model of the theory.

The connection and the potential are not determined by the other quantities in the theory. Although an ordinary Riemannian connection is determined by an ordinary Riemannian metric, the metric in this case is singular and so fails to determine a unique compatible connection. Another way to put this indeterminacy is that the metric, time, and trajectories of free falls do not determine the class of inertial frames.

The upshot is that because the affine connection cannot be determined from the phenomena, not even using the theory, and functions of the connection, such as the curvature tensor, cannot be determined either, many of the equations of Newtonian theory cannot be instantiated in a way that tests them; the theory can be tested in hypothetico-deductive fashion, but that is a fashion different from the one described above. It may occur to some that the theory contains undeterminable quantities only because it is incomplete. Perhaps the indeterminacy arises because, lacking boundary conditions, we cannot get a unique solution of Poisson's equation. If one adds to the theory the natural condition that at infinite distances from sources the gravitational potential vanishes, then it seems the potential and hence the connection will be uniquely determined (because, at arbitrarily large distances from sources, ψ^a must vanish, so $f^k(t)$ must vanish, but $f^k(t)$ is constant throughout space). Even then, however, the most one can say is that in *some* models of the theory the potential is determined. "Full" models, those in which there is an upper bound on the distance between particles, will not determine the potential; in particular every non-empty model of the theory in which the constant time hypersurfaces are compact will leave the potential and connection undetermined.

Consider now another theory, one which permits the very same trajectories as does the Newtonian theory. Save for the absence of the gravitational potential, the new theory has the same kinds of objects as does Newtonian theory, but the field equations and equations of motion are different and some of the objects, the connection in particular, behave differently.

1*) $t_{\{p} \, {}^oR^i_{j\}kl} = 0$

2*) $g^{ip} \, {}^oR^j_{kpl} = g^{jp} \, {}^oR^i_{lpk}$

3*) $t_{i;k} = 0$

4*) $g^{il}_{\;;k} = 0$

5*) $g^{il}t_it_l = 0$

6*) ${}^oR_{lk} = -4\pi\rho t_l t_k$

are the field equations, and the equation of motion is

7*) $\dfrac{d^2x^i}{dt^2} = {}^o\Gamma^i_{lk}\dfrac{dx^1}{dt}\dfrac{dx^k}{dt} = 0$

^oR and $^o\Gamma$ signify the curvature and Christoffel symbols of the connection. The brackets indicate antisymmetrization with respect to the indices between them. In this theory, the affine connection is a dynamical object determined by the distribution of matter through equation 6* which is just the analog of Poisson's equation. The equation of motion, 7*, says that the trajectories of free falls are geodesics of the connection. The Newtonian gravitational potential has, in effect, been geometrized away.

Consider how well the new theory is tested by the same data we considered before. Equations 3*, 4*, 5*, like their Newtonian analogs, imply the existence of inertial coordinates in which spatial components of the connection vanish. So those equations expressed by 7* which have $i \neq 0$ can be tested by determining features of trajectories and congruences. Further, equation 7* says that free falls are geodesics and that the time is an affine parameter. The geodesic spray of a connection and an affine parameter uniquely determine the connection (cf. [1]). The connection can therefore be determined from trajectories by using 7* and thus various of the field equations (e.g., equations 6* and 1*) can be instantiated in a way that tests them.

Informally, it seems clear that the confirmation principles described earlier imply that the second theory is better tested than is the first. But we can here apply the more precise principle developed in the gorce plus morce example. To the first theory we add axioms of definitional form so that the second theory is entailed. But the procedure is not symmetrical. The only object of the second theory that behaves differently from its Newtonian analog is the connection. If to the equations of Newtonian theory we add

$^o\Gamma^i_{lk} = \Gamma^i_{lk} + \phi_{;r}t_l t_k$

then all of the equations of the second theory follow. It does not work in the other direction. We can show that given $\langle M, g, t, {}^o\Gamma, \rho, F \rangle$ satisfying the second theory, there exists a scalar ϕ and connection Γ such that $\langle M, g, t, \Gamma, \rho, \phi, F \rangle$ is a model of the first theory, but we cannot *define* Γ or ϕ from $\langle M, g, t, {}^o\Gamma, \rho, F \rangle$. The two theories do not say the same thing. The relations between the Newtonian theory and the alternative theory with a dynamical connection are exactly like the relations between the gorce plus morce theory and the force theory. Only this time we are dealing with rather more realistic examples. While both theories account for the imagined phenomena, the testing strategy described earlier provides clear reasons for preferring one of these theories to the other on the basis of that body of phenomena.

There are other examples of this kind of relation between competing theories, or of something very close to it. There are many special relativistic theories of gravitation, theories which ascribe to space-time the Minkowski metric, unaffected by the distribution of matter, energy, or momentum, and which treat gravity as a field distinct from the metric field. For various reasons, only those special relativistic gravitational theories which treat the gravitational field as a tensor field have a hope of being empirically adequate. To exaggerate slightly, what many of these flat space-time theories of gravitation do is to divide the dynamical metric field of general relativity into a fixed Minkowski metric and a gravitational field tensor which, of course, is not fixed but dynamical, that is, dependent on the distribution of matter and radiation. If that were exactly what they did, then the relation between such theories and general relativity would be just like the relation between the gorce plus morce theory and the force theory. In fact, the situation is usually a little more complicated. Such theories may, for example, take the metric field of a particular solution or class of solutions of the field equations of general relativity, divide the metric into a Minkowski metric and a gravitational field tensor, and write down new field equations satisfied by these objects. That is just what happens in a flat space-time gravitational theory due to W. Thirring [15]. So far as testing is concerned, the results are generally very much as in the Newtonian case already considered; the special relativistic metric and the gravitational field tensor cannot be determined uniquely, and the field equations, unlike their general relativistic analogs, cannot be instantiated. Thus the authors of a relativity textbook say of Thirring's theory:

> ... there exists a transformation of the potential which leaves all observable quantities unchanged, but which changes the rate of flow of time and the rates of clocks as expressed in terms of "absolute time"....
>
> Thus a fully developed RTGFS (Relativistic Theory of Gravitation in Flat Space) which agrees with GTR (General Theory of Relativity) in the first corrections to Newtonian theory, in order to explain the universality of the action of gravity, is forced to employ the unphysical hypotheses of an unobservable "absolute" time, and of the influence of unobservable quantities—e.g., the gravitational potential—upon all physical processes. ([18]: 69–70).

For "unobservable" in this passage, read "undeterminable". Thirring himself says much the same thing.

R. Sexl [12] has claimed that general relativity says the same thing as Thirring's theory. The sole basis for this claim is that a tensor satisfying Einstein's equations for the metric tensor can be defined from quantities in Thirring's theory. But this is far from sufficient, since the special relativistic metric of Thirring's theory cannot be defined from general relativistic quantities. A quantity satisfying Einstein's equations might be definable from Thirring's theory even if Thirring's theory were inconsistent. (In fact, Thirring's theory *is* inconsistent. Cf. [7]: 186.)

Reichenbach's argument for the general underdetermination of geometry goes like this. Suppose you have an empirically adequate physical theory in which the metric tensor is g and bodies subject to no forces move (or would move) on geodesics of g. Let the theory postulate whatever other fields are necessary, and let g be measured in whatever ways are appropriate, e.g., by congruences of rigid rods. Form an alternative theory as follows. Replace g by any metric you like, call it h, so long as h meets certain topological constraints. Introduce a "universal force" U such that h plus U equals g, and specify that every body is subject, always, to the universal force U, so that bodies subject to no other forces or fields would move on geodesics of the tensor h plus U. Let the other fields and forces, and the criteria for determining where they are acting, be just as in the first theory. Then the two theories should be empirically equivalent and the choice between them underdetermined by all possible evidence.

It is not entirely clear whether Reichenbach meant to be arguing in the context of classical physics, relativistic physics, or both. I believe his arguments have been widely understood to apply to both contexts, and to show that the geometry of space in classical theory and the geometry of space-time in relativistic theory are equally underdetermined. In relativistic contexts, the "universal force" must be a "universal field" but other than that, the argument is most clear for relativity. It tells us, for example, that to obtain a theory equally as good as general relativity we need only replace the general relativistic metric by any other metric we choose and add a "universal field", i.e., a gravitational field tensor. We have seen already, however, that this is exactly the strategy pursued in certain flat space-time theories, and that the result is *not* a theory as well tested as general relativity. In its most direct application, Reichenbach's argument simply fails if we employ the account of confirmation discussed earlier.

What about classical physics? In the context of Newtonian theories it is less clear what a universal force might be, but we can work backwards to arrive at an account. In Newtonian theory with ordinary Euclidean geometry, particles subject to no forces, were there any, would have to move on geodesics of the connection, that is, subject to the equation

$$\frac{d^2x^i}{dt^2} + \Gamma^i_{lk}\frac{dx^l}{dt}\frac{dx^k}{dt} = 0$$

With a non-Euclidean geometry, the motion of particles must be such that if, *per impossible*, they were not subject to a universal force they would move on geodesics of the connection. The actual covariant acceleration then, that is

$$\frac{d^2x^i}{dt^2} + {}^*\Gamma^i_{lk}\frac{dx^l}{dt}\frac{dx^k}{dt}$$

should be equal to the universal force F^i acting on them. So the equation of motion should be

$$\frac{d^2x^i}{dt^2} + {}^*\Gamma^i_{lk}\frac{dx^l}{dt}\frac{dx^k}{dt} = F^i$$

Hence the universal force must be

$$F^i = ({}^*\Gamma^i_{lk} - \Gamma^i_{lk})\frac{dx^l}{dt}\frac{dx^k}{dt}$$

A universal force, then, is feature of the difference in the affine properties of two geometries, and need not involve the metrics directly at all. (Cf. [7]: 186.)

Looking back at the relation between the version of Newtonian theory with a fixed affine connection and the second version, that with a dynamical connection and no potential, it is clear that the former theory is just the latter *with a universal force*. The universal force in that case is $-g^{ir}\phi_{;r}$, i.e., just the gravitational force that enters the equation of motion of the first version. And again, we have already seen that while these two theories may equally save the phenomena, they are not equally well tested or supported by the phenomena.

The examples we have already considered show that Reichenbach's argument is invalid, and that his strategy for generating alternative theories need not result in pairs of theories equally well tested by the phenomena imagined. Considering classical theories which have, besides different connections, different metrics, does not change things at all. Thus if the alternative theory postulates, say, a hyperbolic metric we should expect it to contain field equations such as the following:

$$h^{ik}t_i t_k = 0$$

$$h^{ik}_{;l} = 0$$

$$t^i_{il} = 0$$

$$R_{abcd} = K(Y_{ad}Y_{bc} - Y_{ac}Y_{bd})$$

$$K = -1$$

where h is the singular metric tensor and Y the metric induced on any constant time hypersurface. For the equation of motion of particles subject to no "differential forces" we should have

$$\frac{d^2 x^i}{dt^2} = \Gamma^i_{lk}\frac{dx^l}{dt}\frac{dx^k}{dt} = F^i$$

where F^i is the universal force. The relation between this theory and Newtonian theory is very much the kind we have seen before. Although the Euclidean metric cannot be defined from this theory, the standard connection, Γ, can be by

$$\Gamma^i_{lk} = \Gamma^i_{lk} - F^i\frac{\partial t}{\partial x^l}\frac{\partial t}{\partial x^k}$$

and with this definition (and defining time by time, etc.) the geodesic equation of motion and those field equations of Newtonian theory that do not involve the metric all follow.

An obvious reply to the criticisms I have offered is that the alternative theories described are incomplete, and that more complete versions of them will be equally well tested by the phenomena. The cause of the underdetermination of geometry, allegedly, is that while geometry is supposed to deal with properties of space or of space-time itself, the evidence for a geometry must always be provided by what is material; different assumptions about the connections between geometrical quantities and material systems lead to different geometrical theories. What the theories described so far have left out, the reply continues, is the new assumptions connecting universal force with material systems, or the new metric writh material systems, assumptions which would make the universal force term occurring in a theory determinable, and which would, therefore, permit the testing of various equations in such theories.

I think the reply fails, and does so because it does not take the testing strategy described earlier seriously enough. In the first place, if the demand of covariance be satisfied, the kinds of principles envisioned require that the theories be made rather more complex. Whereas ordinary rods measure, at least approximately, Euclidean congruences or distances, there are no natural relations of material things that can be used to measure, even approximately, distances according to an arbitrary metric. The usual way philosophers have described an alternative metric, therefore, is in terms of functions of some particular set of coordinates, generally Cartesian coordinates such that coordinate differences equal Euclidean distances; the procedure in mind, apparently, for determining the non-Euclidean metric is that one uses material systems to set up Cartesian coordinates and then evaluates the metric as a function of the coordinate description of position. I have no objection to this method of determining a non-Euclidean metric, for it is often the case that we must use some system of coordinates to test hypotheses. But to make the *statement* of the theory independent of coordinates one must in the theory introduce suitable scalar fields (essentially the spatial coordinate fields) and, furthermore, one must introduce the hypothesis that the metric is a suitable function of these scalar fields. And one must claim that material systems, e.g., rigid rods, measure these scalar fields or some feature of them—just as one claims that clocks measure a feature of the time scalar field. With these additions an alternative theory such as the hyperbolic theory described above is covariant and its metric is determinable.

Is such a theory really as good as the ordinary one with ordinary geometry? Introducing a set of hypotheses that link the metric with material systems may make testable various equations, some of the field equations for example, involving the metric. But the equation of motion, since it involves a universal force term, will still not be tested, nor will any equation that involves covariant differentiation. To test these hypotheses, the theory must be expanded still further, and in such a way as to make the universal force term determinable. Perhaps the universal force can be specified as some function of the (coordinate) scalar fields, very much like the metric. The result, one expects, must still be a theory that is less well tested than is the ordinary theory. For while all of the equations written down earlier should be testable in this expanded theory, to test them we will have had to introduce an enormous body of claims in order to permit the determination of the metric, connection and universal force; these claims will either be untested, or else the claims involved in the determination of the metric, say, will only be testable by using the claims that are involved in the determination of the connection and universal force. The theory will be inferior, then, either by reason of untested hypotheses, or by reason of an insufficient variety of evidence.

Suppose it is said that, after all, there is the same kind of interdependence of hypotheses in the ordinary theory. The ordinary theory claims that clocks measure a function of the time scalar, and that rigid rods measure the congruences of the metric—aren't these the same kind of "coordination principles" that the non-Euclidean theory uses? The answer is that they are, but the non-Euclidean theory requires a lot more of them and at best will permit one of them to be tested only by using a lot of others. The case of time is common to all theories we are considering in a Newtonian context. The Euclidean theory must claim that rods (or something) measure congruences; the non-Euclidean theory must claim that there are various scalar fields, that rods (or something) measure functions of these fields, that the metric is a certain function of these fields and, furthermore, that the universal force is another function of these same fields. Nothing less will do. These are all claims which we want tested, and tests of any of them will necessarily involve using all of the others.

It might be said, though not quite accurately, that all I have done is to argue that nonstandard theories must have more theoretical content than standard ones, that nonstandard theories go farther beyond the data. But if that is an objection to the nonstandard theories in comparison to the standard theory, why isn't it equally an objection to the descriptions of actual or possible trajectories and so on? Why not just say: "The possible trajectories are such and such"? Why have theories at all? The answer, I believe, is that actual data on trajectories, etc., can provide better tests of, and better support for, a *theory* of the possible trajectories than it does for the simple claim that the possible trajectories are those the theory claims to be possible. I imagine the latter "simple" claim to be a set of hypotheses of the form: "With such and such initial conditions, the motions satisfy the equation—" where the blank is to be filled by some nondifferential equation in coordinate variables and time, giving the position of a body in the system as a function of time. Clearly, the set of hypotheses of this kind is not going to be finitely axiomatizable. Regard this enormous set of claims as a theory to be tested like any other, and to be compared in particular with the dynamical theory that gives these trajectories as the possible ones. The data, we may suppose, consist of statements as to the locations of various bodies at various times. The data may very well test the dynamical theory better than it tests the set of claims about the trajectories, and for several reasons. Various principles of the dynamical theory may be tested over and over by different pieces of data, whereas data incorporating different sets of initial conditions will generally test but one of the hypotheses explicitly about trajectories. On any finite body of evidence, it will be the case that most of the trajectory hypotheses are untested, but that same data, while not testing every hypothesis of the dynamical theory, may nonetheless test a body of hypotheses of the dynamical theory sufficient to entail every hypothesis of the theory. We may, then have sufficient grounds to accept the dynamical theory even when we would not have anything like sufficient grounds to accept merely that the possible trajectories are those the theory permits.

What if we consider not statements about trajectories but rather just the statements of the data itself. "Body B was at place P at time t." Is not the body of such data claims, whatever they may be, better warranted than the theory, and so do not the principles I used to reject the non-Euclidean theory require that I reject all theories? Clearly not. First, because the data claims are not a theory and cannot serve the purposes of theories, in particular cannot serve for prediction or retrodiction. Second, because while the data as a whole may be better warranted; once we admit that what we call data is no incorrigible body of claims but only claims obtained by methods, whatever they may be, that we believe reliable, it becomes possible that a theory be better supported, better warranted, than some particular piece of evidence for or against it. If data are corrigible, the theory tested and confirmed by·many pieces of evidence may sometimes reasonably be preferred to a datum that conflicts with it. Curve-fitters make such decisions every day.

I think, then, that the criteria by which I have denigrated nonstandard theories of space or of space-time do not require me to denigrate all theories. The sorts of theories Reichenbach and many others have suggested, whether they be understood in classical or in relativistic contexts, are just not as good as the theories they are supposed to prove to be underdetermined. It is still possible, of course, that space-time theories are as radically underdetermined as Poincaré, Reichenbach, and others have believed, but that the alternative theories are simply very different from the kind Reichenbach and subsequent writers envisioned.[6] Even if it is true that our space-time theories are not radically underdetermined, there may still be features of space-time that are underdetermined. There may be quantities or properties which for whatever reasons we believe our theories rightly ascribe to space-time, but which we cannot determine. I have suggested elsewhere [3] that in certain cosmological models the global topology of space-time may be such a feature. Perhaps there are others as well; whatever may turn up, it is bound to be more palatable than is the radical underdetermination of geometry.

Notes

This research was supported, in part, by NSF Grant GS41764.
1. An excellent discussion of covariant formulations of space-time theories is available in [2].
2. An elaboration and defense of these conditions is given in [6].
3. The ideas about confirmation sketched here are given in more detail in [4].
4. An excellent history of Perrin's work is given in [8].
5. A detailed discussion of how the strategy applies to Ptolemaic and Copernican theories and to Newton's argument for universal gravitation is given in [5].
6. In a preprint of [10], Hilary Putnam argues that nonstandard theories can be generated without using "universal forces" by positing an appropriate "interaction force" between differential forces. I do not see how this suggestion can work unless the theory to be undermined already contains two universal forces which are like gravitation in entering the equation of motion without parameters. But a theory with two such forces would already be objectionable for reasons discussed.

References

[1] R. Bishop and S. Goldberg, *Tensor Analysis on Manifolds* (New York: Macmillan, 1968).

[2] Michael, Friedman, "Foundations of Space-Time Theories," 1972 Ph.D. dissertation, Princeton University.

[3] Clark Glymour, "Indistinguishable Space-Times and the Fundamental Group," in *Minnesota Studies in the Philosophy of Science*, Vol. 8, edited by J. Earman, C. Glymour, and J. Stachel (Minneapolis: University of Minnesota Press, 1977).

[4] Clark Glymour, "Relevant Evidence," *The Journal of Philosophy*, LXII (1975).

[5] Clark Glymour, "Physics and Evidence," in *Pittsburgh Series in Philosophy of Science*, ed. by L. Laudan, forthcoming.

[6] Clark, Glymour, "Theoretical Realism and Theoretical Equivalence," *Boston Studies in the Philosophy of Science*, Vol. 8, edited by R. Buck (Dordrecht: D. Reidel, 1971).

[7] C. Misner, K. Thorne, and J. Wheeler, *Gravitation* (San Francisco: W. H. Freeman, 1973).

[8] M. J. Nye, *Molecular Reality* (American Elsevier: 1972).

[9] H. Poincaré, *Science and Hypothesis* (New York: Science Press, 1905).

[10] H. Putnam, "The Refutation of Conventionalism," NOÛS VIII (1974): 25–40.

[11] H. Reichenbach, *The Philosophy of Space and Time* (New York: Dover, 1953).

[12] R. Sexl, "Universal Conventionalism and Space-Time," *General Relativity and Gravitation*, Vol, 1 (1970).

[13] L. Sklar, *Space, Time and Space-Time* (Berkeley: University of California Press, 1974).

[14] J. Sneed, *The Logical Structure of Mathematical Physics* (Dordrecht: D. Reidel, 1971).

[15] W. Thirring, "An Alternative Approach to the Theory of Gravitation," *Annals of Physics*, Vol. XVI (1961): 96–117.

[16] A. Trautman, "Foundation and Current Problems in General Relativity," in *Brandeis Summer Institute in Theoretical Physics, 1964* (New York: Prentice-Hall, 1965).

[17] C. Wilson, "From Kepler's Laws, So-called, to Universal Gravitation," *Archive for the History of Exact Sciences*, Vol. VI (1969): 89–170.

[18] Y. Zeldovich and I. Novikov, *Relativistic Astrophysics* (Chicago: University of Chicago Press, 1971).

Chapter 27

Is the Moon There When Nobody Looks?
Reality and the Quantum Theory

N. David Mermin

Quantum mechanics is magic.[1]

In May 1935, Albert Einstein, Boris Podolsky, and Nathan Rosen published[2] an argument that quantum mechanics fails to provide a complete description of physical reality. Today, fifty years later, the EPR paper and the theoretical and experimental work it inspired remain remarkable for the vivid illustration they provide of one of the most bizarre aspects of the world revealed to us by the quantum theory.

Einstein's talent for saying memorable things did him a disservice when he declared "God does not play dice," for it has been held ever since that the basis for his opposition to quantum mechanics was the claim that a fundamental understanding of the world can only be statistical. But the EPR paper, his most powerful attack on the quantum theory, focuses on quite a different aspect: the doctrine that physical properties have in general no objective reality independent of the act of observation. As Pascual Jordan put it[3]

> Observations not only disturb what has to be measured, they produce it.... We compel [the electron] to assume a definite position.... We ourselves produce the results of measurement.

Jordan's statement is something of a truism for contemporary physicists. Underlying it, we have all been taught, is the disruption of what is being measured by the act of measurement, made unavoidable by the existence of the quantum of action, which generally makes it impossible even in principle to construct probes that can yield the information classical intuition expects to be there.

Einstein didn't like this. He wanted things out there to have properties, whether or not they were measured[4]:

> We often discussed his notions on objective reality. I recall that during one walk Einstein suddenly stopped, turned to me and asked whether I really believed that the moon exists only when I look at it.

The EPR paper describes a situation ingeniously contrived to force the quantum theory into asserting that properties in a space-time region B are the results of an act of measurement in another space-time region A, so far from B that there is no possibility of the measurement in A exerting an influence on region B by any known dynamical mechanism. Under these conditions, Einstein maintained that the properties in A must have existed all along.

Reprinted with permission from the author and *Physics Today*, pp. 38–47 (April 1985). 1985 American Institute of Physics.

Spooky Actions at a Distance

Many of his simplest and most explicit statements of this position can be found in Einstein's correspondence with Max Born.[5] Throughout the book (which sometimes reads like a Nabokov novel), Born, pained by Einstein's distaste for the statistical character of the quantum theory, repeatedly fails, both in his letters and in his later commentary on the correspondence, to understand what is really bothering Einstein. Einstein tries over and over again, without success, to make himself clear. In March 1948, for example, he writes:

> That which really exists in *B* should . . . not depend on what kind of measurement is carried out in part of space *A*; it should also be independent of whether or not any measurement at all is carried out in space *A*. If one adheres to this program, one can hardly consider the quantum-theoretical description as a complete representation of the physically real. If one tries to do so in spite of this, one has to assume that the physically real in *B* suffers a sudden change as a result of a measurement in *A*. My instinct for physics bristles at this.

Or, in March 1947,

> I cannot seriously believe in [the quantum theory] because it cannot be reconciled with the idea that physics should represent a reality in time and space, free from spooky actions at a distance.

The "spooky actions at a distance" (*spukhafte Fernwirkungen*) are the acquisition of a definite value of a property by the system in region *B* by virtue of the measurement carried out in region *A*. The EPR paper presents a wave-function that describes two correlated particles, localized in regions *A* and *B*, far apart. In this particular two-particle state one can learn (in the sense of being able to predict with certainty the result of a subsequent measurement) either the position or the momentum of the particle in region *B* as a result of measuring the corresponding property of the particle in region *A*. If "that which really exists" in region *B* does not depend on what kind of measurement is carried out in region *A*, then the particle in region *B* must have had both a definite position and a definite momentum all along.

Because the quantum theory is intrinsically incapable of assigning values to both quantities at once, it must provide an incomplete description of the physically real. Unless, of course, one asserts that it is only by virtue of the position (or momentum) measurement in *A* that the particles in *B* acquires its position (or momentum): spooky actions at a distance.

At a dramatic moment Pauli appears in the *Born-Einstein Letters*, writing Born from Princeton in 1954 with his famous tact on display:

> Einstein gave me your manuscript to read; he was *not at all* annoyed with you, by only said you were a person who will not listen. This agrees with the impression I have formed myself insofar as I was unable to recognize Einstein whenever you talked about him in either your letter or your manuscript. It seemed to me as if you had erected some dummy Einstein for yourself, which you then knocked down with great pomp. In particular, Einstein does not consider the concept of "determinism" to be as fundametal as it is frequently held to be (as he told me emphatically many times). . . . In the same way, he *disputes* that he uses as criterion for the admissibility of a theory the question: "Is it rigorously determinstic?"

Pauli goes on to state the real nature of Einstein's "philosophy prejudice" to Born, emphasizing that "Einstein's point of departure is 'realistic' rather than 'deterministic'." According to Pauli the proper grounds for challenging Einstein's view are simply that

> One should no more rack one's brain about the problem of whether something one cannot know anything about exists all the same, than about the ancient question of how many angels are able to sit on the point of a needle. But it seems to me that Einstein's questions are ultimately always of this kind.

Faced with spooky actions at a distance, Einstein preferred to believe that things one cannot know anything about (such as the momentum of a particle with a definite position) do exist all the same. In April 1948 he wrote to Born:

> Those physicists who regard the descriptive methods of quantum mechanics as definitive in principle would ... drop the requirement for the independent existence of the physical reality present in different parts of space; they would be justified in pointing out that the quantum theory nowhere makes explicit use of this requirement. I admit this, but would point out: when I consider the physical phenomena known to me, and especially those which are being so successfully encompassed by quantum mechanics, I still cannot find any fact anywhere which would make it appear likely that [the] requirement will have to be abandoned. I am therefore inclined to believe that the description of quantum mechanics ... has to be regarded as an incomplete and indirect description of reality....

A Fact is Found

The theoretical answer to this challenge to provide "any fact anywhere" was given in 1964 by John S. Bell, in a famous paper[6] in the short-lived journal *Physics*. Using a *gedanken* experiment invented[7] by David Bohm, in which "properties one cannot know anything about" (the simultaneous values of the spin of a particle along several distinct directions) are required to exist by the EPR line of reasoning, Bell showed ("Bell's theorem") that the nonexistence of these properties is a direct consequence of the quantitative numerical predictions of the quantum theory. The conclusion is quite independent of whether or not one believes that the quantum theory offers a complete description of physical reality. If the data in such an experiment are in argeement with the numerical predictions of the quantum theory, then Einstein's philosophical position has to be wrong.

In the last few years, in a beautiful series of experiments, Alain Aspect and his collaborators at the University of Paris's Institute of Theoretical and Applied Optics in Orsay provided[8] the experimental answer to Einstein's challenge by performing a version of the EPR experiment under conditions in which Bell's type of analysis applied. They showed that the quantum-theoretic predictions were indeed obeyed. Thirty years after Einstein's challenge, a fact—not a metaphysical doctrine—was provided to refute him.

Attitudes toward this particular fifty-year sequence of intellectual history and scientific discovery vary widely.[9] From the very start Bohr certainly took it seriously. Léon Rosenfeld describes[10] the impact of the EPR argument:

> This onslaught came down upon us as a bolt from the blue. Its effect on Bohr was remarkable.... A new worry could not have come at a less propitious time. Yet, as soon as Bohr had heard my report of Einstein's argument, everything else was abandoned.

Bell's contribution has become celebrated in what might be called semipopular culture. We read, for example, in *The Dancing Wu Li Masters* that "Some physicists are convinced that [Bell's theorem] is the most important single work, perhaps, in the history of physics."[11]

And indeed, Henry Stapp, a particle theorist at Berkeley, writes that "Bell's theorem is the most profound discovery of science."[12]

At the other end of the spectrum, Abraham Pais, in this recent biography of Einstein, writes[13] of the EPR article—that "bolt from the blue," the basis for "the most profound discovery of science":

> The only part of this article which will ultimately survive, I believe, is ... a phrase ["No reasonable definition of reality could be expected to permits this"] which so poignantly summarizes Einstein's views on quantum mechanics in his later years.

I think it is fair to say that more physicists would side with Pais than with Stapp, but between the majority position of near indifference and the minority position of wild extravagance is an attitude I would characterize as balanced. This was expressed to me most succinctly by a distinguished Princeton physicist on the occasion of my asking how he thought Einstein would have reacted to Bell's theorem. He said that Einstein would have gone home and thought about it hard for several weeks—that he couldn't guess what he would then have said, except that it would have been extremely interesting. He was sure that Einstein would have been very bothered by Bell's theorem. Then he added. "Anybody who's not bothered by Bell's theorem has to have rocks in his head."

To this moderate point of view I would only add the observation that contemporary physicists come in two varieties. Type 1 physicists are bothered by EPR and Bell's theorem. Type 2 (the majority) are not, but one has to distinguish two subvarieties. Type 2a physicists explain why they are not bothered. Their explanations tend either to miss the point entirely (like Born's to Einstein) or to contain physical assertions that can be shown to be false. Type 2b are not bothered and refuse to explain why. Their position is unassailable. (There is a variant of type 2b who say that Bohr straightened out[14] the whole business, but refuse to explain how.)

A Gedanken Demonstration

To enable you to test which category you belong to, I shall describe, in black-box terms, a very simple version of Bell's *gedanken* experiment, deferring to the very end any reference whatever either to the underlying mechanism that makes the gadget work or to the quantum-theoretic analysis that accounts for the data. Perhaps this backwards way of proceeding will make it easier for you to lay aside your quantum theoretic prejudices and decide afresh whether what I describe is or is not strange.[15]

What I have in mind is a simple *gedanken* demonstration. The apparatus comes in three pieces. Two of them (*A* and *B*) function as detectors. They are far apart from each other (in the analogous Aspect experiments over 10 meters apart). Each detector has a switch that can be set to one of three positions; each detector responds to an event by flashing either a red light or a green one. The third piece (*C*), midway between *A* and *B*, functions as a source. (See figure 27.1.)

There are no connections between the pieces—no mechanical connections, no electromagnetic connections, nor any other known kinds of relevant connections. (I promise that when you learn what is inside the black boxes you will agree that there are no connections.) The detectors are thus incapable of signaling to each other or to

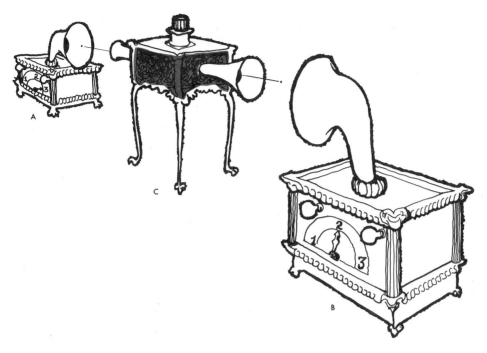

Figure 27.1
An EPR apparatus. The experimental setup consists of two detectors, *A* and *B*, and a source of something ("particles" or whatever) *C*. To start a run, the experimenter pushes the button on *C*; something passes from *C* to both detectors. Shortly after the button is pushed, each detector flashes one of its lights. Putting a brick between the source and one of the detectors prevents that detector from flashing, and moving the detectors farther away from the source increases the delay between when the button is pushed and when the lights flash. The switch settings on the detectors vary randomly from one run to another. Note that there are no connections between the three parts of the apparatus, other than via whatever it is that passes from *C* to *A* and *B*.

the source via any known mechanism, and with the exception of the "particles" described below, the source has no way of signaling to the detectors. The demonstration proceeds as follows:

The switch of each detector is independently and randomly set to one of its three positions, and a button is pushed on the source; a little after that, each detector flashes either red or green. The setting of the switches and the colors that flash are recorded, and then the whole thing is repeated over and over again.

The data consist of a pair of numbers and a pair of colors for each run. A run, for example, in which *A* was set to 3, *B* was set to 2, *A* flashed red, and *B* flashed green, would be recorded as "32RG," as shown in figure 27.2.

Because there are no built-in connections between the source *C* and the detectors *A* and *B*, the link between the pressing of the button and the flashing of the light on a detector can only be provided by the passage of something (which we shall call a "particle," though you can call it anything you like) between the source and that detector. This can easily be tested; for example, by putting a brick between the source and a detector. In subsequent runs, that detector will not flash. When the brick is removed, everything works as before.

Typical data from a large number of runs are shown in figure 27.3. There are just two relevant features:

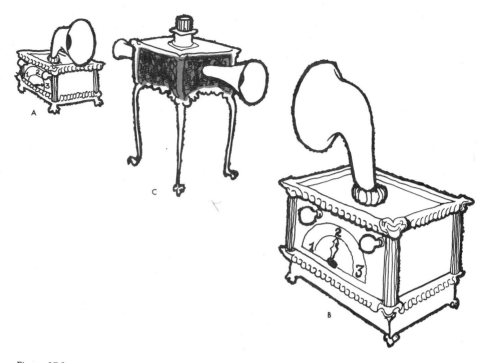

Figure 27.2
The result of a run. Shortly after the experimenter pushed the button on the source in figure 27.1, the detectors flash one lamp each. The experimenter records the switch settings and the colors of the lamps and then repeats the experiment. Here, for example, the record reads 32RG—the switches are in positions 3 and 2 and the lamps flashed R and G, respectively.

• If one examines only those runs in which the switches have the same setting (figure 27.4), then one finds that the lights always flash the same colors.
• If one examines all runs, without any regard to how the switches are set (figure 27.5), then one finds that the pattern of flashing is completely random. In particular, half the time the lights flash the same colors, and half the time different colors.

That is all there is to the *gedanken* demonstration.
Should you be bothered by these data unless you have rocks in your head?

Figure 27.3
Data produced by the apparatus of figure 27.1. This is a fragment of an enormous set of data generated by many, many runs: Each entry shows the switch settings and the colors of the lights that flashed for a run. The switch settings are changed randomly from run to run.

Figure 27.4
Switches set the same: the data of figure 27.3, but highlighted to pick out those runs in which both detectors had the same switch settings as they flashed. Note that in such runs the lights always flash the same colors.

Figure 27.5
Switches set any way: the data of figure 27.3, but highlighted to emphasize only the colors of the lights that flashed in each run, no matter how the switches were set when the lights flashed. Note that the pattern of colors is completely random.

31 GR	22 RR	13 GR	31 GR	22 RR	13 GR	31 GR	13 RR	13 GR
31 GR	32 RR	11 RR	31 GR	32 RR	11 RR	31 GR	32 RR	11 RR
13 RG	13 GR	12 RG	13 RG	13 GR	12 RG	13 RG	13 GR	12 RG
31 RR	22 GG	33 GG	31 RR	22 GG	33 GG	31 RR	22 GG	33 GG
33 GG	11 RR	21 GR	33 GG	11 RR	21 GR	33 GG	11 RR	21 GR
33 RR	33 GG	13 GR	33 RR	33 GG	13 GR	33 RR	33 GG	13 GR
12 GR	31 GR	23 GR	12 GR	31 GR	23 GR	12 GR	31 GR	23 GR
33 GG	12 GG	22 RR	33 GG	12 GG	22 RR	33 GG	12 GG	22 RR
21 GR	21 GR	11 RR	21 GR	21 GR	11 RR	21 GR	21 GR	11 RR
21 RR	33 GG	21 GR	21 RR	33 GG	21 GR	21 RR	33 GG	21 GR
22 RR	21 RR	21 RR	22 RR	21 RR	21 RR	22 RR	21 RR	21 RR
33 GG	12 GR	23 GG	33 GG	12 GR	23 GG	33 GG	12 GR	23 GG
11 GG	22 RR	32 GR	11 GG	22 RR	32 GR	11 GG	22 RR	32 GR
23 RR	13 RG	33 RR	23 RR	13 RG	33 RR	23 RR	13 RG	33 RR
32 GR	12 RG	33 GG	32 GR	12 RG	33 GG	32 GR	12 RG	33 GG
12 GR	23 GG	33 GG	12 GR	23 GG	33 GG	12 GR	23 GG	33 GG
12 RG	11 GG	23 GR	12 RG	11 GG	23 GR	12 RG	11 GG	23 GR
11 GG	13 RG	21 GR	11 GG	13 RG	21 GR	11 GG	13 RG	21 GR
31 RG	21 RG	12 RR	31 RG	21 RG	12 RR	31 RG	21 RG	12 RR
12 RG	33 RR	32 GR	12 RG	33 RR	32 GR	12 RG	33 RR	32 GR
13 GR	32 GR	32 GR	13 GR	32 GR	32 GR	13 GR	32 GR	32 GR
22 GG	32 GG	33 GG	22 GG	32 GG	33 GG	22 GG	32 GG	33 GG
12 RG	33 GG	31 RG	12 RG	33 GG	31 RG	12 RG	33 GG	31 RG
12 GR	21 RR	13 RR	12 GR	21 RR	13 RR	12 GR	21 RR	13 RR
22 GG	12 RG	13 RG	22 GG	12 RG	13 RG	22 GG	12 RG	13 RG
23 GR	22 GG	32 RG	23 GR	22 GG	32 RG	23 GR	22 GG	32 RG
33 RR	11 GG	31 GR	33 RR	11 GG	31 GR	33 RR	11 GG	31 GR
33 GG	23 GR	23 RR	33 GG	23 GR	23 RR	33 GG	23 GR	23 RR
31 RG	22 RR	33 RR	31 RG	22 RR	33 RR	31 RG	22 RR	33 RR
31 RR	11 GG	13 GR	31 RR	11 GG	13 GR	31 RR	11 GG	13 GR
33 RR	32 GR	11 GG	33 RR	32 GR	11 GG	33 RR	32 GR	11 GG
32 RG	13 RG	31 GR	32 RG	13 RG	31 GR	32 RG	13 RG	31 GR
31 RG	13 GR	31 RG	31 RG	13 GR	31 RG	31 RG	13 GR	31 RG
11 RR	23 GG	13 GR	11 RR	23 GG	13 GR	11 RR	23 GG	13 GR
23 GR	33 RR	23 RG	23 GR	33 RR	23 RG	23 GR	33 RR	23 RG
12 GG	31 GR	31 GG	12 GG	31 GR	31 GG	12 GG	31 GR	31 GG
11 GG	13 RG	23 RG	11 GG	13 RG	23 RG	11 GG	13 RG	23 RG
13 RG	23 RR	21 RR	13 RG	23 RR	21 RR	13 RG	23 RR	21 RR
31 RG	12 GR	23 RG	31 RG	12 GR	23 RG	31 RG	12 GR	23 RG
23 GR	31 RG	11 GG	23 GR	31 RG	11 GG	23 GR	31 RG	11 GG
31 GR	32 RG	22 GG	31 GR	32 RG	22 GG	31 GR	32 RG	22 GG
23 RG	21 GR	11 GG	23 RG	21 GR	11 GG	23 RG	21 GR	11 GG
22 RR	22 GG	11 GG	22 RR	22 GG	11 GG	22 RR	22 GG	11 GG
12 GR	22 RR	21 RG	12 GR	22 RR	21 RG	12 GR	22 RR	21 RG
32 GR	13 RR	11 RR	32 GR	13 RR	11 RR	32 GR	13 RR	11 RR
22 RR	21 GG	12 RG	22 RR	21 GG	12 RG	22 RR	21 GG	12 RG
12 GG	23 GR	23 GR	12 GG	23 GR	23 GR	12 GG	23 GR	23 GR
33 RR	22 GG	32 GR	33 RR	22 GG	32 GR	33 RR	22 GG	32 GR
11 RR	22 GG	21 GG	11 RR	22 GG	21 GG	11 RR	22 GG	21 GG
23 GG	31 GG	21 RG	23 GG	31 GG	21 RG	23 GG	31 GG	21 RG
23 GG	13 GR	13 RG	23 GG	13 GR	13 RG	23 GG	13 GR	13 RG
33 RR	21 GR	13 RG	33 RR	21 GR	13 RG	33 RR	21 GR	13 RG
23 GR	33 RR	13 RG	23 GR	33 RR	13 RG	23 GR	33 RR	13 RG
21 GG	23 RR	13 GR	21 GG	23 RR	13 GR	21 GG	23 RR	13 GR
13 GR	22 RR	23 RG	13 GR	22 RR	23 RG	13 GR	22 RR	23 RG
33 GG	12 RR	22 GG	33 GG	12 RR	22 GG	33 GG	12 RR	22 GG
11 GG	23 RG	11 RR	11 GG	23 RG	11 RR	11 GG	23 RG	11 RR
12 RR	23 RG	31 RG	12 RR	23 RG	31 RG	12 RR	23 RG	31 RG
12 GG	32 GR	23 RR	12 GG	32 GR	23 RR	12 GG	32 GR	23 RR
31 GG	31 RG	23 RG	31 GG	31 RG	23 RG	31 GG	31 RG	23 RG
32 RG	22 GG	11 RR	32 RG	22 GG	11 RR	32 RG	22 GG	11 RR
21 GR	11 GG	32 RG	21 GR	11 GG	32 RG	21 GR	11 GG	32 RG
22 GG	11 GG	32 GR	22 GG	11 GG	32 GR	22 GG	11 GG	32 GR
22 RR	21 GR	13 GG	22 RR	21 GR	13 GG	22 RR	21 RG	13 GG
13 RR	11 RR	23 GR	13 RR	11 RR	23 GR	13 RR	11 RR	23 GR
21 GG	12 RG	32 GR	21 GG	12 RG	32 GR	21 GG	12 RG	32 GR
23 GR	23 GR	22 RR	23 GR	23 GR	22 RR	23 GR	32 GR	22 RR
22 GG	32 GR	21 RR	22 GG	32 GR	21 RR	22 GG	32 GR	21 RR
22 GG	21 GG	32 GR	22 GG	21 GG	32 GR	22 GG	21 GG	32 GR
31 GG	21 RG	21 RG	31 GG	21 RG	21 RG	31 GG	21 RG	21 RG
13 GR	13 RG	11 GG	13 GR	13 RG	11 GG	13 GR	13 RG	11 GG
21 GR	13 RG	31 RG	21 GR	13 RG	31 RG	21 GR	13 RG	31 RG
33 RR	13 RG	32 GR	33 RR	13 RG	32 GR	33 RR	13 RG	32 GR
23 RR	13 GR	22 GG	23 RR	13 GR	22 GG	23 RR	13 GR	22 GG
22 RR	23 RG	31 RG	22 RR	23 RG	31 RG	22 RR	23 RG	31 RG

Figure 27.3	Figure 27.4	Figure 27.5

How Could it Work?

Consider only those runs in which the switches had the same setting when the particles went through the detectors. In all such runs the detectors flash the same colors. If they could communicate, it would be child's play to make the detectors flash the same colors when their switches had the same setting, but they are completely unconnected. Nor can they have been preprogrammed always to flash the same colors, regardless of what is going on, because the detectors are observed to flash different colors in at least some of those runs in which their switches are differently set, and the switch settings are independent random events.

How, then, are we to account for the first feature of the data? No problem at all. Born, in fact, in a letter of May 1948, offers such an explanation to Einstein:

> It seems to me that your axiom of the "independence of spatially separated objects A and B" is not as convincing as you make out. It does not take into account the fact of coherence; objects far apart in space which have a common origin need not be independent. I believe that this cannot be denied and simply has to be accepted. Dirac has based his whole book on this.

In our case the detectors are triggered by particles that have a common origin at the source C. It is then easy to dream up any number of explanations for the first feature of the data.

Suppose, for example, that what each particle encounters as it enters its detector is a target (figure 27.6) divided into eight regions, labeled RRR, RRG, RGR, RGG, GRR,

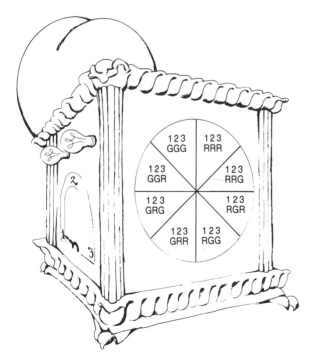

Figure 27.6

Model of a detector to produce data like those in figure 27.4. Particles from the source fall with equal probability into any of the eight bins; for each bin the color flashed depends on the switch as indicated on the back of the box.

GRG, GGR, and GGG. Suppose each detector is wired so that if a particle lands in the GRG bin, the detector flips into a mode in which the light flashes G if the switch is set to 1, R if it is set to 2, and G if it is set to 3; RGG leads to a mode with R for 1 and G for 2 and 3, and so on. We can then easily account for the fact that the lights always flash the same colors when the switches have the same settings by assuming that in each run the source always fires its particles into bins with the same labels.

Evidently this is not the only way. One could imagine that particles come in eight varieties: cubes, spheres, tetrahedra,.... All settings produce R when a cube is detected, a sphere results in R for settings 1 and 2, G for setting 3, and so forth. The first feature of the data is then accounted for if the two particles produced by the source in each run are always both of the same variety.

Common to all such explanation is the requirement that each particle should, in one way or another, carry to its detector a set of instructions for how it is to flash for *each* of the three possible switch settings, and that in *any* run of the experiment both particles should carry the same instruction sets:

- A set of instructions that covers *each* of the three possible settings is required because there is no communication between the source and the detectors other than the particles themselves. In runs in which the switches have the same setting, the particles cannot know whether that setting will be 11, 22, or 33. For the detectors always to flash the same colors when the switches have the same setting, the particles must carry instructions that specify colors for each of the three possibilities.
- The absence of communication between source and detectors also requires that the particles carry such instruction sets in *every* run of the experiment—even those in which the switches end up with different settings—because the particles always have to be prepared: Any run may turn out to be one in which the switches end up with the same settings.

This generic explanation is pictured schematically in figure 27.7.

Alas, this explanation—the only one, I maintain, that someone not steeped in quantum mechanics will ever be able to come up with (though it is an entertaining game to challenge people to try)—is untenable. It is inconsistent with the second feature of the data: There is no conceivable way to assign such instruction sets to the particles from one run to the next that can account for the fact that in all runs taken together, without regard to how the switches are set, the same colors flash half the time.

Pause to note that we are about to show that "something one cannot know anything about"—the third entry in an instruction set—cannot exist. For even if instruction sets did exist, one could never learn more than two of the three entries (revealed in those runs where the switches ended up with two different settings). Here is the argument.

Consider a particular instruction set, for example, RRG. Should both particles be issued the instruction set RRG, then the detectors will flash the same colors when the switches are set to 11, 22, 33, 12, or 21; they will flash different colors for 13, 31, 23, or 32. Because the switches at each detector are set randomly and independently, each of these nine cases is equally likely, so the instruction set RRG will result in the same colors flashing $\frac{5}{9}$ of the time.

Evidently the same conclusion holds for the sets RGR, GRR, GGR, GRG, and RGG, because the argument uses only the fact that one color appears twice and the other

Figure 27.7
Instruction sets. To guarantee that the detectors of figure 27.6 flash the same color when the switches are set the same, the two particles must in one way or another carry instruction sets specifying how their detectors are to flash for each possible switch setting. The results of any one run reveal nothing about the instructions beyond the actual data; so in this case, for example, the first instruction (1R) is "something one cannot know anything about," and I've only guessed at it, assuming that "it exists all the same."

once. All six such instructions sets also result in the same colors flashing $\frac{5}{9}$ of the time.

But the only instruction sets left are RRR and GGG, and these each result in the same colors flashing *all* of the time.

Therefore if instruction sets exist, the same colors will flash in at least $\frac{5}{9}$ of all the runs, regardless of how the instruction sets are distributed from one run of the demonstration to the next. This is Bell's theorem (also known as Bell's inequality) for the *gedanken* demonstration.

But in the actual *gedanken* demonstration the same colors flash only $\frac{1}{2}$ the time. The data described above violate this Bell's inequality, and therefore there can be no instruction sets.

If you don't already know how the trick is done, may I urge you, before reading how the *gedanken* demonstration works, to try to invent some other explanation for the first feature of the data that does not introduce connections between the three parts of the apparatus or prove to be incompatible with the second feature.

Figure 27.8
A realization of the detector to produce the data of figure 27.3. The particles have a magnetic moment and can be separated into "spin up" and "spin down" particles by the Stern-Gerlach magnet inside the detector. Setting the switch to positions 1, 2, or 3 rotates the north pole of the magnet along the coplanar unit vectors $a^{(1)}$, $a^{(2)}$, or $a^{(3)}$, separated by 120°. The vector sum of the three unit vectors is, of course, zero. The switch positions on the two detectors correspond to the same orientations of the magnetic field. One detector flashes red for spin up, green for spin down; the other uses the opposite color convention.

One Way to Do It

Here is one way to make such a device:

Let the source produce two particles of spin $\frac{1}{2}$ in the singlet state, flying apart toward the two detectors. (Granted, this is not all the easy to do, but in the Orsay experiments described below, the same effect is achieved with correlated photons.) Each detector contains a Stern-Gerlach magnet, oriented along one of three directions $(\mathbf{a}^{(1)}, \mathbf{a}^{(2)},$ or $\mathbf{a}^{(3)})$, perpendicular to the line of flight of the particles, and separated by 120°, as indicated in figure 27.8. The three settings of the switch determine which orientation is used. The light on one detector flashes red or green, depending on whether the particle is deflected toward the north (spin up) or south (spin down) pole of the magnet as it passes between them; the other detector uses the opposite color convention.

That's it. Clearly there are no connections between the source and the detectors or between the two detectors. We can nevertheless account for the data as follows:

When the switches have the same setting, the spins of both particles are measured along the same direction, so the lights will always flash the same colors if the measurements along the same direction always yield opposite values. But this is an immediate consequence of the structure of the spin singlet state, which has the form

$$|\psi\rangle = (1/\sqrt{2})[|+-\rangle - |-+\rangle] \tag{1}$$

independent of the direction of the spin quantization axis, and therefore yields $+-$ or $-+$ with equal probability, but never $++$ or $--$, whenever the two spins are measured along any common direction.

To establish the second feature of the data, note that the product $m_1 m_2$ of the results of the two spin measurements (each of which can have the values $+\frac{1}{2}$ or $-\frac{1}{2}$) will have the value $-\frac{1}{4}$ when the lights flash the same colors and $+\frac{1}{4}$ when they flash different colors. We must therefore show that the product vanishes when averaged over all the nine distinct pairs of orientations the two Stern-Gerlach magnets can have. For a given pair of orientations, $\mathbf{a}^{(i)}$ and $\mathbf{a}^{(j)}$, the mean value of this product is just the expectation value in the state ψ of the corresponding product of (commuting) hermitian observables $\mathbf{a}^{(i)} \cdot \mathbf{S}^{(1)}$ and $\mathbf{a}^{(j)} \cdot \mathbf{S}^{(2)}$. Thus the second feature of the data requires:

$$0 = \Sigma_{ij} \langle \psi | [\mathbf{a}^{(i)} \cdot \mathbf{S}^{(1)}][\mathbf{a}^{(j)} \cdot \mathbf{S}^{(2)}] | \psi \rangle \tag{2}$$

But equation 2 is an immediate consequence of the linearity of quantum mechanics, which lets one take the sums inside the matrix element, and the fact that the three unit vectors around an equilateral triangle sum to zero:

$$\Sigma_i \mathbf{a}^{(i)} = \Sigma_j \mathbf{a}^{(j)} = 0 \tag{3}$$

This completely accounts for the data. It also unmasks the *gedanken* demonstration as a simple embellishment of Bohm's version of the EPR experiment. If we kept only runs in which the switches had the same setting, we would have precisely the Bohm-EPR experiment. The assertion that instruction sets exist is then blatant quantum-theoretic nonsense, for it amounts to the insistence that each particle has stamped on it in advance the outcome of the measurements of three different spin components corresponding to noncommuting observables $\mathbf{S} \cdot \mathbf{a}^{(i)}$, $i = 1, 2, 3$. According to EPR, this is merely a limitation of the quantum-theoretic formalism, because instruction sets are the only way to account for the first feature of the data.

Bell's analysis adds to the discussion those runs in which the switches have different settings, extracts the second feature of the data as a further elementary prediction of quantum mechanics, and demonstrates that any set of data exhibiting this features is incompatible with the existence of the instruction sets apparently required by the first feature, quite independently of the formalism used to explain the data, and quite independently of any doctrines of quantum theology.

The Experiments

The experiments of Aspect and his colleagues at Orsay confirm that the quantum-theoretic predictions for this experiment are in fact realized, and that the conditions for observing the results of the experiment can in fact be achieved. (A distinguished colleague once told me that the answer to the EPR paradox was that correlations in the singlet state could never be maintained over macroscopic distances—that anything, even the passage of a cosmic ray in the next room, would disrupt the correlations enough to destroy the effect.)

In these experiments the two spin-$\frac{1}{2}$ particles are replaced by a pair of photons and the spin measurements become polarization measurements. The photon pairs are emitted by calcium atoms in a radiative cascade after suitable pumping by lasers. Because the initial and final atomic states have $J = 0$, quantum theory predicts (and experiment confirms) that the photons will be found to have the same polarizations (lights flashing the same colors in the analogous *gedanken* experiment) if they are measured along the same direction—feature number 1. But if the polarizations are measured at 120° angles, then theory predicts (and experiment confirms) that they will be the same only a quarter of the time [$\frac{1}{4} = \cos^2(120°)$]. This is precisely what is needed to produce the statistics of feature number 2 of the *gedanken* demonstration: The randomly set switches end up with the same setting (same polarizations measured) $\frac{1}{3}$ of the time, so in all runs the same colors will flash $\frac{1}{3} \times 1 + \frac{2}{3} \times (\frac{1}{4}) = \frac{1}{2}$ the time.

The people in Orsay were interested in a somewhat modified version of Bell's argument in which the angles of greatest interest were multiples of 22.5°, but they collected data for many different angles, and except for EPR specialists, the conceptual differences between the two cases are minor.[16].

There are some remarkable features to these experiments. The two polarization analyzers were placed as far as 13 meters apart without producing any noticeable change in the results, thereby closing the loophole that the strange quantum correlations might somehow diminish as the distance between regions A and B grew to macroscopic proportions. At such separations it is hard to imagine that a polarization measurement of photon #1 could, in any ordinary sense of the term, "disturb" photon #2. Indeed, at these large separations, a hypothetical disturbance originating when one photon passed through its analyzer could only reach the other analyzer in time to affect the outcome of the second polarization measurement if it traveled at a superluminal velocity.

In the third paper of the Orsay group's series, bizarre conspiracy theories are dealt a blow by an ingenious mechanism for rapidly switching the directions along which the polarizations of each photon are measured. Each photon passes to its detector through a volume of water that supports an ultrasonic standing wave. Depending on the instantaneous amplitude of the wave, the photon either passes directly into a polarizer with one orientation or is Bragg reflected into another with a different orientation. The standing waves that determine the choice of orientation at each detector are independently driven and have frequencies so high that several cycles take place during the light travel time from one detector to the other. (This corresponds to a refinement of the *gedanken* demonstration in which, to be absolutely safe, the switches are not given their random settings until *after* the particles have departed from their common source.)

What Does It Mean?

What is one to make of all this? Are there "spooky actions at a distance"? A few years ago I received the text of a letter from the executive director of a California thinktank to the Under-Secretary of Defense for Research and Engineering, alerting him to the EPR correlations:

> If in fact we can control the faster-than-light nonlocal effect, it would be possible ... to make an untapable and unjammable command-control-communication system at very high bit rates for use in the submarine fleet. The important point is that since there is no ordinary electromagnetic signal linking the encoder with the decoder in such a hypothetical system, there is nothing for the enemy to tap or jam. The enemy would have to have actual possession of the "black box" decoder to intercept the message, whose reliability would not depend on separation from the encoder nor on ocean or weather conditions. . . .

Heady stuff indeed! But just what is this nonlocal effect? Using the language of the *gedanken* demonstration, let us talk about the "N-color" of a particle (N can be 1, 2, or 3) as the color (red or green) of the light that flashes when the particle passes through a detector with its switch set to N. Because instruction sets cannot exist, we know that a particle cannot at the same time carry a definite 1-color, 2-color and 3-color to its detector. On the other hand, for any particular N (say 3), we can determine the 3-color of the particle heading for detector A before it gets there by arranging things so that the other particle first reaches detector B, where *its* 3-color is measured. If the particle at B was 3-colored red, the particle at A will turn out to be 3-colored red, and green at B means green at A.

Three questions now arise:

• Did the particle at A have its 3-color prior to the measurment of the 3-color of the particle at B? The answer cannot be yes, because, *prior* to the measurement of the 3-color at B, it is altogether possible that the roll of the dice at B or the whim of the B-operator will result in the 2-color or the 1-color being measured at B instead. Barring the most paranoid of conspiracy theories, "prior to the measurement of the 3-color at B" is indistinguishable from "prior to the measurement of the 2- (or 1-) color at B." If the 3-color already existed, so also must the 2- and 1-colors have existed. But instruction sets (which consist of a specification of the 1-, 2-, and 3-colors) do not exist.

• Is the particle at A 3-colored red *after* the measurement at B shows the color red? The answer is surely yes, because under these circumstances it is invariably a particle that will cause the detector at A to flash red.

• Was something (the value of its 3-color) transmitted to the particle at A as a result of the measurement B?

Orthodox quantum metaphysicians would, I believe, say no, nothing has changed at A as the result of the measurement at B; what has changed is our knowledge of the particle at A. (Somewhat more spookily, they might object to the naive classical assumption of localizability or separability implicit in the phrases "at A" and "at B.") This seems very sensible and very reassuring: N-color does not characterize the particle at all, but only what we know about the particle. But does that last sentence sound as good when "particle" is changed to "photon" and "N-color" to "polarization"? And does it really help you to stop wondering why the lights always flash the same colors when the switches have the same settings?

What is clear is that if there is spooky action at a distance, then, like other spooks, it is absolutely useless except for its effect, benign or otherwise, on our state of mind. For the statistical pattern of red and green flashes at detector A is entirely random, however the switch is set at detector B. Whether the particles arriving at A all come with definite 3-colors (because the switch at B was stuck at 3) or definite 2-colors (because the switch was stuck at 2) or no colors at all (because there was a brick in front of the detector at B)—all this has absolutely no effect on the statistical distribution of colors observed at A. The manifestation of this "action at a distance" is revealed only through a comparison of the data independently gathered at A and at B.

This is a most curious state of affairs, and while it is wrong to suggest that EPR correlations will replace sonar, it seems to me something is lost by ignoring them or shrugging them off. The EPR experiment is as close to magic as any physical phenomenon I know of, and magic should be enjoyed. Whether there is physics to be learned by pondering it is less clear. The most elegant answer I have found[17] to this last question comes from one of the great philosophers of our time, whose view of the matter I have taken the liberty of quoting in the form of the poetry it surely is:

We have always had a great deal of difficulty
understanding the world view
that quantum mechanics represents.

At least I do,
because I'm an old enough man
that I haven't got to the point
that this stuff is obvious to me.

Okay, I still get nervous with it. . . .

You know how it always is,
every new idea,
it takes a generation or two
until it becomes obvious
that there's no real problem.

I cannot define the real problem,
therefore I suspect there's no real problem,
but I'm not sure
there's no real problem.

Nobody in the fifty years since Einstein, Podolsky, and Rosen has ever put it better than that.

Notes

Some of the views expressed above were developed in the course of occasional technical studies of EPR correlations supported by the National Science Foundation under grant No. DMR 83-14625.

1. Daniel Greenberger, discussion remarks at the Symposium on Fundamental Questions in Quantum Mechanics, SUNY, Albany, April 1984.
2. A. Einstein, B. Podolsky, N. Rosen, *Phys. Rev.* **47**, 777 (1935).
3. Quoted by M. Jammer, *The Philosophy of Quantum Mechanics*, Wiley, New York (1974) p. 151.
4. A. Pais, *Rev. Mod. Phys.* **51**, 863 (1979).
5. *The Born-Einstein Letters*, with comments by M. Born, Walker, New York (1971).
6. J. S. Bell, *Physics* **1**, 195 (1964).
7. D. Bohm, *Quantum Theory*, Prentice-Hall, Englewood Cliffs, N.J. (1951) pp. 614–619.
8. A. Aspect, P. Grangier, G. Roger, *Phys. Rev. Lett.* **47**, 460 (1981). A. Aspect, P. Grangier, G. Roger, *Phys. Rev. Lett.* **49**, 91 (1982). A. Aspect, J. Dalibard, G. Roger, *Phys. Rev. Lett.* **49**, 1804 (1982).
9. For a discussion of the views of today's physicists toward the meaning of the quantum theory, see the interesting and provocative essay "Cognitive Repression in Contemporary Physics" by E. F. Keller, *Am. J. Phys.* **47**, 718 (1977).
10. L. Rosenfeld in *Niels Bohr, His Life and Work as Seen by His Friends and Colleagues*, S. Rozental, ed., North Holland, Amsterdam (1967) pp. 114–36.
11. G. Zukav, *The Dancing Wu-Li Masters—An Overview of the New Physics*, Morrow, New York (1979) p. 282. On the same page it is also said that "Bell's theorem is a mathematical construct which as such is indecipherable to the non-mathematician," a view that I hope the rest of this article will dispel.
12. H. Stapp, *Nuovo Cimento* **40B**, 191 (1977).
13. A Pais, *"Subtle is the Lord . . ." The Science and the Life of Albert Einstein*, Oxford U. P., New York (1982) p. 456.
14. N. Bohr, *Phys. Rev.* **48**, 696 (1935).
15. What follows is a somewhat refined version of an argument I published a few years ago in *Am. J. Phys.* **49**, 940 (1981), incorporating some improvements suggested by Richard Friedberg. For other elementary treatments see J. S. Bell's beautiful essay, "Bertlemann's Socks and the Nature of Reality," *J.*

Phys. (Paris) **42**, C2-41 (1981), B. d'Espagnat's article in the November 1979 *Scientific American,* or d'Espagnat's book, *In Search of Reality,* Springer-Verlag, New York (1983).

16. For a survey of other attempts to realize the EPR experiment, and the variants of Bell's original argument used to interpret experimental tests, see J. F. Clauser, A. Shimony, *Repts. Prog. Phys.* **41**, 1881 (1978).

17. R. P. Feynman, *Int. J. Theor. Phys.* **21**, 471 (1982).

Chapter 28

Metaphysical Problems in the Foundations
of Quantum Mechanics

Abner Shimony

I propose to summarize a certain line of development in the foundations of quantum mechanics—partly theoretical and partly experimental—and to examine its philosophical implications. The major ideas of this line of development are fairly simple and can be conveyed without complicated calculations. In order to avoid arousing expectations which cannot be fulfilled, I wish to say in advance that the philosophical implications which will be drawn from analyzing the foundations of quantum mechanics are not unequivocal and unqualified. They take the form rather of a disjunction: there appear to be only two options left open by the results of experiments, and we cannot at the present time say which option is correct. I think we can confidently say that either option is momentous, metaphysically or epistemologically; we must recognize either that the intrinsic properties of the real world are very strange indeed, or that scientific theories say much less about the intrinsic properties of things than scientists have commonly assumed.

I. Data and Resulting Problems

Let us begin our analysis by looking at some of the elementary formalism of quantum mechanics. It will be convenient to use the concept of the "state" of a physical system, even though it is a subtle concept that may have to be refined as a result of analysis. Roughly, a state of a physical system is a maximal specification of it—i.e., a specification of the contingencies of the system such that nothing more can be said of it that is not either redundant or contradictory. Quantum mechanics assumes that the set of possible states of a physical system obeys the *superposition principle*, which can roughly be explained as follows.[1] Suppose F is a dynamical variable of the system (often called an "observable") such as the position of the system along a certain axis. Let u_1 be a state of the system in which F has the value f_1 and let u_2 be a state in which F has the value f_2, where f_1 and f_2 are unequal to each other. Then the superposition principle says that there are states of the system achieved by combining u_1 and u_2 (actually, infinitely many such states, by combining u_1 and u_2 in different ways), in which F has no definite value whatsoever. Thus, if u is one of these states, and F is taken to be position along the vertical axis, then a system in the state u does not *have* a definite position along the vertical axis. From the precise way in which u is obtained by combining u_1 and u_2 one can calculate the probability that F will be found to have the value f_1 and the probability that it will have the value f_2 in case F is measured. (The probability that it will be found to have a value other than f_1 or f_2 is 0.) It would not be correct, however, to construe this statement about probabilities as meaning that the

Reprinted from *International Philosophical Quarterly* VIII (1978), pp. 2–17, by permission of the author and the publisher.

value of F is definite but unknown and that the probabilities only refer to the observer's state of knowledge. Such an interpretation would conflict with the assertions that u is a state of the system, and that a state is a maximal specification of the system. Thus the superposition principle has the remarkable, and metaphysically significant, consequence that any dynamical variable which is non-trivial, in the sense that it can take on at least two distinct values, will have *no definite value at all* in some possible states of the system. The combination of the feature that a dynamical variable may have an indefinite value in a given state with the feature that the probabilities of various outcomes are well determined in case the dynamical variable is measured, led Heisenberg to assert that quantum mechanics gives *potentiality* a fundamental status in nature.[2] To be sure, the quantum mechanical concept of potentiality is very different from the Aristotelian concept, but it seems appropriate to borrow Aristotle's terminology in order to characterize a situation of indefiniteness from which passage to a situation of definiteness can take place.

Another remarkable consequence of quantum mechanics is obtained if we consider a composite system consisting of two simpler systems. Let u_1 and u_2 be states of component I in which F has distinct values f_1 and f_2, and let v_1 and v_2 be states of component II in which the dynamical variable G has distinct values g_1 and g_2. One possible state of the composite system I + II can be represented by $u_1 v_1$, which signifies that component I is in state u_1 and component II is in state v_1. (Representing the composite system in this way is not tantamount to denying that the two parts affect each other, for indeed each may exert forces on the other which modify their motions and their internal development. However, the effect of each on the other can be taken into account by considering the dynamical evolution of the composite system I + II after it is prepared in the state $u_1 v_1$ at the initial time.) Similarly the composite system I + II can be prepared in the state $u_2 v_2$ which is to mean that I is in the state u_2 and II is in the state v_2. So far nothing has been said that conflicts either with common sense or with classical physics. Now, however, let us apply the superposition principle to the states $u_1 v_1$ and $u_2 v_2$. There are many ways to combine $u_1 v_1$ with $u_2 v_2$, but no matter how the combination is performed, provided that there is some contribution from both, the resulting state has a remarkable property which has been called "quantum nonseparability": *it does not permit us to attribute to component I by itself a definite state and to component II by itself a definite state.*[3] We thus have a quantum mechanical version of the meta-physical thesis of holism. The thesis is roughly that there are states of composite systems which cannot be fully expressed in terms of the states of the components. Traditionally, this is a thesis maintained by antireductionist biologists, who have asserted that even after one has completely specified every physical atom in an organism, there is something about the organism as a whole which has been omitted. Holism is still maintained by some biologists, but it appears that reductionism is the new orthodoxy, especially among molecular biologists. A very eloquent presentation of the reductionist position in biology is given by Jacques Monod, in his *Chance and Necessity*,[4] and it is interesting that a review of this book was written by d'Espagnat under the title "Une lacune d'importance"[5]—the lacuna being the peculiar quantum mechanical version of holism that appears in the very formalism which Monod relies upon for giving a physical explanation of reproduction, teleonomy, and biological stability. It should be emphasized that the quantum mechanical version of holism is very unlike the traditional versions: it does not say that the state of the whole fails to be exhausted by a specification of the states of the parts but rather that the parts just are not *in* definite states. Even when this modification is recognized, however, it is ironical that tough-minded physicists have become the advocates of a doctrine which historically was defended by tender-minded and romantic writers. But that is precisely what the formalism of quantum mechanics requires, if we are forced to interpret it at face value.

But must we interpret quantum mechanics at face value? Could it be that the apparent implications of *indefiniteness of dynamical variables*, of the *ontological status of potentialities*, and of *quantum nonseparability* all stem from an unwarranted assumption that the quantum mechanical state really is a maximal specification of the physical system? If the indefiniteness that is found in the quantum mechanical state is only an expression of the physicists' ignorance, rather than an intrinsic characteristic of the system, then the bizarre metaphysical implications of quantum mechanics would dissolve. There is indeed nothing paradoxical or strange about our state of *knowledge* being indefinite in certain respects, or consisting of probability evaluations, or about our knowledge of one component of a composite system being correlated with or contingent upon our knowledge of another component. (This last characteristic is exhibited trivially in classical physics when one deals with a conserved quantity which is partitioned in an unknown manner among several parts of a composite system.) Thus, an evident avenue of escape from the bizarre philosophical implications of quantum mechanics is to regard the quantum mechanical description of a physical system, that is, its quantum mechanical state, as being *incomplete*.

II. The EPR Argument

There is a beautiful argument of Einstein, Podolsky, and Rosen (EPR) published in 1935, which purports to show that the incompleteness of the quantum mechanic description is not just a desideratum for the purpose of avoiding strange, or unintuitive, or nonclassical philosophical implications, but that it is actually required by the formalism of quantum mechanics itself.[6] More precisely, their conclusion is required by the formalism of quantum mechanics together with two additional premises, which they regarded as entirely reasonable. I shall briefly summarize their argument, in a somewhat different form from the original presentation, partly in order to expedite the linkage to the later work of Bell and of experimentalists, and partly in order to make explicit the additional premises.

Let us take the two-component system I + II, which was described only in very general terms so far, to be a pair of photons (which are the quanta of light). We shall make use of two quantum mechanical assertions concerning photons. The first is that if a photon is prepared in a state of linear polarization along a certain axis, then its state of polarization along any axis which is neither perpendicular nor parallel to the first is indefinite, and it has non-zero probability of passing and non-zero probability of not passing through an ideal analyzer oriented along the second axis. The second assertion is that a pair of photons can be prepared in a state Ψ with the following characteristics: photon I is propagating in the positive direction along a certain axis, which we shall call the z-axis, and photon II is propagating in the negative direction along this axis. Neither photon I nor photon II is in a definite state of linear polarization, but their polarization properties are correlated, so that if photon I is found to have linear polarization along the x-axis or along the y-axis, then so also will photon II. Here the x- and y-axes are any two axes which are perpendicular to each other and also to the z-axis. There are infinitely many choices of the x- and y-axes, since any pair of perpendicular directions in the plane perpendicular to the z-axis are suitable candidates, and we shall take x', y' and x", y" to be two distinct choices of these axes. It can be shown that the state Ψ exhibits quantum nonseparability, but we shall not insist upon this fact at this point, since one of the motivations for conjecturing the incompleteness of quantum mechanics is to discover a deeper level of description at which nonseparability is eliminated. What cannot be eliminated, however, are the experimental predictions based upon Ψ, which must be correct if Ψ is a correct description on the quantum mechanical level. When Ψ correctly describes the photon pair, one can predict that if photon 1 passes through an ideal polarization analyzer oriented along the x' direction, then photon 2 will also pass through an ideal polarization analyzer oriented in that direction; and failure of the first photon to pass would imply failure of the second to pass. Similarly, photon I will pass through an ideal polarization analyzer oriented in the x" direction if and only if photon 2 will pass through an ideal analyzer oriented in that direction. The argument of EPR now proceeds in the following way. The experimenter can choose to observe the polarization of photon 1 relative either to the axis x'-y' or to x"-y". According to his choice, the polarization of the second photon would be well-determined relative either to the x'-y' or to the x"-y" axes, in view of the correlations implied by Ψ. In neither case is the second photon subjected to any disturbances—*upon assumption that there is no action-at-a-distance*. Consequently, each property of photon 2 which *would be* well-determined, if the experimenter measured the corresponding property of photon 1, must *in fact be* well-determined no matter what observation the experimenter chooses to make upon photon 1. It follows, therefore, that the polarization of photon 2 is well-determined relative to the x'-y'axes, to the x"-y" axes, and indeed to every set of axes perpendicular to the propagation direction. But this conclusion demonstrates the incompleteness of the quantum mechanical description, for the quantum mechanical state of a single photon can at most specify the polarization relative to a single pair of perpendicular axes and must leave polarization relative to any other set of axes indeterminate.

Let us now recapitulate the premises of the argument of EPR.

1. One premise is that it is possible to prepare two-photon systems so that Ψ correctly describes them (yields correct predictions). This premise needs no discussion, because it is implied by quantum mechanics and furthermore is quite strongly supported by experiment.

2. A second premise was already stated explicitly: that there is no action-at-a-distance. If a certain action-at-a-distance does occur the conclusion of EPR does not follow. Specifically, one could imagine that when the two-photon state is represented by Ψ, then the polarization of photon 2 is well-determined in no direction at all; but as soon as the polarization of photon I is determined relative to some definite pair of axes x'-y' by virtue of confronting photon I with a polarization analyzer oriented along one of this pair of axes, then instantaneously photon 2 also acquires a definite polarization relative to x'-y'. EPR assume that no such instantaneous causal sequence occurs.

3. A third premise is implicit in the argument but has not been stated explicitly: it is a strong version of the famous EPR "reality criterion." Their criterion reads as follows: "If, without in any way disturbing a system, we can predict with certainty (i.e., with probability equal to unity) the value of a physical quantity, then there exists an element of physical reality corresponding to this physical quantity."[7] The reason for saying "strong version" is that there is an important ambiguous word in the criterion —the word "can." The word may be used broadly, so that it is true to say that we "can predict" the value of several quantities, which are such that the actual prediction of any one of them is incompatible with the actual prediction of another. In spite of this incompatibility, the word "can" is appropriate because the experimenter is free to make any choice among the quantities in question. On the other hand, the word may be used narrowly, so that we "can predict" the value only of that quantity which will

actually be measured, and it is false to say that we can predict the value of any quantity requiring an experimental arrangement incompatible with that which actually will be used. If "can" is used broadly, then we have a strong form of EPR's criterion; if it is used narrowly, then we have a weak form of the criterion. Unless the strong form of the EPR reality criterion is used, their conclusion does not follow. The weak form of the criterion would permit one to conclude only that the polarization of photon 2 is well determined relative to that set of axes which is picked out by the experimental arrangement actually used in examining photon 1; then there would be no grounds for saying that the quantum mechanical description is incomplete.

Whether the word "can" is used broadly or narrowly is not just a matter of semantical convention; an important issue of metaphysical commitment is involved. If a physical system is conceived to possess a set of intrinsic properties, independently of whether it is observed or not, then the broad sense is appropriate: since we *could* have been in a position to predict with certainty the value of a physical quantity, though actually we made a choice which prevented us from being in that position, we are entitled to say that there is an element of physical reality corresponding to the quantity, for what *we* choose to do is irrelevant to the intrinsic properties of the system. On the other hand, if the set of properties which can be attributed to a system is relative to the experimental arrangement used for observing the system, then the narrow sense of "can" is obligatory. It should be evident, however, that from the realistic point of view of most working scientists the broad sense of "can" is unequivocally the appropriate one, and hence the strong version of EPR's criterion is correct.

I hope that the rigor and beauty of the argument of EPR is apparent. If one does not recognize how good an argument it is—proceeding rigorously from premises which are thoroughly reasonable—then one does not experience an adequate intellectual shock when one finds out that the experimental evidence contradicts their conclusion. The shock should be as great as the one experienced by Frege when he read Russell's set theoretical paradox and said, "Alas, arithmetic totters!"

III. Testing for Hidden Variables

A number of attempts have been made (some of them antedating the argument of EPR) to construct descriptions of physical systems which are more complete than the quantum mechanical description.[8] The generic name for such descriptions is "hidden variables theories." I shall not try to summarize the complex history of these theories, but shall mention only the work of J. S. Bell and his followers, which threw the most light upon the argument of EPR. Bell showed that any hidden variables theory that satisfied a condition which he called "locality," which essentially asserted that there is no action-at-a-distance, must make statistical predictions which disagree with those made by quantum mechanics.[9] Suppose that the polarization analyzer for photon 1 can be oriented either along the x_1' or the x_1'' axes, and that the polarization analyzer for photon 2 can be oriented either along the x_2' or the x_2'' axes. Suppose a collection of photon pairs is prepared in a certain way, so that the statistical behavior of the collection is well determined. Let $P_1(x_1')$ be the probability that photon I from one of these pairs will pass through the first polarization analyzer, if the analyzer is oriented in the direction x_1', and let $P_1(x_1'')$ have a similar meaning. Likewise, let $P_2(x_2')$ be the probability that photon II from one of these pairs will pass through the second analyzer, if it is oriented in the direction x_2', and let $P_2(x_2'')$ be similarly defined. Let $P(x_1', x_2')$ be the probability that photons I and II will pass respectively through the first and second analyzers, if these are respectively oriented in the x_1' and x_2' directions, and let $P(x_1', x_2'')$, $P(x_1'', x_2'')$ have similar meanings. An argument related to Bell's shows that if the collection of photon pairs is governed by *any* local hidden variables theory,[10] then

$$P(x_1', x_2') - P(x_1', x_2'') + P(x_1'', x_2') + P(x_1'', x_2'') - P_1(x_1'') - P_2(x_2') \leq 0. \quad (1)$$

Now let us make a particular choice of the directions: All are to lie in the plane perpendicular to the direction of propagation of the photons, and x_1' can be chosen arbitrarily, but x_2', x_1'', and x_2'' are to make angles respectively $22\frac{1}{2}°$, $45°$, and $67\frac{1}{2}°$ relative to x_1'. It can be shown that if the collection of photon pairs is prepared so that their quantum mechanical description is the state Ψ considered above, then the quantum mechanical values for the probabilities of photon passage through the analyzers are:

$$P_1(x_1'') - P_2(x_2') = \tfrac{1}{2}$$

$$P(x_1', x_2') = P(x_1'', x_2') = P(x_1'', x_2'') = .427$$

$$P(x_1', x_2'') = .074$$

Hence, according to quantum mechanics

$$P(x_1', x_2') - P(x_1', x_2'') + P(x_1'', x_2') + P(x_1'', x_2'') - P_1(x_1'') - P_2(x_2') = .207$$
$$(2)$$

in clear disagreement with the inequality (1) which governs all local hidden variables theories. This result is most remarkable, because of its great generality, for it shows that there is a discrepancy between quantum mechanics and *all* the hidden variables theories of the kind envisaged as physically reasonable by EPR. The existence of this discrepancy made it possible to design and carry out experiments which tested quantum mechanics against the entire family of local hidden-variables theories.[11]

What is the experimental evidence? Well, it is complex. At least seven experiments have been performed to test local hidden variables theories, and the results are not unanimous. Five favor quantum mechanics and two favor local hidden variables theories. This is not a question on which there should be majority rule, and it really is important to look carefully at the experiments and to try to assess the validity of each: the plausibility of assumptions made in each, the possibility of systematic errors, the possibility of random errors. I shall not try to do this, but shall only make three remarks. One is that the preponderance of opinion at a workshop on this question last year at Erice was that the most reliable experiments (those of Freedman and Clauser,[12] Fry and Thompson,[13] and Clauser[14]) were the ones favoring quantum mechanics. A second remark is that even if the score were not five to two in favor of quantum mechanics, but, say, three to four, I would have trusted the experiments favoring quantum mechanics, and this is not just because of conservatism in favor of a highly successful theory. My reason is that the quantum mechanics prediction is both highly correlated and very specific, while the local hidden variables prediction sets a limit on correlations and is relatively unspecific (only an inequality). If quantum mechanics is correct, it is easy to see how experimental errors could wash out high correlations and produce results in agreement with Inequality (1); but if some local hidden variables theory is correct, it would require a most improbable set of coincidences or conspiracies to produce the highly correlated and highly specific quantum mechanical predictions. A third remark is that some loopholes are left even by the experiments which favor quantum mechanics, which leave some hope for advocates of local hidden variable theories: especially, the experimental arrangements actually used in the experiments are such that Bell's locality assumption may not hold. Polarization analyzers are set in place for several minutes at a time, during which the hidden variables of one polarization analyzer could become aware of the orientation of the other analyzer and take appropriate action to allow an incoming photon to pass or not pass. Of course, this sounds like science fiction, but since we are aiming at results of great generality, it is desirable to exclude even such an implausible possibility, and indeed there is an experiment going on which is intended to block this loophole.

IV. Theoretical Implications: Option I

For the rest of this article I shall take it that local hidden variables theories are excluded, so that one or the other of EPR's second and third premises must be false. I think it should be clear that this conclusion is momentous, as claimed at the beginning. If the second premise is false, then there is action-at-a-distance, contrary to the view of space-time structure which we have learned from special and general relativity theory, and contrary to an immense body of experimental evidence. If the third premise is false, then the strong version of the EPR reality criterion must be abandoned, which, as I tried to explain, is tantamount to abandoning the "realistic" view that a physical system is endowed with an intrinsic set of properties independent of what observations one intends to perform upon it. We thus seem to be left with only two philosophical options, both of which are radical.

I shall discuss the latter of these two options first—the abandonment of a realistic interpretation of quantum mechanics of physical systems—since it is the more familiar in the literature and indeed seems to have been the view of Niels Bohr, and with some variations, of various other advocates of the Copenhagen interpretation of quantum mechanics. Bohr's former assistant, Petersen, quotes Bohr as saying, "There is no quantum world. There is only an abstract quantum physical description. It is wrong to think that the task of physics is to find out how nature *is*. Physics concerns what we can say about nature."[15] Petersen says elsewhere that the radical way in which Bohr broke with tradition was to abandon an *ontological* mode of thinking.[16] I am not fully confident that this is the most accurate exegesis of Bohr's rather cryptic philosophical statements, but it does seem to me to be a way in which one can deny the strong version of EPR's reality criterion. It is possible, in my opinion, that we shall be forced to accept this non-ontological philosophy as a last resort, but for several reasons I find it very unappealing.

(1) It is a very anthropocentric view of scientific knowledge, which does not accurately characterize the scientific enterprise. Obviously and trivially, there is no human scientific knowledge without human knowers, but this banal fact does not *by itself* imply that there is any feature of nature which is necessarily hidden from human beings because of human limitations, or that there is any uncorrectable distortion of our representations of things because of peculiarities of human faculties. The history of science has been in part a history of discoveries of corrections to anthropocentricism: of overcoming human limitations by inferring features of nature which are remote from direct perception from features which are directly perceivable, and of taking into account any correcting for peculiarities of our sensory and cognitive faculties. There is no evidence that the microphysics of the twentieth century has been a breakdown or a reversal of this history of corrections to anthropocentrism. It seems quite the contrary. The ingenious utilization by experimentalists of long causal chains has made it possible to measure spatial distances which are ten orders of magnitude or more

smaller than can be discriminated visually. Nor does it seem that we are trapped by our innate intellectual equipment, for such feats as the entertainment of the conception of a superposition of states in which the position of a body is indefinite seems to me to indicate a remarkable elasticity of that equipment.

(2) For the most part, those peculiarities of the quantum mechanial description of phenomena which can be cited against a "realistic" view of physical systems and in favor of a nonontological view do not seem to involve mutually incompatible experimental arrangements. Thus, Heisenberg's position-momentum uncertainty relation shows up in an expression for thermodynamic entropy in which there is no concern with either a position or a momentum measurement. And quantum nonseparability is omnipresent in atomic, nuclear, and solid state physics in situations in which the experimentalists are not overtly measuring correlations. It is hard, therefore, to shake off the impression that these peculiarities of the quantum mechanical description are intrinsic characteristics of the things themselves and not just of our way of looking at or talking about the things.

(3) Most important, I do not believe that a fully worked out and coherent formulation of a nonontological interpretation of quantum mechanics exists in the literature, in writings of Bohr or of any one else. We have a standard of comparison, for there is one great and quite fully worked out non-ontological philosophy which antedates quantum mechanics: namely, the transcendental philosophy of Kant. It is, of course, central to Kant's philosophy that we have no knowledge of things in themselves, but only knowledge of phenomena. But then Kant undertakes the obligation of explaining why our knowledge has the structure that it does have, if that structure cannot be attributed to the things-in-themselves: the structure is imposed by the knowing subject, the faculties of intuition supplying the forms of space and time and the faculty of understanding supplying the categories. I am completely unconvinced by Kant's explanation of the structure of our knowledge, but I do admire him for his sense of responsibility in undertaking to work out a detailed epistemology, instead of elliptically stating a program. What, according to Bohr, plays the role of Kant's transcendental self in establishing the structure of our physical knowledge? It seems not to be the knowing self since Bohr explicitly denies that he is any kind of idealist.[17] If it is the character of experimental apparatus, then a nest of troublesome problems is opened: is the apparatus to be considered as "real" in an unequivocal sense, so that the position is not nonontological at all, but rather is a kind of ontological commitment to macrophysicalism? And is it not strange that the macrophysical apparatus has to be described in microscopic terms, and specifically quantum mechanically, in order to understand how it works—which would be a peculiar kind of macrophysicalism? In short, I am gladly willing to say that Bohr is a great phenomenologist of scientific research—that he has said some profound things about experimental arrangements—but I do not see that he has been able *successfully* to bypass the question of characterizing the intrinsic states of physical systems.

V. Option II

The other option is to admit at least one type of action-at-a-distance. The type that is called for can be seen by referring to the argument of EPR. Suppose that we have a two-component system in a nonseparable quantum state, like the state Ψ of a 2-photon system. The nonseparability is itself a metaphysically radical feature of the composite system, but it is not in contradiction with a "realistic" view of physical systems. It does, however, impose a peculiar understanding of realism. We are forced to say that neither photon by itself can fully be considered to be a system, in the sense of being in a definite state. Only the two-photon system is in a definite state, and like any system in a definite state it is such that certain dynamical variables have definite values whereas others have indefinite ones. But from a "realist" point of view, this peculiar web of actuality and potentialities constitutes the intrinsic character of the two-photon system. When photon I is confronted with a polarization analyzer oriented along the x-axis, then there is a transition from potentiality to a new actuality— the polarization of photon 1 relative to the x-axis becomes definite; and this transition implies that photon 2 also makes the same transition from potentiality to actuality, for it achieves a definite polarization with respect to the same axis. Since we are now construing the properties of physical systems realistically, the transitions in question are events, and they appear to be causally connected in spite of their space-like separation.[18] Here, then, is an action-at-a-distance. But it is a very special action-at-a-distance. It takes place only when one has a composite system exhibiting quantum nonseparability—which means that the potentialities of the components are interconnected—and when a transition from potentiality to actuality is induced in one of those components. One peculiarity of this situation is the following: there exists no dynamical variable (observable) of photon 2 which had one definite value prior to the experiment performed on photon 1 and a different value afterwards. The only changes which have occurred concerning photon 2 are from the indefiniteness of certain dynamical variables to definiteness. This peculiarity is very closely bound up with the fact that there seems to be no way of utilizing quantum nonseparability and the kind of action-at-a-distance that we have just been discussing for the purpose of sending a message faster than light. Upon reflection, we may even question whether it was correct to characterize the transition from potentiality to actuality which occurred in photon 2 as an *event*, just because it fails to share one or more of the classical properties of events. If we understood better just what is involved in the quantum mechanical transition from potentiality to actuality, then we would be in a better position to assess the implications of the kind of nonlocality exhibited in nonseparable quantum systems.

We should like to know what implications quantum nonseparability has for the geometrical structure of space-time. If there is a genuine causal relation between two events with space-like separation, then our present conception of space-time structure must be changed, because in both special and general relativity theory such causal relations are excluded. Can we make any reasonable conjectures about the kind of change in the conception of space-time structure that would be required? Here is one possibility, suggested by Wheeler's idea of "wormholes," which crudely are topological modifications of space-time whereby two points are close to each other by one route and remote by another.[19] (His motivation is entirely different from mine: it is to explain the occurrence of sources of lines of the electric field without postulating charge as a primitive physical entity. But there is no reason why we cannot use his idea for other purposes.) My conjecture is that when we have a system consisting of two apparently spatially separated but correlated components, the microstructure of space-time exhibits a wormhole, and the two components are actually close to each other by one route (via the throat of the wormhole). Hence a causal connection between two events concerning the two components only apparently violates locality, because from a microscopic point of view the events do not have a space-like separation after all. Finally, we may suppose that in the macro-structure of space-time these wormholes cannot be capitalized upon to send messages between two points with apparent space-like separation. Wheeler's own reaction to this speculation was skeptical,[20] and I cannot but agree.

Another possibility is to say that there can be a peaceful coexistence between the causal structure of relativistic space-time and the nonlocality exhibited in the EPR situation, just because different modalities of reality are involved in the two contexts. Classically, the structure of relativistic space-time governs causal relations between events, which are loci of actualities. Quantum mechanically, especially in quantum field theory, the structure of relativistic space-time governs causal relations between potentialities (technically, an observable $A(x)$ constructed out of field operators at point x and an observable $B(x')$ constructed out of field operators are x', commute[21] if x and x' are points with space-like separation). But the "events" in the EPR situation are hybrid entities—they are transitions from potentialities to actualities. Because of the hybrid character of these "events," they may be governed neither by the classical nor by the quantum mechanical versions of the relativistic restrictions upon causal relations. For this reason, there could be peaceful coexistence between relativistic space-time structure and the nonlocality we have been discussing. This is indeed an answer, but is it a solution? It looks suspiciously like a way of avoiding the analysis of an extremely puzzling situation. Again, I would say that if we really understood what goes on in the transition from potentiality to actuality, we would be able to assess better whether or not we have a solution.

I shall consider, finally, one very speculative line of thought on quantum mechanics. Several physicists have suggested that the transition from potentiality to actuality— e.g., from a plane wave state in which position is indefinite to a state in which position is definite—is a real process which requires the intervention of mentality. J. M. Burgers[22] and O. Costa de Beauregard[23] have boldly taken this position, and E. Wigner[24] has quite cautiously considered it. I do not believe that this conjecture is correct, but I think that some considerations on mentality may make us open-minded towards the conjecture. The considerations I have in mind are these: First, mentality does *prima facie* seem to be a fact *in* nature, and not something outside of nature to which nature is presented; the facts of birth, death, sleeping, waking, anaesthesia, shock, inducement of sensations by direct stimulus of nerves, etc., all overwhelmingly support the thesis that mentality is a fact *in* nature. The second consideration is that the general framework of quantum mechanics seems to be *tolerant of* and perhaps even *hospitable to* mentality. The flickering and exploratory character of mentality might somehow be accommodated to the superposition principle, with its implications for the indefinite values of dynamical variables; the interplay between conscious and unconscious levels of mind seems to require a framework in which potentiality plays a crucial role; and the nonlocalization of mentality and its function in coordinating the organs of the body fit naturally into a framework which permits nonseparability and holistic correlations. I do not mean to suggest that we have any clear theories about formulating psychology along quantum mechanical lines. I only want to convey the idea that the quantum mechanical framework has the kind of subtle structure which an adequate naturalistic theory of mentality requires.

These considerations are enough to make us open-minded to the conjecture that the quantum transition from potentiality to actuality involves mentality, but this open-mindedness ought to be balanced by a clear-minded critical attitude. In the spirit of critical open-mindedness, three of my students and I designed and performed a simple experiment to see whether mentality might be involved in a transition from potentiality to actuality.[25] Gamma-rays from a sample of sodium-22 atoms were studied with an apparatus consisting of a scintillation detector, a series of amplifiers for amplifying pulses from the detector, and two scalers in separate rooms on each of which all detection events were registered. In the quantum theory of gamma emission a nucleus is regarded as being in a superposition of an "undecayed" and a "decayed" state, and the relative weights of these two states determine the probability of the decay. After an appropriate time interval the composite system consisting of source and apparatus is in a superposition of two states, one in which a detection of an emitted photon has occurred and one in which it has not. Now according to the speculative hypothesis under consideration, the transition of this superposed state to one in which there is a definite occurrence of a detection or a definite nonoccurrence of a detection takes place only when an observer looks at one of the scalers. Either of the two scalers can be used for this purpose, and if there are two observers A and B, one near each scaler, then presumably the first to look is responsible for the transition. Now suppose that A exercises an option to look or refrain from looking at his scaler, but if he does so, he does it before B looks. If A's looking actually changes the state of the physical system, then possibly B's experience will be different from what it would be if B were responsible for the transition. Now we examine whether A can send a message to B by choosing to look or not to look at his scaler. If A keeps a record of when he looks and when he refrains from looking on successive occasions, and B keeps a record of when he subjectively feels that he is responsible for the transition and when not, then a comparison of the two records should show whether A has communicated with B. It must be emphasized that this is not an ESP experiment. It is an experiment to test a certain type of psycho-physical interaction, and to see whether the action-at-a-distance considered previously could in fact be used to send a message. Without going into details, I report that the experimental result was negative. In 554 trials, exactly half of the decisions made by B about whether A looked were correct, and exactly half were incorrect. This is roughly the result we expected, though the fact that there was 0 deviation from the mean is almost too good.

I do not want to claim too much for the decisiveness of our experiment. Two remarks will suffice. We did want to show that it is possible to be both open-minded to outré hypotheses and very tough-minded in testing them. And the fact that one is drawn into thinking about such speculative hypotheses should underline the bafflement which we feel at this stage in the history of quantum mechanics, in which each easy and commonsensical avenue of interpretation seems to have reached an impasse.

I shall conclude with some wise advice from Hermann Weyl about the puzzling intellectual situation in which we find ourselves: "The example of quantum mechanics has once more demonstrated how the possibilities with which our imagination plays before a problem is ripe for solution are always far surpassed by reality."[26]

Notes

The research for this paper was partly supported by the National Science Foundation.

1. The superposition principle is discussed in all textbooks on quantum mechanics. A very good introductory discussion can be found in J. Andrade e Silva and G. Lochak, *Quanta* (New York: McGraw-Hill, 1969). A more advanced discussion of this principle and of most other topics in the foundations of quantum mechanics may be found in B. d'Espagnat, *Conceptual Foundations of Quantum Mechanics*, 2nd Ed. (Reading: Addison-Wesley, 1976).

2. W. Heisenberg, *Physics and Philosophy* (New York: Harper, 1958), p. 53.

3. E. Shrödinger, "Discussion of probability relations between separated systems," *Proceedings of the Cambridge Philosophical Society*, 31 (1935), 555–562. Also B. d'Espagnat, *op. cit.*

4. J. Monod, *Chance and Necessity* (New York: Knopf, 1971).

5. B. d'Espagnat, "Une lacune d'importance," *Les Nouvelles Littéraires*, May 16, 1977.

6. A. Einstein, B. Podolsky, and N. Rosen, "Can Quantum-Mechanical Description of Physical Reality Be Considered Complete?" *Physical Review*, 47 (1935), 777–780.

7. Ibid., p. 777.

8. An excellent survey article is J. S. Bell, "On the Problem of Hidden Variables in Quantum Mechanics," *Reviews of Modern Physics*, 38 (1966), 447–452.

9. J. S. Bell, "On the Einstein Podolsky Rosen Paradox," *Physics*, 1 (1964), 195–200.

10. R. A. Holt, Ph.D. Thesis, Harvard University, 1973 (unpublished); J. F. Clauser and M. A. Horne," Experimental Consequences of Objective Local Theories," *Physical Review*, D10 (1974), 526–535.

11. J. F. Clauser, M. A. Horne, A. Shimony, and R. A. Holt, "Proposed Experiment to Test Local Hidden-Variable Theories," *Physical Review Letters*, 23, (1969), 880–884.

12. S. J. Freedman and J. F. Clauser, "Experimental Test of Local Hidden-Variable Theories," *Physical Review Letters*, 28 (1972), 938–941.

13. E. S. Fry and R. C. Thompson, "Experimental Test of Local Hidden-Variable Theories," *Physical Review Letters*, 37 (1976), 465–468.

14. J. F. Clauser, "Experimental Investigation of a Polarization Correlation Anomaly," *Physical Review Letters*, 36 (1976), 1223–1226.

15. A. Petersen, "The Philosophy of Niels Bohr," *Bulletin of the Atomic Scientists*, 19, no. 7 (1963), 8–14.

16. A. Petersen, *Quantum Physics and the Philosophical Tradition* (Cambridge: MIT Press, 1968).

17. N. Bohr, *Atomic Physics and Human Knowledge* (New York: Science Editions, 1961), p. 11 and pp. 78–79.

18. Two events have space-like separation if it is impossible to send a signal from one to the other without exceeding the velocity of light.

19. J. A. Wheeler, *Geometrodynamics* (New York: Academic Press, 1962).

20. Private communication.

21. "Commutes" implies that their measurements do not interfere with each other.

22. J. M. Burgers, "The Measuring Process in Quantum Theory," *Reviews of Modern Physics*, 35 (1963), 145–150, and *Experience and Conceptual Activity* (Cambridge: MIT Press, 1965).

23. O. Costa de Beauregard, "Time Symmetry and Interpretation of Quantum Mechanics," *Foundations of Physics*, 6 (1976), 539–59.

24. E. P. Wigner, "Remarks on the Mind-Body Question," in *The Scientist Speculates*, I. J. Good, ed. (London: Heinemann, 1962), reprinted in *Symmetries and Reflections* (Bloomington: Indiana Univ. Press, 1967).

25. J. Hall, C. Kim, B. McElroy, and A. Shimony, "Wave-Packet Reduction as a Medium of Communication," *Foundations of Physics*, 7 (1977), 759–67.

26. H. Weyl, *Philosophy of Mathematics and Natural Science* (Princeton U. Press, 1949), p. 283.

Chapter 29

Is Scientific Realism Compatible with Quantum Physics?

Arthur Fine

The "new" quantum theory that developed in the decade following 1925 was buffeted by two conflicting influences. On the one hand, it inherited the legacy of the old quantum theory, whose machinery was used so skillfully (e.g., by Einstein and Planck) to support the reality of a microworld made up of molecules and atoms. On the other hand, the new quantum theory also grew up alongside the new positivism, a movement that was itself struggling to come to terms with the older "there-are-no-atoms" positivism of Ostwald, Stallo, and Mach. The upshot of these contradictory influences and companions on the quantum theory is a kind of schizophrenia that the theory seems to exhibit over the issue of realism. For the quantum theory of today is reputed to support realism with respect to a variety of entities, including molecules and atoms and electrons and photons, a whole zoo of elementary particles, quarks maybe—and perhaps some even more unlikely things like magnetic monopoles. Yet that very same quantum theory is also reputed to be incompatible with realism, an incompatability suspected by Born as long ago as 1926[1] and recently brought out with clarity and force in the investigations of John Bell and others over hidden variables.

My purpose in this chapter is to examine this schizophrenia over realism. In the best therapeutic tradition, I will try to show that the quantum theory has an integrity of its own which conforms to neither of these opposing images; that is, that quantum theory neither supports that realism of atoms and molecules, etc., to which the old positivism was opposed, nor does it deny it. Thus I will urge the forgotten moral of the new positivism; namely, that realism is metaphysical doctrine that finds neither support nor refutation in scientific theories or investigations. I would not, however, go on to endorse the principle that Carnap generalized from Karl Menger's discussions in the philosophy of mathematics,[2] the principle that one should be tolerant concerning "external questions," like that of realism. For I believe that where ideas can be graded into "better" and "worse" one should always choose the better. And certainly NOA provides a much better framework for science than the metaphysics of so-called scientific realism. [*Ed. note*: Fine's NOA is set out in chapter 14.]

Realism involves a special interpretive stance toward science. It sees science as providing reliable information about the features of a definite world structure, and thus it construes the truth of scientific statements as involving some sort of articulated external-world correspondence. When we come to existence claims, say, the claim that there are quarks, the realist picture is that the truth of the claim corresponds to a certain feature of the world structure (presumably a quarklike part). Obviously, the mere truth of the claim, say, that there are quarks, has nothing specifically to do with realism. That is, we could certainly agree with the physicists that there are quarks without necessarily imposing on that conclusion the special interpretive stance of realism. (We

Reprinted from *The Shaky Game* (Chicago: University of Chicago Press, 1986), Chapter 9, pp. 151–171, by permission of the author and the publisher. Copyright 1986 by University of Chicago Press.

might, for instance, adopt the stance of some antirealist truthmonger or, better still, follow NOA's recommendation and not adopt any special stance at all.) Granting this, the realist might, nevertheless, hope to carry his argument forward by suggesting that there are in fact good grounds for imposing a realist construal. In particular, with respect to existence claims the realist might well suggest that the details of the scientific practice that grounds such claims provides the rationale for his special interpretive stance. The idea is that if we look carefully at the procedures that lead to the general, scientific endorsement of existence claims, then we will discern a practice of assessment, a critical aspect of which involves precisely the interpretive stance of realism.

I am afraid that only immersion in the details of quite lengthy case studies can give one a feel for the texture of decision making over existence claims in a highly structured science like quantum physics. For that procedure involves a truly exquisite balance between experimental and theoretical work. On the experimental side, one has the varied and skillful generation of effect in the laboratory, effects whose very recognition requires intricate data analysis and reduction on a sometimes massive scale, and whose significance is often, at best, only marginal, even at the statistical level. On the theoretical side, there is the calculation of the likelihood of such effects by means of a network of approximations that are only loosely derived from complex and varied theoretical considerations.[3] The most important feature of the whole process, and the one it is most difficult to get a feeling for in the abstract, is that every stage of the experimental design and analysis, as well as every stage of the theoretical reconciliation, involves significant matters of judgment. These are matters not closed by experiment or theory or by any of the modalities that the realist might want to subsume under the rubric of "contact with reality."[4] These judgments express norms, and often transient ones, for pursuing the scientific craft. Thus the decision to accept as true a particular existence claim is the decision to accept the complex network of judgments that ground it. That network itself constitutes an open-ended array of partially overlapping theories and norms. It is precisely the setting of the existence claim within this array that constitutes the scientific practice of truth judging for the claim. The existence claim will be accepted as true just to the extent that the relevant scientific community goes along with the network of normative judgments and the concomitant ranges of theories.[5]

But if this is a fair summary of what goes on when an existence claim is examined and judged to be correct, then the realist ambition to discern in that practice the special interpretive stance of realism is bound to be frustrated. For all that the process displays is how particular judgments of truth are anchored in a network of much more general judgments and normative practices. Hence, when we view this activity without prejudice we do not discern realism; that is, the working through of the realist project for external-world correspondence (or the like). Rather, what we see at work is the critical elaboration of tentative truth claims arising out of locally constrained practical reason and judgment. Thus the realist ambition here is frustrated, for what we see at work in the validation of existence claims is not realism at all but rather NOA.[6]

So far I have been trying to address the following line of thought. When we look at the things that exist, according to quantum physics, we find a large and fascinating variety of objects; in particular, various particles and fields with their attendant properties and relations. A naive inference from this might be that at least with respect to *these* objects, the ones that are supposed to exist, the physics is realist. In order to show that, in fact, no such inference is warranted I have tried to emphasize that realism requires substantially more than just the truth of certain claims. What it requires is that this truth (or these claims) have a certain, special aura—so to speak—an aura that reaches out to reality itself. Since this realist emanation is not to be found in the mere fact of the truth of these existence claims, I have asked whether it might be found to be attached to those claims by the scientific practices that ground their truth. But although those practices are somewhat elusive, they are still definite enough to be seen not to involve the subtle emanations of realism. I conclude that when the realist attaches the aura of his realism to science, he goes well beyond what is warranted either by the truth of specific scientific claims or by the features of scientific practice that ground those claims. In short, realism is unwarranted, even if we restrict it only to the existence claims of quantum physics.

So far, despite some mention of quantum physics and its objects, I have been trying to set out a line of thought that is perfectly general. It is that in the context of any reasonably developed science the realist attempt to ground his special requirements either in the existence claims made by the science or in the practices that certify the correctness of those claims seems bound to fail. The "externality," the reaching out to definite features of a definite world structure, is not found in science itself. It is a kind of overlay to the text of science, an overlay that the realist seems to need in order to direct and focus his own reading of the text. While I am sure the realist would be happy if we were to accept the naive inference from particular existence claims (or even claims of a more general sort) to his realism, I also believe that, in his heart, the realist knows full well that such an inference is fallacious. That is why, in recent years, the patterns of argument for realism have been rather more sophisticated. These recent arguments are the explanationist and coherentist ones for which the "metatheorem" of chapter 7 of *The Shaky Game* provides a powerful rebuttal. But this too is a general consideration and makes no use of special features of the quantum theory that are relevant to the possibility of realism there.

A particular feature of relevance is the prima facie difficulty in reconciling quantum physics with the definiteness that realism requires. For the entities, properties, and relations that enter into the realist world structure are supposed to be observer-independent (or largely so). But the probability-laden formulas of quantum theory all seem to make at least tacit reference to an observer. For the probabilities of the theory are generally understood as probabilities for various measurement outcomes and, so understood, suppose a prearranged apparatus for measurement—and hence a measurer-observer of some sort. Then, too, well-known and densely packed difficulties over the evolution (and collapse) of the state function also appear to involve observer-driven interaction in an essential way. The problem here of whether it is possible to construct a definite world picture on the basis of quantum theory used to be referred to, barbarously, as the problem of "unobjectifiability."[7] I think the consensus of investigators is that "objectifiability" (i.e., the possibility of there being a definite world picture that accords with the detailed predictions of quantum theory), if not actually ruled out, has, at any rate, dim prospects in quantum physics. I must confess, however, that apart from certain recent investigations, including those generated by the work of John Bell, I have never found the various lines of argument for this pessimistic conclusion at all compelling.[8] I will begin to examine the implications of Bell's work for realism in a moment, but first I just want to state the conclusion on realism so far. It is that even without attending to features of observation in quantum theory, realism finds no support there. If it should turn out, in addition, that the role of the observer in the theory actually excludes the possibility for there being a definite world structure compatible with the physics, then so much the worse for realism.

But is realism actually incompatible with quantum physics? That is the conclusion, with one qualification or another, that several investigators have wanted to draw on the basis of Bell's work. The qualifications will turn out to be of central importance. In order to highlight this, let me begin the evaluation of the impact of the Bell literature on realism by sketching a very general argument to show that no theory can actually be incompatible with realism per se, unless the theory is itself inconsistent. The argument is, simply, that—in the logician's sense—every consistent theory has a model. The model automatically provides for referents, via correspondence to the terms in the vocabulary of the theory, and the conditions for truth-in-the-model embody the realist requirements for a correspondence theory of truth. Hence, if we add to the model the realist injunction that the model structure is the real, definite world structure, we get out precisely the desired compatibility of realism with the theory in question.

Now, bracketing off the difficult and interesting logical constructions involved in proving that every consistent theory has a model, one might well think that the argument I have just sketched is really too general, indeed too trivial, to be of much interest in the debate over realism. While I do not want to place *too* much emphasis on this line of argument, I do think it has some genuine interest. In the first place, I think the argument does show that there is no possibility to *refute* realism using some science or scientific practice as a basis. If one combines this conclusion with the one I have been urging up to this point (namely, that there is no way to *support* realism using some science or scientific practice), then the picture of realism that emerges is very much like the one drawn by the neopositivists. Realism emerges as a metaphysical doctrine that transcends human experience and rational support, in a manner similar to that, say, of a religious doctrine. Thus at this level of generality, the only way to support a genuine incompatibility between science and realism would be to attend to a scientific domain whose theory or practice is inconsistent. What comes to mind is a protoscience containing several partially overlapping but irreconcilable-looking theories. For such a domain the possibility of a realist interpretation would not be guaranteed by my model-theoretic argument. Curiously, modern physics may itself be just such a protoscience with quantum physics and general relativistic physics the irreconcilable pairs.[9] Of course, since several lively and different contemporary research programs are moving toward a unified physics,[10] this toehold for antirealism will probably not support it for long.

Related model-theoretic considerations are involved in Hilary Putnam's recent attack on realism (he calls his target "metaphysical realism," as though there were some other, more physical kind).[11] For Putnam wants to attack the idea that realism could actually establish correspondence relations that would pin down the real referents. To this end he uses the observation that a model is only defined up to isomorphism,[12] so that the actual elements in the domain of the definite world structure—considered as a model of some theory—would always elude us, even if we supplement the theory with reference-fixing addenda. It seems to me that Putnam's argument is good enough to make the realist reexamine his vague requirement of substantial epistemic access to features of the world structure. For in the light of Putnam's challenge to the possibility of specifying reference, the realist may want to relativize epistemic access to certain reference-fixing conventions that are not themselves to be considered part of science, and hence not to be thrown into the model at all. Or, the realist may want to reduce the extent of the epistemic access to merely structural features of the world. It is an open question to what extent the consequent conventionalism or the structuralism, which are both familiar moves in the history of epistemology, would support a lively realism. I believe, therefore, that Putnam's argument shows something important about the metaphysical character of realism, insofar as it demonstrates inherent limitations on the specificity of realist correspondence relations. For just this reason, however, Putnam's argument is actually useful to the realist as a means of defense from the "unobjectifiability" that has been urged against realism on behalf of the quantum theory. For those who see difficulties in providing an observer-independent world picture for quantum physics generally agree that if we do bring the observer into the picture then we can indeed find a consistent interpretive scheme. The "Copenhagen interpretation" (in some definite form), for example, might do. But if this were granted, then we could deploy Putnam's strategy to construct out of an observer-laden ontology an observer-independent one isomorphic to the original. Thus if we grant the viability of a Copenhagen-like interpretation for the quantum theory, we can use Putnam's observation to insure the viability of a realist, observer-independent interpretation. This idea, I think, closes what some may have perceived as a gap in my model-theoretic argument for the compatibility of realism with any consistent theory. For how, one might have asked, can we be sure that there is a model that is definite in the sense required by realism? The answer, given above, is this: The realist can always putnamize.

Finally, lest one still think that such general model-theoretic considerations are simply too far-fetched and, perhaps, too easy to attract the interest of genuine realists, I should point out that one realist program for quantum mechanics seems to me to have been derived from precisely such considerations. I have in mind the program of quantum logic in its realist version. In the case of nonrelativistic quantum theory, at any rate, one can construct a model in something much like the logician's sense from the geometry of Hilbert space. Now I do not suppose it would occur to very many people to try to use this fact to declare that reality (i.e., the definite world structure posited by realism) *is* a Hilbert space. But it has certainly occurred to some to contend that the "possibility structure" (or the logical structure) of reality is that of the lattice of closed subspaces of a Hilbert space. (The technical idea is to use that lattice to provide a model for a "quantum logic" of propositions in just the way that the two-element Boolean algebra is used to provide a model for the classical logic of propositions. There are other quantum logical programs that employ somewhat different structures, e.g., the category of partial Boolean algebras. For present purposes I will not distinguish between them.) This is a merely structural realism of the sort one might retreat to in the face of Putnam's argument about reference. It does not attempt to specify what the real possibilities, whose structure is given by the Hilbert space lattice, are really possibilities for. Indeed, one of the persistent anomalies of this quantum logical program has been over the idea of a property and what "having a property" amounts to if the structure is quantum logical. These days the program seems to be a degenerating one, like the program of realism itself. The reasons for that are much like the reasons rehearsed above in connection with realism; namely, that interpreting the application of quantum mechanics as the working out of inferences via a new logic goes well beyond the ordinary practice of the physics, including practices for judging truth. Moreover, as a device for explaining puzzling features of the physics, or puzzling features of experiments (like the tangled statistics of some correlation experiments), quantum logic is clearly sterile for it already assumes that reality contains structural features corresponding to the puzzling explananda. (The technical side is that the probabilistic relations of the theory are already fixed by the lattice structure.) Thus the form of a typical "explanation" proffered by quantum logic is that so-and-so is strange because reality is strange. And that, I think, is the sort of explanation that we usually dismiss as being no explanation at all.[13] If, however, realist quantum logic—like realism more generally—fails to obtain any support from quantum physics, still it remains compatible with the physics; a testament, if you like, to quantum logic's metaphysical status.

Insofar as this discussion of the general compatibility of realism with quantum physics has been persuasive, it will have made as plain as can be that if there actually were a difficulty in reconciling realism with the Bell theorem, that difficulty would be generated by very special assumptions. It should be equally plain that one can indeed make trouble for realism if one does make strong enough background assumptions. For example, suppose we require that our realism be monistic, so that all the things that exist will be of exactly one kind. Suppose, further, that we require the correspondence relations to respect identity. That is, if A and B are distinct according to our science, then the real referent of A must be distinct from the real referent of B. Clearly, if our monism allows for only certain individuating properties and our theory entails sufficient diversity, we may not be able to model the truths of the theory by our monism in a way that respects identity. Of course it would be misleading to advertise this failure as a defeat of realism, or even of monism. For the constraints on correspondence would have played an essential role here. More generally, if our realism is eliminatively reductive, then there will be strong restrictions on the correspondence relations, restrictions that effect the reduction of the "theoretical entities" (to speak picturesquely) to aggregates, or whatever, of the "real stuff." From the difficulties involved in various attempted microreductions of just this sort (for instance, nation-states to aggregates of individuals, genes to DNA structures, or heat to molecules in motion), we have come to expect a mismatch between the reductive base and the original theory-to-be-reduced. Of course the significance of the mismatch is not clear. (Do we conclude that nation-states exist over and above the individuals that they comprise, or that political theory is simply a mistake, or just that our reductive correspondence rules are flawed?) What is clear, I hope, is that an eliminative or reductive realism can be incompatible with a specific theory, and that when this occurs its significance requires careful assessment.

I want to show, now, how the application of the Bell results involves such an eliminatively reductive realism. To see just how eliminative the required reduction is, I want to contrast this reductive realism with a nonreductive sort. Let me begin then by introducing a realist scheme for the quantum theory, a scheme that I shall call *minimal realism*, because it posits a structure that must be reproduced, at least approximately, by any realist construal of the theory.[14] When we contrast Bell's reductive realism with this minimal one, we will be able to pinpoint the reductive constraints, and this will assist us in assessing the significance of the mismatch between quantum theory and the posited reductively realist structure.

Any realist approach to quantum theory will have to specify what (in the real world) corresponds to the systems, observables, states, and probabilities that make up the theoretical apparatus. The nature of the systems is an old and intractable issue. Are they waves or particles or what? Let us not try to decide this issue (keeping in mind, for example, that we could always putnamize from one ontological category to another anyway). Instead let us just say that, according to minimal realism, quantum systems correspond to real objects. The observables of the theory (spin, position, momentum, etc.) will each correspond to some generic feature of the real objects, a feature that can take on any one of several particular forms. We will assume as part of our minimal realism that each real object has (or "possesses") some particular form (or other) of every generic feature. One can think of these particular forms as definite properties of the object. The states, then, will correspond to the various ways of attributing the particular forms of generic features to the real objects. (Formally, a state is a function from real objects to the particular forms of generic features, a function that assigns to each object exactly one form of each generic feature.) Then a system S has a state ψ (or "is in" the state ψ) just in case the real object corresponding to S has the array of particular forms of the generic features that ψ attributes to that object. We must now make some further assumptions about the forms of these features. Suppose A is an observable. Then there will be a number of classical (i.e., Lebesgue) probability measures on the real line that are concentrated on the possible values of A (i.e., on its spectrum). I want to suppose that each particular form of the generic feature that corresponds to A is associated with one such measure on the possible values of A. (You could think of this association as a property of the form; i.e., as a second-order property of the object.) Finally, we call specify the realist truth conditions for the probabilistic assertions of the theory as follows. If system S is in state ψ and A is an observable of S, then ψ attributes to the real object corresponding to S a particular form of the generic feature that corresponds to A. If and only if that particular form is associated with the probability distribution that quantum mechanics assigns for finding values of A, will we say that these various probabilistic assertions are true for system S in state ψ. Roughly speaking, various probabilistic assertions hold just in case the object has the right forms of the features; that is, the right properties.

This minimal realism is, of course, merely a structural realism, a skeleton that could be fleshed out in different ways. In various publications I have suggested some ways to try. One of them is to take each generic feature to be what I call a "statistical variable"; that is, a real-valued function with a probability measure defined on the Borel subsets of its range. This is a concept well known in empirical statistics (to be distinguished from the different concept of a random variable), and which seems just to fit the quantum mechanical uses of probability.[15] Then the particular forms of a statistical variable would just be pairings of the function with a particular measure on its range, which automatically yields the association to probabilities. Another suggestion is to consider the observables as extended entities with variably concentrated extensions.[16] Thus the generic features become functions, associating with each object a set with a probability density over that set (i.e., statistical variable-valued functions). Their particular forms are their "values"; i.e., their variably concentrated extensions (or "spreads"), and this variable concentration is the associated probability measure. Finally, I might mention that quantum logic also fits into the framework of minimal realism—although not necessarily with an interpretation as "logic." For it is sufficient for doing quantum physics to restrict the observables to just those taking 0 or 1 as values. These are called "questions" and correspond to the projection operators (or closed subspaces). Then quantum logic would have the generic features that correspond to these questions understood as "real possibilities." The various probabilities for realizing these possibilities are, then, the particular forms.

Let me now apply this minimal realist framework to the correlation experiments treated in the Bell literature. These involve a system S in a fixed state ψ. The system is composed of two subsystems, which we can refer to as particles—particle (1) and particle (2). On each of the particles we have in mind to perform one of several mutually incompatible measurements, (each of which is maximal on the subsystem); say A_1, A_2, ... on particle (1) and B_1, B_2, ... on particle (2). Further, we will suppose that the particles are spatially separated, and that the measurements on the pair are made simultaneously. (If you prefer, say that each pair of measurement events is spacelike separated.) In typical arrangements, quantum mechanics assigns a probability for each individual measurement outcome. It also assigns probabilities for the various pairs of outcomes. That is, quantum theory determines a single distribution for the outcomes of each measurement separately, and a joint distribution for the simultaneous outcomes of each AB pair. However, quantum mechanics assigns no joint probability to *any* pair of A's nor to any pair of B's. Indeed the joint outcomes of, say, B_1 and B_2 are generally held not to be well defined. They certainly do not enter into the probabilistic formulas of the theory.

From the perspective of minimal realism we can treat the system S as one real object with two parts, the "particles." In state ψ the generic features of the object take particular forms. Let us say that corresponding to the A measurement on particle (1) (technically the observable $A \otimes I$) the object has the form α of the feature corresponding to A. Similarly, the B measurement on particle (2) (the $I \otimes B$ observable) corresponds to the form β. And corresponding to the joint measurements of A on particle (1) and B on particle (2) (the observable $A \otimes B$) let the object have the form $\alpha\beta$, according to ψ. Thus when the system is in state ψ the object already has certain properties (the various α, β, and $\alpha\beta$), and these properties ground the probabilities for the various measurement outcomes. For we have that α is already associated with some definite probability distribution on the outcomes of the A measurement, B with a distribution on the B outcomes, and $\alpha\beta$ with a distribution on the joint AB outcomes. The quantum mechanical description of the system (i.e., single probabilities and joint AB pairs as specified) will be correct just in case it matches these distributions that correspond to the properties of the object. Thus in typical realist fashion we can say that the quantum theory for such a correlated system is correct just to the extent that it matches aspects of the definite world structure. More especially, the probabilities of the theory are correct to the extent to which they actually *are* the probabilities associated with properties of the real object.

There are at least three respects in which this minimal framework may be considered too minimal. First, we have made no provision in the model for the actual outcomes of measurements, only for the likelihood of such. Second, we have made probabilities in the theory correspond to special properties in the model (or in the real world, if you like), and thus taken probability as fundamental. Third, we have not built into the association of the probability measures with properties, the relation of the outcome of the joint measurement to the outcomes of the individual ones.

One could rectify all these omissions, it may seem, if one adopted a standard, eliminative strategy over the probabilities. For one might be motivated to alter the correspondence rules for probability in such a way as to reduce, or eliminate, the correspondents of probabilities as part of the inventory of the world. The standard procedure here is to treat the probabilities as mere averages over a single well-determined ensemble, and to support that treatment as what is forced on us (or, at any rate, reasonable to do) in the face of ignorance of the finer details of things. The probabilistic assertions, then, would signify merely a restriction on the epistemic accessibility of the world. This eliminative strategy could be seen as expressing a deterministic attitude, and in the Bell literature especially it is commonly so labeled.[17] But determinism alone cannot be at the root of the strategy, for the minimal realist framework is already determinist in its regular attribution of a definite array of particular forms of the features in every state. Moreover, one could even sharpen the determinism by enhancing the minimal realism in such a way as to make every outcome of a measurement correspond to some additional property already determined prior to the measurement. This is a feature of the prism models discussed in chapter 4 of *The Shaky Game*, which are deterministic, as above, even over measurement outcomes.[18] Indeed, one point of the models was to show that, in addition to determinism, the Bell results require further constraints. What they in fact require, beyond determinism, is the eliminative strategy for probabilities—or something equivalent to it. More precisely, one can give rigorous content to the following theorem.

The Bell inequalities hold if, and only if, it is possible to reduce the probabilities (for the observables mentioned in the inequalities) to averages over a single ensemble.

Let me use the term *reductive realism* for that type of realism whose concern over the reality of probabilities leads it to adopt the eliminative strategy suggested above.[19] In the context of the quantum theory, reductive realism amounts to requiring, first, that the measures of minimal realism all be dispersion free, and then to changing the correspondence rule for the states to treat them the way statistical mechanics treats macrostates. These modifications result in the probabilistic construct of an ensemble representation which then provides the definite world structure of reductive realism.[20] It follows from this structure that if B and B′ are *any* two observables, then not only do they both have values for each real object but there is always, in the real world, a well-defined joint probability for their values, relative to any ensemble that corresponds to a quantum state. But if B and B′ are incompatible, according to quantum theory, then they are not both assigned values in *any* state, nor do they have a joint distribution. Thus reductive realism necessarily involves features of the world not touched on by the quantum theory. In particular, the way it treats probability has a uniformity to it that one does not find in quantum theory itself. The price of reduction, then, seems to be to make out of the quantum theory an account of the world that is doubly incomplete. It is incomplete descriptively, because it fails to describe the values of incompatible observables. It is incomplete probabilistically, because it fails to specify the well-defined joint distributions for incompatible observables.

I call attention to the way in which the joint probabilities of reductive realism necessarily outstrip those of quantum theory because this particular feature, which is deeply at variance with quantum mechanics, turns out to characterize this special brand of realism *all by itself*. That is, any framework that allows for well-defined joint distributions for the incompatible observables can be given an ensemble representation. Let me restate this more carefully for the correlation experiments.

Recall that in this case we have a single state ψ and, say, observables $A_1 \ldots A_n$; $B_1 \ldots B_m$, where each pair A_i, B_j has a quantum mechanical distribution in state ψ, and no pair A_i, A_j or B_i, B_j has a quantum mechanical distribution. I will say that *there is a well-defined distribution for* $B_1, \ldots B_m$ (relative to the A's) in case (1) for each i, there is a joint distribution for $A_i, B_1, \ldots, B_m$ that returns (as marginals) the quantum mechanical distributions for A_i, B_j ($j = 1, 2, \ldots m$) and (2) each of these distributions just mentioned returns one and the same joint distribution for $B_1 \ldots, B_m$. Then, regardless of the cardinality of the spectra of the observables, of their number, or of their single distributions (i.e., not necessarily all $\frac{1}{2}$), the following theorem holds: *there exists an ensemble representation for* $A_1, \ldots, A_n$; $B_1, \ldots, B_m$ *if and only if there is a well-defined distribution for* $B_1, \ldots, B_m$ *(relative to the A's)*.[20]

The Bell literature generally refers to what I have been calling an "ensemble representation" as a local (or "factorizable") hidden variables theory—more especially, a deterministic one. (The literature also treats a stochastic variety. But it turns out that there is a stochastic, factorizable theory iff there is a deterministic one.[21] So where all that is at stake is the possibility of hidden variables, we can stick with the deterministic kind.) Several special cases of the general situation of the preceding theorem have been studied in some detail. For these cases, quantum mechanical systems have been found whose probabilities cannot be given an ensemble representation. These results can be referred to, collectively, as the *Bell theorem*. (They usually proceed by showing that the quantum probabilities violate some relation necessary for an ensemble representation, a relation like the inequality originally derived by Bell.)

The Bell theorem, then, shows that reductive realism cannot ground the truth of all the probabilistic assertions of quantum theory. This is just the sort of mismatch between a theory and a special sort of realism that, as I suggested earlier, one might well expect in general. In particular, since reductive realism for correlated systems turns out to be fully *equivalent* to the existence of a well-defined distribution for the incompatible observables of each subsystem, quantum mechanics would be seen as incomplete over the most essential features of the world if it *could* be given a realist reduction. That reductive program, it has always seemed to me, is so widely at variance with the theory as to make it a very implausible candidate for shaping a realist worldview for quantum theory. From this perspective, then, the Bell theorem is a welcome result, for it shows that an implausible form of realism for quantum theory is actually numerically inconsistent with the theory.

But there are other perspectives. A common one in the scientific community is to focus on the so-called locality involved in reductive realism and to see the variance between it and quantum theory as a demonstration that a realist construal of quantum theory will have to countenance certain peculiar and suspect nonlocal effects. Recall that the "locality" condition (or as I prefer to call it, "factorizability") is already built into the idea of an ensemble representation. It is the requirement that the quantum correlation for joint measurement outcomes on each pair of particles (i.e., the joint probability for each *A*, *B* pair) arises by averaging over the product of the probability for the outcomes on each particle separately. It is easy to show that this requirement is actually equivalent to the implausible condition already discussed; namely, that all the incompatible observables for one subsystem have a well-defined joint distribution (relative to the observables of the other subsystem). This equivalence certainly ought to make us wonder about the physical grounds for "locality." Indeed, although the required factorizability is related to a condition of stochastic independence, there is no reason to suppose that violations of the independence condition must involve real, nonlocal effects—something like genuine action-at-a-distance.[22]

Nevertheless, the issue of "locality" seems especially hard to deal with, and I think this is because there are deep background beliefs at work. These beliefs, whatever their propositional content, issue in an attitude that makes correlations between spatially separated systems appear puzzling in themselves, and that then restricts the possible ways of explaining the correlations to just two: either they are due to a common background cause that operated when the systems were interacting, or they arise by an exchange of information that occurs after the systems are already separated. The first route here, the common cause idea, is simply equivalent to the existence of an ensemble representation for the correlations.[23] The second route, when we rule out by experimental design all but instantaneous exchanges, is precisely the imputed nonlocality. If one approaches Bell's theorem with the attitude sketched above, then of course, one is going to see it as entailing nonlocality for the correlated systems of quantum mechanics to which the theorem applies. Faced with this attitude, I think there are only two ways to go. One is to try to undermine the suspicion that attaches to distant correlations, to try to see them as an ordinary part of the natural world—a feature to be catalogued rather than explained. Here one might take certain simple varieties of distant correlations as natural paradigms (Toulmin's "ideals of natural order" or Sellars's "unexplained explainers") and try to build the others up from these.[24] A second way of dealing with the suspicion of nonlocality would be to suggest that there are ways of explaining distant correlations other than via common background causes or exchanges of information. Here the realist can point to the explanation embedded in minimal realism. In general, the realist can explain why certain probabilities are found by showing how they are grounded in the particular forms taken by generic features of the real objects. In the case of correlated systems, the real object with the two particles as parts already has, in the fixed state ψ, for any A measurement on one particle and B on the other, a particular form $\alpha\beta$ for the generic feature corresponding to the joint measurement. The correlation between the distant measurement outcomes is due, according to minimal realism, to the presence *in* the real object of this particular property. Not only does minimal realism offer this *explanation* for correlated statistics, an explanation that is free of nonlocal effects, minimal realism could not possibly be convicted of harboring any such effects. For the world of minimal realism includes only objects and particular forms of their features (with associated probabilities). In the world of minimal realism there are no actions at all, certainly none propagating instantaneously across space (or the like).

Of course those suspicious about distant correlations will probably not be satisfied by this minimalist explanation. They may well respond, as I did earlier over quantum logic, that it only explains puzzling features of the theory (or of our observations) by invoking mysterious features of the world. I have considerable sympathy with that response, the general drift of which is to point to the sterility of realism as such. Nevertheless, if the suspicious attitude toward distant correlations makes them stand out as requiring explanation and yet will not accept explanations for them in terms of such structural features of the world, then I think that these particular suspicions could only be addressed by an account of how the correlations are generated in time from uncorrelated, individual outcomes. Since such an explanation would be tantamount to an ensemble representation, Bell's theorem rules it out. The upshot is that one cannot lay the suspicions to rest. Thus there is no help for those who are trapped in this circle; they must struggle, I think, to undo their suspicious nature. But they could, still, be clear enough in their own thinking to see that the difficulties they experience cannot be blamed on realism, but only on their own reductive worldview.

So far I have taken for granted that the incompatibility brought out by Bell's theorem between quantum theory and reductive realism is to be dealt with by abandoning that brand of realism. I am inclined to this attitude because, as I see it, reductive realism should never have been offered in the first place as a plausible candidate for the quantum worldview. But one could be more cautious for, as I pointed out earlier, when one finds a reductive mismatch one ought to be open to asking which side of the reduction should we give up; and not only this, for one can also ask whether the correspondence rules linking the sides may not be at fault. Thus one can certainly wonder, concerning just those areas where reductive realism clashes with the quantum theory, which one will stand the test of experiment. A number of correlation experiments have been run to try to settle this question.[25] On one analysis of experimental error these experiments can be taken as confirming the predictions of quantum theory, and they are generally so regarded. It is, however, also possible to factor in the experimental errors differently to see the experimental results as entirely consistent with reductive realism. Indeed, from the fact that for the range of experiments to date the inequalities of Clauser and Horne (1974) are sufficient (as well as necessary) for an ensemble representation, one can prove that such a representation is always possible for a simple spin-$\frac{1}{2}$ experiment whenever the single-detector efficiency in the experiment is less than, roughly, 90 percent.[26] Since no experiment so far even comes close to this level of efficiency, it follows that there is not yet any really crucial test between quantum mechanics and reductive realism. As of today, then, one could still hope to see quantum theory as a merely approximate account of a reductively realist world structure, an account doubly incomplete and just wrong at certain points. As technology develops, however, highly efficient correlation experiments may remove that way of reconciling the difference.

There would, nevertheless, still be the option of reexamining the reductive correspondence rules. This is precisely the issue treated at length in my essay on Einstein and Bell in chapter 4 of *The Shaky Game*. The argument there was that Einstein's "statistical interpretation" need not be understood as the technical construct of an ensemble representation, but rather it could be understood even better as involving the machinery of prism models. Since Einstein's attitude toward probabilities was certainly reductive, that argument is relevant here, for it shows, constructively, how the elimination of probabilities as fundamental (or "real") need not necessarily lead to an ensemble representation (or, equivalently, to a deterministic hidden variables model). That reductive program could instead, for example, be satisfied by an interpretation based on prism models. Such a shift in the reductive program would certainly avoid the obstacle posed by the Bell theorem. The question of efficiency, however, is also relevant to the survival of the prism models, and it remains to be seen whether the flexible resources of these models will stand up to highly efficient tests.

To sum things up, we can conclude that there is no incompatibility possible between quantum physics and realism as such. We've yet to see whether the possible incompatibility brought out by Bell's theorem between the quantum theory and reductive realism will even go against that peculiar and implausible brand of realism. But the realist should draw no solace from this, because there is no support for realism to be found in quantum physics either. The existence claims of the physics do not support realism, nor does physical practice support the semantics of realism. If my general argument in the first part of this chapter did not persuade you of the extent to which realism transcends the physics, then perhaps my later working out of the structure of minimal realism will have done the job. For what reason do we have to believe that "right out here in the world" there are real objects having particular forms of certain generic features which are associated with special probability measures? Indeed, what sense can we make of this idea?

In formulating such a realism I have pursued the standard procedure for playing the quantum realism game. It consists, to begin with, in taking the salient quantum theoretical apparatus, wholesale, as one big truth. Then it follows up by asking what the world must be like *in order* for the quantum theory to be true. The first step here, the move from successful applications and extensions (what I call local judgments of truth) to the truth of the whole theoretical covering story, is already a controversial one, and one for which there seems to be no general or overriding warrant. But even if we part company with instrumentalism on this score and make this move to truth (perhaps out of special warrant or, maybe, just out of charity), how then do we proceed with the game? Even if we accept the truth of the quantum theory, what now constrains what the world *must* be like? Must it be like minimal realism (with "spreads," or "inexact values," or "disjunctive facts"?), or instead like some viable reductive realism (which one?)? Should the fundamental formulas be read interactively, so that the observables and states are construed as relations (in which particular way?)? Should superpositions be taken as describing nonintersecting branches of many actual worlds, of which we are just one among the many? Or should we take that, perhaps, as just a picturesque way of speaking about an interpretation where the state function never collapses? Now I've said it, *interpretation*; so now, perhaps, we can see what it is. After we have agreed to hold the theory true, or approximately so, the realist still needs to ask, given that, what the world is like. The answer is an "interpretation of the quantum theory"; that is, a model structure plus rules of correspondence (or "satisfaction") according to which the theory comes out to be true, or approximately so. Since these constraints on interpretation are nowhere near specific enough to entail categoricity, there will be nonisomorphic models, as many of them as one likes. Among them the realist, having satisfied the truth constraints, can now only pick and choose according to his needs, desires, or tastes. In the end game, then, we find that the quantum realist, ironically, joins hands with his idealist and constructivist enemies. For just like them, in fashioning his "interpretation of the quantum theory," he is simply constructing his own "real" world according to personal (or social) constraints. As we saw, even Einstein's cautiously hedged and empirically grounded realism was motivational in the end, ultimately universalizing his own felt needs as a scientific investigator. In charging the instrumentalist Copenhagen theorists with playing a shaky game with reality, Einstein was certainly correct. But it would be an error of judgment on our part to suppose that when the realist moves beyond the truth of the quantum theory to constuct its interpretation, he is doing anything other than playing a game himself, and one rather *too* shaky because, granted truth, the rules of this realist game have now been cut loose from any ongoing scientific practice.

To be sure we do have reason to believe that there are molecules and atoms, as well as reason to believe that there are in fact no joint probabilities for incompatible observables (which fact it is reasonable to take as supporting the general validity of the Heisenberg uncertainty formulas). There is growing reason to believe in variously accomplished and decked out quarks, and in the soundness of programs that ground particle properties in the irreducible representations of symmetry transformations of field theories. There is even some reason to believe that certain correlation experiments produce tangled statistics, ones that cannot be modeled by an ensemble representation of the experiment. The reasons here are embedded in the various overlapping and ever-open practices that constitute the judgment of those claims by the community of concerned scientists. They are good reasons, in some cases the best we are likely to find in support of *any* belief. Of course to see such grounds as sufficient for belief in the truth of the claims is a far cry from realism. It has none of realism's splendor, none of that special joy and comfort that realism finds in constructing from the actual scientific endeavor a reaching out to the hidden details of an exquisite and elaborate world structure. Still, although more modest and homely, the attitude that seeks to ground scientific belief in reasonable practice—and to understand that belief in those terms—seems itself a reasonable stance to adopt. I do so, and urge you to do likewise. That is, exactly, NOA—the natural ontological attitude.

Notes

An earlier version of this chapter was presented as a symposium to the Pacific Division of the American Philosophical Association in March 1983. I would like to thank my cosymposiast there, Linda Wessels, for helpful suggestions. I also want to thank a referee for *Noûs*, and Hector Castenada, the editor, who accepted the earlier version for publication but who kindly allowed me to withdraw it for revision and publication here.

1. See the concluding paragraph of Born (1926).
2. Menger (1974), p. 111, contains references to his papers from 1928 to 1933 relating to this point.
3. Galison (1985) gives one a good sense for the complexities on the experimental side, and Cartwright (1983), essay 6 especially, does the same on the side of theory.
4. For the particular case of the existence of quarks this is compellingly documented in a fascinating narrative by Pickering (1984).
5. Simplifying the conclusion of a complex story, Galison writes, "The discovery of the muon was inseparably bound to the resurrection of quantum electrodynamics" (Galison 1983, p. 308).
6. Overlapping considerations lead Hacking (1983) to the same conclusion, in his "experimental argument" for "realism." For insofar as Hacking seems to lean toward a Davidsonian "no-theory" theory

of truth, what Hacking (and perhaps Davidson as well) calls "realism" seems rather a version of NOA. See Rorty (1986a, b) for the suggestion of connecting Davidson with NOA.

7. This is the terminology of von Weizsäcker (1952), who adopts it from Pauli (1933).

8. Fine (1973a) expresses some of my reservations concerning the older literature. Perhaps I inherited this attitude from my teacher in this subject, Henry Mehlberg. See Mehlberg (1960, 1980) who tries to make realism ride piggyback on the idea of treating quantum probabilities as transition probabilities, an idea that had lost its way until Cartwright (1983) found it anew.

9. Joseph (1980) is a nice discussion of this antirealist idea. For those who adopt the semantic approach to theories, a theory is a family of models. Q. E. D. Joseph's puzzle may be an interesting challenge, or growing point, for this semantic approach.

10. See, for example, Fayet and Ferrara (1977) and Levy and Deser (1979).

11. See Putnam (1981a) and references there to his earlier work.

12. Actually, Putnam cites versions of the Löwenheim-Skolem theorem, which do not seem essential to his point.

13. Stairs (1983) is an excellent statement of realist quantum logical ambitions, emphasizing especially how the very rationale for the program is that it is supposed to offer explanatory insight. (The point is that it does not.)

14. The "at least approximately" here is intended to hedge minimal realism by leaving open the possibility of variations in the realist structure; e.g., replacing properties of the real objects by relations, or allowing states to be only partial functions (or even multiple-place functions) on the real objects, and so on. Aficionados will recognize these perennial variations on the realist theme. The openness of these possibilities is significant. I suggest why at the conclusion of the chapter.

15. See Fine (1968) for the background to this idea, and Fine (1973a, 1976, 1982b) for its development.

16. See Fine (1971, 1973b). Teller (1979, 1984) makes up some pretty, motivating stories for this idea, especially for continuous magnitudes, promoting it as an "inexact values interpretation"; and Stairs (1983), focusing on the discrete case, makes it the core of his "M-quantum logic" ("M" for "modest") under the guise of "disjunctive facts." In the article cited, I had anticipated these interpretive moves and criticized them without then realizing that the interpretive dead end here was already precisely the point of the Schrödinger cat paradox. Recall Einstein's "exploding gunpowder" letter to Schrödinger (August 8, 1935) where he puts the difficulty as plainly as can be, "Through no art of interpretation can this psi-function be turned into an adequate description of a real state of affairs; for in reality there is just no intermediary between exploded and not-exploded." Exit my extended entities; a.k.a. "spreads," "disjunctive facts," and "inexact values"!

17. I have in mind the common terminology of "deterministic hidden variables." Recent commentators have noted that the determinism here does not relate to the time evolution of the system but rather to the definiteness of the values of observables at a single time. To make this distinction, Wessels (1985) introduces the useful terminology of "evolutionary determinism" versus "vertical determinism." In her language, the determinism mentioned in my text is vertical not evolutionary.

18. Fine (1982a) also introduces other models for the correlation experiments—synchronization models —with this same deterministic feature.

19. I do not want to suggest by this terminology that concern over the reality of probabilities is a reductive disease to which only quantum realists are susceptible, for that sort of reductionism can infect quantum antirealists as well; witness Leeds (1984).

20. This is a consequence of Theorem 1 of Fine (1982b) and the equivalence of deterministic hidden variables with a suitable joint probability function, demonstrated there on p. 1308.

21. This is shown in Fine (1982c).

22. Perhaps the most important contribution of the Bell literature is just this: it has made us recognize a general problem in connecting the fact of suitably independent causal histories for stochastic processes with the requirement of stochastic independence of their outcomes. This problem is the Achilles' heel of the quantum nonlocality interpretation of the Bell theorem. See Jarrett (1984) and Wessels (1985) for excellent analyses of the options here; Earman (1987) for the many difficulties involved in the requisite concept of "locality"; and Fine (1981b) for several demonstrations of the problem.

23. This follows from results in Suppes and Zannotti (1981) and Fine (1982c).

24. Tolumin (1961) and Sellars (1961). In Fine (1981b) I introduced the idea of "random devices in harmony" as an illustrative paradigm of this sort. Although I was unaware of it at the time, it turns out that a similar concept, called "stochastic coupling," is used in simulation studies. See Fishman (1973).

25. For important, recent ones see Aspect (1982a, b) which also contain references to the literature.

26. See Fine (1982c) and Garg (1983).

27. This issue is discussed in Fine (1981b, 1982d), but general methods for calculating error bounds using the prism idea have yet to be developed. Certainly all extant correlation experiments can be prismed, including the Aspect (1982a, b) experiments, whose symmetries with regard to error rates exactly match the simplest of the prism models.

References

Aspect, A., et al. 1982a. Experimental realization of Einstein-Podolsky-Rosen-Bohm *Gedankenexperiment*: A new violation of Bell's inequalities. *Physical Review Letters* 49: 91–94.

Aspect, A., et al. 1982b. Experimental test of Bell's inequalities using time-varying analyzers. *Physical Review Letters* 49: 1804–7.

Born, M. 1926. Zur Quantenmechanik der Stossvorgange. *Zeitschrift fur Physik* 37: 863–67.

Cartwright, N. 1983. *How the laws of physics lie.* New York: Clarendon Press.

Earman, J. 1987. Locality, nonlocality, and action at a distance: A skeptical review of some philosophical dogmas. In *Kelvin's Baltimore lectures and modern theoretical physics: Historical and philosophical perspectives,* edited by R. Kargon and P. Achinstein, 448–90. Cambridge, MA: MIT Press.

Fayet, P., and S. Ferrara. 1977. Supersymmetry. *Physics Reports* 32(5): 249–334.

Fine, A. 1968. Logic, probability and quantum theory. *Philosophy of Science* 35: 101–11.

Fine, A. 1971. Probability in quantum mechanics and in other statistical theories. In *Problems in the Foundations of Physics,* edited by M. Bunge, 79–92. New York: Springer-Verlag.

Fine, A. 1973a. Probability and the interpretation of quantum mechanics. *British Journal for the Philosophy of Science* 24: 1–37.

Fine, A. 1973b. The two problems of quantum measurement. In *Logic, methodology and philosophy of science,* vol. 4, edited by P. Suppes, 567–81. Amsterdam: North-Holland.

Fine, A. 1976. On the completeness of quantum theory. In *Logic and probability in quantum mechanics,* edited by P. Suppes, 249–81. Dordrecht: Reidel.

Fine, A. 1981. Correlations and physical locality. In *PSA: 1980,* vol. 2, 535–62.

Fine, A. 1982a. Some local models for correlation experiments. *Synthese* 50: 279–94.

Fine, A. 1982b. Joint distributions, quantum correlation, and commuting observables. *Journal of Mathematical Physics* 23: 1306–10.

Fine, A. 1982c. Hidden variables, joint probability and the Bell inequalities. *Physical Review Letters* 48: 291–95.

Fine, A. 1982d. Antinomies of entanglement: The puzzling case of the tangled statistics. *Journal of Philosophy* 79: 733–47.

Fishman, G. S. 1973. *Concepts and methods in discrete event simulation.* New York: Wiley.

Galison, P. 1983. The discovery of the muon and the failed revolution against quantum electrodynamics. *Centaurus* 26: 262–316.

Galison, P. 1985. Bubble chambers and the experimental workplace. In *Observation, experiment, and hypothesis in modern physical science,* edited by P. Achinstein and O. Hannaway. Cambridge, MA: MIT.

Garg, A. 1983. Detector error and Einstein-Podolsky-Rosen correlations. *Physical Review D* 28: 785–90.

Hacking, I. 1983. *Representing and intervening.* Cambridge: Cambridge University Press.

Jarrett, J. 1984. On the physical significance of the locality conditions in the Bell arguments. *Noûs* 12: 569–89 .

Joseph, G. 1980. The many sciences and the one world. *Journal of Philosophy* 77: 773–91.

Leeds, S . 1984. Chance, realism, quantum mechanics. *Journal of Philosophy* 81: 567–78.

Levy, M., and S. Deser. 1979. *Recent developments in gravitation.* New York: Plenum Press.

Mehlberg, H. 1960. The observation problem in quantum theory. *Proceedings XII International Philosophical Congress* 5: 385–91. Florence: Sansoni.

Mehlberg, H. 1980. Philosophical interpretations of quantum physics. In *Time, causality and the quantum theory,* vol. 2, 3–74. Dordrecht: Reidel.

Menger, K. 1974. *Morality, decision and social organization.* Dordrecht: Reidel.

Pauli, W. 1933. Der allgemeinen Prinzipien der Wellenmechanik. In *Handbuch der Physik,* vol. 24, part 1, 83–272. Berlin: Springer-Verlag.

Pickering, A. 1984. *Constructing quarks.* Chicago: University of Chicago Press.

Putnam, H . 1981. *Reason, truth and history.* Cambridge: Cambridge University Press.

Rorty, R. 1986a. Pragmatism, Davidson and truth. In *The philosophy of Donald Davidson: A perspective on inquiry into truth and interpretation,* edited by E. LePore. Oxford: Basil Blackwell.

Rorty, R. 1986b. Beyond realism and anti-realism. In *Wiener Riehe: Themen der Philosophie,* vol. 1, edited by H. Nagl-Docekal et al.

Sellars, W. 1961. The Language of Theories. In *Current issues in the philosophy of science*, edited by H. Feigl and G. Maxwell, 57–77. New York: Holt, Rinehart and Winston.

Stairs, A. 1983. Quantum logic, realism, and value definiteness. *Philosophy of Science* 50: 578–89.

Suppes, P., and M. Zannotti. 1981. When are probabilistic explanations possible? *Synthese* 48: 191–98.

Teller, P. 1979. Quantum mechanics and the nature of continuous physical quantities. *Journal of Philosophy* 76: 345–61.

Teller, P. 1984. The projection postulate: A new perspective. *Philosophy of Science* 51: 369–95.

Toulmin, S. 1961. *Foresight and understanding*. New York: Harper and Row.

von Weizsacker, C. F. 1952. *The worldview of physics*. Translated by M. Grene. Chicago: University of Chicago Press. Originally *Zum Weltbild der Physik*. Leipzig: S. Hirzel, 1945.

Wessels. L. 1985. Locality, factorability and the Bell inequalities. *Noûs* 19: 481–519.

Section II

The Philosophy of Biology

Philip Gasper

For much of this century, philosophers of science have focused most of their attention on theories and developments in the physical sciences. By contrast the biological and social sciences have been far less central. If in retrospect this focus appears one-sided, it is worth remembering that it has not been unmotivated. The revolutionary developments in physics over the last ninety years have raised fundamental philosophical questions and challenged existing conceptions of the nature of science. As Elliott Sober notes, "Einstein's theories of special and general relativity have occupied center stage in philosophy of science for a very good reason: as philosophers, we care about issues of a priori knowledge, conventionalism, and about the general principles that permit radically different scientific theories to be compared and evaluated" (1984, p. 6).

Nevertheless, this preoccupation with physics is now commonly agreed to have had a distorting effect on the philosophy of science. The tendency has been to assume that certain features of physical theories, such as their tractability to mathematical axiomatization, are characteristic of scientific theories in general. To the extent that theories in other areas have not shared these features, it has been assumed that they are incomplete or deficient and that they need to be developed to fit the model derived from physics.

Selections in the first half of this volume have shown that the "received view" of scientific theories articulated by logical empiricists from the 1920s to the 1950s is beset by serious internal difficulties. In other words, the dominant model of scientific theorizing seems inadequate even as a characterization of its central domain. In recent years it has become increasingly apparent that this model is even less appropriate for scientific fields other than physics.

Biology has been an extremely lively area of scientific research for at least the past forty years. There can be no doubt that it is a mature and highly successful area of inquiry, posing sophisticated questions about biological phenomena and developing sophisticated and productive answers to them. In fact, biology is the best example we have of a successful nonphysical science. Yet the structure of biological theories, the standards of biological explanation, and the ways in which biological theories are tested, do not seem to fit the standard model for the physical sciences. This is further reason for doubting the adequacy of the model, at least as a general account of the nature of science.

The continued success of biological research in the context of the crisis of the received view of scientific theories has made philosophy of biology perhaps the most exciting area of inquiry in contemporary philosophy of science. Philosophers of biology have made important contributions to our understanding of the nature of scientific theories, explanation, causation, forces, natural kinds, and many other topics. The selections in this section, however, mainly concentrate on aspects of one issue that is of central importance in biological science: reduction.

For obvious reasons, issues concerning reduction loom large in all the nonphysical sciences (biology, psychology, and the social sciences). It is accepted on all sides that the ultimate constituents of the phenomena discussed by the various special sciences are physical in nature. Biological organisms, for example, are built up of cells, which in their turn are built up of complex molecules, which may be built up of simpler molecules, and so on, until we reach the level of phenomena that it is the aim of the physical sciences to explain. But given that this ontological reductionism is uncontroversial, does this mean that theories in the special sciences ultimately reduce to theories in physics? Should our goal be to find explanations of, for example, biological phenomena using the methods and concepts of the physical sciences? Should we, in other words, embrace some version of explanatory or methodological reductionism? And whether or not we should, what is the relation between theories about "higher-level" domains and theories about "lower-level" domains?

In section 3 of part I, some of the important conceptions of theory reduction were discussed in detail. On the traditional view of theory reduction, theories are regarded as sets of sentences, and one theory is reduced to another roughly when the sentences of the first are derivable from the sentences of the second. A number of able philosophers (see, e.g., Schaffner 1967, 1976; Ruse 1973, 1976) have attempted to apply this model to the relationship between theories of classical biology (cytology, classical genetics, etc.) and theories of molecular biology.

In the first paper in this section, Philip Kitcher raises powerful considerations against this approach. He argues that the standard picture of reduction fails to capture the actual relation between theories of different levels in biology, and that the relevance of molecular genetics for classical genetics can only be understood by carefully examining substantive developments in each area. Kitcher goes on to argue that there are autonomous levels of biological explanation in nature. Attempts to reduce cytology to molecular biology, for example, will thus fail to identify causally relevant properties. He also suggests that explanation may go in both directions, with "higher-level" phenomena sometimes explaining "lower-level" phenomena, as well as vice versa.

The remaining two selections in this section take up the issue of explanatory or methodological reduction in the context of evolutionary theory. The basic idea of Darwinian theory is that evolution takes place by a process of natural selection. Darwin (1859) originally formulated this idea in the following way: Organisms differ from one another in characteristics that are relevant to survival and reproduction, and organisms with certain characteristics will thus tend to leave more offspring than others. Since many of the beneficial characteristics are heritable, successive generations of organisms will tend to differ from their ancestor generations as certain characteristics become more prevalent. As this pattern of development repeats over many generation, evolution takes place.

Darwin took it to be the case that selection operates on individual organisms, but in recent years it has become a matter of dispute whether organisms are always, or ever, the basic unit of selection. The fundamental idea of natural selection can be stated without mentioning organisms at all. Any group of entities that exhibit heritable variation in fitness (where fitness is a measure of an entity's ability to survive and reproduce) could in principle be the subjects of evolutionary change. For Darwin, selection operated on individual organisms, but in principle there seems no reason why, for instance, groups of organisms might not be units of selection. Moving in the other direction, selection could take place at the level of the individual gene, if individual genes can be assigned degrees of fitness.

It is sometimes objected to the possibility that genes might be the units of selection, that selection pressures can only operate directly at the phenotypic level (see, e.g., Mayr 1963, Gould 1980), not at the level of the genotype.[1] Whether or not a particular gene survives to reproduce itself in the next generation depends on the morphology, behavior, and other phenotypic characteristics of the organism of which it is a part. But while this claim is true (at least in most cases), the objection is misplaced. Since it is an organism's genotype that gives rise to its phenotype, any forces that act directly on the latter will act indirectly on the former. If the effect of individual genes on the phenotype can be distinguished, then particular genes will indirectly be objects of selection.

Several influential biologists have argued that not only can the gene be regarded as *a* unit of selection, it should be regarded as *the* unit of selection. In his widely read book *The Selfish Gene* (Dawkins 1976), for example, Richard Dawkins argues that every case of natural selection can be viewed as an instance of genic selection, and that considerations of parsimony thus make it reasonable to see genic selection as basic, with selection at higher levels being merely derivative.

In the second selection in this section, Elliott Sober and Richard Lewontin argue that Dawkins's approach is unsatisfactory. They claim that in many cases, measures of an individual gene's fitness are purely artifactual. The real causal processes that evolutionary biology is trying to pick out do not always take place at the level of the gene.

Sober and Lewontin attempt to show that explanation in terms of individual genes is inadequate even within the field of population genetics. It is uncontroversial that the result of any selection process may be represented by the relative frequencies of the various genes in the total gene pool of a population. Nevertheless, Sober and Lewontin claim that such outcomes cannot always be explained in terms of selection at the genic level. On their view, the basic problem for Dawkins's account is that the effects of individual genes are often context sensitive, depending, for instance, on the nature of the total genomes in which they are embedded. But "if we wish to talk about selection for a single gene, then there must be such a thing as *the* causal upshot of possessing that gene. A gene which is beneficial in some contexts and deleterious in others will have many *organismic* effects. But at *the population level*, there will be no selection for or against that gene." Sober and Lewontin do not rule out genic selection, but they argue that evolutionary processes operate at a number of levels, from genes to whole populations of organisms. Finally, they draw out some of the philosophical implications of their account for questions about the nature of properties and forces.

Whether or not all evolution by natural selection can be seen as taking place at the level of the gene remains a matter of continued debate, as the final paper in this section, by Kim Sterelny and Philip Kitcher, illustrates. Sterelny and Kitcher challenge Lewontin and Sober's conclusions, arguing that Dawkins's proposal, properly construed, remains one legitimate way of representing the workings of natural selection (though perhaps not the only legitimate one).

There are a variety of other important areas of debate in the philosophy of biology that space constraints prevent us from representing here. Two of these, however, at least deserve to be mentioned. The first of these areas concerns the cluster of issues generated by the attempt to construct a human sociobiology. "Sociobiology" is the name given to the study of the biological (and most especially the evolutionary) basis of social behavior. This area of research has attracted the attention of many students of (nonhuman) animal behavior in recent years, and the intense interest in the results of their research has led to attempts to apply related techniques to the study of human behavior.

Work in human sociobiology may be roughly but usefully divided into professional human sociobiology and popular (or "pop") sociobiology (Kitcher 1985, 1987). Professional human sociobiology has been primarily, but not exclusively, concerned with providing evolutionary explanations for features of human social behavior in tribal or other traditional societies—societies living under conditions that might be thought of as approximating the conditions under which human social (and other) traits evolved.

Pop sociobiology, by contrast, has been characterized by efforts to obtain evolutionary insights regarding actual and possible human behavior in modern societies. Almost always, work of this kind has sought to apply methods of evolutionary biology to the problem of assessing the malleability of socially, politically, or morally important features of human behavior. Almost always, the broader aim has been to assess the practicability or likelihood of success of various sorts of social reforms (the elimination of racism and xenophobia, the establishment of more egalitarian social arrangements, etc.). Almost always, the conclusions have been pessimistic: evolutionary theory has been taken to predict the innateness and nonmalleability of behavioral traits that are criticized by reformers (see, e.g., Wilson 1975, 1978; Barash 1979, 1986).

An additional theme runs through much of the popular literature in human sociobiology and through some of the professional literature as well. This is the idea that the project of human sociobiology offers the prospect of reducing the social sciences, and perhaps moral theory as well, to biology. It is an interesting point that the proposed reduction differs substantially from other sorts of reduction achieved or aimed at in the sciences. In general, where reduction has seemed a plausible strategy, the reducing science has been a theory of the constituent parts of the entities or structures that form the subject matter of the reduced science. In the case of sociobiology, the allegedly reduced science studies humans and human societies that are the constituents of human evolutionary lineages, the subject matter of the reducing science.

Many critics (e.g., Allen et al. 1975, Lewontin et al. 1984) have seen in the mainstream of pop sociobiology the sort of influence of social ideology which marked nineteenth-century social Darwinism. Practitioners of pop sociobiology (who are almost all, it is important to note, professional sociobiologists as well) have responded by arguing that their work is informed not by ideology but by new developments in evolutionary theory (e.g., the theory of kin selection; Kitcher 1985 provides a good exposition of these developments). Many also suggest that their critics are themselves driven by left-wing or reform-minded ideological considerations (see, e.g., Wilson 1976).

In response, the critics of pop sociobiology have advanced a number of scientific and methodological criticisms of the ways in which pop sociobiologists apply evolutionary theory to human behavior. It is argued, for instance, that sociobiological hypotheses are frequently based on misplaced analogies between human behavior and the behavior of nonhuman animals, that such hypotheses rely on questionable "adaptationist" assumptions to the effect that all significant behavioral traits have been selected for or that the social behavior of early humans was reproductively optimal, and that, in any case, sociobiologists underestimate the difficulties of extrapolating from claims about the behavior of early hominids to claims about the behavior of humans in modern societies. Sociobiologists have, of course, attempted to rebut all of these criticisms. The interested reader should consult the references cited at the end of this introduction. (Kitcher 1987 is a particularly useful debate between defenders and critics of human sociobiology.)

The second important area not discussed in this section involves questions that arise in systematics, the part of biology concerned with developing a suitable system for the classification of organisms. Disputes within systematics have raised important questions concerning natural kinds and the theory-dependence of scientific method. One important debate concerns the nature of species. Species seem to be paradigm examples of natural kinds—nonarbitrary collections of objects whose boundaries represent objectively existing divisions in the world. But what makes a particular object a member or nonmember of some natural kind? The obvious way to determine membership is in terms of possession of properties (or of a certain number of properties) which define the kind in question. Critics of this approach, however, argue that variation between members of biological species is too great for such an approach to work (Ghiselin 1974, 1981, 1987; Hull 1976). They suggest instead, that species should be regarded as individuals. The species' members are taken to bear the same relation to the species itself as the cells of an organism bear to an organism, that is, the relation of part to whole. Such a view naturally suggests that it is species, not organisms, that are the basic units of selection, and this indeed is what its defenders have argued. The adequacy of this view cannot be discussed here, but if it is correct, it is an interesting question whether the claim that species are natural kinds should be abandoned, or whether the claim should be retained and our conception of natural kinds modified accordingly.

A second area of debate concerns the appropriate framework to employ in classifying species into more general categories, or higher taxa. (The categories in the standard hierarchy are genus, family, order, class, phylum or division, and kingdom.) Some biologists have argued that such classification should proceed without reference to evolutionary theory. Instead, the basis for classification should be the phenotypic similarities and differences between typical members of different species (e.g., Sneath and Sokal 1973). These "phenetic taxonomists" have offered two justifications for their approach: first, that objectivity requires theory-independence and, second, that if evolutionary theory were used as the basis for classification, the resulting classification could not be used to advance our knowledge of evolutionary processes themselves. Neither of these arguments is very impressive, however. Few philosophers of science would now dispute that all aspects of scientific method, including methods of classification, are theory-dependent. But as several papers in the first part of this anthology have argued, this does not preclude such methods from producing objective results. Nor need the fact that relations between species are established on the basis of theoretical considerations rule out the possibility of using such relations to provide further confirmation for the background theory itself (Hull 1970).

An alternative approach to classification takes phylogenetic[2] considerations to be of central importance. We can attempt to determine the evolutionary histories of existing populations by considering alternative possible phylogenies and choosing between them in the same way we choose between any competing scientific hypotheses (Sober 1983, 1988). Phylogenies can be represented in diagrams, known as "cladograms," which show how ancestral populations have branched into various distinct successor populations over time. One influential group of biologists, the "cladists," have argued that answers to classificatory questions can be read off directly from cladograms. Species exist between points of branching on such diagrams. Each time an existing population branches, two new species are formed, while the old species ceases to exist. Cladists insist that higher taxa should be strictly monophyletic—that is, all members of a taxon must be descendants from a common ancestor, and all the descendants must be members of the taxon. The resulting classification, it is argued, will most accurately reflect phylogeny. The classification is constructed by analyzing the characters of species in an attempt to distinguish those that were inherited from an ancestor and those that were not (see, Hennig 1966, Eldredge and Cracraft 1980).

Evolutionary systematists, however, disagree that cladistic classification is satisfactory (e.g., Mayr 1969). They point out that descendants of a common ancestor may diverge considerably from one another, making it in many cases misleading or unnatural to classify all descendants of a common ancestor into the same taxon. For example, crocodiles and other reptiles share many characteristics, which presumably derive from a common ancestor. But if we were to include crocodiles in the same higher taxon as the other reptiles, we would have to include birds as well, since they are descended from the same ancestor, even though they have developed a huge number of new characteristics (Mayr 1981). If we believe that it is more reasonable to classify crocodiles and other reptiles as one category, and birds as a separate sister group, then we must drop the requirement of strict monophyly. Evolutionary systematists do this, requiring only that members of a taxon must share a common ancestor, not that all descendants of the ancestor must be member of the taxon. Which descendants are members of the taxon will depend in part on their specific characteristics.

Although the method of classification used by evolutionary systematists gives rise to apparently natural groupings, its biological justification is not obvious. Evolutionary systematists might allow amphibians to constitute a taxon (even though the common ancestor of all amphibians had many nonamphibian descendants) on the grounds that their common characteristics make it likely that they will undergo similar evolutionary modifications in response to similar selection pressures in the future. But this claim is at best purely speculative and would thus be a weak basis for a system of biological classification.

Moreover, any system of phylogenetic classification suffers from the problem that paucity of evidence may make progress in taxonomy very hard to achieve. Partly in response to this difficulty, and partly in response to the sorts of philosophical considerations mentioned above in connection with phenetic classification, some cladists —known as "pure pattern cladists"—now claim that the cladograms they construct should not be seen as patterns of descent at all, and that what distinguishes cladistic classification are simply its methods of character analysis. Whether such analysis is really all there is to classification remains a matter of dispute (Beatty 1982, Patterson 1978, 1982, Ridley 1986).

Notes

1. An organism's genotype is its set of genes; its phenotype is the totality of its characteristics—physiological, morphological, behavioral, etc.—which arises as a result of the interaction between genotype and environment.
2. A phylogeny is the evolutionary history of an organism or group of organisms.

References

Allen, E., et al., 1975, "Against 'Sociobiology'," *New York Review of Books*. Reprinted in Caplan 1978.
Barash, D., 1979, *The Whisperings Within*, Penguin Books, New York.
Barash, D., 1986, *The Hare and the Tortoise*, Penguin Books, New York.
Beatty, J., 1982, "Classes and Cladists," *Systematic Zoology* 31: 25–34.
Caplan, A., 1978, *The Sociobiology Debate*, Harper and Row, New York.
Darwin, C., 1859, *The Origin of Species*, John Murray, London.
Dawkins, R., 1976, *The Selfish Gene*, Oxford University Press, New York.
Eldredge, N., and Cracraft, J., 1980, *Phylogenetic Patterns and the Evolutionary Process*, Columbia University Press, New York.
Ghiselin, M., 1974, "A Radical Solution to the Species Problem," *Systematic Zoology* 23: 536–544.

Ghiselin, M., 1981, "Categories, Life, and Thinking" (with peer commentary and author's response), *Behavioral and Brain Sciences* 4: 269–313.

Ghiselin, M., 1987, "Species Concepts, Individuality and Objectivity," *Biology and Philosophy* 2: 127–145.

Gould, S. J., 1980, "Caring Groups and Selfish Genes," in *The Panda's Thumb*, Norton, New York.

Hennig, W., 1966, *Phylogenetic Systematics*, University of Illinois Press, Urbana, IL.

Hull, D., 1970, "Contemporary Systematic Philosophies," *Annual Review of Ecology and Systematics* 1: 19–54.

Hull, D., 1976, "Are Species Really Individuals?", *Systematic Zoology* 25: 174–191.

Kitcher, P., 1985, *Vaulting Ambition*, MIT Press, Cambridge, MA.

Kitcher, P., 1987, "Précis of *Vaulting Ambition*" (with peer commentary and author's response), *Behavioral and Brain Sciences* 10: 61–100.

Lewontin, R., et al. 1984, *Not in Our Genes*, Pantheon Books, New York.

Mayr, E., 1963, *Animal Species and Evolution*, Harvard University Press, Cambridge, MA.

Mayr, E., 1969, *Principles of Systematic Zoology*, McGraw–Hill, New York.

Mayr, E., 1981, "Biological Classification: Toward a Synthesis of Opposing Methodologies," *Science* 214: 510–516.

Patterson, C., 1978, "Verifiability in Systematics," *Systematic Zoology* 27: 218–221.

Patterson, C., 1982, "Classes and Cladists or Individuals and Evolution," *Systematic Zoology* 31: 284–286.

Ridley, M., 1986, *Evolution and Classification*, Longman, New York.

Ruse, M., 1973, *The Philosophy of Biology*, Hutchinson, London.

Ruse, M., 1976, "Reduction in Genetics," in Cohen, R., et al., eds., *PSA 1974*, Reidel, Dordrecht, Netherlands.

Schaffner, K., 1967, "Approaches to Reduction," *Philosophy of Science* 34: 137–147.

Schaffner, K., 1976, "Reduction in Biology: Prospects and Problems," in Cohen, R., et al., eds., *PSA 1974*, Reidel, Dordrecht, Netherlands.

Sneath, P., and Sokal, R., 1973, *Principles of Numerical Taxonomy*, 2nd ed., Freeman, San Francisco.

Sober, E., 1983, "Parsimony in Systematics: Philosophical Issues," *Annual Review of Ecology and Systematics* 14: 335–357.

Sober, E., 1984, *The Nature of Selection*, MIT Press, Cambridge, MA.

Sober, E., 1988, *Reconstructing the Past: Parsimony, Evolution and Inference*, MIT Press, Cambridge, MA.

Wilson, E. O., 1975, *Sociobiology: The New Synthesis*, Harvard University Press, Cambridge, MA.

Wilson, E. O., 1976, "Academic Vigilantism and the Political Significance of Sociobiology," *New York Review of Books*. Reprinted in Caplan 1978.

Wilson, E. O., 1978, *On Human Nature*, Harvard University Press, Cambridge, MA.

Further Reading

Alexander, R., 1987, *The Biology of Moral Systems*, de Gruyter, New York.

Brandon, R., and Burian, R., 1984, eds., *Genes, Organisms, Populations: Controversies Over the Units of Selection*, MIT Press, Cambridge, MA.

Brooks, D., and Wiley, E. O., 1986, *Evolution as Entropy*, University of Chicago Press, Chicago.

Dawkins, R., 1982, *The Extended Phenotype*, Freeman, San Francisco.

Dawkins, R., 1986, *The Blind Watchmaker*, Norton, New York.

Depew, D., and Weber, B., 1985, eds., *Evolution at a Crossroads*, MIT Press, Cambridge, MA.

Dupré, J., 1987, ed., *The Latest on the Best*, MIT Press, Cambridge, MA.

Eldredge, N., 1985, *Unfinished Synthesis*, Oxford University Press, New York.

Ghiselin, M., 1969, *The Triumph of the Darwinian Method*, University of California Press, Berkeley.

Gould, S. J., 1977, *Ever Since Darwin*, Norton, New York.

Gould, S. J., 1981, *The Mismeasure of Man*, Norton, New York.

Gould, S. J., 1983, *Hen's Teeth and Horses' Toes*, Norton, New York.

Gould, S. J., 1985, *The Flamingo's Smile*, Norton, New York.

Gould, S. J., and Lewontin, R., 1979, "The Spandrels of San Marco and the Panglossian Paradigm: A Critique of the Adaptationist Programme," *Proceedings of the Royal Society of London* Series B, 205: 581–598. Reprinted in Sober 1984.

Grene, M., 1983, ed., *Dimensions of Darwinism*, Cambridge University Press, New York.

Hookway, C., 1984, ed., *Minds, Machines and Evolution*, Cambridge University Press, New York.

Hull, D., 1974, *The Philosophy of Biological Science*, Prentice-Hall, Englewood Cliffs, NJ.

Kitcher, P., 1982, *Abusing Science*, MIT Press, Cambridge, MA.

Kitcher, P., 1985, "Darwin's Achievement," in N. Rescher, ed., *Reason and Rationality in Science*, University Press of America, Washington, D.C.

Kitcher, P., Sterelny, K., and Waters, C. K., 1990, "The Illusory Riches of Sober's Monism," *Journal of Philosophy* 87 (vol. 3, issue 3): 158–161.

Levins, R., and Lewontin, R., *The Dialectical Biologist*, Harvard University Press, Cambridge, MA.

Lloyd, E. A., 1988, *The Structure and Confirmation of Evolutionary Theory*, Greenwood Press, Westport, CT.

Lumsden, C., and Wilson, E. O., 1981, *Genes, Mind, and Culture*, Harvard University Press, Cambridge, MA.

Maynard, J., Smith 1983, *Evolution and the Theory of Games*, Cambridge University Press, New York.

Mayr, E., 1982, *The Growth of Biological Thought*, Harvard University Press, Cambridge, MA.

Mayr, E., 1988, *Toward a New Philosophy of Biology*, Harvard University Press, Cambridge, MA.

Rose, H., and Rose, S., 1982, eds., *Towards a Liberatory Biology*, Allison and Busby, London.

Rosenberg, A., 1981, *Sociobiology and the Preemption of Social Science*, Johns Hopkins University Press, Baltimore.

Rosenberg, A., 1985, *The Structure of Biological Science*, Cambridge University Press, New York.

Ruse, M., 1979, *The Darwinian Revolution*, University of Chicago Press, Chicago.

Ruse, M., 1982, *Darwinism Defended*, Addison-Wesley, Reading, MA.

Ruse, M., 1988a, *The Darwinian Paradigm*, Routledge and Kegan Paul, Boston.

Ruse, M., 1988b, *Philosophy of Biology Today*, SUNY Press, Albany, NY.

Ruse, M., 1989, ed., *What the Philosophy of Biology Is*, Reidel, Dordrecht, Netherlands.

Sober, E., 1984, ed., *Conceptual Issues in Evolutionary Biology*, MIT Press, Cambridge, MA.

Sober, E., 1990, "The Poverty of Pluralism: A Reply to Sterelny and Kitcher," *Journal of Philosophy* 87 (vol. 3, issue 3): 151–158.

Williams, G., 1966, *Adaptation and Natural Selection*, Princeton University Press, Princeton, NJ.

Wimsatt, W., 1980, "Reductionist Research Strategies and their Biases in the Units of Selection Controversy," in Nickles, T., ed., *Scientific Discoveries*, Reidel, Dordrecht, Netherlands.

Chapter 30

1953 and All That: A Tale of Two Sciences

Philip Kitcher

---

*Must we geneticists becomes bacteriologists, physiological chemists and physicists,
simultaneously with being zoologists and botanists? Let us hope so.*
H. J. Muller, 1922[1]

1. The Problem

Toward the end of their paper announcing the molecular structure of DNA, James
Watson and Francis Crick remark, somewhat laconically, that their proposed structure
might illuminate some central questions of genetics.[2] Thirty years have passed since
Watson and Crick published their famous discovery. Molecular biology has indeed
transformed our understanding of heredity. The recognition of the structure of DNA,
the understanding of gene replication, transcription and translation, the cracking of the
genetic code, the study of gene regulation, these and other breakthroughs have
combined to answer many of the questions that baffled classical geneticists. Muller's
hope—expressed in the early days of classical genetics—has been amply fulfilled.

Yet the success of molecular biology and the transformation of classical genetics
into molecular genetics bequeath a philosophical problem. There are two recent theories which have addressed the phenomena of heredity. One, *classical genetics*, stemming
from the studies of T. H. Morgan, his colleagues and students, is the successful
outgrowth of the Mendelian theory of heredity rediscovered at the beginning of this
century. The other, *molecular genetics*, descends from the work of Watson and Crick.
What is the relationship between these two theories? How does the molecular theory
illuminate the classical theory? How exactly has Muller's hope been fulfilled?

There used to be a popular philosophical answer to the problem posed in these three
connected questions: classical genetics has been reduced to molecular genetics. Philosophers of biology inherited the notion of reduction from general discussions in
philosophy of science, discussions which usually center on examples from physics.
Unfortunately attempts to apply this notion in the case of genetics have been vulnerable to cogent criticism. Even after considerable tinkering with the concept of
reduction, one cannot claim that classical genetics has been (or is being) reduced to
molecular genetics.[3] However, the antireductionist point is typically negative. It denies
the adequacy of a particular solution to the problem of characterizing the relation
between classical genetics and molecular genetics. It does not offer an alternative
solution.

My aim in this paper is to offer a different perspective on intertheoretic relations.
The plan is to invert the usual strategy. Instead of trying to force the case of genetics
into a mold, which is alleged to capture important features of examples in physics, or

Reprinted (with emendations) from *The Philosophical Review* 93 (1984), pp. 335–373, by permission of the
author and the publisher.

resting content with denying that the material can be forced, I shall try to arrive at a view of the theories involved and the relations between them that will account for the almost universal idea that molecular biology has done something important for classical genetics. In so doing, I hope to shed some light on the general questions of the structure of scientific theories and the relations which may hold between successive theories. Since my positive account presupposes that something is wrong with the reductionist treatment of the case of genetics, I shall begin with a diagnosis of the foibles of reductionism.

2. What's Wrong with Reductionism?

Ernest Nagel's classic treatment of reduction[4] can be simplified for our purposes. Scientific theories are regarded as sets of statements.[5] To reduce a theory T_2 to a theory T_1, is to deduce the statements of T_2 from the statements of T_1. If there are nonlogical expressions which appear in the statements of T_2, but do not appear in the statements of T_1, then we are allowed to supplement the statements of T_1 with some extra premises connecting the vocabulary of T_1 with the distinctive vocabulary of T_2 (so-called *bridge principles*). Intertheoretic reduction is taken to be important because the statements which are deduced from the reducing theory are supposed to be explained by this deduction.

Yet, as everyone who has struggled with the paradigm cases from physics knows all too well, the reductions of Galileo's law to Newtonian mechanics and of the ideal gas laws to the kinetic theory do not exactly fit Nagel's model. Study of these examples suggests that, to reduce a theory T_2 to a theory T_1, it suffices to deduce the laws of T_2 from a suitably modified version of T_1, possibly augmented with appropriate extra premises. Plainly, this sufficient condition is dangerously vague. I shall tolerate its vagueness, proposing that we understand the issue of reduction in genetics by using the examples from physics as paradigms of what "suitable modifications" and "appropriate extra premises" are like. Reductionists claim that the relation between classical genetics and molecular biology is sufficiently similar to the intertheoretical relations exemplified in the examples from physics to count as the same type of thing: to wit, as intertheoretical reduction.

It may seem that the reductionist thesis has now become so amorphous that it will be immune to refutation. But this is incorrect. Even when we have amended the classical model of reduction so that it can accommodate the examples that originally motivated it, the reductionist claim about genetics requires us to accept three theses:

> (R1) Classical genetics contains general laws about the transmission of genes which can serve as the conclusions of reductive derivations.
> (R2) The distinctive vocabulary of classical genetics (predicates like '① is a gene', '① is dominant with respect to ②') can be linked to the vocabulary of molecular biology by bridge principles.
> (R3) A derivation of general principles about the transmission of genes from principles of molecular biology would explain why the laws of gene transmission hold (to the extent that they do).

I shall argue that each of the theses is false, offering this as my diagnosis of the ills of reductionism....

Philosophers often identify theories as small sets of general laws. However, in the case of classical genetics, the identification is difficult and those who debate the reducibility of classical genetics to molecular biology often proceed differently. David Hull uses a characterization drawn from Dobzhansky: classical genetics is "concerned with gene differences; the operation employed to discover a gene is hybridization: parents differing in some trait are crossed and the distribution of the trait in hybrid progeny is observed."[6] This is not unusual in discussions of reduction in genetics. It is much easier to identify classical genetics by referring to the subject matter and to the methods of investigation, than it is to provide a few sentences that encapsulate the content of the theory.

Why is this? Because when we read the major papers of the great classical geneticists or when we read the textbooks in which their work is summarized, we find it hard to pick out *any* laws about genes. These documents are full of informative statements. Together, they tell us an enormous amount about the chromosomal arrangement of particular genes in particular organisms, about the effect on the phenotype of various mutations, about frequencies of recombination, and so forth. In some cases, we might explain the absence of formulations of general laws about genes (and even of reference to such laws) by suggesting that these things are common knowledge. Yet that hardly accounts for the nature of the textbooks or of the papers that forged the tools of classical genetics.

If we look back to the pre-Morgan era, we do find two general statements about genes, namely Mendel's Laws (or "Rules"). Mendel's second law states that, in a diploid organism which produces haploid gametes, genes at different loci will be transmitted independently; so, for example, if A, a and B, b are pairs of alleles at different loci, and if an organism is heterozygous at both loci, then the probabilities that a gamete will receive any of the four possible genetic combinations, AB, Ab, aB, ab, are all equal.[7] Once it was recognized that genes are (mostly) chromosomal segments, (as biologists discovered soon after the rediscovery of Mendel's laws), we understand that the law will not hold in general: alleles which are on the same chromosome (or, more exactly, close together on the same chromosome) will tend to be transmitted together because (ignoring recombination) one member of each homologous pair is distributed to a gamete.

Now it might seem that this is not very important. We could surely find a correct substitute for Mendel's second law by restricting the law so that it only talks about genes on nonhomologous chromosomes. Unfortunately, this will not quite do. There can be interference with normal cytological processes so that segregation of nonhomologous chromosomes need not be independent. However, my complaint about Mendel's second law is not that it is incorrect: many sciences use laws that are clearly recognized as approximations. Mendel's second law, amended or unamended, simply becomes irrelevant to subsequent research in classical genetics.

We envisaged amending Mendel's second law by using elementary principles of cytology, together with the identification of genes as chromosomal segments, to correct what was faulty in the unamended law. It is the fact that the application is so easy and that it can be carried out far more generally that makes the "law" it generates irrelevant. We can understand the transmission of genes by analyzing the cases that interest us from a cytological perspective—by proceeding from "first principles," as it were. Moreover, we can adopt this approach whether the organism is haploid, diploid or polyploid, whether it reproduces sexually or asexually, whether the genes with which we are concerned are or are not on homologous chromosomes, whether or not there is distortion of independent chromosomal segregation at meiosis. Cytology not only teaches us that the second law is false; is also tells us how to tackle the problem at which the second law was directed (the problem of determining frequencies for pairs of genes in gametes). The amended second law is a restricted statement of results obtainable using a general technique. What figures largely in genetics after Morgan is the technique, and this is hardly surprising when we realize that one of the major research problems of classical genetics has been the problem of discovering the distribution of genes *on the same chromosome*, a problem which is beyond the scope of the amended law.

Let us now turn from (R1) to (R2), assuming, contrary to what has just been argued, that we can identify the content of classical genetics with general principles about gene transmission. (Let us even suppose, for the sake of concreteness, that the principles in question are Mendel's laws—amended in whatever way the reductionist prefers.) To derive these principles from molecular biology, we need a bridge principle. I shall consider first statements of the form

(*) (x) (x is a gene ↔ Mx),

where 'Mx' is an open sentence (possibly complex) in the language of molecular biology. Molecular biologists do not offer any appropriate statement. Nor do they seem interested in providing one. I claim that no appropriate bridge principle can be found.

Most genes are segments of DNA. (There are some organisms—viruses—whose genetic material is RNA; I shall henceforth ignore them.) Thanks to Watson and Crick, we know the molecular structure of DNA. Hence the problem of providing a statement of the above form becomes that of saying, in molecular terms, which segments of DNA count as genes.

Genes come in different sizes, and, for any given size, we can find segments of DNA of that size that are not genes. Therefore genes cannot be identified as segments of DNA containing a particular number of nucleotide pairs. Nor will it do to give a molecular characterization of those codons (triplets of nucleotides) that initiate and terminate transcription, and take a gene to be a segment of DNA between successive initiating and terminating codons. In the first place, mutation might produce a *single* allele containing within it codons for stopping and restarting transcription. Secondly, and much more importantly, the criterion is not general since not every gene is transcribed on mRNA.

The latter point is worth developing. Molecular geneticists recognize regulatory genes as well as structural genes. To cite a classic example, the operator region in the *lac* operon of *E. coli* serves as a site for the attachment of protein molecules, thereby inhibiting transcription of mRNA and regulating enzyme production. Moreover, it is becoming increasingly obvious that genes are not always transcribed, but play a variety of roles in the economy of the cell.

At this point, the reductionist may try to produce a bridge principle by brute force. Trivially, there are only a finite number of terrestrial organisms (past, present and future) and only a finite number of genes. Each gene is a segment of DNA with a particular structure and it would be possible, in principle, to provide a detailed molecular description of that structure. We can now give a molecular specification of the gene by enumerating the genes and disjoining the molecular descriptions. The point made above, that the segments which we count as genes do not share any structural property can now be put more precisely: any instantiation of (*) which replaces 'M' by a structural predicate from the language of molecular biology will insert a predicate that is essentially disjunctive.

Why does this matter? Let us imagine a reductionist using the enumerative strategy to deduce a general principle about gene transmission. After great labor, it is revealed that all actual genes satisfy the principle. I claim that more than this is needed to reduce a *law* about gene transmission. We envisage laws as sustaining counterfactuals, as applying to examples that might have been but which did not actually arise. To reduce the law it is necessary to show how possible but nonactual genes would have satisfied it. Nor can we achieve the reductionist's goal by adding further disjuncts to the envisaged bridge principle. For although there are only finitely many *actual* genes, there are indefinitely many genes which *might* have arisen.

At this point, the reductionist may protest that the deck has been stacked. There is no need to produce a bridge principle of the form (*). Recall that we are trying to derive a general law about the transmission of genes, whose paradigm is Mendel's second law. Now the gross logical form of Mendel's second law is:

(1) $(x)(y)((Gx \,\&\, Gy) \rightarrow Axy)$.

We might hope to obtain this from statements of the forms

(2) $(x)(Gx \rightarrow Mx)$

(3) $(x)(y)((Mx \,\&\, My) \rightarrow Axy)$

where 'Mx' is an open sentence in the language of molecular biology. Now there will certainly be true statements of the form (2): for example, we can take 'Mx' as 'x is composed of DNA v x is composed of RNA'. The question is whether we can combine some such statement with other appropriate premises—for example, some instance of (3)—so as to derive, and thereby explain (1). No geneticist or molecular biologist has advanced any suitable premises, and with good reason. We discover true statements of the form (2) by hunting for weak necessary conditions on genes, conditions which have to be met by genes but which are met by hordes of other biological entities as well. We can only hope to obtain *weak* necessary conditions because of the phenomenon that occupied us previously: from the molecular standpoint, genes are not distinguished by any common structure. Trouble will now arise when we try to show that the weak necessary condition is jointly sufficient for the satisfaction of the property (independent assortment at meiosis) that we ascribe to genes. The difficulty is illustrated by the example given above. If we take 'Mx' to be 'x is composed of DNA v x is composed of RNA' then the challenge will be to find a general law governing the distribution of all segments of DNA and RNA!

I conclude that (R2) is false. Reductionists cannot find the bridge principles they need, and the tactic of abandoning the form (*) for something weaker is of no avail. I shall now consider (R3). Let us concede both of the points that I have denied, allowing that there are general laws about the transmission of genes and that bridge principles are forthcoming. I claim that exhibiting derivations of the transmission laws from principles of molecular biology and bridge principles would not explain the laws, and, therefore, would not fulfill the major goal of reduction.

As an illustration, I shall use the envisaged amended version of Mendel's second law. Why do genes on nonhomologous chromosomes assort independently? Cytology provides the answer. At meiosis, chromosomes line up with their homologues. It is then possible for homologous chromosomes to exchange some genetic material, producing pairs of recombinant chromosomes. In the meiotic division, one member of each recombinant pair goes to each gamete, and the assignment of one member of one pair to a gamete is probabilistically independent of the assignment of a member of another pair to that gamete. Genes which occur close on the same chromosome are likely to be transmitted together (recombination is not likely to occur between them), but genes on nonhomologous chromosomes will assort independently.

This account is a perfectly satisfactory explanation of why our envisaged law is true to the extent that it is. (We recognize how the law could fail if there were some unusual mechanism linking particular nonhomologous chromosomes.) To emphasize the adequacy of the explanation is not to deny that it could be extended in certain ways. For example, we might want to know more about the mechanics of the process by which the chromosomes are passed on to the gametes. In fact, cytology provides such information. However, appeal to molecular biology would not deepen our understanding of the transmission law. Imagine a successful derivation of the law from principles of chemistry and a bridge principle of the form (*). In charting the details of the molecular rearrangements the derivation would only blur the outline of a simple cytological story, adding a welter of irrelevant detail. Genes on nonhomologous chromosomes assort independently because nonhomologous chromosomes are transmitted independently at meiosis, and, so long as we recognize this, we do not need to know what the chromosomes are made of.

In explaining a scientific law, L, one often provides a deduction of L from other principles. Sometimes it is possible to explain some of the principles used in the deduction by deducing them, in turn, from further laws. Recognizing the possibility of a sequence of deductions tempts us to suppose that we could produce a better explanation of L by combining them, producing a more elaborate derivation in the language of our ultimate premises. But this is incorrect. What is relevant for the purposes of giving one explanation may be quite different from what is relevant for the purposes of explaining a law used in giving that original explanation. This general point is illustrated by the case at hand....

There is a natural reductionist response. The considerations of the last paragraphs presuppose far too subjective a view of scientific explanation. After all, even if *we* become lost in the molecular details, beings who are cognitively more powerful than we could surely recognize the explanatory force of the envisaged molecular derivation. However, this response misses a crucial point. The molecular derivation forfeits something important.

Recall the original cytological explanation. It accounted for the transmission of genes by identifying meiosis as a process of a particular kind: a process in which paired entities (in this case, homologous chromosomes) are separated by a force so that one member of each pair is assigned to a descendant entity (in this case, a gamete). Let us call processes of this kind *PS-processes*. I claim first that explaining the transmission law requires identifying PS-processes as forming a natural kind to which processes of meiosis belong, and second that PS-processes cannot be identified as a kind from the molecular point of view.

If we adopt the familiar covering law account of explanation, then we shall view the cytological narrative as invoking a law to the effect that processes of meiosis are PS-processes and as applying elementary principles of probability to compute the distribution of genes to gametes from the laws that govern PS-processes. If the illumination provided by the narrative is to be preserved in a molecular derivation, then we shall have to be able to express the relevant laws as laws in the language of molecular biology, and this will require that we be able to characterize PS-processes as a natural kind from the molecular point of view. The same conclusion, to wit that the explanatory power of the cytological account can be preserved only if we can identify PS-processes as a natural kind in molecular terms, can be reached in analogous ways if we adopt quite different approaches to scientific explanation—for example, if we conceive of explanation as specifying causally relevant properties or as fitting phenomena into a unified account of nature.

However, PS-processes are heterogeneous from the molecular point of view. There are no constraints on the molecular structures of the entities which are paired or on the ways in which the fundamental forces combine to pair them and to separate them. The bonds can be forged and broken in innumerable ways: all that matters is that there be bonds that initially pair the entities in question and that are subsequently (somehow) broken. In some cases, bonds may be formed directly between constituent molecules of the entities in question; in others, hordes of accessory molecules may be involved. In some cases, the separation may occur because of the action of electromagnetic forces or even of nuclear forces; but it is easy to think of examples in which the separation is effected by the action of gravity. I claim, therefore, that PS-processes are realized in a motley of molecular ways. (I should note explicitly that this conclusion is independent of the issue of whether the reductionist can find bridge principles for the concepts of classical genetics.)

We thus obtain a reply to the reductionist charge that we reject the explanatory power of the molecular derivation simply because we anticipate that our brains will prove too feeble to cope with its complexities. The molecular account objectively fails to explain because it cannot bring out that feature of the situation which is highlighted in the cytological story. It cannot show us that genes are transmitted in the ways that we find them to be because meiosis is a PS-process and because any PS-process would give rise to analogous distributions. Thus (R3)—like (R1) and (R2)—is false.

3. The Root of the Trouble

Where did we go wrong? Here is a natural suggestion. The most fundamental failure of reductionism is the falsity of (R1). Lacking an account of theories which could readily be applied to the cases of classical genetics and molecular genetics, the attempt to chart the relations between these theories was doomed from the start. If we are to do better, we must begin by asking a preliminary question: what is the structure of classical genetics?

I shall follow this natural suggestion, endeavoring to present a picture of the structure of classical genetics which can be used to understand the intertheoretic relations between classical and molecular genetics. As we have seen, the main difficulty in trying to axiomatize classical genetics is to decide what body of statements one is attempting to axiomatize. The history of genetics makes it clear that Morgan, Muller, Sturtevant, Beadle, McClintock, and others have made important contributions to genetic theory. But the statements occurring in the writings of these workers seem to be far too specific to serve as parts of a general theory. They concern the genes of particular kinds of organisms—primarily paradigm organisms, like fruit flies, bread molds, and maize. The idea that classical genetics is simply a heterogeneous set of statements about dominance, recessiveness, position effect, nondisjunction, and so forth, in *Drosophila, Zea mays, E. coli, Neurospora*, etc. flies in the face of our intuitions. The statements advanced by the great classical geneticists seem more like *illustrations* of the theory than *components* of it. (To know classical genetics it is not necessary to know the genetics of any particular organism, not even *Drosophila melanogaster*.) But the only alternative seems to be to suppose that there are general laws in genetics, never enunciated by geneticists but reconstructible by philosophers. At the very least, this supposition should induce the worry that the founders of the field, and those who write the textbooks of today, do a singularly bad job.

Our predicament provokes two main questions. First, if we focus on a particular time in the history of classical genetics, it appears that there will be a set of statements about inheritance in particular organisms, which constitutes the corpus which geneticists of that time accept: what is the relationship between this corpus and the version of classical genetic theory in force at the time? (In posing this question, I assume, contrary to fact, that the community of geneticists was always distinguished by unusual harmony of opinion; it is not hard to relax this simplifying assumption.) Second, we think of genetic theory as something that persisted through various versions: what is the relation among the versions of classical genetic theory accepted at different times (the versions of 1910, 1930, and 1950, for example) which makes us want to count them as versions of the same theory?

We can answer these questions by amending a prevalent conception of the way in which we should characterize the state of a science at a time. The corpus of statements about the inheritance of characteristics accepted at a given time is only one component of a much more complicated entity that I shall call the *practice* of classical genetics at that time. There is a common language used to talk about hereditary phenomena, a set of accepted statements in that language (the corpus of beliefs about inheritance mentioned above), a set of questions taken to be the appropriate questions to ask about hereditary phenomena, and a set of patterns of reasoning which are instantiated in answering some of the accepted questions; (also: sets of experimental procedures and methodological rules, both designed for use in evaluating proposed answers; these may be ignored for present purposes). The practice of classical genetics at a time is completely specified by identifying each of the components just listed.[8]

A pattern of reasoning is a sequence of *schematic sentences*, that is sentences in which certain items of nonlogical vocabulary have been replaced by dummy letters, together with a set of *filling instructions* which specify how substitutions are to be made in the schemata to produce reasoning which instantiates the pattern. This notion of pattern is intended to explicate the idea of the common structure that underlies a group of problem-solutions.

The foregoing definitions enable us to answer the two main questions I posed above. Beliefs about the particular genetic features of particular organisms illustrate or exemplify the version of genetic theory in force at the time in the sense that these beliefs figure in particular problem-solutions generated by the current practice. Certain patterns of reasoning are applied to give the answers to accepted questions, and, in making the application, one puts forward claims about inheritance in particular organisms. Classical genetics persists as a single theory with different versions at different times in the sense that different practices are linked by a chain of practices along which there are relatively small modifications in language, in accepted questions, and in the patterns for answering questions. In addition to this condition of historical connection, versions of classical genetic theory are bound by a common structure: each version uses certain expressions to characterize hereditary phenomena, accepts as important questions of a particular form, and offers a general style of reasoning for answering those questions. Specifically, throughout the career of classical genetics, the theory is directed toward answering questions about the distribution of characteristics in successive generations of a genealogy, and it proposes to answer those questions by using the probabilities of chromosome distribution to compute the probabilities of descendant genotypes.

The approach to classical genetics embodied in these answers is supported by reflection on what beginning students learn. Neophytes are not taught (and never have been taught) a few fundamental theoretical laws from which genetic "theorems" are to be deduced. They are introduced to some technical terminology, which is used to advance a large amount of information about special organisms. Certain questions about heredity in these organisms are posed and answered. Those who understand the theory are those who know what questions are to be asked about hitherto unstudied examples, who know how to apply the technical language to the organisms involved in these examples, and who can apply the patterns of reasoning which are to be instantiated in constructing answers. More simply, successful students grasp general patterns of reasoning which they can use to resolve new cases.

I shall now add some detail to my sketch of the structure of classical genetics, and thereby prepare the way for an investigation of the relations between classical genetics and molecular genetics. The initial family of problems in classical genetics, the family from which the field began, is the family of *pedigree problems*. Such problems arise when we confront several generations of organisms, related by specified connections of descent, with a given distribution of one or more characteristics. The question that arises may be to understand the given distribution of phenotypes, or to predict the distribution of phenotypes in the next generation, or to specify the probability that a particular phenotype will result from a particular mating. In general, classical genetic theory answers such questions by making hypotheses about the relevant genes, their phenotypic effects and their distribution among the individuals in the pedigree. Each version of classical genetic theory contains one or more problem-solving patterns exemplifying this general idea, but the detailed character of the pattern is refined in later versions, so that previously recalcitrant cases of the problem can be accommodated.

Each case of a pedigree problem can be characterized by a set of *data*, a set of *constraints*, and a question. In any example, the data are statements describing the distribution of phenotypes among the organisms in a particular pedigree, or a diagram conveying the same information. The level of detail in the data may vary widely: at one extreme we may be given a full description of the interrelationships among all individuals and the sexes of all those involved; or the data may only provide the numbers of individuals with specific phenotypes in each generation; or, with minimal detail, we may simply be told that from crosses among individuals with specified phenotypes a certain range of phenotypes is found.

The constraints on the problem consist of general cytological information and descriptions of the chromosomal constitution of members of the species. The former will include the thesis that genes are (almost always) chromosomal segments and the principles that govern meiosis. The latter may contain a variety of statements. It may be pertinent to know how the species under study reproduces, how sexual dimorphism is reflected at the chromosomal level, the chromosome number typical of the species, what loci are linked, what the recombination frequencies are, and so forth. As in the case of the data, the level of detail (and thus of stringency) in the constraints can vary widely.

Lastly, each problem contains a question that refers to the organisms described in the data. The question may take several forms: "What is the expected distribution of phenotypes from a cross between a and b?" (where a, b are specified individuals belonging to the pedigree described by the data), "What is the probability that a cross between a and b will produce an individual having P?" (where a, b are specified individuals of the pedigree described by the data and P is a phenotypic property manifested in this pedigree), "Why do we find the distribution of phenotypes described in the data?" and others.

Pedigree problems are solved by advancing pieces of reasoning that instantiate a small number of related patterns. In all cases the reasoning begins from a *genetic hypothesis*. The function of a genetic hypothesis is to specify the alleles that are relevant, their phenotypic expression, and their transmission through the pedigree. From that part of the genetic hypothesis that specifies the genotypes of the parents in any mating that occurs in the pedigree, together with the constraints on the problem, one computes the expected distribution of genotypes among the offspring. Finally, for any mating occurring in the pedigree, one shows that the expected distribution of genotypes among the offspring is consistent with the assignment of genotypes given by the genetic hypothesis.

The form of the reasoning can easily be recognized in examples—examples that are familiar to anyone who has ever looked at a textbook or a research report in genetics. What interests me is the style of reasoning itself. The reasoning begins with a genetic hypothesis that offers four kinds of information: (a) Specification of the number of relevant loci and the number of alleles at each locus; (b) Specification of the relationships between genotypes and phenotypes; (c) Specification of the relations between genes and chromosomes, of facts about the transmission of chromosomes to gametes (for example, resolution of the question whether there is disruption of normal segregation) and about the details of zygote formation; (d) Assignment of genotypes to individuals in the pedigree. After showing that the genetic hypothesis is consistent with the data and constraints of the problem, the principles of cytology and the laws of probability are used to compute expected distributions of genotypes from crosses. The expected distributions are then compared with those assigned in part (d) of the genetic hypothesis.

Throughout the career of classical genetics, pedigree problems are addressed and solved by carrying out reasoning of the general type just indicated. Each version of classical genetic theory contains a pattern for solving pedigree problems with a method for computing expected genotypes which is adjusted to reflect the particular form of the genetic hypotheses that it sanctions. Thus one way to focus the differences among successive versions of classical genetic theory is to compare their conceptions of the possibilities for genetic hypotheses. As genetic theory develops, there is a changing set of conditions on admissible genetic hypotheses. Prior to the discovery of polygeny and pleiotropy (for example), part (a) of any adequate genetic hypothesis was viewed as governed by the requirement that there would be a one-one correspondence between loci and phenotypic traits.[9] After the discovery of incomplete dominance and epistasis, it was recognized that part (b) of an adequate hypothesis might take a form that had not previously been allowed: one is not compelled to assign to the heterozygote a phenotype assigned to one of the homozygotes, and one is also permitted to relativize the phenotypic effect of a gene to its genetic environment.[10] Similarly, the appreciation of phenomena of linkage, recombination, nondisjunction, segregation distortion, meiotic drive, unequal crossing over, and crossover suppression, modify conditions previously imposed on part (c) of any genetic hypothesis. In general, we can take each version of classical genetic theory to be associated with a set of conditions (usually not formulated explicitly) which govern admissible genetic hypotheses. While a general form of reasoning persists through the development of classical genetics, the patterns of reasoning used to resolve cases of the pedigree problem are constantly fine-tuned as geneticists modify their views about what forms of genetic hypothesis are allowable.

So far I have concentrated exclusively on classical genetic theory as a family of related patterns of reasoning for solving the pedigree problem. It is natural to ask if versions of the theory contain patterns of reasoning for addressing other questions. I believe that they do. The heart of the theory is the theory of *gene transmission*, the family of reasoning patterns directed at the pedigree problem. Out of this theory grow other subtheories. The theory of *gene mapping* offers a pattern of reasoning which addresses questions about the relative positions of loci on chromosomes. It is a direct result of Sturtevant's insight that one can systematically investigate the set of pedigree problems associated with a particular species. In turn, the theory of gene mapping raises the question of how to identify mutations, issues which are to be tackled by the *theory of mutation*. Thus we can think of classical genetics as having a central theory, the theory of gene transmission, which develops in the ways I have described above, surrounded by a number of satellite theories that are directed at questions arising from the pursuit of the central theory. Some of these satellite theories (for example, the theory of gene mapping) develop in the same continuous fashion. Others, like the theory of mutation, are subject to rather dramatic shifts in approach.

4. Molecular Genetics and Classical Genetics

Armed with some understanding of the structure and evolution of classical genetics, we can finally return to the question with which we began. What is the relation between classical genetics and molecular genetics? When we look at textbook presentations and the pioneering research articles that they cite, it is not hard to discern major ways in which molecular biology has advanced our understanding of hereditary phenomena. We can readily identify particular molecular explanations which illuminate issues that were treated incompletely, if at all, from the classical perspective. What proves puzzling is the connection of these explanations to the theory of classical genetics. I hope that the account of the last section will enable us to make the connection.

I shall consider three of the most celebrated achievements of molecular genetics. Consider first the question of *replication*. Classical geneticists believed that genes can replicate themselves. Even before the experimental demonstration that all genes are transmitted to all the somatic cells of a developing embryo, geneticists agreed that normal processes of mitosis and meiosis must involve gene replication. Muller's suggestion that the central problem of genetics is to understand how mutant alleles, incapable of performing wild-type functions in producing the phenotype, are nonetheless able to replicate themselves, embodies this consensus. Yet classical genetics had no account of gene replication. A molecular account was an almost immediate dividend of the Watson-Crick model of DNA.

Watson and Crick suggested that the two strands of the double helix unwind and each strand serves as the template for the formation of a complementary strand. Because of the specificity of the pairing of nucleotides, reconstruction of DNA can be unambiguously directed by a single strand. This suggestion has been confirmed and articulated by subsequent research in molecular biology.[11] The details are more intricate than Watson and Crick may originally have believed, but the outline of their story stands.

A second major illumination produced by molecular genetics concerns the characterization of mutation. When we understand the gene as a segment of DNA we recognize the ways in which mutant alleles can be produced. "Copying errors" during replication can cause nucleotides to be added, deleted or substituted. These changes will often lead to alleles that code for different proteins, and which are readily recognizable as mutants through their production of deviant phenotypes. However, molecular biology makes it clear that there can be *hidden* mutations, mutations that arise through nucleotide substitutions that do not change the protein produced by a structural gene (the genetic code is redundant) or through substitutions that alter the form of the protein in trivial ways. The molecular perspective provides us with a general answer to the question, "What is a mutation?" namely that a mutation is the modification of a gene through insertion, deletion or substitution of nucleotides. This general answer yields a basic method for tackling (in principle) questions of form, "Is *a* a mutant allele?" namely a demonstration that *a* arose through nucleotide changes from alleles that persist in the present population. The method is frequently used in studies of the genetics of bacteria and bacteriophage, and can sometimes be employed even in inquiries about more complicated organisms. So, for example, there is good biochemical evidence for believing that some alleles which produce resistance to pesticides in various species of insects arose through nucleotide changes in the alleles naturally predominating in the population.[12]

I have indicated two general ways in which molecular biology answers questions that were not adequately resolved by classical genetics. Equally obvious are a large number of more specific achievements. Identification of the molecular structures of particular genes in particular organisms has enabled us to understand why those genes combine to produce the phenotypes they do....

The claim that genes can replicate does not have the status of a central law of classical genetic theory. It is not something that figures prominently in the explanations provided by the theory (as, for example, the Boyle-Charles law is a prominent premise in some of the explanations yielded by phenomenological thermodynamics). Rather, it is a claim that classical geneticists took for granted, a claim presupposed by explanations, rather than an explicit part of them. Prior to the development of molecular genetics that claim had come to seem increasingly problematic. If genes can replicate, how do they manage to do it? Molecular genetics answered the worrying question. It provided a theoretical demonstration of the possibility of an antecedently problematic presupposition of classical genetics.

We can say that a theory presupposes a statement *p* if there is some problem-solving pattern of the theory, such that every instantiation of the pattern contains statements that jointly imply the truth of *p*. Suppose that, at a given stage in the development of a theory, scientists recognize an argument from otherwise acceptable premises which concludes that it is impossible that *p*. Then the presupposition *p* is problematic for those scientists. What they would like would be an argument showing that it is possible that *p* and explaining what is wrong with the line of reasoning which appears to threaten the possibility of *p*. If a new theory generates an argument of this sort, then we can say that the new theory gives a theoretical demonstration of the possibility of an antecedently problematic presupposition of the old theory....

Because theoretical demonstrations of the possibility of antecedently problematic presuppositions involve derivation of conclusions of one theory from the premises supplied by a background theory, it is easy to assimilate them to the classical notion of reduction. However, on the account I have offered, there are two important differences. First, there is no commitment to the thesis that genetic theory can be formulated as (the deductive closure of) a conjunction of laws. Second, it is not assumed that all general statements about genes are equally in need of molecular derivation. Instead, one particular thesis, a thesis that underlies all the explanations provided by classical genetic theory, is seen as especially problematic, and the molecular derivation is viewed as addressing a specific problem that classical geneticists had already perceived. Where the reductionist identifies a general benefit in deriving all the axioms of the reduced theory, I focus on a particular derivation of a claim that has no title as an axiom of classical genetics, a derivation which responds to a particular explanatory difficulty of which classical geneticists were acutely aware. The reductionist's global relation between theories does not obtain between classical and molecular genetics, but something akin to it does hold between special fragments of these theories.

The second principal achievement of molecular genetics, the account of mutation, involves a conceptual refinement of prior theory. Later theories can be said to provide conceptual refinements of earlier theories when the later theory yields a specification of entities that belong to the extensions of predicates in the language of the earlier theory, with the result that the ways in which the referents of these predicates are fixed are altered in accordance with the new specifications. Conceptual refinement may occur in a number of ways. A new theory may supply a descriptive characterization of the extension of a predicate for which no descriptive characterization was previously available; or it may offer a new description which makes it reasonable to amend characterizations that had previously been accepted....[13]

Finally, let us consider the use of molecular genetics to illuminate the action of particular genes. Here we again seem to find a relationship that initially appears close to the reductionist's ideal. Statements that are invoked as premises in particular problem-solutions—statements that ascribe particular phenotypes to particular genotypes—are derived from molecular characterizations of the alleles involved. On the account of classical genetics offered in section 3, each version of classical genetic theory includes in its schema for genetic hypotheses a clause which relates genotypes to phenotypes.... [W]e might hope to discover a pattern of reasoning within molecular genetics that would generate as its conclusion the schema for assigning phenotypes to genotypes.

It is not hard to characterize the relation just envisioned. Let us say that a theory T' provides an *explanatory extension* of a theory T just in case there is some problem-solving pattern of T one of whose schematic premises can be generated as the conclusion of a problem-solving pattern of T'. When a new theory provides an explanatory extension of an old theory, then particular premises occurring in explanatory derivations given by the old theory can themselves be explained by using arguments furnished by the new theory. However, it does not follow that the explanations provided by the old theory can be improved by replacing the premises in question with the pertinent derivations. What is relevant for the purposes of explaining some statement S may not be relevant for the purposes of explaining a statement S' which figures in an explanatory derivation of S.

Even though reductionism fails, it may appear that we can capture part of the spirit of reductionism by deploying the notion of explanatory extension. The thesis that molecular genetics provides an explanatory extension of classical genetics embodies the idea of a global relationship between the two theories, while avoiding two of the three troubles that were found to beset reductionism. That thesis does not simply assert that some specific presupposition of classical genetics (for example, the claim that genes are able to replicate) can be derived as the conclusion of a molecular argument, but offers a general connection between premises of explanatory derivations in classical genetics and explanatory arguments from molecular genetics. It is formulated so as to accommodate the failure of (R1) and to honor the picture of classical genetics developed in section 3. Moreover, the failure of (R2) does not affect it....

Nevertheless, even born-again reductionism is doomed to fall short of salvation. Although it is true that molecular genetics belongs to a cluster of theories which, taken together, provide an explanatory extension of classical genetics, molecular genetics, on its own, cannot deliver the goods. There are some cases in which the ancillary theories do not contribute to the explanation of a classical claim about gene action. In such cases, the classical claim can be derived and explained by instantiating a pattern drawn from molecular genetics. The example of human hemoglobin provides one such case. [Individuals who are homozygous for a mutant allele for the synthesis of human hemoglobin develop sickle-cell anemia, a phenomenon that can be explained at the molecular level (ed.).] But this example is atypical.

Consider the way in which the hemoglobin example works. Specification of the molecular structures of the normal and mutant alleles, together with a description of the genetic code, enables us to derive the composition of normal and mutant hemoglobin. Application of chemistry then yields descriptions of the interactions of the proteins. With the aid of some facts about human blood cells, one can then deduce that the sickling effect will occur in abnormal cells, and, given some facts about human physiology, it is possible to derive the descriptions of the phenotypes. There is a clear analogy here with some cases from physics. The assumptions about blood cells and physiological needs seem to play the same role as the boundary conditions about shapes, relative positions and velocities of planets that occur in Newtonian derivations of Kepler's laws. In the Newtonian explanation we can see the application of a general pattern of reasoning—the derivation of explicit equations of motion from specifications of the forces acting—which yields the general result that a body under the influence of a centrally directed inverse square force will travel in a conic section; the general result is then applied to the motions of the planets by incorporating pieces of astronomical information. Similarly, the derivation of the classical claims about the action of the normal and mutant hemoglobin genes can be seen as a purely chemical derivation of the generation of certain molecular structures and of the interactions among them. The chemical conclusions are then applied to the biological system under consideration by introducing three "boundary conditions"; first, the claim that the altered molecular structures only affect development to the extent of substituting a different molecule in the erythrocytes (the blood cells that transport hemoglobin); second, a description of the chemical conditions in the capillaries; and third, a description of the effects upon the organism of capillary blockage.

The example is able to lend comfort to reductionism precisely because of an atypical feature. In effect, one concentrates on the *differences* among the phenotypes, takes for granted the fact that in all cases development will proceed normally to the extent of manufacturing erythrocytes—which are, to all intents and purposes, simply sacks for containing hemoglobin molecules—and compares the difference in chemical effect of the cases in which the erythrocytes contain different molecules. *The details of the process of development can be ignored.* However, it is rare for the effect of a mutation to be so simple. Most structural genes code for molecules whose presence or absence make subtle differences. Thus, typically, a mutation will affect the distribution of chemicals in the cells of a developing embryo. A likely result is a change in the timing of intracellular reactions, a change that may, in turn, alter the shape of the cell. Because of the change of shape, the geometry of the embryonic cells may be modified. Cells that usually come into contact may fail to touch. Because of this, some cells may not receive the molecules necessary to switch on certain batteries of genes. Hence the chemical composition of these cells will be altered. And so it goes.

Quite evidently, in examples like this, (which include most of the cases in which molecular considerations can be introduced into embryology) the reasoning that leads us to a description of the phenotype associated with a genotype will be much more complicated than that found in the hemoglobin case. It will not simply consist in a chemical derivation adapted with the help of a few boundary conditions furnished by biology. Instead, we shall encounter a sequence of subarguments: molecular descriptions lead to specifications of cellular properties, from these specifications we draw conclusions about cellular interactions, and from these conclusions we arrive at further molecular descriptions. There is clearly a pattern of reasoning here which involves molecular biology and which extends the explanations furnished by classical genetics by showing how phenotypes depend upon genotypes—but I think it would be folly to suggest that the extension is provided by molecular genetics alone.

In section 2, we discovered that the traditional answer to the philosophical question of understanding the relation that holds between molecular genetics and classical genetics, the reductionist's answer, will not do. Section 3 attempted to build on the diagnosis of the ills of reductionism, offering an account of the structure and evolution of classical genetics that would improve on the picture offered by those who favor traditional approaches to the nature of scientific theories. In the present section, I have tried to use the framework of section 3 to understand the relations between molecular genetics and classical genetics. Molecular genetics has done something important for classical genetics, and its achievements can be recognized by seeing them as instances of the intertheoretic relations that I have characterized. Thus I claim that the problem from which we began is solved.

So what? Do we have here simply a study of a particular case—a case which has, to be sure, proved puzzling for the usual accounts of scientific theories and scientific change? I hope not. Although the traditional approaches may have proved helpful in understanding some of the well-worn examples that have been the stock-in-trade of twentieth century philosophy of science, I believe that the notion of scientific practice sketched in section 3 and the intertheoretic relations briefly characterized here will both prove helpful in analyzing the structure of science and the growth of scientific knowledge *even in those areas of science where traditional views have seemed most successful.* Hence the tale of two sciences which I have been telling is not merely intended as a piece of local history that fills a small but troublesome gap in the orthodox chronicles. I hope that it introduces concepts of general significance in the project of understanding the growth of science.

5. Antireductionism and the Organization of Nature

One loose thread remains. The history of biology is marked by continuing opposition between reductionists and antireductionists. Reductionism thrives on exploiting the charge that it provides the only alternative to the mushy incomprehensibility of vitalism. Antireductionists reply that their opponents have ignored the organismic complexity of nature. Given the picture painted above, where does this traditional dispute now stand?

I suggest that the account of genetics which I have offered will enable reductionists to provide a more exact account of what they claim, and will thereby enable antireductionists to be more specific about what they are denying. Reductionists and antireductionists agree in a certain minimal physicalism. To my knowledge, there are no major figures in contemporary biology who dispute the claim that each biological event, state or process is a complex physical event, state, or process. The most intricate part of ontogeny or phylogeny involves countless changes of physical state. What antireductionists emphasize is the organization of nature and the "interactions among phenomena at different levels." The appeal to organization takes two different forms. When the subject of controversy is the proper form of evolutionary theory, then antireductionists contend that it is impossible to regard all selection as operating at the level of the gene.[14] What concerns me here is not this area of conflict between reductionists and their adversaries, but the attempt to block claims for the hegemony of molecular studies in understanding the physiology, genetics, and development of organisms.

A sophisticated reductionist ought to allow that, in the current practice of biology, nature is divided into levels which form the proper provinces of areas of biological study: molecular biology, cytology, histology, physiology, and so forth. Each of these sciences can be thought of as using certain language to formulate the questions it deems important and as supplying patterns of reasoning for resolving those questions. Reductionists can now set forth one of two main claims. The stronger thesis is that the explanations provided by any biological theories can be reformulated in the language of molecular biology and be recast so as to instantiate the patterns of reasoning supplied by molecular biology. The weaker thesis is that molecular biology provides explanatory extension of the other biological sciences.

Strong reductionism falls victim to the considerations that were advanced against (R3). The distribution of genes to gametes is to be explained, not by rehearsing the gory details of the reshuffling of the molecules, but through the observation that chromosomes are aligned in pairs just prior to the meiotic division, and that one chromosome from each matched pair is transmitted to each gamete. We may formulate this point in the biologists' preferred idiom by saying that the assortment of alleles is to be understood at the cytological level. What is meant by this description is that there is a pattern of reasoning which is applied to derive the description of the assortment of alleles and which involves predicates that characterize cells and their large-scale internal structures. That pattern of reasoning is to be objectively preferred to the molecular pattern which would be instantiated by the derivation that charts the complicated rearrangements of individual molecules because it can be applied across a range of cases which would look heterogeneous from a molecular perspective. Intuitively, the cytological pattern makes connections which are lost at the molecular level, and it is thus to be preferred.

So far, antireductionism emerges as the thesis that there are *autonomous levels of biological explanation*. Antireductionism construes the current division of biology not simply as a temporary feature of our science stemming from our cognitive imperfections but as the reflection of levels of organization in nature. Explanatory patterns that deploy the concepts of cytology will endure in our science because we would foreswear significant unification (or fail to employ the relevant laws, or fail to identify the causally relevant properties) by attempting to derive the conclusions to which they are applied using the vocabulary and reasoning patterns of molecular biology. But the autonomy thesis is only the beginning of antireductionism. A stronger doctrine can be generated by opposing the weaker version of sophisticated reductionism.

In section 4, I raised the possibility that molecular genetics may be viewed as providing an explanatory extension of classical genetics through deriving the schematic sentence that assigns phenotypes to genotypes from a molecular pattern of reasoning. This apparent possibility fails in an instructive way. Antireductionists are not only able to contend that there are autonomous levels of biological explanation. They can also resist the weaker reductionist view that explanation always flows from the molecular level up. Even if reductionists retreat to the modest claim that, while there are autonomous levels of explanation, descriptions of cells and their constituents are always explained in terms of descriptions about genes, descriptions of tissue geometry are always explained in terms of descriptions of cells, and so forth, antireductionists can resist the picture of a unidirectional flow of explanation. Understanding the phenotypic manifestation of a gene, they will maintain, requires constant shifting back and forth across levels. Because developmental processes are complex and because changes in the timing of embryological events may produce a cascade of effects at several different levels, one sometimes uses descriptions at higher levels to explain what goes on at a more fundamental level. . . .

It would be premature to claim that I have shown how to reformulate the anti-treductionist appeals to the organization of nature in a completely precise way. My conclusion is that, to the extent that we can make sense of the present explanatory structure within biology—that division of the field into subfields corresponding to levels of organization in nature—we can also understand the antireductionist doctrine. In its minimal form, it is the claim that the commitment to several explanatory levels does not simply reflect our cognitive limitations; in its stronger form, it is the thesis that some explanations oppose the direction of preferred reductionistic explanation. Reductionists should not dismiss these doctrines as incomprehensible mush unless they are prepared to reject as unintelligible the biological strategy of dividing the field (a strategy which seems to me well understood, even if unanalyzed).

The examples I have given seem to support both antireductionist doctrines. To clinch the case, further analysis is needed. The notion of explanatory levels obviously cries out for explication, and it would be illuminating to replace the informal argument that the unification of our beliefs is best achieved by preserving multiple explanatory levels with an argument based on a more exact criterion for unification. Nevertheless, I hope that I have said enough to make plausible the view that, despite the immense value of the molecular biology that Watson and Crick launched in 1953, molecular studies cannot cannibalize the rest of biology. Even if geneticists must become "physiological chemists" they should not give up being embryologists, physiologists, and cytologists.

Notes

Earlier versions of this paper were read at Johns Hopkins University and at the University of Minnesota, and I am very grateful to a number of people for comments and suggestions. In particular, I would like to thank Peter Achinstein, John Beatty, Barbara Horan, Patricia Kitcher, Richard Lewontin, Kenneth Schaffner, William Wimsatt, an anonymous reader and the editors of *The Philosophical Review*, all of whom have had an important influence on the final version. Needless to say, these people should not be held responsible for residual errors. I am also grateful to the American Council of Learned Societies and the Museum of Comparative Zoology at Harvard University for support and hospitality while I was engaged in research on the topics of this paper.

[This article has been abridged. In the process, much of Professor Kitcher's rich illustrative material has had to be omitted (ed.).]

1. "Variation due to change in the individual gene," reprinted in J. A. Peters ed., *Classic Papers in Genetics* (Englewood Cliffs, N.J.: Prentice-Hall, 1959), pp. 104–116. Citation from p. 115.

2. "Molecular Structure of Nucleic Acids," *Nature* 171 (1953), pp. 737–738; reprinted in Peters, op. cit., pp. 241–243. Watson and Crick amplified their suggestion in "Genetic Implications of the Structure of Deoxyribonucleic Acid" *Nature* 171 (1953), pp. 934–937.

3. The most sophisticated attempts to work out a defensible version of reductionism occur in articles by Kenneth Schaffner. [See the bibliography at the end of the introduction to this section.]

4. E. Nagel, *The Structure of Science* (New York: Harcourt Brace, 1961), Chapter 11. A simplified presentation can be found in Chapter 8 of C. G. Hempel, *Philosophy of Natural Science* (Englewood Cliffs, N.J.: Prentice-Hall, 1966).

5. Quite evidently, this is a weak version of what was once the "received view" of scientific theories, articulated in the works of Nagel and Hempel cited in the previous note.

6. Hull, *Philosophy of Biological Science* (Englewood Cliffs, N.J.: Prentice-Hall, 1974), p. 23, adapted from Theodosius Dobzhansky, *Genetics of the Evolutionary Process* (New York: Columbia University Press, 1970), p. 167.

7. A *locus* is the place on a chromosome occupied by a gene. Different genes which can occur at the same locus are said to be *alleles*. In diploid organisms, chromosomes line up in pairs just before the meiotic division that gives rise to gametes. The matched pairs are pairs of *homologous chromosomes*. If

different alleles occur at corresponding loci on a pair of homologous chromosomes, the organism is said to be *heterozygous* at these loci.

8. My notion of a practice owes much to some neglected ideas of Sylvain Bromberger and Thomas Kuhn. See, in particular, Bromberger. "A Theory about the Theory of Theory and about the Theory of Theories," (W. L. Reese ed., *Philosophy of Science, The Delaware Seminar*, New York, 1963); and "Questions." (*Journal of Philosophy* 63 (1966), pp. 597–606); and Kuhn, *The Structure of Scientific Revolutions* (Chicago: University of Chicago Press, 1962) Chapters II–V. The relation between the notion of a practice and Kuhn's conception of a paradigm is discussed in Chapter 7 of my book *The Nature of Mathematical Knowledge* (New York: Oxford University Press, 1983).

9. *Polygeny* occurs when many genes affect one characteristic; *pleiotropy* occurs when one gene affects more than one characteristic.

10. *Incomplete dominance* occurs when the phenotype of the heterozygote is intermediate between that of the homozygotes; *epistasis* occurs when the effect of a particular combination of alleles at one locus depends on what alleles are present at another locus.

11. See Watson, *Molecular Biology of the Gene* (Menlo Park, CA: W. A. Benjamin, 1976), Chapter 9; and Arthur Kornberg, *DNA Synthesis* (San Francisco: W. H. Freeman, 1974).

12. See. G. P. Georghiou, "The Evolution of Resistance to Pesticides," *Annual Review of Ecology and Systematics* 3 (1972), pp. 133–168.

13. There are numerous examples of such modifications from the history of chemistry. I try to do justice to this type of case in "Theories, Theorists, and Theoretical Change," *The Philosophical Review* 87 (1978), pp. 519–547 and in "Genes," *British Journal for the Philosophy of Science* 33 (1982), pp. 337–359.

14. The extreme version of reductionism is defended by Richard Dawkins in *The Selfish Gene* (New York: Oxford University Press, 1976) and *The Extended Phenotype* (San Francisco: W. H. Freeman, 1982). For an excellent critique, see Elliott Sober and Richard C. Lewontin, "Artifact, Cause, and Genic Selection," *Philosophy of Science* 49 (1982), pp. 157–180 [this volume, chapter 31].

Chapter 31

Artifact, Cause, and Genic Selection

Elliott Sober and Richard Lewontin

Several evolutionary biologists have used a parsimony argument to argue that the single gene is the unit of selection. Since all evolution by natural selection can be represented in terms of selection coefficients attaching to single genes, it is, they say, "more parsimonious" to think that all selection is selection for or against single genes. We examine the limitations of this genic point of view, and then relate our criticisms to a broader view of the role of causal concepts and the dangers of reification in science.

Introduction

Although predicting an event and saying what brought it about are different, a science may yet hope that its theories will do double duty. Ideally, the laws will provide a set of parameters which facilitate computation and pinpoint causes; later states of a system can be predicted from its earlier parameter values, where these earlier parameter values are the ones which cause the system to enter its subsequent state.

In this paper, we argue that these twin goals are not jointly attainable by some standard ideas used in evolutionary theory. The idea that natural selection is always, or for the most part, selection for and against single genes has been vigorously defended by George C. Williams (*Adaptation and Natural Selection*) and Richard Dawkins (*The Selfish Gene*). Although models of evolutionary processes conforming to this view of genic selection may permit computation, they often misrepresent the causes of evolution. The reason is that genic selection coefficients are *artifacts*, not causes, of population dynamics. Since the gene's eye point of view exerts such a powerful influence both within biology and in popular discussions of sociobiology, it is important to show how limited it is. Our discussion will not focus on cultural evolution or on group selection, but rather will be restricted to genetic cases of selection in a single population. The selfish gene fails to do justice to standard textbook examples of Darwinian selection.

The philosophical implications and presuppositions of our critique are various. First, it will be clear that we reject a narrowly instrumentalist interpretation of scientific theories; models of evolutionary processes must do more than correctly predict changes in gene frequencies. In addition, our arguments go contrary to certain regularity and counterfactual interpretations of the concepts of causality and force. To say that *a* caused *b* is to say more than just that any event that is relevantly similar to *a* would be followed by an event that is relevantly similar to *b* (we ignore issues concerning indeterministic causation); and to say that a system of objects is subject to

Reprinted from *Philosophy of Science* 49 (1982) pp. 157–180, by permission of the authors and the Philosophy of Science Association.

certain forces is to say more than just that they will change in various ways, as long as nothing interferes. And lastly, our account of what is wrong with genic selection coefficients points to a characterization of the conditions under which a predicate will pick out a real property. Selfish genes and grue emeralds bear a remarkable similarity.

1. The "Canonical Objects" of Evolutionary Theory

The Modern Synthesis received from Mendel a workable conception of the mechanism of heredity. But as important as this contribution was, the role of Mendelian "factors" was more profound. Not only did Mendelism succeed in filling in a missing link in the three-part structure of variation, selection, and transmission; it also provided a canonical form in which *all* evolutionary processes could be characterized. Evolutionary models must describe the interactions of diverse forces and phenomena. To characterize selection, inbreeding, mutation, migration, and sampling error in a single predictive theoretical structure, it is necessary to describe their respective effects in a common currency. Change in gene frequencies is the "normal form" in which all these aspects are to be represented, and so genes might be termed the canonical objects of evolutionary theory.

Evolutionary phenomena can be distilled into a tractable mathematical form by treating them as preeminently genetic. It by no means follows from this that the normal form characterization captures everything that is biologically significant. In particular, the computational adequacy of genetic models leaves open the question of whether they also correctly identify the causes of evolution. The canonical form of the models has encouraged many biologists to think of all natural selection as genic selection, but there has always been a tradition within the Modern Synthesis which thinks of natural selection differently and holds this gene's eye view to be fundamentally distorted.

Ernst Mayr perhaps typifies this perspective. Although it is clear that selection has an *effect* on gene frequencies, it is not so clear that natural selection is always selection for or against particular genes. Mayr has given two reasons for thinking that the idea of genic selection is wrong. One of the interesting things about his criticisms is their simplicity; they do not report any recondite facts about evolutionary processes but merely remind evolutionary theorists of what they already know (although perhaps lose sight of at times). As we will see, genic selectionists have ready replies for these criticisms.

The first elementary observation is that "natural selection favors (or discriminates against) phenotypes, not genes or genotypes" (1963, p. 184). Protective coloration and immunity from DDT are phenotypic traits. Organisms differ in their reproductive success under natural selection because of their phenotypes. If those phenotypes are heritable, then natural selection will produce evolutionary change (*ceteris paribus*, of course). But genes are affected by natural selection only indirectly. So the gene's eye view, says Mayr, may have its uses, but it does not correctly represent how natural selection works.

Mayr calls his second point *the genetic theory of relativity* (1963, p. 296). This principle says that "no gene has a fixed selective value, the same gene may confer high fitness on one genetic background and be virtually lethal on another." Should we conclude from this remark that there is never selection for single genes or that a single gene simultaneously experiences different selection pressures in different genetic backgrounds? In either case, the lesson here seems to be quite different from that provided by Mayr's first point—which was that phenotypes, not genotypes, are selected for. In this case, however, it seems to be gene complexes, rather than single genes, which are the objects of selection.

Mayr's first point about phenotypes and genotypes raises the following question: if we grant that selection acts "directly" on phenotypes and only "indirectly" on genotypes, why should it follow that natural selection is not selection for genetic attributes? Natural selection is a causal process; to say that there is selection for some (genotypic or phenotypic) trait X is to say that having X causes differential reproductive success (*ceteris paribus*).[1] So, if there is selection for protective coloration, this just means that protective coloration generates a reproductive advantage. But suppose that this phenotype is itself caused by one or more genes. Then having those genes causes a reproductive advantage as well. Thus, if selection is a causal process, in acting on phenotypes it also acts on the underlying genotypes. Whether this is "direct" or not may be important, but it doesn't bear on the question of what is and what is not selected for. Selection, in virtue of its causal character and on the assumption that causality is transitive, seems to block the sort of asymmetry that Mayr demands. Asking whether phenotypes or genotypes are selected for seems to resemble asking whether a person's death was caused by the entry of the bullet or by the pulling of the trigger.

Mayr's second point—his genetic principle of relativity—is independent of the alleged asymmetry between phenotype and genotype. It is, of course, not in dispute that a gene's fitness depends on its genetic (as well as its extrasomatic) environment. But does this fact show that there is selection for gene complexes and not for single genes? Advocates of genic selection tend to acknowledge the relativity but to deny the conclusion that Mayr draws. Williams (1966, pp. 56–7) gives clear expression to this common reaction when he writes:

> Obviously it is unrealistic to believe that a gene actually exists in its own world with no complications other than abstract selection coefficients and mutation rates. The unity of the genotype and the functional subordination of the individual genes to each other and to their surroundings would seem at first sight, to invalidate the one locus model of natural selection. Actually these considerations do not bear on the basic postulates of the theory. No matter how functionally dependent a gene may be, and no matter how complicated its interactions with other genes and environmental factors, it must always be true that a given gene substitution will have an arithmetic mean effect on fitness in any population. One allele can always be regarded as having a certain selection coefficient relative to another at the same locus at any given point in time. Such coefficients are numbers that can be treated algebraically, and conclusions inferred for one locus can be iterated over all loci. Adaptation can thus be attributed to the effect of selection acting independently at each locus.

Dawkins (1976, p. 40) considers the same problem: how can single genes be selected for, if genes build organisms only in elaborate collaboration with each other and with the environment? He answers by way of an analogy:

> One oarsman on his own cannot win the Oxford and Cambridge boat race. He needs eight colleagues. Each one is a specialist who always sits in a particular part of the boat—bow or stroke or cox, etc. Rowing the boat is a cooperative venture, but some men are nevertheless better at it than others. Suppose a coach has to choose his ideal crew from a pool of candidates, some specializing in the bow position, others specializing as cox, and so on. Suppose that he makes his

selection as follows. Every day he puts together three new trial crews, by random shuffling of the candidates, for each position, and he makes the three crews race against each other. After some weeks of this it will start to emerge that the winning boat often tends to contain the same individual men. These are marked up as good oarsmen. Other individuals seem consistently to be found in slower crews, and these are eventually rejected. But even an outstandingly good oarsman might sometimes be a member of a slow crew, either because of the inferiority of the other members, or because of bad luck—say a strong adverse wind. It is only *on average* that the best men tend to be in the winning boat.

The oarsmen are genes. The rivals for each seat in the boat are alleles potentially capable of occupying the same slot along the length of a chromosome. Rowing fast corresponds to building a body which is successful at surviving. The wind is the external environment. The pool of alternative candidates is the gene pool. As far as the survival of any one body is concerned, all its genes are in the same boat. Many a good gene gets into bad company, and finds itself sharing a body with a lethal gene, which kills the body off in childhood. Then the good gene is destroyed along with the rest. But this is only one body, and replicas of the same good gene live on in other bodies which lack the lethal gene. Many copies of good genes are dragged under because they happen to share a body with bad genes, and many perish through other forms of ill luck, say when their body is struck by lightning. But by definition luck, good and bad, strikes at random, and a gene which is consistently on the losing side is not unlucky; it is a bad gene.

Notice that this passage imagines that oarsmen (genes) are good and bad pretty much *in*dependently of their context. But even when fitness is heavily influenced by context, Dawkins still feels that selection functions at the level of the single gene. Later in the book (pp. 91–2), he considers what would happen if a team's performance were improved by having the members communicate with each other. Suppose that half of the oarsmen spoke only English and the other half spoke only German:

What will emerge as the overall best crew will be one of the two stable states—pure English or pure German, but not mixed. Superficially it looks as though the coach is selecting whole language groups *as units*. This is not what he is doing. He is selecting individual oarsmen for their apparent ability to win races. It so happens that the tendency for an individual to win races depends on which other individuals are present in the pool of candidates.

Thus, Dawkins follows Williams in thinking that genic selectionism is quite compatible with the fact that a gene's fitness depends on context.

Right after the passage just quoted, Dawkins says that he favors the perspective of genic selectionism because it is more "parsimonious". Here, too, he is at one with Williams (1966), who uses parsimony as one of two main lines of attack against hypotheses of group selection. The appeal to simplicity may confirm a suspicion that already arises in this context: perhaps it is a matter of taste whether one prefers the single gene perspective or the view of selection processes as functioning at a higher level of organization. As long as we agree that genic fitnesses depend on context, what difference does it make how we tell the story? As natural as this suspicion is in the light of Dawkins's rowing analogy, it is mistaken. Hypotheses of group selection can be genuinely incompatible with hypotheses of organismic selection (Sober 1980), and, as we will see in what follows, claims of single gene selection are at times incompatible with claims that gene complexes are selected for and against. Regardless of one's aesthetic inclinations and regardless of whether one thinks of parsimony as a "real" reason for hypothesis choice, the general perspective of genic selectionism is mistaken for biological reasons.[2]

Before stating our objections to genic selectionism, we want to make clear one defect that this perspective does *not* embody. A quantitative genetic model that is given at any level can be recast in terms of parameters that attach to genes. This genic representation will correctly trace the trajectory of the population as its gene frequencies change. In a minimal sense (to be made clear in what follows), it will be "descriptively adequate". Since the parameters encapsulate information about the environment, both somatic and extrasomatic, genic selectionism cannot be accused of ignoring the complications of linkage or of thinking that genes exist in a vacuum. The defects of genic selectionism concern its distortion of causal processes, not whether its models allow one to predict future states of the population.[3]

The causal considerations which will play a preeminent role in what follows are not being imposed from without, but already figure centrally in evolutionary theory. We have already mentioned how we understand the idea of *selection for X*. Our causal construal is natural in view of how the phenomena of linkage and pleiotropy are understood (see Sober 1981a). Two genes may be linked together on the same chromosome, and so selection for one may cause them both to increase in frequency. Yet the linked gene—the "free rider"—may be neutral or even deleterious; there was no selection *for* it. In describing pleiotropy, the same distinction is made. Two phenotypic traits may be caused by the same underlying gene complex, so that selection for one leads to a proliferation of both. But, again, there was no selection for the free rider. So it is a familiar idea that two traits can attach to exactly the same organisms and yet differ in their causal roles in a selection process. What is perhaps less familiar is that two sets of selection coefficients may both attach to the same population and yet differ in their causal roles—the one causing change in frequencies, the other merely reflecting the changes that ensue.

2. Averaging and Reification

Perhaps the simplest model exhibiting the strategy of averaging recommended by Williams and Dawkins is used in describing heterozygote superiority. In organisms whose chromosomes come in pairs, individuals with different genes (or alleles) at the same location on two homologous chromosomes are called heterozygotes. When a population has only two alleles at a locus, there will be one heterozygote form (*Aa*) and two homozygotes (*AA* and *aa*). If the heterozygote is superior in fitness to both homozygotes, then natural selection may modify the frequencies of the two alleles *A* and *a*, but will not drive either to fixation (i.e., 100%), since reproduction by heterozygotes will inevitably replenish the supply of homozygotes, even when homozygotes are severely selected against. A textbook example of this phenomenon is the sickle cell trait in human beings. Homozygotes for the allele controlling the trait develop severe anemia that is often fatal in childhood. Heterozygotes, however, suffer no deleterious effects, but enjoy a greater than average resistance to malaria. Homozygotes for the other allele have neither the anemia nor the immunity, and so are intermediate in fitness. Human populations with both alleles that live in malarial areas have remained polymorphic, but with the eradication of malaria, the sickle cell allele has been eliminated.

Population genetics provides a simple model of the selection process that results from heterozygotes having greater viability than either of the homozygotes (Li 1955). Let p be the frequency of A and q be the frequency of a (where $p + q = 1$). Usually, the maximal fitness of Aa is normalized and set equal to 1. But for clarity of exposition we will let w_1 be the fitness of AA, w_2 be the fitness of Aa, and w_3 be the fitness of aa. These genotypic fitness values play the mathematical role of transforming genotype frequencies before selection into genotype frequencies after selection:

	AA	Aa	aa
Proportion before selection	p^2	$2pq$	q^2
Fitness	w_1	w_2	w_3
Proportion after selection	$\dfrac{p^2 w_1}{\overline{W}}$	$\dfrac{2pq w_2}{\overline{W}}$	$\dfrac{q^2 w_3}{\overline{W}}$

Here, $\overline{W}$, the average fitness of the population, is $p^2 w_1 + 2pq w_2 + q^2 w_3$. Assuming random mating, the population will move towards a stable equilibrium frequency $\hat{p}$ where

$$\hat{p} = \frac{w_3 - w_2}{(w_1 - w_2) + (w_3 - w_2)}.$$

It is important to see that this model attributes fitness values and selection coefficients to diploid genotypes and not to the single genes A and a. But, as genic selectionists are quick to emphasize, one can always define the required parameters. Let us do so.

We want to define W_A, which is the fitness of A. If we mimic the mathematical role of genotype fitness values in the previous model, we will require that W_A obey the following condition:

$W_A \times$ frequency of A before selection = frequency of A after selection $\times \overline{W}$.

Since the frequency of A before selection is p and the frequency of A after selection is

$$\frac{w_1 p^2 + w_2 pq}{\overline{W}},$$

it follows that

$$W_A = w_1 p + w_2 q.$$

By parity of reasoning,

$$W_a = w_3 q + w_2 p.$$

Notice that the fitness values of single genes are just weighted averages of the fitness values of the diploid genotypes in which they appear. The weighting is provided by their frequency of occurrence in the genotypes in question. The genotypic fitnesses specified in the first model are *constants*; as a population moves toward its equilibrium frequency, the selection coefficients attaching to the three diploid genotypes do not change. In contrast, the expression we have derived for allelic fitnesses says that allelic fitnesses change as a function of their own frequencies; as the population moves toward equilibrium, the fitnesses of the alleles must constantly be recomputed.

Heterozygote superiority illustrates the principle of genetic relativity. The gene a is maximally fit in one context (namely, when accompanied by A) but is inferior when it occurs in another (namely, when it is accompanied by another copy of itself). In spite of this, we can average over the two different contexts and provide the required representation in terms of genic fitness and genic selection.

In the diploid model discussed first, we represented the fitness of the three genotypes in terms of their *viability*, that is, in terms of the proportion of individuals surviving from egg to adult. It is assumed that the actual survivorship of a class of organisms sharing the same genotype precisely represents the fitness of that shared genotype. This assumes that random drift is playing no role. Ordinarily, fitness *cannot* be identified with actual reproductive success (Brandon 1978; Mills and Beatty 1979; Sober 1981a). The same point holds true, of course, for the fitness coefficients we defined for the single genes.[4]

Of the two descriptions we have constructed of heterozygote superiority, the first model is the standard one; in it, *pairs* of genes are the bearers of fitness values and selection coefficients. In contrast to this diploid model, our second formulation adheres strictly to the dictates of genic selectionism, according to which it is *single genes* which are the bearers of the relevant evolutionary properties. We now want to describe what each of these models will say about a population that is at its equilibrium frequency.

Let's discuss this situation by way of an example. Suppose that both homozygotes are lethal. In that case, the equilibrium frequency is .5 for each of the alleles. Before selection, the three genotypes will be represented in proportions 1/4, 1/2, 1/4, but after selection the frequencies will shift to 0, 1, 0. When the surviving heterozygotes reproduce, Mendelism will return the population to its initial 1/4, 1/2, 1/4 configuration, and the population will continue to zig-zag between these two genotype configurations, all the while maintaining each allele at .5. According to the second, single gene, model, at equilibrium the fitnesses of the two genes are both equal to 1 and the selection coefficients are therefore equal to zero. At equilibrium, no selection occurs, on this view. Why the population's *genotypic configuration* persists in zig-zagging, the gene's eye point of view is blind to see; it must be equally puzzling why $\overline{W}$, the average fitness of the population, also zig-zags. However, the standard diploid model yields the result that selection occurs when the population is at equilibrium, just as it does at other frequencies, favoring the heterozygote at the expense of the homozygotes. Mendelism *and selection* are the causes of the zig-zag. Although the models are computationally equivalent in their prediction of gene frequencies, they are not equivalent when it comes to saying whether or not selection is occurring.

It is hard to see how the adequacy of the single gene model can be defended in this case. The biological term for the phenomenon being described is apt. We are talking here about *heterozygote superiority*, and both terms of this label deserve emphasis. The heterozygote—i.e., the diploid genotype (not a single gene)—is superior *in fitness* and, therefore, enjoys a selective advantage. To insist that the single gene is always the level at which selection occurs obscures this and, in fact, generates precisely the wrong answer to the question of what is happening at equilibrium. Although the mathematical calculations can be carried out in the single gene model just as they can in the diploid genotypic model, the phenomenon of heterozygote superiority cannot be adequately "represented" in terms of single genes. This model does not tell us what is patently obvious about this case: even at equilibrium, what happens to gene frequencies is an artifact of selection acting on diploid genotypes.

One might be tempted to argue that in the heterozygote superiority case, the kind of averaging we have criticized is just an example of frequency dependent selection and that theories of frequency dependent selection are biologically plausible and also compatible with the dictates of genic selectionism. To see where this objection goes wrong, one must distinguish genuine from spurious cases of frequency dependent selection. The former occurs when the frequency of an allele has some *biological impact* on its fitness; an example would be the phenomenon of mimicry in which the rarity of a mimic enhances its fitness. Here one can tell a biological story explaining why the fitness values have the mathematical form they do. The case of heterozygote superiority is altogether different; here frequencies are taken into account simply as a mathematical contrivance, the only point being to get the parameters to multiply out in the right way.

The diploid model is, in a sense, more contentful and informative than the single gene model. We noted before that from the *constant* fitness values of the three genotypes we could obtain a formula for calculating the fitnesses of the two alleles. Allelic fitnesses are implied by genotype fitness values and allelic frequencies; since allelic frequencies change as the population moves toward equilibrium, allelic fitnesses must constantly be recomputed. However, the derivation in the opposite direction cannot be made.[5] One cannot deduce the fitnesses of the genotypes from allelic fitnesses and frequencies. This is especially evident when the population is at equilibrium. At equilibrium, the allelic fitnesses are identical. From this information alone, we cannot tell whether there is no selection at all or whether some higher level selection process is taking place. Allelic frequencies plus genotypic fitness imply allelic fitness values, but allelic frequencies plus allelic fitness values do not imply genotypic fitness values. This derivational asymmetry suggests that the genotypic description is more informative.

Discussions of reductionism often suggest that theories at lower levels of organization will be more detailed and informative than ones at higher levels. However, here, the more contentful, constraining model is provided at the higher level. The idea that genic selection models are "deeper" and describe the fundamental level at which selection "really" occurs is simply not universally correct.

The strategy of averaging fosters the illusion that selection is acting at a lower level of organization than it in fact does. Far from being an idiosyncratic property of the genic model of heterozygote superiority just discussed, averaging is a standard technique in modelling a variety of selection processes. We will now describe another example in which this technique of representation is used. The example of heterozygote superiority focused on differences in genotypic *viabilities*. Let us now consider the way differential fertilities can be modelled for one locus with two alleles. In the fully general case, fertility is a property of a mating pair, not of an individual. It may be true that a cross between an *AA* male and *aa* female has an expected number of offspring different from a cross between an *AA* female and an *aa* male. If fitnesses are a unique function of the pair, the model must represent nine possible fitnesses, one for each mating pair. Several special cases permit a reduction in dimensionality. If the sex of a genotype does not affect its fertility, then only six fitnesses need be given; and if fertility depends only on one of the sexes, say the females, the three female genotypes may be assigned values which fix the fertilities of all mating pairs.

But even when these special cases fail to obtain, the technique of averaging over contexts can nevertheless provide us with a fitness value for each genotype. Perhaps an *aa* female is highly fertile when mated with an *Aa* male but is much less so when mated with an *AA* male; perhaps *aa* females are quite fertile on average, but *aa* males are uniformly sterile. No matter—we can merely average over all contexts and find the average effect of the *aa* genotype. This number will fluctuate with the frequency distributions of the different mating pairs. Again, the model appears to locate selection at a level lower than what might first appear to be the case. Rather than assigning fertilities to mating pairs, we now seem to be assigning them to genotypes. This mathematical contrivance is harmless as long as it does not lead us to think that selection really acts at this lower level of organization.[6]

Our criticism of genic selectionism has so far focused on two forms of selection at a single locus. We now need to take account of how a multilocus theory can imply that selection is not at the level of the selfish gene. The pattern of argument is the same. Even though the fitness of a pair of genes at one locus may depend on what genes are found at other loci, the technique of averaging may still be pressed into service. But the selection values thereby assigned to the three genotypes at a single locus will be artifacts of the fitnesses of the nine genotype complexes that exist at the two loci. As in the examples we already described, the lower-level selection coefficients will change as a function of genotype frequencies, whereas the higher-level selection coefficients will remain constant. An example of this is provided by the work of Lewontin and White (reported in Lewontin 1974) on the interaction of two chromosome inversions found in the grasshopper *Moraba scura*. On each of the chromosomes of the EF pair, Standard (ST) and Tidbinbilla (TD) may be found. On the CD chromosome pair, Standard (ST) and Blundell (BL) are the two alternatives. The fitness values of the nine possible genotypes were estimated from nature as follows:

Chromosome EF	Chromosome CD		
	ST/ST	ST/BL	BL/BL
ST/ST	0.791	1.00	0.834
ST/TD	0.670	1.006	0.901
TD/TD	0.657	0.657	1.067

Notice that there is heterozygote superiority on the CD chromosome if the EF chromosome is either ST/ST or ST/TD, but that BL/BL dominance ensues when the EF chromosome is homozygous for TD. Moreover, TD/TD is superior when in the context BL/BL but is inferior in the other contexts provided by the CD pair. These fitness values represent differences in viability, and again the inference seems clear that selection acts on multilocus genotypic configurations and not on the genotype at a single locus, let alone on the separate genes at that locus.

3. Individuating Selection Processes

The examples in the previous section have a common structure. We noted that the fitness of an object (a gene, a genotype) varied significantly from context to context. We concluded that selection was operating at a level higher than the one posited by the model—at the level of genotypes in the case of heterozygote superiority, at the level of the mating pair in the fertility model, and at the level of pairs of chromosome inversions in the *Moraba scura* example. These analyses suggest the following principle: *if the fitness of X is context sensitive, then there is not selection for X; rather, there is selection at a level of organization higher than X.*

We believe that this principle requires qualification. To see why context sensitivity is not a *sufficient* condition for higher level selection, consider the following example. Imagine a dominant lethal gene; it kills any organisms in which it is found unless the organism also has a suppressor gene at another locus. Let's consider two populations. In the first population, each organism is homozygous for a suppressor gene which prevents copies of the lethal gene from having any effect. In the second population, no organism has a suppressor, so, whenever the lethal gene occurs, it is selected against.

A natural way of describing this situation is that there is selection against the lethal gene in one population, but, in the other, there is no selection going on at all. It would be a mistake (of the kind we have already examined) to think that there is a single selection process at work here against the lethal gene, whose magnitude we calculate by averaging over the two populations. However, we do not conclude from this that there is a selection process at work at some higher level of organization than the single gene. Rather, we conclude that there are *two* populations; in one, *genic* selection occurs, and in the other *nothing* occurs. So the context sensitivity of fitness is an ambiguous clue. If the fitness of X depends on genetic context, this may mean that there is a single selection process at some higher level, *or* it may mean that there are several different selection processes at the level of X. Context sensitivity does not suffice for there to be selection at a higher level.[7]

Thus, the fitness of an object can be sensitive to genetic context for at least two reasons. How are they to be distinguished? This question leads to an issue at the foundation of *all* evolutionary models. What unites a set of objects as all being subject to a single selection process? Biological modelling of evolution by natural selection is based on three necessary and sufficient conditions (Lewontin 1970): a given set of objects must exhibit variation; some individuals must be fitter than others; and there must be correlation between the fitness of parents and the fitness of offspring. Here, as before, we will identify fitness with actual reproductive success, subject to the proviso that these will coincide only in special cases. Hence, evolution by natural selection exists when and only when there is heritable variation in fitness.

Using these conditions presupposes that some antecedent decision has been made about which objects can appropriately be lumped together as participating in a single selection process (or, put differently, the conditions are not sufficient after all). Biologists do not talk about a *single* selection process subsuming widely scattered organisms of different species which are each subject to quite different local conditions. Yet, such a gerrymandered assemblage of objects may well exhibit heritable variation in fitness. And even within the same species, it would be artificial to think of two local populations as participating in the same selection process because one encounters a disease and the other experiences a food shortage as its principal selection pressure. Admittedly, the gene frequencies can be tabulated and pooled, but in some sense the relation of organisms to environments is too heterogeneous for this kind of averaging to be more than a mathematical contrivance.

It is very difficult to spell out necessary and sufficient conditions for when a set of organisms experience "the same" selection pressure. They need not compete with each other. To paraphrase Darwin, two plants may struggle for life at the edge of a desert, and selection may favor the one more suited to the stressful conditions. But it needn't be the case that some resource is in short supply, so that the amount expropriated by one reduces the amount available to the other. Nor need it be true that the two organisms be present in the same geographical locale; organisms in the semi-isolated local populations of a species may experience the same selection pressures. What seems to be required, roughly, is that some common causal influence impinge on the organisms. This sameness of causal influence is as much determined by the biology of the organisms as it is by the physical characteristics of the environment. Although two organisms may experience the same temperature fluctuations, there may be no selective force acting on both. Similarly, two organisms may experience the same selection pressure (for greater temperature tolerance, say) even though the one is in a cold environment and the other is in a hot one. Sameness of causal influence needs to be understood biologically.

For all the vagueness of this requirement, let us assume that we have managed to single out the class of objects which may properly be viewed as participating in a single selection process. To simplify matters, let us suppose that they are all organisms within the same breeding population. What, then, will tell us whether selection is at the level of the single gene or at the level of gene complexes? To talk about either of these forms of selection is, in a certain important but nonstandard sense, to talk about "group selection". Models of selection do not concern single organisms or the individual physical copies of genes (i.e., geno*tokens*) that they contain. Rather, such theories are about groups of organisms which have in common certain geno*types*. To talk about selection for *X*, where *X* is some single gene or gene cluster, is to say something about the effect of having *X* and of lacking *X* on the relevant subgroups of the breeding population. If there is selection for *X*, every object which has *X* has its reproductive chances augmented by its possessing *X*. This does not mean that every organism which has *X* has precisely the same overall fitness, nor does it mean that every organism must be affected in precisely the same way (down to the minutest details of developmental pathways). Rather, what is required is that the effect of *X* on each organism be in the same direction as far as its overall fitness is concerned. Perhaps this characterization is best viewed as a limiting ideal. To the degree that the population conforms to this requirement, it will be appropriate to talk about genic selection. To the degree that the population falls short of this, it will be a contrivance to represent matters in terms of genic selection.[8]

It is important to be clear on why the context sensitivity of a gene's effect on organismic fitness is crucial to the question of genic selection. Selection theories deal with groups of single organisms and not with organisms taken one at a time. It is no news that the way a gene inside of a single organism will affect that organism's phenotype and its fitness depends on the way it is situated in a context of background conditions. But to grant this fact of context sensitivity does not impugn the claim of causation; striking the match caused it to light, even though the match had to be dry and in the presence of oxygen for the cause to produce the effect.

Selection theory is about geno*types* not geno*tokens*. We are concerned with what properties are selected for and against in a population. We do not describe single organisms and their physical constituents one by one. It is for this reason that the question of context sensitivity becomes crucial. If we wish to talk about selection for a single gene, then there must be such a thing as *the* causal upshot of possessing that gene. A gene which is beneficial in some contexts and deleterious in others will have many *organismic* effects. But at *the population level*, there will be no selection for or against that gene.

It is not simply the averaging over contexts which reveals the fact that genic selection coefficients are pseudoparameters; the fact that such parameters *change* in value as the population evolves while the biological relations stay fixed also points to their being artifacts. In the case of heterozygote superiority, genotypic fitnesses remain constant, mirroring the fact that the three genotypes have a uniform effect on the viability of the organisms in which they occur. The population is thereby driven to its equilibrium value while genic fitness values are constantly modified. A fixed set of biological relationships fuels both of these changes; the evolution of genic fitness values is effect, not cause.[9]

Are there real cases of genic selection? A dominant lethal—a gene which causes the individual to die regardless of the context in which it occurs—would be selected against. And selection for or against a phenotypic trait controlled by a single locus having two alleles might also be describable in terms of genic selection, provided that the heterozygote is intermediate in fitness between the two homozygotes. In addition, meiotic drive, such as is found in the house mouse *Mus musculus*, similarly seems to involve genic selection (Lewontin and Dunn 1960). Among heterozygote males, the proportion of t-alleles in the sperm pool is greater than 1/2. Chromosomes with the t-allele have enhanced chances of representation in the gamete pool, and this directional effect seems to hold true regardless of what other genes are present at other loci.[10] At this level, but not at the others at which the t-allele affects the population, it is appropriate to talk about genic selection.

We so far have construed genic selection in terms of the way that having or lacking a gene can affect the reproductive chances of organisms. But there is another possibility—namely, that genes differentially proliferate even though they have *no* effect on the phenotypes of organisms. A considerable quantity of DNA has no known function: Orgel and Crick (1980) and Doolittle and Sapienza (1980) suggest that this DNA may in fact be "junk". Such "selfish DNA", as they call it, could nonetheless undergo a selection process, provided that some segments are better replicators than others. Although these authors associate their ideas with Dawkins's selfish gene, their conception is far more restrictive. For Dawkins, *all* selection is genic selection, whereas for these authors, selfish DNA is possible only when the differential replication of genes is not exhaustively accounted for by the differential reproductive success of organisms.

Standard ways of understanding natural selection rule out rather than substantiate the operation of genic selection. It is often supposed that much of natural selection is *stabilizing selection*, in which an intermediate phenotype is optimal (e.g., birth weight in human beings). Although the exact genetic bases of such phenotypes are frequently unknown, biologists often model this selection process as follows. It is hypothesized that the phenotypic value is a monotone increasing function of the number of "plus alleles" found at a number of loci. Whether selection favors the presence of plus genes at one locus depends on how many such genes exist at other loci. Although this model does not view heterozygote superiority as the most common fitness relation *at a locus*, it nevertheless implies that a *heterogeneous genome* is superior in fitness. Exceptions to this intermediate optimum model exist, and the exact extent of its applicability is still an open question. Still, it appears to be widely applicable. If it is generally correct, we must conclude that the conditions in which genic selection exists are extremely narrow. Genic selection is not impossible, but the biological constraints on its operation are extremely demanding.

Although it is just barely conceivable that a critique of a scientific habit of thought might be devoid of philosophical presuppositions, our strictures against genic selectionism are not a case in point. We have described selection processes in which genic selection coefficients are *reifications*; they are artifacts, not causes, of evolution. For this to count as a criticism, one must abandon a narrowly instrumentalist view of scientific theories; this we gladly do, in that we assume that selection theory ought to pinpoint causes as well as facilitate predictions.

But even assuming this broadly noninstrumentalist outlook, our criticisms are philosophically partisan in additional ways. In that we have argued that genic selection coefficients are often "pseudoproperties" of genes, our criticisms of the gene's eye point of view are connected with more general metaphysical questions about the ontological status of properties. Some of these we take up in the following section. And in that we have understood "selection for" as a causal locution, it turns out that our account goes contrary to certain regularity analyses of causation. In populations in which selection generated by heterozygote superiority is the only evolutionary force, it is true that gene frequencies will move to a stable equilibrium. But this law-like regularity does not imply that there is selection for or against any individual gene. To say that "the gene's fitness value caused it to increase in frequency" is not simply to say that "any gene with that fitness value (in a relevantly similar population) would increase in frequency", since the former is false and the latter is true. Because we take natural selection to be a force of evolution, these remarks about causation have implications (explored in section 5) for how the concept of force is to be understood.

4. Properties

The properties, theoretical magnitudes, and natural kinds investigated by science ought not to be identified with the meanings that terms in scientific language possess. Nonsynonymous predicates (like "temperature" and "mean kinetic energy" and like "water" and "H_2O") may pick out the same property, and predicates which are quite meaningful (like "phlogiston" and "classical mass") may fail to pick out a property at all. Several recent writers have explored the idea that properties are to be individuated by their potential causal efficacy (Achinstein 1974; Armstrong 1978; Shoemaker 1980; and Sober 1982b). Besides capturing much of the intuitive content of our informal talk of properties, this view also helps explicate the role of property-talk in science (Sober 1981a). In this section, we will connect our discussion of genic selectionism with this metaphysical problem.

The definitional power of ordinary and scientific language allows us to take predicates which each pick out properties and to construct logically from these components a predicate which evidently does not pick out a property at all. An example of this is that old philosophical chestnut, the predicate "grue". We will say that an object is grue at a given time if it is green and the time is before the year 2000, or it is blue and the time is not before the year 2000. The predicate "grue" is defined from the predicates "green", "blue", and "time", each of which, we may assume for the purposes of the example, picks out a "real" property. Yet "grue" does not. A theory of properties should explain the basis of this distinction.

The difference between real and pseudoproperty is not captured by the ideas that animate the metaphysical issues usually associated with doctrines of realism, idealism, and conventionalism. Suppose that one adopts a "realist" position toward color and time, holding that things have the colors and temporal properties they do independently of human thought and language. This typical realist declaration of independence (Sober 1982a) will then imply that objects which are grue are so independently of human thought and language as well. In this sense, the "reality" of grulers is insured by the "reality" of colors and time. The distinction between real properties and pseudoproperties must be sought elsewhere. Another suggestion is that properties can be distinguished from nonproperties by appeal to the idea of *similarity* or of *predictive power*. One might guess that green things are more similar to each other than grue things are to each other, or that the fact that a thing is green is a better predictor of its further characteristics than the fact that it is grue. The standard criticism of these suggestions is that they are circular. We understand the idea of similarity in terms of shared *properties*, and the idea of predictive power in terms of the capacity to facilitate inference of further *properties*. However, a more fundamental difficulty with these suggestions presents itself: even if grue things happened to be very similar to each other, this would not make grue a real property. If there were no blue things after the year 2000, then the class of grue things would simply be the class of green things before the year 2000. The idea of similarity and the idea of predictive power fail to pinpoint the *intrinsic* defects of nonproperties like grue. Instead, they focus on somewhat accidental facts about the objects which happen to exist.

Grue is not a property for the same reason that genic selection coefficients are pseudoparameters in models of heterozygote superiority. The key idea is not that nonproperties are mind-dependent or are impoverished predictors; rather, they cannot be causally efficacious. To develop this idea, let's note a certain similarity between grue and genic selection coefficients. We pointed out before that genotype fitnesses plus initial genotype frequencies in the population causally determine the gene frequencies after selection. These same parameters also permit the mathematical derivation of genic fitness values, but, we asserted, these genic fitness values are artifacts; they do not cause the subsequent alteration in gene frequencies. The structure of these relationships is as follows.

genotype fitness values and → genic frequencies
  frequencies at time *t*   at *t* + 1
   ⋮
   ↓
genic fitness values at time *t*

Note that there are two different kinds of determination at work here. Genic fitness values at a given time are not *caused* by the genotypic fitness values at the same time. We assume that causal relations do not obtain between simultaneous events; rather, the relationship is one of logical or mathematical deducibility (symbolized by a broken line). On the other hand, the relation of initial genotype fitnesses and frequencies and subsequent gene frequencies is one of causal determination (represented by a solid line).

Now let's sketch the causal relations involved in a situation in which an object's being green produces some effect. Let the object be a grasshopper. Suppose that it matches its grassy background and that this protective coloration hides it from a hungry predator nearby. The relationships involved might be represented as follows.

the grasshopper is green at time *t* → the grasshopper evades
   ⋮   the predator at time *t* + 1
   ↓
the grasshopper is grue at time *t*

Just as in the above case, the object's color at the time *logically implies* that it is grue at that time but is the *cause* of its evading the predator at a subsequent time. And just as genic fitness values do not cause changes in gene frequencies, so the grasshopper's being grue does not cause it to have evaded its predator.

Our assessment of genic selectionism was not that genic fitness values are *always* artifactual. In cases other than that of heterozygote superiority—say, in the analysis of the *t*-allele—it may be perfectly correct to attribute causal efficacy to genic selection coefficients. So a predicate can pick out a real (causally efficacious) property in one context and fail to do so in another. This does not rule out the possibility, of course, that a predicate like "grue" is *globally artifactual*. But this consequence should not be thought to follow from a demonstration that grue is artifactual in a single kind of causal process.

The comparison of grue with genic selection is not meant to solve the epistemological problems of induction that led Goodman (1965) to formulate the example. Nor does the discussion provide any *a priori* grounds for distinguishing properties from nonproperties. Nor is it even a straightforward and automatic consequence of the truth of any scientific model that grue is artifactual, or that the idea of causal efficacy captures the metaphysical distinction at issue. Instead, the point is that a certain natural interpretation of a biological phenomenon helps to indicate how we ought to under-stand a rather abstract metaphysical issue.[11]

5. Forces

Our arguments against genic selectionism contradict a standard positivist view of the concept of force. Positivists have often alleged that Newtonian mechanics tells us that forces are not "things", but that claims about forces are simply to be understood as claims about how objects actually behave, or would behave, if nothing else gets in the way. An exhaustive catalog of the forces acting on a system is to be understood as simply specifying a set of counterfactuals that describe objects.[12]

A Newtonian theory of forces will characterize each force in its domain in terms of the changes it would produce, were it the only force at work. The theory will take pairwise combinations of forces and describe the joint effects that the two forces would have were they the only ones acting on a system. Then the forces would be taken three at a time, and so on, until a fully realistic model is constructed, one which tells us how real objects, which after all are subject to many forces, can be expected to behave. Each step in this program may face major theoretical difficulties, as the recent history of physics reveals (Cartwright 1980b; Joseph 1980).

This Newtonian paradigm is a hospitable home for the modelling of evolutionary forces provided in population genetics. The Hardy-Weinberg Law says what happens to gene frequencies when no evolutionary forces are at work. Mutation, migration, selection, and random drift are taken up one at a time, and models are provided for their effects on gene frequencies when no other forces are at work. Then these (and other) factors are taken up in combination. Each of these steps increases the model's realism. The culmination of this project would be a model that simultaneously rep-resents the interactions of all evolutionary forces.

Both in physics and in population genetics, it is useful to conceive of forces in terms of their *ceteris paribus* effects. But there is more to a force than the truth of counter-factuals concerning change in velocity, or change in gene frequencies. The laws of motion describe the *effects* of forces, but they are supplemented by source laws which describe their *causes*. The standard genotypic model of heterozygote superiority not only says what will happen to a population, but also tells us what makes the popula-tion change.

It is quite true that when a population moves to an equilibrium value, due to the selection pressures generated by heterozygote superiority, the alleles are "disposed" to change in frequency in certain ways.[13] That is, the frequencies *will* change in certain ways, as long as no other evolutionary forces impinge. Yet, there is no force of genic selection at work here. If this is right, then the claim that genic selection is occurring must involve more than the unproblematic observations that gene frequencies are disposed to change in certain ways.

There is something more to the concept of force because it involves the idea of *causality*, and there is more to the idea of causality than is spelled out by such counterfactuals as the ones cited above. Suppose that something pushes (i.e., causally interacts with in a certain way) a billiard ball due north, and something else pushes it due west. Assuming that nothing else gets in the way, the ball will move northwest. There are two "component" forces at work here, and, as we like to say, one "net" force. However, there is a difference between the components and the resultant. Although something pushes the ball due north and something else pushes it due west, nothing pushes it northwest. In a sense, the resultant force is not a force at all, if by force we mean a causal agency. The resultant force is an artifact of the forces at work in the system. For mathematical purposes this distinction may make no difference. But if we want to understand why the ball moves the way it does, there is all the difference in the world between component and net.[14]

The "force" of genic selection in the evolutionary process propelled by heterozygote superiority is no more acceptable than the resultant "force" which is in the northwesterly direction. In fact, it is much worse. The resultant force, at least, is defined from the same conceptual building blocks as the component forces are. Genic selection coefficients, however, are gerrymandered hodgepodges, conceptually and dynamically quite unlike the genotypic selection coefficients that go into their construction. For genic selection coefficients are defined in terms of genotypic selection coefficients *and* gene frequencies. As noted before, they vary as the population changes in gene frequency, whereas the genotypic coefficients remain constant. And if their uniform zero value at equilibrium is interpreted as meaning that no selection is going on, one obtains a series of false assertions about the character of the population.

The concept of force is richer than that of disposition. The array of forces that act on a system uniquely determine the disposition of that system to change, but not conversely. If natural selection is a force and fitness is a disposition (to be reproductively successful), then the concept of selection is richer than that of fitness. To say that objects differ in fitness is not yet to say *why* they do so. The possible causes of such differences may be various, in that many different combinations of selection pressures acting at different levels of organization can have the same instantaneous effect on gene frequencies. Although selection coefficients and fitness values are interdefinable mathematically (so that, typically, $s = 1 - w$), they play different conceptual roles in evolutionary theory (Sober 1980).

Notes

This paper was written while the authors held grants, respectively, from the University of Wisconsin Graduate School and the John Simon Guggenheim Foundation and from the Department of Energy (DE-AS02-76EV02472). We thank John Beatty, James Crow, and Steven Orzack for helpful suggestions.

1. The *"ceteris paribus"* is intended to convey the fact that selection for X can fail to bring about greater reproductive success for objects that have X, if countervailing forces act. Selection for X, against Y, and so on, are component forces that combine vectorially to determine the dynamics of the population.

2. In the passages quoted, Williams and Dawkins adopt a very bold position: any selection process which *can* be represented as genic selection *is* genic selection. Dawkins never draws back from this monolithic view, although Williams's more detailed argumentation leads him to hedge. Williams allows that group selection (clearly understood to be an alternative to genic selection) is possible and has actually been documented once (see his discussion of the t-allele). But *all* selection processes—including group selection—can be "represented" in terms of selection coefficients attaching to single genes. This means that the representation argument proves far too much.

3. Wimsatt (1980) criticizes genic selectionist models for being computationally inadequate and for at best providing a kind of "genetic bookkeeping" rather than a "theory of evolutionary change". Although we dissent from the first criticism, our discussion in what follows supports Wimsatt's second point.

4. We see from this that Dawkins's remark that a gene that is "consistently on the losing side is not unlucky; it's a bad gene" is not quite right. Just as a single genotoken (and the organism in which it is housed) may enjoy a degree of reproductive success that is not an accurate representation of its fitness, so a set of genotokens (which are tokens of the same genotype) may encounter the same fate. Fitness and actual reproductive success are guaranteed to be identical only in models which ignore random drift and thereby presuppose an infinite population.

5. If the heterozygote fitness is set equal to 1, the derivation is possible for the one locus two allele case considered. But if more than two alleles are considered, the asymmetry exists even in the face of normalization.

6. The averaging of effects can also be used to foster the illusion that a group selection process is really just a case of individual selection. But since this seems to be a relatively infrequent source of abuse, we will not take the space to spell out an example.

7. The argument given here has the same form as one presented in Sober (1980) which showed that the following is not a sufficient condition for group selection: there is heritable variation in the fitness of groups in which the fitness of an organism depends on the character of the group it is in.

8. The definition of genic selection just offered is structurally similar to the definition of group selection offered in Sober (1980). There, the requirement was that for there to be selection for groups which are X, it must be the case that every organism in a group that is X has one component of its fitness determined by the fact that it is in a group which is X. In group selection, organisms within the same group are bound together by a common group characteristic just as in genic selection organisms with the same gene are influenced in the same way by their shared characteristic.

9. In our earlier discussion of Mayr's ideas, we granted that selection usually acts "directly" on phenotypes and only "indirectly" on genotypes. But given the transitivity of causality, we argued that this fact is perfectly compatible with the existence of genotypic selection. However, our present discussion provides a characterization of when phenotypic selection can exist without there being any selection at the genotypic level. Suppose that individuals with the same genotype in a population end up with different phenotypes, because of the different microenvironments in which they develop. Selection for a given phenotype may then cross-classify the genotypes, and by our argument above, there will be no such thing as *the* causal upshot of a genotype. Averaging over effects will be possible, as always, but this will not imply genotypic selection. It is important to notice that this situation can allow evolution by natural selection to occur; gene frequencies can change in the face of phenotypic selection that is not accompanied by any sort of genotypic selection. Without this possibility, the idea of phenotypic selection is deprived of its main interest. There is no reason to deny that there can be selection for phenotypic differences that have no underlying genetic differences, but this process will not produce any change in the population (ignoring cultural evolution and the like).

10. Genes at other loci which modify the intensity of segregator distortion are known to exist in *Drosophila*; the situation in the house mouse is not well understood. Note that the existence of such modifiers is consistent with genic selection, as long as they do not affect the *direction* of selection.

11. Another consequence of this analogy is that one standard diagnosis of what is wrong with "grue" fails to get to the heart of the matter. Carnap (1947) alleged that "green", unlike "grue", is purely qualitative, in that it makes no essential reference to particular places, individuals, or times. Goodman (1965) responded by pointing out that *both* predicates can be defined with reference to the year 2000. But a more fundamental problem arises: even if "grue" were, in some sense, not purely qualitative, this would not provide a fully general characterization of when a predicate fails to pick out a real property. Genic selection coefficients are "purely qualitative" if genotypic coefficients are, yet their logical relationship to each other exactly parallels that of "grue" to "green". Predicates picking out real properties can be "gruified" in a purely qualitative way: Let F and G be purely qualitative and be true of all the objects sampled (the emeralds, say). The predicate "$(F$ and $G)$ or $(-F$ and $-G)$" is a gruification of F and poses the same set of problems as Goodman's "grue".

12. Joseph (1980) has argued that this position, in treating the distribution of objects as given and then raising epistemological problems about the existence of forces, is committed to the existence of an asymmetry between attributions of quantities of *mass* to points in space-time and attributions of quantities of *energy* thereto. He argues that this idea, implicit in Reichenbach's (1958) classic argument for the conventionality of geometry, contradicts the relativistic equivalence of mass and energy. If this is right, then the positivistic view of force just described, far from falling out of received physical theory, in fact contradicts it.

13. For the purpose of this discussion, we will assume that attributions of dispositions and subjunctive conditionals of certain kinds are equivalent. That is, we will assume that to say that x is disposed to F is merely to say that if conditions were such-and-such, x would F.

14. This position is precisely the opposite of that taken by Cartwright (1980a), who argues that net forces, rather than component forces, are the items which really exist. Cartwright argues this by pointing out that the billiard ball moves northwesterly and not due north or due west. However, this appears to conflate the *effect* of a force with the force or forces actually at work.

References

Achinstein, P. (1974), "The Identity of Properties," *American Philosophical Quarterly* 11, 4: pp. 257–75.

Armstrong, D. (1978), *Universals and Scientific Realism*. Cambridge: Cambridge University Press.

Carnap, R. (1947), "On the Application of Inductive Logic," *Philosophy and Phenomenological Research* 8: pp. 133–47.

Cartwright, N. (1980a), "Do the Laws of Nature State the Facts?", *Pacific Philosophical Quarterly* 61, 1: pp. 75–84.

Cartwright, N. (1980b), "The Truth Doesn't Explain Much," *American Philosophical Quarterly* 17, 2: pp. 159–63.

Dawkins, R. (1976), *The Selfish Gene*. Oxford: Oxford University Press.

Doolittle, W. and Sapienza, C. (1980), "Selfish Genes, The Phenotype Paradigm, and Genome Evolution," *Nature* 284: 601–3.

Fisher, R. (1930), *The Genetical Theory of Natural Selection*. New York: Dover.

Goodman, N. (1965), *Fact, Fiction, and Forecast*. Indianapolis: Bobbs Merrill.

Joseph, G. (1979), "Riemannian Geometry and Philosophical Conventionalism," *Australasian Journal of Philosophy* 57, 3: pp. 225–36.

Joseph, G. (1980), "The Many Sciences and the One World," *Journal of Philosophy* LXXVII, 12: 773–90.

Lewontin, R. (1970), "The Units of Selection," *Annual Review of Ecology and Systematics* 1, 1: pp. 1–14.

Lewontin, R. (1974), *The Genetic Basis of Evolutionary Change*. New York: Columbia University Press.

Lewontin, R. and Dunn. L. (1960), "The Evolutionary Dynamics of a Polymorphism in the House Mouse," *Genetics* 45: pp. 705–22.

Li, C. (1955), *Populatian Genetics*. Chicago: University of Chicago Press.

Mayr, E. (1963), *Animal Species and Evolution*. Cambridge: Harvard University Press.

Mills, S. and Beatty, J. (1979), "The Propensity Interpretation of Fitness," *Philosophy of Science* 46: 263–86.

Orgel, L. and Crick, F. (1980), "Selfish DNA: The Ultimate Parasite," *Nature* 284: pp. 604–7.

Reichenbach, H. (1958), *The Philosophy of Space and Time*. New York: Dover.

Shoemaker, S. (1980), "Causality and Properties," in P. van Inwagen (ed.), *Essays in Honor of Richard Taylor*. Dordrecht: Reidel.

Sober, E. (1980), "Holism, Individualism, and the Units of Selection," in P. Asquith and R. Giere (eds.) *PSA 1980*, vol. 2, Proceedings of the 1980 Biennial Meeting of the Philosophy of Science Association: East Lansing, Michigan.

Sober, E. (1981a), "Evolutionary Theory and the Ontological Status of Properties," *Philosophical Studies* 40: 147–176.

Sober, E. (1982a), "Realism and Independence," *Noûs*, 16, 3: 369–386.

Sober, E. (1982b), "Why Logically Equivalent Predicates May Pick Out Different Properties," *American Philosophical Quarterly*, 19, 2: 183–189.

Williams, G. (1966), *Adaptation and Natural Selection*. Princeton: Princeton University Press.

Wimsatt, W. (1980), "Reductionistic Research Strategies and Their Biases in the Units of Selection Controversy," in T. Nickles (ed.), *Scientific Discovery*, vol. 2, *Case Studies*. Dordrecht: Reidel.

Chapter 32

The Return of the Gene

Kim Sterelny and Philip Kitcher

We have two images of natural selection. The orthodox story is told in terms of individuals. More organisms of any given kind are produced than can survive and reproduce to their full potential. Although these organisms are of a kind, they are not identical. Some of the differences among them make a difference to their prospects for survival or reproduction, and hence, on the average, to their actual reproduction. Some of the differences which are relevant to survival and reproduction are (at least partly) heritable. The result is evolution under natural selection, a process in which, barring complications, the average fitness of the organisms within a kind can be expected to increase with time.

There is an alternative story. Richard Dawkins[1] claims that the "unit of selection" is the gene. By this he means not just that the result of selection is (almost always) an increase in frequency of some gene in the gene pool. That is uncontroversial. On Dawkins's conception, we should think of genes as differing with respect to properties that affect their abilities to leave copies of themselves. More genes appear in each generation than can copy themselves up to their full potential. Some of the differences among them make a difference to their prospects for successful copying and hence to the number of actual copies that appear in the next generation. Evolution under natural selection is thus a process in which, barring complication, the average ability of the genes in the gene pool to leave copies of themselves increases with time.

Dawkins's story can be formulated succinctly by introducing some of his terminology. Genes are *replicators* and selection is the struggle among *active germ-line* replicators. Replicators are entities that can be copied. Active replicators are those whose properties influence their chances of being copied. Germ-line replicators are those which have the potential to leave infinitely many descendants. Early in the history of life, coalitions of replicators began to construct *vehicles* through which they spread copies of themselves. Better replicators build better vehicles, and hence are copied more often. Derivatively, the vehicles associated with them become more common too. The orthodox story focuses on the successes of prominent vehicles—individual organisms. Dawkins claims to expose an underlying struggle among the replicators.

We believe that a lot of unnecessary dust has been kicked up in discussing the merits of the two stories. Philosophers have suggested that there are important connections to certain issues in the philosophy of science: reductionism, views on causation and natural kinds, the role of appeals to parsimony. We are unconvinced. Nor do we think that a willingness to talk about selection in Dawkinspeak brings any commitment to the adaptationist claims which Dawkins also holds. After all, adopting a particular perspective on selection is logically independent from claiming that selection is omnipresent in evolution.

Reprinted from *Journal of Philosophy* 85, no. 7 (July 1988), pp. 339–361, by permission of the author and the publisher. Copyright 1988 by *Journal of Philosophy*.

In our judgment, the relative worth of the two images turns on two theoretical claims in evolutionary biology:

1. Candidate units of selection must have systematic causal consequences. If Xs are selected for, then X must have a systematic effect on its expected representation in future generations.

2. Dawkins's gene selectionism offers a *more general theory* of evolution. It can also handle those phenomena which are grist to the mill of individual selection, but there are evolutionary phenomena which fit the picture of individual selection ill or not at all, yet which can be accommodated naturally by the gene selection model.

Those skeptical of Dawkins's picture—in particular, Elliott Sober, Richard Lewontin, and Stephen Jay Gould—doubt whether genes can meet the condition demanded in (1). In their view, the phenomena of epigenesis and the extreme sensitivity of the phenotype to gene combinations and environmental effects undercut genic selectionism. Although we believe that these critics have offered valuable insights into the character of sophisticated evolutionary modeling, we shall try to show that these insights do not conflict with Dawkins's story of the workings of natural selection. We shall endeavor to free the thesis of genic selectionism from some of the troublesome excrescences which have attached themselves to an interesting story.

I. Gene Selection and Bean-bag Genetics

Sober and Lewontin[2] argue against the thesis that all selection is genic selection by contending that many instances of selection do not involve selection for properties of individual alleles. Stated rather loosely, the claim is that, in some populations, properties of individual alleles are not positive causal factors in the survival and reproductive success of the relevant organisms. Instead of simply resting this claim on an appeal to our intuitive ideas about causality, Sober has recently provided an account of causal discourse which is intended to yield the conclusion he favors, thus rebutting the proposals of those (like Dawkins) who think that properties of individual alleles can be causally efficacious.[3]

The general problem arises because replicators (genes) combine to build vehicles (organisms) and the effect of a gene is critically dependent on the company it keeps. However, recognizing the general problem, Dawkins seeks to disentangle the various contributions of the members of the coalition of replicators (the genome). To this end, he offers an analogy with a process of competition among rowers for seats in a boat. The coach may scrutinize the relative times of different teams but the competition can be analyzed by investigating the contributions of individual rowers in different contexts (SG 40/1 91/2, EP 239).

Sober's Case

At the general level, we are left trading general intuitions and persuasive analogies. But Sober (and, earlier, Sober and Lewontin) attempted to clarify the case through a particular example. Sober argues that *heterozygote superiority* is a phenomenon that cannot be understood from Dawkins's standpoint. We shall discuss Sober's example in detail; our strategy is as follows. We first set out Sober's case: heterozygote superiority cannot be understood as a gene-level phenomenon, because only pairs of genes can be, or fail to be, heterozygous. Yet being heterozygous can be causally salient in the selective process. Against Sober, we first offer an analogy to show that there must be something wrong with his line of thought: from the gene's eye view, heterozygote superiority is an instance of a standard selective phenomenon, namely *frequency-dependent* selection. The advantage (or disadvantage) of a trait can depend on the frequency of that trait in other members of the relevant population.

Having claimed that there is something wrong with Sober's argument, we then try to say what is wrong. We identify two principles on which the reasoning depends. First is a general claim about causal uniformity. Sober thinks that there can be selection for a property only if that property has a positive uniform effect on reproductive success. Second, and more specifically, in cases where the heterozygote is fitter, the individuals have no uniform causal effect. We shall try to undermine both principles, but the bulk of our criticism will be directed against the first.

Heterozygote superiority occurs when a heterozygote (with genotype *Aa*, say) is fitter than either homozygote (*AA* or *aa*). The classic example is human sickle-cell anemia: homozygotes for the normal allele in African populations produce functional hemoglobin but are vulnerable to malaria, homozygotes for the mutant ("sickling") allele suffer anemia (usually fatal), and heterozygotes avoid anemia while also having resistance to malaria. The effect of each allele varies with context, and the contexts across which variation occurs are causally relevant. Sober writes:

> In this case, the *a* allele does not have a unique causal role. Whether the gene *a* will be a positive or a negative causal factor in the survival and reproductive success of an organism depends on the genetic context. If it is placed next to a copy of *A*, *a* will mean an increase in fitness. If it is placed next to a copy of itself, the gene will mean a decrement in fitness (NS 303).

The argument against Dawkins expressed here seems to come in two parts. Sober relies on the principle

> (A) There is selection for property *P* only if in all causally relevant background conditions *P* has a positive effect on survival and reproduction.

He also adduces a claim about the particular case of heterozygote superiority.

> (B) Although we can understand the situation by noting that the heterozygote has a uniform effect on survival and reproduction, the property of having the *A* allele and the property of having the *a* allele cannot be seen as having uniform effects on survival and reproduction.

We shall argue that both (A) and (B) are problematic.

Let us start with the obvious reply to Sober's argument It seems that the heterozygote superiority case is akin to a familiar type of frequency-dependent selection. If the population consists just of *AAs* and a mutation arises, the *a*-allele, then, initially *a* is favored by selection. Even though it is very bad to be *aa*, *a* alleles are initially likely to turn up in the company of *A* alleles So they are likely to spread, and, as they spread, they find themselves alongside other *a* alleles, with the consequence that selection tells against them The scenario is very similar to a story we might tell about interactions among individual organisms If some animals resolve conflicts by playing hawk and others play dove, then, if a population is initially composed of hawks (and if the costs of bloody battle outweigh the benefits of gaining a single resource), doves will initially be favored by selection.[4] For they will typically interact with hawks, and, despite the fact that their expected gains from these interactions are zero, they will still fare better than their rivals whose expected gains from interactions are negative. But, as doves spread in the population, hawks will meet them more frequently, with the result that the expected payoffs to hawks from interactions will increase. Because they increase more rapidly than the expected payoffs to the doves, there will be a point at which hawks become favored by selection, so that the incursion of doves into the population is halted.

We believe that the analogy between the case of heterozygote superiority and the hawk-dove case reveals that there is something troublesome about Sober's argument. The challenge is to say exactly what has gone wrong.

Causal Uniformity

Start with principle (A). Sober conceives of selection as a *force*, and he is concerned to make plain the effects of component forces in situations where different forces combine. Thus, he invites us to think of the heterozygote superiority case by analogy with situations in which a physical object remains at rest because equal and opposite forces are exerted on it. Considering the situation only in terms of net forces will conceal the causal structure of the situation. Hence, Sober concludes, our ideas about units of selection should penetrate beyond what occurs on the average, and we should attempt to isolate those properties which positively affect survival and reproduction in every causally relevant context.

Although Sober rejects determinism, principle (A) seems to hanker after something like the uniform association of effects with causes that deterministic accounts of causality provide. We believe that the principle cannot be satisfied without doing violence to ordinary ways of thinking about natural selection, and, once the violence has been exposed, it is not obvious that there is any way to reconstruct ideas about selection that will fit Sober's requirement.

Consider *the* example of natural selection, the case of industrial melanism.[5] We are inclined to say that the moths in a Cheshire wood, where lichens on many trees have been destroyed by industrial pollutants, have been subjected to selection pressure and that there has been selection for the property of being melanic. But a moment's reflection should reveal that this description is at odds with Sober's principle. For the wood is divisible into patches, among which are clumps of trees that have been shielded from the effects of industrialization. Moths who spend most of their lives in these areas are at a disadvantage if they are melanic. Hence, in the population comprising all the moths in the wood, there is no uniform effect on survival and reproduction: in some causally relevant contexts (for moths who have the property of living in regions where most of the trees are contaminated), the trait of being melanic has a positive effect on survival and reproduction, but there are other contexts in which the effect of the trait is negative.

The obvious way to defend principle (A) is to split the population into subpopulations and identify different selection processes as operative in different subgroups. This is a revisionary proposal, for our usual approach to examples of industrial melanism is to take a coarse-grained perspective on the environments, regarding the existence of isolated clumps of uncontaminated trees as a perturbation of the overall selective process. Nonetheless, we might be led to make the revision, not in the interest of honoring a philosophical prejudice, but simply because our general views about selection are consonant with principle (A), so that the reform would bring our treatment of examples into line with our most fundamental beliefs about selection.

In our judgment, a defense of this kind fails for two connected reasons. First, the process of splitting populations may have to continue much further—perhaps even to the extent that we ultimately conceive of individual organisms as making up populations in which a particular type of selection occurs. For, even in contaminated patches, there may be variations in the camouflaging properties of the tree trunks and these variations may combine with propensities of the moths to cause local disadvantages for melanic moths. Second, as many writers have emphasized, evolutionary theory is a statistical theory, not only in its recognition of drift as a factor in evolution but also in its use of fitness coefficients to represent the expected survivorship and reproductive success of organisms. The envisaged splitting of populations to discover some partition in which principle (A) can be maintained is at odds with the strategy of abstracting from the thousand natural shocks that organisms in natural populations are heir to. In principle, we could relate the biography of each organism in the population, explaining in full detail how it developed, reproduced, and survived, just as we could track the motion of each molecule of a sample of gas. But evolutionary theory, like statistical mechanics, has no use for such a fine grain of description: the aim is to make clear the central tendencies in the history of evolving populations, and, to this end, the strategy of averaging, which Sober decries, is entirely appropriate. We conclude that there is no basis for any revision that would eliminate those descriptions which run counter to principle (A).

At this point, we can respond to the complaints about the gene's eye view representation of cases of heterozygote superiority. Just as we can give sense to the idea that the trait of being melanic has a unique environment-dependent effect on survival and reproduction, so too we can explicate the view that a property of alleles, to wit, the property of directing the formation of a particular kind of hemoglobin, has a unique environment-dependent effect on survival and reproduction. The alleles form parts of one another's environments, and, in an environment in which a copy of the A allele is present, the typical trait of the S allele (namely, directing the formation of deviant hemoglobin) will usually have a positive effect on the chances that copies of that allele will be left in the next generation. (Notice that the effect will not be invariable, for there are other parts of the genomic environment which could wreak havoc with it). If someone protests that the incorporation of alleles as themselves part of the environment is suspect, then the immediate rejoinder is that, in cases of behavioral interactions, we are compelled to treat organisms as parts of one another's environments.[6] The effects of playing hawk depend on the nature of the environment, specifically on the frequency of doves in the vicinity.[7]

The Causal Powers of Alleles

We have tried to develop our complaints about principle (A) into a positive account of how cases of heterozygote superiority might look from the gene's eye view. We now want to focus more briefly on (B). Is it impossible to reinterpret the examples of heterozygote superiority so as to ascribe uniform effects on survival and reproduction to allelic properties? The first point to note is that Sober's approach formulates the Dawkinsian point of view in the wrong way: the emphasis should be on the effects of properties of alleles, not on allelic properties of organisms (like the property of having an A allele) and the accounting ought to be done in terms of allele copies. Second, although we argued above that the strategy of splitting populations was at odds with the character of evolutionary theory, it is worth noting that the same strategy will be available in the heterozygote superiority case.

Consider the following division of the original population: let P_1 be the collection of all those allele copies which occur next to an S allele, and let P_2 consist of all those allele copies which occur next to an A allele. Then the property of being A (or of directing the production of normal hemoglobin) has a positive effect on the production of copies in the next generation in P_1, and conversely in P_2. In this way, we are able to partition the population and to achieve a Dawkinsian redescription that meets Sober's principle (A)—just in the way that we might try to do so if we wanted to satisfy (A) in understanding the operation of selection on melanism in a Cheshire wood or on fighting strategies in a population containing a mixture of hawks and doves.

Objection: the "populations" just defined are highly unnatural, and this can be seen once we recognize that, in some cases, allele copies in the same organisms (the heterozygotes) belong to different "populations." Reply: so what? From the allele's point of view, the copy next door is just a critical part of the environment. The populations P_1 and P_2 simply pick out the alleles that share the same environment. There would be an analogous partition of a population of competing organisms which occurred locally in pairs such that some organisms played dove and some hawk. (Here, mixed pairs would correspond to heterozygotes.)

So the genic picture survives an important initial challenge. The moral of our story so far is that the picture must be applied consistently. Just as paradoxical conclusions will result if one offers a partial translation of geometry into arithmetic, it is possible to generate perplexities by failing to recognize that the Dawkinsian *Weltanschauung* leads to new conceptions of environment and of population. We now turn to a different worry, the objection that genes are not "visible" to selection.

II. Epigenesis and Visibility

In a lucid discussion of Dawkins's early views, Gould claims to find a "fatal flaw" in the genic approach to selection. According to Gould, Dawkins is unable to give genes "direct visibility to natural selection."[8] Bodies must play intermediary roles in the process of selection, and, since the properties of genes do not map in one-one fashion onto the properties of bodies, we cannot attribute selective advantages to individual alleles. We believe that Gould's concerns raise two important kinds of issues for the genic picture: (i) Can Dawkins sensibly talk of the effect of an individual allele on its expected copying frequency? (ii) Can Dawkins meet the charge that it is the phenotype that makes the difference to the copying of the underlying alleles, so that, whatever the causal basis of an advantageous trait, the associated allele copies will have enhanced chances of being replicated? We shall take up these questions in order.

Do Alleles Have Effects?

Dawkins and Gould agree on the facts of embryology which subvert the simple Mendelian association of one gene with one character. But the salience of these facts to the debate is up for grabs. Dawkins regards Gould as conflating the demands of embryology with the demands of the theory of evolution. While genes' effects blend in embryological development, and while they have phenotypic effects only in concert with their gene-mates, genes "do not blend as they replicate and recombine down the generations. It is this that matters for the geneticist, and it is also this that matters for the student of units of selection" (EP 117).

Is Dawkins right? Chapter 2 of EP is an explicit defense of the meaningfulness of talk of "genes for" indefinitely complex morphological and behavioral traits. In this, we believe, Dawkins is faithful to the practice of classical geneticists. Consider the vast number of loci in *Drosophila melanogaster* which are labeled for eye-color traits—white, eosin, vermilion, raspberry, and so forth. Nobody who subscribes to this practice of labeling believes that a pair of appropriately chosen stretches of DNA, cultured in splendid isolation, would produce a detached eye of the pertinent color. Rather, the intent is to indicate the effect that certain changes at a locus would make against the background of the rest of the genome.

Dawkins's project here is important not just in conforming to traditions of nomenclature. Remember: Dawkins needs to show that we can sensibly speak of alleles having (environment-sensitive) effects, effects in virtue of which they are selected for or selected against. If we can talk of a gene for X, where X is a selectively important phenotypic characteristic, we can sensibly talk of the effect of an allele on its expected copying frequency, even if the effects are always indirect, via the characteristics of some vehicle.

What follows is a rather technical reconstruction of the relevant notion. The precision is needed to allow for the extreme environmental sensitivity of allelic causation. But the intuitive idea is simple: we can speak of genes for X if substitutions on a chromosome would lead, in the relevant environments, to a difference in the X-ishness of the phenotype.

Consider a species S and an arbitrary locus L in the genome of members of S. We want to give sense to the locution 'L is a locus affecting P' and derivatively to the phrase 'G is a gene for P^*' (where, typically, P will be a determinable and P^* a determinate form of P). Start by taking an *environment* for a locus to be an aggregate of DNA segments that would complement L to form the genome of a member of S together with a set of extra-organismic factors (those aspects of the world external to the organism which we would normally count as part of the organism's environment). Let a set of variants for L be any collection of DNA segments, none of which is debarred, on physico-chemical grounds, from occupying L. (This is obviously a very weak constraint, intended only to rule out those segments which are too long or which have peculiar physico-chemical properties). Now, we say that L is a locus affecting P in S relative to an environment E and a set of variants V just in case there are segments s, s^*, and s^{**} in V such that the substitution of s^{**} for s^* in an organism having s and s^* at L would cause a difference in the form of P, against the background of E. In other words, given the environment E, organisms who are ss^* at L differ in the form of P from organisms who are ss^{**} at L and the cause of the difference is the presence of s^* rather than s^{**}. (A minor clarification: while s^* and s^{**} are distinct, we do not assume that they are both different from s.)

L is a locus affecting P in S just in case L is a locus affecting P in S relative to any standard environment and a feasible set of variants. Intuitively, the geneticist's practice of labeling loci focuses on the "typical" character of the complementary part of the genome in the species, the "usual" extra-organismic environment, and the variant DNA segments which have arisen in the past by mutation or which "are likely to arise" by mutation. Can these vague ideas about standard conditions be made more precise? We think so. Consider first the genomic part of the environment. There will be numerous alternative combinations of genes at the loci other than L present in the species S. Given most of these gene combinations, we expect modifications at L to produce modifications in the form of P. But there are likely to be some exceptions, cases in which the presence of a rare allele at another locus or a rare combination of alleles produces a phenotypic effect that dominates any effect on P. We can either dismiss the exceptional cases as nonstandard because they are infrequent or we can give a more refined analysis, proposing that each of the nonstandard cases involves either (a) a rare allele at a locus L' or (b) a rare combination of alleles at loci L', L'' ... such that that locus (a) or those loci jointly (b) affect some phenotypic trait Q that dominates P in the sense that there are modifications of Q which prevent the expression of any modifications of P. As a concrete example, consider the fact that there are modifications at some loci in *Drosophila* which produce embryos that fail to develop heads; given such modifications elsewhere in the genome, alleles affecting eye color do not produce their standard effects!

We can approach standard extra-genomic environments in the same way. If L affects the form of P in organisms with a typical gene complement, except for those organisms which encounter certain rare combinations of external factors, then we may count those combinations as nonstandard simply because of their infrequency. Alternatively, we may allow rare combinations of external factors to count provided that they do not produce some gross interference with the organism's development, and we can render the last notion more precise by taking nonstandard environments to be those in which the population mean fitness of organisms in S would be reduced by some arbitrarily chosen factor (say, 1/2).

Finally, the feasible variants are those which actually occur at L in members of S, together with those which have occurred at L in past members of S and those which are easily attainable from segments that actually occur at L in members of S by means of insertion, deletion, substitution, or transposition. Here the criteria for ease of attainment are given by the details of molecular biology. If an allele is prevalent at L in S, then modifications at sites where the molecular structure favors insertions, deletions, substitutions, or transpositions (so-called "hot spots") should count as easily attainable even if some of these modifications do not actually occur.

Obviously, these concepts of "standard conditions" could be articulated in more detail, and we believe that it is possible to generate a variety of explications, agreeing on the core of central cases but adjusting the boundaries of the concepts in different ways. If we now assess the labeling practices of geneticists, we expect to find that virtually all of their claims about loci affecting a phenotypic trait are sanctioned by all of the explications. Thus, the challenge that there is no way to honor the facts of epigenesis while speaking of loci that affect certain traits would be turned back.

Once we have come this far, it is easy to take the final step. An allele A at a locus L in a species S is for the trait P^* (assumed to be a determinate form of the determinable characteristic P) relative to a local allele B and an environment E just in case (a) L affects the form of P in S, (b) E is a standard environment, and (c) E organisms that are AB have phenotype P^*. The relativization to a local allele is necessary, of course, because, when we focus on a target allele rather than a locus, we have to extend the notion of the environment—as we saw in the last section, corresponding alleles are potentially important parts of one another's environments. If we say that A is for P^* (period), we are claiming that A is for P^* relative to standard environments and common local alleles or that A is for P^* relative to standard environments and itself.

Now, let us return to Dawkins and to the apparently outré claim that we can talk about genes for reading. Reading is an extraordinarily complex behavior pattern and surely no adaptation. Further, many genes must be present and the extra-organismic environment must be right for a human being to be able to acquire the ability to read. Dyslexia might result from the substitution of an unusual mutant allele at one of the loci, however. Given our account, it will be correct to say that the mutant allele is a gene for dyslexia and also that the more typical alleles at the locus are alleles for reading. Moreover, if the locus also affects some other (determinable) trait, say the capacity to factor numbers into primes, then it may turn out that the mutant allele is also an allele for rapid factorization skill and that the typical allele is an allele for factorization disability. To say that A is an allele for P^* does not preclude saying that A is an allele for Q^*, nor does it commit us to supposing that the phenotypic properties in question are either both skills or both disabilities. Finally, because substitutions at many loci may produce (possibly different types of) dyslexia, there may be many genes for dyslexia and many genes for reading. Our reconstruction of the geneticists' idiom, the idiom which Dawkins wants to use, is innocent of any Mendelian theses about one-one mappings between genes and phenotypic traits.

Visibility

So we can defend Dawkins's thesis that alleles have properties that influence their chances of leaving copies in later generations by suggesting that, in concert with their environments (including their genetic environments), those alleles cause the presence of certain properties in vehicles (such as organisms) and that the properties of the vehicles are causally relevant to the spreading of copies of the alleles. But our answer to question (i) leads naturally to concerns about question (ii). Granting that an allele is for a phenotypic trait P^* and that the presence of P^* rather than alternative forms of the determinable trait P enhances the chances that an organism will survive and reproduce and thus transmit copies of the underlying allele, is it not P^* and its competition which are directly involved in the selection process? What selection "sees" are the phenotypic properties. When this vague, but suggestive, line of thought has been made precise, we think that there is an adequate Dawkinsian reply to it.

The idea that selection acts directly on phenotypes, expressed in metaphorical terms by Gould (and earlier by Ernst Mayr), has been explored in an interesting essay by Robert Brandon.[9] Brandon proposes that phenotypic traits screen off genotypic traits (in the sense of Wesley Salmon[10]):

$$\Pr(O_n/G \,\&\, P) = \Pr(O_n/P) \neq \Pr(O_n/G),$$

where $\Pr(O_n/G \,\&\, P)$ is the probability that an organism will produce n offspring given that it has both a phenotypic trait and the usual genetic basis for that trait, $\Pr(O_n/P)$ is the probability that an organism will produce n offspring given that it has the phenotypic trait, and $\Pr(O_n/G)$ is the probability that it will produce n offspring given that it has the usual genetic basis. So fitness seems to vary more directly with the phenotype and less directly with the underlying genotype.

Why is this? The root idea is that the successful phenotype may occur in the presence of the wrong allele as a result of judicious tampering, and, conversely, the typical effect of a "good" allele may be subverted. If we treat moth larvae with appropriate injections, we can produce pseudomelanics that have the allele which normally gives rise to the speckled form and we can produce moths, foiled melanics, that carry the allele for melanin in which the developmental pathway to the emergence of black wings is blocked. The pseudomelanics will enjoy enhanced reproductive success in polluted woods and the foiled melanics will be at a disadvantage. Recognizing this type of possibility, Brandon concludes that selection acts at the level of the phenotype.[11]

Once again, there is no dispute about the facts. But our earlier discussion of epigenesis should reveal how genic selectionists will want to tell a different story. The interfering conditions that affect the phenotype of the vehicle are understood as parts of the allelic environment. In effect, Brandon, Gould, and Mayr contend that, in a polluted wood, there is selection for being dark colored rather than for the allelic property of directing the production of melanin, because it would be possible to have the reproductive advantage associated with the phenotype without having the allele (and conversely it would be possible to lack the advantage while possessing the allele). Champions of the gene's eye view will maintain that tampering with the phenotype reverses the typical effect of an allele by changing the environment. For these cases involve modification of the allelic environment and give rise to new selection processes in which allelic properties currently in favor prove detrimental. The fact that selection goes differently in the two environments is no more relevant than the fact that selection for melanic coloration may go differently in Cheshire and in Dorset.

If we do not relativize to a fixed environment, then Brandon's claims about screening off will not generally be true.[12] We suppose that Brandon intends to relativize to a fixed environment. But now he has effectively begged the question against the genic selectionist by deploying the orthodox conception of environment. Genic selectionists will also want to relativize to the environment, but they should resist the orthodox conception of it. On their view, the probability relations derived by Brandon involve an illicit averaging over environments (see fn. 12). Instead, genic selectionists should propose that the probability of an allele's leaving n copies of itself should be understood relative to the total allelic environment, and that the specification of the total environment ensures that there is no screening off of allelic properties by phenotypic properties. The probability of producing n copies of the allele for melanin in a total allelic environment is invariant under conditionalization on phenotype.

Here too the moral of our story is that Dawkinspeak must be undertaken consistently. Mixing orthodox concepts of the environment with ideas about genic selection is a recipe for trouble, but we have tried to show how the genic approach can be thoroughly articulated so as to meet major objections. But what is the point of doing so? We shall close with a survey of some advantages and potential drawbacks.

III. Genes and Generality

Relatively little fossicking is needed to uncover an extended defense of the view that gene selectionism offers a more general and unified picture of selective processes than can be had from its alternatives. Phenomena anomalous for the orthodox story of evolution by individual selection fall naturally into place from Dawkins' viewpoint. He offers a revision of the "central theorem" of Darwinism. Instead of expecting individuals to act in their best interests, we should expect an animal's behavior "to maximize the survival of genes 'for' that behavior, whether or not those genes happen to be in the body of that particular animal performing it" (EP 223).

The cases that Dawkins uses to illustrate the superiority of his own approach are a somewhat motley collection. They seem to fall into two general categories. First are outlaw and quasi-outlaw examples. Here there is competition among genes which cannot be translated into talk of vehicle fitness because the competition is among cobuilders of a single vehicle. The second group comprises "extended phenotype" cases, instances in which a gene (or combination of genes) has selectively relevant phenotypic consequences which are not traits of the vehicle that it has helped build. Again the replication potential of the gene cannot be translated into talk of the adaptedness of its vehicle.

We shall begin with outlaws and quasi outlaws. From the perspective of the orthodox story of individual selection, "replicators at different loci within the same body can be expected to 'cooperate'." The allele surviving at any given locus tends to be one best (subject to all the constraints) for the whole genome. By and large this is a reasonable assumption. Whereas individual outlaw organisms are perfectly possible in groups and subvert the chances for groups to act as vehicles, outlaw genes seem problematic. Replication of any gene in the genome requires the organism to survive and reproduce, so genes share a substantial common interest. This is true of asexual reproduction, and, granting the fairness of meiosis, of sexual reproduction too.

But there is the rub. Outlaw genes are genes which subvert meiosis to give them a better than even chance of making it to the gamete, typically by sabotaging their corresponding allele (EP 136). Such genes are *segregation distorters* or *meiotic drive* genes. Usually, they are enemies not only of their alleles but of other parts of the genome, because they reduce the individual fitness of the organism they inhabit. Segregation distorters thrive, when they do, because they exercise their phenotypic power to beat the meiotic lottery. Selection for such genes cannot be selection for traits that make organisms more likely to survive and reproduce. They provide uncontroversial cases of selective processes in which the individualistic story cannot be told.

There are also related examples. Altruistic genes can be outlawlike, discriminating against their genome mates in favor of the inhabitants of other vehicles, vehicles that contain copies of themselves. Start with a hypothetical case, the so-called "green beard" effect. Consider a gene Q with two phenotypic effects. Q causes its vehicle to grow a green beard and to behave altruistically toward green-bearded conspecifics. Q's replication prospects thus improve, but the particular vehicle that Q helped build does not have its prospects for survival and reproduction enhanced. Is Q an outlaw not just with respect to the vehicle but with respect to the vehicle builders? Will there be selection for alleles that suppress Q's effect? How the selection process goes will depend on the probability that Q's cobuilders are beneficiaries as well. If Q is reliably associated with other gene kinds, those kinds will reap a net benefit from Q's outlawry.

So altruistic genes are sometimes outlaws. Whether coalitions of other genes act to suppress them depends on the degree to which they benefit only themselves. Let us now move from a hypothetical example to the parade case.

Classical fitness, an organism's propensity to leave descendants in the next generation, seems a relatively straightforward notion. Once it was recognized that Darwinian processes do not necessarily favor organisms with high classical fitness, because classical fitness ignores indirect effects of costs and benefits to relatives, a variety of alternative measures entered the literature. The simplest of these would be to add to the classical fitness of an organism contributions from the classical fitness of relatives (weighted in each case by the coefficient of relatedness). Although accounting of this sort is prevalent, Dawkins (rightly) regards it as just wrong, for it involves double bookkeeping and, in consequence, there is no guarantee that populations will move to local maxima of the defined quantity. This measure and measures akin to it, however, are prompted by Hamilton's rigorous development of the theory of inclusive fitness (in which it is shown that populations will tend toward local maxima of inclusive fitness).[13] In the misunderstanding and misformulation of Hamilton's ideas, Dawkins sees an important moral.

Hamilton, he suggests, appreciated the gene selectionist insight that natural selection will favor "organs and behavior that cause the individual's genes to be passed on, whether or not the individual is an ancestor" (EP 185). But Hamilton's own complex (and much misunderstood) notion of inclusive fitness was, for all its theoretical importance, a dodge, a "brilliant last-ditch rescue attempt to save the individual organism as the level at which we think about natural selection" (EP 187). More concretely, Dawkins is urging two claims: first, that the uses of the concept of inclusive fitness in practice are difficult, so that scientists often make mistakes; second, that such uses are conceptually misleading. The first point is defended by identifying examples from the literature in which good researchers have made errors, errors which become obvious once we adopt the gene selectionist perspective. Moreover, even when the inclusive fitness calculations make the right predictions, they often seem to mystify the selective process involved (thus buttressing Dawkins's second thesis). Even those who are not convinced of the virtues of gene selectionism should admit that it is very hard to see the reproductive output of an organism's relatives as a property of that organism.

Let us now turn to the other family of examples, the "extended phenotype" cases. Dawkins gives three sorts of "extended" phenotypic effects: effects of genes—indeed key weapons in the competitive struggle to replicate—which are not traits of the vehicle the genes inhabit. The examples are of artifacts, of parasitic effects on host bodies and behaviors, and of "manipulation" (the subversion of an organism's normal patterns of behavior by the genes of another organism via the manipulated organism's nervous system).

Among many vivid, even haunting, examples of parasitic behavior, Dawkins describes cases in which parasites synthesize special hormones with the consequence that their hosts take on phenotypic traits that decrease their own prospects for reproduction but enhance those of the parasites (see, for a striking instance, EP 215). There are equally forceful cases of manipulation: cuckoo fledglings subverting their host's parental program, parasitic queens taking over a hive and having its members work for her. Dawkins suggests that the traits in question should be viewed as adaptations—properties for which selection has occurred—even though they cannot be seen as adaptations of the individuals whose reproductive success they promote, for those individuals do not possess the relevant traits. Instead, we are to think in terms of selectively advantageous characteristics of alleles which orchestrate the behavior of several different vehicles, some of which do not include them.

At this point there is an obvious objection. Can we not understand the selective processes that are at work by focusing not on the traits that are external to the vehicle that carries the genes, but on the behavior that the vehicle performs which brings those traits about? Consider a spider's web. Dawkins wants to talk of a gene for a web. A web, of course, is not a characteristic of a spider. Apparently, however, we could talk of a gene for web building. Web building is a trait of spiders, and, if we choose to redescribe the phenomena in these terms, the extended phenotype is brought closer to home. We now have a trait of the vehicle in which the genes reside, and we can tell an orthodox story about natural selection for this trait.

It would be tempting to reply to this objection by stressing that the selective force acts through the artifact. The causal chain from the gene to the web is complex and indirect; the behavior is only a part of it. Only one element of the chain is distinguished, the endpoint, the web itself, and that is because, independently of what has gone on earlier, provided that the web is in place, the enhancement of the replication chances of the underlying allele will ensue. But this reply is exactly parallel to the Mayr-Gould-Brandon argument discussed in the last section, and it should be rejected for exactly parallel reasons.

The correct response, we believe, is to take Dawkins at his word when he insists on the possibility of a number of different ways of looking at the same selective processes. Dawkins's two main treatments of natural selection, SG and EP, offer distinct versions of the thesis of genic selectionism. In the earlier discussion (and occasionally in the later) the thesis is that, for any selection process, there is a uniquely correct representation of that process, a representation which captures the causal structure of the process, and this representation attributes causal efficacy to genic properties. In EP, especially in chapters 1 and 13, Dawkins proposes a weaker version of the thesis, to the effect that there are often alternative, equally adequate representations of selection processes and that, for any selection process, there is a maximally adequate representation which attributes causal efficacy to genic properties. We shall call the strong (early) version *monist genic selectionism* and the weak (later) version *pluralist genic selectionism*. We believe that the monist version is faulty but that the pluralist thesis is defensible.

In presenting the "extended phenotype" cases, Dawkins is offering an alternative representation of processes that individualists can redescribe in their own preferred terms by adopting the strategy illustrated in our discussion of spider webs. Instead of talking of genes for webs and their selective advantages, it is possible to discuss the case in terms of the benefits that accrue to spiders who have a disposition to engage in web building. There is no privileged way to segment the causal chain and isolate the (really) real causal story. As we noted two paragraphs back, the analog of the Mayr-Gould-Brandon argument for the priority of those properties which are most directly connected with survival and reproduction—here the webs themselves—is fallacious. Equally, it is fallacious to insist that the causal story must be told by focusing on traits of individuals which contribute to the reproductive success of those individuals. We are left with the general thesis of pluralism: there are alternative, maximally adequate representations of the causal structure of the selection process. Add to this Dawkins's claim that one can always find a way to achieve a representation in terms of the causal efficacy of genic properties, and we have pluralist genic selectionism.

Pluralism of the kind we espouse has affinities with some traditional views in the philosophy of science. Specifically, our approach is instrumentalist, not of course in denying the existence of entities like genes, but in opposing the idea that natural selection is a force that acts on some determinate target, such as the genotype or the phenotype. Monists err, we believe, in claiming that selection processes must be described in a particular way, and their error involves them in positing entities, "targets of selection," that do not exist.

Another way to understand our pluralism is to connect it with conventionalist approaches to space-time theories. Just as conventionalists have insisted that there are alternative accounts of the phenomena which meet all our methodological desiderata, so too we maintain that selection processes can usually be treated, equally adequately, from more than one point of view. The virtue of the genic point of view, on the pluralist account, is not that it alone gets the causal structure right but that it is always available.

What is the rival position? Well, it cannot be the thesis that the only adequate representations are those in terms of individual traits which promote the reproductive success of their bearers, because there are instances in which no such representation is available (outlaws) and instances in which the representation is (at best) heuristically misleading (quasi-outlaws, altruism). The sensible rival position is that there is a hierarchy of selection processes: some cases are aptly represented in terms of genic selection, some in terms of individual selection, some in terms of group selection, and some (maybe) in terms of species selection. Hierarchical monism claims that, for any selection process, there is a unique level of the hierarchy such that only representations that depict selection as acting at that level are maximally adequate. (Intuitively, representations that see selection as acting at other levels get the causal structure wrong.) Hierarchical monism differs from pluralist genic selectionism in an interesting way: whereas the pluralist insists that, for any process, there are many adequate representations, one of which will always be a genic representation, the hierarchical monist maintains that for each process there is just one kind of adequate representation, but that processes are diverse in the kinds of representation they demand.[14]

Just as the simple orthodoxy of individualism is ambushed by outlaws and their kin, so too hierarchical monism is entangled in spider webs. In the "extended phenotype" cases, Dawkins shows that there are genic representations of selection processes which can be no more adequately illuminated from alternative perspectives. Since we believe that there is no compelling reason to deny the legitimacy of the individualist redescription in terms of web-building behavior (or dispositions to such behavior), we conclude that Dawkins should be taken at face value: just as we can adopt different perspectives on a Necker cube, so too we can look at the workings of selection in different ways (EP ch. 1).

In previous sections, we have tried to show how genic representations are available in cases that have previously been viewed as troublesome. To complete the defense of genic selectionism, we would need to extend our survey of problematic examples. But the general strategy should be evident. Faced with processes that others see in terms of group selection or species selection, genic selectionists will first try to achieve an individualist representation and then apply the ideas we have developed from Dawkins to make the translation to genic terms.

Pluralist genic selectionists recommend that practicing biologists take advantage of the full range of strategies for representing the workings of selection. The chief merit of Dawkinspeak is its generality. Whereas the individualist perspective may sometimes break down, the gene's eye view is apparently always available. Moreover, as illustrated by the treatment of inclusive fitness, adopting it may sometimes help us to avoid errors and confusions. Thinking of selection in terms of the devices, sometimes highly indirect, through which genes lever themselves into future generations may also suggest new approaches to familiar problems.

But are there drawbacks? Yes. The principal purpose of the early sections of this paper was to extend some of the ideas of genic selectionism to respond to concerns that are deep and important. Without an adequate rethinking of the concepts of population and of environment, genic representations will fail to capture processes that involve genic interactions or epigenetic constraints. Genic selectionism can easily slide into naive adaptationism as one comes to credit the individual alleles with powers that enable them to operate independently of one another. The move from the "genes for P" locution to the claim that selection can fashion P independently of other traits of the organism is perennially tempting.[15] But, in our version, genic representations must be constructed in full recognition of the possibilities for constraints in gene-environment coevolution. The dangers of genic selectionism, illustrated in some of Dawkins's own writings, are that the commitment to the complexity of the allelic environment is forgotten in practice. In defending the genic approach against important objections, we have been trying to make this commitment explicit, and thus to exhibit both the potential and the demands of correct Dawkinspeak. The return of the gene should not mean the exile of the organism.[16]

Notes

We are equally responsible for this paper which was written when we discovered that we were writing it independently. We would like to thank those who have offered helpful suggestions to one or both of us, particularly Patrick Bateson, Robert Brandon, Peter Godfrey-Smith, David Hull, Richard Lewontin, Lisa Lloyd, Philip Pettit, David Scheel, and Elliott Sober.

1. The claim is made in The Selfish Gene (New York: Oxford, 1976); and, in a somewhat modified form, in The Extended Phenotype (San Francisco: Freeman, 1982). We shall discuss the difference between the two versions in the final section of this paper, and our reconstruction will be primarily concerned with the later version of Dawkins's thesis. We shall henceforth refer to The Selfish Gene as SG, and to The Extended Phenotype as EP. To forestall any possible confusion, our reconstruction to Dawkins's position does not commit us to the provocative claims about altruism and selfishness on which many early critics of SG fastened.

2. "Artifact, Cause and Genic Selection," Philosophy of Science, XLIX (1982): 157–180 [this volume, chapter 31].

3. See Sober, *The Nature of Selection* (Cambridge: MIT, 1984), chs. 7–9, especially pp. 302–314. We shall henceforth refer to this book as NS.

4. For details, see John Maynard Smith, *Evolution and the Theory of Games* (New York: Cambridge, 1982); and, for a capsule presentation, Philip Kitcher, *Vaulting Ambition: Sociobiology and the Quest for Human Nature* (Cambridge: MIT, 1985), pp. 88–97.

5. The *locus classicus* for discussion of this example is H. B. D. Kettlewell, *The Evolution of Melanism* (New York: Oxford, 1973).

6. In the spirit of Sober's original argument, one might press further. Genic selectionists contend that an *A* allele can find itself in two different environments, one in which the effect of directing the formation of a normal globin chain is positive and one in which that effect is negative. Should we not be alarmed by the fact that the distribution of environments in which alleles are selected is itself a function of the frequency of the alleles whose selection we are following? No. The phenomenon is thoroughly familiar from studies of behavioral interactions—in the hawk-dove case we treat the frequency of hawks both as the variable we are tracking and as a facet of the environment in which selection occurs. Maynard Smith makes the parallel fully explicit in his paper "How To Model Evolution," in John Dupre, ed., *The Latest on the Best: Essays on Optimality and Evolution* (Cambridge: MIT, 1987), pp. 119–131, especially pp. 125/6.

7. Moreover, we can explicitly recognize the co-evolution of alleles with allelic environments. A fully detailed general approach to population genetics from the Dawkinsian point of view will involve equations that represent the functional dependence of the distribution of environments on the frequency of alleles, and equations that represent the fitnesses of individual alleles in different environments. In fact, this is just another way of looking at the standard population genetics equations. Instead of thinking of W_{AA} as the expected contribution to survival and reproduction of (an organism with) an allelic pair, we think of it as the expected contribution of copies of itself of the allele *A* in environment *A*. We now see W_{AS} as the expected contribution of *A* in environment *S* and also as the expected contribution of *S* in environment *A*. The frequencies *p*, *q* are not only the frequencies of the alleles, but also the frequencies with which certain environments occur. The standard definitions of the overall (net) fitnesses of the alleles are obtained by weighting the fitnesses in the different environments by the frequencies with which the environments occur.

   Lewontin has suggested to us that problems may arise with this scheme of interpretation if the population should suddenly start to reproduce asexually. But this hypothetical change could be handled from the genic point of view by recognizing an alteration of the coevolutionary process between alleles and their environments: whereas certain alleles used to have descendants that would encounter a variety of environments, their descendants are now found only in one allelic environment. Once the algebra has been formulated, it is relatively straightforward to extend the reinterpretation to this case.

8. "Caring Groups and Selfish Genes," in *The Panda's Thumb* (New York: Norton, 1980). p. 90. There is a valuable discussion of Gould's claims in Sober, NS 227 ff.

9. Gould, *op. cit.*; Mayr, *Animal Species and Evolution* (Cambridge: Harvard, 1963). p. 184; and Brandon, "The Levels of Selection," in Brandon and Richard Burian, eds., *Genes, Organisms, Populations* (Cambridge: MIT, 1984), pp. 133–141.

10. Brandon refers to Salmon's "Statistical Explanation," in Salmon, ed., *Statistical Explanation and Statistical Relevance* (Pittsburgh: University Press, 1971). It is now widely agreed that statistical relevance misses some distinctions which are important in explicating causal relevance. See, for example, Nancy Cartwright, "Causal Laws and Effective Strategies," *Noûs*, XIII (1979): 419–437; Sober, NS ch. 8; and Salmon, *Scientific Explanation and the Causal Structure of the World* (Princeton: University Press, 1984).

11. Unless the treatments are repeated in each generation, the presence of the genetic basis for melanic coloration will be correlated with an increased frequency of grandoffspring, or of great-grandoffspring, or of descendants in some further generation. Thus, analogs of Brandon's probabilistic relations will hold only if the progeny of foiled melanics are treated so as to become foiled melanics, and the progeny of pseudomelanics are treated so as to become pseudomelanics. This point reinforces the claims about the relativization to the environment that we make below. Brandon has suggested to us in correspondence that now his preferred strategy for tackling issues of the units of selection would be to formulate a principle for identifying genuine environments.

12. Intuitively, this will be because Brandon's identities depend on there being no correlation between O_n and *G* in any environment, except through the property *P*. Thus, ironically, the screening-off relations only obtain under the assumptions of simple bean-bag genetics! Sober seems to appreciate this point in a cryptic footnote (NS 229–230).

   To see how it applies in detail, imagine that we have more than one environment and that the reproductive advantages of melanic coloration differ in the different environments. Specifically, suppose that E_1 contains m_1 organisms that have P (melanic coloration) and G (the normal genetic basis of melanic coloration), that E_2 contains m_2 organisms that have P and G, and that the probabilities $Pr(O_n/G \& P \& E_1)$ and $Pr(O_n/G \& P \& E_2)$ are different. Then, if we do not relativize to environments, we shall compute $Pr(O_n/G \& P)$ as a weighted average of the probabilities relative to the two environments.

$$Pr(O_n/G \& P) = Pr(E_1/G \& P) \cdot Pr(O_n/G \& P \& E_1) + Pr(E_2/G \& P) \cdot Pr(O_n/G \& P \& E_2)$$

$$= m_1/(m_1 + m_2) \cdot Pr(O_n/G \& P \& E_1) + m_2/(m_1 + m_2) \cdot Pr(O_n/G \& P \& E_2)$$

Now, suppose that tampering occurs in E_2 so that there are m_3 pseudomelanics in E_2. We can write $Pr(O_n/P)$ as a weighted average of the probabilities relative to the two environments.

$$Pr(O_n/P) = Pr(E_1/P) \cdot Pr(O_n/P \& E_1) + Pr(E_2/P) \cdot Pr(O_n/P \& E_2).$$

By the argument that Brandon uses to motivate his claims about screening off, we can take $Pr(O_n/G \& P \& E_i) = Pr(O_n/P \& E_i)$ for $i = 1$, 2. However, $Pr(E_1/P) = m_1/(m_1 + m_2 + m_3)$ and $Pr(E_2/P) = (m_2 + m_3)/(m_1 + m_2 + m_3)$, so that $Pr(E_i/P) \neq Pr(E_i/G \& P)$. Thus, $Pr(O_n/G \& P) \neq Pr(O_n/P)$, and the claim about screening off fails.

Notice that, if environments are lumped in this way, then it will only be under fortuitous circumstances that the tampering makes the probabilistic relations come out as Brandon claims. Pseudomelanics would have to be added in both environments so that the weights remain exactly the same.

13. For Hamilton's original demonstration, see "The Genetical Evolution of Social Behavior I," in G. C. Williams, ed., *Group Selection* (Chicago: Aldine, 1971), pp. 23–43. For a brief presentation of Hamilton's ideas, see Kitcher, *op. cit.*, pp. 77–87; and for penetrating diagnoses of misunderstandings, see A. Grafen, "How Not to Measure Inclusive Fitness," *Nature*, CCXCVIII (1982): 425/6; and R. Michod, "The Theory of Kin Selection," in Brandon and Burian, *op. cit.*, pp. 203–237.

14. In defending pluralism, we are very close to the views expressed by Maynard Smith in "How To Model Evolution." Indeed, we would like to think that Maynard Smith's article and the present essay complement one another in a number of respects. In particular, as Maynard Smith explicitly notes, "recommending a plurality of models of the same process" contrasts with the view (defended by Gould and by Sober) of "emphasizing a plurality of processes." Gould's views are clearly expressed in "Is A New and General Theory of Evolution Emerging?" *Paleobiology*, VI (1980): 119–130; and Sober's ideas are presented in NS ch. 9.

15. At least one of us believes that the claims of the present paper are perfectly compatible with the critique of adaptationism developed in Gould and Lewontin, "The Spandrels of San Marco and the Panglossian Paradigm: A Critique of the Adaptationist Programme," in Sober, ed., *Conceptual Problems in Evolutionary Biology* (Cambridge: MIT, 1984). For discussion of the difficulties with adaptationism, see Kitcher, *Vaulting Ambition*, ch. 7; and 'Why Not The Best? in Dupre, *op. cit.*

16. As, we believe, Dawkins himself appreciates. See that last chapter of EP, especially his reaction to the claim that "Richard Dawkins has rediscovered the organism" (251).

Section III

The Philosophy of Psychology

J.D. Trout

When we attempt to predict and explain intelligent behavior, we ordinarily appeal to the actor's beliefs and desires. The idea that these states cause, and that their attribution routinely explains, rational behavior forms the core of a commonsense psychological theory, sometimes called "folk psychology."[1] Intentional state attributions are most evident in lay explanations, but they play a crucial role in a range of social sciences as well, such as microeconomics, sociology, anthropology, and psychology. It might be thought that the integrity of these explanatory domains thus depends on the vindication of commonsense psychology as a scientific theory worthy of the name.

Contemporary work in the philosophy of psychology represents two ways of assessing the scientific status of this folk theory. The first way compares the systematic explanatory power of folk psychology to that of more developed nonpsychological sciences. The second way examines successful areas of professional psychology and compares the theoretical kinds (e.g., states, processes, events, and properties) of the putative scientific psychology to those (e.g., belief, desire, fear, hope, etc.) mentioned in folk psychological generalizations. If folk psychology compares unfavorably (along the relevant dimensions) either to a developed nonpsychological science or to a scientific psychology, its status as a respectable explanatory theory is in doubt. The methodological issues raised in the following chapters bear most directly on disputes in the philosophy of psychology concerning the reliability of folk psychological generalization and the nature of psychological states, but they implicitly or explicitly raise familiar methodological questions in the philosophy of science as well, questions about the role of idealization, the problem of projectability, the identification of theoretical kinds, the epistemic status of explanatory power, and the plausibility of reductionism.[2]

Occasionally a comparison of two neighboring theories reveals both that one theory can explain the phenomena thought to be solely within the purview of another and that the ontology of the explained theory is superseded by that of the more comprehensive theory. In the first chapter of this section, Paul Churchland predicts the discovery of just such a relation between a future neuroscience and our time-worn folk psychology. Naming this bold perspective "eliminative materialism," Churchland argues that "our common-sense conception of psychological phenomena constitutes a radically false theory, a theory so fundamentally defective that both the principles and ontology of that theory will eventually be displaced, rather than smoothly reduced, by completed neuroscience."

Central to Churchland's eliminativist argument is the contention that folk psychology is an empirical theory and, as such, must face the prospect of defeat in empirical battle. Churchland claims that the folk psychological picture of cognitive activity is wedded to a linguistic account of the mental. But this account of cognitive activity, according to Churchland, governs only a superficial and narrow range of interesting psychological phenomena. It is said that folk psychology "cannot explain or fails even to address" such psychological phenomena as mental illness, the function of sleep and dreaming, the construction of 3-D visual representations from 2-D retinal projections, creative imagination, individual intelligence differences, memory, and motor controls of the sort involved in throwing and catching balls. We are thus forced to recognize that folk psychology "suffers explanatory failures on an epic scale."

This list looks pretty formidable. But even if the sentential account of folk psychology is correct,[3] there is some question whether folk psychology *should* address or explain the majority of the mental phenomena recorded here. Folk psychology might be reasonably regarded as a theory of normal, intelligent behavior. As the list of putative explanatory lacunae indicates, Churchland presupposes that folk psychology is defective, apparently on the grounds that it doesn't explain mental illness and subcognitive processes—in short, abnormal and nonintelligent phenomena. In both of these cases, it might be replied that it is no criticism of folk psychology that it fails to explain phenomena it isn't intended to explain. Even our best scientific theories often fall silent about phenomena they identify as abnormal or peripheral, an explanatory silence that is marked by the familiar "normal conditions" and "initial and boundary conditions" clauses in law-statements.

This defense would be quite feeble if folk psychology explained very few mental phenomena, but folk psychology may still make quite substantial claims. First, the balance of Churchland's list—creative imagination, intelligence differences, memory, and learning—includes just four of the areas of research being vigorously pursued with varying degrees of success by professional psychologists. Churchland charges that folk psychology "sheds negligible light" on these phenomena. But it appears that there are established and growing areas of cognitive and social research, such as concept acquisition, learning, semantic memory, problem-solving, expertise, social judgment, and risk and decision under uncertainty, that make unabashed use of the familiar intentional idioms of folk psychology. Second, although it is true that some phenomena, such as those of creative imagination, are not at all understood by our commonsense psychological theories, they are not yet understood by emerging scientific psychological theories either. The areas of professional psychology outlined above are barely 100 years old (Stich 1983, p. 213). Emerging psychological theories in these areas, though recognizably intentional, have just recently begun to study these mental abilities with the sort of rigor and methodological care that is characteristic of scientific inquiry. In light of the fact that neuroscience is no more recent than professional psychology, one might have thought the eliminativist would hold neuroscience to the same explanatory standards as psychology, also counting against eliminativism the fact that neuroscience says little or nothing about these phenomena.

Finally, although Churchland explores the devastating consequences an emerging neuroscience could have on folk psychology, he does not discuss the effect that this elimination would have on other working sciences, such as microeconomics, anthropology, sociology, political theory, social psychology, and history. Theories within these domains make crucial use of ordinary intentional state attribution, and thus the elimination of folk psychology would raise questions about the source of the explanatory successes they enjoy. These successes are represented by the results of decision theory, attitude surveys, economic accounts of social interaction within firms and patterns of consumer behavior, game theory, the dynamics of small group interaction in (say) historical negotiations and historical movements, and projective techniques in anthropology. In the absence of a special argument against the scientific integrity of these theories, the eliminativist must account for whatever successes they achieve in ways that are compatible with his or her contention that the (folk psychological) theory on which they are founded is a "radically false theory."

Churchland characterizes folk psychology as a theory that, though radically false, makes substantial ontological claims, treating mental states such as beliefs and desires as real states with causal properties. In "Three Kinds of Intentional Psychology," Daniel Dennett argues that folk psychology is not a robust, empirical theory of the mind, as Churchland envisions, but rather a semantic thesis[4] about the meanings of mental terms: "[F]olk psychology can best be viewed as a sort of logical behaviorism: *what it means* to say that someone believes that *p*, is that that person is disposed to behave in certain ways under certain conditions." This picture of folk psychology derives from Dennett's intentional-system theory, according to which our folk psychological conceptions of belief and desire are mere *instruments* for the prediction of behavior: "[F]olk psychology can best be viewed as a rationalististic calculus of interpretation and prediction—an idealizing, abstract, instrumentalistic interpretation-method that has evolved because it works, and works because we have evolved."

This interpretation-method—or "intentional stance"—is *abstract* in the sense that its effectiveness is not restricted to the explanation of *human* behavior. We can predict the behavior of a computer as well by the ascription of beliefs and desires; a system is intentional if the ascription of beliefs to that system is instrumental to the "voluminous and reliable" prediction of its behavior. But because intelligent behavior is never optimally rational (we misremember, deny some deductive consequences of our beliefs, etc.), intentional stance predictions will require some degree of idealization: "Folk psychology, then, is *idealized* in that it produces its predictions and explanations by calculating in a normative system; it predicts what we will believe, desire, and do, by determining what we *ought* to believe, desire, and do."

Guided by his instrumentalism, Dennett interprets the role of idealization in folk psychology as supporting the diminished ontological status of central theoretical notions, such as belief and desire. Borrowing a distinction from Reichenbach, Dennett claims that there are "two sorts of referents for theoretical terms: *illata*—posited theoretical entities—and *abstracta*—calculation-bound entities or logical constructs. Beliefs and desires of folk psychology (but not all mental events and states) are *abstracta*." Dennett may well be of two minds about the status of our ordinary notion of belief. Elsewhere in this article he states that "The ordinary notion of belief no doubt does place beliefs somewhere midway between being *illata* and being *abstracta*," and this hybrid character is cited as the reason for thinking that "the concept of belief found in ordinary understanding, i.e., in folk psychology, is unappealing as a scientific concept." He speculates that a future psychology will examine "core-beliefs"—concrete representation tokens (and thus *illata*) explicitly stored in the psychological system—leaving aside implicitly stored "virtual beliefs," calculation-bound states (and thus *abstracta*) routinely attributed across psychological systems. On this view, we can "all use folk psychology knowing next to nothing about what actually happens inside people's skulls" because, as it turns out, our ordinary notions of belief and desire are idealized calculating devices, logical constructions, or *abstracta*. Moreover, the employment of these predictive calculi is effective because in fact we approximate idealized systems of the sort that Dennett's instrumentalism presupposes.

Here Dennett may be too willing to regard an instrumentalist analysis of folk psychology as an inevitable consequence of the presumed fact that idealization plays a role in folk prediction and explanation. We can concede, for example, that no ideal gas actually exists without thereby impugning the full-blooded reality of parts of that idealized model, such as molecules. Indeed, the history of science often enough has recommended the realistic interpretation of theoretical entities *precisely because* an idealization proves so useful a guide to induction in a particular domain.[5]

Dennett's conditions for scientific respectability deserve comment. In his classification of *illata*, Dennett appears to assume that all well-behaved theoretical notions have clear identity conditions. However, many notions of considerable theoretical importance arguably evade such strictures. Taxonomic concepts expressed by terms such as 'species' and 'geosyncline' play important explanatory roles in evolutionary biology and geomorphology. Despite this (or perhaps in virtue of this), no uncontroversial identity conditions have been given for these concepts.

In addition to this restrictive policy regarding identity conditions, Dennett also uses the predictive capacity of a theoretical notion as the measure of its scientific fitness. But this assumption represents a picture of good scientific practice that is both narrow and controversial: narrow, because it rules out as disreputable the successful theoretical notions of largely explanatory sciences such as geology and evolutionary biology, and controversial, because there is a growing consensus emerging from research in the history and philosophy of science that the instrumentalist interpretation of theories faces serious, perhaps fatal, difficulties. For these reasons, we might find it unnecessary to satisfy Dennett's proposal to "create two new theories: one strictly abstract, idealizing, holistic, instrumentalistic—pure intentional system theory—and the other a concrete, microtheoretical science of the actual realization of those intentional systems— ... subpersonal cognitive psychology."

The chapters by Churchland and Dennett are primarily occupied by the issue of the respectability of folk psychology as a systematic scientific theory. A respectable theory should enjoy some degree of explanatory success and reasonable prospects for integration with neighboring theories. These are global theoretical virtues, however, and more specific dimensions of evaluation can also be used, as Dennett suggests in his criticism of the method of mental state identification implicit in folk psychological practice. The scientific status of folk psychology might be in doubt if folk psychology identifies its explanatory kinds (such as beliefs and desires) in a way that is incompatible with standards of individuation applied either in actual professional psychology or, lacking adequately clear standards there, in some envisioned psychology of the future.

Philosophers drawing up this envisioned psychology appeal to standards of kind-individuation putatively employed in sciences other than psychology. Often, these standards are then adapted to, and illustrated by, psychological thought-experiments. In Hilary Putnam's celebrated thought-experiment, you are asked to imagine that you have a neurologically identical twin on a planet called Twin Earth, a place that differs from Earth only in the respect that it has XYZ where Earth has H_2O. Though chemically distinguishable, these substances are phenomenologically identical. Now, if we identify mental states by the truth conditions of the propositional attitudes expressing the mental state, your English claim "Water is wet" is true if and only if H_2O is wet, while the Twin-English claim uttered by your twin is true if and only if XYZ is wet. The intuition this example is supposed to generate is that, because of the chemical differences and despite your neurological identity, the sentence "Water is wet" means something different when expressed by your twin than by you. To the extent that sameness of meaning depends on sameness of psychological state content, then you and your twin are in different psychological states, despite your physical identity.[6] It is these observations that motivate Putnam's famous slogan that "'meanings' just ain't in the head!" (1975, p. 227).

This Twin Earth story has tended to pull philosophers in two different directions, leading many to favor one of two ways of identifying psychological states. *Narrow* psychological states are individuated solely by properties internal to the subject of the psychological state, and *wide* psychological states by their relations to features of the social and physical environment. According to the Twin Earth story just sketched, your twin and you are in the same type of narrow mental state, but in different wide states. Some philosophers have argued that Twin Earth considerations show that a properly scientific psychology would implicate only narrow psychological states in its generalizations; if psychological states depend for their content on brain states, then your neurological identity with your twin guarantees your psychological identity.

The above pattern of reasoning depends on specific metaphysical assumptions about kind individuation and typically ignores available methodological evidence concerning the actual taxonomic practices of psychologists. In "Methodological Solipsism," Fodor contributes to a salient trend set by philosophers of science, appealing to successful methodologies in a particular science—in this case, psychology—to adjudicate disputes within the field. Fodor argues that our best psychological theory—the computational theory of mind—characterizes mental processes as both symbolic and formal: "They are symbolic because they are defined over representations, and they are formal because they apply to representations in virtue of (roughly) the syntax of the representations." Since Fodor sees "no responsible way of saying what, in general, formality amounts to," he offers some rough descriptions of what he calls "The Formality Condition": "Formal operations are the ones that are specified without reference to such semantic properties of representations as, for example, truth, reference, and meaning.... [F]ormal operations apply in terms of the, as it were, shapes of the objects in their domains."

One apparent consequence of this requirement, in Twin Earth parlance, is that my twin and I are in type-identical psychological states when in the presence of that wet, colorless, etc., substance, be it H_2O or XYZ. Our neurological identity guarantees the identity of the form or shape of our respective psychological states and thus, in accordance with the formality condition, ensures the identity of our psychological states.

Fodor states that respecting the formality condition has quite strong consequences for psychological theorizing, warranting both a positive and a negative claim. The positive claim that Fodor defends is that the notion of psychological state content demanded by the formality condition is compatible "plus or minus a bit" with the notion of content implicit in our untutored, commonsense explanations of behavior. The negative claim is that no more ambitious a program in psychology—such as a "naturalistic" one that taxonomizes mental states according to their semantic properties of truth, reference, or meaning—is or will be even remotely plausible.[7]

Although the formality condition might have given clear and systematic voice to some of the commitments implicit in ordinary psychological explanation, it fails to vindicate other considerations we actually make in attributing mental states. For example, it might be argued that the mere "shape" or computational form of an internal psychological state still requires a semantic interpretation in order to determine its content. We can see this by considering that the belief that vampires hate crucifixes could be represented in one person as 'Pa' and in another as 'Sb'. Conversely, 'Na' might represent in one person the belief that Hermann Göring liked doughnuts and in another person the belief that cockatiels breed in captivity. Therefore, the same belief could be represented in different believers by different shapes (just as distinct notations can serve the same function in various systems of first-order logic), and different beliefs could be represented (or "encoded") in different persons by the same formal inscription. Since being in a particular computational relation to a specific internal representation is neither necessary nor sufficient for having a particular belief, identity of computational form or "shape" of internal representations does not entail the identity of their contents (see Rey 1980).

Fodor's negative thesis—that a "wide" or naturalistic psychology of organism-environment relations is doomed to failure—is markedly easier to address. It turns on the claim that properties implicated in a naturalistic psychology aren't in the investigative domain of psychologists, forcing us to "wait forever," or at least until the nonpsychological sciences are completed, to discover whether the proposed psychological laws are true.

Fodor aims to establish that the quest for a naturalistic psychology is seriously flawed as a research strategy. According to Fodor, one of the goals of a naturalistic psychology is to formulate nomological organism-environment relations; but, he continues, the organism/environment relations framed in a naturalistic psychology must describe environmental objects in a projectible vocabulary in order for these relations to be law-instantiating. Sadly, "we have no access to such a vocabulary prior to the elaboration (completion?) of the nonpsychological sciences. 'What Granny likes with her herring' isn't, for example, a description under which salt is law-instantiating; nor, presumably, is 'salt'. What we need is something like 'NaCl,' and descriptions like 'NaCl' are available only after we've done our chemistry."[8] Since such descriptions are outside of the investigative domain of psychologists and currently are incompletely articulated even within the appropriate nonpsychological science, "the naturalistic psychologists will inherit the Earth, but only after everyone else is finished with it. No doubt it's all right to have a research strategy that says 'wait awhile'. But who wants to wait forever?"

Even if we accept Fodor's picture of naturalistic psychology, one might wonder why a naturalistic methodology in psychology must await the completion of the nonpsychological sciences before proposing its generalizations. The naturalistic psychologist can avail herself of the same competence and reference-borrowing procedures used in other sciences. Psychologists could (and should) accept the chemist's testimony regarding the appropriate chemical description of 'salt' and 'water'; this is especially so where such descriptions aid in the development of a psychological theory. Thus, the principle that leads Fodor to criticize the naturalistic research strategy in psychology would also impugn the practices of sciences that Fodor presumably wants to leave unscathed. The membrane biologist relies on the chemist's account of the properties of ions when she forms hypotheses about the transfer of ions across cell membranes. Why should the incompleteness of chemistry pose any more of a problem for the naturalistic psychologist than for the biologist?

Fodor's "methodological" argument for individualism derives more from the theory of computable functions and logical syntax than from the explanatory practices of working psychologists. This impression of Fodor's argument seems further confirmed by the fact that he presents no evidence from human experimental psychology to support the claim that practicing psychologists honor the formality condition. In "Narrow Taxonomy and Wide Functionalism," Patricia Kitcher explicitly addresses the taxonomic concerns of practicing psychologists. Kitcher argues that Fodor's formality condition, along with similar philosophical principles defended by Ned Block and Stephen Stich, depends on philosophical principles that are not motivated by scientific practice.

In just one of a variety of examples, Kitcher considers the motor theory of speech perception (specifically, of phone perception), according to which a speech sound's identity is determined not by some internal metric of acoustic similarity but by the articulatory movements that produced it. At the computational level, psychologists examine features of the environment (in this case, the speaker's vocal gestures) that explain in part our capacity to classify acoustically different signals as instances of a certain articulatory type. Such capacities appear remarkably stable and trustworthy, despite the variability of the signal at the subject's sensory periphery. Moreover, explanations of such psychological capacities essentially appeal to specific features of the environment, making those explanations, on their face, wide or nonindividualistic. On Kitcher's view, the wide explanations of these capacities are tied to their computational (rather than, say, transductive) nature, and thus there is a connection between the nature of psychological content and explanatory level.

In a novel move, Kitcher applies these taxonomic considerations in defense of an influential doctrine in the philosophy of mind: functionalism. Functionalism is the doctrine that a mental state's functional/causal role is determined by its relation to input, output, and other mental states. However, in keeping with the two taxonomic patterns in psychology discussed here—narrow and wide—we can construct two corresponding conceptions of functional role. Some philosophers of mind hold that a mental state's functional role is determined by properties internal to the subject. But once "functional role" is understood in the computational (wide) sense specified above, Kitcher argues, functionalism manages to evade a variety of often clever objections to its narrower ancestor.

The attention paid by Kitcher to traditional philosophical issues and contemporary scientific taxonomy illustrates one of the major themes of this anthology: Scientific practice acts both as an important constraint on, and a crucial source of insight about, the metaphysical and epistemological doctrines entertained by philosophers. In the final chapter of this section, "Individualism and Psychology," Tyler Burge contends that careful analysis of a single theoretically developed and representative psychological theory reveals a profoundly nonindividualistic account of mental processes. According to Burge, Marr's theory of vision appeals to primitive intentional states that are individuated not by their "intrinsic" features (such as their "shape" or "syntax"), but by their relations to the contingently existing, external physical conditions that normally cause those primitive states.

Burge illustrates the theory's invocations of the environment in four examples. The first two describe physical constraints the environment places on the reliable operation of visual mechanisms and processes. Explanations for capacities such as edge-detection depend on assumptions about the normal spatial localization of the features in the world that give rise to changes in illumination. Explanations for stereopsis (the resolution of disparity between the two retinal image signals) depend on (among others) an assumption that the distal object typically has properties such as cohesiveness and relative smoothness that permit the perceiver's distance from the object to vary continuously. These constraints and assumptions make essential reference to the physical environment, and by doing so allow the theory to explain both the successes and failures of visual perception.

The second two examples focus not on explanations for the successes of visual processes, but on the nature of the visual representations implicated in these processes. Here, too, specific features of the environment play an important role, this time in forming the intentional content of "representational primitives" or early-stage visual states. This environmental contribution is registered in the theory's general physical assumptions that constrain the choice of primitive states and identify their normal causal antecedents.

If it has been correctly interpreted, Marr's theory is a living counterexample to Fodor's argument against naturalistic psychology. But even if Burge has correctly interpreted Marr's theory, there is no articulation of a notion of psychological causation that blocks the following individualist move: Facts about the external environment may indeed determine the information content of the internal state, but these environmental determinants can be "factored out" of the organism-environment relation, and a properly scientific psychology would do just that.[9]

This response brings two points clearly into focus. First, it would no longer be for methodological reasons that the individualist insists on a narrow notion of mental state content. If the methodology of Marr's theory is, in its unreconstructed form, non-individualistic, it must be for independent (perhaps metaphysical) reasons that the individualist attempts to sustain a narrow or nonrelational notion of content.[10]

Second, although individualism about psychology is seldom advertised as a reductionist proposal, it is of a piece with traditional reductionist interpretations of other sciences that attempt to specify a theory's explanatory kinds in terms of their intrinsic or nonrelational features. In part I, section 3 of this anthology, "Reductionism and the Unity of Science," we saw similar proposals. There, we observed that materialist conceptions of the special sciences do not entail the type of reducibility to physics anticipated by positivist philosophy of science; reductionist interpretations of a special science must be defended by appeal to special features of that science rather than by sweeping appeal to a general reductionist analysis of materialism. If the causal generalizations of psychology hold not by virtue of intrinsic properties of mental states but instead because of actual relations that those mental states bear to features of the environment, then it would appear that the individualist version of psychological reduction would be rendered implausible.

However, each of the positions discussed in this section represents an ongoing and vigorous research program. We still await resolution of many of the disputes outlined here and the fashioning of new proposals.

Notes

1. Some philosophers deny that folk psychology constitutes a theory. For this dissenting view, see Baker 1987 and Wilkes 1984, 1986. P. S. Churchland (1986, pp. 252-259) and many others (e.g., Fodor 1986, 1987) defend the interpretation of folk psychology as a theory.

2. Relevant issues not raised in this section include functional explanation in psychology and the various research programs adopted in the twentieth century by philosophers and psychologists, such as behaviorism, central-state identity theory, and functionalism. For a good survey, see Fodor 1981. New developments in the area of cognitive science known as parallel distributed processing, particularly connectionist theories of mind, have also been slighted here. Churchland 1989 contains an up-to-date and spirited discussion of these issues. A further area of inquiry not represented here is the recent social and cognitive research on judgment under uncertainty, which has inspired new alliances among psychologists and philosophers interested in the issue of rationality. See Dawes 1988, Goldman 1986, Kornblith 1985, Nisbett and Ross 1980, Stich 1990.

3. Many philosophers have advanced alternatives to the "linguistic" or "sentential" picture of propositional attitude psychology that is assumed by Churchland as the correct analysis. These alternatives distinguish between the information carried by a mental state and the medium (say, a sentence, a wink, or smoke signal) used to express that information. See Stalnaker 1976, Loar 1981, and Dretske 1981. Articulations of this nonlinguistic picture published after Churchland's paper can be found in Stalnaker 1984 and Dretske 1988.

4. I do not mean to suggest that semantics and ontology can be cleanly separated, only that the semantic relations among mental states on Dennett's account of folk psychology are *conceptual*, rather than *causal*, as they are understood in prominent realist accounts of folk psychology.

5. Moreover, we needn't rely solely on the *predictive* resourcefulness of an idealization in order to establish the reality of the theoretical entities that the molecular model mentions; there are independent, converging lines of evidence for the reality of molecules. For a textbook description of the role that Avogadro's number plays in thermodynamics, see Orear 1979, pp. 254–255). Nye 1972 provides an interesting historical supplement to the philosophical discussion of "molecular reality" in Salmon 1984, pp. 214–238. Cartwright 1983, pp. 136–158 contains a provocative argument about the *explanatory* role of idealization in physical theory.

6. You could, of course, hold meaning constant across Earth and Twin Earth, but then it appears that you must give up the traditional view that what you mean determines what you are referring to, or in the technical jargon, that intension determines extension.

7. For other accounts showing the influence of the formality condition, see P. S. Churchland and P. M. Churchland 1983, Dennett 1982, Stich 1978, pp. 161–170.

8. It would be no surprise that physical descriptions don't pick out properties and objects instantiated in psychological generalizations if, as Fodor argued in an earlier paper ("Special Sciences," reprinted here, part I, section 3), psychology is an autonomous science. The idea that psychology is a science autonomous from the physical sciences is motivated by the insight that we would miss important generalizations about behavior if we attempt to translate the predicates in psychological explanations into the vocabulary of chemistry or physics.

9. For an articulation of this factoring strategy, see Fodor 1987, chapter 2; also Block 1986. A general and elegant critique of this approach can be found in Stalnaker 1989.

10. For an opposing interpretation of Marr's theory of vision, see Segal 1989.

References

Baker, L. R., 1987, *Saving Belief*, Princeton University Press, Princeton, NJ.

Block, N., 1986, "Advertisement for a Semantics for Psychology," in French, P., Uehling, T., and Wettstein, H., eds., *Midwest Studies in Philosophy, Vol. 10: Studies in the Philosophy of Mind*, University of Minnesota Press, Minneapolis.

Cartwright, N., 1983, *How the Laws of Physics Lie*, Oxford University Press, New York.

Churchland, P. M., 1989, *A Neurocomputational Perspective: The Nature of Mind and the Structure of Science*, MIT Press, Cambridge, MA.

Churchland, P. S., 1986, "Replies," Inquiry 29: 252–259.

Churchland, P. S., and Churchland, P. M., 1983, "Stalking the Wild Epistemic Engine," *Noûs* 17: 5–18.

Dawes, R. M., 1988, *Rational Choice in an Uncertain World*, Harcourt Brace Jovanovich, New York.

Dennett, D., 1982, "Beyond Belief," in A. Woodfield, ed., *Thought and Object*, Oxford University Press, New York.

Dretske, F., 1981, *Knowledge and the Flow of Information*, MIT Press, Cambridge, MA.

Dretske, F., 1988, *Explaining Behavior*, MIT Press, Cambridge, MA.

Fodor, J., 1981, "The Mind-Body Problem," *Scientific American* 244(1): 124–133.

Fodor, J., 1986, "Banish Discontent," in Butterfield, J., ed., *Language, Mind, and Logic*, Cambridge University Press, New York.

Fodor, J., 1987, *Psychosemantics*, MIT Press, Cambridge, MA.

Fodor, J., 1990, *A Theory of Content and Other Essays*, MIT Press, Cambridge, MA.

Goldman, A., 1986, *Epistemology and Cognition*, Harvard University Press, Cambridge, MA.

Kornblith, H., 1985, ed., *Naturalizing Epistemology*, MIT Press, Cambridge, MA.

Loar, B., 1981, *Mind and Meaning*, Cambridge University Press, New York.

Nisbett, R., and Ross, L., 1980, *Human Inference: Strategies and Shortcomings of Social Judgment*, Prentice-Hall, Englewood Cliffs, NJ.

Nye, M., 1972, *Molecular Reality*, Macdonald, London.

Orear, J., 1979, *Physics*, Macmillan, New York.

Putnam, H., 1975, "The Meaning of 'Meaning'", in *Mind, Language, and Reality: Philosophical Papers*, vol. 2, Cambridge University Press, New York.

Rey, G., 1980, "The Formal and the Opaque," *The Behavioral and Brain Sciences* 30: 90–92.

Salmon, W., 1984, *Scientific Explanation and the Causal Structure of the World*, Princeton University Press, Princeton, NJ.

Segal, G., 1989, "Seeing What is not There," *The Philosophical Review* 98: 189–214.

Stalnaker, R., 1976, "Propositions," in MacKay, A., and Merrill, D., eds., *Issues in the Philosophy of Language*, Yale University Press, New Haven, CT.

Stalnaker, R., 1984, *Inquiry*, MIT Press, Cambridge, MA.

Stalnaker, R., 1989, 'On What's in the Head," in Tomberlin, J., ed., *Philosophical Perspectives, Vol. 3: Philosophy of Mind and Action.*

Stich, S., 1978, "Autonomous Psychology and the Belief-Desire Thesis," *The Monist* 61: 573–591.

Stich, S., 1983, *From Folk Psychology to Cognitive Science*, MIT Press, Cambridge, MA.

Stich, S., 1990, *The Fragmentation of Reason*, MIT Press, Cambridge, MA.

Wilkes, K., 1984, "Pragmatics in Science and Theory in Common Sense," *Inquiry* 27: 339–361.

Wilkes, K., 1986, "Nemo Psychologus nisi Physiologus," *Inquiry* 29: 169–185.

Further Reading

Bechtel, W., 1988, *Philosophy of Mind: An Overview for Cognitive Science*, Erlbaum, Hillsdale, NJ.

Block, N., 1980, ed., *Readings in Philosophy of Psychology*, 2 vols., Harvard University Press, Cambridge, MA.

Burge, T., 1989, "Individuation and Causation in Psychology," *Pacific Philosophical Quarterly* 70: 303–322.

Churchland, P. M., 1988, *Matter and Consciousness*, revised edition, MIT Press, Cambridge, MA.

Churchland, P. S., 1986, *Neurophilosophy*, MIT Press, Cambridge, MA.

Cummins, R., 1983, *The Nature of Psychological Explanation*, MIT Press, Cambridge, MA.

Cummins, R., 1989, *Meaning and Mental Representation*, MIT Press, Cambridge, MA.

Davidson, D., 1980, *Essays on Actions & Events*, Oxford University Press, New York.

Dennett, D., 1978, *Brainstorms*, MIT Press, Cambridge, MA.

Dennett, D., 1987, *The Intentional Stance*, MIT Press, Cambridge, MA.

Dennett, D., 1988, "Précis of *The Intentional Stance*" (with peer commentary and author's reply), *The Behavioral and Brain Sciences* 11: 495–546.

Fodor, J., 1975, *The Language of Thought*, Crowell, Cambridge, MA.

Fodor, J., 1981, *RePresentations*, MIT Press, Cambridge, MA.

Fodor, J., 1983, *The Modularity of Mind*, MIT Press, Cambridge, MA.

Fodor, J., 1985, "Précis of *The Modularity of Mind*" (with peer commentary and author's reply), *The Behavioral and Brain Sciences* 8: 1–42.

Haugeland, J., 1985, *Artificial Intelligence: The Very Idea*, MIT Press, Cambridge, MA.

Lycan, W., 1990, ed., *Mind and Cognition: A Reader*, Blackwell, Cambridge, MA.

Millikan, R. G., 1984, *Language, Thought, and Other Biological Categories*, MIT Press, Cambridge, MA.

Peacocke, C., 1983, *Sense and Content*, Oxford University Press, New York.

Putnam, H., 1987, *Representation and Reality*, MIT Press, Cambridge, MA.

Pylyshyn, Z., 1984, *Computation and Cognition*, MIT Press, Cambridge, MA.

Shoemaker, S., 1984, *Identity, Cause, and Mind*, Cambridge University Press, New York.

Trout, J. D., 1991, "Belief Attribution in Science: Folk Psychology Under Theoretical Stress," *Synthese* 87: 379–400.

Chapter 33

Eliminative Materialism and the Propositional Attitudes

Paul Churchland

Eliminative materialism is the thesis that our commonsense conception of psychological phenomena constitutes a radically false theory, a theory so fundamentally defective that both the principles and the ontology of that theory will eventually be displaced, rather than smoothly reduced, by completed neuroscience. Our mutual understanding and even our introspection may then be reconstituted within the conceptual framework of completed neuroscience, a theory we may expect to be more powerful by far than the commonsense psychology it displaces, and more substantially integrated within physical science generally. My purpose in this paper is to explore these projections, especially as they bear on (1) the principal elements of commonsense psychology: the propositional attitudes (beliefs, desires, etc.), and (2) the conception of rationality in which these elements figure.

This focus represents a change in the fortunes of materialism. Twenty years ago, emotions, qualia, and "raw feels" were held to be the principal stumbling blocks for the materialist program. With these barriers dissolving,[1] the locus of opposition has shifted. Now it is the realm of the intentional, the realm of the propositional attitude, that is most commonly held up as being both irreducible to and ineliminable in favor of anything from within a materialist framework. Whether and why this is so, we must examine.

Such an examination will make little sense, however, unless it is first appreciated that the relevant network of common-sense concepts does indeed constitute an empirical theory, with all the functions, virtues, *and perils* entailed by that status. I shall therefore begin with a brief sketch of this view and a summary rehearsal of its rationale. The resistance it encounters still surprises me. After all, common sense has yielded up many theories. Recall the view that space has a preferred direction in which all things fall; that weight is an intrinsic feature of a body; that a force-free moving object will promptly return to rest; that the sphere of the heavens turns daily; and so on. These examples are clear, perhaps, but people seem willing to concede a theoretical component within common sense only if (1) the theory and the common sense involved are safely located in antiquity, and (2) the relevant theory is now so clearly false that its speculative nature is inescapable. Theories are indeed easier to discern under these circumstances. But the vision of hindsight is always 20/20. Let us aspire to some foresight for a change.

I. Why Folk Psychology Is a Theory

Seeing our commonsense conceptual framework for mental phenomena as a theory brings a simple and unifying organization to most of the major topics in the philo-

Reprinted from *Journal of Philosophy* 78, no. 2 (February 1981), pp. 67–90, by permission of the author and the publisher. Copyright 1981 by *Journal of Philosophy*.

sophy of mind, including the explanation and prediction of behavior, the semantics of mental predicates, action theory, the other-minds problem, the intentionality of mental states, the nature of introspection, and the mind-body problem. Any view that can pull this lot together deserves careful consideration.

Let us begin with the explanation of human (and animal) behavior. The fact is that the average person is able to explain, and even predict, the behavior of other persons with a facility and success that is remarkable. Such explanations and predictions standardly make reference to the desires, beliefs, fears, intentions, perceptions, and so forth, to which the agents are presumed subject. But explanations presuppose laws—rough and ready ones, at least—that connect the explanatory conditions with the behavior explained. The same is true for the making of predictions, and for the justification of subjunctive and counterfactual conditionals concerning behavior. Reassuringly, a rich network of common-sense laws can indeed be reconstructed from this quotidean commerce of explanation and anticipation; its principles are familiar homilies; and their sundry functions are transparent. Each of us understands others, as well as we do, because we share a tacit command of an integrated body of lore concerning the lawlike relations holding among external circumstances, internal states, and overt behavior. Given its nature and functions, this body of lore may quite aptly be called "folk psychology."[2]

This approach entails that the semantics of the terms in our familiar mentalistic vocabulary is to be understood in the same manner as the semantics of theoretical terms generally: the meaning of any theoretical term is fixed or constituted by the network of laws in which it figures. (This position is quite distinct from logical behaviorism. We deny that the relevant laws are analytic, and it is the lawlike connections generally that carry the semantic weight, not just the connections with overt behavior. But this view does account for what little plausibility logical behaviorism did enjoy.)

More importantly, the recognition that folk psychology is a theory provides a simple and decisive solution to an old skeptical problem, the problem of other minds. The problematic conviction that another individual is the subject of certain mental states is not inferred deductively from his behavior, nor is it inferred by inductive analogy from the perilously isolated instance of one's own case. Rather, that conviction is a singular *explanatory hypothesis* of a perfectly straightforward kind. Its function, in conjunction with the background laws of folk psychology, is to provide explanations/predictions/understanding of the individual's continuing behavior, and it is credible to the degree that it is successful in this regard over competing hypotheses. In the main, such hypotheses are successful, and so the belief that others enjoy the internal states comprehended by folk psychology is a reasonable belief.

Knowledge of other minds thus has no essential dependence on knowledge of one's own mind. Applying the principles of our folk psychology to our behavior, a Martian could justly ascribe to us the familiar run of mental states, even though his own psychology were very different from ours. He would not, therefore, be "generalizing from his own case."

As well, introspective judgments about one's own case turn out not to have any special status or integrity anyway. On the present view, an introspective judgment is just an instance of an acquired habit of conceptual response to one's internal states, and the integrity of any particular response is always contingent on the integrity of the acquired conceptual framework (theory) in which the response is framed. Accordingly, one's *introspective* certainty that one's mind is the seat of beliefs and desires may be as badly misplaced as was the classical man's *visual* certainty that the star-flecked sphere of the heavens turns daily.

Another conundrum is the intentionality of mental states. The "propositional attitudes," as Russell called them, form the systematic core of folk psychology; and their uniqueness and anomalous logical properties have inspired some to see here a fundamental contrast with anything that mere physical phenomena might conceivably display. The key to this matter lies again in the theoretical nature of folk psychology. The intentionality of mental states here emerges not as a mystery of nature, but as a structural feature of the concepts of folk psychology. Ironically, those same structural features reveal the very close affinity that folk psychology bears to theories in the physical sciences. Let me try to explain.

Consider the large variety of what might be called "numerical attitudes" appearing in the conceptual framework of physical science: '... has a mass$_{kg}$ of n', '... has a velocity of n', '... has a temperature$_K$ of n', and so forth. These expressions are predicate-forming expressions: when one substitutes a singular term for a number into the place held by 'n', a determinate predicate results. More interestingly, the relations between the various "numerical attitudes" that result are precisely the relations between the numbers "contained" in those attitudes. More interesting still, the argument place that takes the singular terms for numbers is open to quantification. All this permits the expression of generalizations concerning the lawlike relations that hold between the various numerical attitudes in nature. Such laws involve quantification over numbers, and they exploit the mathematical relations holding in that domain. Thus, for example,

(1) $(x)(f)(m)[((x$ has a mass of $m)$ & $(x$ suffers a net force of $f))$
$$\supset (x \text{ accelerates at } f/m)]$$

Consider now the large variety of propositional attitudes: '... believes that p', '... desires that p', '... fears that p', '... is happy that p', etc. These expressions are predicate-forming expressions also. When one substitutes a singular term for a proposition into the place held by 'p', a determinate predicate results, e.g., '... believes that Tom is tall.' (Sentences do not generally function as singular terms, but it is difficult to escape the idea that when a sentence occurs in the place held by 'p', it is there functioning as or like a singular term. On this, more below.) More interestingly, the relations between the resulting propositional attitudes are characteristically the relations that hold between the propositions "contained" in them, relations such as entailment, equivalence, and mutual inconsistency. More interesting still, the argument place that takes the singular terms for propositions is open to quantification. All this permits the expression of generalizations concerning the lawlike relations that hold among propositional attitudes. Such laws involve quantification over propositions, and they exploit various relations holding in that domain. Thus, for example,

(2) $(x)(p)[(x$ fears that $p) \supset (x$ desires that $\sim p)]$

(3) $(x)(p)[(x$ hopes that $p)$ & $(x$ discovers that $p)) \supset (x$ is pleased that $p)]$

(4) $(x)(p)(p)[((x$ believes that $p)$ & $(x$ believes that (if p then $q)))$
$$\supset (\text{barring, confusion, distraction, etc., } x \text{ believes that } q)]$$

(5) $(x)(p)(q)[((x$ desires that $p)$ & $(x$ believes that (if q then $p))$
& $(x$ is able to bring it about that $q))$
$\supset$ (barring conflicting desires or preferred strategies,
x brings it about that $q)]$[3]

Not only is folk psychology a theory, it is so *obviously* a theory that it must be held a major mystery why it has taken until the last half of the twentieth century for philosophers to realize it. The structural features of folk psychology parallel perfectly those of mathematical physics; the only difference lies in the respective domain of abstract entities they exploit—numbers in the case of physics, and propositions in the case of psychology.

Finally, the realization that folk psychology is a theory puts a new light on the mind-body problem. The issue becomes a matter of how the ontology of one theory (folk psychology) is, or is not, going to be related to the ontology of another theory (completed neuroscience); and the major philosophical positions on the mind-body problem emerge as so many different anticipations of what future research will reveal about the intertheoretic status and integrity of folk psychology.

The identity theorist optimistically expects that folk psychology will be smoothly reduced by completed neuroscience, and its ontology preserved by dint of transtheoretic identities. The dualist expects that it will prove *ir*reducible to completed neuroscience, by dint of being a nonredundant description of an autonomous, nonphysical domain of natural phenomena. The functionalist also expects that it will prove irreducible, but on the quite different grounds that the internal economy characterized by folk psychology is not, in the last analysis, a law-governed economy of natural states, but an abstract organization of functional states, an organization instantiable in a variety of quite different material substrates. It is therefore irreducible to the principles peculiar to any of them.

Finally, the eliminative materialist is also pessimistic about the prospects for reduction, but his reason is that folk psychology is a radically inadequate account of our internal activities, too confused and too defective to win survival through intertheoretic reduction. On his view it will simply be displaced by a better theory of those activities.

Which of these fates is the real destiny of folk psychology, we shall attempt to divine presently. For now, the point to keep in mind is that we shall be exploring the fate of a theory, a systematic, corrigible, speculative *theory*.

II. Why Folk Psychology Might (Really) Be False

Given that folk psychology is an empirical theory, it is at least an abstract possibility that its principles are radically false and that its ontology is an illusion. With the exception of eliminative materialism, however, none of the major positions takes this possibility seriously. None of them doubts the basic integrity or truth of folk psychology (hereafter, "FP"), and all of them anticipate a future in which its laws and categories are conserved. This conservatism is not without some foundation. After all, FP does enjoy a substantial amount of explanatory and predictive success. And what better grounds than this for confidence in the integrity of its categories?

What better grounds indeed? Even so, the presumption in FP's favor is spurious, born of innocence and tunnel vision. A more searching examination reveals a different picture. First, we must reckon not only with FP's successes, but with its explanatory failures, and with their extent and seriousness. Second, we must consider the long-term history of FP, its growth, fertility, and current promise of future development. And third, we must consider what sorts of theories are *likely* to be true of the etiology of our behavior, given what else we have learned about ourselves in recent history. That is, we must evaluate FP with regard to its coherence and continuity with fertile and well-established theories in adjacent and overlapping domains—with evolutionary theory, biology, and neuroscience, for example—because active coherence with the rest of what we presume to know is perhaps the final measure of any hypothesis.

A serious inventory of this sort reveals a very troubled situation, one which would evoke open skepticism in the case of any theory less familiar and dear to us. Let me sketch some relevant detail. When one centers one's attention not on what FP can explain, but on what it cannot explain or fails even to address, one discovers that there is a very great deal. As examples of central and important mental phenomena that remain largely or wholly mysterious within the framework of FP, consider the nature and dynamics of mental illness, the faculty of creative imagination, or the ground of intelligence differences between individuals. Consider our utter ignorance of the nature and psychological functions of sleep, that curious state in which a third of one's life is spent. Reflect on the common ability to catch an outfield fly ball on the run, or hit a moving car with a snowball. Consider the internal construction of a 3-D visual image from subtle differences in the 2-D array of stimulations in our respective retinas. Consider the rich variety of perceptual illusions, visual and otherwise. Or consider the miracle of memory, with its lightning capacity for relevant retrieval. On these and many other mental phenomena, FP sheds negligible light.

One particularly outstanding mystery is the nature of the learning process itself, especially where it involves large-scale conceptual change, and especially as it appears in its prelinguistic or entirely nonlinguistic form (as in infants and animals), which is by far the most common form in nature. FP is faced with special difficulties here, since its conception of learning as the manipulation and storage of propositional attitudes founders on the fact that how to formulate, manipulate, and store a rich fabric of propositional attitudes is itself something that is learned, and is only one among many acquired cognitive skills. FP would thus appear constitutionally incapable of even addressing this most basic of mysteries.[4]

Failures on such a large scale do not (yet) show that FP is a false theory, but they do move that prospect well into the range of real possibility, and they do show decisively that FP is *at best* a highly superficial theory, a partial and unpenetrating gloss on a deeper and more complex reality. Having reached this opinion, we may be forgiven for exploring the possibility that FP provides a positively misleading sketch of our internal kinematics and dynamics, one whose success is owed more to selective application and forced interpretation on our part than to genuine theoretical insight on FP's part.

A look at the history of FP does little to allay such fears, once raised. The story is one of retreat, infertility, and decadence. The presumed domain of FP used to be much larger than it is now. In primitive cultures, the behavior of most of the elements of nature were understood in intentional terms. The wind could know anger, the moon jealousy, the river generosity, the sea fury, and so forth. These were not metaphors. Sacrifices were made and auguries undertaken to placate or divine the changing passions of the gods. Despite its sterility, this animistic approach to nature has dominated our history, and it is only in the last two or three thousand years that we have restricted FP's literal application to the domain of the higher animals.

Even in this preferred domain, however, both the content and the success of FP have not advanced sensibly in two or three thousand years. The FP of the Greeks is essentially the FP we use today, and we are negligibly better at explaining human behavior in its terms than was Sophocles. This is a very long period of stagnation and infertility for any theory to display, especially when faced with such an enormous backlog of anomalies and mysteries in its own explanatory domain. Perfect theories, perhaps, have no need to evolve. But FP is profoundly imperfect. Its failure to develop its resources and extend its range of success is therefore darkly curious, and one must query the integrity of its basic categories. To use Imre Lakatos's terms, FP is a stagnant or degenerating research program, and has been for millennia.

Explanatory success to date is of course not the only dimension in which a theory can display virtue or promise. A troubled or stagnant theory may merit patience and solicitude on other grounds; for example, on grounds that it is the only theory or theoretical approach that fits well with other theories about adjacent subject matters, or the only one that promises to reduce to or be explained by some established background theory whose domain encompasses the domain of the theory at issue. In sum, it may rate credence because it holds promise of theoretical integration. How does FP rate in this dimension?

It is just here, perhaps, that FP fares poorest of all. If we approach *homo sapiens* from the perspective of natural history and the physical sciences, we can tell a coherent story of his constitution, development, and behavioral capacities which encompasses particle physics, atomic and molecular theory, organic chemistry, evolutionary theory, biology, physiology, and materialistic neuroscience. That story, though still radically incomplete, is already extremely powerful, outperforming FP at many points even in its own domain. And it is deliberately and self-consciously coherent with the rest of our developing world picture. In short, the greatest theoretical synthesis in the history of the human race is currently in our hands, and parts of it already provide searching descriptions and explanations of human sensory input, neural activity, and motor control.

But FP is no part of this growing synthesis. Its intentional categories stand magnificently alone, without visible prospect of reduction to that larger corpus. A successful reduction cannot be ruled out, in my view, but FP's explanatory impotence and long stagnation inspire little faith that its categories will find themselves neatly reflected in the framework of neuroscience. On the contrary, one is reminded of how alchemy must have looked as elemental chemistry was taking form, how Aristotelean cosmology must have looked as classical mechanics was being articulated, or how the vitalist conception of life must have looked as organic chemistry marched forward.

In sketching a fair summary of this situation, we must make a special effort to abstract from the fact that FP is a central part of our current *lebenswelt*, and serves as the principal vehicle of our interpersonal commerce. For these facts provide FP with a conceptual inertia that goes far beyond its purely theoretical virtues. Restricting ourselves to this latter dimension, what we must say is that FP suffers explanatory failures on an epic scale, that it has been stagnant for at least twenty-five centuries, and that its categories appear (so far) to be incommensurable with or orthogonal to the categories of the background physical science whose long-term claim to explain human behavior seems undeniable. Any theory that meets this description must be allowed a serious candidate for outright elimination.

We can of course insist on no stronger conclusion at this stage. Nor is it my concern to do so. We are here exploring a possibility, and the facts demand no more, and no less, than it be taken seriously. The distinguishing feature of the eliminative materialist is that he takes it very seriously indeed.

III. Arguments against Elimination

Thus the basic rationale of eliminative materialism: FP is a theory, and quite probably a false one; let us attempt, therefore to transcend it.

The rationale is clear and simple, but many find it uncompelling. It will be objected that FP is not, strictly speaking, an empirical theory; that it is not false, or at least not refutable by empirical considerations; and that it ought not or cannot be transcended in the fashion of a defunct empirical theory. In what follows we shall examine these objections as they flow from the most popular and best-founded of the competing positions in the philosophy of mind: functionalism.

An antipathy toward eliminative materialism arises from two distinct threads running through contemporary functionalism. The first thread conserns the *normative* character of FP, or at least of that central core of FP which treats of the propositional attitudes. FP, some will say, is a characterization of an ideal, or at least praiseworthy mode of internal activity. It outlines not only what it is to have and process beliefs and desires, but also (and inevitably) what it is to be rational in their administration. The ideal laid down by FP may be imperfectly achieved by empirical humans, but this does not impugn FP as a normative characterization. Nor need such failures seriously impugn FP even as a descriptive characterization, for it remains true that our activities can be both usefully and accurately understood as rational *except for* the occasional lapse due to noise, interference, or other breakdown, which defects empirical research may eventually unravel. Accordingly, though neuroscience may usefully augment it, FP has no pressing need to be displaced, even as a descriptive theory; nor could it be replaced, qua normative characterization, by any descriptive theory of neural mechanisms, since rationality is defined over propositional attitudes like beliefs and desires. FP, therefore, is here to stay.

Daniel Dennett has defended a view along these lines.[5] And the view just outlined gives voice to a theme of the property dualists as well. Karl Popper and Joseph Margolis both cite the normative nature of mental and linguistic activity as a bar to their penetration or elimination by any descriptive/materialist theory.[6] I hope to deflate the appeal of such moves below.

The second thread conserns the *abstract* nature of FP. The central claim of functionalism is that the principles of FP characterize our internal states in a fashion that makes no reference to their intrinsic nature or physical constitution. Rather, they are characterized in terms of the network of causal relations they bear to one another, and to sensory circumstances and overt behavior. Given its abstract specification, that internal economy may therefore be realized in a nomically heterogeneous variety of physical systems. All of them may differ, even radically, in their physical constitution, and yet at another level, they will all share the same nature. This view, says Fodor, "is compatible with very strong claims about the ineliminability of mental language from behavioral theories."[7] Given the real possibility of multiple instantiations in heterogeneous physical substrates, we cannot eliminate the functional characterization in favor of any theory peculiar to one such substrate. That would preclude our being able to describe the (abstract) organization that any one instantiation shares with all the other. A functional characterization of our internal states is therefore here to stay.

This second theme, like the first, assigns a faintly stipulative character to FP, as if the onus were on the empirical systems to instantiate faithfully the organization that FP specifies, instead of the onus being on FP to describe faithfully the internal activities of a naturally distinct class of empirical systems. This impression is enhanced by the standard examples used to illustrate the claims of functionalism—mousetraps, valve-lifters, arithmetical calculators, computers, robots, and the like. These are artifacts, constructed to fill a preconceived bill. In such cases, a failure of fit between the physical system and the relevant functional characterization impugns only the former, not the latter. The functional characterization is thus removed from empirical criticism in a way that is most unlike the case of an empirical theory. One prominent functionalist—Hilary Putnam—has argued outright that FP is not a corrigible theory at all.[8] Plainly, if FP is construed on these models, as regularly it is, the question of its empirical integrity is unlikely ever to pose itself, let alone receive a critical answer.

Although fair to some functionalists, the preceding is not entirely fair to Fodor. On his view the aim of psychology is to find the *best* functional characterization of ourselves, and what that is remains an empirical question. As well, his argument for the ineliminability of mental vocabulary from psychology does not pick out current FP in particular as ineliminable. It need claim only that *some* abstract functional characterization must be retained, some articulation or refinement of FP perhaps.

His estimate of eliminative materialism remains low, however. First, it is plain that Fodor thinks there is nothing fundamentally or interestingly wrong with FP. On the contrary, FP's central conception of cognitive activity—as consisting in the manipulation of propositional attitudes—turns up as the central element in Fodor's own theory on the nature of thought (*The Language of Thought, op. cit.*). And second, there remains the point that, whatever tidying up FP may or may not require, it cannot be displaced by any naturalistic theory of our physical substrate, since it is the abstract functional features of his internal states that make a person, not the chemistry of his substrate.

All of this is appealing. But almost none of it, I think, is right. Functionalism has too long enjoyed its reputation as a daring and *avant garde* position. It needs to be revealed for the short-sighted and reactionary position it is.

IV. The Conservative Nature of Functionalism

A valuable perspective on functionalism can be gained from the following story. To begin with, recall the alchemists' theory of inanimate matter. We have here a long and variegated tradition, of course, not a single theory, but our purposes will be served by a gloss.

The alchemists conceived the "inanimate" as entirely continuous with animated matter, in that the sensible and behavioral properties of the various substances are owed to the ensoulment of baser matter by various spirits or essences. These non-material aspects were held to undergo development, just as we find growth and development in the various souls of plants, animals, and humans. The alchemist's peculiar skill lay in knowing how to seed, nourish, and bring to maturity the desired spirits enmattered in the appropriate combinations.

On one orthodoxy, the four fundamental spirits (for "inanimate" matter) were named "mercury," "sulphur," "yellow arsenic," and "sal ammoniac." Each of these spirits was held responsible for a rough but characteristic syndrome of sensible, combinatorial, and causal properties. The spirit mercury, for example, was held responsible for certain features typical of metallic substances—their shininess, liquefiability, and so forth. Sulphur was held responsible for certain residual features typical of metals, and for those displayed by the ores from which running metal could be distilled. Any given metallic substance was a critical orchestration principally of these two spirits. A similar story held for the other two spirits, and among the four of them a certain domain of physical features and transformations was rendered intelligible and controllable.

The degree of control was always limited, of course. Or better, such prediction and control as the alchemists possessed was owed more to the manipulative lore acquired as an apprentice to a master, than to any genuine insight supplied by the theory. The theory followed, more than it dictated, practice. But the theory did supply some rhyme to the practice, and in the absence of a developed alternative it was sufficiently compelling to sustain a long and stubborn tradition.

The tradition had become faded and fragmented by the time the elemental chemistry of Lavoisier and Dalton arose to replace it for good. But let us suppose that it had hung on a little longer—perhaps because the four-spirit orthodoxy had become a thumb-worn part of everyman's common sense—and let us examine the nature of the conflict between the two theories and some possible avenues of resolution.

No doubt the simplest line of resolution, and the one which historically took place, is outright displacement. The dualistic interpretation of the four essences—as immaterial spirits—will appear both feckless and unnecessary given the power of the corpuscularian taxonomy of atomic chemistry. And a reduction of the old taxonomy to the new will appear impossible, given the extent to which the comparatively toothless old theory crossclassifies things relative to the new. Elimination would thus appear the only alternative—*unless* some cunning and determined defender of the alchemical vision has the wit to suggest the following defense.

Being "ensouled by mercury," or "sulphur," or either of the other two so-called spirits, is actually a *functional* state. The first, for example, is defined by the disposition to reflect light, to liquefy under heat, to unite with other matter in the same state, and so forth. And each of these four states is related to the others, in that the syndrome for each varies as a function of which of the other three states is also instantiated in the same substrate. Thus the level of description comprehended by the alchemical vocabulary is abstract: various material substances, suitably "ensouled," can display the features of a metal, for example, or even of gold specifically. For it is the total syndrome of occurrent and causal properties which matters, not the corpuscularian details of the substrate. Alchemy, it is concluded, comprehends a level of organization in reality distinct from and irreducible to the organization found at the level of corpuscularian chemistry.

This view might have had considerable appeal. After all, it spares alchemists the burden of defending immaterial souls that come and go; it frees them from having to meet the very strong demands of a naturalistic reduction; and it spares them the shock and confusion of outright elimination. Alchemical theory emerges as basically all right! Nor need they appear too obviously stubborn or dogmatic in this. Alchemy as it stands, they concede, may need substantial tidying up, and experience must be our guide. But we need not fear its naturalistic displacement, they remind us, since it is the particular orchestration of the syndromes of occurrent and causal properties which makes a piece of matter gold, not the idiosyncratic details of its corpuscularian substrate. A further circumstance would have made this claim even more plausible. For the fact is, the alchemists *did* know how to make gold, in this relevantly weakened sense of 'gold', and they could do so in a variety of ways. Their "gold" was never as perfect, alas, as the "gold" nurtured in nature's womb, but what mortal can expect to match the skills of nature herself?

What this story shows is that it is at least possible for the constellation of moves, claims, and defenses characteristic of functionalism to constitute an outrage against reason and truth, and to do so with a plausibility that is frightening. Alchemy is a terrible theory, well-deserving of its complete elimination, and the defense of it just explored is reactionary, obfuscatory, retrograde, and wrong. But in historical context, that defense might have seemed wholly sensible, even to reasonable people.

The alchemical example is a deliberately transparent case of what might well be called "the functionalist strategem," and other cases are easy to imagine. A cracking good defense of the phlogiston theory of combustion can also be constructed along these lines. Construe being highly phlogisticated and being dephlogisticated as functional states defined by certain syndromes of causal dispositions; point to the great variety of natural substrates capable of combustion and calxification; claim an irreducible functional integrity for what has proved to lack any natural integrity; and bury the remaining defects under a pledge to contrive improvements. A similar recipe will provide new life for the four humors of medieval medicine, for the vital essence or archeus of premodern biology, and so forth.

If its application in these other cases is any guide, the functionalist strategem is a smokescreen for the preservation of error and confusion. Whence derives our assurance that in contemporary journals the same charade is not being played out on behalf of FP? The parallel with the case of alchemy is in all other respects distressingly complete, right down to the parallel between the search for artificial gold and the search for artificial intelligence!

Let me not be misunderstood on this last point. Both aims are worthy aims: thanks to nuclear physics, artificial (but real) gold is finally within our means, if only in submicroscopic quantities; and artificial (but real) intelligence eventually will be. But just as the careful orchestration of superficial syndromes was the wrong way to produce genuine gold, so may the careful orchestration of superficial syndromes be the wrong way to produce genuine intelligence. Just as with gold, what may be required is that our science penetrate to the underlying *natural* kind that gives rise to the total syndrome directly.

In summary, when confronted with the explanatory impotence, stagnant history, and systematic isolation of the intentional idioms of FP, it is not an adequate or responsive defense to insist that those idioms are abstract, functional, and irreducible in character. For one thing, this same defense could have been mounted with comparable plausibility no matter *what* haywire network of internal states our folklore had ascribed to us. And for another, the defense assumes essentially what is at issue: it assumes that it is the intentional idioms of FP, plus or minus a bit, that express the important features shared by all cognitive systems. But they may not. Certainly it is wrong to assume that they do, and then argue against the possibility of a materialistic displacement on grounds that it must describe matters at a level that is different from the important level. This just begs the question in favor of the older framework.

Finally, it is very important to point out that eliminative materialism is strictly *consistent* with the claim that the essence of a cognitive system resides in the abstract functional organization of its internal states. The eliminative materialist is not committed to the idea that the correct account of cognition *must* be a naturalistic account, though he may be forgiven for exploring the possibility. What he does hold is that the correct account of cognition, whether functionalistic or naturalistic, will bear about as much resemblance to FP as modern chemistry bears to four-spirit alchemy.

Let us now try to deal with the argument, against eliminative materialism, from the normative dimension of FP. This can be dealt with rather swiftly, I believe.

First, the fact that the regularities ascribed by the intentional core of FP are predicated on certain logical relations among propositions is not by itself grounds for claiming anything essentially normative about FP. To draw a relevant parallel, the fact that the regularities ascribed by the classical gas law are predicated on arithmetical relations between numbers does not imply anything essentially normative about the classical gas law. And logical relations between propositions are as much an objective matter of abstract fact as are arithmetical relations between numbers. In this respect, the law

(4) $(x)(p)(q)[((x$ believes that $p)$ & $(x$ believes that (if p then $q)))$
$\supset$ (barring confusion, distraction, etc., x believes that $q)]$

is entirely on a par with the classical gas law

(6) $(x)(P)(V)(\mu)[((x$ has a pressure $P)$ & $(x$ has a volume $V)$
& $(x$ has a quantity $\mu)) \supset$ (barring very high pressure or density,
x has a temperature of $PV/\mu R)]$

A normative dimension enters only because we happen to *value* most of the patterns ascribed by FP. But we do not value all of them. Consider ,

(7) $(x)(p)[((x$ desires with all his heart that $p)$ & $(x$ learns that $\sim p))$
$\supset$ (barring unusual strength of character,
x is shattered that $\sim p)]$

Moreover, and as with normative convictions generally, fresh insight may motivate major changes in what we value.

Second, the laws of FP ascribe to us only a very minimal and truncated rationality, not an ideal rationality as some have suggested. The rationality characterized by the set of all FP laws falls well short of an ideal rationality. This is not surprising. We have no clear or finished conception of ideal rationality anyway; certainly the ordinary man does not. Accordingly, it is just not plausible to suppose that the explanatory failures from which FP suffers are owed primarily to human failure to live up to the ideal standard it provides. Quite to the contrary, the conception of rationality it provides appears limping and superficial, especially when compared with the dialectical complexity of our scientific history, or with the ratiocinative virtuosity displayed by any child.

Third, even if our current conception of rationality—and more generally, of cognitive virtue—is largely constituted within the sentential/propositional framework of FP, there is no guarantee that this framework is adequate to the deeper and more accurate account of cognitive virtue which is clearly needed. Even if we concede the categorial integrity of FP, at least as applied to language-using humans, it remains far from clear that the basic parameters of intellectual virtue are to be found at the categorial level comprehended by the propositional attitudes. After all, language use is something that is learned, by a brain already capable of vigorous cognitive activity; language use is acquired as only one among a great variety of learned manipulative skills; and it is mastered by a brain that evolution has shaped for a great many functions, language use being only the very latest and perhaps the least of them. Against the background of these facts, language use appears as an extremely peripheral activity, as a racially idiosyncratic mode of social interaction which is mastered thanks to the versatility and power of a more basic mode of activity. Why accept then, a theory of cognitive activity that models its elements on the elements of human language? And why assume that the fundamental parameters of intellectual virtue are or can be defined over the elements at this superficial level?

A serious advance in our appreciation of cognitive virtue would thus seem to *require* that we go beyond FP, that we transcend the poverty of FP's conception of rationality by transcending its propositional kinematics entirely, by developing a deeper and more general kinematics of cognitive activity, and by distinguishing within this new framework which of the kinematically possible modes of activity are to be valued and encouraged (as more efficient, reliable, productive, or whatever). Eliminative materialism thus does not imply the end of our normative concerns. It implies only that they will have to be reconstituted at a more revealing level of understanding, the level that a matured neuroscience will provide.

What a theoretically informed future might hold in store for us, we shall now turn to explore. Not because we can foresee matters with any special clarity, but because it is important to try to break the grip on our imagination held by the propositional kinematics of FP. As far as the present section is concerned, we may summarize our conclusions as follows. FP is nothing more and nothing less than a culturally entrenched theory of how we and the higher animals work. It has no special features that make it empirically invulnerable, no unique functions that make it irreplaceable, no special status of any kind whatsoever. We shall turn a skeptical ear then, to any special pleading on its behalf.

V. Beyond Folk Psychology

What might the elimination of FP actually involve—not just the comparatively straightforward idioms for sensation, but the entire apparatus of propositional attitudes? That depends heavily on what neuroscience might discover, and on our determination to capitalize on it. Here follow three scenarios in which the operative conception of cognitive activity is progressively divorced from the forms and categories that characterize natural language. If the reader will indulge the lack of actual substance, I shall try to sketch some plausible form.

First suppose that research into the structure and activity of the brain, both fine-grained and global, finally does yield a new kinematics and correlative dynamics for what is now thought of as cognitive activity. The theory is uniform for all terrestrial brains, not just human brains, and it makes suitable conceptual contact with both evolutionary biology and nonequilibrium thermodynamics. It ascribes to us, at any given time, a set or configuration of complex states, which are specified within the theory as figurative "solids" within a four- or five-dimensional phase space. The laws of the theory govern the interaction, motion, and transformation of these "solid" states within that space, and also their relations to whatever sensory and motor transducers the system possesses. As with celestial mechanics, the exact specification of the "solids" involved and the exhaustive accounting of all dynamically relevant adjacent "solids" is not practically possible, for many reasons, but here also it turns out that the obvious approximations we fall back on yield excellent explanations/predictions of internal change and external behavior, at least in the short term. Regarding long-term activity, the theory provides powerful and unified accounts of the learning process, the nature of mental illness, and variations in character and intelligence across the animal kingdom as well as across individual humans.

Moreover, it provides a straightforward account of "knowledge," as traditionally conceived. According to the new theory, any declarative sentence to which a speaker would give confident assent is merely a one-dimensional *projection*—through the compound lens of Wernicke's and Broca's areas onto the idiosyncratic surface of the speaker's language—a one-dimensional projection of a four- or five-dimensional 'solid' that is an element in his true kinematical state. (Recall the shadows on the wall of Plato's cave.) Being projections of that inner reality, such sentences do carry significant information regarding it and are thus fit to function as elements in a communication system. On the other hand, being *sub*dimensional projections, they reflect but a narrow part of the reality projected. They are therefore *un*fit to represent the deeper reality in all its kinematically, dynamically, and even normatively relevant respects. That is to say, a system of propositional attitudes, such as FP, must inevitably fail to capture what is going on here, though it may reflect just enough superficial structure to sustain an alchemylike tradition among folk who lack any better theory. From the perspective of the newer theory, however, it is plain that there simply are no law-governed states of the kind FP postulates. The real laws governing our internal activities are defined over different and much more complex kinematical states and configurations, as are the normative criteria for developmental integrity and intellectual virtue.

A theoretical outcome of the kind just described may fairly be counted as a case of elimination of one theoretical ontology in favor of another, but the success here imagined for systematic neuroscience need not have any sensible effect on common practice. Old ways die hard, and in the absence of some practical necessity, they may not die at all. Even so, it is not inconceivable that some segment of the population, or all of it, should become intimately familiar with the vocabulary required to characterize our kinematical states, learn the laws governing their interactions and behavioral projections, acquire a facility in their first-person ascription, and displace the use of FP altogether, even in the marketplace. The demise of FP's ontology would then be complete.

We may now explore a second and rather more radical possibility. Everyone is familiar with Chomsky's thesis that the human mind or brain contains innately and uniquely the abstract structures for learning and using specifically human natural languages. A competing hypothesis is that our brain does indeed contain innate structures, but that those structures have as their original and still primary function the organization of perceptual experience, the administration of linguistic categories being an acquired and additional function for which evolution has only incidentally suited them.[9] This hypothesis has the advantage of not requiring the evolutionary saltation that Chomsky's view would seem to require, and there are other advantages as well. But these matters need not concern us here. Suppose, for our purposes, that this competing view is true, and consider the following story.

Research into the neural structures that fund the organization and processing of perceptual information reveals that they are capable of administering a great variety of complex tasks, some of them showing a complexity far in excess of that shown by natural language. Natural languages, it turns out, exploit only a very elementary portion of the available machinery, the bulk of which serves far more complex activities beyond the ken of the propositional conceptions of FP. The detailed unraveling of what that machinery is and of the capacities it has makes it plain that a form of language far more sophisticated than "natural" language, though decidedly "alien" in its syntactic and semantic structures, could also be learned and used by our innate systems. Such a novel system of communication, it is quickly realized, could raise the efficiency of information exchange between brains by an order of magnitude, and would enhance epistemic evaluation by a comparable amount, since it would reflect the underlying structure of our cognitive activities in greater detail than does natural language.

Guided by our new understanding of those internal structures, we manage to construct a new system of verbal communication entirely distinct from natural language, with a new and more powerful combinatorial grammar over novel elements forming novel combinations with exotic properties. The compounded strings of this alternative system—call them "übersatzen"—are not evaluated as true or false, nor are the relations between them remotely analogous to the relations of entailment, etc., that hold between sentences. They display a different organization and manifest different virtues.

Once constructed, this "language" proves to be learnable; it has the power projected; and in two generations it has swept the planet. Everyone uses the new system. The syntactic forms and semantic categories of so-called natural language disappear entirely. And with them disappear the propositional attitudes of FP, displaced by a more revealing scheme in which (of course) "übersatzenal attitudes" play the leading role. FP again suffers elimination.

This second story, note, illustrates a theme with endless variations. There are possible as many different "folk psychologies" as there are possible differently structured communication systems to serve as models for them.

A third and even stranger possibility can be outlined as follows. We know that there is considerable lateralization of function between the two cerebral hemispheres, and that the two hemispheres make use of the information they get from each other by way of the great cerebral commissure—the corpus callosum—a giant cable of neurons connecting them. Patients whose commissure has been surgically severed display a variety of behavioral deficits that indicate a loss of access by one hemisphere to information it used to get from the other. However, in people with callosal agenesis (a congenital defect in which the connecting cable is simply absent), there is little or no behavioral deficit, suggesting that the two hemisphere have learned to exploit the information carried in other less direct pathways connecting them through the subcortical regions. This suggests that, even in the normal case, a developing hemisphere *learns* to make use of the information the cerebral commissure deposits at its doorstep. What we have then, in the case of a normal human, is two physically distinct cognitive systems (both capable of independent function) responding in a systematic and learned fashion to exchanged information. And what is especially interesting about this case is the sheer amount of information exchanged. The cable of the commissure consists of $\approx$ 200 million neurons,[10] and even if we assume that each of these fibers is capable of one of only two possible states each second (a most conservative estimate), we are looking at a channel whose information capacity is $> 2 \times 10^8$ binary bits/second. Compare this to the < 500 bits/second capacity of spoken English.

Now, if two distinct hemispheres can learn to communicate on so impressive a scale, why shouldn't two distinct brains learn to do it also? This would require an artificial "commissure" of some kind, but let us suppose that we can fashion a workable transducer for implantation at some site in the brain that research reveals to be suitable, a transducer to convert a symphony of neural activity into (say) microwaves radiated from an aerial in the forehead, and to perform the reverse function of converting received microwaves back into neural activation. Connecting it up need not be an insuperable problem. We simply trick the normal processes of dendretic arborization into growing their own myriad connections with the active microsurface of the transducer.

Once the channel is opened between two or more people, they can learn (*learn*) to exchange information and coordinate their behavior with the same intimacy and virtuosity displayed by your own cerebral hemispheres. Think what this might do for hockey teams, and ballet companies, and research teams! If the entire population were thus fitted out, spoken language of any kind might well disappear completely, a victim of the "why crawl when you can fly?" principle. Libraries become filled not with books, but with long recordings of exemplary bouts of neural activity. These constitute a growing cultural heritage, an evolving "Third World," to use Karl Popper's terms. But they do not consist of sentences or arguments.

How will such people understand and conceive of other individuals? To this question I can only answer, "In roughly the same fashion that your right hemisphere 'understands' and 'conceives of' your left hemisphere—intimately and efficiently, but not propositionally!"

These speculations, I hope, will evoke the required sense of untapped possibilities, and I shall in any case bring them to a close here. Their function is to make some inroads into the aura of inconceivability that commonly surrounds the idea that we might reject FP. The felt conceptual strain even finds expression in an argument to the effect that the thesis of eliminative materialism is incoherent since it denies the very conditions presupposed by the assumption that it is meaningful. I shall close with a brief discussion of this very popular move.

As I have received it, the reductio proceeds by pointing out that the statement of eliminative materialism is just a meaningless string of marks or noises, unless that string is the expression of a certain *belief*, and a certain *intention* to communicate, and a *knowledge* of the grammar of the language, and so forth. But if the statement of eliminative materialism is true, then there are no such states to express. The statement at issue would then be a meaningless string of marks or noises. It would therefore *not* be true. Therefore it is not true. Q.E.D.

The difficulty with any nonformal reductio is that the conclusion against the initial assumption is always no better than the material assumptions invoked to reach the incoherent conclusion. In this case the additional assumptions involve a certain theory of meaning, one that presupposes the integrity of FP. But formally speaking, one can as well infer, from the incoherent result, that this theory of meaning is what must be rejected. Given the independent critique of FP leveled earlier, this would even seem the preferred option. But in any case, one cannot simply assume that particular theory of meaning without begging the question at issue, namely, the integrity of FP.

The question-begging nature of this move is most graphically illustrated by the following analogue, which I owe to Patricia Churchland.[11] The issue here, placed in the seventeenth century, is whether there exists such a substance as *vital spirit*. At the time, this substance was held, without significant awareness of real alternatives, to be that which distinguished the animate from the inanimate. Given the monopoly enjoyed by this conception, given the degree to which it was integrated with many of our other conceptions, and given the magnitude of the revisions any serious alternative conception would require, the following refutation of any antivitalist claim would be found instantly plausible.

> The anti-vitalist says that there is no such thing as vital spirit. But this claim is self-refuting. The speaker can expect to be taken seriously only if his claim cannot. For if the claim is true, then the speaker does not have vital spirit and must be *dead*. But if he is dead, then his statement is a meaningless string of noises, devoid of reason and truth.

The question-begging nature of this argument does not, I assume, require elaboration. To those moved by the earlier argument, I commend the parallel for examination.

The thesis of this paper may be summarized as follows. The propositional attitudes of folk psychology do not constitute an unbreachable barrier to the advancing tide of neuroscience. On the contrary, the principled displacement of folk psychology is not only richly possible, it represents one of the most intriguing theoretical displacements we can currently imagine.

Notes

An earlier draft of this paper was presented at the University of Ottawa, and to the *Brain, Mind, and Person* colloquium at SUNY/Oswego. My thanks for the suggestions and criticisms that have informed the present version.

1. See Paul Feyerabend, "Materialism and the Mind-Body Problem," *Review of Metaphysics*, XVII. 1, 65 (September 1963): 49–66; Richard Rorty, "Mind-Body Identity, Privacy, and Categories," *ibid.*, XIX. 1, 73 (September 1965): 24–54; and my *Scientific Realism and the Plasticity of Mind* (New York: Cambridge, 1979).

2. We shall examine a handful of these laws presently. For a more comprehensive sampling of the laws of folk psychology, see my *Scientific Realism and the Plasticity of Mind, op cit.*, ch. 4. For a detailed examination of the folk principles that underwrite action explanation in particular, see my "The Logical Character of Action Explanations." *Philosophical Review*, LXXIX, 2 (April 1970): 214–236.

3. Staying within an objectual interpretation of the quantifiers, perhaps the simplest way to make systematic sense of expressions like ⌜x believes that p⌝ and closed sentences formed therefrom is just to construe whatever occurs in the nested position held by 'p', 'q', etc. as there having the function of a singular term. Accordingly, the standard connectives, as they occur between terms in that nested position, must be construed as there functioning as operators that form compound singular terms from other singular terms, and not as sentence operators. The compound singular terms so formed denote the appropriate compound propositions. Substitutional quantification will of course underwrite a different interpretation, and there are other approaches as well. Especially appealing is the prosentential approach by Dorothy Grover, Joseph Camp, and Nuel Belnap, "A Prosentential Theory of Truth," *Philosophical Studies*, XXVII, 2 (February 1975): 73–125. But the resolution of these issues is not vital to the present discussion.

4. A possible response here is to insist that the cognitive activity of animals and infants is linguaformal in its elements, structure, and processing right from birth. J. A. Fodor, in *The Language of Thought* (New York: Crowell, 1975), has erected a positive theory of thought on the assumption that the innate forms of cognitive activity have precisely the form here denied. For a critique of Fodor's view, see Patricia Churchland, "Fodor on Language Learning," *Synthese*, XXXVIII, 1 (May 1978): 149–159.

5. Most explicitly in "Three Kinds of Intentional Psychology" (forthcoming), but this theme of Dennett's goes all the way back to his "Intentional Systems, this JOURNAL, LXVIII, 4 (Feb. 25, 1971); 87–106; reprinted in his *Brainstorms* (Montgomery, Vt.: Bradford Books, 1978).

6. Popper, *Objective Knowledge* (New York: Oxford, 1972); with J. Eccles, *The Self and Its Brain* (New York: Springer Verlag, 1978). Margolis, *Persons and Minds* (Boston: Reidel, 1978).

7. *Psychological Explanation* (New York: Random House, 1968), p. 116.

8. "Robots: Machines or Artificially Created Life?", *Journal of Philosophy*, LXI, 21 (Nov. 12, 1964): 668–691, pp. 675, 681 ff.

9. Richard Gregory defends such a view in "The Grammar of Vision," *Listener*, LXXXIII, 2133 (February 1970): 242–246; reprinted in his *Concepts and Mechanisms of Perception* (London: Duckworth, 1975), pp. 622–629.

10. M. S. Gazzaniga and J. E. LeDoux, *The Integrated Mind* (New York: Plenum Press, 1975).

11. "Is Determinism Self-Refuting?" *Mind*, 90 (1981): 99–101.

Chapter 34

Three Kinds of Intentional Psychology

Daniel Dennett

1

Suppose you and I both believe that cats eat fish. Exactly what feature must we share for this to be true of us? More generally, recalling Socrates' favorite style of question, what must be in common between things truly ascribed an *intentional* predicate—such as 'wants to visit China' or 'expects noodles for supper'?[2] As Socrates points out, in the *Meno* and elsewhere, such questions are ambiguous or vague in their intent. One can be asking on the one hand for something rather like a definition, or on the other hand for something rather like a theory. (Socrates of course preferred the former sort of answer.) What do all magnets have in common? First answer: they all attract iron. Second answer: they all have such-and-such a microphysical property (a property that explains their capacity to attract iron). In one sense people knew what magnets were —they were things that attracted iron—long before science told them what magnets were. A child learns what the word 'magnet' means not, typically, by learning an explicit definition, but by learning the 'folk physics' of magnets, in which the ordinary term 'magnet' is embedded or implicitly defined as a theoretical term.[3]

Sometimes terms are embedded in more powerful theories, and sometimes they are embedded by explicit definition. What do all chemical elements with the same valence have in common? First answer: they are disposed to combine with other elements in the same integral ratios. Second answer: they all have such-and-such a microphysical property (a property which explains their capacity so to combine). The theory of valences in chemistry was well in hand before its microphysical explanation was known. In one sense chemists knew what valences were before physicists told them.

So what appears in Plato to be a contrast between giving a definition and giving a theory can be viewed as just a special case of the contrast between giving one theoretical answer and giving another, more 'reductive' theoretical answer. Fodor (1975) draws the same contrast between 'conceptual' and 'causal' answers to such questions, and argues that Ryle (1949) champions conceptual answers at the expense of causal answers, wrongly supposing them to be in conflict. There is justice in Fodor's charge against Ryle, for there are certainly many passages in which Ryle seems to propose his conceptual answers as a bulwark against the possibility of *any* causal, scientific, psychological answers, but there is a better view of Ryle's (or perhaps at best a view he ought to have held) that deserves rehabilitation. Ryle's 'logical behaviorism' is composed of his steadfastly conceptual answers to the Socratic questions about matters mental. If Ryle thought these answers ruled out psychology, ruled out causal (or reductive) answers to the Socratic questions, he was wrong, but if he thought only

Reprinted from *Reduction, Time and Reality*, ed. R. Healey (New York: Cambridge University Press, 1981), pp. 37–61, by permission of the author and the publisher. Copyright 1981 by Cambridge University Press.

that the conceptual answers to the questions were not to be given by a microreductive psychology, he was on firmer ground. It is one thing to give a causal explanation of some phenomenon and quite another to cite the cause of a phenomenon in the analysis of the concept of it.

Some concepts have what might be called an essential causal element.[4] For instance, the concept of a genuine Winston Churchill *autograph* has it that how the trail of ink was in fact caused is essential to its status as an autograph. Photocopies, forgeries, inadvertently indistinguishable signatures but perhaps not carbon copies—are ruled out. These considerations are part of the *conceptual* answer to the Socratic question about autographs.

Now some, including Fodor, have held that such concepts as the concept of intelligent action also have an essential causal element; behavior that appeared to be intelligent might be shown not to be by being shown to have the wrong sort of cause. Against such positions Ryle can argue that even if it is true that every instance of intelligent behavior is caused (and hence has a causal explanation), exactly *how* it is caused is inessential to its being intelligent—something that could be true even if all intelligent behavior exhibited in fact some common pattern of causation. That is, Ryle can plausibly claim that no account in causal terms could capture the class of intelligent actions except *per accidens*. In aid of such a position—for which there is much to be said in spite of the current infatuation with causal theories—Ryle can make claims of the sort Fodor disparages ('it's not the mental activity that makes the clowning clever because what makes the clowning clever is such facts as that it took place out where the children can see it') without committing the error of supposing causal and conceptual answers are incompatible.[5]

Ryle's logical behaviourism was in fact tainted by a groundless anti-scientific bias, but it need not have been. Note that the introduction of the concept of valence in chemistry was a bit of *logical chemical behaviorism*: to have valence *n* was 'by definition' to be disposed to behave in such-and-such ways under such-and-such conditions, *however* that disposition to behave might someday be explained by physics. In this particular instance the relation between the chemical theory and the physical theory is now well charted and understood—even if in the throes of ideology people sometimes misdescribe it—and the explanation of those dispositional combinatorial properties by physics is a prime example of the sort of success in science that inspires reductionist doctrines. Chemistry has been shown to reduce, in some sense, to physics, and this is clearly a Good Thing, the sort of thing we should try for more of.

Such progress invites the prospect of a parallel development in psychology. First we will answer the question 'What do all believers-that-*p* have in common?' the first way, the 'conceptual' way, and then see if we can go on to 'reduce' the theory that emerges in our first answer to something else—neurophysiology most likely. Many theorists seem to take it for granted that *some* such reduction is both possible and desirable, and perhaps even inevitable, even while recent critics of reductionism, such as Putnam and Fodor, have warned us of the excesses of "classical" reductionist creeds. No one today hopes to conduct the psychology of the future in the vocabulary of the neurophysiologist, let alone that of the physicist, and principled ways of relaxing the classical "rules" of reduction have been proposed. The issue, then, is *what kind* of theoretical bonds can we expect—or ought we to hope—to find uniting psychological claims about beliefs, desires, and so forth with the claims of neurophysiologists, biologist, and other physical scientists?

Since the terms 'belief' and 'desire' and their kin are parts of ordinary language, like 'magnet', rather than technical terms like 'valence', we must first look to "folk psychology' to see what kind of things we are being asked to explain. *What do we learn beliefs are when we learn how to use the words 'believe' and 'belief'?* The first point to make is that we do not really learn what beliefs are when we learn how to use these words.[6] Certainly no one *tells us* what beliefs are, or if someone does, or if we happen to speculate on the topic on our own, the answer we come to, wise or foolish, will figure only weakly in our habits of thought about what people believe. We learn to *use* folk psychology—as a vernacular social technology, a craft—but we don't learn it self-consciously as a theory—we learn no metatheory with the theory—and in this regard our knowledge of folk psychology is like our knowledge of the grammar of our native tongue. This fact does not make our knowledge of folk psychology entirely unlike human knowledge of explicit academic theories, however; one could probably be a good practising chemist and yet find it embarrassingly difficult to produce a satisfactory textbook definition of a metal or an ion.

There are no introductory textbooks of folk psychology (although Ryle's *The Concept of Mind* might be pressed into service), but many explorations of the field have been undertaken by ordinary language philosophers (under slightly different intentions), and more recently by more theoretically minded philosophers of mind, and from all this work an account of folk psychology—part truism and the rest controversy can be gleaned. What are beliefs? *Roughly*, folk psychology has it that *beliefs* are information-bearing states of people that arise from perceptions, and which, together with appropriately related *desires*, lead to intelligent *action*. That much is relatively uncontroversial, but does folk psychology also have it that nonhuman animals have beliefs? If so, what is the role of language in belief? Are beliefs constructed of parts? If so, what are the parts? Ideas? Concepts? Words? Pictures? Are beliefs like speech acts or maps or instruction manuals or sentences? Is it implicit in folk psychology that beliefs enter into causal relations, or that they don't? How do decisions and intentions intervene between belief-desire complexes and actions? Are beliefs introspectible, and if so, what authority do the believer's pronouncements have?

All these questions deserve answers, but one must bear in mind that there are different reasons for being interested in the details of folk psychology. One reason is that it exists as a phenomenon, like a religion or a language or a dress code, to be studied with the techniques and attitudes of anthropology. It may be a myth, but it is a myth we live in, so it is an 'important' phenomenon in nature. A different reason is that it seems to be a *true* theory, by and large, and hence is a candidate—like the folk physics of magnets and unlike the folk science of astrology—for incorporation into science. These different reasons generate different but overlapping investigations. The anthropological question should include in its account of folk psychology whatever folk actually include in their theory, however misguided, incoherent, gratuitous some of it may be.[7] The protoscientific quest, on the other hand, as an attempt to prepare folk theory for subsequent incorporation into or reduction to the rest of science, should be critical, and should *eliminate* all that is false or ill-founded, however well-entrenched in popular doctrine. (Thales thought that lodestones had souls, we are told. Even if most people agreed, this would be something to eliminate from the folk physics of magnets prior to 'reduction'.) One way of distinguishing the good from the bad, the essential from the gratuitous, in folk theory is to see what must be included in the theory to account for whatever predictive or explanatory success it seems to have in ordinary use. In this way we can criticize as we analyze, and it is even open to us in the end to discard folk psychology if it turns out to be a bad theory, and with it the presumed theoretical entities named therein. If we discard folk psychology as a theory, we would have to replace it with another theory, which while it did violence to many ordinary intuitions would explain the predictive power of the residual folk craft.

We use folk psychology all the time, to explain and predict each other's behaviour; we attribute beliefs and desires to each other with confidence—and quite unselfconsciously—and spend a substantial portion of our waking lives formulating the world —not excluding ourselves—in these terms. Folk psychology is about as pervasive a part of our second nature as is our folk physics of middle-sized objects. How good is folk psychology? If we concentrate on its weaknesses we will notice that we often are unable to make sense of particular bits of human behavior (our own included) in terms of belief and desire, even in retrospect; we often cannot predict accurately or reliably what a person will do or when; we often can find no resources within the theory for settling disagreements about particular attributions of belief or desire. If we concentrate on its strengths we find first that there are large areas in which it is extraordinarily reliable in its predictive power. Every time we venture out on a highway, for example, we stake our lives on the reliability of our general expectations about the perceptual beliefs, normal desires, and decision proclivities of the other motorists. Second, we find that it is a theory of great generative power and efficiency. For instance, watching a film with a highly original and unstereotypical plot, we see the hero smile at the villain and we all swiftly and effortlessly arrive at the same complex theoretical diagnosis: 'Aha!' we conclude (but perhaps not consciously), 'he wants her to think he doesn't know she intends to defraud his brother!' Third, we find that even small children pick up facility with the theory at a time when they have a very limited experience of human activity from which to induce a theory. Fourth, we find that we all use folk psychology knowing next to nothing about what actually happens inside people's skulls. 'Use your head' we are told, and we know some people are brainier than others, but our capacity to use folk psychology is quite unaffected by ignorance about brain processes—or even by large-scale misinformation about brain processes.

As many philosophers have observed, a feature of folk psychology that sets it apart from both folk physics and the academic physical sciences is the fact that explanations of actions citing beliefs and desires normally not only describe the provenance of the actions, but at the same time defend them as reasonable under the circumstances. They are reason-giving explanations, which make an ineliminable allusion to the rationality of the agent. Primarily for this reason, but also because of the pattern of strengths and weaknesses just described, I suggest that folk psychology might best be viewed as a rationalistic calculus of interpretation and prediction—an idealizing, abstract, instrumentalistic interpretation-method that has evolved because it works, and works because we have evolved. We approach each other as *intentional systems*,[8] that is, as entities whose behavior can be predicted by the method of attributing beliefs, desires and rational acumen according to the following rough and ready principles:[9]

> (1) A system's beliefs are those it *ought to have*, given its perceptual capacities, its epistemic needs, and its biography. Thus, in general, its beliefs are both true and relevant to its life, and when false beliefs are attributed, special stories must be told to explain how the error resulted from the presence of features in the environment that are deceptive relative to the perceptual capacities of the system.
>
> (2) A system's desires are those it *ought to have*, given its biological needs and the most practicable means of satisfying them. Thus intentional systems desire survival and procreation, and hence desire food, security, health, sex, wealth, power, influence, and so forth, and also whatever local arrangements tend (in

their eyes—given their beliefs) to further these ends in appropriate measure. Again, 'abnormal' desires are attributable if special stories can be told.

(3) A system's behavior will consist of those acts that *it would be rational* for an agent with those beliefs and desires to perform.

In (1) and (2) 'ought to have' means 'would have if it were *ideally* ensconced in its environmental niche'. Thus all dangers and vicissitudes in its environment it will *recognize as such* (i.e. *believe* to be dangers) and all the benefits—relative to its needs, of course—it will *desire*. When a fact about its surroundings is particularly relevant to its current projects (which themselves will be the projects such a being ought to have in order to get ahead in its world) it will *know* that fact, and act accordingly. And so forth and so on. This gives us the notion of an ideal epistemic and conative operator or agent, relativized to a set of needs for survival and procreation and to the environment(s) in which its ancestors have evolved and to which it is adapted. But this notion is still too crude and overstated. For instance, a being may come to have an epistemic need that its perceptual apparatus cannot provide for (suddenly all the green food is poisonous but alas it is colorblind), hence the relativity to perceptual capacities. Moreover, it may or may not have had the occasion to learn from experience about something, so its beliefs are also relative to its biography in this way: it will have learned what it ought to have learned, *viz.* what it had been given evidence for in a form compatible with its cognitive apparatus—providing the evidence was 'relevant' to its project then.

But this is still too crude, for we understand that evolution does not give us a best of all possible worlds, but only a passable jury-rig, so we should look for design shortcuts that in specifiably abnormal circumstances yield false perceptual beliefs, etc. (We are not immune to illusions—which we would be if our perceptual systems were *perfect*.) To offset the design shortcuts we should also expect design bonuses: circumstances in which the 'cheap' way for nature to design a cognitive system has the side benefit of giving good, reliable results even outside the environment in which the system evolved. Our eyes are well adapted for giving us true beliefs on Mars as well as on Earth—because the cheap solution for our Earth-evolving eyes happens to be a more general solution.

I propose that we can continue the mode of thinking just illustrated *all the way in*—not just for eye-design, but for deliberation-design and belief-design and strategy-concocter-design. In using this optimistic set of assumptions (nature has built us to do things right; look for systems to believe the truth and love the good) we impute no occult powers to epistemic needs, perceptual capacities and biography, but only the powers common sense already imputes to evolution and learning.

In short, we treat each other as if we were rational agents, and this myth—for surely we are not all that rational—works very well because we are *pretty* rational. This single assumption, in combination with home truths about our needs, capacities and typical circumstances, generates both an intentional interpretation of us as believers and desirers and actual predictions of behavior in great profusion. I am claiming, then, that folk psychology can best be viewed as a sort of logical behaviorism: *what it means* to say that someone believes that *p*, is that that person is disposed to behave in certain ways under certain conditions. What ways under what conditions? The ways it would be rational to behave, given the person's other beliefs and desires. The answer looks in danger of being circular, but consider: an account of what it is for an element to have a particular valence will similarly make ineliminable reference to the valences of other elements. What one is given with valence-talk is a whole system of interlocking attributions, which is saved from vacuity by yielding independently testable predictions.

I have just described in outline a *method* of predicting and explaining the behaviour of people and other intelligent creatures. Let me distinguish two questions about it: (1) is it something we could do and (2) is it something we in fact do? I think the answer to (1) is obviously yes, which is not to say the method will always yield good results. That much one can ascertain by reflection and thought experiment. Moreover, one can recognize that the method is familiar. Although we don't usually use the method self-consciously, we do use it self-consciously on those occasions when we are perplexed by a person's behavior, and then it often yields satisfactory results. Moreover, the ease and naturalness with which we resort to this self-conscious and deliberate form of problem-solving provide some support for the claim that what we are doing on those occasions is not *switching methods* but simply becoming self-conscious and explicit about what we ordinarily accomplish tacitly or unconsciously.

No other view of folk psychology, I think, can explain the fact that we do so well predicting each other's behavior on such slender and peripheral evidence; treating each other as intentional systems works (to the extent that it does) because we really are well designed by evolution and hence we *approximate* to the ideal version of ourselves exploited to yield the predictions. But not only does evolution not guarantee that we will always do what is rational; it guarantees that we won't. If we are designed by evolution, then we are almost certainly nothing more than a bag of tricks, patched together by a *satisficing*[11] nature, and no better than our ancestors had to be to get by. Moreover, the demands of nature and the demands of a logic course are not the same. Sometimes—even *normally* in certain circumstances—it pays to jump to conclusions swiftly (and even to forget that you've done so), so by most philosophical measures of rationality (logical consistency, refraining from invalid inference) there has probably been some positive evolutionary pressure in favor of 'irrational' methods.[12]

How rational are we? Recent research in social and cognitive psychology suggests we are *minimally* rational, appallingly ready to leap to conclusions or be swayed by logically irrelevant features of situations,[13] but this jaundiced view is an illusion engendered by the fact that these psychologists are deliberately trying to produce situations that provoke irrational responses—inducing pathology in a system by putting strain on it—and succeeding, being good psychologists. No one would hire a psychologist to prove that people will choose a paid vacation to a week in jail if offered an informed choice. At least not in the better psychology departments. A more optimistic impression of our rationality is engendered by a review of the difficulties encountered in artificial intelligence research. Even the most sophisticated AI programs stumble blindly into misinterpretations and misunderstandings that even small children reliably evade without a second thought.[14] From this vantage point we seem marvellously rational.

However rational we are, it is the myth of our rational agenthood that structures and organizes our attributions of belief and desire to others, and that regulates our own deliberations and investigations. We aspire to rationality, and without the myth of our rationality the concepts of belief and desire would be uprooted. Folk psychology, then, is *idealized* in that it produces its predictions and explanations by calculating in a normative system; it predicts what we *will* believe, desire, and do, by determining what we *ought* to believe, desire, and do.[15]

Folk psychology is *abstract* in that the beliefs and desires it attributes are not— or need not be—presumed to be intervening distinguishable states of an internal behavior-causing system. (The point will be enlarged upon later.) The role of the concept of belief is like the role of the concept of a centre of gravity, and the calculations that yield the predictions are more like the calculations one performs with a parallelo-gram of forces than like the calculations one performs with a blueprint of internal levers and cogs.

Folk psychology is thus *instrumentalistic* in a way the most ardent realist should permit: people really do have beliefs and desires, on my version of folk psychology, just the way they really have centers of gravity and the earth has an equator.[16] Reichenbach distinguished between two sorts of referents for theoretical terms: *illata* —posited theoretical entities—and *abstracta*—calculation-bound entities or logical constructs.[17] Beliefs and desires of folk psychology (but not all mental events and states) are *abstracta*.

This view of folk psychology emerges more clearly in contrast to a diametrically opposed view, each of whose tenets has been held by some philosopher, and at least most of which have been espoused by Fodor:

> Beliefs and desires, just like pains, thoughts, sensations and other episodes, are taken by folk psychology to be real, intervening, internal states or events, in causal interaction, subsumed under covering laws of causal stripe. Folk psychol-ogy is not an idealized, rationalistic calculus but a naturalistic, empirical, descrip-tive theory, imputing causal regularities discovered by extensive induction over experience. To suppose two people share a belief is to suppose them to be ulti-mately in some structurally similar internal condition, e.g. for them to have the same words of Mentalese written in the functionally relevant places in their brains.

I want to deflect this head-on collision of analyses by taking two steps. First, I am prepared to grant a measure of the claims made by the opposition. *Of course* we don't all sit in the dark in our studies like mad Leibnizians rationalistically excogitating behavioral predictions from pure, idealized concepts of our neighbors, nor do we derive all our readiness to attribute desires from a careful generation of them from the ultimate goal of survival. We may observe that some folks seem to desire cigarettes, or pain, or notoriety (we observe this by hearing them tell us, seeing what they choose, etc.) and without any conviction that these people, given their circumstances, ought to have these desires, we attribute them anyway. So rationalistic generation of attribu-tions is augmented and even corrected on occasion by empirical generalizations about belief and desire that guide our attributions and are learned more or less inductively. For instance, small children believe in Santa Claus, people are inclined to believe the more self-serving of two interpretations of an event in which they are involved (unless they are depressed), and people can be made to want things they don't need by making them believe that glamorous people like those things. And so forth in familiar profu-sion. This folklore does not consist in *laws*—even probabilistic laws—but some of it is being turned into science of a sort, e.g., theories of 'hot cognition' and cognitive dissonance. I grant the existence of all this naturalistic generalization, and its role in the normal calculations of folk psychologists—i.e., all of us. People do rely on their own parochial group of neighbours when framing intentional interpretations. That is why people have so much difficulty understanding foreigners—their behavior, to say noth-ing of their languages. They impute more of their own beliefs and desires, and those of their neighbors, than they would if they followed my principles of attribution slavishly. Of course this is a perfectly reasonable shortcut for people to take, even when it often leads to bad results. We are in this matter, as in most, satisficers, not optimizers, when it comes to information gathering and theory construction. I would insist, however, that all this empirically obtained lore is laid over a fundamental generative and normative framework that has the features I have described.

My second step away from the conflict I have set up is to recall that the issue is not what folk psychology as found in the field truly is, but what it is at its best, what deserves to be taken seriously and incorporated into science. It is not particularly to the point to argue against me that folk psychology is *in fact* committed to beliefs and desires as distinguishable, causally interacting *illata*; what must be shown is that it *ought* to be. The latter claim I will deal with in due course. The former claim I *could* concede without embarrassment to my overall project, but I do not concede it, for it seems to me that the evidence is quite strong that our ordinary notion of belief has next to nothing of the concrete in it. Jacques shoots his uncle dead in Trafalgar Square and is apprehended on the spot by Sherlock; Tom reads about it in the *Guardian* and Boris learns of it in *Pravda*. Now Jacques, Sherlock, Tom, and Boris have had remarkably *different* experiences—to say nothing of their earlier biographies and future prospects—but there is one thing they share: they all believe that a Frenchman has committed murder in Trafalgar Square. They did not all *say* this, not even 'to themselves'; *that proposition* did not, we can suppose, 'occur to' any of them, and even if it had, it would have had entirely different import for Jacques, Sherlock, Tom, and Boris. Yet they all believe that a Frenchman committed murder in Trafalgar Square. This is a shared property that is, as it were, visible only from one very limited point of view—the point of view of folk psychology. Ordinary folk psychologists have no difficulty imputing such useful but elusive commonalities to people. If they then insist that in doing so they are postulating a similarly structured object, as it were, in each head, this is a gratuitous bit of misplaced concreteness, a regrettable lapse in ideology.

But in any case there is no doubt that folk psychology is a mixed bag, like folk productions generally, and there is no reason in the end not to grant that it is much more complex, variegated (and in danger of incoherence) than my sketch has made it out to be. The *ordinary* notion of belief no doubt does place beliefs somewhere midway between being *illata* and being *abstracta*. What this suggests to me is that the concept of belief found in ordinary understanding, i.e. in folk psychology, is unappealing as a scientific concept. I am reminded of Anaxagoras' strange precursor to atomism: the theory of seeds. There is a portion of everything in everything, he is reputed to have claimed. Every object consists of an infinity of seeds, of all possible varieties. How do you make bread out of flour, yeast, and water? Flour contains bread seeds in abundance (but flour seeds predominate—that's what makes it flour), and so do yeast and water, and when these ingredients are mixed together, the bread seeds form a new majority so bread is what you get. Bread nourishes by containing flesh and blood and bone seeds in addition to its majority of bread seeds. Not good theoretical entities, these seeds, for as a sort of bastardized cross between properties and proper parts they have a penchant for generating vicious regresses, and their identity conditions are problematic to say the least.

Beliefs are rather like that. There seems no comfortable way of avoiding the claim that we have an infinity of beliefs, and common intuition does not give us a stable answer to such puzzles as whether the belief that 3 is greater than 2 is none other than the belief that 2 is less than 3. The obvious response to the challenge of an infinity of beliefs with slippery identity conditions is to suppose these beliefs are not all 'stored separately'; many—in fact *most* if we are really talking about infinity—will be stored *implicitly* in virtue of the *explicit* storage of a few (or a few million—the *core beliefs*.[18] The core beliefs will be 'stored separately', and they look like promising *illata* in contrast to the *virtual* or *implicit* beliefs which look like paradigmatic *abstracta*. But although this might turn out to be the way our brains are organized, I suspect things will be more complicated than this: there is no reason to suppose the core *elements*, the concrete, salient, separately stored representation-tokens (and there must be some such elements in any complex information processing system), will explicitly represent (or *be*) a subset of our *beliefs* at all. That is, if you were to sit down and write out a list of a thousand or so of your paradigmatic beliefs, *all* of them could turn out to be virtual, only implicitly stored or represented, and what was explicitly stored would be information (e.g., about memory addresses, procedures for problem-solving, or recognition, etc.) that was entirely unfamiliar. It would be folly to prejudge this empirical issue by insisting that our core representations of information (whichever they turn out to be) are beliefs *par excellence*, for when the facts are in our intuitions may instead support the contrary view: the least controversial self-attributions of belief may pick out beliefs that from the vantage point of developed cognitive theory are invariably virtual.[19]

In such an eventuality what could we say about the *causal* roles we assign ordinarily to beliefs (e.g. 'Her belief that John knew her secret caused her to blush')? We could say that whatever the core elements were in virtue of which she virtually believed that John knew her secret, they, the core elements, played a direct causal role (somehow) in triggering the blushing response. We would be wise, as this example shows, not to tamper with our *ordinary* catalog of beliefs (virtual though they might all turn out to be), for these are predictable, readily understandable, manipulable regularities in psychological phenomena in spite of their apparent neutrality with regard to the explicit/implicit (or core/virtual) distinction. What Jacques, Sherlock, Boris, and Tom have in common is probably only a virtual belief 'derived' from largely different explicit stores of information in each of them, but virtual or not, it is their sharing of *this* belief that would explain (or permit us to predict) in some imagined circumstances their all taking the same action when given the same new information. ('And now for one million dollars, Tom [Jacques, Sherlock, Boris], answer our jackpot question correctly: has a French citizen ever committed a major crime in London?')

At the same time we want to cling to the equally ordinary notion that beliefs can cause not only actions, but blushes, verbal slips, heart attacks, and the like. Much of the debate over whether or not intentional explanations are causal explanations can be bypassed by noting how the core elements, *whatever they may be*, can be cited as playing the causal role, while belief remains virtual. 'Had Tom not believed that p and wanted that q, he would not have done A.' Is this a causal explanation? It is tantamount to this: Tom was in some one of an indefinitely large number of structurally different states of type B that have in common just that each one of them licenses attribution of belief that p and desire that q in virtue or its normal relations with many other states of Tom, and this state, whichever one it was, was causally sufficient, given the 'background conditions' of course, to initiate the intention to perform A, and thereupon A was performed, and had he not been in one of those indefinitely many type B states, he would not have done A. One can call this a causal explanation because it talks about causes, but it is surely as unspecific and unhelpful as a causal explanation can get. It commits itself to there being some causal explanation or other falling within a very broad area (i.e, the intentional interpretation is held to be supervenient on Tom's bodily condition), but its true informativeness and utility in actual prediction lie, not surprisingly, in its assertion that Tom, however his body is currently structured, has a particular set of these elusive intentional properties, beliefs, and desires.

The ordinary notion of belief is pulled in two directions. If we want to have *good* theoretical entities, good *illata*, or good logical constructs, good *abstracta*, we will have to jettison some of the ordinary freight of the concepts of belief and desire. So I propose a divorce. Since we seem to have both notions wedded in folk psychology, let's split them apart and create two new theories: one strictly abstract, idealizing, holistic, instrumentalistic—pure intentional system theory—and the other a concrete, microtheoretical science of the actual realization of those intentional systems—what I will call subpersonal cognitive psychology. By exploring their differences and inter-relations, we should be able to tell whether any plausible 'reductions' are in the offing.

2

The first new theory, intentional system theory, is envisaged as a close kin of—and overlapping with—such already existing disciplines as decision theory and game theory, which are similarly abstract, normative and couched in intentional language. It borrows the ordinary terms, 'belief' and 'desire' but gives them a technical meaning within the theory. It is a sort of holistic logical behaviorism because it deals with the prediction and explanation from belief-desire profiles of the actions of whole systems (either alone in environments or in interaction with other intentional systems), but treats the individual realizations of the systems as black boxes. The *subject* of all the intentional attributions is the whole system (the person, the animal, or even the corporation or nation)[20] rather than any of its parts, and individual beliefs and desires are not attributable in isolation, independently of other belief and desire attributions. The latter point distinguishes intentional system theory most clearly from Ryle's logical behaviorism, which took on the impossible burden of characterizing individual beliefs (and other mental states) as particular individual dispositions to outward behavior.

The theory deals with the 'production' of new beliefs and desires from old, *via* an interaction among old beliefs and desires, features in the environment, and the system's actions, and this creates the illusion that the theory contains naturalistic descriptions of internal processing in the systems the theory is about, when in fact the processing is all in the manipulation of the theory, and consists in updating the intention characterization of the whole system according to the rules of attribution. An analogous illusion of process would befall a naive student who, when confronted with a parallelogram of forces, supposed that it pictured a mechanical linkage of rods and pivots of some kind instead of being simply a graphic way of representing and plotting the effect of several simultaneously acting forces.

Richard Jeffrey (1970), in developing his concept of probability kinematics, has usefully drawn attention to an analogy with the distinction in physics between kinematics and dynamics. In kinematics,

> you talk about the propagation of motions throughout a system in terms of such constraints as rigidity and manner of linkage. It is the physics of position and time, in terms of which you can talk about velocity and acceleration, but not about force and mass. When you talk about forces—*causes* of accelerations—you are in the realm of dynamics (172).

Kinematics provides a simplified and idealized level of abstraction appropriate for many purposes—e.g. for the *initial* design development of a gearbox—but when one must deal with more concrete details of systems—e.g. when the gearbox designer must worry about friction, bending, energetic efficiency, and the like—one must switch to dynamics for more detailed and reliable predictions, at the cost of increased complexity and diminished generality. Similarly one can approach the study of belief (and desire and so forth) at a highly abstract level, ignoring problems of realization and simply setting out what the normative demands on the design of a believer are. For instance, one can ask such questions as 'What must a system's epistemic capabilities and propensities be for it to survive in environment A?'[21] or 'What must this system already know in order for it to be able to learn B?' or 'What intentions must this system have in order to mean something by saying something?'[22]

Intentional system theory deals just with the performance specifications of believers while remaining silent on how the systems are to be implemented. In fact this neutrality with regard to implementation is the most useful feature of intentional characterizations. Consider, for instance, the role of intentional characterizations in evolutionary biology. If we are to explain the evolution of complex behavioral capabilities or cognitive talents by natural selection, we must note that it is the intentionally characterized capacity (e.g., the capacity to acquire a belief, a desire, to perform an intentional action) that has survival value, however it happens to be realized as a result of mutation. If a particularly noxious insect makes its appearance in an environment, the birds and bats with a survival advantage will be those that come to believe this insect is not good to eat. In view of the vast differences in neural structure, genetic background and perceptual capacity between birds and bats, it is highly unlikely that this useful trait they may come to share has a common description at any level more concrete or less abstract than intentional system theory. It is not only that the intentional predicate is a projectible predicate in evolutionary theory; since it is more general than its species-specific counterpart predicates (which characterize the successful mutation just in birds, or just in bats), it is preferable. So from the point of view of evolutionary biology, we would not want to 'reduce' all intentional characterizations even if we knew in particular instances what the physiological implementation was.

This level of generality is essential if we want a theory to have anything meaningful and defensible to say about such topics as intelligence in general (as opposed, say, to just human or even terrestrial or natural intelligence), or such grand topics as meaning or reference or representation. Suppose, to pursue a familiar philosophical theme, we are invaded by Martians, and the question arises: do they have beliefs and desires? Are they that much *like us*? According to intentional system theory, if these Martians are smart enough to get here, then they most certainly have beliefs and desires—in the technical sense proprietary to the theory no matter what their internal structure, and no matter how our folk psychological intuitions rebel at the thought.

This principled blindness of intentional system theory to internal structure seems to invite the retort:[23] but there has to be *some* explanation of the *success* of intentional prediction of the behavior of systems. It isn't just magic. It isn't a mere coincidence that one can generate all these *abstracta*, manipulate them *via* some version of practical reasoning, and come up with an action prediction that has a good chance of being true. There must be some way in which the internal processes of the system mirror the complexities of the intentional interpretation, or its success would be a miracle.

Of course. This is all quite true and important. Nothing without a great deal of structural and processing complexity could conceivably realize an intentional system of any interest, and the complexity of the realization will surely bear a striking resemblance to the complexity of the instrumentalistic interpretation. Similarly, the success of valence theory in chemistry is no coincidence, and people were entirely right to expect that deep microphysical similarities would be discovered between elements with the same valence, and that the structural similarities found would explain the dispositional similarities. But since people and animals are unlike atoms and molecules not only in being the products of a complex evolutionary history, but also in being the products of their individual learning histories, there is no reason to suppose that individual (human) believers that *p*—like individual (carbon) atoms with valence 4—regulate their dispositions with *exactly* the same machinery. Discovering the constraints on design and implementation variation, and demonstrating how particular species and individuals in fact succeed in realizing intentional systems is the job for the third theory: subpersonal cognitive psychology.

3

The task of subpersonal cognitive psychology is to explain something that at first glance seems utterly mysterious and inexplicable. The brain, as intentional system theory and evolutionary biology show us, is a *semantic engine*; its task is to discover what its multifarious inputs *mean*, to discriminate them by their significance and 'act accordingly'.[24] That's what brains *are for*. But the brain, as physiology or plain common sense shows us, is just a *syntactic engine*; all it can do is discriminate its inputs by their structural, temporal, and physical features, and let its entirely mechanical activities be governed by these 'syntactic' features of its inputs. That's all brains *can do*. Now how does the brain manage to get semantics from syntax? How could *any* entity (how could a genius, or an angel, or God) get the semantics of a system from nothing but its syntax? It couldn't. The syntax of a system doesn't determine its semantics. By what alchemy, then, does the brain extract semantically reliable results from syntactically driven operations? It cannot be designed to do an impossible task, but it could be designed to *approximate* the impossible task, to *mimic* the behavior of the impossible object (the semantic engine) by capitalizing on close (close enough) fortuitous correspondences between structural regularities—of the environment and of its own internal states and operations—and semantic types.

The basic idea is familiar. An animal needs to know when it has satisfied the goal of finding and ingesting food, but it settles for a friction-in-the-throat-followed-by-stretched-stomach detector, a mechanical switch turned on by a relatively simple mechanical condition that *normally* co-occurs with the satisfaction of the animal's 'real' goal. It's not fancy, and can easily be exploited to trick the animal into either eating when it shouldn't or leaving off eating when it shouldn't, but it does well enough by the animal in its normal environment. Or suppose I am monitoring telegraph transmissions and have been asked to intercept all *death threats* (but only death threats in English to make it 'easy'). I'd like to build a machine to save me the trouble of interpreting semantically every message sent, but how could this be done? No machine could be designed to do the job perfectly, for that would require defining the semantic category *death threat in English* as some tremendously complex feature of strings of alphabetic symbols, and there is utterly no reason to suppose this could be done in a principled way. (If somehow by brute-force inspection and subsequent enumeration we could list all and only the English death threats of, say, less than a thousand characters, we could easily enough build a filter to detect them, but we are looking for a principled, projectible, extendable method.) A really crude device could be made to discriminate all messages containing the symbol strings

... I will kill you ...

or

... you ... die ... unless ...

or

... (for some finite disjunction of likely patterns to be found in English death threats).

This device would have some utility, and further refinements could screen the material that passed this first filter, and so on. An unpromising beginning for constructing a sentence understander, but if you want to get semantics out of syntax (whether the syntax of messages in a natural language or the syntax of afferent neuron impulses), variations on this basic strategy are your only hope.[25] You must put together a bag of tricks and hope nature will be kind enough to let your device get by. Of course some tricks are elegant, and appeal to deep principles of organization, but in the end all one can hope to produce (all natural selection can have produced) are systems that *seem* to discriminate meanings by actually discriminating things (tokens of no doubt wildly disjunctive types) that co-vary reliably with meanings.[26] Evolution has designed our brains not only to do this but to evolve and follow strategies of self-improvement in this activity during their individual lifetimes.[27]

It is the task of subpersonal cognitive psychology to propose and test models of such activity—of pattern recognition or stimulus generalization, concept learning, expectation, learning, goal-directed behavior, problem-solving—that not only produce a simulacrum of genuine content-sensitivity, but that do this in ways demonstrably like the way people's brains do it, exhibiting the same powers and the same vulnerabilities to deception, overload, and confusion. It is here that we will find our good theoretical entities, our useful *illata*, and while some of them may well resemble the familiar entities of folk psychology—beliefs, desires, judgments, decisions—many will certainly not.[28] The only similarity we can be sure of discovering in the *illata* of subpersonal cognitive psychology is the intentionality of their labels.[29] They will be characterized as events with content, bearing information, signaling this and ordering that.

In order to give the *illata* these labels, in order to maintain any intentional interpretation of their operation at all, the theorist must always keep glancing outside the system, to see what normally produces the configuration he is describing, what effects the system's responses normally have on the environment, and what benefit normally accrues to the whole system from this activity. In other words the cognitive psychologist cannot ignore the fact that it is the realization of an intentional system he is studying on pain of abandoning semantic interpretation and hence psychology. On the other hand, progress in subpersonal cognitive psychology will blur the boundaries between it and intentional system theory, knitting them together much as chemistry and physics have been knit together.

The alternative of ignoring the external world and its relations to the internal machinery (what Putnam has called psychology in the narrow sense, or methodological solipsism, and Keith Gunderson lampoons as black world glass box perspectivalism)[30] is not really psychology at all, but just at best abstract neurophysiology—pure internal syntax with no hope of a semantic interpretation. Psychology 'reduced' to neurophysiology in this fashion would not be psychology, for it would not be able to provide an explanation of the regularities it is psychology's particular job to explain: the reliability with which 'intelligent' organisms can cope with their environments and thus prolong their lives. Psychology can, and should, work towards an account of the

Black Box Behaviorism   Black World Glass Box Perspectivalism

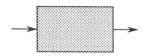
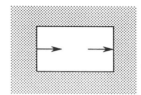

physiological foundations of psychological processes, not by eliminating psycho-logical or intentional characterizations of those processes, but by exhibiting how the brain implements the intentionally characterized performance specifications of sub-personal theories.[31]

Friedman, discussing the current perplexity in cognitive psychology, suggests that the problem

> is the direction of reduction. Contemporary psychology tries to explain *individual* cognitive activily independently from *social* cognitive actitity, and then tries to give a *micro* reduction of social cognitive activity—that is, the use of a public language—in terms of a prior theory of individual cognitive activity. The op-posing suggestion is that we first look for a theory of social activity, and then try to give a *macro* reduction of individual cognitive activity—the activity of applying concepts, making judgments, and so forth—in terms of our prior social theory.[32]

With the idea of macroreduction in psychology I largely agree except that Fried-man's identification of the macro level as explicitly *social* is only part of the story. The cognitive capacities of non-language-using animals (and Robinson Crusoes, if there are any) must also be accounted for, and not just in terms of an analogy with the practices of us language users. The macro level *up* to which we should relate microprocesses in the brain in order to understand them as psychological is more broadly the level of organism-environment interaction, development and evolution. That level includes social interaction as a particularly important part,[33] but still a proper part.

There is no way to capture the semantic properties of things (word tokens, dia-grams, nerve impulses, brain states) by a microreduction. Semantic properties are not just relational but, you might say, superrelational, for the relation a particular vehicle of content, or token, must bear in order to have content is not just a relation it bears to other similar things (e.g., other tokens, or parts of tokens, or sets of tokens, or causes of tokens) but a relation between the token and the whole life—and counterfactual life[34]—of the organism it 'serves' *and* that organism's requirements for survival *and* its evolutionary ancestry.

4

Of our three psychologies—folk psychology, intentional system theory, and subper-sonal cognitive psychology—what then might reduce to what? Certainly the one-step microreduction of folk psychology to physiology alluded to in the slogans of the early identity theorists will never be found—and should never be missed, even by staunch friends of materialism and scientific unity. A prospect worth exploring, though, is that folk psychology (more precisely, the part of folk psychology worth caring about) reduces—conceptually—to intentional system theory. What this would amount to can best be brought out by contrasting this proposed conceptual reduction with more familiar alternatives: 'type-type identity theory' and 'Turing machine functionalism'. According to type-type identity theory, for every mentalistic term or predicate '*M*', there is some predicate '*P*' *expressible in the vocabulary of the physical sciences* such that a creature is *M* if and only if it is *P*. In symbols:

(1) (x)(Mx ≡ Px)

This is reductionism with a vengeance, taking on the burden of replacing, in principle, all mentalistic predicates with coextensive predicates composed truth-functionally from the predicates of physics. It is now widely agreed to be hopelessly too strong a demand. Believing that cats eat fish is, intuitively, a *functional* state that might be variously implemented physically, so there is no reason to suppose the commonality referred to on the left-hand side of (1) can be reliably picked out by any predicate, however complex, of physics. What is needed to express the predicate on the right-hand side is, it seems, a physically neutral language for speaking of functions and functional states, and the obvious candidates are the languages used to describe automata—for instance, Turing machine language.

The Turing machine functionalist then proposes

(2) (x)(Mx ≡ x realizes some Turing machine k in logical state A)

In other words, for two things both to believe that cats eat fish they need not be physically similar in any specifiable way, but they must both be in a 'functional' condition specifiable in principle in the most general functional language; they must share a Turing machine description according to which they are both in some particular logical state. This is still a reductionist doctrine, for it proposes to identify each mental type with a functional type picked out in the language of automata theory. But this is still too strong, for there is no more reason to suppose Jacques, Sherlock, Boris, and Tom 'have the same program' in *any* relaxed and abstract sense, considering the differences in their nature and nurture, than that their brains have some crucially identical physico-chemical feature. We must weaken the requirements for the right-hand side of our formula still further.

Consider

(3) (x)(x believes that p ≡ x can be predictively attributed the belief that p)

This appears to be blatantly circular and uninformative, with the language on the right simply mirroring the language on the left. But all we need to make an informative answer of this formula is a systematic way of making the attributions alluded to on the right-hand side. Consider the parallel case of Turing machines. What do two different realizations or embodiments of a Turing machine have in common when they are in the same logical state? Just this: there is a system of description such that according to it both are described as being realizations of some particular Turing machine, and according to this description, which is predictive of the operation of both entities, both are in the same state of that Turing machine's machine table. One doesn't *reduce* Turing machine talk to some more fundamental idiom; one *legitimizes* Turing machine talk by providing it with rules of attribution and exhibiting its predictive powers. If we can similarly legitimize 'mentalistic' talk, we will have no need of a reduction, and that is the point of the concept of an intentional system. Intentional systems are supposed to play a role in the legitimization of mentalistic predicates parallel to the role played by the abstract notion of a Turing machine in setting down rules for the interpretation of artifacts as computational automata. I fear my concept is woefully informal and un-

systematic compared with Turing's, but then the domain it attempts to systematize—
our everyday attributions in mentalistic or intentional language—is itself something
of a mess, at least compared with the clearly defined field of recursive function theory,
the domain of Turing machines.

The analogy between the theoretical roles of Turing machines and intentional
systems is more than superficial. Consider that warhorse in the philosophy of mind,
Brentano's thesis that intentionality is the mark of the mental: all mental phenomena
exhibit intentionality and no physical phenomena exhibit intentionality. This has been
traditionally taken to be an *irreducibility* thesis: the mental, in virtue of its intentionality,
cannot be reduced to the physical. But given the concept of an intentional system, we
can construe the first half of Brentano's thesis—all mental phenomena are intentional
—as a *reductionist* thesis of sorts, parallel to Church's thesis in the foundation of
mathematics.

According to Church's thesis, every 'effective' procedure in mathematics is recursive, that is, Turing-computable. Church's thesis is not provable, since it hinges on
the intuitive and informal notion of an effective procedure, but it is generally accepted,
and it provides a very useful reduction of a fuzzy-but-useful mathematical notion to a
crisply defined notion of apparently equal scope and greater power. Analogously, the
claim that every mental phenomenon alluded to in folk psychology is *intentional-
system-characterizable* would, if true, provide a reduction of the mental as ordinarily
understood—a domain whose boundaries are at best fixed by mutual acknowledgment and shared intuition—to a clearly defined domain of entities, whose principles of
organization are familiar, relatively formal and systematic, and entirely general.[35]

This reductive claim, like Church's thesis, cannot be proven, but could be made
compelling by piecemeal progress on particular (and particularly difficult) cases—a
project I set myself elsewhere (in *Brainstorms*). The final reductive task would be to
show not how the terms of intentional system theory are eliminable in favor of
physiological terms via subpersonal cognitive psychology, but almost the reverse: to
show how a system described in physiological terms could warrant an interpretation
as a realized intentional system.

Notes

1. I am grateful to the Thyssen Philosophy Group, the Bristol Fulbright Workshop, Elliot Sober, and Bo
   Dahlbom for extensive comments and suggestions on an earlier draft of this paper.
2. Other 'mental' predicates, especially those invoking episodic and allegedly *qualia*-laden entities—
   pains, sensations, images—raise complications of their own which I will not consider here, for I have
   dealt with them at length elsewhere, especially in *Brainstorms* (1978). I will concentrate here on the
   foundational concepts of belief and desire, and will often speak just of belief, implying, except where
   I note it, that parallel considerations apply to desire.
3. The child need learn only a portion of this folk physics, as Putnam argues in his discussion of the
   'division of linguistic labour' (1975).
4. Cf. Fodor 1975: 7n.
5. This paragraph corrects a misrepresentation of both Fodor's and Ryle's positions in my critical notice
   of Fodor's book in *Mind*, 1977, reprinted in *Brainstorms*, pp. 90–108.
6. I think it is just worth noting that philosophers' use of 'believe' as the standard and general ordinary
   language term is a considerable distortion. We *seldom* talk about what people *believe*; we talk about
   what they *think* and what they *know*.
7. If the anthropologist marks part of the catalogue of folk theory as false, as an inaccurate or unsound
   account of the folk craft, he may speak of *false consciousness* or *ideology*; the role of such false theory
   in constituting a feature of the anthropological phenomenon is not diminished by its falseness.
8. See my "Intentional Systems" (1971).
9. For a more elaborate version of similar principles, see Lewis 1974.
10. Cf. Sober (unpublished) for useful pioneering exploration of these topics.

11. The term is Herbert Simon's (e.g. 1969).

12. While in general true beliefs have to be more useful than false beliefs (and hence a system ought to have true beliefs), in special circumstances it may be better to have a few false beliefs. For instance it might be better for beast B to have some false beliefs about whom B can beat up and whom B can't. Ranking B's likely antagonists from ferocious to pushover, we certainly want B to believe it can't beat up all the ferocious ones, and can beat up all the obvious pushovers, but it is better (because it 'costs less' in discrimination tasks and protects against random perturbations such as bad days and lucky blows) for B to extend 'I can't beat up x' to cover even some beasts it can in fact beat up. *Erring on the side of prudence* is a well recognized good strategy, and so Nature can be expected to have valued it on occasion when it came up. An alternative strategy in this instance would be to abide by the rule: avoid conflict with penumbral cases. But one might have to 'pay more' to implement that strategy than to implement the strategy designed to produce, and rely on, some false beliefs.

13. See, e.g. Tversky and Kahneman 1974; and Nisbett and Ross 1980.

14. Roger Schank's (1977; Schank and Abelson 1977) efforts to get a computer to 'understand' simple but normally gappy stories is a good illustration.

15. It tests its predictions in two ways: action predictions it tests directly by looking to see what the agent does; belief and desire predictions are tested indirectly by employing the predicted attributions in further predictions of eventual actions. As usual, the Duhemian thesis holds: belief and desire attributions are under-determined by the available data.

16. Michael Friedman's "Theoretical Explanation" in R. Healey, ed., *Reduction, Time and Reality*. Cambridge: Cambridge University Press, 1981, provides an excellent analysis of the role of instrumentalistic thinking within realistic science. Scheffler (1963) provides a useful distinction between *instrumentalism* and *fictionalism*. In his terms I am characterizing folk psychology as instrumentalistic, not fictionalistic.

17. Reichenbach 1938: 211–12. 'Our observations of concrete things confer a certain probability on the existence of *illata*—nothing more ... Second, there are inferences to *abstracta*. These inferences are ... equivalences, not probability inferences. Consequently, the existence of abstracta is reducible to the existence of concreta. There is, therefore, no problem of their objective existence; their status depends on a convention.'

18. See my "Brain Writing and Mind Reading," 1975. See also Fodor 1975, and Field 1978.

19. See Field 1978: 55, n. 12 on 'minor concessions' to such instrumentalistic treatments of belief.

20. See my "Conditions of Personhood" (1976).

21. Cf. Campbell 1973, and his William James lectures (Harvard U.P., forthcoming).

22. The questions of this variety are familiar, of course, to philosophers, but are now becoming equally familiar to researchers in artificial intelligence.

23. From Ned Block and Jerry Fodor, *inter alia*, in conversation.

24. More accurately if less picturesquely, the brain's task is to come to produce internal mediating responses that reliably vary in concert with variation in the actual environmental significance (the natural and non-natural meanings, in Grice's (1957) sense) of their distal causes and independently of meaning—irrelevant variations in their proximal causes, and moreover to respond to its mediating responses in ways that systematically tend to improve the creature's prospects in its environment if the mediating responses are varying as they ought to vary.

25. One might think that while *in principle* one cannot derive the semantics of a system from nothing but its syntax, *in practice* one might be able to cheat a little and exploit syntactic features that don't *imply* a semantical interpretation, but strongly suggest one. For instance, faced with the task of deciphering isolated documents in an entirely unknown and alien language, one might note that while the symbol that *looks like* a duck doesn't *have* to mean 'duck', there is a good chance that it does, especially if the symbol that look like a wolf seems to be eating the symbol that looks like a duck, and not *vice versa*. Call this *hoping for hieroglypics* and note the form it has taken in psychological theories from Locke to the present: we will be able to tell which mental representations are which (which idea is the idea of *dog* and which of *cat*) because the former will look like a dog and the latter like a cat. This is all very well as a crutch for us observers on the outside, trying to assign content to the events in some brain, but it is of no use to the brain ... because brains don't know what dogs look like! Or better, this cannot be the brain's fundamental method of eking semantic classes out of raw syntax, for any brain (or brain part) that could be said—in an extended sense—to know what dogs look like would be a brain (or brain part) that had already solved its problem, that was already (a simulacrum of) a semantic engine. But this is still misleading, for brains in any event do not *assign* content to their own events in the way observers might: brains *fix* the content of their internal events in the act of reacting as they do. There are good reasons for positing *mental images* of one sort or another in cognitive theories (see

'Two Approaches to Mental Images' in *Brainstorms*, pp. 174–89) but hoping for hieroglyphics isn't one of them, though I suspect it is covertly influential.

26. I take this point to be closely related to Davidson's reasons for claiming there can be no psychophysical laws, but I am unsure that Davidson wants to draw the same conclusions from it that I do. See Davidson 1970.

27. This claim is defended in my "Why the law of effect will not go away" (1974).

28. See, for instance, Stephen Stich's (1978) concept of subdoxastic states.

29. See my "Reply to Arbib and Gunderson", in *Brainstorms*, pp. 23–38.

30. In his reply to Fodor's 'Methodological Solipsism as a Research Strategy in Psychology' at the Cincinnati Colloquium on Philosophy of Psychology, February 1978.

31. I treat methodological solipsism in (much) more detail in 'Beyond Belief', in Andrew Woodfield, ed. *Thought and Object*.

32. Michael Friedman, "Theoretical Explanation," in R. Healey, ed., (1981), pp. 15–16.

33. See Tyler Burge 1979.

34. What I mean is this: counterfactuals enter because content is in part a matter of the *normal* or *designed* role of a vehicle whether or not it ever gets to play that role. Cf. Sober (unpublished).

35. Ned Block (1978) presents arguments supposed to show how the various possible functionalist theories of mind all slide into the sins of 'chauvinism' (improperly excluding Martians from the class of possible mind-havers) or 'liberalism' (improperly including various contraptions, imagined human puppets, and so forth among the mind-havers). My view embraces the broadest liberalism, gladly paying the price of a few recalcitrant intuitions for the generality gained.

References

Block, N. 1978. "Troubles with functionalism." *Perception and Cognition: Issues in the Foundations of Psychology*, ed. C. Wade Savage, pp. 261–326. Minnesota Studies in Philosophy of Science, vol. IX. Minneapolis: Minnesota University Press.

Burge, T. 1979. "Individualism and the mental." *Midwest Studies in Philosophy*, vol . IV pp. 73–121 .

Campbell, D. 1973. "Evolutionary epistemology." *The Philosophy of Karl Popper*, ed . Paul A. Schilpp. La Salle, Illinois: Open Court.

Davidson, D. 1970. "Mental events." *Experience and Theory*, ed. L. Foster and J. Swanson, pp. 79–102. Amherst: University of Massachusetts Press.

Dennett, D. C. 1971. "Intentional systems." *Journal of Philosophy* 68, 87–106. Reprinted (with other essays on intentional systems) in Brainstorms, pp. 3–22.

Dennett, D. C. 1974. "Why the law of effect will not go away." *Journal of the Theory of Social Behaviour* 5, 169–187. Reprinted in *Brainstorms*, pp. 71–89.

Dennett, D. C. 1975. "Brain writing and mind reading." *Language, Mind and Knowledge*, ed. K. Gunderson. Minnesota Studies in Philosophy of Science, vol. VII. Minneapolis: Minnesota University Press. Reprinted in *Brainstorms*, pp. 39–50

Dennett, D. C. 1976. "Conditions of personhood." *The Identities of Persons*, ed. A. Rorty. Reprinted in *Brainstorms*, pp. 267–85.

Dennett, D. C. 1978. *Brainstorms*. Montgomery, Vermont: Bradford Books; Hassocks, Sussex: Harvester Press.

Field, H. 1978. "Mental representation." *Erkenntnis* 13, 9–61.

Fodor, J. 1975. *The Language of Thought*. Hassocks, Sussex: Harvester Press; Scranton, Pa.: Crowell.

Grice, H. P. 1957. "Meaning." *Philosophical Review* 66, 377–88.

Healey, R., ed., 1981. *Reduction, Time & Reality*. Cambridge: Cambridge University Press.

Jeffrey, R. 1970. "Dracula meets Wolfman: acceptance vs. partial belief." *Induction, Acceptance and Rational Belief*, ed. Marshall Swain. Dordrecht: Reidel.

Lewis, D. 1974. "Radical interpretation." *Synthèse* 23, 331–44.

Nisbett, R. E. and Ross, L. D. 1980. *Human Inference: Strategy and Shortcomings*. Englewood Cliffs, N.J.: Prentice Hall.

Putnam, H. 1975. "The meaning of 'meaning'." *Mind, Language and Reality (Philosophical Papers*, vol. II), pp. 215–71. Cambridge: Cambridge University Press.

Reichenbach, H. 1938. *Experience and Prediction*. Chicago: University of Chicago Press.

Ryle, G. 1949. *The Concept of Mind*. London: Hutchinson.

Schank, R. 1977. "Sam—a story understander." Research Report 43, Yale University Dept. of Computer Science.

Schank, R. and Abelson, R. 1977. *Scripts, Plans, Goals and Understanding*. Hillside, N.J.: Erlbaum.

Scheffler, I. 1963. *The Anatomy of Inquiry*. New York: Knopf.

Simon, H. 1969. *The Sciences of the Artificial.* Cambridge, Mass.: MIT Press.

Sober, E. (unpublished) 'The Descent of Mind.'

Stich, S. 1978. "Belief and subdoxastic states." *Philosophy of Science* 45, 499–518.

Tversky, A. and Kahneman, D. 1974. "Judgement under uncertainty: heuristics and biases." *Science* 185, 1124–31.

Woodfield, A., ed., 1982. *Thought and Object.* Oxford: Oxford University Press.

Chapter 35

Methodological Solipsism Considered as a Research Strategy in Cognitive Psychology

Jerry Fodor

... to form the idea of an object and to form an idea simply is the same thing; the
reference of the idea to an object being an extraneous denomination, of which in itself it
bears no mark or character.
Hume, *Treatise*, book I

Your standard contemporary cognitive psychologist—your throughly modern menta-list—is disposed to reason as follows. To think (e.g.) that Marvin is melancholy is to represent Marvin in a certain way; viz., as being melancholy (and not, for example, as being maudlin, morose, moody, or merely moping and dyspeptic). But surely we cannot represent Marvin as being melancholy except as we are in some or other relation to a representation of Marvin; and not just to *any* representation of Marivn, but, in particular, to a representation the content of which is *that* Marvin is melancholy; a representation which, as it were, expresses the proposition that Marvin is melan-choly. So, a fortiori, at least some mental states/processes are or involve at least some relations to at least some representations. Perhaps, then, this is the *typical* feature of such mental states/processes as cognitive psychology studies; perhaps all such states can be viewed as relations to representations and all such processes as operations defined on representations.

This is, prima facie, an appealing proposal since it gives the psychologist two degrees of freedom to play with and they seem, intuitively, to be the right two. On the one hand, mental states are distinguished by the *content* of the associated rep-resentations, so we can allow for the difference between thinking that Marvin is melancholy and thinking that Sam is (or that Albert isn't, or that it sometimes snows in Cincinnati); and, on the other hand, mental states are distinguished by the *relation* that the subject bears to the associated representation (so we can allow for the difference between thinking, hoping, supposing, doubting and pretending that Marvin is melancholy). It's hard to believe that a serious psychology could make do with fewer (or less refined) distinctions than these, and it's hard to believe that a psychology that makes these distinctions could avoid taking the notion of mental representation seri-ously. Moreover, the burden of argument is clearly upon anyone who claims that we need *more* degrees of freedom than just these two: the least hypothesis that is remotely plausible is that a mental state is (type) individuated by specifying a relation and a representation such that the subject bears the one to the other.[2]

I'll say that any psychology that takes this line is a version of the *representational theory of the mind*. I think that it's reasonable to adopt some such theory as a sort of working hypothesis, if only because there aren't any alternatives which seem to be even remotely plausible and because empirical research carried out within this framework has, thus far, proved interesting and fruitful.[3] However, my present concern is neither to attack nor to defend this view, but rather to distinguish it from something other—and stronger—that modern cognitive psychologists *also* hold. I shall put this stronger doctrine as the view that mental states and processes are *Computational*. Much of what is characteristic of cognitive psychology is a consequence of adherence to this stronger view. What I want to do in this paper is to say something about what this stronger view is, something about why I think it's plausible, and, most of all, something about the ways in which it shapes the cognitive psychology we have.

I take it that computational processes are both *symbolic* and *formal*. They are symbolic because they are defined over representations, and they are formal because they apply to representations, in virtue of (roughly) the *syntax* of the representations. It's the second of these conditions that makes the claim that mental processes are computational stronger than the representational theory of the mind. Most of this paper will be a meditation upon the consequences of assuming that mental processes are formal processes.

I'd better cash the parenthetical "roughly." To say that an operation is formal isn't the same as saying that it is syntactic since we could have formal processes defined over representations which don't, in any obvious sense, *have* a syntax. Rotating an image would be a timely example. What makes syntactic operations a species of formal operations is that being syntactic is a way of *not* being semantic. Formal operations are ones that are specified without reference to such semantic properties of representations as, for example, truth, reference and meaning. Since we don't know how to complete this list (since, that is, we don't know what semantic properties there are), I see no responsible way of saying what, in general, formality amounts to. The notion of formality will thus have to remain intuitive and metaphoric, at least for present purposes: formal operations apply in terms of the, as it were, "shapes" of the objects in their domains.[4]

To require that mental processes be computational (viz., formal-syntactic) is thus to require something not very clear. Still, the requirement has some clear consequences, and they are striking and tendentious. Consider that we started by assuming that the *content* of representations is a (type) individuating feature of mental states. So far as the *representational* theory of the mind is concerned, it's possibly the *only* thing that distinguishes Peter's thought that Sam is silly from his thought that Sally is depressed. But, now, if the *computational* theory of the mind is true (and if, as we may assume, content is a semantic notion par excellence) it follows that content alone cannot distinguish thoughts. More exactly, the computational theory of the mind requires that two thoughts can be distinct in content only if they can be identified with relations to formally distinct representations. More generally: fix the subject and the relation, and then mental states can be (type) distinct only if the representations which constitute their objects are formally distinct.

Again, consider that accepting a formality condition upon mental states implies a drastic narrowing of the ordinary ontology of the mental; all sorts of states which look, prima facie, to be mental states in good standing are going to turn out to be none of the psychologist's business if the formality condition is endorsed. This point is one that philosophers have made in a number of contexts, and usually in a deprecating tone of voice. Take, for example, knowing that such-and-such, and assume that you can't know what's not the case. Since, on that assumption, knowledge is involved with truth, and since truth is a semantic notion, it's going to follow that there can't be a psychology of *knowledge* (even if it is consonant with the formality condition to hope for a psychology of *belief*). Similarly, it's a way of making a point of Ryle's to say that, strictly speaking, there can't be a psychology of perception if the formality condition is to be complied with. Seeing is an achievement; you can't see what's not there. From the point of view of the representational theory of the mind, this means that seeing involves relations between mental representations *and their referents*; hence, semantic relations within the meaning of the act.

I hope that such examples suggest (what, in fact, I think is true) that even if the formality condition isn't very clear, it is quite certainly very strong. In fact, I think it's not all *that* anachronistic to see it as the central issue which divides the two main traditions in the history of psychology: "Rational psychology" on the one hand, and "Naturalism" on the other. Since this is a mildly eccentric way of cutting the pie, I'm going to permit myself a semihistorical excursus before returning to the main business of the paper.

Descartes argued that there is an important sense in which how the world is makes no difference to one's mental states. Here is a well-known passage form the *Meditations*:

> At this moment it does indeed seem to me that it is with eyes awake that I am looking at this paper; that this head which I move is not asleep, that it is deliberately and of set purpose that I extend my hand and perceive it.... But in thinking over this I remind myself that on many occasions I have been deceived by similar illusions, and in dwelling on this reflection I see so manifestly that there are no certain indications by which we may clearly distinguish wakefulness from sleep that I am lost in astonishment. And my astonishment is such that it is almost capable of persuading me that I now dream. (Descartes 1931)

At least three sorts of reactions to this kind of argument are distinguishable in the philosophical literature. First, there's a long tradition, including both Rationalists and Empiricists, which takes it as axiomatic that one's experiences (and, a fortiori, one's beliefs) might have been just as they are even if the world had been quite different from the way that it is. See, for example, the passage from Hume which serves as an epigraph to this paper. Second, there's a vaguely Wittgensteinian mood in which one argues that it's just *false* that one's mental states might have been what they are had the world been relevantly different. For example, if there had been a dagger there, Macbeth would have been *seeing*, not just hallucinating. And what could be more different than that? If the Cartesian feels that this reply misses the point, he is at least under an obligation to say precisely which point it misses; in precisely *which* respects the way the world is is irrelevant to the character of one's beliefs, experiences, etc. Finally there's a tradition which argues that—epistemology to one side—it is at best a strategic mistake to attempt to develop a psychology which individuates mental states without reference to their environmental causes and effects; (e.g., which counts the state that Macbeth *was* in as type-identical to the state he would have been in had the dagger been supplied.) I have in mind the tradition which includes the American Naturalists (notably Peirce and Dewey), all the learning theorists, and such contemporary representatives as Quine in philosophy and Gibson in psychology. The recurrent theme here is that psychology is a branch of biology, hence that one must view the organism as embedded in a physical environment. The psychologist's job is to trace those organism/environment interactions which constitute its behavior. A passage from William James (1890, p. 6) will serve to give the feel of the thing:

On the whole, few recent formulas have done more service of a rough sort in psychology than the Spencerian one that the essence of mental life and of bodily life are one, namely, 'the adjustment of inner to outer relations.' Such a formula is vagueness incarnate; but because it takes into account the fact that minds inhabit environments which act on them and on which they in turn react; because, in short, it takes mind in the midst of all its concrete relations, it is immensely more fertile than the old-fashioned 'rational psychology' which treated the soul as a detached existent, sufficient unto itself, and assumed to consider only its nature and its properties.

A number of adventitious intrusions have served to muddy the issues in this long-standing dispute. On the one hand, it may well be that Descartes was relying on a specifically introspectionist construal of the claim that the individuation of mental states is independent of their environmental causes. That is, Descartes's point may have been that (a) mental states are (type) identical if and only if (iff) they are introspectively indistinguishable, and (b) introspection cannot distinguish (e.g.) perception from hallucination, or knowledge from belief. On the other hand, the naturalist, in point of historical fact, is often a behaviorist as well. He wants to argue not only that mental states are individuated by reference to organism/environment relations, but also that such relations constitute the mental. In the context of the present discussion he is arguing for the abandonment not just of the formality condition, but of the notion of mental representation as well.

If, however, we take the computational theory of the mind as what's central to the issue, we can reconstruct the debate between rational psychologists and naturalists in a way that does justice to both their points; in particular, in a way that frees the discussion from involvement with introspectionism on the one side and behaviorism on the other.

Insofar as we think of mental processes as computational (hence as formal operations defined on representations) it will be natural to take the mind to be, inter alia, a kind of computer. That is, we will think of the mind as carrying out whatever symbol manipulations are constitutive of the hypothesized computational processes. To a first approximation, we may thus construe mental operations as pretty directly analogous to those of a Turing machine. There is, for example, a working memory (corresponding to a tape) and there are capacities for scanning and altering the contents of the memory (corresponding to the operations of reading and writing on the tape). If we want to extend the computational metaphor by providing access to information about the environment, we can think of the computer as having access to "oracles" which serve, on occasion, to enter information in the memory. On the intended interpretation of this model these oracles are analogs to the senses. In particular, they are assumed to be transducers in that what they write on the tape is determined solely by the ambient environmental energies that impinge upon them. (For elaboration of this sort of account, see Putnam [1960]; it is, of course, widely familiar from discussions in the field of artificial intelligence.)

I'm not endorsing this model, but simply presenting it as a natural extension of the computational picture of the mind. Its present interest is that we can use it to see how the formality condition connects with the Cartesian claim that the character of mental processes is somehow independent of their environmental causes and effects. The point is that, so long as we are thinking of mental processes as purely computational, the bearing of environmental information upon such processes is exhausted by the formal character of whatever the oracles write on the tape. In particular, it doesn't matter to such processes whether what the oracles write is *true*; whether, for example, they really are transducers faithfully mirroring the state of the environment, or merely the output end of a typewriter manipulated by a Cartesian demon bent on deceiving the machine. I'm saying, in effect, that the formality condition, viewed in this context, is tantamount to a sort of methodological solipsism. If mental processes are formal, then they have access only to the formal properties of such representations of the environment as the senses provide. Hence, they have no access to the *semantic* properties of such representations, including the property of being true, of having referents, or, indeed, the property of being representations *of the environment*.

That some such methodological solipsism really is implicated in much current psychological practice is best seen by examining what researchers actually do. Consider, for example, the well-known work of Professor Terry Winograd. Winograd was primarily interested in the computer simulation of certain processes involved in the handling of verbal information; asking and answering questions, drawing inferences, following instructions and the like. The form of his theory was a program for a computer which "lives in" and operates upon a simple world of blocklike geometric objects (see Winograd 1971). Many of the capacities that the device exercises vis-à-vis its environment seem impressively intelligent. It can arrange the blocks to order, it can issue "perceptual" reports of the present state of its environment and "memory" reports of its past states, it can devise simple plans for achieving desired environmental configurations, and it can discuss its undertakings (more or less in English) with whoever is running the program.

The interesting point for our purposes, however, is that the machine environment which is the nominal object of these actions and conversations actually isn't there. What actually happens is that the programmer so arranges the memory states of the machine that the available data are whatever they would be *if* there were objects for the machine to perceive and manipulanda for it to operate upon. In effect the machine lives in an entirely notional world; all its beliefs are false. Of course, it doesn't matter to the machine that its beliefs are false since falsity is a semantic property and, qua computer, the device satisfies the formality condition; viz., it has access only to formal (nonsemantic) properties of the representations that it manipulates. In effect, the device is in precisely the situation that Descartes dreads; it's a mere computer which dreams that it's a robot.

I hope that this discussion suggests how acceptance of the computational theory of the mind leads to a sort of methodological solipsism as a part of the research strategy of contemporary cognitive psychology. In particular, I hope it's clear how you get that consequence from the formality condition alone, without so much as raising the introspection issue. I stress this point because it seems to me that there has been considerable confusion about it among the psychologists themselves. People who do machine simulation, in particular, very often advertise themselves as working on the question how thought (or language) is related to the world. My present point is that, whatever else they're doing, they certainly aren't doing *that*. The very assumption that defines their field—viz., that they study mental processes *qua* formal operations on symbols—guarantees that their studies won't answer the question how the symbols so manipulated are semantically interpreted. You can, for example, build a machine that answers baseball questions in the sense that (e.g.) if you type in "Who had the most wins by a National League pitcher since Dizzy Dean?" it will type out "Robin Roberts, who won 28." But you delude yourself if you think that a machine which in this sense answers baseball questions, is thereby answering questions *about* baseball (or that the machine has somehow referred to Robin Roberts). If the *programmer* chooses to interpret the machine inscription "Robin Roberts won 28" as a statement about Robin Roberts (e.g., as the statement that he won 28), that's all well and good, but it's no business of the machine's. The machine has no access to that interpretation, and its computations are in no way affected by it. The machine doesn't know what it's talking about, it doesn't care; *about* is a semantic relation.[5]

This brings us to a point where, having done some sort of justice to the Cartesian's insight, we can also do some sort of justice to the naturalist's. For, after all, mental processes are supposed to be operations on representations, and it is in the nature of representations to represent. We have seen that a psychology which embraces the formality condition is thereby debarred from raising questions about the semantic properties of mental representations; yet surely such questions ought *somewhere* to be raised. The computer which prints out "RR won 28" is not thereby referring to RR. But, surely, when I think: *RR won 28*, I *am* thinking about RR, and if not in virtue of having performed some formal operations on some representations, then presumably in virtue of something else. It's perhaps borrowing the least tendentious fragment of causal theories of reference to assume that what fixes the interpretation of my mental representations of RR is something about the way that he and I are embedded in the world; perhaps not a causal chain stretching between us, but anyhow *some* facts about how he and I are causally situated; *Dasein*, as you might say. Only a *naturalistic* psychology will do to specify these facts, because here we are explicitly in the realm of organism/environment transactions.

We are on the verge of a bland and ecumenical conclusion that there is room both for a computational psychology—viewed as a theory of formal processes defined over mental representations—*and* a naturalistic psychology, viewed as a theory of the (presumably causal) relations between representations and the world which fix the semantic interpretations of the former. I think that, in principle, this is the right way to look at things. In practice, however, I think that it's misleading. So far as I can see, it's overwhelmingly likely that computational psychology is the only one that we are going to get. I want to argue for this conclusion in two steps. First, I'll argue for what I've till now only assumed: that we must *at least* have a psychology which accepts the formality condition. Then I'll argue that there's good reason to suppose that that's the most that we can have; that a naturalistic psychology isn't a practical possibility and isn't likely to become one.

The first move, then, is to give reasons for believing that at least some part of psychology should honor the formality condition. Here too the argument proceeds in two steps. I'll argue first that it is typically under an *opaque* construal that attributions of propositional attitudes to organisms enter into explanations of their behavior; and second that the formality condition is intimately involved with the explanation of propositional attitudes so construed: roughly, that it's reasonable to believe that we can get such explanations only within computational theories. *Caveat emptor*: the arguments under review are, in large part, nondemonstrative. In particular, they will assume the perfectibility in principle of the kinds of psychological theories now being developed, and it is entirely possible that this is an assumption contrary to fact.

Thesis: when we articulate the generalizations in virtue of which behavior is contingent upon mental states, it is typically an opaque construal of the mental state attributions that does the work; for example it's a construal under which believing that *a is F* is logically independent from believing that *b is F*, even in the case where $a = b$. It will be convenient to speak not only of opaque construals of propositional attitude ascriptions, but also of *opaque taxonomies* of mental state types; e.g., of taxonomies which, inter alia, count the belief that the morning star rises in the east as type distinct from the belief that the evening star does. (Correspondingly, *transparent* taxonomies are such as, inter alia, would count these beliefs as type-identical). So, the claim is that mental states are typically opaquely taxonomized for purposes of psychological theory.[6]

The point doesn't depend upon the examples, so I'll stick to the most informal sorts of cases. Suppose I know that John wants to meet the girl who lives next door, and suppose I know that this is true when "wants to" is construed opaquely. Then, given even rough-and-ready generalizations about how people's behaviors are contingent upon their utilities, I can make some reasonable predictions (guesses) about what John is likely to do: he's likely to say (viz., utter), "I want to meet the girl who lives next door." He's likely to call upon his neighbor. He's likely (at a minimum, and all things being equal) to exhibit next-door-directed behavior. None of this is frightfully exciting, but it's all I need for present purposes, and what more would you expect from folk psychology?

On the other hand, suppose that all I know is that John wants to meet the girl next door where "wants to" is construed transparently; i.e., all I know is that it's true of the girl next door that John wants to meet her. Then there is little or nothing that I can predict about how John is likely to proceed. And this is not just because rough and ready psychological generalizations want ceteris paribus clauses to fill them in; it's also for the deeper reason that I can't infer from what I know about John to any relevant description of the mental causes of his behavior. For example, I have no reason to predict that John will say such things as "I want to meet the girl who lives next door" since, let John be as cooperative and as truthful as you like, and let him be utterly a native speaker, still, he *may* believe that the girl he wants to meet languishes in Latvia. In which case, "I want to meet the girl who lives next door" is the last thing it will occur to him to say. (The contestant wants to say "suspender," for "suspender" is the magic word. Consider what we can predict about his probable verbal behavior if we take this (a) opaquely and (b) transparently. And, of course, the same sorts of points apply, mutatis mutandis, to the prediction of *non*verbal behavior).

Ontologically, transparent readings are stronger than opaque ones; for example, the former license existential inferences which the latter do not. But psychologically opaque readings are stronger than transparent ones; they tell us more about the character of the mental causes of behavior. The representational theory of mind offers an explanation of this anomaly. Opaque ascriptions are true in virtue of the way that the agent represents the objects of his wants (intentions, beliefs, etc.) *to himself*. And, by assumption, such representations function in the causation of the behaviors that the agent produces. So, for example, to say that it's true *opaquely* that Oedipus did such-and-such because he wanted to marry Jocasta, is to say something like (though not, perhaps, very like; see Fodor 1978b): "Oedipus said to himself, 'I want to marry Jocasta,' and his so saying was among the causes of his behavior." Whereas to say (only) that it's true transparently that O. wanted to marry J. is to say no more than that among the causes of his behavior was O.'s saying to himself "I want to marry ..." where the blank was filled by *some* expression that denotes J.[7] But now, what O. *does*, how he in the proprietary sense behaves, will depend on which description he (literally) had in mind.[8] If it's "Jocasta," courtship behavior follows ceteris paribus. Whereas, if it's "my Mum," we have the situation towards the end of the play and Oedipus at Colonus eventually ensues.

I dearly wish that I could leave this topic here, because it would be very convenient to be able to say, without qualification, what I strongly implied above: the opaque readings of propositional attitude ascriptions tell us how people represent the objects of their propositional attitudes. What one would like to say, in particular, is that if two people are identically related to formally identical mental representations, then they are in opaquely type-identical mental states. This would be convenient because it yields a succinct and gratifying characterization of what a computational cognitive psychology is about: such a psychology studies propositional attitudes opaquely taxonomized.

I think, in fact, that this is *roughly* the right thing to say since what I think is *exactly* right is that the construal of propositional attitudes which such a psychology renders is nontransparent. (It's nontransparency that's crucial in all the examples we have been considering). The trouble is that nontransparency isn't quite the same notion as opacity, as we shall now see.

The question before us is: "What are the relations between the pretheoretic notion of type identity of mental states opaquely construed and the notion of type identity of mental states that you get from a theory which strictly honors the formality condition?" And the answer is complicated. For one thing, it's not clear that we have *a* pretheoretic notion of the opaque reading of a propositional attitude ascription: I doubt that the two standard tests for opacity (failure of existential generalization and failure of substitutivity of identicals) even pick out the same class of cases. But what's more important are the following considerations. While it's notorious that extensionally identical thoughts may be opaquely type distinct (e.g., thoughts about the morning star and thoughts about the evening star) there are nevertheless some semantic conditions on opaque type identification. In particular:

> (a) there are some cases of formally distinct but coextensive token thoughts which count as tokens of the same (opaque) type (and hence as identical in content at least on one way of individuating contents); and
> (b) *non*coextensive thoughts are ipso facto, type-distinct (and differ in content, at least on one way of individuating contents).

Cases of type (a): 1. I think I'm sick and you think I'm sick. What's running through my head is "I'm sick"; what's running through your head is "he's sick." But we are both having thoughts of the same (opaque) type (and hence of the same content).

2. You think: "that one looks edible"; I think: "this one looks edible." Our thoughts are opaquely type-identical if we are thinking about the same one.

It connects with the existence of such cases that pronouns and demonstratives are typically (perhaps invariably) construed as referring, even when they occur in what are otherwise opaque constructions. So, for example, it seems to me that I can't report Macbeth's hallucination by saying: "Macbeth thinks that's a dagger" if Macbeth is staring at nothing at all. Which is to say that "that's a dagger" doesn't report Macbeth's mental state even though "that's a dagger" may be precisely what is running through Macbeth's head (precisely the representation his relation to which is constitutive of his belief).

Cases of type (b): 1. Suppose that Sam feels faint and Misha knows he does. Then what's running through Misha's head may be "he feels faint." Suppose too that Misha feels faint and Alfred knows he does. Then what's running through Alfred's head, too, may be "he feels faint." I have no, or rather no univocal, inclination to say, in this case, that Alfred and Misha are having type identical thoughts even though the principle of type individuation is, by assumption, opaque and even though Alfred and Misha have the same things running through their heads. But if this is right, then formal identity of mental representations cannot be sufficient for type identity of opaquely taxonomized mental states.[9] (There is an interesting discussion of this sort of case in Geach

[1957]. Geach says that Aquinas says that there is no "intelligible difference" between Alfred's thought and Misha's. I don't know whether this means that they are having the same thought or that they aren't).

2. Suppose that there are two Lake Eries (two bodies of water so-called). Consider two tokens of the thought "Lake Erie is wet," one of which is, intuitively speaking, about the Lake Erie in North America and one of which is about the other one. Here again, I'm inclined to say that the aboriginal, uncorrupted pretheoretical notion of type-wise same thought wants these to be tokens of *different* thoughts and takes these thoughts to differ in content. (Though in this case, as in the others, I think there's also a countervailing inclination to say that they count as type-identical—and as identical in content—for some relevant purposes and in some relevant respects. How like aboriginal, uncorrupted, pretheoretical intuition!)

I think, in short, that the intuitive opaque taxonomy is actually what you might call "semitransparent." On the one hand, certain conditions on coreference are in force (Misha's belief that he's ill is type distinct from Sam's belief that *he's* ill and my thought *this is edible* may be type identical to your thought *that is edible*.) On the other hand, you don't get free substitution of coreferring expressions (beliefs about the morning star are type-distinct from beliefs about the evening star) and existential generalization doesn't go through for beliefs about Santa Claus.

Apparently, then, the notion of same mental state that we get from a theory which honors the formality condition is related to, but not identical to, the notion of same mental state that unreconstructed intuition provides for opaque construals. And it would certainly be reasonable to ask whether we actually need both. I think the answer is probably: yes, if we want to capture all the intuitions. For if we restrict ourselves to either one of the taxonomies, we get consequences that we don't like. On the one hand, if we taxonomize *purely* formally, we get identity of belief compatible with difference of truth value. (Misha's belief that he's ill will be type-identical to Sam's belief that *he's* ill, but one may be true while the other is false.) On the other hand, if we taxonomize solely according to the pretheoretic criteria, we get trouble with the idea that people act out of their beliefs and desires. We need, in particular, some taxonomy according to which Sam and Misha have the *same* belief in order to explain why it is that they exhibit the same behaviors. It is, after all, *part* of the pretheoretic notion of belief that difference in belief ought ceteris paribus to show up in behavior *somewhere*; ("ceteris paribus" means "given relevant identities among other mental states"). Whereas, it's possible to construct cases where differences like the one between Misha's belief and Sam's can't show up in behavior even in principle (see note 9). What we have, in short, is a tension between a partially semantic taxonomy and an entirely functional one, and the recommended solution is to use both.

Having said all this, I now propose largely to ignore it and use the term "opaque taxonomy" for principles of type individuation according to which Misha and Sam are in the same mental state when each believes himself to be ill. When I need to distinguish this sense of opaque taxonomy from the pretheoretic one, I'll talk about *full* opacity and fully opaque type identification.

My claim has been that, in doing our psychology, we want to attribute mental states fully opaquely because it's the fully opaque reading which tells us what the agent has in mind, and it's what the agent has in mind that causes his behavior. I now need to say something about how, precisely, all this is supposed to constitute an argument for the formality condition.

Point one: it's just as well that it's the fully opaque construal of mental states that we need since, patently, that's the only one that the formality condition permits us. This is because the formality condition prohibits taxonomizing psychological states by reference to the semantic properties of mental representations and, at bottom, transparency is a semantic (viz., nonformal; viz., nonsyntactic) notion. The point is sufficiently obvious: if we count the belief that the evening star is F as (type) identical to the belief that the morning star is F, that must be because of the coreference of such expressions as "the morning star" and 'the evening star." But coreference is a semantic property, and not one which could conceivably have a formal doppelganger; it's inconceivable, in particular, that there should be a system of mental representations such that, in the general case, coreferring expressions are formally identical in that system. (This might be true for God's mind, but not, surely, for anybody else's [and not for God's either unless he is an extensionalist; which I doubt.]) So if we want transparent taxonomies of mental states, we will have to give up the formality condition. So it's a good thing for the computational theory of the mind that it's not transparent taxonomies that we want.

What's harder to argue for (but might, nevertheless, be true) is point two: that the formality condition *can* be honored by a theory which taxonomizes mental states according to their content. For, barring caveats previously reviewed, it may be that mental states are distinct in content only if they are relations to formally distinct mental representations; in effect, that aspects of content can be reconstructed as aspects of form, at least insofar as appeals to content figure in accounts of the mental causation of behavior. The main thing to be said in favor of this speculation is that it allows us to explain, within the context of the representational theory of mind, how beliefs of different content *can* have different behavioral effects, even when the beliefs are transparently type-identical. The form of explanation goes: it's because different content implies formally distinct internal representations (via the formality condition) and formally distinct internal representations can be functionally different; can differ in their causal role. Whereas, to put it mildly, it's hard to see how internal representations could differ in causal role *unless* they differed in form.

To summarize: transparent taxonomy is patently incompatible with the formality condition; whereas taxonomy in respect of content *may* be compatible with the formality condition, plus or minus a bit. That taxonomy in respect of content is compatible with the formality condition, plus or minus a bit, is perhaps *the* basic idea of modern cognitive theory. The representational theory of mind and the computational theory of mind merge here for, on the one hand, it's claimed that psychological states differ in content only if they are relations to type-distinct mental representations; and, on the other, it's claimed that only formal properties of mental representations contribute to their type individuation for the purposes of theories of mind/body interaction. Or, to put it the other way 'round, it's allowed that mental representations affect behavior in virtue of their content, but it's maintained that mental representations are distinct in content only if they are also distinct in form. The first clause is required to make it plausible that mental states are relations to mental representations and the second is required to make it plausible that mental processes are computations. (Computations just are processes in which representations have their causal consequences in virtue of their form.) By thus exploiting the notions of content and computation *together*, a cognitive theory seeks to connect the *intensional* properties of mental states with their *causal* properties vis-à-vis behavior. Which is, of course, exactly what a theory of the mind ought to do.

As must be evident from the preceding, I'm partial to programmatic arguments: ones that seek to infer the probity of a conceptual apparatus from the fact that it plays a role in some prima facie plausible research enterprise. So, in particular, I've argued that a taxonomy of mental states which honors the formality condition seems to be required by theories of the mental causation of behavior, and that that's a reason for taking such taxonomies very seriously.

But there lurks, within the general tradition of representational theories of mind, a deeper intuition: that it is not only *advisable* but actually *mandatory* to assume that mental processes have access only to formal (nonsemantic) properties of mental representations; that the contrary view is not only empirically fruitless but also conceptually unsound. I find myself in sympathy with this intuition, though I'm uncertain precisely how the arguments ought to go. What follows is just a sketch.

I'll begin with a version that I *don't* like, an epistemological version:

> Look, it makes no *sense* to suppose that mental operations could apply to mental representations in virtue of (e.g.) the truth or falsity of the latter. For, consider: truth value is a matter of correspondence to the way the world is. To determine the truth value of a belief would therefore involve what I'll call 'directly comparing' the belief with the world; i.e., comparing it with the way the world is, not just with the way the world is represented as being. And the representational theory of mind says that we have access to the world only via the ways in which we represent it. There is, as it were, nothing that corresponds to looking around (behind? through? what's the right metaphor?) one's beliefs, to catch a glimpse of the things they represent. Mental processes can, in short, compare representations, but they can't compare representations with what they're representations of. Hence mental processes can't have access to the truth value of representations or, mutatis mutandis, to whether they denote. Hence the formality condition.

This line of argument could, certainly, be made a good deal more precise. It has been in, for example, some of the recent work of Nelson Goodman (see especially Goodman 1978). For present purposes, however, I'm content to leave it *im*precise so long as it sounds familiar. For I suspect that all versions of the argument suffer from a common deficiency: they assume that you can't run a *correspondence* theory of truth together with a *coherence* theory of evidence. Whereas I see nothing compelling in the inference from "truth is a matter of the correspondence of a belief with the way the world is" to "*ascertaining* truth is a matter of 'directly comparing' a belief with the way the world is." Perhaps we ascertain the truth of our beliefs by comparing them with one another, appealing to inference to the best explanation whenever we need to do so.

Anyhow, it would be nice to have a *non*epistemological defence of the formality condition; one which saves the intuition that there's something conceptually wrong with its denial but doesn't acquire the skeptical/relativistic commitments with which the traditional epistemic versions of the argument have been encumbered. Here goes:

Suppose, just for convenience, that mental processes are algorithms. So, we have rules for the transformation of mental representations, and we have the mental representations that constitute their ranges and domains. Think of the rules as being like hypothetical imperatives; they have antecedents which specify conditions on mental representations, and they have consequents which specify what is to happen if the antecedents are satisfied. And now consider rules (a) and (b):

    (a) Iff it's the case that P, do such and such.
    (b) Iff you believe it's the case that P, do such and such.

Notice, to begin with, that the compliance conditions on these injunctions are quite different. In particular, in the case where P is *false but believed true*, compliance with

(b) consists in doing such and such, whereas compliance with (a) consists in *not* doing it. But despite this difference in compliance conditions, there's something *very* peculiar (perhaps *pragmatically* peculiar, whatever precisely that may mean) about supposing that an organism might have different ways of going about attempting to comply with (a) and (b). The peculiarity is patent in (c). To borrow a joke from Professor Robert Jagger, (c) is a little like the advice "buy low, sell high." One knows just what it would be *like* to comply with either, but somehow knowing that doesn't help much.

(c) Do such and such iff it's the case that P, *whether or not* you believe that it's the case that P.[10]

The idea is this: when one has done what one can to establish that the belief that P is warranted, one has done what one can to establish that the antecedent of (a) is satisfied. And, conversely, when one has done what one can do to establish that the antecedent of (a) is satisfied, one has done what one can to establish the warrant of the belief that P. Now, I suppose that the following is at least *close* to being true: to have the belief that P is to have the belief that the belief that P is warranted; and conversely, to have the belief that the belief that P is warranted is to have the belief that P. And the upshot of *this* is just the formality condition all over again. Given that mental operations have access to the fact that P is believed (and hence that the belief that P is believed to be warranted, and hence that the belief that the belief that p is warranted is believed to be warranted, . . . etc.) there's nothing further left to do; there is nothing that corresponds to the notion of a mental operation which one undertakes to perform just in case one's belief that P is *true*.

This isn't, by the way, any form of skepticism, as can be seen from the following: there's nothing wrong with Jones having one mental operation which he undertakes to perform iff it's the case that P and another *quite different* mental operation which he undertakes to perform iff *Smith* ($\neq$ Jones) believes that it's the case that P. (Cf. "I promise . . . though I don't intend to . . ." vs. "I promise . . . though Smith doesn't intend to . . .") There's a first person/third person asymmetry here, but it doesn't impugn the semantic distinction between "P is true" and "P is believed true." The suggestion is that it's the tacit recognition of this pragmatic asymmetry that accounts for the traditional hunch that you can't both identify mental operations with transformations on mental representations and at the same time flout the formality condition; that the representational theory of mind and the computational theory of mind are somehow conjoint options.

So much, then, for the formality condition and the psychological tradition which accepts it. What about Naturalism? The first point is that none of the arguments for a rational psychology is, in and of itself, an argument *against* a Naturalistic psychology. As I remarked above, to deny that mental operations have access to the semantic properties of mental representations is *not* to deny that mental representations *have* semantic properties. On the contrary, beliefs are *just* the kinds of things which exhibit truth and denotation, and the Naturalist proposes to make science out of the organism/environment relations which (presumably) fix these properties. Why, indeed, should he not?

This all *seems* very reasonable. Nevertheless, I now wish to argue that a computational psychology is the only one that we are likely to get; that qua research strategy, the attempt to construct a *naturalistic* psychology is very likely to prove fruitless. I think that the basis for such an argument is already to be found in the literature, where it takes the form of a (possibly inadvertent) reductio ad absurdum of the contrary view.

Consider, to begin with, a distinction that Professor Hilary Putnam introduces in "The Meaning of Meaning" (1975) between what he calls "psychological states in the wide sense" and "psychological states in the narrow sense." A psychological state in the *narrow* sense is one the ascription of which does not "(presuppose) the existence of any individual other than the subject to whom that state is ascribed" (p. 10). All others are psychological states in the wide sense. So, for example, *x's jealousy of y* is a schema for expressions which denote psychological states in the wide sense since such expressions presuppose the existence, not only of the *x*s who are in the states, but also of the *y*s who are its objects. Putnam remarks that methodological solipsism (the phrase, by the way, is his) can be viewed as the requirement that only psychological states in the narrow sense are allowed as constructs in psychological theories.

Whereas, it's perhaps Putnam's main point that there are at least *some* scientific purposes (e.g., semantics and accounts of intertheoretical reference) which demand the wide construal. Here, rephrased slightly, is the sort of example that Putnam finds persuasive.

There is a planet (call it "Yon") where things are very much like here. In particular, by a cosmic accident, some of the people on Yon speak a dialect indistinguishable from English and live in an urban conglomerate indistinguishable from the greater Boston area. Still more, for every one of our greater Bostonians, there is a doppelganger on Yon who has precisely the same neurological structure down to and including microparticles. We can assume that, so long as we're construing "psychological state" narrowly, this latter condition guarantees type identity of our psychological states with theirs.

However, Putnam argues, it doesn't guarantee that there is a corresponding identity of psychological states, hither and Yon, if we construe "psychological state" *widely*. Suppose that there is this difference between Yon and Earth; whereas, over here, the stuff we call "water" has the atomic structure H_2O, it turns out that the stuff that they call "water" over there has the atomic structure XYZ ($\neq H_2O$). And now, consider the mental state *thinking about water*. The idea is that, so long as we construe that state widely, it's one that we, but not our doppelgangers, can reasonably aspire to. For, construed widely, one is thinking about water only if it is water that one is thinking about. But it's water that one's thinking about only if it is H_2O that one's thinking about; water is H_2O. But since, by assumption, they never think about H_2O over Yon, it follows that there's at least one wide psychological state that we're often in and they never are, however neurophysiologically like us they are, and however much our narrow psychological states converge with theirs.

Moreover, if we try to say what they speak about, refer to, mention, etc.; if, in short, we try to supply a semantics for their dialect, we will have to mention XYZ, not H_2O. Hence it would be wrong, at least on Putnam's intuitions, to say that they have a word for water. A fortiori, the chemists who work in what they call "M.I.T." don't have theories about *water*, even though what runs through their heads when they talk about XYZ may be identical to what runs through our heads when we talk about H_2O. The situation is analogous to the one that arises for demonstratives and token reflexives, as Putnam insightfully points out.

Well, what are we to make of this? Is it an argument against methodological solipsism? And, if so, is it a *good* argument against methodological solipsism?

To begin with, Putnam's distinction between psychological states in the narrow and wide sense looks to be very intimately related to the traditional distinction between psychological state ascriptions opaquely and transparently construed. I'm a bit wary about this since what Putnam says about wide ascriptions is only that they "presuppose the existence" of objects other than the ascribee; and, of course *a believes Fb and b exists* does not entail *b is such that a believes F of him*, or even ∃x (*a believes Fx*). Moreover, the failure of such entailments is notoriously important in discussions of quantifying in. For all that, however, I don't *think* that it's Putnam's intention to exploit the difference between the existential generalization test for transparency and the presupposition of existence test for wideness. On the contrary, the burden of Putnam's argument seems to be precisely that "John believes (widely) that water is F" is true only if water (viz., H_2O) is such that John believes it's F. It's thus unclear to me why Putnam gives the weaker condition on wideness when it appears to be the stronger one that does the work.[11]

But whatever the case may be with the wide sense of belief, it's pretty clear that the narrow sense must be (what I've been calling) fully opaque. (This is because only full opacity allows type identity of beliefs that have different truth conditions [Sam's belief that he's ill with Misha's belief that *he* is; Yon beliefs about XYZ with hither beliefs about H_2O.]) I want to emphasize this correspondence between narrowness and full opacity, and not just in aid of terminological parsimony. Putnam sometimes writes as though he takes the methodological commitment to a psychology of narrow mental states to be a sort of vulgar prejudice: "Making this assumption is, of course, adopting a *restrictive program*—a program which deliberately limits the scope and nature of psychology to fit certain mentalistic preconceptions or, in some cases, to fit an idealistic reconstruction of knowledge and the world" (p. 137). But, in light of what we've said so far, it should be clear that this is a methodology with malice aforethought. Narrow psychological states are those individuated in light of the formality condition; viz., without reference to such semantic properties as truth and reference. And honoring the formality condition is part and parcel of the attempt to provide a theory which explains (a) how the belief that the morning star is F could be different from the belief that the evening star is F despite the well-known astronomical facts; and (b) how the behavioral effects of believing that the morning star is F could be different from those of believing that the evening star is F, astronomy once again apparently to the contrary notwithstanding. Putnam is, of course, dubious about this whole project: "... The three centuries of failure of mentalisic psychology is tremendous evidence against this procedure, in my opinion" (p. 137). I suppose this is intended to include everybody from Locke and Kant to Freud and Chomsky. I should have such failures.

So much for background. I now need an argument to show that a naturalistic psychology (a psychology of mental states transparently individuated; hence, presumably, a psychology of mental states in the wide sense) is, for practical purposes, out of the question. So far as I can see, however, Putnam has given that argument. For, consider: a naturalistic psychology is a theory of organism/environment transactions. So, to stick to Putnam's example, a naturalistic psychology would have to find some stuff S and some relation R, such that one's narrow thought that water is wet is a thought about S in virtue of the fact that one bears R to S. Well, *which* stuff? The natural thing to say would be "Water, of course." Notice, however, that if Putnam is right, it may not even be *true* that the narrow thought that water is wet is a thought about water; it *won't* be true of tokens of that thought which occur on Yon. Whether the narrow thought that water is wet is about water depends on whether it's about H_2O; and whether it's about H_2O depends on "how science turns out"—viz., on what chemistry is true. (Similarly, mutatis mutandis, "water" refers to water is *not*, on this view, a truth of any branch of linguistics; it's chemists who tell us what it is that "water" refers to.) Surely, however, characterizing the objects of thought is methodologically prior to characterizing the causal chains that link thoughts to their objects.

But the theory which characterizes the objects of thought is the theory of *everything*; it's all of science. Hence, the methodological moral of Putnam's analysis seems to be the naturalistic psychologists will inherit the Earth, but only after everybody else is finished with it. No doubt it's alright to have a research strategy that says "wait awhile." But who wants to wait *forever*?

This sort of argument isn't novel. Indeed, it was anticipated by Bloomfield (1933). Bloomfield argues that, for all practical purposes, you can't do semantics. The reason that you can't is that to do semantics you have to be able to say, for example, what "salt" refers to. But what "salt" refers to is NaCl, and that's a bit of chemistry, not linguistics:

> The situations which prompt people to utter speech include every object and happening in their universe. In order to give a scientifically accurate definition of meaning for every form of a language, we would have to have a scientifically accurate knowledge of everything in the speaker's world. The actual extent of human knowledge is very small compared to this. We can define the meaning of a speech-form accurately when this meaning has to do with some matter of which we possess scientific knowledge. We can define the names of minerals, as when we say that the ordinary meaning of the English word *salt* is 'sodium chloride (NaCl),' and we can define the names of plants or animals by means of the technical terms of botany or zoology, but we have no precise way of defining words like *love* or *hate*, which concern situations that have not been accurately classified.... The statement of meanings is therefore the weak point in language-study, and will remain so until knowledge advances very far beyond its present state. (pp 139–140)

It seems to me as though Putnam ought to endorse all of this *including the moral*: the distinction between wanting a naturalistic semantics (psychology) and not wanting any is real but academic.[12]

The argument just given depends, however, on accepting Putnam's analysis of his example. But suppose that one's intuitions run the other way. Then one is at liberty to argue like this:

1. They do too have water over Yon; all Putnam's example shows is that there could be two kinds of water, our kind ($= H_2O$) and their kind ($= XYZ$).
2. Hence, Yon tokens of the thought that water is wet are thoughts about water after all.
3. Hence, the way chemistry turns out is irrelevant to whether thoughts about water are about water.
4. Hence, the naturalistic psychology of thought need not wait upon the sciences of the objects of thought.
5. Hence, a naturalistic psychology may be in the cards after all.

Since the premises of this sort of reply may be tempting (since, indeed, they may be *true*) it's worth presenting a version of the argument which doesn't depend on intuitions about what XYZ is.

A naturalistic psychology would specify the relations that hold between an organism and an object in its environment when the one is thinking about the other. Now, think how such a theory would have to go. Since it would have to define its generalizations over mental states on the one hand and environmental entities on the other, it will need, in particular, some canonical way of referring to the latter. Well, *which* way? If one assumes that what makes my thought about Robin Roberts a thought *about*

Robin Roberts is some causal connection between the two of us, then we'll need a description of RR such that the causal connection obtains in virtue of his satisfying that description. And that means, presumably, that we'll need a description under which the relation between him and me instantiates a law.

Generally, then, a naturalistic psychology would attempt to specify environmental objects in a vocabulary such that environment/organism relations are law-instantiating when so described. But here's the depressing consequence again: we have no access to such a vocabulary prior to the elaboration (completion?) of the nonpsychological sciences. "What Granny likes with her herring" isn't, for example, a description under which salt is law-instantiating; nor, presumably, is "salt." What we need is something like "NaCl," and descriptions like "NaCl" are available only *after* we've done our chemistry. What this comes down to is that, at a minimum, "x's being F causally explains ..." can be true only when "F" expresses nomologically necessary properties of the xs. Heaven knows it's hard to say what *that* means, but it presumably rules out both "Salt's being what Granny likes with herring ..." and "Salt's being salt ..."; the former for want of being necessary, and the latter for want of being nomological. I take it, moreover, that Bloomfield is right when he says (a) that we don't know relevant nomologically necessary properties of most of the things we can refer to (think about) and (b) that it isn't the linguist's (psychologist's) job to find them out.

Here's still another way to put this sort of argument. The way Bloomfield states his case invites the question: "Why *should* a semanticist want a definition of 'salt' that's 'scientifically accurate' in your sense? Why wouldn't a 'nominal' definition do?" There is, I think, some point to such a query. For example, as Hartry Field has pointed out (1972), it wouldn't make much difference to the way that truth-conditional semantics goes if we were to say only " 'salt' refers to whatever it refers to." All we need for this sort of semantics is some way or other of referring to the extension of "salt"; we don't, in particular, need a "scientifically accurate" way. It's therefore pertinent to do what Bloomfield notably does not: distinguish between the goals of *semantics* and those of a naturalistic psychology of language. The latter, by assumption, purports to explicate the organism/environment transactions in virtue of which relations like reference hold. It therefore requires, at a minimum, lawlike generalizations of the (approximate) form: *X's utterance of 'salt' refers to salt iff x bears relation R to*—Since this whole thing is supposed to be lawlike, what goes in for "   " must be a projectible characterization of the extension of "salt." But, in general, we discover which descriptions are projectible only a posteriori; in light of how the sciences (including the nonpsychological sciences) turn out. We are back where we started. Looked at this way, the moral is that we can do (certain kinds of) semantics if we have a way of referring to the extension of "salt." But we can't do the naturalistic psychology of reference unless we have some way of saying what salt is; which of its properties determine its causal relations.

It's important to emphasize that these sorts of arguments do *not* apply against the research program embodied in "Rational psychology"; viz., to the program which envisions a psychology that honors the formality condition. The problem we've been facing is: under what description does the object of thought enter into scientific generalizations about the relations between thoughts and their objects? It looks as though the naturalist is going to have to say: under a description that's law instantiating; e.g., under physical description. Whereas the rational psychologist has a quite different answer. What *he* wants is *whatever description the organism has in mind* when it thinks about the object of thought, construing "thinks about" fully opaquely. So, for a theory of psychological states narrowly construed, we want such descriptions of Venus as, e.g., "the morning star," "the evening star," "Venus," etc., for it's these sorts of descriptions which we presumably entertain when we think that the morning star is F. In particular, it's our relation to these sorts of descriptions that determines what psychological state type we're in insofar as the goal in taxonomizing psychological states is explaining how they affect behavior.

A final point under the general head: the hopelessness of naturalistic psychology. Practicing naturalistic psychologists have been at least dimly aware all along of the sort of bind that they're in. So, for example, the "physical specification of the stimulus" is just about invariably announced as a requirement upon adequate formulations of S-R generalizations. We can now see why. Suppose, wildly contrary to fact, that there exists a human population (e.g., English speakers) in which pencils are, in the technical sense of the notion, discriminative stimuli controlling the verbal response "pencil." The point is that, even if some such generalization were true, it wouldn't be among those enunciated by a naturalistic psychology; the generalizations of naturalistic psychology are presumably supposed to be nomological, and there aren't any *laws* about pencils qua pencils. That is: expressions like "pencil" presumably occur in no true, lawlike sentences. Of course, there presumably is *some* description in virtue of which pencils fall under the organism/environment laws of a naturalistic psychology, and everybody (except, possibly, Gibson) has always assumed that those descriptions are, approximately, physical descriptions. Hence, the naturalist's demand, perfectly warranted by his lights, that the stimulus should be physically specified.

But though their theory has been consistent, their practice has uniformly not. In practice, and barring the elaborately circumscribed cases that psychophysics studies, the requirement that the stimulus be physically specified has been ignored by just about all practitioners. And, indeed, they were well advised to ignore it; how else could they get on with their job? If they really had to wait for the physicists to determine the description(s) under which pencils are law-instantiators, how would the psychology of pencils get off the ground?

So far as I can see, there are really only two ways out of this dilemma:

1: We can fudge, the way that learning theorists usually do. That is, we can "read" the description of the stimulus from the character of the organism's response. In point of historical fact, this has led to a kind of naturalistic psychology which is merely a solemn paraphrase of what everybody's grandmother knows: e.g., to saying "pencils are discriminative stimuli for the utterance of "pencil"" where Granny would have said "pencil" refers to pencils. I take it that Chomsky's review of *Verbal Behavior* (1959) demonstrated, once and for all, the fatuity of this course. What *would* be interesting— what would have surprised Grandmother—is a generalization of the form Δ *is the discriminative stimulus for utterances of "pencil"* where Δ is a description which picks out pencils in some projectible vocabulary (e.g., in the vocabulary of physics). Does anybody suppose that such descriptions are likely to be forthcoming in, say, the *next* three hundred years?

2. The other choice is to try for a computational psychology; which is, of course, the burden of my plaint. On this view, what we can reasonably hope for is a theory of mental states fully opaquely type-individuated. We can try to say what the mental representation is, and what the relation to a mental representation is, such that one believes that the morning star is F in virtue of bearing the latter to the former. And we can try to say how that representation, or that relation, or both, differ from the representation and the relation constitutive of believing that the evening star is F. A naturalistic psychology, by contrast, remains a sort of ideal of pure reason; there must *be* such a psychology since, presumably, we do sometimes think of Venus and, presumably, we do so in virtue of a causal relation between it and us. But there's no

practical hope of making science out of this relation. And, of course, for methodology, practical hope is *everything*.

One final point, and then I'm through. Methodological solipsism isn't, of course, solipsism *tout court*. It's not part of the enterprise to assert, or even suggest, that you and I are actually in the situation of Winograd's computer. Heaven only knows what relation between me and Robin Roberts makes it possible for me to think of him (refer to him, etc.), and I've been doubting the practical possibility of a science whose generalizations that relation instantiates. But I *don't* doubt that there *is* such a relation or that I do sometimes think of him. Still more: I have reasons not to doubt it; precisely the sorts of reasons I'd supply if I were asked to justify my knowledge claims about his pitching record. In short: it's true that Roberts won twenty-eight, and it's true that I know that he did, and nothing in the preceding tends to impugn these truths. (Or, contrariwise, if he didn't and I'm mistaken, then the reasons for my mistake are philosophically boring; they're biographical, not epistemological or ontological). My point, then, is *of course* not that solipsism is true; it's just that truth, reference and the rest of the semantic notions aren't psychological categories. What they are is: they're modes of *Dasein*. I don't know what *Dasein* is, but I'm sure that there's lots of it around, and I'm sure that you and I and Cincinnati have all got it. What more do you want?

Notes

1. I've had a lot of help with this one. I'm particularly indebted to: Professors Ned Block, Sylvain Bromberger, Janet Dean Fodor, Keith Gundersen, Robert Richardson, Judith Thomson; and to Mr. Israel Krakowski.

2. I shall speak of "type identity" (distinctness) of mental states to pick out the sense of "same mental state" in which, for example, John and Mary are in the same mental state if both believe that water flows. Correspondingly, I shall use the notion of "token identity" (distinctness) of mental state to pick out the sense of "same mental state" in which it's necessary that if x and y are in the same mental state, then $x = y$.

3. For extensive discussion, see Fodor (1975; 1978b).

4. This is *not*, notice, the same as saying "formal operations are the ones that apply mechanically"; in this latter sense, *formality* means something like *explicitness*. There's no particular reason for using "formal" to mean both "syntactic" and "explicit," though the ambiguity abounds in the literature.

5. Some fairly deep methodological issues in Artifical Intelligence are involved here. See Fodor (1978a) where this surface is lightly scratched.

6. I'm told by some of my friends that this paragraph could be read as suggesting that there are *two kinds* of beliefs: opaque ones and transparent ones. That is not, of course, the way that it is intended to be read. The idea is rather that there are two kinds of conditions that we can place on determinations that a pair of belief tokens count as tokens of the same belief type. According to one set of conditions (corresponding to transparent taxonomy) a belief that the morning star is such and such counts as the same belief as a belief that the evening star is such and such; whereas, according to the other set of conditions (corresponding to opaque taxonomy), it does not.

7. I'm leaving it open that it may be to say still less than this (e.g., because of problems about reference under false descriptions). For purposes of the present discussion, I don't need to run a line of the truth conditions for transparent propositional attitude ascriptions. Thank Heaven, since I do not have one.

8. It's worth emphasizing that the sense of "behavior" *is* proprietary, and that that's pretty much what you would expect. Not every true description of an act can be such that a theory of the mental causation of behavior will explain the act under that description. (In being rude to Darcy, Elizabeth is insulting the man whom she will eventually marry. A theory of the mental causation of her behavior might have access to the former description, but not, surely, to the latter.)

   Many philosophers—especially since Wittgenstein—have emphasized the ways in which the description of behavior may depend upon its context, and it is a frequent charge against modern versions of Rational psychology that they typically ignore such characterizations. So they do, but so what? You can't have explanations of everything under every description, and it's a question for empirical determination which descriptions of behavior reveal its systematicity vis-à-vis its causes.

The Rational psychologist is prepared to bet that—to put it *very* approximately—behavior will prove to be systematic under some of the descriptions under which it is intentional.

At a minimum, the present claim goes like this: there is a way of taxonomizing behaviors and a way of taxonomizing mental states such that, given these taxonomies, theories of the mental causation of behavior will be forthcoming. And that way of taxonomizing mental states construes them nontransparently.

9. One might try saying: what counts for opaque type individuation is what's *in* your head, not just what's running through it. So, for example, though Alfred and Misha are both thinking "he feels faint," nevertheless different counterfactuals are true of them: Misha would cash his pronoun as: "he, Sam" whereas Alfred would cash *his* pronoun as: "he, Misha." The problem would then be to decide *which* such counterfactuals are relevant since, if we count all of them, it's going to turn out that there are few, if any, cases of distinct organisms having type-identical thoughts.

    I won't, in any event, pursue this proposal since it seems clear that it won't, in principle, cope with all the relevant cases. Two people would be having different thoughts when each is thinking "I'm ill" even if *everything* in their heads were the same.

10. I'm assuming, for convenience that all the Ps are such that either they or their denials are believed. This saves having to relativize to time (e.g., having (b) and (c) read "... you believe or come to believe ...").

11. I blush to admit that I had missed some of these complexities until Sylvain Bromberger kindly rubbed my nose in them.

12. It may be that Putman *does* accept this moral. For example, the upshot of the discussion around p. 153 of his article appears to be that a Greek semanticist prior to Archimedes *could* not (in practice) have given a correct account of what (the Greek equivalent of) "gold" means; viz., because the theory needed to specify the extension of the term was simply not available. Presumably *we* are in that situation vis-à-vis the objects of many of *our* thoughts and the meanings of many of our terms; and, presumably, we will continue to do so into the indefinite future. But, then, what's the point of defining psychology (semantics) so that there can't be any?

References

Bloomfield, L. (1933) *Language*. New York: Holt, Rinehart & Winston.

Chomsky, N. (1959) Review of Skinner's *Verbal Behavior*. *Language* 35: 26–58.

Descartes, R. (1931) *Meditations on first philosophy*, trans. E. S. Haldane and G. R. T. Ross. Cambridge: Cambridge Univ. Press.

Field, H. (1972) Tarski's theory of truth. *Journal of Philosophy* 69: 347–375.

Fodor, J. A. (1975) *The language of thought*. New York: Thomas Y. Crowell.

Fodor, J. A. (1978a) Tom Swift and his procedural grandmother. *Cognition* 6: 229–247.

Fodor, J. A. (1978b) Propositional attitudes. *The Monist* 61: 501–523.

Geach, P. (1957) *Mental acts*. London: Routledge & Kegan Paul.

Goodman, N. (1978) *Ways of worldmaking*. Indianapolis: Hackett.

James, W. (1890) *Principles of psychology*, vol. I (repr. New York: Dover, 1950) New York: Henry Holt.

Putnam, H. (1960) Minds and machines. In Hook, S. (ed.), *Dimensions of mind*. New York: New York Univ. Press.

Putnam, H. (1975) The meaning of meaning. In Gunderson, K. (ed.), *Minnesota studies in the philosphy of science. 7. Language, mind and knowledge*. Minneapolis: Univ. of Minnesota Press.

Winograd, T. (1971) *Procedures as a represenation for data in a computer program for understanding natural language*. Cambridge, Mass.: MIT Project MAC.

Chapter 36
Narrow Taxonomy and Wide Functionalism
Patricia Kitcher

1. Introduction

Cognitive psychology has become a respectable and exciting field. This is largely because cognitive psychology has become computational psychology. Hilary Putnam offers a cogent diagnosis of why computational psychology is so appealing: it turns out that the best, if not the only, way to simulate intelligent performance is to provide the computer with a formalized language; but it has always been obvious that we think by utilizing some innate or acquired model that represents our environment; so all things conspire to support the idea that we think by using a formalized language both as medium of representation and as medium of computation (Putnam ms., pp. 1–3).

With its new status, cognitive psychology has properly become an object of critical philosophical evaluation. The analyses I am going to consider focus on the central theoretical construct of a psychological state. All turn on fundamentally the same consideration: There is a problem for cognitive psychology, because the various tasks on its agenda put conflicting pressures on its theoretical constructs. Unless something is done, the inevitable result will be confusion or outright incoherence. Stephen Stich, Jerry Fodor, and Ned Block present different versions of this worry and each proposes a different remedy (Stich 1978; Stich 1983; Fodor 1981c; Block 1980). Stich wants the central notion of belief to be jettisoned if it cannot be shown to be sound. Fodor tries to reduce confusion in cognitive psychology, by dismissing some putative tasks as impossible. Block argues that the widely shared expectation that some variety of functionalism (e.g., computational functionalism) will provide a correct account of mentality is just not warranted, given the relative weights of the evidence and the anomalies.

I think these appraisals are wrong. The argument will be that these doubts about the integrity of cognitive psychology are unfounded, because they rest on overly restrictive views about psychological classifications and psychological constructs. So the problem lies in implicit taxonomic principles and not in cognitive psychology. Besides the confusions about taxonomy, I will object to some details in the analyses provided by Stich, Fodor, and Block.

2. Stich's Attack on Belief

In "Autonomous Psychology and the Belief-Desire Thesis," Stephen Stich offers a fairly straightforward argument against the coherence of the belief construct.[1] A standard mode of explanation in cognitive psychology adverts to content-bearing inner states. One obvious way to individuate these theoretical constructs is by refer-

Reprinted from *Philosophy of Science* 52 (1985), pp. 78–97, by permission of the author and the Philosophy of Science Association.

ence to the type of attitude—belief, desire, fear, hope and so forth—and by reference to the content of the inner state. So, for example, the belief that P is distinguished from the desire that P, and the fear that P is distinguished from the fear that Q. Leaving aside worrisome questions about whether the contents of mental attitudes are best understood as propositions or neural sentences, Stich grounds his objection on an apparently innocuous point: two beliefs, for example, cannot be type-identical in content if one is true, while the other is false (Stich 1978, p. 578). However, there is another principle about individuating psychological states that has enjoyed widespread support. What Stich calls the "principle of psychological autonomy" claims that if two systems are physically identical, down to the last microparticle, then they must share all the same psychological states. I find this terminology confusing, since the name suggests a principle about the autonomy of psychology from, say, neurophysiology. Stich eschews Jaegwon Kim's more traditional nomenclature of "supervenience," because, on Kim's account, one type of property is supervenient on a second type if the second class of properties completely determines what the properties of the first type will be (Kim 1978). Stich wants a stricter notion. The principle he has in mind claims that psychological properties are supervenient on *current* physical properties. I will refer to this principle as that of "simultaneous" supervenience. According to Stich, all the psychologists he knows accept the simultaneous supervenience principle (Stich 1978, p. 576, n. 8).

Stich aims to reveal an internal tension in belief-desire psychology by presenting cases where it is impossible to honor both the principle of simultaneous supervenience and the principle that type-identical beliefs must have the same truth value. Although he presents four different types of cases, self-referential beliefs, beliefs about one's spatio-temporal location, beliefs about other people, and beliefs involving natural kind predicates, all turn on the same point. So I will combine them into one communal case. Queen Elizabeth II believes correctly that the Duke of Edinburgh gave her a gold ring in 1947. Following the current vogue in philosophical science fiction, we assume that in a thousand years a new planet is created that is almost exactly like earth today, except for some superficially undetectable differences in natural substances, including gold. Like everyone else, the Queen has a molecule-for-molecule replica on Twin Earth. Now, according to the principle of simultaneous supervenience, the Queen's replica will believe that the Duke of Edinburgh gave her a gold ring in 1947. But this belief will be false on all counts: it was not the Duke, it was not 1947, her ring is not gold. So by the principle that type-identical beliefs cannot differ in truth value, the Queen and her replica cannot share the same belief. Yet, by the principle of narrow supervenience, they must. Thus, insofar as cognitive psychology is committed to both principles of individuation for content-bearing inner states, its central theoretical construct is incoherent.

Stich notes that he has not produced a refutation of the possibility of belief-desire psychology. Rather, he has offered a challenge. Faced with inconsistency, cognitive psychologists must give up one of two attractive principles, without abandoning anything central to their theory. I disagree with Stich's glum appraisal of the future of belief-desire psychology, because I believe this challenge can be met.

To begin with, the same-content-same-truth-value principle is suspect. As Stich notes in an appendix to the paper, without some additional assumptions the principle breaks down for indexicals anyway (Stich 1978, pp. 586–88). Are two candidates saying the same thing when each confidently asserts, "I will win"? The same-content-same-truth-value principle exerts negative pressure, but it still seems obvious that there is some sense in which these utterances have type-identical contents. On the other side, the principle of simultaneous supervenience cannot be ranked among the obvious eternal verities either. After all, if you really accept the principle of *simultaneous* supervenience, then you are committed to the consequence that there will be no learning theories in psychology. By definition, a learning theory will provide some account of how the organism has changed over time, how its states have altered as a result of interaction with the environment. But Stich's principle maintains that only current properties can be psychological properties, can play a role in explanatory psychology. So a properly scientific explanatory psychology will have no learning theory. While learning theory may have occupied an excessively prominent place in past psychological theories, it is hard to believe that psychologists are committed now to a program that would eliminate learning theory altogether. I will pursue this objection to the principle of simultaneous supervenience by focusing on Jerry Fodor's closely related doctrine of Methodological Solipsism. Having attacked both principles that Stich attributes to cognitive psychology, I will suggest that they are related to two important ideas that set legitimate constraints on this discipline. However, it will turn out that both requirements can be met.

Some terminology introduced by Hilary Putnam will be helpful (Putnam 1975). Among other purposes, Putnam originally used Twin Earth cases to dramatize a distinction between "narrow" and "wide" construals of psychological states. The Queen and her molecule-for-molecule replica are exactly alike "on the inside"; so on the "narrow construal," they share the same psychological states. If one views psychological states more "widely", as representing external objects, then the Queen and her *doppelgänger* have different psychological states, for their thoughts are directed upon disjoint sets of objects. For a variety of reasons, which I will discuss below, Fodor believes that cognitive psychologists should construe psychological states narrowly. He believes that the laws, true generalizations, and principles of computational psychology will all be stated in a vocabulary pegged only to internal differences among psychological states. Since this approach eschews the wide world, Fodor adopts Putnam's characterization of it as "Methodological Solipsism." In effect, Fodor's position represents a decision to honor the principle of simultaneous supervenience—or at least the principle of supervenience—and to reject worldly, i.e., semantic, considerations in individuating psychological states. Since simultaneous supervenience is a more restrictive principle than Methodological Solipsism, any argument showing that the latter is inadequate for the needs of psychology will apply a fortiori to the former.

The obvious objection to Methodological Solipsism is that it sets *a priori* limits on the forms that a future science can take. That seems like a bad idea in general, and there is particular reason for concern in this case. The problem is that it is relatively easy to imagine developments in cognitive psychology where solipsistic scruples should be ignored. Here is a plausible scenario. One moral of Chomsky's work in psycholinguistics is that it may be useful to model mental systems by thinking of them as having some universal features (possessed by every normal member of the species) and as having "free parameters" that are set by the environmental context. To take a well-worn example, the human language faculty seems to have some universal characteristics that rule out otherwise possible word orders. But whether or not you will standardly produce, e.g., VSO or SVO sentences depends on which natural language you have acquired. A parallel story could be true about concepts. Suppose the standard human conceptual repertoire consists of a set of concepts that have both universal features and free parameters. This might be true of the set as a whole, but it is somewhat easier to think of a situation where each concept has universal features and free parameters. Under these circumstances, particular concepts would be functions of universal features and the environmental factors which "set" the parameters. Using U's to indicate universal features (the subscripts specify different concept schemata) and E's for environments (the superscripts specify different environments), the following sorts of principles would be true: C_1 is the product of U_1 and E^1, D_1 is the product of U_1 and E^2, D_2 is the product U_2 and E^2 and so forth.

Before discussing the implications of this possibility for Methodological Solipsism, let me note explicitly that the details do not matter. They are there only to illustrate a range of possibilities. Two crucial assumptions support this range: (1) within computational psychology, to have a concept is to have inner formulae that play certain computational roles; and (2) the program(s) in which we do our thinking can be affected by environmental factors. While these claims are not obviously true, they are plausible and that is all that is needed. Given that they may be true, cognitive psychology could include principles like those I have sketched, or other principles characterizing concepts in relation to universal and environmental determinants. Of course, the idea that the principles of psychology might refer to organism-environment interactions is hardly novel. My point is that this account can be applied to the new model of thinking as the exercise of a computational repertoire. As I read Chomsky's account of language acquisition, he endorses this view (Chomsky 1980).

If a future cognitive psychology contains etiological principles like those presented, then it will violate the maxim of methodological solipsism. I think there are two ways to state Fodor's canon: (a) do psychology without ever referring to anything outside the head; (b) type-individuate psychological states by construing them narrowly. Clearly (a) will be violated, but one might think (a) is merely a picturesque and overly strong way of expressing (b). One could try to preserve (b) by pressing the following line. I have been excessively vague about what those E's, or environmental factors, are. In a scientific psychology, vagueness would be eliminated. Obviously, etiological principles would be useless unless precise features of the environments that set the free parameters are specified. Now, an environmental factor can set a free parameter only insofar as it is registered in the sensory system. No difference which fails to be reflected in the sensorium can make a difference to the resulting computational repertoire. Hence, it will always be possible to type-identify psychological states—even for the purpose of providing etiologies—by referring to inputs *from* transducers, as well as other internal relations. So while (a) cannot be honored strictly, since we must refer to *some* external cause affecting the senses, we could type-identify psychological states by reference only to factors inside the head. The etiological principles sketched above would be formulated, using descriptions of transducer outputs in the place of the "E's." Thus we could explain why some people have the concept C_1, others the concept D_1.

I think this reply is a good illustration of what is objectionable about setting *a priori* restrictions on a science. To begin with, there would still be generalizations that would be missed by the solipsist, to wit, that certain aspects of psychological development are invariant across two or more different E's. There are two subcases. Psychological development might be insensitive to the differences between two environments simply because those differences are not reflected across the sensorium. Presumably, a methodological solipsist would handle this case by arguing that principles about what environmental differences make a difference at the sensory level belong to psychophysics and not to cognitive psychology proper. However, the other subcase resists this treatment. It is well known that many differences in inputs to the senses that are reflected at the first transducer level are invisible to later stages of processing. That is, some differences in transducer outputs make no difference to later operations, and this could be true of the processes that set free parameters. A concrete example may clarify the sort of possibility I have in mind. The "motor theory' of phone perception claims that we classify acoustic signals as different phones on the basis of articulatory considerations.[2] Roughly, we will classify a range of acoustic signals as "ba's" not in virtue of their intrinsic acoustic similarity, but on the basis of whether all of the sounds would be produced by certain articulatory movements. I do not know whether this is true or not, but let us assume that we have a good taxonomy of articulatory movements. In that case, we would have a good scientific description of the environmental factors, namely, the taxonomy that enables us to classify articulatory movements, even though the story at the transducer level is hopelessly messy. Thus, the proposed rejoinder that a precise account of the environmental factors that set free parameters would have to be reformulable in terms describing transducer outputs fails.

A methodological solipsist might be tempted by the following reply. Although a taxonomy of environmental factors plays a certain role in this explanation, that role is compatible with the canon of methodological solipsism. For, if the general approach of computational psychology is correct, then a complete motor theory of phone perception must advert to some inner program which enables hearers to decode incoming acoustic signals in such a way that they can be matched up against their own stored programs for producing articulatory movements. Or, if the details here are wrong, some such further story must be right. As in this case, a methodological solipsist may permit reference to external factors to serve as clues to the discovery of the narrow computational account. The claim is only that the ultimate explanatory burden must be borne by factors inside the head.

This defense of methodological solipsism is not only wrong, but wrongheaded. It is wrong on two counts. First, the basic theory of phone perception might be widely accepted even if we never fill in the computational details. We might be indifferent to the details, or the task might be virtually impossible. So the suggestion that the external taxonomy will have merely heuristic value is jejune. Second, even if we had a detailed computational account, it hardly follows that the wide theory would become explanatorily otiose. The inner story would tell us how various symbols are rearranged to produce other strings of symbols. Nowhere would that story reveal the surprising fact (if it is a fact) that we classify incoming speech on the basis of factors involved in speech production, as opposed to the obvious suggestion that what matters are purely acoustic properties of the signal. In cleaving to methodological solipsism, we lose explanatory power.

This attempt to save methodological solipsism reveals a striking parallel with behaviorism, which should be very disturbing to the theory's admirers. In actual cases, behaviorists permitted themselves and others to use mentalistic language in describing human behavior, for, without that latitude, there would have been no explanations. Their rationale was that mentalese description was merely heuristic, something that would be replaced without loss by behavioral descriptions. At this point in the history of the philosophy of psychology, that sort of account can only be run on a cash basis. Since there is no reason to believe that a narrow computational account can bear the entire explanatory burden of a theory like the motor theory of phone perception—and excellent reasons to believe that it cannot—I conclude that this case is a counterexample to the principle of methodological solipsism. Further, this theory, and the more abstract theory of concept acquisition with which I began, are representative of a large range of actual and potential cognitive theories. We do not want a methodological canon that would so limit research in cognitive psychology.

Had they realized the implications of supervenience and, consequently, of simultaneous supervenience, it is hard to believe that Stich's respondents would have professed adherence. As we saw above, the same-content-same-truth-value principle also looks less obvious on closer inspection. Nevertheless, while these principles are questionable as stated, they reflect two important ideas. The approaches of Methodological Solipsism and simultaneous supervenience try to give full weight to the strong intuition that originals and *doppelgängers*, are, in some sense, psychologically identical.[3] On the other hand, it is equally obvious that beliefs are intentional representations, and that if two creatures have the same belief about a common world, then their beliefs must have a common truth value. It seems to me that such intuitions are required to give direction to computational psychology. Hence—at least at the beginning—they set legitimate constraints on the enterprise.

Where Stich errs is in thinking that these intuitions cannot both be honored. His rejoinder to a potential defense of belief-desire psychology is instructive. Stich thinks that the most attractive option for cognitive psychologists is to cleave to the principle of simultaneous supervenience and sacrifice the same-content-same-truth-value principle. But, Stich suggests, the cost of this move may be prohibitive. By his lights, conceding that the content-bearing inner states of your psychology do not refer to external objects and do not contain truth-valuable contents amounts to giving up the idea that these things are beliefs or the scientific successors of beliefs. So the assumption that computational psychology extends ordinary psychological explanation, and is a science of *belief*, would be abandoned (Stich 1978, p. 586). This argument recurs as the central theme of Stich's book, *From Folk Psychology to Cognitive Science* (Stich 1983). If cognitive science wants to be a science, it should taxonomize states narrowly. Ordinary psychological explanation standardly employs a wide construal of psychological states. Thus cognitive science cannot be thought of as an extension of folk psychology, because the approaches are inconsistent at a rather fundamental level.

In fact, the dilemma that Stich constructs for belief-desire psychology is not as dire as it first appears. It would be quite consistent to hold that although cognitive psychology *individuates* psychological states by construing them narrowly, it does not deny that psychological states refer to objects or have truth-valuable contents. The claim is only that wide content is not used in type-identifying psychological states. Stich considers this possibility in his new book, calling it the "Weak Representational Theory of Mind." He counters by scouting various arguments for the claim that we ought to attribute external reference to psychological states even though such reference plays no role in psychological explanation. Regardless of the merits of his particular arguments, it is easy to sympathize with Stich's general antipathy to weak RTM, as he presents that view. There is something prima facie perverse in attributing external reference to psychological states while denying it any role in explanatory psychology. In the cases I raise against Fodor, psychological states are construed widely in order to allow the psychological explanation to go through.[4] Such cases suggest a more compelling solution to Stich's dilemma than weak RTM.

A very popular approach has been to type-identify psychological states by reference to typical environmental inputs, computational role, and typical behavioral outputs.[5] When applied to sensory states, the typical environmental inputs are usually occurrent events. This model does not generalize to cognitive states like belief very well, because our thoughts are fairly independent of immediate environmental influences. In the case of non-episodic psychological states like belief or possession of a conceptual repertoire, the environmental connections also extend over time. If, for example, you acquired the concept 'water' in an environmental context that features H_2O, then your present beliefs utilizing the concept 'water' will have external reference to H_2O, even if you are in an H_2O-less region right now (as long as no new systematic connection has been set up). A number of accounts of environmental context have been proposed, including the causal theory of reference, Gareth Evans's dominance theory (Evans 1973), and Tyler Burge's linguistic community account (Burge 1979). I do not wish to choose among these accounts or even to presume that a monolithic theory of environmental context is possible.[6] Without prejudging these issues, the suggestion is that psychological states be individuated by the typical environmental contexts in which they arise, computational role, and typical behavioral outputs. (Of course, this proposal does assume that the environmental parameter can be specified in particular cases.) A final note: like the environmental parameter, the behavioral parameter should not be restricted to present behavior, or, for that matter, to actual behavior.

Since it is an explicitly "wide" version of (an explicitly computational) functionalism, I call this approach "wide functionalism." The broadly shared expectation is that by using these resources we can attribute content to psychological states. The same-content-same-truth-value principle would guide and constrain these attributions. What happens to the principle of simultaneous supervenience? I think there are two reasons for endorsing a principle of supervenience, or simultaneous supervenience. A historically important reason was the desire for ontological parsimony, specifically, the wish to dispel the illusion that the mental was anything in addition to a complex arrangement of physical entities. That reason is less compelling now, simply because the opposing position has largely been abandoned. As noted above, the strongest contemporary motivation is the recognition that a *doppelgänger* is, to say the least, very like the original person. In particular, every prediction of bodily movement that is true of the person is true of his *doppelgänger*. However, wide functionalism can easily be elaborated to accommodate this fact. Let us suppose that a wide taxonomy identifies psychological states P_1 through P_n. Given that set of psychological states, we could easily construct a set of superordinate categories of states by dropping the first parameter, the typical environmental contexts. We could label these $P_1^* - P_n^*$. The generalizations that hold across people and their *doppelgängers*, which explain, among other things, why they move in exactly the same ways, could all be expressed in terms of the P^*'s. At first, this may seem like equivocation, as if I have surreptitiously reintroduced the narrow construal. I am allowing cognitive psychology to use different taxonomies for different purposes: a finer-grained taxonomy to explain cognitive abilities, conceptual repertoire and the like, a coarser set of divisions to explain activities. However, this practice is very common in science and completely innocuous when the relation between the taxonomies is clear. Cognitive psychologists would be exactly as vulnerable to a charge of vicious ambiguity as are chemists who distinguish among neon, argon and krypton to assign melting points, and yet treat them all together to express generalizations about the noble gases.

To sum up my case against Stich: The two principles that are supposed to impale belief-desire psychology on the horns of a dilemma are open to serious criticism. More importantly, the sense that cognitive psychology is threatened by incoherence, because its theoretical constructs must be responsive to diverse explanatory pressures, would appear to rest on overly restrictive principles of taxonomy. If cognitive psychologists are permitted to use standard taxonomic methods, then we have been given no reason to think that they will fail to meet their goals. Do the Queen and her *doppelgänger* have the same belief? Wide functionalism implies that, in one clear sense, they do, and, in another clear sense, they do not. Surely, this is the correct answer to Stich's puzzle.

3. Fodor's Defense of Methodological Solipsism

Unlike Stich, Fodor's aim is not to bury traditional belief-desire psychology, but to save it. Still, Fodor agrees with Stich that the dual nature of inner formulae—being both medium of computation and medium of representation—raises special difficulties for cognitive psychology. As a merely historical claim, Fodor's seems to be right. A subgroup within artificial intelligence, the "procedural semanticists," have apparently let the dual nature of representations gull them into accepting a hopeless, and familiar, semantic theory.[7] The idea is to assign meanings to complex formulae by reference to the computational subroutines they call up. The definition by decomposition continues until we reach the most basic expressions of the formal language. These expressions are to be assigned meanings in virtue of their relations to transducer outputs (i.e., sense-data). In "Tom Swift and His Procedural Grandmother," Fodor gives procedural semanticists a stern, if witty lecture on how the empiricist theory of meaning is faring these days, namely, poorly (Fodor 1981b).

Fodor's central claim is correct. Knowing the computational or syntactic relations among formulae of the inner system of representation will not enable us to determine what they represent. I think he is also right to suspect that the strong prima facie plausibility of cashing out mental contents in terms of sensations makes it very tempting to believe that only a few short steps stand between a computational theory and a full semantic interpretation of thought processes. So, perhaps, each new generation of cognitive psychologists is in danger of falling into the empiricist trap. The problem is that Fodor tries to push this moral too far: computational psychologists must not only acknowledge the gulf between theories of interpretation and theories of computation, they must limit themselves to the latter. Computational psychologists should forswear the world beyond the subject and consider only the formal relations among inner formulae. They should become methodological solipsists. I have explained why I think Fodor's canon is a mistake, but I will also note that it gives him a rather perverse view. Fodor's most general claim is that the representational theory of mind is true. Yet, this methodological directive tells us that we will never have a scientific theory of representation!

Fodor offers what seems to be two distinct arguments for methodological solipsism. First he attempts to draw out straightforward consequences of computational psychology. If you believe thinking is computing, then you must recognize thought processes as operating only on formal or syntactic properties of representations. For, all the internal operations have access to are the "shapes" of internal representations. However, it seems obvious that content must play a role in type-individuating cognitive representations. Notice, however, that content can affect thinking (i.e., computing) only insofar as differences in content are mirrored in formal differences among representations. "[Hence] ... the computational theory of mind requires that two thoughts can be distinct in content only if they can be identified with relations to *formally distinct representations*" (Fodor 1981c, p. 227, my emphasis). Thus, any wide construal of psychological states is banned from computational psychology. I hope it is already clear why Fodor's conclusion does not follow. Computational psychology could perfectly well use a wide functionalist taxonomy to assign content, and so to type-individuate inner representations. Some distinctions among representations, namely, those grounded solely on environmental or behavioral parameters, would be irrelevant to computational relations among psychological states. Such a taxonomy would provide more distinctions than those required to work out a computational theory. But problems arise only if a taxonomy provides fewer than the necessary distinctions. We can reach Fodor's conclusion only by assuming: (1) Occam's razor; and (2) *only* inner computational relations among psychological states are of interest to computational psychology. The reasoning here is circular, because (2) is tantamount to the conclusion. Further, there is no way to patch up the argument, because, basically, Fodor is trying to derive the conclusion that computational psychology must only deal with inner computations from the premise that it must at least deal with computational relations among inner states.

Like Stich, Fodor also seems to make tacit appeal to a very restrictive approach to taxonomy. For Fodor, what matters inside the organism is the formulae; for Stich, it is the physical states. That substantive difference aside, Fodor makes a methodological assumption exactly like that needed by Stich to pose his dilemma: Since the narrow construal of psychological states is most appropriate when constructing a theory of computational relations, the computational psychologist is wedded to it. He cannot have both his computations and the world, so the world must be renounced. At times, Fodor seems to recognize that he has constructed a false dilemma. A dual taxonomy to serve the varied purposes of cognitive psychology would be fine. Still, Fodor is not prepared to accept this "bland and ecumenical conclusion," because he thinks a taxonomy based on construing states widely is actually impossible (Fodor 1981c, p. 233).

Since the argument just canvassed does not cut any ice, Fodor should view his entire brief for methodological solipsism as resting on his objection to the wide construal. Again, the argument takes the form of a dilemma. For a taxonomy which construes psychological states widely to be feasible, it must have some way of specifying the environmental conditions that enter into the organism-environment interaction. Fodor sees just two possibilities: either the specification of the stimulus will give its proper scientific description (e.g., H_2O, NaCl) or that specification will be couched in the language of laymen. Proceeding on the first alternative leads to an interminable impasse, because a scientific psychology could only follow the completion of every other science. The second option fares no better, however, for there are no laws to be discovered which link inner states to pencils, salt, or the Grand Canyon.

Both halves of this argument seem rather weak. *Any* science is going to be stymied if it refrains from explaining some phenomena until it is in a position to provide complete accounts of all the phenomena in its domain. Second, it is unclear why the obvious (let alone only) alternative to scientific description is ordinary description. Let us say that a description that specifies a stimulus by placing it in its basic scientific category is "object-centered." It is also possible to have a "viewer-centered" description that captures those features of the object which are salient for a particular class of viewers. To cite one of the most famous psychological experiments in recent years, Lettvin, Maturana, McCulloch, and Pitts (1959) explained that frogs are able to detect flies because any small moving speck within a given range causes a certain group of neurons to fire. While we have an accurate scientific taxonomy of (many kinds of) flies, this was irrelevant to Lettvin et al.'s work. For their purposes, the crucial description did not place flies in their basic scientific category, but in a class of geometrically and aerodynamically similar objects.

Fodor is explicit about why he would reject a taxonomy based on viewer-centered descriptions. He believes that theoretical terms used in psychology must occur in exceptionless laws (Fodor 1981c, e.g., pp. 249 and 251). Lay terminology and viewer-centered descriptions will almost certainly fail to meet this requirement. Presumably, sleeping frogs do not detect flies. Certainly we do not usually take note of stimuli unless we are awake, alert, facing the right direction, and so forth. Given the likely complexity of organism-environment interactions, it is improbable that they can be described by appeal to exceptionless laws. However, that does not render them unfit subjects for scientific study. Even if Lettvin et al. could not list all the potential contributing or interfering factors for fly-detecting in frogs, they still isolated the most salient factor and so explained the phenomenon.

This pattern of explanation is common throughout the life sciences. Ernst Mayr summarizes the practice of biologists: "Instead of fomlulating laws, biologists usually organize their generalizations into a framework of concepts ... [So, for example] the progress ... of evolutionary science [advanced by; such concepts as descent, selection, and fitness" (Mayr 1982, p. 43). These concepts earn their keep because of the number and diversity of phenomena that can be explained by appeal to them.[8] It seems to me that Lettvin et al.'s work fits this pattern. While there may be no exceptionless laws using viewer-centered descriptions, this conception of stimuli and receptors has enabled us to explain numerous perceptual phenomena (although, perhaps not as many as early adherents had hoped).

Fodor's demand for no taxonomy without strict nomologicality puts a requirement on cognitive psychology that is not met by the rest of science. This principle is crucial to his case against a wide construal. It enables him to reject the obvious suggestions of viewer-centered descriptions for the environmental parameter, and to reject lay terminology as well, leaving the hapless wide taxonomist to wait until the end of science. Like Stich's dilemma, Fodor's first argument against the wide construal tacitly imposes a requirement of strict monogamy on taxonomy; again, this is not a canon honored in the rest of science. I conclude that Stich and Fodor make the difficult job of type-individuating contentful psychological states appear impossible only by placing extravagant constraints on psychological taxonomy.

4. Block's "Troubles with Functionalism"

In "Troubles with Functionalism," Ned Block argues that current approaches to psychological classification will fail, not just for beliefs, but for all psychological states. Block thinks that the fundamental problem with all versions of functionalism, including computational functionalism, is that they must be either too "liberal" or too "chauvinistic" (Block 1980, e.g., p. 293).[9] A "liberal" functionalism counts too many things as mental systems; a "chauvinistic" functionalism is inappropriately exclusive. In rough outline, this is Block's argument. Some versions of functionalism type-individuate psychological states by reference to input-output functions and to relatively gross similarities in internal state transitions. Thus, two systems would share psychological states if a common machine table describes both systems. These versions are too liberal, because they would count a suitably organized Bolivian economy as exemplifying mentality, or a well-drilled army of Chinese as instantiating a single qualitative state. It would seem that there are just two ways to tighten admission requirements to the realm of the psychological. A functionalist could avoid the counterexamples by adding constraints about having a sensory system and/or having appropriate behavioral capacities. Or, he could require that putative psychological systems resemble human thought processes at a more detailed level of analysis. Either way, Block argues, the price of ruling out bogus psychological systems is that bona fide cases will be rejected as well.

This argument probably begs too many questions. As William Lycan has argued, the population of China case is not a clear counterexample (Lycan 1979, 1981). Were the Bolivian economy example given in more detail, I think our intuition that there is no mental life involved would also become clouded. However, my concern is not with the charge of liberalism, but with the chauvinism half of the argument. In Block's terms, computational psychology would be a version of "psychofunctionalism," that is, a theory that individuates psychological states by reference to future psychological theories (as opposed to "analytic functionalism," which type-identifies states by reference to common sense platitudes). He thinks that psychofunctionalisms will always be chauvinistic, because they will be modeled on the human case. Yet, one project for computational psychology is to offer a general theory of thought processes. This project comes to computational psychology through its logical behaviorist lineage, although the idea goes back at least to Kant. Block's worry is that if the goal is a general theory, yet man is to be the measure of psychological theories then the inevitable result will be chauvinism.

He dramatizes the problem by way of another hypothetical case. We are to envision the possibility of a race of Martians who are enough like us so that we can engage in significant cultural exchanges, but whose thinking differs from ours at what might be called the level of engineering decisions. The point is that the same task may be performed in a variety of different ways: for example, one engineer might implement a computation by adding greater computational capacity, another by increasing the amount of memory. We are to imagine that "... Martians and Earthians differ as if they were the end products of maximally different design choices ..." (Block 1980, p. 291), even though at the level of common-sense psychology both groups appear to have the same sorts of beliefs and desires. Block's claim is that, having based his taxonomy of psychological states on the human case, a psychofunctionalist could not attribute any psychological states to the Martians; and that is clearly chauvinism, since they in fact have mental lives.

I will suggest two replies to this argument, one of which Block considers himself. The first point is that we need to distinguish three levels of psychological description: (1) the common-sense level of beliefs and desires; (2) the computational level that presents a more fine-grained analysis of the molar capacity; (3) the algorithmic level which describes algorithms or heuristics by which subtasks underlying the capacity are actually carried out. This hierarchy enables me to make a needed clarification of the second term of the wide functionalist schema for psychological classification. By "computational role" I mean a description of the role the state plays at the computational level. One could have a theory that individuates states at the level of algorithms. That level of description seems unattractive for the reason Block gives: in concentrating on the specifics of how a task is implemented, we miss regularities concerning the common capacities of diverse systems. This clarification permits the following line of rebuttal to Block's charge that psychofunctionalisms are chauvinistic. The differences between Martians and Earthlings occur at the algorithmic level. But a wide functionalist classification scheme is tied to the computational level, so the example does not run counter to the thesis. The problem with this reply is that it invites new counterexamples. However, I think it requires greater ingenuity to construct the examples at this level. It is easy to describe cases at the level of algorithmic implementation, because there are many ways to do a given task. The computational level is different. At this level, the concern is not with how a capacity is realized, but with a more precise description of what a given capacity is. So, for example, a computational theory of stereoscopic perception asserts that what this capacity really amounts to is, among other things, the ability to calculate surface discontinuities from the intensity changes in an image.[10] Were dissimilarities to be present at this level—suppose an imagined system were just given 3-D information as inputs, for example—then I think that we would be less eager to admit that such systems were really like us from a psychological point of view.

Nevertheless, this reply merely eases the problem of the amiable Martians. It does not solve it, because even if the Martians were unlike us psychologically—they might still be like us in having a psychology. Block thinks that the psychofunctionalist has boxed himself in. Having used humans as paradigms, it will turn out that maximally different Martians will not exemplify any of the psychological states listed in our science. But, what follows? Block feels that the psychofunctionalist must either deny that Martians have any psychological states or try to construct a "universal psychology," a functional theory that covers all creatures and systems that have psychological properties (Block 1980, pp. 291–93). However, I think the obvious response for the psychofunctionalist is to suggest that Martians do not have the *same* psychological states we do, but different states of the *same type*: for example, states that are most perspicuously type-identified by the typical environmental context-computational role-typical behavioral output schema.[11] It is clear how Block would reply to this move: Although the wide functionalism (version of psychofunctionalism) has avoided commitment to one type of universal psychology—one computational theory for all psychological entities—it is still presupposing that a kind of universal psychology is possible. Specifically, it is presupposing that all and only psychological systems can be characterized by some wide functionalist theory. But, Block sensibly remarks, "Perhaps life in the universe is such that we shall simply have no basis for reasonable decisions about what systems are in the domain of psychology and what systems are not" (Block 1980, p. 293).

If universal psychology must answer that question, then I share Block's doubts about feasibility. However, I do not see why any psychofunctionalist must be committed to a universal psychology with that portfolio. Computational psychology operates on the assumption that central cases of psychological systems are best characterized by computational theories. Thus, at most, this program is committed to the existence of some sufficient conditions for the presence of cognition. The "at most" is appropriate because specific theories could be modified by adding defeating conditions. In general, psychofunctionalisms will be vulnerable to the charge of chauvinism only if they make falling within the purview of a particular theory or a particular type of theory a necessary and sufficient condition for being a psychological entity. Then the genuine possibility of unexpected cases and indeterminate cases makes the enterprise look dubious. However, there is no reason for a psychofunctionalist to buy into this project. It is perfectly reasonable for a wide functionalist, for example, to develop and use his classifications of psychological states without harboring the belief that he has hit upon the one and only true mark of the mental. He may even be committed to the view that, in general, thinking is best characterized by such theories, without presuming that this holds for absolutely every actual or possible mental system.

I think the theoretical stance I have presented as available for the psychofunctionalist, specifically, for the wide functionalist, is very common in science. However, I will try to make this attitude toward theory both clearer and more plausible by illustrating it with an actual case from biology. Sutton, Boveri, and Morgan all adopted the working hypothesis that the chains of matter inside the cell that became discernible in staining—the chromosomes—carried the genetic material.[12] This hypothesis is now universally accepted. Nevertheless, one could object to the program with an argument that parallels Block's. The problem is that there are no necessary and sufficient conditions for being a chromosome. A theory which tried to press the original criterion, namely, taking on color in staining, would be chauvinistic, inappropriately excluding the chromosomes of bacteria and viruses, which are too small to stain. On the other hand, a theory that tried to identify chromosomes with whatever carries genetic material would be too liberal. It would count the fragments of genetic material that float in the cytoplasm of some organisms (plasmids) as chromosomes. Despite the lack of a definition for "chromosome," the view that chromosomes carry the genetic material is the foundation of a fruitful program in which numerous genes have been identified with various bits of chromosomes. I see no reason why the computational approach could not play the same enviable role in the development of psychology, even if we can never define "psychological."

Block's other objection to psychofunctionalism turns on exactly the same point. He notes that theories like wide functionalism advert to sensory systems and behavior, even though it may never be possible to provide necessary and sufficient conditions for something's being behavior or being a sensorium (Block 1980, p. 293).[13] By the argument just given, this prospect only becomes a problem if a psychofunctionalist tries to claim that the theory he has modelled on known cases covers all actual and possible cases. Nothing compels him to make the leap, however. He can maintain that cognition is ineluctably connected with perception and action in central cases of thought processes. He can even maintain that it is hard to understand how cognition could occur without what we think of as perception and action, all without committing himself to an absolutely universal generalization.

The point I have been urging against Block is that computational psychology can offer theories of great scope and power without denying the actual or potential diversity of nature. For an approach can be the great unifying idea for a large range of phenomena, without claiming absolutely exclusive dominion. Computational psychology has nothing to fear from unexpected or indeterminate cases. As with other ambitious programs, the danger is that either some new approach to psychology will prove to have greater scope or the phenomena will turn out to be so fragmentary that no general approach can succeed. Once again, the claim that current approaches will never produce an adequate classification of psychological phenomena depends on holding psychology to a standard other sciences routinely rise above. In this case, the erroneous principle is that a theory can adequately identify members of a range of phenomena only if it can provide a universally applicable definition for membership in that range. I should emphasize that this standard is not Block's idea; it is very prevalent among functionalists. I agree with Block that there are numerous, insurmountable troubles with bad philosophical versions of functionalism. As far as I can tell, however, computational psychology is not vulnerable to his attack, even though it is an explicitly functional approach.

Computational psychology may develop into a genuine science of psychology. Or, the approach could be completely barren, like so many of its forerunners. I have tried to save the program only from premature obituaries—which, I fear, might lead to a premature demise. Throughout, my claim has been that the problems do not lie with the new mode in cognitive psychology, but with an outmoded philosophy of science. Sciences can flourish, even though they must meet competing demands, even though they do not formulate exceptionless laws, even though they cannot delimit their domains with absolute precision. The mistake is to expect a tidy little theory, when the subject is as complex as thought processes of living systems produced over vast stretches of time by evolutionary forces.

Notes

I am grateful to Ned Block, Philip Kitcher, Hilary Kornblith, and Joe Owens for helpful conversations, and to the MIT Department of Linguistics and Philosophy for its hospitality during a valuable sabbatical visit. The helpful criticisms of two referees for *Philosophy of Science* enabled me to make a number of improvements in an earlier version.

1. Stich (1983) offers a more complex argument against the belief construct. For reasons of space, I will not discuss some of the interesting additional points Stich raises there. Still, the argument I consider provides much of the motivation for the book's indictment of belief so, where appropriate, I will note how my criticisms would bear on that more extended argument.

2. Cited in Springer and Deutsch 1981, pp. 201–2.

3. The importance of this point was made clear to me by Ned Block in conversation.

4. I should note that, in his book, Stich offers independent arguments against the wide construal. Stich's claim (made originally in Stich 1982) is that our ordinary notion of content is incoherent because it involves at least reference similarity, ideological similarity, and causal-functional role similarity. In particular cases, one or another of these factors dominate or, worse, they compete. In other words, folk psychology has no univocal way of assigning content. Given my other concerns, I cannot provide an adequate treatment of this chain of argumentation here. Stich forsees the form the opposition will take. Since he aims to show the incoherence of our ordinary notion of belief and belief-content, he must engage in conceptual analysis—"what we would say" in bizarre cases. By contrast, defenders of content are not limited to considering the theories implied, or apparently implied, in ordinary usage. Since they think the phenomenon exists, they are free to explore different ways of capturing its nature (Stich 1983, p. 76). That is exactly the approach I take in the text. Despite appearances, this does not amount to arguing past Stich. I take his description of his dialectical position to be an admission that all he can hope to show is that our ordinary ascriptions of content are fairly inconsistent, so we should not infer the existence of content from the ubiquity or apparent success of the content-construct in ordinary psychological explanation. I do not make this assumption. My argument is that serious psychological explanations require the wide construal of psychological states.

5. See, for example, Field 1977, 1978; Harman 1970, 1973. For an early version of this view, see Wilfrid Sellars, "Empiricism and the Philosophy of Mind," "Truth and Correspondence," and "Naming and Saying," in his 1963 book.

6. I am grateful to Joe Owens for a very useful discussion on this point.

7. Fodor's particular targets are Philip Johnson-Laird (1977) and Terry Winograd (1971).

8. This view of scientific concepts is described in Philip Kitcher 1982. For a more technical discussion, see Kitcher 1981.

9. I should note that Block thinks the twin earth problem dooms any wide functionalism, so he sees his attack as being directed at the remnants of functionalism, i.e., at narrow versions. However, if his objections were cogent, they would doom wide functionalism as well.

10. For a general discussion of the computational level, see David Marr 1976; and Marr and Poggio 1976.

11. The qualifier "most perspicuously" is necessary because if the psychology of Martians could be described adequately by reference to physiological states then the functional account would be otiose.

12. For a general account of this work, see Carlson 1966. I am grateful to Philip Kitcher for drawing my attention to this example.

13. Block would also object to such accounts on the grounds that they are chauvinistic with respect to brains in vats and paralytics. I am not terribly confident about our intuitions in such cases. However, the strategy I develop to deal with Stich's puzzle could be applied here. Starting with the wide functionalist taxonomy of psychological states, form superordinate categories by dropping the sensory and/or behavioral parameter(s). These superordinate categories will then describe the states shared by us and brains in vats if—which I doubt—brains in vats really think the way we do.

References

Block, Ned (1980), "Troubles with Functionalism," in *Readings in Philosophy of Psychology*, Ned Block (ed.). Vol. 1. Cambridge: Harvard University Press. (First published in *Perception and Cognition: Issues in the Foundations of Psychology*, C. Wade Savage [ed.] Minnesota Studies in the Philosophy of Science, vol. 9 Minneapolis University of Minnesota Press, 1978.)

Burge, Tyler (1979), "Individualism and the Mental," in *Studies in Epistemology*, P. French. T. Uehling, and H. Wettstein (eds.). Midwest Studies in Philosophy, vol. 4. Minneapolis University of Minnesota Press.

Carlson, E. A. (1966), *The Gene: A Critical History*. Philadelphia: Saunders.

Chomsky, Noam (1980), *Rules and Representations*. New York: Columbia University Press.

Evans, Gareth (1973). "The Causal Theory of Names," *Proceedings of the Aristotelian Society*, n.s., supp. vol. 47, pp. 187–208.

Field, Hartry (1977), "Logic, Meaning and Conceptual Role," *Journal of Philosophy* 74: 370–409.

Field, Hartry (1978), "Mental Representation," *Erkenntnis 13*: 9–61.

Fodor, Jerry (1981a), *Representations*. Cambridge: MIT Press.

Fodor, Jerry (1981b), "Tom Swift and his Procedural Grandmother," in *Representations*. (First published in *Cognition 6*, 1978.)

Fodor, Jerry (1981c), "Methodological Solipsism considered as a research strategy in cognitive psychology," in *Representations*. (First published in *The Behavioral and Brain Sciences 3*, 1980.)

Harman, Gilbert (1970), "Language and Learning," *Noûs* 4: 33–43.

Johnson-Laird, Philip (1977), "Procedural Semantics," *Cognition* 5: 189–214.

Kim, Jaegwon (1978), "Supervenience and Nomological Incommensurables," *American Philosophical Quarterly 15*: 149–56.

Kitcher, Philip (1981), "Explanatory Unification," *Philosophy of Science 48*: 507–31.

Kitcher (1982), *Abusing Science*. Cambridge: MIT Press.

Lettvin, J.; Maturana, R. R.; McCulloch, W. S.; and Pitts, W. H. (1959), "What the frog's eye tells the frog's brain," *Proceedings of the Institute for Radio Engineers 47*: 1940–51.

Lycan, William (1979), "A New Lilliputian Argument against Machine Functionalism," *Philosophical Studies 35*: 379–87.

Lycan (1981), "Form, Function, and Feel," *The Journal of Philosophy 77*: 24–50.

Marr, David (1976), "Early Processing of Visual Information," *Philosophical Transactions of the Royal Society of London*. Vol. 275, 942, pp. 483–534.

Marr, David, and Poggio, Tomasso (1976), "Cooperative Computation of Stereo Disparity," *Science 194*: 283–87.

Mayr, Ernst (1982), *The Growth of Biological Thought*. Cambridge: Harvard University Press.

Putnam, Hilary (n.d.), "Computational Psychology and Interpretation Theory". Manuscript.

Putnam, Hilary (1975), "The meaning of 'meaning'," in *Language, Mind, and Knowledge*, K. Gunderson (ed.). Minnesota Studies in the Philosophy of Science, vol. 7. Minneapolis: University of Minnesota Press.

Sellars, Wilfrid (1963), *Science, Perception, and Reality*. London: Routledge and Kegan Paul.

Springer, Sally P., and Deutsch, Georg (1981), *Left Brain, Right Brain*. San Francisco: W. H. Freeman and Company.

Stich, Stephen (1978), "Autonomous Psychology and the Belief-Desire Thesis," *The Monist 61*: 573–91.

Stich, Stephen (1982), "On the Ascription of Content," in *Thought and Object*, A. Woodfield (ed.). Oxford: Oxford University Press.

Stich, Stephen (1983), *From Folk Psychology to Cognitive Science: The Case Against Belief*. Cambridge: MIT Press.

Winograd, Terry (1971), *Procedures as a Representation for Data in a Computer Program for Understanding Natural Language*. Cambridge: MIT Project MAC.

Chapter 37

Individualism and Psychology

Tyler Burge

Recent years have seen in psychology—and overlapping parts of linguistics, artificial intelligence, and the social sciences—the development of some semblance of agreement about an approach to the empirical study of human activity and ability. The approach is broadly mentalistic in that it involves the attribution of states, processes and events that are intentional, in the sense of 'representational'. Many of these events and states are unconscious and inaccessible to mere reflection. Computer jargon is prominent in labeling them. But they bear comparison to thoughts, wants, memories, perceptions, plans, mental sets and the like—ordinarily so-called. Like ordinary propositional attitudes, some are described by means of that-clauses and may be evaluated as true or false. All are involved in a system by means of which a person knows, represents, and utilizes information about his or her surroundings.

In the first part of this paper, I shall criticize some arguments that have been given for thinking that explanation in psychology is, and ought to be, purely "individualistic." In the second part of the paper, I shall discuss in some detail a powerful psychological theory that is not individualistic. The point of this latter discussion will be to illustrate a nonindividualistic conception of explanatory kinds. In a third section, I shall offer a general argument against individualism, that centers on visual perception. What I have to say, throughout the paper, will bear on all parts of psychology that attribute intentional states. But I will make special reference to explanation in cognitive psychology.

Individualism is a view about how kinds are correctly individuated, how their natures are fixed. We shall be concerned primarily with individualism about the individuation of mental kinds. According to individualism about the mind, the mental natures of all a person's or animal's mental states (and events) are such that there is no necessary or deep individuative relation between the individual's being in states of those kinds and the nature of the individual's physical or social environments.

This view owes its prominence to Descartes. It was embraced by Locke, Leibniz, and Hume. And it has recently found a home in the phenomenological tradition and in the doctrines of twentieth-century behaviorists, functionalists, and mind-brain identity theorists. There are various more specific versions of the doctrine. A number of fundamental issues in traditional philosophy are shaped by them. In this paper, however, I shall concentrate on versions of the doctrine that have been prominent in recent philosophy of psychology.

Current individualistic views of intentional mental states and events have tended to take one of two forms. One form maintains that an individual's being in any given intentional state (or being the subject of such an event) can be *explicated* by reference to states and events of the individual that are specifiable without using intentional

Reprinted from *The Philosophical Review* 95 (1986), pp. 3–46, by permission of the author and the publisher.

vocabulary and without presupposing anything about the individual subject's social or physical environments. The explication is supposed to specify—in nonintentional terms—stimulations, behavior, and internal physical or functional states of the individual. The other form of individualism is implied by the first, but is weaker. It does not attempt to explicate anything. It simply makes a claim of *supervenience*: an individual's intentional states and events (types and tokens) could not be different from what they are, given the individual's physical, chemical, neural, or functional histories, where these histories are specified nonintentionally and in a way that is independent of physical or social conditions outside the individual's body.

In other papers I have argued that both forms of individualism are mistaken. A person's intentional states and events could (counterfactually) vary, even as the individual's physical, functional (and perhaps phenomenological) history, specified nonintentionally and individualistically, is held constant. I have offered several arguments for this conclusion. Appreciating the strength of these arguments, and discerning the philosophical potential of a nonindividualist view of mind, depend heavily on reflecting on differences among these arguments. They both reinforce one another and help map the topography of a positive position.

For present purposes, however, I shall merely sketch a couple of the arguments to give their flavor. I shall not defend them or enter a variety of relevant qualifications. Consider a person A who thinks that aluminum is a light metal used in sailboat masts, and a person B who believes that he or she has arthritis in the thigh. We assume that A and B can pick out instances of aluminum and arthritis (respectively) and know many familiar general facts about aluminum and arthritis. A is, however, ignorant of aluminum's chemical structure and microproperties. B is ignorant of the fact that arthritis cannot occur outside of joints. Now we can imagine counterfactual cases in which A and B's bodies have their same histories considered in isolation of their physical environments, but in which there are significant environmental differences from the actual situation. A's counterfactual environment lacks aluminum and has in its places a similar-looking light metal. B's counterfactual environment is such that no one has ever isolated arthritis as a specific disease, or syndrome of diseases. In these cases, A would lack "aluminum thoughts" and B would lack "arthritis thoughts." Assuming natural developmental patterns, both would have different thoughts. Thus these differences from the actual situation show up not only in the protagonist's relations to their environments, but also in their intentional mental states and events, ordinarily so-called. The arguments bring out variations in obliquely (or intensionally) occurring expressions in literal mental state and event ascriptions, our primary means of identifying intentional mental states.[1]

I believe that these arguments use literal descriptions of mental events, and are independent of conversational devices that may affect the form of an ascription without bearing on the nature of the mental event described. The sort of argument that we have illustrated does not depend on special features of the notions of arthritis or aluminum. Such arguments go through for observational and theoretical notions, for percepts as well as concepts, for natural-kind and non-natural kind notions, for notions that are the special preserve of experts, and for what are known in the psychological literature as "basic categories." Indeed, I think that, at a minimum, relevantly similar arguments can be shown to go through with any notion that applies to public types of objects, properties, or events that are typically known by empirical means.[2]

I shall not elaborate or defend the arguments here. In what follows, I shall presuppose that they are cogent. For our purposes, it will be enough if one bears firmly in mind their conclusion: mental states and events may in principle vary with variations in the environment, even as an individual's physical (functional, phenomenological) history, specified nonintentionally and individualistically, remains constant.

A common reaction to these conclusions, often unsupported by argument, has been to concede their force, but to try to limit their effect. It is frequently held that they apply to common-sense attributions of attitudes, but have no application to analogous attributions in psychology. Nonindividualistic aspects of mentalistic attribution have been held to be uncongenial with the purposes and requirements of psychological theory. Of course, there is a tradition of holding that ordinary intentional attributions are incapable of yielding any knowledge at all. Others have held the more modest view that mentalistic attributions are capable of yielding only knowledge that could not in principle be systematized in a theory.

I shall not be able to discuss all of these lines of thought. In particular I shall ignore generalized arguments that mentalistic ascriptions are deeply indeterminate, or otherwise incapable of yielding knowledge. Our focus will be on arguments that purport to show that nonindividualistic mentalistic ascriptions cannot play a systematic role in psychological explanation—*because* of the fact that they are not individualistic.

There are indeed significant differences between theoretical discourse in psychology and the mentalistic discourse of common sense. The most obvious one is that the language of theoretical psychology requires refinements on ordinary discourse. It not only requires greater system and rigor, and a raft of unconscious states and events that are not ordinarily attributed (though they are, I think, ordinarily allowed for). It also must distill out descriptive-explanatory purposes of common attributions from uses that serve communication at the expense of description and explanation. Making this distinction is already common practice. Refinement for scientific purposes must, however, be systematic and meticulous—though it need not eliminate all vagueness. I think that there are no sound reasons to believe that such refinement cannot be effected through the development of psychological theory, or that effecting it will fundamentally change the nature of ordinary mentalistic attributions.

Differences between scientific and ordinary discourse survive even when ordinary discourse undergoes the refinements just mentioned. Although common sense discourse—both about macrophysical objects and about mental event—yields knowledge, I believe that the principles governing justification for such discourse differ from those that are invoked in systematic scientific theorizing. So there is, *prima facie*, room for the view that psychology is or should be fully individualistic—even though ordinary descriptions of mental states are not. Nevertheless, the arguments for this view that have been offered do not seem to me cogent. Nor do I find the view independently persuasive.

Before considering such arguments, I must articulate some further background assumptions, this time about psychology itself. I shall be taking those parts of psychology that utilize mentalistic and information-processing discourse pretty much as they are. I assume that they employ standard scientific methodology, that they have produced interesting empirical results, and that they contain more than a smattering of genuine theory. I shall not prejudge what sort of science psychology is, or how it relates to the natural sciences. I do, however, assume that its cognitive claims and, more especially, its methods and presuppositions are to be taken seriously as the best we now have in this area of inquiry. I believe that there are no good reasons for thinking that the methods or findings of this body of work are radically misguided.

I shall not be assuming that psychology *must* continue to maintain touch with common sense discourse. I believe that such touch will almost surely be maintained. But I think that empirical disciplines must find their own way according to standards that they set for themselves. Quasi-*apriori* strictures laid down by philosophers count for little. So our reflections concern psychology as it is, not as it will be or must be.

In taking psychology as it is, I am assuming that it seeks to refine, deepen, generalize and systematize some of the statements of informed common sense about people's mental activity. It accepts, for example, that people see physical objects with certain shapes, textures, and hues, and in certain spatial relations, under certain specified conditions. And it attempts to explain in more depth what people do when they see such things, and how their doing it is done. Psychology accepts that people remember events and truths, that they categorize objects, that they draw inferences, that they act on beliefs and preferences. And it attempts to find deep regularities in these activities, to specify mechanisms that underly them, and to provide systematic accounts of how these activities relate to one another. In describing and, at least partly, in explaining these activities and abilities, psychology makes use of interpreted that-clauses and other intensional constructions—or what we might loosely call "intentional content."[3] I have seen no sound reason to believe that this use is merely heuristic, instrumentalistic, or second class in any other sense.

I assume that intentional content has internal structure—something like grammatical or logical structure—and that the parts of this structure are individuated finely enough to correspond to certain individual abilities, procedures, or perspectives. Since various abilities, procedures, or perspectives may be associated with any given event, object, property, or relation, intentional content must be individuated more finely than the entities in the world with which the individual interacts. We must allow different ways (even, I think, different primitive ways) for the individual to conceive of, or represent any given entity. This assumption about the fine grainedness of content in psychology will play no explicit role in what follows. I note it here to indicate that my skepticism about individualism as an interpretation of psychology does not stem from a conception of content about which it is already clear that it does not play a dominant role in psychology.[4]

Finally, I shall assume that individualism is prima facie wrong about psychology, including cognitive psychology. Since the relevant parts of psychology frequently use attributions of intentional states that are subject to our thought experiments, the language actually used in psychology is not purely individualistic. That is, the generalizations with counterfactual force that appear in psychological theories, given their standard interpretations, are not all individualistic. For ordinary understanding of the truth conditions, or individuation conditions, of the relevant attributions suffices to verify the thought experiments. Moreover, there is at present no well-explained, well-understood, much less well-tested, individualistic language—or individualistic reinterpretation of the linguistic forms currently in use in psychology—that could serve as surrogate.

Thus individualism as applied to psychology must be revisionistic. It must be revisionistic at least about the language of psychological theory. I shall be developing the view that it is also revisionistic, without good reason, about the underlying presuppositions of the science. To justify itself, individualism must fulfill two tasks. It must show that the language of psychology should be revised by demonstrating that the presuppositions of the science are or should be purely individualistic. And it must explain a new individualistic language (attributing what is sometimes called "narrow content") that captures genuine theoretical commitments of the science.

These tasks are independent. If the second were accomplished, but the first remained unaccomplishable, individualism would be wrong; but it would have engendered a new level of explanation. For reasons I will mention later, I am skeptical about such wholesale supplementation of current theory. But psychology is not a monolith. Different explanatory tasks and types of explanation coexist within it. In questioning the view that psychology is individualistic, I am not *thereby* doubting whether there are some subparts of psychology that conform to the strictures of individualism. I am doubting whether all of psychology as it is currently practiced is or should be individualistic. Thus I shall concentrate on attempts to fulfill the first of the two tasks that face someone bent on revising psychology along individualistic lines. So much for preliminaries.

I

We begin by discussing a general argument against non-individualistic accounts. It goes as follows. The behavior of the physiologically and functionally identical protagonists in our thought experiments is identical. But psychology is the science (only) of behavior. Since the behavior of the protagonists is the same, a science of behavior should give the *same* explanations and descriptions of the two cases (by some Ockhamesque principle of parsimony). So there is no room in the discipline for explaining their behavior in terms of different mental states.[5]

The two initial premises are problematic. To begin with the first: it is not to be assumed that the protagonists are behaviorally identical in the thought experiments. I believe that the only clear, general interpretation of 'behavior' that is available and that would verify the first premise is 'bodily motion'. But this construal has almost no relevance to psychology as it is actually practiced. 'Behavior' has become a catch-all term in psychology for observable activity on whose description and character psychologists can reach quick "pretheoretical" agreement. Apart from methodological bias, it is just not true that all descriptions that would count as "behavioral" in cognitive (social, developmental) psychology would apply to both the protagonists. Much behavior is intentional action; many action specifications are nonindividualistic. Thought experiments relevantly similar to those which we have already developed will apply to them.

For example, much "behavioral" evidence in psychology is drawn from what people say or how they answer questions. Subjects' utterances (and the questions asked them) must be taken to be interpreted in order to be of any use in the experiments; and it is often assumed that theories may be checked by experiments carried out in different languages. Since the protagonists' sayings in the thought experiments are different, even in nontransparent or oblique occurrences, it is prima facie mistaken to count the protagonists "behaviorally" identical. Many attributions of nonverbal behavior are also intentional and non-individualistic, or even relational: she picked up the apple, pointed to the square block, tracked the moving ball, smiled at the familiar face, took the money instead of the risk. These attributions can be elaborated to produce non-individualist thought experiments. The general point is that many relevant specifications of behavior in psychology are intentional, or relational, or both. The thought experiments indicate that these specifications ground nonindividualist mental attributions. An argument for individualism cannot reasonably *assume* that these specifications are individualistic or ought to be.

Of course, there are non-individualistic specifications of behavior that are unsuitable for any scientific enterprise ('my friend's favorite bodily movement'). But most of these do not even appear to occur in psychology. The problem of providing reasonable specifications of behavior cannot be solved from an armchair. Sanitizing the notion of behavior to meet some antecedently held methodological principle is an old game, never won. One must look at what psychology actually takes as "behavioral" evidence. It is the responsibility of the argument to show that nonindividualistic notions have no place in psychology. Insofar as the argument assumes that intentional, nonindividualistic specifications of behavior are illegitimate, it either ignores obvious aspects of psychological practice or begs the question at issue.

The second step of the argument also limps. One cannot assume without serious discussion that psychology is correctly characterized as a science (only) of behavior. This is, of course, particularly so if behavior is construed in a restrictive way. But even disregarding how behavior is construed, the premise is doubtful. One reason is that it is hardly to be assumed that a putative science is to be characterized in terms of its evidence as opposed to its subject matter. Of course, the subject matter is to some extent under dispute. But cognitive psychology appears to be about certain molar abilities and activities some of which are propositional attitudes. Since the propositional attitudes attributed do not seem to be fully individuable in individualistic terms, we need a direct argument that cognitive psychology is not a science of what it appears to be a science of.

A second reason for doubting the premise is that psychology seems to be partly about relations between people, or animals, and their environment. It is hard to see how to provide a natural description of a theory of vision, for example, as a science of behavior. The point of the theory is to figure out how people do what they obviously succeed in doing—how they see objects in their environment. We are trying to explain relations between a subject and a physical world that we take ourselves to know something about. Theories of memory, of certain sorts of learning, of linguistic understanding, of belief formation, of categorization, do the same. It is certainly not obvious that these references to relations between subject and environment are somehow inessential to (all parts of) psychological theory. They seem, in fact, to be a large part of the point of such theory. In my view, these relations help motivate nonindividualistic principles of individuation (cf. section II). In sum, I think that the argument we have so far considered begs significant questions at almost every step.

There is a kindred argument worth considering: the determinants of behavior supervene on states of the brain. (If one is a materialist, one might take this to be a triviality: "brain states supervene on brain states.") So if propositional attitudes are to be treated as among the determinants of behavior, they must be taken to supervene on brain states. The alternative is to take propositional attitudes as behaviorally irrelevant.[6]

This argument can, I think, be turned on its head. Since propositional attitudes are among the determinants of our "behavior" (where this expression is as open-ended as ever), and since propositional attitudes do not supervene on our brain states, not all determinants of our "behavior" supervene on our brain states. I want to make three points against the original argument, two metaphysical and one epistemic or methodological. Metaphysics first.

The ontological stakes that ride on the supervenience doctrine are far less substantial than one might think. It is simply not a "trivial consequence" of materialism about mental states and events that the determinants of our behavior supervene on the states of our brains. This is because what supervenes on what has at least as much to do with how the relevant entities are individuated as with what they are made of. If a mental event m is individuated partly by reference to normal conditions outside a person's body, then, regardless of whether m has material composition, m might vary even as the body remains the same.

Since intentional phenomena form such a large special case, it is probably misleading to seek analogies from other domains to illustrate the point. To loosen up the imagination, however, consider the Battle of Hastings. Suppose that we preserve every human body, every piece of turf, every weapon, every physical structure and all the physical interactions among them, from the first confrontation to the last death or withdrawal on the day of the battle. Suppose that, counterfactually, we imagine all these physical events and props placed in California (perhaps at the same time in 1066). Suppose that the physical activity is artifically induced by brilliant scientists transported to earth by Martian film producers. The distal causes of the battle have nothing to do with the causes of the Battle of Hastings. I think it plausible (and certainly coherent) to say that in such circumstances, not the Battle of Hastings, but only a physical facsimile would have taken place. I think that even if the location in Hastings were maintained, sufficiently different counterfactual causal antecedents would suffice to vary the identity of the battle. The battle is individuated partly in terms of its causes. Though the battle does not supervene on its physical constituents, we have little hesitation about counting it a physical event.

Our individuation of historical battles is probably wrapped up with intentional states of the participants. The point can also be made by reference to cases that are clearly independent of intentional considerations. Consider the emergence of North America from the ocean. Suppose that we delimit what count as constituent (say, micro) physical events of this larger event. It seems that if the surrounding physical conditions and laws are artfully enough contrived, we can counterfactually conceive these same constituent events (or the constituent physical objects' undergoing physically identical changes in the same places) in such a way that they are embedded in a much larger land mass, so that the physical constituents of North America do not make up any salient part of this larger mass. The emergence of North America would not have occurred in such a case, even though its "constituent" physical events were, in isolation, physically identical with the actual events. We individuate the emergence of continents or other land masses in such a way that they are not supervenient on their physical constituents. But such events are nonetheless physical.

In fact, I think that materialism does not provide reasonable restrictions on theories of the role of mentalistic attributions in psychology. The relation of physical composition presently plays no significant role in any established scientific theory of mental events, or of their relations to brain events. The restrictions that physiological considerations place on psychological theorizing, though substantial, are weaker than those of any of the articulated materialisms, even the weak compositional variety I am alluding to. My point is just that rejecting individualistic supervenience does not entail rejecting a materialistic standpoint. So materialism per se does nothing to support individualism.[7]

The second "metaphysical" point concerns causation. The argument we are considering in effect simply assumes that propositional attitudes (type and token) supervene on physico-chemical events in the body. But many philosophers appear to think that this assumption is rendered obvious by bland observations about the etiology of mental events and behavior. It is plausible that events in the external world causally affect the mental events of a subject only by affecting the subject's bodily surfaces; and that nothing (not excluding mental events) causally affects behavior except by affecting (causing or being a causal antecedent of causes of) local states of the subject's body. One might reason that in the anti-individualistic thought experiments these principles are violated insofar as events in the environment are alleged to differentially "affect" a person's mental events and behavior without differentially "affecting" his or her body: only if mental events (and states) supervene on the individual's body can the causal principles be maintained.

The reasoning is confused. The confusion is abetted by careless use of the term 'affect', conflating causation with individuation. Variations in the environment that do not vary the impacts that causally "affect" the subject's body may "affect" the individuation of the information that the subject is receiving, of the intentional processes he or she is undergoing, or of the way the subject is acting. It does not follow that the environment causally affects the subject in any way that circumvents its having effects on the subject's body.

Once the conflation is avoided, it becomes clear that there is no simple argument from the causal principles just enunciated to individualism. The example from geology provides a useful counter-model. It shows that one can accept the causal principles and thereby experience no bewilderment whatsoever in rejecting individualism. A continent moves and is moved by local impacts from rocks, waves, molecules. Yet we can conceive of holding constant the continent's peripheral impacts and chemically constituent events and objects, without holding identical the continent or certain of its macrochanges—because the continent's spatial relations to other land masses affect the way we individuate it. Or take an example from biology. Let us accept the plausible principle that nothing causally affects breathing except as it causally affects local states of the lungs. It does not follow, and indeed is not true, that we individuate lungs and the various subevents of respiration in such a way as to treat those objects and events as supervenient on the chemically described objects and events that compose them. If the same chemical process (same from the surfaces of the lungs inside, and back to the surfaces) were embedded in a different sort of body and had an entirely different function (say, digestive, immunological, or regulatory), we would not be dealing with the same biological states and events. Local causation does not make more plausible local individuation, or individualistic supervenience.

The intended analogy to mental events should be evident. We may agree that a person's mental events and behavior are causally affected by the person's environment only through local causal effects on the person's body. Without the slightest conceptual discomfort we may individuate mental events so as to allow distinct events (types or tokens) with indistinguishable chemistries, or even physiologies, for the subject's body. Information from and about the environment is transmitted only through proximal stimulations, but the information is individuated partly by reference to the nature of normal distal stimuli. Causation is local. Individuation may presuppose facts about the specific nature of a subject's environment.

Where intentional psychological explanation is itself causal, it may well presuppose that the causal transactions to which its generalizations apply bear some necessary relation to some underlying physical transactions (or other). Without a set of physical transactions, none of the intentional transactions would transpire. But it does not follow that the kinds invoked in explaining causal interactions among intentional states (or between physical states and intentional states—for example, in vision or in action) supervene on the underlying physiological transactions. The same physical transactions in a given person may in principle mediate, or underly, transactions involving different intentional states—if the environmental features that enter into the individuation of the intentional states and that are critical in the explanatory generalizations that invoke those states vary in appropriate ways.

Let us turn to our epistemic point. The view that propositional attitudes help determine behavior is well entrenched in common judgments and in the explanatory practices of psychology. Our arguments that a subject's propositional attitudes are not fixed purely by his or her brain states are based on widely shared judgments regarding *particular* cases that in relevant respects bring out familiar elements in our actual psychological and common sense practices of attitude attribution. By contrast, the claim that none of an individual's propositional attitudes (or determinants of his behavior) could have been different unless some of his brain states were different is a metaphysical conjecture. It is a modal generalization that is not grounded in judgments about particular cases, or (so far) in careful interpretation of the actual explanatory and descriptive practices of psychology. Metaphysical ideology should either conform to and illuminate intellectual praxis, or produce strong reasons for revising it.

What we know about supervenience must be derived, partly, from what we know about individuation. What we know about individuation is derived from reflecting on explanations and descriptions of going cognitive practices. Individuative methods are bound up with the explanatory and descriptive needs of such practices. Thus justified judgments about what supervenes on what are *derivative* from reflection on the nature of explanation and description in psychological discourse and common attitude attributions. I think that such judgments cannot be reasonably invoked to restrict such discourse. It seems to me therefore that, apart from further argument, the individualistic supervenience thesis provides no reason for requiring (pan-) individualism in psychology. In fact, the argument from individualistic supervenience begs the question. It *presupposes* rather than establishes that *individuation—hence explanation and description* —in psychology should be fully individualistic. It is simply the wrong sort of consideration to invoke in a dispute about explanation and description.

This remark is, I think, quite general. Not just questions of supervenience, but questions of ontology, reduction, and causation generally, are epistemically posterior to questions about the success of explanatory and descriptive practices.[8] One cannot reasonably criticize a purported explanatory or descriptive practice primarily by appeal to some prior conception of what a "good entity" is, or of what individuation or reference should be like, or of what the overall structure of science (or knowledge) should turn out to look like. Questions of what exists, how things are individuated, and what reduces to what, are questions that arise by reference to going explanatory and descriptive practices. By themselves, proposed answers to these questions cannot be used to criticize an otherwise successful mode of explanation and description.[9]

Of course, one might purport to base the individualist supervenience principle on what we know about good explanation. Perhaps one might hope to argue from inference to the best explanation concerning the relations of higher-level to more basic theories in the natural sciences that the entities postulated by psychology should supervene on those of physiology. Or perhaps one might try to draw analogies between nonindividualistic theories in psychology and past, unsuccessful theories. These two strategies might meet our methodological strictures on answering the question of whether nonindividualistic explanations are viable in a way that an unalloyed appeal to a supervenience principle does not. But philosophical invocations of inference to the best explanation tend to conceal wild leaps supported primarily by ideology. Such considerations must be spelled out into arguments. So far they do not seem very promising.

Take the first strategy. Inductions from the natural sciences to the human sciences are problematic from the start. The problems of the two sorts of sciences look very different, in a multitude of ways. One can, of course, reasonably try to exploit analogies in a pragmatic spirit. But the fact that some given analogy does not hold hardly counts against an otherwise viable mode of explanation. Moreover, there are nonindividualistic modes of explanation even in the natural sciences. Geology, physiology, and other parts of biology appeal to entities that are not supervenient on their underlying physical makeup. Kind notions in these sciences (plates, organs, species) presuppose individuative methods that make essential reference to the environment surrounding instances of those kinds.

The second strategy seems even less promising. As it stands, it is afflicted with a bad case of vagueness. Some authors have suggested similarities between vitalism in biology, or action-at-a-distance theories in physics, and nonindividualist theories in psychology. The analogies are tenuous. Unlike vitalism, nonindividualist psychology does not ipso facto appeal to a new sort of force. Unlike action-at-a-distance theories, it does not appeal to action at a distance. It is true that aspects of the environment that do not differentially affect the physical movement of the protagonists in the thought experiments do differentially affect the explanations and descriptions. This is not, however, because some special causal relation is postulated, but rather because environmental differences affect what kinds of laws obtain, and the way causes and effects are individuated.

Let us now consider a further type of objection to applying the thought experiments to psychology. Since the actual and counterfactual protagonists are so impressively *similar* in so many psychologically relevant ways, can a theoretical language that cuts across these similarities be empirically adequate? The physiological and non-intensional "behavioral" similarities between the protagonists seem to demand similarity of explanation. In its stronger form this objection purports to indicate that nonindividualistic mentalistic language has no place in psychology. In its weaker form it attempts to motivate a new theoretical language that attributes intensional content, yet is individualistic. Only the stronger form would establish individualism in psychology. I shall consider it first.

The objection is that the similarities between the protagonists render implausible any theory that treats them differently. This objection is vague or enthymemic. Filling it out tends to lead one back toward the arguments that we have already rejected. On any view, there are several means available (neurophysiology, parts of psychology) for explaining in similar fashion those similarities that are postulated between protagonists in the thought experiments. The argument is not even of the right form to produce a reason for thinking that the differences between the protagonists should not be reflected somewhere in psychological theory—precisely the point at issue.

The objection is often coupled with the remark that nonindividualistic explanations would make the parallels between the behavior of the protagonists in the thought experiments "miraculous": explaining the same behavioral phenomena as resulting from different propositional attitudes would be to invoke a "miracle." The rhetoric about miracles can be deflated by noting that the protagonists' "behavior" is not straightforwardly identical, that nonindividualistic explanations postulate no special forces, and that there are physical differences in the protagonists' environments that help motivate describing and explaining their activity, at least at one level, in different ways.

The rhetoric about miracles borders on a fundamental misunderstanding of the status of the nonindividualistic thought experiments, and of the relation between philosophy and psychology. There is, of course, considerable empirical implausibility, which we might with some exaggeration call "miraculousness," in two person's having identical individualistic physical histories but different thoughts. Most of this implausibility is an artifact of the two-person version of the thought experiments—a feature that is quite inessential. (One may take a single person in two counterfactual circumstances.) This point raises a caution. It is important not to think of the thought experiments as if they were describing actual empirical cases. Let me articulate this remark.

The kinds of a theory, and its principles of individuation, evolve in response to the world as it actually is found to be. Our notions of similarity result from attempts to explain actual cases. They are not necessarily responsive to preconceived philosophical ideals.[10] The kind terms of propositional attitude discourse are responsive to broad, stable similarities in the actual environment that agents are taken to respond to, operate on, and represent. If theory had been frequently confronted with physically similar agents in different environments, it might have evolved different kind terms. But we are so far from being confronted by even rough approximations to global physical similarities between agents that there is little plausibility in imposing individual physical similarity by itself as an ideal sufficient condition for sameness of kind terms throughout psychology. Moreover, I think that local physical similarities between the psychologically relevant activities of agents are so frequently intertwined with environmental constancies that a psychological theory that insisted on entirely abstracting from the nature of the environment in choosing its kind terms would be empirically emasculate.

The correct use of counterfactuals in the thought experiments is to explore the scope and limits of the kind notions that have been antecedently developed in attempts to explain actual empirical cases. In counterfactual reasoning we assume an understanding of what our language expresses and explore its application conditions through considering nonactual applications. The counterfactuals in the philosophical thought experiments illumine individuative and theoretical principles to which we are already committed.

The empirical implausibility of the thought experiments is irrelevant to their philosophical point—which concerns possibility, not plausibility. Unlikely but limiting cases are sometimes needed to clarify the modal status of presuppositions that govern more mundane examples. Conversely, the highly counterfactual cases are largely irrelevant to *evaluating* an empirical theory—except in cases (not at issue here) where they present empirical possibilities that a theory counts impossible. To invoke a general philosophical principle, like the supervenience principle, or to insist in the face of the thought experiments that only certain sorts of similarity can be relevant to psychology—without criticizing psychological theory on empirical grounds or showing how the kind notions exhibited by the thought experiments are empirically inadequate—is either to treat counterfactual circumstances as if they were actual, or to fall into *apriorism* about empirical science.

Let us turn to the weaker form of the worry that we have been considering. The worry purports to motivate a new individualistic language of attitude attribution. As I have noted, accepting such a language is consistent with rejecting (pan-) individualism in psychology. There are a variety of levels or kinds of explanation in psychology. Adding another will not alter the issues at stake here. But let us pursue the matter briefly.

There are in psychology levels of individualistic description above the physiological but below the attitudinal that play a role in systematic explanations. Formalistically described computational processes are appealed to in the attempt to specify an algorithm by which a person's propositional information is processed. I think that the protagonists in our thought experiments might, for some purposes, be said to go through identical algorithms formalistically described. Different information is processed in the "same" ways, at least at this formal level of description. But then might we not want a whole level of description, between the formal algorithm and ordinary propositional attitude ascription, that counts "information" everywhere the same between protagonists in the thought experiments? This is a difficult and complex question, which I shall not attempt to answer here. I do, however, want to mention grounds for caution about supplementing psychology wholesale.

In the first place, the motivation for demanding the relevant additions to psychological theory is empirically weak. In recent philosophical literature, the motivation rests largely on intuitions about Cartesian demons or brains in vats, whose relevance and even coherence have been repeatedly challenged; on preconceptions about the supervenience of the mental on the neural that have no generalized scientific warrant; on misapplications of ordinary observations about causation; and on a sketchy and unclear conception of behavior unsupported by scientific practice.[11] Of course, one may reasonably investigate any hypothesis on no more than an intuitively based hunch. What is questionable is the view that there are currently strong philosophical or scientific grounds for instituting a new type of individualistic explanation.

In the second place, it is easy to underestimate what is involved in creating a relevant individualistic language that would be of genuine use in psychology. Explications of such language have so far been pretty makeshift. It does not suffice to sketch a semantics that says in effect that a sentence comes out true in all worlds that chemically identical protagonists in relevant thought experiments cannot distinguish. Such an explication gives no clear rules for the *use* of the language, much less a demonstration that it can do distinctive work in psychology. Moreover, explication of the individualistic language (or language component) only for the special case in which the language-user's physiological or (individualistically specified) functional states are held constant, is psychologically useless since no two people are ever actually identical in their physical states.

To fashion an individualist language it will not do to limit its reference to objective properties accessible to perception. For our language for ascribing notions of perceptually accessible physical properties is not individualistic. More generally, as I have argued elsewhere (last *op. cit.* note 1), any attitudes that contain notions for physical objects, events and properties are non-individualistic.[12] The assumptions about objective representation needed to generate the argument are very minimal. I think it questionable whether there is a coherent conception of objective representation that can support an individualistic language of intentional attitude attribution. Advocates of such a language must either explain such a conception in depth, or attribute intentional states that lack objective physical reference.

II

I have been criticizing arguments for revising the language of psychology to accord with individualism. I have not tried to argue for nonindividualistic psychological theories from a standpoint outside of psychology. The heart of my case is the observation that psychological theories, taken literally, are not purely individualistic, that there are no strong reasons for taking them nonliterally, and that we currently have no superior standpoint for judging how psychology ought to be done than that of seeing how it *is* done. One can, of course, seek deeper understanding of nonindividualistic aspects of psychological theory. Development of such understanding is a multifaceted task. Here I shall develop only points that are crucial to my thesis, illustrating them in some detail by reference to one theory.

Ascription of intentional states and events in psychology constitutes a type of individuation and explanation that carries presuppositions about the specific nature of the person's or animal's surrounding environment. Moreover, states and events are individuated so as to set the terms for specific evaluations of them for truth or other types of success. We can judge directly whether conative states are practically success-ful and cognitive states are veridical. For example, by characterizing a subject as visu-ally representing an X, and specifying whether the visual state appropriately derives from an X in the particular case, we can judge whether the subject's state is veridical. Theories of vision, of belief formation, of memory, learning, decision-making, catego-rization, and perhaps even reasoning all attribute states that are subject to practical and semantical evaluation *by reference to standards partly set by a wider environment.*

Psychological theories are not themselves evaluative theories. But they often in-dividuate phenomena so as to make evaluation readily accessible *because* they are partly motivated by such judgments. Thus we judge that in certain delimitable con-texts people get what they want, know what is the case, and perceive what is there. And we try to frame explanations that account for these successes, and correlative failures, in such a way as to illumine as specifically as possible the mechanisms that underly and make true our evaluations.

I want to illustrate and develop these points by considering at some length a theory of vision. I choose this example primarily because it is a very advanced and impres-sive theory, and admits to being treated in some depth. Its information-processing approach is congenial with mainstream work in cognitive psychology. Some of its intentional aspects are well understood—and indeed are sometimes conceptually and mathematically far ahead of its formal (or syntactical) and physiological aspects. Thus the theory provides an example of a mentalistic theory with solid achievements to its credit.

The theory of vision maintains a pivotal position in psychology. Since perceptual processes provide the input for many higher cognitive processes, it is reasonable to think that if the theory of vision treats intentional states nonindividualistically, other central parts of cognitive psychology will do likewise. Information processed by more central capacities depends, to a large extent, on visual information.

Certain special aspects of the vision example must be noted at the outset. The arguments that I have previously published against individualism (cf. note 1) have centered on "higher" mental capacities, some of which essentially involve the use of language. This focus was motivated by an interest in the relation between thought and linguistic meaning and in certain sorts of intellectual responsibility. Early human vision makes use of a limited range of representations—representations of shape, texture, depth and other spatial relations, motion, color, and so forth. These representations (percepts) are formed by processes that are relatively immune to correction from other sources of information; and the representations of early vision appear to be fully in-dependent of language. So the thought experiments that I have previously elaborated will not carry over simply to early human vision. (One would expect those thought experiments to be more relevant to social and developmental psychology, to concept learning, and to parts of "higher" cognitive psychology.) But the case against in-dividualism need not center on higher cognitive capacities or on the relation between thought and language. The anti-individualistic conclusions of our previous arguments can be shown to apply to early human vision. The abstract schema which those thought experiments articulate also applies.

The schema rests on three general facts. The first is that what entities in the objec-tive world one intentionally interacts with in the employment of many representa-tional (intentional) types affects the semantic properties of those representational types, what they are, and how we individuate them.[13] A near consequence of this first fact is that there can be slack between, on the one hand, the way a subject's representational types apply to the world, and on the other, what that knows about, and how he or she can react to, the way they apply. It is possible for representational types to apply differently, without the person's physical reactions or discriminative powers being different. These facts, together with the fact that many fundamental mental states and events are individuated in terms of the relevant representational types, suffice to generate the conclusion that many paradigmatic mental states and events are not individualistically individuated: they may vary while a person's body and discriminative powers are conceived as constant. For by the second fact one can conceive of the way a person's representational types apply to the objective world as varying, while that person's history, nonintentionally and individualistically specified, is held constant. By the first fact, such variation may vary the individuation of the person's representational types. And by the third, such variation may affect the individuation of the person's mental states and events. I shall illustrate how instances of this schema are supported by Marr's theory of vision.[14]

Marr's theory subsumes three explanatory enterprises: (a) a theory of the computation of the information, (b) an account of the representations used and of the algorithms by which they are manipulated, and (c) a theory of the underlying physiology. Our primary interest is in the first level, and in that part of the second that deals with the individuation of representations. Both of these parts of the theory are fundamentally intentional.

The theory of the computation of information encompasses an account of what information is extracted from what antecedent resources, and an account of the reference-preserving "logic" of the extraction. These accounts proceed against a set of biological background assumptions. It is assumed that visual systems have evolved to solve certain problems forced on them by the environment. Different species are set different problems and solve them differently. The theory of human vision specifies a general information processing problem—that of generating reliable representations of certain objective, distal properties of the surrounding world on the basis of proximal stimulations.

The human visual system computes complex representations of certain visible properties, on the basis of light intensity values on retinal images. The primary visible properties that Marr's theory treats are the shapes and locations of things in the world. But various other properties—motion, texture, color, lightness, shading—are also dealt with in some detail. The overall computation is broken down into stages of increasing complexity, each containing modules that solve various subproblems.

The theory of computation of information clearly treats the visual system as going through a series of intentional or representational states. At an early stage, the visual system is counted as representing objective features of the physical world.[15] There is no other way to treat the visual system as solving the problem that the theory sees it as solving than by attributing intentional states that represent objective, physical properties.

More than half of Marr's book is concerned with developing the theory of the computation of information and with individuating representational primitives. These parts of the theory are more deeply developed, both conceptually and mathematically, than the account of the algorithms. This point is worth emphasizing because it serves to correct the impression, often conveyed in recent philosophy of psychology, that intentional theories are regressive and all of the development of genuine theory in psychology has been proceeding at the level of purely formal, "syntactical" transformations (algorithms) that are used in cognitive systems.

I now want, by a series of examples, to give a fairly concrete sense of how the theory treats the relation between the visual system and the physical environment.

Understanding this relation will form essential background for understanding the non-individualistic character of the theory. The reader may skip the detail and still follow the philosophical argument. But the detail is there to support the argument and to render the conception of explanation that the argument yields both concrete and vivid.

Initially, I will illustrate two broad points. The *first* is that the theory makes essential reference to the subject's distal stimuli and makes essential assumptions about contingent facts regarding the subject's physical environment. Not only do the basic questions of the theory refer to what one sees under normal conditions, but the computational theory and its theorems are derived from numerous explicit assumptions about the physical world.

The *second* point to be illustrated is that the theory is set up to explain the reliability of a great variety of processes and subprocesses for acquiring information, at least to the extent that they are reliable. Reliability is presupposed in the formulations of the theory's basic questions. It is also explained through a detailed account of how in certain specified, standard conditions, veridical information is derived from limited means. The theory explains not merely the reliability of the system as a whole, but the reliability of various, stages in the visual process. It begins by assuming that we see certain objective properties and proceeds to explain particular successes by framing conditions under which success would be expected (where the conditions are in fact typical). Failures are explained primarily by reference to a failure of these conditions to obtain. To use a phrase of Bernie Kobes, the theory is not success-neutral. The explanations and, as we shall later see, the kinds of theory presuppose that perception and numerous subroutines of perception are veridical in normal circumstances.

> *Example 1:* In an early stage of the construction of visual representation, the outputs of channels or filters that are sensitive to spatial distributions of light intensities are combined to produce representaions of local contours, edges, shadows, and so forth. The filters fall into groups of different sizes, in the sense that different groups are sensitive to different bands of spatial frequencies. The channels are primarily sensitive to sudden intensity changes, called "zero-crossings," at their scales (within their frequency bands). The theoretical question arises: How do we combine the results of the different sized channels to construct representations with physical meaning—representations that indicate edge segments or local contours in the external physical world? There is no *a priori* reason why zero-crossings obtained from different sized filters should be related to some one physical phenomenon in the environment. There is, however, a physical basis for their being thus related. This basis is identfed by *the constraint of spatial localization*. Things in the world that give rise to intensity changes in the image, such as changes of illumination (caused by shadows, light sources) or changes in surface reflectance (caused by contours, creases, and surface boundaries), are spatially localized, not scattered and not made up of waves. Because of this fact, if a zero-crossing is present in a channel centered on a given frequency band, there should be a corresponding zero-crossing at the same spatial location in larger-scaled channels. If this ceases to be so at larger scales, it is because a) two or more local intensity changes are being averaged together in the larger channel (for example, the edges of a thin bar may register radical frequency changes in small channels, but go undetected in larger ones); or b) because two independent physical phenomena are producing intensity changes in the same area but at different scales (for example, a shadow superimposed on a sudden reflectance change; if the shadow is located in a certain way, the positions of the zero-

crossings may not make possible a separation of the two physical phenomena). Some of these exceptions are sufficiently rare that the visual system need not and does not account for them—thus allowing for possible illusions; others are reflected in complications of the basic assumption that follows. The spatial coincidence constraint yields *the spatial coincidence assumption:*

If a zero-crossing segment is present in a set of independent channels over a contiguous range of sizes, and the segment has the same position and orientation in each channel, then the set of such zero-crossing segments indicates the presence of an intensity change in the image that is due to a single physical phenomenon (a change in reflectance, illumination, depth, or surface orientation).

Thus the theory starts with the observation that physical edges produce roughly coincident zero-crossings in channels of neighboring sizes. The spatial coincidence assumption asserts that the coincidence of zero-crossings of neighboring sizes is normally sufficient evidence of a real physical edge. Under such circumstances, according to the theory, a representation of an edge is formed.[16]

Example 2: Because of the laws of light and the way our eyes are made, positioned, and controlled, our brains typically receive similar image signals originating from two points that are fairly similarly located in the respective eyes or images, at the same horizontal level. If two objects are separated in depth from the viewer, the relative positions of their image signals will differ in the two eyes. The visual system determines the distance of physical surfaces by measuring the angular discrepancy in position (disparity) of the image of an object in the two eyes. This process is called stereopsis. To solve the problem of determining distance, the visual system must select a location on a surface as represented by one image, identify the same location in the other image, and measure the disparity between the corresponding image points. There is, of course, no *a priori* means of matching points from the two images. The theory indicates how correct matches are produced by appealing to three *Physical Constraints* (actually the first is not made explicit, but is relied upon): (1) the two eyes produce similar representations of the same external items; (2) a given point on a physical surface has a unique position in space at any given time; (3) matter is cohesive—separated into objects, the surfaces of which are usually smooth in the sense that surface variation is small compared to overall distance from the observer. These three physical constraints are rewritten as three corresponding *Constraints on Matching:* (1) two representational elements can match if and only if they normally could have arisen from the same physical item (for example, in stereograms, dots match dots rather than bars); (2) nearly always, each representational element can match only one element from the other image (exceptions occur when two markings lie along the line of sight of one eye but are separately visible by the other—causing illusions); (3) disparity varies smoothly almost everywhere (this derives from physical constraint (3) because that constraint implies that the distance to the visible surface varies, approximately continuously except at object boundaries, which occupy a small fraction of the area of an image). Given suitable precisifications, these matching constraints can be used to prove the *Fundamental Theorem of Stereopsis:*

If a correspondence is established between physically meaningful representational primitives extracted from the left and right images of a scene that contains a sufficient amount of detail (roughly 2% density for dot stereograms) and if the correspondence satisfies the three matching constraints, then that correspondence is physically correct—hence unique.

The method is again to identify general physical conditions that give rise to a visual process, then to use those conditions to motivate constraints on the form of the process that, when satisfied, will allow the process to be interpreted as providing reliable representations of the physical environment.[17]

These examples illustrate theories of the computation of information. The critical move is the formulation of general physical facts that limit the interpretation of a visual problem enough to allow one to interpret the machinations of the visual system as providing a unique and veridical solution, at least in typical cases. The primary aim of referring to contingent physical facts and properties is to enable the theory to explain the visual system's reliable acquisition of information about the physical world: to explain the success or veridicality of various types of visual representation. So much for the first two points that we set out to illustrate.

I now turn to a *third* that is a natural corollary of the second, and that will be critical for our argument that the theory is non-individualistic: the information carried by representations—their intentional content—is individuated in terms of the specific distal causal antecedents in the physical world that the information is about and that the representations normally apply to. The individuation of the intentional features of numerous representations depends on a variety of physical constraints that our knowledge of the external world gives us. Thus the individuation of intentional content of representational types, presupposes the verdicality of perception. Not only the explanations, but the intentional kinds of the theory presuppose contingent facts about the subject's physical environment.

Example 3: In building up informational or representational primitives in the primal sketch, Marr states six general physical assumptions that constrain the choice of primitives. I shall state some of these to give a sense of their character: (a) the visible world is composed of smooth surfaces having reflectance functions whose spatial structure may be complex; (b) markings generated on a surface by a single process are often arranged in continuous spatial structures—curves, lines, etc.; (c) if direction of motion is discontinuous at more than one point—for example, along a line—then an object boundary is present. These assumptions are used to identify the physical significance of—the objective information normally given by—certain types of patterns in the image. The computational theory states conditions under which these primitives form to carry information about items in the physical world (Marr, *op. cit.,* pp. 44–71). The theory in Example 1 is a case in point: conditions are laid down under which certain patterns may be taken as representing an objective physical condition; as being edge, boundary, bar, or blob detectors. Similar points apply for more advanced primitives.

Example 4: In answering the question "what assumptions do we reasonably and actually employ when we interpret silhouettes as three-dimensional shapes?" Marr motivates a central representational primitive by stating physical constraints that lead to the proof of a theorem. *Physical Constraints:* (1) Each line of sight from the viewer to the object grazes the object's surface at exactly one point. (2) Nearby points on the contour in an image arise from nearby points on the contour generator on the viewed object. (That is, points that appear close together in the image actually are close together on the object's surface.) (3) The contour generator lies wholly in a single plane. Obviously these are conditions of perception that may fail, but they are conditions under which we seem to do best at solving the problem of deriving three-dimensional shape descriptions from representations of silhouettes. *Definition:* A *generalized cone* is a three-dimensional object generated by moving a cross section along an axis; the cross section may vary smoothly in size, but its shape remains the same. (For example footballs, pyramids, legs, stalagmites are or approximate generalized cones.) *Theorem:* If the surface is smooth and if physical constraints (1)–(3) hold for all distant viewing positions in any one plane, then the viewed surface is a generalized cone. The theorem indicates a natural connection between generalized cones and the imaging process. Marr infers from this, and from certain psycho-physical evidence, that representations of generalized cones—that is, representations with intentional content concerning, generalized cones—are likely to be fundamental among our visual representations of three-dimensional objects. (Marr, *op. cit.*, pp. 215–225)

Throughout the theory, representational primitives are selected and individuated by considering specific, contingent facts about the physical world that typically hold when we succeed in obtaining veridical visual information about that world. The information or content of the visual representations is always individuated by reference to the physical objects, properties, or relations that are seen. In view of the success-orientation of the theory, this mode of individuation is grounded in its basic methods. If theory were confronted with a species of organism reliably and successfully interacting with a different set of objective visible properties, the representational types that the theory would attribute to the organism would be different, regardless of whether an individual organism's physical mechanisms were different.

We are now in a position to argue that the theory is not individualistic: (1) The theory is intentional. (2) The intentional primitives of the theory and the information they carry are individuated by reference to contingently existing physical items or conditions by which they are normally caused and to which they normally apply. (3) So if these physical conditions and, possibly, attendant physical laws were regularly different, the information conveyed to the subject and the intentional content of his or her visual representations would be different. (4) It is not incoherent to conceive of relevantly different physical conditions and perhaps relevantly different (say, optical) laws regularly causing the same non-intentionally, individualistically individuated physical regularities in the subject's eyes and nervous system. It is enough if the differences are small; they need not be wholesale. (5) In such a case (by (3)) the individual's visual representations would carry different information and have different representational content, though the person's whole non-intentional physical history (at least up to a certain time) might remain the same. (6) Assuming that some perceptual states are identified in the theory in terms of their informational or intentional content, it follows that individualism is not true for the theory of vision.

I shall defend the argument stepwise. I take it that the claim that the theory is intentional is sufficiently evident. The top levels of the theory are explicitly formulated in intentional terms. And their method of explanation is to show how the problem of arriving at certain veridical representations is solved.

The second step of the argument was substantiated through Examples 3 and 4. The intentional content of representations of edges or generalized cones is individuated in terms of *specific* reference to those very contingently instantiated physical properties, on the assumption that those properties normally give rise to veridical representations of them.

The third step in our argument is supported both by the way the theory individuates intentional content (cf. the previous paragraph and Examples 3 and 4), and by the explanatory method of the theory (cf. the second point illustrated above, and Examples 1–2). The methods of individuation and explanation are governed by the assumption that the subject has adapted to his or her environment sufficiently to obtain veridical information from it under certain normal conditions. If the properties and relations that *normally* caused visual impressions were regularly different from what they are, the individual would obtain different information and have visual experiences with different intentional content. If the regular, law-like relations between perception and the environment were different, the visual system would be solving different information-processing problems; it would pass through different informational or intentional states; and the explanation of vision would be different. To reject this third step of our argument would be to reject the theory's basic methods and questions. But these methods and questions have already borne fruit, and there are presently no good reasons for rejecting them.

I take it that step four is a relatively unproblematic counterfactual. There is no metaphysically necessary relation between individualistically individuated processes in a person's body and the causal antecedents of those processes in the surrounding world.[18] (To reject this step would be self-defeating for the individualist.) If the environmental conditions were different, the same proximal *visual* stimulations could have regularly had different distal causes. In principle, we can conceive of some regular variation in the distal causes of perceptual impressions with no variation in a person's individualistically specified physical processes, even while conceiving the person as *well adapted* to the relevant environment—though, of course, not uniquely adapted.

Steps three and four, together with the unproblematic claim that the theory individuates some perceptual states in terms of their intentional content or representational types, entail that the theory is nonindividualistic.

Steps two and three are incompatible with certain philosophical approaches that have no basis in psychological theory. One might claim that the information content of a visual representation would remain constant even if the physical conditions that lead to the representation were regularly different. It is common to motivate this claim by pointing out that one's visual representations remain the same, whether one is perceiving a black blob on a white surface or having an eidetic hallucination of such a blob. So, runs the reasoning, why should changing the distal causes of a perceptual representation affect its content? On this view, the content of a given perceptual representation is commonly given as that of "the distal cause of *this* representation," or "the property in the world that has *this* sort of visual appearance." The content of these descriptions is intended to remain constant between possible situations in which the microphysical events of a person's visual processes remain the same while distal causes of those processes are regularly and significantly different. For it is thought that the representations themselves (and our experiences of *them*) remain constant under these circumstances. So as the distal antecedents of one's perceptual representations vary, the reference of those representations will vary, but their intentional content will not.[19]

There is more wrong with this line than I have room to develop here. I will mention some of the more straightforward difficulties. In the first place, the motivation from perceptual illusion falls far short. One is indeed in the same perceptual state whether one is seeing or hallucinating. But that is because the intentional content of one's visual state (or representation) is individuated against a background in which the relevant state is *normally* veridical. Thus the fact that one's percepts or perceptual states remain constant between normal perception and hallucinations does not even tend to show that the intentional visual state remains constant between circumstances in which different physical conditions are the normal antecedents of one's perceptions.

Let us consider the proposals for interpreting the content of our visual representations. In the first place both descriptions ('the distal cause of *this* representation' *et al.*) are insufficiently specific. There are lots of distal causes and lots of things that might be said to appear "thus" (for example, the array of light striking the retina as well as the physical surface). We identify the relevant distal cause (and the thing that normally appears thus and so) as the thing that we actually see. To accurately pick out the "correct" object with one of these descriptions would at the very least require a more complex specification. But filling out the descriptive content runs into one or both of two difficulties: either it includes kinds that are tied to a specific environment ('the convex, rough textured object that is causing this representation'). In such case, the description is still subject to our argument. For these kinds are individuated by reference to the empirical environment. Or it complicates the constraints on the causal chain to the extent that the complications cannot plausibly be attributed to the content of processes in the early visual system.

Even in their unrevised forms, the descriptions are overintellectualized philosophers' conceits. It is extremely implausible and empirically without warrant to think that packed into every perceptual representation is a distinction between distal cause and experiential effect, or between objective reality and perceptual appearance. These are distinctions developed by reflecting on the ups and downs of visual perception. They do not come in at the ground, animal level of early vision.

A further mistake is the view that our perceptual representations never purport to specify particular physical properties *as such*, but only via some relation they bear to inner occurrences, which are directly referred to. (Even the phrase 'the convex object causing this percept' invokes a specification of objective convexity as such.) The view will not serve the needs of psychological explanation as actually practiced. For the descriptions of information are too inspecific to account for specific successes in solving problems in retrieving information about the actual, objective world.

The best empirical theory that we have individuates the intentional content of visual representations by specific reference to specific physical characteristics of visible properties and relations. The theory does not utilize complicated, self-referential, attributively used role descriptions of those properties. It does not individuate content primarily by reference to phenomenological qualities. Nor does it use the notions of cause or appearance in specifying the intentional content of early visual representations.[20]

The second and third steps of our argument are incompatible with the claim that the intentional content of visual representations is determined by their "functional role" in each person's system of dispositions, nonintentionally and individualistically specified. This claim lacks any warrant in the practice of the science. In the first place, the theory suggests no reduction of the intentional to the nonintentional. In the second, although what a person can do, nonvisually, constitutes evidence for what he or she can see, there is little ground for thinking that either science or common sense takes an individual person's nonvisual abilities fully to determine the content of his or her early visual experience. A person's dispositions and beliefs develop by adapting to what the person sees. As the person develops, the visual system (at least at its more advanced stages—those involving recognition) and the belief and language systems affect each other. But early vision seems relatively independent of these nonvisual systems. A large part of learning is accommodating one's dispositions to the information carried by visual representations. Where there are failures of adaptation, the person does not know what the visual apparatus is presenting to him or her. Yet the presentations are there to be understood.

III

There is a general argument that seems to me to show that a person's nonintentional dispositions could not fix (individuate) the intentional content of the person's visual presentations. The argument begins with a conception of objectivity. As long as the person's visual presentations are of public, objective objects, properties, or relations, it is possible for the person to have mistaken presentations. Such mistakes usually arise for a single sensory modality—so that when dispositions associated with other modalities (for example, touch) are brought into play, the mistake is rectified. But as long as the represented object or property is objective and physical, it is in principle possible, however unlikely, that there be a confluence of illusions such that all an individual person's sensory modalities would be fooled and all of the person's nonintentional dispositions would fail to distinguish between the normal condition and the one producing the mistaken sensory representations. This is our first assumption. In the argument, we shall employ a corollary: our concept of objectivity is such that no one objective entity that we visually represent is such that it must vary with, or be typed so as necessarily to match exactly, an individual's proximal stimuli and discriminative abilities. The point follows from a realistic, and even from a nonsubjectivistic, view of the objects of sight.[21]

We argued earlier that intentional representational types are not in general individuated purely in terms of an attributive role-description of a causal relation, or a relation of appearance-similarity, between external objects and qualitative perceptual representatives of them. For present purposes, this is our second assumption: some objective physical objects and properties are visually represented as such; they are specifically specified.

Third, in order to be empirically informative, some visual representations that represent objective entities as such must have the representational characteristics that they have partly *because* instances regularly enter into certain relations with those objective entities.[22] Their carrying information, their having objective intentional content, consists partly in their being the normal causal products of objective entities. And their specific intentional content depends partly on their being the normal products of the specific objective entities that give rise to them. That is why we individuate intentional visual representations in terms of the objective entities that they normally apply to, for members of a given species. This is the core of truth in the slogan, sometimes misapplied I think, that mistakes presuppose a background of veridicality.

The assumptions in the three preceding paragraphs enable us to state a general argument against individualism regarding visual states. Consider a person P who normally correctly perceives instances of a particular objective visible property O. In such cases, let the intentional type of P's perceptual representation (or perceptual state) be O'. Such perceptual representations are normally the product of interaction with instances of O. But imagine that for P, perceptual representations typed O' are on some few occasions the product of instances of a different objective property C. On such occasions, P mistakenly sees an instance of C as an O; P's perceptual state is of type O'. We are assuming that O' represents any instance of O as such (as an O), in the sense of our second premise, not merely in terms of some attributive role description. Since O' represents an objective property, we may, by our first premise, conceive of P as lacking at his or her disposal (at every moment up to a given time) any means of discriminating the instances of C from instances of O.

Now hold fixed both P's physical states (up to the given time) and his or her discriminative abilities, nonintentionally and individualistically specified. But conceive of the world as lacking O altogether. Suppose that the optical laws in the counter-factual environment are such that the impressions on P's eyes and the normal causal processes that lead to P's visual representations are explained in terms of C's (or at any rate, in terms of some objective, visible entities other than instances of O). Then by our third premise, P's visual representation (or visual state) would not be of intentional type O'. At the time when in the actual situation P is misrepresenting a C as an O, P may counterfactually be perceiving something (say, a C) correctly (as a C)—if the processes that lead to that visual impression are normal and of a type that normally produces the visual impression that P has on that occasion. So the person's intentional visual states could vary while his or her physical states and non-intentionally specified discriminative abilities remained constant.

The first premise and the methodology of intentional-content individuation articu-lated in the third premise entail the existence of examples. Since examples usually involve shifts in optical laws, they are hard to fill out in great detail. But it is easiest to imagine concrete cases taken from early but still conscious vision. These limit the number of an individual's dispositions that might be reasonably thought to bear on the content of his or her visual states. Early vision is relatively independent of linguistic or other cognitive abilities. It appears to be relatively modular.

Suppose that the relevant visible entities are very small and not such as to bear heavily on adaptive success. An O may be a shadow of a certain small size and shape on a gently contoured surface. A C may be a similarly sized, shallow crack. In the actual situation P sees O's regularly and correctly as O's: P's visual representations are properly explained and specified as shadow representations of the relevant sort. We assume that P's visual and other discriminative abilities are fairly normal. P encounters C's very rarely and on those few occasions not only misperceives them as O's, but has no dispositions that would enable him or her to discriminate those instances from O's. We may assume that given P's actual abilities and the actual laws of optics, P would be capable, in ideal circumstances, of visually discriminating some instances of C's (relevantly similar cracks) from instances of O (the relevant sort of shadows). But our supposition is that in the actual cases where P is confronted by instances of C's, the circumstances are not ideal. All P's abilities would not succeed in discriminating those instances of relevant cracks, in those circumstances, from instances of relevant shad-ows. P may not rely on touch in cases of such small objects; or touch may also be fooled. P's ability to have such mistaken visual states is argued for by the objectivity premise.

In the counterfactual case, the environment is different. There are no instances of the relevant shadows visible to P; and the laws of optics differ in such a way that P's physical visual stimulations (and the rest of P's physical makeup) are unaffected. Suppose that the physical visual stimulations that in the actual case are derived from instances of O—at the relevant sort of shadows—are counterfactually caused by and explained in terms of C's, relevantly sized cracks. Counterfactually, the cracks take the places of the shadows. On the few occasions where, in the actual case, P misperceives shadows as cracks, P is counterfactually confronted with cracks; and the optical circum-stances that lead to the visual impressions on those occasions are, we may suppose, normal for the counterfactual environment.[23] On such counterfactual occasions, P would be visually representing small cracks as small cracks. P would never have visual representations of the relevant sort of shadows. One can suppose that even if there were the relevant sort of shadows in the counterfactual environment, the different laws of optics in that environment would not enable P ever to see them. But since P's visual states would be the normal products of normal processes and would provide as good an empirical basis for learning about the counterfactual environment as P has for learning about the actual environment, it would be absurd to hold that (counterfactually) P misperceives the prevalent cracks as shadows on gently contoured surfaces. Counterfactually, P correctly sees the cracks as cracks. So P's intentional perceptual states differ between actual and counterfactual situations. This general argument is independent of the theory of vision that we have been discussing. It supports and is further supported by that theory.

IV

Although the theory of vision is in various ways special, I see no reason why its nonindividualistic methods will not find analogs in other parts of psychology. In fact, as we noted, since vision provides intentional input for other cognitive capacities, there is reason to think that the methods of the theory of vision are presupposed by other parts of psychology. These nonindividualistic methods are grounded in two natural assumptions. One is that there are psychological states that represent, or are about, an objective world. The other is that there is a scientific account to be given that presupposes certain successes in our interaction with the world (vision, hearing, memory, decision, reasoning, empirical belief formation, communication, and so forth), and that explains specific successes and failures by reference to these states.

The two assumptions are, of course, interrelated. Although an intention to eat meat is "conceptually" related to eating meat, the relation is not one of entailment in either direction, since the representation is about an objective matter. An individual may be, and often is, ignorant, deluded, misdirected, or impotent. The very thing that makes the nonindividualistic thought experiments possible—the possibility of certain sorts of ignorance, failure, and misunderstanding—helps make it possible for explanations using nonindividualistic language to be empirically informative. On the other hand, as I have argued above, some successful interaction with an objective world seems to be a precondition for the objectivity of some of our intentional representations.

Any attempt to produce detailed accounts of the relations between our attitudes and the surrounding world will confront a compendium of empirically interesting problems. Some of the most normal and mundane successes in our cognitive and conative relations to the world must be explained in terms of surprisingly complicated intervening processes, many of which are themselves partly described in terms of intentional states. Our failures may be explained by reference to *specific* abnormalities in operations or surrounding conditions. Accounting for environmentally specific successes (and failures) is one of the tasks that psychology has traditionally set itself.

An illuminating philosophy of psychology must do justice not only to the mechanistic elements in the science. It must also relate these to psychology's attempt to account for tasks that we succeed and fail at, *where these tasks are set by the environment and represented by the subject him- or herself.* The most salient and important of these tasks are those that arise through relations to the natural and social worlds. A theory that insists on describing the states of human beings purely in terms that abstract from their relations to any specific environment cannot hope to provide a completely satisfying explanation of our accomplishments. At present our best theories in many domains of psychology do not attempt such an abstraction. No sound reason has been given for thinking that the nonindividualistic language that psychology now employs is not an appropriate language for explaining these matters, or that explanation of this sort is impossible.

Notes

A version of this paper was given at the Sloan Conference at MIT in May 1984. I have benefited from the commentaries by Ned Block, Fred Dretske, and Stephen Stich. I have also made use of discussion with Jerry Fodor, David Israel, Bernie Kobes, and Neil Stillings.

1. "Individualism and the Mental," *Midwest Studies* 4 (1979), pp. 73–121; "Other Bodies," in *Thought and Object*, Woodfield, ed. (Oxford: Oxford University Press, 1982); "Two Thought Experiments Reviewed," *Notre Dame Journal of Formal Logic* 23 (1982), pp. 284–293; "Cartesian Error and the Objectivity of Perception," in *Subject, Thought, and Context*, MacDowell and Pettit, eds. (Oxford: Oxford University Press, 1986); "Intellectual Norms and Foundations of Mind" *The Journal of Philosophy* vol. 83, 1986). The aluminum argument is adapted from an argument in Hilary Putnam, "The Meaning of Meaning'," *Philosophical Papers* Vol. II (Cambridge, England: Cambridge University Press, 1975). What Putnam wrote in his paper was, strictly, not even compatible with this argument. (Cf. the first two cited papers in this note for discussion). But the aluminum argument lies close to the surface of the argument he does give. The arthritis argument raises rather different issues, despite its parallel methodology.

2. On basic categories, cf., e.g., Rosch, E., Mervis, Gray, Johnson, Boyes-Graem, "Basic Objects in Natural Categories," *Cognitive Psychology* 8 (1976), pp. 382–439. On the general claim in the last sentence, cf. "Intellectual Norms," *op. cit.* and the latter portion of this paper.

3. Our talk of intentional "content" will be ontologically colorless. It can be converted to talk about how that-clauses (or their components) are interpreted and differentiated—taken as equivalent or nonequivalent—for the cognitive purposes of psychology. Not all intentional states or structures that are attributed in psychology are explicitly propositional. My views in this paper apply to intentional states generally.

4. Certain approaches to intensional logic featuring either "direct reference" or some analogy between the attitudes and necessity have urged that this practice of fine-structuring attitudinal content be revised. I think that for purely philosophical reasons these approaches cannot account for the attitudes. For example, they do little to illumine the numerous variations on Frege's "paradox of identity." They seem to have even less to recommmend them as prescriptions for the language of psychology. Some defenses of individualism have taken these approaches to propositional content to constitute the opposition to individualism. I think that these approaches are not serious contenders as accounts of propositional attitudes and thus should be left out of the discussion.

5. Stephen Stich, *From Folk Psychology to Cognitive Science* (Cambridge, Mass.: MIT Press, 1983), chapter VIII. Although I shall not discuss the unformulated Ockhamesque principle, I am skeptical of it. Apart from question-begging assumptions, it seems to me quite unclear why a science should be required to explain two instances of the same phenomenon in the same way, particularly if the surrounding conditions that led to the instances differ.

6. I have not been able to find a fully explicit statement of this argument in published work. It seems to inform some passages of Jerry Fodor's "Methodological Solipsism Considered as a Research Strategy in Cognitive Psychology" in Fodor's *Representations* (Cambridge, Mass.: MIT Press, 1981), e.g., pp. 228–232. It lies closer to the surface in much work influenced by Fodor's paper. Cf., e.g., Colin McGinn, "This Structure of Content" in Woodfield ed. *Thought and Object* (Oxford: Clarendon Press, 1982), pp. 207–216. Many who like McGinn concede the force of the arguments against individualism utilize something like this argument to maintain that individualistic "aspects" of intentional states are all that are relevant to psychological explanation.

7. In "Individualism and the Mental," *op. cit.*, pp. 109–113, I argue that token *identity* theories are rendered implausible by the nonindividualistic thought experiments. But token identity theories are not the last bastion for materialist defense policy. Composition is what is crucial.

It is coherent, but I think mistaken, to hold that propositional-attitude attributions nonrigidly pick out physical events: so the propositional attributions vary between the actual and counterfactual protagonists in the thought experiments, though the ontology of mental event tokens remains identical. This view is compatible with most of my opposition to individualism. But I think that there is no good reason to believe the very implausible thesis that mental events are not individuated ("essentially" or "basically") in terms of the relevant propositional-attitude attributions. (cf. ibid.) So I reject the view that the same mental events (types or tokens) are picked out under different descriptions in the thought experiments. These considerations stand behind my recommending, to the convinced materialist, composition rather than identity as a paradigm. (I remain unconvinced.)

8. The points about ontology and reference go back to Frege, *Foundations of Arithmetic*, Austin trans. (Northwestern University Press, Evanston, 1968). The point about reduction is relatively obvious, though a few philosophers have urged conceptions of the unity of science in a relatively aprioristic spirit. At least as applied to ontology, the point is also basic to Quine's pragmatism. There are, however, strands in Quine's work and in the work of most of his followers that seem to me to let a preoccupation with physicalism get in the way of the Fregean (and Quinean) pragmatic insight. It is simply an illusion to think that metaphysical or even epistemic preconceptions provide a standard for judging the ontologies or explanatory efforts of particular sciences, deductive or inductive.

9. Even more generally, I think that epistemic power in philosophy derives largely from reflections on particular implementations of successful cognitive practices. By a cognitive practice, I mean a cognitive enterprise that is stable, that conforms to standard conditions of inter-subjective checkability, and that incorporates a substantial core of agreement among its practitioners. Revisionistic philosophical hypotheses must not, of course, be rejected out of hand. Sometimes, but rarely nowadays, such hypotheses influence cognitive practices by expanding theoretical imagination so as to lead to new discoveries. The changed practice may vindicate the philosophical hypothesis. But the hypothesis waits on such vindication.

10. For an interesting elaboration of this theme in an experimental context, see Amos Tversky, "Features of Similarity," *Psychological Review* 84 (1977), pp. 327–352. Cf. also Rosch et al., *op cit.*

11. The most careful and plausible of several papers advocating a new language of individualist explanation is Stephen White, "Partial Character and the Language of Thought," *Pacific Philosophical Quarterly* 63 (1982), pp. 347–365. It seems to me, however, that many of the problems mentioned in the text here and below, beset this advocacy. Moreover, the positive tasks set for the new language are already performed by the actual nonindividualist language of psychology. The brain-in-vat intuitions raise very complex issues that I cannot pursue here. I discuss them further in "Cartesian Error and the Objectivity of Perception," *op. cit.*

12. See especially "Intellectual Norms and Foundations of Mind," *op. cit.*, but also "Individualism and the Mental," *op. cit.*, pp. 81–82.

13. 'Representational type' (also 'intentional type') is a relatively theory-neutral term for intentional content, or even intentional state-kinds. Cf. note 3. One could about as well speak of concepts, percepts, and the representational or intentional aspects of thought contents—or of the counterpart states.

14. In what follows I make use of the important book *Vision*, by David Marr, (San Francisco: W. H. Freeman and Company, 1982). Marr writes:

> The purpose of these representations is to provide useful descriptions of aspects of the real world. The structure of the real world therefore plays an important role in determining both the nature of the representations that are used and the nature of the processes that derive and maintain them. An important part of the theoretical analysis is to make explicit the physical constraints and assumptions that have been used in the design of the representations and processes ... (p. 43).
>
> It is of critical importance that the token [representational particulars] one obtains [in the theoretical analysis] correspond to real physical changes on the viewed surface; the blobs, lines, edges, groups, and so forth that we shall use must not be artifacts of the imaging process, or else inferences made from their structure backwards to the structure of the surface will be meaningless. (p. 44)

Marr's claim that the structure of the real world figures in determining the nature of the representations that are attributed in the theory is tantamount to the chief point about representation or reference that generates our nonindividualist thought experiments—the first step in the schema. I shall show that these remarks constitute the central theoretical orientation of the book.

Calling the theory Marr's is convenient but misleading. Very substantial contributions have been made by many others; and the approach has developed rapidly since Marr's death. Cf. for example, Ballard, Hinton, and Sejnowski, "Parallel Vision Computation," *Nature* 306 (November 1983), pp. 21–26. What I say about Marr's about applies equally to more recent developments.

15. It is an interesting question when to count the visual system as having gone intentional. I take it that information is in a broad sense, carried by the intensity values in the retinal image; but I think that

this is too early to count the system as intentional or symbolic. I'm inclined to agree with Marr that where zero-crossings from different sized filters are checked against one another (cf. Example 1), it is reasonable to count visual processes as representational of an external physical reality. Doing so, however, depends on seeing this stage as part of the larger system in which objective properties are often discriminated from subjective artifacts of the visual system.

16. Marr, op. cit., pp. 68–70; cf. also Marr and Hildreth, "Theory of Edge Detection," *Proceedings of Royal Society of London* B 207 (1980), pp. 187–217, where the account is substantially more detailed.

17. Marr, op. cit., pp. 111–116; Marr and Poggio "A Computational Theory of Human Stereo Vision," *Proceedings of Royal Society of London* B 204 (1979), pp. 301–328. Marr, op. cit., pp. 205–212; Shimon Ullman, *The Interpretation of Visual Motion*, (Cambridge, Mass.: MIT Press, 1979).

18. As I have intimated above, I doubt that all biological, including physiological, processes and states in a person's body are individualistically individuated. The failures of individualism for these sciences involve different, but related considerations.

19. Descartes went further in the same direction. He thought that the perceptual system, and indeed the intellect, could not make a mistake. Mistakes derived from the will. The underlying view is that we primarily perceive or make perceptual reference to our own perceptions. This position fails to account plausibly for various visual illusions and errors that precede any activity of the will, or even intellect. And the idea that perceptions are in general what we make perceptual reference to has little to recommend it and, nowadays, little influence. The natural and, I think, plausible view is that we have visual representations that specify external properties specifically, that these representations are predoxastic in the sense they are themselves objects of belief, and that they sometimes fail to represent correctly what is before the person's eyes: when they result from abnormal processes.

20. Of course, at least in the earliest stages of visual representation, there are analogies between qualitative features of representations in the experienced image and the features that those representations represent. Representations that represent bar segments are bar-shaped, or have some phenomenological property that strongly tempts us to call them "bar-shaped." Similarly for blobs, dots, lines, and so forth. (Marr and Hildreth, op. cit., p. 211, remark on this dual aspect of representations). These "analogies" are hardly fortuitous. Eventually they will probably receive rigorous psychophysical explanations. But they should not tempt one into the idea that visual representations in general make reference to themselves, much less into the idea that the content of objective representation is independent of empirical relations between the representations and objective entities that give rise to them. Perhaps these qualitative features are constant across all cases where one's bodily processes, nonintentionally specified, are held constant. But the information they carry, their intentional content, may vary with their causal antecedents and causal laws in the environment.

21. There is no need to assume that the abnormal condition is unverifiable. Another person with relevant background information might be able to infer that the abnormal condition is producing a perceptual illusion. In fact, another person with different dispositions might even be able to perceive the difference.

22. Not all perceptual representations that specify objective entities need have their representational characteristics determined in this way. The representational characters of *some* visual representations (or states) may depend on the subject's background theory or primarily on interaction among other representations. There are hallucinations of purple dragons. (Incidentally, few if any of the perceptual representations—even the conscious perceptual representations—discussed in Marr's theory depend in this way on the subject's conceptual background.) Here, I assume only that *some* visual representations acquire their representational characters through interaction. This amounts to the weak assumption that the formation of some perceptual representations is *empirical*.

Some of the interaction that leads to the formation and representational characters of certain innate perceptual tendencies (or perhaps even representations) may occur in the making of the species, not in the learning histories of individuals. Clearly this complication could be incorporated into a generalization of this third premise—without affecting the anti-individualistic thrust of the argument.

23. What of the nonintentionally specified dispositions that in the actual environment (given the actual laws of optics) would have enabled P to discriminate C's from O's in ideal circumstances? In the counterfactual environment, in view of the very different optical laws and different objects that confront P, one can suppose that these dispositions have almost any visual meaning that one likes. These dispositions would serve to discriminate C's from some other sort of entity. In view of the objectivity premise, the non-intentional dispositions can always be correlated with different, normal antecedent laws and conditions—in terms of which their intentional content may be explained.

The argument of this section is developed in parallel but different ways in "Cartesian Error and Objectivity of Perception," op. cit.

Section IV

The Philosophy of Social Science

Philip Gasper

The philosophy of social science addresses questions concerning interpretation, confirmation, explanation, and reduction that arise in relation to theories of human society. Earlier sections of this anthology have examined various aspects of these questions in some detail, but distinctive issues arise in the context of the social sciences. The essays in this section address some of these issues and add new twists to the earlier discussions.[1]

It is worth noting at the outset that philosophical issues have generally had a greater urgency for practitioners of the social sciences than for their counterparts in the natural sciences. The main reason for this is that, when compared to the outstanding advances of the natural sciences, the social sciences seem to have been relatively unsuccessful. No overarching predictive or explanatory social theories have achieved the status of, for example, general relativity theory or quantum mechanics in physics, or the neo-Darwinian synthesis in biology. This apparent failure has prompted methodological reflection: social scientists have attempted to root out mistakes in method that may be responsible for holding back their disciplines. And they have offered a wide variety of explanations for the differences in results between the natural and social sciences. Some have pointed to the relative youth of the social sciences, others to the greater susceptibility of social inquiry to ideological distortion, still others to the special complexity of the social scientist's subject matter. Some have even argued that the search for systematic explanations of social phenomena is itself misguided. We lack the space to provide a full and direct discussion of these issues, but a number of them are examined in the selections that follow.

Perhaps the most influential social scientist of the present century has been the German sociologist Max Weber. Weber frequently wrote on questions of method. In the essay reprinted here (which is abridged from a longer discussion), Weber discusses the role of (nonscientific) value judgments in the social sciences, arguing that social inquiry is hindered unless questions about empirical fact and questions about how such facts should be evaluated are firmly distinguished. In Weber's view, only questions of the first sort are part of the province of social science proper, and qua scientist the social enquirer must set aside any partisan moral or political views that she happens to hold. This may seem sound methodological advice, but Weber's argument for value-free social science may not be as compelling as it initially appears. One line of criticism is developed in Richard Miller's article, discussed below.

In our second selection, "Historical Explanation in the Social Sciences," John Watkins defends another methodological principle that has been immensely influential in social scientific research. Watkins claims that rules of method are "insufficient to guarantee success" in the scientific enterprise, but that they "are necessary to prohibit some wrong-headed moves." He distinguishes formal rules, which apply to all fields of inquiry, and material requirements, which say something about the content of satisfactory theories. Material requirements reflect special features of a particular subject matter and are thus domain specific. It is just such a requirement that Watkins defends for social science.

The particular principle Watkins advocates is *methodological individualism*. On Watkins's interpretation, this principle tells us that we have not "arrived at rock-bottom explanations of ... large-scale phenomena [such as inflation or full employment] until we have deduced an account of them from statements about the dispositions, beliefs, resources and inter-relations of individuals." According to Watkins, the principle follows from the recognition that "human beings are ... the only moving agents in history" and that there are no "superhuman agents or factors ... at work in history." He defends this perspective in two ways. First, he argues that it does not have various implausible consequences that are often attributed to it. Methodological individualism neither prohibits explanations of how psychological characteristics are formed nor claims that "all large-scale characteristics are ... a *reflection* of, individual characteristics." Second, Watkins argues that methodological individualism has proved to be more fruitful than its denial, which he terms "sociological holism."

One peculiarity of Watkins's argument is the status which he attributes to the principle of methodological individualism. He apparently does not believe that the principle can be known a priori, but he does not regard it as clearly empirical either. Watkins compares methodological individualism with mechanism "a metaphysical theory which governed thinking in the physical sciences from the seventeenth century until it was largely superseded by a wave or field worldview. According to mechanism, the ultimate constituents of the physical world are impenetrable particles which obey simple mechanical laws." The theory places restrictions on the content of acceptable accounts of the physical world, ruling out nonmechanical explanations of such phenomena. Since mechanism was eventually superseded, it seems that it cannot be an a priori truth. But although "it is confirmed, even massively confirmed, by the huge success of mechanical theories which conform to its requirements," mechanism itself "is untestable."

Obviously, Watkins is employing a rather peculiar notion of testability here. He apparently holds, following Popper, that a theory is testable only if it can be conclusively falsified by observational evidence. Yet, as he rightly points out, "[i]f certain phenomena ... seem refractory to this mechanistic sort of explanation, this refractoriness can always ... be attributed to our inability to find a successful mechanical model." So mechanism is "compatible with any *observation* whatever" and is thus an "unempirical principle." If this is the definition of testability, however, then it will quickly turn out that no scientific theory at all is testable, since any theory is *logically* compatible with any observation.[2] And once we loosen the notion of testability sufficiently to allow theories of particular phenomena to count as empirical, there seems no reason to think that an overarching theory like mechanism will not be empirical too. Similar considerations apply to the principle of methodological individualism, which we should consequently regard as a very general empirical doctrine, capable of being both confirmed and disconfirmed.

Thus modified, Watkins's discussion of rules of method is consonant with Richard Miller's claim (selection 3) that "[t]he questions defining the subject matter of methodology cannot be answered a priori .... [M]ethodology does not stand above social science, unalterable by it .... It includes principles governing science that might be changed in light of changes in science." Miller argues that the alternative view, which takes rules of method to be a priori and empirically uncontroversial, "has crippled the social sciences."

Miller defends this view of methodology through an examination of the doctrines discussed by Weber and Watkins in their essays: value freedom and methodological individualism. With respect to the issue of value freedom, Miller argues first that Weber's arguments for the exclusion of evaluative components from the content of scientific explanations, and for the illegitimacy of relying on nonscientific commitments in theory acceptance, are nonempirical and inadequate. He then outlines an empirical case for "the conclusion that certain kinds of partisanship are sometimes the best scientific policy, even though the best explanations do not evaluate." Miller's case is based on a plausible principle of social psychology, namely that when "social forces create strong pressure away from the truth, the counterpressure of certain partisan commitments to change the status quo may be more scientifically productive than neutrality." Miller goes on to argue that in present circumstances, for those concerned to establish scientifically adequate theories of society, a commitment to social change may be an important defense against truth-distorting, conservative social forces. None of this, however, supports the conclusion that such theories will themselves contain evaluative elements. Indeed, according to Miller, "[t]here is evidence from the history of social science that the best explanations do not evaluate."[3]

Miller's discussion of methodological individualism depends on isolating a version of this doctrine that is neither obviously true nor totally implausible. In fact the principle defended by Watkins—that explanations of social phenomena must ultimately refer only to the psychologies, resources, and interrelations of individuals—fits the bill nicely. Watkins's main argument in favor of this thesis was based on its fruitfulness in leading to explanations. But while this fruitfulness should not be ignored, the critic of individualism may well reject the adequacy of explanations couched in individualistic terms. Instead, Miller argues that the critical issue for evaluating the doctrine is whether "objective interests which guide a person's behavior, even though they are not his reasons for acting as he does, play a crucial social role." Methodological individualism, on this view, thus stands or falls on the resolution of this straightforwardly empirical issue.

Miller goes on to consider two related but much more general issues: "What makes a hypothesis, if true, an adequate explanation?" and "What makes it rational to accept an explanation, in light of available data?" With respect to the first question, Miller rejects both the positivist's covering-law model and the criterion of hermeneutic understanding advocated in the interpretative tradition running from Dilthey to Habermas, as satisfactory guides to acceptable social explanations. Neither of these approaches recognizes the relevance of empirical issues to the evaluation of explanations. On Miller's alternative view, the adequacy of an explanation depends on background empirical principles, but "there is no framework of empirical principles determining what counts as an explanation in all social sciences. Rather, there are particular frameworks for particular fields." Similarly, explanation testing "is almost always a comparison of an alleged explanation with its current rivals. Moreover, the background against which this comparison is performed does not just consist of the supremely general realm of logic and the highly specific realm of particular observed facts, the data. A whole spectrum of intermediate kinds of knowledge is relevant." Thus, principles of both explanation and confirmation are themselves open to empirical refutation or refinement. Miller's examination of both these issues extends the discussion begun in part I.

The final essay in this section, Peter Railton's "Marx and the Objectivity of Science," takes up a somewhat different set of issues. The articles by Weber, Watkins, and Miller discuss issues that arise from a consideration of efforts to acquire a scientific understanding of society. But it has become a commonplace that science itself is a social institution that can become the subject of scientific research. Indeed, there is a flourishing branch of inquiry, known as the sociology of knowledge, which aims to construct an account of the scientific enterprise considered in its social context. Such an inquiry might naturally be expected to yield important information about how scientific investigation is conducted; but sociologists of science have often gone further, suggesting that by uncovering the social roots of scientific developments, or the social interests they serve, the objectivity or impartiality of scientific claims is thereby undermined.[4] This idea has been pursued from a number of perspectives. It is, for instance, one theme in recent feminist critiques of science.[5] But in its strong form, the suggestion is both disquieting and paradoxical, since it presumably must apply to the claims of the sociology of knowledge just as much as to the claims of any other science.

One version of this strong sociology of knowledge thesis is often thought to follow from a Marxist account of ideology, according to which the dominant ideas in society, including its scientific ideas, exist to serve the interests of the dominant class. It is this version of the thesis that Railton discusses, although the general points he makes are relevant to non-Marxist versions of the thesis as well. Railton offers a naturalistic solution to the apparent paradox, arguing that even if "scientific inquiry is driven by the instrumental and narrow . . . interests of industrial capitalism," this need not undermine its claims to objectivity, since it would "increase the possibility of receiving and responding to causal feedback from natural phenomena." Like Miller, then, Railton recognizes the possibility of social forces that guide us toward the truth, as well as social forces that are truth-distorting. At least in the case of the natural sciences, it is plausible to maintain that it is forces of the first sort that are dominant, although the social sciences may be more susceptible to truth-distorting pressures.

In defending this analysis, Railton offers a careful account of the notion of objectivity, arguing that objective knowledge is not ruled out by the theory-dependence of method. Railton's discussion of science considered in its social context thus brings this anthology full circle, returning us to issues examined in the first section of part I.

Notes

1. This section deals with only a few of the many issues that arise in the philosophy of social science. For discussions of problems that arise with respect to specific social sciences, and of some of the various traditions of social inquiry, the reader is referred to the bibliography at the end of this introduction.
2. See Putnam, "The 'Corroboration' of Theories," this volume, chapter 6.
3. For arguments that evaluative properties can legitimately figure in social explanations, see Moore 1978 and Sturgeon 1985.
4. See for example, Barnes 1974, 1977, Barnes and Bloor 1982, and Bloor 1976. For a criticism of these views, see Newton-Smith 1981, chapter X.
5. For one example, see Gergen 1988.

References

Barnes, B., 1974, *Scientific Knowledge and Sociological Theory*, Routledge & Kegan Paul, London.

Barnes, B., 1977, *Interests and the Growth of Knowledge*, Routledge & Kegan Paul, London.

Barnes, B., and Bloor, B., 1982, "Relativism, Rationalism and the Sociology of Knowledge," in Hollis, M., and Lukes, S., eds., *Rationality and Relativism*, MIT Press, Cambridge, MA.

Bloor, D., 1976, *Knowledge and Social Imagery*, Routledge & Kegan Paul, London.

Gergen, M., "Toward a Feminist Metatheory and Methodology in the Social Sciences," in Gergen, M., ed., *Feminist Thought and the Structure of Knowledge*, New York University Press, New York.

Moore Jr., B., 1978, *Injustice: The Social Bases of Obedience and Revolt*, Sharpe, White Plains, NY.

Newton-Smith, W., 1981, *The Rationality of Science*, Routledge and Kegan Paul, London.

Sturgeon, N., 1985, "Moral Explanations," in Copp, D., and Zimmerman, D., eds., *Morality, Reason and Truth*, Rowman and Allanheld, Totowa, NJ.

Further Reading

Benton, T., 1977, *Philosophical Foundations of the Three Sociologies*, Routledge & Kegan Paul, London.

Bhaskar, R., 1979, *The Possibility of Naturalism*, Humanities Press, Atlantic Highlands, NJ.

Callinicos, A., 1988, *Making History: Agency, Structure and Change in Social Theory*, Cornell University Press, Ithaca, NY.

Carr, E. H., 1961, *What is History?* Vintage Books, New York.

Cohen, G. A., 1978, *Karl Marx's Theory of History: A Defence*, Princeton University Press, Princeton, NJ.

Dray, W., 1957, *Laws and Explanation in History*, Oxford University Press, New York.

Durkheim, E., 1901, *The Rules of Sociological Method* (trans. W. D. Hall and ed. S. Lukes), Free Press, New York.

Elster, J., 1983, *Sour Grapes*, Cambridge University Press, New York.

Elster, J., 1989, *Solomonic Judgments: Studies in the Limitations of Rationality*, Cambridge University Press, New York.

Emmet, D., and MacIntyre, A., 1970, eds., *Sociological Theory and Philosophical Analysis*, Macmillan, New York.

Fiske, D., and Shweder, R., eds., 1986, *Metatheory and Social Science*, University of Chicago Press, Chicago, IL.

Foucault, M., 1970, *The Order of Things: An Archeology of the Human Sciences*, Vintage, New York.

Gardiner, P., 1974, ed., *The Philosophy of History*, Oxford University Press, New York.

Garfinkel, A., 1981, *Forms of Explanation*, Yale University Press, New Haven, CT.

Geertz, C., 1973, *The Interpretation of Cultures*, Harper Colophon, New York.

Gibbon, G., 1989, *Explanation in Archaeology*, Blackwell, Oxford, England.

Gilbert, A., 1981, *Marx's Politics*, Rutgers University Press, New Brunswick, NJ.

Habermas, J., 1971, *Knowledge and Human Interests* (trans. J. Shapiro), Beacon, Boston, MA.

Hahn, F., and Hollis, M., 1979, eds., *Philosophy and Economic Theory*, Oxford University Press, New York.

Hausman, D., 1984, ed., *The Philosophy of Economics: An Anthology*, Cambridge University Press, New York.

Hollis, M., 1987, *The Cunning of Reason*, Cambridge University Press, New York.

Hollis, M., and S. Lukes 1982, eds., *Rationality and Relativism*, MIT Press, Cambridge, MA.

Keat, R., and J. Urry 1981, *Social Theory as Science*, 2nd ed., Routledge & Kegan Paul, London.

Kincaid, H., 1986, "Reduction, Explanation, and Individualism," *Philosophy of Science* 53: 492–513.

Levine, A., Sober, E., and Wright, E. O., 1987, "Marxism and Methodological Individualism," *New Left Review* 162: 67–84.

Little, D., 1990, *Varieties of Social Explanation*, Westview, Boulder, CO.

Lloyd, C., 1986, *Explanation in Social History*, Blackwell, Oxford, England.

Luce, R. H., and Raiffa, H., 1957, *Games and Decisions*, Wiley, New York.

Manicas, P., 1987, *A History and Philosophy of the Social Sciences*, Blackwell, Oxford, England.

Miller, R., 1978, "Methodological Individualism and Social Explanation," *Philosophy of Science* 45: 387–414.

Miller, R., 1979, "Reason and Commitment in the Social Sciences," *Philosophy and Public Affairs* 8: 241–266.

Miller, R., 1984, *Analyzing Marx*, Princeton University Press, Princeton, NJ.

Nielsen, J. M., 1990, ed., *Feminist Research Methods*, Westview, Boulder, CO.

Olson, M., 1965, *The Logic of Collective Action*, Harvard University Press, Cambridge, MA.

Roemer, J., 1986, ed., *Analytical Marxism*, Cambridge University Press, New York, NY.

Roemer, J., 1988, *Free to Lose*, Cambridge University Press, New York.

Rosenberg, A., 1989, *Philosophy of Social Science*, Westview, Boulder, CO.

Ruben, D.-H., 1985, *The Metaphysics of the Social World*, Routledge and Kegan Paul, Boston, MA.

Ryan, A., 1973, ed., *The Philosophy of Social Explanation*, Oxford University Press, New York.

Skinner, Q., 1985, ed., *The Return of Grand Theory in the Human Sciences*, Cambridge University Press, New York.

Taylor, C., 1985, *Philosophy and the Human Sciences*, Cambridge University Press, New York.

Wilson, B., 1970, ed., *Rationality*, Blackwell, Oxford, England.

Chapter 38

Value-judgments in Social Science

Max Weber

In what follows, except where a different sense is either explicitly mentioned or obvious from the context, the term 'value-judgment' is to be understood as referring to 'practical' evaluations of a phenomenon which is capable of being influenced by our actions as worthy of either condemnation or approval. The problem of the 'freedom' of a particular science from value-judgments of this kind—that is, the acceptability and meaning of this logical principle—is in no way identical with the entirely different question ... whether, in the academic context, the teacher's practical value-judgments (whether based on ethical standards, cultural ideals, or some other kind of 'world view') ought or ought not to be 'acknowledged'. This question cannot be discussed in scientific terms, since it is itself entirely dependent on practical value-judgments and so irresoluble .... The sciences, both normative and empirical, can perform only one invaluable service for the politicians and the opposing parties, and that is to say to them: (i) there are such and such conceivable 'ultimate' positions to be taken on this practical problem; (ii) such and such are the facts which you must take account of in choosing between these positions. At this point, we have arrived at our 'topic'.

Endless misunderstanding and, above all, terminological (and therefore sterile) de-bate has arisen over the term 'value-judgment', and this has obviously contributed nothing at all toward settling the issue. It is, as was said at the beginning, perfectly clear that the issue in these discussions, as far as our discipline is concerned, is one of the practical evaluation of social facts as practically desirable or undesirable, whether on ethical grounds or on the basis of some attitude to culture or for some other reason. In spite of all that has been said on the matter,[1] such 'objections' have been raised (in all seriousness) as that science seeks to attain 'valuable' results, (i) in the sense of logically and factually correct results and (ii) in the sense of results which are important from the point of view of scientific interest, and that the very selection of material implies a 'value-judgment'. Then again, there is the constantly recurring and almost incredibly wrong-headed misunderstanding of those who think it is being maintained that empirical science cannot treat men's 'subjective' value-judgments as objects (whereas the whole of sociology and, in economics, the whole theory of marginal utility are based on the opposite assumption). What is at issue, however, is exclusively the requirement, utterly trivial in itself, that anyone engaged in research or in presenting its results should keep two things absolutely separate, because they involve different kinds of problem: first, the statement of empirical facts (including facts established by him about the 'evaluative' behavior of the empirical human beings whom he is studying); and secondly, his own practical value-position, that is, his judgment and, in this sense, 'evaluation' of these facts (including possible 'value-

Reprinted with emendations from *Weber: Selections in Translation* (New York: Cambridge University Press, 1978), ed. W. G. Runciman, selections from pp. 69–98, by permission of the publisher and editor. Copyright 1978 by Cambridge University Press.

judgments' made by empirical human beings, which have themselves become an object of investigation) as satisfactory or unsatisfactory.

The author of an otherwise valuable paper asserts that a researcher can take even his own value-judgment as 'fact' and proceed to draw the consequences from it. What is meant here is as indisputably correct as the chosen form of expression is misleading. It is of course possible to agree before a discussion that a particular practical measure, such as a plan to meet the costs of an increase in the army out of the pockets of the propertied classes alone, should be 'assumed' in the discussion and that the only topic for discussion should be the means of carrying it out. That is often a perfectly useful thing to do. But a practical purpose which is mutually taken for granted in this way is not called a 'fact', but an 'end fixed *a priori*'. That even this is essentially ambiguous would very soon become apparent in the discussion of the 'means', unless the 'assumed end' held to be outside the scope of the discussion was something as concrete as lighting a cigar now. In that case, admittedly, the means too would only rarely require any discussion. In almost every case of a purpose formulated in more general terms (for example, in the illustration just used), it will be found that in the discussion of the means, not only does it become apparent that the different individuals understand something quite different by the supposedly clear end, but in particular it may happen that precisely the same end is desired for very different ultimate reasons and that this has some influence on the discussion of the means. Still, this is by the way. For it has never so far occurred to anyone to dispute that it is possible to start from a certain mutually agreed end and discuss only the means of achieving it and that this *can* result in a discussion which can be settled by purely empirical methods. Rather, the whole discussion turns precisely on the choice of ends (not on that of the 'means' to an already accepted end)—in other words, precisely on the question of the sense in which the individual's fundamental value-judgment can be, not taken as a 'fact', but made the object of a scientific critique. If this is not accepted, then all further discussion is in vain.

The topic for discussion is not really the question of the extent to which practical value-judgments, in particular ethical judgments, may claim for themselves normative status—in other words, whether they are different in character from, for instance, the often cited example of the question whether blondes are preferable to brunettes or any other similarly subjective judgment of taste. These are problems for moral philosophy, not for the methodology of the empirical disciplines. What is important from the methodological point of view is that the validity of a practical imperative as a norm, on the one hand, and the truth claims of a statement of empirical fact, on the other, create problems at totally different levels, and that the specific value of each of them will be diminished if this is not recognized and if the attempt is made to force them into the same category. In my opinion, this is to a large extent what has been done, especially by Professor von Schmoller.[2] It is precisely respect for our Master which makes it impossible to ignore these points at which I believe we should not follow him.

First, I should like to oppose the view that the proponents of 'value-freedom' take the mere fact of the historical and individual variability of the value-positions accepted at particular times to be proof of the necessarily merely 'subjective' character of, for instance, ethics. Statements of empirical fact, too, are often very much disputed, and there may often be considerably greater general agreement about whether someone is to be considered a scoundrel than there is (among the very experts themselves) about the question of the interpretation of a mutilated inscription. Von Schmoller's assumption of an increasing conventional unanimity among all religious denominations and individuals about the most important values is in marked contrast to my impression, which is quite the opposite. However, that seems to me to have no bearing on the present issue. For it would still be necessary to oppose the view that the fact that certain practical values, however widely held, had come, simply by convention, to be accepted in fact as self-evident could count as an adequate scientific proof. The specific function of science seems to me to be exactly the opposite: for science, what is conventionally 'self-evident' becomes a problem. This is just what von Schmoller and his friends themselves have done in their time. The fact that one investigates the causal influence on economic life of the actual existence of certain ethical or religious convictions, and in certain cases assesses it highly, certainly does not imply that one must therefore share these convictions, which have, perhaps, had a considerable causal influence, or even that one must consider them merely as 'valuable'. Similarly, a high valuation of some ethical or religious phenomenon does not in the least imply a similar positive evaluation of the unexpected consequences which its realisation has had or would have. Such questions cannot be settled by citing facts, and the individual's judgment on them would vary considerably, depending on his own religious and other practical values. All this is completely irrelevant to the question at issue.

On the other hand, I am emphatically opposed to the view that a 'realistic' science of morality, in the sense of a demonstration of the factual influences exercised on the ethical convictions which prevail at any given time in a group of human beings by their other conditions of life and in turn by the ethical convictions on the conditions of life, would produce an 'ethics' which could ever say anything about what *ought* to be the case. Any more than a 'realistic' account of the astronomical ideas of, for instance, the Chinese—one which would show what their practical motives were for studying astronomy and how they went about it, what results they achieved and why—could ever have as its goal to prove the correctness of this Chinese astronomy. Or again, any more than an account of the way in which Roman surveyors or Florentine bankers (the latter even when apportioning quite large inherited fortunes) very often arrived by their methods at results which are incompatible with trigonometry or the multiplication table could ever make it a matter for discussion whether the latter were valid. The one and only result which can ever be achieved by empirical psychological and historical investigation of a particular value-system, as influenced by individual, social and historical causes, is its *interpretative explanation*. That is no small achievement. Not only is it desirable because of its personal (though not scientific) by-product, of making it easier for the individual to 'do justice to' those who really or apparently think differently. But it is also extremely important from the scientific point of view, in two respects: (i) for the purpose of an empirical causal study of human action, in learning to recognise what are really its ultimate motives; (ii) when one is engaged in discussion with someone who (really or apparently) has a different set of values from oneself, in determining which value-positions are genuinely opposed. For this is the real meaning of any debate about values: to understand what one's opponent (or oneself) really means, in the sense of the value which really, and not just apparently, is important to each of the two parties, and in this way to make it possible to decide one's attitude to this value in general.

Thus, far from its being the case that, from the point of view of the requirement of 'value-freedom' in discussions of empirical matters, debates about value-judgments would be sterile or even meaningless, awareness of the meaning of this requirement is a presupposition of all fruitful discussions of this kind. They presuppose an appreciation, quite simply, of the possibility that ultimate values might diverge, in principle and irreconcilably. For neither is it the case that 'to understand all' means 'to forgive all', nor is there in general any path leading from mere understanding of someone else's point of view to approval of it. Rather, it leads, at least as easily and often with much greater reliability, to an awareness of the impossibility of agreement, and of the reasons why and the respects in which this is so. This very awareness, however, is the recognition of a truth and it is just this recognition which is advanced by 'discussion of values'. What can certainly not be achieved in this way, since it lies in precisely the opposite direction, is any kind of normative ethic or in general any kind of binding 'imperative'. Quite the contrary: everyone knows that the achievement of such a goal is rather made more difficult by the (at least apparently) 'relativizing' effect of such discussions. Again, this is naturally not to say that such discussions should be avoided. Quite the opposite. For an 'ethical' conviction which can be undermined by psychological 'understanding' of divergent value-judgments is worth no more than religious opinions which are overthrown, as sometimes happens, by scientific knowledge. Finally, when von Schmoller takes it for granted that the advocates of 'value-freedom' in the empirical disciplines could recognise only 'formal' ethical truths (which obviously means 'formal' in the sense of Kant's *Critique of Practical Reason*), some discussion of his claim is called for, even though the problem is not absolutely relevant to the present issue.

First, the identification which is implicit in von Schmoller's view of ethical imperatives and 'cultural values' must be rejected—even when they are said to be the highest cultural values. For there may be a point of view from which cultural values can be seen as 'given', even insofar as they conflict, inevitably and irreconcilably, with all the requirements of ethics. And contrariwise an ethics which rejects all cultural values is possible without internal contradiction. In any event, the two types of value are not identical. Again, it is a grave (though widespread) misunderstanding to think that 'formal' propositions, like those of Kantian ethics, imply no substantive guidance. The possibility of a normative ethics is by no means called in question merely because there are problems of a practical kind for which normative ethics cannot by itself provide any clear guidance (a very specific example being, in my opinion, certain problems connected with institutions, and so precisely with 'social policy'). Nor is it called in question because ethics is not the only area of values in the world—because, besides ethics, there are other kinds of value, which can in certain cases be realised only by someone who will accept ethical 'responsibility'. A prime example is the area of political action. It would be feeble-minded, in my opinion, to wish to deny the tension with ethics which is inherent precisely in political activity. But it is by no means peculiar to politics, as the usual antithesis of 'private' and 'political' morality would have us believe. Let us go beyond some of the 'limits' of ethics mentioned above.

Among those questions which cannot be clearly resolved by *any* system of ethics are those concerning the consequences of the postulate of 'justice'. For instance, is much owed to the man who achieves much (a view which comes closest to the opinion expressed by von Schmoller in his day)? Or, on the contrary, is much required from the man who can achieve much? Should one then, in the name of justice (for other considerations, such as the necessary 'incentive', would have to be set aside in this case), ensure that those with great talent have the best chances? Or should one rather, like Babeuf, try to compensate for the injustice involved in the unequal distribution of intellectual abilities by making absolutely sure that talent, the very possession of which already confers a beneficial feeling of prestige, cannot also take advantage of its better chances in the world for itself? Such questions would seem to be unanswerable in purely 'ethical' terms. But the ethical aspects of most questions of social policy conform to this type.

Even when purely individual action is concerned, however, there are fundamental problems, of a specifically ethical kind, which cannot be resolved on the basis of purely ethical presuppositions. One example in particular is the fundamental question whether the intrinsic value of a moral action (usually referred to as the 'pure will' or the 'intention') is in itself sufficient to justify the action: this follows the maxim formulated by Christian moralists as, 'The Christian acts rightly and leaves the outcome to God'. Or should some account also be taken of responsibility for the possibly or probably foreseeable *consequences* of the action, once it becomes enmeshed with the ethically irrational world? In the social sphere, all radical revolutionary political tendencies, especially so-called 'syndicalism', base themselves on the former postulate, while all forms of 'political realism' follow the latter. Both appeal to ethical maxims. But these maxims are in permanent conflict with each other, of a kind which simply cannot be resolved by the means of an ethics which relies entirely on its own resources.

Both these ethical maxims are of a severely 'formal' character, and so are similar in that respect to the well-known axioms of the *Critique of Practical Reason*. Because of this formal character, it is widely held that these latter did not in general contain any substantive guidance for the assessment of action. That, as was said above, is by no means true. Suppose we deliberately take an example which is as far removed as possible from anything to do with 'politics': such an example may perhaps clarify the real meaning of the much-discussed 'merely formal' character of Kantian ethics. Suppose a man says of his sexual relationship with a woman, 'At first, our affair was for both of us merely a passion, but now it is a value'. In terms of the cool objectivity of the Kantian ethic, the first half of this sentence would be expressed as 'At first, we were both merely a means for each other', and the whole sentence would thus be claimed as an instance of that well-known principle, which there has been a curious eagerness to represent as a purely historically conditioned expression of 'individualism', whereas in reality it is an extremely original formulation of an enormous number of ethical situations—though one must understand this formulation correctly. In its negative form, and leaving out of account any statement of what is being positively contrasted with treating someone else, in the morally disapproved fashion, 'merely as a means', it evidently contains three elements: (i) the recognition of kinds of values which are independent of ethics; (ii) the demarcation of the ethical domain from these others; and finally (iii) a statement of the fact that, and the sense in which, action in the service of extra-ethical values may nevertheless be connected with differences in ethical worth. In fact, the kinds of values which permit or prescribe the treatment of others 'merely as a means' are quite different in character from ethical values. This matter cannot be pursued any further here, but it is at any rate clear that the 'formal' character of even that, highly abstract, ethical proposition is not indifferent to the content of action.

At this point, however, the problem becomes even more complex. The negative attitude embodied in the words 'merely a passion' may be represented from a certain standpoint as a blasphemy against all that is most authentic and real in life, against the only, or at least the royal, road away from impersonal or *supra*personal and so life-denying 'value'-mechanisms, from bondage to the lifeless petrification of routine existence and the pretensions of inauthentic values taken as 'given'. At all events, it is possible to conceive of such a view which, although it would certainly disdain to use the word 'value' to describe the kind of totally concrete experience which it has in mind, would yet constitute a domain of values, which, while totally alien and hostile to all conceptions of sanctity or goodness, all forms of ethical or aesthetic legalism, all ideas of the importance of culture or the value of the individual, would yet, and for that very reason, claim its own kind of 'immanent' worth, in the most extreme sense of that word. Whatever our attitude to this claim may be, it is at all events not one which could be either proved or disproved by the methods of any 'science'.

Any empirical consideration of this situation would, as John Stuart Mill remarked, lead to acknowledgment of absolute polytheism as the only metaphysic which would fit the case. A nonempirical approach, concerned more with the interpretation of meanings (in other words, a genuine moral philosophy), would go further than this: it could not fail to recognise that a conceptual scheme of 'values', however well ordered, would fail to do justice to precisely that aspect of the situation which is most decisive. That is to say, it is in the last resort always, and again and again, more than a mere matter of choosing between alternative values: it is rather a matter of an irreconcilable struggle to the death like the conflict between 'God' and the 'Devil'. Between these rivals there can be no question of relativism or compromise—or not, as must be insisted, in the real sense. For, as everyone finds in the course of life, such compromises are made in fact, and so in outward appearance: indeed, they are made at every step. The different domains of value are entwined and entangled in virtually every single important attitude which real men adopt. It is here that we find the levelling effect of 'everyday life' in the truest sense of that word: in the context of everyday routine a man does not become aware (above all, does not even *want* to become aware) of this partly psychological, partly pragmatic confusion of mortally opposed values, and evades the choice between 'God' and the 'Devil' and the decision, which ultimately lies with him, about which of the conflicting values is under the sway of the one and which of the other. The fruit of the Tree of Knowledge, so disturbing to human complacency yet so inescapable, is nothing but this recognition of these oppositions, and of the consequent necessity to accept that every important individual action, indeed life as a whole, if it is not to slip by like a merely natural process but to be lived consciously, is a series of ultimate decisions, by means of which the soul, as in Plato, chooses its own destiny, in the sense of the meaning of what it does and is. The crudest misunderstanding to which the intentions of those who argue for an ultimate conflict of values are occasionally subject is thus that contained in the interpretation of their view as a form of 'relativism', or in other words as a view of life which is based on precisely the opposite conception of the relations between the different value-spheres and is only meaningfully tenable (in any coherent form) on the basis of a metaphysic which is structured in a very special ('organic') fashion.

If we return to our special case, it seems to me to be possible to establish without a shadow of a doubt that, in the area of practical political value-judgments (especially in the fields of economics and social policy), as soon as guidance for a valued course of action is to be sought, all that an empirical discipline with the means at its disposal can show is (i) the unavoidable means; (ii) the unavoidable side-effects; (iii) the resulting conflict of several possible value-judgments with each other in their practical consequences. *Philosophical* disciplines can go further, determining by means of reasoning the 'meaning' of the value-judgments, and so their ultimate structure and consequences from the point of view of meaning: in this way they can assign them their 'place' within the totality of possible 'ultimate' values and mark out their spheres of application from the point of view of meaning. Even such simple questions as: how far should the end justify the necessary means? or again, how far should unintended consequences be taken into account? or finally, how are conflicts between a number of intended or obligatory ends which clash in a particular case to be resolved?—All are entirely matters of choice or of compromise. There is no scientific procedure, either rational or empirical, of any kind which could provide a decision in such cases. Least of all can *our* strictly empirical science presume to spare the individual the necessity of making this choice, and so it should not even give the impression of being able to do so.

One further point which should be explicitly made in conclusion is that the recognition of this state of affairs in relation to our disciplines is completely independent of any attitude one might adopt towards the extremely brief outline of value theory given above. For there is in general no logically tenable point of view from which it could be denied, apart from that of a hierarchy of values clearly prescribed by religious dogmas. I must wait and see whether there are really people who maintain that there is *no* basic distinction in meaning between such questions as: are the facts in a particular case such and such or are they not? why did the particular situation develop as it did, and not in some other way? is a given state of affairs usually succeeded, in accordance with a factual rule, by another state of affairs, and if so with what degree of probability? and such questions as: what should a man do in practice in a particular situation? from which points of view might that situation seem practically desirable or undesirable? are there any general propositions or axioms, of whatever form, to which these points of view are reducible? Again, is there anyone who will maintain that there is the slightest connection in meaning between the question: in which direction will a particular given factual situation (or more generally, a situation of a particular, sufficiently determinate, type) probably develop, and how great is the probability that it will develop in that direction (or typically tends so to develop)? and the question: should one assist a particular situation to develop in a particular direction (whether that which is inherently probable or the precise opposite or some other)?; or, lastly, between the question: what view will probably (or even certainly) be formed on a problem, of whatever kind, by certain people in particular circumstances, or by an indefinite number of people in similar circumstances? and the question: is this view, which will probably or certainly be formed, *correct*? Can it really be contended that they are, as is said time and time again, 'inseparable from each other'? Or that this latter contention is *not* incompatible with the requirements of scientific thought? Whether someone who admits that the two sorts of question are absolutely heterogeneous in character nevertheless claims the right to express his views on both sorts of problem in one and the same book, on one and the same page, or even in the principal and subordinate clauses of one and the same sentence, is entirely his own affair. What *can* be required of him is simply that he should not unintentionally (or even intentionally, out of a wish to be clever) mislead his readers about the absolute heterogeneity of the problems. Personally I am of the opinion that no means whatsoever is too 'pedantic' to be used in avoiding confusions.

The point of discussions of practical value-judgments (those, that is, of the parties to such discussions) can only be:

(*a*) To work out the ultimate internally 'coherent' value-axioms, from which the opposing opinions are derived. Frequently enough we deceive ourselves, not only about our opponent's fundamental axioms, but also about our own. This procedure essentially begins with the particular value-judgment and its analysis in terms of meaning, and then ascends by stages to more and more fundamental evaluative attitudes. It does not use the methods of any empirical discipline and does not increase our knowledge of facts. It is 'valid' in the same way as logic.

(*b*) To deduce the 'consequences', in terms of evaluative attitudes, which would follow from particular ultimate value-axioms if they and they alone were made the basis of the practical evaluation of factual states of affairs. The argumentation in this case is entirely at the level of meanings, but the procedure depends on empirical enquiry for the most exhaustive possible analysis of those empirical states of affairs which might be generally relevant to a practical evaluation.

(c) To ascertain the consequences which would necessarily follow in fact from the practical realization of a particular practically evaluative attitude to a problem (i) as a result of its being limited to the use of certain unavoidable means, and (ii) as a result of the inevitability of certain, not directly intended, side-effects. This purely empirical inquiry may have the following results, among others: (i) that it is absolutely impossible to realize the value-postulate, to however slight a degree of approximation, because no way of realising it can be discovered; (ii) that it becomes more or less improbable that it should be realized, either completely or approximately, either for the same reason or because it is probable that there will be certain unintended consequences of such a kind as directly or indirectly to make its realization illusory; (iii) that it is necessary to take into account means or indirect side-effects of a kind which the advocate of the practical postulate in question had not considered, so that, even in his own eyes, his evaluative decision between end, means, and side-effects becomes a new problem and loses its compelling power over others.

Finally (d) new value-axioms, and the postulates derivable from them, may emerge from the discussion, of a kind which the advocate of a practical postulate had not noticed and toward which he had as a result not adopted any attitude, although the realization of his own postulate conflicts with them either (i) in principle or (ii) because of its practical consequences—in other words, either at the level of meaning or in practice. In case (i) further discussion will concern problems of type (a), in case (ii) of type (c).

It is thus very far from being the case that discussions of this type about value-judgments are 'pointless'. Rather, it is precisely when their purposes are rightly understood (and in my opinion only then) that they have considerable point.

The utility of a discussion of practical value-judgments, in the right place and in the right sense, is, however, by no means exhausted by the direct 'yield' which it may produce in this way. Rather, when properly conducted, it bears lasting fruit in empirical work, in that it supplies the basic questions for investigation.

The problems posed in the empirical disciplines are, of course, to be answered in a 'value-free' way. They are not 'evaluative problems'. But in the field of our disciplines they are influenced by the relationship of reality 'to' values. For the meaning of the expression 'value-relevance' I must refer to my own earlier discussions and above all the well-known works of Heinrich Rickert. It would be impossible to enter into the discussion again here, so it should simply be recalled that the expression 'value-relevance' refers merely to the philosophical interpretation of that specifically scientific *interest* which governs the selection and formulation of the object of an empirical enquiry.

Within empirical enquiry, this fact, with its purely logical import, does not license any kind of 'practical value-judgments'. But this fact shows, as does all historical experience, that it is cultural (that is, value-) interests which indicate the direction even of empirical scientific work. Clearly, these value-interests may become explicit in the course of discussions about value-judgments. Such discussions may to a large extent remove the need for, or at least facilitate, the scientific researcher's (especially the historian's) task of 'value-interpretation', which is for him such an important preliminary to his genuinely empirical work. Since the distinction, not only between evaluation and value-relevance, but also between evaluation and value-interpretation (in the sense of the development of possible positions at the level of meaning toward a given phenomenon) is often not made with complete clarity, with the result that obscurities arise which have a special bearing on the assessment of the logical character of history, I refer the reader in this regard to the remarks in my paper "Critical Studies in the Logic of the Cultural Sciences"[3] (without claiming in any way that this is a definitive account).

Instead of entering into yet another discussion of this fundamental methodological problem, I should like to consider in more detail a few specific points of practical importance for our discipline.

There is a recurrent and widespread belief that guidance in practical decisions ought to be, must be, or even may be derived from 'developmental trends'. From such 'trends', however, clear as they may be, clear imperatives for action can be obtained only in regard to the means which will probably be appropriate given a certain end, not in regard to the end itself. The concept of a 'means' which is being used here is, admittedly, as broad as it can conceivably be. For instance, someone whose ultimate end was the power-political interests of the state would, according to the situation, have to regard an absolutist constitution as much as a radical-democratic one as the (relatively) more appropriate means, and it would be ludicrous if a possible change in his assessment of these constitutional contrivances as a means were to be regarded as a change in his 'ultimate' value-position. Obviously, however, as was said earlier, the individual is constantly faced anew with the problem whether to abandon his hopes of realizing his practical values in the light of his awareness that there is a clear developmental trend which would either make it possible for him to achieve his end only by using new means which perhaps seem to him morally or otherwise objectionable, or force him to take into account side-effects which he finds abhorrent, or make it so unlikely that he will achieve his end that his work, judged by its chances of success, is bound to seem like fruitless tilting at windmills. But there is nothing very special about the role played by awareness of such more or less easily modifiable developmental 'trends' in all this. Any single new fact may equally mean that a new adjustment has to be made between end and necessary means, intended end and unavoidable side-effects. But whether this is to happen, and what practical conclusions are to be drawn from it if it does, are questions which not only no empirical science of whatever kind but, as was said earlier, no science at all, however it is constituted, can answer. For instance, one may use the most cogent arguments to show the convinced syndicalist that his action is not only socially 'useless' in that it does not hold out any prospect of success in changing the external class situation of the proletariat, but will undoubtedly make that position worse by creating a 'reactionary' mood: he will still see absolutely no force in such arguments, if he is really committed to his view down to its ultimate consequences. And this would not be because he was mad, but because he may from his own point of view be 'right', as will presently be explained.

On the whole, people have a rather marked tendency to adapt themselves mentally to success, or to what at a particular time holds out the prospect of it, not only, as goes without saying, in regard to the means with which or the extent to which they seek to realize their ultimate ideals at that time, but in their abandonment of these ideals themselves. In Germany, it is thought proper to dignify this attitude with the name of *Realpolitik*. At all events it is incomprehensible why precisely the representatives of an empirical science should feel the need to give this attitude their support, by constituting themselves into a claque of supporters of the current 'developmental trend' and transforming the question of 'adaptation' to the trend from an ultimate problem of values, to be settled only by the individual in the individual case and so a matter for the individual's own conscience, into a principle supposedly guaranteed by the authority of a 'science'.

It is true to say, provided it is rightly understood, that successful politics is always 'the art of the possible'. It is no less true, however, that the possible is very often achieved only by reaching out toward the impossible which lies beyond it. It was not, finally, the only truly consistent ethic of 'adaptation' to the possible (the Confucian bureaucratic morality) which produced the specific qualities of our civilization, which we probably all (subjectively) value more or less positively, despite all our other differences. I at least should not like to see the nation, as further explained above, systematically deprived of the sense that the value of an action does not only lie in its 'consequences' but also in its 'intentions'—least of all in the name of science. Anyway, failure to appreciate this impedes our understanding of realities. For—to stick to our earlier example of the syndicalist—it is, even from the logical point of view, absurd to 'criticize' a course of action which must, if consistent, take as its guiding thread the value of the agent's intentions by confronting it merely with the value of its consequences. The genuinely consistent syndicalist seeks as much merely to preserve in himself a certain intention which seems to him to be of absolute value, indeed sacred, as he does to arouse, whenever possible, such an intention in someone else. His external actions, in particular those which are doomed from the outset to be totally ineffectual, ultimately have the purpose of assuring him in his own mind that this intention is genuine, that is, has the strength to 'stand the test' in action, and is not an idle boast. That end can (perhaps) only be achieved in the real world by means of such actions. For the rest, his kingdom, if he is consistent, is, like that of any ethics of intention, 'not of this world'. All that can be said from the 'scientific' point of view is that this conception of his own ideals is the only one which is internally coherent and that it cannot be contradicted by external 'facts'.

I should like to think that, in saying this, I have performed a service for supporters and opponents of syndicalism alike, and exactly the service which they rightly require of science. On the other hand, nothing seems to me to be achieved in the sense of any science, however constituted, by 'on the one hand—on the other hand', by seven reasons 'for' and six reasons 'against' a particular phenomenon (such as the General Strike), which are then set against each other in the manner of ancient public admin- istration or modern Chinese memoranda. Once the syndicalist view has been reduced in this way to as rational and internally consistent a form as possible, and once the empirical conditions of its realization, its chances of success and empirically predictable practical consequences have been stated, the task of value-free science, at any rate in relation to it, is complete. That one should, or should not, be a syndicalist is something that can never be proved in the absence of very definite metaphysical premises, which are not demonstrable, and certainly not by any science of whatever form. Again, for an officer to blow himself and his trench up rather than surrender may in a particular case be absolutely futile in all respects, judged by its consequences. It should not be a matter of indifference, however, whether the intention to act without asking about the usefulness of doing so does or does not exist in general. At any rate, it is no more 'senseless' than that of the consistent syndicalist. If a professor wanted to recommend such Catonism from the comfortable heights of his academic chair, it would not, admittedly, look in particularly good taste. But neither is it necessary for him to extol the opposite attitude and make it into an obligation to adapt one's ideals to the opportunities afforded precisely by current trends and situations.

The expression 'adaptation' has repeatedly been used just now, and in any given case its meaning is sufficiently clear because of the form of expression which has been chosen. But clearly the term is in itself ambiguous: it may refer to the adaptation of the means used in the pursuit of some ultimate end to given situations ('*Realpolitik*' in the narrower sense) or to adaptation, in the choice from among the possible ultimate ends themselves, to the real or apparent momentary chances of one of them at any given time (the form of 'Realpolitik' which has been so remarkably successful in our policies for the last twenty-seven years). But this is far from exhausting its possible meanings. Hence it would in my opinion be best to avoid employing this much misused concept in any discussions of our problems, whether of questions of 'value' or of questions of any other kind. It is readily liable to misunderstanding as an expression of a scientific argument, as which it is constantly used, both in 'explanation' (for instance, of the empirical emergence of certain ethical views in certain human groups at particular periods) and in 'evaluation' (for example, of the ethical views just referred to as having emerged in practice as objectively 'appropriate' and so objectively 'correct' and valuable). In neither of these respects, however, does it perform any useful function, since it always requires interpretation itself first of all. Its original home is in biology. If it were really understood in the biological sense as referring to the relatively determinable chances, resulting from the environment, which a human group has to preserve its own psycho-physical genetic inheritance through abundant procreation, then, for instance, those social classes which are economically most affluent and regulate their lives in the most rational fashion would be, in terms of the familiar empirical statistics of birth rate, the 'least well adapted'. The few Indians who lived around Salt Lake before the Mormon immigration were as well or as poorly 'adapted' to the conditions of the environment as were the later densely populated Mormon settlements, both in the biological sense and in any other of the numerous possible genuinely empirical senses. Thus we do not increase our empirical understanding in the slightest by using this concept, though it is easy to imagine that we do. And—let it be said at this point—it is only where there are two organizations which are in every other respect absolutely identical that one can say that a concrete difference of detail creates a situation for one of them which is empirically better 'suited' to its continued existence, and is in this sense better 'adapted' to the given conditions. As for evaluation, one person might take the view that the greater numbers of Mormons and the material and other achievements and qualities which they brought to the area and developed there were evidence of their superiority to the Indians; another, who was utterly revolted by the means used by the Mormons and the side-effects of their ethical code, which was at least partly responsible for those achievements, might be just as likely to prefer the plains even if there had been no Indians there, and so to prefer the romantic existence which the Indians led there. No science in the world, however constituted, could claim to be able to convert them. For the issue here is the irresoluble one of balancing ends, means, and side-effects against each other.

Only where it is a question of finding the appropriate means to an absolutely unambiguously given end is the problem one which can really be decided empirically. The proposition 'x is the only means to y' is in fact merely the converse of the proposition 'y follows x'. The concept of 'adaptedness', however (and all those linked to it), does not, and this is the main point, give us the slightest information about the ultimate underlying value-judgments, which it rather merely conceals—as does, for instance, the recently fashionable concept of 'human economy', which in my view is fundamentally confused. In the domain of 'culture', either everything is 'adapted' or nothing is, depending on how the concept is used. For no form of civilized life can be without conflict. Its methods, its object, even its basic direction and the people involved in it can be altered, but it cannot be eliminated itself. It may take the form, not of an external struggle between enemies for external things, but of an internal struggle between friends for internal goods, and in the process external compulsion may be replaced by internal control (even in the form of devotion inspired by sexual or charitable feelings). It may, finally, mean an inner struggle of the individual with himself within his own soul. In whatever form, it is always with us. Often, it is all the more fraught with consequence the less it is noticed and the more it appears in the form of apathetic or easygoing tolerance or the illusions of self-deception or takes the form of 'selection'. 'Peace' means nothing more than a shift in the forms of conflict or the parties to conflict or the objects of conflict or, finally, in the chances of selection. Whether and when such shifts stand the test of ethical or other value-judgments is a question about which, obviously, absolutely no generalization is possible. Only one conclusion undoubtedly follows: without any exception, every ordering of social relationships, whatever its structure, must, if its value is to be assessed, ultimately be judged by the type of human being to which it gives the best chances of becoming dominant in its processes of selection, whether they operate by external criteria or by the internal criterion of motive. For otherwise the empirical inquiry is not exhaustive, nor is there the necessary factual basis for a general evaluation, whether it is consciously subjective or claims objective validity....

The total separation of the domain of values from the empirical sphere is typically revealed in the fact that the use of a particular technique, however 'advanced', implies nothing at all about the aesthetic value of the work of art. Aesthetically, works which employ the most 'primitive' techniques (for instance, paintings produced without any awareness of perspective) may be completely equal in value to the most sophisticated works, created by a rational technique, provided that the artist's intentions have been limited to those forms which are appropriate to such a 'primitive' technique. The invention of new technical means means in the first instance only an increase in differentiation and creates only the possibility of an increase in 'richness' in art, in the sense of heightened value. In practice it has fairly often had the reverse effect, of 'impoverishing' the feeling for form. But from the point of view of an empirical, causal inquiry it is precisely changes in 'technique' (in the highest sense of that word) which constitute the most important generally determinable factor in the development of art.

Not only art historians, but also historians in general, tend to retort that they will neither allow their right of political, cultural, ethical, and aesthetic evaluation to be taken away nor are they in a position to be able to do their work without it. Methodology has neither the power nor the intention to dictate to anyone what he should have it in mind to offer in a literary work. It merely claims for its part the right to point out that certain problems are different in nature from each other, that to confuse them with each other results in the parties to a discussion talking at cross purposes, and that a meaningful discussion about the one kind of problem, using the methods either of empirical science or of logic, is possible, but not about the other. Perhaps at this point one further general observation ought to be added, without any proofs being offered for the moment: a careful analysis of historical works shows very easily that the historian's relentless search for empirical causal connections, right to the end of the causal chain, tends almost always to come to a halt, to the detriment of the scientific results, at the point at which the historian begins to 'evaluate'. He runs the risk at this point of, for example, trying to 'explain' something as the result of a 'fault' or of 'decadence', when it was really perhaps an expression of the agent's ideals, which are simply different from his own: in this way he fails in his essential task of 'understanding'. The misunderstanding can be explained by two causes. First, it is a result of the fact that (to remain in the area of art) the field of art may be approached, not only from the point of view of pure aesthetic evaluation on the one hand and from that of purely empirical causal analysis on the other, but also from a third point of view, that of the interpretation of values: what has been already said in other places on the nature of this third point of view will not be repeated here. Of its inherent value and indispensability for every historian there can be not the slightest doubt. Nor can there be any doubt that the ordinary reader of works of art history expects to be offered this too—indeed this above all. But it is not identical in its logical structure with the empirical approach .

In that case, however, anyone who wants to achieve anything in art history, in however purely empirical a vein, must also have the capacity to 'understand' artistic activity, and this is of course inconceivable if he does not also have the capacity for aesthetic judgment, or in other words the *ability* to evaluate. Parallel things might of course be said of the political or literary historian, or of the historian of religion or philosophy. But obviously this tells us nothing at all about the logical character of historical work.

Notes

This is a revised version of a paper presented for internal discussion in the committee of the Association for Social Policy in 1913, and circulated in manuscript form. As far as possible, everything of interest only to this association has been omitted, while the general discussion of methodology has been expanded. Of the other papers presented for discussion in that committee, that by Professor Spranger has been published in *Schmollers Jahrbuch für Gestzgebung, Verwaltung und Volkswirtschaft*. I confess I find this work, by a philosopher whom I greatly esteem, curiously weak, because insufficiently clear: however, for reasons of space, I shall avoid polemics with him and content myself with presenting my own point of view.

1. I must here refer to what I have said elsewhere, in my essays on " 'Objectivity' in Social Science and Social Policy," "The Logic of the Cultural Sciences" and "R. Stammlers' 'Victory' over the Materialist Interpretation of History" [*Weber: Selections in Translation* (New York: Cambridge University Press, 1978), ed. by W. G. Runciman, pp. 99–131]. Occasional deficiencies in accuracy in the individual formulations in these papers, which are more than likely, should not affect any essential point. On the 'undecidability' of certain ultimate value-judgments in a particular important problem area, I should like to refer to Gustav Radbruch's *Einführung in die Rechtswissenschaft*, 2nd ed. (1913) in particular. I differ from him on a number of points, but they are not important for the problem here being discussed.

2. In his article on "Volkswirtschaftslehre" in *Handwörterbuch der Staatswissenschaften*, 3rd ed., VIII, pp. 426–501.

3. Original reference: *Archiv für Sozialwissenschaft und Sozialpolitik*, XXII, pp. 168f [see *Weber: Selections in Translation* (New York: Cambridge University Press, 1978) ed. by W. G. Runciman, pp. 111–131].

Chapter 39

Methodological Individualism and Social Tendencies

John Watkins

Introduction

The hope which originally inspired methodology was the hope of finding a method of inquiry which would be both necessary and sufficient to guide the scientist unerringly to truth. This hope has died a natural death. Today, methodology has the more modest task of establishing certain rules and requirements which are necessary to prohibit some wrong-headed moves but insufficient to guarantee success. These rules and requirements, which circumscribe scientific inquiries without steering them in any specific direction, are of the two main kinds, formal and material. So far as I can see, the formal rules of scientific method (which comprise both logical rules and certain realistic and fruitful stipulations) are equally applicable to all the empirical sciences. You cannot, for example, deduce a universal law from a finite number of observations whether you are a physicist, a biologist, or an anthropologist. Again, a single comprehensive explanation of a whole range of phenomena is preferable to isolated explanations of each of those phenomena, whatever your field of inquiry. I shall therefore confine myself to the more disputable (I had nearly said 'more disreputable') and metaphysically impregnated part of methodology which tries to establish the appropriate *material* requirements which the *contents* of the premises of an explanatory theory in a particular field ought to satisfy. These requirements may be called regulative principles. Fundamental differences in the subject-matters of different sciences—differences to which formal methodological rules are impervious—ought, presumably, to be reflected in the regulative principles appropriate to each science. It is here that the student of the methods of the social sciences may be expected to have something distinctive to say.

An example of a regulative principle is mechanism, a metaphysical theory which governed thinking in the physical sciences from the seventeenth century until it was largely superseded by a wave or field worldview. According to mechanism, the ultimate constituents of the physical world are impenetrable particles which obey simple mechanical laws. The existence of these particles cannot be explained—at any rate by science. On the other hand, every complex physical thing or event is the result of a particular configuration of particles and can be explained in terms of the laws governing their behavior in conjunction with a description of their relative positions, masses, momenta, etc. There may be what might be described as unfinished or halfway explanations of large-scale phenomena (say, the pressure inside a gas container) in terms of other large-scale factors (the volume and temperature of the gas); but we shall not have arrived at rock-bottom explanations of such large-scale phenomena until we have deduced their behavior from statements about the properties and relations of particles.

Reprinted from *British Journal for the Philosophy of Science* 8 (1957), pp. 104–117, originally appearing under the title "Historical Explanation in the Social Sciences," by permission of the author.

This is a typically metaphysical idea (by which I intend nothing derogatory). True, it is confirmed, even massively confirmed, by the huge success of mechanical theories which conform to its requirements. On the other hand, it is untestable. No experiment could overthrow it. If certain phenomena—say, electromagnetic phenomena—seem refractory to this mechanistic sort of explanation, this refractoriness can always (and perhaps rightly) be attributed to our inability to find a successful mechanical model rather than to an error in our metaphysical intuition about the ultimate constitution of the physical world. But while mechanism is weak enough to be compatible with any *observation* whatever, while it is an untestable and unempirical principle, it is strong enough to be incompatible with various conceivable physical *theories*. It is this which makes it a *regulative*, nonvacuous metaphysical principle. If it were compatible with everything it would regulate nothing. Some people complain that regulative principles discourage research in certain directions, but that is a part of their purpose. You cannot encourage research in one direction without discouraging research in rival directions.

I am not an advocate of mechanism but I have mentioned it because I am an advocate of an analogous principle in social science, the principle of methodological individualism.[1] According to this principle, the ultimate constituents of the social world are individual people who act more or less appropriately in the light of their dispositions and understanding of their situation. Every complex social situation, institution, or event is the result of a particular configuration of individuals, their dispositions, situations, beliefs, and physical resources and environment. There may be unfinished or halfway explanations of large-scale social phenomena (say, inflation) in terms of other large-scale phenomena (say, full employment); but we shall not have arrived at rock-bottom explanations of such large-scale phenomena until we have deduced an account of them from statements about the dispositions, beliefs, resources, and interrelations of individuals. (The individuals may remain anonymous and only typical dispositions, etc., may be attributed to them.) And just as mechanism is contrasted with the organicist idea of physical fields, so methodological individualism is contrasted with sociological holism or organicism. On this latter view, social systems constitute 'wholes' at least in the sense that some of their large-scale behavior is governed by macro-laws which are essentially *sociological* in the sense that they are *sui generis* and not to be explained as mere regularities or tendencies resulting from the behavior of interacting individuals. On the contrary, the behavior of individuals should (according to sociological holism) be explained at least partly in terms of such laws (perhaps in conjunction with an account, first of individuals' rôles within institutions and secondly of the functions of institutions within the whole social system). If methodological individualism means that human beings are supposed to be the only moving agents in history, and if sociological holism means that some superhuman agents or factors are supposed to be at work in history, then these two alternatives are exhaustive. An example of such a superhuman, sociological factor is the alleged long-term cyclical wave in economic life which is supposed to be self-propelling, uncontrollable, and inexplicable in terms of human activity, but in terms of the fluctuations of which such large-scale phenomena as wars, revolutions, and mass emigration, and such psychological factors as scientific and technological inventiveness can, it is claimed, be explained and predicted.

I say 'and predicted' because the irreducible sociological laws postulated by holists are usually regarded by them as laws of social development, as laws governing the dynamics of a society. This makes holism well-nigh equivalent to historicism, to the idea that a society is impelled along a predetermined route by historical laws which cannot be resisted but which can be discerned by the sociologist. The holist-historicist position has, in my view, been irretrievably damaged by Popper's attacks on it. I shall criticise this position only in so far as this will help me to elucidate and defend the individualistic alternative to it. The central assumption of the individualistic position—an assumption which is admittedly counterfactual and metaphysical—is that no social tendency exists which could not be altered *if* the individuals concerned both wanted to alter it and possessed the appropriate information. (They might want to alter the tendency but, through ignorance of the facts and/or failure to work out some of the implications of their action, fail to alter it, or perhaps even intensify it.) This assumption could also be expressed by saying that no social tendency is somehow imposed on human beings 'from above' (or 'from below')—social tendencies are the product (usually undesigned) of human characteristics and activities and situations, of people's ignorance and laziness as well as of their knowledge and ambition. (An example of a social tendency is the tendency of industrial units to grow larger. I do not call 'social' those tendencies which are determined by uncontrollable physical factors, such as the alleged tendency for more male babies to be born in times of disease or war.)[2]

My procedure will be: first, to delimit the sphere in which methodological individualism works in two directions; second, to clear methodological individualism of certain misunderstandings; third, to indicate how fruitful and surprising individualistic explanations can be and how individualistic social theories can lead to sociological discoveries; and fourth, to consider in somewhat more detail how, according to methodological individualism, we should frame explanations, first for social regularities or repeatable processes, and secondly for unique historical constellations of events.

Where Methodological Individualism Does Not Work

There are two areas in which methodological individualism does not work. The first is a probability situation where accidental and unpredictable irregularities in human behavior have a fairly regular and predictable overall result.[3] Suppose I successively place 1,000 individuals facing north in the centre of a symmetrical room with two exits, one east, the other west. If about 500 leave by one exit and about 500 by the other I would not try to explain this in terms of tiny undetectable west-inclining and east-inclining differences in the individuals, for the same reason that Popper would not try to explain the fact that about 500 balls will topple over to the west and about 500 to the east, if 1,000 balls are dropped from immediately above a north-south blade, in terms of tiny undetectable west-inclining and east-inclining differences in the balls. For in both cases such an 'explanation' would merely raise the further problem: why should these west-inclining and east-inclining differences be distributed approximately *equally* among the individuals and among the balls?

Those statistical regularities in social life which are inexplicable in individualistic terms for the sort of reason I have quoted here are, in a sense, inhuman, the outcome of a large number of sheer *accidents*. The outcome of a large number of decisions is usually much less regular and predictable because variable human factors (changes of taste, new ideas, swings from optimism to pessimism) which have little or no influence on accident rates are influential here. Thus stock exchange prices fluctuate widely from year to year, whereas the number of road accidents does not fluctuate widely. But the existence of these actuarial regularities does not, as has often been alleged, support the historicist idea that defenseless individuals like you and me are at the chance mercy of the inhuman and uncontrollable tendencies of our society. It does not support a secularized version of the Calvinist idea of an Almighty Providence who picks people at random to fill His fixed damnation quota. For we can control these statistical regularities insofar as we can alter the conditions on which they depend. For example, we could obviously abolish road accidents if we were prepared to prohibit motor traffic.

The second kind of social phenomenon to which methodological individualism is inapplicable is where some kind of physical connection between people's nervous systems short-circuits their intelligent control and causes automatic, and perhaps in some sense appropriate, bodily responses. I think that a man may more or less literally smell danger and instinctively back away from unseen ambushers; and individuality seems to be temporarily submerged beneath a collective physical *rapport* at jive sessions and revivalist meetings and among panicking crowds. But I do not think that these spasmodic mob organisms lend much support to holism or constitute a very serious exception to metholological individualism. They have a fleeting existence which ends when their members put on their mufflers and catch the bus or otherwise disperse, whereas holists have conceived of a social whole as something which endures through generations of men; and whatever holds together typical long-lived institutions, like a bank or a legal system or a church, it certainly is not the physical proximity of their members.

Misunderstandings of Methodological Individualism

I will now clear methodological individualism of two rather widespread misunderstandings.

It has been objected that in making individual dispositions and beliefs and situations the terminus of an explanation in social science, methodological individualism implies that a person's psychological make-up is, so to speak, God-given, whereas it is in fact conditioned by, and ought to be explained in terms of, his social inheritance and environment.[4] Now methodological individualism certainly does not prohibit attempts to explain the formation of psychological characteristics; it only requires that such explanations should in turn be *individualistic*, explaining the formation as the result of a series of conscious or unconscious responses by an individual to his changing situation. For example, I have heard Professor Paul Sweezy, the Harvard economist, explain that he became a Marxist because his father, a Wall Street broker, sent him in the 1930s to the London School of Economics to study under those staunch liberal economists, Professors Hayek and Robbins. This explanation is perfectly compatible with methodological individualism (though hardly compatible, I should have thought, with the Marxist idea that ideologies reflect class positions) because it interprets his ideological development as a human response to his situation. It is, I suppose, psychoanalysts who have most systematically worked the idea of a thorough individualist and historical explanation of the formation of dispositions, unconscious fears and beliefs, and subsequent defense mechanisms, in terms of responses to emotionally charged, and especially childhood, situations.

My point could be put by saying that methodological individualism encourages *innocent* explanations but forbids *sinister* explanations of the widespread existence of a disposition among the members of a social group. Let me illustrate this by quoting from a reply I made to Goldstein's criticisms.

> Suppose that it is established that Huguenot traders were relatively prosperous in seventeenth-century France and that this is explained in terms of a widespread disposition among them (a disposition for which there is independent evidence) to plough back into their businesses a larger proportion of their profits than was customary among their Catholic competitors. Now this explanatory disposition

might very well be explained in its turn—perhaps in terms of the general thriftiness which Calvinism is said to encourage, and/or in terms of the fewer alternative outlets for the cash resources of people whose religious disabilities prevented them from buying landed estates or political offices. (I cannot vouch for the historical accuracy of this example.)

I agree that methodological individualism allows the formation, or 'cultural conditioning,' of a widespread disposition to be explained only in terms of other human factors and not in terms of something *in*human, such as an alleged historicist law which impels people willy-nilly along some pre-determined course. But this is just the anti-historicist point of methodological individualism.

Unfortunately, it is typically a part of the program of Marxist and other historicist sociologies to try to account for the formation of ideologies and other psychological characteristics in strictly sociological and nonpsychological terms. Marx for instance professed to believe that feudal ideas and bourgeois ideas are more or less literally generated by the water mill and the steam engine. But no description, however complete, of the productive apparatus of a society, or of any other nonpsychological factors, will enable you to deduce a single psychological conclusion from it, because psychological statements logically cannot be deduced from wholly nonpsychological statements. Thus whereas the mechanistic idea that explanations in physics cannot go behind the impenetrable particles is a prejudice (though a very understandable prejudice), the analogous idea that an explanation which begins by imputing some social phenomenon to human factors cannot go on to explain those factors in terms of some inhuman determinant of them is a necessary truth. That the human mind develops under various influences the methodological individualist does not, of course, deny. He only insists that such development must be explained 'innocently' as a series of responses by the individual to situations and not 'sinisterly' and illogically as a direct causal outcome of nonpsychological factors, whether these are neurological factors, or impersonal sociological factors alleged to be at work in history.

Another cause of complaint against methodological individualism is that it has been confused with a narrow species of itself (Popper calls it 'psychologism') and even, on occasion, with a still narrower subspecies of this (Popper calls it the "Conspiracy Theory of Society").[5] Psychologism says that all large-scale social characteristics are not merely the intended or unintended result of, but a *reflection* of, individual characteristics.[6] Thus Plato said that the character and make-up of a *polis* is a reflection of the character and makeup of the kind of soul predominant in it. The conspiracy theory says that all large-scale social phenomena (do not merely reflect individual characteristics but) are deliberately brought about by individuals or groups of individuals.

Now there are social phenomena, like mass unemployment, which it would not have been in anyone's interest deliberately to bring about and which do not appear to be large-scale social reflections or magnified duplicates of some individual characteristic. The practical or technological or therapeutic importance of social science largely consists in explaining, and thereby perhaps rendering politically manageable, the unintended and unfortunate consequences of the behavior of interacting individuals. From this pragmatic point of view, psychologism and the conspiracy theory are unrewarding doctrines. Psychologism says that only a change of heart can put a stop to, for example, war (I think that this is Bertrand Russell's view). The conspiracy theory, faced with a big bad social event, leads to a hunt for scapegoats. But methodological individualism, by imputing unwanted social phenomena to individuals' responses to their situations, in the light of their dispositions and beliefs, suggests that we may be able to make the phenomena disappear, not by recruiting good men to fill the posts hitherto occupied by bad men, nor by trying to destroy men's socially unfortunate dispositions while fostering their socially beneficial dispositions, but simply by altering the situations they confront. To give a current example, by confronting individuals with dearer money and reduced credit the government may (I do not say will) succeed in halting inflation without requiring a new self-denying attitude on the part of consumers and without sending anyone to prison.

Factual Discoveries in Social Science

To explain the unintended but *beneficial* consequences of individual activities—by 'beneficial consequences' I mean social consequences which the individuals affected *would* endorse *if* they were called on to choose between their continuation or discontinuation—is usually a task of less practical urgency than the explanation of undesirable consequences. On the other hand, this task may be of greater theoretical interest. I say this because people who are painfully aware of the existence of unwanted social phenomena may be oblivious of the unintended but beneficial consequences of men's actions, rather as a man may be oblivious of the good health to which the smooth functioning of his digestion, nervous system, circulation, etc., give rise. Here, an explanatory social theory may surprise and enlighten us not only with regard to the connections between causes and effect but with regard to the existence of the effect itself. By showing that a certain economic system contains positive feedback leading to increasingly violent oscillations and crises an economist may explain a range of well-advertised phenomena which have long been the subject of strenuous political agitation. But the economists who first showed that a certain kind of economic system contains negative feedback which tends to iron out disturbances and restore equilibrium, not only explained, but also revealed the existence of phenomena which had hardly been remarked upon before.[7]

I will speak of organic-like social behavior where members of some social system (that is, a collection of people whose activities disturb and influence each other) mutually adjust themselves to the situations created by the others in a way which, without direction from above, conduces to the equilibrium or preservation or development of the system. (These are again evaluative notions, but they can also be given a 'would-be-endorsed-if' definition.) Now such far-flung organic-like behavior, involving people widely separated in space and largely ignorant of each other, cannot be simply observed. It can only be theoretically reconstructed—by deducing the distant social consequences of the typical responses of a large number of interacting people to certain repetitive situations. This explains why individualistic-minded economists and anthropologists, who deny that societies really are organisms, have succeeded in piecing together a good deal of unsuspected organic-like social behavior, from an examination of individual dispositions and situations, whereas sociological holists, who insist that societies really are organisms, have been noticeably unsuccessful in convincingly displaying any organic-like social behavior—they cannot observe it and they do not try to reconstruct it individualistically.

There is a parallel between holism and psychologism which explains their common failure to make surprising discoveries. A large-scale social characteristic should be explained, according to psychologism, as the manifestation of analogous small-scale psychological tendencies in individuals, and according to holism as the manifestation of a large-scale tendency in the social whole. In both cases, the *explicans* does little more than duplicate the *explicandum*. The methodological individualist, on the other hand, will try to explain the large-scale effect as the *indirect*, unexpected, complex product of individual factors none of which, singly, may bear any resemblance to it at all. To use hackneyed examples, he may show that a longing for peace led, in a certain international situation, to war, or that a government's desire to improve a bad economic situation by balancing its budget only worsened the situation. Since Mandeville's *Fable of the Bees* was published in 1714, individualistic social science, with its emphasis on unintended consequences, has largely been a sophisticated elaboration on the simple theme that, in certain situations, selfish private motives may have good social consequences and good political intentions bad social consequences.[8]

Holists draw comfort from the example of biology, but I think that the parallel is really between the biologist and the methodological individualist. The biologist does not, I take it, explain the large changes which occur during, say, pregnancy, in terms of corresponding large teleological tendencies in the organism, but physically, in terms of small chemical, cellular, neurological, etc., changes, none of which bears any resemblance to their joint and seemingly planful outcome.

How Social Explanations Should Be Framed

I will now consider how regularities in social life, such as the trade cycle, should be explained according to methodological individualism. The explanation should be in terms of individuals and their situations; and since the process to be explained is repeatable, liable to recur at various times and in various parts of the world, it follows that only very general assumptions about human dispositions can be employed in its explanation. It is no use looking to abnormal psychology for an explanation of the structure of interest rates—everyday experience must contain the raw material for the dispositional (as opposed to the situational) assumptions required by such an explanation. It may require a stroke of genius to detect, isolate, and formulate precisely the dispositional premises of an explanation of a social regularity. These premises may state what no one had noticed before, or give a sharp articulation to what had hitherto been loosely described. But once stated they will seem obvious enough. It took years of groping by brilliant minds before a precise formulation was found for the principle of diminishing marginal utility. But once stated, the principle—that the less, relatively, a man has of one divisible commodity the more compensation he will be disposed to require for foregoing a small fixed amount of it—is a principle to which pretty well everyone will give his consent. Yet this simple and almost platitudinous principle is the magic key to the economics of distribution and exchange.

The social scientist is, here, in a position analogous to that of the Cartesian mechanist.[9] The latter never set out to discover new and unheard-of physical principles because he believed that his own principle of action-by-contact was self-evidently ultimate. His problem was to discover the typical physical configurations, the mechanisms, which, operating according to this principle, produce the observed regularities of nature. His theories took the form of models which exhibited such regularities as the outcome of 'self-evident' physical principles operating in some hypothetical physical situation. Similarly, the social scientist does not make daring innovations in psychology but relies on familiar, almost 'self-evident' psychological material. His skill consists, first in spotting the relevant dispositions, and secondly in inventing a simple but realistic model which shows how, in a precise type of situation, those dispositions generate some typical regularity or process. (His model, by the way, will also show that in this situation certain things cannot happen. His negative predictions of the form, 'If you got this you can't have that as well' may be of great practical importance.)

The social scientist can now explain in principle historical examples of this regular process, provided his model does in fact fit the historical situation.

This view of the explanation of social regularities incidentally clears up the old question on which so much ink has been spilt about whether the so-called laws of economics apply universally or only to a particular 'stage' of economic development. The simple answer is that the economic principles displayed by economists' models apply only to those situations which correspond with their models; but a single model may very well correspond with a very large number of historical situations widely separated in space and time.

In the explanation of regularities the same situational scheme or model is used to reconstruct a number of historical situations with a similar structure in a way which reveals how typical dispositions and beliefs of anonymous individuals generated, on each occasion, the same regularity.[10] In the explanation of a unique constellation of events the individualistic method is again to reconstruct the historical situation, or connected sequence of situations, in a way which reveals how (usually both named and anonymous) individuals, with their beliefs and dispositions (which may include peculiar personal dispositions as well as typical human dispositions), generated, in this particular situation, the joint product to be explained. I emphasize *dispositions*, which are open and law-like, as opposed to *decisions*, which are occurrences, for this reason. A person's set of dispositions ought, under varying conditions, to give rise to appropriately varying decisions. The subsequent occurrence of an appropriate decision will both confirm, and be explained by, the existence of the dispositions. Suppose that a historical explanation (of, say, the growth of the early Catholic Church) largely relies on a particular decision (say, the decision of Emperor Constantine to give Pope Silvester extensive temporal rights in Italy). The explanation is, so far, rather *ad hoc*: an apparently arbitrary *fiat* plays a key role in it. But if this decision can in turn be explained as the offspring of a marriage of a set of dispositions (for instance, the emperor's disposition to subordinate all rival power to himself) to a set of circumstances (for instance, the emperor's recognition that Christianity could not be crushed but could be tamed if it became the official religion of the empire), and if the existence of these dispositions and circumstances is convincingly supported by independent evidence, then the area of the arbitrarily given, of sheer brute fact in history, although it can never he made to vanish, will have been significantly reduced.

Notes

1. Both of these analogous principles go back at least to Epicurus. In recent times methodological individualism has been powerfully defended by Professor F. A. Hayek in his *Individualism and Economic Order* and *The Counter-Revolution of Science*, and by Professor K. R. Popper in his *The Open Society and its Enemies* and 'The Poverty of Historicism.' *Economica*, 1944–45, **11–12**. Following in their footsteps I have also attempted to defend methodological individualism in 'Ideal Types and Historical Explanation,' *British Journal for the Philosophy of Science*, 1952, **3**, 22, reprinted in *Readings in the Philosophy of Science*, ed. Feigl and Brodbeck, New York, 1953. This article has come in for a good deal of criticism, the chief items of which I shall try to rebut in what follows.

2. The issue of holism *versus* individualism in social science has recently been presented as though it were a question of the existence or nonexistence of irreducibly social *facts* rather than of irreducibly sociological *laws*. [See M. Mandelbaum 'Societal Facts,' *The British Journal of Sociology*, 1955, **6**, (reprinted in *Theories of History*, P. Gardiner, ed., The Free Press, New York, 1959, pp. 476–488) and E. A. Gellner, "Explanations in History,' *Aristotelian Society*, Supplementary Volume **30**, 1956. This way of presenting the issue seems to me to empty it of most of its interest. If a new kind of beast is discovered, what we want to know is not so much whether it falls outside existing zoological categories, but how it behaves. People who insist on the existence of social facts but who do not say whether they are governed by sociological laws, are like people who claim to have discovered an

unclassified kind of animal but who do not tell us whether it is tame or dangerous, whether it can be domesticated or is unmanageable. If an answer to the question of social facts could throw light on the serious and interesting question of sociological laws, then the question of social facts would also be serious and interesting. But this is not so. On the one hand, a holist may readily admit (as I pointed out in my "Ideal Types" paper, which Gellner criticizes) that all observable social facts *are* reducible to individual facts and yet hold that the latter are invisibly governed by irreducibly sociological laws. On the other hand, an individualist may readily admit (as Gellner himself says) that some large social facts are simply too complex for a full reduction of them to be feasible, and yet hold that individualistic explanations of them are in principle possible, just as a physicist may readily admit that some physical facts (for instance, the precise blast effects of a bomb explosion in a built-up area) are just too complex for accurate prediction or explanation of them to be feasible and yet hold that precise explanations and predictions of them in terms of existing scientific laws are in principle possible.

This revised way of presenting the holism *versus* individualism issue does not only divert attention from the important question. It also tends to turn the dispute into a purely verbal issue. Thus Mandelbaum is able to prove the existence of what he calls 'societal facts' because he defines psychological facts very narrowly as 'facts concerning the thoughts and actions of specific human beings' (*op. cit.*). Consequently, the *dispositions* of *anonymous individuals* which play such an important rôle in individualistic explanations in social science are 'societal facts' merely by definition.

3. Failure to exclude probability situations from the ambit of methodological individualism was an important defect of my "Ideal Types" paper. Here, Gellner's criticism (*op. cit.*) does hit the nail on the head.

4. Thus Gellner writes: 'The real oddity of the reductionist [i.e., the methodological individualist's] case is that it seems to preclude *a priori* the possibility of human dispositions being the dependent variable in an historical explanation—when in fact they often or always are' (*op. cit*). And Leon J. Goldstein says that in making human dispositions methodologically primary I ignore that cultural conditioning (*The Journal of Philosophy*, 1956, **53**, 807).

5. See K. R. Popper, *The Open Society and its Enemies*, 2nd ed., 1952, ch. 14.

6. I am at a loss to understand how Gellner came to make the following strange assertion: '... Popper refers to both "psychologism" which he condemns, and "methodological individualism," which he commends. When in the articles discussed [i.e., my "Ideal Types" paper] "methodological individualism" is worked out more fully than is the case in Popper's book, it seems to me to be indistinguishable from "Psychologism."' Finding no difference between methodological individualism and a caricature of methodological individualism, Gellner has no difficulty in poking fun at the whole idea: 'Certain tribes I know have what anthropologists call a segmentary patrilineal structure, which moreover maintains itself very well over time. I could "explain" this by saying that the tribesmen have, all or most of them, dispositions whose effect is to maintain the system. But, of course, not only have they never given the matter much thought, but it also might very well be impossible to isolate anything in the characters and conduct of the individual tribesmen which *explains* how they come to maintain the system' (*op. cit.*). Yet this example actually suggests the lines along which an individualistic explanation might be found. The very fact that the tribesmen *have never given the matter much thought*, the fact that they accept their inherited system uncritically, may constitute an important part of an explanation of its stability. The explanation might go on to pinpoint certain rules—that is firm and widespread dispositions—about marriage, inheritance, etc., which help to regularize the tribesmen's behavior toward their kinsmen. How they come to share these common dispositions could also be explained individualistically in the same sort of way that I can explain why my young children are already developing a typically English attitude toward policemen.

7. This sentence, as I have learnt from Dr. A. W. Phillips, is unduly complacent, for it is very doubtful whether an economist can ever *show* that an economic system containing negative feedback will be stable. For negative feedback may produce either a tendency toward equilibrium, or increasing oscillations, according to the numerical values of the parameters of the system. But numerical values are just what economic measurements, which are usually ordinal rather than cardinal, seldom yield. The belief that a system which contains negative feedback, but whose variables cannot be described quantitatively, is stable may be based on faith or experience, but it cannot be shown mathematically. See A. W. Phillips, 'Stabilisation Policy and the Time-Forms of Lagged Responses,' *The Economic Journal*, 1957, **67**.

8. A good deal of unmerited opposition to methodological individualism seems to spring from the recognition of the undoubted fact that individuals often run into social obstacles. Thus the conclusion at which Mandelbaum arrives is 'that there are societal facts which exercise external constraints over individuals' (*op. cit.*). This conclusion is perfectly harmonious with the methodological individualist's insistence that plans often miscarry (and that even when they do succeed, they almost invariably have

other important and unanticipated effects). The methodological individualist only insists that the social environment by which any particular individual is confronted and frustrated and sometimes manipulated and occasionally destroyed is, if we ignore its physical ingredients, made up of other *people*, their habits, inertia, loyalties, rivalries, and so on. What the methodological individualist denies is that an individual is ever frustrated, manipulated or destroyed or borne along by irreducible sociological or historical *laws*.

9. I owe this analogy to Professor Popper.

10. This should rebut Gellner's conclusions that methodological individualism would transform social scientists into 'biographers *en grande série*' (*op. cit.*).

Chapter 40

Fact and Method in the Social Sciences

Richard W. Miller

At one and the same time, we think about methodology in the social sciences in two different ways. These ways of thinking conflict, and that conflict has crippled the social sciences.

On the one hand, we think of methodology as consisting of principles describing what a social scientist should do in pursuing his or her explanations. This first way of thinking about methodology is unavoidable. If there are no principles describing what research and explanation should be like, there is no methodology.

The second way of thinking about methodology almost always accompanies the first, though it is usually unannounced. In the first and unavoidable view, methodology consists of principles regulating empirical social-scientific research. In the second view, avoidable but nearly universal, methodology consists of social-scientific principles requiring no research. We limit ourselves to statements about social reality that require no controversial empirical commitments. We only rely on principles of logic and the analysis of such concepts as "adequate explanation," "fact," and "value," together, perhaps, with thoroughly obvious factual considerations and armchair reflections giving rise to intuitions of the truth. The methodological, here, is the a priori.

The unavoidable conception of the goals of methodology conflicts with the pervasive conception of the basis for methodology. The questions defining the subject matter of methodology cannot be answered a priori. In the contrary view, which I shall be defending, methodology does not stand above social science, unalterable by it, like the law of the excluded middle. It includes principles governing science that might be changed in light of changes in science, like principles of telescopic observation in astronomy.

My argument will be a survey of some leading issues in the methodology of the social sciences. First, I shall consider the status of value freedom and of methodological individualism. Despite the assumptions to the contrary shared by both their partisans and their opponents, these doctrines, I shall argue, are empirical theses. They depend on controversial theories concerning the impact of social circumstances on individual psychology (including, in the case of value freedom, the social scientist's own psychology). Certain extremely plausible aspects of Marxist social theory, usually neglected in these debates, suggest nontraditional outcomes for these traditional methodological disputes.

Finally, I will discuss the two related questions: "What makes a hypothesis, if true, an adequate explanation?", and "What makes it rational to accept an explanation, in light of available data?" In the covering-law model of Hempel, Popper, and other positivists, the capacity of a true hypothesis to explain a phenomenon is just a matter of its logical relations to that phenomenon. Similarly, at least in standard and central

Reprinted with revisions by the author from *Changing Social Science*, ed. D. Sabia and J. Wallulis (Albany, NY: SUNY Press, 1983), pp. 73–101, by permission of the author and the publisher.

cases, an explanation is confirmed by a body of data because of its logical relations to that data. I shall argue that this division of labor between logic and empirical theory needs to be shifted. In typical cases, adequacy and confirmation depend on empirical principles not part of the hypothesis itself or included in the data. While I shall usually contrast this approach to the logic of explanation with the positivist model, I shall also discuss its great distance from critical theory. Here, much more than elsewhere, critical theory resembles its positivist rival, basing explanation on a repertoire of a priori principles, and accepting the positivist analysis of explanation in the natural sciences.

Value Freedom

That the social sciences should be value free is the closest thing to a methodological dogma in Anglo-American social science. It has a sacred text of sorts, Weber's methodological writings. Like many dogmas, it is often misunderstood by orthodox believers and heretics alike.

Value freedom, for Weber, includes two claims, which he constantly mixes together. On the one hand, evaluations are excluded from the content of explanations. A valid explanation of a social phenomenon never makes a value judgment.[1] A social scientist respecting this rule cannot, for example, explain the downfall of the Stuarts, in Whig fashion, as due to Stuart injustice. Note, however, that nothing in this antimoralizing principle precludes describing people's evaluations in an explanation so long as one does not endorse or disapprove them. The downfall of Stuart autocracy may well have been due to the widespread *belief* in its injustice.

Along with this constraint on the content of explanations, value freedom calls for a constraint on the context in which social-scientific explanations are pursued. Once he or she has chosen what explanatory questions to answer, the social scientist should, so far as possible, try to forget his or her extrascientific commitments in pursuing the answer.[2] The timing of nonpartisanship is crucial, here. Weber is well aware that the choice of a question guides subsequent research, that it is rational to choose more important questions over less important ones, and that judgments of importance depend on moral and political judgments.[3] Once the choice of questions has been made, however, the researcher should try to pursue the answers dispassionately, or, more precisely, warmed only by the passion for the truth as such.

Value freedom has always had its critics. But both critics and defenders have accepted common, a priorist rules of debate. They assume that value freedom, if true, depends on logical distinctions and mere common sense; if false, it depends on logical confusions or *obvious* distortions of reality.

Weber bases the exclusion of evaluation from the content of social-scientific explanation mainly on an alleged characteristic of all scientific propositions. A scientific proposition, if valid, must be demonstrable, in principle, to everyone possessing all relevant data. Value judgments, Weber claims, are not universally demonstrable, as scientific propositions should be.[4]

Depending on how demonstrability is understood, either the denial of this characteristic to all value judgments is wrong empirically, or undeniably scientific propositions cannot meet the test of demonstrability any better than some value judgments. When he speaks of demonstrability to all, Weber seems to have in mind demonstrability to all actual rational people. His examples always refer to actual cultural and political differences.[5] With typical ethnocentricity (and its political equivalent), he denies that there is hope of establishing socially significant value judgments for everyone, "even" a Chinese or a revolutionary socialist.[6]

Fact and Method in the Social Sciences 745

In fact, there seem to be a number of value judgments that any actual rational person could be brought to accept, if he or she knew all relevant facts. There is no evidence of any moral framework in which chattel slavery or the Nazis' Final Solution is less than evil, when all the facts are in. Indeed, even Nazis and slaveholders speaking among themselves had to rely on false statements of fact concerning Jews and enslaved peoples to justify their actions. A justification based on the real facts, "German Jews typically have a slightly different culture from non-Jews; though a small minority, they are a somewhat disproportionate one in banking and the arts; therefore they should be killed," is as blatant a non sequitur as any blunder in scientific inference.

Perhaps, though, Weber meant to require that a scientific proposition be demonstrable (if true) not just to all actual but to all possible rational beings. In this conception, the bare possibility of an ultimate Nazi for whom the death of Jews is an intrinsic good, standing in need of no justification, makes the condemnation of the Final Solution relevantly nondemonstrable.

Perhaps no value judgment can pass this test. If not, neither can the most important explanatory hypotheses in the social sciences. In the realm of bare possibility, there exists an ultimate anti-Weberian for whom it is fundamental truth, requiring no justification, that businessmen do not let religious beliefs interfere with their business practices. Weber's own social-scientific thesis about Calvinism and the rise of capitalism could not be demonstrated to this possible being. Surely, his resistance should not deprive Weber's thesis of scientific status. Perhaps the ultimate anti-Weberian is irrational, because he does not see that this separation of religion from business requires justification. There are no grounds, however, for denying rationality to him, but not to the ultimate Nazi, who does not recognize that killing people with a certain family background requires justification.

Weber offers some other arguments for value freedom, along similar lines. I have argued elsewhere[7] that they fail for similar reasons. They depend either on a far-fetched estimate of the actual diversity among the moral outlooks of rational people, or on a standard of scientific status so high that even the most interesting and important social-scientific propositions cannot meet it.

Weber's denial that value judgments are subject to scientific argument has harmed not just the official methodology, but the practice of the social sciences. If stated at all, the value judgments that guide an investigator are usually treated as stipulations, not requiring the theoretical or empirical justification that equally basic social-scientific claims would need. Yet, often, the questioning of these evaluative assumptions is the most obvious, urgent, and coherent means of developing alternatives to the explanatory hypothesis which the investigator supports.

Consider, for example, the discussion of United States foreign policy after World War II in Theodore Lowi's *The End of Liberalism*. The failures of United States foreign policy after the Second World War are traced to the dispersal of leadership among a variety of cabinet and subcabinet departments and government agencies, allied in turn with diverse interest groups. Central to Lowi's argument is the claim that crises, which dictate temporary unification of leadership, "tend to bring out the very best in Americans," in contrast to the normal dispersal of leadership. This claim is only supported through a brief list of "postwar examples of exemplary behavior in crisis": "Greek-Turkish aid and the Truman Doctrine, the Berlin Airlift, the response to the Korean invasion, the Dienbienphu crisis of 1954, the Arab-Israeli intervention of 1956, and 1962 Cuban missile crisis, the 1967 and 1973 Arab-Israeli Wars." Lowi acknowledges in a footnote that here, as elsewhere, he makes value judgments, based, essentially, on the belief that effective United States action in foreign affairs has reflected "vital," "legitimate," and "rational" interests.[8]

Lowi's acknowledgment of his value judgments is typical of that combination of forthrightness and theoretical sophistication that have made his writings so influential. But here, as usual, labelling judgments as evaluative serves as a license for avoiding crucial arguments. What about responses to crises missing from the list: interventions in Guatemala, Lebanon, Iran, and the Dominican Republic, the response to the uprising in South Vietnam of 1956, or the response to the demonstrations which brought down the Shah in 1978? Did these crises produce initiatives reflecting a legitimate, vital and rational interest involving the people of the United States as a whole? Even among the crises on Lowi's list, is it obvious that vital and legitimate interests were rationally served by providing massive material aid for the French empire in Indochina or by bringing the world to the brink of war over the missiles in Cuba?

Of course, an investigator must choose which issues to discuss in detail, and has a right to brief pronouncements on questions outside the chosen subject matter. But in fact it is the evaluative challenge to the legitimacy of United States foreign policy, both in crisis and in between, that has been the impetus for arguments in support of a major alternative to Lowi's own thesis: Failure and drift in United States foreign policy have reflected conflicts between the interests dominating foreign policy, on the one hand, and, on the other, the interests and fundamental moral convictions of most people in the United States and most people in the world.

In practice, Weber assumes that the exclusion of evaluation from the content of explanations entails nonpartisanship in the pursuit of explanations, as well. Certainly he offers no independent argument for the latter aspect of value freedom. But the inference does not work. Even if valid explanations did not evaluate, there could be contexts in which a researcher is most apt to arrive at valid explanations when committed to certain value judgments. In general, the absence of certain kinds of propositions from the content of explanations does not dictate their absence from maxims governing the pursuit of such explanations. Valid astronomical hypotheses do not refer to drunkenness or sobriety. We do not explain an eclipse as due to the moon's being drunk. But it is a sound maxim only to make astronomical observations while sober.

Arguments to the effect that the social sciences should be value-laden are, typically, just as nonempirical as Weber's that they should be value-free. Often, partisans of values oversimplify Weber's thesis, then knock down their straw man with truisms. In particular, Weber's acknowledgement of the importance of values in choosing questions is widely ignored.[9] Another common strategy is to attack Weber's fact-value distinction, arguing that value judgments may be factual statements as well.[10] This is a necessary preliminary to introducing value judgments into the realm of social-scientific explanations. But it is hardly sufficient. Statements about the stars are factual, too. But few social scientists are so astrological as to suppose that they should figure in social scientific explanations.

The question of whether the social sciences should be value-free is an empirical question. I shall try to show this by sketching a particular empirical case for a nontraditional resolution of the question of value freedom: certain kinds of partisanship are sometimes the best scientific policy; nonetheless, the best explanations do not evaluate; yet evaluative explanations are often true. While I do not have space to establish the relevant empirical claims, I shall try to make them relevant and plausible. That is enough to show that value freedom is an empirical issue, and to indicate what it is like to approach methodological issues in an empirical spirit.

In their prejudices and hunches, self-ignorance and self-criticism, enthusiasms and hesitations, scientists are influenced by social forces outside of science. In the social sciences, these social forces may have an important influence on typical expectations as to what projects are apt to produce definitive, scientifically useful results. They may determine what research techniques and bodies of data are elaborated and refined. They may determine, in important ways, who becomes a famous and influential figure. When these social forces create strong pressure away from the truth, the counter-pressure of certain partisan commitments to change the status quo may be more scientifically productive than neutrality.

Consider the situation of an anthropologist in the 1880s. According to the reigning ideology, the cultures of nonliterate nonwhite peoples were perhaps subhuman, at best crude simplifications of European culture. Indeed, this ideology was even embedded in grammar. In European languages in the 1880s, there is no plural for "culture," a word reserved for the traditions stemming from the ancient Greeks. As a result, research techniques and professional rewards in the investigation of nonwhite non-literate peoples centered on geography and physical anthropology, above all the intensive measurement of skulls to determine how low such peoples stood on the ladder of evolution.[11]

Along with more important costs, this ideology was the main barrier to scientific progress in anthropology. There, progress depended on the insight that nonliterate societies are held together by social and symbolic structures of great complexity. The anthropologists such as Boas who made this discovery did so through projects that were widely regarded as doomed to failure, that employed few established research tools, that challenged the views of respected figures in the profession, sometimes people of undeniable competence. Having embarked on the investigation of the social systems and mythologies of nonliterate nonwhites, these pioneers were under great pressure to give up prematurely or to come up with the wrong answers.

How are such truth-distorting pressures best resisted? One strategy is the Weberian one. The anthropologist should passionately commit himself to pursuing the truth, and should otherwise forget all moral and political commitments, whether racist or anti-racist. But perhaps this vaccine would be too weak to prevent the disease I have described. If slander against someone is pervasive enough, you may have to like him and hate his enemies, if you are not to succumb to it. Perhaps, typically and over the long run, an anthropologist of the 1880s could not clearly see the complexity and ingenuity of nonliterate nonwhites if he did not sympathize with them, feel outrage at the contempt in which they were held, or hate their oppression by the colonial system. More precisely, the probable scientific gains of keeping alive one's attachment to antiracist value judgments in doing research might outweigh the associated risks of wishful thinking and sentimentality. If so, then an injunction to cultivate antiracist sentiments in the course of research would be better methodology than the injunction to be neutral.

There is evidence from the history of anthropology that the partisan maxim would be scientifically superior. The pioneers of modern anthropology were typically sustained by antiracist commitments during their years of fieldwork and bitter controversy. Boas, for example, always regarded the survival in his childhood home of "the ideals of the Revolution of 1848" as a crucial influence on his scientific activity.[12]

The scientific usefulness of egalitarian commitments is not only plausible for the *eighteen*-eighties. In the present-day United States, the people in one percent of the spending units who own two-thirds of the individually held corporate stock (and especially in the .1 percent who own one third) have disproportionate influence on the media, the foundations, and government, and therefore have important indirect influence on large scale projects, research tools, and the roads to fame in the social sciences. These extrascientific forces, among others, strongly support a consensus that present-day hierarchies cannot be changed and have many hidden benefits. As a result, in the real-life social setting of social science no political scientist is forced to defend the view that the United States working class (referred to by some euphemism) is extremely conservative. No economist is forced to defend the view that racism is against the interests of corporations. In these and other cases, consensus reigns in spite of contrary evidence offering substantial grounds for doubt.[13] Scientists operating outside the consensus are usually consigned to marginal status in a "left-wing" fringe. Perhaps a commitment to the truth is a sufficient defense against social pressures to conform. But alternatively, a lively commitment to social change could be an important scientific good in the 1980s, as it was in the 1880s.

This argument for partisanship does not imply in the least that explanations of social phenomena should ever themselves include evaluations. There is evidence from the history of social science that the best explanations do not evaluate. Evaluative explanation is most promising where large social changes are explained as due to moral defects of the old arrangements. However, at least since the time of Harrington and Hobbes, the most productive framework for explaining social change has appealed to the interests, resources, social relations, and cultural traditions of social groups, described in nonevaluative terms.

A social scientist operating in this framework need not be totally Weberian. He need not (indeed he should not) deny that an evaluation may yield a *true* explanation. But he will, at a minimum, regard such explanations as more vague and less fruitful than those that are yielded by the study of interests, resources, and cultural traditions. Thus, histories of slavery in the United States emphasizing the shifting resources and interests of plantation owners, slaves, farmers, industrialists, and merchants do not contradict the appeal to the injustice of slavery as a source of its overthrow. Typically, they provide at least some evidence supporting it. But the study of the political economy of the westward expansion of slavery has yielded more explanations, and more precise ones, of the history of its overthrow than the study of slavery's immorality, as such. This contrast is typical of the study of change, from English constitutional history to current debates over the Nazi seizure of power.

At the same time, causal processes ascribed in empirically valid explanations of moral outlooks often constitute sources of heightened moral insight. For example, modern ways of assessing the justice of institutions developed as they did partly because they were a means of finding a basis for stable, voluntary interaction among people with conflicting interests but increasing equality of disruptive power. Such a process is a source of increased access to moral truth, regardless of whether the claim that this is so is made in the best explanations. As we shall see, an empirically justified hypothesis must be a better explanation than any current *rival*, but the claim that our ways of assessing justice are due to the pursuit of terms of cooperation for those of equal power hardly excludes the hypothesis that they are due to a process of moral learning. On the other hand, there are debunking explanations that really do conflict with claims to moral insight. Thus, the question of our access to moral truths (including true explanations in terms of moral insight, depravity, and the like) is itself empirical.

I have barely sketched some elements of a case for commitment to fighting inequality in the course of social rsearch together with a preference for explanations that do not evaluate. All sorts of factual questions might be raised. That is my point, for present purposes. Value freedom is an empirical issue, not a refuge from the factual debates that dominate political controversy.

Methodological Individualism

The debate over methodological individualism raises very different issues from the value freedom controversy. But, here too, a dispute that should be empirical is traditionally based instead on conceptual analysis and the assertion of truisms.

By methodological individualism, I mean whatever methodologically useful doctrine is asserted in the vague claim that social explanations should be ultimately reducible to explanations in terms of people's beliefs, dispositions, and situations. Karl Popper, his student J.W.N. Watkins, and George Homans argue explicitly for this claim.[14] It is a working doctrine of most economists, political scientists, and political historians in North America and Britain. This commitment is sometimes expressed in protests against the mysteriousness of hypotheses in which someone's political behavior has sources of which he is not aware. "The Marxist assessment of fascism," writes one historian, "stands on metaphysical or at least transhistorical grounds and as such ordinary historical analysis can scarcely challenge it. The imputation of a class basis to diverse groups which themselves were usually supraclass in conscious ('subjective') orientation [is a hypothesis] which one must ... either accept on faith or reject out of hand as unrealistic."[15] Two political theorists, as it happens leading critics of the pluralist establishment, ask, "Suppose there appears to be universal acquiescence in the status quo. Is it possible, in such circumstances, to determine whether the consensus is genuine or instead has been enforced by nondecision-making [i.e., the restriction of opportunities for political controversy]? The answer must be negative. Analysis of this problem is beyond the reach of the political analyst and perhaps can only be fruitfully analyzed by a philosopher."[16]

Methodological individualism is an extemely influential idea. Yet the debate over it has been dreary, in a way that is typical of methodological disputes. Partisans of individualism usually claim that it amounts to some truism, that, say, social change is the result of what people do, or that we could reverse any social process if we had appropriate beliefs and resources and the will to do so.[17] But these truistic claims are so obvious that no social theorist, not even the most holistic, not Durkheim or Marx or even Hegel, has ever violated them.

On the other side, opponents of individualism argue to the opposite effect in much the same style. They associate methodological individualism with some totally implausible doctrine, then show it is wrong. For example, it is easy to show that the vocabulary of social science cannot be defined entirely using basic terms which could refer to isolated individuals. "Bank check" cannot be so defined, much less "the state".[18]

In fact, there is an interesting doctrine which is sometimes advanced by explicit partisans of methodological individualism, and which is an important influence on the practice of much economics, history, and political science. It is the sort of methodological individualism which is worth debating. According to this thesis, large-scale social phenomena, those affecting the characteristics of enduring institutions, should be explained as due to people's reasons for acting as they do together with the resources available to them. More precisely, those explanations should refer either solely to those reasons and resources or in addition only to processes and causal connections which can be explained in turn as due to participants' reasons and resources.

This thesis cannot be dismissed a priori. It is the framework of Weber's encyclopedic *Economy and Society*, where sociology is restricted to the explanation of social phenomena in terms of the subjective meanings that participants attach to their behavior. At the same time, it is not obviously right. In particular, it is wrong if objective interests which guide a person's behavior, even though they are not his reasons for acting as he does, play a crucial social role.

The power of objective interests to guide someone's actions when they are not his reasons for so acting is a common enough phenomenon in everyday life. A friend of mine has a brother who is a nuclear engineer. He says his brother believes that nuclear plants are quite safe. In my friend's view, the reason why his brother believes this is that he wants to see his profession as socially useful. He thinks his brother has overwhelming evidence that the plants are not safe, and "should know better." At the same time, my friend is very far from saying that an interest in serene professional pride is his brother's *reason* for asserting the safety of nuclear plants. The technical considerations to which his brother appeals really *are* his reasons.

The question of methodological individualism has now become thoroughly empirical: Does a sort of mechanism that could, a priori, play a crucial role in large-scale social processes actually do so? Once again, current yet nonstandard theories suggest a different answer from the one that dominates Anglo-American social science. For example, according to Marxist accounts of ideology, beliefs and conduct of great social significance are molded by class interests in ways of which the bearers of those interests are often not aware. If this thesis is true in significant cases, then methodological individualism is wrong.

The truth, in important cases, of such a theory of ideology is surely worthy of empirical investigation. Consider the spread of the so-called positive good doctrine of slavery in the antebellum South. Around 1820, Southern plantation owners rather suddenly stopped portraying slavery as a temporarily necessary evil, which should be allowed to die out. They began to defend it as a positive good, above all for the benefits it brought to the slaves. There is no basis for supposing the typical plantation owner lied when he or she extolled the civilizing influence of slavery. But it is not plausible that this sudden shift in opinion was actually due to an influx of evidence of the civilizing influence of slavery. A more likely candidate is the cotton gin. The gin turned slavery from an archaic relic to the basis of a thriving industry for cotton planters in the Deep South, and for the Old South slave breeders who supplied them with victims. This was not the slaveowners' reason for believing in the doctrine of "positive good." Yet, quite plausibly, it is the reason why they had this belief.

This example can stand for many others. No one can read the political and social debates under Cromwell's Commonwealth and doubt the sincerity of the religious reasoning of all sides. But historians from Hobbes to Hume to Marx to Macpherson have noticed what different conclusions were often derived from virtually identical religious premises, and have explained the divergent tendencies on the basis of rival objective interests. Closer to our time, Eisenhower, Kennedy, and Johnson may not have been lying when they based United States involvement in Indochina on the defense of freedom. But the Pentagon Papers suggest that the reason for their behavior was, primarily, an interest in continued American domination over the so-called underdeveloped countries.

Empirical claims about how people behave are the right basis for judging methodological individualism. That thesis is neither a truism nor a confusion. It is either an empirically valid means of simplifying the range of hypotheses which social scientists must consider, or, based on empirical falsehoods, a factually inappropriate device for excluding explanations which may well be the best.

The Logic of Explanation

When is a set of propositions an adequate explanation of why a social phenomenon occurred? Obviously, an adequate explanation ought to provide true descriptions of prior conditions. Almost as obviously, this requirement is not enough. That the Kaiser sneezed before World War I broke out is hardly an explanation of the outbreak of the First World War. The argument as to what further qualifications make a set of true propositions a valid explanation is the most enduring, the most fundamental, and perhaps the fiercest dispute in the philosophy of the social sciences.

In this century, the center of the dispute has been an analysis of explanation developed by positivist philosophers out of Hume's discussion of causality. In rough outline, this analysis makes explanation, whether in the social sciences or the natural sciences, a matter of subsumption under general laws. A valid explanation of an event must describe (or, at least, implicitly sketch) general characteristics of the situation leading up to the event and general empirical laws dictating that when such characteristics are realized, an event of that kind always (or almost always) follows. Carl Hempel, in particular, has elaborated this so-called covering-law model in great detail, and defended it with unparalleled resourcefulness.[19]

Except in the writing of history, the covering-law model dominates the practice of the social sciences. The major precursors of the current academic consensus in sociology, anthropology, and economics—Weber and Durkheim, Radcliffe-Brown and Malinowski, Menger, Jevons, and Walras—all regarded subsumption under general laws as the essence of scientific explanation, and took the discovery of such laws to be the means for making the social sciences truly scientific. Commitment to the covering-law model has a powerful influence on the direction of social research. For example when social anthropologists discovered that their fieldwork yielded few interesting general laws involving such relatively concrete characteristics as "grandfather," they did not abandon the pursuit of general laws. Many responded by seeking such general relationships among more abstract structural characteristics, such as "binary opposition." Many economists elaborate the internal logic of some general model, serenely accepting that their work makes no appreciable contribution to explaining specific episodes of inflation or unemployment, or trends in world trade. The intellectual justification is, basically, that the elaboration of general models is the most promising route to the discovery of general laws, in turn an essential aspect of explanations.

Most opponents of the covering-law model work in a tradition, going at least as far back as Dilthey, that emphasizes the existence of autonomous methods in history that are radically different from those in the natural sciences. The covering-law model is regarded as an accurate analysis of natural science explanation. The crucial positivist mistake is said to be its extension of the model to the realm of social explanation. Thus for Habermas the covering-law model does describe the goal of natural science inquiry, a pursuit of general laws through experiments, guided by an interest in instrumental control over the environment. But it fails to validate the insights yielded by other sources of knowledge more important for social explanation: hermeneutic understanding, that is, the capacity to interpret the words, acts, and symbols of others in the interest of mutual understanding, and self-reflection, that is, the ability to achieve the moral knowledge and self-awareness of a responsible person through self-analysis.[20]

Despite the furious controversy between positivists and those working in Dilthey's and Habermas's hermeneutic tradition, both sides share two important common assumptions. In each framework, once we know that a set of propositions is true we can tell whether they constitute an adequate explanation without committing ourselves to further, controversial claims about social reality, based on empirical research. In the covering-law model, we need only analyze the logical relations between the hypothesis and the statement of what is to be explained. In the hermeneutic approach, we mull the hypothesis over in appropriate ways, to determine whether it satisfies relevant human faculties. Also, in both approaches, the covering-law model is accepted as an accurate analysis of natural science explanation.

These common assumptions are wrong, and disastrously wrong. They bar the way to a more accurate understanding of what counts as a valid explanation and of how explanations should be chosen in the real world of social and of natural science.

In arguing against the positivist approach and (in passing) the hermeneutic one, and in constructing an alternative model, my methods will be less empirical and my goals more modest than my earlier ones. I will be using a priori arguments to reveal the inadequacy of a priori logics of explanation. By analyzing judgments as to the circumstances in which true propositions should serve as explanations, I will try to show that such judgments depend on empirical principles. I will describe the functions that those principles fulfill. But I will not make the necessarily empirical arguments as to what those principles should be.

This modesty is dictated by the diversity of the empirical principles that give true hypotheses explanatory status. According to the alternative model I will sketch, there is no framework of empirical principles determining what counts as an explanation in all social sciences. Rather, there are particular frameworks for particular fields. Each specific framework is, in turn, highly complex, with components serving many functions. Whether a true hypothesis explains, or whether a hypothesis should be accepted as explaining, in light of given data, is determined by facts specific, say, to the study of power structures or investment decisions. My present arguments are a preliminary to an indefinite series of partial discussions, which will look more like debates over pluralist versus elite theories in political science or over Keynesian versus neoclassical versus Marxist theories in economics than disputes over the covering-law model as such.

Beyond the Covering-Law Model

Valid departures from the covering-law model always turn out to be of two general kinds. The Dilthey-Habermas tradition to the contrary, these departures occur in both the social and the natural sciences. The adequacy of these explanations to explain phenomena without covering laws suggests a new theory of explanation.

In one enormous class of valid departures from the covering-law model, the true generalizations, to which one might point as establishing the explanatory role of the particular facts in question, are not empirical laws, but tautologies, truths as nonempirical as, "All bachelors are single." Suppose we discover Robert E. Lee's secret diary and read the entry for that famous morning at Appomatox: "Today, I heard that Sherman has reached Savannah, cutting the Confederacy in two. I despair of our cause. I have therefore sent a message of surrender to Grant." Surely, we are now in a position to explain Lee's surrender as due to his despair over Sherman's reaching Savannah. But to what true empirical law can we appeal as the generalization linking despair and surrender, here? Surely not, "When a general despairs of success, he surrenders." Even among Confederate generals, others, such as Thomas Hunt Morgan, well aware that their cause was lost, fought on for weeks after Appomatox. Other potential covering laws are, similarly, either false or not known to be true.[21] This should not be surprising. We do not even have a sketch of a general theory of despair with laws describing conditions in which surrender must occur.

A true generalization, showing how facts established by Lee's diary explain his surrender, might take this form: "If a general despairs of success, and if the despair is intense enough to produce surrender, given the kind and degree of stubbornness, pride, and other countervailing factors, then he surrenders." However, this generalization is not an empirical truth. "Lee despaired, his despair was intense enough to produce surrender, countervailing factors were not of a kind or degree to prevent surrender, and he did not surrender" is as absurd, a priori, as "Lee was a husband and a bachelor." What is empirical and has explanatory force is not the generalization about despair but the particular fact that Lee's despair was intense enough to produce surrender, under the circumstances.

In the explanation of human behavior, the generalization revealing the connection between cause and effect is, very often, a tautology. This is almost always so when we explain someone's actions as due to his having information that gave him good reason to act in that way. We may, for example, be guided by the tautology: "If a person who is acting rationally sees that a course of action is the best means, on balance, of satisfying his or her total interests, he or she chooses that course of action."

The central role of such tautologies in explanations of human behavior might suggest that only these explanations depart from the covering-law model by relying solely on nonempirical generalizations. Nothing could be further from the facts of natural science explanation.

After a standard examination of a sore throat, a physician takes a throat culture, and discovers a streptococcal infection. She now has a warrant for explaining the inflammation as due to the infection. But present knowledge of immunology is so primitive that she cannot even sketch a general empirical law describing conditions in which streptococci always or almost always produce inflammation. Of the typical causes of sore throats, only one, an infection, has been found. The indication that this particular infection was strong enough under the circumstances at hand to produce a sore throat is simply the sore throat itself. The generalization connecting cause and effect is a tautology: "If a bacterial infection is virulent enough to produce inflammation, given the state of the tissue infected and the rest of the body (e.g., the immunological system), then it will."

The other departures from the covering-law model are of a different kind. In these cases, we point to an empirical principle as giving the particular facts their explanatory role. But that principle is not general in the way the covering-law model requires. It is restricted to a certain time or place or person referred to by name, not marked off by general characteristics. Suppose a historian seeks to explain why a counterrevolutionary uprising with popular support occurred in the Vendée region of France, in 1793. No other such uprising occurred elsewhere. The historian finds only one relevant difference. The clergy of the rural Vendée had, uniquely, virtual monopoly over access to the outside world. As the Parisian government became increasingly anticlerical, the Vendean clergy mobilized the peasantry in support of the royalists. That is why a royalist uprising occurred.

This explanation (actually suggested by Charles Tilly, *The Vendée*) might be acceptable even though we are very far from being given a general description of conditions under which a counter-revolutionary uprising must in general occur. If sufficiently philosophical, the historian might link cause and effect by appealing to some tautology. But another tactic is also acceptable. He might assert that in late eighteenth-century France, clerical monopoly of access to the outside world was sufficient to produce peasant conformity to the clergy's political interests. For all he knows, the same connection does not exist in other societies, in which peasant attitudes, relations between town and country, or other social facts are relevantly different. Sketching a general description of the difference between societies obeying this law of clerical power and those that don't is not a job he needs to perform to explain the Vendée rebellion. If in tenth-century Japan the clergy dominated peasant access to the outside world, but could not get peasants to conform to their political interests, this is not a fact he needs to explain away before he can ask us to accept his explanation of the Vendée uprising.

Many natural sciences depart from generality in the same way. Geologists explain mountain formation on the earth. They do not expect Martian mountain formation to obey the same laws. Indeed, they now have good evidence that it does not. Perhaps there are or might be other planets on which the buckling of continental plates which creates mountains here, creates ravines or great sheets of debris. At present, geologists cannot sketch the general conditions under which the buckling of continental plates is bound to create mountains. Still, data from the Earth justify their claims that this process, occurring under earthly circumstances, explains the formation of earthly mountains.

That the above departures from the covering-law model are valid has considerable negative importance. Going a step further, and understanding why the imagined explainers are justified in their explanatory claims, provides the raw materials for a positive alternative theory of explanation.

In explaining Lee's surrender as due to his despair over Sherman's success, our historian relied on a diary entry and on the fact that Lee did surrender. To reach his explanatory conclusion, he employed ideas concerning the evaluation of autobiographical statements. For example, he must have been committed to some such principle as this: An intelligent general's private description of his motives for a deed actually performed is likely to be accurate, unless there is a strong motive for self-deception specific to the case at hand. This statement might be called an auxiliary hypothesis. It is a hypothesis in that it is not a statement of particular observed facts. It is auxiliary in that it is not part of the proposed explanation itself, any more than principles governing the use of telescopes are partial explanations of why the planets move in ellipses.

The use of auxiliary hypotheses is not just characteristic of particular departures from the covering-law model. It blocks an important general argument used to support the model. The assertion that an event does not merely precede another but, in addition, explains it, is often said to be unverifiable except by the testing of an implicit covering law. That is plausible so long as we view verification as the direct confrontation of a proposed explanation and a body of data. How could the explanatory connection be tested, then, except by seeking a counterinstance to the covering law of the explanation among the facts in the data? In reality, however, there are many other actors in the drama of explanation-testing, part of neither the proposed explanation nor the data by which it is confronted. They may make acceptance or rejection rational without supporting or overturning a law-like part of the explanation. Thus, though general itself, the principle for interpreting autobiographical claims supports explanations of surrenders without affirming any general law of surrendering. The role of auxiliary hypotheses changes the whole logic of explanation-testing. An adequate theory of such testing must describe these functions at the outset, not treat them as mere elaborations of the central theme, the direct confrontation of explanatory hypothesis and data.

The explanation of the Vendée uprising illustrates a related point. The division of labor between the logical and the empirical in the analysis of explanatory adequacy needs to be shifted. Judgments which might seem to depend on logical relations turn out to require commitments concerning empirical facts.

Consider a general argument often used in support of the covering-law model. A rational explainer (the argument states) must either sketch a covering law or abandon his explanation when he considers the counterexamples from other situations that might refute his explanation of the phenomenon at hand. Either our French historian abandons his explanation in light of the existence of societies in which clerical dominance of access to the outside world does not produce political dominance. Or he explains those cases away by describing relevant general properties distinguishing those societies from France in 1793. In the latter case, he has arrived at a general law of political dominance of the covering-law type.

This argument depends on the principle that anything with the logical form of a counterexample is a genuine counterexample. If someone explains the presence of G in a certain case as due to the presence of F, he must explain away every case of F without G, or abandon his initial explanation. In fact, whether a formal counterexample is a real one depends on whether the respective situations are so similar that the same cause is likely to have similar effects in both. And that is an empirical question.

There is no reason to suppose that ninth-century Japan and eighteenth-century France are so similar that if clerical news-monopoly produces political domination in one society it will in the other. The French historian need not explain away the purported counterexample from ninth-century Japan. On the other hand, a counterexample from seventeenth-century England cannot simply be ignored. Here, the societies are quite similar, and are passing through similar revolutionary transformations. If High Church clergymen dominated access to the outside world in rural counties under the Commonwealth, and could not instigate counterrevolutionary activity, the explanation of the Vendée really is challenged. In general, the theory of explanation must allow such abstract questions as, "Does this count as a counterexample?" to be resolved, in part, by reliance on empirical claims.

The Causal Definition of Explanation

A theory of explanation that does justice to the expanded role of the empirical and to the many qualitatively different roles of empirical hypotheses will be more complex than the covering-law model. It is best seen as consisting of two different theories, an analysis of what a true hypothesis has to do in order to be an adequate explanation, and a description of general rules for deciding when a hypothesis is doing this job.

The proposed definition of adequate explanation employs causal notions, not notions of regularity or of accessibility to a hermeneutic faculty. The definition is: An adequate explanation is a true description of underlying causal factors sufficient to bring about the phenomenon in question.

By a causal factor I mean something necessary under the circumstances for the occurrence of the phenomenon in question. If Lee's surrender would not have occurred if he had not despaired over the news from Savannah, then that despair was a causal factor.[22]

A further task in the definition of explanatory adequacy is the analysis of the relevant sort of causal sufficiency. When have we described factors sufficient to bring about the phenomenon in question? The factors must be sufficient to bring it about in the circumstances at hand. But to require merely that is to require too little. In the circumstances at hand, a wave of selling in the Stock Market in 1929 produced the Great Depression. But no economic historian supposes that the Great Depression is explained by that wave of selling. The task of explaining why the Great Depression occurred largely consists of describing the circumstances in which a stockmarket crash would trigger a general economic collapse. On the other hand, to require a description of all the causally relevant factors, factors that taken together would produce the phenomenon in question no matter what the further circumstances, is to require too much. This demand would reimpose the covering-law model.

There seems to be no general rule valid a priori for distinguishing causal factors that need to be described from those which can be consigned to an undescribed background of "circumstances at hand." Rather, particular rules of causal sufficiency are part of specific theoretical frameworks, subject to empirical debate.

The history of natural science is a story of shifts from one rule of causal sufficiency to another. For example, in Aristotelian physics, there are two patterns of adequate explanation of motion. In one, the scientist derives the motion of an object from the inherent tendencies of its component elements. In the other, he or she attributes to episodes of interference any deviations from this guidance by inherent tendencies. In the latter case of deviation from the course of nature, the derivation of precise trajectories is unnecessary, indeed impossible. That this obstacle, say, produced that deviation from the course of nature in the case at hand is an adequate explanation. In the seventeenth century, a new physics arose in which an adequate explanation must describe the pushes, pulls, and impacts of matter on matter producing the trajectory in question, no matter what the circumstances. Aristotelian laxity in explaining departures from the course of nature is regarded as an admission of defeat.[23]

Sometimes, however, greater laxity is the way of progress. In many Greek and Renaissance theories of disease, disease is an imbalance among bodily fluids. An explanation of symptoms describes the increase or diminution of fluids, including all relevant circumstances, i.e., all relevant changes in ratios of fluids. In these theories, causal factors must be described which are bound to produce the symptoms in all circumstances. Later, in the germ theory of the late nineteenth century, many symptoms are ascribed to the invasion of microorganisms. Obviously, appropriate circumstances are required for infection to produce disease. A description of those circumstances is not required. In this period, scientific progress typically requires willingness to break off the task of explanation when the infectious agent has been identified.

In the social sciences, rules of adequacy are also a part of theoretical frameworks. For example, many political historians operate in a framework in which adequate explanations may simply describe actions of political leaders sufficient to bring about the event to be explained in the circumstances at hand. Thus, the downfall of the French Bourbons can be attributed to the blunders of individual kings and ministers. But other historians employ frameworks which require, in addition, the description of the social conditions which gave individual actions their power to produce large-scale effects. For them, an explanation of the downfall of the Bourbons as due to a series of mistakes is inadequate, since it does not describe the social conditions which made those blunders lethal for a whole system.

Different rules of adequacy govern the same subject matter at different times or among different explainers. But all are not equally valid. A valid rule must single out as crucial a causal factor that really does exist, as Aristotelian inherent tendencies do not. More distinctively, a rule is invalid if practice guided by it is an inferior source of further discoveries. Thus, historians who tend to confine themselves to decisions of kings and ministers argue that the investigation of the social conditions giving those decisions their effects has mostly produced falsehoods and trivialities while directing attention away from important unresolved questions about the actions of the famous. If they are right, their narratives are adequate explanations of large-scale social events.

An explanation must describe causal factors sufficient to bring about the phenomenon in question under the circumstances at hand. In doing so, it must describe at least as many causal factors as required by a relevant *empirically justified* rule of adequacy. Thus, the adequacy of a true explanatory description is not determined by logic alone, but by empirical considerations. Also, preference for one rule over another may depend on rating the explanatory progress to which one contributes more effectively as more important than the progress better promoted by the other. Here, value judgements may properly affect the assessment of explantory adequacy, not just the choice of the question to be asked or the research leading to an explanatory proposal.

The task of explanation has a further aspect. A description of causal factors sufficient to bring about a phenomenon is not an explanation if those causal factors lack sufficient depth. In the definition of explanation, I indicated the importance of depth by requiring that *underlying* causal factors be described.

A causal description may fail to explain through shallowness of two kinds. The factor described may be too shallow in that, had it not occurred, something else would have occurred, filling the same causal role, in a process producing the same effect. Thus, Hindenburg's invitation to Hitler to become Chancellor is sometimes portrayed as a senile blunder, involving a stupid underestimate of Hitler's political ability. Suppose this was the case. Certainly, in the actual course of events, the offer of the Chancellorship was a crucial stage in the Nazi seizure of power. Still, it may be, as some historians have argued, that the political needs and powers of German big business and of the military would have led to state power for the Nazis, even if Hindenburg had been brighter. The same destination would have been reached by a different route. In that case, Hindenburg's mistake does not explain why the Nazis came to power. Rather, the needs and powers of big business and the military are the underlying cause. (It is because of this causal depth requirement that methodological individualists are wrong to infer the explanatory adequacy of their apparatus from the premise that the links in a causal chain that led to an outcome consisted of agents' reasons and resources.)

The other sort of depth depends on a kind of causal priority. Often, there are causal relations among the concurrent causal factors producing a phenomenon. Perhaps a cause is only sufficient to bring about the phenomenon on account of the presence of another causal factor, which causes that cause, as well. The shallower cause is, as it were, a means by which the deeper cause produces its effect. Then, the shallower one is too shallow to be explanatory. Among explanations of the Nazi seizure of power that appeal to broad social forces, some explain the Nazi regime as a revolt of the middle classes, a product of the radical rightward drift of German middle class opinion during the Great Depression. This was the initial explanation offered by the leaders of the German Social Democratic Party. Others, left-wing Social Democrats such as Neumann and Communists such as Palme Dutt, argued that the rightward turn of middle-class opinion was a result of the ideological political power of German big business, a power that resulted in the Nazi seizure of power in the conditions of the Great Depression. Both sides in this furious debate (which still continues) accept that the more Marxist explanation is not just a supplement to the "revolt of the middle classes" explanation, but a rival. If the revolt of the middle classes was just one of the means by which big business domination of Germany produced a fascist response to German economic crisis, then the Nazi seizure of power cannot be explained as due to the rightward turn of the middle class.

There is an attractive picture of explanation according to which the explainer tries to piece together an unbroken causal chain between one event and another. The requirements of depth make it clear that this picture is too simple. Whether a description of a causal chain explains depends on the location of the chain in the whole network of causal relations. To put it another way, an explanatory claim is intrinsically comparative. It does not merely describe how a phenomenon was produced. It denies that any other casual process is deeper in the two relevant ways.

How to Choose an Explanation

If this is, in rough outline, what an explanation must do, how should we choose an explanation in light of the evidence available to us? The complexity of the causal definition of explanatory adequacy makes it unlikely that the associated theory of explanation-testing will be as simple as the traditional ones. Radically different sorts of phenomena can function as causal factors. The realm of causal sufficiency changes from subject matter to subject matter. Considerations of depth introduce complex comparative presuppositions into the simplest explanatory claims. In the brief space remaining, I can only sketch some of the main features of a theory of explanation-testing, features sharp enough to provide some guidance for social scientists.

In positivist models, explanation testing is the confrontation of a hypothesis with a body of observed facts, a confrontation whose outcome depends on logical relations between the two sides. This conception is excessively narrow along two dimensions. Explanation-testing almost always has an array of rival hypotheses as its object. More specifically, it is almost always a comparison of an alleged explanation with its current rivals. Moreover, the background against which this comparison is performed does not just consist of the supremely general realm of logic and the highly specific realm of particular observed facts, the data. A whole spectrum of intermediate kinds of knowledge is relevant.

The testing of a hypothesis typically consists of comparing it with its current rivals to see if it is superior. Thus, a scientist may accumulate all sorts of observations implied by a hypothesis without in any way confirming it. For those observations may be implied as well by a rival hypothesis. Robert Dahl's book, *Who Governs?*, is an attempt to show that independently functioning politicians, maneuvering among a wide variety of social forces, determine the direction of political change. He points to many facts entailed by this hypothesis, mainly the political triumphs of Mayor Richard C. Lee of New Haven. As it happens, these innovations and maneuvers are of the sort one would expect on most of the ruling-elite theories of political power, the rivals in the background. On these theories, one would expect a mayor to fare at least as well as local economic notables when issues are discussed in official forums. A major result of bourgeois or power-elite dominance is supposed to be the exclusion of social decisions worth fighting about from official forums. For example, the dispositions of major firms and banks toward relevant investment and credit decisions are supposed to provide a powerful constraint on governmental discussions, removing options from the agenda as unrealistic. For these and related reasons, the rich data of *Who Governs?* do not confirm Dahl's hypothesis, because they are not an adequate basis for comparison.

Popper's theory of confirmation, an important variant of positivism, does account for the possible irrelevance of even a vast body of positive instances. On this view, testing is the pursuit of negative instances, observations incompatible with the hypothesis. Confirmation is the unsuccessful though strenuous pursuit of such observations. However, this theory neglects the important role of comparison in falsification. It is perfectly normal and rational for someone to remain committed to a hypothesis that conflicts with observations, i.e., is logically incompatible with some observation when the latter is combined with relevant beliefs about auxiliary hypotheses and factual circumstances. Every important explanatory hypothesis generates some anomalies of this sort. Anomalies only disconfirm when the anomaly is best explained as due to the falsehood of the hypothesis. Typically, that argument is made by showing that a rival hypothesis better explains the data. In the natural sciences, for example, a numerical result which is precisely that predicted by a hypothesis being tested is an uncommon fluke, mostly of interest for the suspicions it arouses. Deviations are interesting when they are crucial evidence for a rival hypothesis, like the small deviations from Newtonian values of the orbit of Mercury, which became of fundamental importance when they become a way of comparing Newtonian and relativist physics.

Rival hypotheses are compared against a background of beliefs occupying the whole spectrum stretching from the utterly general and a priori principles of logic to the most concrete and empirical observational beliefs. Most of these background beliefs are empirical. Most are concerned with an indefinite number of situations other than the immediate object of investigation, and are held on account of diverse evidence drawn from those other situations. Unlike hermeneutic principles, they are not valid a priori. Yet they are not, typically, either covering laws or descriptions of initial conditions. The practicing scientist ignores these empirical principles at great peril. For example, in pursuing disagreements with others, he or she may simply miss the point at issue, unless he or she is aware that propositions all along the spectrum may be at stake.

Here are the main kinds of background beliefs intermediate between particular facts and a priori principles that play a crucial role in the choice of explanations. Auxiliary principles guiding the interpretation of different kinds of data are usually crucial. They include, for example, the principle for interpreting generals' autobiographical testimony that was sketched before, and principles for interpreting images in telescopes or microscopes. They also include principles of empathy like the ones given prominence in the hermeneutic tradition.

The spectrum of relevant knowledge also includes theories, laws, and vague generalities concerning the behavior of the kind of situation in question. Some may function as covering laws. But other functions are at least as important for explanation choice. For example, principles asserting that certain situations are sufficiently similar that similar causes are likely to have similar effects function, as we have seen, as certificates of authenticity for counterexamples. An apparent counterexample drawn from outside the case at hand must be certified as genuine by such a principle.

Generalizations may also serve as measures of depth, telling us whether a causal description is deep enough to serve as an explanation. For example, some social scientists are committed to the vague principle that ruling classes are willing to resort to war to resolve basic but uncertain questions of dominance. They are led by this principle to deny that the aggressive temperaments of Kaiser Wilhelm, Lord Grey, and Clemenceau explain the outbreak of World War I. The particular facts about these leaders need not be in dispute. Rather, a general principle is at work, implying, in light of other generally accepted facts, that less rambunctious leaders would have adopted essentially the same policies, or would have passed from the scene or become irrelevant.

Finally, generalizations may function as criteria of causal likelihood, telling us when it is plausible to consider that something operates as a causal factor. Such a generalization may assert that a certain kind of phenomenon is likely to have one of a limited number of causes. For example, it might tell us that a disastrous decision by a usually competent general is likely to be the result of inadequate information, pressure of time, a rigid adherence to inappropriate tactics, or an inappropriate attitude toward risk. If we discover that just one of these causal factors is present, we are justified in supposing that it explains the disaster even if we do not go on to investigate such further possibilities as psychotic break or an unbearable toothache. Of course, such principles always presuppose that there is no special evidence already available, specific to the case at hand, that a nonstandard causal factor was operating.

Another sort of criterion of causal likelihood tells us that a certain kind of causal factor is usually the most important influence on a certain kind of behavior. Thus, in Keynesian economics, investment decisions in manufacturing are typically dominated by expectations concerning effective demand for consumers. This principle does not rule out a monetarist explanation of a slump as due to tight credit for business ventures. After all, the unusual does sometimes happen. The typically secondary may be primary, at times. But the general principle does put the monetarist explanation at a disadvantage, in competition with an explanation appealing to declining demand. Unless it is further elaborated, the monetarist explanation creates an explanatory loose end: Why were businessmen so sensitive to credit restrictions in this particular case?

Using this motley background of generalizations, the scientist chooses among rival hypotheses. The question he or she poses is itself explanatory and historical: "Would an explanation of the history of data gathering and theorizing up until now that entails the basic truth of this hypothesis explain that history better than any alternative entailing the basic falsehood of the hypothesis and the truth of a current rival?"

In effect, the discussion of explanation testing so far has been limited to an ideal case in which background beliefs are uncontroversial bits of knowledge. But what about the real world? How should rival explanations be compared when background beliefs are themselves controversial? Here, a leading principle is a maxim of fair play. Arguments for the superiority of a hypothesis should ultimately rely on background principles common to all the competing rational frameworks that actually guide inquiry. In contrast, Dahl's argument that a coalition centered on the mayor, rather than dominance by an economic elite, shaped New Haven urban renewal, is invalid if it assumes measures of influence which conflict with the framework principles that generate the hypothesis of a ruling economic elite. Who among us has not sinned in this way? The path of righteousness, here, is to identify the crucial framework differences, and to conduct the argument over these differences using facts and principles acceptable in both frameworks.

This description of a logic of explanation has been sketchy and tentative. Whatever the problems of detail, if the underlying theory is basically right, traditional expectations are thoroughly wrong. The logic of explanation is traditionally expected to be a useful tool for excluding proposals as pseudoexplanations, unworthy of empirical research. In fact, the principles enabling us to judge whether a set of true propositions really explains are themselves empirical. Rather than helping scientists avoid empirical controversy, the logic of explanation should show them how their explanations depend on a variety of controversial empirical principles, usually resting on evidence far afield from the immediate object of explanation.

Conclusion

I will end with a historical speculation. I have defended a series of methodological principles which are not implausible, when stated, and which are often followed in practice by social scientists. Yet in the United States and Great Britain, explicit discussions of methodology almost always deny or ignore the scientific uses of partisanship, the role of nonsubjective interests, or the possibility of empirical but nonrelativist standards of explanatory adequacy. That is a puzzle.

Part of the answer may lie in a social effect of these denials. Methodological condemnation has often been used in universities as a way of excluding from discussion socially disreputable hypotheses that, at least implicitly, challenge the status quo—that is excluding them without engaging in empirical controversy. These hypotheses, Marxist and otherwise, are apt to result from partisan inquiries, to emphasize the role of objective interests, and to claim objective validity for explanations that are neither covered by general laws nor validated by empathy. Methodology may have been significantly shaped by a tendency to avoid certain factual controversies. If so, no wonder that the irrelevance of facts has become an underlying principle of methodology itself.

Notes

1. "Causal analysis provides absolutely no value judgment and a value judgment is absolutely not a causal explanation," contends Weber in "Critical Studies in the Logic of the Cultural Sciences," *The Methodology of the Social Sciences*, ed. and trans. Edward A. Shils and Henry A. Finch (Glencoe, Ill.: Free Press, 1949), p. 123. And in "The Meaning of 'Ethical Neutrality' in Sociology and Economics," [reprinted as "Value-judgments in Social Science," this volume, chapter 38] ibid., p. 33, he contends: "[T]he treatment of one of these types of problems with the means afforded by science or by logic is meaningful, but ... the same procedure is impossible in the case of the other. A careful examination of historical works quickly shows that when the historian begins to 'evaluate', causal analysis almost always ceases—to the prejudice of the scientific results." [Cf. this volume, p. 730.]
2. In "The Meaning of 'Ethical Neutrality' in Sociology and Economics," p. 5, Weber argues: "Every professional task has its own 'inherent norms' and should be fulfilled accordingly. In the execution of his professional responsibility, a man should confine himself to it alone, and should exclude whatever is not strictly proper to it—particularly his own loves and hates." And in '"Objectivity' in Social Science and Social Policy," ibid., p. 60, he maintains: "In the social sciences, personal value-judgments have tended to influence scientific arguments without being explicitly admitted. They have brought about continual confusion and have caused various interpretations to be placed on scientific arguments even in the sphere of simple causal connections among facts, according to whether the results increased or decreased the chances of realizing one's personal ideals. ...'"
3. Indeed, Weber's most extensive and vigorous discussion of value freedom is largely occupied with the explanation and illustration of the role of "value-relevance" in the choice of questions and in the stipulation of definitions for the vague terms which social science borrows from ordinary usage. See ibid., pp. 72–112.
4. See, for example, ibid., pp. 58ff.
5. See, for example, ibid., pp. 3, 18 and 58. Also "Science as a Vocation," in *From Max Weber*, ed. H. H. Gerth and C. Wright Mills (New York: Oxford University Press, 1958), pp. 148, 156.
6. Weber, "'Objectivity' in Social Science and Social Policy," p. 58, and "Politics as a Vocation," in *From Max Weber*, pp. 121ff.
7. "Reason and Commitment in the Social Sciences," *Philosophy and Public Affairs*, 8 (1979), pp. 241–266.
8. Theodore J. Lowi, *The End of Liberalism* (New York: Norton, 1969), p. 159.
9. For example, Alvin W. Gouldner, "Anti-Minotaur: The Myth of a Value-Free Sociology," in *Sociology on Trial*, ed. Maurice Stein and Arthur Vidich (Englewood Cliffs, N. J.: Prentice-Hall, 1963).
10. For example, Leo Strauss, "The Social Science of Max Weber," *Measure*, 2 (Spring 1951), pp. 204–230.
11. See George W. Stocking, *Race, Culture and Evolution* (New York: Free Press, 1968).
12. "An Anthropologist's Credo," in *I Believe*, ed. Clifton Fadiman (New York: Simon and Schuster, 1939), p. 19.

13. On the political views of workers in the contemporary United States see Richard Hamilton, *Class and Politics in the United States* (New York: Wiley, 1972), and Robert Gilmour and Robert Lamb, *Political Alienation in Contemporary America* (New York: St. Martin's Press, 1975); on the economics of racism see Robert Cherry, "Economic Theories of Racism," and Michael Reich, "The Economics of Racism," both in *Problems in Political Economy: An Urban Perspective*, ed. David Gordon (Lexington, Mass.: Heath, 1977 ed.). I am not, of course, suggesting that these writings definitively establish the falsehood of dominant assumptions about class, politics, and ideology. However, depending as they do on widely accepted data and standard analytical techniques, they show, by implication, that conservative social forces, not rational inference or mere misinformation, remove the burden of argument from those who assume that blue-collar workers are extremely conservative or that white workers, rather than their employers, benefit from racism. By right, these safe and standard propositions should be controversial in the extreme.

14. See Karl R. Popper, *The Open Society*, II (Princeton: Princeton University Press, 1963); J. W. N. Watkins, "Historical Explanation in the Social Sciences," *British Journal for the Philosophy of Science*, 8 (1957), pp. 104–117 [reprinted as "Methodological Individualism and Social Tendencies," this volume, chapter 39]; George Homans, "Bringing Men Back In," *American Sociological Review*, 29 (1964), pp. 809–818.

15. G. M. Wilson, "A New Look at the Problem of 'Japanese Fascism'," in *Reappraisals of Fascism*, ed. Henry A. Turner (New York: Watts, 1975), p. 202.

16. Peter Bachrach and Morton Baratz, *Power and Poverty* (New York: Oxford University Press, 1970), p. 49.

17. See Watkins, pp. 104–117 [this volume, pp. 733–742].

18. See Steven Lukes, "Methodological Individualism Reconsidered," *British Journal of Sociology*, 29 (1968), pp. 119–129, and M. Mandelbaum, "Societal Facts," *British Journal of Sociology*, 6 (1955), pp. 305–317, both reprinted in *The Philosophy of Social Explanation*, ed. Alan Ryan (New York: Oxford University Press, 1973).

19. His initial, highly influential statement is "The Function of General Laws in History," *The Journal of Philosophy*, 39 (1942), pp. 35–48. His more-or-less final elaboration, refinement, and defense is the title essay of *Aspects of Scientific Explanation* (New York: Free Press, 1965).

20. See, for example, Jürgen Habermas, *Knowledge and Human Interests*, trans. Jeremy J. Shapiro (Boston: Beacon Press, 1971), pp. 308–311.

21. The covering-law model requires, for good reason, that the laws in question employ only general, qualitative predicates, referring to no particular time, place, or person, for example, "male," "plantation-owner," "intelligent," but not "Confederate" or "nineteenth-century." After all, the model would be neither valid nor informative if "Whoever is Napoleon Bonaparte becomes Emperor of France" is counted as a law. But, among purely logical constraints, only the requirement of generality distinguishes that pseudo-law from real ones. Thus, the relevant covering-law connecting despair with surrender must be valid throughout the universe of military leaders, applying to Etruscan warrior-kings and Iroquois war chiefs, quite as much as Lee's compeers. At present, it is mere wishful thinking to suppose that such a law exists. On the requirement of qualitativeness, see Carl G. Hempel and P. Oppenheim, "Studies in the Logic of Explanation," originally written in 1948, in Hempel, *Aspects of Scientific Explanation*, pp. 268ff.

22. [Note added 1990.] I now think that the counterfactual treatment of causality implicit in this sentence (based on powerful writings by David Lewis) is no better than a simplication appropriate to special circumstances. So this essay showed residual lust for topic-neutral a priori principles. For an alternative view of causality, see my *Fact and Method: Explanation, Confirmation and Reality in the Natural and the Social Sciences* (Princeton: Princeton University Press, 1987), chapter 2. Also, the account of confirmation as fair explanatory comparison, later in the present essay, fails to confront the "Bayesian" project of regulating comparison by topic-neutral, a priori principles derived through an appropriate interpretation of probability theory. In *Fact and Method*, chapters 6–7, I argue that all such regulating principles are wrong and that the relevant explanatory comparisons are not analyzable in terms of conditional probabilities.

23. See Thomas S. Kuhn, "Concepts of Cause in the Development of Physics," in his *The Essential Tension* (Chicago: University of Chicago Press, 1977), pp. 21–30.

Chapter 41

Marx and the Objectivity of Science

Peter Railton

Karl Marx has written that "modern industry ... makes science a productive force distinct from labor and presses it into the service of capital" (1867, p. 361). Moreover, according to Marx, "The ideas of the ruling class are in every epoch the ruling idea," which are "nothing more than the 'ideal expression' of the dominant material relationships" (1846, p. 64). Part of what Marx means by 'ideal expression' is revealed when he argues that ruling ideas have a legitimating function: a ruling class must "represent its interest as the common interest," "give its ideas the form of universality, and represent them as the only rational, universally valid ones" (1846, pp. 65–66).

The idea that scientific inquiry is objective is unquestionably among the ruling ideas of our epoch, and it represents science as serving not the interests of a particular class, but a purely general interest in the understanding of nature. Indeed, the idea of scientific objectivity has often been invoked on behalf of the claim that the attitude of modern science is "the only rational, universally valid" one. This idea thus appears to be a target of opportunity for Marxist *Ideologiekritik*.

At the same time, however, Marx seems to claim something like scientific objectivity for his own theory. In methodological remarks scattered through the various prefaces and afterwords to *Capital*, for example, Marx compares himself to the physicist, biologist, and natural historian, and repeatedly characterizes his method as scientific in the sense that theirs is. Paradox looms. Marx's purportedly scientific theory seems to call into question the objectivity of science: if we accept the theory, it would appear, we must doubt its objectivity.

My aim in this paper is to indicate a way out of this seeming paradox that is available to a philosopher who accepts a fair amount of Marx's empirical theory—including the theory of ideology—but who believes that there is an important sense in which scientific inquiry is objective. I recognize in advance that someone who accepts still more of Marx's theory might deny that the resolution I suggest is possible. Perhaps, then, the account offered here is better termed 'Marxish' than 'Marxist'.

Marxist, Marxish, or other, no discussion of ideology and objectivity can assume that these notions are antecedently well understood, and so we must begin by saying something, if only in a preliminary way, about how these notions will be understood in the argument that follows.

Ideology

It seems to be widely agreed that the root concept of an ideology is that of a system of ideas that owes its existence at least in part to the fact that it serves certain interests. Controversy and complication arise when one attempts to say what sort of service is

Reprinted from *PSA 1984*, Vol. 2, ed. P. Asquith and P. Kitcher (East Lansing, MI: Philosophy of Science Association), pp. 813–825, by permission of the author and the Philosophy of Science Association.

involved, and what implications this has for the nature or validity of the ideas in question.

This is hardly the place to attempt a full-scale theory of ideology. What is needed instead is simply a set of criteria such that a system of ideas satisfying those criteria is *prima facie* ideological. It will strengthen, not weaken, the argument if it turns out that these criteria are stricter than the most general notion of an ideology. With this in mind, let us lay down the following criteria as relevant to whether a set of beliefs held by a group is ideological for that group, in the sense of being part of its ideology:

> 1. The explanation of the prevalence of the beliefs among group members, and perhaps also among other segments of the population, assigns an important role to the fact that holding these beliefs, and perhaps also acting upon them, promotes (or is believed by members of the group to promote) the interests of the group.
>
> 2. One of the effects of holding these beliefs is directly or indirectly to encourage belief, on the part of members of the group and perhaps also others, that this group's practices (or other features of it) are legitimate with reference to some normative scheme that extends beyond the group's interests.
>
> 3. This legitimating function of these beliefs for the group is served in part because these beliefs represent particular institutions, interests, or practices as general or universal in some way that they are not.[1]

A general theory of ideology might modify any of the criteria 1–3.[2] Perhaps, however, they come close enough to stating a sufficient condition to serve our purposes.

It is important to see that it is beliefs, and not propositions as such, that are ideological. Indeed, the same proposition may be believed by one individual as a piece of ideology, and by another for quite nonideological reasons.[3]

Objectivity

Despite its central role in philosophical debates, the notion of objectivity has received surprisingly little analysis, especially in comparison to some of the notions whose company it keeps, for example, rationality. Perhaps it has been assumed that we all know what objectivity consists in, and perhaps, too, that objectivity follows automatically once we proceed rationally.

Since there is no standard view upon which to draw, let us review some of the things objectivity, and specifically scientific objectivity, has been thought to involve: (i) objective inquiry is value-free; (ii) objective inquiry is not biased by factual or theoretical preconceptions—e.g., it does not adopt a theory until the evidence is in, and it refuses to interpret evidence in light of the theory at issue; and (iii) objective inquiry uses procedures that are intersubjective and independent of particular individuals or circumstances—for example, its experiments are reproducible, its methods are determinate, its criteria are effective, and it makes no essential use of introspective or subjectively privileged evidence in theory assessment.

These three features have the characteristics needed to generate a conflict between ideology and objectivity, since all three seem incompatible with ideological belief: ideological belief is significantly influenced by interests and values, contrary to the first; ideological belief seems to be a form of bias or preconception, a tendency to develop and retain certain beliefs for reasons quite independent of the balance of the evidence, contrary to the second; and, for these reasons, people in different social or historical locations who find themselves in disagreement on central questions may be unable, even if they are fully rational, to find mutually agreeable procedures for resolving their disagreement, contrary to the third.

The Ideological Character of Belief in the Objectivity of Science

Certainly scientific inquiry has often enough been claimed to be objective in one or more of the three senses just mentioned, but are these claims plausible? Let us take them up in order.

(i) It now seems impossible to accept the once widely held view that scientific inquiry is value-free, or even that value-freedom constitutes an ideal that it approximates. Let us set aside issues about the values that lead individual scientists to focus their research in one area rather than another, or about whether scientific inquiry aims at hypothesis acceptance or at the adjustment and readjustment of epistemic probabilities. The general point to be made is that rational experimental and theoretical practice must, like any other rational activity, be regulated by the goals of the agent or agents. If we accept the dominant, instrumental view of rationality, it is clear that these goals cannot themselves be given by rationality.[4] But even if we do not accept this view, it seems highly implausible to believe that all of the various goals that figure in theory testing and development—explanatory power, empirical adequacy, scope, well-confirmedness, simplicity, conservatism, and so on—are goals intrinsic to rationality, or that even if they were, that rationality would dictate a unique weighting among them sufficient to guide actual scientific practice without the embarrassment of asking scientists to make judgments about these goals.

If we cannot expect rationality to tell us which goals should be pursued in theory testing and development, must theory assessment be irrational? Not if rationality is in part a matter of choosing appropriate means to considered ends. According to what is perhaps the dominant view of science, a controlling end of the scientific enterprise is the attainment of theories capable of yielding successful prediction and control over a wide range of experience. If we grant that the scientific community has achieved unparalleled success at realizing this goal, and that belief formation in this community has been regulated by such criteria as explanatory unity, empirical adequacy, scope, well-confirmedness, conservatism, etc., then it is rational of scientists (qua scientists, as the phrase goes) to allow such criteria of theory assessment to shape their belief formation.

However, what matters for our purposes is not whether it is rational of scientists to use the criteria of theory assessment they do, but whether it would necessarily be irrational of others to use different criteria. And surely it is not intrinsic to rationality that one adopt as one's dominant end the prediction and control of experience. To be sure, people with widely divergent ends would find the capacity to predict and control experience highly useful, but it does not follow that they rationally must assign overriding priority to the attainment of this capacity. For to cultivate this capacity has certain costs, and devotion to cultivating it would exclude devotion to a great many competing ends that rational individuals might have, even upon reflection.

(ii) If rational choice, and thus the rational assessment of theories, cannot be value-free, neither can it be innocent of factual or theoretical assumptions. Theory testing is to a considerable degree holistic, and as a result there can be little hope for the idea that an isolated body of nontheoretical evidence could confer upon an isolated hypothesis any specific degree of evidential support. To arrive at values for degree of evidential support, we need to invoke a quantity of background assumptions that cannot themselves be tested independent of background theory.

At the most basic level, perception itself would be impossible without presuppositions or values. It is a commonplace to remark that without *some* theory—perhaps implicit—of what one is seeing, perception could only be a blur. It should be equally obvious that without *some* values—perhaps implicit—regarding the importance of what one might see, perception could never be sufficiently focused to make sense. It is not enough to be able to notice something merely to expect it—the perceiver must also be interested.

(iii) The third notion of objectivity, as freedom from any dependence upon person or circumstance, also seems problematic. Not only is there little reason to think that methods of theory evaluation in science could be formalized algorithmically, so as to remove any need for unformalizable judgment, but it follows from what has already been said that two inquirers, equally rational, careful, and committed to publicly scrutinizable procedures, but belonging to research traditions that adopt different normative and substantive assumptions, might come up with different degrees of belief for a given hypothesis and be unable to find neutral grounds upon which to resolve their disagreement.

So it cannot be claimed that scientific inquiry (or any significant form of inquiry about the world, for that matter) is objective in any of the senses thus far distinguished. Yet the belief that scientific inquiry is objective in some such sense, and perhaps uniquely so, is among the dominant ideas of our age. This is not sufficient to justify the claim that such belief is ideological, however, for it remains to be shown that this ruling belief satisfies our criteria 1–3.

Any serious attempt to show this would take us much farther into the history of science and society than I am able to go. But what is needed here is not so much a genuine historical account as a Marxish one, since the question before us is not whether Marxish historical analyses are correct, but whether, if correct, they would undermine talk of scientific objectivity. We can pose this question most sharply by assuming that the Marxish account clearly meets criteria 1–3.

No special difficulty attends this assumption in the case of criteria 2 and 3. Belief that scientific inquiry is objective in senses thus far distinguished plainly has helped to legitimate science, and the purported basis for this legitimation is not narrow class interests but rather such perfectly general notions as value-freedom, absence of bias, and rational agreement, as criterion 2 requires. Moreover, once it is seen that scientific inquiry cannot be value-free, innocent of bias, etc., and that scientific inquiry is rational only relative to particular normative and substantive assumptions, it can also be seen that the appeal to objectivity to legitimate science involves a misrepresentation of the particular as the general, as criterion 3 requires.

Criterion 1 poses something of a problem. It is not implausible to assume that belief in the objectivity of science has promoted the interests of capital in various ways—helping to weaken the conceptual foundations of feudalism, promoting the growth of science and associated technological development, and so on. But can we assume that on the most plausible version of a Marxish account this contribution to interests of capital will have played an important role in the explanation of the prevalence of belief in the objectivity of science? Certainly science would never have undergone such explosive development without the support of capital and the political and social institutions that arose under capitalism: culturally and practically advanced civilizations that did not undergo capitalist revolutions, such as China and India, did not undergo indigenous scientific revolutions, either. And certainly it is doubtful that scientific inquiry would have received such support under capitalism had it not served the interests of capital. And certainly it is doubtful that belief in the objectivity of science would have become as widespread as it has if scientific and technological development had been less impressive. But is this enough to satisfy criterion 1? Let us simply assume so. As Marx would have it: "Where would natural science be without industry and commerce? Even this 'pure' natural science is provided with an aim, as with its material, only through trade and industry" (1846, p. 63).

We now have the elements necessary to present the Marxish theorist with the unhappy choice mentioned at the outset. Is he to defend his view using a piece of bourgeois ideology about the objectivity of science of which his own theory tells him to be suspect? Or is he to renounce the claim of scientific objectivity, and the special epistemic status associated with it?

Objectivity Regained

Perhaps a mistake has been made. If we cannot distinguish scientific inquiry from any arbitrary bit of ideology using criteria thus far distinguished, the problem may be that these criteria fail to capture something that is part of our notion of objectivity.

We may approach this question by asking what epistemic worries objectivity was thought to address. Perhaps the main such worry can be put as follows. Values are thought to damage inquiry into the nature of the world because they are held to be subjective—they come from us, not the world. Therefore to allow values to influence inquiry into the nature of the world is to allow such inquiry to be subject to a control other than the world itself. Similarly, a theoretical bias seems threatening when viewed as an insertion of substantive beliefs between us and the world. Unless we can find some access to reality unmediated by prior belief, we can never determine which elements of such belief come from within us (i.e., subjectively) and which from without (i.e., objectively). Objectivity becomes linked to such conditions as publicity, inter-subjectivity, and effectiveness through the hope that when these conditions are met, subjective contributions and biases will be excluded as far as possible, or, where not excluded, will tend to cancel one another out or to become sufficiently manifest that we may proceed to reduce their influence.

The worry about objectivity, then, was in part a worry about having the evolution of our beliefs controlled by uncorrected-for and potentially arbitrary subjective factors rather than by the objects of inquiry themselves. Since our aim is to determine the nature of the objects, it is clear why objectivity is a central term of epistemic evaluation. It is also clear why objectivity has seldom been fully distinguished from other epistemic desiderata, for example, rationality. Reason has often been thought of as the faculty by which we inquire into the nature of things. Failure of objectivity is failure to prevent factors other than "the nature of things" from influencing one's thought. Thus, success at rationality is success at objectivity. But if we think of reason as a practical faculty, directing action relative to goals, then we can see how rationality and objectivity might come apart—one might have interests not best served by being objective in representing the world. This, in fact, is one of the bases of the theory of ideology.

Let us now ask not what a general theory of objectivity would look like, but whether anything can be done to capture this underlying concern about objectivity. We need not require freedom from all value and bias in order to have objective inquiry if there nonetheless exist mechanisms that would operate to make one's factual pre-suppositions more factual over time, or that would shape values in such a way that the norms governing inquiry come to approximate norms that would, if followed, permit or encourage this sort of self-correction. That is, although we cannot, even in principle, have direct access to the objects of inquiry, there may yet exist mechanisms of belief formation that incorporate feedback from the object to the inquiring subject. This feedback would force us, if we are to realize our goals, to reexamine our theory and values in such a way that our beliefs are appropriately controlled over time by the object as well as by our subjectivity.

This sort of objectivity is possible even though all perceptions of and inferences about the object are mediated by theory and norms because the object nonetheless has a direct way of affecting us: causally. To have no "conceptual niche" for a given phenomenon does not in general prevent that phenomenon from influencing our fate through all-too-familiar causal mechanisms.

Feedback operates upon norms as well. For example, in twentieth-century science operationalist criteria for the admissibility of concepts have been relaxed and relaxed again as it proved impossible to reformulate scientific theories within operationalist confines while at the same time preserving their power to guide scientific practice and theory development. Something had to give, and in this case it was a methodological canon that had great initial intuitive appeal.

To be most effective in achieving this sort of objectivity, we must regularly and ambitiously insert ourselves into the causal nexus, operating on the basis of our beliefs and norms. When anticipated outcomes are not realized, we may experiment with various different beliefs and norms to see if we fare better, shifting our allegiance toward beliefs and norms that let us do as much as possible as successfully as possible. This process gives objects ample opportunity to affect us causally, and the fact that we find reversals frustrating, but continue to hold onto our ambitions, has been decisive in producing whatever degree of objectivity we have achieved. There is no guarantee that our readjustments, even when they lessen frustration while feeding ambition, will carry us away from error and toward truth. The most that can be said is that if we extend our ambitions and practical activity further and further, forcing ourselves upon the world in ways ever more removed from the commonsense world of ordinary needs and objects, and if we meet unprecedented success, then we are not simply reifying our beliefs when we suppose that their evolution has been shaped by the nature of things as well as by our preconceptions.

The component of objectivity under consideration here is shamelessly *externalist*, and this is a source of difficulties both for the epistemic agent and for our evaluation of him. There certainly is no internal "sign" that infallibly distinguishes genuine feedback from mere noise, or that distinguishes appropriate versus inappropriate adjustments among those that lessen the negative effects of feedback. Yet while there are no infallible internal signs of objectivity, there are some suggestive internal symptoms, and these may figure in internal evaluation of the rationality of agents concerned about objectivity in continuing to use certain methods of belief formation. Lack of genuine theoretical innovation in response to failure, lack of success in improving our practical capacities, and reduction of ambition could be signs that feedback from the object is not playing the desired role in continuing to shape beliefs and norms. Moreover, at any given time we may appeal to our theory to ask whether we are doing what we can to achieve feedback, for example, by making novel predictions, using experimental controls, varying our samples in random ways, requiring reproducibility, and so on. It will be contingent—that is, it will depend upon what sort of world we are in and what our relation is to it—whether such methods do contribute to the component of objectivity now under consideration. But what we are after is the possibility of objectivity, not its guarantee.

Scientific Interests, Objectivity, and Warrant

Equipped with this conception of a central component of objectivity, we may be able to remove the paradox that appears to face the Marxish theorist, for it may be possible to show that even though belief that science is objective in the original sense of value-freedom, and so on, is ideological, still scientific inquiry may achieve substantial objectivity in a sense that gives its results a special epistemic status.

According to Marxish suppositions, scientific inquiry is driven by the instrumental and narrow, albeit highly ambitious, interests of industrial capitalism, interests in the prediction and control of natural phenomena. Moreover, under capitalism, scientific inquiry is conducted through rationalized, quantitative, technique-oriented, ard competitive means within a community that has a special role in the capitalist division of labor, that of enlarging our capacity for "the practical subjugation of Nature" (Marx 1867, p. 390n). Our question now becomes: Could we expect the practices of such a community to exhibit the sort of objectivity just discussed?

If one's goal is to bend nature to one's will, and if one has the strongest possible incentive for doing so in novel and efficient ways, and if one is provided with the very large resources necessary to pursue this goal through a practice of constant experimentation and technical development, then one can expect that one's practice will rapidly reveal deficiencies in one's understanding of natural phenomena, make these deficiencies hard to live with, and provide rewards for modifying one's theories or practices in ways that yield greater success. The demonic character of capitalist competition and the pervasiveness of capitalist penetration of social institutions only intensifies this. Universities become ever more thoroughly absorbed into the capitalist division of labor, converting many of the men and women of science into "paid wage-laborers" (Marx 1848, p. 82) set to work on technical and theoretical projects by those who control access to resources and positions; ideas become commoditized, converting still other men and women of science into vigorous entrepreneurs; and the pressure for constant expansion of our capacity for technical manipulation creates an entire sector of non-university-based research and development institutions. In contrast to the contemplative or speculative ideals of precapitalist intellectual elites and the heavily restricted possibilities for competition and innovation under feudal modes of production or within such feudal institutions as the early universities, the rise of capitalism gives enormous impetus and scope to the pursuit of inquiry in ways that increase the possibility of receiving and responding to causal feedback from natural phenomena.

Thus, even if one accepts Marx's view that modern science serves the interests of capital and owes much of its shape and success to the development of modern commerce and industry, science can be regarded as attaining substantial objectivity in virtue of its particular position and function within the capitalist division of labor.

This conclusion is of epistemic interest because a mode of inquiry that is objective in the reformulated sense could be expected to be reliable, and thus capable of contributing to at least one important component of epistemic warrant. Since we cannot assume a priori conformity between our beliefs and the world, and we do not have access to magical means of revealing knowledge, a mechanism that strongly promotes the sort of feedback characteristic of objective modes of inquiry is likely to be more reliable than alternative mechanisms that lack this feature or possess it to a lesser extent. We arrive at a special epistemic status for science despite—in fact, in part because of—strong Marxish assumptions.[5]

Marx

This may be an interesting tale, but what has it to do with Karl Marx? For one thing, it shows how one could accept certain Marxish premises and yet still, while holding recognizable philosophical views, say that scientific inquiry is to a considerable extent warranted and objective. For another, it seems to me—although I won't attempt to argue it in detail—that these philosophical views are compatible with views plausibly attributed to Marx.

Perhaps the most difficult aspect of the present account to reconcile with Marx is the extent to which it incorporates externalism into epistemic assessment. Isn't this the sort of thing that Marx meant to dismiss with his ruthless insistence upon the contextual character of all belief, or with his "Second Thesis on Feuerbach": "The question whether objective truth can be attributed to human thinking is not a question of theory but is a *practical* question. Man must prove the truth, that is, the reality and power, the this-sidedness of his thinking in practice. The dispute over the reality or non-reality of thinking which is isolated from practice is a purely *scholastic* question"? (1845, p. 121).

However, the appeal made to externalism here might be quite congenial to Marx—he may even be making a similar appeal at various places. Throughout Marx's discussions of method, even in his early struggles with Hegelianism, Marx emphasizes the need for real premises. "Of course," he writes, "in all this the priority of external nature remains unassailed" (1846, p. 63). He agrees with Feuerbach on the need for "sensuous objects, really distinct from the thought objects" (1845, p. 121), and his talk of the unity of man with nature, or of the mutual contribution of subject and object to our thinking, is not at all intended to deny that reality has a determinate character prior to conceptualization. Rather, it is meant to emphasize that despite the role of our creations (1846, p. 62) and expectations (1845, p. 121) in shaping our perception of the world, still, we are natural beings who operate within nature—"human activity itself (is) *objective* activity" (ibid.) (*that*, I take it, is part of the point about Feuerbach and the cherry tree (ibid))—and our real properties, like those of "external nature," are not a matter of what we believe to be the case (1846, p. 67).

It is important in understanding the "Second Thesis on Feuerbach" to note that Marx speaks of "objective truth," and of the epistemic problem of "prov(ing) the truth, that is, the reality and power, the this-sidedness of (our) thinking in practice." I take Marx to be assuming that truth is a matter of possessing ideas that correspond to reality, not of pragmatics or coherence—indeed, in an afterword to *Capital* Marx notoriously says that in an adequate description "the life of the subject matter is ideally reflected as in a mirror" (1867, p. 19)—even though there can be no question of developing true ideas or testing their reality except by demonstrating through practical application that these ideas really have "power" or "this-sidedness". The *Theses* as a whole can be understood as centrally concerned with suggesting how an epistemic link between objective reality and subjective experience can be forged through active human intervention in the world. True criticism and self-criticism thus involve efforts to bring about actual, directed change. Marx charges that although Feuerbach wants "sensuousness" to replace "abstract thinking," he fails to see that "sensuousness" must be conceived not as "contemplation" of the object but as change-oriented "practical activity"—Feuerbach "does not grasp the significance of 'revolutionary', of 'practical-critical' activity" (1845, p. 121). The celebrated Eleventh Thesis, so often seen as a call to forgo theorizing for political activism, can also be seen as making an epistemic recommendation: even when one is concerned with *theoretical* comprehension, the point is not merely to propose interpretations of the world that cohere with what we see, but to test the adequacy of our interpretations by showing that we are able to change the world in systematic and fundamental ways by acting upon them.

With all this said, it is important to point out that Marx also believes that the specific character of the practical interests that shape our activities in the world will have a definite and in some ways distorting effect upon the beliefs acquired through practice. As he wrote in the *Economic and Philosophic Manuscripts*, "Industry is the *actual* historical relation of nature, and therefore of natural science, to man," so that "the history of *industry* and the established *objective* existence of industry are the *open* book of *man's essential powers*, the exposure to the senses of human *psychology*" (1844, pp. 142–143, 142). Or, as he wrote in *The German Ideology*, "the restricted relation of men to nature determines their restricted relation to one another, and their restricted relation to one another determines men's restricted relation to nature" (1846, p. 51). Several easy examples emerge for modern industry. Thus, Marx claims that "Descartes, in defining animals as mere machines, saw with the eyes of the manufacturing period" (1867, p. 390n). We might add that mechanism came to pervade thought about nature in general and man in particular as well, unselfconsciously assimilating the whole world to that of a manufacturer. As Duhem wrote in criticism of nineteenth-century British physics, with its obsession with mechanical models, "We thought we were entering the tranquil and neatly ordered abode of reason, but we find ourselves in a factory" (Duhem 1906, p. 71). Similar points can be made with respect to biology and especially medicine, where, in the latter case, not only has the body been viewed as a machine, but curing disease has been viewed as a process of physical intervention and mechanical repair—psychologically caused illness, and even the psychological components of illness, have been regarded as in some sense unreal or epiphenomenal ("psychosomatic"). Even evolutionary biology, which Marx much admired, can be seen as borrowing from the conceptual vocabulary of economic competition in developing a theory of natural selection (perhaps excessively, if proponents of the importance of genetic drift are right), and certainly the success of this view in both the scientific and popular imagination owes much to this socially based conceptual preconditioning. It may be odd in this context to say so, but a Marxist can argue that the delayed assimilation of the concept of kin selection into evolutionary theory can be explained in part by the hold an essentially economic model of competition had on the imagination: economic agents as classically conceived are indeed atomic, but everything in genetic theory argues that biological agents are not.

The point is not to blame an epoch for failure to escape its conceptual horizons. This in any event is hardly a criticism Marx would be in a position to make. Nor is the point to discredit modern science for its material and conceptual origins in a form of practical activity that can hardly be viewed as "disinterested." Quite the contrary, Marx takes Feuerbach to task for seeing such practical activity as beneath regard from a scientific standpoint (Marx 1845, p. 121), whereas in fact it is the very thing that has made the development of science possible. To view nature and man mechanically, and to treat both instrumentally, is to come at the world with definite preconceptions and values, but that need not prevent this approach from having been highly productive of objective, warranted belief.

The point instead is to emphasize that, despite this productivity, there is reason to believe that some features of the world will be much harder—perhaps virtually impossible—to discover if one's framework is constrained by the conceptual vocabularly of a given stage in the development of production and if one's approach to nature reflects narrowed interests. The eventual emergence of a social dimension to evolutionary theory, the growing recognition in medicine of the need to view illness and cure as more than a problem of fixing the plumbing, the movement beyond purely mechanical models in physics, and the emergence of such fields as ethology and ecology, suggest that despite its narrowness, the instrumental goal of prediction and control may, if vigorously pursued, lead us to reject certain preconceptions. Yet some preconceptions may be harder to overcome than others, and some may continue to exert themselves in new forms (as the actual development of sociobiology seems to indicate). We have no trouble seeing this when we look at the science of ancient or feudal society; naturally, we have great trouble seeing it in our own case.

One final implication of this Marxish account is that we should expect less objectivity—and ultimately less warrant and knowledge—in those areas of inquiry where dominant preconceptions and interests are less likely to prompt change-oriented activity that would promote genuine feedback and challenge preconceptions. This is famously the case in the social sciences. One might argue from Marxish premises that the ruling class interests served by constant, revolutionary improvement of our understanding of physical reality are served in the social sphere by the protection of bourgeois political and economic theory from the embarrassment of negative feedback. There is no inconsistency, then, in Marx's acceptance of so much of bourgeois natural science and so little of bourgeois social science: where "revolutionizing practice" is absent, so is genuine objectivity. Engels did, I think, get Marx right when he said over a grave in Highgate Cemetery that Marx was both a "man of science" and "above all else a revolutionist," for "Science was for Marx a historically dynamic, revolutionary force."

Notes

I am indebted to Garland Allen, Allan Gibbard, Joseph Hanna, and Richard Lewontin for helpful remarks in response to an earlier version of this paper. I follow a familiar convention in attributing the ideas expressed in such works as *The German Ideology* and *The Communist Manifesto* to Marx alone, rather than to Marx and Engels.

1. Cf. the remarks of Marx quoted in the second sentence of this paper. It is not clear to me whether criterion 3 should be stated in terms of the *falsity* of the representation of the particular as the general or its *unwarrantedness* (perhaps combined with the condition that the proneness on the part of the group to accept this unwarranted—though not necessarily inaccurate—representation stems significantly from the fact that it serves that group's interests). The argument to be made below could be made using either version of 3, although the warrant-based version makes for more elaboration. A general theory of ideology might treat the representation of the particular as the general as but one form of "ideological inversion". For example, Marx claims that "in all ideology men and their circumstances appear upside-down as in *camera obscura*," and has in mind inversions of cause and effect, of the natural and the social, and of the necessary and the contingent as well as of the particular and the general (1846, p. 47).

2. For one example, it may be theoretically important to have a broadly descriptive notion of ideology that dropped any reference to the epistemic status or falsity of ideological beliefs, so that criterion 3 would be thought of as characterizing a special case. For another, Richard Boyd has pointed out to me that a general theory would have to encompass cases in which an ideology that serves the interests of a dominant group is widely believed by other groups, but not by the group itself.

3. I am speaking loosely here, since holism about propositional content may make it unlikely that a belief expressed by a given sentence that plays different roles in two perhaps quite different conceptual schemes will have exactly the same content in both.

4. Isn't there a special problem about assimilating belief formation to a general model of rational choice? If rational people choose according to expected value, then they must already have (something like) epistemic probabilities. If we try to imagine that they choose what to do about belief formation, we seem to be caught in a circle. But instead it is a spiral. Any rational choice of strategies in belief formation will make use of (something like) epistemic probabilities, but these will constitute a prior probability assignment relative to the choice, and the question facing the belief-forming agent is: Where to go from here?

5. It might be thought that this argument is question-begging, since it presupposes something like the worldview of modern science in characterizing what sorts of mechanisms of belief formation are likely to be reliable, for example, in assuming that what purports to be divine revelation is not a genuine source of knowledge. Wouldn't a religious individual disagree? Yes, but we must not lose sight of the externalism of the argument. We have no choice but to use the best available theory (by our own lights) when attempting to determine how we should answer the question "Which mechanisms of belief formation are reliable?" If, however, it should turn out that this best available theory is quite wrong, then it could be that our beliefs about reliability are wrong and that our beliefs in general are not well warranted. Recall that we are concerned with a hypothetical: "If we give a Marxish explanation for belief in the objectivity of science, but do not otherwise challenge the substantive claims of science, can it be shown that scientific inquiry is objective and scientific beliefs warranted?"

References

Duhem, P. (1906). *The Aim and Structure of Physical Theory.* Trans. by P. P. Wiener. Princeton: Princeton University Press, 1954.

Marx, K. (1844). *Economic and Philosophic Manuscripts.* Trans. by M. Milligan. Ed. by D. J. Struik. New York: International Publishers, 1964.

Marx, K. (1845). *Theses on Feuerbach.* As reprinted in Marx 1846, pp. 121–123.

Marx, K. (1846). With F. Engels. *The German Ideology: Part I.* Trans. by W. Lough. Ed. by C. J. Arthur. New York: International Publishers, 1970.

Marx, K. (1848). With F. Engels. *The Communist Manifesto.* Trans. by S. Moore. New York: Penguin, 1967.

Marx, K. (1867). *Capital: A Critique of Political Economy.* Volume I. Trans. by S. Moore and E. Aveling. New York: International Publishers, 1967.

Glossary

A posteriori   An epistemological classification about the sources of knowledge; *a posteriori* knowledge is dependent on experience.

A priori   An epistemological classification about the sources of knowledge; *a priori* knowledge is independent of experience.

Abduction   A term used by C. S. Peirce for a special pattern of inference; see Inference to the best explanation.

Artifact   An unintended experimental product of an unmeasured variable, which can be confounded with results of the variable(s) that the experiment was designed to measure.

Auxiliary statement   Any claim conjoined with a hypothesis that is under test, in order to derive observable predictions from the hypothesis. (Auxiliary statements are sometimes called "auxiliary hypotheses"; this name is misleading, since in a good test, the auxiliary statements are typically already well confirmed.) (Cf. Hypothesis, Hypothetico-deductive method.)

Behaviorism   The view that all behavior (both intelligent and reflexive) can be adequately explained in terms of observable responses to stimuli. *Radical behaviorism*, associated with the psychologists John Watson and B. F. Skinner, is the view that there are no mental causes; psychological laws invoke only relations between stimuli and responses. *Logical behaviorism*, associated most prominently with the philosopher Gilbert Ryle, is a semantic thesis about the meaning of mental terms: mental terms express behavioral dispositions.

Bivalence   The property of a sentence that has only two possible truth values (truth or falsity). The term can also be used to describe linguistic or logical systems, all of whose sentences are bivalent.

Cause   A central notion in science, often simply defined in the following way: X caused Y just in case Y would not have occurred unless X had occurred. Elaborations, limitations, and difficulties of this simple account can be found in the selections in part I, section 2.

Confirmation   The process of showing a claim to be supported by the evidence.

Constructivism   The view that the subject matter of scientific research is wholly or partly constructed by the background theoretical assumptions of the scientific community and thus is not, as realists claim, largely independent of our thoughts and theoretical commitments. (Cf. Neo-Kantianism.)

Convention   A method or practice adopted for reasons of simplicity or convenience.

Convergence   The relation between a theoretical tradition and the world, by virtue of which a particular theory is said to be getting closer to the truth.

Corroboration   A term introduced by Popper to refer to the enhanced status of a hypothesis after it has survived falsification attempts. Popper does not regard a well-corroborated hypothesis as more likely to be true than an uncorroborated (but unfalsified) one. (Cf. Falsification, Falsificationism.)

Counterfactuals   Types of conditional (if ... then ...) statements whose antecedents or if-clauses express circumstances that are contrary-to-fact, such as "If it *were* raining ..." or "If it *had* rained ...". Scientific laws are said to support counterfactuals.

Covering-Law Model   An account of scientific explanation as (ideally) the process of inferring a description of the phenomenon to be explained from premises that essentially include the statement of a law of nature and (typically) a description of relevant initial and/or boundary conditions.

Deduction   The process of deriving statements (conclusions) that follow necessarily from an initial set of statements. A *deductive* argument is one in which the truth of the premises guarantees the truth of the conclusion. Example:

> All dogs are mammals.
> All mammals are warm-blooded.
> ∴ All dogs are warm-blooded.

Deductive-nomological explanation   A covering-law explanation in which the inference is deductive. (Cf. Covering-law Model.)

Determinism   The view that the final state of a system is completely fixed by its initial state. For example, the Newtonian particle system, as a theoretical model, is considered by most to be a deterministic system. The masses, momenta, and positions of all of the particles in the system (the "total state") at a given time uniquely fixes the total state at any later time.

Dialectical   In the philosophy of science, a process of interactive development by which scientists regulate their beliefs and practices in response to critical reflection and feedback from the world.

Disquotation   A linguistic technique that allows us to move from talking about language to talking about the world; that is, to move from mention to use of language. The Tarski truth predicate (see Truth) is defined by using this technique, which equates the meaning of a quoted (or mentioned) sentence followed by 'is true' with the unquoted (or used) version of the sentence. (Example: "Grass is green" is true if and only if grass is green.) This procedure is said to provide the truth-conditions of the quoted sentence and was used in an attempt by Tarski to define the predicate "is true" in a metaphysically innocuous way.

Disposition   A characteristic of an object that causes it to behave in a certain way if placed in specific conditions. (Example: salt's solubility is a disposition to dissolve when placed in water.) Other dispositions include fragility, ductility, etc. The object possesses the disposition whether or not it is actually displaying the property at the time. For instance, an object can be fragile even if it has never been broken. By contrast, there are properties of objects that are nondispositional, such as hardness, which do not require special "precipitating conditions" for their display.

Dualism   An ontological doctrine that comes in two forms: *Substance dualism* is the view, most closely associated with Descartes, that there are two irreducibly distinct types of substances in the world, mental and physical. *Property dualism* is the view that although the brain is the seat of the mind, the brain has a special class of properties characteristic of conscious intelligence—belief, desire, pain, fear, etc.—that cannot be explained entirely in physical terms.

Eliminativism   The stance that the entities postulated by a specified area of inquiry do not exist. Eliminativism typically involves the further claim that this area of enquiry is replaceable by a more sophisticated account. Its most popular contemporary expression is found in the work of Patricia Smith Churchland and Paul Churchland, in which it is predicted that folk psychology will be replaced by a mature neuroscience.

Empirical adequacy   The property of a theory all of whose observable consequences are true.

Empirical equivalence   The relation between two or more theories when all of their observable consequences are identical.

Empiricism   The view that all knowledge is based on or exhausted by what is known by sensory experience.

Entailment   A logical relation between a statement and the consequences it implies. In statements such as '*p* implies *q*', *q* is said to be *entailed* by *p*.

Epistemology   The study of the nature, origins, objects, and limitations of knowledge.

Essentialism   The view that certain substances have characteristics necessary to their identity. (Cf. Nominalism.)

Extension   A semantic notion that concerns the class of objects that a term picks out. For example, a particular triangle falls in the *extension* of the term 'triangle'. The extension of a proper name is its bearer.

Falsification   The process of showing a claim to be false.

Falsificationism   The view, advocated by Popper, that for a claim to be scientific it must be possible to specify which observation would falsify it or, more generally, the circumstances in which it would be abandoned. Popper also holds that scientific claims can never be verified or positively confirmed to any degree and that science progresses by systematically attempting to falsify previously advanced hypotheses. (Cf. Corroboration.)

Feminism   An intellectual and political current which argues that women have been systematically denied an equal role in society and that women's distinctive intellectual contributions have been undervalued or ignored, and which seeks to correct the imbalance.

Foundationalism   The epistemological doctrine that holds that some favored beliefs are not dependent for their justification on other beliefs and that these "basic beliefs" are the fundamental source of justification for all of our other beliefs.

Functionalism   1. In philosophy of psychology, the view that psychological states can be individuated functionally, in terms of sensory inputs, behavioral outputs, and relations to other psychological states. 2. In sociology and social anthropology, the view that social institutions and practices can be explained in terms of their role in promoting social stability.

Hermeneutics   The study of the principles of interpretation of texts or of other objects of inquiry.

Holism   1. In ontology, the view that emergent entities (entities that only come into existence when combinations of simpler phenomena have reached a certain level of complexity) are more than the sums of their parts. 2. In semantics, the view that the meanings of individual linguistic expressions are determined by their roles in a larger linguistic system. 3. In epistemology, the view that only groups of beliefs can be tested and that individual beliefs can thus only be assessed in the context of a larger system.

Hypothesis   The status of a scientific claim after it has been advanced but before there is sufficient evidence to accept (or reject) it.

Hypothetico-deductive method   An account of theory confirmation as a process of deducing from the hypothesis under test (together with appropriate auxiliary statements) predictions whose truth or falsity can be directly observed. Theories are confirmed by their true observational consequences. (Cf. Auxiliary statement, Hypothesis.)

Idealism   An ontological view that holds that the world depends on the nature or existence of minds, or that the only things that exist are ideas.

Incommensurability   1. Methodological: a relation claimed to hold between theoretical frameworks such that, because of the deeply theory-dependent character of observation and scientific method, no rational method for resolving theoretical disputes acceptable to defenders of both sides can be found. 2. Semantic: a relation claimed to to hold between instances of the same term as it occurs in theories before and after a scientific revolution. In such a revolution, fundamental laws are revised, and it can be argued that this requires a corresponding change in the definitions of fundamental theoretical terms. Scientists before and after a scientific revolution can therefore be claimed to be talking about different theoretical entities—or talking past one another—even when they use the same terms. According to Kuhn (1970), for example, instances of the term 'mass' in Newtonian and relativistic mechanics are incommensurable.

Individualism   1. In social theory, the view that only individuals exist; entities such as classes or nations are seen as at best useful fictions with no reality independent of the individuals by whom they are constituted. (Cf. Methodological individualism.) 2. In philosophy of psychology, the view that the content of mental states is fixed entirely by the internal properties of such states, independent of their relations to the physical and/or social environment.

Induction   Simple induction is the process of drawing a conclusion, or estimating the support for a hypothesis, on the basis of observed instances of past events. Example:

> All hitherto observed carnivores have canines.
> Therefore, all carnivores probably have canines.

However, the term 'inductive' is often used more broadly to refer to any plausible nondeductive inference.

Inference   The process of drawing a conclusion from a set of premises; this relation between premises and conclusion can be either inductive or deductive.

Inference to the best explanation   A pattern of reasoning by which one infers that a hypothesis is true from the fact that the hypothesis offers the most plausible or satisfactory explanation of the evidence.

Instrumentalism   The view that a theory is merely a device or tool for producing accurate observational predictions; theories so construed are not said to be true or false, but effective or ineffective.

Intension   A semantic notion that concerns the defining properties common to all objects in a class designated by a particular term. Having interior angles that sum to 180 degrees is the *intension* of 'triangle'.

Intentionality   The property of mental states by virtue of which they have representational content.

Law   A causal or statistical relation between at least two factors, or the statement used to express such a relation. Examples are the ideal gas law, $PV = NkT$, and Newton's second law, $F = ma$. Normally, laws tell us something about counterfactual situations. (Cf. Counterfactuals.)

Logical positivism (or Logical empiricism)   A doctrine originally articulated by Schlick, Carnap, Neurath, and other members of the Vienna Circle in the 1920s and 1930s, which primarily attempts to interpret science and philosophy in terms of the verificationist theory of meaning. (Cf. Verificationism.)

Materialism   The ontological doctrine that states that everything that exists is, or depends on, matter. Nonreductionist philosophers sometimes prefer to use the term 'materialism' rather than 'physicalism' to express their view about the material or physical nature of the universe.

Mechanism   The view that all phenomena can ultimately be explained in terms of simple mechanical relations of cause and effect.

Metaphysics   Traditionally understood as the study of the fundamental nature of reality; used pejoratively by logical positivists to indicate a type of statement (or encompassing worldview, such as materialism or determinism), whose factual status was thought to be undecidable solely on observational grounds and was thus considered meaningless. (Cf. Logical positivism.)

Methodological individualism   The view that all social phenomena can be explained in terms of the properties of and relations between individuals.

Methodology   The procedures and techniques governing inquiry, or the study of such procedures and techniques.

Naturalism   The view that all phenomena are subject to natural laws, and/or that the methods of the natural sciences are applicable in every area of inquiry.

Natural kind   A type of property, process, state, event, or object studied by science, mentioned in scientific laws, and assumed to be a causal feature of the world. The primary instances of natural kinds are objects of scientific taxonomy, such as electrons in physics, zinc in chemistry, and species in biology.

Natural kinds are contrasted with phenomena that are assigned no such systematic, organizing role, such as an event's occurring after I drop this pen, or an object's being located 34 miles west of the Liberty Bell.

Necessity   A modal property expressed by statements that describe states of affairs that could not be otherwise or that could not be the case. Logical and mathematical truths are typical examples of necessarily true statements, and logically contradictory statements are examples of necessarily false statements. (Cf. Possibility.)

Neo-Kantianism   Another name for constructivism, the view that the reality described by our scientific theories is a social and intellectual construct and thus is not, as realists claim, largely independent of our thoughts and theoretical commitments. The name suggests an association with the views of the eighteenth-century philosopher Immanuel Kant, but this association is exegetically controversial.

Nominalism   The view that only individual (or token) objects exist, and that reference to abstract objects or *universals*, such as properties, classes, numbers, and modalities (possibility and necessity) can be eliminated.

Objectivity   The property of a theory or claim that accurately reflects—or of a method that yields knowledge of—phenomena that exist independently of our beliefs about them.

Observable   Capable of being perceived by the (typically unaided) senses.

Ontology   Used in two senses: 1. a branch of metaphysics that studies the nature of existence; 2. the entities postulated by a particular theory.

Operationalism   The view that terms and concepts are defined by a set of operations. For example, the total meaning of the concept of length is given by a specification of the operations used to determine the length of an object. This doctrine was first explicitly formulated by the physicist P. W. Bridgman (see his selection in part I, section 1).

Paradigm   A set of general background assumptions (usually unarticulated and grounded in a piece of exemplary scientific research) that shapes the methodology employed in subsequent inquiry. The term was originally introduced by Kuhn.

Parsimony   Property of a theory that posits a relatively small number of theoretical entities, processes, mechanisms, or other such phenomena.

Phenomenalism   *Linguistic version*: All statements about the world are properly understood as statements about actual and possible sense experiences. *Ontological version*: Objects are groups of possible and actual sense experiences. Philosophers such as Mill, Mach, Russell, Ayer, and C. I. Lewis all held a version of phenomenalism during some period in their careers.

Physicalism   An ontological doctrine that holds that the world is entirely composed of physical phenomena. Physicalism is often understood as the stronger, reductionist thesis that the world can be entirely described in the vocabulary of physics.

Positivism   The view, originally advanced by Comte, that "positive facts" concerning observable phenomena and their relations are all that can be known, and that inquiry into causes, origins, and purposes should be abandoned. (Cf. Logical positivism.)

Possibility   A modal property expressed by statements that describe states of affairs that could have been otherwise or that might have been the case. A statement is said to be *logically* possible so long as it is not logically contradictory. Therefore, a statement that is necessarily true is also possible. (See Necessity.)

Pragmatics   The area of the study of language concerned with the communicative effects of using linguistic expressions in particular circumstances.

Predicate   A term that expresses a property; the predicate 'tall' expresses the property of tallness. According to some views, however, not all predicates express *genuine* properties.

Probability   The chance that a certain event will occur. Probability theory is used to estimate the chance that some selected sample of individuals belongs to a certain population.

Projectibility   A feature 1. of terms that makes them suitable for framing generalizations capable of receiving evidential support or 2. of generalizations such that they are capable of receiving evidential support. A generalization is projectible if it represents a theoretically important pattern that might be exhibited in the data.

Proposition   The content or meaning expressed by a sentence. (Example: though couched in different languages, "It is raining" and "Es regnet" express the same proposition.)

Radical skepticism   The view that no belief is better warranted than any other, and hence that we have no reason to believe any claim in preference to its negation.

Realism   The view that phenomena of a specified sort exist independently of being thought about and/or are largely nonmental in character. (Cf. Scientific realism.)

Reference   The relation between a word and the thing in the world that the word denotes or picks out. The term 'dog' *refers* to the class of dogs, or to some particular dog.

Relativism   In epistemology, the view that the acceptability or unacceptability of knowledge claims is relative to a particular group or community, and that there are no objective epistemological standards.

Reliabilism   The view that knowledge consists of true belief produced or regulated by processes that reliably lead to the truth in appropriate circumstances.

Scientific realism   The view that the subject matter of scientific research and scientific theories exists independently of our knowledge of it, and that the goal of science is the description and explanation of both the observable and unobservable aspects of an independently existing world.

Semantics   Area of the study of language concerned with the meaning or content of linguistic expressions and with their relation to nonlinguistic reality.

Simplicity   Property of a theory that is either more parsimonious or computationally less cumbersome than its rivals. (Cf. Parsimony.)

Skepticism   The view that knowledge claims in a specified area have not been, or cannot be, established. (Cf. Radical skepticism.)

Solipsism   The view that only one's own consciousness exists.

Soundness   The property a valid argument has when its premises are *in fact* true.

Stochastic   The name for a process that is *nondeterministic*. In stochastic systems, the initial state of the system only determines the *probability* of the final state, but does not completely ensure its occurrence. For example, the model of Mendelian heritability represents a stochastic system. Features such as parental eye color do not in general determine the eye color of the offspring, but only the probability that the offspring will have a particular eye color.

Structuralism   An eclectic intellectual movement, associated with Saussure, Althusser, and others, holding that linguistic and social systems constitute domains of inquiry that are autonomous from the physical sciences and whose behavior is best explained by often ignored superstructural relations among parts of the system.

Subjectivity   Property of a claim or method that largely reflects aspects of the particular individual who makes or uses it, rather than aspects of a world existing independently of the individual.

Supervenience   The relation of dependence of macrophenomena on microphenomena, such as the dependence of brain states on chemical states, or of economic relations on psychological relations. One set of phenomena supervenes on another just in case a change in the former requires a change in the latter.

Appealed to variously to capture the doctrine of physicalism, the notion of cause, mind-body interaction, a naturalistic conception of moral properties, etc.

Syntax   Area of the study of language concerned with the ways in which linguistic expressions can be legitimately combined.

Systematics   See Taxonomy.

Taxonomy (or systematics)   In general, the science of classification. In biology, the classification and examination of living things in terms of their natural relations.

Teleology   The examination of or appeal to goals or ends as fundamental principles of explanation.

Theory   A general, systematic account of a subject matter. Theories frequently posit the existence of unobservable (or "theoretical") entities and often have the status of hypotheses, since by their nature they are harder to confirm than less general claims. (Cf. Hypothesis.)

Theory-laden   A feature that scientific terms, methods, practices, and judgments are said to have by virtue of occurring within the context of a particular theory or theoretical tradition, and whose significance or meaning can be fairly assessed only within that theory or tradition. Scientific terms such as 'mass', and practices such as observation and explanation, are often called 'theory-laden'.

Truth   There are three influential but conflicting theories of truth. *Correspondence theory*: A statement is true if and only if it corresponds with the facts. *Coherence theory*: A statement is true if and only if it coheres with some specific set of other statements we hold. *Disquotational or redundancy theory*: A quoted statement followed by 'is true' says the same thing as the unquoted version without the appended 'is true'. For example, 'Mastiffs are the best pets' is true = Mastiffs are the best pets. Tarski presented a formal and rigorous version of the redundancy theory of truth. On Tarski's account, for every sentence *s* in language L there is a provable theorem of the following form: The sentence *s* in language L is true if and only if *p*, where *s* is replaced by the name of a sentence in L, and *p* by a sentence in the language in which the theory is stated. For example, the German sentence 'Schnee ist weiss' is true if and only if snow is white. According to the disquotational approach, a theory of truth is materially adequate only if all such provable sentences are in fact true.

Type/token distinction   The distinction between a kind of thing and an instance of the kind. For example, a particular dog will be a token of the general type "dog".

Validity   A formal property of deductive arguments such that, *if* the premises are true, the conclusion must also be true. Example:

> All plants are vertebrates.
> All vertebrates are bipeds.
> ∴ All plants are bipeds.

N.B. Valid arguments do not need to have either true premises or a true conclusion.

Value-neutralism   The view that the desirability or undesirability of a state of affairs is irrelevant to scientific inquiry about it, and that in their role as scientists, inquirers should refrain from making such evaluations.

Verification   Conclusively showing a claim to be true.

Verificationism   A theory of meaning according to which all meaningful sentences are either analytic (true or false in virtue of the meanings of the terms involved) or empirically verifiable.

Verisimilitude   The truth-content of a theory; the degree of "truth-likeness" a theory or statement is said to have. Truth-likeness has sometimes been characterized as a syntactic property of theories construed as formal systems, but it might alternatively be cast as a type of semantic property relating a theory to the world.

Bibliography

Achinstein, P., 1983, *The Nature of Explanation*, New York, Oxford University Press.

Achinstein, P., and Hannaway, O., eds., 1985, *Observation, Experiment, and Hypothesis in Modern Physical Science*, Cambridge, MIT Press.

Anderson, J. L., 1967, *Principles of Relativity Physics*, New York, Academic.

Armstrong, D. M., 1983, *What is a Law of Nature?* New York, Cambridge University Press.

Aune, B., 1985, *Metaphysics*, Minneapolis, University of Minnesota Press.

Ayer, A. J., 1946, *Language, Truth and Logic*, 2nd ed., New York, Dover.

Baker, L. R., 1987, *Saving Belief*, Princeton, NJ, Princeton University Press.

Barwise, J., and Perry, J., 1983, *Situations and Attitudes*, Cambridge, MA, MIT Press.

Bechtel, W., 1988, *Philosophy of Science: An Overview for Cognitive Science*, Hillsdale, NJ, Erlbaum.

Benacerraf, P., and Putnam, H., 1983, *Philosophy of Mathematics*, 2nd ed., New York, Cambridge University Press.

Bennett, J., 1964, *Rationality*, London, Routledge & Kegan Paul. (Reprinted 1989, Indianapolis, Hackett.)

Bernal, J. D., 1971, *Science in History*, 3rd ed., 4 vols., Cambridge, MA, MIT Press.

Block, N., and Dworkin, G., eds., 1976, *The IQ Controversy*, New York, Pantheon.

Block, N., ed., 1980, *Readings in Philosophy of Psychology*, 2 vols., Cambridge, MA, Harvard University Press.

Block, N., 1986, Advertisement for a Semantics for Psychology. In P. A. French, T. Uehling, and H. Wettstein, eds., *Studies in the Philosophy of Mind: Midwest Studies in Philosophy*, Vol. 10 , Minneapolis, University of Minnesota Press.

BonJour, L., 1985, *The Structure of Empirical Knowledge*, Cambridge, MA, Harvard University Press.

Boolos, G., and Jeffrey, R., 1989, *Computability and Logic*, 3rd ed., New York, Cambridge University Press.

Boyd, R., 1973, "Realism, Underdetermination, and a Causal Theory of Evidence," *Noûs* 7: 1–12.

Boyd, R., 1979, "Metaphor and Theory Change," in A. Ortony, ed., *Metaphor and Thought*, New York, Cambridge University Press.

Boyd, R., 1981, "Scientific Realism and Naturalistic Epistemology," in P. Asquith and R. Giere, eds., *PSA 1980*, vol. 2, East Lansing, MI, Philosophy of Science Association.

Boyd, N., 1985, "The Logician's Dilemma: Deductive Logic, Inductive Inference and Logical Empiricism," *Erkenntnis* 22: 197–252.

Braithwaite, R. B., 1953, *Scientific Explanation*, New York, Cambridge University Press.

Brodbeck, M., 1968, *Readings in Philosophy of Social Science*, New York, Macmillan.

Brown, H. I., 1977, *Perception, Theory and Commitment*, Chicago, University of Chicago Press.

Brush, S., 1989, "Prediction and Theory Evaluation: The Case of Light Bending," *Science* 246: 1124–1129.

Burge, T., 1979, "Individualism and the Mental," in P. A. French, T. E. Uehling, and H. K. Wettstein, eds., *Midwest Studies in Philosophy, vol. IV: Studies in Metaphysics*. Minneapolis, University of Minnesota Press.

Byerly, H. and Lazara, V., 1973, "Realist Foundations of Measurement," *Philosophy of Science* 40:10–28.

Bynum, W. F., Browne, E. J., and Porter, R., eds., 1984, *Dictionary of the History of Science*, Princeton, NJ, Princeton University Press.

Carnap, R., 1934, *The Unity of Science*, London, Kegan Paul, Trench, Trubner and Co.

Carnap, R., 1966, *An Introduction to the Philosophy of Science*, ed. M. Gardner, New York, Basic Books.

Cartwright, N., 1983, *How the Laws of Physics Lie*, Oxford, Clarendon Press.

Cartwright, N., 1989, *Nature's Capacities and Their Measurement*, New York, Oxford University Press.

Churchland, P. M., 1979, *Scientific Realism and the Plasticity of Mind*, New York, Cambridge University Press.

Churchland, P. M., 1985, "Reduction, Qualia, and the Direct Introspection of Brain States," *Journal of Philosophy* 82: 8–28.

Churchland, P. M., 1988, *Matter and Consciousness*, 2nd ed., Cambridge, MA, MIT Press.

Churchland, P. M., and Hooker, C., eds., 1985, *Images of Science*, Chicago, University of Chicago Press.

Churchland, P. S., 1980, "Language, Thought, and Information Processing," *Noûs* 14: 147–170.

Churchland, P. S., 1982, "Mind-Brain Reduction: New Light from the Philosophy of Science," *Neuroscience*, 7/5: 1041–1047.

Churchland, P. S., 1986, *Neurophilosophy*, Cambridge, MA, MIT Press.

Coleman, W., 1971, *Biology in the Nineteenth Century: Problems of Form, Function, and Transformation*, New York, John Wiley & Sons.

Crossley, J. N. et al., eds., 1972, *What is Mathematical Logic?* New York, Oxford University Press.

Davidson, D., 1980, *Essays on Actions and Events*, New York, Oxford University Press.

Davies, P., 1977, *Space and Time in the Modern Universe*, New York, Cambridge University Press.

Dennett, D., 1969, *Content and Consciousness*, London, Routledge & Kegan Paul.

Dennett, D., 1978, *Brainstorms*, Cambridge, MA, MIT Press.

Dennett, D., 1984, *Elbow Room*, Cambridge, MA, MIT Press.

Dennett, D., 1987, *The Intentional Stance*, Cambridge, MA, MIT Press.

Devitt, M., 1984, *Realism and Truth*, Princeton, NJ, Princeton University Press.

Devitt, M., and Sterelny, K., 1987, *Language and Reality*, Cambridge, MA, MIT Press.

Dretske, F., 1981, *Knowledge and the Flow of Information*, Cambridge, MA, MIT Press.

Dretske, F., 1988, *Explaining Behavior*, Cambridge, MA, MIT Press.

Duhem, P., (1906, reprinted 1981), *The Aim and Structure of Physical Theory*, New York, Atheneum.

Durbin, P. T., 1980, *A Guide to the Culture of Science, Technology, and Medicine*, New York, Free Press.

Edelson, M., 1984, *Hypothesis and Evidence in Psychoanalysis*, Chicago, University of Chicago Press.

Evans-Pritchard, E. E., 1976, *Witchcraft, Oracles, and Magic among the Azande*, Oxford, Oxford University Press.

Faust, D., 1984, *The Limits of Scientific Reasoning*, Minneapolis, University of Minnesota Press.

Feigl, H., and Brodbeck, M., eds., 1953, *Readings in the Philosophy of Science*, New York, Appleton-Century-Crofts, Inc.

Feyerabend, P., 1975, *Against Method*, London, Verso.

Feyerabend, P., 1981a, *Realism, Rationalism and Scientific Method*, New York, Cambridge University Press.

Feyerabend, P., 1981b, *Problems of Empiricism*, New York, Cambridge University Press.

Field, H., 1972, "Tarski's Theory of Truth," *Journal of Philosophy* 69: 347–375.

Field, H., 1973, "Theory Change and the Indeterminacy of Reference," *Journal of Philosophy* 70: 462–481.

Field, H., 1974, "Quine and the Correspondence Theory," *Philosophical Review* 83: 200–228.

Field, H., 1975, "Conventionalism and Instrumentalism in Semantics," *Noûs* 9: 375–405.

Field, H., 1980, *Science Without Numbers*, Princeton, NJ, Princeton University Press.

Fine, A., 1986, *The Shaky Game*, Chicago, University of Chicago Press.

Fiske, D. W., and Shweder, R. A., eds., 1986, *Metatheory and Social Science*, Chicago, University of Chicago Press.

Fodor, J. A., 1975, *The Language of Thought*, Cambridge, MA, Crowell.

Fodor, J. A., 1981, *Representations*, Cambridge, MA, MIT Press.

Fodor, J. A., 1982, "Cognitive Science and the Twin-Earth Problem," *Notre Dame Journal of Formal Logic* 23: 98–118.

Fodor, J. A., 1983, *The Modularity of Mind*, Cambridge, MA, MIT Press.

Fodor, J. A., 1984, "Observation Reconsidered," *Philosophy of Science*, 51: 23–43.

Fodor, J. A., 1984, "Semantics, Wisconsin Style," *Synthese* 59: 231–250.

Fodor, J. A., 1986, "Banish Discontent," in J. Butterfield, ed., *Language, Mind and Logic*, New York, Cambridge University Press.

Fodor, J. A., 1987, *Psychosemantics*, Cambridge, MA, MIT Press.

Fodor, J. A., 1990, *A Theory of Content and Other Essays*, Cambridge, MA, MIT Press.

Fodor, J. A., and Pylyshyn, Z., 1981, "How Direct is Visual Perception? Some Reflections on Gibson's 'Ecological Approach'," *Cognition* 9: 139–196.

Friedman, M., 1983, *Foundations of Space-Time Theories*, Princeton, NJ, Princeton University Press.

Galison, P., 1987, *How Experiments End*, Chicago, University of Chicago Press.

Garfield, J., 1988, *Belief in Psychology*, Cambridge, MA, MIT Press.

Garfinkel, A., 1981, *Forms of Explanation*, New Haven, CT, Yale University Press.

Giere, R., 1984, *Understanding Scientific Reasoning*, 2nd ed., New York, Holt, Rinehart, and Winston.

Giere, R., 1988, *Explaining Science*, Chicago, University of Chicago Press.

Gillispie, C. C., ed., 1970–1980, *Dictionary of Scientific Biography*, 16 vols., New York, Charles Scribners Sons.

Glass, A., and Holyoak, K., 1986, *Cognition*, 2nd ed., New York, Random House.

Glymour, C., 1980, *Theory and Evidence*, Princeton, NJ, Princeton University Press.

Goldman, A., 1986, *Epistemology and Cognition*, Cambridge, MA, Harvard University Press.

Goodman, N., 1978, *Ways of Worldmaking*, Indianapolis, Hackett.

Goodman, N., 1983, *Fact, Fiction, and Forecast*, 4th ed. Cambridge, MA, Harvard University Press.

Gould, S. J., 1981, *The Mismeasure of Man*, New York, Norton.

Grant, E., 1971, *Physical Science in the Middle Ages*, New York, John Wiley & Sons.

Hacking, I., 1965, *The Logic of Statistical Inference*, New York, Cambridge University Press.

Hacking, I., 1983, *Representing and Intervening*, New York, Cambridge University Press.

Hamlyn, D. W., 1984, *Metaphysics*, New York, Cambridge University Press.

Hanson, N., 1958, *Patterns of Discovery*, New York, Cambridge University Press.

Harding, S., 1986, *The Science Question in Feminism*, Ithaca, NY, Cornell University Press.

Hardwig, J., 1985, "Epistemic Dependence," *Journal of Philosophy* 87: 335–349.

Haugeland, J., 1982, "Weak Supervenience," *American Philosophical Quarterly* 19: 93–103.

Haugeland, J., 1984, "Ontological Supervenience," *The Southern Journal of Philosophy* 22 (supplement): 1–12.

Haugeland, J., 1985, *Artificial Intelligence: The Very Idea*, Cambridge, MA, MIT Press.

Hempel, C., 1965, *Aspects of Scientific Explanation*, New York, Free Press.

Hempel, C., 1966, *Philosophy of Natural Science*, Englewood Cliffs, NJ, Prentice-Hall.

History of Science Society, 1971–1980, *The ISIS Cumulative Bibliography*, 4 vols., London, Mansell.

Hooker, C., 1981, "Towards a General Theory of Reduction," *Dialogue* 20: 38–60, 201–235, 496–529.

Horgan, T., 1982, "Supervenience and Microphysics," *Pacific Philosophical Quarterly* 63: 29–43.

Horgan, T. and Woodward, J., 1985, "Folk Psychology is Here to Stay," *The Philosophical Review* 94: 197–226.

Horwich, P., 1982, *Probability and Evidence*, New York, Cambridge University Press.

Howson, C., and Urbach, P., 1989, *Scientific Reasoning: The Bayesian Approach*, La Salle, IL, Open Court.

Huck, S., and Sandler, H., 1979, *Rival Hypotheses: Alternative Interpretations of Data Based Conclusions*, New York, Harper & Row.

Hull, D., 1974, *Philosophy of Biological Science*, Englewood Cliffs, NJ, Prentice-Hall.

Jarrett, J., 1984, "On the Physical Significance of the Locality Conditions in the Bell Arguments," *Noûs* 18: 569–589.

Jaspars, J. et al., eds., 1983, *Attribution Theory and Research: Conceptual, Developmental and Social Dimensions*, New York, Academic Press.

Jeffrey, R., 1983, *The Logic of Decision*, 2nd ed., Chicago, University of Chicago Press.

Keller, E. F., 1985, *Reflections on Gender and Science*, New Haven, CT, Yale University Press.

Kim, J., 1982, "Psychophysical Supervenience," *Philosophical Studies* 41: 51–70.

Kitcher, Philip, 1978, "Theories, Theorists and Theoretical Change," *Philosophical Review* 87: 519–547.

Kitcher, Philip, 1982, *Abusing Science*, Cambridge, MA, MIT Press.

Kitcher, Philip, 1984, *The Nature of Mathematical Knowledge*, New York, Oxford University Press.

Kitcher, Philip, 1985, *Vaulting Ambition*, Cambridge, MA, MIT Press.

Kornblith, H., ed., 1985, *Naturalizing Epistemology*, Cambridge, MA, MIT Press.

Kripke, S., 1980, *Naming and Necessity*, Cambridge, MA, Harvard University Press.

Kuffler, S. et al., 1984, *From Neuron to Brain*, 2nd ed., Sunderland, MA, Sinauer.

Kuhn, T. S., 1970, *The Structure of Scientific Revolutions*, 2nd ed., Chicago, University of Chicago Press.

Kuhn, T. S., 1977, *The Essential Tension: Selected Studies in Scientific Tradition and Change*, Chicago, University of Chicago Press.

Kyburg, H., 1983, *Epistemology and Inference*, Minneapolis, University of Minnesota Press.

Lakatos, I., 1978, *Philosophical Papers*, 2 vols., New York, Cambridge University Press.

Lakatos, I., and Musgrave, A., eds., 1970, *Criticism and the Growth of Knowledge*, New York, Cambridge University Press.

Latour, B., and Woolgar, S., 1986, *Laboratory Life*, Princeton, NJ, Princeton University Press.

Laudan, L., 1977, *Progress and Its Problems*, Berkeley, CA, University of California Press.

Laudan, L., 1984, *Science and Values*, Berkeley, CA, University of California Press.

Laudan, L., 1986, "Progress or Rationality? The Prospects for Normative Naturalism," *American Philosophical Quarterly*, 24: 19–31.

Leeds, S. 1978, "Theories of Reference and Truth," *Erkenntnis*, 13: 111–129.

Leiber, L. R., and Leiber, H. G., 1945, *The Einstein Theory of Relativity*, New York, J. J. Little & Ives.

Lenin, V. I., 1927, *Materialism and Empirio-Criticism*, New York, International Publishers.

Leplin, J., ed., 1984, *Scientific Realism*, Berkeley, CA, University of California Press.

Levi, I., 1980, *The Enterprise of Knowledge*, Cambridge, MA, MIT Press.

Levins, R., and Lewontin, R., 1985, *The Dialectical Biologist*, Cambridge, MA, Harvard University Press.

Lewis, D., 1973, *Counterfactuals*, Cambridge, MA, Harvard University Press.

Livingston, P., 1988, *Literary Knowledge*, Ithaca, NY, Cornell University Press.

Loar, B., 1981, *Mind and Meaning*, New York, Cambridge University Press.

Lycan, W. G., 1988, *Judgment and Justification*, New York, Cambridge University Press.

Marr, D., 1982, *Vision*, San Francisco, W. H. Freeman.

Maxwell, G., 1962, "The Ontological Status of Theoretical Entities," in H. Feigl and G. Maxwell, eds., *Minnesota Studies in the Philosophy of Science*, vol. III, Minneapolis, University of Minnesota Press.

Miller, R., 1984, *Analyzing Marx*, Princeton, NJ, Princeton University Press.

Miller, R., 1987, *Fact and Method*, Princeton, NJ, Princeton University Press.

Millikan, R. G., 1984, *Language, Thought, and Other Biological Categories*, Cambridge, MA, MIT Press.

Misner, C. W. et al., 1973, *Gravitation*, San Francisco, W. H. Freeman.

Nagel, E., 1961, *The Structure of Science*, New York, Harcourt, Brace and World.

Needham, J., 1954, *Science and Civilisation in China*, 6 vols., Cambridge, Cambridge University Press.

Newton-Smith, W., 1981, *The Rationality of Science*, Boston, Routledge & Kegan Paul.

Nidditch, P. H., ed., 1968, *The Philosophy of Science*, New York, Oxford University Press.

Nisbett, R., and Ross, L., 1980, *Human Inference: Strategies and Shortcomings of Social Judgment*, Englewood Cliffs, NJ, Prentice-Hall.

Nye, M., 1972, *Molecular Reality*, London, Macdonald.

Oldroyd, D., 1986, *The Arch of Knowledge*, New York, Methuen.

Orear, J., 1979, *Physics*, New York, Macmillan.

Platts, M., ed., 1980, *Reference, Truth and Reality*, Boston, Routledge & Kegan Paul.

Popper, K. R., 1959, *The Logic of Scientific Discovery*, London, Hutchison.

Popper, K. R., 1963, *Conjectures and Refutations*, New York, Harper & Row.

Putnam, H., 1975a, *Mathematics, Matter and Method*, New York, Cambridge University Press.

Putnam, H., 1975b, *Mind, Language and Reality*, New York, Cambridge University Press.

Putnam, H., 1978, *Meaning and the Moral Sciences*, Boston, Routledge & Kegan Paul.

Putnam, H., 1981, *Reason, Truth and History*, New York, Cambridge University Press.

Putnam, H., 1983, *Realism and Reason*, New York, Cambridge University Press.

Quine, W. V., 1960, *Word and Object*, Cambridge, MA, MIT Press.

Quine, W. V., 1969, *Ontological Relativity*, New York, Columbia University Press.

Reichenbach, H., 1958, *The Philosophy of Space and Time*, New York, Dover.

Reichenbach, H., 1959, *Modern Philosophy of Science*, London, Routledge & Kegan Paul.

Rey, G., 1983, "Concepts and Stereotypes," *Cognition* 15: 237–262.

Rosch, E., 1973, "On the Internal Structure of Perceptual and Semantic Categories," in T. Moore, ed., *Cognitive Development and the Acquisition of Language*, New York, Academic.

Salmon, W., 1984, *Scientific Explanation and the Causal Structure of the World*, Princeton, NJ, Princeton University Press.

Sarton, G., 1927–1948, *An Introduction to the History of Science*, 3 vols., Baltimore, Williams & Wilkins.

Scheffler, I., 1967, *Science and Subjectivity*, Indianapolis, Bobbs-Merrill.

Scheffler, 1981, *The Anatomy of Inquiry*, Indianapolis, Hackett.

Schwartz, S., ed., 1977, *Naming, Necessity, and Natural Kinds*, Ithaca, NY, Cornell University Press.

Shapere, D., 1984, *Reason and the Search for Knowledge*, Hingham, MA, Reidel.

Shoemaker, S., 1984, *Identity, Cause, and Mind*, New York, Cambridge University Press.

Shoemaker, S., 1985, "Churchland on Reduction, Qualia, and Introspection," in *PSA 1984*, vol. 2, East Lansing, MI, Philosophy of Science Association.

Sidelle, A.,1989, *Necessity, Essence, and Individuation: A Defense of Conventionalism*, Ithaca, NY, Cornell University Press.

Simon, H., 1983, *Reason in Human Affairs*, Stanford, CA, Stanford University Press.

Sklar, L., 1974, *Space, Time, and Space-Time*, Berkeley, CA, University of California Press.

Sklar, L., 1985, *Philosophy and Space-Time Physics*, Berkeley, CA, University of California Press.

Skyrms, B., 1975, *Choice and Chance: An Introduction to Inductive Logic*, Belmont, CA, Wadsworth.

Skyrms, B., 1980, *Causal Necessity*, New Haven, CT, Yale University Press.

Smart, J. J. C., 1963, *Philosophy and Scientific Realism*, London, Routledge and Kegan Paul.

Sober, E., 1982, "Realism and Independence," *Noûs*, 16: 369–386.

Sober, E., 1984, *The Nature of Selection*, Cambridge, MA, MIT Press.

Sober, E., ed., 1984, *Conceptual Issues in Evolutionary Biology*, Cambridge, MA, MIT Press.

Sober, E., 1988, *Reconstructing the Past*, Cambridge, MA, MIT Press.

Spiegel-Rosing, I., and de Solla Price, D., 1977, eds., *Science, Technology and Society: A Cross-Disciplinary Perspective*, London, Sage.

Stalnaker, R., 1984, *Inquiry*, Cambridge, MA, MIT Press.

Stich, S., 1983, *From Folk Psychology to Cognitive Science*, Cambridge, MA, MIT Press.

Stich, S., 1990, *The Fragmentation of Reason*, Cambridge, MA, MIT Press.

Stockman, N., 1983, *Anti-Positivist Theories of the Sciences*, Dordrecht, Reidel.

Suppe, F., ed., 1977, *The Structure of Scientific Theories*, 2nd ed., Urbana, IL, University of Illinois Press.

Suppe, F., 1989, *The Semantic Conception of Theories and Scientific Realism*, Urbana, IL, University of Illinois Press.

Taton, R., 1963–1966, *A General History of the Sciences*, 4 vols., London, Thames and Hudson.

Teller, P., 1984, "A Poor Man's Guide to Supervenience and Determination," *The Southern Journal of Philosophy* 22 (supplement): 137–162.

Teller, P., 1986, "Relational Holism and Quantum Mechanics," *British Journal for the Philosophy of Science* 37: 71–81.

Thagard, P., 1988, *Computational Philosophy of Science*, Cambridge, MA, MIT Press.

Thorndyke, L., 1923–1958, *A History of Magic and Experimental Science*, 8 vols., New York, Columbia University Press.

Toulmin, S., 1953, *The Philosophy of Science*, New York, Harper & Row.

Trout, J. D., 1991, "Belief Attribution in Science: Folk Psychology Under Theoretical Stress," *Synthese* 87: 379–400.

Trout, J. D., 1991, "Theory-Conjunction and Mercenary Reliance," *Philosophy of Science*, 59: 231–245.

van Fraassen, B., 1980, *The Scientific Image*, New York, Oxford University Press.

van Fraassen, B., 1989, *Laws and Symmetries*, New York, Oxford University Press.

Wartofsky, M., 1968, *Conceptual Foundations of Scientific Thought*, New York, Macmillan.

Westfall, R. S., 1971, *The Construction of Modern Science: Mechanisms and Mechanics*, New York, John Wiley & Sons.

Whewell, W., 1840, *The Philosophy of the Inductive Sciences, Founded upon their History*, 2 vols., London, J. W. Parker.

Whewell, W., (1989, ed. R. E. Butts), *Theory of Scientific Method*, Indianapolis, Hackett.

White, L.,1962, *Medieval Technology and Social Change*, New York, Oxford University Press.

Williams, T. I., ed., 1969, *A Biographical Dictionary of Scientists*, London, Black.

Wylie, M. A., 1986, "Arguments for Scientific Realism: The Ascending Spiral," *American Philosophical Quarterly* 23: 287–297.

Name Index

Subject Index